Mary L. Courage
Memorial University of Newfoundland
Chapter 6

Richard N. LaLonde
York University
Chapter 16

Jeanette McGlone
Dalhousie University
Chapter 2

Raymond P. Perry
University of Manitoba
Chapter 17

Kenneth M. Prkachin
University of Northern British Columbia
Chapter 10

Michelle K. Surbey
Mount Allison University
Chapter 9

Paul T. Wong
Trent University
Chapter 10

Psychology

CANADIAN EDITION

Psychology

CANADIAN EDITION

ROBERT A. BARON
RENSSELAER POLYTECHNIC INSTITUTE

BRUCE EARHARD
DALHOUSIE UNIVERSITY

MARCIA OZIER
DALHOUSIE UNIVERSITY

ALLYN & BACON CANADA

Scarborough, Ontario

Canadian Cataloguing in Publication Data

Baron, Robert A.
    Psychology

Canadian ed.
Includes bibliographical references and index.
ISBN 0–205–17232–6

1. Psychology. I. Ozier, Marcia
II. Earhard, Bruce. III. Title.

BF121.B37 1995   150   C95–930215–8

© 1995 Allyn & Bacon Canada
A Division of the Simon & Schuster Publishing Higher Education Group
1870 Birchmount Road
Scarborough, Ontario, M1P 2J7

ISBN 0–205–17232–6

Executive Editor: Clifford J. Newman
Managing Editor: Marta Tomins
Copy Editor: Matthew Kudelka
Production Editor: Imogen Brian
Assistant Editor: Emily Meetsma
Photo Research: Angelika Baur
Cover Illustration: J.W. Stewart
Cover Design: Bruce Bond
Page Layout: Zena Denchik/Steve Lewis

Original English language edition published by Allyn and Bacon, Needham Heights, MA
Copyright © 1995, 1992, 1989.

Every reasonable effort has been made to obtain permissions for all articles and data used in this edition. If errors or omissions have occurred, they will be corrected in future editions provided written notification has been received by the publisher.

1 2 3 4 5 A/H 99 98 97 96 95
Printed and bound in the United States of America

For Mark Daniel, Sean Jeremy, and Rachel Ann Earhard

Contents-at-a-Glance

1   PSYCHOLOGY: ITS NATURE, SCOPE, AND METHODS   2

2   BIOLOGICAL BASES OF BEHAVIOR: A LOOK BENEATH THE SURFACE   46

3   SENSATION AND PERCEPTION: MAKING CONTACT WITH THE WORLD AROUND US   92

4   CONSCIOUSNESS: AWARENESS OF OURSELVES AND THE EXTERNAL WORLD   142

5   LEARNING: HOW EXPERIENCE CHANGES US   184

6   MEMORY: OF THINGS REMEMBERED ... AND FORGOTTEN   226

7   COGNITION: THINKING, DECIDING, COMMUNICATING   268

8   HUMAN DEVELOPMENT I: THE CHILDHOOD YEARS   312

9   HUMAN DEVELOPMENT II: ADOLESCENCE, ADULTHOOD, AND AGING   356

10   MOTIVATION AND EMOTION   398

11   INDIVIDUAL DIFFERENCES I: INTELLIGENCE AND GENDER   442

12   INDIVIDUAL DIFFERENCES II: PERSONALITY—CONSISTENCY IN THE BEHAVIOR OF INDIVIDUALS   488

13   HEALTH PSYCHOLOGY: HEALTH, STRESS, AND COPING   530

14   PSYCHOLOGICAL DISORDERS: THEIR NATURE AND CAUSES   574

15   THERAPY: DIMINISHING THE PAIN OF PSYCHOLOGICAL DISORDERS   618

16   SOCIAL THOUGHT, HOW WE THINK ABOUT OTHERS ... AND THE SOCIAL WORLD   658

17   PSYCHOLOGY AT WORK: INDUSTRIAL/ORGANIZATIONAL PSYCHOLOGY AND HUMAN FACTORS   712

Appendix   STATISTICS: USES—AND POTENTIAL ABUSES   763

Contents

Preface   xxii
Acknowledgments   xxviii

1 Psychology: Its Nature, Scope, and Methods   2

PSYCHOLOGY: WHAT IT IS AND HOW IT DEVELOPED   5
  Philosophy and Science: The Dual Roots
    of Modern Psychology   6
  Psychology: Some Early Views   7
  Psychology During the Twentieth Century:
    How It Developed and Grew   8
  Modern Psychology: Some Key Perspectives   9
  Psychology in a Diverse World: Multicultural
    and Gender Issues   14
  Psychology: Some Basic Questions   16

PSYCHOLOGY: WHO AND WHAT   18
  Who: The Background and Training of
    Psychologists   19
  What: Specialties Within Psychology   19

ADDING TO WHAT WE KNOW: THE PROCESS OF
PSYCHOLOGICAL RESEARCH   21
  Naturalistic Observation: Scientists as Explorers   21
  Case Studies: Generalizing from the Unique   22
  Surveys: The Science of Self-Report   22
  The Correlational Method: Knowledge Through
    Systematic Observation   23
  Experimentation: Knowledge Through
    Systematic Intervention   25
  Interpreting Research Results: Statistics as a Tool 29

  Key Concept:
  Correlational and Experimental Research
  Methods   30
  The Role of Theory in Psychological Research   31

ETHICAL ISSUES IN PSYCHOLOGY   33
  Deception: Is It Ever Appropriate for
    Psychologists to Lie to Research Participants?   34
  Research with Animals: Is It Acceptable?   35
  Ethical Issues in the Practice of Psychology   37

USING THIS BOOK: A NOTE ON ITS FEATURES   39
  Using the Knowledge in This Book: Some Tips
    on How to Study   40

MAKING PSYCHOLOGY PART OF YOUR LIFE:
  Practice in Critical Thinking: The Hidden Bonus
  in Introductory Psychology   42

SUMMARY AND REVIEW OF KEY POINTS   44
CRITICAL THINKING QUESTIONS   45

2 Biological Bases of Behavior: A Look Beneath the Surface   46

NEURONS: BUILDING BLOCKS OF THE NERVOUS
SYSTEM   49
  Neurons: Their Basic Structure   50
  Neurons: Their Basic Function   51

  Key Concept:
  Communication in the Nervous System:
  Putting It All Together   54
  Neurotransmitters: Chemical Keys to the
    Nervous System   55

  The Point of It All:
  Using Knowledge of Synaptic Transmission to
  Treat Addictions: Fighting Fire with Fire   57

THE NERVOUS SYSTEM: ITS BASIC STRUCTURE AND
FUNCTIONS   59
  The Nervous System: Its Major Divisions   60
  The Nervous System: How It Is Studied   62

  The Point of It All:
  High-Tech Snoopers: Putting Brain Imaging
  Devices to Work   64

THE BRAIN: WHERE CONSCIOUSNESS IS MANIFEST   66
  Survival Basics: The Brain Stem   66
  Emotion and Motivation: The Hypothalamus,
    Thalamus, and Limbic System   67
  The Cerebral Cortex: The Hub of Complex
    Thought   68

Canadian Focus:
Music and the Right Hemisphere   71

Language and the Cerebral Cortex: Models of Human Speech   72

LATERALIZATION OF THE CEREBRAL CORTEX: TWO MINDS IN ONE BODY?   73

Research with Intact Individuals   74

Research with Split-Brain Participants: Isolating the Two Hemispheres   75

THE ENDOCRINE SYSTEM: CHEMICAL REGULATORS OF BODILY PROCESSES   77

Hormones and Behavior: Is the Premenstrual Syndrome Real?   79

Perspectives on Diversity:
The Biological Basis of Gender Differences   80

HEREDITY AND BEHAVIOR   81

Genetics: Some Basic Principles   82

Disentangling Genetic and Environmental Effects: Research Strategies   84

The Research Process:
Sexual Orientation—Genetically Determined or Lifestyle Choice?   85

MAKING PSYCHOLOGY PART OF YOUR LIFE:
Traumatic Brain Injury: Using Psychology to Enhance Quality of Life   87

SUMMARY AND REVIEW OF KEY POINTS   89
CRITICAL THINKING QUESTIONS   91

3   *Sensation and Perception: Making Contact with the World Around Us*   92

SENSATION: THE RAW MATERIALS OF UNDERSTANDING   95

Sensory Thresholds: How Much Stimulation Is Enough?   95

Sensory Adaptation: "It Feels Great Once You Get Used to It!"   99

VISION   100

The Eye: Its Basic Structure   100

Light: The Physical Stimulus for Vision   102

Basic Functions of the Visual System: Acuity, Dark Adaptation, and Eye Movements   103

Color Vision   104

Vision and The Brain: Processing Visual Information   106

HEARING   107
The Ear: Its Basic Structure   108

Sound: The Physical Stimulus for Hearing   108

Pitch Perception   109

Sound Localization   110

TOUCH AND OTHER SKIN SENSES   111

Pain: Its Nature and Control   112

Perspectives on Diversity:
Culture and the Perception of Pain   114

SMELL AND TASTE: THE CHEMICAL SENSES   115

Smell and Taste: How They Operate   115

Smell and Taste: Some Interesting Findings   116

KINESTHESIA AND VESTIBULAR SENSE   118

PERCEPTION: PUTTING IT ALL TOGETHER   120

Perception: The Focus of Our Attention   120

Perception: Some Organizing Principles   121

The Research Process:
DANGER—Warnings are Effective Only Under Certain Conditions: They Have to Be Developed and Applied with Great Care   122

Constancies and Illusions: When Perception Succeeds—and Fails   124

Key Concept:
Figure-Ground   125

Some Key Perceptual Processes: Pattern and Distance   129

THE PLASTICITY OF PERCEPTION: TO WHAT EXTENT IS IT INNATE OR LEARNED THROUGH EXPERIENCE?   132

Perception: Evidence That It's Innate   132

Perception: Evidence for the Importance of Learning and Experience 133

Must We Try to Resolve the Nature–Nurture Controversy? 133

Canadian Focus:
Testing the Limits of Perceptual Plasticity 134

EXTRASENSORY PERCEPTION: PERCEPTION WITHOUT SENSATION? 134

Psi: What Is It? 135

Psi: Does It Really Exist? 135

MAKING PSYCHOLOGY PART OF YOUR LIFE:
The Danger of Stereo Headsets: Let's Turn Down the Volume 137

SUMMARY AND REVIEW OF KEY POINTS 138
CRITICAL THINKING QUESTIONS 140

4 *Consciousness:*
Awareness of Ourselves and the External World *142*

BIOLOGICAL RHYTHMS: TIDES OF LIFE—AND CONSCIOUS EXPERIENCE 144

Circadian Rhythms: Their Basic Nature 145

Circadian Rhythms: What Mechanism Underlies Them? 146

Canadian Focus:
Seasonal Sadness 147

Individual Differences in Circadian Rhythms: Of Larks and Owls 148

Disturbances in Circadian Rhythms: Jet Lag and Shift Work 148

The Point of It All:
Countering the Negative Effects of Shift Work 149

WAKING STATES OF CONSCIOUSNESS: EVERYDAY EXPERIENCE 150

Controlled and Automatic Processing: The Limits of Attention 151

Daydreams and Fantasies: Self-Induced Shifts in Consciousness 152

Self-Consciousness: Some Effects of Looking Inward 153

SLEEP: THE PAUSE THAT REFRESHES? 156

Sleep: How It Is Studied 156

Sleep: Its Basic Nature 156

Sleep: What Functions Does It Serve? 158

Sleep Disorders: No Rest for the Weary 160

Dreams: Stimulation in the Midst of Sleep 162

Perspectives on Diversity:
Culture and the Interpretation of Dreams 164

HYPNOSIS: ALTERED STATE OF CONSCIOUSNESS OR SOCIAL ROLE PLAYING? 166

Hypnosis: What It Is and Who Is Susceptible to It 167

Hypnosis: Contrasting Views About Its Nature 168

The Research Process:
Does Hypnosis Produce Changes in Memory and Perception? 169

CONSCIOUSNESS-ALTERING DRUGS: WHAT THEY ARE AND WHAT THEY DO 171

Consciousness-Altering Drugs: Some Basic Concepts 172

Psychological Mechanisms Underlying Drug Abuse: Contrasting Views 172

Consciousness-Altering Drugs: An Overview 174

Key Concept:
Effects of Consciousness-Altering Drugs 178

The Psychology of Drug Effects 179

MAKING PSYCHOLOGY PART OF YOUR LIFE:
Meditation: A Technique for Inducing Potentially Beneficial Shifts in Consciousness 179

SUMMARY AND REVIEW OF KEY POINTS 182
CRITICAL THINKING QUESTIONS 183

5 Learning: How Experience Changes Us 184

CLASSICAL CONDITIONING: LEARNING THAT SOME STIMULI SIGNAL OTHERS 186

Pavlov's Early Work on Classical Conditioning: Does This Ring a Bell? 188

Classical Conditioning: Some Basic Principles 188

Classical Conditioning: Exceptions to the Rules 193

Classical Conditioning: A Cognitive Perspective 195

The Point of It All:
Conditioned Taste Aversions: Breaking All the Rules? 195

Classical Conditioning: Turning Principles into Action 198

OPERANT CONDITIONING: LEARNING BASED ON CONSEQUENCES 200

The Nature of Operant Conditioning: Consequential Operations 202

Operant Conditioning: Some Basic Principles 203

Key Concept:
The Difference Between Negative Reinforcement and Punishment 204

Canadian Focus:
Gambling: The Psychological Downside 209

Operant Conditioning: A Cognitive Perspective 210

The Research Process: Stimulus Control in Action: Promoting Paper Waste Recycling on a University Campus 212

Applying Operant Conditioning: Can We Make a Difference? 215

OBSERVATIONAL LEARNING: LEARNING FROM THE BEHAVIOR AND OUTCOMES OF OTHERS 217

Observational Learning: Some Basic Principles 218

Observational Learning and Aggression 220

Perspectives on Diversity:
Learning to Avoid Culture Shock 221

MAKING PSYCHOLOGY PART OF YOUR LIFE:
Getting in Shape: Applying Psychology to Get Fit and Stay Fit 222

SUMMARY AND REVIEW OF KEY POINTS 224

CRITICAL THINKING QUESTIONS 225

6 Memory: Of Things Remembered ... and Forgotten 226

HUMAN MEMORY: THE INFORMATION PROCESSING APPROACH 229

Human Memory: One Influential Model—and an Emerging New Approach 229

Types of Information in Memory 232

SENSORY MEMORY: GATEWAY TO CONSCIOUSNESS 233

Canadian Focus:
The Story of a Man Without Episodic Memory 233

SHORT-TERM MEMORY: THE WORKBENCH OF CONSCIOUSNESS 235

Evidence for the Existence of Short-Term Memory 235

Short-Term Memory: Its Basic Operation 236

LONG-TERM MEMORY: THE STOREHOUSE OF CONSCIOUSNESS 237

Long-Term Memory: Its Basic Operation 238

Retrieval: Locating Information in Long-Term Memory 240

FORGETTING FROM LONG-TERM MEMORY 242

The Trace-Decay Hypothesis: Forgetting with the Passage of Time 242

Forgetting as a Result of Interference 243

The Point of It All:
Repression: Do We Sometimes Forget Because We Want to Forget? 244

Prospective Memory: Forgetting to Do What We're Supposed to Do 246

MEMORY IN NATURAL CONTEXTS 247

Autobiographical Memory: Remembering the Events of Our Own Lives 247

Canadian Focus:
Why Can We Remember so Little of Our Very Early Childhood? 250

Key Concept:
Different Kinds of Memory: An Overview 251

Distortion and Construction in Memory of
Natural Events   252

Perspectives on Diversity:
Culture and Memory: Remembering What Fits
with Our Cultural Schemas   254

The Research Process:
Eyewitness Testimony: How Accurate Is It?
What Factors Affect It?   256

THE BIOLOGICAL BASIS OF MEMORY: HOW THE
BRAIN STORES KNOWLEDGE   258
Amnesia and Other Memory Disorders: Keys
to Understanding the Nature of Memory   259
Memory and the Brain: A Modern View   262

MAKING PSYCHOLOGY PART OF YOUR LIFE:
Improving Your Memory: Some Useful Steps   263

SUMMARY AND REVIEW OF KEY POINTS   265
CRITICAL THINKING QUESTIONS   267

7 Cognition: Thinking, Deciding, Communicating   268

THINKING: FORMING CONCEPTS AND REASONING
TO CONCLUSIONS   270
Basic Elements of Thought: Concepts,
Propositions, Images   271

REASONING: TRANSFORMING INFORMATION TO
REACH CONCLUSIONS   275

Perspectives on Diversity:
When Culture Shapes Reasoning—or at Least
Influences Its Outcomes   276

ANIMAL COGNITION: DO THEY REALLY THINK?   279

The Research Process:
Animal Cognition: Tales of Intelligence   280

MAKING DECISIONS: CHOOSING AMONG
ALTERNATIVES   282
Heuristics: Using Quick—but Fallible—
Rules of Thumb to Make Decisions   282

Key Concept:
Factors That Influence the Decision-Making
Process   285
Framing in Decision Making   286
Escalation of Commitment: Getting Trapped
in Bad Decisions   287

PROBLEM SOLVING AND CREATIVITY: FINDING
PATHS TO DESIRED GOALS   289
Problem Solving: An Overview   289

The Point of It All:
The Education Crisis in North America:
Practice May Be the Key   291
Methods for Solving Problems: From Trial
and Error to Heuristics   291
Factors That Interfere with Effective Problem
Solving   292
Creativity: Innovative Problem Solving   294
Artificial Intelligence: Can Machines Really
Think?   296

LANGUAGE: THE COMMUNICATION OF
INFORMATION   298
Language: Its Basic Nature   298
The Development of Language   300

Canadian Focus:
*Do Some Kinds of Language Impairment Result
from a Genetic Abnormality?*   301
Language and Thought: Do We Think What
We Say or Say What We Think?   304
Language in Other Species   304

MAKING PSYCHOLOGY PART OF YOUR LIFE:
Making Better Decisions   308

SUMMARY AND REVIEW OF KEY POINTS   309
CRITICAL THINKING QUESTIONS   311

8 Human Development I: The Childhood Years   312

PHYSICAL GROWTH AND DEVELOPMENT   315

The Prenatal Period   315

Prenatal Influences on Development: When Trouble Starts Early   316

Physical and Perceptual Development During Our Early Years: Infancy and Childhood   319

Perspectives on Diversity:
Maternal Responsiveness and Diversity   319

The Research Process:
Lullabies and Good Night   322

COGNITIVE DEVELOPMENT: CHANGES IN HOW WE KNOW THE EXTERNAL WORLD ... AND OURSELVES   323

The Research Process:
Basic Methods for Studying Human Development   324

Piaget's Theory: An Overview   326

Piaget's Theory: A Modern Assessment   328

Cognitive Development: An Information Processing Perspective   330

The Point of It All:
Attention-Deficit Hyperactivity Disorder: Kids Who Really Can't Sit Still   332

Moral Development: Reasoning About Right and Wrong   335

Key Concept:
Two Views of Cognitive Development   336

Perspectives on Diversity:
Moral Development: Universal or Culture-Related?   341

SOCIAL AND EMOTIONAL DEVELOPMENT: FORMING RELATIONSHIPS WITH OTHERS   342

Emotional Development and Temperament   342

Attachment: The Beginnings of Love   345

Canadian Focus:
Is Day Care a Threat to Secure Attachment?   347

GENDER: THE DEVELOPMENT OF GENDER IDENTITY AND SEX-STEREOTYPED BEHAVIOR   350

Gender Identity: Some Contrasting Views   350

Sex-Stereotyped Beliefs and Behavior   351

MAKING PSYCHOLOGY PART OF YOUR LIFE:
Being a Successful Parent   353

SUMMARY AND REVIEW OF KEY POINTS   354

CRITICAL THINKING QUESTIONS   355

9 Human Development II: Adolescence, Adulthood, and Aging   356

ADOLESCENCE: BETWEEN CHILD AND ADULT   358

Physical Development During Adolescence   359

The Research Process:
Puberty and Gender Identity   360

Cognitive Development During Adolescence   362

Social and Emotional Development During Adolescence   363

Key Concept:
Erikson's Eight Stages of Psychosocial Development   366

Adolescence in the 1990s: A Generation at Risk   367

The Point of It All:
Overcoming the Odds: Adolescents in High-Risk Environments   370

ADULTHOOD AND AGING   371

Contrasting Views of Adult Development: Internal Crises or External Life Events?   371

Physical Change During Our Adult Years   373

Perspectives on Diversity:
Menopause: The Role of Cultural Factors   375

Cognitive Change During Adulthood   378

The Research Process:
Age, Intelligence, Wisdom, and Creativity: Change or Stability Across the Life Span?   381

Social Change in Adulthood: Tasks and Stages of Adult Life   382

Crises of Adult Life   385

Gender and the Adult Years: How Men and
    Women Differ   388

AGING AND DEATH: THE END OF LIFE   389

    Why Do We Die?   389

    Theories of Aging: Contrasting Views About
        Why We Grow Old   389

    Meeting Death: Facing the End of Life   390

    Bereavement: Mourning the Death of Loved
        Ones   391

MAKING PSYCHOLOGY PART OF YOUR LIFE:

    Preparing for Tomorrow's Job Market Today   393

SUMMARY AND REVIEW OF KEY POINTS   395

CRITICAL THINKING QUESTIONS   396

The Point of It All:
Turning Work into Play: Intrinsic Motivation
in the Classroom   424

EMOTIONS: THEIR NATURE, EXPRESSION, AND
IMPACT   426

    The Nature of Emotions: Some Contrasting
        Views   426

The Research Process:
Support for Schachter and Singer   428

    The Physiology of Emotion   428

Key Concept:
Three Major Theories of Emotion   429

    The External Expression of Emotion: Outward
        Signs of Inner Feelings   430

The Point of It All:
Can Physiological Reactions Be Used to
Detect Lies?   431

    Emotion and Cognition: How Feelings Shape
        Thoughts and Thoughts Shape Feelings 435

The Research Process:
Are People in a Good Mood Easier to Influence?
Effects of Mood on Information Processing   436

MAKING PSYCHOLOGY PART OF YOUR LIFE:
    Getting Motivated: Some Practical Techniques 439

SUMMARY AND REVIEW OF KEY POINTS   440

CRITICAL THINKING QUESTIONS   441

10. *Motivation and Emotion*   *398*

MOTIVATION: THE ACTIVATION AND PERSISTENCE
OF BEHAVIOR   401

    Theories of Motivation: Diverse Views of a
        Complex Process   401

    Hunger: Regulating Our Caloric Intake   406

Canadian Focus:
*Serious Eating Disorders: Anorexia Nervosa and
Bulimia*   409

    Sexual Motivation: The Most Intimate Motive 411

    Aggressive Motivation: The Most Dangerous
        Motive   418

Perspectives on Diversity:
The Role of Cultural Factors in Aggression:
The Social Context of Violence   420

    Achievement and Power: Two Complex
        Human Motives   421

    Gender Differences in Achievement Motivation:
        Do They Really Exist?   422

    Intrinsic Motivation: How (Sometimes) to Turn
        Play into Work   423

11. *Individual Differences I: Intelligence and Gender*   *442*

INTELLIGENCE: ITS NATURE AND MEASUREMENT   444

    Human Intelligence: Some Contrasting Views   445

Canadian Focus:
*Studies of the Savant Syndrome: Islands of Superior
Functioning in a Sea of General Impairment*   446

    Measuring Human Intelligence   450

    Reliability and Validity: Basic Requirements
        for All Psychological Tests   455

Intelligence Testing and Public Policy: Are
Intelligence Tests Fair?   459

Key Concept:
Major Types of Test Validity   458

The Point of It All:
Individual Tests of Intelligence: Their
Practical Uses   461

HUMAN INTELLIGENCE: THE ROLE OF HEREDITY
AND THE ROLE OF ENVIRONMENT   463
    Evidence for the Influence of Heredity   463
    Evidence for the Influence of Environmental
    Factors   465
    Environment, Heredity, and Intelligence:
    Summing Up   467

GENDER: HOW MALES AND FEMALES DIFFER   467
    Gender Differences in Social Behavior   468
    Mate Selection, Relationships, and Sexuality   473

The Research Process:
Integrating the Evolutionary and Social
Exchange Models of Mate Preferences:
Taking Account of Our Own "Market Value"   475

    Gender Differences in Psychological
    Adjustment   478
    Cognitive Abilities   480
    Gender Differences: A Note on Their Possible
    Origins   481

Canadian Focus:
The Montreal Massacre: Gender Hatred   483

MAKING PSYCHOLOGY PART OF YOUR LIFE:
Measuring Attitudes Towards Women:
A Short Test for Sexism   484

SUMMARY AND REVIEW OF KEY POINTS   486
CRITICAL THINKING QUESTIONS   487

12 *Individual Differences II: Personality—Consistency in the Behavior of Individuals*   488

THE PSYCHOANALYTIC APPROACH: MESSAGES
FROM THE UNCONSCIOUS   491
    Freud the Person: A Life in Summary   491
    Freud's Theory of Personality   492
    Research Evidence Concerning Freud's Theory:
    Freudian Slips   497
    Freud's Theory: An Overall Evaluation   498

Canadian Focus:
Cultural Variations in Love and Intimacy   499

OTHER PSYCHOANALYTIC VIEWS: FREUD'S
DISCIPLES ... AND DISSENTERS   500
    Jung: The Collective Unconscious   501
    Horney: The Importance of Social and
    Cultural Factors   501
    Adler: Striving for Superiority   503
    The Neo-Freudians: An Evaluation   504

HUMANISTIC THEORIES: EMPHASIS ON GROWTH   505
    Roger's Self Theory: Becoming a Fully
    Functioning Person   505
    Maslow and the Study of Self-Actualizing
    People   507
    Humanistic Theories: An Evaluation   507
    The Research Process—Self-Disclosure: The
    Potential Benefits of Revealing Ourselves to
    Others   508

TRAIT THEORIES: SEEKING THE KEY DIMENSIONS OF
PERSONALITY   510
    Allport's Central, Secondary, and Cardinal
    Traits   510
    Cattell's Surface and Source Traits   511
    Five Robust Factors: A Modern Framework   511
    Trait Theories: An Evaluation   513

LEARNING APPROACHES TO PERSONALITY   514

  Social Cognitive Theory: Reciprocal Causality
    in Human Behavior   515
  Evaluation of the Learning Approach   516

  The Point of It All:
  The Atlas Personality   516

KEY ASPECTS OF PERSONALITY: A SAMPLE OF
RECENT RESEARCH   517

  Key Concept:
  Major Theories of Personality: An Overview   518
  Aspects of the Self: Self-Perception,
    Self-Esteem, and Self-Motivation   519
  Sensation Seeking: The Desire for Stimulation   523

  Canadian Focus:
  The Role of Personality Factors in Adjusting to
  Life in a New Culture   524

MAKING PSYCHOLOGY PART OF YOUR LIFE:
  How Accurate Is Your Self-Concept?   526

SUMMARY AND REVIEW OF KEY POINTS   527
CRITICAL THINKING QUESTIONS   529

13 Health Psychology: Health, Stress, and Coping 530

HEALTH PSYCHOLOGY: AN OVERVIEW   532

STRESS: ITS CAUSE , EFFECTS AND CONTROL   534

  Stress: Its Basic Nature   534

  Key Concept:
  Two Sides of Stress   538

  Stress: Some Major Causes   539

  The Point of It All:
  Putting Psychology to Work: Reducing Stress
  in the Workplace   544

  Stress: Some Major Effects   545

UNDERSTANDING AND COMMUNICATING OUR
HEALTH NEEDS   550

  Symptom Perception: How Do We Know
    When We're Ill?   550
  Health Beliefs: When Do We Seek Medical
    Advice?   551
  Doctor-Patient Interactions: Why Can't We
    Talk to Our Doctors?   552

BEHAVIORAL AND PSYCHOLOGICAL CORRELATES   553
OF ILLNESS: COGNITION AND HEALTH
  Risky for You and Everyone Around You   554

  Perspectives on Diversity:
  Global Equality: Susceptibility to the
  Adverse Effects of Smoking   556
  Diet and Nutrition: What You Eat May Save
    Your Life   558
  Alcohol Consumption: Here's to Your Health   558
  Emotions: Mood and Health   558
  AIDS: The New War for Public Health   561

  The Research Process:
  Changing Risky Behaviors: An Ounce of
  Prevention Is the Only Known Cure   563

PROMOTING WELLNESS: DEVELOPING A HEALTHIER
LIFESTYLE   565

  Primary Prevention: Decreasing the Risks of
    Illness and Injury   565
  Secondary Prevention: Early Detection of
    Disease and Illness   568

MAKING PSYCHOLOGY PART OF YOUR LIFE:
  Managing Stress—Some Useful Tactics   569

SUMMARY AND REVIEW OF KEY POINTS   571
CRITICAL THINKING QUESTIONS   573

14 Psychological Disorders: Their Nature and Causes 574

CHANGING CONCEPTIONS OF PSYCHOLOGICAL
DISORDERS: A BRIEF HISTORICAL PERSPECTIVE   577

  From Demons to Disease: Changing Concepts
    of Abnormal Behavior   577

The Biological/Medical Perspective: Psychological Disorders as Disease 578

The Psychodynamic Perspective: Desires, Anxieties, and Defenses 579

The Modern Psychological Approach: Recognizing the Multiple Roots of Abnormal Behavior 579

IDENTIFYING PSYCHOLOGICAL DISORDERS: THE DSM-IV 580

Key Concept:
Contrasting Perspectives on Abnormal Behavior 581

Perspectives on Diversity:
Taking Account of Cultural Factors in Psychological Disorders: Improvements in the DSM-IV 584

Canadian Focus:
Assessing the Prevalence of Psychological Disorders in Canada 585

MOOD DISORDERS: THE DOWNS AND UPS OF LIFE 587
Depressive Disorders: Probing the Depths of Despair 587

Bipolar Disorders: Riding the Emotional Roller Coaster 588

The Causes of Depression: Its Biological and Psychological Roots 588

Suicide: When Life Becomes Unbearable 589

Why Suicide? A Host of Contributing Factors 591

ANXIETY DISORDERS: WHEN DREAD DEBILITATES 592
Panic Attack: the Body Signals "Danger!" But Is It Real? 592

Phobias: Fear That Is Focused 593

Obsessive-Compulsive Disorder: Behaviors and Thoughts Outside One's Control 594

Post-Traumatic Stress Disorder 594

Anxiety: The Role of Subliminal Processing 595

SOMATOFORM DISORDERS: PHYSICAL SYMPTOMS WITHOUT PHYSICAL CAUSES 596

DISSOCIATIVE DISORDERS: WHEN MEMORY FAILS 597

The Point of It All:
Dissociative Identity Disorder: Multiple Personalities in a Single Body? 598

Canadian Focus:
The Cause and Character of Dissociative Identity Disorder 599

SEXUAL AND GENDER IDENTITY DISORDERS 600
Sexual Dysfunctions: Disturbances in Desire and Arousal 601

Paraphilias: Disturbances in Sexual Object or Behavior 601

Gender Identity Disorders 601

Eating Disorders 602

PERSONALITY DISORDERS: TRAITS THAT PROVE COSTLY 603
Paranoid and Schizoid Personality Disorders: Cut Off from Human Contact 603

The Antisocial Personality Disorder 604

The Research Process:
The Antisocial Personality Disorder: Anomalous Emotional Reactivity and Irregularities in Allocation of Attention and Learning 605

SCHIZOPHRENIA: OUT OF TOUCH WITH REALITY 607
The Basic Nature of Schizophrenia 607

Subtypes of Schizophrenia 609

The Origins of Schizophrenia 610

MAKING PSYCHOLOGY PART OF YOUR LIFE:
Preventing Suicide: Some Basic Steps 614

SUMMARY AND REVIEW OF KEY POINTS 615

CRITICAL THINKING QUESTIONS 617

15 Therapy: Diminishing the Pain of Psychological Disorders 618

PSYCHOTHERAPIES: PSYCHOLOGICAL APPROACHES TO PSYCHOLOGICAL DISORDERS 620
Psychodynamic Therapies: From Repression to Insight 621

Humanistic Therapies: Emphasizing the Positive 624

Behavior Therapies: Psychological Disorders
and Faulty Learning 626
Cognitive Therapies: Changing Disordered
Thought 629

Canadian Focus:
Coping with Anxiety: Meichenbaum's Stress
Inoculation Training Program 632

GROUP THERAPIES: WORKING WITH OTHERS TO
SOLVE PERSONAL PROBLEMS 633
Psychodynamic Group Therapies 633
Behavioral Group Therapies 633
Humanistic Group Therapies 634
Self-Help Groups: Help from Our Peers 634

The Research Process:
Subliminal Self-Help Audiotapes: Do They
Deliver What They Promise? 635

THERAPIES FOCUSED ON INTERPERSONAL
RELATIONS: MARITAL AND FAMILY THERAPY 637
Marital Therapy: When Spouses Become the
Intimate Enemy 637
Family Therapy: Changing Environments That
Harm 638

PSYCHOTHERAPY: SOME CURRENT ISSUES 639
Does Psychotherapy Really Work? An
Optimistic Conclusion 639

Key Concept:
Major Forms of Psychotherapy 640
Are Some Forms of Therapy More Successful
Than Others? Solving a Persistent Puzzle 642

Canadian Focus:
Addressing Mental Health Problems in
Canada's North 643

BIOLOGICALLY BASED THERAPIES 645
Early Forms of Biological Therapy 645
Electroconvulsive Therapy 645
Psychosurgery 646
Drug Therapy: The Pharmacological
Revolution 646
Antipsychotic Drugs 647

THE SETTING FOR MAJOR THERAPY 650
Treatment Locations: The Shift from Hospitals
to the Community 650

Community Services: What Are They? And
Why Are They Needed? 651
Prevention: Heading Off Trouble Before It
Begins—or Becomes Serious 651
MAKING PSYCHOLOGY PART OF YOUR LIFE:
How to Choose a Therapist: A Consumer's
Guide 653

SUMMARY AND REVIEW OF KEY POINTS 655
CRITICAL THINKING QUESTIONS 657

16 Social Thought:
How We Think About Others ... and the Social World 658

SOCIAL THOUGHT: THINKING ABOUT OTHER
PEOPLE 661
Attribution: Understanding the Causes of
"Their" Behavior 661
Social Cognition: How We Process Social
Information 667
Basic Aspects of Social Thought: How We
Think About Other People 667
Automatic Vigilance: Noticing the Negative 669
Attitudes: Evaluating the Social World 672

The Point of It All:
Practical Uses of Dissonance Theory:
Hypocrisy and the Alteration of Societally
Important Attitudes 678

GROUP BEHAVIOR: INTERACTING WITH OTHERS 679
Prejudice: Distorted Views of the Social World 679

Challenging Prejudice: Some Potential Plans
of Action 682

Perspectives on Diversity:
The Effects of Prejudice: Group Identification
Among African Americans 685
Social Influence: Changing Behavior 687

The Research Process:
Lineups and Lines   688

Gender Differences and Conformity:
The Myth of Female/Male Differences   690

Compliance: To Ask—Sometimes—Is to
Receive   690

Key Concept:
Major Forms of Social Influence   696

Prosocial Behavior: When We Help ... and
When We Don't   697

Canadian Focus:
Where Charity Begins ... and Continues   697

Feeling Good and Feeling Bad and Helping:
Mood and Prosocial Behavior   699

ATTRACTION, LOVE, AND CLOSE RELATIONSHIPS   701

The Research Process:
Is Physical Attractiveness Only Skin Deep?   703

Love: The Most Intense Form of Attraction   704

MAKING PSYCHOLOGY PART OF YOUR LIFE:
Enhancing the Accuracy of Your Social
Judgments   708

SUMMARY AND REVIEW OF KEY POINTS   709
CRITICAL THINKING QUESTIONS   711

17 *Psychology at Work: Industrial/Organizational Psychology: Human Factors, the Environment, and the Law*   *712*

INDUSTRIAL/ORGANIZATIONAL PSYCHOLOGY:
THE SYSTEMATIC STUDY OF BEHAVIOR AT WORK   715

Work Motivation: Theories and Techniques   716

Key Concept:
Theories of Work Motivation   721

The Point of It All:
Computers at Work   723

Performance Appraisal: Tying Rewards to
Performance   724

Perspectives on Diversity:
Negative Effects of Gender Stereotypes:
Why Men Often Get the Job   727

Performance Appraisals: Techniques for
Reducing Errors   730

Work-Related Attitudes: The Prevalence,
Causes, and Effects of Job Satisfaction   732

The Research Process:
Job Satisfaction and Task Performance   736

Leadership: Its Nature and Impact   738

APPLIED PSYCHOLOGY: PUTTING KNOWLEDGE
ABOUT BEHAVIOR TO WORK   741

Environmental Psychology: The Physical
Environment and Behavior   741

Crowding: The Effects of Close Encounters
with Other People   742

Canadian Focus:
Ethnic Differences in Reactions to Crowding   743

Other Aspects of the Physical Environment:
Noise, Temperature and Light   743

HUMAN FACTORS: DESIGNING FOR EFFECTIVENESS
AND SAFETY   745

Visual Displays: Principles and Applications   746

Controls: "What Happens When I Turn This
Dial..."?   749

Workplace Environments: Planning for
Productivity and Well-Being   751

The Research Process:
Computers and Stress   754

PSYCHOLOGY AND THE LEGAL SYSTEM: WHERE
LAW AND PSYCHOLOGY MEET   756

Sources of Bias in Legal Proceedings:
Characteristics of Defendants   756

Sources of Bias in Legal Proceedings: The
Procedures Themselves   757

MAKING PSYCHOLOGY PART OF YOUR LIFE:
Computers and Repetitive Strain Injury:
Keyboards Can Hurt You   758

SUMMARY AND REVIEW OF KEY POINTS   761
CRITICAL THINKING QUESTIONS   762

Appendix
Statistics: Uses—and Potential Abuses 763

DESCRIPTIVE STATISTICS: SUMMARIZING DATA 763
Measures of Central Tendencies: Finding the Center 764
Measures of Dispersion: Assessing the Spread 765
The Normal Curve: Putting Descriptive Statistics to Work 766

INFERENTIAL STATISTICS: DETERMINING WHETHER DIFFERENCES ARE OR ARE NOT REAL 768

CORRELATION AND PREDICTION 770

THE MISUSE OF STATISTICS: NUMBERS DON'T LIE ... OR DO THEY? 771
Random Events Don't Always Seem Random 771
Large Samples Provide a Better Basis for Reaching Conclusions Than Small Ones 772

Unbiased Samples Provide a Better Basis for Reaching Conclusions Than Biased Ones 772
Unexpressed Comparisons are Often Meaningless 773
Some Differences Aren't Really There 773
Graphs May Distort (or at Least Bend) Reality 773

SUMMARY AND REVIEW OF KEY POINTS 775

REFERENCES 777

GLOSSARY 817

NAME INDEX 830

SUBJECT INDEX 839

PHOTO CREDITS 847

Preface

Psychology is much more than a scientific field or a collection of findings and principles: It is also an invaluable perspective for understanding ourselves, other people, our relationships with them, and just about everything else that really matters to most of us most of the time. It is, in short, an eminently useful field, with important practical benefits for anyone wise enough to use it, or at least to adopt it as a personal framework. It is no exaggeration to state that psychology should be part of everyone's education and, ultimately, everyone's life. With it, and the knowledge it provides, we gain enhanced insight into virtually every aspect of our experience. Without it, we must struggle along, constantly puzzled by our own reactions, others' behavior, and many aspects of daily existence.

Because of the practical as well as the scientific value of psychology, this text is designed to do more than simply present a broad and up-to-date introduction to the field. It seeks to bring the *usefulness* of psychology sharply into focus, to illustrate its relevance and application to daily life—everyone's daily life. In order to attain this goal, this text has incorporated many new features. These and other changes are summarized below.

SPECIAL FEATURES RELATED TO THE BOOK'S MAJOR THEME

This new edition has many features designed to contribute to the theme described above. The most important of these are as follows.

MAKING PSYCHOLOGY PART OF YOUR LIFE

These special sections illustrate how readers can actually apply the information presented in each chapter to their own lives. The features cover a wide range of topics, including the following:

Chapter 3   The Danger of Stereo Headsets: Let's Turn Down the Volume

Chapter 6   Improving Your Memory: Some Useful Steps

Chapter 9   Preparing for Tomorrow's Job Market Today

Chapter 10   Getting Motivated: Some Practical Techniques

Chapter 12   How Accurate Is Your Self-Concept?

Chapter 16   Enhancing the Accuracy of Your Social Judgments

CANADIAN FOCUS

These special sections outline distinctive contributions in applications, problem analysis, and research made by psychologists in Canada.

THE POINT OF IT ALL

These special sections—virtually all of which are new to this edition—illustrate the implications and applications of psychology's findings and principles to important practical issues. Here are a few examples:

Chapter 2   Using Knowledge of Synaptic Transmission to Treat Addictions: Fighting Fire with Fire

Chapter 6   Repression: Do We Sometimes Forget Because We Want to Forget?

Chapter 8   Attention-Deficit Hyperactivity Disorder: Kids Who Really *Can't* Sit Still

Chapter 9   Overcoming the Odds: Adolescents in High-Risk Environments

Chapter 12   The Atlas Personality

Chapter 16   Practical Uses of Dissonance: Hypocrisy and the Alteration of Societally Important Attitudes

Chapter 17   Computers at Work

PERSPECTIVES ON DIVERSITY

This new feature takes account of the growing interest among psychologists in cultural diversity, and the fact that most readers of this text are likely to encounter increasing cultural diversity themselves in the years ahead. Understanding the role of cultural and ethnic factors in behavior, therefore, is crucial to applying psychology to everyday life. Here is a sampling of topics covered in the new diversity sections:

Chapter 2   The Biological Basis of Gender Differences

Chapter 4   Culture and the Interpretation of Dreams

Chapter 6   Culture and Memory: Remembering What Fits with Our Cultural Schemas

Chapter 7   When Culture Shapes Reasoning—or At Least Influences Its Outcomes

Chapter 9   Menopause: The Role of Cultural Factors

Chapter 10   The Role of Cultural Factors in Aggression: The Social Context of Violence

Chapter 14   Taking Account of Cultural Factors in Psychological Disorders: Improvements in the DSM-IV

Chapter 17   Negative Effects of Gender Stereotypes: Why Men Often Get the Job

SPECIAL FEATURES DESIGNED TO ENHANCE LEARNING

In addition to the features described above, this new edition incorporates many features designed to enhance learning.

KEY POINTS

Each major section ends with a capsule overview of the key points covered, designed to catch the reader's attention. These points provide readers with frameworks for organizing—and hence retaining—chapter content.

THE RESEARCH PROCESS

These sections are designed to illustrate the process of psychological research:

- How psychologists use research to answer important questions about human behavior
- Why one line of research leads to others
- How the findings of psychological research are interpreted and contribute to the development of accurate theories

Most Research Process sections now include critical thinking questions designed to get students actively thinking about the process of psychological research and how it is used to add to our knowledge of human behavior. Again, a wide range of topics is covered in these sections, for example:

Chapter 3   DANGER—Warnings Are Effective Only under Certain Conditions; Develop Them with CAUTION

Chapter 5   Stimulus Control in Action: Promoting Paper Waste Recycling on a University Campus

Chapter 7   Animal Cognition: Tails of Intelligence

Chapter 9   Age, Intelligence, Wisdom, and Creativity: Change or Stability Across the Lifespan?

Chapter 11   Integrating the Evolutionary and Social Exchange Models of Mate Preferences: Taking Account of Our Own "Market Value"

Chapter 13   Changing Risky Behaviors: An Ounce of Prevention Is the Only Known Cure

Chapter 15   Subliminal Self-Help Audiotapes: Do They Deliver What They Promise?

KEY CONCEPT PAGES

The special Key Concept pages are designed to accomplish two goals:

1. They illustrate concepts and principles students often find difficult to understand (for example, the difference between punishment and negative reinforcement).
2. They summarize and integrate topics covered in the text—for example, contrasting theories of emotion.

In short, they are graphically appealing, informative, and useful aids to learning.

CHAPTER OPENINGS

Chapters typically start by asking readers to consider a number of interesting questions about the topics being covered. This engages their interest immediately. A detailed road map to the chapter contents also is provided.

CRITICAL THINKING QUESTIONS

Critical Thinking Questions typically appear in three locations:

1. Integrated within the regular text (readers are often asked to think about various aspects of behavior and predict what they or others might do in a given situation)
2. Within Research Process sections
3. At the end of each chapter

These questions are designed to stimulate critical thinking—an important goal for any psychology text.

NEW TOPICS WITHIN CHAPTERS

So many new topics have been included that we could not possibly list all of them here. Here is a sampling:

Evolutionary Perspective
Ethical Issues in the Practice of Psychology

Interpreting Diverse Results: Meta-Analysis and
the Search for an Overall Pattern

Multiple (Cognitive) Resource Theory

Warning Labels: When Are They Effective?

New Findings on the Effects of Pleasant
Fragrances on Behavior

Potential Benefits of Increased Self-Consciousness

Dreams of Absent-Minded Transgression: Their
Role in Quitting Smoking and Reducing
Alcohol Consumption

Stimulus Control of Behavior and Protecting the
Environment

Operant Conditioning and Seat Belt Use

Memory for the Time When a Past Event Occurred

Repression of Memories of Childhood Sexual
Abuse

The Oversight Bias in Reasoning

Artificial Intelligence and Neural Networks

Information Processing and Cognitive
Development

Cognitive Variability and Cognitive Development

Fathers and Attachment

Adolescent Invulnerability

Successful Development in High-Risk
Environments

Gender Differences in Sexual Jealousy

Effects of Mood on Information Processing

Gender Differences in Social Behavior, Mate
Selection, and Psychological Adjustment

The Neuroscience Approach to Intelligence

Sensation Seeking

The Potential "Downside" of High Self-Esteem

Stress from Natural and Human-Caused Disasters

Changing Risky Behaviors

DSM-IV

Post Traumatic Stress Disorder

Chronic Mental Illness and the Homeless

Settings for Therapy

Prevention of Psychological Disorders

Tilts in Social Cognition: Automatic Vigilance,
Motivated Skepticism

Troubled Relationships: When Love Dies

Human Factors: Design of Controls and Displays

Workplace Environments

In addition, coverage of genetic factors in behavior
and what has come to be termed *evolutionary psychology* has been increased considerably. These topics
are discussed in several chapters (including 2, 3, 8,
10, and 17).

ANCILLARIES

A complete teaching and learning package accompanies this text. The key elements are described below.

LEARNING AIDS FOR STUDENTS

- *Study Guide* offers a comprehensive, carefully structured learning guide to all of the important concepts in this text. Organized around chapter learning objectives, it includes a variety of book-specific exercises, review sections, and exercises to strengthen readers' critical thinking and application skills. In addition, the study guide contains practice tests for each chapter, which are coordinated with the test bank that accompanies the book.
- *Studying Psychology: A Manual for Success*, by Robert T. Brown, is a brief how-to manual designed to help students develop the skills needed to succeed in psychology and in other college-level courses. The down-to-earth techniques and ideas in this manual will help students develop effective strategies for studying, listening, learning from lectures, and preparing for exams.
- *Evaluating Psychological Information: Sharpening Your Critical Thinking Skills*, by James Bell, focuses on helping students evaluate research as they build their critical thinking skills through step-by-step exercises.
- *Psychology and Culture*, edited by Walter Lonner and Roy Malpass, is an entry-level, broad-based book of readings that serves as an introduction to the role of culture and ethnicity in human behavior. It features original articles by experts in the field.

SUPPLEMENTS FOR INSTRUCTORS

The *Instructor's Resource Manual* is designed to encourage student involvement and understanding. It includes teaching suggestions, examples, demonstrations, visual aids, learning objectives, critical thinking exercises, and more. The *Instructor's Resource Manual* provides step-by-step instructions, as well as ready-to-duplicate handouts for over 150 activities and demonstrations. It also includes detailed notes on lecture launchers, Chapter-at-a-Glance tables that show how to organize the many supplementary materials available for each chapter, and an array of additional teaching aids.

Also available are a superb set of acetate transparencies, an extensive computerized test item file; PsychScience, interactive computer simulations of real-life experiments; and CNN videos, Allyn and Bacon's exclusive Video Disc series related to various topics in psychology.

Please see your Allyn and Bacon sales representative for information about these ancillaries and more.

WHY PSYCHOLOGY MATTERS: REFLECTIONS OF ROBERT BARON— LONG-TERM BELIEVER

In the mid-1970s, when I was on the faculty of Purdue University, I had a friend named Sam. Sam was an analytical chemist and one of the most brilliant people I have ever known. But what Sam didn't know about *people* would fill several books. Let me give you an example.

Sam was perpetually having problems with his department's copy room. Many jobs he sent there were not done on time—a real problem for him since he constantly worked against tight deadlines. After listening to Sam moan about this problem over and over again, I asked him the following questions: (1) Did he ever bring his really important jobs to the copy room himself rather than sending them down with his secretary? (2) Did he ever thank the people involved when copies were ready on time? Sam was puzzled by my questions. He couldn't see any purpose in visiting the copy room in person, and his attitude about on-time jobs was simple: Why should he thank someone for simply doing his or her job?

When I suggested that both of these steps might help, Sam seemed doubtful. But he was open-minded; so he promised to give them a try.

Several weeks later, he reported that they did seem to help. In fact, he said, after he thanked the copy-room staff in person a few times, a miraculous change occurred: They began to put his work on top of the stack rather than on the bottom. Sam was happy about this change, but confused about *why* it had occurred. When I described the basic principles of reinforcement to him, he listened in rapt attention. Here, I could tell, was something entirely new for Sam, world-class scientist though he was. Yes, Sam was brilliant, but as he himself admitted, he almost never thought about people.

I haven't seen my friend Sam in many years, but I'm tempted to dedicate this book to him. To me, he is a perfect illustration of the importance of psychology and of why everyone—top-notch scientists included—needs a basic, working knowledge of it. Psychology, I have long believed, is much more than a scientific field or a collection of findings and principles: It is also an invaluable perspective for understanding ourselves, other people, our relationships with them, and just about everything else that really matters to most of us most of the time. It is, in short, an eminently useful field, with important practical benefits for anyone wise enough to use it, or at least to adopt it as a personal framework. So, it's no exaggeration to state that I strongly believe in the theme of this new edition: *making psychology part of your life*.

Preface to the Canadian Edition

At the present time, an instructor in introductory psychology has many choices in selecting a textbook. The decision is not easy because most of the texts are remarkably similar in character and in content. This is hardly surprising. There is a common consensus about the basic body of material that is to be covered in an introductory course. It follows that a marked degree of similarity among texts is as certain as tomorrow.

All currently available texts also have in common the fact that they are standard American editions. The illustrations, demographics, place names, allusions to current events are inevitably set within the American context.

Is the present text simply another addition to the towering pile of introductory texts in the offices of most introductory psychology instructors? We think not. This one has been specifically tailored to meet the needs of students being introduced to psychology in Canada. That is because be believe students will be more attentive, comfortable and responsive to material that is directly relevant to them.

Let us make clear our objectives in tailoring the book lest our intentions be misunderstood. We recognize that the vast majority of research that continues to enrich the discipline is carried out in the United States and elsewhere, and these realities are well entrenched within this book. The coverage of traditional problems, theories and practices is complete.

What we have to offer that is special is a textbook set within the Canadian context. First, this means Canadian demographics, law, public figures, scientists, and even Canadian entertainers appear throughout. Canadian place names, institutions, culture and language are very apparent. There are graphs, charts, images and illustrations drawn from Canadian sources.

Bruce Earhard

Marcia Ozier

Second, there are significant differences in the development and practice of psychology in Canada and the United States. Psychology came later to Canada than to the United States, and different significant figures populate the early Canadian landscape. We think Canadian students should know something about the development and practice of psychology in Canada. We think they should know something about who the psychologists in Canada are, and what they do. There are other differences. For example, ethical codes, and the legal system within which they operate are not the same in Canada and in the United States. Forces influencing deinstitutionalization of mental hospitals and community service organizations available to deal with these changes are different in Canada than in the United States. Canada has mental health services in isolated areas of the far North that are not shared by the United States. There are problems with respect to outrageous suicide rates in isolated areas that are unique to Canada. In short, there are many distinctly Canadian issues and problems that are both relevant and important.

Third, wherever possible, and appropriate, we have referred to the findings of Canadian researchers. You will find their studies and their faces from cover to cover. Our objective is not, however, to exaggerate the contributions of Canadian psychologists. We are not trying to Canadianize psychology. Our purpose is to offer students studying in Canada an opportunity to appreciate the degree to which the study of psychology flourishes in this country, and to gain some insight into the scope, diversity, and character of psychological research carried out at Canadian institutions.

We recognize that there are some who will look upon efforts to provide a Canadian edition of an introductory psychology textbook with misgivings. We had ours when we began to prepare this material. We have since come to believe that providing a Canadian textbook to introduce students in Canada to the science of psychology is important.

What reinforced that belief was a survey of introductory psychology students at Dalhousie University. We asked them to indicate in writing whether they preferred an American text similar to the one they were currently using or a comparable text that used Canadian demographics, place names, illustrations and examples and singled out, where possible, significant contributions of Canadian researchers. Of 399 students, 337 expressed a preference for a Canadian edition.

Students are often not consulted about textbook adoptions. We suggest, however, that you ask your students what they would prefer. Our hope is that you and your students gain as much from reading this Canadian edition as we did from writing it.

Bruce Earhard and Marcia Ozier
Halifax, N.S., December 1994.

Acknowledgments

It took the combined efforts of many special people to produce this Canadian adaptation of Robert Baron's *Psychology*.

First, there are our colleagues in psychological science who contributed, through their publications and prepublications, their hypotheses, their results, and their conclusions, and in many cases their faces as well.

Second, there are the student researchers: Janice Lantz, Derrick Enslow, Jennifer Bird, and Pamela Cochrane. Each in their own way, these senior undergraduates took ownership of this project. Their ingenuity, their initiative, and their collective energy carried us along when we might have faltered. Their expertise on Psychlit, Medline, CBCA, and other databases (also Telnet and Gopher) is incredible. No subject is safe from their search strategies: no e-mail address/addresse electronique is too difficult to find. As well, their good humor was constant. We had fun together, and we thank them for that. Jan MacQuarrie, Rachel Earhard and Jeff Strug (with legal research) helped too.

Third, there are the people connected with Allyn and Bacon Canada: Yolanda de Rooy, Cliff Newman, Marta Tomins, Imogen Brian, Matthew Kudelka, Emily Meetsma, Bruce Bond, Carole Giguère, Theresa Thomas, and Glen Gordon are the ones we know about. Likely there are others whom we never met.

These are outstanding professionals to whom we credit the initiative, the development, the editing, the coordination, the photographs, the art, the design, and the production of this textbook. The talent of Matthew Kudelka is evident on every page.

We recognize with special thanks also the cooperation of Robert A. Baron, and the support of Bill Barke, Susan Badger, and many others at Allyn & Bacon (USA). The work of Emer Andrews at the Memorial University of Newfoundland for the Study Guide and the Instructor's Testbank is acknowledged here as well.

Fourth, there are the librarians: at the Killam, MacDonald Science, Weldon Law, and Kellog Medical libraries at Dalhousie; and at St. Mary's University, Mount Saint Vincent University, Halifax Regional Library (main branch reference room), the Nova Scotia legislature; and at Statistics Canada in Halifax.

Fifth, there are the associations and societies that provided information as fast as a fax could fly: The Addiction Research Foundation (Toronto), the Canadian Heart and Stroke Foundation (Nova Scotia), the Nova Scotia, Ontario, and British Columbia Head Injury Associations, the Canadian Mental Health Association (Nova Scotia), the Canadian Cancer Society (Nova Scotia Division), the American Cancer Society (Washington, D.C., and Portland, Oregon), AIDS Nova Scotia and AIDS Canada, Sport Nova Scotia, the National Eating Disorder Information Centre, the Nova Scotia Confederation of University Faculty Associations, the Nova Scotia Heart Health Program, the Nova Scotia Department of Health, Drug Dependency Services. The staff at the Ontario Psychological Association, and the Registry of Ontario Psychologists helped too.

Sixth, there are many of Canada's newspapers, each of which is remarkable in its own way. In particular, however, we single out *The Globe and Mail* and the *Vancouver Sun* for the breadth and depth of their coverage. We thank them for their obvious respect for Canadian readers and for their welcome assumption that we are bright, interested, and open to all kinds of new information.

For extraordinary assistance, we acknowledge the editorial staff of the *Express* (in St. John's) and the *Whitehorse Star Daily*, and the photography departments of *Yellowknife News/North*, the *Ottawa Citizen* and the *San Antonio Examiner News*.

For his unique contribution, we acknowledge the outstanding work of Paul Taylor, medical reporter for *The Globe and Mail*.

Finally, we thank the students of Psychology 1000 at Dalhousie who told us—in numbers we could not have imagined when we began—that a project like this was well worth doing.

Bruce Earhard and Marcia Ozier

Special Request to Readers of This Book

Here are our e-mail addresses.
Please: Let us know how you like the book and how
we can make it better.

BEARHARD@AC.DAL.CA

MOZIER@AC.DAL.CA

Psychology

Its Nature, Scope, and Methods

Psychology: What It Is and How It
Developed 5
Philosophy and Science: The Dual Roots of
  Modern Psychology
Psychology: Some Early Views
Psychology During the Twentieth Century:
  How It Developed and Grew
Modern Psychology: Some Key
  Perspectives
Psychology in a Diverse World:
  Multicultural and Gender Issues
Psychology: Some Basic Questions

Psychology: Who and What 18
Who: The Background and Training of
  Psychologists
What: Specialties Within Psychology

Adding to What We Know: The Process of
Psychological Research 21
Naturalistic Observation: Scientists as
  Explorers
Case Studies: Generalizing from the Unique
Surveys: The Science of Self-Report
The Correlational Method: Knowledge
  Through Systematic Observation
Experimentation: Knowledge Through
  Systematic Intervention
Interpreting Research Results: Statistics as
  a Tool
The Role of Theory in Psychological
  Research

Ethical Issues in Psychology 33
Deception: Is It Ever Appropriate for
  Psychologists to Lie to Research
  Participants?
Research with Animals: Is It Acceptable?
Ethical Issues in the Practice of Psychology

Using This Book: A Note on Its Features 39
Using the Knowledge in This Book: Some
  Tips on How to Study

Summary and Review of Key Points 44

Key Concept—Correlational and
Experimental Research Methods 30

Making Psychology Part of
Your Life—Practice in Critical Thinking:
The Hidden Bonus in Introductory
Psychology 42

BEING NUMBER 1—WITH A SINGLE-HOLER

MacLean's Magazine:
June 8, 1992

In 1992, for the first time, Canada was rated by the United Nations as the best place in the world to live.

Maclean's judged this a "most stunning event," although Canada has won

world championships before: in hockey, in olympic-sized pumpkins, in cross-border shopping, and in producing Saskatoon berries.

In Chapter 1 you will begin a very special introduction to psychology—one that is clearly Canadian.

You will find that for those of us who live north of the 49th Parallel—in the best place in the world to live—psychological science is alive and well, and relevant to every one of our very own lives.

PSYCHOLOGISTS SEEK
TO OBTAIN SCIENTIFIC
INFORMATION ON
VIRTUALLY EVERY
IMAGINABLE ASPECT
OF HUMAN BEHAVIOR.

Do the things other people do and say ever surprise you? Are you sometimes puzzled by your own thoughts, feelings, or reactions? Do you wonder what you'll be like in five years or ten years? Or think about how you compare with other people in terms of your intelligence, personality traits, happiness, or psychological adjustment? If so, then welcome to the club: Most people spend a lot of time pondering just such issues.

What most of us do on a part-time basis with respect to our own lives and experiences, psychologists pursue as a full-time career. They seek to obtain scientific information on virtually every imaginable aspect of human behavior—everything from how our senses function and how memory operates to why we fall in love, what factors or conditions motivate us to work hard, and why we become depressed. In fact, as you can see in Table 1.1, the field of psychology is so broad in scope that one can claim, with some confidence, that psychologists are currently studying every question about human behavior you have ever contemplated—and many you have probably not yet considered.

One major goal of this book, therefore, is to acquaint you with the knowledge psychologists have attained through the systematic study of human behavior. There are many specialties in psychology, and psychologists in these subfields have focused on different aspects of behavior—on memory, human development, and psychological disorders, to name just three major areas. Reflecting this fact, each chapter will focus on a different aspect of behavior. But since the overall objective is to present an integrated view of psychology, this text will also try to indicate how these various aspects of behavior are related, and how ideas and concepts reported in one portion of the book are related to those in other portions.

A second, and equally important, goal stems from the assumption that psychology is not just a scientific field of study—it is also an eminently *useful* and *practical* one. In other words, you should be able to profit greatly from applying to your own life the information presented in this text. In keeping with this view, we will draw attention consistently to the practical aspects of psychology's findings, and how, perhaps, you can apply them. Thus, an important theme of this book is **Making Psychology Part of Your Life,** and you'll see this theme reflected in many ways in every chapter.

Before turning to the findings of modern psychology and its potential uses, we must first acquaint you with some basic facts about the nature and scope of the field. One important reason for doing so is suggested by the findings of psychological research on memory and thinking (covered in Chapters 6 and 7). This research indicates that having a mental framework in which to place new information makes it easier to understand, remember, and use. The goal of this chapter is to provide you with the background material you need to construct a framework that will help you to organize and understand new information about psychology as it is presented. To make the material covered familiar and meaningful to you, we will use, wherever possible, Canadian examples, practices, and statistics. Let's begin with an overview of this chapter.

First, we will provide a brief summary of psychology's history, followed by an outline of the scope and nature of present-day psychology. We will make note of psychology's growing sensitivity to multicultural and gender issues. Key questions that many students ask when encountering psychology for the first time will be answered (for example, is it really scientific?). Second, we will comment briefly on modern psychologists—who they are and what they do. Third, and perhaps most important, we will describe the methods psychologists use in their research—the techniques used to gain

TOPIC/ISSUE	CHAPTER
Why do some people have so much difficulty regulating their weight?	2
How can we perform two activities at once—such as driving while talking to a friend?	3
What is hypnotism? Is everyone susceptible to it?	4
Can we learn simply by watching others?	5
Does being in a good mood increase creativity?	7
How do children acquire a sense of morality?	8
Do people become less intelligent as they age?	9
Can changes In our facial expressions influence our moods?	10
What factors influence our self-image and our self-esteem?	11
What are the most important dimensions of personality—the most central traits?	12
Why are some people so much more resistant to stress than others?	13
What is schizophrenia? What are its causes?	14
Does psychoanalysis really work? Or are there more effective kinds of therapy?	15
Can our attitudes be changed by information of which we are not aware?	16
Why do people often do better at various tasks when they have specific goals for their own performance?	17

TABLE 1.1

The Breadth of Psychological Research

As shown here, psychologists are currently investigating almost every imaginable aspect of human behavior.

new insights into various aspects of behavior. At this point, we will consider some of the *ethical issues* psychologists face in their research and in the practice of their profession. We will follow this with a description of this text—how it is organized, some special features it contains, and how these can help your studying. Finally, we will consider what you, as an individual, can hope to gain from your first exposure to psychology. Included here will be a discussion of **critical thinking**—the ability to make objective judgments about statements and claims, judgments based on careful reasoning and close scrutiny of available facts. As you'll see throughout this text, critical thinking is an essential ingredient in psychology, and learning to think like a psychologist (at least where questions about behavior are concerned) is one of the most important benefits you will gain from this text and from your first course in this field.

Psychology: What It Is and How It Developed

What, exactly, is psychology? As you'll soon see, the definition has changed and evolved during its relatively short history. Today we define **psychology** as *the science of behavior and cognitive processes*. In other words, psychologists are concerned with obtaining scientific information on everything we (and other living organisms) think, feel, and do. They examine observable behavior, cognitive processes, physiological events, social and cultural influences, and hidden and largely unconscious processes. They also look at the complex interactions between all of these different factors in order to understand behavior.

Critical Thinking: *Careful assessment of available evidence in order to evaluate claims and statements in an objective and reasoned manner.*

Psychology: *The science of behavior and cognitive processes.*

How did the field of psychology come to exist? In movies and television shows, scientists are sometimes represented as magnificent loners—geniuses who work in isolation and develop major breakthroughs out of their own creative spirit. While this sometimes occurs, another pattern is more frequent: Progress flows naturally from what went before. Modern psychology is no exception to this general rule. When it emerged as an independent field of study in the late nineteenth century, it had important roots in several other disciplines, ranging from philosophy on the one hand to biology and physiology on the other.

Philosophy and Science: The Dual Roots of Modern Psychology

From philosophy came two important influences: (1) the logical underpinnings of science—that is, ideas concerning the ways in which we can acquire valid knowledge about the natural world; and (2) ideas concerning the relationship between mind (mental events) and body. With respect to the philosophy of science, two very important ideas were *empiricism,* the view that knowledge can be gathered through careful observation, and *rationalism,* the view that knowledge can be gained through logic and careful reasoning. During the eighteenth and early nineteenth centuries these two traditions combined with other lines of philosophical thought to yield the basic ground rules of modern science. Psychology took shape as an independent field of study when a number of scientists with training in such fields as biology, physiology, and medicine concluded that the methods of science could be applied to the understanding of many aspects of behavior.

Turning to the mind–body issue, seventeenth-century philosophers rejected the idea that mind and body are separate (a view known as *dualism*) and suggested, instead, that they interact: Mental events can influence physical ones and physical events can influence mental ones. This view, known as *interactionism,* is a key principle in modern psychology, as you'll see when we consider the complex relationship between feelings and thought in Chapter 10.

In short, psychology emerged when (1) ideas in philosophy—especially ideas about how new knowledge can be acquired and about the relationship

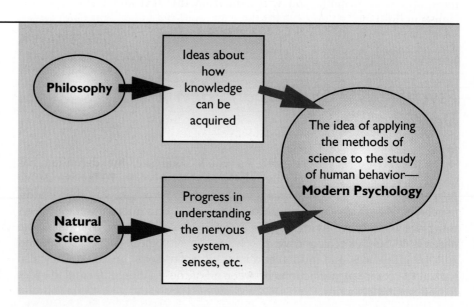

FIGURE 1.1

The Dual Roots of Psychology

Psychology emerged as an independent field of study when ideas from philosophy (about how valid knowledge of the natural world can be obtained) were applied by scientists in other fields to the task of understanding human behavior.

Philosophy → Ideas about how knowledge can be acquired

Natural Science → Progress in understanding the nervous system, senses, etc.

The idea of applying the methods of science to the study of human behavior—**Modern Psychology**

**Wilhelm Wundt
(1832–1920)**

Wundt is considered by many to be the founder of psychology. He developed the first widely accepted school of thought, structuralism, which focused on the inner workings of consciousness. In 1879 he opened the first psychology laboratory at the University of Leipzig in Germany.

**William James
(1842–1910)**

James is known as the first North American psychologist. He authored the first widely used psychology textbook, *Principles of Psychology*, in 1890. He led the movement of *functionalism*, which focused on how and why the mind functions.

**John B. Watson
(1878–1958)**

Watson, one of the most preeminent North American psychologists, moved psychology away from studying the contents of the mind to studying only observable behavior, an approach known as *behaviorism*.

PSYCHOLOGISTS OF NOTE

between mind and body—and (2) progress in several scientific fields combined to create an environment in which the idea of the scientific study of human behavior could emerge (see Figure 1.1).

As is true of all new fields, however, psychology did not spring into existence fully formed; nor was there agreement among its early founders as to just what the new science should be or what it should study. On the contrary, early psychologists disagreed sharply about these issues. These disagreements played an important role in shaping the nature of our modern field.

Psychology: Some Early Views

Perhaps a useful way of illustrating important shifts in how psychologists have defined their field is to imagine a conversation between three major figures in the history of the field. Wilhelm Wundt was the founder of the first psychological laboratory (1879); William James wrote an early influential text, *Principles of Psychology,* and had a lasting impact on the field; and John B. Watson founded an approach that dominated the field until well into the twentieth century. (Please note that this conversation is purely imaginary. There is no indication that these people ever met face to face. If they had, however, they might well have made comments such as these.)

WUNDT   In my opinion, psychology should focus on the study of conscious experience. Our task is that of analyzing sensations, feelings, and images in their most basic parts, just as chemists analyze complex substances. In that way, we'll come to understand the nature of the human mind—what it is. We can accomplish this through introspection—asking individuals to describe what is going on in their own minds as they perform various tasks or have specific experiences.

JAMES   I disagree. The mind isn't static. It is always changing. Also, it is useful—probably the most useful thing we possess. So the key task for psychology should be understanding how the mind functions in everyday life—how it works, and how it helps us adapt to a complex and ever-changing world. To understand the human mind, we have to study how it functions. We need to know how people form habits, how they form their ideas of their own selves, and how they experience emotions. Identifying the basic components of the mind is interesting, but it provides only part of the total picture.

WATSON   You're both all wet. We can't see "mind" or "conscious experience." All we can observe is overt behavior. And people can't report accurately what goes on in their "minds"—whatever those are! The idea of using introspection as a research method to build our new science is ridiculous. Overt behavior is the only thing we can observe or measure scientifically, so that should be the focus of psychology.

As you can readily see, these three individuals held sharply contrasting beliefs about the nature of psychology. Wundt was the chief advocate of **structuralism**: the view that psychology should focus on conscious experience and on the task of breaking down such experience into its basic parts. In contrast, James was a vigorous supporter of **functionalism**: the view that psychology should study the ways in which our ever-changing stream-of-conscious experience helps us adapt to, and survive in, a complex and challenging world. And Watson was the foremost spokesperson for **behaviorism**: the view that psychology should focus solely on observable, overt activities, ones that can be measured in a scientific manner. Events and processes going on "inside," such as thoughts, images, feelings, and intentions, have no place in the field.

Which view prevailed? For many years, Watson's behaviorism was dominant—the view that psychology should focus solely on aspects of behavior that can be directly observed and measured. Indeed, for almost sixty years psychology was defined, by and large, as the science of behavior. While this strong emphasis on observable behavior persists, the scope of modern psychology broadened considerably during the 1960s and 1970s, to include many topics Watson and other early behaviorists would not have included in the field. What are these topics, and how did psychology evolve into its present, eclectic, form? To see, let's briefly consider the history of psychology during the twentieth century.

Structuralism: An early view suggesting that psychology should focus on conscious experience and on the task of analyzing such experience into its basic parts.

Functionalism: An early view of psychology suggesting that psychology should study the ways in which the ever-changing stream of conscious experience helps us adapt to a complex and challenging world.

Behaviorism: The view that psychology should study only observable behavior.

Psychology During the Twentieth Century: *How It Developed and Grew*

Watson unfurled the banner of behaviorism in the early 1920s. Yet much important work had been completed by psychologists before that time. For example, tests to measure intelligence and other human characteristics had already been devised and put to practical use (Binet & Simon, 1905). Sigmund Freud had already published much of his famous work on human personality and psychological disorders (Freud, 1901, 1915). And much had already been learned about the functioning of our senses (Fechner, 1860) and the operation of human memory (Ebbinghaus, 1913).

In the decades that followed, the pace of progress within psychology accelerated sharply. During the 1930s and 1940s, C.L. Hull, B.F. Skinner, and other behaviorists uncovered much new information about learning and related topics (Hull, 1943; Skinner, 1953). Important work on conformity, leadership, and other aspects of social behavior was done during the same period (e.g., Sherif, 1935; Lewin, 1947). In the 1950s the scope of psychology expanded greatly, and major advances were made in human development (Piaget, 1954), motivation (McClelland et al., 1953), functioning of the human brain (Lashley, Chow, & Semmes, 1951), and many other subfields.

The 1960s brought the emergence of many new interests and subfields. One of these was *environmental psychology*—the study of how behavior is affected by the physical world around us (see Chapter 17). Another was *psychology and law*—a field that focuses on how basic psychological processes (such as memory, perception, and social influence) can, and do, affect the legal process (see Chapter 6). In addition, of course, rapid progress continued in existing areas of research.

During the 1970s and 1980s, psychology, in a sense, came fully into its own. It gained increasing recognition as an active and valuable branch of science. Moreover, its scope expanded even further with the emergence of such new fields and specialties as *adult development* (development and change during the adult years; see Chapter 9), *gender differences* (differences between the sexes; see Chapters 2 and 11), and *health psychology* (the impact of various psychological factors on physical health; see Chapter 13). Many other lines of research, too numerous to mention here, also emerged during these exciting decades. The result is that psychology has now expanded its scope to the point where it studies virtually every question about human behavior you can possibly imagine—and then some.

By design, this capsule overview of the history of psychology is extremely brief. However, the information presented here should provide you with at least a rough idea of how the field has grown and developed during the twentieth century. See Figure 1.2 for a capsule summary of the historical development of psychology in Canada.

Modern Psychology: Some Key Perspectives

Psychology is the science of behavior and cognitive processes. Psychologists seek to obtain systematic information about all aspects of behavior—with behavior being very broadly defined—through the use of scientific methods. In order to obtain complete and accurate answers to the complex questions with which they grapple (refer to Table 1.1), psychologists have found it useful to study behavior from several different perspectives. The most important of these are described next.

THE BEHAVIORAL PERSPECTIVE   In an important sense, the behaviorist tradition is still very much alive and well in modern psychology. Indeed, most psychologists agree that only aspects of behavior that can be carefully measured, either directly or indirectly, have a place in the scientific field of psychology. Further, most agree that only concepts that can be related to observable

FIGURE 1.2

Canadian Focus: Highlights in the Growth of Canadian Psychology

1838 The first course in psychology, focusing on the philosophical writings of Thomas Reid, is taught by Thomas McCulloch of Dalhousie College in Halifax (Wright & Myers, 1982).

1850s Teaching of pre-scientific psychology begins at McGill University and the University of Toronto.

1885 The first psychology text to be written in Canada is published: *The Intellect, the Emotions and the Moral Nature* by the Rev. William Lyall of the Free Church College in Halifax.

1889 James Mark Baldwin, considered to be Canada's first modern psychologist, joins the University of Toronto. Schooled in experimental procedures by Wundt, he develops a psychological laboratory and an experimental psychology curriculum at Toronto.

1909 Psychology courses are introduced by the philosophy departments of the universities of Alberta and Saskatchewan.

1915 The University of British Columbia opens its doors, but resources permit only a single psychology course to be offered (through the Department of Philosophy) for the next eleven years.

1920s In central Canada, psychology departments begin to separate from philosophy departments and emerge as distinct academic entities. McGill and Toronto make this separation first. Other universities do not follow until decades later (Wright & Myers, 1982).

1939 The Canadian Psychological Association, a national organization of psychologists, is founded. Up to this time, research in Canadian psychology tended to focus on applied issues, especially in the area of mental health. With the outbreak of World War II, research is directed to problems associated with the war effort, particularly personnel selection and training.

1941 The University of Ottawa establishes the first bilingual program in psychology. A year later, the first French-language program in psychology is introduced by the Institute of Psychology at the University of Montreal (Granger, 1993).

---

aspects of behavior are useful to their work. For example, consider the question of what motivates people to work hard—to expend effort on their jobs. This is a key question studied by *industrial/organizational psychologists*, who are interested in all aspects of behavior in work settings. As you'll see in Chapter 10, we can't observe such *work motivation* directly; it is an internal state that we assume exists inside people and affects their overt behavior— for example, how long and hard they work at a given task. But we *can* observe the conditions we believe may influence motivation, such as the extent to which good performance is rewarded, and the changes in overt behavior that appear to be linked to motivation, such as actual output, number of errors, and so on. In sum, modern psychology still focuses a great deal of attention on overt behavior, which remains an important perspective within the field.

THE COGNITIVE PERSPECTIVE   Consider the following incident. You have been asked to write a letter of recommendation for someone. How do you proceed? Probably, by thinking about this individual and bringing many incidents to mind. From these you try to extract some basic themes (e.g., she is intelligent; she is conscientious). Notice that you don't select just any themes or bring just any incidents to mind. Rather, since this is a letter of recommendation, you tend to focus on positive experiences and events—ones that will help you write a good, supportive letter. If for some reason you have great

1946–60 Returning veterans strain the resources of Canadian universities, especially their psychology departments. The Macleod Report decries the "premature professionalization" of psychology. Hebb and others champion a return to basic scientific research at the Opinicon Conference on Research Training in Psychology. Increased federal funding becomes available to support basic research.

1960s In the late 1950s and 1960s, unparalleled growth occurs in Canadian universities. A strong economy, and a flood of applications from the children of World War II veterans and the immigrants who entered Canada in large numbers after the war, forces expansion. In Ontario, ten new universities are opened. In Atlantic Canada, Memorial University and the University of Prince Edward Island assume their present form. In British Columbia, construction of Simon Fraser University begins, and Victoria College becomes the University of Victoria. A corresponding growth in community colleges takes place across the country. The availability of funding for research permits Canadian researchers to achieve international significance, and there is an explosive growth of interest in psychology as an area of study (Wright & Myers, 1982).

1990s Canadian researchers continue to distinguish themselves in the world of science. Psychology department enrollments are now among the largest in most colleges and universities. In 1966 a total of 1,337 undergraduate degrees in psychology were granted (Appley & Rickward, 1967). In 1991–92, according to Statistics Canada, 7,369 degrees were awarded, and 23,184 undergraduates and 2,411 graduate students were enrolled in psychology programs. Since the late 1970s, when Statistics Canada began reporting the gender of students registered in psychology programs, women have outnumbered men. There are three times as many women in undergraduate programs and more than twice as many in graduate programs. This has yet to be reflected among university instructors. An examination of staffing figures provided by twenty-eight Canadian departments of psychology for the 1992 graduate studies guide of the American Psychological Association shows that women held only about 19 percent of full-time faculty positions.

---

difficulty in remembering favorable incidents, your friend is in serious trouble! In any case, since you can only include in the letter information you recall, the workings of your memory are crucial to carrying out this task in the way you (and your friend) desire.

Events like this one indicate that if we wish to understand people and how they behave, we must pay careful attention to **cognitive processes**: the ways in which people think, remember, decide, and so on. Indeed, many would argue that attempting to understand behavior without attention to cognitive processes is akin to trying to solve a complex jigsaw puzzle from which many of the most important pieces have been removed.

THE PSYCHODYNAMIC PERSPECTIVE   Do dreams have any meaning? Why do people often experience slips of the tongue, saying, for example, "I could have killed him!" when they meant to say, "I could have kissed him"? What accounts for the bizarre forms of behavior often attributed to "psychological disorders" or "mental illness"? According to the **psychodynamic perspective,** these and many other puzzling aspects of behavior stem from continuous, and largely unconscious, struggles among hidden forces deep within our personalities. The most famous advocate of this perspective, of course, was Sigmund Freud, whose views we'll discuss at several points in this book (Chapters 12, 14, and 15). However, even psychologists who disagree strongly with Freud's theories of human personality and mental disorders

Cognitive Processes: Mental activities involving the acquisition, representation, storage, retrieval, or use of information.

Psychodynamic Perspective: An approach suggesting that many aspects of behavior stem from hidden forces within our personalities.

PSYCHOLOGY: ITS NATURE, SCOPE, AND METHODS   **11**

accept the notion that behavior is often affected by forces, urges, and tendencies largely outside our conscious recognition. Consideration of these, too, is a part of modern psychology.

THE HUMANISTIC PERSPECTIVE   Is there such a thing as free will? For behaviorists this question is irrelevant, since they contend that behavior is *determined* by a wide range of internal and external factors. Other psychologists, however, believe that such factors do *not* rigidly shape our actions, feelings, or thoughts. Rather, they contend, we can choose how we behave, regardless of the pressures exerted by the environment in which we live. Further, psychologists who adhere to the **humanistic perspective** emphasize the importance of *personal growth*, which is that tendency in each of us to try to become the best person we can be. Only when external obstacles interfere is the growth process interrupted; in such cases, humanistic psychologists contend, we may experience various psychological disorders stemming from disruption of our normal growth.

While some psychologists find the optimism of the humanistic perspective appealing, many feel that the approach is somewhat vague and difficult to test. However, it has called attention to several key issues, such as the importance of a favorable self-concept and of continued growth and development throughout life. In these respects, humanistic psychology has been influential; it is certainly part of the rich tapestry of modern psychology.

THE BIOPSYCHOLOGICAL OR NEUROSCIENCE PERSPECTIVE   What happens inside your body when you think, listen to music, grow hungry, or become angry? And what takes place when you dream, experience anxiety, become sexually aroused, or simply read a text such as this one? Obviously, *something* must be occurring in all these cases; we are living beings, and every experience we have must be accompanied, at some level, by biological events. Activity in our brains and other parts of the nervous system, hormones released by our glands and the bodily changes these induce—such processes are intimately linked to everything we do, think, feel, and say (Carlson, 1993). Psychologists have long recognized this fact and generally agree that understanding these biological roots is an essential component of the field.

THE EVOLUTIONARY PERSPECTIVE   Does behavior stem primarily from inherited tendencies and related biological factors, or primarily from experience and learning? This question—often described as the **nature-nurture controversy**—has long been of interest to psychologists. Early behaviorists, of course, adopted a strict "nurture" position: They argued that behavior is entirely shaped by experience and the effects of learning. Indeed, in a famous quotation, Watson boasted that he could make any healthy infant into virtually any kind of adult simply by controlling all of that infant's experiences (Watson, 1924).

Modern psychologists generally reject such extreme views and adopt a much more balanced position with respect to the nature–nurture controversy. They realize that like all other species on our planet, human beings have an evolutionary history, which equips them with inherited tendencies or dispositions. It would be surprising if such tendencies played little or no role in our behavior. And in fact, growing evidence suggests that inherited dispositions do, indeed, exert important effects. Recognition of this fact has led to the emergence of the field of **evolutionary psychology**—a branch of psychology that studies the adaptive problems humans have faced over the course of evolution, and the behavioral mechanisms that have evolved in response to such environmental pressures (e.g., Nisbett, 1990).

Humanistic Perspective: A perspective in modern psychology suggesting that human beings have free will and are not simply under the control of various internal and external factors.

Nature-Nurture Controversy The question whether behavior stems from inherited tendencies and related biological factors, or from experience and learning.

Evolutionary Psychology: A branch of psychology that studies the adaptive problems humans faced over the course of evolution and the behavioral mechanisms that evolved in response to these environmental pressures.

CULTURE HAS A MAJOR IMPACT ON OUR BEHAVIOR

For example, the distance between two people holding a conversation varies across cultures. In some, a distance of about 1.3 meters is considered appropriate. In others, a much smaller distance is preferred.

Much of the research pointing to the potentially important role of genetic factors in human behavior is provided by the systematic study of identical twins who were separated very early in life. Even though such individuals are often raised in sharply contrasting environments and have very different life experiences, they tend to show a considerable—sometimes amazing—amount of similarity with respect to many aspects of behavior. Indeed, they are far more similar with respect to various personality traits, interests, and even attitudes than pairs of unrelated persons or even nonidentical twins (who, of course, don't share all the same genes as identical twins do) (e.g., Keller et al., 1992). We'll review additional evidence pointing to the potentially important role of genetic factors in human behavior at several points in this book (e.g., see Chapters 2, 8, 9, and 14).

THE SOCIOCULTURAL PERSPECTIVE   Imagine the following situation. A Canadian real estate agent is asked to find a suitable home for a high-ranking executive of a Japanese company that has just opened a plant in a large Canadian city. Confidently, she takes the vice-president and his wife to see a house in the fanciest subdivision in town. As they enter the subdivision, the executive becomes nervous; and as they approach the house, both he and his wife become visibly upset. In fact, they tell the agent that they do not wish to see the house but would prefer to see another one on the opposite side of town. The real estate agent is puzzled, because this house seems to be precisely what the executive and his wife are seeking. Why do they refuse to consider it? Later she finds out: The executive's boss lives in this subdivision, just down the block. From the Japanese perspective, buying a house in the same location would be viewed as inappropriate; in fact, it could be interpreted as an insult to the higher-ranking executive!

This incident provides one illustration of the fact that culture is a very important determinant of human behavior. In many cases, individuals' perceptions, feelings, and actions are strongly influenced by the social and cultural systems in which they live. In order to fully understand many aspects of behavior, therefore, one must take such factors into careful account. Psychologists have become increasingly aware of this fact in recent years and, as a result, have adopted an increasingly **multicultural perspective** on all of the topics they study (e.g., Smith & Bond, 1993). We'll return to some of the implications of this perspective below. (See Table 1.2 for an overview of these different perspectives.)

> **KEY POINTS**
>
> - Psychology is the science of behavior and cognitive processes.
> - Early psychologists differed sharply over the scope of their new field: Structuralists felt that psychology should seek to identify the basic parts of consciousness. Functionalists believed that psychology should focus on the adaptive value of the human mind. Behaviorists felt that psychology should focus primarily on observable behavior.
> - In their efforts to answer complex questions about behavior, psychologists have adopted several different perspectives, including the behavioral, cognitive, psychodynamic, humanistic, biopsychological, evolutionary, and sociocultural perspectives.

Multicultural Perspective: In modern psychology, a perspective that takes note of the fact that many aspects of behavior are strongly influenced by factors related to culture and ethnic identity.

TABLE 1.2

Major Perspectives of Modern Psychology

As indicated here, modern psychology includes many different perspectives or approaches within its boundaries.

PERSPECTIVE	MAJOR INTERESTS
Behavioral	Focuses on overt, observable behavior; concepts are viewed as useful only if they can be related to overt behavior.
Cognitive	Focuses on cognitive processes such as memory, thinking, decision-making. Often adopts an information-processing approach.
Psychodynamic	Emphasizes the role of internal forces and conflicts in behavior. Views many actions, and many forms of psychological disorders, as stemming from unconscious impulses or forces.
Humanistic	Emphasizes the importance of tendencies toward personal growth. Assumes that individuals have free will with respect to their own behavior.
Biopsychological	Relates behavior to biological and physiological events and processes, especially those occurring in the nervous system.
Evolutionary	Suggests that behavior is shaped to some extent by inherited tendencies and dispositions. Often focuses on the task of determining the relative importance of genetic factors and experience with respect to specific aspects of behavior.
Sociocultural	Focuses on the impact of cultural factors on various aspects of behavior. Recognizes that behavior is often strongly determined by such factors.

Psychology in a Diverse World: Multicultural and Gender Issues

The world has changed radically in the past century. One dramatic development has been the growth of cultural and ethnic diversity in the countries of the world. An equally profound change within many societies has been in the character of traditional gender roles. These changes are quite clear in Canada and the United States.

Shortly after Confederation, most Canadians were of either British (61 percent) or French (31 percent) background. By 1991, the proportion claiming British descent had dropped to 28 percent, and claiming French descent to 23 percent. Of the remaining population, 18 percent claimed French or English origin in combination with some other background, and 31 percent an ethnic origin that was neither French nor English. It is clear that Canada is no longer primarily an English and French country. No single group is a majority in the country as a whole (Dreidger, 1989; Kerr & Ram, 1994). Similar patterns are evident in the United States and Western Europe. For example, in 1960, approximately 90 percent of Americans were of European descent. At present, in the mid-1990s, this figure is about 80 percent and dropping quickly. It is projected that by the year 2050, it will be only 53 percent.

As far as changing gender roles are concerned, it should be remembered that in 1917 Canadian women could not vote in federal elections or run for federal office. In this period, less than 20 percent of women were involved in the workforce and domestic service was their most common paid occupation. The present situation is far different. In 1993, Canada had its first woman prime minister, and the current deputy prime minister is a woman. Involvement of women in the workforce had increased to 35 percent by the mid-1960s and to 58 percent by 1992.

What are the implications for psychology of this change in gender roles and this growing cultural diversity? In the view of many psychologists, they are

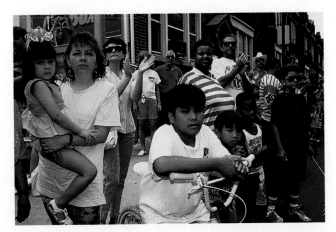

certain to be profound. Psychology has till now been primarily a North American- and European-based field: the major figures in psychology have been European and North American men. This is not likely to continue.

Changes have occurred already, especially in the area of gender equality. Psychology is no longer primarily a white male domain. As you will see shortly, most psychologists in modern Canada are women, and most of the advanced degrees granted in both Canada and the United States are now being awarded to women. This change was not achieved without struggle. Women psychologists encountered difficulties in both countries in the process of achieving full professional stature.

To briefly illustrate some of the difficulties encountered by Canadian women psychologists, consider the following account drawn from articles by Pyke and Stark-Ademac (1981) and Pyke (1992). They observe that as late as the early 1970s, program committees of the Canadian Psychological Association were reluctant to support presentation and discussion of issues relating to the psychology of women, gender issues, and sex role stereotyping at annual meetings. Editors of journals controlled by the association were similarly reluctant to publish papers on these issues.

Influential in changing these policies was the decision made by a group of women from York University to organize their own independent "underground" symposium in Montreal, to be held at the same time as the regular association meeting in 1972. The symposium proved popular, and signaled, as Kimball (1986) notes, that women members of the association were no longer going to remain silent about women's issues. Further steps were taken through the Committee on the Status of Women, formed in 1975. Many of the recommendations this committee made to the association were accepted. By the late 1970s, convention programming issues had been resolved and a permanent Status of Women Committee had been established. Other changes followed: Journal policies were changed to eliminate sexist language, and editorial practices were updated so that blind reviews were now required. Also, women were now entitled to representation on journal editorial boards, and on committees of the association, in numbers more in keeping with their membership in the association. In recent years more and more women have been assuming senior administrative functions. Between 1939 and 1975 only two women had been president of the association; by 1990, six had held this position.

The representation of various minority groups has not yet shown any substantial increase. There is, nevertheless, a growing awareness of multicultural issues within the field. Increased attention is being paid to the concerns of these groups and to all aspects of cultural diversity (e.g., Smith & Bond,

Norma V. Bowen
University of Guelph

Connie Stark-Adamec
University of Regina

1993). This attention has taken the form of an increased volume of research on the effects of ethnic and cultural factors on many aspects of behavior. Indeed, there is hardly an area of psychology in which research on such issues is not currently being conducted.

In addition, growing concern with multicultural diversity on the part of psychologists has led to the formulation of ethical guidelines in both Canada and the United States emphasizing the need to pay particular attention to ethnic and cultural factors in carrying out all professional and research activities. The code of ethics of the Canadian Psychological Association requires that psychologists "engage in self-reflection regarding how their own values, attitudes, experience and social context (e.g., culture, ethnicity, colour, religion, gender, sexual orientation, physical and mental ability level, age, and socioeconomic status) influence their actions, interpretations, choices, and recommendations." [Canadian Psychological Association, 1991]

A growing sensitivity to gender issues and cultural diversity does not imply that the situation is perfect, however—far from it. Recent evidence indicates that although there has been major change, there is still room for improvement. In one recent study, Gannon and her colleagues (1992) examined almost 5,000 articles published in major psychological journals between 1970 and 1990 to determine whether barriers against women had decreased during that period. Some of their results were highly encouraging. For example, as shown in Figure 1.3, the proportion of articles in which a female was first author increased dramatically during this period. Similarly, the use of sexist language (for example, using "he" to refer to both males and females) dropped to almost zero during these years. However, there was still some indication of sex bias even in 1990: Sex of participants was not specified in some articles, sexist language was used, and findings with one gender were extended to the other in an inappropriate fashion. Approximately 29 percent of the articles published in 1990 showed one or more of these flaws.

Psychology: *Some Basic Questions*

Definitions, it has often been said, are made to be challenged. Given that fact, we'll now consider some of the questions you may have about the suggestion that psychology be viewed as the science of behavior and cognitive processes.

Is PSYCHOLOGY REALLY SCIENTIFIC?   To start at the beginning, let's address a question often raised by students: Is psychology really scientific? Even today, some people seem to feel that this is not a science in the same sense as chemistry, physics, or biology. Such reservations may stem mainly from a basic misunderstanding about the meaning of the word *science*.

Some people assume that the term *science* refers to specific fields of study, such as chemistry or physics, and that only these are truly scientific in nature. In fact, the word actually refers mainly to a general approach to acquiring knowledge—one involving the use of certain methods as well as adherence to several key values or standards. The methods consist primarily of *systematic observation* and direct *experimentation* and will be described in detail in a later section. The standards involve commitment to such goals as objectivity (evaluating information on the basis of its merits rather than according to one's personal preferences), accuracy (gathering information as carefully and precisely as possible), and skepticism (accepting findings as true only after they have been verified over and over again and all inconsistencies have been resolved).

As you can see, these methods and values are largely independent of the content of any specific field. In fact, they can be used to study a wide range of

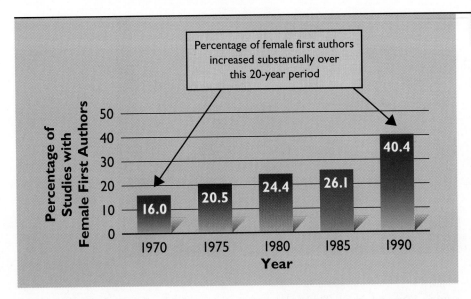

FIGURE 1.3

Women: A Growing Role in Psychology

As shown here, the proportion of articles in major psychological journals authored by women increased substantially between 1970 and 1990. (Based on data from Gannon et al., 1992.)

topics. In determining whether a field is or is not scientific, then, the crucial question is this: Does the field make use of scientific methods and accept scientific values? To the extent it does, it may be viewed as scientific in nature. To the extent it does not, it should be seen as basically nonscientific in its approach. In short, it is the methods and values, not the topics being studied, that are the central issue.

Given the criteria just described, is psychology really scientific? The answer is a firm yes. In their efforts to understand behavior and cognitive processes, psychologists rely heavily on scientific methods and adhere closely to the standards mentioned above. It is appropriate to define psychology as "the science of behavior and cognitive processes," because in their research psychologists are firmly committed to the scientific method and to the values of science. The topics they seek to study certainly differ from those in the older and more traditional fields of science, but the approach they follow is basically the same. And that, as has already been noted, is really the central issue.

IS PSYCHOLOGY MERELY COMMON SENSE? In a very real sense, everyone is an amateur psychologist. We all think about our own behavior, and that of other people, on a regular basis. Because we do, we often feel that we already know the answers to many of the questions studied by psychology, and that we can predict the results of psychological research on this basis. Are such impressions correct? In other words, is psychology merely a rehashing of what our common sense and informal experience already tell us? Before you conclude this is so, consider these two points.

First, if you stop and think about it for a moment, you'll quickly realize that common sense isn't quite as useful a guide to human behavior as you might initially assume. Often it yields contradictory answers about important issues. For example, according to common sense, "absence makes the heart grow fonder" (separation strengthens bonds of affection). But common sense also notes, "out of sight, out of mind" (separation weakens bonds of affection). Can both be true? Perhaps, but common sense doesn't explain why or how. As another example, consider these two statements: "Birds of a feather flock together" (similar individuals are attracted to one another), and "Opposites attract" (dissimilar individuals are mutually attracted). Again, we are left with contradictory suggestions. This is where a scientific field like psychology

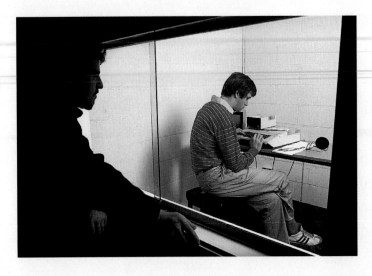

comes into its own. Through systematic research, it can help determine whether any of these commonsense suggestions are true. Going further, it can also find out why such effects occur—why, for example, the more similar two people are, the more they tend to like each other. (Evidence will be presented in Chapter 16 that this is actually the case; there's very little support for the view that opposites attract; Smeaton, Byrne, & Murnen, 1989.)

Second, before concluding that many of the findings of psychology are merely common sense, you should consider a phenomenon known as the hindsight, or "I knew it all along" effect. This refers to our tendency to assume, on learning of some event, that we knew it would happen all along and that therefore it is not all that surprising (Mazursky & Ofir, 1990). Why do we tend to do this? Because doing so puts us in a favorable light in our own eyes. After all, if we perceive that new information is not really very new and that, in fact, we knew it all along (or at least would have predicted it), this confirms the vast scope of our personal wisdom. In any case, because of the hindsight effect, people often perceive the results of psychological research as something they would have predicted if asked in advance. In fact, however, several studies indicate that when people are asked to predict the results of actual research, they are often dead wrong. So before you decide that the knowledge gathered by psychologists is usually something you really knew all along (or something your grandmother could have told you if you had asked), remember that in such cases, as in many others, hindsight is often a lot more accurate than foresight (Wasserman, Lempert, & Hastie, 1991).

KEY POINTS

- Today, psychologists conduct research on cultural differences and take account of them in providing psychological services.
- Psychology is scientific in nature because it adopts the methods and values of science in its efforts to understand all aspects of behavior.
- Psychology is not mere common sense: the results of systematic research are a much more reliable guide to understanding human behavior than informal observation or the "wisdom of the ages."

Psychology: Who and What

*H*aving defined the field of psychology and addressed some questions about its basic nature, let's turn to two related topics: who psychologists are and what they actually do.

Who: The Background and Training of Psychologists

The terms *psychiatrist* and *psychologist* are quite similar, so it is not surprising that many people think they mean the same thing. Actually, they refer to two different groups of professionals. Psychiatrists are physicians who, after completing medical studies, specialize in the treatment of mental disorders. In contrast, psychologists receive their training in graduate programs of psychology, where they earn both a master's degree and, in most cases, a Ph.D. The latter degree usually requires a minimum of four to five years of study. In addition, psychologists who choose to specialize in certain areas of their field, such as the treatment of psychological disorders, must also complete one or more years of practical training in a hospital, clinic, school, or business. Throughout their graduate education, psychologists focus mainly on the principles and findings of their field. However, most also complete extensive training in statistics, in research methods, and in related fields such as physiology, sociology, or management sciences.

It should be clear, then, that psychologists and psychiatrists receive different kinds of training. So why are the two fields often confused? In part because many psychologists specialize in the diagnosis, study, and treatment of psychological (mental) disorders. This means that they focus on many of the same problems and perform many of the same activities as psychiatrists. In fact, members of the two fields often work closely together in the same mental health facilities. Since only some psychologists focus on mental disorders, the two fields overlap only partially and remain largely independent.

Now that we've clarified the difference between psychologists and psychiatrists, here are a few facts about Canadian psychologists:

1. The most recent 1991 census figures show that 14,160 Canadians are engaged in the profession of psychology.

2. The majority of those listing psychology as a profession are women, who outnumber men 9,010 to 5,150.

3. Most psychologists (70 percent) practice in Ontario and Quebec.

4. In 1991–92, 1,271 students were pursuing a doctoral degree in psychology. Women outnumbered men 813 to 458.

What: Specialties Within Psychology

Before going farther, stop and answer the following question: What exactly do psychologists do? If you are like most people, you probably said "conduct therapy," "help people with problems," or perhaps "conduct research." In a sense, the first two replies are not inaccurate, for nearly half of all psychologists are *clinical* or *counseling* psychologists, who do indeed focus on mental problems and disorders. But there are many other specialties within psychology, so in reality psychologists do many different things and investigate a wide range of topics. Here are brief descriptions of several of psychology's major subfields:

Clinical psychology Studies the diagnosis, causes, and treatment of mental disorders. For example, clinical psychologists have recently devised effective forms of treatment for reducing aggression among highly assaultive children (e.g., Bienert & Schneider, 1993).

Counseling psychology Assists individuals in dealing with many personal problems that do not involve psychological disorders. For example, counseling psychologists assist individuals in career planning and in developing more effective interpersonal skills.

Developmental psychology Studies how people change physically, cognitively, and socially over their entire life span. For example, developmental psychologists have found that the patterns of attachment children form with their parents can influence the nature of the romantic relationships they form as adults (Vormbrock, 1993).

Educational psychology Studies all aspects of the educational process, from techniques of instruction to learning disabilities. For example, educational psychologists are working to develop classroom procedures designed to help minority children overcome the environmental disadvantages they face.

Cognitive psychology Investigates all aspects of cognition—memory, thinking, reasoning, language, decision-making, and so on. For example, cognitive psychologists have recently found evidence suggesting that the reason we can't remember events that happen to us before we are about three years old is that we lack a clearly developed self-concept prior to this age (Howe & Courage, 1993).

Industrial/organizational psychology Studies all aspects of behavior in work settings—selection of employees, evaluation of performance, work motivation, leadership. For example, industrial/organizational psychologists have found that work performance often decreases sharply when employees feel that they are being treated unfairly—that they are receiving fewer benefits than they deserve. Indeed, professional basketball players who feel underpaid actually score fewer points than those who feel that their salaries are fair (Harder, 1992).

Psychobiology (physiological psychology) Investigates the biological bases of behavior—the role of biochemical events within our nervous systems and bodies in everything we do, sense, feel, or think. For example, psychobiologists have recently investigated the possible role in gender differences in behavior of subtle differences in the structure of female and male brains (Law, Pellegrino, & Hunt, 1993). An applied offshoot of this area is *neuropsychology*, which focuses on brain–behavior relationships, especially those associated with various clinical disorders.

Social psychology Studies all aspects of social behavior and social thought—how we think about and interact with others. For example, social psychologists have recently found that while both women and men use complaints to change others' behavior, the two genders use this technique in slightly different ways (Klotz & Alicke, 1993).

Experimental psychology Studies all aspects of basic psychological processes such as perception, learning, and motivation. For example, research by experimental psychologists has recently added much to our understanding of attention—the process of directing portions of our information-processing capacity to specific stimuli. This knowledge is now being applied to the design of more effective warnings about various hazards (e.g., Duffy, Kalsher, & Wogalter, 1993).

To gain an idea of the variety of different areas in which psychologists work, have a look at Figure 1.4. It shows the different areas in which Ontario's licenced psychologists work, and the relative percentage of psychologists employed in these various areas.

The exact percentages are not crucial to remember; rather, keep in mind two facts: (1) Psychologists do a number of very different things; and

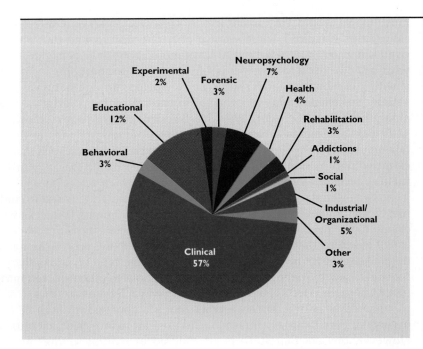

FIGURE 1.4

Specialty areas of licenced psychologists in Ontario

Source: Based on membership lists of the College of Psychologists of Ontario.

(2) despite the existence of many subfields or specialties, psychology remains a unified field with shared values, goals, and overall methods.

Adding to What We Know: The Process of Psychological Research

*S*o far, this chapter has considered some basic questions about psychology and has indicated why it can be defined as a scientific field. Now let's turn to what is perhaps the most important question in this chapter: How do psychologists perform the task of adding to our knowledge about behavior and cognitive processes? How do they move beyond common sense in seeking answers to puzzling questions about human behavior? Psychologists use several different techniques for conducting systematic research. This section will describe the most important of these procedures. The next section will examine some of the complex ethical issues these procedures sometimes raise.

Naturalistic Observation: Scientists as Explorers

Almost everyone finds the giant panda of China fascinating. Here, at least in outward appearance, is a teddy bear come to life. For many years zoos throughout the world sought eagerly to add these appealing animals to their collections. Unfortunately, these efforts usually produced disappointing results. The pandas, when finally obtained, seemed to pine away in captivity. Even worse, they adamantly refused to mate, despite the best efforts of the experts and the pandas' keepers. Given the small and declining number of pandas present in the wild, all of this seemed to spell disaster for a species

KEY POINTS

- Psychologists receive their advanced training in graduate departments of psychology. Most receive a Ph.D. after at least five years of advanced study.
- There are many subfields in psychology, including cognitive psychology, developmental psychology, and psychobiology.

THE GIANT PANDA

In recent years, naturalistic observation has been used effectively to gain valuable information about the habits of the giant panda. This knowledge is crucial if pandas are to be saved from extinction.

most people would very much like to preserve. Could anything be done to change this situation? There seemed only one way to find out: observe the pandas in their natural habitat to learn more about their behavior and about what could be done to save them from extinction. In short, this seemed to be a situation in which research should be conducted through **naturalistic observation**—systematic study of behavior in natural settings. Fortunately, efforts along these lines (Schaller, 1986) have added greatly to our knowledge of giant pandas. Scientists have spent months observing pandas in the mountainous regions of western China where they live and, from such study, have extracted information about their diet and mating habits that may prove useful in assuring their survival.

As this example suggests, naturalistic observation is often used to study animal behavior. However, it is sometimes applied to human beings as well. For example, an ingenious study of this type conducted by Murdoch and Pihl (1988) observed the behavior of male patrons drinking beer or liquor in randomly selected Montreal bars. Information on the type of drinks the patrons consumed and the aggressiveness of their reactions to others offered intriguing insights into the effects of alcohol on behavior in at least one setting.

It should be added that sometimes the data obtained through naturalistic observation are relatively informal, and this can reduce their scientific value. However, the fact that subjects are studied in natural settings and so are likely to act in the ways they normally do is an important advantage that makes this method useful in some contexts.

Case Studies: *Generalizing from the Unique*

As you already know from your own experience, human beings are unique: Each possesses a distinctive combination of traits, abilities, and characteristics. Given this fact, is it possible to learn anything about human behavior in general from detailed study of one or perhaps a few individuals? Several famous figures in the history of psychology have contended that it is. Thus, they have adopted the **case method,** in which detailed information is gathered on specific individuals. For example, Freud based his entire theory of personality on the case method. Is the case method really useful? In the hands of talented researchers such as Freud, it does seem capable of yielding valuable insights about behavior. Moreover, when the behavior involved is very unusual, the case method can be quite revealing. In Chapter 6 you'll see how detailed study of several unique cases has added greatly to our understanding of the biological bases of memory. These cases involve individuals who have experienced specific kinds of damage to the brain and, as a result, show certain kinds of memory deficits. By studying the pattern of such memory losses, psychologists have been able to piece together a more complete picture of how memories are stored in the brain (Graf & Schachter, 1985; Squire, 1991). So, despite its obvious drawbacks—for example, the possibility that researchers' emotional attachments to people with whom they work closely for months or even years may reduce their objectivity—the case method does appear to have its uses. When used with considerable caution, it can prove helpful in the investigation of at least some aspects of behavior.

Surveys: *The Science of Self-Report*

You are probably already familiar with another research method often used by psychologists—the **survey method.** This involves asking large numbers of indi-

Naturalistic Observation: A research method in which various aspects of behavior are carefully observed in the settings where such behavior naturally occurs.

Case Method: A method of research in which detailed information about individuals is used to develop general principles about behavior.

Survey Method: A research method in which large numbers of people answer questions about aspects of their views or their behavior.

viduals to complete questionnaires designed to yield information on specific aspects of their behavior or attitudes. Such surveys (or polls) are often conducted to measure a wide range of attitudes and behaviors. Examples include surveys on free trade in Canada or economic reform in Russia, on voting preferences prior to elections, on consumer reactions to various products, on health practices, and on public compliance with safety regulations.

Surveys are often repeated over long periods of time in order to track shifts in public opinion or actual behavior. For example, some surveys of job satisfaction—individuals' attitudes toward their jobs—have continued for several decades. And changing patterns of sexual behavior and sexual attitudes have been tracked by the Kinsey Institute since the 1940s.

The survey method offers some very real advantages. Large amounts of information can be gathered with relative ease, and shifts over time can be readily noted. And when conducted carefully, surveys can provide highly accurate predictions with respect to the outcome of elections and other events. However, the disadvantages are also quite apparent. People may fail to respond accurately or truthfully, providing answers that place them in a favorable light rather than ones that reflect their true views. In addition, the results of surveys are useful only if the people questioned are truly representative of the larger groups to which the findings are to be generalized. For example, imagine that a survey conducted with 1,000 young men and women indicates that more than 99 percent are strongly opposed to the foreign policies of the current federal government. Should you conclude that there is widespread unrest among the youth in the country with regard to the foreign policies now in place? Perhaps. But not if you learn that all of the 1,000 individuals who responded to the survey are members of the youth wing of an opposition political party. The fact that they are would raise serious questions about the extent to which they are representative of the larger group about which we wish to generalize, that group being the entire youth population of the country. The moral is clear: Unless the people who respond to a survey are similar to the larger group to which we wish to extend the results, generalizations are on very shaky ground.

PREDICTION: A KEY SCIENTIFIC PRINCIPLE

Like psychologists, meteorologists rely on the principle of prediction: the fact that information about some variables can be used to predict other variables accurately. How do you use prediction in your own life?

The Correlational Method: *Knowledge Through Systematic Observation*

Prediction—the ability to forecast future events from present ones—is an important goal of science; psychologists, too, often seek to make predictions. Consider, for instance, how useful it would be if we could predict from current information such future outcomes as a person's success in school or various occupations, effectiveness as a parent, length of life span, or likelihood of developing a serious mental disorder. How can we learn to do so? One answer involves efforts to determine whether various aspects of the world (termed *variables* because they can take different values) are related to one another. That is, we try to determine whether changes in one variable are associated with changes in another so that, for example, as one rises, the other does too. The stronger such relationships (*correlations*) are, the more successfully one variable can be predicted from the other. (Appendix A provides more information about correlations and how they are computed.)

As you already know from your own experience, some events are indeed closely related to others and so can be used as effective predictors. For example, meteorologists (scientists who specialize in the prediction of weather) have found that the greater the number of disturbances on the face of the sun (sunspots), the more unsettled the world's weather will be in the coming months in several different respects. Similarly, it has been observed that the greater the number of hours of violent television shows watched by children, the greater their likelihood of behaving aggressively as teenagers (Eron, 1987).

While these examples involve only two variables, you should bear in mind that in many cases accurate predictions can be obtained only when several factors (and the correlations between them) are taken into account at once. For example, if you wish to predict the likelihood that a given student will have a distinguished academic career, you will have to take many different factors into consideration: intelligence, motivation, long-term goals, degree of family support, financial resources, and many other variables.

How do psychologists use correlations in their research? How do they search for relationships between variables so that they can make accurate predictions about important aspects of behavior? Perhaps the best way of illustrating the nature and value of this research approach—known as the correlational method—is through an actual example.

THE CORRELATIONAL METHOD: AN EXAMPLE Instructors of large introductory courses frequently express concern about poor attendance (e.g., Gunn, 1993). If these concerns are expressed to students, a common response is that it is just as effective, or more effective, to skip class and study the textbook independently. Does attending class increase the likelihood of obtaining better marks? Gunn (1993) carried out a simple experiment to test the **hypothesis** (an as yet untested prediction about some aspect of behavior) that students taking psychology at Laurentian University in Sudbury would have a greater likelihood of performing well on examinations if they attended class. To carry out this study, he first informed his introductory classes that attendance would be taken at different times over the term; he emphasized, however, that attendance information would not be considered in calculating final grades. He then examined the relationship between attendance and the final grades obtained by the students. An appropriate statistical procedure was used to obtain a correlation coefficient. Correlation coefficients range between -1.00 and +1.00; the greater their departure from 0.00, the stronger the relationship between the variables being considered. So if a correlation of +0.80 was found between class attendance and grades, this would indicate a stronger link between two variables than a correlation of +0.30. Similarly, a correlation of -0.60 would indicate a stronger correlation than one of -0.20. In this case, however, a negative sign would indicate that the fewer classes attended, the better the final grade. Gunn actually found a correlation of +.66, indicating a fairly strong positive correlation between attendance and grades. Students who attended classes did tend to achieve higher grades.

As a research device, the **correlational method** offers several major advantages. For one thing, it can be used to study behavior in many real-life settings. For another, it is often highly efficient and can yield a large amount of interesting data in a short time. Moreover, it can be extended to include many different variables at once. Thus, in the simple study described above, information on age, gender, note-taking practices, and extracurricular involvement might also be obtained. Then these variables could also be related to final grades, to determine if they too influenced the outcome. (See Appendix A for more detailed discussion of correlational methods.)

Unfortunately, the correlational method suffers from one major drawback that lessens its appeal, at least to a degree: The findings it yields are not conclusive with respect to cause-and-effect relationships. That is, the fact that two variables are correlated (even highly correlated) does not guarantee that there is a causal link between them—that changes in the first cause changes in the second. Rather, in many cases, the fact that two variables tend to rise or

Hypothesis: In psychology, a prediction about behavior that is to be investigated in a research project.

Correlational Method: A research method in which investigators observe two or more variables in order to determine whether changes in one are accompanied by changes in the other.

OBSERVED RELATIONSHIP	POSSIBLE UNDERLYING CAUSE
(1) The more people weigh, the higher their salaries.	_____
(2) The greater the degree of crowding in cities, the higher the crime rate.	_____
(3) The colder the winter, the greater the number of births the next fall.	_____

Possible answer to Table 1.3: (1) Weight and earnings both increase with age and experience. (2) Crowding and crime are both related to poverty. (3) Cold weather makes people stay indoors and increases their tendency to cuddle—with predictable results.

fall together simply reflects the fact that both are caused by a third variable.

Consider, for example, the positive correlation between attendance and final grades found in Gunn's study. Does it mean that classroom attendance causes higher final grades? Not necessarily. It may be that students who attend class regularly study more than those who do not. If so, it would be, not attendance, but studying practices that determined grade level. Table 1.3 offers a few additional examples of correlations that do not indicate causation. Can you identify the third factors that may underlie each relationship shown in the table?

Experimentation: *Knowledge Through Systematic Intervention*

While psychologists use all of the research methods described so far, they often prefer the approach we will now consider: **experimentation** (or *the experimental method*). This involves determining whether variables are related to one another by systematically changing one (or more) and observing the effects of such variations on the other (or others). There are several reasons why psychologists prefer this basic approach, but perhaps the most important is this: In contrast to the other methods we have considered, experimentation yields relatively clear-cut evidence on causality. If systematic variations in one factor produce changes in another (and if additional conditions, which we'll soon consider, are also met), we can conclude with reasonable certainty that there is a causal link between the factors: that changes in one caused changes in the other. Establishing such causality is extremely valuable from the perspective of one major goal of science: *explanation*. Briefly, scientists do not wish merely to describe the world around them and the relationships between different variables or factors in it. They also wish to be able to explain why such relationships exist—why, for example, people find some gauges easier to read than others, why individuals with certain personality traits are more likely than others to suffer a heart attack, why some people gain weight readily while others do not. Experimentation, because it often yields information that is useful in answering such questions, is frequently the method of choice in psychology. But bear in mind that there are no hard-and-fast rules in this regard. Rather, most psychologists select the research technique that seems most suited to the topic they wish to study and the resources available to them.

KEY POINTS

- Psychologists use many different research methods, including naturalistic observation, the case method, and the survey approach.
- The correlational method examines relationships between variables.
- The stronger the correlation between two variables, the more accurately one variable can predict the other. However, correlations cannot prove causation.

Experimentation: A research method where investigators systematically alter one or more variables in order to determine whether such changes will influence some aspect of behavior.

EXPERIMENTATION: ITS BASIC NATURE   Reduced to its bare essentials, the experimental method involves two basic steps: (1) The presence or strength of some variable believed to affect behavior is systematically altered, and (2) the effects of such alterations (if any) are measured. The logic behind these steps is as follows: If the factor varied does indeed influence behavior or cognitive processes, then individuals exposed to different levels or amounts of that factor should differ in terms of their behavior. Thus, exposure to a small amount of the variable should result in one level of behavior, exposure to a larger amount should result in a different level, and so on.

The factor systematically varied by the researcher is termed the **independent variable,** while the aspect of behavior or cognitive processes studied is termed the **dependent variable.** In a simple experiment, then, different groups of participants are exposed to different levels of the independent variable (such as low, moderate, and high). The participants' behavior is then carefully measured to determine whether it does in fact vary with different levels or amounts of the independent variable. If it does—and if two other conditions described below are met—the researcher can tentatively conclude that the independent variable does indeed cause changes in the aspect of behavior being studied.

To illustrate the basic nature of experimentation in psychological research, let's imagine that a researcher wishes to test the following hypothesis: The faster people speak (up to a point), the more persuasive they are. How could the investigator proceed? The first step would be to recognize that the independent variable is the speed at which would-be persuaders speak. The dependent variable is some measure of the persuader's success in influencing an audience. The second step would involve some way of directly testing the hypothesized relationship between these two variables.

There are many different ways of testing the hypothesis that fast talkers are more persuasive than slow ones, but for the sake of illustration, let's assume that the researcher arranges to have an assistant deliver a speech designed to alter listeners' views on a specific issue: legislation to limit the use of chemicals known to deplete the earth's ozone layer. The speaker presents this speech to different groups of participants at different speeds. For example, for participants in one group, the speech is presented at a slow pace (150 words per minute); for those in another group, it is presented at a moderate pace (170 words per minute); and for those in the third group, it is presented at a fast pace (190 words per minute). The audience members' attitudes toward the legislation are then measured in some way. If rate of speech does make a difference, then data something like those shown in Figure 1.5 should be obtained. As this figure shows, the faster the persuader speaks, the more favorable are the audience members' attitudes toward the pending legislation. We must assume, by the way, that the individuals in the three groups start out with similar attitudes toward the legislation; if they do not, serious complications can arise when the results are interpreted. (Actually, several studies have been conducted to investigate the relationship between speed of speech and persuasion which Figure 1.5 shows quite clearly.

EXPERIMENTATION: TWO REQUIREMENTS FOR ITS SUCCESS   Earlier, we saw that before we can conclude that an independent variable has caused some change in behavior, two conditions must be met. The first condition involves **random assignment** of participants to experimental conditions. According to the principle of random assignment, all participants in an experiment must have an equal chance of being exposed to each level of the independent variable. The reason for this rule is simple: If participants are *not* randomly assigned to each group, it may later be impossible to determine whether differences in their

Independent Variable: The variable that is systematically altered in an experiment.

Dependent Variable: The aspect of behavior that is measured in an experiment.

Random Assignment of Participants to Experimental Conditions: Assuring that all research participants have an equal chance of being assigned to each of the experimental conditions.

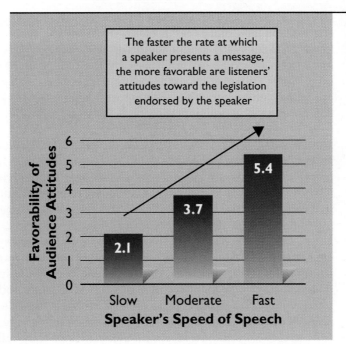

FIGURE 1.5

Results of a Simple Experiment

The results shown here indicate that the faster would-be persuaders speak, the greater their impact on the attitudes of an audience.

The faster the rate at which a speaker presents a message, the more favorable are listeners' attitudes toward the legislation endorsed by the speaker

Favorability of Audience Attitudes

2.1

3.7

5.4

Slow   Moderate   Fast

Speaker's Speed of Speech

behavior stem from differences they brought with them, from the impact of the independent variable, or from both. For instance, continuing with our study of speed of speech and persuasion, imagine that participants in the proposed study are drawn from two different groups: first-year law students and a group of high school dropouts enrolled in a special course designed to provide them with basic vocational skills. Now imagine that because of differences in the two groups' schedules, most of the participants exposed to the slow talker are law students, while most of the people exposed to the fast talker are high school dropouts. Suppose that results indicate that participants exposed to the fast talker show much more agreement with the views expressed than participants exposed to the slow talker. What can we conclude? Not much, because it is entirely possible that the difference stems from the different mixes of participants in the two experimental conditions. In the "slow talker" condition, 85 percent of the participants are law students and 15 percent are high school dropouts, while in the "fast talker" condition, the opposite is the case. Since law students may be somewhat harder to persuade than high school dropouts, we can't really tell why these results occurred. Did they derive from differences in the persuader's rate of speech? From different proportions of the two groups of participants in each condition? From both factors? It's impossible to tell. To avoid such problems, it is crucial that all subjects have an equal chance of being assigned to each experimental group.

The second condition referred to above may be stated as follows: Insofar as possible, all other factors that might also affect participants' behavior, aside from the independent variable, must be held constant. To see why this is so, consider what will happen if, in the study on speed of speech and persuasion, different speakers are used in the two conditions. Further, imagine that one of these speakers—the fast talker—has a pleasant, cultivated voice, while the slow talker has an irritating voice. Now assume that participants express greater agreement with the fast talker than the slow one. What is the cause of this result? The difference in the speakers' speed of speech? Differences in the pleasantness of their voices? Both factors? Obviously, it's impossible to tell. In this situation, the independent variable of interest (speed of speech) is *confounded* with another variable—the pleasantness of the speaker's voice—that is not a planned part of the research. That is, another factor changes as the independent variable changes, so we can't tell whether any effects observed are produced by the independent variable or by this other factor. When such confounding occurs, the findings of an experiment are largely uninterpretable. (See Figure 1.6 for an overview of the nature of confounding in experimentation.)

EXPERIMENTER EFFECTS AND DEMAND CHARACTERISTICS: HOW TO GET POSITIVE RESULTS WITHOUT REALLY TRYING Before concluding this discussion of experimentation, we should consider two additional pitfalls lying in wait for careless researchers. The first of these is the risk of **experimenter effects**—the fact that sometimes researchers influence the behavior of subjects without intending to do so. Such effects can occur in several ways. First, researchers usually have expectations about how participants in their studies may behave. These expectations, in turn, may influence their behavior toward participants and so alter the results obtained. For example, if an experimenter expects fast talkers to be more persuasive than slow ones, she may nod or smile at participants when they express agreement with the speaker's views in the fast-speech condition, but show disapproval when they express agreement in the slow-speech condition. The result: Her reactions may influence participants and lead to greater agreement with the speaker's views in the fast-speech than in the slow-speech condition.

Experimenter Effects:
Unintentional influence exerted by researchers on research participants.

FIGURE 1.6

Confounding of Variables: A Fatal Flaw in Experimentation

In an imaginary study designed to investigate the effects of speed of speech on persuasion, the person who speaks quickly has a pleasant, cultivated voice, while the person who speaks slowly has an irritating voice. As a result, two variables—speed of speech and pleasantness of speech—are *confounded*. Because of this fact, it is impossible to interpret the results.

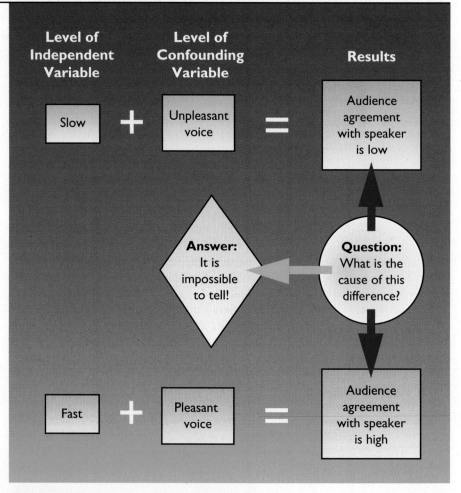

A second potential snare for unwary researchers is the fact that experimenters may sometimes communicate the hypothesis behind the study to participants. Once they do, participants' behavior may be affected even if the researchers have no direct contact with them and cannot provide subtle cues of approval and disapproval such as those described above. The effects of such communication are known as **demand characteristics,** since they place subtle demands on participants to "help" the researcher by confirming his or her hypothesis. Research findings indicate that experimenter effects and demand characteristics can both exert powerful effects on participants' behavior. Thus, it is crucial that these effects be minimized in all psychological research. One way of doing this is through a **double-blind procedure.** Here, those who have contact with participants (often research assistants) are unfamiliar with the hypothesis under investigation and don't know the condition to which the participants have been assigned. Under these conditions, they can't readily communicate the hypothesis being studied and can't have clear expectations about how a given participant "should" behave. Another technique for avoiding experimenter effects and demand characteristics is to minimize direct contact between participants and the researcher. This can be accomplished through the use of computerized procedures, in which subjects receive instructions and perform experimental tasks by means of a computer terminal. Through these and related procedures, the impact of several potential pitfalls can be reduced and the validity or accuracy of experimental findings can be enhanced. For an overview of the correlational and experimental methods of research, see the **Key Concept** page.

Interpreting Research Results: *Statistics as a Tool*

Once an experiment has been completed, researchers must turn to the next crucial task: interpreting the results. Suppose that in the study we have been discussing throughout this section, results like those in Figure 1.5 are obtained: The faster speakers talk, the more successful they are at persuading listeners. How much confidence can we place in these results? In other words, are the differences observed real ones—ones that would be observed again if the study were repeated with other participants? This is a crucial question, for unless we can be confident that the differences are real, the results really tell us little about human behavior.

One way of dealing with this question, of course, would be to repeat the study over and over again. This would do the trick, but, as you can well imagine, it would be costly in terms of time and effort. Another approach is to use **inferential statistics.** This is a special form of mathematics designed, in part, to evaluate the likelihood that a given pattern of findings, such as differences between experimental groups, is due to chance alone. Thus, to determine whether the findings of a study are indeed real (are unlikely to have occurred by chance alone), psychologists perform appropriate statistical analyses on the data they collect. If these analyses suggest that the likelihood of obtaining the observed findings by chance is low (usually, fewer than five times in a hundred), the results are described as being *significant.* Only then are they interpreted as being of value in the task of understanding some aspect of behavior.

Please note: The likelihood that a given pattern of findings is a chance event is never zero. This probability can be very low—for example, one chance in ten thousand or even one chance in a million—but there is always some possibility, however small, that a pattern occurred by chance. For this reason, actual replication of results by different researchers in different laboratories is

Demand Characteristics:
Implicit pressure on research participants to act in ways consistent with a researcher's expectations.

Double-Blind Procedure:
Procedure in which neither the individuals collecting data nor research participants have knowledge of the experimental conditions to which they have been assigned.

Inferential Statistics:
Statistical procedures that provide information on the probability that an observed event is due to chance.

Correlational and Experimental Research Methods

Question: Do people act more aggressively when the temperature goes up?

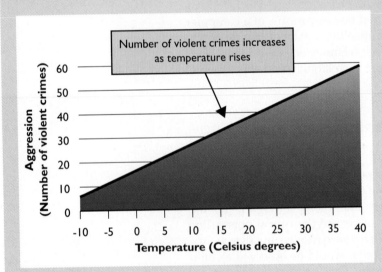

Number of violent crimes increases as temperature rises

Aggression (Number of violent crimes) / Temperature (Celsius degrees)

CORRELATIONAL METHOD

• Records of temperature are obtained for each day for two years in several large cities.
• The number of violent crimes committed on these days is also recorded.
• These two sets of numbers are correlated.

Conclusion: As temperature rises, aggression increases.

EXPERIMENTAL METHOD

• Participants are exposed to comfortably cool (20°C) and very hot (35°C) conditions.
• After thirty minutes of exposure to one of these conditions, members of each group are given an opportunity to aggress against a stranger by evaluating his or her work. (Poor ratings will prevent this person from being reappointed to a position as research assistant.)
• Mean ratings assigned to the stranger's work are obtained for the two experimental groups and compared.

Conclusions: Exposure to uncomfortably high temperatures increases aggression. Since temperature was systematically varied, there is some evidence of a causal link between heat and aggression.

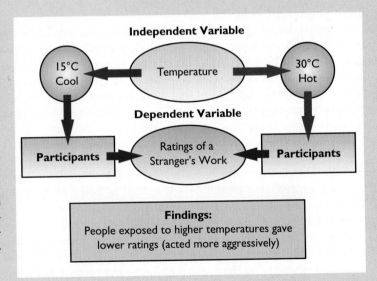

Independent Variable

15°C Cool ← Temperature → 30°C Hot

Dependent Variable

Participants → Ratings of a Stranger's Work ← Participants

Findings:
People exposed to higher temperatures gave lower ratings (acted more aggressively)

usually necessary before the findings of any research project can be accepted with confidence, even if statistical analysis indicates that the findings are unlikely to be a chance event. Still, inferential statistics is a valuable tool of tremendous help to psychologists in evaluating research findings.

META-ANALYSIS AND THE SEARCH FOR AN OVERALL PATTERN Before this discussion is concluded, one more complexity in the process should be mentioned. Because the results of a single experiment are rarely sufficiently clear to warrant strong conclusions, most hypotheses are subjected to independent testing by many different researchers. When they are, the results are not always consistent. Some studies may find support for a given hypothesis while others do not. For example, imagine that over the years fifty different studies are conducted to examine the effects of speed of speech on persuasion. Of these, thirty-five yield results supporting the hypothesis that the faster people talk, the greater their success in influencing others. However, ten report exactly the opposite findings, and five report no difference in persuasiveness between slow and fast talkers. How can we reach any firm conclusions in this situation? In other words, how can we combine the results obtained by all these studies to determine whether speed of speech does or does not influence persuasion? In recent years a very powerful technique for doing precisely this has been developed. This technique, known as **meta-analysis** (e.g., Dillard, 1991; Eagly, Makhijani, & Klonsky, 1992), has gained increasing acceptance among researchers in all areas of psychology. The complex statistical procedures of meta-analysis are far beyond the scope of this discussion. In essence, however, these procedures combine the results of many different studies in order to estimate both the direction and the magnitude of the effects of independent variables of interest. For example, a meta-analysis on the results of the fifty studies on speed of speech and persuasion would combine the findings of all of these investigations in order to determine whether, across all fifty, speed has any effect on persuasion. Meta-analysis is especially useful because it helps to counteract the all-too-human tendency for researchers to be strongly influenced by results that are especially interesting or well presented. It utilizes statistical formulas that are free from such influences to combine the results of all available studies. Incidentally, meta-analysis of the many studies that have investigated the effect of speed of speech on persuasion indicates that fast talkers do indeed appear to be more persuasive than slow ones (Smith & Shaffer, 1991).

In sum, because of their commitment to scientific skepticism, psychologists are reluctant to accept the results of any research project—even their own—as valid. Only when the data have been subjected to appropriate mathematical (statistical) analysis and significant effects have been obtained do psychologists view experimental findings as useful in understanding various aspects of behavior. And only when the results of many different studies, combined through meta-analysis, point to specific conclusions, are findings accepted as valid and informative.

The Role of Theory in Psychological Research

Now that we have considered basic aspects of the research process in psychology, we can turn to a question students often ask: Just how do psychologists come up with the ideas for all those studies anyway? As you can probably guess, there is no simple answer, for several factors play a role. Some research projects are suggested by informal observation of the world around us.

Meta-Analysis: Statistical procedures for combining the results of many studies in order to determine whether their findings provide support for specific hypotheses.

Psychologists take note of some puzzling aspect of behavior or cognition and plan investigations to increase their understanding of it. At other times the idea for a research project is suggested by the findings of earlier studies. Successful experiments do not simply answer questions; they often raise additional ones as well. Thus, the problem facing psychologists is usually not that of coming up with interesting ideas for research. Rather, the difficulty is in choosing among the many intriguing possibilities. Perhaps the most important single basis for research in psychology, however, is formal theories.

Theories represent efforts by scientists in any field to answer the question "Why?" In more formal terms, theories consist of two major parts: (1) basic concepts, and (2) statements concerning relationships between these concepts. Scientists use these parts to generate testable propositions—ones that can be examined in actual research and found to be either true or false. The development of accurate theories is a major goal of all sciences, and psychology is no exception to this rule (Howard, 1985; Popper, 1959). Psychologists, like other scientists, wish not merely to observe or describe the phenomena they study (i.e., aspects of behavior); they wish to explain them as well. Thus, a great deal of research in psychology consists of efforts to construct, refine, and test specific theories. Perhaps the best way of illustrating the central role of theory in ongoing research is, again, through a concrete example.

Consider the following: When individuals make a decision, they tend to stick to it even in the face of growing signs that it was wrong. For example, they remain in romantic relationships even after these continue to yield more pain than joy. Or they continue to "throw good money after bad" by repairing an automobile that requires one repair after another. This pattern is sometimes known as "escalation of commitment," and we'll consider it in more detail in Chapter 7 (Garland & Newport, 1991).

Certainly, knowing about this tendency is useful in itself. It allows us to predict what may happen in situations where people invest resources or effort in failing courses of action: All things being equal, they will continue to stick to their initial bad decisions. Further, it also suggests the possibility of intervening in some manner to prevent such outcomes. For example, informing people about this tendency to throw good money after bad may prove helpful in lessening its occurrence. These two outcomes—prediction and intervention (or control)—are major goals of science. Knowing about the occurrence of escalation of commitment, however, does not explain why it occurs. It is at this point that theory enters the picture, for as noted above, providing such explanation is its foremost goal.

In fields such as physics and chemistry, theories often take the form of mathematical equations. While this is also true to some extent in psychology, many of the theories we will consider in later chapters involve verbal statements. For example, a theory designed to account for escalation of commitment might be stated this way: "When individuals make decisions that result in losses, they are reluctant to admit their mistake, for this admission causes them to 'lose face' (look foolish) in the eyes of others. As a result, they feel they have no choice but to stick to their original commitment in order to make up for initial losses and so justify their decision." Note that this theory, like all others, consists of the two parts mentioned above: basic concepts (such as losses, pressures to justify past actions) and assertions about the

---

KEY POINTS

- Experimentation involves systematically changing one or more variables in order to determine whether changes in these variables affect various aspects of behavior.

- Participants must be randomly assigned, and confounding of variables must be prevented.

- The results of an experiment can be invalidated by experimenter effects and demand characteristics.

- Theories consist of (1) basic concepts and (2) statements about the relationships between the concepts.

- The results of an experiment are informative only if they are significant; that is, if the probability is low that they occurred by chance alone.

- Meta-analysis can be used to combine the results of many different studies in order to determine whether, when combined, they provide support for a given hypothesis.

relationships between these concepts (as losses mount, pressures to justify previous decisions intensify).

Once a theory has been formulated, a critical process begins. First, predictions are derived from the theory. These predictions, known as *hypotheses*, are formulated in accordance with basic principles of logic. Then the hypotheses are tested in actual research. If they are confirmed, confidence in the theory's accuracy is increased. If, instead, such predictions are disconfirmed, confidence in the theory's accuracy is reduced. The theory itself may be altered so as to generate new predictions. These are subjected to test and the process continues. If the modified predictions are confirmed, confidence in the revised theory is increased. If they are disconfirmed, the theory may be modified again or, ultimately, rejected. See Figure 1.7 for a summary of this process.

It's important to remember, by the way, that theories are useful only to the extent that they lead to testable predictions. If a theory does not generate hypotheses that can be examined in actual research, it cannot be viewed as scientific in nature.

Ethical Issues in Psychology

Strange as it may seem, the phrase "psychological research" has an ominous ring for some people. When they hear it, they visualize unsettling scenes in which all-knowing psychologists somehow force unwary subjects to reveal their deepest secrets and wildest fantasies. Do such concerns have

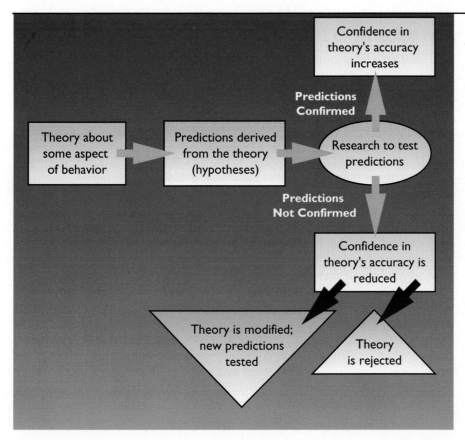

FIGURE 1.7

The Role of Theory in Psychological Research

Once a theory has been formulated, predictions derived from it are tested through research. If these predictions are confirmed, confidence in the theory's accuracy is increased. If they are disconfirmed, confidence in the theory's accuracy is reduced. The theory may then be modified so as to generate new predictions, or, ultimately, be rejected.

any basis in fact? Is psychological research really harmful to the people and animals who participate in it, and therefore unethical?

Given that it is dangerous to gloss over a complex and serious issue, the answer is a firm no. Virtually all psychological research conducted today is performed in accordance with ethical principles acceptable both to society and to science. Indeed, in Canada, the conduct of psychological research is monitored at a variety of levels. The Canadian Psychological Association has a code of ethical standards to which members must adhere. In addition, provincial licencing boards have special ethical codes governing psychologists in private practice. Further, government granting agencies such as the National Science and Engineering Research Council, the Medical Research Council, and the Social Science and Humanities Research Council all require careful ethical review of the research projects they support. These standards seek to guarantee the safety, privacy, and well-being of all research participants and are strictly enforced in universities and other organizations in which research takes place by special review panels called institutional ethics review committees. These boards review all proposed research projects, and such projects can proceed only when final approval is granted. Government agencies and private foundations that fund psychological research will not provide funding for projects until they have received review board approval. Given these safeguards, it seems clear that the frightening picture of psychological research sketched above has little connection to reality.

Despite such precautions, however, two ethical issues deserving of our attention persist. One has to do with the use of deception—withholding information about a study from research participants or, in some cases, giving false information about it. The other has to do with the use of animals in psychological research.

Deception: Is It Ever Appropriate for Psychologists to Lie to Research Participants?

Suppose that before becoming involved in a research project, participants were informed that the purpose was to determine how readily they could be influenced by a stranger. Then, suppose they were actually exposed to efforts by another person to change their attitudes or their behavior. Would the study yield any valid results? In all probability, it would not. Having learned that they would soon be exposed to influence, many participants would probably dig in their heels and resist—even if, without this information, they might have yielded. Similarly, imagine that before taking part in a study concerned with willingness to help others in an emergency, participants were informed of this purpose. If they were then exposed to a simulated emergency, could anything be learned about their reactions to such events? Again, probably not, for the knowledge that this aspect of their behavior was being studied might well alter their reactions.

In situations such as these, many psychologists feel that it is appropriate to withhold information about a study from participants, or even to give them misleading information, on a temporary basis. The reason behind such procedures—for which the term is **deception**—is straightforward: Researchers believe that if participants have complete information about the purposes and procedures of an investigation, their behavior will be changed from what it would otherwise be and the study will fail to yield any valid new information.

Yet employing deception raises important ethical issues. Deception, even when temporary, may result in some type of harmful outcome for the indi-

Deception: Withholding information about a study from participants. Deception is used in situations where the information that is withheld is likely to alter participants' behavior.

viduals exposed to it (Kelman, 1967). For example, they may experience discomfort, stress, negative shifts in their self-esteem, or related effects. In addition, there is the question of whether scientists, committed to the search for knowledge, should place themselves in the position of deceiving those who are kind enough to assist them in this undertaking.

Given such possibilities, is it ever appropriate to employ temporary deception in psychological research? Consider a series of recent experiments by Baron (e.g., Baron, 1990; Baron & Bronfen, 1994). These experiments focus on the question of whether pleasant scents can affect people's behavior—for example, influence their performance on various tasks or, by putting them in a positive mood, increase their willingness to help others. It seems clear that if participants received full information about the purposes of the research, their behavior would be changed by this information. In such cases, most psychologists would conclude that it is appropriate to temporarily withhold some information from research participants. However, this is only acceptable if two important conditions are met: (1) **informed consent** is employed—before agreeing to take part in a study, subjects must be given as much information as possible about it, and about all the events and procedures it will involve; and (2) thorough **debriefing** is provided—after the study is over, subjects must be provided with full information about all of the study's aspects and purposes. Both informed consent and thorough debriefing are required by the ethical standards for conducting behavioral research, so these are essentially built into the process.

Despite this fact, however, not all psychologists accept the view that deception is sometimes acceptable in research projects (Baumrind, 1985). These critics feel that the use of such procedures diminishes participants' faith in science generally, and in psychology in particular, and so jeopardizes public support for psychological research. While such arguments cannot be ignored, existing evidence seems to point to more optimistic conclusions. When surveyed, an overwhelming majority of participants report that they view temporary deception as acceptable and do not resent its use (Rogers, 1980). Further, individuals who have participated in studies involving deception do not report more negative feelings about psychological research, and actually may sometimes report more favorable feelings in this regard (Sharpe, Adair, & Roese, 1992; Smith & Richardson, 1983). Finally, it appears that effective debriefing does eliminate many negative effects experienced by subjects as a result of temporary deception (Smith & Richardson, 1985). Of course, even in the light of such findings it is unwise to take the safety or suitability of deception for granted (Rubin, 1985), and Canadian ethical codes do not. The code of the Canadian Psychological Association forbids the use of deception in service activities. Deception is countenanced in research only if no alternative procedure is available and no negative effects can be predicted, or such predicted negative effects can be offset. The Social Science and Humanities Research Council guidelines go further and insist that deception be allowed only when no other methodology is available, and when a review committee is satisfied that scientific advance could result from the project.

Research with Animals: *Is It Acceptable?*

If you were given a tour through the research facilities of any large psychology department, you would soon encounter rooms filled with rats, pigeons, or monkeys, as well as equipment used in studying their behavior. At the present time approximately 8 percent of all research projects in psychology are

Informed Consent: Participants' agreement to take part in a research project after they are provided with information about the nature of such participation.

Debriefing: In psychological research, the provision of complete and accurate information about a study to participants after they have taken part in it.

Research with animals is only a small part of psychological research, but it is invaluable for exploring many topics, including learning, attachment, and social behavior.

conducted with animal subjects—primarily with rodents such as white rats (Beckstead, 1991). There are several compelling reasons for this state of affairs.

First, and probably foremost, it is often impossible (for health or safety reasons) to conduct certain types of research with human participants. For obvious ethical and legal reasons, researchers cannot perform operations on healthy human beings in order to study the role of various parts of the brain in important aspects of behavior. And researchers cannot place human beings on diets lacking in certain nutrients to determine how such deficits influence their learning, or give them addictive drugs to study the neural basis for substance abuse. Under certain conditions, however, it is permissible to employ such procedures with animals.

Other reasons for conducting research with animals include their relatively short life spans, which make investigations of various aspects of development (changes over time) more feasible, and the fact that they can be bred over many generations so as to be genetically homogeneous. Such homogeneity, in turn, makes it easier to investigate the impact of many different variables upon behavior, since individual differences relating to genetic factors are minimized. Finally, knowledge of animal behavior can be of great practical value. For example, understanding the behavior of various pests can help us to combat them more effectively, perhaps without resorting to dangerous chemicals.

In view of these and other important considerations, many psychologists believe that it is appropriate to conduct at least some research projects with animals. Moreover, it should be noted that most psychological projects conducted with animals involve absolutely no harm or discomfort to the animals; indeed, in many cases they involve such procedures as observing the animals' social interaction with members of their own species or the rate at which they learn to perform various activities. Despite this fact, however, research with animals has generated intense controversy. Supporters of animal rights contend that the procedures employed in research with animals often expose them to harsh or cruel treatment. Most of these protests have been directed against medical research, in which, for example, animals may be injected with lethal microbes or given potentially dangerous drugs. And vigorous objections have been raised against the use of animals in the development and testing of commercial products such as cosmetics. As you might guess, most people find this last type of research especially objectionable—far less acceptable than research in which the results may, potentially, contribute to human health and welfare (Beckstead, 1991). Although psychologists do not typically conduct medical or marketing research, they too have been criticized for exposing animals to dangerous or harmful treatments in their studies of various aspects of behavior, and opponents of animal research have broken into laboratories in both Canada and the United States (Bowd, 1990).

Animal research practices in Canada are largely regulated by the Canadian Council on Animal Care, a broad-based committee with representatives from humane societies, professional associations (including the Canadian Psychological Association), governments, and granting agencies. It was formed in an effort to establish uniform treatment practices in all Canadian research institutions, and it specifies, in detail, procedures to be followed in the care and treatment of research animals. Although compliance is not mandated by law, public institutions almost invariably follow its guidelines (Bowd, 1990).

Animal experimentation is a complex issue with no simple solutions. It does seem cruel to expose animals to conditions that are deemed unsafe or unethical for humans. Yet important breakthroughs have often been produced by such research. For example, studies conducted by psychologists with animals have contributed to the development of effective forms of therapy for treating emotional problems, controlling high blood pressure, reducing chronic pain, and rehabilitating those with neuromuscular disorders (such as disorders that prevent normal walking). They have also enhanced understanding of the neural mechanisms underlying memory loss, senility, and various addictions (Miller, 1985).

Do such benefits justify research with animals—even research that exposes subjects to conditions to which humans would not be subjected? Clearly, this is a value judgment, outside the realm of science. However, many psychologists believe that if every possible precaution is taken to minimize harm or discomfort to subjects, the potential benefits do outweigh the very real costs. It is for you as an individual to decide whether—and in what circumstances—you agree.

Ethical Issues in the Practice of Psychology

While psychologists often confront complex ethical issues when conducting research, it would be wrong not to mention here that they may also face such issues in the normal practice of their profession, when they deliver psychological services to clients. Indeed, since a large majority of psychologists are engaged in applied work rather than in research, the ethical issues that arise in such work are probably far more common than the ones described earlier.

A survey of practicing psychologists (Pope & Vetter, 1992) indicates that, as you might well expect, there are many different situations in which ethical issues or dilemmas arise. The most frequent of these center on questions of *confidentiality*—situations in which psychologists receive information from their clients that professional ethics require them to hold confidential, but which they also feel obligated to reveal to legal authorities. The confidentiality issue is especially complicated in Canada. In the United States, a large number of states have laws according privileged communication status to psychologist–client relationships; psychologists in Canada have no such protection. Moreover, according to Canadian law, certain information—such as information about child abuse—must be reported to authorities, even when the psychologist believes that reporting this information is not in the best interest of the client. There are those who argue that, rightly or wrongly (depending on the circumstances), this tantamount to converting a therapist into a police informant. Others see reporting in such circumstances as the

CONFIDENTIALITY AND ETHICS

Ethical standards require that psychologists hold in strict confidence information provided by their clients during therapy. However, what should be done when such information relates to illegal actions? Should therapists reveal their knowledge to legal authorities? There is no easy or simple answer to such dilemmas.

only appropriate course of action. It is not possible to deal with all the legal and ethical issues this chapter. (A good summary of the confidentiality issue in Canada is provided by Cram and Dobson, 1993.)

One psychologist reported a distressing situation in which a client reported being raped but could not get police to believe her story. Shortly afterward, another client of the same psychologist admitted committing this crime (Pope & Vetter, 1992, p. 399). Clearly, the psychologist in question faced a difficult ethical dilemma. What would *you* do in the same situation? (We don't know how this dilemma was resolved, because the psychologist chose to keep the decision itself confidential.)

Another frequent ethical concern involves situations in which psychologists find themselves in dual or conflicted relationships with clients. That is, the psychologist's professional role as healer is somehow inconsistent with other relationships he or she may have with a client. One of the most troublesome situations of this type centers on sexual issues. An illustration of the such a situation is provided by Weinberger (1989), who is employed in a mental health center in Weyburn, Saskatchewan. He describes a case in which a male client became sexually infatuated with his female therapist. This not only threatened to shatter the normal professional distance that has to be maintained in a therapeutic setting but also began to disrupt the therapist's personal life. The patient repeatedly attempted to meet with the therapist outside of the office and to talk with her by telephone at night and on weekends. Only with great difficulty was the therapist able to convince the patient to transfer to another case worker. The code of ethics of the Canadian Psychological Association forbids sexual relationships between therapists and clients, yet such attraction still occurs, and it is not always the patient who is the aggressor. Such relationships can be very distressing to all parties concerned.

These are just a few of the ethical dilemmas and problems faced by psychologists in their efforts to assist individuals. Many others, ranging from concerns over providing expert testimony in criminal trials through the use of advertising to build one's practice, exist as well. In short, efforts to help individuals cope with life problems and psychological disorders raise many ethical issues and require adherence to the highest professional standards. Truly, working as a psychologist can be a demanding job.

KEY POINTS

- The use of deception in psychological research is controversial, but most researchers agree that it is acceptable provided that certain safeguards are strictly implemented.
- Research with animals raises complex ethical issues and must always involve strenuous efforts to minimize discomfort to the subjects.
- Practicing psychologists also face ethical dilemmas, such as client confidentiality.

Using This Book: A Note on Its Features

Are all textbooks alike? Not at all. Textbooks, like individuals, are all unique and reflect the experience, perspectives, and goals of their authors. The goals for this book have already been outlined: to provide you with a broad yet integrated overview of the findings of modern psychology, *and* to call your attention to how you, personally, can benefit from this knowledge. In order to achieve these goals, a number of special features have been incorporated into this book. These will be briefly described at this point so that you'll have a better idea of what's coming and an awareness of how to make maximum use of these features.

First, several steps have been taken to make the text easier to read and more convenient to use. Each chapter begins with an outline and ends with a summary. Within the text, key terms are printed in **dark type like this** and are accompanied by a definition. These terms are also defined in a running marginal glossary, as well as in a glossary at the end of the book. In addition, important principles that lie at the very heart of our field are highlighted in the margins under the heading **Key Points.** If you understand and retain these, you will be off to a very good start in your efforts to profit from this first course in psychology. All figures and tables are as clear as possible, and most contain special labels and notes designed to help you interpret them. Finally, to help you understand concepts that many students find difficult to grasp, special **Key Concept** pages illustrate these ideas in an attractive graphic format.

Second, an attempt has been made, wherever possible, to include references to experiences, situations, and problems that will get you thinking about ways in which the topics and materials discussed are relevant to your own experiences. Please watch for them throughout the book.

Third, this version of the text has been augmented, and (we hope) improved, to meet the needs of Canadian students. As was mentioned earlier in the chapter, wherever possible, Canadian demographics will be cited and reference will be made to Canadian places, traditions, and cultures. The basic objective is to present modern developments in psychology in a Canadian context. It is our view that you will be more comfortable, and responsive, to material presented in that context. The point is not to exaggerate the role of Canadian traditions, or the contributions of Canadian psychologists; rather, it is to offer you, as a student studying in Canada, an opportunity to appreciate and understand the degree to which the study of psychology flourishes in Canada, and to gain some insight into the scope, diversity, and character of psychological research carried out at various Canadian institutions.

Fourth, this text includes several types of special sections that you should find both interesting and informative. Sections labeled **The Research Process** discuss active lines of research in psychology—current efforts by psychologists to understand specific aspects of behavior. They are designed to help you understand how research actually unfolds in psychology and to provide you with practice in critical thinking. Sections labeled **Canadian Focus** appear in almost all chapters. These will outline distinctive contributions in applications, problem analysis, and research made by Canadian psychologists, and give you a sense of the enormous variety of problems being dealt with, and the significant contributions being made, by contemporary Canadian practitioners and researchers. Special sections titled **The Point of It All** seek to accomplish two goals: to try to help you see the "big picture"— that is, understand why specific topics are important and why psychologists are interested in them; and to describe for you how the findings and principles of psychology are currently being used to solve a wide range of practical problems. Sections headed **Perspectives on Diversity** appear in many chapters. These examine the impact of ethnic and cultural factors on many aspects of behavior and bring into focus psychology's growing concern about multicultural issues. Finally, all chapters conclude with a section titled **Making Psychology Part of Your Life.** These sections indicate how you personally can apply the information presented in this text to enhance your own life.

It is hoped that all of the features of this text will help you understand psychology and get you excited about the field. In any case, may your first contact with psychology be as stimulating, enjoyable, and beneficial as it was for the authors many years ago.

Using the Knowledge in This Book:
Some Tips on How to Study

Three topics that have long been of major interest to psychologists are learning, memory, and motivation. (We'll consider them in detail in Chapters 5, 6, and 10.) Indeed, all three topics can probably be listed with those about which psychology currently knows most. From your perspective as a postsecondary student, this is a positive state of affairs, for all three are closely related to one activity you must perform—and perform well—which is studying. After all, you must be motivated to study, must learn new materials, and must remember them accurately in order to succeed. Knowledge gained by psychologists can be very useful to you in accomplishing these tasks. In this section, we will drawn upon existing knowledge about learning, memory, and motivation to offer some concrete tips on how you can get the most out of the time you spend studying.

1. *Begin with an overview* Research on memory indicates that it is easier to retain information if it can be placed within a cognitive framework—in other words, if it is clear how different pieces of information or topics relate to one another. So when you begin to study, it is very helpful to start with an overview. Examine the outline provided at the start of each chapter and thumb through the chapter itself once or twice. That way, you'll know what to expect and will already have an initial framework for holding the information in mind when you get down to more serious studying.

2. *Eliminate (or at least minimize) distractions* In order for information to be entered into memory accurately, close attention is necessary; it won't make sense or flow into your mind unless you focus on it. This means you should take care to avoid distractions—that is, stimuli or events that will disrupt your attention and cause you to focus on something other than your studying. So when you get down to serious studying, try to do it in a quiet, secluded place. Turn off the television or radio, put those magazines out of sight, and unhook your telephone. You may find this hard to do, but remember: If you don't eliminate distractions, it will take you longer to cover the same ground. And where studying is concerned, efficiency—covering the most you can in the shortest period of time—is a key goal.

3. *Recognize the limitations of your own span of concentration* Students sometimes tell instructors that they have studied for six or seven hours without a break. Instructors tend to be dubious: they know that they could not study that long without a break. We are, after all, human; and this means that we get hungry or bored after performing one activity for a long time. How long should you study without taking a break? People differ greatly in this.

However, it is important to recognize your own span of concentration and to avoid exceeding it. Yes, you should certainly try to stretch it a bit: This kind of self-discipline can help you increase the length of your study sessions. But no, you should not try to study for many hours without a break. Your learning efficiency will decrease, and you will get diminishing returns from forcing yourself to continue well beyond your own personal limits.

4. *Set specific, challenging but attainable goals for your studying* Industrial/organizational psychologists have long been interested in the topic of work motivation—that is, people's willingness to expend effort on various tasks (Locke & Latham, 1990). One of the key findings of their research is that setting certain kinds of goals can help greatly in this regard. When individuals set specific goals, ones that are challenging yet attainable, both motivation and task performance often increase. What does this mean with respect to studying? First, that you should set concrete goals for each session—for example, "I'll read twenty pages and review my class notes," or "I'll read an entire chapter." Merely telling yourself "I'll do as much as I can" is far less effective. Second, you should set challenging but feasible goals. If you know that you can't sit still for more than an hour, then it is silly to set as a goal, "I'll read two chapters." You simply won't be able to do so before you get restless and can't continue. It is much more effective to set somewhat difficult goals that you can, with effort, attain. Such goals are within your reach, and you will experience a sense of accomplishment when you attain them. So begin by setting appropriate goals; the motivation you increase will almost certainly be your own!

5. *Reward yourself for progress* As you'll see in Chapter 5, people often perform various activities to attain external rewards, ones administered to them by others. But in many cases we provide our own rewards. We pat ourselves on the back for accomplishments, eat a favorite dessert as a reward for dieting successfully all week, and so on. You can put this process to good use where studying is concerned. Studying is certainly hard work. So, after completing an assignment or reaching one of your self-set goals, you should definitely give yourself a reward. What rewards should you select? This depends on what you like. The basic rules are simply these: (a) provide yourself with something you enjoy, whatever that may be; and (b) do so only after you have completed your studying and reached the goals you set.

IMPROVING YOUR STUDY SKILLS: HOW PSYCHOLOGY CAN HELP

Research findings in the areas of learning, memory, and motivation can help you become a more effective learner.

6. *Engage in active, not passive, studying* As you probably know, it is quite possible to sit in front of a book or set of notes for hours without accomplishing much—except daydreaming. And even when you keep your mind on what you read, it is difficult to remember it if all you do is follow the printed words. Many studies on memory and related aspects of cognition suggest that in order truly to master new information, we must do more than merely be exposed to it. We must also think about it, relate it to information we already know, ask questions about it, and so on (Baddeley, 1990; Craik & Tulving, 1975). With respect to studying, this implies that when you read new material, you should think actively about it as you progress. Ask questions about it, try to generate examples of the principles or concepts covered, and relate the material to what you already know. Taking notes of key points and reviewing these later can also be helpful. (This is one reason why we have included the **Key Points** feature in this text.) Finally, you should actively review your notes and the material, quizzing yourself in various ways.

Following these guidelines sounds like a lot of effort. But doing so can greatly increase the effectiveness with which you study. Moreover, once you gain practice with these procedures and form good study habits, the whole process will tend to get easier. The ultimate result, then, will be that you learn and remember more information in shorter periods of time. Certainly, reaching that outcome is well worth the effort.

MAKING PSYCHOLOGY PART OF YOUR LIFE

Practice in Critical Thinking: The Hidden Bonus in Introductory Psychology

If we asked a large group of students to indicate why they had enrolled in introductory psychology, we'd obtain a wide range of answers. Among the most common, though, would be replies such as these: "I wanted to know more about people," "I want to know more about myself," "I thought it would be interesting." In other words, most would indicate that they enrolled in the course because of its content. They expected to learn a lot of interesting facts about people—things they didn't know before taking the course.

Such expectations are fully warranted; you will acquire a great deal of intriguing information about behavior and cognitive processes from this book and from your course. Yet there is another major benefit you will derive from your first exposure to psychology—one that is often overlooked. In brief, not only

will you acquire facts about psychology, but you will also learn to think critically about human behavior. To illustrate this hidden value of introductory psychology, we must first define the term *critical thinking* (Paul, 1990).

First, let's note what critical thinking is not. Critical thinking does not mean negative, fault-finding, nitpicking thinking. It does not imply an automatic rejection of all arguments, hypotheses, or theories. What it does involve is the ability to cast a skeptical mental eye on claims, assertions, and arguments until they have been carefully assessed and objectively examined. In other words, critical thinking means the ability to resist being stampeded, emotionally or otherwise, into accepting statements or arguments that are not actually supported by the facts. (See Table 1.4 for a summary of key aspects of critical thinking.)

For example, suppose that one day you pick up a newspaper and read the following headline: PERSONALITY FLAWS KEEP PEOPLE FROM PROMOTION. You read on and learn that according to a management "expert," people who demonstrate certain personal characteristics—such as constant complaining, aloofness, arrogance, and overconfidence—don't get promotions. "More people lose jobs or promotions because of personality problems than from an inability to do the work," states the expert. How should you react to these claims? Your first reaction may be, "Hmm ... that makes sense. I'd better watch out for these problems in my own behavior." If you stop and think more carefully, however, you may ask questions such as these: How does the expert know that these things keep people from getting promotions? What data did he or she collect? How do you measure complaining, being a loner, or being overconfident? What kinds of jobs were involved? Are these really the traits that matter most? In other words, you would approach the whole issue with a healthy degree of skepticism—and reserve judgment until you have better answers to your questions.

But what, specifically, does introductory psychology have to do with development of the capacity for critical thinking? In fact, a great deal. First, such critical thinking is part and parcel of the scientific approach in our field. Time and time again in this text, we'll consider instances in which common sense suggests a simple answer to an important question about behavior—an answer which is then shown to be false by systematic research. In the absence of science-based critical thinking, the commonsense conclusion, false as it is, might well persist. Indeed, the question of its accuracy might never even be raised. For this reason, many examples of critical, scientific thinking will appear in later chapters.

Second, discussions of such topics as memory, decision-making, problem-solving, and creativity will provide you with new insights into these important processes—and especially with insights into the many forms of bias and error that can affect them. Realizing that your memory can indeed play tricks on you and that your decisions can be influenced by many forms of bias will help alert you to these potential problems. And as one old saying goes, "Forewarned is forearmed."

Third, and perhaps most important, exposure to psychology will provide you with experience in thinking critically about behavior. Many individuals who are quite capable of thinking clearly and critically about the physical world lapse into far less careful and sophisticated patterns of thought when they contemplate their own feelings, others' behavior, or their social relationships. As you'll see throughout this book, critical thinking can be applied to virtually any topic—including all aspects of behavior. Thus, once you become proficient at it, you can apply it to almost any situation or question you encounter in later life.

As you will soon see, your first course in psychology will provide you with much practice in critical thinking. And this is definitely a skill you will take with you—and use—long after the course, and this book, are just memories of days long past.

TABLE 1.4	**ASPECT**	**VALUE/PURPOSE**
Critical Thinking: Some Basic Components Critical thinking involves considerable effort. However, since it can help you avoid serious errors of judgment, bad decisions, and many other pitfalls, it is a skill well worth developing.	Define the issue of the problem clearly, including key terms.	We can't think clearly about an issue unless we know just what it involves.
	Examine all relevant evidence; avoid jumping to premature conclusions.	Avoid the temptation to go with "gut level" feelings. Better decisions and judgments can be made if all available evidence is taken into account.
	Carefully consider assumptions and biases.	All arguments are based on assumptions. These must be brought out into the open so that you can determine their validity.
	Avoid the tendency to oversimplify.	Simple answers or solutions are very misleading and ignore important complexities.
	Avoid the tendency to overgeneralize.	Avoid leaping from a single event or experience to all related events or experiences.

PSYCHOLOGY: WHAT IT IS AND HOW IT DEVELOPED critical thinking 5 psychology 5 structuralism 8 functionalism 8 behaviorism 8 cognitive processes 11 psychodynamic perspective 11 humanistic perspective 12 nature–nurture controversy 12 evolutionary psychology 12 multicultural perspective 13	• Psychology is defined as the science of behavior and cognitive processes. • Psychology studies behavior from many different perspectives: behavioral, cognitive, psychodynamic, humanistic, biopsychological, evolutionary, and sociocultural. • Early psychologists differed sharply over the scope of their new field. Structuralists felt that it should identify the basic parts of consciousness. Functionalists believed that psychology should focus on the adaptive value of the human mind. Behaviorists felt that psychology should focus primarily on observable behavior. • Until recently, the field of psychology did not focus much attention on cultural or ethnic differences. This situation has now changed greatly, and such differences are the focus of an increasing amount of research attention. • Psychology is scientific in nature because it adopts the methods and values of science in its efforts to understand behavior. Psychology is not mere common sense: The results of systematic research are a much more reliable guide to understanding human behavior than informal observation.
PSYCHOLOGY: WHO AND WHAT	• Psychologists receive their advanced training in graduate departments of psychology. Most receive a Ph.D. after at least five years of advanced study. • There are many subfields in psychology, including cognitive psychology, developmental psychology, and psychobiology. All share a commitment to advancing our knowledge of behavior through scientific means.
ADDING TO WHAT WE KNOW: THE PROCESS OF PSYCHOLOGICAL RESEARCH naturalistic observation 22 case method 22 survey method 22 hypothesis 24 correlational method 24 experimentation 25 independent variable 26 dependent variable 26 random assignment 26 experimenter effects 28 demand characteristics 29 double-blind procedure 29 inferential statistics 29 meta-analysis 31 theories 32	• Psychologists use many different research methods, including *naturalistic observation*, the *case method*, and the *survey approach*. • In the *correlational method of research*, efforts are made to determine whether relationships (correlations) exist between variables—that is, whether changes in one variable are accompanied by changes in another. • The stronger the correlation between two variables, the more accurately one variable can be predicted from the other. However, even strong correlations do not indicate that changes in one variable cause changes in another. • *Experimentation* involves systematically altering one or more variables in order to determine whether changes in these variables affect behavior. • The results of an experiment are valid only to the extent that participants are randomly assigned to conditions and that confounding of the independent variable with other factors is prevented. • Research results can also be invalidated by subtle cues that reveal a researcher's expectations about participants' behavior (*experimenter effects*) or that reveal the hypothesis of the study to participants (*demand characteristics*). • The results of an experiment are informative only if they are significant—that is, if the probability is low that they occurred by chance. • Combining and evaluating the results of many different studies through *meta-analysis* can help researchers determine whether the studies provide support for a specific hypothesis. • *Theories* consist of (1) basic concepts and (2) statements concerning relationships between these concepts. They are frameworks designed to help explain various aspects of the natural world. Only theories that can be tested and confirmed (or perhaps disconfirmed) are scientifically useful.

ETHICAL ISSUES IN PSYCHOLOGY deception 34 informed consent 35 debriefing 35	• In some cases, psychologists withhold information about a study from participants. This kind of deception is used when the withheld information might change participants' behavior from what it would normally be. • Research with animals raises complex ethical issues and must always involve strenuous efforts to minimize discomfort or risk to the subjects. • Psychologists also face many complex ethical issues with respect to the practice of their field—for example, assuring confidentiality of sensitive information for individuals receiving therapy.

CRITICAL THINKING QUESTIONS

APPRAISAL	Most psychologists view their field as being scientific in nature. Do you agree? Explain why you do or do not accept this view.
CONTROVERSY	Research with animals is a very controversial topic. Some people believe that it is never appropriate to conduct such research, while others feel that such research is often justified. What are your views on this issue? Is research with animals ever justified? If so, when? If not, why?
MAKING PSYCHOLOGY PART OF YOUR LIFE	Now that you know the basic ground rules of psychological research, do you think this knowledge will lead you to evaluate claims about human behavior differently than in the past? Think of one statement about people you have read in newspapers or magazines or heard on television in recent days; in the light of appropriate research methods, do you think it is accurate?

Biological Bases of Behavior

A Look Beneath the Surface

NEURONS: BUILDING BLOCKS OF THE NERVOUS SYSTEM 49
Neurons: Their Basic Structure
Neurons: Their Basic Function
Neurotransmitters: Chemical Keys to the Nervous System

THE NERVOUS SYSTEM: ITS BASIC STRUCTURE AND FUNCTIONS 59
The Nervous System: Its Major Divisions
The Nervous System: How It Is Studied

THE BRAIN: WHERE CONSCIOUSNESS IS MANIFEST 66
Survival Basics: The Brain Stem
Emotion and Motivation: The Hypothalamus, Thalamus, and Limbic System
The Cerebral Cortex: The Hub of Complex Thought
Language and the Cerebral Cortex: Models of Human Speech

LATERALIZATION OF THE CEREBRAL CORTEX: TWO MINDS IN ONE BODY? 73
Research with Intact Individuals
Research with Split-Brain Participants: Isolating the Two Hemispheres

THE ENDOCRINE SYSTEM: CHEMICAL REGULATORS OF BODILY PROCESSES 77
Hormones and Behavior: Is the Premenstrual Syndrome Real?

HEREDITY AND BEHAVIOR 81
Genetics: Some Basic Principles
Disentangling Genetic and Environmental Effects: Research Strategies

SUMMARY AND REVIEW OF KEY POINTS 89

KEY CONCEPT—COMMUNICATION IN THE NERVOUS SYSTEM: PUTTING IT ALL TOGETHER 54

THE POINT OF IT ALL—USING KNOWLEDGE OF SYNAPTIC TRANSMISSION TO TREAT ADDICTIONS: FIGHTING FIRE WITH FIRE 57

THE POINT OF IT ALL—HIGH-TECH SNOOPERS: PUTTING BRAIN IMAGING DEVICES TO WORK 64

CANADIAN FOCUS—MUSIC AND THE RIGHT HEMISPHERE 70

PERSPECTIVES ON DIVERSITY—THE BIOLOGICAL BASIS OF GENDER DIFFERENCES 80

THE RESEARCH PROCESS—SEXUAL ORIENTATION: GENETICALLY DETERMINED OR LIFESTYLE CHOICE? 85

MAKING PSYCHOLOGY PART OF YOUR LIFE—TRAUMATIC BRAIN INJURY: USING PSYCHOLOGY TO ENHANCE QUALITY OF LIFE 87

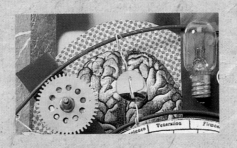

CLUES SHARED INTO HOW BRAIN LEARNS MUSIC

The Chronicle Herald (Halifax): November 19, 1993

Three hundred experts from various fields—psychiatry, psychology, music, education and communications—gathered to exchange ideas about music and brain function. In one presentation, reported in The Chronicle Herald, the participants learned about the case of Maurice Ravel, a famous composer who lived around the turn of this century. Apparently, toward the end of his career, Ravel suffered a mysterious brain affliction that left him able to compose music in his head but no longer able to sing his compositions or play them on a musical instrument.

Chapter 2 begins your introduction to the science of psychology. You will learn how brain function and normal behavior are intricately coupled, and how the effects of brain damage tell us a great deal about normal behavior.

What happens to your body when you feel joy or hunger? What does your brain do when you dream, make plans, or remember events that took place ages ago? How does your body know where to move when you want to get somewhere? All these questions are about the relationship between biology, brain, and behavior. And they are of central concern not only in **biopsychology** (the study of biology and behavior), but also in more specialized disciplines such as neuropsychology (the study of the brain, brain damage, and behavior) and neuroscience (which is the general term applied to any research into how brain cells work).

The 1990s have been the "Decade of the Brain." This recognizes the great progress that world scientists are making toward understanding how our brains work. The human brain is the most complex organ of all—and the most mysterious. Its abilities—reading, feeling, understanding, computing, deciding, planning, strumming, slam-dunking, tasting, sleeping, predicting, and in essence, living are without equal.

Research into brain-behavior relationships has vital practical applications. Statistics tell us that about 5 million Canadians suffer from some kind of brain damage, often resulting from stroke, from diseases such as Alzheimer's (see Chapter 6), or from traumatic brain injury or spinal cord damage (often the result of a car accident). Brain damage has not only a serious emotional impact on the individual, their family and friends, but also a significant economic impact on society. For this reason, Canada's federal government has earmarked $25.5 million to establish a "center of excellence" to develop new research in this field. That center is actually a network of over one hundred Canadian scientists at sixteen different universities. Many of these scientists have training and expertise in psychology and perform all kinds of research, the general purpose of which is to discover how the nervous system works, and how it recovers from damage.

Psychological research turned a corner in 1949 with the publication of a book called *The Organization of Behaviour: A Neuropsychological Theory*. Its author, D.O. Hebb, a Nova Scotian who spent his scientific career at McGill University in Montreal, changed the direction of psychology and his ideas became very influential in brain science. In his book, Hebb predicted that in order to understand human behavior, it would be necessary to understand

Biopsychology: *The branch of psychology concerned with discovering the biological bases of our thoughts, feelings, and behaviors.*

THE "DECADE OF THE BRAIN"

Although scientists have not yet succeeded in constructing the thinking cap of Calvin's active imagination, they are making great strides toward understanding the biological bases of behavior.

CALVIN AND HOBBES

By Bill Watterson

the nervous system and its functions. This sounds reasonable today, but forty years ago it was considered radical. In those days, the biology of the individual responding to stimuli was deliberately ignored!

Hebb recognized, however, that human behavior could never be explained fully by knowledge of how the brain functions. Rather, he acknowledged that our physical, psychological, social, and emotional experiences affect the state of our nervous system, and thus the way we behave. Research by biopsychologists confirms that environmental factors can offset the effects of nature. Thus, while biological factors are powerful, they are not always immutable.

Hebb was not the first to suggest that behavior is a product of brain function. That idea already had a long history. A full 2,400 years before Hebb, the Greek physician Hippocrates had concluded, "From the brain, and from the brain only, arise our pleasures, joys, laughter and jests, as well as our sorrows, pains, griefs and fears. Through [the brain], in particular, we think, see, hear, and distinguish the ugly from the beautiful, the bad from the good, the pleasant from the unpleasant." Hippocrates, however, lacked both knowledge of the principles of scientific investigation and the know-how to test those ideas scientifically. Today, because of rapid advances in technology, researchers can actually construct computer images of the nervous systems of people, while they are awake and following instructions, in order to see how the brain's structure and function are related to behavior. Such advances would have been viewed as science fiction a generation ago. Today they are a reality.

We will begin by examining the structure and function of neurons, the building blocks of the nervous system. Research about how neurons function—and especially how they communicate with one another—provides important insights into such diverse topics as how drugs exert their effects and how serious forms of mental illness develop. Next, we will turn to the structure and function of the nervous system, devoting special attention to the human brain, the marvelous organ that is ultimately responsible for consciousness—and for the fact that you are now reading and understanding these words! Discussion of the structure and function of the brain will lead us to several special topics, including the biological basis of addictions and the unique abilities of the two sides of the brain. After this, we will turn briefly to the endocrine system—the internal glands regulated by the nervous system that also play an important role in behavior. We'll conclude by reviewing the role genetic factors play in physical and mental disorders, and even sexual preference.

Neurons: Building Blocks of the Nervous System

*H*ow does the sound of the words "It's time for supper!" produce rumbles in the stomach, feelings of hunger, and a dash to the dinner table? In other words, how can information reaching our ears produce sensations of hunger, and overt actions relating to these? The answer involves the activity of **neurons**—cells within our bodies that are specialized for the tasks of receiving, moving, and processing information.

Neurons: Cells specialized for communicating information, the basic building blocks of the nervous system.

**D.O. Hebb
(1904–1985)**

D.O. Hebb insisted that behavior is a function of the brain. He gained international recognition, receiving the Distinguished Scientific Contribution Medal of the APA among other rewards.

**Justine Sergent
(1950–94)**

Justine Sergent explored right and left brain hemisphere function, such as how the brain processes words and music, at both the Montreal Neurological Institute and McGill University.

PSYCHOLOGISTS OF NOTE

Neurons: *Their Basic Structure*

Neurons are tremendously varied in appearance. Yet most consist of three basic parts: (1) a *cell body*, (2) an **axon**, and (3) one or more **dendrites**. Dendrites carry information toward the cell body, whereas axons carry information away from it. Thus, neurons are one-way channels of communication. Information moves from dendrites to the cell body and then on along the axon to its terminals. A simplified diagram of a neuron and actual neurons is shown in Figure 2.1.

In many neurons the axon is covered by a sheath of fatty material known as *myelin*. This myelin "wrapping" is interrupted by small gaps. Both the sheath and its gaps play an important role in the neuron's ability to transmit information rapidly. The myelin sheath is actually produced by other cells within the nervous system, **glial cells**. Glial cells, which outnumber neurons by about ten to one, form the myelin sheath by wrapping themselves around axons.

Near its end, the axon divides into several small branches. These, in turn, end in **axon terminals**, which closely approach, but do not actually touch, other cells (other neurons, muscles, or glands). The region between an axon terminal and another neuron is known as a **synapse**. The manner in which neurons communicate across this space is described below.

Axon: The part of the neuron that conducts action potential away from the cell body.

Dendrites: The parts of neurons that conduct action potentials toward the cell body.

Glial Cells: Cells in the nervous system that surround, support, and protect neurons.

Axon Terminals: Structures at the end of axons that contain transmitter substances.

Synapse: A region where the axon of one neuron closely approaches other neurons or the cell membrane of other types of cells such as muscle cells.

Donald T. Stuss

Donald Stuss contributes both to research and to real-life applications in neuropsychology. The 1994 President of the International Neuropsychological Society, Stuss is the Director of the Rotman Research Institute in Toronto.

Bryan Kolb

Bryan Kolb studies the links between brain and behavior. Kolb is the current president of the Canadian Society for Brain, Behavior and Cognitive Science and the Psychology department chair at the University of Lethbridge.

Neurons: *Their Basic Function*

As we consider how neurons function, two questions arise: How does information travel from point to point within a single neuron? And how is information transmitted from one neuron to another, and from neurons to other cells of the body?

Communication within neurons: The action potential The answer to the first question is complex. When a neuron is at rest, there is an electrical charge across the cell membrane. This electrical charge is due to the fact that several types of ions (positively or negatively charged particles) exist in different concentrations outside and inside the cell. As a result, the interior of the cell has a negative electric charge relative to the outside. This *resting potential* does not occur by accident; the neuron works to maintain the resting potential by actively pumping positively charged ions back out while retaining negatively charged ions in greater concentrations inside the cell.

When the neuron is stimulated, either directly (by light, heat, or pressure) or by chemical messages from other neurons, the situation may change radically. If the stimulation exceeds the set *threshold* level of the neuron in question—complex biochemical changes occur in the cell membrane. The result of these changes is that some types of *positively charged ions* are briefly allowed to enter the neuron through specialized pores called *ion channels*. This influx of positive ions reduces and then eliminates the resting potential. Indeed, for a brief period of time, the interior of the cell becomes positively charged.

FIGURE 2.1

Neurons: Their Basic Structure

(A) Neurons appear in many forms, but all possess the basic structures shown here: a cell body, an axon (with axon terminals), and one or more dendrites. (B) Actual human neurons, greatly magnified.

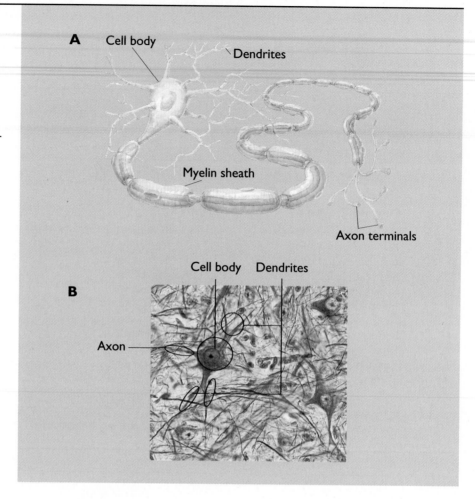

After a very brief period (1 or 2 milliseconds), the neuron actively pumps the positive ions back outside and allows other ions to reenter. Once the resting potential is restored, the cell is ready to "fire" once again. Together, these swings in electric charge—from negative to positive and back again—are termed the **action potential**. It is the passage of this electrical disturbance along the cell membrane that constitutes the basic transmission within the nervous system.

The action potential is an *all-or-none response*. Either it occurs at full strength or it does not occur at all; there is nothing in between. The speed of conduction is very rapid, especially in neurons possessing a myelin sheath. The action potential along myelinated axons jumps from one small gap in this sheath to another, instead of passing along the whole length of the axon. These gaps are known as **nodes of Ranvier**. Speeds along myelinated axons can reach 450 kilometers an hour. At the University of Toronto in 1991, Reed and Jensen measured the neural transmission rate in the arms of male students. The point of this study was to learn whether the speed of neural transmission (in the arm) could predict how well the students did on a nonverbal intelligence test. The answer was "no."

Another kind of signal that passes information between neurons is called the **graded potential** and results from the stimulation of the dendrite or cell

Action Potential: A rapid shift in the electrical charge across the cell membrane of neurons. This disturbance along the membrane communicates information within neurons.

Nodes of Ranvier: Small gaps in the myelin sheath surrounding the axons of many neurons.

Graded Potential: A potential that varies in magnitude with the size of the stimulus that produced it.

body (refer to Figure 2.2). Unlike the action potential, which is all-or-nothing, a graded potential varies in magnitude with the size of the stimulus that produced it. Because graded potentials weaken quickly, they function primarily to convey incoming information over short distances, usually along the dendrite toward the neuron's cell body. Since neurons typically receive information from thousands of other cells, it is the overall pattern of graded potentials reaching the cell body that determines whether or not an action potential will occur.

COMMUNICATION BETWEEN NEURONS: SYNAPTIC TRANSMISSION   Earlier we saw that neurons closely approach, but do not actually touch, other neurons. How, then, does the action potential cross the gap? Existing evidence points to the following answer.

When a neuron "fires," the action potential travels along the membrane to the axon terminals. Within the axon terminals are many biochemical containers known as **synaptic vesicles**. Arrival of the action potential causes these vesicles to approach the cell membrane, where they fuse with the membrane and then empty their chemical contents into the synapse (see Figure 2.2). Some of the molecules thus released—known as **neurotransmitters**—cross the synaptic gap and reach special receptor sites in the membrane of the other cell.

These receptors are complex protein molecules into which transmitter substances fit—like chemical keys into locks. Specific transmitters can deliver signals only at certain locations on cell membranes, and this introduces precision into the nervous system's complex communication system. Upon binding to their receptors, neurotransmitters produce their effects either directly, or indirectly through other substances called neuromodulators.

Synaptic Vesicles: Structures in the axon terminals that contain various neurotransmitters.

Neurotransmitters: Chemicals, released by neurons, that carry information across the synapse.

FIGURE 2.2

Synaptic Transmission: An Overview

The axon terminals found on the ends of axons contain many synaptic vesicles. When an action potential reaches the axon terminal, these vesicles move toward the cell membrane. Once there, the vesicles fuse with the membrane and release their contents (neurotransmitters) into the synapse.

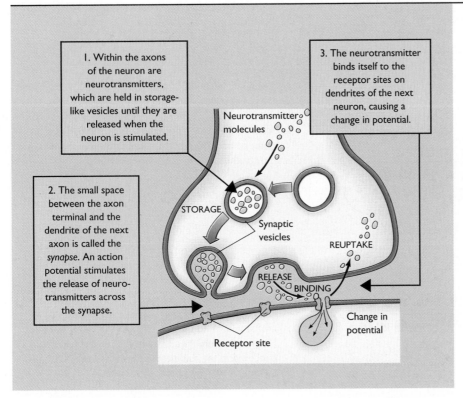

1. Within the axons of the neuron are neurotransmitters, which are held in storage-like vesicles until they are released when the neuron is stimulated.

2. The small space between the axon terminal and the dendrite of the next axon is called the *synapse*. An action potential stimulates the release of neurotransmitters across the synapse.

3. The neurotransmitter binds itself to the receptor sites on dendrites of the next neuron, causing a change in potential.

Neurotransmitter molecules

STORAGE

Synaptic vesicles

REUPTAKE

RELEASE

BINDING

Receptor site

Change in potential

Communication in the Nervous System: Putting It All Together

The key to understanding communication in the nervous system is to understand that information transmission depends on the movement of positively and negatively charged ions across the membrane that covers the neuron.

As shown in the diagram, a resting neuron has a slight negative charge –70 millivolts) across the cell membrane—that is, the inside is negative relative to the outside. The nervous system expends a great deal of energy to maintain this state of readiness. This is because the neuron's cell membrane is not a perfect barrier. Rather, it leaks a little, allowing some particles to slip in and others to slip out.

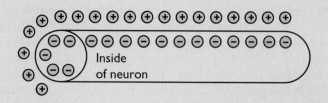

Steps in the Transmission Mechanism

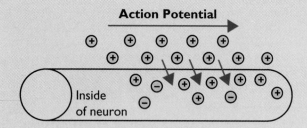

1. When the neuron is stimulated either by an external stimulus or by another neuron, positively charged particles enter the membrane through specialized ion channels, thereby momentarily eliminating the neuron's membrane. Movement of this disturbance along the membrane constitutes the action potential.

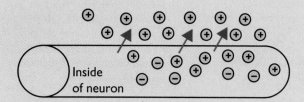

2. After a brief period, positively charged particles are pumped back outside the neuron's membrane via the ion channels.

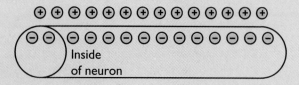

3. As a result of this active process, the inside of the neuron's membrane regains the negative charge (–70 millivolts) relative to the outside, and the cell is ready to "fire" once more. The passage of this electrical disturbance along the cell membrane serves as the basis for communication in the nervous system.

Directly or indirectly, neurotransmitters produce one of two effects. If their effects are *excitatory*, they cause a *depolarization* in the membrane of the second cell, making it more likely for that cell to fire. Or the transmitter substances may be *inhibitory*. In this case, they *hyperpolarize* (increase the negative charge of) the membrane of the second cell, thereby making it less likely that the cell will fire. Key Concept on page 54 diagrams the nervous system's information transmission mechanisms.

What happens to neurotransmitter substances after synaptic transmission? Either they are taken back for recycling into the axon terminals of the neuron that released them—a process known as *reuptake*—or they are deactivated by various enzymes in the synapse. The used neurotransmitters must be cleared away; otherwise, activation will reoccur when it should not.

Neurons actually form synapses with many other cells—ten thousand or more in some cases. Therefore, at any given moment, neurons are receiving a complex pattern of excitatory and inhibitory influences from many neighbors. Whether a neuron conducts an action potential or not, depends on the total pattern—for example, whether excitatory or inhibitory input predominates. Further, the effects of excitatory and inhibitory input can accumulate over time, in part because such effects do not dissipate instantaneously. Thus, if a neuron that has recently been stimulated, but not sufficiently to produce an action potential, is stimulated again soon afterwards, the two sources of excitation may combine so that an action potential is generated. In one sense, then, neurons are *decision-making* cells, firing only when the pattern of information reaching them is just right. As we will see further on, it is this intricate web of neural excitation that generates the richness and complexity of our conscious experience.

Neurotransmitters: Chemical Keys to the Nervous System

The fact that transmitter substances produce either excitation or inhibition might suggest that there are two types of neurotransmitters. In fact, there are at least nine universally recognized substances known to act as neurotransmitters, and forty or more peptides (amino acid combinations) that *appear* to act as neurotransmitters. Several known neurotransmitters and their functions are summarized in Table 2.1.

Although the specific role of many transmitter substances remains unclear, several have been studied extensively. For example, *acetylcholine* is an important neurotransmitter found throughout the nervous system. Acetylcholine is the neurotransmitter at junctions between motor neurons (neurons which carry instructions about movement) and muscle cells. Thus, anything that interferes with the action of acetylcholine can have dramatic effects on normal control of movement. These effects may vary from total paralysis to muscular convulsions. Acetylcholine is also believed to play a role in attention, arousal, and memory processes (Beninger et al., 1988). Scientists believe that the severe memory loss characteristic of individuals suffering from *Alzheimer's disease* results from a degeneration of cells that produce acetylcholine. Examinations of the brains of people who have died from this disease show unusually low levels of this substance (Coyle, Price, & DeLong, 1983).

TABLE 2.1

Neurotransmitters: A Summary

The neurons have been found to communicate by means of many different neurotransmitters. This table presents several known neurotransmitters, their locations, and their known or supposed effects on the body.

NEUROTRANSMITTER	LOCATION	EFFECTS
Acetylcholine	Found throughout the central nervous system, in the autonomic nervous system, and at all neuromuscular junctions.	Involved in muscle action, earning, and memory.
Norepinephrine	Found in neurons in the autonomic nervous system.	Principally involved in control of alertness and wakefulness.
Dopamine	Produced by neurons located in a region of the brain called the substantia negra.	Involved in movement, attention, and learning. Degeneration of dopamine-producing neurons is linked to Parkinson's disease. Too much dopamine has been linked to schizophrenia.
Serotonin	Found in neurons in the brain and spinal cord.	Plays a role in the regulation of mood and in the control of eating, sleep, and arousal. Has also been implicated in the regulation of pain and in dreaming.
GABA (gamma-amino butyric acid)	Found throughout the brain and spinal cord.	GABA is the major inhibitory neurotransmitter in the brain. Abnormal levels of GABA have been implicated in sleep and eating disorders.

ENDORPHINS Perhaps the most dramatic discoveries about neurotransmitters and their effects were first reported in the mid-1970s (Hughes et al., 1975). At that time, many researchers who were studying the impact of *morphine* and other opiates on the nervous system found receptor sites for these drugs within the brain. Since morphine and opiates are not natural to the brain, this was indeed a puzzle. Why should such receptor sites exist? The answer was this: Within the brain there are naturally occurring substances that, in their chemical structure, closely resemble morphine. These substances, known as *endorphins,* seem to act as neurotransmitters. But this finding, in turn, raised another question: Why should the brain produce such substances? Research now suggests that endorphins are released in response to pain and so help reduce sensations of pain that might otherwise interfere with our ongoing behavior (Fields & Basbaum, 1984; Henry, 1982). Additional evidence indicates that the release of endorphins may also serve to intensify positive sensations—for example, the "runner's high" many people experience after vigorous exercise.

In short, it appears that the brain possesses an internal mechanism for moderating unpleasant sensations and magnifying positive ones. The effects of morphine and other opiates stem, at least in part, from the fact that these drugs exploit the receptor sites of this natural system.

Research efforts are now aimed at identifying drugs that will alter synaptic transmission for practical purposes. As we'll see in **The Point of It All**, it is very possible that understanding the process of synaptic transmission will lead researchers to successful treatment of a variety of disorders, including addictions to alcohol and other drugs.

KEY POINTS

- Neurotransmitters produce one of two effects: excitatory effects cause a depolarization in the nerve cell membrane, making it more likely that a graded potential will be generated; inhibitory effects hyperpolarize the cell membrane, making it less likely that the cell will fire.

- Growing evidence suggests that knowledge of neurotransmitter systems can be applied to solve important practical problems, including drug and alcohol abuse.

THE POINT OF IT ALL

Using Knowledge of Synaptic Transmission to Treat Addictions: Fighting Fire with Fire

D rugs are big business—*very* big business—and the medical portion of this huge industry is by no means the largest part. Each day, hundreds of millions of people all over the world take drugs not to combat illness or improve their health, but to change the way they feel. People have come to use drugs to combat insomnia and to fight fatigue; to calm jittery nerves or increase their energy; to chase away the blues; or—perhaps most questionable of all—simply to get high.

The explosion in recreational drug use (and abuse) during the past several decades has had devastating effects, both economic and social. The amount of money involved is astonishing. In February 1994 the RCMP raided a small New Brunswick–registered fishing boat just off Canada's east coast, at Shelburne, Nova Scotia. There they found a "monster shipment" of more than 1000 kilograms of cocaine with a street value of $100 million. The cocaine had come from South America and was for wide North American distribution.

In Canada, illegal drugs are used by a relatively small percentage of the population. For example, in the 1993 Ontario Student Survey of Drug Use (Adlaf, Smart, & Walsh, 1993), there was good news and bad with respect to drug abuse among students in grades 7 to 13. The good news was that there had been a long-term increase in the percentage of Ontario students reporting that they used *no drugs in the previous year* (from 17.4 percent in 1979 to 36.9 percent in 1993). Unfortunately, there was also a disturbing age-related shift in drug use—at the grade 7 level there were *increases* in use of tobacco, alcohol, and cannabis (i.e., marijuana). In addition, students' use of cannabis had doubled in Northern Ontario, and the use of LSD-type substances had increased among older students. Although the overall percentage of drug use in the general population of students in Ontario was low, some of the numbers were alarming. For example, about 1 percent of the students in this survey (that is, 9,200 of them) reported using cannabis every day, and the same number were using crack. As for the legal drugs like tobacco and alcohol, 157,200 students reported smoking daily, and 22,000 reported having five or more drinks on the same occasion at least once a week.

It is estimated that at least 100,000 Canadians have been experimenting with over-the-counter "brain boosters" or "smart drugs." These are nutrients and vitamins which, it is claimed, increase your brain power and intelligence, make you more alert, and improve your concentration and memory. There is no evidence that any of these substances work, and their side effects are unknown. Using them involves taking a risk, as is always the case when special substances are utilized to alter the chemical balance of the body and the brain.

Unfortunately, the methods traditionally used to treat drug addictions have been only marginally successful. This has led researchers in recent years to consider fighting fire with fire—in other words, using knowledge of how drugs exert their effects on the nervous system to develop effective drug therapies. Here is how that is done.

There is an important link between the structure and function of neurons and the effects of many drugs. Stated simply, the link is this: In many cases, drugs affect us by altering the process of synaptic transmission. They produce their effects—including the feelings of pleasure that many addicts strongly crave—by changing the complex biochemical events that occur when one neuron communicates with another. In the most basic terms, such effects take one of two main forms. If a particular drug *mimics* (i.e., copies the effect of) a

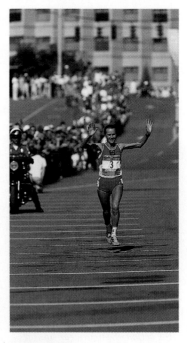

ENDORPHINS: NEUROTRANSMITTERS AS PAIN RELIEVERS?

Endorphins are released by the body in response to pain and may also intensify positive bodily sensations, as in the "runner's high."

specific neurotransmitter, it is said to be an **agonist** of the neurotransmitter. If, in contrast, a drug interferes with or *inhibits* the impact of a neurotransmitter, it is said to be an **antagonist** of the neurotransmitter. The specific ways in which drugs can function as agonists or antagonists in synaptic transmission are summarized in Figure 2.3.

Many drugs exert their effects on behavior through one or more of these mechanisms (e.g., Kalivas & Samson, 1992). For example, nicotine, a drug found in tobacco, influences neural receptors sensitive to acetylcholine. The effect is agonistic—nicotine excites these receptors and so acts as a mild stimulant. Atropine is used by physicians use to dilate the pupils of your eyes so that they can examine the insides of your eyeballs. Atropine occupies receptors that normally respond to acetylcholine; as a result, the pupils do not respond to messages delivered by that neurotransmitter, and remain dilated. Curare is a poison used for hunting by native people in South America. Curare occupies acetylcholine receptors at synapses between neurons and muscles. When shot with an arrow or dart tipped with this substance, an animal loses its ability to move. Total paralysis soon results—including paralysis of the respiratory muscles, which leads to death. Cocaine (Roberts, 1993; Phillips & Fibiger, 1990) and amphetamines produce their effects by inhibiting reuptake of such neurotransmitters as *dopamine* and *norepinephrine*. As a result of this inhibition, the neurotransmitter remains in the synapse, where they cause continued activity in many neurons. This is one reason why individuals taking such drugs often experience feelings of tremendous excitement and energy. Agonists and antagonists to the neurotransmitter dopamine have contributed to our understanding of electrical events in the brain (Nakajima & O'Regan, 1991). With various

Agonist: *A drug that mimics the action of a neurotransmitter.*

Antagonist: *A drug that inhibits the impact of a neurotransmitter.*

FIGURE 2.3

Drugs: How They Influence Synaptic Transmission

Various drugs produce their effects either by mimicking (agonistic) or by interfering with (antagonistic) the operations of specific transmitter substances.

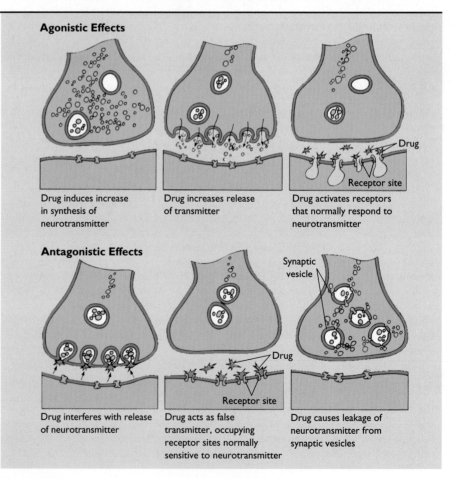

Agonistic Effects

Drug induces increase in synthesis of neurotransmitter

Drug increases release of transmitter

Drug activates receptors that normally respond to neurotransmitter

Drug

Receptor site

Antagonistic Effects

Drug interferes with release of neurotransmitter

Drug acts as false transmitter, occupying receptor sites normally sensitive to neurotransmitter

Drug causes leakage of neurotransmitter from synaptic vesicles

Synaptic vesicle

Drug

Receptor site

opiates, yet another mechanism is involved. Morphine and heroin are agonists. These drugs engage the receptor sites that normally fit endorphins and opiate peptides—that is, they mimic those naturally occurring substances, lessen pain and stress, and produce a feeling of wonderful well-being.

Still more complex is the action of benzodiazepines, which have an indirect effect on the action of GABA, another important neurotransmitter. GABA's inhibitory effects are increased by benzodiazepines; the outcome is a decrease in anxiety.

Several converging lines of evidence (Reid, 1990) point to the conclusion that the addicting properties of some drugs may derive, at least in part, from their impact on *naturally occurring reward* circuits deep within the brain. This may well apply to morphine (Corbett, 1992), heroin (Roberts & Bennett, 1993), and cocaine (Corrigall & Coen, 1991). In these studies, it has been found that the neurotransmitter dopamine is involved in complex ways (Nakajima et al., 1993; Bozarth, 1987; Phillips & Fibiger, 1989), and one proposed way of combating such addictions is to administer drugs that prevent substances which are often abused from stimulating the reward circuits.

Some success along these lines has been reported by Volpicelli and his colleagues (1992). These researchers administered either the drug naltrexone or a placebo to individuals suffering from alcohol dependence. They used naltrexone to block receptors in the brain—that is, to prevent alcohol from having an effect. If alcohol produces pleasurable effects by stimulating these receptors, naltrexone should prevent those effects from occuring. To the extent it does, the motivation for drinking alcohol should be reduced and its consumption should also fall. Volpicelli and his colleagues found that participants who received naltrexone reported much weaker cravings for alcohol than those in the control group. They also indicated that they drank less alcohol, and—most importantly—were less likely to resume drinking after the study had ended.

Understanding how drugs affect the nervous system, and thereby also affect behavior, can be important in developing useful techniques for treating their harmful effects, especially drug addictions. Knowledge of how various drugs produce their effects has also proved valuable for determining the causes of serious psychological disorders. For example, drugs that combat depression are known as *antidepressants*. Studies designed to determine exactly how these drugs work are shedding new light on the neural basis of the serious psychological problem of depression itself (e.g., McNeal & Cimbolic, 1986; Linesman, 1989), as well as on anorexia nervosa and bulimia (Kennedy & Garfinkel), and on chronic low back pain (Sullivan et al., 1992). In these and other ways, basic knowledge about how neurons function has turned out to be of considerable practical value. This information is already making substantial contributions to the enhancement of human health and well-being.

The Nervous System: *Its Basic Structure and Functions*

Neurons are the building blocks; the **nervous system** is the structure they form, along with other types of cells. Since this system regulates our internal bodily functions and permits us to react to the external world in countless ways, it deserves very careful attention. In this section we will describe the basic structure of the nervous system and introduce several techniques psychologists use to study its complex functions.

Nervous System: The complex structure that regulates bodily processes and is responsible, ultimately, for all aspects of conscious experience.

The Nervous System: *Its Major Divisions*

While the nervous system functions as an integrated whole, it is often viewed as having two major divisions—the **central nervous system** and the **peripheral nervous system**. Figure 2.4 diagrams these and other divisions of the nervous system.

THE CENTRAL NERVOUS SYSTEM (CNS)　This system consists of the brain and the spinal cord. The spinal cord runs through a column of hollow bones known as *vertebrae*. You can feel these by moving your hand up and down the middle of your back.

The spinal cord has two major functions. First, it carries sensory information to the brain via *afferent* nerve fibers, and relays information via *efferent* nerve fibers from the brain to muscles and glands. Second, it plays a key role in various *reflexes*. Withdrawing your hand from a hot object, and blinking your eye in response to a rapidly approaching object, are common examples of reflex actions. In their simplest form, reflexes involve neural circuits in which information from various receptors is carried to the spinal cord, where it stimulates *interneurons*. These send the information to afferent neurons, which in turn

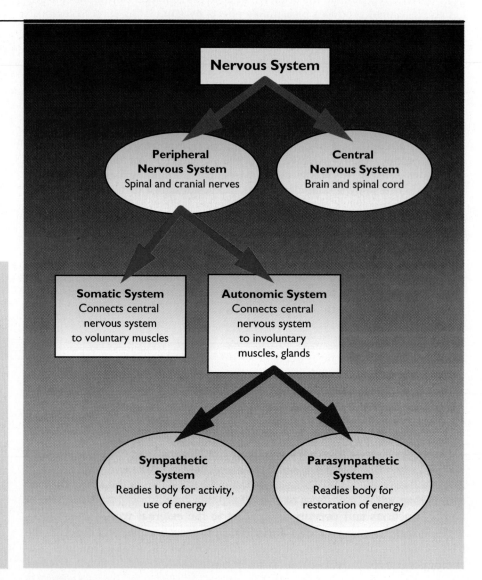

FIGURE 2.4

Major Divisions of the Nervous System

The nervous system consists of several major parts.

Central Nervous System: The brain and the spinal cord.

Peripheral Nervous System: The portion of the nervous system that connects internal organs and glands, as well as voluntary and involuntary muscles, to the central nervous system.

Somatic Nervous System: The portion of the peripheral nervous system that connects the brain and spinal cord to voluntary muscles.

Autonomic Nervous System: The part of the peripheral nervous system that connects internal organs, glands, and involuntary muscles to the central nervous system.

relay instructions to muscles, thus producing reflex actions. This is called a reflex arc, but please take note: Spinal reflexes are usually much more complex than this. Hundreds or even thousands of neurons may influence a reflex, and input from certain areas of the brain may be influential as well. However they arise, spinal reflexes offer an obvious advantage: They permit us to react to potential dangers much more rapidly than if we had to use our brains to decide how to respond.

THE PERIPHERAL NERVOUS SYSTEM (PNS) This system consists primarily of *nerves*—bundles of axons from many neurons—which connect the central nervous system with sense organs and with muscles and glands throughout the body. These *spinal nerves* serve all of the body below the neck. Other nerves, known as *cranial nerves,* carry sensory information from receptors in the eyes and ears and other sense organs above the neck. They also carry information from the brain to the muscles of the face, neck, and head.

The peripheral nervous system has two further subdivisions: the **somatic nervous system** and **autonomic nervous system**. The somatic nervous system connects the central nervous system to voluntary muscles throughout the body. Thus, when you engage in almost any voluntary action, such as making a line pass or hauling in the jib, portions of your somatic nervous system are involved. In contrast, the autonomic nervous system connects the central nervous system to internal organs and glands and to muscles over which we have little voluntary control—for instance, the muscles in our digestive system.

Still, we can't stop dividing things here. The autonomic nervous system, too, consists of two distinct parts. The first is known as the **sympathetic nervous system**. In general, this system prepares the body for using energy, as in vigorous physical actions. Stimulation of this system increases heartbeat, raises blood pressure, releases sugar into the blood for energy, and increases the flow of blood to muscles. The second portion of the autonomic system, known as the **parasympathetic nervous system,** operates in the opposite manner: It stimulates processes that conserve the body's energy. Activation of this system slows heartbeat, lowers blood pressure, and diverts blood away from skeletal muscles (e.g., muscles in the arms and legs) and to the digestive system. Figure 2.5 summarizes the structure and many of the functions of the autonomic nervous system.

At first glance it might appear that these two parts of the autonomic system compete with each other head-on. In fact, this is far from the case. The sympathetic and parasympathetic systems actually function in a coordinated manner by taking turns. Otherwise, there would be a lot of discomfort. For example, after a person eats a large meal on a warm day, the parasympathetic system stimulates digestion; at the same time, the sympathetic system increases sweating in order to eliminate excess heat. Also, both systems are involved at different stages of sexual intercourse.

While the autonomic nervous system plays an important role in regulating internal bodily processes, it does so mainly by transmitting information to and from the central nervous system. Thus, the CNS, ultimately, has all the information to run the show.

KEY POINTS

- The central nervous system (CNS) consists of the brain and spinal cord.

- The spinal cord carries sensory information from receptors of the body to the brain via afferent nerve fibers, and carries information from the brain to muscles and glands via efferent nerve fibers. It also plays a key role in reflexes.

- Many drugs produce their effects by influencing synaptic transmission. Drugs that mimic the impact of a neurotransmitters at specific receptors are termed agonists; drugs that inhibit their impact are termed antagonists.

- The peripheral nervous system consists of the somatic and autonomic nervous systems. The somatic nervous system connects the CNS to voluntary muscles throughout the body; the autonomic nervous system connects the CNS to internal organs and glands and to muscles over which we have little voluntary control.

- The sympathetic nervous system prepares the body for using energy; the parasympathetic nervous system activates processes that conserve the body's energy.

- Psychologists use several methods to study the nervous system, including observing the effects of damage, and of electrical or chemical stimulation of the brain, and several modern imaging techniques.

- PET scans have been used to show how the brain's activities change in response to experience in certain language tasks. The brain appears to expend less energy as it masters a task.

Sympathetic Nervous System: The portion of the autonomic nervous system that readies the body for expenditure of energy.

Parasympathetic Nervous System: The portion of the autonomic nervous system that readies the body for restoration of energy.

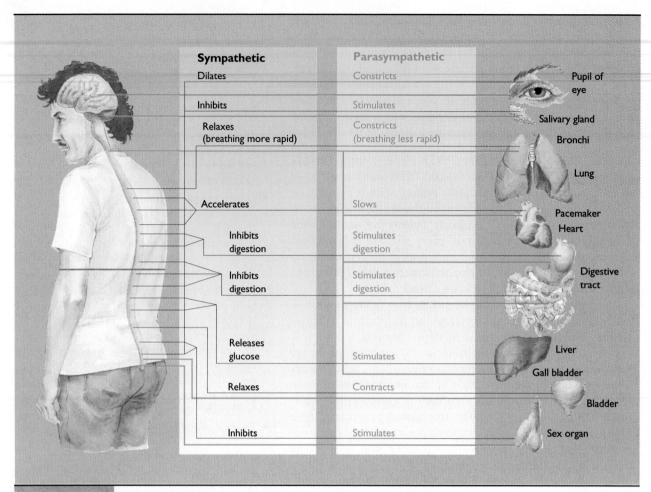

Sympathetic	Parasympathetic	
Dilates	Constricts	Pupil of eye
Inhibits	Stimulates	Salivary gland
Relaxes (breathing more rapid)	Constricts (breathing less rapid)	Bronchi
		Lung
Accelerates	Slows	Pacemaker Heart
Inhibits digestion	Stimulates digestion	Digestive tract
Inhibits digestion	Stimulates digestion	
Releases glucose	Stimulates	Liver
		Gall bladder
Relaxes	Contracts	Bladder
Inhibits	Stimulates	Sex organ

FIGURE 2.5

The Autonomic Nervous System: An Overview

The autonomic nervous system consists of two major parts: the sympathetic and parasympathetic nervous systems. Some of the functions of each are shown here.

The Nervous System: *How It Is Studied*

Suppose that you are a psychologist interested in creating a map of the brain, one that identifies the brain structures involved in various behaviors. How do you obtain the information to construct your map? There is no simple way, but biopsychologists and others have devised several ingenious methods.

OBSERVING THE EFFECTS OF DAMAGE One of the earliest sources of information for researchers was clinical observation of people who had suffered damage to their brain through disease or accident. Then, following their death—sometimes years later—researchers examined these brains to identify the location and extent of the injury. In a related approach, researchers operate on different brain structures of laboratory animals and then carefully observe the behavioral effects.

PSYCHOPHARMACOLOGICAL METHODS: INTRODUCING DRUGS INTO THE BRAIN Psychologists have also mapped the brain's functions by using minute quantities of drugs to damage specific brain sites, or to stimulate or anesthetize specific sets of neurons. If, for example, a drug that anesthetizes neurons is introduced into an area of the brain believed to play a role in speech production, we might expect the person's ability to speak to decrease while the drug's effects persist.

ELECTRICAL RECORDING AND BRAIN STIMULATION   Biopsychologists also study the nervous system by examining the electrical activity of the brain in the behaving organism. Sometimes this involves recording the electrical activity of the entire brain by means of electrodes placed on the skull—a procedure called **electroencephalography**, or **EEG**. EEG studies have examined specific responses of the brain to various external conditions. For example, Fowler and Lindeis (1992) used EEG recordings to determine whether breathing a low oxygen mixture slowed down reactions to odd sounds and sights. (Yes, it did.) In other cases EEG studies involve the precise implantation of fine electrodes in specific brain locations to *record* the activity of single neurons or groups of neurons. In addition, accurately implanted electrodes can be used to stimulate specific areas of the brain electrically, to determine their particular role in various forms of behavior.

MRI: A HIGH-TECH TOOL TO PEEK INSIDE THE BRAIN
Magnetic resonance imaging provides detailed images of the brain and is expecially useful in diagnosing brain disorders.

IMAGES OF THE LIVING BRAIN: MRIs, SQUIDs, AND PETs   Perhaps most exciting, however, is the alphabet soup of techniques that provide detailed images of the living brain's structures and functions. One of these techniques is **magnetic resonance imaging**, or **MRI**. MRI is a way of creating an image of an individual's internal state—that is, of examining the subject's biochemical and physical well-being without actually invading the body or the brain. At the Institute for Biodiagnostics, established in Winnipeg by the National Research Council of Canada, and at about thirty other centers across the country, MRI technology is being used to advance our knowledge of the basic biology of the body and of disease—for example, to pinpoint tumors and to diagnose injuries.

Here is how MRI works: It is known that hydrogen atoms, which are found in all living tissue, emit measurable waves of energy when exposed to strong magnetic fields. In MRI, these waves are measured and transformed by computer into images of cross-sections of the brain. These MRI images are impressively clear and therefore extremely useful in diagnosing many brain disorders. In basic research, MRI may be used to compare the size (volume) of various brain structures in patients with particular disorders, such as epilepsy (Watson, et al., 1992). *Functional MRI* displays detailed images of the brain in action. For example, functional MRI has revealed where the brain plans and produces movements. MRI scanning uses no radioactive substances. It is a way of studying how the brain works that has no known risk.

A second imaging device is called **SQUID**—short for **superconducting quantum interference device**. Here is how SQUID works: Recall that when neurons fire, they produce electrical currents that flow along the axon of the cell. Those currents give rise to weak magnetic fields, which the SQUID is able to detect. A supercomputer can then interpret and image that information for us. Researchers have used SQUID to locate various brain functions—for example, to create a tonal map of the brain's response to different musical notes. The SQUID tonal map closely resembles the keys on a piano—one tiny group of cells reacts to middle C, an adjacent group to C sharp, and so on.

A third high-tech method neuroscientists use to snoop on the living brain is **positron emission tomography**, or **PET** scans. PET scans were originally meant to reveal the brain at work. To that purpose, they provide information about the metabolic activity of the brain—that is, the level of activity of its various parts—at a given moment in time. The idea here is this: Blood flow is greatest to the most active areas of the brain. Also, glucose (the brain's natural fuel) is taken up by brain cells in proportion to their level of activity, so that the most active cells take up the greatest amount of glucose. PET scans use the rate of blood flow to various areas of the brain, and the rate at which glucose is taken up, to produce an image of relative levels of activity in different brain locations. Scientists are able to create a map of the parts of a person's brain

Electroencephalography (EEG): A technique for measuring the electrical activity of the brain via electrodes placed at specified locations on the skull.

Magnetic Resonance Imaging (MRI): A method for studying the intact brain in which images are obtained by exposure of the brain to a strong magnetic field.

SQUID (Superconducting Quantum Interference Device): An imaging device that captures images of the brain through its ability to detect tiny changes in magnetic fields in the brain.

Positron Emission Tomography (PET): An imaging technique that detects the activity of the brain by measuring glucose utilization or blood flow.

Obsessive-compulsive disorder: Mental disorder characterized by persistent, uncontrollable intrusions of unwanted thoughts and urges to engage in ritualistic behavior.

involved in activities such as reading, listening to music, or performing other mental activities (such as solving math problems). Needless to say, these images can contribute much to our understanding of the brain and how it works. Since abnormal cells metabolize glucose at a higher rate than normal, PET has come to be a diagnostic tool in the detection of cancer, and of heart problems such as blocked arteries. PET has also been used to identify which AIDS patients will benefit from particular kinds of drugs. For more information on practical uses of imaging techniques, refer to **The Point of It All**.

THE POINT OF IT ALL

High-Tech Snoopers: Putting Brain Imaging Devices to Work

Advances in technology have made it possible to create dynamic images of the living brain. Researchers apply these techniques in useful ways. For example, when brain scans have been performed on normal individuals and on those with mental disorders, differences in brain activity have been detected (e.g., Seeman & Seeman, 1988; Resnick, 1992). For example, as we'll see in Chapter 14, **obsessive-compulsive disorder** is characterized by persistent, uncontrollable intrusions of unwanted thoughts and urges to engage in ritualistic behaviors. The PET scans of people with obsessive-compulsive disorder consistently show elevated activity in several areas of the brain, including the frontal lobe of the cerebral cortex—a brain region believed to be involved in impulse control and response inhibition (see Figure 2.6). After successful pharmacologic or psychosurgical treatment, PET scans of these patients' brains show decreased activity in these areas. Thus, imaging techniques may play a useful role in monitoring the effects of treatments for some mental disorders.

Imaging techniques may also reveal how the brain delegates mental tasks. In one study, researchers used a PET scanner to monitor participants' brains while they performed a fairly simple task—signing their name with their dominant hand (Nadis, 1992). The PET scan showed a low level of activity in the

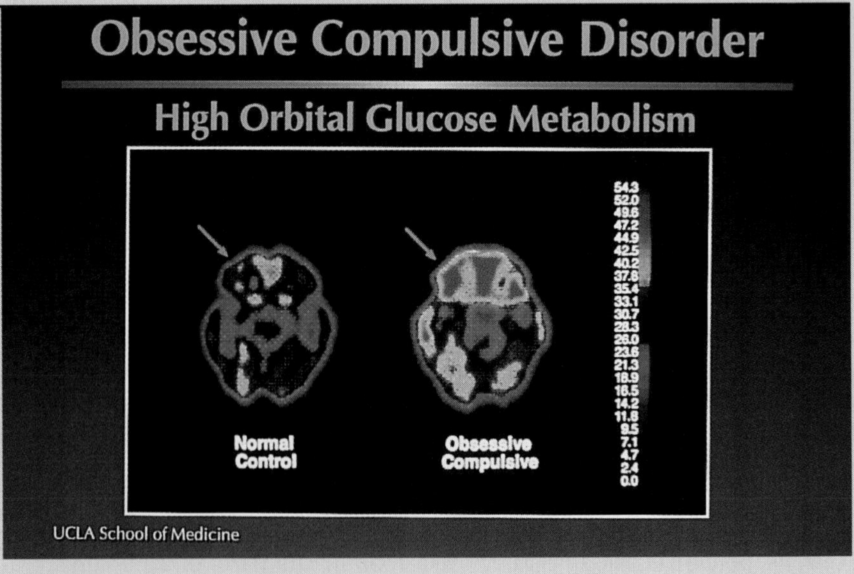

FIGURE 2.6

PET Scanners: A Useful Device for Detecting Mental Disorders

PET scans provide color-coded maps of the brain's activity. These PET scans shows the brain activity of a normal person (left) and of a patient with obsessive-compulsive disorder (right). Note the increased brain activity in the frontal area of the brain on the right.
(Source: Courtesy of Lewis Baxter, UCLA. From Resnick, 1992.)

Obsessive Compulsive Disorder

High Orbital Glucose Metabolism

Normal Control

Obsessive Compulsive

UCLA School of Medicine

prefrontal cortex—the region of the brain associated with higher cognitive functions such as thinking, planning, and reasoning. In contrast, a high level of activity was present in the basal ganglia, an area responsible for coordination of motor activity. When participants were asked to write their names with their *nondominant* hand, however, another pattern emerged: decreased activity in the basal ganglia, but increased activity in the brain's cortex. This simple example reveals an important principle regarding how the brain delegates its resources: When we undertake a novel or complex task, a greater overall amount of mental activity is required—especially in the brain's cortex. Later, as we master a task, less cortical activity is required, and responsibility for the task is shifted to more automatic brain regions.

Recent evidence suggests that this principle applies to other aspects of information processing, including how the brain processes language (Fiez & Petersen, 1993; Posner & McCandliss, 1993). In one study, researchers asked participants to say aloud an appropriate verb for each of several nouns (e.g., baseball–throw, money–spend) at three different times: once before they had practice with the task (*naive* condition); after they had several opportunities to practice with the same set of nouns (*practiced* condition); and following practice with the task, but with a new set of nouns (*novel* condition). As shown in Figure 2.7, a PET scan of their brains revealed that the brain delegates language-processing tasks based on experience: Higher activity in the brain's cortex was observed during the naive and novel conditions, but not in the practiced condition. The findings of these and related studies demonstrate that modern imaging techniques are useful tools for increasing our understanding of normal brain-behavior relationships.

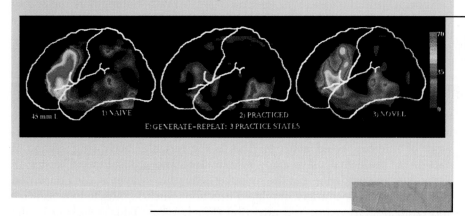

FIGURE 2.7

PET Scanners: A Research Tool for Exploring Important Brain Processes

Brain imaging tools are proving to be important research tools—in this case, for determing how the pattern of activity in the brain changes with experience on a language task.
(Source: Fiez & Peterson, 1993)

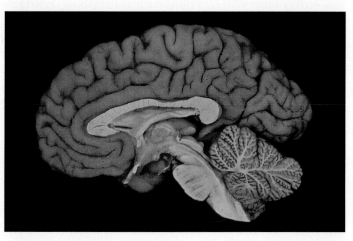

THE HUMAN BRAIN

An actual human brain split in half to reveal its inner structure.

The Brain: *Where Consciousness Is Manifest*

*I*f there can be said to be a "governing organ" of the body, it is definitely the brain. And what an amazing structure it is! The brain is the envy of computer scientists. What computer, no matter how huge or advanced, is currently capable of storing seemingly *unlimited* amounts of information for years or decades, and rewriting its own programs in response to new input and experience, while simultaneously controlling a vast number of complex internal processes and external activities. Moreover, even if such a computer existed, it could not, as far as we can tell, reproduce the emotional experience, imagery, insight, flexibility, and creativity of the human brain.

The brain is a complex structure and can be described in many different ways. Often, though, it is said to have three major divisions: the first concerned with basic bodily functions and survival, the second with motivation and emotion, and the third with such complex activities as language, planning, foresight, and reasoning.

Survival Basics: *The Brain Stem*

Let's begin with the basics: the structures in the brain that regulate the bodily processes we share with many other life forms on earth. These structures are located in the *brain stem*, which sits at the top of the spinal cord (refer to Figure 2.8).

The **medulla** is located where the spinal cord joins the brain. Major sensory and motor pathways pass through both this structure and the **pons**, which is the next structure, on their way up to higher brain centers or down to effectors (muscles or glands) in other parts of the body. In addition, the medulla and the pons contain a special central core consisting of a dense network of interconnected neurons. This is the **reticular activating system,** a part of the brain that plays a key role in sleep and arousal (see Chapter 4). There is recent evidence that the reticular activating system is also concerned with many other seemingly unrelated functions, such as muscle tone, cardiac and circulatory reflexes, and attention (Pinel, 1993). Thus, referring to the RAS as a single "system," which implies a unitary function, may be somewhat misleading.

The medulla also contains several *nuclei*—collections of neuron cell bodies—that control vital functions such as breathing, heart rate, and blood pressure, as well as reflexes such as coughing and sneezing.

Behind the medulla and pons is the **cerebellum** (refer again to Figure 2.8). It is primarily concerned with coordination and synchronization of muscular activities. Damage to the cerebellum results in jerky, poorly coordinated movement. Also involved in movement are subcortical structures called the *basal ganglia*. Recent evidence suggests that the cerebellum may also play a role in nonmotor cognitive activities, such as memory and learning (e.g., Daum et al., 1993; Lalonde & Botez, 1990).

Above the medulla and pons is the **midbrain**. It contains an extension of the reticular activating system as well as primitive centers concerned with vision and hearing: the *superior colliculi* (vision) and the *inferior colliculi* (hearing). The midbrain also contains structures that play a role in other brain functions, such as the relief of pain and the guidance and control of movement by sensory information from vision, hearing, and touch.

Medulla: *A brain structure concerned with the regulation of vital bodily functions such as breathing and heartbeat.*

Pons: *A portion of the brain through which sensory and motor information passes and which contains structures relating to sleep, arousal, and the regulation of muscle tone and cardiac reflexes.*

Reticular Activating System: *A structure within the brain concerned with sleep, arousal, and the regulation of muscle tone and cardiac reflexes.*

Cerebellum: *A part of the brain concerned with the regulation and coordination of basic motor activities.*

Midbrain: *A part of the brain containing primitive centers for vision and hearing. It also plays a role in the regulation of visual reflexes.*

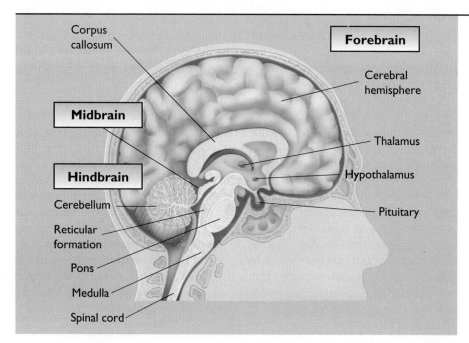

FIGURE 2.8

Corpus callosum

Forebrain

Cerebral hemisphere

Midbrain

Thalamus

Hypothalamus

Hindbrain

Cerebellum

Pituitary

Reticular formation

Pons

Medulla

Spinal cord

Basic Structure of the Human Brain

In this simplified drawing, the brain has been split down the middle to reveal its inner structure.

Emotion and Motivation: The Hypothalamus, Thalamus, and Limbic System

Ancient philosophers identified the heart as the center of our emotions. While this poetic belief is still reflected on many valentine cards, modern science indicates that it is wrong. If there is indeed a center for appetites, emotions, and motives, it actually lies deep within the brain in several interconnected structures.

Perhaps the most fascinating of these is the **hypothalamus**. Less than one cubic centimeter in size, this tiny structure exerts a profound influence on our behavior. First, it regulates the autonomic nervous system, thus influencing a range of reactions, from sweating and salivating to altering blood pressure. Second, it plays a key role in *homeostasis*—the maintenance of the body's internal environment at optimal levels. For example, the hypothalamus plays a role in the regulation of eating and drinking, primarily through its influence on metabolism. Animals that have suffered damage to the ventromedial hypothalamus tend to overeat; their bodies store calories as fat much more than is normally the case. As a result, they must keep eating to maintain sufficient stores of available energy in their blood to meet immediate requirements (Gray & Morley, 1986; Powley et al., 1980). Damage to the lateral hypothalamus *reduces* food intake, perhaps because of a more general reduction in responsiveness to *all* sensory input. In other words, subjects with lesions in the lateral hypothalamus lose interest in many stimuli, including food and drink. (See Chapter 10 for further discussion of the regulation of eating and of several eating disorders.)

The hypothalamus also plays a role in other forms of motivated behavior such as mating and aggression. Adamec (1990) found that he could relate predatory aggression and defensive behavior in animals to electrical transmissions from the amygdala (about which you will read more below) to the hypothalamus. It exerts this influence, at least in part, by regulating the release of hormones from the **pituitary gland,** which we'll consider in more detail further on.

Hypothalamus: A small structure deep within the brain that plays a key role in the regulation of the autonomic nervous system and of several forms of motivated behavior such as eating and aggression.

Pituitary Gland: An endocrine gland that releases hormones to regulate other glands and several basic biological processes.

Above the hypothalamus, quite close to the center of the brain, is another important structure, the **thalamus**. The thalamus has sometimes been called the great relay station of the brain, and with good reason: It receives input from all of our senses except olfaction (smell), performs preliminary analyses, and then directs those messages to various parts of the brain.

Finally, there is a set of structures that together are known as the **limbic system**. The functions of this system—and whether it should even be considered a unitary system—are unclear, but several of the subcortical structures have been studied a great deal, most notably the amygdala and the hippocampus. At McGill University, McDonald and White (1993) have hypothesized that these special structures may have evolved for remembering different kinds of emotion-based information. For example, the amygdala is important for remembering whether to approach or avoid an object in the environment, and whether that object is for eating (like a burger—that may be a veggieburger) or not (like wood chips). The hippocampus provides information about our current experience to other structures engaged in the creation of new memory traces. Thus, the structures that make up the limbic system play an important role in emotion and in motivated behaviors such as feeding, fleeing, fighting, and sex (remembered by some undergraduates as "the four f's).

The Cerebral Cortex: The Hub of Complex Thought

The **cerebral cortex**—the thin outer covering of the brain—is the part of the brain responsible for our impressive capacity to assemble, combine, and transform data gathered by the senses into behavior—that is, into action.

The cerebral cortex contains billions of neurons, each connected to many thousands of others. Because it is composed mostly of brownish-gray cell bodies, it is often referred to as gray matter. Beneath the cortex are myelin-sheathed axons connecting the neurons of the cortex with those of other parts of the brain. The large concentrations of myelin give this tissue an opaque appearance, and hence it is often referred to as white matter. It is important to note that the cortex is divided into two nearly symmetrical halves, the *cerebral hemispheres*. Thus, the structures described below appear in both the left and the right cerebral hemispheres. As we'll soon see, however, this similarity in appearance is not entirely matched by similarity in function—the two hemispheres are also specialized in the functions they perform.

The cerebral hemispheres are folded into many ridges and grooves, and this greatly increases their surface area. Each hemisphere is usually described as having four regions or lobes, divided by the largest of these grooves or *fissures*.

THE FRONTAL LOBE   The rear boundary of the **frontal lobe** is the deep *central fissure*. Lying along this fissure, just within the frontal lobe, is the *motor cortex*, an area concerned with the control of body movements (see Figure 2.9). Typically, the right motor cortex controls the movement of the left limbs; the left motor cortex controls the movement of the right limbs. Damage to this area often results in a loss of control over fine movements, especially independent movements of the fingers of the contralateral hand—that is, the hand on the side of the body opposite to the motor cortex that has been injured. Much research had been done on the front third of this lobe (called the prefrontal cortex) and on its involvement in the planning, timing,

Thalamus: A structure deep within the brain that receives sensory input from other portions of the nervous system and then transmits this information to the cerebral hemispheres and other parts of the brain.

Limbic System: Several structures deep within the brain that play a role in emotional reactions and behavior.

Cerebral Cortex: The outer covering of the cerebral hemispheres.

Frontal Lobe: The portion of the cerebral cortex that lies in front of the central fissure.

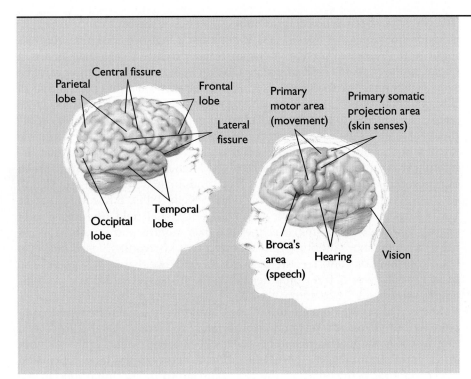

FIGURE 2.9

Major Regions of the Cerebral Cortex

The cerebral cortex is divided into four major lobes (left drawing). Specific areas in these lobes are concerned with sensory and motor functions (right drawing).

sequencing, and flexibility of behavior, the control of impulses, and the management of interference (Stuss & Benson, 1984). Moreover, there may be a connection between alcoholism, antisocial behavior, and the functions of the frontal lobe (Giancola et al., 1993).

THE PARIETAL LOBE   Across the central fissure from the frontal lobe is the **parietal lobe**. The anterior portion of the parietal lobe contains the *somatosensory cortex*, to which information from the skin senses—touch, temperature, pressure, and possibly pain—is carried (see Figure 2.9). One of the most amazing phenomena in psychology is "the phantom limb," attributable in large part to this area of the parietal lobe. In some cases of accident or injury, individuals may lose a limb or part of a limb. Almost all of these people have the impression that their lost limb is still part of their body, even though they can see that it has been removed. Moreover, the pain that they experienced in connection with that limb persists after the operation (this is "phantom limb" pain). Researchers have suggested that the set of neurons in the brain that represents our body-self continues to signal the presence of the limb (Melzack, 1989), so that the sensory memory of the limb and its pain continues to exist (Katz, 1992), even though both are gone.

Damage to the posterior (rear) area of the parietal lobe produces a variety of defects, depending in part on whether the injury has occurred to the left or the right cerebral hemisphere. If the damage involves the left hemisphere, individuals may be no longer able to point to various parts of their body. That is, they no longer "know," for example, where their limbs are. For some patients, putting on clothes is quite a chore, with the left arm ending up in the right pant leg, and so on. If it occurs in the right hemisphere, individuals may be unaware of the left side of space. For example, a person may eat only what is on the right side of a dinner plate and neglect the food on the left, write on the right side of a page and not the left, and make up or shave the right side of the face and not the left.

Parietal Lobe: A portion of the cerebral cortex, lying behind the central fissure, that plays a major role in the skin senses: touch, temperature, pressure.

THE OCCIPITAL LOBE   The **occipital lobe** is located at the back of the brain. Its primary functions are visual, and it contains a sensory area that receives input from the eyes. Damage to this area may produce a scotoma—that is, a "hole" in the person's field of vision: Objects in a particular location can't be seen, but the rest of the visual field is unaffected. A notable case is that of B.K., a Canadian professor of psychology who, in 1986, suffered an occipital stroke. This is how B.K. described his own experience: "I arose early on the morning of Jan. 9 in order to prepare a lecture. Upon rising, I walked into the kitchen in the dark and turned the lights on. My first reaction was that the lighting was rather dim, and that one of the kitchen lights must have burned out. I proceeded to open a can of cat food, and, in so doing, I was startled to discover that I could not see my left hand" (Kolb, 1990). B.K. found that he had a large "scintillating" scotoma in the left visual field (the left side of space). The scotoma shrank over the next two months and remained about the same thereafter, although B.K. reported that his reading speed and eye-hand coordination continued to improve. As evidence that he has adjusted to his new visual world, B.K. continues his distinguished scientific work and his tennis, squash, and badminton as well.

In cases of severe damage to the occipital lobes, people may report complete loss of vision, yet respond appropriately to certain visual stimuli as if they *had* seen them. This phenomenon has been called "blindsight." As with other brain structures, the effects of injury to the occipital lobe depend on which cerebral hemisphere is affected. Damage to the occipital lobe in the right hemisphere produces loss of vision in the left visual field (side of space), whereas damage to the occipital lobe in the left hemisphere produces loss of vision in the right visual field.

THE TEMPORAL LOBE   Finally, the **temporal lobe** is located along the side of each hemisphere (see Figure 2.9). The location makes sense, for this lobe is concerned primarily with hearing. It is to an area on the upper surface of this lobe that sensory input from the ears is first sent. Damage to the left temporal lobe can result in different symptoms from damage to the right. When such injuries occur in the left hemisphere, people may lose the ability to understand spoken words. When damage is restricted to the right hemisphere, they may lose the ability to recognize other kinds of sounds—for example, melodies, tones, or rhythms.

It is worth noting that the primary regions of the brain which either directly control motor movements (*motor cortex*) or receive direct sensory input (*sensory cortex*) account in total for only 20 to 25 percent of the cortex's area. The remainder is known as the *association cortex*. As its name suggests, this region is assumed to play a role in integrating the activities in the various sensory systems and in translating sensory input into programs for motor output. For example, vision and movement must work together for us to reach toward objects in the visual world (Goodale, 1990). It is the pathway from the visual cortex to the rear of the parietal lobe that provides essential information for visually guided actions, such as picking up something you see (Goodale et al., 1992). When accurate aiming is required, other areas of the frontal lobe get involved too (Whishaw et al., 1992). It is worth noting that these may be damaged independently. A woman in London, Ontario, who suffered brain damage from breathing too much carbon monoxide lost the ability to perceive objects, yet she retained the ability to aim her arm and grasp them (Goodale et al., 1991). In addition, the association cortex is involved in complex cognitive activities such as speaking, reading, writing, and spelling.

Occipital Lobe: A portion of the cerebral cortex involved in vision.

Temporal Lobe: The lobe of the cerebral cortex that is involved in hearing.

Music and the Right Hemisphere

Jimi Hendrix said, "Music is a safe kind of high." Writing in the *Vancouver Sun* in October 1993, Trevor Lautens described a concert of the Vancouver Symphony Orchestra he attended with his niece, who was a McGill student. The concert took place, in the rain and fog, 1900 meters up Whistler Mountain. To Lautens, it seemed as if he was at a "phantom concert [that was] deliriously beautiful." If that strikes you as an overstatement, consider the long lines for tickets to concerts by Bryan Adams, the Rankin Family, David Foster, Céline Dion, or any one of the many other Canadian megastars, and the faces of the fans at those happenings. Music exists in every culture; it is central to our human lives, and we come by it naturally. Music is also a consequence of brain function.

Imagine your favorite movie without the music. What is lost? That question was studied by Annabel Cohen at Dalhousie University in the early 1990s. In her experiments, subjects watched the same short movie excerpt with different musical soundtracks. What was measured was how the meaning of the visual images and their emotional impact, varied with the musical accompaniment. In the earliest days of the film industry, music was introduced to drown out the noise of the projector. The chief consideration then was that it be loud enough. Now, the sound track has other functions: to provide meaning, to arouse emotional responses, and to draw our attention to particular events on the screen.

Other psychologists have studied how the brain handles the comprehension and production of music (e.g., Sergent, 1993; Peretz, 1993; Polk & Kertesz, 1993; Zatorre et al., 1992; Cohen, 1992). When we make music, the notes, melody, rhythm, harmony, loudness, quality, and emotion, and the skilled breathing, lip, and hand movements, are all put together (synthesized) by the brain. Data from MRI and PET scans of professional musicians reading music while playing their instruments, and reading without playing, support the conclusion that many different parts of the brain are engaged in a special neural network that includes visual, auditory, space, and motor areas as well as emotional systems. That special network enables us to read music independently of reading words. It is well worth noting that brain damage which affects our speech may still leave us able to sing a song (words and music).

MRI scans have been used to produce images of the brain engaged in various musical activities (e.g., Sergent et al., 1992). MRI scans of highly trained musicians reveal a thicker *corpus callosum*, which is the bundle of nerve fibers connecting the two hemispheres of the brain. This bundle may contribute to musical skill by allowing the rapid flow of information from one hemisphere to another, thus allowing the coordination of the right and left hand movements required. Musicians who began their training before the age of seven had the greatest advantage in the size of the bridge between the hemispheres.

Patients with brain damage in various locations have been studied as well by Robert Zatorre and his colleagues at the Montreal Neurological Institute. When patients with right and left temporal-lobe damage were tested for recognition of songs (Samson & Zatorre, 1991; Zatorre & Halpern, 1993), the words, with or without the melody, were most difficult for the left-damaged patients; the melodies, without the words, were most difficult for the right-damaged patients. These and other data suggest that the right hemisphere, particularly the right temporal lobe, is specialized for various musical activities, such as imagining a song, and for the perception and production of music; the left hemisphere has a different role—it memorizes the words. The musical competence of the brain seems relatively immune to damage to the left hemisphere (Zatorre, 1989).

Language and the Cerebral Cortex:
Models of Human Speech

Many complex mental activities take place in the cerebral cortex. Much research has been directed toward understanding where and how the brain handles language. We first present a relatively simple model that was initially proposed to explain the neural bases of language. Then you will read about an idea that has emerged more recently (Peterson et al., 1989).

THE WERNICKE-GESCHWIND MODEL   Writing in the mid-nineteenth century in France, Paul Broca suggested that an area of the left frontal lobe, just in front of the primary motor cortex, played a key role in the production of speech. Specifically, he noted that damage to this area left people still able to understand speech, but less able to produce it. Broca concluded, *"On parle avec l'hémisphère gauche."*

Some years later, in 1874, another physician, Karl Wernicke, suggested that a second area, in the left temporal lobe just behind the primary auditory cortex, also played a key role in language. Wernicke noticed that damage to this region left people still able to speak but less able to understand spoken words. In other words, these individuals could produce fluent speech, but they could not understand what was said to them.

Almost one hundred years later, Norman Geschwind combined these into a unified model known as the **Wernicke-Geschwind theory** (Geschwind, 1972). According to this model, both areas of the cortex identified by Broca and Wernicke, as well as the pathways connecting them and several other regions of the cortex (including the primary visual and primary motor areas) function together in the production and comprehension of language. By way of illustration, here is how the theory describes what happens in the brain when language is actually used—when, for example, you have a conversation with another person. According to the Wernicke-Geschwind model, auditory signals produced by the other person's speech are received by your primary auditory cortex and conducted to Wernicke's area, where they are comprehended. For your reply, neural information proceeds from Wernicke's area to Broca's area via a pathway known as the *arcuate fasciculus*. In Broca's area, the set movements needed to produce speech are selected. This information is transmitted to the primary motor cortex, which in turn activates the appropriate muscles in your larynx and elsewhere. The result: overt speech (see Figure 2.10).

Is this model accurate? Careful study of people suffering from aphasia—disturbances in the ability to produce or comprehend language—argue against accepting this model as it stands. Why is that? For one thing, when crucial parts of the cortex are removed for medical reasons, some patients show little disruption in their language skills (Rasmussen & Milner, 1975).

One study examined the brains of 214 individuals who had experienced lesions in Broca's and Wernicke's areas. Not one of these people demonstrated the kind of language deficits predicted by the model (Hecaen & Angelergues, 1964).

If the Wernicke-Geschwind theory is not correct, how then is language represented in the brain? Here is the 1990s view.

PARALLEL MODELS OF THE NEURAL BASIS OF LANGUAGE   The Wernicke-Geschwind theory is sometimes described as a *ser-*

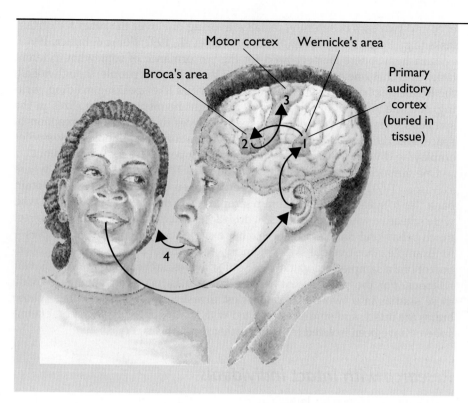

FIGURE 2.10

The Wernicke-Geschwind Model of Human Speech

The Wernicke-Gescwhind model of speech suggests that information received by the ears is transmitted to the primary auditory cortex (1). From there it moves to Wernicke's area, where it is comprehended. Neural information is then sent from this area to Broca's area (2). There it activates information concerned with the muscular movements needed to produce speech. When this information is transmitted to the motor cortex (3), actual speech occurs.

ial model: It assumes that neural events relating to language occur one step at a time and along one route. Many psychologists believe that such models are wrong. Instead, they suggest that language and other complex mental processes are more accurately represented by *parallel processing models*—that is, models which assume that neural information can move along several routes at once and be processed simultaneously in different ways in different areas of the brain. Given that there are many different kinds of language deficits that can occur independently, such models seem to make much more sense. More importantly, they are supported by a growing body of evidence (Petersen et al., 1989).

Current studies of aphasia are designed to focus upon different components of language. One study may focus on the timing of speech sounds in aphasic patients (e.g., Baum & Ryan, 1993), or on which damaged structures recover and which do not (e.g., Kertesz et al., 1993).

Lateralization of the Cerebral Cortex: *Two Minds in One Body?*

A simple visual inspection of the two halves of the human brain would lead casual observers to conclude that they are mirror images of one another. Yet the cerebral hemispheres of the human brain are quite different, at least with respect to what they do—that is, the brain shows a considerable degree of **lateralization of function**. That should not surprise you too much—after all, you know that the two sides of our bodies look the same, yet they often serve different purposes. Think of the contribution of each hand when you tie up your sneakers. We rely on our two hands and feet differently, and on our two

Lateralization of Function: Specialization of the two hemispheres of the brain for the performance of different functions.

eyes and two ears differently, usually favoring one over the other for certain tasks (e.g., Porac, 1993; Coren, 1993; Bryden et al., 1991; Porac & Buller, 1990).

Each hemisphere is specialized for the performance of somewhat different tasks. Speech is one of the most obvious of these. In most people, though not all, the left hemisphere specializes in verbal activities like speaking, reading, writing, and the analysis of information. The right hemisphere specializes in the synthesis of information (putting separate pieces together), the perception of space, and the comprehension and communication of emotion. Many studies employing diverse methods and procedures support these basic conclusions.

One important center for these studies is McMaster University, where Witelson (1991) has assembled a large collection of brain samples—a "brain bank," so to speak. Since these brain samples were donated by individuals who were still alive when they made the donation, Witelson has been able to collect much behavioral data in advance of her examination of their brain samples—for example, about verbal skills, memory, and general intelligence. This collection of brain samples is a valuable resource for researchers into brain–behavior relations. For the purposes of summarizing, it is most convenient to divide these studies into two major categories: investigations of individuals whose brains are intact, and studies conducted with individuals whose cerebral hemispheres have been isolated from each other through surgery.

Research with Intact Individuals

Convincing evidence for lateralization of function in the cerebral hemispheres has been provided by research employing the drug *sodium amytal*. When injected into an artery, the drug quickly anesthetizes (i.e., deactivates) the cerebral hemisphere on the side of the injection. During the few minutes that follow before the anesthesia passes, a person can be tested on a number of different tasks. Recent reports that have used this procedure have investigated sex differences in brain organization (Strauss et al., 1992), risk of global amnesia in epileptic patients (Smith et al., 1993; Rouleau et al., 1989), memory (McGlone & MacDonald, 1989), hand–hemisphere coordination (Kosaka, 1993), and multiple-personality disorder and obsessive-compulsive disorder (Ross & Anderson, 1988). When the right hemisphere is anesthetized, participants can—with their left hemisphere—recite letters of the alphabet or days of the week, name familiar objects, and repeat sentences. In contrast, when the left hemisphere is anesthetized and only the right hemisphere is available, participants have difficulty performing such tasks. Further, the more complex the tasks, the greater the deficits in performance (Milner, 1974).

Additional evidence for lateralization of brain function is provided by studies using PET scan procedures. These studies indicate that when individuals speak or work with numbers, activity in the left hemisphere increases. In contrast, when they work on spatial perceptual tasks—for instance, when they compare various shapes—activity increases in the right hemisphere (e.g., Springer & Deutsch, 1985). Interestingly, while individuals are making up their minds about some issue, EEG activity is higher in the left than in the right hemisphere (Cacioppo, Petty, & Quintanar, 1982). However, once logical thought is over and a decision has been made, heightened activity occurs in the right hemisphere.

A third line of evidence points to differences between the left and right hemispheres and that relates to recognition of emotions and our ability to communicate them. Several studies (e.g., Bryden, Ley, & Sugarman, 1982) have suggested that the right hemisphere is faster than the left at recognizing signs of emotional arousal in the facial expressions of other people. In a relevant study (Lalande, et al., 1992), post-stroke patients performed three tasks. First, they pointed to the appropriate emotion name (on a list) when they heard a sentence read in a neutral emotional tone. That was to see if they understood the emotional sense of a spoken sentence from the words only. Second, they identified the emotion being conveyed when all that they heard was a humming sound of the sentence being produced. Third, they identified the tone of the sentence when the words were said clearly, both when the tone was consistent with the meaning of the sentence and when it was not. Those patients with damage to the right hemisphere were significantly impaired when they had to rely on the emotional tone of voice for the correct response. One result of this study is shown in Figure 2.11, in which you can see the clear relationship between right- and left-hemisphere damage and verbal content and emotional tone.

In addition, some findings indicate that the two hemispheres have different roles in emotional experiences (Springer & Deutsch, 1985)—that is, that the left hemisphere is more active during positive emotions, whereas the right is more active during negative ones (Miller, 1987). However, others (e.g., Bryden & MacRae, 1988; McLaren & Bryson, 1987) find that processing of all emotional information involves the right hemisphere. Since the two hemispheres work together of course, and the matter is complex, the contribution of the left hemisphere to our comprehension and expression of emotion remains a matter for continuing research.

Research with Split-Brain Participants:
Isolating the Two Hemispheres

Under normal conditions, the two hemispheres of the brain communicate with each other primarily through the **corpus callosum**. On occasion, the corpus callosum may be absent from birth (see Lassonde et al., 1990; and others) or disconnected as a result of damage (Jason & Pajurkova, 1992). Sometimes it is necessary to sever this link deliberately—for example, in order to prevent the spread of epileptic seizures from one hemisphere to the other. Careful study of individuals who have undergone such surgery (and of animals as well; e.g., Adelstein & Crowne, 1991) has provided intriguing information about the lateralization of brain function (Corballis & Sergent, 1992; Sergent & Corballis, 1990; Gazzaniga, 1984, 1985; Sperry, 1968).

Corpus Callosum: A band of nerve fibers connecting the two hemispheres of the brain.

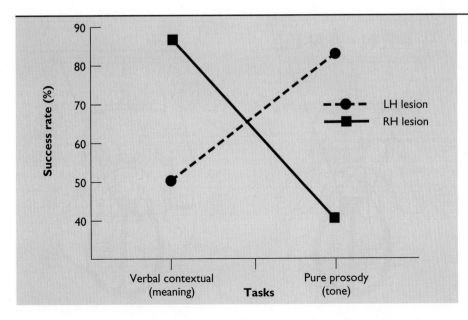

FIGURE 2.11

The relationship between right- and left-hemisphere damage and content and tone of speech.

When the right hemisphere is down (RH-lesion), the problem is identifying emotions from the *tone* of speech; when the left hemisphere is down (LH-lesion), the problem is identifying emotions from the *meanings* of words.
(Source: Lalande, Braun, Charlbois, & Whitaker 1992)

For example, consider the following demonstration. A woman whose corpus callosum has been cut is seated before a screen and told to stare, with her eyes as motionless as possible, at a central point on the screen. Then simple words such as *tenant* are flashed across the screen so that the letters *ten* appear to the left of the central point and the letters *ant* appear to the right. Which word does the woman report seeing? Before you guess, consider the following fact: Because of the way our visual system is constructed, stimuli presented in the *left* part of space stimulate only the *right* hemisphere of the brain; items on the *right* side of space stimulate only the *left* hemisphere (refer to Figure 2.12).

Now, what do you think the split-brain woman reports? If you said "ant," you are correct. This would be expected, since only the left hemisphere can answer verbally. When asked to *point* to the word she saw on a list of words, she points with her left hand to the word *ten*. So the right hemisphere had indeed seen and recognized this stimulus; it simply could not say the word. Moreover, in the case of partial disconnection of the corpus callosum, a patient may experience various kinds of conflict between the two sides of the body.

Perhaps even more dramatic evidence that differences exist between the left and right hemispheres is what happens when the split cerebral hemispheres are provided with different information. In one study, pictures of two different objects were presented on a screen. One picture was presented only in the left visual field (to the right hemisphere), while the other was presented only in the right (to the left hemisphere) (refer again to Figure 2.12). Participants were then asked to reach into two bags simultaneously, pick the objects they were shown, and name the items in their hands. Almost invariably, they named the object shown to the right visual field, which, of course, stimulated the verbal left hemisphere. Imagine their surprise when, on looking in their hands, they found that they actually held two different objects.

FIGURE 2.12

Some Intriguing Effects of Severing the Corpus Callosum

If a simple word such as TENANT is shown to a person whose corpus callosum has been severed, the letters TEN stimulate only the right hemisphere while the letters ANT stimulate only the left hemisphere; the person reports seeing ANT (left drawing). This is because only the left hemisphere can respond to the verbal question. If shown the word TENANT in a list of several words, however, the person can point to this word as the one seen previously (right drawing). This indicates that the right hemisphere recognizes this word and can respond to it in a nonverbal manner (i.e., by pointing).

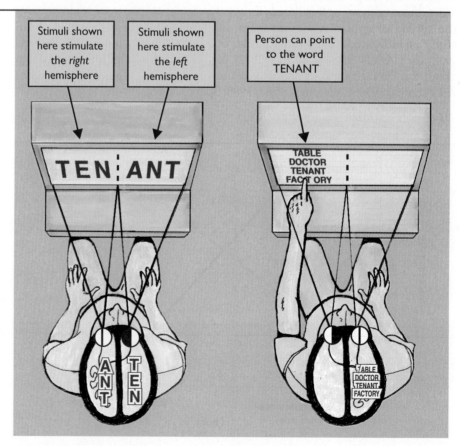

CHAPTER 2

PUTTING THE BRAIN BACK TOGETHER AGAIN: MULTIPLE RESOURCE THEORY The two hemispheres of the brain show differences that are often striking. This raises interesting questions about how these separate systems coordinate their efforts to produce consciousness—the understanding that we are one person, in other words, the unity that we feel about ourselves and our own identity. The manner in which responsibility for brain function is divided between the two hemispheres is not always easily predicted. Some information-processing tasks require the combined efforts of both hemispheres of the brain; others may be carried out independently by the right or left hemisphere.

Several recent investigations (Sergent, 1990) suggest that whether the two sides of the brain collaborate on a particular task is based on efficiency—that is, on the relative costs and benefits of interhemispheric cooperation (Hellige, 1993). One relevant factor may be the difficulty of the task; performance on cognitively difficult tasks is enhanced by cooperation *between* the brain's hemispheres, while simple tasks are carried out more efficiently *within* a single hemisphere (Banich & Belger, 1990).

This may be how the brain delegates its resources in situations involving *one* task. But how about more complex situations involving multiple tasks? After all, most often, daily life involves doing two or more things at once. Recent evidence suggests that the brain delegates its resources not only between its two hemispheres but also *within* each hemisphere (Boles, 1992).

Each side of the brain contains multiple cognitive resources. It *is* possible to do two things at once—however, Boles's data say that tasks should not require the same cognitive resource in the same hemisphere.

The Endocrine System: *Chemical Regulators of Bodily Processes*

*T*he hypothalamus plays a key role in the activities of important glands. These are the **endocrine glands,** which release chemicals called **hormones** directly into the bloodstream. Hormones exert profound effects on a wide range of processes relating to basic bodily functions. Of special interest to psychologists are *neurohormones*, which interact with and affect the nervous system. Neurohormones, like neurotransmitters, influence neural activity. However, because they are released into the circulatory system rather than into synapses, they exert their effects more slowly, at a greater distance, and often for longer periods than neurotransmitters. The locations of the major endocrine glands are shown in Figure 2.13.

The relationship between the hypothalamus and the endocrine glands is complex. Basically, though, the hypothalamus exerts its influence through the *pituitary gland* (refer to Figure 2.13). This gland is located just below the hypothalamus and is closely connected to it. The pituitary is sometimes described as the body's master gland, for the hormones it releases control and regulate the actions of other endocrine glands.

The pituitary is really two glands in one, the *posterior pituitary* and the *anterior pituitary*. It is the anterior pituitary that releases the hormones that regulate the activity of other endocrine glands. One such hormone, ACTH, stimulates

Endocrine Glands: Glands that secrete hormones directly into the bloodstream.

Hormones: Substances secreted by endocrine glands that regulate a wide range of bodily processes.

FIGURE 2.13

Location of the Endocrine Glands

Endocrine glands are found in several locations throughout the body. The hormones they produce exert important effects on many bodily functions.

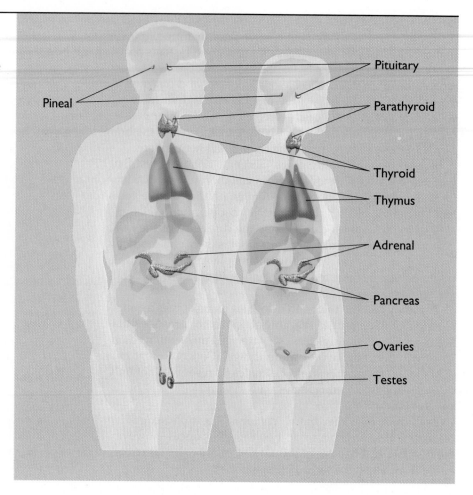

Pineal · Pituitary · Parathyroid · Thyroid · Thymus · Adrenal · Pancreas · Ovaries · Testes

the outer layer of the adrenal gland, the *adrenal cortex*, causing it to secrete cortisone. Cortisone, in turn, affects cells in many parts of the body. The pituitary also secretes hormones that affect sexual development, govern the functioning of the sexual glands (by regulating the amount of hormones they release), and help control basic bodily functions relating to metabolism and excretion. The posterior pituitary releases hormones that regulate reabsorption of water by the kidneys and, in females, the production and release of milk.

A dramatic illustration of hormones affecting sexual development is a disorder known as *congenital adrenogenital syndrome*. In this condition, excessive levels of adrenal androgens (hormones that typically exist in higher concentrations in males than in females) are produced. In males this hormonal imbalance accelerates the onset of puberty. In females, however, the infant is born with external sexual organs that are distinctly masculine in appearance. If her condition is recognized at birth and she receives corrective surgery as well as hormonal treatment to reduce her levels of androgens, the girl's development may proceed normally.

In another disorder, known as *adrenogenic insensitivity syndrome*, the cells of genetic males lack receptors for androgens. Although such people lack the internal female organs, they are born with genitalia that are distinctly female. As noted by Money and Ehrhardt (1972), their childhood play, goals, sexual behavior, and maternal interests all conform to patterns traditionally seen among females.

Together, these syndromes highlight the contribution of the endocrine glands, and the hormones they secrete, to physical and cognitive development.

As we'll see in Chapter 8, the development of *gender identity*—individuals' recognition of their sex and the effects of such recognition on later development—is also influenced by many social and environmental variables. Nevertheless, the endocrine glands and their various different hormones are central to our biopsychological well-being. Table 2.2 summarizes the major endocrine glands and their effects.

Hormones and Behavior: *Is the Premenstrual Syndrome Real?*

Gonadal hormone levels remain fairly constant in males, but change in a rhythmic manner in young to middle-aged females. This is the *menstrual cycle*, which occurs regularly over about twenty-eight days. As you know, this pattern is related to shifts in fertility.

Because there are shifts in gonadal hormones during the course of this cycle, these shifts may be related in some way to behavior or emotions. And indeed, there are women who report that their moods, energy level, and even sexual desire shift over the course of their menstrual cycle. For some women, these changes are most pronounced in the days just before the start of menstruation—an effect known as the *premenstrual syndrome* (PMS; Hopson & Rosenfeld, 1984). Are these changes strictly hormonal? Perhaps, but

GLAND	EFFECTS OR FUNCTIONS IT REGULATES
Adrenal Glands	
Adrenal medulla	Produces **epinephrine** or **norepinephrine**. Both play an important role in reactions to stress (e.g., increased heartbeat, raised blood sugar).
Adrenal cortex	Produces hormones that promote release of sugar stored in the liver. Also regulates the excretion of sodium and potassium.
Gonads	
Ovaries	Produce hormones responsible for secondary sex characteristics of females (e.g., breast development); also regulate several aspects of pregnancy.
Testes	Produce hormones responsible for secondary sex characteristics of males (e.g., beard growth); also affect sperm production and male sex drive.
Pancreas	Produces hormones (e.g., insulin) that regulate metabolism.
Parathyroid	Produces hormones that regulate levels of calcium and phosphate within the body (these substances play an important role in the functioning of the nervous system).
Pituitary Gland	
Anterior	Controls activity of gonads; regulates timing and amount of body growth; stimulates milk production in females.
Posterior	Releases hormones that control contractions of the uterus during birth and the release of milk from mammary glands; also regulates excretion of water.
Thyroid	Produces thyroxin, which regulates the rate of metabolism and controls growth.

TABLE 2.2

The Endocrine System: A Summary of Its Major Effects

Hormones of the endocrine glands and their major roles in bodily processes.

research evidence suggests that in many cases they may be smaller and less clear-cut than is often assumed. In fact, it appears that in many cases, reports of shifts in mood, energy, and symptoms may relate to *beliefs* about such changes, not just the hormonal changes themselves. This point is illustrated by a revealing study by McFarland, Ross, and DeCourville (1989).

These researchers asked women at the University of Waterloo to rate each day for several weeks various physical discomforts (e.g., headaches, back-aches, or cramps) and mood states (e.g., crying, anxiety, or tension). Their beliefs about the physical and psychological impact of menstruation were assessed separately. Later, all of the subjects were asked to recall their ratings for a particular day two weeks previous. For half the subjects, that was a day they had been menstruating; for the others, it was not. The results were these: "The more a woman believed menstruation to have a negative influence on her, the more negatively she recalled her menstrual symptoms." Memories for days on which they had not been menstruating were not biased in this way.

These findings by no means imply that shifts in hormonal levels do not influence moods or behavior; on the contrary, such effects do occur (Pinel, 1993). There are changes in sleep patterns (Mauri et al., 1988), and mood, aggressiveness, and trust (Bisson & Whissell, 1989), and there are different types of cyclic symptoms (Chisholm et al., 1990). However, the results obtained by McFarland and her colleagues indicate that the psychological and physical impact of hormones can be influenced by expectations, beliefs, and other cognitive factors. For information on the possible role of biological factors in sex differences, see **Perspectives on Diversity**.

PERSPECTIVES ON DIVERSITY

The Biological Basis of Gender Differences

Throughout this chapter, we've noted that basic biological processes underlie cognition and behavior. One age-old biological fact that has sparked a great deal of controversy in recent years is the relative contribution of a person's sex to differences in the ways that men and women think, feel, and behave. (We'll consider such differences in detail in Chapter 11). During the past several decades, research has found social and cultural factors that might explain these differences. Changing these factors should lead to the elimination of many gender-related differences. Consistent with these predictions, gender-related differences *have* narrowed somewhat over the past few decades, reflecting an evolution in socialization, education, and employment practices.

Yet recent research suggests that sex differences remain in certain cognitive behaviors of males and females (e.g., Law, Pellegrino, & Hunt, 1993). On average, men score slightly higher on tests of spatial ability, such as the ability to mentally rotate three-dimensional figures, and show greater language lateralization than women. Women, on average, tend to have a slight advantage over men on certain verbal tasks. How do psychologists explain such differences? One new possibility is that there are differences in the sizes of certain structures in the brains of men and women.

Sex Differences in Brain Structure and Cognitive Processes

Recent evidence suggests that men and women do, in fact, differ in brain structure. After correcting for body size differences, men's brains remain, on average, about 100 grams heavier than women's (Ankney, 1992). We do not know what those extra grams of brain weight are good for, though it is known that more brain does not result in more intelligence (McGlone, 1993). Other potential brain differences have been studied. There are reports of differences between men's and women's brains in the areas of brain development (Strauss et al., 1992; Witelson, 1991; Kimura, 1987), serotonin receptor sites (Arato et al.), cerebral ventricle size (Smith et al., 1991), schizophrenia (Flor-Henry, 1990; Kopala et al., 1989), language organization (Kertesz & Benke, 1989), and decline in intelligence following brain injury (Snow et al., 1986). What exactly do these differences say about brain function differences between the sexes? We do not yet know (Peters, 1991). Here is some research involving the relative sizes of various regions of the corpus callosum that, although controversial, may illustrate the reasoning.

The corpus callosum is a massive structure, made up of more than 200 million nerve fibers, all of them dedicated to the transmission of neural messages back and forth between the two cerebral hemispheres. There are a few other connections or bridges between the hemispheres (Gloor, 1993), but they are very much smaller. The rear third of the corpus callosum carries messages from the area where the temporal–parietal–occipital lobes of both hemispheres are contiguous with each other. That might make you suspect, correctly as it turns out, that it is a region of the corpus callosum which is involved in cognitive processing.

As part of a larger study, Hines and her colleagues (1992) gave twenty-eight women a number of tests of cognitive abilities, including a verbal one. Then they measured the various regions of the corpus callosum of these subjects, using MRI (the brain-imaging technique you studied earlier). Hines found that the larger the rear third of the corpus callosum, the better was the woman's verbal ability score. Hines suggested that the difference in size might result in greater transmission back and forth between the two hemispheres. Men have, on average, a smaller corpus callosum in this region (though it is larger elsewhere), and this may account for the common observation that women do better than men on verbal tests. This does not prove that differences in brain structure are the cause of the cognitive differences observed in this or any other study. Still, it raises interesting questions regarding the relationship between sex differences in brain structure and sex differences in behavior.

HORMONES: SHAPING GENDER-SPECIFIC BEHAVIORS

Researchers are studying the effects of basic biological processes—including hormonal influences—on the development of sex-typed behaviors among children.

The Role of Hormones in Gender-Related Behaviors

What, then, is the biological basis for sex differences in brain structure? Recent evidence suggests that basic biological events that occur very early in our development—in fact, before we are born—are involved. As you have learned already, congenital adrenogenital syndrome results from hormonal influences present before birth, but it is also possible that environmental influences play a role as well. Berenbaum and Hines (1992) assessed differences in children's preferences for three types of toys: traditional boys' toys, girls' toys, and toys that are gender neutral. The participants in the study were boys and girls between the ages of three and eight—including girls with congenital adrenogenital syndrome. Which toys would these girls prefer to play with if given equal access to all three types? The results showed that their preferences closely matched those of boys.

An alternative explanation for these results is that because of their masculine features at birth, the parents of these girls may have inadvertently treated them like boys. However, measures taken to assess this possibility showed there were no differences among the parents in their tendencies to encourage their children to behave in gender-specific ways. These results suggest that biological processes may play a significant role in important aspects of human behavior during child development.

Heredity and Behavior

*T*he basic theme of this chapter is straightforward: that behavior is the product of complex biological processes. It makes sense, then, to consider the relationship between **heredity**—biologically determined characteristics—and

Heredity: Biologically inherited characteristics.

behavior. After all, many aspects of our biological nature are inherited, so in an indirect way, and always through the filter of our experience and environmental factors, heredity can indeed influence behavior. In this final section we'll examine several aspects of heredity that appear to be relevant to understanding the biological bases of behavior.

Genetics: *Some Basic Principles*

Every cell of the body contains a set of biological blueprints that enable it to perform its essential functions. This information is contained in **chromosomes,** strandlike structures found in the nuclei of all cells. Chromosomes are composed of deoxyribonucleic acid, DNA. In turn, DNA is made up of several simpler components arranged in the form of a double helix. Chromosomes contain thousands of **genes**—segments of DNA that serve as basic units of heredity. Our genes, working in complex combinations with each other, with our environment, and with our experiences, ultimately determine our biological make-up (see Figure 2.14).

Remarkable progress has been made toward identifying the genetic basis of a variety of physical and mental disorders. For example, researchers recently discovered the gene that causes **Huntington's disease,** a rare neuromuscular disorder. People afflicted with Huntington's disease experience a gradual onset of uncontrollable, jerky movements in their limbs. The children of those affected have a 50 percent chance of inheriting the gene that causes this disorder. Ironically, the symptoms usually appear after the age of forty, long after many parents have their children. Although scientists are not yet sure how the gene actually causes the disease, and there is not yet a cure, it is now possible to detect its presence before the onset of symptoms and, more importantly, in time for parents to choose whether they wish to risk passing the gene on. DNA testing for the Huntington's gene does have psychological consequences for those who are so identified.

Merely possessing a particular gene does not ensure that a specific effect will follow. Genes do not control behavior or other aspects of life directly—they exert their influence only indirectly, through chemical reactions in the brain and other organs. These reactions may depend on certain environmental conditions. For example, consider **phenylketonuria (PKU),** a genetically based disorder in which the body lacks the enzyme necessary to break down *phenylalanine*, a substance present in many foods. Affected individuals on a normal diet tend to accumulate phenylalanine in their bodies. This in turn

Chromosomes: *Threadlike structures containing genetic material, found in nearly every cell of the body.*

Genes: *Biological "blueprints" that shape development and all basic bodily processes.*

Huntington's Disease: *A genetically based fatal neuromuscular disorder characterized by the gradual onset of jerky, uncontrollable movements.*

Phenylketonuria (PKU): *A genetically based disorder in which a person lacks the enzyme to break down phenylalanine, a substance present in many foods. The gradual buildup of phenylalanine contributes to subsequent outcomes that include retardation.*

FIGURE 2.14

DNA: Mapping Our Genetic Heritage

Chromosomes are composed of DNA (deoxyribonucleic acid). Each human cell contains twenty-three pairs of chromosomes. The twenty-third pair determines sex. In males, the twenty-third pair contains one X and one Y chromosome (shown here); in females, the twenty-third pair contains two X chromosomes.

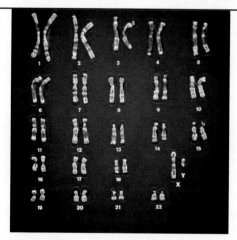

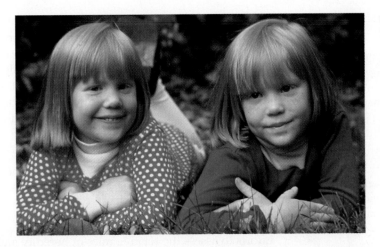

interferes with normal development of the brain; mental retardation, seizures, and hyperactivity follow (Nyhan, 1987). Altering environmental conditions, however, can prevent this chain of events. Hospitals now routinely screen infants' blood for high levels of phenylalanine. If PKU is detected during the first few weeks of life, babies placed on a diet low in phenylalanine do not develop the PKU symptoms (Archer et al., 1988). Dietary restrictions can be relaxed in late childhood after brain development is mostly complete (Clarke et al., 1987).

Most human traits, however, are determined by more than one gene. In fact, hundreds of genes, acting in concert with environmental forces, may be involved in shaping complex physical or cognitive abilities (Lerner, 1993; McClearn et al., 1991). At this point we can almost hear you wondering, "Then how do psychologists tell which aspects of behavior are determined by genetic factors—by heredity—and which by experience?" This question has been the source of debate among psychologists for many years and is often referred to as the *nature-nurture controversy*, an issue we will consider in greater detail now, and again in later chapters.

Most cells in the human body contain forty-six chromosomes, arranged in pairs (refer to Figure 2.14). When such cells divide, the chromosome pairs split; then, after the cells have separated, each chromosome replicates itself so that the full number is restored. This kind of cell division is known as **mitosis**. In contrast, sperm and ova, the male and female sex cells, or *gametes*, contain only twenty-three chromosomes. Thus, when they join to form a fertilized ovum from which a new human being will develop, the full number (forty-six) is attained. For each of us, then, half of our genetic material comes from our mother and half from our father.

These basic mechanisms explain why people who are related resemble one another more than those who are totally unrelated, and also why the closer the familial tie between individuals, the more similar they tend to be physically. The closer such links are, the greater the proportion of chromosomes and genes family members share. And since genes determine many aspects of physical appearance, similarity increases with closeness of relationship. Thus, siblings tend to be more alike than cousins. In the case of identical or *monozygotic twins*, a single fertilized egg splits in two and forms two children. Because identical twins share all of their genes, they look remarkably alike. They are surprisingly similar in other respects as well, including their religious beliefs, their television-viewing preferences, their grief responses (e.g., Segal & Bouchard, 1993), and even their risk for divorce. Psychologists have long known that there is an increased risk of divorce among the children of divorced parents, and data

Mitosis: Cell division in which chromosome pairs split and then replicate themselves so that the full number is restored in each of the cells produced by division.

- Biological blueprints are contained in chromosomes, which, in turn, contain thousands of genes that can affect physical characteristics and aspects of behavior.
- Two well-known genetically based diseases are Huntington's disease and phenylketonuria (PKU).
- Research comparing identical twins raised apart suggests that genetic factors play a role in many aspects of behavior.

reported recently by McGue and Lykken (1992) indicate that genetic factors may play a role in this outcome. Briefly, they found that if one identical (monozygotic) twin was divorced, the probability that her or his twin would also divorce was higher than among nonidentical (dizygotic) twins. This suggests that there may be inherited tendencies that contribute to the likelihood of divorce. We'll consider what these might be in a more detailed discussion of this study (see Chapter 9).

Disentangling Genetic and Environmental Effects: *Research Strategies*

Efforts to assess the relative roles of heredity and the environment in complex forms of behavior have often involved comparisons between identical twins who were separated early in life and raised in contrasting environments. As we've already noted, since such twins have identical genes, any differences between them must be due to contrasting experiences and environments. And to the extent that identical twins behave alike, despite being raised in different environments, there are genetic contributions to such behaviors. Research of this type (e.g., Bouchard, 1987; Bouchard et al., 1990) has yielded some surprising findings. Even identical twins reared in very different environments show similarities (Lykken et al., 1992).

Perhaps the most startling evidence for such similarities was provided by a study conducted by Arvey and his colleagues in 1989. These researchers asked thirty-four sets of identical twins to complete standard measures of job satisfaction. Each twin pair (average age forty-two) had been separated since infancy. Since then, each sibling in each pair had always lived in a different home and led a different life. Despite all this, and despite the fact that the siblings held different jobs, there were significant similarities in their rated job satisfaction. The higher the satisfaction reported by one twin, the higher the satisfaction reported by the other. Moreover, this statistical relationship occurred even when adjustments were made for possible similarities in the twins' jobs. (If they held similar jobs, then it would not be surprising for them to report similar levels of satisfaction.)

Arvey and his colleagues suggest that tendencies to be positive and enthusiastic—characteristics already known to be partly determined by genetic factors—may explain these data (Tellegen et al., 1988). In other words, because of genetic factors, some people tend to experience positive moods more often than others, and these positive moods contribute to their level of satisfaction with their work. Whatever the biochemical mechanism involved here, it seems clear that there may be a genetic component in many aspects of behavior, including sexual orientation—a possibility we'll consider in greater detail in **The Research Process**.

Sexual Orientation: Genetically Determined or Lifestyle Choice?

Determining the causes of behavior can be a complicated business. Doing so requires careful examination of both environmental and biological factors. What about sexuality? Is a person's sexual orientation determined by genes and, therefore, immutable? Or does it stem from powerful influences in our environment? If the latter, it is subject to change. These and similar questions form the basis of one of the most public issues of the 1990s—sexual orientation.

Most people are *heterosexual;* they direct their sexual energies toward members of the opposite sex. However, about 6 percent of the adult population in Canada is *homosexual*. That is, they direct their sexual behavior predominantly to members of their own sex (Haas & Haas, 1993).

The Search for Precursors to Homosexuality

How is a person's sexual orientation established? Researchers initially focused on ways in which homosexuals might differ from their heterosexual counterparts: hormonal levels, quality of family and social relationships, and the nature of early sexual experiences were all studied. None of these factors seemed to differentiate reliably between homosexuals and heterosexuals. In fact, most research has shown that homosexuals as a group are very similar to heterosexuals, except in their sexual orientation (Haas & Haas, 1993).

Then the results of a large-scale survey suggested a new possibility. Bell, Weinberg, and Hammersmith (1981) interviewed homosexual and heterosexual men and women, who answered questions about aspects of their childhood, adolescence, and adult life. Most of the survey items found no difference between homosexuals and heterosexuals. But there *was* one important difference: Homosexual women and men consistently expressed the feeling that they *knew they were different* in some way from their same-sex peers, even during their early childhood.

Evidence for a Biological Basis of Sexual Orientation

That hinted at the possiblity of a biological or genetic component in sexual preference. As a result, researchers began to devise ways to explore this hypothesis.

In one intriguing study, LeVay (1991) enlisted the assistance of some very unlikely research participants—forty-one cadavers, including nineteen homosexual men, sixteen heterosexual men, and six heterosexual women. His purpose? To compare the relative sizes of small clusters of cells located in the hypothalamus of their brains. Prior research had revealed that damage to this region of the hypothalamus in male monkeys destroyed their interest in female monkeys—

but *not* their sex drive. LeVay reasoned that if a similar mechanism existed in humans, there could be differences in the relative sizes of brain structures in his research participants. LeVay's measurements showed that this cluster of cells in the human hypothalamus was more than twice as large in heterosexual men as in females or homosexual men. Other brain structures have been compared in size, and some differences have been revealed. For example, the size of one of the smaller bridges (or commissures) between the right and left hemispheres, the anterior commissure, has been found to be significantly larger in heterosexual males than in females or in homosexual males (whose commissures are about the same size).

But does this finding prove that the observed differences in homosexual men's brain structures *caused* their sexual orientation? No, since it is possible that the reverse is true—that their sexual orientation led to a change in brain structure. LeVay's findings also leave a key question unanswered: How did the size difference develop? One possibility is that the men differed biologically—perhaps in terms of their genes.

To explore this prospect, Bailey and Pillard (1991) recruited 161 gay men, each of whom had an identical twin, a nonidentical male twin, or an adopted brother. Bailey and Pillard reasoned that if homosexuality had a genetic component, then concordance for homosexuality would be highest among the identical twins. As shown in Figure 2.15, 52 percent of the identical twins were both gay, compared with 22 percent of the nonidentical twins and 11 percent of the adopted brothers. Would these findings also apply to gay women? Using similar procedures, Bailey and Pillard (1993) found similar results for a group of 147 gay women: 48 percent of the identical twins were both gay, compared with 16 percent of the nonidentical twins and 6 percent of the adopted sisters (see Figure 2.15). While these results strongly suggest a genetic component in sexual orientation, genetics cannot be the whole story, since nearly half of the gay identical twins were *not* both gay.

Other evidence in this regard comes from a recent study (Hamer et al., 1993) that attempted to locate a possible homosexuality gene. Hamer and his colleagues traced the family histories of seventy-six gay men to determine which, if any, of their male relatives were also gay. Homosexuality was much more common among male relatives on the mother's side of the family. This finding suggested that there may be a gene that is passed on by female members of the family and that the gene may be located on the X chromosome—the only chromosome inherited exclusively from the mother. Next, the researchers obtained DNA

FIGURE 2.15

The Role of Heredity in Sexual Orientation

Recent evidence suggests that sexual orientation may have a genetic component. Here, the probability that identical twins were both gay or lesbian was higher than for people less closely related, including nonidentical twins and adopted siblings. (Source: Based on data from Bailey & Pillard, 1993.)

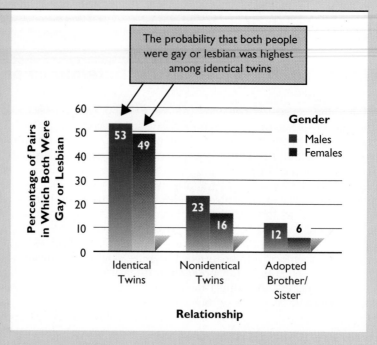

The probability that both people were gay or lesbian was highest among identical twins

samples from forty pairs of homosexual brothers and performed a **genetic linkage analysis**—a procedure used to determine the location of specific genes based on their proximity to known reference points on the chromosome referred to as "genetic markers." On average, two brothers have about half the DNA on their chromosomes in common. Thus, if brothers are homosexual because they inherit a common gene from their mother, then the gene must be located somewhere in a shared section of the X chromosome. The shared section, in turn, can be identified via the location of known markers.

Interestingly, 33 of the 40 pairs of brothers shared a set of markers located in an area of the X chromosome named Xq28—a much higher rate than would be expected to occur by chance. These results provide the strongest evidence to date for genetic involvement in sexual orientation. However, they should be viewed as preliminary, and require replication by other researchers in different laboratories. Moreover, it is unlikely that all homosexuality is related to a single gene. Because seven of the pairs did not share a common set of markers, it is likely that genetic *and* environmental factors contribute to sexual orientation.

Critical Thinking Questions:

1. LeVay's results and, therefore, the conclusions he reached regarding the role of the hypothalamus in sexual orientation were based on a small sample of subjects. Also, most of the males had died from AIDS. In your view, do these limitations negate the value of LeVay's findings?

2. The findings of the studies by Bailey and Pillard and by Hamer and his colleagues converge on the idea that biological processes are involved in shaping sexual orientation. What other factors not considered by these studies may contribute to sexual orientation?

3. The discovery of a genetic marker for homosexuality raises several ethical issues. For example, it is possible that prospective parents could use genetic tests as screening devices. Some might even choose to terminate a pregnancy. Should genetic information be made available to parents? If so, why? If not, why?

Genetic Linkage Analysis: A procedure used to determine the location of specific genes based on their proximity to known reference points on chromosomes.

Traumatic Brain Injury:
Using Psychology to Enhance Quality of Life

A ccording to the World Health Organization, compared with the rest of the world, the number of Canadians who die each year in motor vehicle accidents is very low. However, this section is not about the brains of people who die in car crashes; rather, it is about the many more individuals who are fortunate enough to survive, yet suffer permanent damage to the nervous system, particularly to the brain, as a result of a severe blow to the head—that is, traumatic brain injury, or TBI.

There are less common causes of traumatic brain injury—falls, illness, assault, work-related accidents, and others. One of the rarer of these is dementia pugilistica, a brain disorder found in boxers who have been punched in the head too many times. However, about 68 percent of TBI cases are caused by motor vehicle accidents. According to a study done in Nova Scotia, the incidence of TBI is highest among men. In fact, Malloy (1990) found that his youngest group of patients (aged 15 to 24) accounted for 83 percent of all these cases. These statistics are similar in Ontario and probably in the rest of Canada as well. To get a sense of how many people might be affected, consider that in the first two months of 1994, there were 17,000 injury claims made to the Insurance Corporation of British Columbia. Of course, not all of those claims were for brain injury. Nevertheless, according to American statistics, about one-quarter of people injured in this way suffer psychologically for a year or more afterwards.

TBI has emotional, cognitive, and social consequences. A common emotional reaction, found in 70 percent of patients, is irritability—a tendency to get annoyed easily. Another common reaction is impulsivity—that is, a tendency to act without considering the consequences. Because they lack awareness of their deficits, patients may become quite disturbed—for example, when their new limitations are pointed out (Prigitano, 1992). Typically, these patients are apathetic, but they may also explode in anger, or act silly.

There are cognitive changes as well. After suffering a TBI, patients may process information more slowly (Stuss et al., 1989), and their memory—for example, for where they learned something or who told them—may be poor, especially if they were in a coma for an extended period of time (Dwyan et al., 1993). Moreover TBI patients act inappropriately in social situations and seem unable to learn from their experiences with other people.

Of course, each TBI case is different. For example, the consequences of TBI may be focal—that is, localized to a particular brain structure. In such cases, it may be possible to predict with some accuracy what behavioral disturbances will occur. However, brain damage is often diffuse, extending to many regions throughout the brain. When that is the case, it is more difficult for psychologists and other health professionals to predict exactly what psychological disturbances are likely to follow. This, in turn, makes the design of effective treatments for individual patients a real challenge (Armstrong, 1991).

The behavior changes that follow a TBI affect not only the patient personally but also his or her relationships with family, friends, employer, co-workers, and so on (Stambrook et al., 1989). For this reason, a treatment team that includes neuropsychologists and physical, occupational, and speech therapists as well as specialist social workers is usually called on to design a rehab program that accommodates the unique changes that have taken place within the patient (Armstrong, 1991). There will likely be a neurophysiological assessment to determine the strengths that remain and the deficits that have

Injuries to the brain can often produce widespread physical and psychological problems. New insights into the relationship between biological processes and behavior have led to exciting new programs to enhance the quality of life of brain injured people.

resulted from the trauma (Stuss & Buckle, 1992; Stuss, 1989). After this, a program is planned that may include specialized rehabilitation, such as speech therapy. Vocational assessment may be necessary, as well as retraining for occupations in which the individual may reasonably expect to succeed. Interactive computer software has been created for this retraining.

One of the most important features of a TBI treatment program is the creation of an environment that is structured in such a way that frustration is minimal and success is likely. Brain-injured people commonly feel frustrated by their inability to think ahead; a carefully structured environment allows them to attend to one thing at a time, thus reducing the confusion they experience when there are choices to be made. Another variable that affects the success of rehabilitation after a TBI is how firmly patients believe they have the ability to determine their own progress (Moore et al., 1989). Their confidence in the difference they themselves can make is very important to rehabilitation.

Of course, family members are also involved. In particular, their expectations are discussed, and they are taught not only how to help when difficulties occur, but also how to cope (themselves) with the stresses of becoming caregivers to individuals whose behavior has changed (Segatore, 1991; Moore et al., 1991; Jackson & Haverkamp, 1991). Psychological counseling may be in order, or there may be a need for marital or family therapy. The most effective treatment begins soon after injury, involves family members actively, and continues consistently over time.

Thanks to advances in our understanding of the complex interactions between biological processes and behavior, psychologists can improve the quality of the lives of those who suffer a TBI. It is important to realize, however, that at present, the best we can do is help people deal with their disabilities effectively. We cannot restore their former physical and cognitive strengths. Much basic research is now being performed on the mechanisms of recovery of function after brain damage, both in people (e.g., Goodale et al., 1990) and in animals (e.g., Kolb & Gibb, 1993). Many of the animal experiments compare recovery of function in young animals with recovery in mature animals. For example, Kolb and Whishaw (1991) showed that brain damage inflicted upon adult rats affected their ability to navigate in space; however, in rats who were damaged as infants but tested as adults, spatial navigation was satisfactory. In another study, Kolb and Gibb (1991) compared the effects of enriched and isolated housing conditions on rats with damaged brains. They found that the enriched environment had a positive effect on brain-damaged animals; there were increases in their brain weight and other neuronal changes, similar to those which occurred in normal rats. These are the kinds of basic studies that may one day in the far future make it possible to recover fully from traumatic brain injury.

Neurons: Building Blocks of the Nervous System

biopsychology 48

neurons 49

axon 50

dendrites 50

glial cells 50

axon terminals 50

synapse 50

action potential 52

nodes of Ranvier 52

graded potential 52

synaptic vesicles 53

neurotransmitters 53

agonist 58

antagonist 58

- Biopsychology is the field in psychology concerned with discovering the biological processes that give rise to our thoughts, feelings, and actions.
- Neurons are cells specialized for receiving, processing, and moving information. They are made up of a cell body, an axon, and one or more dendrites. Information transmission in the nervous system depends on the movement of positively and negatively charged ions across the neuron's cell membrane. Glial cells produce each neuron's myelin sheath.
- Action potentials—rapid changes in the electrical properties of the cell membranes of neurons—are the basic mechanism by which information moves through the nervous system.
- Graded potentials vary in proportion to the size of the stimulus that produced them and function over relatively short distances, usually along the dendrite toward the cell body.
- Neurons communicate across the tiny gaps that separate them by means of neurotransmitters—complex chemicals that can depolarize or polarize the membranes of other cells they reach.
- Neurotransmitters produce one of two effects: excitatory effects cause a depolarization in the nerve cell membrane, making it more likely that the cell will "fire"; inhibitory effects hyperpolarize the cell membrane, making a graded potential less likely.
- Many drugs produce their effects by influencing *synaptic transmission*. Drugs that mimic the effects of neurotransmitters are called *agonists*; drugs that inhibit their effects are called *antagonists*.
- Growing evidence suggests that knowledge of neurotransmitter systems can be applied to solve important practical problems, including drug and alcohol abuse and certain mental disorders.

The Nervous System: Its Basic Structure and Functions

nervous system 59

central nervous system 60

peripheral nervous system 60

somatic nervous system 61

autonomic nervous system 61

sympathetic nervous system 61

parasympathetic nervous
system 61

electroencephalography (EEG) 63

magnetic resonance imaging
(MRI) 63

SQUID (superconducting quantum interference device) 63

positron emission tomography
(PET) 63

obsessive-compulsive disorder 64

- The central nervous system (CNS) consists of the brain and spinal cord.
- The spinal cord carries sensory information to the brain via afferent nerve fibers and carries information from the brain to muscles and glands via efferent nerve fibers. It also plays a key role in reflexes.
- The peripheral nervous system consists of the somatic and autonomic nervous systems. The somatic nervous system connects the CNS to voluntary muscles throughout the body. The autonomic nervous system connects the CNS to internal organs and glands and to muscles over which we have little voluntary control.
- The autonomic nervous system consists of two parts: the sympathetic nervous system prepares the body for using energy, while the parasympathetic nervous system activates processes that conserve the body's energy.
- Psychologists use a variety of methods to study the nervous system, including observing the effects of damage, applying electrical or chemical stimulation to the brain, and modern imaging techniques. Imaging techniques have proved useful in detecting brain abnormalities associated with certain mental disorders.
- PET scans have been used to show how the brain's activities change with experience. For example, the brain appears to expend less energy as it learns to master a task.

THE BRAIN: WHERE CONSCIOUSNESS IS MANIFEST medulla 66 pons 66 reticular activating system 66 cerebellum 66 midbrain 66 hypothalamus 67 pituitary gland 67 thalamus 68 limbic system 68 cerebral cortex 68 frontal lobe 68 parietal lobe 69 occipital lobe 70 temporal lobe 70 Wernicke-Geschwind theory 72	• The brain stem, which includes the medulla, pons, and cerebellum, is concerned primarily with the regulation of basic bodily functions. • The hypothalamus and thalamus are involved in the regulation of motivated behavior and in emotion. • The hypothalamus plays a role in the regulation of eating. Damage to the ventromedial hypothalamus increases food intake because of its dramatic impact on metabolism. Damage to the lateral hypothalamus reduces food intake because of a general reduction in responsiveness to all sensory stimuli. • The cerebral cortex is the hub for higher mental processes, such as thinking, language, planning, reasoning, and memory. The association areas of the cerebral cortex may play an important role in integrating the input from many other areas of the brain. • The way in which the brain processes language and other complex mental events is most accurately represented by *parallel models*—ones suggesting that neural information moves along several routes and is processed in different regions of the brain simultaneously.
LATERALIZATION OF THE CEREBRAL CORTEX: TWO MINDS IN ONE BODY? lateralization of function 73 corpus callosum 75	• The two hemispheres of the brain are somewhat specialized for performing different functions, but this specialization is far from absolute. • In most people, the left hemisphere specializes in verbal activities and in logical thought and analysis. The right hemisphere specializes in the comprehension and communication of emotion, and in the synthesis of information. • Evidence for specialization of the cerebral hemispheres has been obtained both from studies of individuals with intact brains and from studies of those whose corpus callosum has been separated through surgical operation. • Within each hemisphere of the brain, cognitive processes may operate independently, allowing us to do two or more things at once—as long as the tasks do not depend on the same cognitive resource.
THE ENDOCRINE SYSTEM: CHEMICAL REGULATORS OF BODILY PROCESSES endocrine glands 77 hormones 77	• Hormones released by the endocrine glands exert far-reaching effects on bodily processes and also on aspects of behavior. • Research findings suggest that women's beliefs and expectations concerning PMS may play a more important role than hormones. • Congenital adrenogenital syndrome (CAS) results from the excess production of androgen by the adrenal glands. Females born with CAS may have masculinized sexual organs. Left untreated, these girls take on masculine features. • Some evidence suggests a relationship between sex differences in the size of regions of the corpus callosum and sex differences in several cognitive abilities, including verbal fluency and language lateralization. • Genetically based hormonal disturbances such as CAS may play a role in shaping gender-specific behaviors.

HEREDITY AND BEHAVIOR	• Each of the body's cells has a set of biological blueprints that enable it to perform its essential functions. This information is contained in chromosomes, which in turn contain thousands of genes that can strongly affect physical characteristics and aspects of behavior.
heredity 81 chromosomes 82 genes 82 Huntington's disease 82 phenylketonuria (PKU) 82 mitosis 83 genetic linkage analysis 86	• Two well-known genetically based diseases are Huntington's disease and phenylketonuria. Huntington's disease is a fatal, progressive neuromuscular disorder that causes uncontrollable movements. In phenylketonuria (or PKU), the body lacks the enzyme to break down phenylalanine. PKU can cause retardation, seizures, and hyperactivity, but can be prevented by a diet that restricts phenylalanine. • The relative contribution of genetic and environmental factors to aspects of behavior has been assessed through studies of identical twins raised apart. • Converging lines of research—twin research, anatomical studies of the hypothalamus, and genetic linkage analysis—provide evidence that sexual orientation may be influenced by genetic factors.

CRITICAL THINKING QUESTIONS

APPRAISAL	Throughout this chapter, we've seen our thoughts, feelings, and actions all stem from basic biological processes. Do you think that all of our conscious experience can be reduced to electrochemical events? If so, why? If not, offer an alternative view.
CONTROVERSY	Growing evidence suggests that sexual orientation may be linked to genetic processes and may not simply be a lifestyle choice. Given this strong possibility, what ethical and social implications does this hold? A related issue pertains to the possibility that scientists will soon be able to determine if genetic abnormalities are present in the developing fetus. What ethical issues does this raise? What are your views on these issues?
MAKING PSYCHOLOGY PART OF YOUR LIFE	Perhaps you know someone who has suffered traumatic brain injury. Now that you understand the difficult path such a person faces during rehabilitation, can you think of ways in which you can use the information in this chapter to improve the TBI patient's quality of life?

Sensation
and Perception

Making Contact with
the World Around Us

SENSATION: THE RAW MATERIALS OF UNDERSTANDING 95
Sensory Thresholds: How Much Stimulation Is Enough?
Sensory Adaptation: "It Feels Great Once You Get Used to It!"

VISION 100
The Eye: Its Basic Structure
Light: The Physical Stimulus for Vision
Basic Functions of the Visual System: Acuity, Dark Adaptation, and Eye Movements
Color Vision
Vision and the Brain: Processing Visual Information

HEARING 107
The Ear: Its Basic Structure
Sound: The Physical Stimulus for Hearing
Pitch Perception
Sound Localization

TOUCH AND OTHER SKIN SENSES 111
Pain: Its Nature and Control

SMELL AND TASTE: THE CHEMICAL SENSES 115
Smell and Taste: How They Operate
Smell and Taste: Some Interesting Findings

KINESTHESIA AND VESTIBULAR SENSE 118

PERCEPTION: PUTTING IT ALL TOGETHER 120
Perception: The Focus of Our Attention
Perception: Some Organizing Principles
Constancies and Illusions: When Perception Succeeds—and Fails

Some Key Perceptual Processes: Pattern and Distance

THE PLASTICITY OF PERCEPTION: TO WHAT EXTENT IS IT INNATE OR LEARNED THROUGH EXPERIENCE? 132
Perception: Evidence That It's Innate
Perception: Evidence for the Importance of Learning and Experience
Must We Try to Resolve the Nature–Nurture Controversy?

EXTRASENSORY PERCEPTION: PERCEPTION WITHOUT SENSATION? 134
Psi: What Is It?
Psi: Does It Really Exist?

SUMMARY AND REVIEW OF KEY POINTS 138

PERSPECTIVES ON DIVERSITY—CULTURE AND THE PERCEPTION OF PAIN 114

THE RESEARCH PROCESS—RESEARCH ON WARNINGS 122

KEY CONCEPT—FIGURE–GROUND 125

CANADIAN FOCUS—TESTING THE LIMITS OF PERCEPTUAL PLASTICITY 134

MAKING PSYCHOLOGY PART OF YOUR LIFE —THE DANGER OF STEREO HEADSETS: LET'S TURN DOWN THE VOLUME 137

DRIVERS' EYES FOOLED BY CHILDREN

The Globe and Mail: Friday, June 17, 1994

Using computers to simulate driving conditions, volunteer drivers responded as fast as they could when they saw someone cross in front of their "car." Oddly enough, these drivers braked earlier when they saw an adult in the distance, than they did when they saw a child.

Why would that be? As reported by The Globe, *the reason turned out to be that these drivers thought the children were further away, when actually, they were at the same distance as the adults.*

As you proceed through Chapter 3, you will learn more about the sensory/perceptual systems that tell us about the world in which we live—and about how, sometimes, those systems deliver the wrong information.

MAKING SENSE OF THE WORLD AROUND US IS A COMPLICATED BUSINESS.

*H*ave you ever wondered why certain smells trigger scenes long since forgotten? Why does bathwater that initially "scalds" us feel soothing only moments later? Do you know why the moon appears large on the horizon, but smaller overhead? Do you believe in ESP? If you've wondered about phenomena like these, then you're already aware that making sense of the world around us is a complicated business. Indeed, the mystery of how we sense and interpret events in our environment constitutes one of the oldest fields of study in psychology. Careful psychological research conducted over several decades has shown that we do not understand the external world in a simple, automatic way. Rather, we actively construct our interpretation of sensory information through several complex processes.

Making sense of the world around us is a complicated business. To clarify how we do it, psychologists distinguish between two key concepts: sensation and perception. The study of **sensation** is concerned with the initial contact between organisms and their physical environment. It focuses on describing the relationship between various forms of sensory stimulation (including electromagnetism, sound waves, and pressure) and how these inputs are registered by our sense organs (the eyes, ears, nose, tongue, and skin). In contrast, the study of **perception** is concerned with identifying the processes through which we interpret and organize sensory information to produce our conscious experience of objects and object relationships. It is important to remember that perception is not simply a passive process of decoding incoming sensory information. If this were the case, we would lose the richness of our everyday stream-of-conscious experiences. For example, consider the picture in Figure 3.1. At first glance, you may see a red fox in the snow among the aspen trees. Closer inspection, however, reveals native people on horseback quietly making their way through the wintry scene. This is an example of the active and complex process of perception. The information supplied by our senses remained constant, yet our interpretation of this sensory input shifted dramatically.

Sensation: Input about the physical world provided by our sensory receptors.

Perception: The process through which we select, organize, and interpret input from our sensory receptors.

The dual processes of sensation and perception play a role in virtually every topic we will consider in later chapters. For this reason, we will devote careful attention to them here. We'll begin by exploring in detail how the receptors for each sensory system transduce raw physical energy into an electrochemical code. As we'll soon note, our sensory receptors are exquisitely designed to detect various aspects of the world around us. As part of our discussion, we'll consider the role of cultural factors in one very important aspect of our sensory processes—the sensation of pain. Next, we'll turn our

FIGURE 3.1

The Active and Complex Process of Perception

"Woodland Encounter" by Bev Doolittle illustrates how the dual processes of sensation and perception help us make sense of the world around us.
(Source: *Visions: the Art of Bev Doolittle*, 1989)

attention to the active process of perception. Here, we'll focus on how the brain integrates and interprets the constant flow of information it receives from our senses. In our discussion of perception, we'll also consider the relative contributions of heredity and experience to our perception of the world around us. Finally, we'll examine the evidence supporting one intriguing aspect of perception—the possibility of extrasensory perception, or *psi*.

Sensation: The Raw Materials of Understanding

*T*he sight of a breathtaking sunset, the taste of ice-cold lemonade on a hot day, the piercing sound of heavy metal music, the soothing warmth of a steamy bath … exactly how are we able to experience these events? As you may recall from Chapter 2, all of these sensory experiences are based on complex processes occurring within the nervous system. This fact highlights an intriguing paradox: Although we are continually bombarded by various forms of physical energy, including light, heat, sound, and smells, our brain cannot directly detect the presence of these forces. Rather, it can only respond to intricate patterns of action potentials conducted by *neurons*, special cells that receive, move, and process sensory information. Thus, a critical question is how the many forms of physical energy impacting our sensory systems are converted into signals our nervous system can understand.

Highly specialized cells known as **sensory receptors,** located in our eyes, ears, nose, tongue, and elsewhere, are responsible for accomplishing this coding task. The sights, sounds, and smells that we experience are actually the product of **transduction**, a process in which the physical properties of stimuli are converted into neural signals that are then transmitted to our brain via specialized sensory nerves. To illustrate how our nervous system makes sense out of the surging sea of physical energies in our environment, we'll begin by focusing on two critical concepts: *thresholds* and *sensory adaptation*.

Sensory Thresholds: How Much Stimulation Is Enough?

Although we are immersed in sensory information, we thrive rather than drown. Our bodies seem so well prepared to deal with this ocean of information that if, for some reason, the flow of sensory input is diminished, we sometimes hallucinate to fill the void. To illustrate, consider the complex visual hallucinations that some people experience when their eyesight deteriorates. This disorder is called Bonnet's syndrome after Charles Bonnet, who described the elaborate hallucinations reported by his grandfather, who, although well in all other respects, was losing his sight. Schulz and Melzack (1991) of McGill University attribute these hallucinations to spontaneous internal patterns of neural activity generated by the visual system in the face of diminished external sensory stimulation.

Although we are normally bombarded by sensory information, there are times when it is important for us to discern the faintest of sensations. What is the slightest amount of stimulation that our sensory systems can detect? In other words, how much physical stimulation is necessary in order for us to experience a sensation? Actually, surprisingly little for most aspects of sensation. As shown in Table 3.1, we can hear a watch tick six meters away in a

Sensory Receptors: Cells specialized for the task of transduction—converting physical energy (light, sound) into neural impulses.

Transduction: The translation of physical energy into electrical signals by specialized receptor cells.

quiet room; we can smell a single drop of perfume in an empty three-room apartment; and on a clear, dark night, we can see a dim candle 48 kilometers away (Galanter, 1962).

Although our receptors are remarkably efficient, they do not register all the information available in the environment at any given moment. We are able to smell and taste certain chemicals but not others, we hear sound waves only at certain frequencies, and our ability to detect light energy is restricted to a relatively narrow band of wavelengths. However, as Coren & Ward (1989) of the University of British Columbia point out, the range of physical stimuli that we and other species can detect seems to be designed in a way that maximizes survival potential.

TABLE 3.1	SENSE	ABSOLUTE THRESHOLD EQUIVALENT
	Vision	Candle 48 kilometers away on a clear, dark night
Absolute Thresholds for Each of Our Senses	Hearing	Tick of a watch 6 meters away in a quiet room
	Taste	Teaspoon of sugar dissolved in 9 liters of water
The sensitivity of each of our senses is remarkable. (Source: Based on Galanter, 1962.)	Smell	One drop of perfume in a three-room apartment; a single molecule of an odorous substance
	Touch	A bee's wing falling on the cheek from a height of 1 centimeter
	Warmth or cold	A 1- to 2-degree (Celsius) change in skin temperature

ABSOLUTE THRESHOLDS: "WAS IT REALLY THERE?"   For more than a century, psychologists have conducted studies to determine the level of sensitivity in each sensory system. To do this, they have used a variety of procedures called *psychophysical methods*. These procedures allow psychologists to determine the smallest magnitude of a stimulus that can be reliably discriminated from no stimulus at all 50 percent of the time; this is called the **absolute threshold.** To understand how absolute thresholds for our sensory systems have been explored, consider the following example. Suppose researchers at the Jaw Breaker Chewing Gum Company have discovered a new way to make the flavor in gum last forever. The process is simple and inexpensive but has a minor flaw: A critical ingredient, substance SOUR, escapes detection in low concentrations, but in larger concentrations makes the gum taste terrible.

To determine the absolute threshold for detection of SOUR, Jaw Breaker researchers select several concentrations; the lowest is clearly below threshold (nobody tastes the SOUR), and the highest causes the tasters to spit out the gum. Then volunteers chew many samples of gum with different concentrations of SOUR. The concentration at which the volunteers detect SOUR 50 percent of the time is the absolute threshold; it follows that the concentration of SOUR in the final product should fall *below* this level.

ABSOLUTE THRESHOLDS: SOME COMPLICATIONS   We often assume there is a direct relationship between the presence of a physical stimulus and the resulting sensation. Thus, given a stimulus of sufficient intensity, we should always be able to detect its presence. Unfortunately, as shown in the SOUR example, this relationship is not so simple. Why? One reason is that our sensitivity to stimuli changes from moment to moment. A stimulus we can detect at one time will not necessarily be detected by us later. For this reason, psychologists have arbitrarily defined the absolute threshold as that magnitude of physical energy we can detect 50 percent of the time.

Although this definition takes account of fluctuations in our sensitivity to various stimuli, it does not explain *why* such fluctuations occur. There are actually several reasons. First, our bodies are constantly adjusting in order to maintain their internal environment at optimal levels, a state termed *homeostasis*. It is not surprising that as a result of these adjustments, the sensitivity of our sensory organs to external stimuli also varies. Second, motivational factors such as the rewards or costs associated with detecting various stimuli play a role. For example, the outcome of the SOUR study might have been different if the participants had been faced with the prospect of being fired for a "wrong" decision.

Signal detection theory suggests that complex decision mechanisms are involved whenever we try to determine if we have or have not detected a specific stimulus (Swets, 1992). For instance, imagine that you are a radiologist. While scanning a patient's X-ray, you think you detect a faint spot on the film, but you're not quite sure. What should you do? If you conclude that the spot is an abnormality, you must order more scans or tests—an expensive and time-consuming alternative. If further testing reveals an abnormality, such as cancer, you may have saved the patient's life. If no abnormality is detected, though, you'll be blamed for wasting resources and unnecessarily upsetting the patient. Alternatively, if you decide the spot is *not* an abnormality, there's no reason to order more tests. If the patient remains healthy, then you've done the right thing. If the spot is really cancerous tissue, however, the results could be fatal.

Your decision in this scenario is likely to be influenced by the rewards and costs associated with each alternative. Because of the potentially deadly consequences, you may be tempted to order more tests, even if the spot on

Absolute Threshold: The smallest amount of a stimulus that we can detect 50 percent of the time.

Signal Detection Theory: A theory suggesting that there are no absolute thresholds for sensations. Rather, detection of stimuli depends on their physical energy and on internal factors such as the relative costs and benefits associated with detecting their presence.

the X-ray is extremely faint. But what if you are new in the field and you have just gone deeply into debt buying a house for your growing family? The fear of making a decision that could jeopardize your position may weigh more heavily in the balance; you may avoid reporting the spot unless you are quite certain you saw it.

In summary, deciding whether we have detected a given stimulus is not always easy. These decisions often involve much more than a simple determination of the relationship between the amount of physical energy present in a stimulus and the resulting psychological sensations.

DIFFERENCE THRESHOLDS: ARE TWO STIMULI THE SAME OR DIFFERENT? A good cook tastes a dish, then adds salt to it, then tastes it again to measure the change. This suggests another basic question relating to our sensory capacities: How much change in a stimulus is required before a shift can be noticed? Psychologists refer to the amount of change in a stimulus required for a person to detect it as the **difference threshold.** Obviously, the smaller the change we can detect, the greater our sensitivity. In other words, the difference threshold is the amount of change in a physical stimulus necessary to produce a **just noticeable difference (jnd)** in sensation. As it turns out, our ability to detect differences in stimulus intensity depends on the magnitude of the initial stimulus; we easily detect even small changes in weak stimuli, but we require much larger changes before we notice differences in strong stimuli. If you are listening to your favorite tunes at a low sound intensity, even small adjustments to the volume are noticeable. But if you are listening to very loud music, much larger changes are required before a difference is apparent. As you might guess, we are also more sensitive to changes in some types of stimuli than to changes in others. For example, we are able to notice very small shifts in temperature (less than 1 degree Celsius) and in the pitch of sounds (a useful ability for people who tune musical instruments), but we are somewhat less sensitive to changes in loudness or in smells.

STIMULI BELOW THRESHOLD: CAN THEY HAVE AN EFFECT? For decades **subliminal perception** has been a source of controversy. The question is whether we can sense or be affected by subthreshold stimuli that remain outside our conscious awareness (Greenwald, 1992; Merikle, 1992). Subliminal perception first captured the public's attention in the 1950s when a clever marketing executive announced he had embedded subliminal messages like "Eat popcorn" and "Drink Coke" into a then-popular movie. Supposedly, the embedded messages were flashed on the movie screen so briefly (a fraction of a second) that audience members were not aware of them. Popular press reports claimed that sales of both products in theater lobbies increased substantially right after the messages (Brean, 1958). Although the executive later confessed to the hoax (no messages were actually presented), many people remained convinced that subliminal messages could be powerful sources of persuasion.

During the 1980s, public attention was again drawn to the issue of subliminal perception when concerned parents and religious leaders expressed outrage over the possibility that "evil messages" had been recorded backward and embedded into songs on rock albums. The issue came to a head in a highly publicized trial in which the heavy metal band *Judas Priest* was accused of embedding subliminal satanic messages promoting suicide on their album *Stained Class*. The subliminal messages—which told listeners to "do it"—were alleged to have been instrumental in the suicides by shotgun of two young men. The judge dismissed the case against the rock band, citing a lack of scientific evidence that the subliminal messages actually *caused* the shootings (*Vance et al. v. Judas Priest et al.*, 1990).

Difference Threshold: The amount of change in a stimulus required before a person can detect the shift.

Just Noticeable Difference (jnd): The smallest amount of change in a physical stimulus necessary for an individual to notice a difference in the intensity of the stimulus.

Subliminal Perception: The presumed ability to perceive a stimulus that is below the threshold for conscious experience.

Is it possible that subliminal satanic messages can lead unsuspecting young listeners down a path of loose morality and aberrant behavior? A study carried out at McMaster University in 1993 suggests that this is unlikely. Begg, Needham, and Mookbinder found that students in their study were capable of discriminating, and even remembering, the sound patterns of backward messages, but that the meaning contained in these sentences did not "leak through" to influence their subsequent behavior.

Given that it is unlikely backward messages on recordings can influence behavior, what are we to make of other efforts to use subliminal messages to influence behavior? Consider the current explosion of self-help materials that offer to help you lose weight, stop smoking, get smarter, or improve your memory. Their manufacturers often claim that the effectiveness of these products is due to the presence of subliminal messages. Are these claims true? The results of careful research suggest that the answer is no. (Greenwald et al., 1991; Urban, 1992). Any improvements appear to stem from other factors, such as motivation and expectations—not from the effects of subliminal perception. So rest easy; there's little danger that we will soon be coaxed down a path of loose morality by satanic moguls in the recording industry, or that advertisers will send us marching to the nearest store in robotlike fashion to purchase products they wish to sell.

Sensory Adaptation: "It Feels Great Once You Get Used to It!"

Nova Scotia is very nearly surrounded by the Atlantic Ocean. Anyone putting a toe in the ocean water on a Nova Scotia beach is in for a shock—it's cold! This does not stop native Nova Scotians, and some brave tourists, from plunging in for a swim on warm summer days … and claiming to enjoy the experience. The initial shock of the icy water is traumatic, but eventually it feels refreshing. This type of experience illustrates the process of **sensory adaptation**—the fact that our sensitivity to an unchanging stimulus tends to decrease over time. When we first encounter a stimulus, like icy water, our temperature receptors fire vigorously. Soon, however, they fire less vigorously, and through the process of sensory adaptation, the water begins to feel just right.

Sensory adaptation has some practical advantages. If it did not occur, we would constantly be distracted by the stream of sensations we experience each day. We would not adapt to our clothing rubbing our skin, to the feel of our tongue in our mouth, or to bodily processes such as eye blinks and swallowing. However, sensory adaptation is not always beneficial and can even

Sensory Adaptation: Reduced sensitivity to unchanging stimuli over time.

SENSORY ADAPTATION

Have you ever jumped into the icy waters of a mountain lake or ocean? At first the water feels freezing, but later it feels refreshing. This is an example of sensory adaptation.

be dangerous. For instance, after about a minute our sensitivity to most odors drops by nearly 70 percent. Thus, in situations where smoke or harmful chemicals are present, sensory adaptation may actually reduce our awareness of existing dangers. In general, though, the process of sensory adaptation allows us to focus on changes in the world around us, and that ability to focus on and respond to stimulus change is usually what is most important for survival.

Now that we've considered some basic aspects of sensation, let's examine in detail each of the major senses.

Vision

Light, in the form of energy from the sun, is part of the fuel that drives the engine of life on earth. Thus, it is not surprising that we possess exquisitely adapted organs for detecting this stimulus: our eyes. Indeed, for most of us, sight is the most important way of gathering information about the world. Figure 3.2 shows a simplified diagram of the human eye.

The Eye: Its Basic Structure

How is light energy converted into signals our brain can understand? The answer lies in the basic structure of the eye. It is in the eye that light energy is converted into a neural code understandable to our nervous system. Light rays first pass through a transparent protective structure called the **cornea** and then enter the eye through the **pupil,** a round opening whose size varies with lighting conditions: the less light present, the wider the pupil opening (refer to Figure 3.3). These adjustments are executed by the **iris,** the colored part of the eye, which is actually a circular muscle that contracts or expands to let in varying amounts of light. After entering through the pupil, light rays pass through the **lens,** a clear structure whose shape adjusts to permit us to focus on objects at varying distances. When we look at a distant object the muscles of the lens relax, allowing it to become thinner and flatter; when we look at a nearby object those muscles contract, making the lens thicker and rounder. Light rays leaving the lens are projected on the **retina** at the back of the eyeball. As illustrated in Figure 3.3, the lens bends light rays in such a way that the image projected onto the retina is actually upside down and reversed; but the brain reverses this image, letting us see objects and people correctly.

The retina is actually a postage-stamp-sized structure that contains two types of light-sensitive receptor cells: about 6.5 million **cones** and about 100 million **rods.** Cones, located primarily in the center of the retina in an area called the **fovea,** function best in bright light and play a key role both in color vision and in our ability to notice fine detail. In contrast, rods are found only outside the fovea and function best under lower levels of illumination, so they help us to see in a darkened room or at night. At increasing distances from the fovea, the density of cones decreases and the density of rods increases. When stimulated, the rods and cones transmit

Cornea: The curved, transparent layer through which light rays enter the eye.

Pupil: An opening in the eye, just behind the cornea, through which light rays enter the eye.

Iris: The colored part of the eye that adjusts the amount of light that enters by constricting or dilating the pupil.

Lens: A curved structure behind the pupil that bends light rays, focusing them on the retina.

Retina: The surface at the back of the eye containing the rods and cones.

Cones: Sensory receptors in the eye that play a crucial role in sensations of color.

KEY POINTS

- Sensory receptors transduce raw physical energy into neural impulses, which are then interpreted by our central nervous system.
- The absolute threshold is the smallest magnitude of a stimulus that can be detected 50 percent of the time.
- Signal detection theory helps to separate sensitivity from motivational factors.
- Sensory adaptation allows us to focus on important changes in our environment.

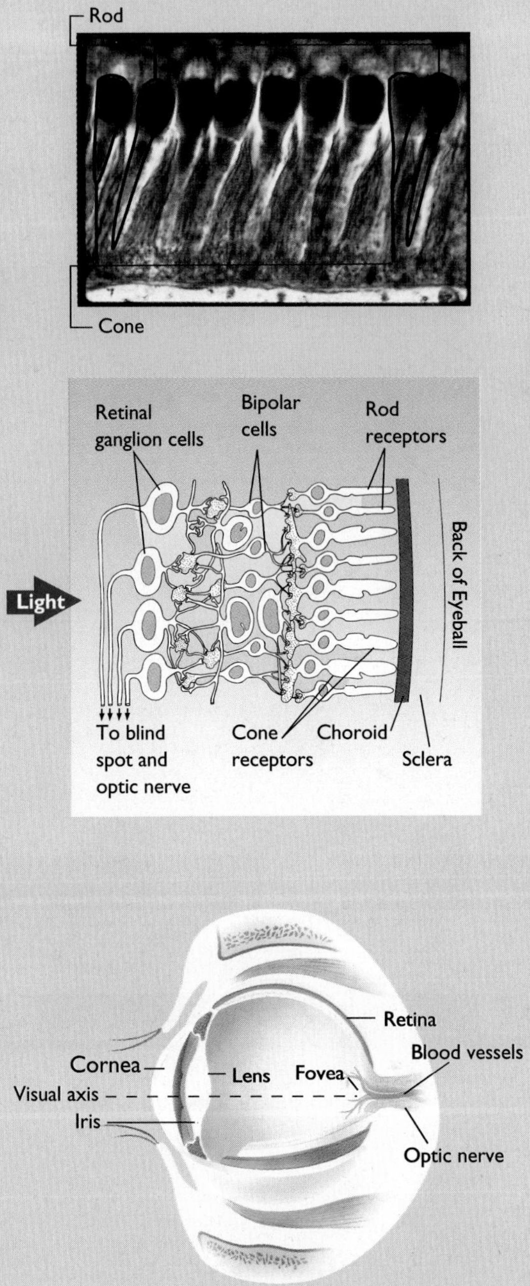

FIGURE 3.2

The Human Eye

The photoreceptors of the retina connect to higher brain pathways through the optic nerve. Light filters through layers of retinal cells before hitting the receptors (rods and cones), which are located at the back of the eye and pointed away from the incoming light. The rods and cones pass an electrical impulse to bipolar cells. Rods assist in night vision; cones are necessary to day vision, color vision, and fine discrimination. Rods and cones relay the impulse to the ganglion cells. The axons of the ganglion cells form the fibers of the optic nerve.

Rod

Cone

Retinal ganglion cells

Bipolar cells

Rod receptors

Back of Eyeball

Light

To blind spot and optic nerve

Cone receptors

Choroid

Sclera

Retina

Blood vessels

Cornea

Lens

Fovea

Visual axis

Iris

Optic nerve

Rods: One of the two types of sensory receptors for vision found in the eye.

Fovea: The area in the center of the retina in which cones are highly concentrated.

Optic Nerve: A bundle of nerve fibers that exit the back of the eye and carry visual information to the brain.

Blind Spot: The point in the back of the retina through which the optic nerve exits the eye. This exit point contains no rods or cones and is therefore insensitive to light.

neural information to other neurons called *bipolar cells.* These cells, in turn, contact other neurons, called *ganglion cells.* Axons from the ganglion cells converge to form the **optic nerve** and carry visual information to the brain. Interestingly, no receptors are present where this nerve exits the eye, so there is a **blind spot** at this point in our visual field. Try the exercise in Figure 3.4 to check your own blind spot.

FIGURE 3.3

The Upside-Down and Reversed Image Projected onto Our Retina

The lens of our eye bends light rays entering our eye so that the image projected onto our retina is actually upside down and reversed: The light from the top of an object is projected onto receptors at the bottom of the retina, and light rays from the left side of an object are projected onto receptors on the right side of the retina. Our brain rearranges this information so that we can see the object correctly.

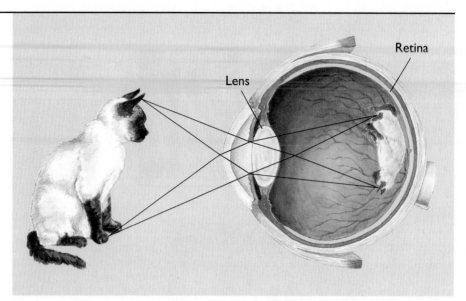

FIGURE 3.4

The Blind Spot

To find your blind spot, close your left eye and focus your right eye on the "A". Slowly move the page toward and away from your right eye until the dark spot on the right disappears. The image of this dot is now being projected onto the blind spot—the region of the retina where the nerve fibers group together and leave the eye. There are no rods or cones in this area of the retina. Now, follow the same procedure for "B" and "C". What do you see?

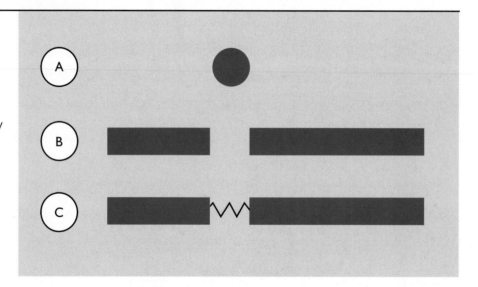

Wavelength: The peak-to-peak distance in a sound or light wave.

Hue: The color that we experience due to the dominant wavelength of a light.

Light: The Physical Stimulus for Vision

At this point we will consider some important facts about light, the physical stimulus for vision. First, the light that is visible to us is only a small portion of the electromagnetic spectrum. This spectrum ranges from radio waves at the slow or long-wave end to cosmic rays at the fast or short-wave end (refer to Figure 3.5). Visible light occupies only a narrow band in the entire spectrum.

Second, certain physical properties of light contribute to our psychological experiences of vision. **Wavelength,** the distance between successive peaks and valleys of light energy, determines what we experience as **hue** or color. As shown in Figure 3.5, as wavelength increases from about 400 to 700 nanometers (a nanometer is one-billionth of a meter), our sensations shift from violet through blue (shorter wavelengths), green, yellow, orange

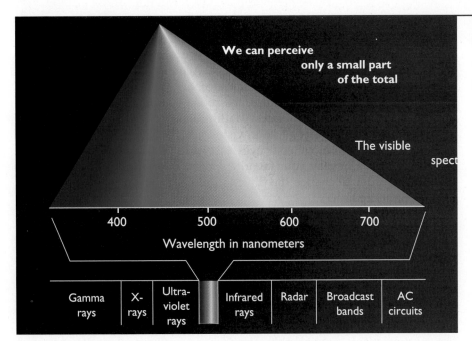

FIGURE 3.5

The Electromagnetic
Spectrum

(medium wavelengths), and finally red (longer wavelengths). The intensity of light—the amount of energy it contains—is experienced as **brightness.** The extent to which light contains only one wavelength, rather than many, determines our experience of **saturation;** the fewer the number of wavelengths mixed together, the more saturated or "pure" a color appears. For example, the deep red of an apple is highly saturated, whereas the pale pink of an apple blossom is low in saturation.

Basic Functions of the Visual System:
Acuity, Dark Adaptation, and Eye Movements

Our visual system is remarkably sensitive and can detect even tiny amounts of light. However, another important aspect of vision is **acuity,** the ability to resolve fine details. Two types of visual acuity are measured. The first is *static visual acuity (SVA),* our ability to discriminate different objects when they are stationary or static, as on the familiar chart at an eye doctor's office. The second measure of acuity is *dynamic visual acuity (DVA),* our ability to resolve detail when either the test object or the viewer, or both, is in motion (Houfman, House, & Ryan, 1981). In general, our ability to discriminate objects decreases as the *angular velocity*—the speed at which an object's image moves across our retina—of the object increases. This aspect of our visual capacity is important in, for example, a professional baseball player's ability to detect a sizzling fastball out of the corner of his eye just before hitting a grand slam. If you wear eyeglasses or contact lenses designed to improve your visual acuity, chances are that your visual deficit stems from a slight abnormality in the shape of your eye. If your eyeball is too long, you suffer from **nearsightedness,** in which you see near objects clearly but distant objects appear blurry. This occurs because the image entering your eye is focused slightly in front of the retina rather than directly on it. Similarly, in **farsightedness,** your eyeball is too short and the lens focuses the image behind the retina.

Brightness: *The physical intensity of light.*

Saturation: *The degree of concentration of the hue of light. We experience saturation as the purity of a color.*

Acuity: *The visual ability to see fine details.*

Nearsightedness: *A condition in which the visual image of a distant object is focused slightly in front of our retina rather than directly on it. Therefore distant objects appear fuzzy or blurred, whereas near objects can be seen clearly.*

Farsightedness: *A condition in which the visual image of a nearby object is focused behind rather than directly on the retina. Therefore close objects appear out of focus, while distant objects are in clear focus.*

Another aspect of visual sensitivity is **dark adaptation,** the increase in sensitivity that occurs when we move from bright light to a dim environment, such as a movie theater. The dark-adapted eye is about 100,000 times more sensitive to light than the light-adapted eye. Actually, dark adaptation occurs in two steps. First, within five to ten minutes, the cones reach their maximum sensitivity. After about ten minutes, the rods begin to adapt; they complete this process in about thirty minutes (Matlin & Foley, 1992).

Eye movements also play a role in visual acuity. To appreciate the importance of the ability to move your eyes, just imagine how inefficient it would be to read a book or play your favorite sport if your eyes were stuck in one position. In order to change the direction of your gaze, you would have to move your entire head.

Eye movements are of two basic types: *version movements,* in which the eyes move together in the same direction, and *vergence movements,* in which the lines of sight for the two eyes converge or diverge. As we'll discover later in this chapter, vergence movements are crucial to our ability to perceive distance and depth. Three types of version movements are *involuntary movements, saccadic movements,* and *pursuit movements.*

At the end of this sentence, stop reading and stare at the last word for several seconds. Did your eyes remain motionless or did they tend to move about? The eye movements you probably experienced were *involuntary;* they occurred without your conscious control. These movements ensure that the stimuli reaching our rods and cones are constantly changing. Like other sensory receptors, those in our retina are subject to the effects of sensory adaptation; if involuntary movements did not occur we would experience temporary blindness whenever we fixed our gaze on any object for more than a few seconds.

Saccadic movements are fast, frequent jumps by the eyes from one fixation point to the next. Saccadic movements are apparent in reading or driving. Careful research has shown that both the size of the jumps and the region seen during each fixation affect the amount of information we glean while reading (McConkie et al., 1989; McConkie & Zola, 1984; Just & Carpenter, 1987). Moreover, the saccadic movements of good readers move smoothly across the materials being read; those of poor readers are shorter and move backward as well as forward (Schiffman, 1990). Finally, *pursuit movements* are smooth eye movements used to track moving objects, as when you watch a plane fly overhead and out of sight.

Color Vision

A world without color would be sadly limited, for color—vivid reds, glowing yellows, restful greens—is a crucial part of our visual experience. For many people, though, some degree of color deficiency is a fact of life. Nearly 8 percent of males and 0.4 percent of females are less sensitive than the rest of us either to red and green or to yellow and blue (Nathans, 1989). And a few individuals are totally color blind, experiencing the world only in varying shades of white, black, and gray. Intriguing evidence on how the world appears to people suffering from color weakness has been gathered from rare cases in which individuals have normal color vision in one eye and impaired color vision in the other (e.g., Graham & Hsia, 1958). For example, one such woman indicated that to her color-impaired eye, all colors between red and green appeared yellow, while all colors between green and violet seemed blue. See Figure 3.6 to check your own color vision.

There are two leading theories to explain our rich sense of color. The first, **trichromatic theory,** suggests that we have three different types of cones in our retinas, each of which is maximally sensitive, though not exclusively so, to a

Dark Adaptation: The process through which our visual system increases its sensitivity to light under low levels of illumination.

Saccadic Movements: Quick movements of the eyes from one point of fixation to another.

Trichromatic Theory: A theory of color perception suggesting that we have three types of cones, each primarily receptive to particular wavelengths of light.

particular range of light wavelength—a range roughly corresponding to blue (450–500 nanometers), green (500–570 nanometers), or red (620–700 nanometers). Careful study of the human retina suggests that we do possess three types of receptors, although as Figure 3.7 shows, there is a great deal of overlap in each receptor type's sensitivity range (DeValois & DeValois, 1975; Rushton, 1975).

According to trichromatic theory, our ability to perceive colors results from the joint action of the three receptor types. Thus, light of a particular wavelength produces differential stimulation of each receptor type, and it is the overall pattern of stimulation that produces our rich sense of color. This differential sensitivity may be due to genes that direct different cones to produce pigments sensitive to blue, green, or red (Nathans, Thomas, & Hogness, 1986).

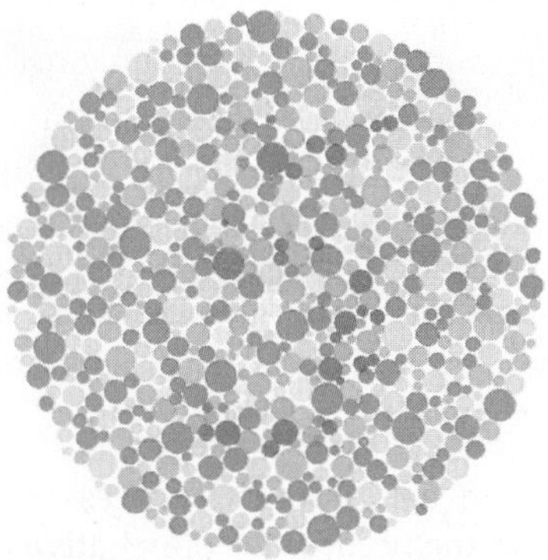

Trichromatic theory, however, fails to account for certain aspects of color vision, such as the occurrence of **negative afterimages**—sensations of complementary colors that occur after one stares at a stimulus of a given color. For example, after you stare at a red object, if you shift your gaze to a neutral background, sensations of green may follow. Similarly, after you stare at a yellow stimulus, sensations of blue may follow. (Figure 3.8 demonstrates negative afterimage.)

The **opponent process theory** addresses phenomena like afterimages more effectively than the trichromatic theory, by accounting for what happens after the cones in the retina transmit their information to the *bipolar* and *ganglion cells*. Opponent process theory suggests that we possess six kinds of cells that play a role in sensations of color (DeValois & DeValois, 1975). Two of these handle red and green: one is stimulated by red light and inhibited by green light, whereas the other is stimulated by green light and inhibited by red. This is where the phrase *opponent process* originates. Two additional types of cells handle yellow and blue; one is stimulated by yellow and inhibited by blue, while the other shows the opposite pattern. The remaining two types handle black and white—

FIGURE 3.6

A Simple Test of Color Vision

What do you see in this circle? People who have normal color vision see the number 5; those who have a color weakness may not.

Negative Afterimage: A sensation of complementary color that we experience after staring at a stimulus of a given hue.

Opponent Process Theory: A theory that describes the processing of sensory information related to color at levels above the retina. The theory suggests that we possess six different types of neurons, each of which is either stimulated or inhibited by red, green, blue, yellow, black, or white.

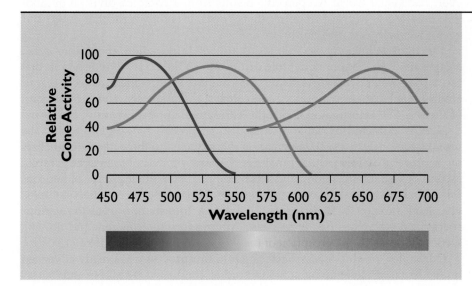

FIGURE 3.7

Three Types of Receptors Contribute to Our Perception of Color

Color vision appears to be mediated by three types of cones, each maximally sensitive—but not exclusively so—to wavelengths corresponding to blue (450–500 nm), green (500–570 nm), and red (620–700 nm).

FIGURE 3.8

Demonstration of a Negative Afterimage

Stare at the object on the left for about one minute. Then shift your gaze to the blank space at the right. Do you see a negative afterimage?

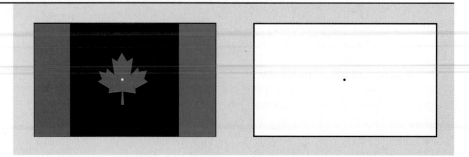

again, in an opponent process manner. Opponent process theory can help explain the occurrence of negative afterimages (Jameson & Hurvich, 1989). The idea is that, when stimulation of one cell in an opponent pair is terminated, the other is automatically activated. Thus, if the original stimulus viewed was yellow, the afterimage seen would be blue. Each opponent pair is stimulated in different patterns by the three types of cones. It is the overall pattern of such stimulation that yields our complex and eloquent sensation of color.

Although these theories competed for many years, we now know that both are necessary to explain our impressive ability to respond to color. Trichromatic theory explains how color coding occurs in the cones of the retina, whereas opponent process theory accounts for processing in higher-order nerve cells (Coren & Ward; 1989; Hurvich, 1981; Matlin & Foley, 1992).

Vision and the Brain: Processing Visual Information

Our rich sense of vision does not result from the output of single neurons, but instead from the overall pattern of our sensory receptors. In other words, there is more to vision than meets the eye. But how, then, do the simple action potentials of individual neurons contribute to our overall conscious experience? To help answer this question, let's consider how the brain "invents" our visual world.

Until recently scientists believed that visual scenes in our environment were impressed onto our retinas, much like images on photographic plates, and then sent directly to the brain. We now know this view is incorrect, however. The visual world we perceive results from a complex division of labor that only *begins* in the retina. In other words, it is only light that enters our eyes—we really see with our brains.

The light falling on our retinas is full of information about the world around us. There is so much information, and so little time to interpret it, that the visual system must pluck out information about salient aspects of our environment (e.g., form, motion, and color) simultaneously. The current point of view is that information about the various salient properties of the visual domain is extracted by separate and distinct processing systems within the visual system (Zeki, 1992). Information is conducted to these specialized areas by a process of hierarchical analysis. Groups of neurons analyze simpler aspects of visual information and send their results to other groups of neurons for further analysis. At successive stages in this process, increasingly complex visual information is analyzed and compiled. Information from the various specialized systems is finally assembled to produce the coherent and flowing scenes that constitute perception of the world around us (Zeki, 1992).

Our understanding of the initial stages of this process was greatly advanced by the Nobel Prize-winning series of studies conducted by Hubel and Wiesel

(1979). These researchers conducted studies on **feature detectors**—neurons at various levels in the visual cortex that respond primarily to stimuli possessing certain features. Their work revealed the existence of three types of feature detectors. One group of neurons, known as **simple cells**, responds to bars or lines presented in certain orientations (horizontal, vertical, and so on). A second group, **complex cells**, responds most strongly to moving stimuli such as a vertical bar moving from left to right, or a tilted bar moving from right to left. Finally, **hypercomplex cells** respond to even more complex features of the visual world, such as length, width, and even aspects of shape, like corners and angles. These cells may fail to respond to a thin bar moving from right to left, but may respond strongly to a thick bar moving from lower to higher regions of the visual field. Or they may respond to a shape containing a right angle but fail to respond to one containing an acute angle. It seems quite possible that by extrapolating from information provided by the basic detector mechanisms, specialized systems within the visual cortex generate a representation of the objects and forms that populate our visual world (Marr, 1982).

It can be argued that the visual system operates not like a camera but more like a computer, assembling bits of visual information associated with different specialty systems at various locations in the brain to make a composite representation. This "computer" model would explain why we sometimes lose certain visual abilities—like the ability to recognize faces—while similar abilities, like the ability to perceive form, motion, or color, remain largely unaffected (Mestre et al., 1992; Zeki, 1992). Presumably, a specific specialty system has been injured, or access to that system cannot be gained in certain circumstances. Research into specialty systems is now being conducted using modern imaging techniques. These tools create detailed visual images that help researchers pinpoint areas of the brain that, when damaged, produce predictable visual abnormalities.

From all of this, what overall conclusions can be drawn about how the visual system works? First, the visual system seems to be highly selective; certain types of visual features stand a greater chance of reaching the brain and undergoing further processing. Second, since nature is rarely wasteful, the existence of cells that are specially equipped to detect certain features of the external world implies that these features likely constitute the building blocks for the production of the complex visual shapes and forms of everyday existence. A final conclusion is that "seeing" the world requires the careful assembly of material from a number of separate specialty systems within the visual cortex.

Hearing

*T*he clamor of laughing voices, the roar of a jet plane, the rustling of leaves, and that quintessential sound of the late twentieth century—the "beep, beep" of a personal computer … Clearly, we live in a world full of sound. And, as with vision, human beings are well equipped to receive many sounds in their environment. A simplified diagram of the human ear is shown in Figure 3.9; refer to it as you proceed through the discussion below.

KEY POINTS

- The physical stimulus for vision consists of electromagnetic wavelengths that stimulate the rods and cones in the retina.

- Two theories that explain how we perceive color are trichromatic theory and opponent process theory.

- There are specialty areas in the brain that analyze salient aspects of our visual environment such as form, shape, and motion.

- Visual information is conveyed to the specialty areas in a hierarchical fashion. At successive stages, increasingly complex visual information is analyzed and compiled.

- Visual perception begins with feature detectors and continues with integration, at higher levels in the brain, of the information they provide.

Feature Detectors: Neurons at various levels within the visual cortex that respond primarily to stimuli possessing certain features.

Simple Cells: Cells within the visual system that respond to specific shapes presented in certain orientations (horizontal, vertical, etc.).

Complex Cells: Neurons in the visual cortex that respond to stimuli moving in a particular direction and having a particular orientation.

Hypercomplex Cells: Neurons in the visual cortex that respond to complex aspects of visual stimuli, such as width, length, and shape.

FIGURE 3.9

The Human Ear

A simplified diagram of the human ear. Sound waves (alternating compressions and expansions in the air) enter through the external auditory canal and produce slight movements in the eardrum. This motion, in turn, produces movements in fluid within the cochlea. As this fluid moves, tiny hair cells shift their position, thus generating the nerve impulses we perceive as sound.

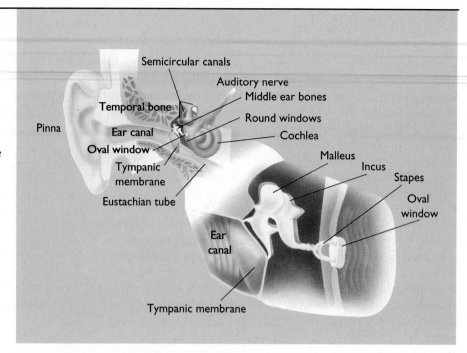

Pinna: The external portion of the ear.

Cochlea: A portion of the inner ear containing the sensory receptors for sound.

Pitch: The characteristic of a sound that is described as high or low. Pitch is mediated by the frequency of a sound.

The Ear: *Its Basic Structure*

Try asking a friend, "When did you get your pinna pierced?" The response will probably be a blank stare. **Pinna** is the technical term for the visible part of our hearing organ, the *ear*. However, this is only a small part of the entire ear. Inside the ear is an intricate system of membranes, small bones, and receptor cells that transform sound waves into neural information for the brain. The *eardrum*, a thin piece of tissue just inside the ear, moves ever so slightly in response to sound waves striking it. When it moves, the eardrum causes three tiny bones within the *middle ear* to vibrate. The third of these bones is attached to a second membrane, the *oval window*, which covers a fluid-filled, spiral-shaped structure known as the **cochlea.** Vibration of the oval window causes movements of the fluid in the cochlea. Finally, the movement of fluid bends tiny *hair cells*, the true sensory receptors of sound. The neural messages they create are then transmitted to the brain via the *auditory nerve*.

Sound: *The Physical Stimulus for Hearing*

In discussing light, we noted that relationships exist between certain of its physical properties, such as wavelength and intensity, and psychological aspects of vision, including hue and brightness. Similar relationships exist for sound, at least with respect to two of its psychological qualities: *loudness* and *pitch*.

Sound waves are compressions of the air, or, more precisely, of the molecules that compose air. The greater the *amplitude* (magnitude) of these waves, the greater their loudness to us (see Figure 3.10). The rate at which air is expanded and contracted constitutes the *frequency* of a sound wave, and the greater the frequency, the higher the **pitch.** Frequency is measured in cycles per second, or hertz (Hz), and humans can generally hear sounds ranging

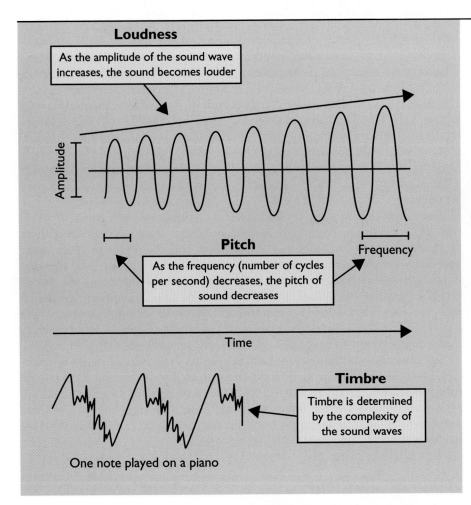

Loudness

As the amplitude of the sound wave increases, the sound becomes louder

Amplitude

Pitch

As the frequency (number of cycles per second) decreases, the pitch of sound decreases

Frequency

Time

Timbre

Timbre is determined by the complexity of the sound waves

One note played on a piano

FIGURE 3.10

Physical Characteristics of Sound

Our perception of sounds is determined by three characteristics. *Loudness* depends on the amplitude, or height, of the sound waves; as amplitude increases, the sound seems louder. *Pitch* is determined by the frequency of the sound waves—that is, the number of sound waves that pass a given point per second. *Timbre* refers to the quality of the sound we perceive and is the characteristic that helps us distinguish the sound of a flute from the sound of a saxophone.

from about 20 Hz to about 20,000 Hz. In **Making Psychology Part of Your Life**, we'll explore how the loudness of your stereo headset can dramatically affect your ability to hear certain sound frequencies.

A third psychological aspect of sound, its **timbre**, refers to a sound's quality and depends on the mixture of frequencies and amplitudes that make up the sound. For example, a piece of chalk squeaking across a blackboard may have the same pitch and amplitude as a note played on a clarinet, but it will certainly have a different quality. In general, the timbre of a sound is related to its complexity—how many different frequencies it contains. However, other physical aspects of the source of the sound may be involved, too, so the relationship is not simple (refer to Figure 3.10).

Pitch Perception

When we tune a guitar or sing in harmony with other people, we demonstrate our ability to detect differences in pitch. Most individuals can easily tell when two sounds have the same pitch and when they do not. But how does a person manage to make such fine distinctions? Two explanations, based on two different mechanisms, seem to provide the answer.

Place theory (also called the *traveling wave theory*) suggests that sounds of different frequencies cause different places along the *basilar membrane* (the floor of the cochlea) to vibrate. These vibrations, in turn, stimulate the hair cells—the sensory receptors for sound. Actual observations have shown that

Timbre: The quality of a sound, resulting from the complex makeup of a sound wave; timbre helps us to distinguish the sound of a trumpet from that of a saxophone.

Place Theory: A theory suggesting that sounds of different frequency stimulate different areas of the basilar membrane.

SOUND WAVES: THE PHYSICAL STIMULUS FOR HEARING

Like light, sound has a range of intensities—from very soft to very loud.

sound does produce pressure waves and that these waves peak, or produce maximal displacement, at various distances along the basilar membrane, depending on the frequency of the sound (Békésy, 1960). High-frequency sounds cause maximum displacement at the narrow end of the basilar membrane near the oval window, whereas lower frequencies cause maximum displacement toward the wider, farther end of the basilar membrane (see Figure 3.11). Unfortunately, place theory does not explain our ability to discriminate between sounds of very low frequency—of only a few hundred cycles per second—for which displacement on the basilar membrane is nearly identical. Another problem is that place theory does not account for our ability to discriminate sounds whose frequencies differ by as little as 1 or 2 Hz; basilar membrane displacement for these sounds is also nearly identical.

Frequency theory suggests that sounds of different pitch cause different rates of neural firing. Thus, high-pitched sounds produce high rates of activity in the auditory nerve, whereas low-pitched sounds produce lower rates. Frequency theory seems to be accurate up to sounds of about 1,000 Hz—the maximum rate of firing for individual neurons. Above that level, the theory must be modified to include the *volley principle:* the assumption that sound receptors for other neurons begin to fire in volleys. For example, a sound with a frequency of 5,000 Hz might generate a pattern of activity in which each of five groups of neurons fires 1,000 times in rapid succession—that is, in volleys.

Since our daily activities regularly expose us to sounds of many frequencies, both theories are needed to explain our ability to respond to this wide range of stimuli. Frequency theory explains how low-frequency sounds are registered, whereas place theory explains how high-frequency sounds are registered. In the middle ranges, between 500 and 4,000 Hz, the range that we use for most daily activities, both theories apply.

Sound Localization

You are walking down a busy street filled with many sights and sounds. Suddenly a familiar voice calls your name. You instantly turn in the direction of this sound and spot one of your friends. How do you know where to turn? Research on **localization**—the ability of the auditory system to locate the source of a given sound—suggests that several factors play a role.

The first is the fact that we have two ears, placed on opposite sides of our head. As a result, our head creates a *sound shadow*, a barrier that reduces the

Frequency Theory: A theory of pitch perception suggesting that sounds of different frequencies, heard as differences in pitch, induce different rates of neural activity in the hair cells of the inner ear.

Localization: The ability of our auditory system to determine the direction of a sound source.

FIGURE 3.11

The Basilar Membrane

The cochlea is unwound and cut open to reveal the basilar membrane, which is covered with thousands of hair cells.
Pressure waves in the fluid filling the cochlea cause oscillations to travel in waves down the basilar membrane, stimulating the hair cells.

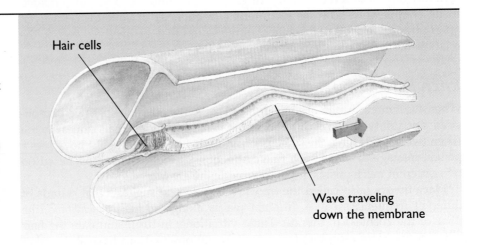

Hair cells

Wave traveling down the membrane

intensity of sound on the "shadowed" side. Thus, a sound behind us and to our left will be slightly louder in our left ear. The shadow effect is strongest for high-frequency sounds, which have difficulty bending around the head and may produce a difference in intensity of 30 decibels or more in the ear farthest away (Phillips & Brugge, 1985). The placement of our ears also produces a slight difference in the time it takes for a sound to reach each ear. Although this difference is truly minute—often less than one millisecond—it provides an important clue to sound localization.

What happens when sound comes from directly in front or directly in back of us? At these times, we often have difficulty determining the location of the sound source, since the sound reaches both our ears at the same time. Head movements can help resolve a problem like this. By turning your head, you create a slight difference in the time it takes for the sound to reach each of your ears—and now you can determine the location of the sound and take appropriate action (Moore, 1982).

In summary, the human auditory system is ideally constructed to take full advantage of a variety of subtle cues. When you consider how rapidly we process and respond to such information, the whole system seems nothing short of marvelous in its efficiency.

KEY POINTS

- Sound waves that stimulate tiny hair cells in the cochlea are the physical stimulus for hearing.
- Place theory and frequency theory help explain how we perceive pitch.
- The sound shadow created by our head helps us localize the source of sound.

Touch and Other Skin Senses

What is the largest sensory organ you possess? If you said anything except "my skin," think again. The skin is the largest sensory organ and produces the most varied experiences: everything from the pleasure of a soothing massage to the pain of injury. Actually, there are several skin senses, including touch (or pressure), warmth, cold, and pain.

Since there are specific sensory receptors for vision and hearing, it seems reasonable to expect this to be true for the various skin senses as well—one type of receptor for touch, another for warmth, and so on. Microscopic examination reveals several different receptor types, which led early researchers to suggest that each receptor type produced a specific sensory experience. Several researchers attempted to test this prediction. They located sensitive patches of their own skin, then snipped these patches out and examined them under a microscope. The results were disappointing; specific types of receptors were *not* found at spots highly sensitive to touch, warmth, or cold. Other studies have also shown that many different types of receptors often respond to a particular stimulus. It follows that the skin's sensory experience is probably determined by the total pattern of nerve impulses reaching the brain.

The physical stimulus for sensations of touch is a stretching of or pressure against the receptors in or near the skin. But have you ever wondered why certain areas are more sensitive than others? As it turns out, the receptors in skin are not evenly distributed; the touch receptors in areas highly sensitive to touch, such as the face and fingertips, are much more densely packed than receptors in less sensitive areas, such as our legs (See Figure 3.12). Additionally, areas of the skin with greater sensitivity also have greater representation in higher levels of the brain.

FIGURE 3.12

The Distribution of Pain Sensitivity over Various Regions of the Skin.

Pain receptors are not distributed evenly on our skin.

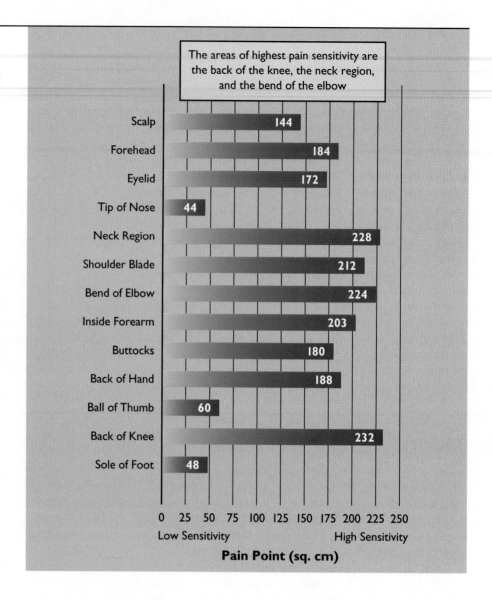

The areas of highest pain sensitivity are the back of the knee, the neck region, and the bend of the elbow

Region	Pain Point (sq. cm)
Scalp	144
Forehead	184
Eyelid	172
Tip of Nose	44
Neck Region	228
Shoulder Blade	212
Bend of Elbow	224
Inside Forearm	203
Buttocks	180
Back of Hand	188
Ball of Thumb	60
Back of Knee	232
Sole of Foot	48

0 25 50 75 100 125 150 175 200 225 250

Low Sensitivity   High Sensitivity

Pain Point (sq. cm)

Most of us have experienced the soft texture of a baby's skin, the sleek feel of silk, or the grittiness of sandpaper. In most instances we discover the texture of an object through active exploration, using our fingertips or other sensitive areas of our body. Psychologists distinguish between *passive touch*, in which an object comes in contact with the skin, and *active touch*, in which we place our hand or other body part in contact with an object. We are considerably more accurate at identifying objects through active than through passive touch, in part because of the feedback we receive from the movement of our fingers and hands when we explore an object (Matlin & Foley, 1992). Our understanding of active touch has been especially important in the development of reading aids. For example, visually impaired people find the **braille alphabet** (a series of raised dots recognizable through touch) much easier to use than raised versions of standard letters.

Braille Alphabet: Representation of letters by a system of raised dots, used in reading materials for blind persons.

Pain: Its Nature and Control

Pain plays an important adaptive role; without it, we would be unaware that something is amiss with our body or that we have suffered some type of injury. Determining the mechanisms for sensing pain has been particularly difficult, because unlike the other sensory processes that we have studied, pain sensation has no specific stimulus (Besson & Chaouch, 1987). However, sensations of pain do seem to originate in *free nerve endings* located throughout the body: in the skin, around muscles, and in internal organs. Apparently, painful stimuli cause damage to body tissues. The tissues damaged release chemical substances, including a neurotransmitter called *substance P*, that stimulate specialized pain neurons; the messages from these neurons are responsible for the sensation of pain.

Actually, two types of pain seem to exist. One can best be described as quick and sharp—the kind of pain we experience when we receive a cut. The other is dull and throbbing—the pain we experience from a sore muscle or an injured back. The first type of pain seems to be transmitted through large myelinated sensory nerve fibers (Campbell & LaMotte, 1983). As you may recall from Chapter 2, impulses travel faster along myelinated fibers, so it makes sense that sharp sensations of pain are carried via these fibers. In contrast, dull pain is carried by smaller, unmyelinated nerve fibers, which conduct neural impulses more slowly. Both fiber types synapse with neurons in the spinal cord that carry pain messages to the thalamus and other parts of the brain (Willis, 1985).

The discovery of the two pain systems described above led to the development, by researchers at McGill University in Montreal, of what is probably the most influential view of pain—the gate-control theory (Melzack, 1976). **Gate control theory** suggests that there are neural mechanisms in the spinal cord that sometimes close, thus preventing pain messages from reaching the brain. Apparently, pain messages carried by the large fibers cause this "gate" to close, while messages carried by the smaller fibers—the ones related to dull, throbbing pain—cannot. This may explain why sharp pain is relatively brief, but an ache persists. The gate control theory also helps to explain why vigorously stimulating one area to reduce pain in another sometimes works (Matlin & Foley, 1992). Presumably, tactics such as rubbing the skin near an injury, applying ice packs or hot-water bottles, and even acupuncture stimulate activity in the large nerve fibers, thus closing the spinal gate and reducing sensations of pain.

This theory has been revised to account for the importance of several brain mechanisms in the perception of pain (Melzack & Wall, 1982). For example, our emotional state at the time may interact with the onset of a painful stimulus to alter the intensity of pain we experience. The brain, in other words, may affect pain perception by transmitting messages that either close the spinal gate or keep it open. The result: When we are anxious (as many people are when sitting in a dentist's chair), pain is intensified; when we are calm and relaxed, pain may be reduced. We will explore the influence of other contextual factors, including culture, on the experience of pain in **Perspectives on Diversity**.

Endorphins, the opiatelike chemicals our body produces, discussed in Chapter 2, may also interact with the spinal gate to lessen sensations of pain (Akil et al., 1984; Millan, 1986). Researchers have found that certain areas of the spinal cord are highly enriched in opiate receptors and endorphin-containing neurons; thus, these substances may close the spinal gate by inhibiting the release of excitatory substances for neurons carrying information about pain (Snyder, 1977; Neale et al., 1978).

Drugs such as morphine can also be effective in relieving pain. Physicians often avoid prescribing these medications, or administer them in levels too small to provide any benefit, because of their potentially addictive properties. However, under certain conditions and under close medical supervision, morphine can be used safely to relieve pain (Melzack, 1990). Apparently,

Research in Canada

Ronald Melzack
McGill University

Gate-Control Theory: A theory suggesting that the spinal cord contains a mechanism that can block transmission of pain signals to the brain.

Endorphins: Morphine-like substances produced by the body.

- The physical stimulus for touch is a stretching of or pressure against receptors in the skin.
- Sensations of pain originate in free nerve endings throughout the body.
- Cultural differences in pain perception result from learning, not physical differences.

context is the key: the chances of addiction are high when morphine is taken for "recreational" purposes, but low when it is taken for pain.

In cases of persistent excruciating pain, people sometimes seek relief through measures as extreme as surgery to sever nerve pathways. But because our perception of pain involves both physical *and* psychological factors (Fernandez & Turk, 1992), psychologists have developed less drastic means of relief, collectively termed *cognitive-behavioral procedures*. Evidence suggests that changing our thoughts and feelings—as well as our overt responses—before, during, and after painful episodes can dramatically influence our perceptions of pain (Turk & Rudy, 1992). Although the specific mechanisms accounting for the success of cognitive–behavioral procedures remain unclear, an important element seems to be the extent to which we think negative thoughts while in pain. Some intriguing research has shown that reducing or interrupting such thoughts can greatly improve our ability to cope with pain (Chaves & Brown, 1987; Turner & Clancy, 1986). Other techniques that involve cognitive mechanisms, such as hypnosis, distraction, and social modeling, have also been successfully applied to relieve pain (Bellisimo & Tunks, 1984; Craig & Prkachin, 1978).

PERSPECTIVES ON DIVERSITY

Culture and the Perception of Pain

European winters are not as harsh as Canadian winters. The early explorers had no means of knowing this and arrogantly dismissed information from native informants who knew quite well what winter would bring. Jacques Cartier, for example, ridiculed his new Iroquois neighbors when they predicted that so much ice and snow would come that all would perish; because of his arrogance, he and his followers almost did perish. Making the winter experience even more difficult for the early explorers and settlers was the indifference of the native people to cold-induced pain. Cartier described how the Iroquois visited his ship by marching in a near-naked state across the ice and snow in the most severe cold, and held this sight to be "something which is unbelievable for those who have not seen it" (Trudel, 1973, p. 28). The indifference to pain that some people sometimes display in these and other circumstances has led to many interesting discussions about the nature of pain (e.g., Weisenberg, 1992). Although we commonly view pain as something automatic and universal, large cultural differences exist in how pain is interpreted and expressed. But what is the basis for these differences?

At first glance it is tempting to conclude that cultural differences in *pain threshold*—physical differences—are the cause. Those of us who have grown accustomed to down jackets and central heating have a hard time believing that we could display the indifference to cold that so amazed Cartier. However, there is no consistent experimental evidence to support the notion that there are cultural differences in pain thresholds (Zatzick & Dimsdale, 1990). Rather, observed cultural differences in the capacity to withstand pain (or not) seem to be perceptual in nature and to reflect the powerful effects of social learning (Morse & Morse, 1988). For example, honor and social standing among the Bariba of West Africa are tied closely to stoicism and the ability to withstand great pain (Sargent, 1984). Bariba men and women are expected to suffer pain silently. As you might expect,

CULTURE AND PAIN

Pain is a universal sensation, but pain perception can be strongly influenced by one's culture.

their language contains few words for the expression of pain. Additional environmental factors may also play a role in determining our perceptions of pain. For example, some evidence suggests that individuals exposed to harsh living or working conditions become more stoical than those who work or live in more comfortable circumstances (Clark & Clark, 1980).

Taken together, the evidence suggests that pain may, in fact, be universal—at least in some respects. Specifically, differences in pain perception seem to result from the powerful effects of social learning, not from physical differences.

Smell and Taste: The Chemical Senses

Although smell and taste are separate senses, we'll consider them together for two reasons. First, both respond to substances in solution—that is, substances that have been dissolved in a fluid or gas, usually water or air. Second, in everyday life, smell and taste are interrelated.

Smell and Taste: How They Operate

SMELL   The stimulus for sensations of smell consists of molecules of various substances contained in the air. Such molecules enter the nasal passages, where they dissolve in moist nasal tissues. This brings them in contact with receptor cells contained in the *olfactory epithelium* (see Figure 3.13). Human

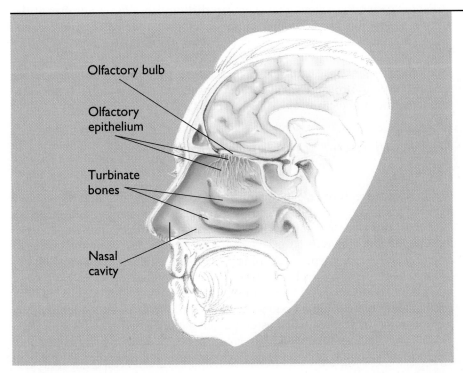

Olfactory bulb

Olfactory epithelium

Turbinate bones

Nasal cavity

FIGURE 3.13

Location of Receptors for Smell

Receptors for our sense of smell are located in the olfactory epithelium, at the top of the nasal cavity. Molecules of odorous substances are dissolved in moisture present in the nasal passages. This brings them into contact with *receptor cells,* whose neural activity gives rise to sensations of smell.

beings possess only about 10 million of these receptors. (Dogs, in contrast, possess more than 200 million receptors.) Nevertheless, our ability to detect smells is impressive. To appreciate this, consider a "scratch and sniff" smell survey that was done in which six different odors were embedded separately onto panels measuring about 4 by 3 centimeters. Amazingly, less than 30 grams of each odor was needed to place these smells onto 11 million copies of the survey (Gibbons, 1986; Gilbert & Wysocki, 1987).

Our olfactory senses are restricted, however, in terms of the range of stimuli to which they are sensitive, just as our visual system can detect only a small portion of the total electromagnetic spectrum. Our olfactory receptors can detect only substances with a molecular weight—the sum of the atomic weights of all atoms in an odorous molecule—between 15 and 300 (Carlson, 1994). This explains why we can smell the alcohol contained in a mixed drink, which has a molecular weight of 46, but cannot smell table sugar, which has a molecular weight of 342.

Several theories have been proposed for how smell messages reach the brain. *Stereochemical theory* suggests that substances differ in smell because they have different molecular shapes (Amoore, 1970; 1982). Unfortunately, support for this theory has been mixed; nearly identical molecules can have extremely different fragrances, whereas substances with very different chemical structures can produce very similar odors (Engen, 1982; Wright, 1982). Other theories have focused on isolating "primary odors," similar to the basic hues in color vision. But these efforts have been unsuccessful, because there is often disagreement in people's perceptions of even the most basic smells.

TASTE The sensory receptors for taste are located inside small bumps on the tongue known as *papillae*. Within each papilla is a cluster of *taste buds* (Figure 3.14). Each taste bud contains several receptor cells. Human beings possess about 10,000 taste buds. In contrast, chickens have only 24, while catfish would win any taste-bud-counting contest—they possess more than 175,000, scattered over the surface of their body. In a sense, they can "taste" with their entire skin (Pfaffmann, 1978).

People generally believe that they can distinguish a large number of flavors in foods. But in fact, there appear to be only four basic tastes: sweet, salty, sour, and bitter (see Figure 3.14). Why, then, do we perceive many more? The answer lies in the fact that we are aware not only of the taste of the food but of its smell, its texture, its temperature, the pressure it exerts on our tongue and mouth, and many other sensations. When these factors are removed from the picture, only the four basic tastes remain.

Smell and Taste: Some Interesting Findings

Perhaps because they are more difficult to study, smell and taste have received far less attention from researchers than vision and hearing. However, this does not imply that these senses are not important. Indeed, individuals who have lost their sense of smell (a state known as *anosmia*) often become deeply depressed; some even commit suicide (Douek, 1988).

Despite the relative lack of research, many interesting facts have been uncovered about smell and taste. For example, it appears that we are not very good at identifying different odors (Engen, 1986). When asked to identify thirteen common fragrances (such as grape, smoke, mint, pine, and soap), individuals were successful only 32 percent of the time. Even when brand-name products or common odors are used, accuracy is still less than 50 percent.

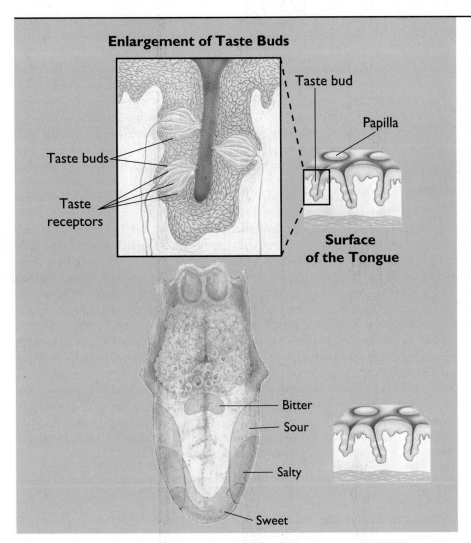

Enlargement of Taste Buds

Taste bud

Taste buds

Papilla

Taste receptors

Surface of the Tongue

Bitter

Sour

Salty

Sweet

FIGURE 3.14

Sensory Receptors for Taste

Taste buds are located inside small bumps on the surface of the tongue known as papillae. Within each taste bud are individual receptor cells. Also shown are the areas of the tongue most sensitive to the four basic tastes: sweet, salty, sour, and bitter.

Some research suggests that we lack a well-developed representational system for describing olfactory experiences (Engen, 1987). In other words, we may recognize a smell without being able to name the odor in question—a condition sometimes called the "tip of the nose" phenomenon (Lawless & Engen, 1977; Richardson & Zucco, 1989). Some experiments have shown that when odorants are associated with experimenter-provided verbal and visual cues, participants' long-term ability to recognize odors is enhanced (Lyman & McDaniel, 1986; 1987).

Actually, although our ability to identify specific odors is limited, our memory of them is impressive (Schab, 1991). Once exposed to a specific odor, we can recognize it months or even years later (Engen & Ross, 1973; Rabin & Cain, 1984). This may be due, in part, to the fact that our memory for odors is often coded as part of memories for more complex and significant life events (Richardson & Zucco, 1989). For example, the delicious aroma of freshly made popcorn may elicit images of your favorite movie theater.

Knowledge about the chemical senses, especially smell, can also have important practical implications—a fact that has not escaped manufacturers of scented products. In North America, sales of fragranced products exceed $19 billion annually (Foderaro, 1988). Commercial success has led to numerous claims regarding the potential benefits of fragrance. For example, practitioners of a field called *aromatherapy* claim that they can successfully treat a wide range of psychological problems and physical ailments by means of specific fragrances (Tisserand, 1977). Moreover, a growing number of companies have installed equipment that introduces various fragrances into the heating and air-conditioning systems of their buildings. Supposedly, the fragrances yield a variety of benefits: Fragrances such as lemon, peppermint, and basil lead to increased alertness and energy, whereas lavender and cedar promote relaxation and reduced tension after high-stress work periods (Iwahashi, 1992). Although little scientific evidence for such claims exists, the concept poses an intriguing question: Can fragrance influence human behavior in measurable ways? A growing body of evidence indicates that the answer is yes. Several studies indicate that individuals who wear perfume or cologne to job interviews can strongly affect the ratings they receive—and not always positively (Baron, 1983, 1986). Other evidence suggests that simply introducing pleasant fragrances (i.e., *ambient fragrances*) into the air of work settings can often produce beneficial effects (Baron & Thomley, 1994; Warm, Dember, & Parasuraman, 1991). In one study, popular brands of air freshener were either sprayed or not sprayed into rooms where people worked on various tasks. Initial results showed that the presence of a pleasant aroma increased the participants' confidence in their own ability to perform various tasks and led them to raise the goals they set for themselves on these tasks. Additionally, the presence of pleasant scents enhanced the mood of the participants and increased their willingness to compromise with opponents during negotiations. These results suggest that introducing pleasant scents into work settings may be one inexpensive and noncontroversial tactic for improving employee performance and satisfaction.

Kinesthesia and Vestibular Sense

Kinesthesia: The sense that gives us information about the location of our body parts with respect to each other and allows us to perform movement.

Vestibular Sense: Our sense of balance.

Vestibular Sacs: Fluid-filled sacs in our inner ear that provide information about the positions and changes in linear movement of our head and body.

Semicircular Canals: Fluid-filled structures that provide information about rotational acceleration of the head or body around three principal axes of rotation.

*O*ne night, while driving along a solitary stretch of the Trans-Canada Highway, you notice flashing lights on the roadside ahead. You slow to a crawl and get a close look at the situation as you pass by. A mountie is in the process of administering a sobriety test to the driver of a car he has pulled over. The driver's head is tilted back at an angle, and he is trying to touch each of his fingers to his nose but is having great difficulty doing so. This example illustrates the importance of our *kinesthetic* and *vestibular senses*—two important but often ignored aspects of our sensory system.

Kinesthesia is the sense that gives us information about the location of our body parts with respect to each other and allows us to perform movements—from simple ones like touching our nose with our fingertips to more complex ones required for gymnastics, dancing, or driving an automobile. Kinesthetic information comes from receptors in joints, ligaments, and muscle fibers (Matlin & Foley, 1992). When we move, these receptors register the rate of change of movement speed as well as the rate of change of the angle of the bones in our limbs; then they transform this mechanical information into neural signals for the brain. We also receive important kinesthetic information from our other senses, especially vision and touch. To demonstrate how your kinesthetic sense system draws on other senses, try the following experiment:

Close your eyes for a moment and hold your arms down at your sides. Now without looking, touch your nose with each of your index fingers—one at a time. Can you do it? Most people can, but only after missing their nose a time or two. Now, try it again with your eyes open. Is it easier this way? In most instances it is, because of the added information we receive from our visual sense.

Whereas kinesthesia keeps our brain informed about the location of our body parts in relation to each other, the **vestibular sense** gives us information about body position, movement, and acceleration—factors critical for maintaining our sense of balance (Schiffman, 1990). We usually become aware of our vestibular sense after activities that make us feel dizzy, like the rides at amusement parks that involve rapid acceleration or spinning.

The sensory organs for the vestibular sense are located in the inner ear (see Figure 3.15). Two fluid-filled **vestibular sacs** provide information about the body's position relative to the earth by tracking changes in linear movement. When our body accelerates (or decelerates) along a straight line, as when we are on a bus that is starting and stopping, or when we tilt our head or body to one side, hair cells bend in proportion to the rate of change in our motion. This differential bending of hair cells causes attached nerve fibers to discharge neural signals that are sent to the brain.

Three fluid-filled **semicircular canals,** also in the inner ear, provide information about rotational acceleration of the head or body along the three principle axes, one of which is shown in Figure 3.15. Whenever we turn or rotate our head, the fluid in these canals begins to move and causes a bending of hair cells. Since these structures are arranged at right angles to each other, bending is greatest in the semicircular canal corresponding to the axis along which the rotation occurs.

Note that the vestibular system is designed to detect *changes* in motion rather than constant motion. For example, it helps us to detect the change in acceleration that accompanies takeoff in an airplane, but not the constant velocity that follows.

THE VESTIBULAR SENSE
A spinning ice skater provides an example of rotational acceleration around one of the three axes monitored in the semicircular canals.

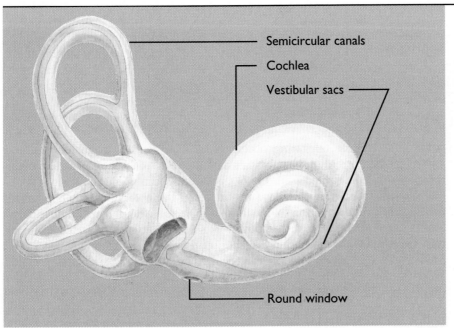

Semicircular canals

Cochlea

Vestibular sacs

Round window

FIGURE 3.15

The Structures Underlying Our Sense of Balance

Shown here are the organs of our kinesthetic and vestibular senses. Structures in the two *vestibular sacs* provide information about the positions of our head and body with respect to gravity by tracking changes in linear movement; those in the *semicircular canals* provide information about *rotational acceleration* around three principal axes. An example of rotational acceleration around one of the three axes.

We also receive vestibular information from our other senses, especially vision—a fact that can produce queasy consequences if the information from these senses is in conflict (Jefferson, 1993). Developers of a realistic Back to the Future ride at Universal Studios in Florida discovered this fact when riders in their DeLorean simulator lost their cookies. Apparently, the visual effects were not synchronized with the movements the riders felt. Once reprogrammed, however, the simulator conveyed the developers' initial intent—the sensation of flying through space and time.

Perception: *Putting It All Together*

Up to this point we have focused on the sensory processes that convert raw physical stimulation into usable neural codes. But you may be wondering how this array of neural action potentials contributes to the richness of conscious experience. Stop for a moment and look around you. Do you see a meaningless swirl of colors, brightnesses, and shapes? Probably not. Now turn on the radio and tune it to any station. Do you hear an incomprehensible babble of sounds? Certainly not (unless, of course, you've tuned to a foreign-language or heavy metal station). In both cases, you "see" and "hear" more than the raw sensations that stimulate the receptors in your eyes, ears, and other sense organs; you see recognizable objects and hear understandable words or music. In other words, transmission of sensory information from sensory receptors to the brain is only part of the process. Equally important is the process of perception—the way in which we *select*, *organize*, and *interpret* sensory input to achieve a grasp of our surroundings. The remainder of this chapter is about some of the basic principles that influence perception.

Perception: *The Focus of Our Attention*

Our attention, or mental focus, captures only a small portion of the stimuli available at a given moment. But what about all of the other available information? For example, by shifting our attention away from visual and auditory stimuli, we may suddenly notice smells, tastes, and tactile sensations that were outside our awareness only moments before.

One thing is certain: We cannot absorb all of the available sensory information in our environment. Thus, we *selectively attend* to certain aspects of our environment while relegating others to the background (Johnston & Dark, 1986). Selective attention has obvious advantages, in that it allows us to maximize information gained from the object of our focus while reducing sensory interference from other, irrelevant sources (Matlin & Foley, 1992). Unfortunately, selective attention to one thing may involve neglecting another. For a firsthand understanding of the power of selective attention, watch someone who is completely absorbed in a suspenseful novel or a thrilling sports event. Studies have shown that people can focus so intently on one task that they fail to notice other events occurring simultaneously—even very salient ones (Becklen & Cerone, 1983; Cherry, 1953). We are, however, faced with many everyday situations in which we must cope with multiple conflicting inputs. Think back to the last time you were at a crowded party with many conversations going on at once. Were you able to shut out all voices except for that of the person you were talking to? Probably not. Our attention often shifts to other aspects of our environment, such as a juicy bit of conversation or a mention of our own name (Moray, 1959). This is often referred to as the *cocktail party phenomenon* and illustrates one way in which we deal with the demands of divided attention.

Although we control the focus of our attention, at least to some extent, certain characteristics of stimuli can cause our attention to shift suddenly. Features such as contrast, novelty, stimulus intensity, color, and sudden change tend to attract our attention. Indeed, advertisers have capitalized on attention-getting strategies for years. Additionally, if you recall the discussion of signal detection theory early in this chapter, it should not surprise you that the focus of our attention is dramatically affected by higher-level cognitive processes; in other words, motivation and expectancy factors have a lot to do with selective attention.

As it turns out, our attentional processes play a crucial survival role in aspects of our everyday life by alerting us to immediate natural dangers in our environment. They enable us, for example, to leap back onto the curb when we glimpse a speeding car out of the corner of our eye. You can probably imagine hundreds of ways in which attentional processes help us to avoid peril. But what about hazards for which there are no sensory cues available? One of the most deadly examples of this is radioactivity. The radioactive particles emitted by certain materials are colorless and odorless and thus cannot be detected through our normal sensory receptors; even a limited exposure, however, can have deadly consequences. In **The Research Process**, we'll examine how aspects of our attentional processes have figured prominently in the development of effective *warnings*—information displays that attempt to influence our behavior through the information they present.

Perception: *Some Organizing Principles*

Look at the illustrations in Figure 3.16. Instead of random smatterings of black and white, you can probably discern a familiar figure in each. But how does our brain allow us to interpret these confused specks as a dog and a horseback rider? The process by which we structure the input from our sensory receptors is called *perceptual organization*. Aspects of perceptual organization were first

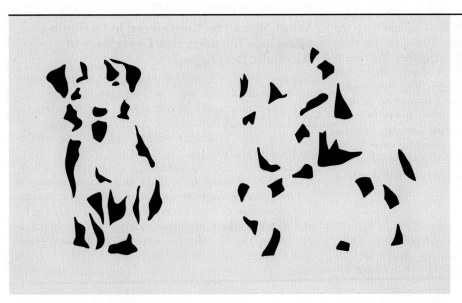

FIGURE 3.16

Perceptual Organization

Look carefully at each of the figures. What do you see? Our perceptual processes often allow us to perceive shapes and forms from incomplete and fragmented stimuli.

DANGER—Warnings are Effective Only Under Certain Conditions: They Have to Be Developed and Applied with Great Care

Y ou are undoubtedly familiar with warnings. They are everywhere and on everything— including network TV. In response to public criticism over high levels of violence shown on TV—even in children's programs—Canadian television executives have deemed it prudent to precede transmission of certain programs with warnings. We have all seen this warning: THIS PROGRAM IS INTENDED FOR A MATURE AUDIENCE: VIEWER DISCRETION ADVISED.

Television Warnings: Are They Effective?

Warnings alone may be inadequate to counteract the potential effects of violence on TV.
(Source: MacNelly, *Chicago Tribune*)

A critical question is whether the use of this warning, and of the hundreds of others currently flooding our environment, is justified. Even the experts cannot agree (McCarthy et al., 1984). Those opposed to the use of warnings argue that their excessive use may cause people to ignore warnings altogether. This point of view is consistent with what we know about our *information processing* limitations: As you may recall, we can only attend to and process a limited amount of sensory information before becoming overwhelmed. Also, using warnings for low-risk hazards, or for those with a low probability of occurring, may teach people to ignore them, since these warnings are rarely associated with an aversive outcome such as death or serious injury.

Research on Warnings

Warnings can be effective, but their ability to influence behavior is greatly affected by many factors, including the physical features of the warnings themselves and the way in which the warnings are presented (Wogalter & Young, 1993). In a 1991 study, Wogalter and Young examined the effects of warning modality (i.e., whether the warning was visual or auditory) on compliance behavior. Participants performed a chemistry demonstration task involving the measuring and mixing of what they thought were hazardous chemicals. Included in the instructions was the following message: WARNING: WEAR GLOVES AND MASK WHILE PERFORMING THE TASK TO AVOID IRRITATING FUMES AND POSSIBLE IRRITATION OF SKIN.

Participants received this warning in one of three ways: in printed form, or as an oral presentation (by the experimenter or through audiotape), or both (printed instructions *and* oral presentation). Not surprisingly, compliance was highest when the warning was presented in both printed and oral form. Why? Since our conscious experience depends on input from *all* of our senses, presentation of critical information to more than one of the senses may enhance a warning's effectiveness.

But the use of warnings has not been universally successful, in part because of a failure to recognize that their effectiveness depends on our sensory *and* perceptual processes. To illustrate, let's look at what Canadians, who are considering the use of warning labels on alcoholic beverage containers, can learn from the American experience with such labels.

CANADIAN PERSPECTIVE

What Should be Considered in Designing Warnings for Canadian Containers of Alcoholic Beverages?

In June 1992, the federal Minister of Health proposed a pilot study to determine whether warnings on Canadian alcoholic beverage containers could help protect the health of unborn fetuses. Current discussions suggest that the Canadian warning will likely be similar to the one used in the United States. In that country, containers of alcoholic beverages are required to bear a small cautionary note. This note warns pregnant women that consumption of alcoholic beverages during the course of a pregnancy can lead to birth defects; it also warns the population at large that alcohol consumption impairs driving and machinery operation and may contribute to health problems.

Should Canada simply adopt a similar warning label? Much research suggests that broader consideration of the objectives and of the warning's design is required. A basic difficulty with the American warning is that large-scale research has generally shown that it does not work, either in changing perceptions of risk or in changing behavior (Hilton, 1993). The reason? Developers of the warning apparently failed to recognize the importance of both *sensation*—the physical features of the warning—and *perception*—the characteristics of individuals exposed to the warning (Wogalter & Young, 1993). First, because of the small size of the current alcohol warning message, drinkers may be unable to read or even see it, especially as they become more intoxicated. Second, the warning is indistinguishable from other information on the label, such as the ingredients. Third, the warning lacks sufficient detail to convey the intended information effectively. Fourth, the American warning is found only on bottles and cans, which can be a definite problem when beer is served from kegs.

Additional difficulties stem from the fact that the designers of the American labeling system failed to consider important aspects of perception—how we organize and interpret the warning information. For example, the first part of the message focuses on the risks of drinking while pregnant. Although important, this information is not relevant to the experience and interests of high-risk groups other than pregnant women (e.g., college and university students). Further, the fact that the American label is written in English means that those lacking an adequate level of literacy,

or who speak a foreign language, cannot be influenced by such labels.

Whether Canadian designers of warning labels for alcoholic beverages will profit from the apparent deficiencies in the American labeling system—perhaps by adding stimulus features, such as international symbols, illustrations that show a hazard to be avoided, and other "language-free" warning stimuli—remains to be seen. The essential point is that well-designed warnings can be effective (Kalsher, Clarke, & Wogalter, 1993), but that Canadian designers will have to focus on stimulus properties that engage the attention of consumers, and also convey the warning message not to just a subset of consumers but to the entire consuming population. (See Chapter 17 for more information on the design of effective warnings.)

Critical Thinking Questions

1. What are some of the implications of overusing warnings or using warnings for low-risk hazards?

2. Under what conditions would you recommend the use of warnings?

3. In light of the findings described in this special section, do you believe that warnings can be effective in increasing knowledge of alcohol-related hazards? Can they change behavior?

4. Suppose you were called upon to design a warning that would be effective in changing the behavior of your peers. What steps would you follow in its development and implementation?

studied systematically in the early 1900s by **Gestalt psychologists**—early German psychologists who were intrigued by certain innate tendencies of the human mind to impose order and structure on the physical world and to perceive sensory patterns as well-organized wholes rather than as separate, isolated parts (*Gestalt* means "whole" in German). These scientists outlined several principles that describe how we organize basic sensory input into whole patterns (gestalts). Some of these are described below. You could say that the Gestalt psychologists changed our perceptions about the nature of perception.

FIGURE AND GROUND: WHAT STANDS OUT?   By looking carefully at Figure 3.17, you can experience a principle of perceptual organization known as the **figure-ground relationship.** What this means, simply, is that we tend to divide the world around us into two parts: *figure*, which has a definite shape and a location in space; and *ground*, which has no shape, seems to continue behind the figure, and has no definite location. The figure-ground relationship helps clarify the distinction between sensation and perception. While the pattern of sensory information generated in our receptors remains constant, our perceptions shift between the two figure-ground patterns in Figure 3.17; thus, we may see either

Gestalt Psychologists: Early German psychologists intrigued by our tendency to perceive sensory patterns as well-organized wholes rather than as separate, isolated parts.

Figure-Ground Relationship: Our tendency to divide the perceptual world into two distinct parts: discrete figures and the background against which they stand out.

FIGURE 3.17

A Demonstration Of Figure-Ground

What do you see when you look at this drawing? You probably see either an old woman or a young woman. Since this is an ambiguous figure, your perceptions may switch back and forth between these two possibilities.

the young or the old woman, but not both. Note that the principles of perceptual organization apply to the other senses, too. For instance, consider how the figure-ground relationship applies to audition. During a complicated lecture, you become absorbed in whispered gossip between two students sitting next to you; the professor's voice becomes background noise. Suddenly you hear your name and realize the professor has asked you a question; her voice has now become the sole focus of your attention, while the conversation becomes background noise.

GROUPING: WHICH STIMULI GO TOGETHER? The Gestaltists also called attention to a number of principles known as the **laws of grouping**—basic ways in which we group items together perceptually. Several of these laws, including a more recently discovered perceptual grouping principle called *common region*, are shown in the Key Concept illustration on page 125 (Palmer, 1992). As you can see from this feature, laws of grouping do offer a good description of our perceptual tendencies.

The principles outlined by Gestalt psychologists are not, however, hard-and-fast rules. They are merely descriptions of ways in which we perceive the world around us. Whether these principles are innate, as the Gestaltists believed, or learned, as some newer evidence suggests, is still open to debate. In any case, principles of perceptual organization are readily visible in the natural world, and they are effective in helping us organize our perceptual world.

Constancies and Illusions: When Perception Succeeds—and Fails

Perception, we have seen, is more than the sum of all the sensory input supplied by our eyes, ears, and other receptors. It is the active selection, organization, and interpretation of such input. It yields final products that differ from raw, unprocessed sensations in important ways. Up till now, this discussion has focused on the benefits of this process. But perception, like any other powerful process, can be a double-edged sword. On the one hand, perception helps us adapt to a complex and ever-changing environment. On the other hand, perception sometimes leads us into error. To see how, let's consider *constancies* and *illusions*.

Laws of Grouping: Simple principles describing how we tend to group discrete stimuli together in the perceptual world.

Constancies: Our tendency to perceive physical objects as unchanging despite shifts in the pattern of sensations these objects induce.

Size Constancy: The tendency to perceive a physical object as having a constant size even when the size of the image it casts on the retina changes.

PERCEPTUAL CONSTANCIES: STABILITY IN THE FACE OF CHANGE Try this simple demonstration. Hold your right hand in front of you at arm's length. Now, move it toward and away from your face several times. Does it seem to change in size? Probably not. Now hold your left hand in front of your face at a distance of about 20 centimeters; again, move your right hand in and out. Does it seem to change in size now? Again, probably not. The purpose of this demonstration is to illustrate the principles of perceptual **constancies**—our tendency to perceive aspects of the world as unchanging despite changes in the sensory input we receive from them. The principle of **size constancy** relates to the fact that the perceived size of an object remains the same when the distance is varied, even though the size of the image it casts on the retina changes greatly.

Figure–Ground

The tendency to view the world in two parts: *figure*, which has definite shape and location in space, and *ground*, background stimuli with no specific shape or location in space.

Laws of Grouping

Law of Similarity
Tendency to perceive similar items as a group.

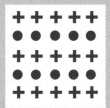

Law of Proximity
Tendency to perceive items located ogether as a group.

Law of Common Region
Tendency to perceive objects as a group if they occupy the same place within a plane.

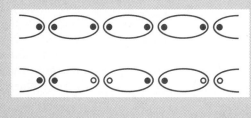

Law of Good Continuation
Tendency to perceive stimuli as part of a continuous pattern.

Law of Closure
Tendency to perceive objects as whole entities, despite the fact that some parts may be missing or obstructed from view.

Law of Simplicity
Tendency to perceive complex patterns in terms of simpler shapes.

Under normal circumstances, such constancy is impressive. Consider, for example, what you see when you notice a friend walking toward you from several blocks away. Distant objects—cars, trees, people—cast tiny images on our retina. Yet we perceive them as being of normal size. Two factors seem to account for this tendency—distance invariance and relative size.

The principle of *size-distance invariance* suggests that when estimating the size of an object, we take into account both the size of the image it casts on our retina and the apparent distance to the object. From these data we almost instantly calculate the object's size. Only when the cues that normally reveal an object's distance are missing do we run into difficulties in estimating the object's size (as we'll see in the discussion of illusions that follows). In the same way, we judge the **relative size** of an object by comparing it with objects of known size. This mechanism is especially useful for estimating the size of unfamiliar things.

But size is not the only perceptual feature of the physical world that does not correspond directly with the information transmitted by our sensory receptors. The principle of **shape constancy** refers to the fact that the perceived shape of an object does not alter as the image it casts on the retina changes. For example, all of us know that coins are round; yet we rarely see them that way. Flip a coin into the air: although you continue to perceive the coin as being round, the image that actually falls onto your retina constantly shifts from a circle to various forms of an ellipse.

The principle of **brightness constancy** refers to the fact that we perceive objects as constant in brightness and color whatever the lighting conditions. Thus, we will perceive a sweater as dark green whether we are indoors or outdoors in bright sunlight. Brightness constancy apparently prevails because objects and their surroundings are usually lighted by the same illumination source, so changes in lighting conditions occur simultaneously for both the object and its immediate surroundings. As long as the changes in lighting remain constant for both object and surround, the neural message reaching the brain is unchanged. Brightness constancy breaks down, however, when changes in lighting are not equivalent for both the object and its surroundings (Sekuler & Blake, 1990).

Although most research on perceptual constancies has focused on size, shape, and brightness, constancy pervades nearly every area of perception, including our other senses. For example, imagine listening to elevator music while riding on an elevator en route to a dental appointment on the thirtieth floor of an office building. When one of your favorite oldies from the mid-1970s begins, you can't believe what they've done to "your song." Nonetheless, you are still able to recognize it, despite differences in its loudness, tone, and pitch.

Whatever their basis, perceptual constancies are highly useful. Without them, we would spend a great deal of time and effort reidentifying sensory information in our environment each time we experienced the information from a new perspective. The gap between our sensations and the perceptions provided by the constancies is clearly beneficial.

ILLUSIONS: WHEN PERCEPTION FAILS Perception can also, however, provide false interpretations of sensory information. Such cases are known as **illusions,** a term used by psychologists to refer to incorrect perceptions. Actually, there are two types of illusions: those due to physical processes and those due to cognitive processes (Matlin & Foley, 1992). Illusions due to distortion of physical conditions include *mirages*, in which you perceive things that aren't really there—like the water you often seem to see on the dry road ahead of you. Our focus, however, will be on the latter type of illusions—those involving cognitive processes.

Countless illusions related to cognitive processes exist, but most fall into two categories: illusions of *size* and illusions of *shape* or *area* (Coren et al.,

Relative Size: A visual cue based on comparison of the size of an unknown object to one of known size.

Shape Constancy: The tendency to perceive a physical object as having a constant shape even when the image it casts on the retina changes.

Brightness Constancy: The tendency to perceive objects as having a constant brightness even when they are viewed under different conditions of illumination.

Illusions: Instances in which perception yields false interpretations of physical reality.

1976). Natural examples of two well-known size illusions are presented in Figure 3.18, and as you can see, their effects are powerful. But why do illusions occur? What causes our interpretation of such stimuli to be directly at odds with physical reality? Recent evidence suggests that illusions generally have multiple causes (Schiffman, 1990). However, one explanation is provided by the *theory of misapplied constancy*, which suggests that when looking at illusions, we interpret certain cues as suggesting that some parts are farther away than others. Our powerful tendency toward size constancy then comes into play, with the result that we perceptually distort the length of various lines (refer to Figure 3.19). Learning also plays an important role in illusions, as shown in the architectural examples of the *Müller-Lyer illusion* in Figure 3.19. Past experience tells us that the corner shown in the photo on the right is usually farther away than the corner in the photo on the left. Since the size of the retinal image cast by the vertical lines in both photos is identical, we interpret the vertical line as longer in the photo on the right. Moreover, learning seems to affect the extent to which our perception is influenced by illusions, since many visual illusions decline in magnitude following extended exposure—although they do not decline altogether (Greist-Bousquet, Watson, & Schiffman, 1990).

Another type of illusion is that of *shape* or *area*. If you've ever wondered why the moon looks bigger at the horizon (about 30 percent bigger!) than at its highest point in the sky, then you are familiar with the most famous area illusion—the *moon illusion*. Why does the moon illusion occur? In part, because when the moon is near the horizon, we can see that it is farther away than trees, houses, and other objects. When it is overhead at its zenith, such cues are lacking. Thus, the moon appears larger near the horizon because there are cues available that cause us to perceive that it is very far away. Once again, our tendency toward size constancy leads us astray.

Like illusions of size or area, shape illusions (see Figure 3.20) too can influence perception, sometimes with unsettling consequences. Consider a real-world example involving the *Poggendorf illusion* (see drawing A in Figure 3.20). In this illusion, a line disappears at an angle behind a solid figure, then reappears on the other side—at what seems to be the incorrect position. As reported by Coren and Girgus (1978), in 1965 two airplanes were about to arrive in New York City, and because of the Poggendorf illusion, they thought that they were on a collision course. Both pilots changed direction to correct

A   **B**

FIGURE 3.18

Illusions of Size

Natural examples of two powerful illusions of size. (A) The horizontal-vertical illusion stems from our tendency to perceive objects higher in our visual field as more distant. This illusion helps explain·why the St. Louis Gateway falsely appears taller than it is wide (its height and width are actually equal). (B) In the Ponzo illusion, the object in the distance appears larger, although both objects are actually the same size.

FIGURE 3.19

The Müller-Lyer Illusion

(a) In the Müller-Lyer illusion, lines of equal length appear unequal; the line with the wings pointing outward looks longer than the line with the wings pointing inward. (b) Now carefully examine the vertical line in each of the photographs. Which line is longer? Most people perceive the vertical line in the photo on the right as longer, although careful measurement shows that the two lines are exactly the same length!

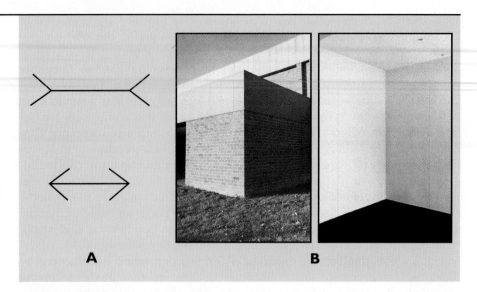

A   B

FIGURE 3.20

Illusions of Area or Shape

Illusions of area or shape can be quite powerful. (a) In this drawing, known as the Poggendorf illusion, which of the three lines on the right continues the line on the left? Check your answer with a ruler. (b) In this drawing, are the horizontal lines straight or bent in the middle? Again, check for yourself. (c) Finally, in this drawing are the letters tilted or vertical? When you check, you'll see why sometimes you can't believe what you think you see.

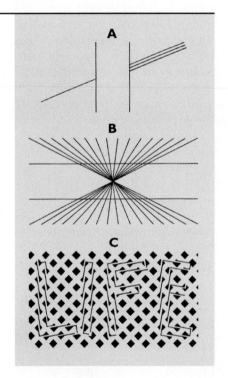

A

B

C

for what they perceived as an error, and their planes thus collided. The result was four deaths and forty-nine injuries—all because of an illusion.

One final point: illusions are not limited to visual processes. Indeed, there are numerous examples of illusions involving our other senses, including touch and audition (Sekuler & Blake, 1990; Shepard, 1964). One well-known illusion that you can demonstrate for yourself is that of touch temperature. First place one hand in a container of hot water and the other hand in cold water. Then place *both* hands in a container of lukewarm water. What do you feel? Most people experience a dramatic difference in perceived temperature between the two hands; the hand initially placed in hot water feels the lukewarm water as cool, while the hand initially placed in cold water feels it as hot. How do we explain this illusion? When we touch an object, the temperature of the area of our skin in contact with it shifts toward that of the object's surface. So, when we perceive an object to be warm or cool, our experience stems partly from the temperature difference between the object and our skin, not solely from the actual temperature of the object.

Some Key Perceptual Processes: *Pattern and Distance*

It can be argued that perception is a practical process, for it provides living organisms with information essential to survival in their normal habitat. The specific nature of this information varies greatly with different species. For example, frogs must be able to detect small moving objects in order to feed on insects, whereas porpoises require sensory input that enables them to navigate turbulent and murky ocean waters. Nonetheless, it is probably safe to say that virtually all living creatures need information concerning (1) what's out there and (2) how far away it is. Humans are no exception to this general rule, and we possess impressive perceptual skills in both areas.

PATTERN RECOGNITION: WHAT'S OUT THERE?   Our ability to read the words on this page depends on our ability to recognize small black marks as letters and collections of such marks as words. How do we accomplish this task? An early explanation for this phenomenon was the *template-matching theory*. According to this theory, we have many **templates,** or specific patterns, stored in our memories for various visual stimuli that we encounter. Thus, if a visual stimulus—say, a letter—matches one of the templates, we recognize it; if it does not, we search for another that does match. As you may have already guessed, this theory is impractical, since it requires that we store an almost infinite number of these templates in memory in order to be able to recognize even variants of the same letter. Additionally, the template-matching theory does not explain our ability to read at rates exceeding hundreds of words per minute or to recognize visual stimuli almost instantly, even when they're tilted or viewed upside down (Pinker, 1984).

A related but more viable explanation, referred to as *prototype-matching theory*, suggests that we automatically compare each letter (and perhaps word) to abstract representations of these stimuli in our memories. These representations are known as **prototypes.** According to this view, we have a prototype in memory for each letter of the alphabet, based on all examples of the letter previously encountered. Thus, recognition depends on finding a correct match between the stimulus letter or word and a previously seen prototype. Please note that a prototype is not an exact match or a template for some visual stimulus, but a general pattern that lets us recognize a letter even when it is distorted. While some evidence supports this view (e.g., Franks & Bransford, 1971), the physiological details of this theory are not well developed (Matlin & Foley, 1992). For example, it is not yet clear how these stimuli are internally represented in our cognitive structure.

Two other approaches are the bottom-up and top-down theories of pattern recognition. As their names imply, these adopt somewhat opposite perspectives on the basic question of how we recognize patterns of visual stimuli. The *bottom-up approach* suggests that our ability to recognize specific patterns, such as letters of the alphabet, is based on simpler capacities to recognize and combine correctly lower-level features of the letters, such as lines, edges, corners, and angles. For example, our ability to recognize an A and distinguish it from other letters depends on activation of *feature detectors*, which when stimulated activate other neurons that may be described as *letter detectors*. Bottom-up theories suggest that pattern recognition is constructed from simpler perceptual abilities

Templates: *Specific patterns stored in our memories for various visual stimuli that we encounter.*

Prototypes: *Representations in memory of various objects or stimuli in the physical world.*

FIGURE 3.21

Bottom-Up Theories Do Not Explain Perception of Reversible Figures

Bottom-up theories based on feature analysis cannot explain how we can see both faces and a vase in this reversible ambiguous figure.

through a discrete series of steps (Marr, 1982). Unfortunately, bottom-up theories based on feature analysis do not explain well how people perceive ambiguous stimuli. For example, in Figure 3.21, we can see either a vase or a face, despite the fact that the stimulus pattern remains the same in both instances.

In contrast, the *top-down approach* emphasizes the fact that our expectancies play a critical role in shaping our perceptions. We often proceed in accordance with what our past experience tells us to expect, and therefore we don't always analyze every feature of most stimuli we encounter. Although top-down processing can be extremely efficient (think about the speed with which you can read this page), it can also lead us astray. Nearly everyone has had the experience of rushing over to another person who appears to be an old friend, only to realize that he or she is actually a stranger. In such cases, our tendency to process information quickly from the top down can indeed produce errors.

Which of these theories is correct? Current evidence indicates that both play a role in pattern recognition (Matlin & Foley, 1992). When we have strong expectations or we are in a familiar context, we often opt for speed and adopt a top-down approach. However, when we are dealing with unfamiliar situations or stimuli, bottom-up processing often dominates. In many situations, both processes may occur at once. In summary, our efforts to make sense out of the world around us tend to take whatever form is most efficient in a given context.

DISTANCE PERCEPTION: HOW FAR AWAY IS IT?   Our ability to judge depth and distance is impressive because we make use of many different cues in forming such judgments. These cues are *monocular* or *binocular*, depending on whether they can be seen with only one eye or require the use of both eyes.

Monocular cues to depth or distance include the following:

1. *Size cues* The larger the image of an object on the retina, the larger the object is judged to be; in addition, if an object is larger than other objects, it is often perceived as closer.

2. *Linear perspective* Parallel lines appear to converge in the distance; the greater this effect, the farther away an object appears to be.

3. *Texture gradient* The texture of a surface appears smoother as distance increases.

4. *Atmospheric perspective* The farther away objects are, the less distinctly they are seen—smog, dust, haze, and so on get in the way.

5. *Overlap (or interposition)* If one object overlaps another, it is seen as being closer than the one it covers.

Monocular Cues: Cues to depth or distance provided by one eye.

6. *Height cues (aerial perspective)* Below the horizon, objects lower down in our field of vision are perceived as closer; above the horizon, objects higher up are seen as closer.

7. *Motion parallax* When we travel in a vehicle, objects far away appear to move in the same direction as the observer, whereas close objects move in the opposite direction. Objects at different distances appear to move at different velocities.

As you can see, much of our ability to perceive depth is based on the use of *monocular cues*. However, we also rely heavily on **binocular cues**—depth information based on the coordinated efforts of both eyes. Binocular cues for depth perception stem from two primary sources:

1. *Convergence* In order to see close objects, our eyes turn inward, toward one another; the greater this movement, the closer such objects appear to be.

2. *Retinal disparity (binocular parallax)* Our two eyes observe objects from slightly different positions in space; the difference between the two images provides our brain with another cue to depth. Figure 3.22 contains a *stereogram:* a pattern of dots in which we can perceive 3-D images—thanks in part to retinal disparity.

These lists of monocular and binocular cues are by no means exhaustive. By using the wealth of information provided by these and other cues (Schiffman, 1990), we can usually perceive depth and distance with great accuracy.

Binocular Cues: *Cues to depth or distance provided by the use of both eyes.*

FIGURE 3.22

Retinal Disparity and Stereograms

Retinal disparity is the basis for perceiving 3-D images in stereograms. (1) Hold the book about a foot away from your eyes. (2) Note the pair of circles at the top of the stereogram. (3) Relax your gaze as if you were looking beyond the page, until you see each mark split in two. (4) Widen the split until the two central marks meet and merge. Depth should pop out at you! Now move your gaze slowly into the image. Do you see the train engines?
(Source: *Games,* 1993)

The Plasticity of Perception: To What Extent Is It Innate or Learned Through Experience?

*I*magine a man blind from birth who is suddenly provided with sight through a miraculous operation. Will his visual world be the same as yours or mine? Will it be orderly and consistent with his expectations? Or will he experience a chaotic swirl of colors, brightnesses, and meaningless shapes? This intriguing question has often served as the basis for exploring the nature–nurture controversy. In other words, to what extent are aspects of perception learned or hereditary?

Perception: Evidence That It's Innate

Evidence that perception is innate stems from two lines of research. The first involves people like the one described above, who were born blind but later gained their sense of sight (or were blinded soon after birth and whose sight was later restored). If perception is innate, then such individuals should be able to see clearly immediately after recovery from surgery. Although cases like this are few in number and the results often vary, many of these individuals can make at least partial sense out of the visual world soon after their sight is provided or restored. For example, they can detect and follow moving objects, suggesting that some aspects of visual perception may indeed be innate (Von Senden, 1960). However, certain complications require us to be cautious in making even limited interpretation of these findings. For example, it is difficult to know precisely when recovery from a medical procedure is sufficient to allow for "normal" vision. This leaves open the question of when the patient should be tested for perceptual abilities.

Additional evidence suggesting that perception is innate is provided by research with very young subjects, such as babies only a few hours or days old. Studies have explored numerous perceptual abilities, particularly auditory and visual abilities, that are present at birth or shortly afterward (Schiffman, 1990). In one such study, infants slightly more than three days old were exposed to squares of colored light (blue, green, yellow, red) and to gray light of equal brightness. These infants spent more time looking at every one of the colored stimuli than at the gray—an indication that ability to perceive color is present soon after birth (Adams, 1987).

In another study, Balogh and Porter (1986) exposed babies only a few hours old to one of two aromas—ginger or cherry—for about twenty-four hours. One odor was present on a gauze pad in each infant's bassinet. After the initial exposure, two pads, each containing a different one of the two original aromas, were placed in each bassinet, and the amount of time the infant spent orienting toward each one during brief test periods was observed. Female infants showed a marked preference for the familiar odor—the one to which they had previously been exposed—while male infants showed no preference. It is not certain why this gender difference occurred; other research suggests, however, that at all ages females are superior to males in identifying specific odors (Doty et al., 1984). Thus, our perception of smell may also be present at or soon after birth. In any case, studies like these suggest that some aspects of perception are innate, or at least that they appear early in life.

Perception: *Evidence for the Importance of Learning and Experience*

At the same time, there is considerable evidence for the view that learning and experience play a key role in perception. Consider a 1974 study by Muir and Mitchell at Dalhousie University that involved raising kittens in selective visual environments. They raised kittens in darkness except for brief periods, during which they were exposed to either horizontal or vertical stripes. When later transferred to a normal visual environment, it was clear that these animals had been markedly affected by the visual experience they had encountered during rearing. They were quite responsive to linear objects—such as a long black rod—if the rod was oriented in the same direction as the stripes to which they had been exposed during rearing. When, however, the same rod was rotated ninety degrees, they appeared completely blind to it. The exact opposite was true for animals exposed to horizontal lines during rearing. After a substantial period of adjustment to a normal visual environment, these kittens continued to show enduring differences. For as long as six months after the rearing experience, they had difficulty "seeing" linear arrangements oriented differently from the ones they had been exposed to. Clearly, the early learning experience can influence the development of visual functions.

Research in Canada

Darwin Muir (1974)
Dalhousie University

Additional evidence for the role of learning and experience in perception comes from studies in which human volunteers wear special goggles that invert their view of the world and reverse right and left. The participants at first have difficulty carrying out normal activities with their goggles on, but they soon adapt and do everything from reading a book to flying a plane (Kohler, 1962). These findings, and others, suggest that we do indeed learn to interpret the information supplied by our sensory receptors.

Must We Try to Resolve the Nature–Nurture Controversy?

The findings we've reviewed thus far offer no simple resolution to the nature–nurture issue; other studies involving both animals and humans are equally inconclusive. Some studies show that certain aspects of visual perception seem to be present without previous sensory experience, whereas other aspects develop only through experience with the external world (Wiesel, 1982).

Confronted with this mixed evidence, most psychologists accept that perception is influenced both by innate factors *and* by experience. For example, consider the strange case of Virgil—a fifty-year-old man who regained his sight after forty-five years of blindness (Sacks, 1993). The fact that Virgil could immediately detect visual features, such as letters, objects and colors, suggested the influence of nature. However, Virgil could not "see" in the true sense. Learning even simple visual relationships required great effort, since most of his knowledge of the world had come to him through the sense of touch.

In sum, there is no way that we can resolve the nature-nurture question. Perception is plastic in the sense that it can be, and often is, modified by our encounters with physical reality. But there are biological limits to that plasticity. The best we can do is try and tease out, through clever experimentation, the relative roles played by innate mechanisms and by learning and experience in various different perceptual phenomena.

KEY POINT

- Both nature and nurture are important determinants of the ways we perceive the world around us.

Testing the Limits of Perceptual Plasticity

Our visual perceptual apparatus is designed to respond to visual information in the environment. We rapidly acquire the capacity to respond to that information and to use it effectively to understand objects and events we encounter in our daily activities. An interesting and extremely useful research strategy involves testing the limits of our capacity to adapt to changes in perceptual information. Such research can tell us much about the flexibility, or plasticity, of our perceptual system.

A particularly interesting study of perceptual plasticity was undertaken by Stuart Anstis and his associates at York University in Toronto in the early 1990s (Anstis & Hutahajan, 1991; Anstis, 1992). In his study, Anstis used a video device that generated a negative image of the visual world: Black became white, and white became black, and colors appeared in complementary hues—yellows were conveyed as blues, and blues as yellows, and greens as reds or purples, and so on.

For three days Anstis viewed the world through this device, carefully closing or masking his eyes when away from the device so as not to interfere with the adaptive process. At first the world was very unsettling: The normally blue sky appeared as a dark yellow. Moving into bright sunshine caused a darkening of the visual world and produced white shadows. As night closed in, the world appeared as a "daylit snowscape." People had a strange appearance. A research assistant had black teeth, white hair, and dark-blue skin. The pupils of her eyes were white, her irises silvery white. Recognition of individuals was difficult, and facial expressions were difficult to read.

After three days, some adaptation had taken place. Gross movements became readily discernible. Shapes and shadows could be separated if the shadows were sharp-edged. (Fuzzy shadows were harder to interpret.) Some improvement in reading facial expressions had been acquired, but profound difficulties in face recognition remained. Even very familiar figures were hard to identify. Anstis reports watching an old movie in which Bob Hope danced, and being quite able to follow the movements but totally unable to recognize the person making them.

The Anstis study shows that it isn't enough to be exposed to all the necessary visual information. To be effective, that information has to be in a form that the visual system is programmed to read and interpret. Anstis had all the visual information that we have under normal viewing conditions; the only change he experienced was a reversal of color and brightness. The fact that his visual system could adapt only to certain aspects of this reversal is informative with respect to the limits of perceptual plasticity. His inability to deal with the changes that colour and brightness reversal made to face recognition, and the difficulties he experienced in interpreting shading, suggest that there is something very special, and very difficult to change, about the way our system has evolved to cope with these aspects of our visual environment.

Extrasensory Perception: Perception Without Sensation?

*H*ave you ever wondered if we have a "sixth sense"? In other words, can we gain information about the external world without using our five basic senses? Many people believe we can, and accept the existence of **extrasensory perception**—literally, perception without a basis in sensation. The first and most basic question we can ask about ESP is, "Does it really exist?" Recently this question has been recast by Bem and Hornton (1994) in terms of a hypothetical process known as **psi**. These researchers define psi as unusual processes of information or energy transfer that are currently unexplained in

Exrasensory Perception (ESP): Perception without a basis in sensory input.

terms of known physical or biological mechanisms. In short, psi underlies and forms the basis for what has generally been referred to as ESP. In the discussion that follows, we'll use this newer term—psi—instead of the older term, ESP. What precisely is psi? And is there any evidence for its existence? In this section, we will discuss some of the evidence on this intriguing topic.

Psi: What Is It?

Parapsychologists, who study psi and other *paranormal events* (i.e., events outside our normal experience or knowledge), suggest that there are actually several distinct forms of psi (or ESP). One form of psi is *precognition*—the ability to foretell future events. Fortune-tellers and even stock market analysts often earn their living from their supposed ability to make such predictions. *Clairvoyance,* the ability to perceive objects or events that do not directly stimulate your sensory organs, is another form. While playing cards, if you somehow know which one will be dealt next, you are experiencing clairvoyance. *Telepathy,* a skill used by mind readers, involves the direct transmission of thought from one person to the next. Another phenomenon often associated with psi is *psychokinesis,* the ability to affect the physical world purely through thought. Bending spoons, and moving objects with your mind, and performing feats of levitation (making objects rise into the air) are examples of psychokinesis.

Psi: Does It Really Exist?

The idea of a mysterious sixth sense is intriguing, and many people are passionately convinced of its existence (Bowles & Hynds, 1978). But does it really exist? Most psychologists are skeptical about the existence of psi for several reasons. The first, and perhaps the most important, reason for doubting its existence is the repeated failure of researchers to replicate instances of psi; that is, certain procedures yield evidence for psi at one time but not at others. Indeed, one survey failed to uncover a single instance of a paranormal phenomenon that could be reliably produced after ruling out alternative explanations such as fraud, methodological flaws, and normal sensory functioning (Hoppe, 1988). Moreover, it appears that the more controlled studies of psi are, the less evidence for psi they provide (Blackmore, 1986).

Second, present-day scientific understanding states that all aspects of our behavior must ultimately stem from biochemical events, yet it is not clear what physical mechanism could account for psi. In fact, the existence of such a mechanism would require restructuring our view of the physical world. Nevertheless, major changes in our knowledge are still occurring, and it is still possible that a mechanism accounting for psi could be discovered.

Third, much of the support for psi has been obtained by people who are already deeply convinced of its existence. As we noted in Chapter 1, scientists are not immune to being influenced in their observations by their own beliefs. Thus, while studies suggesting that psi exists may represent a small sample of all research conducted on this topic, perhaps only the few experiments yielding positive results find their way into print; perhaps the many "failures" are simply not reported.

One set of recent studies has caused some investigators to look anew at psi. These studies employ a ganzfield procedure to test for telepathic communication between a *sender* and a *receiver.* Parapsychologists are using this procedure in an attempt to eliminate the flaws that cause scientists to criticize much of the earlier research on psi. Receivers in the ganzfield procedure are placed

Psi: Unusual processes of information or energy transfer that are currently unexplained in terms of known physical or biological mechanisms. Included under the heading of psi are such supposed abilities as telepathy (reading others' thoughts) and clairvoyance (perceiving unseen objects or unknowable events).

Parapsychologists: Individuals who study psi and other paranormal events.

- Most psychologists remain skeptical about the existence of psi (ESP).

in a comfortable chair in a soundproof room. Translucent Ping-Pong ball halves are taped over the receivers' eyes, and headphones are placed over their ears. A red floodlight directed toward the eyes produces a homogenous visual field, and white noise is played through the headphones to mask any outside noises.

The sender is usually secluded in a separate room and asked to concentrate on a "target" visual stimulus, such as a photograph or a brief videotape. Simultaneously, the receiver provides an ongoing verbal report of the mental images that he or she experiences. After about thirty minutes, the receiver is presented with several stimuli and, without knowing which was the "target" stimulus on which the sender concentrated, is asked to rate the extent to which each stimulus matches the imagery he or she experienced during the ganzfield period. If a high proportion of the receivers' ratings are assigned to "target" stimuli, it is assumed to be evidence for psi. A recent evaluation of studies that used the ganzfield procedure suggest that receivers are significantly more accurate in selecting target stimuli than would be explained by chance (Bem & Hornton, 1994). Critics of psi theories remain skeptical and await the results of additional research in this area (Hyman, 1994).

The Danger of Stereo Headsets: Let's Turn Down the Volume

If you've experienced the clamor of traffic during rush hour, the deafening roar of a jet taking off, or the piercing blast of a jackhammer digging up city streets, you're already familiar with the growing problem of *noise pollution*. Noise has become a pervasive part of everyday living, and increasing evidence suggests that noise pollution affects aspects of our physical and mental health, task performance, and social behavior (Matlin & Foley, 1992).

Although many sources of noise in our environment are beyond our control, people often bring hearing-related problems on themselves. Psychologists and other health professionals are becoming increasingly concerned with the rapid increase in use of portable stereo headset radios and CD players. Millions of these devices are sold each year in North America primarily to young people (Monroe, 1990). One problem with their use is that these headsets produce sound intense enough to cause varying degrees of hearing loss (Rice, Breslin, & Roper, 1987).

Three types of hearing loss are usually distinguished: *temporary threshold shift* (TTS), a short-term and reversible elevation of the level at which sounds are first heard; *permanent threshold shift* (PTS), nonreversible hearing loss from long-term exposure to noise; and *acoustic trauma*, permanent hearing loss stemming from brief exposures to extremely intense noise, such as an explosion (Jones & Broadbent, 1987). Even brief exposure to certain levels of sound intensity can cause a measurable shift in hearing ability. For example, exposure to 90-decibel sound levels—the level of noise that might be present in a crowded restaurant—can produce a TTS of nearly 20 decibels after only ninety minutes of sound exposure.

So why all the fuss over stereo headsets? Consider, for example, the results of a study by Navarro (1990) in which researchers examined fifty portable stereo headsets to determine if they had the potential to damage hearing. The decibel levels were measured at three volume settings: one-third, two-thirds, and full volume. The results showed that headsets produce an average of 87 decibels at one-third of their full volume, 100 decibels at two-thirds, and 108 decibels at full volume. Thus, it should be clear that portable stereo headsets have the potential to produce serious hearing loss even at seemingly low volume settings, particularly among those who listen to them often and for extended periods of time. Indeed, some evidence suggests that habitual use of portable headsets at high volumes does result in temporary threshold shifts and *tinnitus*, or ringing of the ears, and increases the risk of permanent hearing loss (Rice, Breslin, & Roper, 1987; Lee et al., 1985).

So next time you get the urge to crank up the volume of your portable headset while walking, jogging, or performing some other activity—do yourself a favor by turning down the sound. The hearing you save may be your own.

Stereo headsets, one source of noise that *can* be controlled, have the potential to cause permanent damage to the ears.

Summary and Review of Key Points

SENSATION: THE RAW MATERIALS OF UNDERSTANDING	• *Sensory receptors* transduce raw physical energy into neural impulses, which are then interpreted by our central nervous system.

sensation 94
perception 94
sensory receptors 95
transduction 95
absolute threshold 97
signal detection theory 97
difference threshold 98
just noticeable difference (jnd) 98
subliminal perception 98
sensory adaptation 99

• The *absolute threshold* is the smallest magnitude of a stimulus that can be detected 50 percent of the time.
• *Signal detection theory* helps to separate sensitivity from motivational factors.
• *Sensory adaptation* serves a useful function by allowing us to focus on important changes in our environment.

VISION

cornea 100
pupil 100
iris 100
lens 100
retina 100
cones 100
rods 100
fovea 100
optic nerve 101
blind spot 101
wavelength 102
hue 102
brightness 103
saturation 103
acuity 103
nearsightedness 103
farsightedness 103
dark adaptation 104
saccadic movements 104
trichromatic theory 104
negative afterimage 105
opponent process theory 105
feature detectors 107
simple cells 107
complex cells 107
hypercomplex cells 107

• The physical stimulus for vision consists of electromagnetic wavelengths that stimulate the rods and cones in the retina.
• Our rich sense of color stems from mechanisms at several levels of our nervous system. Two leading theories that explain how we perceive color are *trichromatic theory* and *opponent process theory*.
• The basic building blocks of visual perception begin with *feature detectors*—neurons in the visual cortex that respond when particular types of stimuli, with characteristic features, are registered.
• Visual perception is a hierarchical process. At successive stages, increasingly complex visual information is analyzed and compiled, eventually yielding a coherent and flowing visual world.
• Specialized systems in the brain are dedicated to the analysis of specific important aspects of our visual environment such as form, motion, and color.
• Information from the various specialized systems is assembled, at higher levels in the brain, to produce a coherent and structured perception of the world about us.

HEARING pinna 108 cochlea 108 pitch 108 timbre 109 place theory 109 frequency theory 110 localization 110	• The physical stimulus for hearing consists of sound waves that stimulate tiny hair cells in the cochlea. • *Place theory* and *frequency theory* help explain how we perceive pitch. • The sound shadow created by our head helps us localize the source of sound.
TOUCH AND OTHER SKIN SENSES braille alphabet 112 gate-control theory 113 endorphins 113	• The physical stimulus for sensations of touch is a stretching of or pressure against receptors in the skin. • Sensations of pain originate in free nerve endings throughout the body. • Observed cultural differences in pain perception result from the powerful forces of learning—not from physical differences.
SMELL AND TASTE: THE CHEMICAL SENSES	• The physical stimulus for sensations of smell consists of molecules of various substances contained in the air; these molecules stimulate receptor cells in the *olfactory epithelium*. • The sensory receptors for taste are located in papillae on the tongue. • The presence of a pleasant fragrance in the workplace can have beneficial effects on work-related behaviors.
KINESTHESIA AND VESTIBULAR SENSE kinesthesia 118 vestibular sense 119 vestibular sacs 119 semicircular canals 119	• *Kinesthesia* informs the brain about the location of body parts in relation to each other. The physical stimulus for kinesthesia is movement, which is registered in receptors in joints and ligaments. • The *vestibular sense* provides information about body position, movement, and acceleration. Receptors for the vestibular sense are hair cells inside the fluid-filled *semicircular canals*.
PERCEPTION: PUTTING IT ALL TOGETHER Gestalt psychologists 123 figure–ground relationship 123 laws of grouping 124 constancies 124 size constancy 124 relative size 126 shape constancy 126 brightness constancy 126 illusions 126 templates 129 prototypes 129 monocular cues 130 binocular cues 131	• *Selective attention* helps us maximize information gain by reducing interference from irrelevant sensory sources. • The effectiveness of warnings depends on both sensory and perceptual processes. • The Gestalt principles of *perceptual organization* help us to structure the input from our sensory receptors. • Because of *perceptual constancies*, our perceptions of the world do not change as much as variations in the sensory information registered by our receptors might lead us to expect. • The top-down theory of pattern recognition emphasizes the role that expectancies play in shaping our perceptions. • Bottom-up processing suggests that pattern recognition stems from the ability to recognize and combine basic visual features, such as lines, edges, corners, and angles. • Judgments of depth and distance result from binocular and monocular cues.

THE PLASTICITY OF PERCEPTION: TO WHAT EXTENT IS IT INNATE OR LEARNED?	• Both nature and nurture are important determinants of the ways we perceive the world around us.
EXTRASENSORY PERCEPTION: PERCEPTION WITHOUT SENSATION? extrasensory perception 134 psi 134 parapsychologists 135	• Most psychologists remain skeptical about the existence of psi, because careful research has failed to reproduce these phenomena reliably and because no currently known physical mechanism can account for them.

CRITICAL THINKING QUESTIONS

APPRAISAL	At present, many psychologists would agree that our conscious experience is nothing more than the result of the brain's efforts to integrate information received from our sensory systems. Do you agree? If so, why? If not, offer an alternative view.
CONTROVERSY	The possibility of extrasensory perception has long enjoyed widespread popularity with the public, although most psychologists remain skeptical. Recent studies employing the ganzfield procedure have eliminated many of the methodological flaws uncovered in earlier research and have demonstrated weak, but consistent, evidence for psi. Does psi exist? Or is it more likely that subsequent research will uncover methodological flaws with these procedures? Please explain your views on this issue.
MAKING PSYCHOLOGY PART OF YOUR LIFE	Knowing something about the way in which we receive and process sensory information is very useful for a variety of practical reasons. For example, knowing that our sensitivity to smell decreases rapidly through habituation is critical, especially if a person has just detected the odor of a poisonous gas! Can you think of other ways in which you can benefit from such knowledge? (Hint: How would you explain to your friend that listening to stereo headsets at high volumes—even for brief periods—is a bad idea?)

Consciousness

Awareness of Ourselves and the External World

BIOLOGICAL RHYTHMS: TIDES OF LIFE—AND CONSCIOUS EXPERIENCE 144
Circadian Rhythms: Their Basic Nature
Circadian Rhythms: What Mechanism Underlies Them?
Individual Differences in Circadian Rhythms: Of Larks and Owls
Disturbances in Circadian Rhythms: Jet Lag and Shift Work

WAKING STATES OF CONSCIOUSNESS: EVERYDAY EXPERIENCE 150
Controlled and Automatic Processing: The Limits of Attention
Daydreams and Fantasies: Self-Induced Shifts in Consciousness
Self-Consciousness: Some Effects of Looking Inward

SLEEP: THE PAUSE THAT REFRESHES? 156
Sleep: How It Is Studied
Sleep: Its Basic Nature
Sleep: What Functions Does It Serve?
Sleep Disorders: No Rest for the Weary
Dreams: Stimulation in the Midst of Sleep

HYPNOSIS: ALTERED STATE OF CONSCIOUSNESS OR SOCIAL ROLE PLAYING? 166
Hypnosis: What It Is and Who Is Susceptible to It
Hypnosis: Contrasting Views About Its Nature

CONSCIOUSNESS-ALTERING DRUGS: WHAT THEY ARE AND WHAT THEY DO 171
Consciousness-Altering Drugs: Some Basic Concepts
Psychological Mechanisms Underlying Drug Abuse: Contrasting Views
Consciousness-Altering Drugs: An Overview
The Psychology of Drug Effects

SUMMARY AND REVIEW OF KEY POINTS 182

CANADIAN FOCUS: SEASONAL SADNESS 147

THE POINT OF IT ALL—COUNTERING THE NEGATIVE EFFECTS OF SHIFT WORK 149

PERSPECTIVES ON DIVERSITY—CULTURE AND THE INTERPRETATION OF DREAMS 164

THE RESEARCH PROCESS—DOES HYPNOSIS PRODUCE CHANGES IN MEMORY AND PERCEPTION? 169

KEY CONCEPT—EFFECTS OF CONSCIOUSNESS-ALTERING DRUGS 178

MAKING PSYCHOLOGY PART OF YOUR LIFE—MEDITATION: A TECHNIQUE FOR INDUCING POTENTIALLY BENEFICIAL SHIFTS IN CONSCIOUSNESS 179

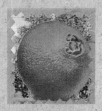

OUR WEATHER ISN'T DEPRESSING, UNLESS YOU THINK IT IS

The Express (St. John's): July 21, 1993

Why do more people feel sad in winter than at any other time of the year? Are there fluctuations in mood that are tied to the seasons? The Express reported that researchers have found the answer to be yes—in some people.

 Biochemical reactions to the reduction in light during the winter season produce mood disorders, the collective name for which is seasonal affective disorder, or SAD. The symptoms inlude "lower productivity, less interest and energy, lower motivation and not much vitality."

 In Chapter 4 you will learn how the nature of the world around us—including the amount of light during a particular season—interacts with our biological rhythms to affect much of our behavior. You will also learn about different states of conscious-ness—for example, day-dreaming and sleep—and about altered states of con-sciousness that result from psychoactive drugs, hypnosis, and meditation.

WE ALL EXPERIENCE
DIFFERENT STATES OF
CONSCIOUSNESS—
LEVELS OF AWARENESS
OF INTERNAL AND
EXTERNAL
STIMULI—EVERY DAY.

Do you feel more alert and energetic at some times of the day? Have you ever daydreamed in class so that later you had no idea what the teacher or professor said? Have you ever stood in front of a mirror brushing your teeth while your thoughts were an ocean away? If you have, you already know that we all experience different **states of consciousness**—levels of awareness of internal and external stimuli—every day. And when we go to sleep at night, or take some drug that affects the way we feel, these changes in consciousness are even more dramatic. Being familiar with these shifts, however, doesn't necessarily help us understand them. *Why* are we more alert at some times during the day than at others? What happens when we fall asleep? What, precisely, *are* dreams? And how do various drugs affect our emotions, perceptions, and cognition?

Given its obvious impact on many aspects of our behavior, consciousness is clearly an important topic in psychology. You may be surprised to learn, therefore, that from about the 1920s until as recently as the 1960s, consciousness was largely ignored by psychologists. In fact, some viewed it as a slightly shady topic—one to be avoided by serious scientists. Many factors contributed to this unsettling state of affairs, but perhaps the most important was the dominance of behaviorism. As you may recall from Chapter 1, Watson and other early behaviorists believed that psychology should focus only on overt, observable actions. Since consciousness could not be directly seen or measured, they literally ruled it out as a legitimate topic of research.

On the contrary, some early psychologists—the structuralists—viewed consciousness as the core topic on which psychology should focus. In recent decades consciousness has reemerged as an important field of study.

Although consciousness has returned as a topic of systematic research in psychology relatively recently, we have already acquired a great deal of interesting—and often provocative—knowledge about it. Much of this knowledge will be summarized in this chapter. We'll begin by considering the biological roots of consciousness: *biological rhythms*. These are naturally occurring, cyclical changes in many basic bodily processes and mental states that occur regularly (de-Koninck, 1991). Next, we'll consider several aspects of normal, *waking consciousness*. Here, we'll examine three major topics: (1) *controlled* and *automatic processing*, which are shifts between conscious attention to our current behavior and the kind of "automatic pilot" that seems to operate when we perform well-practiced actions such as grooming or driving; (2) the nature and impact of *daydreams* and *fantasies*; and (3) changing levels of *self-consciousness*, and how we focus on ourselves rather than the external world. After this, we'll turn to what is perhaps the most profound, regular shift in consciousness we experience: *sleep*. Finally, we'll examine two external factors that sometimes produce altered states of consciousness: *hypnosis*, and various *consciousness-altering drugs*.

Biological Rhythms: *Tides of Life— and Conscious Experience*

Suppose that you must schedule an appointment for a very important interview. The interviewer has a number of time slots available, so you can choose to meet with her at almost any time of day. What time will you select? Probably you have little difficulty in making a choice. Most of us are well aware of the fact that we are at our best—most alert and energetic—at certain times of the day. Thus, all other things being equal, you'll probably schedule the meeting for a time when you think you're most likely to make a good impression (Monk & Folkard, 1983).

States of Consciousness:
Varying degrees of awareness of ourselves and the external world.

CHANGING STATES OF CONSCIOUSNESS

As shown here, our states of consciousness change during the course of a single day.
(Source: *The New Yorker*)

Regular shifts in our alertness or energy are examples of **biological rhythms**—regular fluctuations in our bodily processes over time. Many of these fluctuations occur over the course of a single day and are known as **circadian rhythms** (from the Latin words for "around" and "day"). As we'll soon see, such rhythms can affect us profoundly in many respects. Other biological rhythms take place within shorter periods of time (e.g., Klein & Armitage, 1979); they are known as *ultradian rhythms.* For example, many people become hungry every two or three hours (at least while they are awake). And during sleep, periods of dreaming seem to occur at roughly ninety-minute intervals. Finally, some biological rhythms occur over longer periods, such the menstrual cycle experienced by women, which spans approximately twenty-eight days. Such rhythms often have a relationship to states of consciousness. Since circadian rhythms have received the most research attention, we'll focus primarily on these, describing their basic nature, individual differences among them, and some of their practical implications.

Circadian Rhythms: *Their Basic Nature*

Most people are aware of fluctuations in their alertness, energy, and mood over the course of a day. Do such shifts reflect actual changes in underlying bodily states? There is much evidence that they do (e.g., Moore-Ede, Sulzman, & Fuller, 1982). Careful study has revealed that many bodily processes do indeed show daily cyclical changes. To mention just a few, it has been found that the production of various hormones fluctuates across the day; their levels are high at some times but much lower at others. Similarly, for many people, core body temperature, blood pressure, and several other processes are highest in the late afternoon or evening and lowest in the early hours of the morning—although, as we'll see below, there are large individual differences in these measures.

These cyclical fluctuations in basic bodily functions affect our performance on many tasks. Tasks requiring physical activity are performed best at times when body temperature and other processes are at or near their peak. The same is true for simple cognitive (mental) tasks. However, as the complexity of cognitive tasks increases, the closeness of the link between them and circadian rhythms seems to weaken.

For example, Daniel and Potasova (1989) asked workers at a chemical factory (in what was then Czechoslovakia) to perform several different tasks. One was a tapping task that required rapid hand movements. Another was a relatively simple cognitive task in which participants searched for a target letter among a series of letters and, when they found it, pushed a button as quickly as possible. A third task required complex mental effort; it involved making grammatical transformations on a series of sentences. Each participant's body

Biological Rhythms: Cyclic changes in bodily processes.

Circadian Rhythms: Cyclic changes in bodily processes occurring within a single day.

CONSCIOUSNESS: AWARENESS OF OURSELVES AND THE EXTERNAL WORLD

temperature was recorded at several times during the day. As shown in Figure 4.1, there was a clear relationship between body temperature and performance on the tapping task. This relationship also held for the simple visual search task. The relationship disappeared, however, for the complex sentence transformation. This pattern of findings suggests that daily fluctuations in body temperature may have a stronger impact on relatively simple tasks than on more complex cognitive ones.

Circadian Rhythms: What Mechanism Underlies Them?

If bodily processes, mental alertness, and performance fluctuate regularly over the course of the day, it seems reasonable to suggest that there is an internal biological mechanism for regulating such changes. In other words, we must possess a biological clock that times various circadian rhythms. While there is not as yet total agreement on the nature of this clock, many scientists believe that it is located in a portion of the hypothalamus—specifically, in the **suprachiasmatic nucleus** (Rusak, 1990). This nucleus responds to visual input from the eyes and either stimulates or inhibits activity in the pineal gland. This gland, in turn, secretes *melatonin*, a hormone that exerts a far-reaching sedative effect, reducing activity and increasing fatigue.

Exposure to daylight stimulates the suprachiasmatic nucleus, and this in turn reduces the secretion of melatonin. In contrast, darkness enhances it. Interestingly, only fairly intense light (three to five times that of ordinary room lighting) is sufficient to stimulate the suprachiasmatic nucleus. Thus, if you spent all of your time in a dimly lit environment, your biological clock would respond as if you were living in perpetual night. Melatonin secretion would be increased, and you would probably feel quite tired most of the time. Evidence that the suprachiasmatic nucleus acts as a biological clock is provided by research indicating that when it is damaged, or when neural pathways connecting it to the eyes are destroyed, circadian rhythms disappear. Some continue to work, however, so that (according to researchers at Simon Fraser and the University of Toronto) there may be not just one but several biological clocks for different purposes, in different locations in the brain (Mistlberger, 1992; Mrosovsky, 1986).

Suprachiasmatic Nucleus: A portion of the hypothalamus that seems to play an important role in the regulation of circadian rhythms.

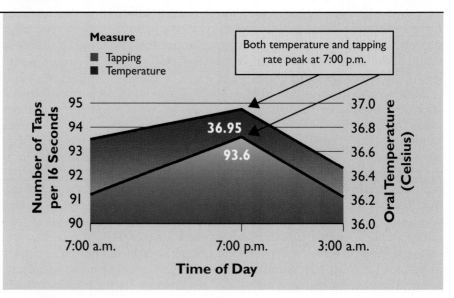

FIGURE 4.1

Circadian Rhythms, Body Temperature, and Task Performance

On both a tapping task and a relatively simple cognitive task, performance rose and fell with daily changes in body temperature. However, there was no relationship between body temperature and performance on a more complex cognitive task. (Source: Based on data from Daniel & Potasova, 1989.)

Another intriguing fact is that when left to its own devices, our internal biological clock seems to operate on a twenty-five-hour rather than a twenty-four-hour day. This is indicated by research in which volunteers have lived in caves or other environments totally removed from clocks, the rising and setting of the sun, and other cues we normally use to keep track of time. Under these conditions, most people shifted to a "day" of about twenty-five hours (Moore-Ede, Sulzman, & Fuller, 1982). In other words, each day they rose and went to sleep a little later, and all their activities shift accordingly. Their basic bodily functions, too, shifted from a twenty-four-hour cycle to this slightly longer one.

Seasonal Affective Disorder (SAD): Depression experienced during the winter months, supposedly stemming from a lack of exposure to sunlight.

CANADIAN FOCUS

Seasonal Sadness

Many Canadians feel down in winter, when the amount of sunlight is drastically reduced. If the symptoms include recurring episodes of deep depression during winter, and anxiety, withdrawal, decreased energy levels and sex drive, increased appetite, craving for carbohydrates, and weight gain, the depression may be winter **seasonal affective disorder, or SAD** (Levitt et al., 1993; Lam et al., 1992). Studies of animal behavior indicate that winter depression may involve a disturbance in some circadian rhythms (Surridge et al., 1987), including those for body temperature, sleep–wakefulness, REM sleep, melatonin secretion, and levels of some neurotransmitters. Another finding is that people with SAD may have abnormal retinal sensitivity (too low or too high) to light. Animals that hibernate in the winter—chipmunks, for example—may help us understand this type of depressive reaction (Mrosovsky, 1988).

Since melatonin disturbance and lack of sunlight are both thought to be involved, the therapy for winter SAD may include melatonin pills (an experimental approach) or light therapy, or both. According to research at the Clarke Institute in Toronto, an antidepressant response occurs in at least half of winter SAD patients who are treated with light therapy (Joffe et al., 1993) and as high an improvement rate as 85 percent of patients has been reported. The light therapy may be provided by a bank of lights or by a helmet with a light visor that the SAD patient wears. There may be some temporary side effects of light therapy, such as "feeling wired," early in treatment (Levitt et al., 1993), and there is some concern for retinal damage if too-bright light is used. Antidepressant drugs are known to change the response of the retinas to light, and that may be one of the ways they are effective in relieving depression.

Yukoners have created their own version of preventive light therapy. There, in winter, people use timers to turn on lights in the morning to mimic the dawn each day. Along the same lines, a new dawn simulator is being tested. This simulator emits low-intensity light in the early morning, while the patient is asleep and tries to convince the brain to "pretend that it is spring."

The farther north one goes from the equator, the less sunlight there is in winter. In Inuvik, in the Northwest Territories, for example, in December the sun does not shine at all. It makes some sense to predict, then, that SAD will become more and more common the closer to the North Pole you get. The frequency of winter SAD at different latitudes has been studied (e.g., Rosen et al., 1990); these frequencies may vary from 1.4 percent of the population in southern Florida, to 8 percent in New Hampshire, to 12 percent in Edmonton, to an estimated 18 percent in Inuvik, the largest community in the Western Arctic.

Some patients suffer from a different seasonal disorder: summer SAD. The symptoms of summer and winter depression are quite opposite (Wehr et al., 1991). Where summer depressives most often report decreased appetite and insomnia, winter depressives most often report increased appetite and hypersomnia (excessive sleepiness). In June, in Inuvik, the sun does not set. Patients complain then that they have too much energy (hypomania) and that they feel unable to slow themselves down. The more we understand biological rhythms, the better we will be able to solve the puzzle of these changes in mood over the course of the seasons.

Individual Differences in Circadian Rhythms: *Of Larks and Owls*

Before reading further, please answer the questions in Table 4.1.

How did you score? If you answered "Day" to eight or more questions, the chances are good that you are a morning person (a lark). If, instead, you answered "Night" to eight or more questions, you are probably a night person (an owl). Morning people feel most alert and active early in the day, while night people experience peaks in alertness and energy in the afternoon or evening. Such differences are more than purely subjective. Studies comparing larks and owls indicate that the two groups differ in several important ways. For example, morning people have a higher overall level of adrenaline than night people; thus, they seem to operate at a higher overall level of activation (e.g., Akerstedt & Froberg, 1976). Similarly, as you might expect, morning people experience peaks in body temperature earlier in the day than night people (Wallace, 1993). Morning people have temperature peaks before noon; night people often experience those peaks in the evening, around six p.m. or even later.

In addition, larks and owls also differ with respect to relatively subtle fluctuations in cognitive states. Not surprisingly, morning people report feeling more alert and do better on many cognitive tasks early in the day. In contrast, night people report feeling more alert and do better on such tasks later in the day. More surprising is the fact that these two groups also differ with respect to the times at which they are most susceptible to *hypnotism*—a topic we'll consider later in this chapter. Morning people seem to be most susceptible to hypnosis in the morning and early afternoon, while night people are most susceptible to hypnosis in the afternoon and evening (Wallace, 1993).

How did larks and owls become different in these ways? The answer to that question is not known, but at Simon Fraser University, Ralph Mistlberger (1991) did make some hamsters into "night owls" and others into "early birds" by varying the times the animals did exercise (i.e., in the late dark or in midlight) or the times they were fed, or both.

Disturbances in Circadian Rhythms: *Jet Lag and Shift Work*

Under normal conditions, the existence of circadian rhythms poses no special problems. Most people are aware of their personal highs and lows and try to schedule their activities accordingly. Unfortunately, though, there are circumstances in which circadian rhythms may get badly out of phase with our daily activities.

TABLE 4.1

Are You a Lark or an Owl?

If you answer "Day" to eight or more of these questions, you are probably a morning person. If you answer "Night" to eight or more, you are probably a night person. (Source: Based on items from Wallace, 1993.)

Please respond to each of the following items by circling either "Day" or "Night".

	Day	Night
1. I feel most alert during the	Day	Night
2. I have most energy during the	Day	Night
3. I prefer to take classes during the	Day	Night
4. I prefer to study during the	Day	Night
5. I get my best ideas during the	Day	Night
6. I prefer to study during the	Day	Night
7. I am most productive during the	Day	Night
8. I feel most intelligent during the	Day	Night
9. I enjoy leisure-time activities most during the	Day	Night
10. I prefer to work during the	Day	Night

The first of these situations occurs as a result of modern travel—especially by jet plane. When individuals cross several time zones, they often experience considerable difficulty in adjusting to their new location. The reason for this is clear: Their internal biological clocks are calling for one level or type of activity, while the external world is calling for another one. For example, suppose you were flying nonstop from St. John's to Vancouver. If you left the east at one p.m. local time, you would arrive in the west about nine hours later. Back in Newfoundland it would be dark, and for your internal biological clock, it would be eleven p.m., just about time to hit the sack, perhaps. In B.C., however, it would be 6:30 p.m., still light and a little early to go to sleep, no matter what your brain was telling your body. This conflict between your internal clock and your external environment may produce jet lag.

Current wisdom has it that an efficient way to reduce the discomfort of jet lag—and to readjust your internal clock—is to immediately adopt the time on the external clock (the one in B.C., in the example above) and behave accordingly. For a few days, that may mean eating at times when you do not feel hungry and going to bed when you do not feel sleepy, until your internal clock adjusts to the external world. For frequent fliers, there is a new technology. Alternately wearing a light visor and dark goggles, at specific times, can shift the setting of your biological clock (Gallo & Eastman, 1993).

A second cause of difficulties with respect to circadian rhythms is *shift work*. Here, individuals must work at times when they would normally be sleeping (say midnight to eight a.m.). To make matters worse, shift workers often face a schedule in which they work on one shift for a fairly short period (say a week), get two days off, and then work on another shift. The results are, for many people, quite unsettling. Even if you've never had a job involving shift work, you have probably experienced such effects after winter or spring break. During these vacation periods, you may have stayed up late and slept in every day. When you returned to school, you probably found readjusting to early morning classes a drag, to say the least. Shift workers, who must constantly reset their biological clocks, suffer even stronger effects, such as high levels of fatigue and serious sleep disorders. In addition, they may suffer other adverse effects, such as increased rates of heart disease and ulcers; increased rates of automobile and industrial accidents; and increased use of alcohol, sleeping pills, and other drugs, relative to non-shift workers (Lidell, 1982; Angerspach et al., 1980). The economic loss resulting from these effects is staggering. Can anything be done to reduce such costs? For encouraging information on this issue, see **The Point of It All**.

THE POINT OF IT ALL

Countering the Negative Effects of Shift Work

Shift work is a growing trend in many industries. The costs of modern industrial equipment make it almost a necessity to operate many factories on a round-the-clock basis. Individuals who face shift-work schedules, however, often report high levels of dissatisfaction. And it is little wonder that they do, given the havoc such schedules play with their biologically driven circadian rhythms. This leads to a practical question: If shift work is a reality of modern

CIRCADIAN RHYTHMS AND SHIFT WORK

Many factories operate twenty-four hours a day. People who work night shifts must adjust their circadian rhythms to fit these schedules.

life, can anything be done to lessen its potentially harmful effects? In fact, basic knowledge about the nature of circadian rhythms points to some simple steps that might be of considerable help in this respect.

First, research on circadian rhythms suggests that it is easier for individuals to get their biological clocks back into phase with the external world when they have to *delay* them rather than advance them. In other words, it is easier to stay up a few hours later and to reset one's biological clock than to go to sleep earlier and try to move it ahead. Second, it is easier for individuals to reset their biological clocks if they work on a particular shift for a longer period of time (Cunningham, 1989), and then have several days in between shifts. This is because human beings seem able to reset their internal clocks by about one hour each day.

Does taking account of these findings in planning shift work actually help employees adjust to changing shifts? A study by Czeisler, Moore-Ede, and Coleman (1982) indicates that it does. These researchers exposed a group of male shift workers either to a standard rotating-shift pattern of seven days on one shift followed by rotation to the earlier (rather than later) shift; or to a revised pattern in which they stayed on a particular shift for several weeks and then were rotated to a later one. Results indicated that the workers were much more satisfied with the revised schedule than with the standard one. Further, their productivity increased, their health improved, and their rate of turnover (voluntary quitting) dropped appreciably. In other words, the findings indicated that a work schedule that took account of the basic properties of the circadian system was much more effective than one that ignored them.

More recent efforts to help people cope with the stress of shift work have adopted a somewhat different approach that is based on the role of the suprachiasmatic nucleus in regulating circadian rhythms. In order to help night workers at nuclear power plants to stay awake in the early morning hours, one company—Light Sciences, Inc.—has developed a lighting system that simulates the normal cycle of strengthening and weakening sunlight during the day (Noble, 1993). In this system, which is currently being tested in several generating plants in the United States, the lighting gradually brightens and then dims during the eleven p.m. to seven a.m. shift. It is hoped that these changes will "trick" the visual system into reversing the times of peak alertness and drowsiness that are part of the normal circadian cycle. To help strengthen such effects, the workers wear dark glasses when they have to leave the light-controlled areas of the plant for ones that are more brightly lit during the "dim" part of their shift. And they wear sunglasses when going home in the morning to avoid exposure to direct sunlight. While final results are not yet available, early findings are encouraging with respect to increased alertness—and decreased errors.

The moral of this project is clear: Human beings are adaptive and can, to an extent, cope with almost any kind of work schedule. However, schedules designed to coordinate with rather than challenge employees' basic biological rhythms are almost certain to prove more cost effective, as well as more compassionate, in the long run.

Waking States of Consciousness:
Everyday Experience

*A*s a new professor, one of the first things you learn about teaching university students is this: No matter what you are saying and no matter how interesting it is, only some of the class is listening at any given time. Why? One answer relates back to the topic of this chapter: While many members of the class are paying attention to your words, others are off somewhere in their own thoughts, daydreaming, planning dinner, and so on. After a while, they may tune in again to what you're saying, but then they may shift back into some other state of consciousness. Such fluctuations are a normal part of life, for during our waking hours, we shift frequently between contrasting states of consciousness. In this section we'll focus on several of these recurring or routine states of consciousness.

Controlled and Automatic Processing: The Limits of Attention

Have you ever tried to carry on conversations with two different people at once? If so, you already know a basic fact about human consciousness: Our attentional or *information-processing* capacities are quite limited. We simply don't have the ability to focus on several different stimuli or events at once. Rather, we find it necessary to shift back and forth between events that we wish to make the center of our current attention. If this is so, how do we manage to perform two or more activities at once—for example, brushing your teeth while thinking about the day's coming events? The answer seems to be that there are two contrasting ways of controlling ongoing activities—different levels of attention to, or conscious control over, our own behavior (Logan, 1985, 1988).

The first level is the kind of "automatic pilot" mentioned at the start of this chapter. Psychologists describe this as **automatic processing** because it is the performance of activities with relatively little conscious awareness. Such processing seems to make little demand on our attentional capacity. Thus, several activities, each under automatic control, can occur at the same time (Shiffrin & Schneider, 1977; Shiffrin & Dumais, 1981). You are demonstrating automatic processing when you drive your car and listen to the radio at the same time. Automatic processing, with respect to a given activity, tends to develop with practice, as the components of the activity become well learned and become associated with specific stimuli.

In contrast, **controlled processing** requires more effortful and more conscious control of behavior. While it is occurring, you direct careful attention to the task at hand and concentrate on it. Obviously, processing of this type does use significant attentional capacity. As a result, tasks requiring controlled processing can usually only be performed one at a time. Automatic processing has been studied in memory and reading (Jennings & Jacoby, 1993; Jacoby, Levy, & Steinbach, 1992) and in listening to music (Unyk, 1990), and in special populations (e.g., autistic children and those with attention deficit hyperactivity disorder).

Research on the nature of automatic and controlled processing suggests that they differ in several important respects. First, as you might guess, behaviors that have come under the control of automatic processing are performed more quickly and with less effort than those which require controlled processing (Logan, 1988, 1992; Newell & Rosenbloom, 1981). In addition, automatized acts, but not controlled ones, can be initiated without conscious intention; they are triggered in a seemingly automatic manner, by specific stimuli or events (Norman & Shallice, 1985). In fact, it may be difficult to inhibit automatized actions once they are initiated. Finally, within limits, neither the accuracy nor the speed of automatic processing is strongly affected by *attentional load*—the number of different items, objects, or operations with which we must deal.

This fact was first demonstrated by Schneider and Shiffrin (1977) in a famous series of experiments. In one of these studies, participants were asked to search for numbers contained in a list of letters. On some trials they searched

Automatic Processing:
Processing of information with minimal conscious awareness.

Controlled Processing:
Processing of information with relatively high levels of conscious awareness.

for a single target (for instance, the number 7). On others, they searched for as many as four different targets at once (such as the numbers 1, 4, 7, and 8). After many practice trials, participants were able to search for the four targets almost as quickly as they could search for one. This was interpreted as evidence that the participants had shifted to automatic processing in performing this task.

Taking these differences into account, it is clear that neither controlled nor automatic processing necessarily has an edge; both offer a mixed pattern of advantages and disadvantages. As we have seen, automatic processing is rapid and efficient but relatively inflexible. Controlled processing is slower but is more flexible and open to change. Clearly, both have their place in our efforts to deal with information from the external world.

One final point: Automatic and controlled processing are not hard-and-fast categories. Rather, they represent the ends of a continuum. On any given task, individuals may be operating in a relatively controlled or a relatively automatic manner.

It seems that we have a strong tendency to adopt automatic processing whenever feasible. Given our limited capacity for attending to many simultaneous stimuli or for processing information generally (see Chapters 6 and 7), this tendency offers major benefits. At the same time, though, our readiness to use our automatic pilot can exact important costs. Whatever the balance between the relative pluses and minuses, the important point to remember is this: Even during waking activities, we can and often do shift back and forth between levels of awareness or states of consciousness.

Daydreams and Fantasies: *Self-Induced Shifts in Consciousness*

Sigmund Freud once said: "A happy person never fantasizes; only an unsatisfied one" (1908, p. 136). If that comment is true, most of us must be very unhappy, for most of us regularly have **daydreams** or **fantasies**—imaginary events that we experience while we are awake (Singer, 1975). Further, it is clear that for many people such experiences can be quite intense, blotting out the external world at least temporarily. But what do people daydream about? And do these self-generated shifts of consciousness serve any function? It is on these questions that we will now focus.

THE CONTENT OF DAYDREAMS AND FANTASIES: MAJOR THEMES What was the content of your last daydream? If you are like most people, it can probably be placed under one of the following headings: success or failure (you imagined receiving straight A's or failing an important test); aggression or hostility (you fantasized about evening the score with someone who had angered or annoyed you); sexual or romantic fantasies; guilt (you tortured yourself once again over something you should or shouldn't have done); or problem solving (you imagined yourself working on some task or solving some problem). Of course, many other themes exist; these are merely the most common ones for many people.

While most people report daydreaming at least occasionally, there are large individual differences. First, people differ greatly in the frequency with which they daydream or fantasize (Lynn & Rhue, 1986). While some report spending up to half their free time in this activity, others indicate that they rarely have fantasies or daydreams (Silva & Kirsch, 1992). Second, the intensity of such experiences also varies greatly. Some people report that their fantasies and daydreams are so vivid and lifelike that they are almost real and may even become confused with reality itself. If they are, and if such experiences are not readily controlled by those who have them, they may be said to border on being **hallucinations**—vivid perceptual experiences that occur in

Daydreams (or Fantasies): Imaginary scenes and events that occur while a person is awake.

Hallucinations: Sensory experiences that occur in the absence of external stimuli yet have the full force of impact of real events or stimuli.

the absence of an external stimulus. Such experiences are usually associated with severe psychological disorders, but they also sometimes occur among people who are not mentally ill (Bentall, 1990). For most people, however, fantasies and daydreams are much less intense and far less involving. Interestingly, as we'll note in a later section, people who have intense and frequent fantasies turn out to be more susceptible to hypnotism than those who do not (Lynn, Rhue, & Weekes, 1990).

Daydreams and fantasies: What function do they serve? If people spend a considerable amount of time engaging in daydreams and fantasies—changing their own consciousness, if you will—then these activities must serve some useful function. But what, precisely, do these activities accomplish? No clear-cut answer to this question has as yet emerged, but existing evidence points to several interesting possibilities.

First, daydreams and fantasies may serve as a kind of safety valve, permitting people to escape, however briefly, from the stresses and boredom of everyday life. Perhaps this is one reason why many students tend to daydream in class or while reading their textbooks.

Second, daydreams and fantasies often provide us with a ready means of altering our own moods, primarily in a positive direction. If you've ever felt happier after a daydream filled with desirable activities and events, you are already familiar with these benefits (Forgas & Bower, 1988).

Third, it is possible that daydreams and fantasies help people find solutions to actual problems in their lives. By imagining various behaviors and the outcomes they may produce, we can examine potential courses of action carefully and from the safe perspective of our own mind. This can help us formulate useful plans of action.

Finally, fantasies may play an important role in the self-regulation of behavior. By imagining negative outcomes, people may strengthen their inhibitions against dangerous or prohibited behaviors (Bandura, 1986). Similarly, by dreaming about potential rewards, people may enhance their own motivation and performance. In sum, fantasies and daydreams may be much more than a pleasant diversion; they may actually yield substantial benefits to those who choose to induce them.

HEIGHTENED SELF-CONSCIOUSNESS

What do you do when you pass a mirror? If you are like most people, you glance at your reflection, thus experiencing increased awareness of yourself and your appearance.

Self-Consciousness: *Some Effects of Looking Inward*

What do you do when you pass a mirror? If you are like most people, you stop, however briefly, and examine your appearance. When you do, you are also, in a sense, changing your current state of consciousness. Before you passed the mirror, you were probably thinking about something other than yourself. Now, at least while you stand in front of the glass, your thoughts are focused on you. Psychologists term this focus **self-consciousness,** and they have uncovered much about its causes and effects. First, we'll consider one influential theory concerning self-consciousness; then, we'll turn to some of the surprising effects about this state.

The control theory of self-consciousness: Self-regulation of behavior Think for a moment about how the thermostat in your house or apartment works. In essence, the thermostat continuously compares the level of temperature you have set to the actual temperature in the room. When the temperature is too cold or too hot, the thermostat closes a circuit that turns on your furnace or your air conditioner. In the **control theory of self-consciousness,** Carver and Scheier (1981, 1990) suggest that self-consciousness operates in a

Self-Consciousness: Increased awareness of oneself as a social object or of one's own values and attitudes.

Control Theory of Self-Consciousness: A theory suggesting that people compare their current behavior and states with important goals and values. They then alter their behavior to close any gaps they observe.

similar manner. Once we focus our attention on ourselves, we compare our current state with important goals and values. If the gap between reality and these goals and values is too large, we make adjustments in our behavior to move closer to these desired states. In this sense, self-consciousness is an important component in the self-regulation of our own behavior.

Scheier and Carver (1986, 1987), and many other psychologists (e.g., Britt, 1992), also draw a distinction between two forms of self-consciousness: *private self-consciousness* and *public self-consciousness*. Private self-consciousness is our tendency to reflect on private aspects of the self—our own feelings, attitudes, and values. In contrast, public self-consciousness has to do with our tendency to think about aspects of the self that are presented to others—about how we appear in others' eyes. When you look into a mirror or at a photograph of yourself, you almost certainly experience public self-consciousness; after all, you are seeing yourself (physically) the way others do. But if seeing your own reflection causes you to think about how you are feeling or about what kind of person you really are, you may experience heightened private self-consciousness as well. In fact, in much of the research being done on self-awareness, the experimenters induce this state by having people work on various tasks in front of a mirror or with a camera aimed in their direction. Many different studies offer support for the basic assumptions of the control theory proposed by Carver and Scheier. This theory is a useful framework for thinking about the nature of self-consciousness and its impact upon behavior.

FACTORS THAT PRODUCE HEIGHTENED SELF-CONSCIOUSNESS That mirrors and cameras induce heightened self-consciousness is obvious. There are many other things, however, that may cause us to enter this state. One of these is a personal disposition to become self-conscious. In other words, some people spend more time than others thinking about themselves—about their feelings and reactions, the kind of impression they are making on strangers. Where do you fall on this dimension?

To find out, answer the questions in Table 4.2. These are items from a psychological test designed to measure both private and public self-consciousness

---

TABLE 4.2	
Private Self-Consciousness	Please indicate how characteristic or uncharacteristic of you each of these items is by placing a number in the blank space next to each.

Are you high in private self-consciousness? To find out, add the numbers you entered for items 1, 3, 4, 5, 6, and 8; then subtract the numbers you entered for items 2 and 7. The higher your score, the more you tend to be aware of your own inner feelings and reactions.
(Source: Based on items from Britt, 1992.)

0 = extremely uncharacteristic

1 = uncharacteristic

2 = neither characteristic nor uncharacteristic

3 = characteristic

4 = extremely characteristic

_____ 1 I'm always trying to figure myself out.

_____ 2. Usually, I'm not very aware of myself.

_____ 3. I think about myself a lot.

_____ 4. I'm often the subject of my own fantasies or daydreams.

_____ 5. I usually pay close attention to my inner feelings.

_____ 6. I'm aware of the way my mind works when I try to solve a problem or reason something out.

_____ 7. I never reflect on myself.

_____ 8. I frequently examine my own motives.

(Scheier & Carver, 1986). Their revised self-consciousness scale has been translated and adapted by Pelletier and Vallerand (1991) at the University of Ottawa, for use with French-Canadian high school students, university students, and working adults. As you can probably guess, the items in the table measure private self-consciousness; people who score high on these items have a greater-than-average tendency to think about themselves and their inner feelings or reactions (Britt, 1992). Other items on the self-consciousness scale measure public self-consciousness.

Another factor that influences self-consciousness is the familiarity of a given situation. In general, the more familiar and comfortable with a situation people are, the greater their tendency to think about themselves, and so the greater their self-consciousness.

A third factor is our mood at the time. Research indicates that people who are feeling either happy or sad are more likely to focus their attention inward than those in a neutral mood, presumably because they wish to understand their feelings and the factors responsible for them (Conway et al., 1993; Salovey, 1992).

THE EFFECTS OF SELF-CONSCIOUSNESS: REDUCED PERFORMANCE BUT INCREASED SELF-INSIGHT

That we often experience self-consciousness is obvious: This state is a regular part of daily life. But what are the effects of this inward focus? On the negative side of the ledger is a phenomenon known as **choking under pressure** (Baumeister & Scher, 1988). This term refers to the fact that sometimes people, when confronted with strong pressures to perform, do worse than they could have. For example, athletes who do very well in practice, when pressure is low, may choke up during important games or contests. Growing evidence indicates that heightened self-consciousness may contribute to such effects. The reasoning goes something like this. Many highly skilled activities are performed under automatic control. For example, consider keyboarding. Once you have mastered this skill, you don't think about the keys. If you do, such cognition may actually interfere with your performance and cause you to make errors. Similar effects occur with respect to many other skilled actions, from skiing or diving to pitching a baseball or swinging a golf club. When people performing such actions think too much about what they are doing, their performance may suffer. For example, heightened self-consciousness produced by a huge audience of cheering fans leads to precisely this kind of problem. The result: Performance suffers. Several studies offer support for this reasoning (e.g., Baumeister & Steinhilber, 1984). It has been found that more private self-consciousness goes along with lower self-esteem (Conway & Giannopoulos, 1993). Moreover, damage to the prefrontal lobe can cause a personality change in which the patient's self-awareness is no longer normal (Stuss, Gow, & Hetherington, 1992).

This is not the entire story, however. There are also potential benefits to be gained from entering a state of increased self-consciousness. In particular, doing so can sometimes increase our *self-insight*. For example, consider research conducted by Hixon and Swann (1993). These researchers asked pairs of friends to rate themselves on several different dimensions, such as intelligence, athletic ability, and social skills. Participants in half of the pairs (those in the *high self-reflection* condition) performed this task under conditions that allowed them to reflect on their own traits—to experience increased self-consciousness. Participants in the other half (those in the *low self-reflection* condition) performed the task under conditions that prevented such reflection; they were asked to

PRESSURE TO PERFORM

Performing in front of a large crowd can cause many people—even professional athletes—to experience increased self-consciousness.

Choking Under Pressure: The tendency to perform less well at times when pressures for excellent performance are especially high.

KEY POINTS

- Automatic processing involves performing many activities without conscious attention. In contrast, controlled processing requires conscious attention.

- Daydreams and fantasies are common and may serve several useful functions for us.

- When we focus our attention on ourselves, we enter a state of self-consciousness.

- Increased self-consciousness can interfere with the performance of skilled activities (choking under pressure). However, self-consciousness can also serve as an important first step toward increased self-insight.

remember an eight-digit number while they worked. Trying to remember the number, of course, used up cognitive resources and interfered with (or at least reduced) self-consciousness. While participants performed these tasks, their friends rated them on the same dimensions. When participants were prevented from experiencing heightened self-consciousness, their accuracy in assessing their own traits was reduced. These findings and those of related studies (e.g., Swann et al., 1992) suggest that increased self-consciousness may sometimes contribute to enhanced self-insight. This is not always the case: Other evidence indicates that if we think about ourselves *too* much, we can become confused and experience reduced rather than increased self-insight (Wilson & Schooler, 1991). But as Hixon and Swann note (1993, p. 4), it appears that self-reflection may often be an essential ingredient in increased self-knowledge.

Sleep: The Pause That Refreshes?

What single activity occupies more of your time than any other? While you may be tempted to say "studying" or "working," think again. If you are like most people, the answer is probably **sleep**. Most human beings spend one-third of their lives asleep, and for some the proportion is even higher (Dement, 1975; Webb, 1975). Any activity that occupies so much of our time must be important, so the nature of sleep has been studied by psychologists for several decades. What has this research revealed? What happens when we sleep and when we dream? And what are the functions of these behaviors? These are some of the questions we will now explore.

Sleep: How It Is Studied

Everyone would agree that when we sleep, we are in a different state of consciousness than when we are awake. But what is sleep really like? This is a difficult question to answer, since during sleep we are far less aware of ourselves and our surroundings than at other times. For this reason, asking people about their own experience with sleep is not a very useful technique for studying it. Fortunately, there is another approach that is much more informative. As a person moves from a waking state to deep sleep, complex changes in the electrical activity of the brain occur. These changes can be measured with great precision, and the resulting **electroencephalograms (EEGs)** reveal much about the nature of sleep. In research on sleep, volunteers are fitted with electrodes so that researchers can record their brain activity as well as other changes in bodily functions such as respiration, muscle tone, heart rate, and blood pressure. The changes that occur as the volunteers fall asleep and continue sleeping are then studied. In this way researchers can obtain information about the normal course of sleep.

Sleep: Its Basic Nature

What has sleep research revealed? Perhaps the best way of answering is by describing the changes in brain activity and other bodily processes that occur during a single night of sleep. As we will soon see, these changes progress through several different stages. In a sense, these are normal circadian rhythms, so it is reasonable to view sleep as part of this overall cycle.

When you are fully awake and alert, your EEGs contain many *beta waves*, which are of relatively high frequency (14 to 30 Hz) and low voltage. As you

Sleep: A process in which important physiological changes (including shifts in brain activity and slowing of basic bodily functions) are accompanied by major shifts in consciousness.

Electroencephalogram (EEG): A record of electrical activity within the brain. EEGs play an important role in the scientific study of sleep.

enter a quiet, resting state (for example, just after getting into bed and turning out the light), these beta waves are replaced by **alpha waves**, which are of somewhat lower frequency (8 to 13 Hz) but slightly higher voltage. As you begin to fall asleep, alpha waves are replaced by even slower, higher-voltage **delta waves**. The appearance of delta waves seems to reflect the fact that increasingly large numbers of neurons are firing together, in a synchronized manner.

Although such phrases as "drifting off to sleep" suggest that the onset of sleep is gradual, it is actually quite sudden. One instant you are awake and aware of your surroundings; the next you are asleep, no longer experiencing such awareness. Sleep is not entirely an "either/or" type of phenomenon, however. EEG records obtained from thousands of volunteers in sleep research indicate that sleep can actually be divided into four different stages. The transition from wakefulness to sleep occurs with the onset of Stage 1 sleep. During this stage, a mixed but relatively slow, low-voltage EEG pattern emerges. Breathing slows, muscle tone decreases, and the body generally relaxes. At this point, individuals can still be easily awakened by external stimuli. If they are not, they move into Stage 2 (Webb, 1975). During this stage the brain emits occasional short bursts of rapid, high-voltage waves known as sleep spindles. In Stage 2, sleepers are much more difficult to awaken than they were during Stage 1. Stage 2 is followed by Stages 3 and 4. As shown in Figure 4.2, these stages are marked by the increasing appearance of slow, high-voltage delta waves, and by a further slowing of all major bodily functions (Dement, 1975). Almost everyone shows the same pattern when asleep; indeed, a departure from this pattern is often a sign of some physical or psychological disorder, such as Alzheimer's disease (Petit et al., 1992) or adolescent depression (Kutcher et al., 1992).

So far, the picture presented here probably sounds consistent with your own subjective experience of sleep; you change from being awake to being more and more deeply asleep. About ninety minutes after the process begins, however, several dramatic changes occur. First, most people enter a highly distinct phase known as **REM (rapid eye movement) sleep**. During this phase, the electrical activity of the brain changes rapidly; it now closely resembles that shown when people are awake. Delta waves disappear, and fast, low-voltage activity returns.

Alpha Waves: Brain waves that occur when individuals are awake but relaxed.

Delta Waves: High-amplitude, slow brain waves that occur during several stages of sleep, but especially during Stage 4.

REM Sleep: A state of sleep in which brain activity resembling waking restfulness is accompanied by deep muscle relaxation and movements of the eyes. Most dreams occur during periods of REM sleep.

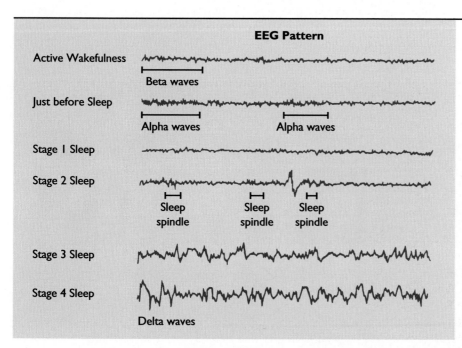

FIGURE 4.2

Sleep Stages

As an individual falls asleep, the electrical activity of his or her brain changes in an orderly manner. Note the contrasting patterns of activity shown before sleep begins and during each of the succeeding stages.

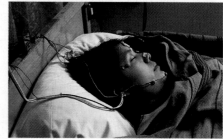

Second, sleepers' eyes begin to move about rapidly beneath their closed eyelids. Third, there is an almost total suppression of activity in the body muscles. Indeed, muscle relaxation is so great that a state bordering on paralysis seems to exist. Yet at the same time, males may experience erections and females corresponding changes in their sexual organs. This combination of signs of activation and signs of profound relaxation has led some researchers to describe REM sleep as *paradoxical* in nature; in several respects this description seems apt.

These observable shifts in brain activity are accompanied, in many cases, by one of the most fascinating phenomena of sleep: *dreams*. An individual awakened during REM sleep often reports dreaming. In some cases, eye movements during such sleep seem to be related to the content of dreams (Dement, 1974). It is as if the individual is following the action in a dream with his or her eyes. The relationship between rapid eye movements and dream content is uncertain, however, so it is best to view this as an intriguing but as yet unverified possibility.

Periods of REM sleep continue to alternate with the other stages of sleep throughout the night. Their duration is variable, but the REM periods tend to increase in length toward morning, while the amount of time spent in Stage 4 tends to decrease (see Figure 4.3). Thus, while the first REM period may last only five to ten minutes, the final one—from which many people awake—may last thirty minutes or more (Hartmann, 1973; Kelly, 1991).

Sleep: *What Functions Does It Serve?*

Any activity that fills as much of our lives as sleep must serve important functions. But what, precisely, are these? What benefits do we gain from the hours we spend asleep? Several theories exist.

The first, and perhaps most obvious, is the restorative or recuperative theory. It suggests that sleep provides the rest we require to recover from the wear and tear of the previous day's activities. While this view seems consistent with our subjective impressions (we often report feeling irritable and out of sorts after a poor night's sleep), there is little direct evidence for it. Even prolonged deprivation of sleep does not seem to produce large or clear-cut effects on behavior. For example, in one demonstration seventeen-year-old Randy Gardner stayed awake for precisely 264 hours and 12 minutes—eleven entire days! His motivation for doing so was simple: He wanted to earn a place in the *Guinness Book of Records*, and he did. Although he had some difficulty staying

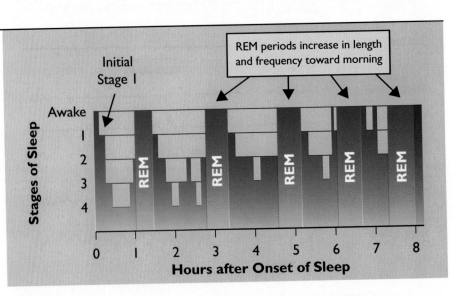

FIGURE 4.3

Time Spent in Various Stages of Sleep During a Single Night

Periods of REM sleep alternate with other stages of sleep during the night. The duration of the REM periods tends to increase toward morning, while the amount of time spent in stage 4 decreases.

REM periods increase in length and frequency toward morning

Initial Stage 1

Awake

Stages of Sleep

Hours after Onset of Sleep

CHAPTER 4

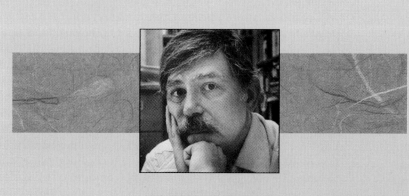

**Nicholas P. Spanos
(1942–1994)**

Nicholas Spanos wrote over 200 articles, book chapters and books on behavior under hypnosis. This research gained international recognition for the late Carleton professor. During his distinguished career, he was awarded the Carleton University Scholarly Achievement Award several times.

PSYCHOLOGISTS OF NOTE

awake this long, he remained generally alert and active throughout the entire period. After completing his ordeal, Randy slept a mere fourteen hours. Then he returned to his usual eight-hour cycle. Further, he seemed to suffer no lasting physical or psychological harm from his long sleepless period.

More systematic studies of the effects of sleep deprivation have been conducted with both animals and people (e.g., Rechtschaffen et al., 1983). With respect to humans, several long-term studies have been performed in which volunteers gradually reduce their nightly sleep—for example, by thirty minutes every two or three weeks. These procedures continue until the volunteers report that they do not want to reduce their sleep any further. Results indicate that most people can reduce their amount of sleep to about five hours per night (Mullaney et al., 1977). No reductions in their performance on various tasks, no negative shifts in mood, and no harmful effects on health seem to result from such reductions. The major changes observed are in the sleep itself. After reducing their sleep to five hours or less, participants demonstrate an increased *sleep efficiency*. They fall asleep very quickly, and they spend a higher proportion of time in Stage 4 sleep. It is as if they have learned to compress their sleep into a shorter period of time. In sum, research on sleep deprivation does not support the view that sleep serves primarily a restorative or recuperative function.

A second theory emphasizes the relationship between sleep and basic circadian rhythms. According to this view, sleep evolved to encourage various species, including human beings, to remain inactive during those times of day when they were not usually engaged in activities necessary for survival. As one well-known sleep researcher (Webb, 1975) has put it, sleep is nature's way of keeping us quiet at night—a dangerous time for our ancestors, and, given current crime statistics, for many North Americans.

Yet another possibility is that only certain components of sleep are crucial. For example, it has been suggested that perhaps it is REM sleep that is essential

- The EEG is an important method for studying sleep.

- As we sleep, we pass through several different stages, in which patterns of brain activity change and our awareness of the external world decreases.

- During REM sleep, the EEG shows a pattern very similar to that of waking, but there is almost total suppression of activity in body muscles. Most dreams occur during REM sleep.

- Although they report feeling tired and irritable, most people can function quite well even after prolonged periods of sleep deprivation.

- However, growing evidence indicates that sleep does serve important functions relating to restoration of bodily resources and circadian rhythms.

to our health and well-being, and that being deprived of REM will induce harmful effects. Unfortunately, efforts to test this possibility have yielded mixed results. On the one hand, a few studies have indicated that selectively depriving individuals of REM sleep (by waking them up whenever their EEG indicates that they have entered this phase) may interfere with their ability to retain newly learned information (McGrath & Cohen, 1978). These findings suggest that REM sleep may play an important role in the integration of newly acquired information with existing memories. On the other hand, additional studies indicate that the only effect of depriving individuals of REM sleep is to increase the amount of REM sleep they have on subsequent nights (Webb & Agnew, 1967).

So where does all this leave us? Does sleep really serve important functions? Or is it merely a holdover from our more primitive past, like facial hair and the appendix? Most sleep researchers reject this conclusion. They believe that sleep probably serves both the restorative and the circadian functions noted above (Borbely et al., 1989). In support of this reasoning, some findings suggest that the amount of time people spend in slow-wave sleep is related to how long they have been awake, while the amount of time spent in REM sleep is determined mainly by circadian rhythms—our daily cycles of activity and rest (Webb, 1975). Further, there is an important relationship between sufficient sleep and moods. The more effectively people sleep, the more positive are their waking moods, and the less anxiety they experience (Berry & Webb, 1985). So, in sum, sleep does seem to serve important functions for us. Falling asleep is a function of both restorative and circadian factors, and sleep itself fulfills needs related to both.

Sleep Disorders: *No Rest for the Weary*

Do you ever have trouble falling or staying asleep? If so, you are in good company: Almost 40 percent of adults report that they sometimes have this problem—generally known as **insomnia** (Bixler et al., 1979). Further, such problems seem to increase with age and are somewhat more common among women than men. While many people report insomnia, it is not clear that the problem actually exists in all cases. When the sleep habits of people who claim to be suffering from insomnia are carefully studied, it turns out that many of them sleep as long as people who do not complain of such problems (Empson, 1984). As pointed out by Trinder (1988), this does not necessarily imply that these people are faking their disorder or complaining about a problem they don't really have. For example, the amount of sleep they get may be within what experts consider to be normal limits (6.5 hours or more per night), but this may still not be enough to meet their individual needs. Further, the quality of their sleep may be disturbed in ways not yet measured in research. Still, these arguments aside, it does appear that many people who believe that their sleep is somehow inadequate may actually be getting as much sleep—and sleeping about as well—as others who don't report such problems. Some people who complain of insomnia may really be suffering from depression or drug misuse (Fleming, 1993).

Several approaches to the treatment of insomnia have been studied at Canadian sleep disorder clinics (e.g., in Ottawa, Toronto, and Vancouver). These approaches include behavior modification (Sloan et al., 1993), group therapy (Kupych, MacFarlane, & Shapiro, 1993), and substitution of drugs (Shapiro, MacFarlane, & MacLean, 1993).

Insomnia: Disorder involving the inability to fall asleep or maintain sleep once it is attained.

Unfortunately, no totally effective cure for insomnia exists. However, you may well find the following tactics helpful:

1. Read something pleasant or relaxing just before going to sleep.

2. Arrange your schedule so that you go to sleep at the same time each night.

3. Take a warm bath, massage, or other relaxing treatment at bedtime.

4. If you find yourself tossing and turning, get up and read, work, or watch television until you feel drowsy. Lying in bed for hours worrying about loss of sleep is definitely *not* the best procedure to follow.

5. Whatever else you do, don't worry. Almost everyone experiences difficulty falling asleep sometimes, so don't be overly concerned unless the problem persists for more than a few days.

By the way, despite what advertisements promise, sleeping pills—prescription as well as nonprescription—are *not* effective at inducing sleep. They may be at first, but drug tolerance quickly develops so that larger and larger doses are soon needed. Further, some drugs used for this purpose interfere with REM sleep, and can lead to other sleep disturbances.

Unfortunately, insomnia is far from the only problem associated with sleep. Several other *disorders of initiating and maintaining sleep* (DIMS for short) exist. First, there are disorders of arousal. The most dramatic of these is **somnambulism**—walking in one's sleep. This is less rare than you might guess; almost 25 percent of children experience at least one sleepwalking episode (Empson, 1984). A second, related sleep disorder is **night terrors**. Here, children awaken from deep sleep with signs of intense arousal—such as a racing pulse and rapid respiration—and powerful feelings of fear. Yet they have no memory of any dream relating to these feelings. Night terrors occur primarily during Stage 4 sleep. In contrast, *nightmares*, which most of us experience at some point in our lives (most often as children) occur during late night or early morning, when REM sleep is longer. Most nightmares involve recall of vivid dreams, which may include a specific danger (Leung & Robson, 1993). Both somnambulism and night terrors appear to be related to disturbances of the autonomic nervous system, which plays a key role in regulating brain activity during sleep.

Another highly disturbing type of sleep disorder is **apnea**. Those who suffer from sleep apnea actually stop breathing when they are asleep. Needless to say, this often causes them to wake up. Since this process can be repeated literally hundreds of times during the night, apnea can seriously affect the health of those who suffer from it, and efforts are being made to find a remedy (e.g., Bedard et al., 1993).

Have you ever felt yourself twitch suddenly as you were sleeping, or while falling asleep? If so, you have had a small taste of what people suffering from another sleep disorder—*nocturnal myoclonus*—experience. These individuals endure periodic and repeated episodes of body twitching all through the night. Little wonder that their sleep is greatly disturbed.

Finally, there are several disorders known as **hypersomnias,** in which those affected sleep too much. The most serious of these is **narcolepsy,** a condition in which individuals suddenly fall deeply asleep during their waking activities. Such attacks are sometimes accompanied by almost total paralysis and are often triggered by a strong emotion. Thus, when a person with narcolepsy becomes excited or upset, he or she may suddenly fall down in a deep sleep. Once there was a professor who suffered from narcolepsy. During a lecture he would sit down, lean forward, and suddenly be asleep—often in the middle of a sentence. Needless to say, both he and the students in

Somnambulism: A sleep disorder in which individuals actually get up and move about while still asleep.

Night Terrors: Extremely frightening dream-like experiences that occur during non-REM sleep.

Apnea: Cessation of breathing during sleep.

Hypersomnias: Disorders involving excessive amounts of sleep or an overwhelming urge to fall asleep.

Narcolepsy: A sleep disorder in which individuals are overcome by uncontrollable periods of sleep during waking hours.

"DREAM OF OSSIAN"
BY JEAN INGRES

Artists throughout history have attempted to capture the essence of dreams in their work.

his classes found this disturbing. The impact of narcolepsy on the psychological and social life of the individual is serious (Broughton, 1992).

What causes such sleep disorders? With some people, insomnia seems to involve disturbances in the internal mechanisms that regulate body temperature. As noted in our discussion of circadian rhythms, core body temperature usually drops to low levels during sleep. This conserves energy and permits many bodily functions to proceed at reduced rates. In those suffering from insomnia, however, these mechanisms fail to operate normally, so that the body temperature remains relatively high (Sewitch, 1987).

Other causes of sleep disorders may involve disturbances of the biological clock within the hypothalamus (the suprachiasmatic nucleus). This clock interacts with other structures of the brain—such as serotonin-producing portions of the reticular activating system and parts of the forebrain just in front of the hypothalamus—to regulate all circadian rhythms, including the sleep–waking cycle. Any disturbance in these complex and delicately balanced mechanisms, then, can result in a sleep disorder. More specifically, Mamelak (1992) has reported particular differences in the levels of certain neurotransmitters (serotonin, noradrenaline, and dopamine).

Dreams: Stimulation in the Midst of Sleep

Without a doubt, the most dramatic aspect of sleep is that of **dreams**—those jumbled, vivid, sometimes enticing and sometimes disturbing images that fill the sleeper's mind. What are these experiences? Why do they happen? While psychologists are still seeking final answers to these puzzling questions, we already know much more about dreams than we did only a few decades ago (Moffitt, 1993; Koulack, 1992). Here, we'll first consider some basic facts about dreams, and then turn to three contrasting views concerning their nature and function.

DREAMS: SOME BASIC FACTS   Try answering each of the following questions. Then consider the answers given, which reflect current knowledge about the nature of these encounters with the workings of our own nervous systems.

1. *Does everybody dream?* The answer seems to be yes. While not all people remember dreaming, EEG recordings and related data indicate that everyone experiences REM sleep. Moreover, if awakened during such periods, even people who normally don't recall dreaming may report vivid dreams.

2. *How long do dreams last?* Many people believe that dreams last only an instant, no matter how long they may seem. In fact, though, dreams seem to run on "real time": the longer they seem to last, the longer they really are (Dement & Kleitman, 1957).

3. *Can external events be incorporated into dreams?* Common sense suggests that they can, and this seems to be correct, at least to a degree: external events are sometimes incorporated into dreams. For example, Dement

Dreams: Cognitive events, often vivid but disconnected, that occur during sleep. Most dreams take place during REM sleep.

and Wolpert (1958) sprayed water on sleeping people who were experiencing REM sleep. Then they woke them up. In more than half the cases, participants reported water in their dreams. Nielsen (1993) applied pressure to either the right or the left leg of volunteers during their REM sleep. In the subjects' dream reports were not only sensations of pressure or squeezing, but also effects of that pressure upon their posture and/or movement in the dream.

4. *If a man experiences an erection or a woman experiences vaginal secretions during sleep, does this mean that the sleeper is having a sexy dream?* The answer to this one seems to be no. When male and female volunteers are awakened at such times, they are no more likely to report dreams with sexual content than they would be at other times (Karacan et al., 1966). So signs of sexual arousal during dreams seem to be a mere by-product of other bodily events that occur during dreaming.

5. *Do dreams really express unconscious wishes?* Many people believe they do, but there is no convincing evidence for it. (See the discussion of this topic below.)

6. *When people cannot remember their dreams, does this mean that they are purposely forgetting them, perhaps because they find the content too disturbing?* Probably not. Research on why people can or cannot remember their dreams indicates that this is primarily a function of what they do when they wake up; for instance, whether they lie quietly in bed, actively trying to remember the dream, or leap up and start the day's activities. While we can't totally rule out the possibility of some kind of repression—that is, of active, motivated forgetting—there is little evidence for its occurrence.

Now that we've considered some basic facts about dreams, let's turn to several views concerning their nature and function.

DREAMS: THE PSYCHODYNAMIC VIEW Perhaps the most dramatic answers to the questions posed at the start of this section were those proposed by Sigmund Freud. He felt that dreams provide an important means of probing the unconscious—all those thoughts, impulses, and wishes that lie outside the realm of conscious experience. In dreams, he believed, we can give expression to impulses and desires we find unacceptable during our waking hours. Thus, we can dream about gratifying illicit sexual desires or about inflicting painful tortures on those who have made us angry, although we actively repress such thoughts during the day.

Freud contended that no matter how vague, jumbled, or strange dreams may seem to be, they always contain important messages. Often these are disguised, either in the dreams themselves or in our memories of them. But if we search diligently enough, we will be able to uncover them. Freud incorporated careful analysis of dreams into his treatment of patients suffering from a wide range of psychological problems. He claimed that this often provided him with just the insight he needed to understand and help them. His reports of such interpretations make provocative reading—but, alas, there is virtually no scientific evidence for their accuracy, or for Freud's more general assertions about dreams. He left us with no clear-cut rules for interpreting dreams and no way of knowing whether such interpretations are accurate. Further, as we'll note in **Perspectives on Diversity**, dreams, and their meanings, may be strongly influenced by cultural factors; dreams differ greatly not only from one individual to another, but from culture to culture. In view of all this, psychologists are currently reluctant to accept Freud's view that dreams offer a unique means for exploring the unconscious. Instead, most accept one of the alternative views we will now consider.

Culture and the Interpretation of Dreams

As mentioned earlier, Freud believed that dreams contain important messages from the *unconscious*—that they reflect impulses and thoughts that are hidden from our view while we are awake. More specifically, he contended that the **manifest content** of a dream—what we actually remember about it—may not, at first glance, reveal its **latent content**—the underlying, hidden meaning. How can the latent content of dreams be determined? Here is Freud's answer: Through careful application of his theories!

For example, consider Freud's interpretations of dreams that were reported to him by several of his male patients. In these dreams, the patient's father was somehow harmed, much to the patient's grief and horror. In fact, when describing such dreams, some patients lost control and burst into tears. How did Freud interpret these dreams? In his view, dreams serve a wish-fulfilling function, allowing people to express desires they cannot express while awake. Within this framework, dreams in which male patients' fathers are harmed represent unconscious anger or resentment toward the parents. According to Freud, these feelings, in turn, stem from what he termed the *Oedipus complex*—the male's jealousy about his father's sexual relationship with his mother.

These are certainly provocative suggestions, but are they actually correct? One way to find out would be to determine whether males in cultures other than the one in which Freud worked (nineteenth-century Vienna) also report such dreams. If they do, this might provide support for the view that the *Oedipus complex* is universal, and for Freud's interpretation of such dreams.

Such research has been conducted, and in general it has failed to confirm the universality of "Oedipus complex" dreams. For example, in one famous study, Malinowksi (1927) found that boys in the Trobriand culture of New Guinea often reported dreams in which the maternal uncle (the mother's brother), not the father, was hurt. Why did they have such dreams? Their uncles didn't have sexual relationships with their mothers, so that was not the cause of the resentment toward the uncles expressed in these dreams. Consider that in Trobriand culture, it is the maternal uncles, not the fathers, who train and discipline boys. So it seems possible that the dreams reported by Trobriand boys reflected resentment toward the adult males who disciplined them. This interpretation is strengthened by the fact that Trobriand boys did *not* have such dreams about their fathers, while none of Freud's Viennese patients had such dreams about their uncles. Put in other terms, in Viennese culture, the two roles "mother's lover" and "source of discipline" are filled by a single person: boys' fathers. In Trobriand culture, in contrast, these two roles are filled by different people: boys' fathers and maternal uncles. Comparing the two cultures permits us to determine which of these roles is related to a specific kind of dream (Segall et al., 1990).

The findings of cross-cultural research indicate that Freud may well have been correct in suggesting that dreams may sometimes function as an outlet for expressing unacceptable impulses, but also that he was wrong in suggesting that the content of dreams is universal across cultures. Rather, it appears that the content of dreams—and their specific meaning—is strongly influenced by the dreamer's culture. Further, comparing dreams in different cultures can help us understand a dream's meaning and the impact of cultural factors upon it. Even at this very basic level, therefore, adopting a *multicultural perspective* is valuable and informative.

CULTURE AND DREAMS

If dreams represent universal human themes, as Freud asserted, then they should be similar in all cultures. Research with the Trobriand culture in New Guinea has shown that they are not.

Manifest Content: In Freud's theory, the overt or reported content of dreams.

Latent Content: In Freud's theory, the hidden content of dreams.

DREAMS: THE PHYSIOLOGICAL VIEW   If dreams aren't reflections of hidden wishes or impulses, what are they? Another answer is provided by what is sometimes called the *physiological view* of dreams. According to this perspective (Hobson, 1988; McCarley & Hobson, 1981) dreams are simply our subjective experience of what is, in essence, random neural activity in the brain. Such activity may reflect ongoing information-processing tasks, as described below, or may occur simply because a minimal amount of stimulation is necessary for the normal functioning of the brain and nervous system. In other words, dreams merely represent efforts by our cognitive systems to make sense out of this neural activity (Foulkes, 1985; Hobson, 1988). As Hobson has put it, the brain "is so ... bent on the quest for meaning that it attributes and even creates meaning when there is little or none to be found in the data it is asked to process."

DREAMS: THE COGNITIVE VIEW   A third view carries somewhat further these suggestions about our efforts to interpret neural activity during sleep. This perspective, proposed by Antrobus (1991), suggests that two facts about REM sleep are crucial to understanding the nature of dreams: First, during REM sleep areas of the brain in the cerebral cortex that play a key role in waking perception, thought, and regulation of motor processes are highly active; and second, at the same time, there is massive inhibition of input from sensory systems and muscles (which, as you may recall, are suppressed during REM sleep). As a result, Antrobus (1991) reasons, the cortical structures or systems that normally regulate perception and thought have only their own output as input. It is this activity which forms the basis for the imagery and ideas in dreams (see Figure 4.4).

Does this mean that dreams are meaningless? Not at all. Since they represent interpretations of neural activity by our own brains, they reflect aspects of our memories and waking experience. Convincing evidence for this connection between dreams and important events in our lives is provided by the fact that people attempting to make important changes in their own behavior—for example, to quit smoking or drinking—often report having **dreams of absent-minded transgression**—DAMIT dreams, for short (e.g., Gill, 1985). In such dreams, people suddenly notice that they are smoking or drinking, and that they have slipped into this behavior in an absent-minded or careless manner—without planning to do so. This realization leads to feelings of panic or guilt in the dream. In many cases, the dreamer wakes up at that point, feeling very disturbed. A study conducted by Hajek and Belcher (1991) yielded intriguing data on the nature of such dreams and their relationship to waking behavior. These researchers asked several hundred people enrolled in a stop-smoking program to report on the kinds of dreams they had before and during the program. They found that about 33 percent of the participants reported having DAMIT dreams while trying to quit, and that they had not had such dreams in the past, while still smoking. Further, and of even greater importance, it was found that having such dreams was positively related to the participants' success at quitting smoking. A higher proportion of those who reported such dreams were still not smoking one year after the training program.

Why was the occurrence of DAMIT dreams related to success in efforts to refrain from smoking? Hajek and Belcher (1991) suggest that the guilt and panic

Dreams of Absent-Minded Transgression: Dreams in which individuals attempting to change their own behavior, as in quitting smoking, see themselves slipping into the unwanted behavior in an absent-minded or careless manner.

FIGURE 4.4

Dreams: One Modern View

According to a model proposed by Antrobus (1991), dreams occur because during REM sleep, areas of the brain that play a key role in waking perception and thought are highly active while at the same time there is massive inhibition of input from sensory systems and muscles. As a result, the cortical systems that normally regulate perception and thought have only their own output as input. The interpretation of this activity forms the basis for dreams.

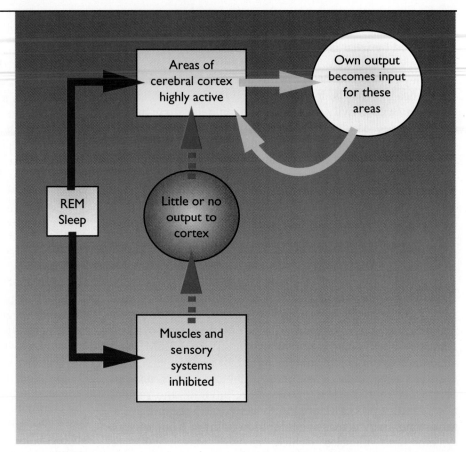

produced by such dreams are so unpleasant that they help strengthen smokers' resolve to break their habit. The fact that smoking in these dreams is *not* accompanied by the pleasurable feelings of smoking helps to strengthen such effects. To the extent that this interpretation is correct, it suggests not only a clear link between what is happening in people's lives at the moment and the contents of their dreams, but a link between the content of dreams and subsequent behavior. In this sense, the content of dreams does have meaning; and, what's more, such meaning may have strong effects upon dreamers' overt behavior.

Hypnosis: Altered State of Consciousness or Social Role Playing?

*A*t one time in the past, every traveling fair and circus included at least one hypnotist among its performers. The hypnotist would ask for volunteers from the audience and then, before the eyes of hundreds of onlookers, put these people in what seemed to be a deep trance. Once they were hypnotized, the volunteers would be made to do an assortment of amazing and sometimes embarrassing things. They might be told to imagine that they were someone else, or even an animal. Under the hypnotist's commands, they would then act this part. Or, having been told that a glass of ammonia contained a delightful perfume, they would proceed to sniff it with apparent delight. Sometimes they would be instructed to perform strange actions after they were awakened from their trance, whenever the hypnotist said a particular word or clapped his hands. Later, the volunteers would obey these previously issued commands, even though they claimed they could not remember the hypnotist's instructions.

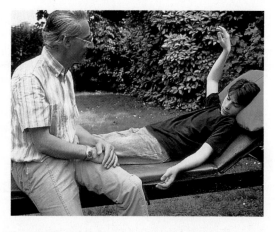

HYPNOSIS: HOW IT'S DONE
Psychologists interested in studying hypnosis have developed highly standardized methods for hypnotizing susceptible research participants.

Are such seemingly amazing feats actually possible? In other words, is **hypnosis** real? And if it is, what is it, and how does it work?

Hypnosis: What It Is and Who Is Susceptible to It

Let's start with two basic questions: How is hypnotism actually performed? And is everyone susceptible to it? With respect to the first, standard hypnotic inductions usually involve *suggestions* by the hypnotist that the person being hypnotized feels relaxed, is getting sleepy, and is unable to keep his or her eyes open. Speaking continuously, in a calm voice, the hypnotist gradually suggests to the subject that he or she is sinking deeper and deeper into a relaxed state—not sleep, but a state in which the person will not be able to do, think, or say anything without input from the hypnotist. Another technique involves having people concentrate on a small object, often one that sparkles and can be rotated by the hypnotist. Hypnosis is definitely not sleep, by the way. EEG recordings of hypnotized individuals resemble those of normal waking, not any of the sleep stages described previously (Wallace & Fisher, 1987).

Now for the second question: Can anyone be hypnotized, or are some individuals more susceptible to this process than others? The answer seems clear: Large individual differences in hypnotizability exist. About 15 percent of adults are highly susceptible (as measured by their response to a graded series of suggestions by the hypnotist), while 10 percent are highly resistant; the rest are somewhere in between. In addition, it appears that several traits are related to hypnotic susceptibility (Lynn & Rhue, 1986; Silva & Kirsch, 1992). Specifically, those who are highly susceptible to hypnotism tend to show the following characteristics:

- They have vivid, frequent fantasies.

- They are high in visual imagery.

- They are high in the trait of absorption—the tendency to become deeply involved in sensory and imaginative experiences.

- They are dependent on others and seek direction from them.

- They expect to be influenced by hypnotic suggestions and believe that these will have a powerful effect on them.

Hypnosis: An interaction between two individuals in which one (the hypnotist) induces changes in the behavior, feelings, or cognition of the other (the subject) through suggestions. Hypnosis involves subjects' expectations and their attempts to conform to the role of the hypnotized person.

The greater the extent to which individuals possess these characteristics, the greater, in general, is their susceptibility to hypnosis. And recent evidence suggests that this is the case because such people can more readily imagine the effects suggested by the hypnotist and (it follows) translate them into their own overt behavior (Silva & Kirsch, 1992). In contrast, there is little evidence that hypnosis-susceptible people intentionally set out to obey these suggestions in a purely voluntary manner. To what extent do *you* possess the characteristics listed above? To the degree you do, you may be a suitable subject for hypnosis.

Hypnosis: Contrasting Views About Its Nature

Now that we have described how hypnotism is performed, we'll consider a more complex question: What does hypnosis involve? In other words, what changes—if any—does it produce in consciousness and other psychological processes? Systematic research has led to the formulation of two major theories of the nature of hypnosis.

THE SOCIAL–COGNITIVE OR ROLE-PLAYING VIEW   The first of these views suggests that the seemingly strange and mysterious effects of hypnosis can best be understood by studying the relationship between the hypnotized person and the hypnotist. Specifically, this theory argues that hypnotized individuals are actually playing a special *social role*—that of *hypnotic subject.* Having seen movies and read stories about hypnosis, most people have an idea of what it supposedly involves. They believe that when hypnotized they will lose control over their own behavior and be unable to resist strong suggestions from the hypnotist. When exposed to hypnotic inductions (instructions to behave in a certain way or to experience specific feelings), therefore, many people tend to obey, since this is what the social role they are enacting suggests *should* happen. Further, they often report experiencing the changes in perceptions and feelings that they *expect* to experience (e.g., Lynn, Rhue, & Weekes, 1990; Spanos, 1991).

This does not mean that those who undergo hypnosis engage in a conscious effort to fool other people. On the contrary, they sincerely believe that they are experiencing an altered state of consciousness and that they have no choice but to act and feel as the hypnotist suggests. Thus, in an important sense, their behavior and their reports of their experiences while hypnotized are genuine. These behaviors and experiences, however, reflect beliefs about hypnosis and the role of the hypnotic subject as much as—perhaps even more than—the special skills of the hypnotist or the effects of hypnosis on consciousness.

Spanos (and others working at Carleton University in Ottawa) have developed the Carleton Training Program for people who are low-hypnotizable—that is, who are difficult to hypnotize. That program has increased hypnotizability successfully, even when the hypnosis occurred as long as eighteen weeks after the original training had been given (Spanos, DuBreuil, & Gabora, 1991). The attitudes of students toward hypnosis became more positive as a result of the training program and this may be part of the explanation for the change in their hypnotizability. For more on hypnosis, see **The Research Process**.

THE NEODISSOCIATION THEORY   The second major theory of hypnosis is very different. The **neodissociation theory** suggests that hypnosis operates by inducing two kinds of splits or *dissociations* in consciousness (Bowers, 1990; Hilgard, 1977). The first of these, *dissociated experience*, raises an amnesialike barrier that

Neodissociation Theory: A theory of hypnosis suggesting that hypnotized individuals enter an altered state of consciousness in which consciousness is divided.

prevents experiences during hypnosis from entering normal consciousness. The second split, known as *dissociated control*, implies a split in normal control over behavior. Individuals who have been hypnotized, the theory argues, obey suggestions from the hypnotist in a direct, uncritical fashion; the higher centers of control are essentially cut out of the picture. According to Hilgard (1977), then, people who have been hypnotized are in an altered state of consciousness in which one part of their mind accepts suggestions from the hypnotist while the other part (which Hilgard terms "the hidden observer") observes the procedures without participating in them. So, for example, when hypnotized individuals are told to put an arm into icy water but told that they will experience no pain, they will obey and report no discomfort. However, when asked to describe their feelings in writing, they may indicate that they did experience feelings of intense cold (Hilgard, 1979). It seems as if one part of consciousness obeys hypnotic suggestions while another does not.

Which of these theories is correct? While support for both views exists (e.g., Miller & Bowers, 1993), most psychologists believe that the social–cognitive view is more accurate. It appears that most of the unusual or bizarre effects observed under hypnosis can be explained by the hypnotized person's belief in hypnotism's effects and of his or her efforts— not necessarily conscious—to behave in accordance with those expectations and the hypnotist's suggestions. What kind of research findings point to these conclusions? For information, see **The Research Process**.

THE RESEARCH PROCESS

Does Hypnosis Produce Changes in Memory and Perception?

N*ow you* say *you see it; now you* say *you don't.* Under hypnosis, people may see and hear things that others do not, or deny that they heard or saw things that actually happened. Does hypnosis change our perceptions and our memories in some way? What are the current ideas about the dramatic events that occur on stage when an entertainer like Reveen or Doug Henning plays Saskatoon or Brandon, Sherbrooke or Thunder Bay?

As you already know, there are at least two theories here. One of these, the neodissociation theory, proposes that people under hypnosis enter a special state of consciousness in which they do or say, perceive or remember, things that they otherwise could not. The other one, the social–cognitive theory, proposes that how people behave under hypnosis is determined by the social demands of the situation.

Hypnosis and Sensory Hallucinations

Now you see it, now you don't. Does hypnosis really change what we see, hear, or feel? Nicholas Spanos and other researchers at Carleton University conducted numerous investigations into the apparent changes in perception that occur under hypnosis. For this, they used an ingenious experimental design. For example, in one experiment, hypnotized subjects (Carleton undergraduate volunteers) were told that they were being shown a blank piece of paper. On the paper, however, there was a number "8". After hypnosis was ended, those who said the paper they saw was blank were told that only fakers said that. Then they were given a chance to draw what had been on the paper. Of the fifteen subjects, fourteen drew the number "8" (Spanos, Flynn, & Gabora, 1989). Clearly, these students had seen what was on the paper while they were hypnotized. In a subsequent study, subjects reported that, under hypnosis, they had used several different strategies *not to see properly*. For example, they unfocused their eyes, crossed their eyes, or looked above, below, or away from what was written on the paper (Spanos, Burgess, Cross, & MacLeod, 1992).

In another study, subjects heard a clearly audible tone, three times. The first time they heard the tone, they rated how loud it sounded to them. Then they were hypnotized and given the hypnotic suggestion that they would not be able to hear the second tone. The second tone was presented, and again they rated its loudness. Before the third and final presentation, the hypnotic suggestion was cancelled. For some subjects,

however, misinformation was added: They were told that they had probably slipped back into hypnosis and would not be able to hear the tone very well. Then the tone was played and all subjects rated it a third time. (As you might have guessed by now, the three tones were actually identical in every way.)

You will find the results of this experiment (Spanos, Burgess, & Perlini, 1992) in Figure 4.5. The misinformed subjects rated the third tone as less loud than the others did. Was that because, under hypnosis, their hearing was impaired? Not at all.

Similar results have been obtained with individuals who reported little or no reaction to pain under hypnosis—for example, to placing their arms in icy water (Spanos, Perlini, Patrick, Bell, & Gwynn, 1990—and

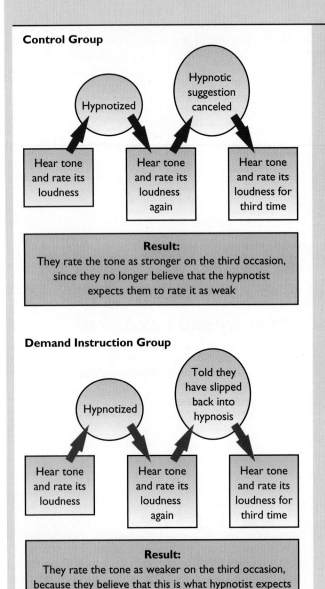

Control Group

Hypnotized

Hypnotic suggestion canceled

Hear tone and rate its loudness

Hear tone and rate its loudness again

Hear tone and rate its loudness for third time

Result:
They rate the tone as stronger on the third occasion, since they no longer believe that the hypnotist expects them to rate it as weak

Demand Instruction Group

Hypnotized

Told they have slipped back into hypnosis

Hear tone and rate its loudness

Hear tone and rate its loudness again

Hear tone and rate its loudness for third time

Result:
They rate the tone as weaker on the third occasion, because they believe that this is what hypnotist expects

FIGURE 4.5

Procedures for Determining Whether Hypnotically Induced Deafness Is Real

People who are hypnotized and told that they will not hear a tone will rate it as lower in loudness than those who are not given this hypnotic suggestion. To determine whether such effects represent actual changes in perception or merely changes in what hypnotized individuals report hearing, Spanos and his colleagues use the procedures shown here.
(Source: Based on procedures used by Spanos et al., 1992.)

with those who regressed into a past life under hypnosis (Spanos, Menary, Gabora, DuBreuil, & Dewhirst, 1991). From all of these results, it seems clear that what appear to be changes in the perceptual experiences of hypnotized people may really be changes in what these people *report* they experienced.

Hypnosis and Memory

Can hypnotized people tell fact from fiction? Some investigators believe that the "extra" details recalled by eyewitnesses who have been hypnotized are distortions of memory rather than a result of improved recall. Several studies have examined memory for events that occur under hypnosis. For example, Murrey, Cross, & Whipple (1992) had students watch a videotape of a mock robbery. Then, under hypnosis, all of the students listened to an audiotape containing false and misleading suggestions about the robbery. Later, they were asked to answer ten questions about the robbery shown on the videotape.

Before the subjects actually answered the questions, however, some were offered an incentive to be as accurate as possible (a cash prize for the student with the most accurate set of answers). These students recalled the details of the robbery as they were on the original videotape. The students who were *not* offered the cash prize for accuracy misremembered the details as they had heard them on the audiotape. Clearly, the false details heard under hypnosis did not produce genuine changes in the memories of these students.

Why would subjects misrepresent what they saw, heard, felt, and remembered? Spanos argues that there are three kinds of pressures here: expectations and beliefs about how to behave under hypnosis;

motivation to comply with the suggestions of the hypnotist; and concerns about how they are seen by those watching them.

In summary, then, there are strong reasons to believe that the effects of hypnosis stem from pressures on hypnotized individuals to meet the expectations of the hypnotist, and to conform to their own beliefs—and those of others—concerning the powerful impact of hypnosis. This does not mean that hypnotism is a hoax, or that all of its effects are the result of calculated fraud on the part of the subjects. Whichever theory you support, it is clear that the power of suggestion is indeed great. However, these kinds of findings do suggest strongly that hypnotism is better understood in terms of expectations and beliefs than in terms of the supposedly mystical powers of hypnotists.

Critical Thinking Questions:

1. Do you think hypnosis can be used to boost the memory of eyewitnesses? Would you recommend this procedure for use by the police? If so, why? If not, why not?

2. Suppose that the participants in research using the methods developed by Spanos rejected the suggestion that they had "slipped back into hypnosis." Would that change the results? How?

3. In light of the findings reported in this special section, do you think that hypnosis can provide a useful technique for reducing pain? In other words, can it be used to reduce the discomfort experienced by people suffering from chronic pain? If so, why? If not, why not?

Consciousness-Altering Drugs:
What They Are and What They Do

*I*n Chapter 2, we saw that drugs are big business in the late twentieth century. Each day, many millions of human beings use drugs to change the way they feel—to alter their moods or states of consciousness. Much of this use of consciousness-altering drugs is completely legal; indeed, many people take such drugs under a physician's supervision. In many other instances, however, people turn to drugs that are illegal, or use legal ones to excess, contrary to medical advice. Drug use—and abuse—is clearly a serious social problem in the 1990s. In this final section, therefore, we'll consider several issues relating to the use of consciousness-altering drugs.

DRUGS AT HOME

Does your medicine cabinet look like this one? Most people have a variety of consciousness-altering drugs in their home.

Drugs: *Chemical substances that change the structure or function of biological systems.*

Drug Abuse: *Instances in which individuals take drugs purely to change their moods, and in which they experience impaired behavior or social functioning as a result of doing so.*

Dependence: *Strong physiological or psychological need for particular drugs.*

Physiological Dependence: *Strong urges to continue using a drug based on organic factors such as changes in metabolism.*

Psychological Dependence: *Strong desires to continue using a drug even though it is not physiologically addicting.*

Tolerance: *Habituation to a drug, causing larger and larger doses to be required to produce effects of the same magnitude.*

Cross-Tolerance: *Increased tolerance for one drug that develops as a result of taking another drug.*

Consciousness-Altering Drugs: Some Basic Concepts

First, what are **drugs?** One widely accepted definition is that they are compounds which, because of their chemical structure, change the structure or function of biological systems (Grilly, 1994). Thus, *consciousness-altering drugs* are drugs that produce changes in consciousness when introduced into the body (Wallace & Fisher, 1987).

Suppose you went to your family medicine cabinet and conducted a careful inventory of all the drugs present. How many would you find? Unless your family is very unusual, quite a few. To the extent these drugs were prescribed by a physician and were used for medical purposes, taking them would probably be appropriate. The term **drug abuse,** therefore, is usually restricted to instances in which people take drugs purely to change their mood, and in which they experience impaired behavior or social functioning as a result of doing so (Wallace & Fisher, 1987).

Unfortunately, when people take consciousness-altering drugs on a regular basis, they often develop **dependence**—they come to need the drug and cannot function without it. Two types of dependence exist. One, **physiological dependence,** occurs when the need for the drug is based on biological factors, such as changes in metabolism. This type of dependence is what is usually meant by the term drug addiction. However, people can also experience **psychological dependence,** in which case they experience a strong desire to continue using the drug even though, physiologically, their body does not need it. As we'll soon see, several psychological mechanisms probably contribute to this dependence. Physiological and psychological dependence often occur together and magnify the individual's craving for and dependence on specific drugs.

Continued use of a drug over a prolonged period of time often leads to drug **tolerance**—a physiological reaction in which the body requires larger and larger doses in order to experience the same effects. Drug tolerance has been observed in connection with many different consciousness-altering drugs and often increases the dangers of these substances. In some cases, the use of one drug increases tolerance for a different drug; this is known as **cross-tolerance** (Pinel, 1993). In current research (e.g., Kim, Pinel, & Roese, 1992), experimenters are testing ways in which one drug may be used in a positive way, to allow safe use of a second drug, which taken alone would have serious side effects.

Psychological Mechanisms Underlying Drug Abuse: Contrasting Views

On the face of it, drug abuse is a puzzling form of behavior. Recreational use of drugs, after all, carries considerable risk of harm, and long-term drug abuse usually undermines the physical and psychological health of those who adopt such practices. Why, then, do so many people engage in this behavior? Several different explanations have been proposed.

THE LEARNING PERSPECTIVE: REWARDING PROPERTIES OF CONSCIOUSNESS-ALTERING DRUGS Several explanations for why people use consciousness-altering drugs derive from basic principles of learning—principles we'll consider in detail in Chapter 5. One approach suggests that people use such drugs because doing so feels good; in other words, the effects produced by the drugs are somehow rewarding (Wise & Bozarth, 1987). Evidence supporting this view is provided by many studies indicating that animals will self-administer many of the same drugs that people abuse, presumably because they find the effects of these drugs rewarding (Young & Herling, 1986).

On the other hand, these substances reduce *negative* feelings, such as stress, anxiety, or physical discomfort. Thus, people take drugs to reduce negative feelings rather than simply to generate positive ones (Tiffany, 1990). This explanation is especially applicable to cases in which individuals have become physiologically dependent on a drug; the negative symptoms they experience when it is no longer used—known as *withdrawal*—may provide a powerful incentive to obtain the drug again at all costs.

THE PSYCHODYNAMIC PERSPECTIVE: COPING WITH UNCONSCIOUS FEARS AND DESIRES
As we saw in Chapter 1, the psychodynamic perspective views human behavior as stemming from unconscious conflicts among hidden aspects of personality. This perspective points to another, and very different, explanation for drug abuse: Perhaps individuals use drugs to reduce or at least conceal the anxiety generated by such inner turmoil. While this is an intriguing idea, it is very difficult to test empirically. For this reason, it currently receives little attention from psychologists.

THE SOCIAL PERSPECTIVE: DRUG ABUSE AND SOCIAL PRESSURE   A third perspective suggests that drug abuse can be understood largely in terms of social factors. According to this view, individuals—especially adolescents and young adults—use consciousness-altering drugs because it is the "in" thing to do. They observe their friends using these substances and experience pressure—subtle or overt—to join them (Mann, Chassin, & Sher, 1987). You may well have experienced such pressure yourself; if so, you know hard it can be to resist. We'll examine social influences in detail in Chapter 16.

THE COGNITIVE PERSPECTIVE: DRUG ABUSE AS AUTOMATIC BEHAVIOR   Another perspective on the use of consciousness-altering drugs—and a very intriguing one—has been proposed by Tiffany (1990). He suggests that in many cases, drug abuse represents a kind of automatic processing or automatic behavior on the part of the individuals involved. As individuals use various drugs, Tiffany contends, many aspects of obtaining the drugs and consuming them take on the character of automatic processes. As you may recall from our earlier discussion, this implies that drug use becomes quick and relatively effortless, occurs without conscious intention, is difficult to inhibit, and may even take place in the absence of conscious awareness. Once they have used a drug on a considerable number of occasions, individuals may find themselves responding almost automatically to external cues—for example, a specific environment (such as a bar) in which the drug has often been enjoyed (Davis & Tunks, 1990–91), or specific sights and smells associated with drug use, such as the aroma of a burning cigarette. In a similar manner, they may respond automatically to internal cues or emotions, such as wanting to celebrate or feeling tired or out of sorts. These cues may trigger people's tendencies to use drugs, and they may find themselves doing so before they realize it, even without any strong urge to take a drug.

Do you remember the DAMIT dreams—dreams of absent-minded transgression—reported by many individuals who are trying to give up the use of tobacco or alcohol? The content of such dreams captures the kind of automatic drug use suggested by Tiffany. Note that according to Tiffany (1990), strong urges or cravings are not necessary for drug use to occur; such behavior may be initiated in the absence of these urges by appropriate internal or external stimuli.

Tiffany's model has not yet been subjected to extensive tests. However, many findings concerning drug abuse appear to be consistent with it. For example, it has often been noted that individuals who were once addicted to a drug and stopped using it are more likely to relapse into using it when

- People often use drugs to change the way they feel—their state of consciousness.
- Continued use of a given drug may result in growing tolerance to it and psychological or physiological dependence on it.
- The learning perspective suggests that drug abuse stems from the fact that people find the effects of consciousness-altering drugs rewarding, or that these drugs help reduce stress, anxiety, and other negative feelings.
- The social perspective suggests that people abuse drugs because of strong social pressures to do so.
- The cognitive perspective proposes that drug abuse may be at least in part an automatic behavior triggered by the presence of external cues.

experiencing high levels of stress than at other times (Bliss et al., 1989). Tiffany explains these relapses by suggesting that at such times, individuals must use part of their cognitive resources to deal with the stress, thus leaving fewer resources to focus on continued abstinence. The result: They resort to patterns of automatic processing, and this leads them to their drug relapse. Despite such indirect support, Tiffany's theory must be subjected to additional, systematic testing before it can be accepted. Still, it seems to offer important insights into the nature of drug abuse and drug addiction, and deserves further careful attention.

Consciousness-Altering Drugs: An Overview

While many different drugs affect consciousness, most seem to fit under one of four major headings: *depressants, stimulants, opiates,* and *psychedelics and hallucinogens.* Please note that these categories are based on the psychological effects of various drugs, not their chemical nature. Several drugs can exert similar effects on mood or consciousness though they have fundamentally different chemical formulas, and some drugs with similar chemical formulas can exert very different psychological effects (Pinel, 1993).

DEPRESSANTS Drugs that reduce both behavioral output and activity in the central nervous system are called **depressants.** According to the reports of the Addiction Research Foundation in Toronto, perhaps the most important of these is *alcohol,* undoubtedly the most widely consumed drug in the world (Smart, 1991). Small doses of alcohol seem, subjectively, to be stimulating— they induce feelings of excitement and activation. Larger doses, however, act as a depressant. They dull the senses so that pain, cold, and other forms of discomfort become less intense. This is why alcohol was widely used to deaden the pain of medical operations before more effective anesthetics became available. Large doses of alcohol also interfere with coordination and normal functioning of our senses—often with tragic results for motorists— and may disrupt information processing in several respects. (Table 4.3 summarizes these effects.) Alcohol also lowers social inhibitions. After consuming large quantities of this drug, people often become more prone to engage in dangerous forms of behavior as well as more generally unrestrained in their words and actions (see Chapter 10 for more information on these effects). Alcohol may produce its pleasurable effects by stimulating special receptors in the brain. Its depressant effects may stem from the fact that it interferes with the capacity of neurons to conduct nerve impulses, perhaps by affecting the cell membrane directly.

Barbiturates, which are contained in sleeping pills and relaxants, are a second type of depressant. First manufactured in the late nineteenth century, these drugs depress activity in the central nervous system and reduce activation and mental alertness. How these effects are produced is not certain, but existing evidence suggests that barbiturates may reduce the release of excitatory neurotransmitters by neurons in many different locations. Initially, high doses of barbiturates can produce feelings of relaxation and euphoria—a kind of drunkenness without alcohol. They often go on to produce serious confusion, slurred speech, memory lapses, and reduced ability to concentrate. Wide

Depressants: Drugs that reduce activity in the nervous system and therefore slow many bodily and cognitive processes. Depressants include alcohol and barbiturates.

Barbiturates: Drugs that act as depressants, reducing activity in the nervous system and behavior output.

BLOOD ALCOHOL LEVEL (IN MILLIGRAMS OF ALCOHOL PER MILLIMETER OF BLOOD)	BEHAVIORAL EFFECTS
0.05	Lowered alertness, impaired judgment, release of inhibitions, good feeling
0.10	Slowed reaction times and impaired motor function, less caution
0.15	Large, consistent increases in reaction time
0.20	Marked depression in sensory and motor capability, decidedly intoxicated behavior
0.25	Severe motor disturbance and impairment of sensory perceptions
0.30	In a stupor but still conscious—no comprehension of events in the environment
0.35	Surgical anesthesia; lethal dose for about 1 percent of the population
0.40	Lethal dose for about 50 percent of the population

TABLE 4.3

Behavioral Effects of Various Blood Alcohol Levels

swings of emotion, from euphoria to depression, are also common. Extremely large doses can be fatal, because they result in paralysis of centers of the brain that regulate respiration. This is a real danger, since tolerance to barbiturates gradually develops, so that individuals find it necessary to increase the doses they consume to obtain the same effects.

Because some barbiturates induce sleep, people often try to use them to treat sleep disorders such as insomnia. However, these drugs do not seem to produce normal sleep. In particular, they suppress REM sleep, which may rebound after individuals stop taking the drugs.

STIMULANTS   Drugs that produce the opposite effects of depressants—feelings of energy and activation—are known as **stimulants**. Amphetamines and cocaine are stimulants. Others, in common use, include caffeine (found in coffee, tea, and many soft drinks) and nicotine (in tobacco). Drugs like **cocaine** and **amphetamines** raise the user's blood pressure, heart rate, and respiration—in effect, they mimic all the signs of activation or arousal that the sympathetic nervous system produces. They also yield short periods of pleasurable sensations, twenty to forty minutes long, during which the user feels incredibly powerful and energetic. As the drug wears off, the user often experiences an emotional crash marked by strong anxiety, depression, and fatigue. This has happened because the drug has stripped the body of its natural chemical supply.

Freud believed that cocaine was useful in treating various illnesses such as asthma, indigestion, and even addiction to alcohol or morphine. Cocaine is usually consumed by snorting—that is, by inhaling it through the nostrils. It is absorbed through the mucous lining of the nose directly into the blood stream. When cocaine is heated and treated chemically, an even more powerful form known as **crack** is produced. Smoking crack produces an instant high, during which the individual experiences powerful feelings of energy, confidence, and excitement. While cocaine is not usually considered to be addictive, it often produces strong psychological dependence, and crack even more so.

Stimulants: Drugs that increase activity in the nervous system, including amphetamines, caffeine, and nicotine.

Cocaine: A powerful stimulant that produces pleasurable sensations of increased energy and self-confidence.

Amphetamines: Drugs that act as stimulants, increasing feelings of energy and activation.

Crack: A cocaine derivative that can be smoked. It acts as a powerful stimulant.

RIVER PHOENIX (1970–1993)
This actor's life was tragically cut short by a lethal combination of drugs.

In most parts of Canada, cocaine use is relatively rare, except among street youth (Smart & Adlef, 1992). In 1991, in Ontario, fewer than 2 in every 100 post-secondary students reported having used cocaine in the past year.

Very recently, studies at the ARF have found that cocaine and nicotine use the same receiving sites in the brain (Shrier, 1994). That means we may ultimately be able to use a nicotine-like drug to help cocaine addicts kick their habit.

OPIATES   Among the most dangerous drugs in widespread use are the **opiates**, which include *opium, morphine, heroin,* and related synthetic drugs. Opium is derived from the opium poppy—remember the scene in *The Wizard of Oz* where Dorothy falls asleep in a field of beautiful poppies? Morphine is produced from opium, while heroin is produced from morphine. Opiates produce lethargy and a pronounced slowing of almost all bodily functions. They also alter consciousness, producing a dreamlike state and, for some people, intensely pleasurable sensations. The costs associated with these sensations are high, however. Heroin and other opiates are extremely addicting, and withdrawal from them often results in agony. Growing evidence indicates that the brain produces substances closely related to the opiates in chemical structure—*opioid peptides* or *endorphins*—and contains special receptors for them (Phillips & Fibiger, 1989; 1992). This suggests one possible explanation for the discomfort opiate users experience during withdrawal. Regular use of opiates soon overloads endorphin receptors in the brain. As a result, the brain stops producing these substances. When the drugs are withdrawn, endorphin levels remain depressed. Thus, an important internal mechanism for regulating pain is disrupted (Reid, 1990).

Since tolerance for opiates such as heroin increases rapidly with use, physiological addiction can occur very quickly. The withdrawal symptoms are so painful that addicts will go to incredible lengths, and take incredible risks, to obtain a steady supply of the drug.

PSYCHEDELICS AND HALLUCINOGENS   The drugs with the most profound effects upon consciousness may well be the **psychedelics**, which alter sensory perception, and the **hallucinogens**, which generate sensory perceptions when there are no external stimuli.

The most widely used psychedelic drug is marijuana. Medicinal use of marijuana dates back to a Chinese guide to medicines written more than 4,700 years ago. The world's earliest confirmed marijuana user was a pregnant teenager who lived 1,700 years ago. Her skeleton was found near Jerusalem in 1993; she may have been given the drug as an anesthetic during childbirth (Mechoulam et al., 1993). Until this century, marijuana was advised for pain, headaches, cramps, and even ulcers. At the present time, some physicians suggest that marijuana prevents nausea associated with chemotherapy, reduces eye pressure in glaucoma, promotes weight gain in AIDS patients, decreases muscle spasm in multiple sclerosis, and suppresses the immune system in organ transplant operations.

Since 1961, marijuana has been illegal under Canada's Narcotics Control Act. Illegal or not, it is grown and used as a recreational drug across the country and is the most common illicit drug. In 1992, it was a multimillion-dollar Canadian cash crop. In one study of about 500 undergraduates at Concordia College in Edmonton, it was found that while the overall rate of drug use was low, of the drugs used, marijuana was the most common (Campbell & Svenson, 1992).

When smoked or eaten (e.g., baked in cookies or cakes), marijuana produces moderate arousal in the form of increased blood pressure and pulse

Opiates: *Drugs that induce a dreamy, relaxed state and, in some individuals, intense feelings of pleasure. Opiates exert their effects by stimulating special receptor sites within the brain.*

Psychedelics: *Drugs that alter sensory perception and so may be considered mind-expanding.*

Hallucinogens: *Drugs that profoundly alter consciousness, such as marijuana and LSD.*

rate; a perceived increase in the intensity of sounds, colors, tastes, and smells; and distorted judgement of time and distance. Other effects reported by some users (though not all) include reduced inhibitions, increased sexual pleasure (which may simply reflect increased sensitivity to all sensations), and feelings of relaxation.

Marijuana smoke contains over 400 chemicals, many of which may affect the brain. The one that is psychoactive, and causes perceptual and other changes, is THC. Although THC is not found naturally in the body, it matches up with receptor sites in the brain, such as the hippocampus, cerebral cortex, and basal ganglia, and in other body locations, such as the spleen (which filters our complete blood supply every twenty-four hours). What these receptor sites normally do is a puzzle; but in 1992, a substance that uses the same receptors was discovered in pigs' brains. That substance was named anandamine ("bliss"), and it seems to have the same effects as THC in mice and hamsters. In humans, anandamine may relieve pain, control appetite and motor coordination, and regulate moods.

The use of marijuana poses certain dangers. First, the perceptual distortions it produces may result in tragedy—when users attempt to drive or to operate power machinery, for example. Second, because it is illegal, marijuana purchasers never know exactly what they are getting. For example, the designer drug "Skunk" may have ten times the usual THC content and produce terrifying paranoia. Third, there is some indication that long-term use of marijuana may result in shifts in the personality toward passivity and a general lack of motivation (Baumrind, 1984). Finally, some find that marijuana interferes with memory (Miller, Cornelius, & McFarland, 1978).

There have been few studies of the long-term effects of marijuana on individual users, or on children whose mothers used marijuana while pregnant (Fried, Watkinson, & Gray, 1992). Some research has reported few long-lasting adverse effects for users (e.g., Page, Fletcher, & True, 1988). However, Cynader and Chen at the University of British Columbia have found that there are many more THC receptors in newborn kitten and monkey brains than in adults. This has led them to suggest that exposure to the THC in marijuana smoke at a very young age may affect how well the brain will function throughout the person's life. These are all matters to be considered before you decide whether to use this drug for recreation.

Much more dramatic effects are produced by *hallucinogens*—drugs that produce vivid hallucinations and other perceptual shifts. Of these, the most famous is **LSD** (lysergic acid diethylamide), or *acid*. After taking LSD, many people report profound changes in perceptions of the external world. Objects and people seem to change color and shape; walls may sway and move; and many sensations seem more intense than normal. There may also be a strange blending of sensory experiences known as *synesthesia*. Music yields visual sensations, while colors produce feelings of warmth or cold. These effects may sound exciting or even pleasant, but many others produced by LSD are quite negative. Objects, people, and even one's own body may seem distorted or threatening. Users may experience deep sorrow or develop intense fear of close friends and relatives. Perhaps worst of all, the effects of this drug are unpredictable; there is no way of determining in advance whether LSD will yield mostly pleasant or mostly unpleasant sensations. In fact, the same person may experience radically different effects at different times. Unless you are willing to gamble with your own health, therefore, LSD is a drug to avoid. An overview of various drugs and their effects is provided in **Key Concept** on page 178.

LSD: A powerful hallucinogen that produces profound shifts in perception; many of these are frightening in nature.

Effects of Consciousness-Altering Drugs

DEPRESSANTS

Reduce behavioral output and activity in the central nervous system

Alcohol

- Deadening of pain
- Reduced coordination
- Interference with normal functioning of senses
- Reduced social inhibitions

Barbiturates

- Reduced mental alertness
- Sleep
- Confusion
- Euphoria
- Memory lapses, inability to concentrate
- Suppression of REM sleep

STIMULANTS

Induce feelings of energy and activation.

Amphetamines

- Elevation of blood pressure, heart rate, respiration
- Feelings of alertness and energy, followed by depression as effect wears off

Caffeine

- Mild feelings of increased alertness

- Mild diuretic effect (increased urination)

Cocaine and derivatives (including crack)

- Feelings of tremendous power and energy
- Intense pleasurable sensations
- Psychological dependence (cocaine)
- Powerful addiction (crack)

OPIATES

Produce lethargy and pronounced slowing of almost all bodily functions; induce a dreamlike state and pleasurable sensations.

Opium

- Deadening of pain
- Induced dreamlike state
- Inducing of pleasurable sensations, feelings
- Highly addicting

Morphine

- Similar to opium but even more pronounced

Heroin

- Like opium and morphine, but pleasurable sensations are intensified; described by some users as a whole-body orgasm
- Extremely addicting

PSYCHEDELICS AND HALLUCINOGENS

Psychedelics alter sensory perception; sometimes viewed as mind-expanding. Hallucinogens generate sensory perceptions for which there are no external stimuli.

Psychedelics (e.g., marijuana)

- Moderate arousal
- Increased intensity of various stimuli
- Distortions in sense of time
- Diminished ability to judge distances
- Feelings of increased sexual pleasure, for some people
- Feelings of relaxation

Hallucinogens (e.g., LSD)

- Profound changes in perceptions of external world
- Blending of sensory experiences
- Objects seem to change shape
- Ordinary situations may become threatening or frightening
- Effects of drugs vary greatly on different people

The Psychology of Drug Effects

While specific drugs do generally produce the effects just described, their impact may vary, depending on many other factors.

First, the impact of drugs is often determined by expectations. If users expect a drug to produce certain effects (increase their sex drive, reduce their inhibitions, put them in a good mood), these effects are much more likely to happen than if users do not anticipate them.

Second, a drug's effects depend on the user's physical state. Some people are naturally more tolerant of various drugs than others. Also, the influence of a specific drug may depend on whether the person taking it is fatigued or well rested, whether he or she has recently eaten, and many other factors.

Third, the effects of various drugs depend on previous experience. First-time users of alcohol or tobacco generally report very different reactions to these substances than people who have used them for quite some time. The same is true for many other drugs that alter mood or consciousness.

Finally, the influence of a given drug depends on what other drugs the user is also taking. In medicine, careful physicians consider the possibility of drug interactions before issuing prescriptions. People who take various illegal drugs, however, rarely do this—sometimes with tragic results.

In sum, the influence of drugs on feelings, behavior, and consciousness is neither certain nor fully predictable. Many factors can determine the magnitude and direction of their effects. This is yet another reason why, where drugs are concerned, the byword should be *caution*.

KEY POINTS

- Depressants reduce both behavioral output and activity in the central nervous system. Important depressants include alcohol and barbiturates.

- Stimulants produce feelings of energy and activation. Amphetamines and cocaine fall into this category.

- Opiates produce lethargy and pronounced slowing of almost all bodily functions. They also produce pleasurable sensations for some people, and so are highly addicting.

- Psychedelics such as marijuana alter sensory perception, while hallucinogens such as LSD produce vivid hallucinations and other bizarre perceptual shifts.

- A specific dose of a given drug may produce very different effects on the same person at different times, depending on such factors as physical condition, expectations, other drugs taken recently, and other factors.

MAKING PSYCHOLOGY PART OF YOUR LIFE

Meditation: A Technique for Inducing Potentially Beneficial Shifts in Consciousness

For centuries, travelers from the West who visited India returned with tales of the amazing feats performed by *yogis*—members of special religious orders who seemed to possess incredible powers. These people, it was reported, could walk barefoot over hot coals and lie on beds of nails without experiencing pain. Perhaps even more astounding, some seemed able to enter a self-induced trance in which they could bring their own heart to a virtual stop!

Were such reports actually true? Existing evidence is mixed, at best, but one fact *is* clear: there are techniques by which some individuals can alter their consciousness and enter a state in which their contact with and awareness of the external world is reduced (Shapiro, 1980).

Several techniques for producing these changes exist, but of these, meditation is by far the most popular.

Many different varieties of meditation exist. One of these, transcendental meditation (TM for short), has gained wide popularity. For example, in 1993, the *Toronto Star* reported that there were more than 500 members of the Toronto Association of Professionals Practicing the Transcendental Meditation Program. Practitioners of TM repeat a word or set of words, known as their mantra, over and over again, focusing their attention entirely on this activity and on the mantra rather than on the world around them. If they find their thoughts beginning to wander to something else, they attempt to bring them back to the mantra.

This requires considerable cognitive discipline, which must be acquired if meditation is to be successful.

Why should anyone bother to meditate? Research designed to investigate the physiological effects of meditation suggests that there are some benefits. During meditation, and especially during TM, significant and potentially beneficial changes do occur in basic biological processes. For example, in one well-known study on the effects of TM, Wallace and Benson (1972) found that during meditation people's oxygen consumption decreased, their heartbeat slowed, and they showed stronger alpha brain waves (see Figure 4.6). In other words, they experienced several signs of relaxation and reduced tension. While some researchers suggest that one can obtain similar effects simply by resting (Holmes, 1984), others contend that greater and more general shifts in physiological processes are produced by meditation (Benson & Friedman, 1985). Further, additional evidence indicates that after adopting TM, many people report

finding it easier to give up the use of various drugs, including marijuana, amphetamines, and barbiturates (Marzetta, Benson, & Wallace, 1972). So meditation does seem to have several potential benefits.

Can you enjoy these benefits yourself, without special training and without joining a religious group that makes meditation the center of its philosophy? Yes: TM is a relatively simple technique and requires only a few minutes each day. To put it into practice, follow these steps:

1. *Find a quiet, isolated location* TM doesn't require lots of time, but it *does* require you to focus your attention inward, away from the outside world. So the first requirement is that you find a quiet location where you can be alone for twenty minutes to half an hour.

2. *Choose an appropriate mantra* Meditation derives historically from Buddhism and Hinduism. In its original form, TM involved choosing a mantra from religious writings. This is not necessary; your

---

FIGURE 4.6   **Physiological Changes During Meditation**

During meditation, individuals experience changes in several basic physiological processes. Oxygen consumption decreases and the intensity of alpha waves increases.
(Source: Based on data from Wallace & Benson, 1972.)

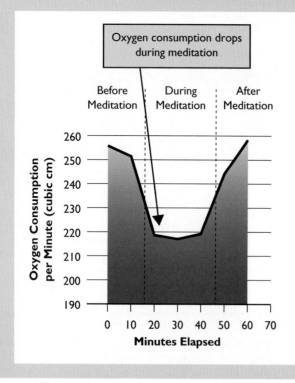
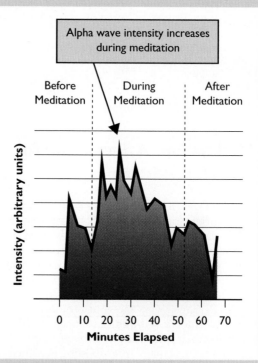

mantra can be almost any word or phrase on which you can concentrate.

3. *Meditate* Repeat your mantra silently, over and over again, and focus your attention only on this word. The hardest part of meditation is learning to keep your thoughts from slipping away from the mantra and back to the normal worries, cares, and concerns of everyday life. At first you may find this difficult, but if you practice and really try, you can readily acquire such discipline.

4. *Continue meditating for fifteen to twenty minutes* As you master the skill of focusing your attention on the mantra and screening out other distracting thoughts, gradually increase your period of medi-tation to fifteen or twenty minutes. (Initially, five to ten minutes will suffice.) If possible, meditate sev-eral times each week, in moderation, especially on days when you feel especially stressed.

What benefits can you expect to obtain from medi-tating? Research suggests that the benefits may include reduced feelings of tension, increased ability to express your feelings freely, and reduced levels of anx-iety (Greenberg, 1991). Of course, TM is not for every-one, and it does have detractors (Persinger, 1993). If you find it difficult or unappealing, you should con-sider other techniques for gaining these benefits. If you do find meditation to your liking, however, you may wish to make it part of your daily life.

BIOLOGICAL RHYTHMS: TIDES OF LIFE—AND CONSCIOUS EXPERIENCE

states of consciousness 144
biological rhythms 145
circadian rhythms 145
suprachiasmatic nucleus 146
seasonal affective disorder (SAD) 147

- Biological rhythms involve regular fluctuations in our bodily processes.
- We possess a biological clock that places many of our bodily processes on a twenty-four-hour cycle. Basic components of this clock involve the eyes and a portion of the hypothalamus.
- Large individual differences in circadian rhythms exist. Some people are "larks," most active early in the day, while others are "owls" and are most active later in the day.
- Disturbances in circadian rhythms can be produced by travel across time zones and by shift work. Knowledge of circadian rhythms suggests effective ways of countering such disturbances.

WAKING STATES OF CONSCIOUSNESS: EVERYDAY EXPERIENCE

automatic processing 151
controlled processing 151
daydreams (or fantasies) 152
hallucinations 152
self-consciousness 153
control theory of self-consciousness 153
choking under pressure 155

- We are capable of performing many activities without directing conscious attention to them. This automatic processing does not require much, if any, of our limited attention capacity. In contrast, controlled processing requires conscious attention and does use information-processing capacity.
- Daydreams and fantasies are a common experience for most people. These alterations in consciousness while we are awake may serve several useful functions for us.
- When we focus our attention on ourselves, we enter a state of self-consciousness. We then compare our current states with important goals and values. Heightened self-consciousness can be induced by many factors, including personal disposition and happy or sad moods. Self-consciousness can reduce performance on skilled tasks; however, it is also an important first step toward increased self-insight.

SLEEP: THE PAUSE THAT REFRESHES?

sleep 156
electroencephalogram (EEG) 156
alpha waves 157
delta waves 157
REM sleep 157
insomnia 160
somnambulism 161
night terrors 161
apnea 161
hypersomnias 161
narcolepsy 161
dreams 162
manifest content 164
latent content 164
dreams of absent-minded transgression 165

- An important method for studying sleep involves making EEGs, which are recordings of electrical activity in the brain during sleep. As we sleep, we pass through several different stages in which changes occur in brain activity and awareness of the external world.
- During REM sleep the EEG shows a pattern similar to that of waking, but body muscle activity is almost totally suppressed. Most dreams occur during REM sleep.
- Although people undergoing sleep deprivation report feeling tired, they can function quite well even after long periods without sleep. However, growing evidence indicates that sleep does serve important functions relating to restoration of bodily resources and to circadian rhythms that are a function of our biological evolution.
- Several different sleep disorders exist. Insomnia is difficulty in falling asleep; somnambulism is walking in one's sleep; narcolepsy is a tendency to fall suddenly into a deep sleep during waking activities.
- Dreams occur primarily during REM sleep. Everyone dreams, but not all dreams are remembered. Several different explanations for the occurrence of dreams have been offered. Freud believed that dreams reflect suppressed thoughts, impulses, and wishes. A physiological interpretation suggests that dreams reflect the brain's interpretation of random neural activity during sleep. A cognitive view suggests that dreams result from the fact that many systems of the brain are active during sleep while input from muscles and sensory systems is inhibited.
- Hypnosis involves a condition in which individuals are highly susceptible to suggestions from others.

HYPNOSIS: ALTERED STATE OF CONSCIOUSNESS OR SOCIAL ROLE PLAYING? hypnosis 167 neodissociation theory 168	• One theory of hypnosis, the social–cognitive view, suggests that the effects of hypnosis stem from the hypnotized person's expectations and his or her efforts to play the role of hypnotized subject. • Another view, the neodissociation theory, suggests that hypnotism involves splits in consciousness; hypnotized people are unaware of experiences during hypnosis and cannot exert normal control over their own behavior. • Cross-cultural research indicates that the content and meaning of dreams are strongly influenced by the dreamer's culture.
CONSCIOUSNESS-ALTERING DRUGS: WHAT THEY ARE AND WHAT THEY DO drugs 172 drug abuse 172 dependence 172 physiological dependence 172 psychological dependence 172 tolerance 172 cross-tolerance 172 depressants 174 barbiturates 174 stimulants 175 cocaine 175 amphetamines 175 crack 175 opiates 176 psychedelics 176 hallucinogens 176 LSD 177	• People often use drugs to alter their state of consciousness. Continued use of a given drug may result in growing tolerance to it and psychological or physiological dependence upon it. • There are several perspectives concerning the nature of drug abuse. The learning perspective suggests that drug abuse stems from the fact that people find the effects of consciousness-altering drugs rewarding, or that these drugs help to lessen stress, anxiety, and other negative feelings. • The social perspective suggests that people abuse drugs because of strong social pressures to do so. • The cognitive perspective proposes that drug abuse may be at least in part an automatic behavior triggered by the presence of external cues. • Depressants reduce both behavioral output and activity in the central nervous system. Important depressants include alcohol and barbiturates. • Stimulants produce feelings of energy and activation. Amphetamines and cocaine fall within this category. • Opiates produce lethargy and pronounced slowing of almost all bodily functions. They also produce pleasurable sensations for some people, and so are highly addicting. • Psychedelics such as marijuana alter sensory perception, while hallucinogens such as LSD produce vivid hallucinations and other bizarre perceptual shifts. • A specific dose of a given drug may produce very different effects on the same person at different times, depending on such factors as physical condition, expectations, and other drugs taken recently.

CRITICAL THINKING QUESTIONS

APPRAISAL	Today, most psychologists believe that states of consciousness can be studied in a scientific manner. Do you agree? Or do you feel that this is stretching the banner of science beyond the breaking point? Why do you hold the opinion that you do?
CONTROVERSY	Hypnotism is one of the most controversial topics of research in modern psychology. Many psychologists doubt that hypnosis represents an altered state of consciousness, while others believe that it does. What are your views on this topic?
MAKING PSYCHOLOGY PART OF YOUR LIFE	Now that you have some basic understanding of biological rhythms, states of consciousness, self-consciousness, and the nature of sleep, try to think of ways in which you can put this knowledge to practical use. For example, what steps might you take to schedule your day so as to take advantage of high points in your own circadian rhythm? How can you help ensure that you get a good night's sleep as often as possible? List at least three ways in which you can benefit from your increased understanding of various states of consciousness.

Learning
How Experience Changes Us

CLASSICAL CONDITIONING: LEARNING THAT SOME STIMULI SIGNAL OTHERS 186
Pavlov's Early Work on Classical Conditioning: Does This Ring a Bell?
Classical Conditioning: Some Basic Principles
Classical Conditioning: Exceptions to the Rules
Classical Conditioning: A Cognitive Perspective
Classical Conditioning: Turning Principles into Action

OPERANT CONDITIONING: LEARNING BASED ON CONSEQUENCES 200
The Nature of Operant Conditioning: Consequential Operations
Operant Conditioning: Some Basic Principles
Operant Conditioning: A Cognitive Perspective
Applying Operant Conditioning: Can We Make a Difference?

OBSERVATIONAL LEARNING: LEARNING FROM THE BEHAVIOR AND OUTCOMES OF OTHERS 217
Observational Learning: Some Basic Principles
Observational Learning and Aggression

SUMMARY AND REVIEW OF KEY POINTS 224

THE POINT OF IT ALL—CONDITIONED TASTE AVERSIONS: BREAKING ALL THE RULES? 195

KEY CONCEPT—THE DIFFERENCE BETWEEN NEGATIVE REINFORCEMENT AND PUNISHMENT 204

CANADIAN FOCUS—GAMBLING: THE PSYCHOLOGICAL DOWNSIDE 209

THE RESEARCH PROCESS—STIMULUS CONTROL IN ACTION: PROMOTING PAPER WASTE RECYCLING ON A UNIVERSITY CAMPUS 212

PERSPECTIVES ON DIVERSITY—LEARNING TO AVOID CULTURE SHOCK 221

MAKING PSYCHOLOGY PART OF YOUR LIFE—GETTING IN SHAPE: APPLYING PSYCHOLOGY TO GET FIT AND STAY FIT 222

BOUNCE BACK SAFELY

The Winnipeg Free Press: January 2, 1994

A feature in the Free Press—just after New Year's Day—provided some tips on how to "get back into the swing of fitness."

Most of us make resolutions around the turn of the year, but they don't last. When February rolls around—and sometimes sooner than that—we slip back to December of the previous year, or even earlier.

What does it take to produce a relatively permanent change in our behavior?

That is what researchers in learning study. You will survey their findings in Chapter 5 of this introduction to psychology.

THE LEARNING
PROCESS IS CRUCIAL
TO ALL ORGANISMS,
INCLUDING PEOPLE,
SINCE IT HELPS US
ADAPT TO CHANGING
CONDITIONS IN THE
WORLD AROUND US.

*H*ave you ever gotten ill after eating a favorite food—and wondered why, even years later, just the thought of it makes you feel sick? How do animals at Marineland in Niagara Falls, Ontario, learn to perform complex sequences of behaviors, while your dog does not seem to comprehend even simple commands like "sit"? Does watching violence on television cause children to perform violent acts? Why do gamblers continue to put money into slot machines, even after losing a bundle?

If you've wondered about issues like these, then you are already familiar with one of the most basic topics in psychology—*learning*. Indeed, the learning process is crucial to all organisms, not just people, as a mechanism for adapting to changing conditions in the world.

In this chapter we'll examine several basic principles that help to explain how many forms of behavior change as a result of experience. Psychologists refer to these effects on behavior as learning. Specifically, they define **learning** as *any relatively permanent change in behavior, or behavior potential, produced by experience*. Several aspects of this definition are especially worth noting. First, the term *learning* does not apply to temporary changes in behavior such as those stemming from fatigue, drugs, or illness. Second, it does not refer to changes resulting from maturation—the fact that you change in many ways as you grow and develop. Third, learning can result from *vicarious* as well as from direct experiences; in other words, you can change by observing events and behavior in your environment as well as by participating in them (Bandura, 1986). Finally, the changes produced by learning are not always positive in nature. As you well know, people are as likely to acquire bad habits as good ones.

There is no doubt that learning is a key process in human behavior. It plays an important role in virtually every activity we perform, from mastering complex skills to falling in love. Although the effects of learning are diverse, many psychologists believe that it occurs in several basic forms: *classical conditioning*, *operant conditioning*, and *observational learning*. We'll begin with *classical conditioning*, a form of learning in which two stimulus events become associated in such a way that the occurrence of one event reliably predicts the occurrence of the other. Classical conditioning is the basis for many learned fears and also helps explain how we acquire taste aversions. Next, we'll turn to *operant conditioning*, a form of learning in which organisms learn associations between behaviors and their consequences. Here, we'll see how psychologists have applied basic operant principles to promote certain behaviors, such as obeying signs at pedestrian crosswalks, conserving energy, and recycling. Finally, we'll explore *observational learning*, a process by which organisms learn through watching the behaviors—and the consequences of those behaviors—of others around them.

Classical Conditioning: Learning That Some Stimuli Signal Others

*C*onsider the following situation: During a particularly hectic term, you find yourself with a timetable that leaves absolutely no time for lunch. After a few days, you lose your ability to concentrate during your afternoon classes because all you can think about is food. A friend tells you about a vending area where she buys microwavable snacks, including popcorn (without coconut oil, of course). As it turns out, this solution works out well; you love popcorn, it is

Learning: *Any relatively permanent change in behavior (or behavior potential) resulting from experience.*

ready in only a few minutes, and you find that it is even possible to do other things while the popcorn is popping—like cram for tests—since a loud beep from the microwave signals when the popcorn is done. When you open the door of the microwave, the delightful aroma of freshly popped popcorn rushes out, causing you to salivate in anticipation of eating it. After several days, however, your mouth waters immediately after the beep, before you actually open the door to the microwave. Why should this occur? After all, at this point you can neither see nor smell the popcorn. The reason is actually fairly simple: Since the beep is always followed by the aroma and taste of the popcorn, the beep comes to serve as a signal. Just hearing the beep, you expect the smell and taste of the popcorn to follow, and you react accordingly (see Figure 5.1).

The situation just described is a common example of **classical conditioning,** the first type of learning we will consider. In classical conditioning, a physical event—termed a **stimulus**—that initially does not elicit a particular

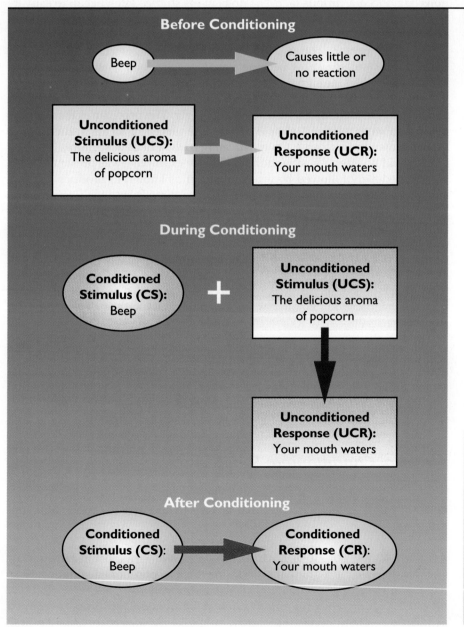

Before Conditioning

Beep → Causes little or no reaction

Unconditioned Stimulus (UCS): The delicious aroma of popcorn → **Unconditioned Response (UCR):** Your mouth waters

During Conditioning

Conditioned Stimulus (CS): Beep + **Unconditioned Stimulus (UCS):** The delicious aroma of popcorn → **Unconditioned Response (UCR):** Your mouth waters

After Conditioning

Conditioned Stimulus (CS): Beep → **Conditioned Response (CR):** Your mouth waters

FIGURE 5.1

Classical Conditioning: A Simple Example

At first, the sound of the microwave's beep may startle you and cause you to look toward its source, but it will probably not cause you to salivate. However, after the beep has been paired with the aroma and taste of the popcorn on several occasions, you may find that you salivate to the beep alone. This "mouth-watering" reaction is a result of classical conditioning.

Classical Conditioning: A basic form of learning in which one stimulus comes to serve as a signal for the occurrence of a second stimulus. During classical conditioning, organisms acquire information about the relationships between various stimuli, not simply associations between them.

Stimulus: A physical event capable of affecting behavior.

response gradually acquires the capacity to elicit that response as a result of repeated pairing with a stimulus that *can* elicit a reaction. Learning of this type is quite common and seems to play a role in such varied reactions as strong fears, taste aversions, some aspects of sexual behavior, racial or ethnic prejudice (Baron & Byrne, 1994), and even visual illusions (Allen & Siegel, 1993). Classical conditioning became the subject of careful study in the early twentieth century, when Ivan Pavlov, a Nobel Prize-winning physiologist from Russia, identified it as an important behavioral process.

Pavlov's Early Work on Classical Conditioning: *Does This Ring a Bell?*

In one of those strange twists of fate that seem so common in the history of science, Pavlov did not set out to investigate classical conditioning. Rather, his research focused on the process of digestion in dogs. During his investigations he noticed a curious fact: The dogs in his studies often began to salivate when they saw or smelled food but before they actually tasted it. Some even salivated at the sight of the pan where their food was kept, or at the sight or sound of the person who usually brought it. This suggested to Pavlov that these stimuli had somehow become signals for the food itself: The dogs had learned that when the signals were present, food would soon follow.

Pavlov quickly recognized the potential importance of this observation and shifted the focus of his research accordingly. The procedures that he now developed were relatively simple. Dogs were placed in an apparatus similar to that shown in Figure 5.2. On *conditioning trials*, a neutral stimulus that previously had no effect on salivation—a bell, for example—was presented. This was immediately followed by a second stimulus known to produce a strong effect on salivation: dried meat powder placed directly into the dog's mouth. The meat powder was termed the **unconditioned stimulus** (**UCS**), because its ability to produce salivation was automatic and did not depend on the dog's having learned the response. Similarly, the response of salivation to the meat powder was termed an **unconditioned response** (**UCR**); it too did not depend on previous learning. The bell was termed a **conditioned stimulus** (**CS**), because its ability to produce salivation depended on its being paired with the meat powder. Finally, salivation in response to the bell was termed a **conditioned response** (**CR**).

The basic question was whether the sound of the bell would elicit salivation in the dogs as a result of its repeated pairing with the meat powder. In other words, would the bell elicit a conditioned response when it was presented alone? The answer was clearly *yes*. After the bell had been paired repeatedly with the meat powder, the dogs salivated upon hearing it, even when the bell was not followed by the meat powder.

Classical Conditioning: *Some Basic Principles*

Let's turn now to the principles that govern the occurrence of classical conditioning.

ACQUISITION: *THE COURSE OF CLASSICAL CONDITIONING*   In most instances, classical conditioning is a gradual process in which a conditioned stimulus gradually acquires the capacity to elicit a conditioned response as a result of repeated pairing with an unconditioned stimulus. This process—termed **acquisition**—often occurs as shown in panel A of Figure 5.3. At first,

Unconditioned Stimulus (UCS): In classical conditioning, a stimulus that can evoke an unconditioned response the first time it is presented.

Unconditioned Response (UCR): In classical conditioning, the response evoked by an unconditioned stimulus.

Conditioned Stimulus (CS): In classical conditioning, the stimulus that is repeatedly paired with an unconditioned stimulus.

Conditioned Response (CR): In classical conditioning, the response to the conditioned stimulus.

Acquisition: The process by which a conditioned stimulus acquires the ability to elicit a conditioned response through repeated pairings of an unconditioned stimulus with the conditioned stimulus.

FIGURE 5.2

Pavlov's Apparatus for Studying Classical Conditioning

Pavlov used equipment similar to this in his early experiments on classical conditioning. He attached a tube to a dog's salivary gland, which had been surgically moved to the outside of the dog's cheek to allow easy collection of saliva. He then measured the number of drops of saliva that occurred naturally when a bell was sounded. Next, he measured the number of drops of saliva that occurred when a bell was sounded along with the presentation of food. Pavlov found that after repeated presentations of the bell followed by the food, the dog's saliva increased as soon as the bell was sounded, indicating that it had learned to associate the food and the bell.

conditioning proceeds quite rapidly, the speed increasing as the number of pairings between conditioned and unconditioned stimulus increases. However, there is a limit to this effect; after a number of pairings of CS and UCS, acquisition slows down and finally levels off.

Although psychologists initially believed that conditioning was determined primarily by the number of conditioned–unconditioned stimulus pairings, we now know that this process is affected by other factors. As shown in Figure 5.4, one factor that matters is *temporal arrangement* of the CS-UCS pairings (e.g., Davey & Biederman, 1991). Temporal means time-related, and refers to the extent to which a conditioned stimulus precedes or follows the presentation of an unconditioned stimulus. The first two temporal arrangements shown, **delayed conditioning** and **trace conditioning,** are examples of forward conditioning, since the presentation of the conditioned stimulus (light) always precedes the presentation of the unconditioned stimulus (shock). They differ, however, in that the CS and the UCS overlap to some degree in *delayed* conditioning, but not in *trace* conditioning. Two other temporal arrangements are **simultaneous conditioning,** in which the conditioned and unconditioned stimuli begin and end at the same time; and **backward conditioning,** in which the unconditioned stimulus precedes the conditioned stimulus.

Delayed conditioning is generally the most effective method for establishing a conditioned response. This is because the conditioned stimulus often plays an important role in predicting forthcoming presentations of the unconditioned stimulus (Lieberman, 1990). Consider a real-life situation. The sound of a siren warns us of the arrival of an ambulance or a fire truck. The purpose of the siren is to make sure that cars get out of the way of the approaching emergency vehicle. If we hear the siren just before these vehicles arrive, as in

Delayed Conditioning: A form of forward conditioning in which the onset of the conditioned stimulus begins while the unconditioned stimulus is still present.

Trace Conditioning: A form of forward conditioning in which the onset of the conditioned stimulus precedes and does not overlap with the onset of the unconditioned stimulus and the presentation of the CS.

Simultaneous Conditioning: A form of conditioning in which the conditioned stimulus and the unconditioned stimulus begin and end at the same time.

Backward Conditioning: A type of conditioning in which the presentation of the unconditioned stimulus precedes the presentation of the conditioned stimulus.

FIGURE 5.3

The Course of Conditioning

The strength of the conditioned response rapidly increases during *acquisition* (panel A). The process of *extinction* begins once the conditioned stimulus is no longer paired with the unconditioned stimulus (panel B). As shown in panels C and D, extinction can be disrupted through the processes of *spontaneous recovery* and *reconditioning*. Finally, although not shown in the figure, if no subsequent conditioned stimulus–unconditioned stimulus pairings occur, the conditioned response will decrease once again.

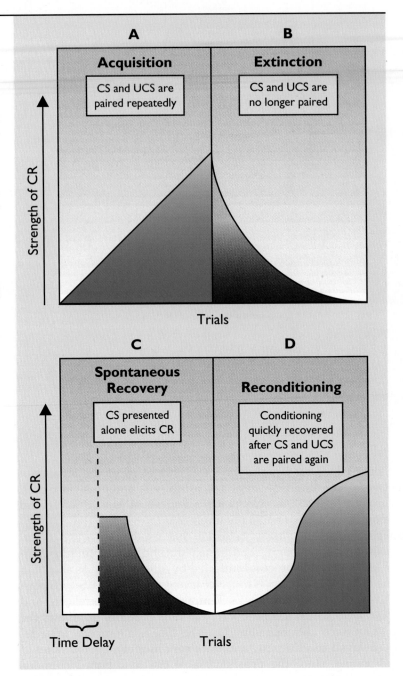

delayed conditioning, we quickly pull over. In contrast, if we do not hear the siren until the emergency vehicle has appeared (as in simultaneous conditioning), or until after it has passed (as in backward conditioning), we have no reason to respond, since the siren provides no additional information to help us predict that an emergency vehicle is coming.

Conditioning also depends on the *conditioned stimulus–unconditioned stimulus interval:* the time interval between presentation of the two stimuli. Extremely short intervals—less than 0.2 seconds—rarely produce conditioning. In animal research, the optimal CS-UCS interval usually seems to be between 0.2 and 2 seconds; intervals longer than that make it difficult for animals to recognize the conditioned stimulus as a signal for some future event (Gordon, 1989; Wall et al., 1990).

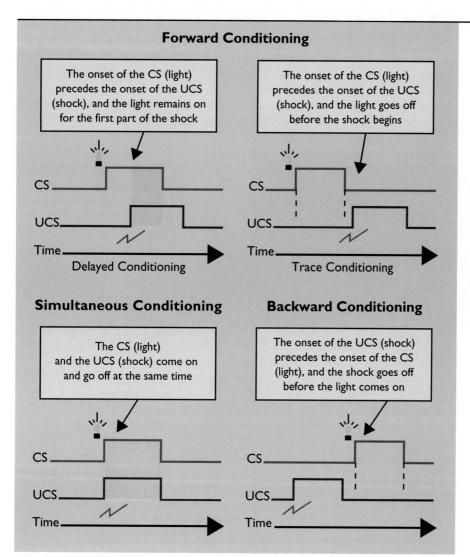

Forward Conditioning

The onset of the CS (light) precedes the onset of the UCS (shock), and the light remains on for the first part of the shock

CS

UCS

Time

Delayed Conditioning

The onset of the CS (light) precedes the onset of the UCS (shock), and the light goes off before the shock begins

CS

UCS

Time

Trace Conditioning

Simultaneous Conditioning

The CS (light) and the UCS (shock) come on and go off at the same time

CS

UCS

Time

Backward Conditioning

The onset of the UCS (shock) precedes the onset of the CS (light), and the shock goes off before the light comes on

CS

UCS

Time

FIGURE 5.4

Temporal Arrangement of the CS and UCS Affects the Acquisition of a Conditioned Response

Four CS-UCS temporal arrangements commonly used in classical conditioning procedures are shown. *Temporal* means time-related: the extent to which a conditioned stimulus precedes or follows the presentation of an unconditioned stimulus. *Delayed conditioning* generally produces the most rapid learning. *Simultaneous conditioning* and *backward conditioning* are usually the least effective procedures.

In general, conditioning is faster when the *intensity* of either the conditioned or the unconditioned stimulus increases. However, it is not necessarily the absolute intensity of stimuli that is most important to the conditioning process, but rather the intensity relative to other background stimuli. A classic study done by Kamin at McMaster University in 1965 helps illustrate this point. In this study, the conditioned stimulus was not a discrete stimulus; instead, it was a contrast created by a reduction in the usual level of background noise. All subjects in the study (laboratory rats) were first exposed to "white noise" at a level of 80 decibels. Then the subjects were divided into groups that received varying reductions in this noise level as the conditioned stimulus. The reduction in noise was always followed by an unconditioned stimulus—an electrical shock. The rats receiving the largest reduction in noise level as a conditioned stimulus—which, interestingly, was also the least intense level of noise in absolute terms—demonstrated the greatest evidence of conditioning. The results of this study show that conditioning is more likely when conditioned stimuli stand out relative to other background stimuli.

Finally, *familiarity* can greatly affect conditioning. In a modern laboratory, the stimuli selected for study may be two drugs—for example, one drug (pentobarbital) as the UCS, and another drug (amphetamine) as the CS, with heart rate as the response (Revusky & Reilly, 1990). In nature, however, many of the potential conditioned stimuli are ones with which we are already familiar. Our day-to-day experiences often teach us that certain conditioned stimuli, such as the background noise usually present in an office setting, or the odors ordinarily present in our homes, do not predict anything unusual. In other words, once we learn that these stimuli are largely irrelevant, future conditioning of them is more difficult (Baker & Mackintosh, 1977).

Extinction: Once conditioning is acquired, how do we get rid of it? You are one of several executive assistants in the head office of a large supermarket chain. You and your co-workers have been working night and day to prepare a proposal crucial to the company's survival, and things are not going well. Over the past week, the president of the company has chewed you out at least a dozen times. Now, whenever you hear the unmistakable sound of his approaching footsteps, your heart starts racing and your mouth gets dry, even though he has not yet reached your office. Fortunately, this story has a happy ending—the company's directors are impressed with the proposal, and your boss is no longer angry when he enters your office. Will you continue to react strongly to his footsteps? Perhaps you will at first, but gradually his footsteps will cease to elicit the original conditioned response from you. The eventual decline and disappearance of a conditioned response in the absence of an *un*conditioned stimulus is known as **extinction** (refer to Figure 5.3). Extinction plays an important role, for if it did not occur, we would soon become walking collections of useless—but persistent—conditioned responses.

The course of extinction, however, is not always entirely smooth. To see why, let's consider the behavior of one of Pavlov's dogs. After many presentations of a bell (conditioned stimulus) in the absence of meat powder (unconditioned stimulus), the dog no longer salivates in response to the bell. In other words, extinction has occurred. But after the conditioned response of salivation has been extinguished, if the conditioned stimulus (the bell) and the unconditioned stimulus (the meat powder) are again paired, salivation will return very quickly—a process termed **reconditioning**.

Or suppose that after extinction, the experiment is interrupted: Pavlov is caught up in another project that keeps him away from his laboratory, and the dog, for several weeks. Now will the sound of the bell, the conditioned stimulus, elicit salivation? The answer is yes, but the reaction will be in a weakened form. The reappearance of the reaction after a time interval is referred to as **spontaneous recovery.** If extinction is then allowed to continue—that is, if the sound of the bell is presented many times in the absence of meat powder—salivation to the sound of the bell will eventually disappear.

Generalization and discrimination: Responding to similarities and differences Suppose that because of several painful experiences, a child has acquired a strong conditioned fear of hornets: Whenever she sees one or hears one buzzing, she shows strong emotional reactions and runs away. Will she also experience similar reactions to other flying insects, such as flies? She almost certainly will, because of a process called **stimulus generalization,** the tendency of stimuli similar to a conditioned stimulus to elicit similar conditioned responses (Honig & Urcuioli, 1981; Pearce, 1986). As you can readily see, stimulus generalization often serves a useful function. In this example, it may indeed save the girl from additional stings. The red lights that we encounter at certain intersections while driving also illustrate the important function performed by stimulus generalization: Even though these signals often vary in height, brightness or shape, or all of the above, we learn to stop in response to all of them, and it's a good thing we do.

Extinction: The process through which a conditioned stimulus gradually loses the ability to evoke conditioned responses when it is no longer followed by the unconditioned stimulus.

Reconditioning: The rapid recovery of a conditioned response to a CS-UCS pairing following extinction.

Spontaneous Recovery: Following extinction, return of a conditioned response upon reinstatement of CS-UCS pairings.

Stimulus Generalization: The tendency of stimuli similar to a conditioned stimulus to evoke conditioned responses.

Many other species turn stimulus generalization to their advantage. For example, some totally harmless insects resemble more dangerous species in coloring and in this way ward off would-be predators. Similarly, some harmless frogs show markings highly similar to those of poisonous species, thus increasing their chances of survival.

Although stimulus generalization can serve an important adaptive function, it is not always beneficial and in some cases can be dangerous. For example, because of many pleasant experiences with her parents and other adult relatives, a young child may become trusting of all adults through the process of stimulus generalization. Unfortunately, generalization in this instance will not be beneficial if it extends to certain strangers. You can understand why stimulus generalization can be maladaptive—even deadly. Fortunately, most of us learn to avoid potential problems like these through **stimulus discrimination**—the process of learning to respond to certain stimuli but not to others. You have probably encountered many instances of stimulus discrimination. Perhaps this incident will serve as an example. About a year ago, the driver for a local pizza palace was badly bitten by a dog. Until that incident, he had no fear of dogs. Because he was so badly frightened by the attack, there was concern that his fear would generalize to dogs of all breeds—perhaps even to his own dog. Fortunately, because of stimulus discrimination, this didn't happen. He becomes tense only when he encounters the breed of dog that bit him.

Classical Conditioning: Exceptions to the Rules

When psychologists began the systematic study of learning, around the turn of the century, they noticed that some species could master certain tasks more quickly than others. Such findings sparked little interest, though, because early researchers saw their task as to establish general principles of learning—principles that applied equally well to all organisms and to all stimuli. For several decades it was widely assumed that such universal principles existed. Beginning in the 1960s, however, some puzzling findings began to accumulate, which suggested that not all organisms learn all responses or all associations between stimuli with equal ease.

The most dramatic evidence pointing to this conclusion was reported by Garcia and his colleagues (Garcia, Hankins, & Rusiniak, 1974; Braverman & Bronstein, 1985). In perhaps the most famous of these studies, Garcia and Koelling (1966) allowed two groups of rats to drink from a device that emitted a bright flashing light and a loud clicking noise (conditioned stimuli) whenever the rats licked the saccharin-flavored water. While both groups were drinking, one group was exposed to X-rays that later made them sick (an unconditioned stimulus); the other received painful shocks to their feet (an unconditioned stimulus). Traditional principles of classical conditioning suggest that *both* groups of rats should have learned to avoid all three stimuli—the flavored water, the bright light, and the clicking noise. After all, for both groups, these stimuli were followed by a strong unconditioned stimulus (either X-rays or a painful shock). But this was not what Garcia and Koelling found. Rats exposed to the pain learned to avoid the light and noise, but not the flavored water; rats made to feel ill learned to avoid the flavored water, but not the light or noise (see Figure 5.5). In short, it seems that rats—and other organisms—are predisposed to associate nausea and dizziness with something they've consumed (the flavored water), and to associate pain with something they've seen or heard (the bright light and clicking noise). Similar findings from many different studies (e.g., Braverman & Bronstein, 1985) suggest that acquisition of a

Stimulus Discrimination: The process by which organisms learn to respond to certain stimuli but not to others.

FIGURE 5.5

Biological Constraints and Characteristics of the CS and UCS Affect the Acquisition of a Conditioned Response

Rats quickly acquired an aversion to a flavored water when it was followed by X-rays that made them ill, but they did *not* readily acquire an aversion to the flavored water when it was followed by an electric shock. In contrast, rats learned to avoid a light-noise combination when it was paired with shock, but *not* when it was followed by X-rays. These findings indicate that classical conditioning cannot be established with equal ease for all stimuli and for all organisms. (Source: Based on data from Garcia & Koelling, 1966.)

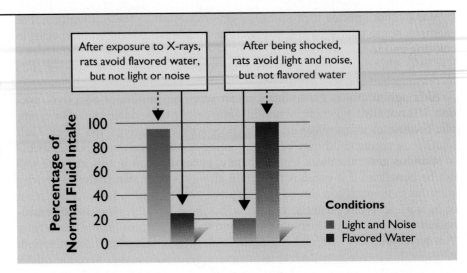

Biological Constraints on Learning: Tendencies of some species to acquire some forms of conditioning less readily than other species do.

conditioned response does *not* occur with equal ease for different stimuli. For instance, in 1990, Holder and his colleagues at Memorial University found that taste and odor were easier to condition than taste and noise.

Another intriguing outcome that emerged from Garcia and Koelling's classic study is also noteworthy: Although the rats who received the X-rays did not get sick immediately, they still acquired an aversion to the flavored water. This finding contradicted the widely held assumption that classical conditioning can occur only if the unconditioned stimulus follows the conditioned stimulus within a very short interval. In the decades since this discovery, much information about conditioned taste aversion has been collected (e.g., Lett, 1992). There are now studies of flavor neophobia—that is, the fear of new tastes. At the University of British Columbia in 1993, Wong and McBride found that when they offered their gerbils and hamsters their usual peanuts, but with the flavor changed to sweet, salty, sour, or bitter, there was a neophobic response. For forty undergraduates at Erindale College, what most affected their willingness to eat "dangerous" food was the taste of the novel food. If the taste was O.K., they were less likely to become neophobic than if it was bad (Pliner et al., 1993). At McMaster in 1990, Galef and his colleagues contributed a different experiment. Observer rats watched a conditioned taste aversion response being established in demonstrator rats; the demonstrator rats did not learn conditioned taste aversion simply by observing that others were eating a particular food and getting sick. However, the researchers did find that conditioned aversions that animals had already acquired were reduced when those animals watched other animals eat the food for which an aversion had been established. In other laboratories, there have been studies of the brain changes that occur in conditioned taste aversion; dopamine receptors may be involved (Hoffman & Beninger, 1988).

Further research has also shown that in regard to conditioning, important differences exist not only among stimuli, but also among species. Because of these **biological constraints on learning,** types of conditioning readily accomplished by some species are only slowly acquired by others. And often, the types of conditioning most readily accomplished by a particular species are the very ones it needs to survive in its normal habitat (Shettleworth, 1993). For example, rats eat a varied diet and are most active at night. Thus, it is especially useful for them to be able to associate specific tastes with later illness, since in many cases they can't see the foods they eat. In contrast, birds depend heavily on vision for finding food. For a bird it is more useful to be able to form associations between visual cues and later illness (Wilcoxon, Dragoin, & Kral, 1971).

One of the clearest demonstrations of an exception to the rules of traditional classical conditioning, however, involves what is called conditioned taste aversion. We'll explore this interesting aspect of learning in **The Point of It All**.

Classical Conditioning: *A Cognitive Perspective*

During his early conditioning experiments, Pavlov (1927) observed a curious thing. A dog was conditioned to the ticking of a metronome, which had been previously paired with the presentation of food. When the metronome was turned off, the dog sat in front of the machine and proceeded to whine and beg. Why? If conditioning involves only the development of an association between conditioned and unconditioned stimuli, the dog should have responded only when the conditioned stimulus was presented. The fact that the dog appeared to beg for the ticking sound suggested that classical conditioning involves more than just association. In fact, this and several related findings point to the following conclusion: Regular pairing of a conditioned stimulus with an unconditioned stimulus provides subjects with valuable predictive information— when a conditioned stimulus is presented, an unconditioned stimulus will shortly follow. Thus, as conditioning proceeds, subjects acquire an *expectation* that the conditioned stimulus will be followed by the unconditioned stimulus.

That cognitive processes involving expectation play a role in classical conditioning is supported by several types of evidence (Rescorla & Wagner, 1972). First, conditioning fails to occur when unconditioned and conditioned stimuli are paired at some times but not at others—that is, in a random manner. With random pairing, subjects cannot acquire any firm expectation that an unconditioned stimulus will indeed follow presentation of a conditioned stimulus. This means that for conditioning to occur, the CS–UCS pairing must be reliable.

THE POINT OF IT ALL

Conditioned Taste Aversions: Breaking All the Rules?

Y ou are at a "pot luck supper," and to your delight someone has brought lasagna—a favorite dish that you haven't tasted in ages. The first few bites are delicious, but as the meal progresses you begin to feel dreadful. For the next two days you have a fever and can't keep anything down. Months later, you still experience the same awful feelings whenever you see, smell, or even think about lasagna. In other words, you have developed what is termed a **conditioned taste aversion** to what was once your favorite meal.

Conditioned Taste Aversion: A type of conditioning in which the UCS (usually internal cues associated with nausea or vomiting) occurs several hours after the CS (often a novel food), leading to a strong CS–UCS association in a single trial.

LEARNED TASTE AVERSIONS: PUTTING CLASSICAL CONDITIONING TO WORK

Classical conditioning has been used to solve many practical problems, including saving ranchers' livestock from predators.

For animals in their natural environment, conditioned taste aversions are important for survival because they inhibit the repeated ingestion of dangerous and toxic substances. Surveys show that food or beverage aversions are also quite common among humans, with most people reporting at least one such learned aversion (Logue, Ophir, & Strauss, 1981; Logue, Logue, & Strauss 1983). Although many conditioned taste aversions are the result of overindulgence, some are established when we eat just before the onset of an illness like the flu (Garb & Stunkard, 1974). Interestingly, many people report that even when they are convinced that a particular food or beverage was not the cause of the illness that followed, they still continue to experience a taste aversion to that substance. This evidence suggests that conditioned food aversions are unusually strong and can occur despite our thoughts about the cause of our illness (Seligman & Hager, 1972).

Research also shows that the way in which these powerful associations are established differs from most instances of classical conditioning in several important respects. First, a conditioned taste aversion can usually be established with a single CS-UCS pairing—that is, with *one-trial learning*; in contrast, many pairings are involved in most Pavlovian conditioning. Second, conditioned taste aversions have been reported in circumstances in which the conditioned stimulus was presented hours before the unconditioned stimulus occurred; in contrast, most instances of conditioning require a CS-UCS interval of no more than a few seconds. Finally, conditioned taste aversions are extremely resistant to extinction. Indeed, some evidence suggests that everyday taste aversions may last a lifetime (Garb & Stunkard, 1974; Logue, 1979), although previous exposure to the conditioned stimulus may prevent the establishment of a taste aversion (Droungas & LoLordo, 1991).

Unfortunately, conditioned taste aversions can create serious problems for some individuals. For example, radiation and chemotherapy used in the treatment of cancer often cause nausea or vomiting as a side effect (Burish & Carey, 1986). As a result, cancer patients receiving these therapies may acquire taste aversions to foods they ingested before therapy sessions. Several studies have in fact shown that conditioned taste aversions are common among patients receiving chemotherapy (Bernstein, 1978; Challis & Stam, 1972). These effects help explain the lack of appetite often reported by chemotherapy patients.

Radiation and chemotherapy patients can take a number of steps to reduce the likelihood of developing a conditioned taste aversion. First, as we have seen, the strength of a conditioned response depends partly on the temporal relationship between the conditioned stimulus and the unconditioned stimulus. Patients receiving chemotherapy should therefore arrange their meal schedules to decrease the chances of establishing an association between ingestion of the food and illness; the interval between their meals and chemotherapy should be as long as possible. Second, since in most instances of classical conditioning, the strength of a conditioned response is directly related to novelty, patients should also eat familiar foods, avoiding new or unusual foods before therapy. Because familiar foods have already been associated with feeling good, rather than feeling ill, it is less likely that cancer patients will acquire an aversion for these foods. Finally, since the strength of a conditioned response is related to the intensity of the conditioned stimulus, patients should eat bland foods and avoid strongly flavored foods. By following these steps, patients receiving radiation or chemotherapy can minimize the possibility of developing a conditioned taste aversion.

Our understanding of acquired taste aversions has also been used to help Western ranchers in their efforts to prevent the loss of sheep and cattle to predators such as wolves and coyotes (Garcia, Rusiniak & Brett, 1977; Gustavson et al., 1974). By establishing in predators a conditioned taste aversion for cattle and sheep, ranchers have been able to save their livestock without actually having to kill these animals. To create the taste aversion, ranchers lace small amounts of mutton or beef with lithium chloride, a substance that causes dizziness and nausea, but not death, in the predators. The predators eat the bait, become sick several hours later, and as a result, learn to avoid sheep or cattle in the future.

The point of it all, then, is that a solid understanding of processes like learned taste aversion—a clear exception to the traditional rules of classical conditioning—can be applied toward solving important real-life problems.

Second, conditioning to one stimulus may be prevented by previous conditioning to another stimulus. This phenomenon is known as blocking. For example, suppose that a dog is initially conditioned to a tone. After repeated pairings with presentation of meat powder, the tone becomes a conditioned stimulus, capable of causing the dog to salivate. Then a second stimulus, a light, is added to the situation. It too occurs just before the presentation of food. If classical conditioning occurs in an automatic manner, simply as a result of repeated pairings of a conditioned stimulus with an unconditioned stimulus, then the light too should become a conditioned stimulus: It should elicit salivation when presented alone. In fact, this does not happen. Why not? Again, an explanation in terms of expectancies is helpful. Since the meat powder is already predicted by the tone, the light provides no new information. Since it is of little predictive value to the subjects, it fails to become a conditioned stimulus.

These findings suggest that classical conditioning involves much more than the formation of simple associations between specific stimuli. Indeed, modern views of classical conditioning conceive of it as a complex process in which organisms form rich representations of the relationships among a variety of factors—including many aspects of the physical setting or context in which the conditioned and unconditioned stimuli are presented (Rescorla, 1988; Swartzentruber, 1991). Pavlovian conditioning is "the learning of relations among events so as to allow the organism to represent its environment" (Furedy, 1992).

This cognitive perspective on classical conditioning has also been extended to several of its basic aspects. For example, one theory of stimulus generalization suggests that memory and other cognitive processes play an important role (Pearce, 1986; Shettleworth, 1993). During conditioning, organisms form a representation in memory of the stimuli that preceded the unconditioned stimulus. When they then encounter different stimuli at later times, they compare these with the information stored in memory. The greater the similarity between current stimuli and such memory representations, the stronger the response evoked. In short, both memory and active comparison processes play a role in what might at first seem to be an automatic function. For Shettleworth (1993) there are two basic research questions here. The first has to do with whether humans and nonhumans process information in the same ways. The second has to do with the differences among nonhuman species— for example, the differences among species of birds in their songs and in their memories for where they have stored their food (Brodbeck et al., 1992).

The suggestion that cognitive processes are important in human classical conditioning is not surprising. After all, we all have expectations about what events go together or are likely to follow others. But it may surprise you to learn that processes like memory and active comparison also occur in animals. Although this possibility would have been considered absurd even as recently as the 1970s, growing evidence suggests that animals, like humans, form mental representations of events in the world around them (Cook, 1993; Wasserman, 1993). We'll consider cognitive processes in greater detail in Chapter 7.

Research in Canada

Shepard Siegel
McMaster University

Classical Conditioning: *Turning Principles into Action*

Much of this chapter has focused on basic principles of classical conditioning, many of them derived from laboratory research involving animals. However, knowledge of these principles has been put to many practical uses to help people.

One of the earliest applications was reported in a study, now a classic in psychology, conducted by John B. Watson and his assistant, Rosalie Raynor, in 1920. Watson and Raynor (1920) demonstrated that human beings can sometimes acquire strong fears—termed **phobias**—through classical conditioning. In their study, an eleven-month-old child named Albert was shown a white laboratory rat. His initial reactions to the rat were positive: He smiled and attempted to play with it. Just as he reached out for the rat, though, an iron bar was struck to make a loud noise right behind his ear. Albert jumped, obviously very upset by the startling noise. After several more pairings of the rat (conditioned stimulus) and the loud noise (unconditioned stimulus), Albert cried loudly and tried to crawl away whenever he saw the rat—even when it was not accompanied by the noise.

Knowledge of how phobias like little Albert's occur has led to the development of several effective procedures for reducing these reactions (Davey, 1992; Rachman, 1990). In one procedure, termed emotional **flooding,** a person suffering from a specific fear may be forced to confront the fear-eliciting stimulus directly, without an avenue of escape (e.g., Gordon, 1989; Morganstern, 1973). For example, a therapist may persuade a person who has an irrational fear of heights to walk onto a high bridge for a while—under careful supervision, of course. When no harm results from this intense experience, the person may become less fearful of heights. Contrary evidence was found in 1993 at the University of Alberta by Treit and his colleagues—flooding did not help alleviate rats' fear of an elevated maze. In fact, the subjects avoided the feared open arms of the maze even more. In cases where fear-provoking thoughts are too painful to deal with directly, *systematic desensitization*—a progressive technique designed to replace anxiety with a relaxation response—has been effective (Wolpe, 1958; 1969). A person undergoing this procedure is asked to describe fearful situations. Then, starting with the least anxiety-producing situation, the person alternately visualizes situations and relaxes. Gradually, the individual learns to relax while imagining situations that are increasingly more threatening. Chapter 15 will discuss these procedures in more detail.

Phobias: Intense, irrational fears of objects or events.

Flooding: Procedure for eliminating conditioned fears based on principles of classical conditioning. During flooding an individual is exposed to fear-inducing objects or events. Since no unconditioned stimulus then follows, extinction of fears eventually takes place.

CLASSICAL CONDITIONING: A HUMAN EXAMPLE

John B. Watson and his graduate assistant Rosalie Raynor used classical conditioning to teach "Little Albert" to fear various small, furry objects. What ethical problems were involved in these studies?

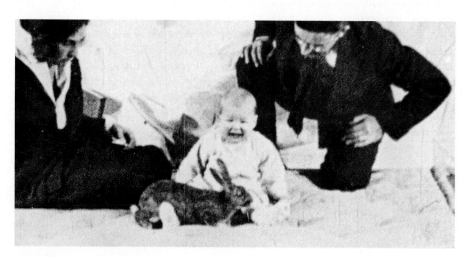

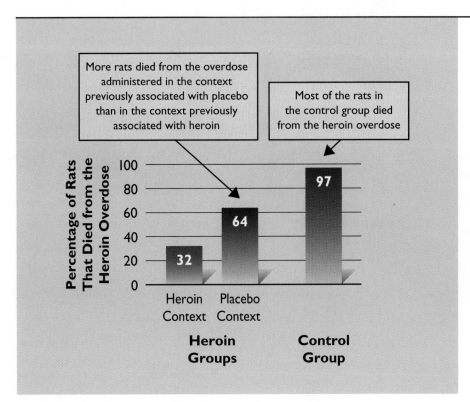

FIGURE 5.6

More rats died from the overdose administered in the context previously associated with placebo than in the context previously associated with heroin

Most of the rats in the control group died from the heroin overdose

Classical Conditioning Can Help Explain Deaths Following Drug Overdose

The results of this study lead to two conclusions: (1) Control group subjects—those with no previous experience with heroin—were more likely to die after receiving a potentially lethal dose of heroin than subjects with previous drug experience. (2) Subjects who received the potentially lethal dose of heroin in an environment previously associated with drug injections were more likely to survive than those who received the same injection in an environment not previously associated with the drug. (Source: Based on data from Siegel, Hinson, Krank, & McCully, 1982.)

Knowledge of conditioning processes gained from basic research has also led to another contemporary application. Research evidence suggests that some instances of drug overdose can be explained, at least in part, by principles of classical conditioning. For example, when a user does drugs in a particular place (such as in a particular room), the stimuli in that place become conditioned stimuli. When the addict is in that environment, a conditioned physiological response occurs. For certain drugs, that response is quite different from the unconditioned response of the body to the injection of the drug itself. With morphine, for example, although the unconditioned response is a *decreased* sensitivity to pain, the conditioned response to a conditioned stimulus associated with the drug is *increased* sensitivity to pain (Siegel, 1975). Apparently, these conditioned stimuli signal the body to prepare for morphine by suppressing the response to it.

In a related study (Siegel et al., 1982), rats received, every other day in alternating environments, heroin on one day and placebo on another. Then all subjects received a single high—potentially fatal—dose of heroin. Some animals received the high dose in the environment where they had been injected with heroin, and the others received it in the environment where they had been injected with the placebo. Mortality was highest among those receiving the injection in the environment previously associated with the placebo—*not* heroin. Cues in the heroin environment served as conditioned stimuli and prepared the rats' bodies to counteract the effects of the potentially lethal injection; the placebo environment did not provide such cues. Indeed, human drug users

KEY POINTS

- Modern views of classical conditioning emphasize the important role of cognitive processes.

- In blocking, conditioning to one stimulus is prevented by previous conditioning to another stimulus.

- Basic principles of classical conditioning can be used to increase our understanding of phobias and drug overdoses.

- In flooding, a person is forced to experience the intense emotion that occurs in the presence of the fearful stimulus—without the possibility of escape.

- Cases in which fearful thoughts are too painful to deal with directly are treated by systematic desensitization—a progressive technique designed to replace anxiety with a relaxation response.

who have nearly died following drug use commonly report that the environment in which they took the drug was not usual (Siegel, 1984). These environmental differences may be quite subtle—a fact that emphasizes the powerful effects produced by conditioning.

Siegel's findings may have implications for drug treatment. Recent evidence has shown that the environments to which former drug users return often contain cues that may produce drug-related conditioned responses, such as withdrawal symptoms and drug cravings (Krank & Perkins, 1993; Ehrman et al., 1992). Knowledge of classical conditioning processes may help health professionals arrange environments that minimize relapse among former drug users, by eliminating the cues that trigger these classically conditioned responses.

Operant Conditioning: Learning Based on Consequences

*I*t was the first day of school, and Jeff was already off to a bad start. Barely there an hour, he had already landed himself in the principal's office. Before

**B.F. Skinner
(1904–1990)**

Skinner was a professor emeritus at Harvard University and a leader in the field of *behaviorism*. His work focused on explaining the causes of behavior by looking at events in the environment (stimuli) and the organism's response.

Albert Bandura

Bandura has focused on observational learning and the role of thought in establishing and maintaining behavior. Some of his most notable research includes studies of the ways in which children learn to be aggressive.

starting the first grade, Jeff had always gotten his way. Although they knew it was wrong, his parents eventually gave in to his demands because of the tantrums Jeff was sure to throw if they did not. Jeff's behavior had become unbearable—even in school.

Much to Jeff's surprise, however, his teacher did not react to his misbehaviors as he expected. In fact, each time Jeff misbehaved, he received "time out"—a few minutes in a quiet corner of the room, away from his classmates. At first Jeff tried his usual routine: He kicked and screamed all the way to the corner. After all, this strategy always worked at home. The teacher's reaction to these outbursts, however, remained consistent, despite the fact that Jeff's tantrums initially worsened. As the weeks went by, Jeff's outbursts seemed to lose some of their steam. Jeff also began to notice that on days when he was well behaved, the teacher smiled at him more and rewarded his good behavior with sports cards or status jobs, like being in charge of the classroom VCR. After just a few weeks, Jeff's outbursts disappeared completely.

What happened here? The answer is probably obvious: Jeff's behaviors changed consistent with the nature of the consequences they produced. Behaviors that produced positive consequences increased in frequency, while those that were ignored (or resulted in time out) decreased. In short, the teacher had used the principles of *operant* (or *instrumental*) *conditioning* to change Jeff's behavior.

The Nature of Operant Conditioning:
Consequential Operations

In situations involving instrumental or **operant conditioning**, the probability that a given response will occur changes depending on the consequences that follow it. Psychologists generally agree that these probabilities are determined through four basic procedures, two of which strengthen or increase the rate of behavior and two of which weaken or decrease the rate of behavior. Procedures that *strengthen* behavior are termed *reinforcement*, while those that *suppress* behavior are termed *punishment*.

REINFORCEMENTS   There are two types of **reinforcement**: positive reinforcement and negative reinforcement. *Positive* reinforcement is the impact of **positive reinforcers**, which are stimulus events or consequences that strengthen the responses that precede them. In other words, if the consequence of some action increases the probability that the action will occur again, that consequence is functioning as a positive reinforcer. Some positive reinforcers seem to exert these effects because they are related to basic biological needs. Such *primary reinforcers* include food when we are hungry, water when we are thirsty, and sexual pleasure. Other consequences acquire their capacity to act as positive reinforcers through association with primary reinforcers. Among such *conditioned reinforcers* are money, status, grades, trophies, and praise from others. At Lakehead University in 1992, Hume and Crossman used musical reinforcement to increase productive practice behaviors in competitive swimmers at the Thunderbolt Swim Club.

In this connection, several Canadian researchers (Nakajima, 1986; Beninger, 1992) have reported a link between dopamine receptors and the rewarding effects of food, water, and saccharin.

Preferred activities can also be used to reinforce behavior. This is the **Premack principle**. If you recall hearing, "You must clean your room before you can watch TV" when you were growing up, then you're already familiar with this principle. Jeff's teacher could use the Premack principle to reinforce a *less* preferred behavior—like doing school work or behaving appropriately—with a *more* preferred activity, such as going out for recess. As you can guess, the Premack principle is a powerful tool for changing behavior.

Please note that a stimulus event that functions as a positive reinforcer at one time (or in one context) may have a different effect at another time or in another place. For example, food may serve as a positive reinforcer when you are hungry, but not when you are ill or just after you finish a large meal. Also, at least where people are concerned, many individual differences exist. Clearly, a stimulus that functions as a positive reinforcer for one person may fail to operate in a similar manner for another person. We will return to this important point later.

Negative reinforcement is the impact of **negative reinforcers**—aversive stimulus events that strengthen behaviors that either terminate or postpone those events. Thus, when we take an action that allows us to escape from a negative reinforcer that is already present, or to avoid the threatened application of one, our tendency to take that action in the future increases. Some negative reinforcers, such as intense heat, extreme cold, or electric shock, exert their effects the first time they are encountered, while others acquire their impact through repeated association.

There are many examples of negative reinforcement in our everyday lives. For example, imagine the following scene. On a particularly cold and dark winter morning, you're sleeping soundly in a warm, comfortable bed. Suddenly, the "alarm from hell" begins to wail from across the room. Although getting out of your cozy bed is the last thing on your mind, you

USING REINFORCEMENT IN THE BOARDROOM

Many businesses offer employee rewards for outstanding performance. According to the principles of operant conditioning, if these rewards increase employee efforts to improve performance, they are functioning as positive reinforcers. What positive reinforcers do you respond to?

Operant Conditioning: A process through which organisms learn to repeat behaviors that yield positive outcomes or permit them to avoid or escape from negative outcomes.

Reinforcement: The application or removal of a stimulus so as to increase the strength of a behavior.

Positive Reinforcers: Stimuli that strengthen responses that precede them.

Premack Principle: The principle that a more preferred activity can be used to reinforce a less preferred activity.

Negative Reinforcers: Stimuli that strengthen responses that permit an organism to avoid or escape from their presence.

find the noise intolerable. What do you do? If you get up to turn off the alarm—or, on subsequent mornings, get up early enough to avoid hearing the sound of the alarm altogether—your behavior has been *negatively* reinforced. In other words, your tendency to perform actions that allow you to escape from or avoid the sound of the alarm clock has increased.

Another everyday example of negative reinforcement occurs when parents give in to their children's tantrums—especially in public places, such as restaurants and shopping centers. Over time, the parents' tendency to give in may increase, because doing so stops the screaming.

To repeat, then, both positive and negative reinforcement are procedures that strengthen or increase behavior. Positive reinforcers are stimulus events that strengthen responses that precede them, while negative reinforcers are aversive stimulus events that strengthen responses that lead to their termination or avoidance. The Key Concept illustration on page 204 summarizes the difference between negative reinforcement and punishment.

THE PREMACK PRINCIPLE: A POWERFUL BEHAVIOR CHANGE TECHNIQUE

The Premack principle is a powerful tool to encourage desired behaviors—including eating one's veggies!

PUNISHMENT AND OMISSION TRAINING   Sometimes behaviors are followed by consequences that are nasty or unpleasant—events called punishers. In such instances, we learn not to perform these behaviors, since there will be an undesirable consequence. This highlights a point about which there is often much confusion. Contrary to what common sense seems to suggest, **punishment** is not the same as negative reinforcement. Here is an example to illustrate the difference.

Imagine that you are driving home in a hurry. Suddenly, you become aware of flashing lights and a siren. An RCMP officer has detected you speeding. You see how much the ticket will cost you; and after paying that fine, you obey the posted speed limit. This is an example of how punishment works: An unpleasant outcome follows your speeding, so that afterwards the probability that you will speed decreases.

Now imagine that a year later you are again caught speeding. (Apparently the punishment suppressed your speeding behavior only temporarily.) Because you are a past offender, the judge gives you a choice: attend a month-long series of driver education classes or lose your driver's licence. In order to avoid losing your licence, you attend every class. This is an example of how negative reinforcement works: You attend the driver education classes to avoid an aversive event—the loss of your driver's licence.

Omission training is the weakening of a behavior when the consequence is the removal of something pleasurable. For example, parents frequently attempt to combat certain behaviors of their teenage sons or daughters by withdrawing privileges, such as access to the car or the bank card. In basic research with animals, omission may mean that a peck on a key cancels the delivery of food (e.g., Eldridge & Pear, 1987). Both punishment and omission training weaken or decrease behavior. Table 5.1 summarizes positive reinforcement, negative reinforcement, punishment, and omission training.

KEY POINTS

- In operant conditioning, organisms learn the relationships between certain behaviors and the consequences they produce.
- Both positive and negative reinforcement strengthen or increase behavior. Punishment and omission training aim to weaken or suppress behavior.
- Primary reinforcers include food, water, and sexual pleasure; conditioned reinforcers include money, status, and praise.
- According to the Premack principle, preferred activities can be used to reinforce less preferred activities.

Punishment: The application or removal of a stimulus so as to decrease the strength of a behavior.

Omission Training: A procedure in which a response is weakened through the removal of a desired object or activity.

Operant Conditioning: *Some Basic Principles*

In classical conditioning, organisms learn that certain stimulus events predict the occurrence of others, which then naturally trigger a specific response. Unconditioned responses are generally involuntary. They occur in response

KEY CONCEPT

The Difference Between Negative Reinforcement and Punishment

Negative reinforcement and punishment are definitely not the same. In fact, one of the few similarities between them is that both involve an aversive stimulus. The examples here illustrate ways in which negative reinforcement and punishment differ.

NEGATIVE REINFORCEMENT

• Negative reinforcement *motivates* behavior—organisms perform behaviors that allow them to *escape* or *avoid* aversive stimuli.

• In negative reinforcement, aversive stimuli *precede* the escape or avoidance response.

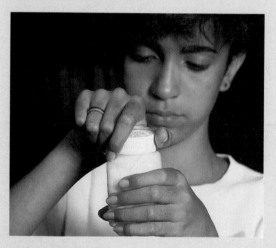

Avoidance behavior

Sometimes, events in our environment reliably signal an impending aversive event. These stimuli provide us with advance warning and motivate behavior that allows us to avoid experiencing the aversive event altogether.

Escape behavior

Organisms engage in behaviors that allow them to escape or terminate an unpleasant, or aversive, event that has already occurred.

PUNISHMENT

• Punishment decreases or suppresses behavior— organisms stop doing behaviors that produce aversive consequences.

• In punishment, an aversive stimulus *follows* a response and decreases the likelihood the response will occur again.

PROCEDURE	STIMULUS EVENT	EFFECTS	BEHAVIORIAL OUTCOMES
Positive reinforcement	Application of desirable (appetitive) stimulus (e.g., food, sexual pleasure, praise)	Strengthens responses that precede occurrence of stimulus	Organisms learn to perform responses that produce positive reinforcers
Negative reinforcement	Removal or postponement of undesirable (aversive) stimulus (e.g., heat, cold, harsh criticism)	Strengthens responses that permit escape from or avoidance of stimulus	Organisms learn to perform responses that permit them to avoid or escape from negative reinforcers
Punishment	Application of undesirable (aversive) stimulus	Weakens responses that precede occurrence of stimulus	Organisms learn to suppress responses that lead to unpleasant consequences
Omission training	Removal of desirable (appetite) stimulus	Weakens responses that precede occurrence of stimulus	Organisms learn to suppress responses that lead to the removal of pleasant consequences

TABLE 5.1

Positive Reinforcement, Negative Reinforcement, Punishment, and Omission Training: An Overview

Positive and negative reinforcement are both procedures that strengthen behavior. Positive reinforcers strengthen responses that precede them, whereas negative reinforcers strengthen responses that allow us to escape from or avoid aversive events. Punishment and omission training are procedures that weaken behavior. Punishers weaken behaviors that precede them by applying an aversive stimulus, whereas omission training weakens responses through the removal of desirable stimuli.

to a specific unconditioned stimulus, in an automatic manner—for example, salivation to the taste of food, blinking in response to a puff of air in the eye.

In operant conditioning, in contrast, organisms learn associations between particular *behaviors* and the consequences that follow them. The responses involved in operant conditioning are more voluntary and are *emitted* by organisms in a given environment. In order to understand the nature of operant conditioning, then, we must address two basic questions: Why are certain behaviors emitted in the first place? And once they occur, what factors determine the frequency with which they are repeated?

SHAPING AND CHAINING: GETTING BEHAVIOR STARTED AND THEN PUTTING IT ALL TOGETHER In order to study instrumental or operant conditioning under laboratory conditions, psychologists often use two basic types of apparatus. The first is known as a maze (or runway). Here, subjects (usually rats) must learn which ways to turn in order to receive a reward, usually food, at the end of the maze. Since making correct responses yields a reward, the speed and accuracy of such responses usually increase over successive trials.

The second type of equipment is known as the *Skinner box*, after its originator, B.F. Skinner. Skinner was a major figure in the history of psychology, well known both for his research and for his outspoken support of a behavioristic point of view, which he called the *experimental analysis of behavior*. We will consider his substantial contributions to psychology at several points in this chapter. Animals (usually rats or pigeons) in a Skinner box must perform a response (press a lever or peck a bar) in order to obtain small pellets of food. Since this is the only response that yields reinforcement, it quickly increases in frequency, and subjects may spend long periods of time working for their reward. A cumulative recorder, developed by Skinner, provides a permanent record of how the rate of a particular response, whether pecks or presses, changes over time. Although simple by today's technical standards, Skinner's tools allowed him to observe systematically the relationship between operant responses and the consequences they produced. This led to the discovery of important principles of learning that we'll consider later in this discussion.

The responses that occur in mazes and Skinner boxes are both simple and natural for the organisms involved; rats often run through tunnels and pecking

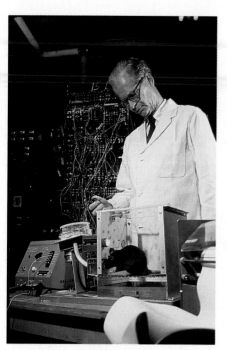

B.F. SKINNER WITH HIS SKINNER BOX

Animals in the Skinner box learn to press a lever in order to obtain small pellets of food. The animal's responses are recorded by a device called a *cumulative recorder*.

Shaping: A technique in which closer and closer approximations of desired behavior are required for the delivery of positive reinforcement.

Chaining: A procedure that establishes a sequence of responses, which lead to a reward following the final response in the chain.

is common among pigeons. But how can behaviors that organisms *don't* spontaneously emit be established? The answer involves a procedure known as shaping, which was first systematically studied by Skinner. In essence, **shaping** is based on the principle that a little can eventually go a long way. Subjects receive a reward for each small step toward a final goal—the target response. That is, at first, actions even remotely resembling the target behavior—termed *successive approximations*—are followed by a reward. Gradually, closer and closer approximations of the final target behavior are required before the reward is given. This sounds simple, but does it actually work? Consider this example. When a baby suddenly blurts out the sound "Mmmuuhh," the parents are ecstatic; they immediately lavish attention and affection on the child and do so each time the baby repeats the sound; all the baby's other relatives do the same. But what happens over time? Although initially the family responds enthusiastically to any sound the child makes, gradually they respond only to sounds that approximate actual words. Shaping, then, contributes to our acquiring, or constructing, new and more complex forms of behavior from simpler behavior.

What about even more complex or unusual sequences of behavior, such as the exciting water routines performed by dolphins and killer whales at public aquariums? These behaviors can be cultivated by a procedure called **chaining**, in which trainers establish a sequence, or chain, of responses, the last of which leads to a reward. Trainers usually begin by shaping the last response in the chain. When this terminal response is well established, the trainer shapes responses earlier and earlier in the chain.

Shaping and chaining have important implications for human behavior. For example, when working with a beginning student, a skilled ski instructor may use shaping techniques to establish basic skills, such as standing on the skis without falling down. At first, the instructor praises small improvements. As training progresses, however, the student may receive praise only when he or she has successfully completed an entire sequence or chain of actions, such as skiing down a small slope.

Shaping and chaining techniques can produce dramatic effects. But can they be used to establish virtually any form of behavior in any organism? If you recall our earlier discussion of biological constraints on classical conditioning, you can probably guess the answer: no. Just as there are biological constraints on classical conditioning, there are constraints on operant learning based on consequences, or on shaping.

Perhaps this is most clearly illustrated by the experience of two psychologists, Keller and Marian Breland (1961), who attempted to put their expertise in operant conditioning to commercial use by training animals to perform unusual tricks. At first, things went well. Using standard shaping techniques, the Brelands trained chickens to roll plastic capsules holding prizes down a ramp and then peck them into the hands of waiting customers; they also taught pigs to deposit silver dollars into a piggy bank. As time went by, though, these star performers gradually developed some unexpected behaviors. The chickens began to seize the capsules and pound them against the floor, and the pigs began to throw coins onto the ground and root them about instead of making "deposits" in their bank. In short, despite careful training, the animals showed what the Brelands termed *instinctive drift*—a tendency to return to the type of behavior they would show under natural conditions. So operant conditioning, like classical conditioning, is subject to biological constraints. While the power of positive and negative reinforcers is great, natural tendencies are important, too, and can influence the course and results of operant conditioning in many cases.

THE SIZE OF REINFORCEMENT AND DELAY: BIGGER OR SMALLER, SOONER OR LATER In most instances, operant conditioning proceeds faster as *magnitude* of the reward that follows each response increases. But does this mean the absolute size of each reward? Or does it mean the number of rewards received? One study shows that if two groups of rats receive the same absolute amount of reward for each response, but one group receives this amount in a greater number of smaller pieces, the group receiving the most pieces will respond faster (Campbell, Batsche, & Batsche, 1972). This suggests that the rats preferred to receive smaller, more numerous rewards rather than larger, fewer rewards.

Reward delay also affects operant conditioning, with longer delays producing poorer levels of performance. A study by Capaldi (1978), for example, examined how reward delay affected running behavior in two groups of rats rewarded on every trial. Although both groups received the same amount and quality of food reward on each trial, one group received the reward immediately, while the other group received the reward following a ten-second delay. As you might guess, subjects in the immediate-reward group performed better than subjects in the delayed-reward group. In another study, experimenters used a delay procedure to show how rats' accuracy decreased when reward was postponed over intervals that varied from 4, 15, 60, 120, to 600 seconds (Mumby, Pinel, & Wood, 1990).

The effects of reward delay are also evident in humans. For example, children will often choose smaller, immediate rewards over rewards of greater value that they must wait to receive. Adults, too, often choose immediate rewards, even if the delayed consequences for doing so are aversive. Smokers, for instance, choose the immediate pleasures they derive from smoking over the potentially negative consequences they may suffer later on, such as cancer. It may be new to you to learn that alcoholic beverages can also affect the way we evaluate short-term as opposed to delayed consequences (Steele & Josephs, 1990), a result that researchers have called "alcoholic myopia" (i.e., alcoholic shortsightedness). For example, drinking the night before an exam may reduce the influence of inhibiting cues associated with long-term consequences, such as failing the next day's test, and may increase the influence of environmental cues associated with short-term consequences, such as friends or good music.

SHAPING AND CHAINING

The dual processes of shaping and chaining help explain the development of complex behaviors in animals, including these water-skiing squirrels.

SCHEDULES OF REINFORCEMENT: DIFFERENT RULES FOR THE DELIVERY OF PAYOFFS

Through experience, you may already realize that under natural conditions reinforcement is often an uncertain event. Sometimes a given response yields a reward every time it occurs, but sometimes it does not. For example, smiling at someone you don't know may produce a return smile and additional positive outcomes. On other occasions it may produce a suspicious frown, or other rejection. Similarly, putting a loonie in a pop machine usually produces a soft drink. Sometimes, though, you merely lose the money.

In these examples, the occurrence or nonoccurrence of reinforcement seems to be random or unpredictable. In many other instances, though, it is governed by rules. For example, paycheques are delivered on certain days of the month; free pizzas or car washes are provided to customers who have purchased a specific amount of products or services. Do such rules—known as **schedules of reinforcement**—affect behavior? Several decades of research by Skinner and other psychologists suggest that they do. Many different types of schedules of reinforcement exist (Ferster & Skinner, 1957; Honig & Staddon, 1977). We'll concentrate on several of the most important ones here.

The simplest is called the **continuous reinforcement schedule** (CRF), in which every occurrence of a particular behavior is reinforced. For example, if a rat receives a food pellet each time it presses a lever, or a small child receives a quarter each time she ties her shoes correctly, both are on a continuous reinforcement schedule. As you might imagine, continuous reinforcement is useful for establishing or strengthening new behaviors.

Schedules of Reinforcement: Rules determining when and how reinforcements will be delivered.

Continuous Reinforcement Schedule: A schedule of reinforcement in which every occurrence of a particular behavior is reinforced.

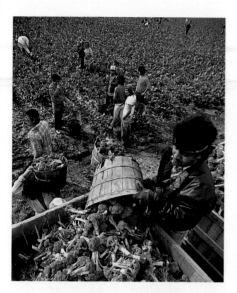

SCHEDULES OF REINFORCEMENT AT WORK

Migrant workers are paid on a fixed-rate schedule. Because each worker's pay depends on the amount of produce picked, this type of schedule generally yields a high rate of response. Which type of payment schedule would you prefer?

Fixed-Interval Schedule: A schedule of reinforcement in which a specific interval of time must elapse before a response will yield reinforcement.

Variable-Interval Schedule: A schedule of reinforcement in which a variable amount of time must elapse before a response will yield reinforcement.

Fixed-Ratio Schedule: A schedule of reinforcement in which reinforcement occurs only after a fixed number of responses have been emitted.

Variable-Ratio Schedule: A schedule of reinforcement in which reinforcement is delivered after a variable number of responses have been performed.

Other types of schedules, however, termed *partial* or *intermittent reinforcement*, are often more powerful in maintaining behavior. In the first of these, known as a **fixed-interval schedule**, the occurrence of reinforcement depends on the passage of time; the first response made after a specific period has elapsed brings the reward. When placed on schedules of this type, people generally show a pattern in which they respond at low rates immediately after delivery of a reinforcement, but then gradually respond more and more as the time of the next reward approaches. A good example of behavior on a fixed-interval schedule is provided by students' study habits. After a big exam, little if any studying takes place. As the time for the next test approaches, the rate of this behavior increases dramatically.

In a **variable-interval schedule**, reinforcement is also controlled mainly by the passage of time. Here, though, the period that must elapse before a response will again yield reinforcement varies around some average value. An example of behavior on a variable-interval schedule of reinforcement is provided by employees whose supervisor checks their work at irregular intervals but perhaps every two hours, on average. Since the employees never know when these checks will occur, they must perform in a consistent manner in order to obtain positive outcomes, such as praise, or to avoid negative ones, such as criticism. This is precisely what happens on variable-interval schedules: Organisms respond at a steady rate, without the pauses observed on fixed-interval schedules. An important procedure that is arranged according to a variable-interval schedule is random drug testing of individuals in safety-sensitive jobs—people whose impaired performance could endanger the lives of others, such as airline pilots or operators at nuclear reactors. Because they cannot predict the day on which the next test will occur, these individuals may be more likely to refrain from using drugs that could impair their on-the-job performance.

Reinforcement is determined in a very different manner on a **fixed-ratio schedule**. Here, reinforcement occurs only after a fixed number of responses. Individuals who are paid for each piece of work completed (i.e., on a piece-work basis), at a fixed amount for each item produced, are being rewarded according to a fixed-ratio schedule. Generally, these schedules yield a high rate of response, though with a tendency toward a brief pause immediately after each reinforcement. The pauses occur because individuals take a slight breather after earning each unit of reinforcement. People who collect bottles, cans, and other recyclables by the dozen for the money they bring are behaving according to a fixed-ratio schedule.

Finally, on a **variable-ratio schedule**, reinforcement occurs after completion of a number of responses, this number varying around a set average. Since organisms confronted with a variable-ratio schedule cannot predict how many responses are required before reinforcement will occur, they usually respond at high and steady rates.

Variable-ratio schedules result in behaviors that are highly resistant to extinction—that persist even when reinforcement is no longer available. In fact, resistance to extinction is much higher. (Pigeons prefer the continuous schedule when given the choice; Spetch et al., 1990). This persistence of behavior is known as the *partial reinforcement effect*. Many golfers are well acquainted with this effect; for each great shot they hit, they hit many more poor ones, yet they continue to play the game. Suppose that golfers fail to hit even one good shot over the course of an entire season—will they continue to play? Probably yes. This is because when reinforcement is infrequent and intermittent in its delivery, people have difficulty recognizing that it is no longer available. The effect of variable-ratio schedules on human behavior is readily apparent in gambling casinos, video arcades and other public places (which in some provinces include bowling alleys and corner stores) where high rates of responding occur.

As summarized in Figure 5.7 and as was evident throughout the preceding discussion, different schedules of reinforcement produce distinct patterns of responding. In Quebec, an analysis of arcade video games by Braun and Giroux (1989) found that the most popular games provided rewards on fixed-ratio, continuous, reward and punishment schedules. However, consequences are not the only determinants of behavior. The stimuli that precede our behavior and signal the availability of certain consequences are also important.

STIMULUS CONTROL OF BEHAVIOR: SIGNALS ABOUT THE USEFULNESS (OR USELESSNESS) OF RESPONSES   Imagine you are a rat in a Skinner box. Over the past few days, you have learned to press a lever in order to receive food pellets. One morning you notice the presence of a light in the box, which is turned

❉ CANADIAN FOCUS

Gambling: The Psychological Downside

In July 1994, *The Globe and Mail* reported that two new casinos were being proposed in Canada—one in Toronto (estimated cost: $1 billion), the other in Vancouver ($750 million). There are already casinos in Winnipeg, Windsor, and Montreal. In some provinces, such as Saskatchewan, gambling machines have been installed in hotels and bars. The potential economic gain is enormous—for example, $40 to 60 million from a casino proposed for Nova Scotia. Yet residents of Toronto, Halifax, and Vancouver are strongly opposed to these casinos. In Quebec, the Mohawks of the Kahnawake reserve have already rejected a similar but smaller project. So, what is the downside to gambling casinos?

Whether it is on bingo or horses, with video lottery terminals or slot machines, gambling is potentially addictive. In one recent case, an American basketball superstar may have lost as much as $1.25 million betting at golf. An unemployed Halifax man reported losing $40,000 on Nova Scotia's video gambling machines (this was before the province removed the machines). In a 1993 study done in Edmonton, Bland and his colleagues estimated that 0.45 percent of the population were lifetime pathological gamblers. Among these people, there were three times more men than women. Most often, they began gambling between 25 and 29 years of age; 80 percent of them had problems at work or at home, and 60 percent stole or borrowed money so that they could continue

gambling. More recently, it has been estimated that 5 percent of Albertans have gambling difficulties, and that 1.4 percent more have severe problems. These percentages total 125,000 Albertans.

How are we to account for compulsive gambling? The fact that people become addicted to gambling, as they do to nicotine, to alcohol, to heroin, and sometimes even to starving or to jogging, suggests that there may be a biological basis to compulsive gambling. Perhaps the biochemical changes that accompany risk taking reinforce gambling behavior. One recent study has identified excitement as the most important motivational factor among regular videopoker players (Dumont & Ladouceur, 1990).

When Saskatchewan installed its 3,500 gambling machines, the provincial government set aside $500,000 for the treatment of compulsive gambling. Alberta has set aside twice that much. Treatments for pathological gambling may include help lines, behavior modification (Sylvain & Ladouceur, 1992), support groups such as Gamblers Anonymous, some drugs, and psychotherapy. The cost of treatment per gambler is expensive—an estimated at $18,000 a year. That projects to just under $600 million for the taxpayers of Nova Scotia alone. Prevention programs for adolescents are being designed; however, recent studies by Gaboury and Ladouceur at Laval University found that the usefulness of at least one such program was uncertain at best.

FIGURE 5.7

Schedules of Reinforcement: A Summary of Their Effects

Rates of responding vary under different schedules of reinforcement. The steeper each line in the graph, the higher the rate at which responses are performed.

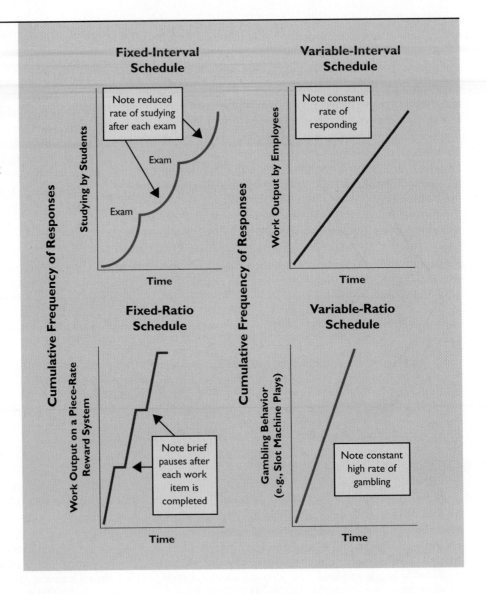

on and off with some regularity. The light is actually a signal: You will be rewarded with food if you press the lever when the light is on, but not when the light is off. Over time, you learn to press the lever in the presence of the light—termed a **discriminative stimulus**—but not when the light is turned off. In short, your lever-pressing behavior has come under **stimulus control** of the light: You are obeying the light's signal as to whether lever pressing should be performed or omitted (Skinner, 1938).

Stimulus control has important implications for people—for example, it has been used in the treatment of insomnia (Sloan et al., 1993). In **The Research Process**, we'll consider additional ways in which psychologists have applied the concept of stimulus control.

Discriminative Stimulus: Stimulus that signals the availability of reinforcement if a specific response is made.

Stimulus Control: Consistent occurrence of a behavior in the presence of a discriminative stimulus.

Operant Conditioning: A Cognitive Perspective

Do cognitive processes play a role in operant conditioning as they do in classical conditioning? This continues to be a point on which psychologists

FIGURE 5.8

Mr. Yuk Means NO!

Put Mr. Yuk stickers on products like these:

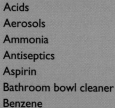

Acids	Drain cleaners	Oven cleaner
Aerosols	Drugs	Paint
Ammonia	Epoxy glue	Paint thinner
Antiseptics	Eye makeup	Permanent wave solution
Aspirin	Furniture polish	Pesticides
Bathroom bowl cleaner	Garden sprays	Petroleum distilates
Benzene	Gun cleaners	Pine oil
Bubble bath	Hair dyes	Rodenticides
Carbon tetrachloride	Herbicides	Shaving lotion
Cigarettes	Insecticides	Silver polish
Cleaning fluids	Iodine	Strychnine
Clinitest tablets	Kerosene	Turpentine
Cologne	Mace (chemical)	Typewriter cleaner
Copper & brass cleaners	Model cement	Vitamins
Corn & wart removers	Nail polish	Window wash solvent
Dandruff shampoo	Nail polish remover	
Dishwasher detergents	Narcotics	

Applying Stimulus Control to Prevent Accidental Poisonings

Stimulus control can be applied to solve important problems of everyday life—in this case, preventing accidental poisonings among very small children. (Source: Permission to use Mr. Yuk symbol given by Children's Hospital of Pittsburgh)

disagree. Skinner and his supporters have contended that there is no need to introduce cognition into the picture: If we understand the nature of the reinforcers available in a situation and the schedules on which they are delivered, we can accurately predict behavior. But many other psychologists—a majority, it appears—believe that no account of operant conditioning can be complete without attention to cognitive factors (e.g., Colwill, 1993). Several types of evidence support this conclusion.

First, and perhaps most dramatic, is the phenomenon known as *learned helplessness:* the lasting effects produced by exposure to situations in which no response yields reinforcement or provides escape from negative events—in other words, nothing the organism does works. After such exposure, both people and animals seem literally to give up. And here is the unsettling part: If the situation changes so that some of their abandoned responses would work, they never discover that fact, because they have stopped trying; rather, they remain in a seemingly passive state and simply don't check (Seligman, 1975; Tennen & Eller, 1977). Although it is not clear why learned helplessness occurs (McReynolds, 1980), it seems too simple to explain it entirely in terms of contingent relationships between individual responses and the consequences they produce. Some evidence suggests that organisms learn a general expectation of helplessness that transfers across situations, even after they do gain control over their environment (Maier & Jackson, 1979).

As we'll see in later chapters, learned helplessness may play a key role in depression, a serious psychological disorder. The onset of learned helplessness seems to suggest this: When we begin to believe that we have no control over our environment or our lives, we stop trying to improve our situation (Dweck & Licht, 1980). For example, many children perceive that they have

Stimulus Control in Action: Promoting Paper Waste Recycling on a University Campus

A s we've already seen, B.F. Skinner was a major proponent of the importance of operant conditioning. In Skinner's view, learning results from the interaction between an organism's behavior and the environment in which it behaves. He suggested that a complete understanding of the environment–behavior interaction requires knowledge of three things: (1) the characteristics of stimulus events that precede a particular response, or *antecedents*; (2) the characteristics of the response or behavior itself; and (3) the reinforcing consequences that maintain the response (Skinner, 1969). The development by Skinner of this *three-term contingency* led to an explosion of research, and behavioral researchers have developed a broad range of conditioning techniques to promote beneficial behavior change, from improving the performance of children at school, to getting people to buckle their automobile safety belts, to promoting recycling.

Most of the research on recycling has focused on manipulating the consequences for this behavior. Recently, however, psychologists have broadened their focus to include the control of antecedent stimuli—in other words, how to make recycling easy (Austin et al., 1993; Geller, Winett, & Everett, 1982).

Why is it so important to get people to recycle? One reason is that increased recycling will mean less demand on the natural resources necessary to produce new paper containers and packaging materials. There is a great deal of room for improvement.

Reluctance on the part of consumers to recycle is due, at least in part, to the availability of disposable products. Manufacturers make it easier for people to throw empty containers in the trash than to recycle them. When people can pay a deposit on buying a container and get the deposit back when they return it, recycling is dramatically increased—at least for beverage containers.

While this practice works splendidly for beverage containers, it does not address other important recycling problems, such as office paper. Although most forms of office paper can readily be turned into other useful paper products, it is nearly impossible to reward individuals for recycling paper. That is why most office paper ends up in the trash. How can we

FIGURE 5.9

Stimulus Control in Action: Promoting Recycling Behaviors

Poster used to promote correct placement of paper wastes. The bins depicted in the poster were colored to correspond to each bin's purpose—red for white paper, yellow for colored paper, and blue for computer paper. (Source: Kalsher et al., 1993)

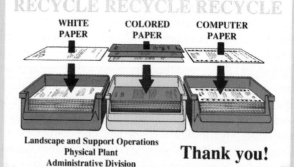

solve this problem? Psychologists have recently used their knowledge of Skinner's three-term contingency to address this issue. Specifically, they have explored the possibility of arranging aspects of the environment to support recycling behavior.

Can we really get people to recycle in this way? Several recent studies suggest that we can (Austin et al., 1993; Dwyer et al., 1993). In one large study, about 400 participants in each of Edmonton, Calgary, and the rest of Alberta were interviewed regarding their views about the environment and their recycling behaviors. In all groups, the vast majority were concerned about issues relating to the environment (water quality, pollution, and so on) and about recycling in particular. Yet Edmontonians recycled more than others. In Edmonton, there was a curbside "blue box" program that made it convenient to recycle such things as beverage cans and bottles, newspapers and cardboard, household plastics, milk cartons, food cans, and the like. That was not the case in the other two areas. It is notable (in light of the American study cited next) that one of the largest differences in Edmonton related to the recycling of other paper products (Derksen & Gartrell, 1993).

In another study of this particular topic, it was observed that office environments (on a university campus) discouraged the recycling of paper wastes (Kalsher et al., 1993). The employees' wastebaskets were next to their desks or work stations, but the recycling bins were in dingy basements or on another floor of the building. While both the waste baskets and recycling bins were discriminative stimuli, they signaled very different consequences. Throwing paper into the trash was quick, easy, and convenient. In contrast, recycling bins signaled a long walk, lost time, and much inconvenience.

Kalsher and his colleagues redesigned the office environments to be more conducive to recycling. The researchers equipped the offices of four campus buildings with sets of colored bins for the purpose of sort-separating three types of recyclable paper waste (refer to Figure 5.9). Colorful posters above each set of bins gave specific instructions for correctly placing the papers. Brochures describing the program and recycling procedures were distributed to all employees. This program was successful: Both the average daily weight of paper recycled and the percentage of paper correctly sorted increased dramatically. Moreover, the cost of the program was minimal.

Clearly, operant conditioning and the three-term contingency are powerful tools for solving a variety of important social problems, including recycling.

Critical Thinking Questions:

1. Rearranging the work environment appeared to increase recycling behavior in the study just described—without the use of external rewards. Which approach—stimulus control or rewards—do you believe would be more effective in producing long-term behavior change?

2. In what ways could knowledge of stimulus control be applied to solve other environmental problems? Give an example.

little control over their environment and even less hope of escaping it. As a result of learned helplessness, they may simply resign themselves to a lifetime of inactivity, denial, and isolation.

Second, several studies indicate that in some cases people's beliefs about schedules of reinforcement may have greater effects on behavior than the schedules themselves. For example, in one study (Kaufman, Baron, & Kopp, 1966), three groups of participants performed a manual response on a variable-interval schedule; the period between reinforcements varied, but averaged one minute. One group was told about the schedule that would be in effect. The other two groups were given false information: one was told that they would be rewarded every minute (a fixed-interval schedule); the other was told that they would be rewarded after an average of 150 responses (a variable-ratio schedule). Although all groups actually worked on the same schedule, large differences in their behavior emerged. Those who thought they were working on a variable-ratio schedule showed a high rate of responses: 259 per minute. Those who were told they would be rewarded on a fixed-interval schedule showed a very low rate of 6 responses per minute; and those who were correctly informed that they would work on a variable-interval schedule showed an intermediate rate of 65 responses per minute. As suggested by Bandura (1986, p. 129), people's behavior may sometimes be more accurately predicted from their beliefs than from the actual rewards they experience.

Third, our behavior is influenced not only by the level of rewards we receive, but also by our evaluation of rewards, relative to our experiences with previous rewards. Studies have shown that a shift in the amount of reward we receive can dramatically influence performance. That temporary behavior shift is called the *contrast effect* (e.g., Crespi, 1942; Flaherty & Largen, 1975; Shanab & Spencer, 1978). For example, when laboratory animals are shifted from a small reward to a larger reward, there is an increase in their performance to a level greater than that of subjects consistently receiving the larger reward. This increase is known as a positive contrast effect. Conversely, when subjects are shifted from a large reward to a smaller reward, their performance decreases to a level lower than that of subjects receiving only the smaller reward—a negative contrast effect.

But positive and negative contrast effects are transient. Thus, the elevated or depressed performances slowly give way to performance levels similar to those of control animals that receive only one level of reward. The existence of contrast effects indicates that level of reward alone cannot always explain our behavior, and that experience with a previous level of reward—and consequent expectancies—can dramatically affect our performance. Contrast effects have also been studied in human fear (Samson & Rachman, 1992) and human impatience (Lupker et al., 1988). Contrast effects also help explain some of our everyday behaviors. For example, following an unexpected raise in salary or a promotion, a person is initially elated, and his or her performance skyrockets—at least for a while. Then, after the novelty wears off, performance falls to levels equal to that of others already being rewarded at the same level.

Finally, evidence suggests that cognitive processes play an important role in learning among animals, as well. In a classic study by Tolman and Honzik (1930), rats were trained to run through a complicated maze. One group, the reward group, received a food reward in the goal box at the end of the maze on each of their daily trials. A second group, the no-reward group, never received a reward. The third group, the no-reward/reward group, did not receive a food reward until the eleventh day of training. As illustrated in Figure 5.10, rats in the *reward group* showed a steady improvement in performance, decreasing the number of errors they made in reaching the goal box. Rats in the *no-reward group* showed only a slight improvement in performance. Rats in the *no-reward/reward* group showed performance similar to those in the no-reward group—for the first ten days. Their performance improved dramatically immediately after the food reward was introduced. In fact, their performance was as good as that of rats who had been rewarded for their performance all along.

How do we account for these results? An explanation based on reinforcement alone is not sufficient; the performance of the third group improved too suddenly. Obviously, the rats had learned something about what to expect in the previous trials. Tolman and others take these data, and other results (e.g., Colwill & Rescorla, 1985; 1988), as evidence for the importance of cognitive processes in animal learning. In fact, Tolman theorized that his rats may have formed a *cognitive map*—that is, a mental representation of the maze. Although the existence of such maps has not yet been confirmed (e.g., Dyer, 1991), a large body of evidence supports the view that nonhuman species form mental representations that include spatial and temporal features of their environment (Poucet, 1993).

At the University of Alberta, Marcia Spetch and others are investigating what pigeons know about time—that is, the duration of an event (e.g., Spetch & Grant, 1993), and what pigeons know about where they are located in space. These researchers are seeking to understand how it is that animals (such as many species of birds) use natural landmarks to guide them in their environment. For that purpose, they have developed a touch-screen task, in which pigeons peck at an outdoor scene shown on a video monitor. The latest

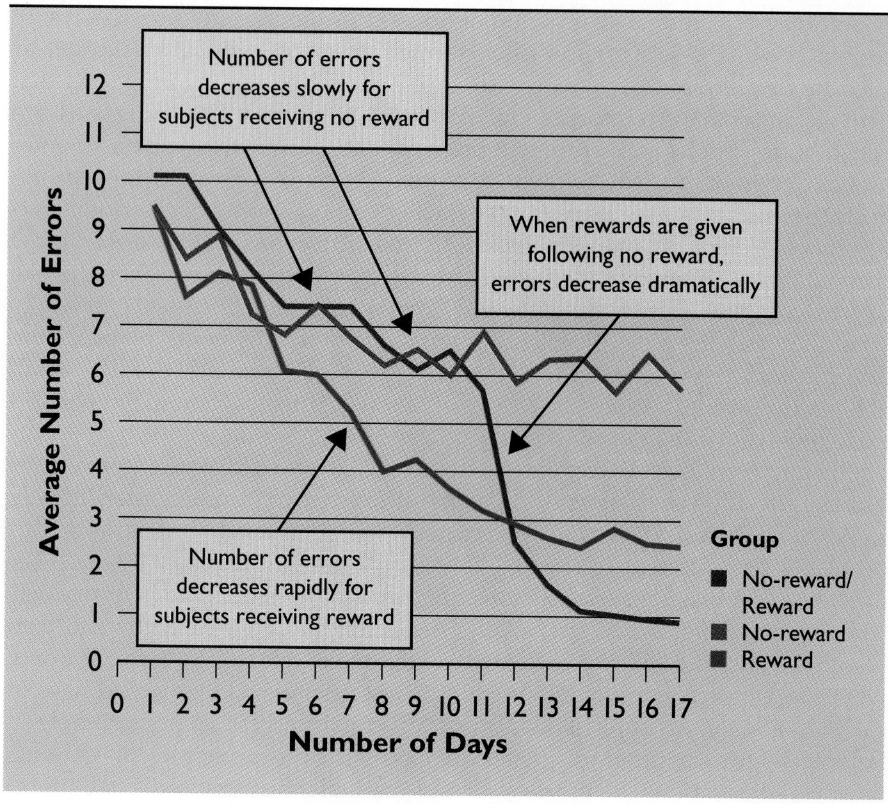
Number of errors decreases slowly for subjects receiving no reward
When rewards are given following no reward, errors decrease dramatically
Number of errors decreases rapidly for subjects receiving reward
Average Number of Errors
Number of Days
Group
No-reward/ Reward
No-reward
Reward
0
1
2
3
4
5
6
7
8
9
10
11
12
13
14
15
16
17

FIGURE 5.10

The Role of Cognitive Processes in Learning

Performance for rats in the no-reward/reward group improved dramatically immediately after the introduction of the food reward. Because the improvement was so dramatic, these data suggest that the animals "learned" something during previous trials—even though they received no reward for their efforts. Tolman used this as evidence for the importance of cognitive processes in learning, suggesting that the rats may have formed a "cognitive map." (Source: Based on data from Tolmen & Honik, 1930.)

results show that, given the opportunity to use one, two, or three landmarks, pigeons choose to use only one. Different pigeons, however, chose different landmarks. We don't know why a particular pigeon chooses a particular landmark. It may be that, even in pigeons, some matters are decided by individual taste. The cognitive maps of bees and ants have also been studied (Wehner & Menzel, 1990). For example, bees choose individual flowers by flower size and flower depth (Harder, 1988). Although we do not yet fully understand their precise nature, one thing is clear: Cognitive processes play an important and active role in animal learning.

Applying Operant Conditioning: Can We Make a Difference?

Because positive and negative reinforcement exert powerful effects on behavior, procedures based on operant conditioning have been applied in many practical settings—so many that it would be impossible to describe them all here. Here is an overview of some of these applications.

First, principles of operant conditioning have been applied to the field of education. One of the most impressive operant-based teaching techniques is termed *precision teaching* (Lindsley, 1992). In this approach, the "precision teacher" rarely lectures; instead, she acts like a coach, organizing materials and methods for the students to teach themselves and each other. The students are taught to measure and chart their own daily progress on standard charts. The charts provide students with immediate feedback and facilitate more efficient learning. The tools and methods used in precision teaching permit even primary-grade students to project, improve, and summarize their own learning (Bates & Bates, 1971).

Another educational application of operant techniques involves the use of computers in the classroom—often termed *computer-assisted instruction*, or *CAI*. In CAI, students interact with sophisticated computer programs that provide immediate reinforcement of correct responses. The programs are paced according to each student's progress and permit the student to enter branch programs for special help in areas of weakness. Some evidence suggests that students may learn to take greater responsibility for their own performance under CAI than under teacher-led instruction, because they view computers as impersonal and therefore fairer. CAI technology includes the use of computer-based simulation exercises that allow students to apply what they've learned in the classroom to solve problems under realistic conditions. With the color graphics, synthesized speech, and other effects available on increasingly sophisticated equipment, CAI instruction may help add excitement and enhance motivation for learning.

Operant conditioning can also be used to treat eating disturbances such as *anorexia nervosa* (see Chapter 10). People suffering from this disorder literally starve themselves. How can operant techniques be used to deal with this problem? Consider an individual who has been hospitalized because her unwillingness to eat is seriously affecting her health. In order to help this person, we might first ask her to monitor her eating behavior carefully and then identify something she likes. Then we would make this activity available only when she eats a minimum amount of food. At first, the patient would have to eat only a small amount of food in order to gain access to (for example) a favorite television program. In accordance with the principles of shaping, however, the amount she must eat would gradually be increased. Such procedures, when used as part of a comprehensive treatment plan, have been successful (Bemis, 1987; Schmidt, 1989 ; Steiger, 1989; Garner et al., 1986, 1990).

Principles of operant conditioning have also been applied to socially significant issues in our communities, such as energy conservation and recycling, health care, crime, consumer affairs, and safety promotion. Here are two examples. First, at crosswalks in St. John's, Fredericton, and Moncton, Malenfant and Van Houten (1989) studied the effects of various stimuli—among them signs, lines, and lighting—on pedestrian safety. One of these stimuli was a large sign displaying the percentage of motorists who yielded properly to pedestrians each week; the point of this was to provide motorists with feedback as to whether, as a group, they were improving or not. The program resulted in large increases in compliance by drivers and a 50 percent decrease in the number of accidents.

Second, Transport Canada reported in 1992 that 87 percent of adults used seat belts while driving or riding in a car, and also, that efforts like the Quebec Selective Traffic Enforcement Program (a combination of public education, enforcement of the law, and incentives for compliance) had been very successful in promoting the use of seat belts (Dussault, 1990). Why, then, did some drivers still not buckle up? Wilson (1990) studied committed nonusers of seat belts. He found that "nonusers were higher sensation seekers, more impulsive, consumed more alcohol and other drugs and accumulated more traffic violations"; he suggested, therefore, that special programs were needed for these particular offenders. Analysis must now focus on another population of Canadian car riders: children five and under, fewer than 50 percent of whom are properly restrained when riding in moving automobiles.

Operant conditioning principles have been applied to a severe disorder in which individuals inflict injury on themselves—*self-injurious behavior*, or *SIB* (Carr, 1977; Lovaas, 1982). SIB occurs frequently in the developmentally handicapped and those with autism or brain damage. Common SIBs are head hitting, self-biting, severe scratching, eye gouging, and hair pulling (known as trichotillomania; Maurice & Trudel, 1982). How can care givers use operant techniques to treat self-injury? Using a unique observational assessment procedure, Iwata and his colleagues discovered that individuals engage in self-injury for a variety of reasons (Iwata et al., 1982). Some individuals engage in SIB to attract the attention of people around them, while others do so to avoid or terminate demands placed on them. For still others, SIB was a form of self-generated sensory reinforcement. This principle was applied to the case of a ten-year-old boy who injured himself by slapping his own face. Van Houten (1993) reasoned that wrist weights would reduce the face slapping by making the action more effortful and by changing the sensory consequences—that is, by changing the way it felt. The behavior was modified using learning principles; in the five-month follow-up period, no face slapping occurred.

Finally, techniques of operant conditioning have been applied to work (Latham & Huber, 1992)—to improve the flexibility of work schedules (Winett & Neale, 1981), the performance of retail clerks (Luthans, Paul, & Baker, 1981), the productivity of waiters (George & Hopkins, 1989), and the effectiveness of work groups (Petty, Singleton, & Connell, 1992). Why are some people more effective in the role of leader or manager than others? Researchers have carefully observed and then analyzed the actual on-the-job behavior of managers within the framework of operant conditioning (e.g., Komacki, 1986). Effective managers pay close attention to their subordinates' performance and then provide contingent rewards and punishments. That approach may sound like common sense, but in fact it doesn't come naturally in many work settings. Often, instead of yielding rewards, good performance is "recognized" only by higher expectations, more work, and tougher challenges. Clearly, both employers and employees can profit greatly from closer attention to the basic principles of operant conditioning.

Observational Learning: Learning from the Behavior and Outcomes of Others

You are at a formal dinner. Next to your plate are five different forks, including two of a shape you've never seen before. Which ones do you use for which dishes? You have no idea. As the first course arrives, you watch the other guests. When several reach unhesitatingly for one of the unfamiliar forks, you do the same. Now, thank goodness, you can concentrate on the food.

Even if you have not had an experience quite like this, you probably have encountered situations in which you have acquired new information, forms of behavior, or even abstract rules and concepts by watching other people. Such **observational learning** is a third major way we learn, and it is a common part of everyday life (Bandura, 1977, 1986). Indeed, observational learning can play a role in almost every aspect of behavior (Grusec & Goodnow, 1994). Here are a few examples:

- A student chef watches while a master chef prepares a soufflé; she then tries to prepare one herself.

Observational Learning: The acquisition of new information, concepts, or forms of behavior through exposure to others and the consequences they experience.

- A man and a woman watch a television program (probably "Home Improvements") that shows step by step how to remodel a bathroom. The following day, they remodel their own.

- A child sees both of his parents wash dishes, do laundry, cook meals, and go to work each morning. From such observations, he learns that people share the responsibilities of running a household.

In these and countless other instances, we appear to learn vicariously, by watching the actions of other people and the consequences they experience. Observational learning occurs in fish, birds, and mammals (Robert, 1990). For example, Galef (1990) showed that, when given a choice, "observer" rats preferred the food that had been fed to their "demonstrator" partners, even when there was no physical contact between them. Evidence that observational learning exists in humans has been provided by hundreds of studies, many of them performed with children. Perhaps the most famous of these studies were the "Bobo doll" experiments conducted by Bandura and his colleagues (e.g., Bandura, Ross, & Ross, 1963). In these studies, one group of nursery-school children saw an adult engage in aggressive actions against a large inflated Bobo doll. The adult, who was serving as a model—that is, setting an example—knocked the doll down, sat on it, insulted it verbally, and repeatedly punched it in the nose. Another group of children were exposed to a model who behaved in a quiet, nonaggressive manner.

Later, both groups of children were placed in a room with several toys, including a Bobo doll. Those children who had seen the aggressive adult model often imitated that behavior: they too punched the toy, sat on it, and even uttered verbal comments similar to those the model had made. In contrast, children in the control group rarely, if ever, demonstrated such actions. While you may not find these results surprising, they may be significant in relation to the enduring controversy over whether children acquire new methods of aggression through exposure to violent video games, television programs, and movies. We'll return to this issue soon. For the moment, let's consider the nature of observational learning itself.

Observational Learning: Some Basic Principles

Given that observational learning exists, what do we know about how we acquire behaviors, information, and concepts by observing others? According to Bandura (1986), who is still the leading expert on this process, four factors are most important.

First, in order to learn through observation, you must direct your *attention* to appropriate *models*—that is, to other people performing an activity. As you might expect, you don't choose such models at random but focus the most attention on people who are attractive to you—on people who possess signs (such as status or success) of knowing what they're doing, and on people whose behavior seems relevant to your own needs and goals (Baron, 1970).

Second, you must be able to *remember* what the people have said or done. Only if you can retain some representation of their actions in memory can you perform similar actions at later times or acquire useful information from them.

Third, you need to be able to convert these memory representations into appropriate actions. Bandura terms this aspect of observational learning *production processes*. Production processes depend on two things: your own physical abilities—if you can't perform the behavior in question, having a clear representation of it in memory is of little use; and your capacity to monitor your own performance and adjust it until it matches that of the model.

Finally, *motivation* plays a role. We often acquire information through observational learning but do not put it into immediate use in our own behavior. You may have no need for the information, as when you watch someone tie a bow tie but have no plans to wear one yourself. Or the observed behaviors may involve a high risk of punishment or be repugnant to you personally, as when you observe an ingenious way of cheating during an exam but don't want to try it yourself. Only if the information or behavior acquired is useful will observers put it to actual use. Figure 5.11 summarizes the factors affecting observational learning.

As you can see, observational learning is a complex process—far more complex than mere imitation—and plays an important role in many aspects of behavior. This point is perhaps most forcefully illustrated by the controversy that has persisted in psychology, and in society as a whole, since the early 1960s: whether children, and perhaps even adults, are made more aggressive by long-term exposure to violence on television shows or in movies, and now in video games. In Canadian cities and in more remote centers, television is a common bond. In Igloolik, for example, of 139 households, 134 have TV sets. Studies show that one in five Canadian teens watches more than five hours a day, two out of five watch three or four hours, and two out of five watch one or two hours. By the time they enter junior high, these teens have already seen 100,000 violent acts and 8,000 murders (81 in "Robocop" alone) on television or in the movies (Biddy & Postersky, 1992). Many of the most popular video games involve players in gruesome acts of violence, such as decapitation with spine attached ("Mortal Kombat") and hanging from a meat hook by a hole drilled in the neck by a vampire ("Night Moves"). What do we learn by observing all of that?

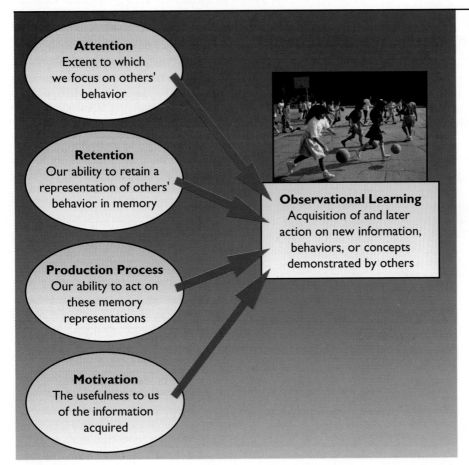

FIGURE 5.11

Key Factors in Observational Learning

Observational learning is affected by several factors or subprocesses. The most important of these are summarized here.

Attention
Extent to which we focus on others' behavior

Retention
Our ability to retain a representation of others' behavior in memory

Production Process
Our ability to act on these memory representations

Motivation
The usefulness to us of the information acquired

Observational Learning
Acquisition of and later action on new information, behaviors, or concepts demonstrated by others

Observational Learning and Aggression

Aggression can be learned through observation (Baron & Richardson, 1994; Centerwall, 1989; Snyder, 1991; Wood, Wong, & Chachere, 1991). Moreover, when children and adults are exposed to new ways of aggressing against others—techniques they have not previously seen—they may add these new behaviors to their repertoire. Later, when angry, irritated, or frustrated, they may put these behaviors to actual use in assaults against others.

Of course, media violence has other effects as well. It may convey the message that violence is an acceptable means of handling interpersonal difficulties; after all, if heroes and heroines can do it, why not viewers? It may elicit additional aggressive ideas and thoughts—convincing viewers, for example, that violence is even more common in real life than it is (Berkowitz, 1984). And it may also lessen emotional reactions to aggression and the harm it produces, so that such outcomes seem less upsetting or objectionable (Thomas, 1982). This process is known as desensitization. When these effects are coupled with new behaviors and skills acquired through observational learning, the overall impact for many people may be an increased tendency to engage in acts of aggression (Eron, 1987).

It is important to note that not all findings support such conclusions (Freedman, 1986; Widom, 1989) Even so, many children spend more time watching television or playing violent video games than at any other single activity. And those who have experienced childhood abuse learn vicariously to behave specifically in the ways they had observed early in their lives (Dutton & Hart, 1990). For at least these reasons, the potential influence of TV and video violence on behavior seems worthy of careful attention.

Research has also studied the potential real-life benefits of television for other areas of life. For instance, in the United States, a study was conducted of automobile safety-belt use among stars on prime-time television shows (1984–86). The results of this study (Geller, 1988) showed that drivers and their passengers were rarely belted, and that the most probable consequences of crashes for unbelted vehicle occupants—serious injury or death—were almost never shown.

So, Geller and his students initiated a campaign designed to bring public attention to the nonuse of safety belts by television stars. More than 800 students from Olympia, Washington, wrote buckle-up requests to Mr. T, a star on a popular action program called "The A-Team." Mr T went from wearing his seat belt 0 percent of the time in 1984 to wearing it 70 percent of the time in 1985.

Safety-belt use on television *increased* over the three-year period of the study, consistent with changes in the statistics for safety-belt use in the United States. Because TV shows enjoy such a massive viewing audience—often millions of viewers—efforts to depict exemplary behavior among network stars—like safe driving behaviors—could potentially save many lives.

Observational learning, then, plays an important role in many aspects of behavior, including our language and customs. **Perspectives on Diversity** explores this point further.

KEY POINTS

- Observational learning is more complex than simple imitation.
- Several factors determine the extent to which we acquire new information through observation: We must pay attention to those modeling the behavior, remember the modeled speech or action, possess the ability to act upon this memory, and have the motivation to do so.
- Observational learning plays a role in many forms of behavior, including aggression.
- Observational learning may play an important role in the training of workers to interact more effectively with people from different cultural backgrounds.

Learning to Avoid Culture Shock

Recently, psychologists have applied principles of observational learning to help solve a problem of growing concern: preparing people for the "culture shock" that sometimes occurs when they live and work in another country with a different language and unfamiliar customs.

As the world moves toward a global economy and freer trade, companies everywhere are facing a difficult challenge. They must prepare their employees for a business environment that requires them to communicate effectively with people from other cultures (Adler & Bartholomew, 1992; Feldman & Tompson, 1993). Behaviors that are acceptable and encouraged in one country may be offensive and intolerable to people from another country; dramatic differences in language, customs, dress, climate, and lifestyle often lead to unintended slights. Indeed, ignorance of these differences has long been cited as the biggest cause of misunderstandings between people from different cultures (Harris, 1979). These misunderstandings may arise from a matter as simple as the making of eye contact—which is taken as a good thing in Canada, but improper in some parts of Asia.

All of this is true not only for other countries, but also within Canada, where cultural diversity is the norm everywhere. In one company in Richmond, B.C., fifty different ethnic backgrounds and nationalities are represented in the workforce of 820. Diversity and multiculturalism are fundamental to the Canadian fabric, and knowledge of other cultures is normal for most of us. That is seen as a benefit for Canadian companies doing business internationally.

Nevertheless, there are cultural gaps, and to help close these, companies that conduct business abroad have scrambled to develop cross-cultural training programs. The goal of these programs is to teach appropriate, sensitive, and consistent behavior in cross-cultural interactions. Earlier efforts to prepare employees for cross-cultural assignments had taken a cognitive approach—trainees received factual information (government, religion, customs, weather, and so on) about a particular country (Fielder et al., 1971).

More recently, however, experts in cross-cultural training have advocated an "experiential" approach based on observational learning—that is, a behavioral modeling approach (Black & Mendenhall, 1990). Trainees first watch films in which models exhibit the correct behaviors in a problem situation. Then they participate in role-playing exercises to test their knowledge. Finally, they receive constructive feedback regarding their performance.

OBSERVATIONAL LEARNING: ADAPTING TO DIVERSITY

Observing the behaviors of others can help us acquire important social skills that will be needed as we move rapidly toward a global economy.

LEARNING: HOW EXPERIENCE CHANGES US

Are these programs effective? Recent evidence suggests that they are. In one study, Harrison (1992) compared the effectiveness of several approaches to cross-cultural training. One experimental group received culture-relevant information only; another received behavioral modeling training only; a third received both components; and a fourth was a no-training control group. The results showed that participants who received both forms of training—information and behavioral modeling—performed best on measures of culture-specific knowledge and on a behavioral measure.

These findings, and those of related studies, illustrate the important role that observational learning plays in alleviating the effects of culture shock. This form of learning at first enables us to perform behaviors appropriate to our own cultures, but later helps us adapt to the demands of a rapidly changing world.

MAKING PSYCHOLOGY PART OF YOUR LIFE

Getting in Shape: Applying Psychology to Get Fit and Stay Fit

Research has shown that exercise relieves stress; also, that it improves resistance to diseases (such as colds, heart attack, and diabetes) and physical problems (including high blood pressure and back pain). Yet surveys show that only one Canadian in three works out enough to gain these benefits.

Need to get back into shape? Establishing your fitness program using the learning principles we've discussed in this chapter will help you succeed.

First, set your sights realistically. Don't try to lose all twenty pounds in one week or run ten kilometers the first time out. Why not? Recall reinforcement and punishment: setting impossible goals will lead to failure, and failure will actually punish your efforts, making it even more difficult to stay with your program. If you've tried to exercise in the past and failed for this reason, you can probably appreciate the point.

Instead, set yourself up for small wins by taking advantage of the principle of *shaping*—rewarding yourself with modest rewards for successive steps toward your ultimate goals. Then slowly increase the amount of exercise you do, building on each of your previous successes. Also, take care to choose rewards that are desirable but consistent with your goals. For example, rent a movie you want to see badly, or buy a CD you can no longer live without, or call a friend who is far away.

Also, specify the amount and intensity of the exercise you will do and write it down. Some people find it helpful to chart their progress in order to have accurate and immediate feedback that will serve to reinforce or punish their behavior. By placing the chart in

Charting the progress of an exercise or weight-loss program may help keep you on track because it provides accurate and immediate feedback.

a prominent place that you and your friends and family can see, you will be taking advantage of both positive and negative reinforcement. For example, you can work to receive the positive attention that will come your way when your chart shows progress. Negative reinforcement may also help you, in that by posting your progress publicly, you can work to avoid the negative comments you may get if you are tempted to "take a day off … just because."

Stimulus control can help set the stage for healthy responses. So avoid situations where you may be tempted to consume unhealthy food or beverages, and instead begin going to places that are likely to occasion healthy responses. For example, by joining a health club, YMCA, or other *active* organization, you will be more likely to exercise and eat healthy.

Finally, take advantage of the principles of observational learning by identifying people who have traits and skills you admire. By observing and then emulating their behavior, you may become more efficient in reaching your goals. So get fit and stay fit, by making psychology a part of your fitness program.

CLASSICAL CONDITIONING: LEARNING THAT SOME STIMULI SIGNAL OTHERS

learning 186
classical conditioning 187
stimulus 187
unconditioned stimulus (UCS) 188
unconditioned response (UCR) 188
conditioned stimulus (CS) 188
conditioned response (CR) 188
acquisition 188
delayed conditioning 189
trace conditioning 189
simultaneous conditioning 189
backward conditioning 189
extinction 192
reconditioning 192
spontaneous recovery 192
stimulus generalization 192
stimulus discrimination 193
biological constraints on learning 194
conditioned taste aversion 195
phobias 198
flooding 198

- Learning is any relatively permanent change in behavior (or behavior potential) produced by experience.
- Classical conditioning is a basic and powerful form of learning in which neutral stimuli come to cause a response through their association with stimuli that naturally elicit a response.
- Acquisition of classically conditioned responses depends on many factors: temporal arrangement of the conditioned stimulus–unconditioned stimulus pairings, intensity of the conditioned stimulus and unconditioned stimulus relative to other background stimuli, and familiarity of potential conditioned stimuli present in the conditioning environment. Delayed conditioning and a brief CS-UCS interval are generally the most effective.
- Although a conditioned stimulus gradually ceases to elicit a conditioned response through extinction, it can quickly regain this ability through reconditioning: a renewed pairing of the conditioned stimulus with the unconditioned stimulus.
- Stimulus generalization and discrimination are essential tools for survival. Generalization allows us to apply our learning to many other situations; in contrast, discrimination allows us to differentiate among similar but different stimuli.
- Classical conditioning is not equally easy to establish with all stimuli for all organisms. There are important biological constraints on such learning, and members of a given species may acquire some types of conditioning more readily than others.
- Conditioned taste aversions can be established in one trial when a food or beverage (conditioned stimulus) is paired with a stimulus that naturally produces feelings of illness (unconditioned stimulus).
- Classical conditioning involves more than the formation of simple associations between stimuli. Some modern views of classical conditioning emphasize the importance of cognitive processes such as expectancies about the occurrence of various stimuli
- In blocking, conditioning to one stimulus is prevented by previous conditioning to another stimulus.
- Basic principles of classical conditioning can be used to treat serious problems, such as phobias and drug abuse.
- In flooding, a person is forced to come into contact with fear-eliciting stimuli without an avenue of escape.
- Cases in which fearful thoughts are too painful to deal with directly are treated by systematic desensitization—a progressive technique designed to replace anxiety with a relaxation response.

OPERANT CONDITIONING: LEARNING BASED ON CONSEQUENCES

operant conditioning 202
reinforcement 202
positive reinforcers 202
Premack principle 202
negative reinforcers 202

- In operant conditioning, organisms learn the relationships between behaviors and the consequences they produce.
- Both positive and negative reinforcement strengthen or increase behavior, whereas punishment and omission training aim to weaken or suppress behavior.
- Primary reinforcers include food, water, and sexual pleasure. Conditioned reinforcers—such as money, status, and praise—acquire their ability to act as positive reinforcers through association with primary reinforcers.
- The Premack principle suggests that preferred activities can be used to reinforce less preferred activities.
- Shaping involves reinforcing successive approximations of the final desired behavior.

punishment 203

omission training 203

shaping 206

chaining 206

schedules of reinforcement 207

continuous reinforcement
  schedule 207

fixed-interval schedule 208

variable-interval schedule 208

fixed-ratio schedule 208

variable-ratio schedule 208

discriminative stimulus 210

stimulus control 210

- Chaining involves teaching a complex sequence of behaviors by first shaping the final response in the sequence, then working backwards until a chain of behaviors is learned.
- Schedules of reinforcement are rules that determine the occasion on which a response will be reinforced.
- Schedules of reinforcement can be time-based (interval schedules) or event-based (ratio schedules). They can also be fixed or variable.
- A continuous reinforcement schedule is desirable for establishing new behaviors, since it reinforces each instance of a behavior; partial or intermittent schedules of reinforcement, however, are often more powerful in maintaining behavior over time.
- Discriminative stimuli signal the availability of reinforcement if a certain response is made. When a behavior occurs consistently in the presence of a discriminative stimulus, it is said to be under stimulus control.
- Several types of evidence, including studies of learned helplessness and contrast effects, support the conclusion that cognitive factors play an important role in operant conditioning. For example, people's beliefs about reinforcement schedules and people's evaluation of rewards may exert strong effects.
- Procedures based on operant conditioning principles can be applied to help solve many practical real-world problems.

OBSERVATIONAL LEARNING: LEARNING FROM THE BEHAVIOR AND OUTCOMES OF OTHERS

observational learning 217

- Observational learning is more complex than simple imitation.
- Several factors determine the extent to which we acquire new information through observation: We must pay attention to those modeling the behavior, remember the modeled speech or action, possess the ability to do act upon this memory, and have the motivation to do so.
- Observational learning plays a role in many forms of behavior. For example, individuals may acquire new ways of aggressing against others through exposure to media violence. In contrast, other evidence suggests that television stars can be used to promote prosocial behaviors.
- Observational learning may play an important role in the training of workers to interact more effectively with people from different cultural backgrounds.

CRITICAL THINKING QUESTIONS

APPRAISAL	At the present time, many psychologists are moving increasingly toward a cognitive view of the learning process. Do you think this movement is appropriate, or is there still a role for the views of operant psychologists?
CONTROVERSY	Growing evidence suggests that animals do indeed form mental representations of their environment that are analogous to those formed by human beings. Does this mean that animals think? What are your views on this issue? What are the implications of this theory of animal learning?
MAKING PSYCHOLOGY PART OF YOUR LIFE	Knowing something about important principles of learning is very useful to people who wish to get into shape or lose weight. But these are only two ways in which knowledge of learning can be applied to help people. Can you think of others?

Memory

Of Things Remembered …
and Forgotten

HUMAN MEMORY: THE INFORMATION PROCESSING APPROACH 229
Human Memory: One Influential Model—and an Emerging New Approach
Types of Information in Memory

SENSORY MEMORY: GATEWAY TO CONSCIOUSNESS 233

SHORT-TERM MEMORY: THE WORKBENCH OF CONSCIOUSNESS 235
Evidence for the Existence of Short-Term Memory
Short-Term Memory: Its Basic Operation

LONG-TERM MEMORY: THE STOREHOUSE OF CONSCIOUSNESS 237
Long-Term Memory: Its Basic Operation
Retrieval: Locating Information in Long-Term Memory

FORGETTING FROM LONG-TERM MEMORY 242
The Trace-Decay Hypothesis: Forgetting with the Passage of Time
Forgetting as a Result of Interference
Prospective Memory: Forgetting to Do What We're Supposed to Do

MEMORY IN NATURAL CONTEXTS 247
Autobiographical Memory: Remembering the Events of Our Own Lives
Distortion and Construction in Memory of Natural Events

THE BIOLOGICAL BASES OF MEMORY: HOW THE BRAIN STORES KNOWLEDGE 258
Amnesia and Other Memory Disorders: Keys to Understanding the Nature of Memory
Memory and the Brain: A Modern View

SUMMARY AND REVIEW OF KEY POINTS 265

CANADIAN FOCUS—THE STORY OF A MAN WITHOUT EPISODIC MEMORY 233

THE POINT OF IT ALL—REPRESSION: DO WE SOMETIMES FORGET BECAUSE WE WANT TO FORGET? 244

CANADIAN FOCUS—WHY CAN WE REMEMBER SO LITTLE OF OUR VERY EARLY CHILDHOOD? 250

KEY CONCEPT—DIFFERENT KINDS OF MEMORY: AN OVERVIEW 251

PERSPECTIVES ON DIVERSITY—CULTURE AND MEMORY: REMEMBERING WHAT FITS WITH OUR CULTURAL SCHEMAS 254

THE RESEARCH PROCESS—EYEWITNESS TESTIMONY: HOW ACCURATE IS IT? WHAT FACTORS AFFECT IT? 256

MAKING PSYCHOLOGY PART OF YOUR LIFE—IMPROVING YOUR MEMORY: SOME USEFUL STEPS 263

WITNESS DESCRIBES MURDER SCENE

**The Journal-Pioneer
(Prince Edward Island):
September 3, 1994**

This article reported the testimony of the only eyewitness to a murder that took place in Charlottetown. The death was the result of a struggle at the top of a second-floor staircase. The alleged murderer hacked the victim repeatedly with a hatchet, repeating, "Be nice or be ice."

How accurate are human observers in such circumstances? How well do we remember precisely what happened? Is eyewitness testimony reliable? These questions relate to how people remember and why they forget. This topic has been the focus of much research in psychology. You will learn about what we know about memory as you proceed through Chapter 6.

Memory, people often say, is a very funny thing, and our life experience tends to confirm this. Have you ever forgotten a phone number you looked up in the directory before you could manage to dial it? Have you ever taken a wrong turn while driving because your memory told you that your destination was off in one direction, when, as you learned later, it was really in the opposite one? Have you ever had your mind go blank when you were about to introduce two people to each other, or during an exam? Nearly everyone has had such experiences. In these situations we come face to face with the imperfect nature of our own **memory**—our cognitive system for storing and retrieving information.

We often retain vivid—and accurate—memories of events and scenes from months, years, or even decades in the past. Your high school days are still recent memories. As time passes, and you begin your career, marry, and start a family, your high school days will become experiences of the distant past. If you come upon your high school graduation picture thirty years from now, will you recognize your friends' pictures? Without question! Bahrick, Bahrick, and Wittlinger (1975) found that even after thirty-four years, memory for faces of high school friends remained unimpaired. It is equally likely that you will still be able to ride a bicycle thirty years from now, even if you never go near one in the intervening years. In these and other respects, memory truly *is* impressive.

Because it is clearly a crucial aspect of cognition, memory has long occupied a central place in psychological research. In fact, memory was the focus of some of the earliest systematic work in the field—studies conducted more than one hundred years ago, in 1885, by Hermann Ebbinghaus. Using himself as a subject, Ebbinghaus memorized and then recalled hundreds of nonsense syllables—meaningless combinations of letters, such as TEG or XOT. Some of his findings about the nature of forgetting are valid even today. For example, he found that at first we forget materials we have memorized quite rapidly. Later, forgetting proceeds more slowly.

While Ebbinghaus's studies were ingenious in many respects, modern research on memory has gone far beyond these simple beginnings. It is probably safe to say that psychologists now know more about memory than about any other basic aspect of cognition. To provide you with an overview of this diverse and intriguing body of knowledge we'll proceed in the following manner. First, we'll consider a basic model of human memory—one that is currently

Memory: *The capacity to retain and later retrieve information.*

WHEN MEMORY FAILS—OR DOES IT?

While Calvin is obviously pulling one of his usual tricks, he's right about one thing: Memory is indeed far from perfect.
(Source: CALVIN AND HOBBES copyright 1987 & 1993 Watterson. Dist. by UNIVERSAL PRESS SYNDICATE. Reprinted with permission. All rights reserved.)

accepted by many psychologists. This model suggests that we actually possess three distinct memory systems. After describing the model, we'll examine these systems, indicating how each carries out the basic tasks of memory: (1) entering information into storage, (2) retaining such input for varying periods of time, and (3) retrieving it when it is needed. Next, we'll explore the operation of memory in natural contexts—how memory operates in daily life, outside the confines of the experimental laboratory. We will consider such issues as *autobiographical memory*, or memory of events and experiences in our own lives; *distortion* and *construction* in memory; and *eyewitness testimony*. We'll conclude by examining several memory disorders and what these disorders (and other research) tell us about the biological nature of memory.

Human Memory: The Information Processing Approach

*H*ave you ever operated a personal computer? If so, you already know that computers, like people, have memories. In fact, most have two different types of memory: a temporary working memory (known as random access memory), and a larger and more permanent memory in which information is stored for longer periods of time (a hard drive). Do computers' memories operate like those of human beings? Almost certainly not. Consider the following differences. Unless you correctly specify the precise nature and location of information you want to find, computers are unable to recover it. They merely flash an error message such as INVALID PATH. In contrast, you can often find information in your own memory even on the basis of a partial description. Similarly, information that is lost from a computer is often permanently gone. In contrast, you can fail to remember a fact or information at one time but remember it readily at another. And you can often remember part of the information you want, even if you can't remember all of it. Clearly, human memory and computer memory are not identical.

Even so, many researchers have concluded that there is sufficient similarity between computer memory and human memory for the former to serve as a rough working model for the latter. Both types of memory, after all, must accomplish the same basic tasks: (1) **encoding**—converting information into a form that can be entered into memory; (2) **storage**—retaining information over varying periods of time; and (3) **retrieval**—locating and accessing specific information when it is needed later. Please don't misunderstand: The fact that computers and human memory deal with the same basic tasks in no way implies that they operate in an identical manner. They certainly do not. You should view this **information processing approach** primarily as a useful means for drawing a bead on the key issues. It is a convenient way of discussing memory, not a fully developed representation of how memory operates.

Human Memory: One Influential Model—and an Emerging New Approach

Having issued these cautions, we should quickly note that in psychology the study of memory has proceeded, since the late 1960s, largely within the context of the information processing approach. Thus, it makes good sense to organize much of this chapter around that basic theme. Further, several important models of memory rest firmly on this basic approach. Of these, a model proposed by Atkinson and Shiffrin (1968) has been perhaps the most influential.

Encoding: The process through which information is converted into a form that can be entered into memory.

Storage: The process through which information is retained in memory.

Retrieval: The process through which information stored in memory is located.

Information Processing Approach: *An approach to understanding human memory that emphasizes the encoding, storage, and later retrieval of information.*

THE MODAL MODEL: THREE KINDS OF MEMORY SYSTEMS The Atkinson–Shiffrin model is sometimes described as the modal (i.e., most representative) model. Its central feature is the contention that in fact we possess not one but *three* distinct memory systems. One of these, known as *sensory memory*, provides temporary storage of information brought by our senses. If you've ever watched someone wave a flashlight in a dark room and perceived what seem to be trails of light behind it, you are familiar with the operation of sensory memory. A second type of memory is known as *short-term memory* (STM). STM holds relatively small amounts of information for brief periods of time, usually thirty seconds or less. This is the type of memory system you use when you look up a phone number and dial it immediately. Our third memory system, *long-term memory*, allows us to retain vast amounts of information for very long periods of time. For example, consider the following incident (Marek, 1975). Once, just before the beginning of a concert, the noted conductor Arturo Toscanini was approached by a member of the orchestra, who said that the lowest note on his bassoon was broken. Toscanini thought for a moment and then replied: "It is all right; that note does not occur in tonight's concert." In other words, in just a few moments he had mentally run through the entire score for all the instruments! Clearly, from the point of view of duration and capacity, long-term memory can be impressive. As we'll soon see, its key problem is often retrieval: finding a specific piece of information in this huge storage system.

How does information move from one memory system to another? We'll return to this complex question in more detail below; but here we can note that the modal model (Atkinson & Shiffrin, 1968) suggests the operation of *active control processes* that act as filters, determining which information will be retained. Information in sensory memory enters short-term memory when it becomes the focus of our attention; sensory impressions that do not engage attention fade and quickly disappear. So, where memory is concerned, **selective attention**—our ability to pay attention to only some aspects of the world around us while largely ignoring others—often plays a crucial role.

In contrast, information in short-term memory enters long-term storage through *elaborative rehearsal*—that is, by our thinking about its meaning and relating it to other information already in long-term memory. (Figure 6.1 provides a summary of the Atkinson–Shiffrin model.)

PARALLEL DISTRIBUTED PROCESSING: AN EMERGING PERSPECTIVE While the modal model and related views remain important in psychology, other influential perspectives on memory exist as well (Craik & Lockhart, 1972). Of these, perhaps the one now receiving the greatest amount of attention is the **parallel distributed processing model** (Lewandowsky & Murdock, 1989). According to this model, information is not processed in the step-by-step manner proposed by the Atkinson–Shiffrin model. In other words, it does not move from sensory to short-term and from short-term to long-term memory. The parallel distributed processing model suggests rather that information is actually processed simultaneously in several different parts of our total memory system. These parts or units operate in parallel, working on the same information at once. This means that many copies or representations of given information are present simultaneously at numerous locations within memory and can be accessed from any of these.

Why do many psychologists find this model so appealing? Because something like parallel processing of information is in fact necessary to account for many daily activities involving memory. For example, consider reading. This task, which most of us can perform with ease, includes recognizing the vertical, horizontal, and curved lines that combine to make up letters, identifying letters

Selective Attention: Our ability to pay attention to only some aspects of the world around us while largely ignoring others.

Parallel Distributed Processing Model: A model suggesting that our memory systems process information in several different ways simultaneously.

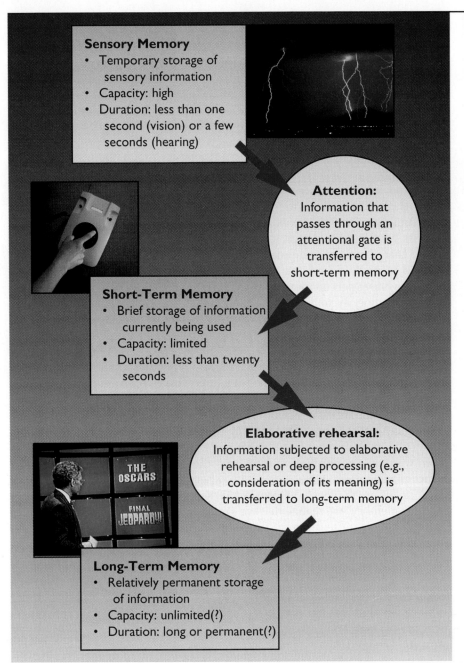

FIGURE 6.1

Sensory Memory
- Temporary storage of sensory information
- Capacity: high
- Duration: less than one second (vision) or a few seconds (hearing)

Attention: Information that passes through an attentional gate is transferred to short-term memory

Short-Term Memory
- Brief storage of information currently being used
- Capacity: limited
- Duration: less than twenty seconds

Elaborative rehearsal: Information subjected to elaborative rehearsal or deep processing (e.g., consideration of its meaning) is transferred to long-term memory

Long-Term Memory
- Relatively permanent storage of information
- Capacity: unlimited(?)
- Duration: long or permanent(?)

One Widely Accepted Model of Memory

According to a model proposed by Atkinson and Shiffrin (1968), we actually possess three distinct memory systems. Information moves between these through *active control processes* such as attention and elaborative rehearsal.

themselves, understanding words, and comprehending combinations of words. It is difficult to see how all these tasks could be performed so quickly and smoothly in the absence of something like parallel processing. In short, we must possess some mechanism for processing, at the same time, complex information from what we read *and* complex information already stored in memory. So models of memory based on parallel processing seem consistent with the ways in which memory actually operates—and also, as we'll see in a later section, with growing evidence about how the human brain functions. To the extent it helps us establish such links between cognitive and neural activity, the distributed parallel processing model may prove to be valuable.

Types of Information in Memory

If memory is a system (or, as we have seen, a set of systems) for retaining information, the next question is obvious: What types of information does it store? The world, and our experience in it, is incredibly diverse, so this is a more complex question than you might at first assume. After careful study, however, psychologists have concluded that most, if not all, information in memory can be placed in one of three distinct categories.

The first is **semantic memory**: the sum total of each individual's general, abstract knowledge about the world. What is the population of Canada? Is Alberta larger or smaller than New Brunswick? Are clams crustaceans or mollusks? And, whatever their place in the animal kingdom, how long does it take to cook them? The answers to these and countless other questions are contained in semantic memory. The people who win large prizes on television quiz shows are ones who have managed to expand the scope of their semantic memory beyond that of most other human beings. Semantic memory allows us to represent and mentally operate on objects or situations that are not present to our senses. As one expert on memory puts it (Tulving, 1993, p. 67), "The owner of a semantic memory system can think about things that are not here now."

A second type of information we retain relates to specific events that we have experienced personally. This is **episodic memory** (sometimes known as autobiographical memory), which allows us, in a sense, to travel back in time. When was the last time you went to a movie? How did you feel on the day of your most recent graduation? What was it like to drive a car for the first time? Information pertaining to these and countless other aspects of your own experience is contained in episodic memory.

Another way to understand the difference between semantic and episodic memory is to think about the conscious experiences associated with them. When we retrieve information from episodic memory, we experience this as the act of remembering; in a sense, we experience again something that happened to us in the past. In contrast, when we retrieve information from semantic memory, we realize that we know this information—we can bring it to mind. This is quite different from the conscious experience of remembering events in our lives (Tulving, 1993).

Finally, we retain information relating to the performance of various tasks. Do you know how to ice skate? Tie a necktie? Play the saxophone? If you do, then you are well aware of the operation of our third type of memory, known as **procedural memory**. Procedural memories are the result of the basic learning processes discussed in Chapter 5. In contrast to semantic and episodic memories, these memories are difficult to put into words; indeed, as we saw in Chapter 4, trying to do so and becoming overly self-conscious can interfere with smooth performance. Yet such memories are extremely important, for without them we would be unable to retain many skills once we have learned them.

As you might readily guess, we often require—and use—information of all three types at once. Consider a student taking a final examination. Obviously, as she takes the exam, she is drawing on facts stored in semantic memory. In addition, she is using complex motor skills such as writing, which are represented in procedural memory. And she may be thinking about experiences with other examinations. For example, she may remember that recently she actually lowered her grade on an exam by changing many correct answers to wrong ones. Having recalled this, she may refrain

SEMANTIC MEMORY IN ACTION

People who are highly successful on television quiz shows, like "Jeopardy," have stored a tremendous amount of general knowledge in semantic memory.

Semantic Memory: The content of our general, abstract knowledge about the world.

Episodic Memory: Memories of events that we have experienced personally (sometimes termed autobiographical memory).

Procedural Memory: A memory system that retains information we cannot readily express verbally—for example, information necessary to perform skilled motor activities such as riding a bicycle.

KEY POINTS

- Several influential models of human memory suggest that we possess three distinct memory systems: sensory memory, short-term memory, and long-term memory.

- Evidence indicates that in at least some memory systems, information is processed in a parallel manner rather than step by step.

- Several different types of information are stored in memory: semantic memory holds general information about the world; episodic memory holds information about experiences from our own lives; and procedural memory holds nonverbal information that allows us to perform various motor tasks.

from revising several answers. In this and many other situations, all three types of information are used at once.

How do we know that these different forms of memory exist? Important information about this is provided by memory disabilities that emerge after injury. In **Canadian Focus**, an injury-induced defect in episodic memory is described.

Sensory Memory: Gateway to Consciousness

You are waiting in a busy airport. Many different activities are occurring around you. People are rushing about; passengers are moving through security gates; people are talking, laughing, crying, hugging. You glance at a large video monitor containing flight information. You look away, but then, almost instantly, you look back to it. Something seemed different—what was it?

CANADIAN FOCUS

The Story of a Man Without Episodic Memory

Since 1983, researchers in the Unit for Memory Disorders at the University of Toronto have been studying a man with a quite remarkable memory deficit. In October 1981, K.C., as he is known in the psychological literature, ran off the road on his motorcycle on his way home from work and received a severe closed-head injury. He was unconscious for seventy-two hours and in intensive care for a month. As a consequence of the accident, he suffered very extensive memory impairment. In this discussion we are going to focus on only one aspect of the memory problems of K.C.—his loss of episodic memory (Tulving, 1989; Tulving, Schacter, McLachlan, & Moscovitch, 1988).

If you were to meet K.C., you would find him to be cooperative and responsive. He has normal intelligence. His speech and reading abilities are largely unimpaired. He has a reasonable knowledge of the world and of events that occurred prior to his injury. He also has memories about experiences that he, as an individual, had before the accident. His memory tends to be better for events that are remoter from the time of his accident. There is, however, a peculiar character to his descriptions of these experiences: They are strangely detached and factual, as if he were describing his past from the point of view of an observer rather than a participant. He knows that his family owns a cottage in Ontario and that he has spent substantial time there, but he can recall nothing about any experiences he had at the cottage. He knows that he has owned a car and two motorcycles, and can even provide physical descriptions of these vehicles, but he is quite unable to provide information about any specific trips or experiences that he had with these vehicles. He knows that he can play chess and change a tire, but he has no recollection of any particular chess game or any tire-changing episode. In short, he has a reasonable knowledge of what he can and cannot do, and of things he has done and places he has gone; but he has no recollection of the subjective experience associated with the learning or doing of any of these things.

The case of K.C. provides compelling support for the claims of Tulving and his associates that episodic memory can be distinguished from semantic and procedural memory. K.C. has retained substantial factual material about the nonpersonal aspects of events that took place prior to the accident—his semantic memory is relatively intact. He has lost, however, all information about the personal experiences he had as an individual in living through this period of his life—his episodic memory has vanished.

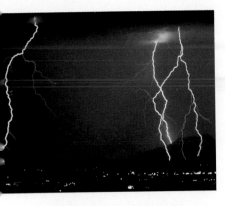

VISUAL SENSORY MEMORY

Visual sensory memory holds an image, such as a flash of lightning, for only a fraction of a second—just long enough for us to determine if it is worthy of further attention.

Sensory Memory: A memory system that retains representations of sensory input for brief periods of time.

Groaning, you realize that your flight has been delayed—again. Discouraged, you settle back in your chair for an even longer wait.

This incident may seem at first to have more to do with the difficulties of modern travel than with memory; but think again: What made you glance back at the screen? The answer involves what is in a sense our simplest memory system: **sensory memory**. This system holds representations of information from our senses very briefly—just long enough, it appears, for us to determine that some aspect of this input is worthy of further attention. Without such memory, you would have had no reason to look back at the video monitor. As soon as your eyes moved away from it, all traces of the screen and its contents would have vanished. In this and countless other situations, sensory memory is useful indeed. Without it, we'd be able to react only to those stimuli reaching us at a given instant.

How much can sensory memory hold? And how long does such information last? Existing evidence suggests that the capacity of sensory memory is quite large—indeed, it may hold fleeting representations of virtually everything we see, hear, taste, smell, or feel (Reeves & Sperling, 1986). These representations are retained for only brief periods, however. Visual sensory memory seems to last for less than a second, while acoustic sensory memory lasts for no more than a few seconds (Cowan, 1984). Convincing evidence for these conclusions was first gathered by Sperling (1960) in a series of now well-known experiments.

In one of these studies, participants were shown nine letters arranged in rows of three on a card. These stimuli were shown very briefly—for only fifty milliseconds (0.05 seconds). Participants were then asked to report all the letters they could remember. Under these procedures, their memory was not impressive: They could recall only about four or five of the nine letters shown. However, they also reported the impression that right after seeing the card, they could remember all of the letters; the visual image faded quickly, however, so that by the time they had named four or five letters, the rest were completely gone.

To determine if this was actually happening, Sperling devised an ingenious technique. Immediately after presenting the letters, he sounded a tone that was either high, medium, or low in pitch. The high tone meant that participants should report the first row, the medium tone indicated that they should report the second, and so on. The results were clear: Under these conditions, participants demonstrated near-perfect scores. Just how quickly does such information fade? To answer this question, Sperling repeated the above procedures, but delayed presentation of the tone for various periods of time. The results indicated that sensory memory is indeed brief: When the tone was delayed only 0.10 seconds (100 milliseconds), participants' performance dropped sharply; when it was delayed for an entire second, their ability to remember the letters all but disappeared.

These findings, confirmed in many later studies, point to two conclusions. Sensory memory exists, and it can store an impressive amount of information. But it is very short-lived. Where sensory memory is concerned, then, it appears to be a matter of, "Now you see (or hear) it, now you don't."

Short-Term Memory: The Workbench of Consciousness

*I*magine that you are in an ethnic restaurant tasting foods you've never had before. One of the dishes is truly delicious, so you ask the waiter for its name in his native language. He tells you, and you repeat it several times until you get it right. A couple of minutes later, you decide to write it down so you won't forget. You get out your pen and paper, only to find that it is already too late—you've forgotten the name of the dish. Have you ever had an experience like this? If not, remember the last time you looked up the spelling of a word in the dictionary only to forget it before you could write it down; or the last time you met someone, only to forget his or her name within seconds of hearing it. Such experiences point to the existence of our second memory system: **short-term memory,** which holds a limited amount of information for a short period of time. Despite its limitations, short-term memory, like sensory memory, is very important. Indeed, many experts view it as a kind of workbench for consciousness—a system for temporarily holding information you are using or processing right now. Thus, another term for short-term memory is *working* memory.

Evidence for the Existence of Short-Term Memory

Everyday experience strongly supports the view that short-term memory exists and is distinct from long-term memory. Before turning to some of the basic characteristics of this memory system, let's look briefly at some of the scientific evidence for its presence.

THE SERIAL POSITION CURVE   Suppose that someone read you a list of unrelated words and asked you to recall as many as possible in any order you wished. Which words would you be most likely to remember? Research findings indicate that you would be more likely to remember words at the beginning and at the end of the list than words in the middle (see Figure 6.2). Why does this effect, known as the **serial position curve,** occur? One possible answer has to do with the existence of two memory systems. Presumably, you remember the last words you heard quite well—a *recency* effect—because they are still in short-term memory when you are asked to recall them. And you remember the words at the start of the list because they have already been entered into long-term memory. Words in the middle, in contrast, have vanished from short-term memory and are not yet fully present in long-term memory. Several different studies have obtained results consistent with this reasoning (Postman & Phillips, 1965). The serial position curve, then, provides support for the existence of two distinct memory systems.

ACOUSTIC AND SEMANTIC CODING   Additional evidence that short-term memory is distinct from long-term memory comes from studies indicating that people have more difficulty immediately recalling words or letters whose names sound alike (such as P, D, V, C, and T) than ones whose names sound different (such as K, Y, Z, W, and R) (e.g, Wickelgren, 1965). This finding suggests that information is entered into immediate short-term memory in terms of acoustic coding—how it sounds. In contrast, when asked to recall words over longer periods, people have more difficulty remembering ones that sound different but are similar in meaning (such as big, huge, broad, long,

Short-Term Memory: A memory system that holds limited amounts of information for relatively short periods of time.

Serial Position Curve: The greater accuracy of recall of words or other information early and late in a list than in the middle of the list.

FIGURE 6.2

The Serial Position Curve

When people try to recall a list of unrelated words, they usually remember more words from the beginning and end of the list than from the middle. This serial position curve provides evidence for the existence of two distinct memory systems: short-term and long-term.

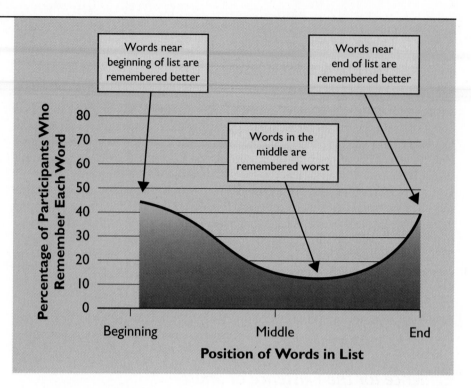

tall) than ones that are dissimilar in meaning but sound alike (such as man, mad, cap, can). These latter findings suggest that information may be entered into long-term memory primarily in terms of its meaning. While other evidence suggests that this distinction is not as clear-cut as was once believed (Baddeley, 1990), the fact that information is coded differently when remembered for short periods than when remembered for longer ones supports the existence of two distinct memory systems.

Short-Term Memory: *Its Basic Operation*

Now let's turn to some of the basic features of short-term memory. What kind of information does it hold? How much? And for how long?

First, in sensory memory, information is represented in a form similar to that reported by our senses. In short-term memory, information is represented somewhat differently. There, most verbal input—both the words we read and the words others speak—seems to be stored acoustically, by how it sounds (Salame & Baddeley, 1982). There is some indication, however, that information is also represented semantically, in terms of its meaning. When asked to recall words they have just memorized, people often confuse ones with similar meanings as well as ones that sound alike. So, it appears that we can store information in different ways in short-term memory.

Second, how much can this memory system hold? The answer seems to be something like seven to nine separate pieces of information. However, each of these "pieces" can contain several separate bits of information, when they are somehow related and can be grouped together in a meaningful way. In such cases, each piece of information is described as a **chunk**, and the total amount of information held in chunks can be quite large. For example, consider the following list of letters: RNCATAFNPDNVTCPMCR. After hearing or reading it once, would you remember it? Probably not. But imagine that instead, the letters were presented as follows: CNR, NAFTA, NDP, CTV,

Chunk: Stimuli perceived as a single unit or a meaningful grouping. Most people can retain seven to nine chunks of information in short-term memory at a given time.

RCMP. Could you remember them now? The chances are much better that you could, because now you could combine them into meaningful chunks—in this case, well-known acronyms. Because of the process of *chunking*, short-term memory can hold a large amount of information, even though it can retain only seven to nine separate items at once.

Third, how long does information in short-term memory last? The answer is clear: not very long. Unless it is actively *rehearsed* (repeated again and again), information entered into short-term memory fades quickly. Indeed, if individuals are prevented from rehearsing—for example, by being asked to count backwards—the information may be almost totally gone within twenty seconds (e.g., Peterson & Peterson, 1959).

Additional evidence suggests that the greater the extent to which rehearsal is prevented—for example, by tasks even more distracting than counting backwards—the more rapid is the fading of short-term memory (Reitman, 1974). Further, most people, when left to their own devices, actively rehearse information they wish to retain in short-term memory. The moral of such findings is clear: If you want to keep a phone number, a licence plate, a new acquaintance's name, or any other piece of information in short-term memory, there's only one solution—rehearse, rehearse, and then rehearse some more.

- Short-term memory retains information for a few seconds.

- The existence of short-term memory is supported by the finding that words near the end of a list are remembered better than words near the middle. This is the serial position curve.

- Additional evidence for the distinction between short-term and long-term memory is the finding that people have more difficulty keeping words or letters that sound alike in short-term memory than retaining ones that do not.

Long-Term Memory: The Storehouse of Consciousness

Can you remember your first trip to the dentist? Your first-grade teacher? Your first date? Even though these events occurred long ago, the chances are good that you have vivid memories of them. The fact that you do points to the existence of a third memory system—one that permits us to store vast quantities of information in a relatively permanent manner. This is **long-term memory,** and evidence concerning its accuracy is nothing short of startling. For example, in a study carried out by Standing (1973) at Bishop's University in Quebec, students were shown 10,000 pictures over the course of five days. They were then presented with pairs of slides, each pair in the sample consisting of one slide they had already seen and one they had not. Their task was to indicate the slide they had seen earlier. Despite the enormous number of items shown, they had an 83 percent accuracy rate on the sample pairs tested.

Yet we have all had experiences in which we could not remember some item or piece of information, no matter how hard we tried. To make matters worse, at such times we often feel that the fact, name, or item we want is somewhere "in there" but just beyond our reach. This is the **tip-of-the-tongue phenomenon,** and research findings indicate that it is quite real. When individuals are given the definition of an uncommon English word such as *sampan*, *geode*, or *charisma* and report that they can almost think of the word, they are quite successful in supplying its first letter and indicating how many syllables it has (Brown & McNeill, 1966). To add to our frustration at such times, we often find ourselves repeatedly coming up with related but incorrect responses (Reason & Lucas, 1984). These tend to be words that are more common than the one we want; and as we think of them repeatedly, they tend to strengthen still further until they totally block all efforts to

Long-Term Memory: A memory system for retaining large amounts of information over long periods of time.

Tip-of-the-Tongue Phenomenon: The feeling that we can almost remember some information we wish to retrieve from memory.

remember the word we really want. If we then give up, however, some kind of search often continues, so that later, quite unexpectedly, the missing item suddenly appears in consciousness. These everyday experiences indicate that the information being sought is indeed present in memory but can't be located. As we'll soon see, *retrieval* is a crucial process where long-term memory is concerned; after all, information that can't be found is as useless to us, in a practical sense, as information that is no longer present.

So we are left with a mixed picture of long-term memory. On the one hand, it is impressive in its capacity to store huge quantities of information for long periods of time. On the other hand, it often lets us down just when we seem to need it most—for example, while we are taking exams or delivering an important speech. How does this memory system operate? How is information entered into long-term memory and later retrieved? These are among the questions we'll now consider.

Long-Term Memory: *Its Basic Operation*

The first question we should address is this: How does information enter long-term memory from short-term memory? The answer seems to involve a process we have already discussed: rehearsal. In this case, though, the rehearsal does not consist simply of repeating what we wish to remember, as in simply restating a phone number over and over again. Rather, for information to enter long-term memory, **elaborative rehearsal** seems to be required. This is rehearsal requiring significant cognitive effort; it can include thinking about the meaning of the new information and attempting to relate it to information already in memory (see Figure 6.3). For example, if you wish to enter into long-term memory the facts and findings presented in a section of this chapter, it is not sufficient merely to state them over and over again. Instead, you should think about what they mean and how they relate to things you already know.

If elaborative rehearsal is required for information to enter long-term memory, then anything that interferes with such rehearsal should also interfere with long-term memory. Many factors create such interference. One with which many people have had direct experience is alcohol. Informal observation suggests that when consumed in sufficient quantities, this drug interferes with long-term memory, and research findings lend support to this claim: Alcohol does seem to impair human memory (Birnbaum & Parker, 1977).

Elaborative Rehearsal:
Rehearsal in which the meaning of information is considered and the information is related to other knowledge already present in memory.

CHAPTER 6

FIGURE 6.3

Entering Information into Long-Term Memory

In order for information to move from short-term memory to long-term memory, *elaborative rehearsal* is required. Such rehearsal involves thinking about the meaning of new information and attempting to relate it to information already in memory. If this cognitive effort is not expended, the new information may fail to enter long-term memory and be rapidly forgotten.

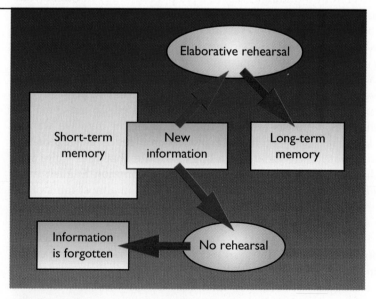

Specifically, it seems to interfere with the processes through which information is entered into long-term memory. We'll return to this topic in more detail in a later discussion of eyewitness testimony (Yuille & Tollestrup, 1990).

LEVELS OF PROCESSING: COGNITIVE EFFORT AND LONG-TERM MEMORY We have been focusing on the concept of elaborative rehearsal as it relates to long-term memory; but now let's consider one of the alternative models of memory we mentioned earlier: the **levels of processing view.** Like many influential models of memory processes, it emerged from research carried out at the University of Toronto. Craik and Lockhart (1972), who were the proponents of this approach, suggested that rather than concentrating on the *structure* of memory and the different systems it involves, it might be more useful to concentrate on the *processes* that contribute to remembering. They noted that information can be processed in several different ways, ranging from relatively superficial *shallow processing* to more effortful and lasting *deep processing*. Shallow processing might consist of merely repeating a word or making a simple sensory judgment about it—for example, do two words or letters look alike? A deeper level of processing might involve more complex comparisons—for example, do two words rhyme? A much deeper level of processing would include attention to meaning—for example, do two words have the same meaning? Does a word make sense when used in a specific sentence?

Considerable evidence suggests that the deeper the level of processing that takes place when we encounter new materials, the more likely the materials are to enter long-term memory. For example, in a well-known study, Craik and Tulving (1975) presented unrelated words and asked participants one of three kinds of questions about each word. For example, was the word written in capital or lower-case letters? Did the word rhyme with another word? Did the word fit within a given sentence? After answering a large number of such questions, participants were asked whether each word in a list was one they had already seen or was new. The results offered clear support for the levels of processing view. The deeper the level of processing performed by subjects, the slower their responses—but the more accurate their decisions (see Figure 6.4).

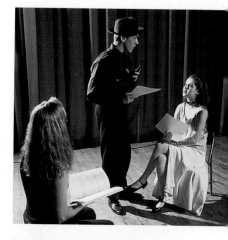

THE ROLE OF REHEARSAL

In order to pass from short-term to long-term memory, information must be rehearsed repeatedly.

Levels of Processing View: A view of memory suggesting that the greater the effort expended in processing information, the more readily it will be recalled at later times.

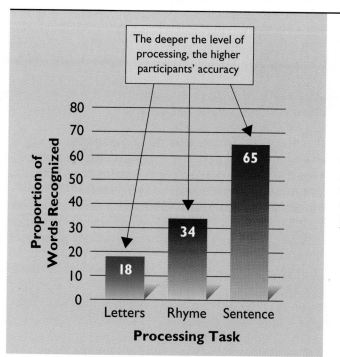

The deeper the level of processing, the higher participants' accuracy

Proportion of Words Recognized

Letters — 18
Rhyme — 34
Sentence — 65

Processing Task

FIGURE 6.4

Levels of Processing and Memory

Individuals were asked one of three kinds of questions with respect to unrelated words. These questions required varying levels of processing. The deeper the level of processing required, the more accurately the participants could later identify the words. (Source: Based on data from Craik & Tulving, 1975.)

Why does deeper and more effortful processing of information lead to better long-term memory? One possibility is that such cognitive effort leads us to encode more features of the items in question. This, in turn, makes it easier to locate the information later. Supporting this view is the fact that in general, when people not only see a series of objects but actually perform some action upon them, they can later remember the names of the objects better in a test of free recall—a test in which they are simply asked to recall as many of the objects as possible (Nilsson & Cohen, 1988).

While such findings are compatible with the levels of processing model, there are still some difficulties with this model that cannot be overlooked. For example, it is difficult to specify in advance just what constitutes a deep rather than a shallow level of processing. Second, it is not clear that a person can read a word over and over again and not be aware of, or think about, its meaning. In fact, several forms of processing (such as acoustic and semantic) may occur at once. So it is difficult to speak about discrete levels of processing.

Despite such problems, there can be little doubt that the levels of processing view has added to our understanding of long-term memory, and especially to our knowledge of how information is entered into this system.

Retrieval: *Locating Information in Long-Term Memory*

As noted earlier, the limitations of short-term memory are all too obvious: it has limited capacity, and information is quickly lost unless it is continually rehearsed. Long-term memory, of course, does not have these problems. It has a seemingly limitless capacity and can retain information for very long periods, perhaps indefinitely. Is it, then, a perfect system? Definitely not. All too often we are unable to remember information we need just when we need it. Only later—maddeningly!—does it sometimes appear effortlessly in our mind (Payne, 1987). What is the cause of this? The answer involves the process of *retrieval*—our ability to locate information that has previously been stored in memory.

Where long-term memory is concerned, it is difficult to separate retrieval from the issue of *storage*—the way information is initially placed in long-term memory. Storage plays an important role in determining how readily information can later be retrieved. In general, the better organized materials are, the easier they are to retrieve (Bower et al., 1969). One key to the effective retrieval of information from long-term memory, then, is *organization*. Organizing information requires extra effort, but it appears that the benefits in terms of later ease of retrieval make this effort well worthwhile.

RETRIEVAL CUES: STIMULI THAT HELP US REMEMBER   Imagine that after an absence of several years, you return to a place where you used to live. On your arrival, memories of days gone by come flooding back, with no apparent effort on your part to bring them to mind. You remember incidents you had totally forgotten, conversations with people you haven't seen in years, even the weather during your last visit. Have you ever had this kind of experience? If so, you are already familiar with the effects of what psychologists term **retrieval cues**. These are stimuli that are associated with information stored in memory and so can help bring it to mind at times when it cannot be recalled spontaneously. Such cues can be aspects of the external environment—a place, sights or sounds, even smells. Indeed, some evidence suggests that odors are particularly effective in evoking memories of events in our lives (Richardson & Zucco, 1989).

Many studies point to the strong impact that retrieval cues have on long-term memory. Perhaps the most intriguing research on this topic involves the

Retrieval Cues: Stimuli associated with information stored in memory that can aid in its retrieval.

concept of **context-dependent memory**: the fact that material learned in one environment is more difficult to remember in a very different context than it is in the original one. An ingenious study performed by Godden and Baddeley (1975) illustrates context-dependent memory.

In this study, the participants were practiced deep-sea divers. They learned a list of words either on the beach or beneath fifteen feet of water; then they tried to recall the words either in the same environment in which they had learned them or in the other setting. As shown in Figure 6.5, the results offered striking evidence for the importance of context—in this case, physical setting. Words learned on land were recalled much better in that location than under water, and vice versa. Interestingly, such effects were not found with respect to recognition—merely deciding whether they had seen the words before or not (Godden & Baddeley, 1980). Thus, it appears that context-related retrieval cues help mainly with respect to actual recall. Additional findings suggest that it is not necessary actually to be in the location or context where storage in long-term memory occurred; merely imagining this setting may be sufficient (Smith, 1979). In other words, we seem capable of generating our own context-related retrieval cues.

Finally, our own internal state can serve as a retrieval cue in some cases. The concept of **state-dependent retrieval** refers to the fact that it is often easier to recall information in long-term memory when our internal state resembles the one we were in at the time the information was first learned than when our state is different. For example, suppose that while studying for an exam you drink lots of coffee. Thus, the effects of caffeine are present while you memorize the materials in question. On the day of the test, should you also drink lots of coffee so that the effects of caffeine will again be present? Will these effects act as a retrieval cue and enhance your memory? The results of several studies indicate that they will indeed (Eich, 1980). Again, as with context-related memory, state-dependent retrieval seems to apply only to free recall; recognition is not necessarily enhanced.

Context-Dependent Memory:
The greater ease of recall of information entered into memory in one context or setting in that same context than in others.

State-Dependent Retrieval:
Retrieval of information stored in long-term memory cued by aspects of one's physical state.

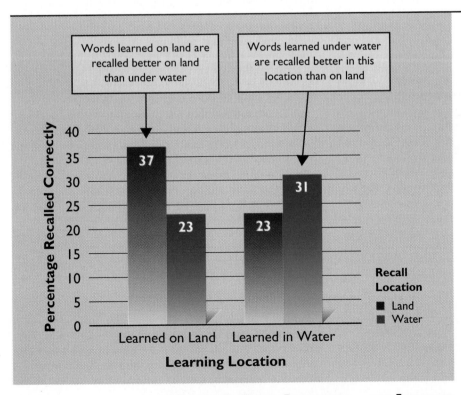

FIGURE 6.5

Context-Dependent Memory

Participants learned a list of words either on the beach or when under water. Later, they recalled the words more successfully in the same physical setting (context) where the learning took place.
(Source: Based on data from Godden & Baddeley, 1975.)

- Information moves from short-term to long-term memory through elaborative rehearsal.
- The levels of processing view suggests that the greater the cognitive effort we expend in processing information, the better it will be remembered.
- Retrieval cues are stimuli that help bring to mind information stored in long-term memory.

In sum, many different stimuli can serve as retrieval cues. Which do we actually use, and which are most helpful? According to the **encoding specificity principle** (Tulving & Thomson, 1973), this depends on what information we enter into memory in the first place. If, when learning some information, you encode certain aspects of your physical surroundings as part of the "package," these will later serve as useful retrieval cues. If your internal state is part of what is encoded, this will later serve as an effective retrieval cue. The key seems to be a close match between the conditions in which you first acquire some information and the conditions in which you attempt to recall it. The specific nature of individual retrieval cues seems to be of less importance.

Forgetting from Long-Term Memory

When are we most aware of memory? Typically, when it fails—when we are unable to remember information that we need at a particular moment. Given this fact, it is not surprising that the first systematic research on memory, conducted by Ebbinghaus, was concerned with forgetting. As you may recall, Ebbinghaus experimented on himself and studied the rate at which he forgot nonsense syllables. The results of his investigations suggested that forgetting is rapid at first but slows down with the passage of time.

Modern research has generally confirmed Ebbinghaus's findings as they relate to meaningless materials such as nonsense syllables, but suggests that we are much better at remembering other and more meaningful types of information. For example, Bahrick (1984) asked college professors to identify the names and faces of former students who had taken a single course with them. Even after more than eight years, the professors were quite successful in recognizing the students' names and in matching their names to photos. Similarly, it is clear that many complex skills, such as swimming or driving, are retained over long periods of time, even if we have little opportunity to practice them. In contrast, discrete skills—ones requiring associations between specific stimuli and responses—are subject to a much greater degree of forgetting. Thus, a few months after learning how to perform a procedure for reviving heart attack victims, most individuals have forgotten many of the steps and actions it involves (McKenna & Glendon, 1985). Many other complex skills, such as typing, show a similar pattern. What, then, accounts for forgetting? Why is information that was firmly entered in long-term memory sometimes lost, at least in part, with the passage of time? Several explanations have been offered. Here we'll focus on the two that have received the most attention. Then, we'll examine a far different view of forgetting—*repression*—and its bearing on the tragedy of childhood sexual abuse (Loftus, 1993).

Encoding Specificity Principle: *The fact that only cues encoded at the time information is entered into memory can later contribute to the retrieval of such information.*

The Trace-Decay Hypothesis: *Forgetting with the Passage of Time*

Perhaps the simplest view of forgetting is that information entered into long-term memory fades or decays with the passage of time. This suggestion is consistent with our informal experience: Often, information we acquired quite some time ago is more difficult to remember than information learned only recently. Yet considerable evidence suggests that decay is probably not the key mechanism in forgetting.

First, consider a famous study conducted by Jenkins and Dallenbach (1924). They asked two participants to learn a list of ten nonsense syllables. In one condition, both individuals then went directly to sleep. In another, they continued with their normal activities. The participants' recall of the nonsense syllables was tested after one, two, four, and eight hours. The results indicated that forgetting was more rapid when the participants stayed awake than when they went to sleep. These findings argue against the suggestion that forgetting is primarily the result of gradual decay of information over time.

Can you see any problems with this study—problems that raise complexities with respect to these seemingly straightforward results? Here's one: The participants who went to sleep learned the nonsense syllables in the evening, while those who stayed awake learned them in the morning. This means that differences in circadian rhythms may have played a role in the obtained results. And indeed, sleep during the day does not seem to reduce forgetting as reported by Jenkins and Dallenbach.

However, other research, in which animals have been kept awake but prevented from moving about and engaging in normal activities, also indicates that forgetting is not merely a matter of the passage of time. In one such study, Minami and Dallenbach (1946) taught cockroaches to avoid a dark compartment by giving them an electric shock whenever they entered it. After the participants had mastered this simple task, they were either restrained in a paper cone or permitted to wander around a darkened cage at will. The results again argued against the trace decay hypothesis: Roaches permitted to move about showed substantially more forgetting over a given period of time.

Forgetting as a Result of Interference

If forgetting is not a function of the passage of time and the weakening of materials stored in memory, then what *is* its source? The answer currently accepted by most psychologists focuses on *interference* between items of information stored in memory. Such interference can take two different forms. In **retroactive interference**, information being learned now interferes with information already present in memory. If learning the rules of a new board game causes you to forget the rules of a similar game you learned to play last year, you are the victim of retroactive interference. In contrast, **proactive interference** occurs when previously learned information interferes with information you are acquiring at present. If information you acquired about operating an old VCR interferes with your ability to operate a new one that has very different controls, you are experiencing proactive interference (see Figure 6.6).

A large body of evidence offers support for the view that interference plays a key role in forgetting from long-term memory (e.g., Tulving & Psotka, 1971). For example, in many laboratory studies, the more similar the words or nonsense syllables learned on different lists, the more interference among them, and the poorer participants' ability to remember these materials (Gruneberg, Morris, & Sykes, 1988). What remains unclear, however, is precisely *how* interference causes forgetting. Does it actively push information out of memory? Or does it merely impede our ability to retrieve information? A final answer to such questions must await the completion of additional research.

Retroactive Interference:
Interference with retention of information already present in memory by new information being entered into memory.

Proactive Interference:
Interference with the learning or storage of current information by information previously entered into memory.

FIGURE 6.6

Retroactive and Proactive Interference: Important Factors in Forgetting

In *retroactive interference,* information currently being learned interferes with retention of previously acquired information. In *proactive interference,* information learned previously interferes with retention of new information.

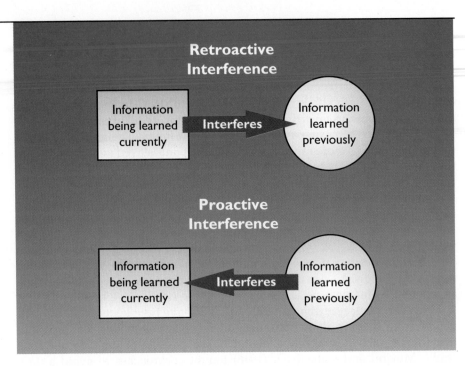

THE POINT OF IT ALL

REPRESSION AND MEMORY

In the trial of George Franklin, his daughter testified that she witnessed the murder, which had taken place more than twenty years earlier. She claimed that she had repressed the memory in the years since the traumatic event.

Repression: Do We Sometimes Forget Because We Want to Forget?

In 1991, George Franklin Sr. was convicted of sexually attacking and then murdering an eight-year-old girl who was a friend of his daughter. The crime had occurred in 1969—more than twenty years earlier. How had he escaped prosecution for all these years, and why was he finally placed on trial so long after this tragic crime? The answer is that in 1990 his daughter Eileen came forward and accused her father of being the murderer. Further—and this is directly related to our discussion of forgetting—she claimed that she had not come forward sooner because she had not remembered these events until shortly before she made her accusations. How could she "forget" such a traumatic event for so long a period?

One answer is provided by a third theory of forgetting from long-term memory—the theory of **repression**. According to this theory, which plays a key role in Freud's views of personality and mental illness (see Chapters 12 and 14), traumatic events such as the one here described are so shocking that all memory of them is forced from consciousness—*repressed*—into hidden recesses of the unconscious. There, the memories lie hidden until they are brought back into consciousness by some specific event—for example, by the probings of a therapist. In short, the theory of repression suggests that we forget some information and experiences because we find them too frightening or threatening to bear.

The existence of repression is widely accepted by psychologists and psychiatrists, as well as by society generally (Loftus & Herzog, 1991). Thus, Eileen Franklin's charges carried great weight with the jury who tried her father—so much weight, in fact, that he was convicted primarily on this evidence.

Repression has featured prominently in many dramatic trials focusing on charges of *early childhood sexual abuse*. In these trials, repression has been put forward to explain the fact that the victims failed to remember their terrible experiences until many years after they occurred. Only when these individuals were exposed to careful questioning by trained therapists did memories of their abuse during early childhood come flooding back into consciousness. Such trials, and the accounts of the people involved, certainly make for dramatic reading. Indeed, in recent years, many public figures—entertainers, famous athletes, and even Miss America—have reported the sudden emergence of traumatic memories of childhood abuse.

The growing frequency of these reports raises a question: Are the frightening "memories" always—or even usually—accurate? Did the people reporting them actually experience the devastating events? This is a complex question, because often the alleged events occurred so long ago that concrete, objective evidence of them is difficult to obtain. In addition, as noted recently by Loftus (1993), a leading expert on memory, there are several reasons for viewing at least some of these claims with a healthy degree of skepticism.

First, and most important, there is still very little scientific evidence that repression exists. Most support for the theory of repression derives from case studies. While these are often quite impressive, they do not, as we saw in Chapter 1, generally provide conclusive evidence on the issues they address. Indeed, so weak is present evidence for the existence of repression that one researcher (Holmes, 1990, p. 97) has suggested that use of the concept of repression in psychological reports should be preceded by the following statement: "Warning: The concept of repression has not been validated with experimental research and its use may be hazardous to the accurate interpretation of behavior."

Second, the fact that many therapists believe strongly in the existence of repression and its role in psychological disorders indicates that in at least some instances, therapists may act in ways that lead clients to report repressed memories even if they don't really have them. For example, a therapist who believes in the powerful impact of repressed memories might say something like this: "You know, in my experience a lot of people who are struggling with the same kind of problems as you had painful experiences as kids—they were beaten or even molested. I wonder if anything like that ever happened to you." Faced with such questions and their corresponding *demand characteristics* (refer to Chapter 1), clients may begin to search their memories for traces of traumatic early events. This search, in turn, may sometimes lead them to generate memories that weren't there, or to distort ones that do exist. As we'll see later in this chapter, there is growing evidence to suggest that memories can be generated or altered in precisely this fashion (e.g., Haugaard, et al., 1991; Loftus & Coan, in press).

Third, even if they are not undergoing therapy and do not hear their therapist suggest repressed memories, many people may be influenced by media accounts indicating that both early sexual abuse and repressed memories of these experiences are quite common. After exposure to such accounts, people suffering from depression, sexual dysfunction, or other psychological problems may be all too ready to attribute these difficulties to traumatic childhood events that they can no longer remember.

This is not to suggest that repressed memories never exist or that they can't be accurate. And there is certainly no doubt that childhood sexual abuse is disturbingly common (Kutchinsky, 1992). However, there do seem to be sufficient questions concerning both the nature and the occurrence of repression—to go with clear evidence that memories of traumatic events can

Repression: A theory of forgetting that suggests that memories of experiences or events we find threatening are sometimes pushed out of consciousness so that they can no longer be recalled.

be unintentionally fabricated—to suggest the need for caution. Many reports of repressed memories of early sexual abuse may indeed be accurate. But careful research indicates that memory is sometimes highly susceptible to distortion by misleading questions or false information (Loftus, 1992). Even worse, once such errors and distortions of memory occur, they may be accepted as the truth by the person involved.

Thus, as Loftus (1993) has put it, we must be careful to avoid letting false memories of early childhood abuse take on the certainty of unalterable fact. Falling into this trap, it seems, could ultimately be as dangerous and unfair to the ostensible perpetrators as closing our eyes to the existence and frequency of abuse was, in the past, to its victims.

Prospective Memory: *Forgetting to Do What We're Supposed to Do*

So far, we have focused on what can be termed *retrospective forgetting*—an inability to remember specific information entered into memory at an earlier time. Such forgetting is important, but often it is not the most annoying type we experience. Much worse, from this perspective, are those occasions on which we forget to keep an appointment or forget to perform some chore or errand we promised to complete. Such incidents involve **prospective memory**—remembering that we are supposed to perform some action at a certain time. This type of memory has important practical implications. Missing an important meeting can have serious consequences for one's career; forgetting to take a prescribed medication at certain times of the day can adversely affect one's health (Ley, 1988).

Why do we experience such forgetting? The answer seems to involve at least two factors. First, such forgetting is closely related to motivation. We tend to forget appointments or errands that are relatively unimportant to us, or which we view as unpleasant burdens, while remembering the ones we judge to be important or pleasurable (Winograd, 1988). For example, many dentists have to phone their patients the day before to remind them of their appointments, though few hairdressers find this necessary.

Second, prospective memory, like other forms of memory, involves retrieval cues. We remember to perform those activities that we build into the structure of our days in such a way that we are reminded of them by various cues. Thus, we remember to go to the supermarket, the dry cleaner's, and the bank on the way home by taking a route that passes each of these establishments; the route itself provides vivid reminders for prospective memory. Other cues we use for prospective memory are internal, and relate to the passage of time (Harris & Wilkins, 1982). At first we check our watch or nearby clocks frequently, to "calibrate" our internal time-measuring mechanism. In the middle of the waiting period, we perform fewer checks. Later, as the time for performing some activity—such as removing a cake from the oven or departing for a meeting—approaches, we check clocks and watches with increasing frequency. The result: We have a continuing series of cues to remind us of the activity we must perform (Ceci, Baker, & Bronfenbrenner, 1988). If retrieval cues are absent, prospective memory may fail us.

Prospective Memory:
Remembering to perform certain activities at specific times.

KEY POINTS

- Forgetting from long-term memory appears to result primarily from interference, not from the weakening of memories over time.

- In retroactive interference, information being learned now interferes with information already in memory.

- In proactive interference, information already in memory interferes with acquisition of new information.

- There is little direct evidence for the existence of repression. Individuals who suddenly "remember" painful events from long ago may not be providing accurate descriptions of actual events.

- Prospective forgetting is related to both motivation and the presence of retrieval cues.

Memory in Natural Contexts

Much of the research mentioned so far has involved the performance of relatively artificial tasks: memorizing nonsense syllables, lists of words, or lists of numbers. While we do have to remember some such items in real life, this kind of research seems fairly remote from many situations in our daily experience. In this section, we'll turn to the operation of memory in natural contexts and see how it operates in our daily lives (Loftus, 1991).

Autobiographical Memory:
Remembering the Events of Our Own Lives

How do we remember information about our own lives? Autobiographical memory, also known as episodic memory, has long been of interest to psychologists and has been studied in several different ways. For example, Baddeley and his colleagues (Kopelman, Wilson, & Baddeley, cited in Baddeley, 1990) have developed an *autobiographical memory schedule*, in which individuals are systematically questioned about different periods of their lives. Questions about childhood ask them to supply the names of their teachers and friends and the addresses at which they lived, and to describe incidents in their early lives. Additional questions are asked about other periods in their lives. The information obtained is then checked for accuracy against objective records. In this way, the accuracy of autobiographical memory can be assessed.

DIARY STUDIES: RECALLING THE DAILY EVENTS OF OUR LIVES Another technique for studying autobiographical memory involves efforts by individuals to keep detailed diaries of events in their own lives (Linton, 1975). In one such study, the Dutch psychologist Willem Wagenaar (1986) kept a diary for six years. On each day he recorded one or two incidents, carefully indicating who was involved, what happened, where it happened, and when it took place. He rated each incident in terms of whether it was something that happened frequently or rarely, and he also indicated the amount of emotional involvement he experienced.

During the course of the study, he recorded a total of 2,400 incidents. Then he tested his own memory for each, over a period of twelve months. To do so, he took each incident and, after cueing himself with one piece of information, tried to recall the rest. Thus, he might provide the *who* and then try to recapture the *what, where,* and *when*. Needless to add, he randomly selected the cue; for some incidents it involved *what*, for others *where*, and so on.

The findings Wagenaar reported are intriguing. First, he found that cues relating to *who, what,* and *where* were about equally effective in prompting memory. Information about *when* an incident took place was far less useful. This not surprising. Can you remember where you were last June 12 or October 15? Probably not, unless these dates are personally significant for you—your birthday or anniversary, for instance. You probably have a much better chance of remembering where you were during a particular incident if you know *whom* you were with or what you were doing.

In addition, and as expected, Wagenaar found that the more cues he provided himself, the more successful he was in answering correctly. Thus, if he knew who, what, and when, he was more successful in supplying the where than if he knew only who or what alone. He also found—again, far from surprisingly—that incidents that were unusual, emotionally involving, or pleasant were easier to recall than ones that were unpleasant. Finally, he appeared to forget fewer items than did other people who have conducted similar studies (e.g., Linton,

Endel Tulving

A dominant figure in memory research, Endel Tulving received the APA Gold Medal Award for Life Achievement in Psychological Science. He currently holds the Tannenbaum Chair in Cognitive Neuroscience at the Rotman Research Institute in Toronto.

Brenda A. L. Milner

Brenda Milner contributes to the understanding of memory and brain activity. Her awards include Officer of the Order of Canada and APA's Distinguished Scientific Contribution Award as well as several honorary degrees in Canada, the United States, and Scotland.

Elizabeth Loftus

Loftus is well known for her research in the areas of cognition, memory, eyewitness testimony, and psychology and the law. She advises students considering a career in psychology to "work closely with faculty mentors to get a good look at how they conduct their professional lives."

PSYCHOLOGISTS OF NOTE

1975), perhaps because he used a more detailed procedure for recording incidents and remembering them—one that provided him with more retrieval cues.

Keep in mind that there was only one subject in Wagenaar's (1986) study, and that the study was essentially observational in nature. As noted in Chapter 1, while such research is often informative, it cannot establish causal relationships or test hypotheses with the same degree of precision as experimentation. But Wagenaar's project, and the results of similar studies, indicate that autobiographical memory is affected by many of the same variables— such as retrieval cues and emotional states—that have been found to affect memory for abstract information presented under controlled laboratory conditions. This is valuable information in itself, and it suggests that further efforts to investigate autobiographical memory may indeed prove fruitful.

MEMORY FOR TIMES OF PAST EVENTS: WHEN DID YOU DO WHAT YOU REMEMBER DOING? Consider the following events:

- your last visit to the dentist
- the most recent federal election
- your most recent date
- the last time you ate Chinese food
- your most recent midterm exam

Can you place these events in chronological order from the one that occurred earliest to the one that occurred most recently? Of course; in fact, this sounds like a very trivial request. But the fact that you can do this with such ease and certainty points to an important fact about autobiographical memory: It involves a strong sense of time. Looking back over our lives, we do not see a jumble of unrelated events. Rather, we perceive a "story" that unfolds in time, with one event following another. We have a sense of how long ago each event occurred. We know its general location in the patterns of our life—for example, that it happened while we were in high school rather than college or university. And we know each event's relative position—whether it occurred before or after other events in our lives (Friedman, 1993).

How do we manage to keep track of time in this impressive manner? Research findings offer support for the following conclusions. As events occur, they are associated in memory with general contextual information and with other events. For example, consider your memories of your first date. At the time this event took place and information about it was entered into memory, it was associated with information about the environment (for example, you had just moved to a new house, it was a blazingly hot day) and about your own internal state (you were just recovering from the flu, you were feeling anxious about entering a new school), and so on. Later, when you think about your first date, you retrieve this contextual information along with information about the date. Since you know when you moved, that it is hot only in the summer, and that you tend to worry about the coming school year only during August, you immediately have lots of useful information at your disposal (e.g., Brown, Shevell, & Rips, 1986; Friedman, 1993). It is this kind of information which forms the basis for our ability to determine fairly accurately the timing of past events (see Figure 6.7). Apparently, it is by examining past events in the context of a wealth of other information about our own lives, and of a rich knowledge of social, natural, and personal time patterns, that we know when events took place. See the Key Concept illustration on page 251 for an overview of the different kinds of memory we possess.

People tend to be quite adept at remembering what they did and when they did it, except for one period in life—-early childhood. In **Canadian Focus**, reasons are offered for this observation.

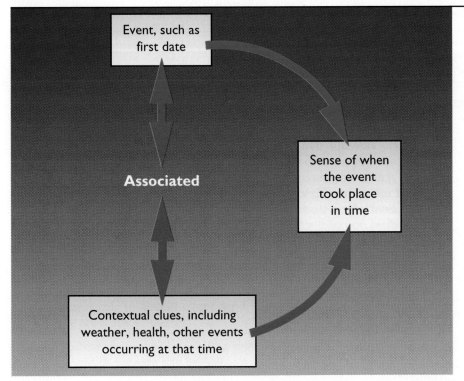

FIGURE 6.7

Memory for the Timing of Past Events

Research findings suggest that we keep track of the timing of events in our own lives by associating them with a broad range of contextual information. For example, we remember when our first date took place because it is associated with information about the weather on that day, the way we felt at the time, and other events in our lives.
(Source: Based on suggestions by Friedman, 1993.)

Why Can We Remember So Little of Our Very Early Childhood?

What is your earliest memory? If you are like most people, it probably dates from your third or fourth year of life, although some people seem capable of recalling events that occurred when they were as young as two (Usher & Neisser, 1993). This inability to recall events that happened to us during the first two or three years of life is known as **infantile amnesia**. An analysis of this phenomenon by Howe and Courage (1993) of Memorial University in Newfoundland offers an interesting explanation for why our memories do not extend back to the very early days of infancy.

It is obvious that we do retain information we acquired during the first years of life, for it is then that we learned to walk and to speak. Why, then, is *autobiographical* memory absent for this period? Why are we unable to recall events that happened to us at specific times and in specific places? Until recently, two explanations were widely accepted. According to the first, autobiographical memory is absent early in life because the brain structures necessary for such memories are not sufficiently developed at this time (Moscovitch, 1985). A second possibility has to do with the absence of language skills. Since we can't verbalize very effectively during the first two years of life, and since language plays a key role in long-term memory, it is not surprising that we cannot remember specific events from this period (Baddeley, 1990).

More recent findings, however, suggest that neither of these explanations is entirely accurate. Contrary to widespread belief, infants appear to possess relatively well-developed memory abilities. For example, as we'll see in Chapter 8, infants can imitate actions shown by an adult even after a twenty-four-hour delay (Meltzoff, 1990). It has been shown also that children

as young as two years can recount events that happened as long as six months earlier (Fivush, Gray, & Fromhoff,1987). It seems unlikely, therefore, that underdeveloped brain structures, or limited linguistic resources, are responsible for infantile amnesia.

How, then, do Howe and Courage explain the phenomenon? They contend that infants cannot store autobiographical memories until they have developed a clear self-concept. Without a self-concept, they lack the necessary personal frame of reference necessary for autobiographical memory. In other words, we cannot remember events that happened to us because we had no clear sense of ourselves as distinct individuals.

When do we acquire a clear self-concept? Not until we are about two years of age. Before this time, for example, babies show considerable interest in their own reflection in a mirror, but will not attempt to clean a spot of rouge that has been placed on their nose and is visible in their reflection. They do not appreciate that it is their own image that is being reflected in the mirror. By the time they are eighteen months to two years of age, however, they do attempt to clean the spot, thus indicating that they do recognize themselves (Lewis et al., 1989).

In summary, the researchers at Memorial University contend that infantile amnesia may actually be a misleading term. Our inability to report autobiographical memories from the first few years of life seems to reflect the absence of a clearly defined self-concept during this period, *not* a deficit in our memory system. In light of this evidence, it may be more appropriate to refer to this gap in our autobiographical memory not as a period of infantile amnesia, but rather as a period of infantile non-self.

Infantile Amnesia: Inability to remember the first two or three years of our life, probably because we did not possess a well-developed self-concept during that period.

Different Kinds of Memory: An Overview

Primary Memory Systems

Sensory memory
Holds information from our senses for brief periods of time.

An image of a flash of lightning is held in visual sensory memory for just a fraction of a second.

Short-Term Memory
Holds a limited amount of information—about seven to nine "chunks"—for short periods of time—less than a minute

Short-term memory allows us to remember a phone number we have just looked up long enough to dial it.

Long-Term Memory
Holds seemingly unlimited amounts of information for long periods of time—perhaps indefinitely.

The wide range of information representing correct answers to quiz show questions is held in long-term memory.

Aspects of Long-Term Memory

Prospective Memory
Memory for actions that we are supposed to perform at a certain time.

Autobiographical memory
Memory for information about our own lives, including information about the *who, what, where,* and *when* of events we have experienced.

Memory for the timing of past events
Memories for when various events in our lives occurred.

Flashbulb memories
Memories of where we were or what we were doing at the time of significant or unusual events.

- Autobiographical memory is memory of information about our own lives.
- Our inability to recall events from the first three years of life is often called infantile amnesia. This term is misleading, because memory does function during that period.
- Flashbulb memories—memories connected to dramatic events in our lives—are less accurate than we generally believe.

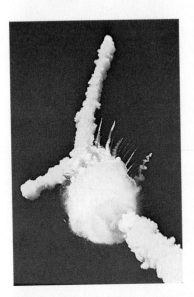

THE CHALLENGER EXPLOSION

For many of us, the tragic explosion of the space shuttle *Challenger* represents a flashbulb memory—we remember where we were and what we were doing when we heard the news in 1986. Can you think of other flashbulb memories?

Flashbulb Memories: Vivid memories of what we were doing at the time of an emotion-provoking event.

Schemas: Cognitive frameworks representing our knowledge about aspects of the world.

FLASHBULB MEMORIES: MEMORIES THAT DON'T FADE—OR DO THEY? Think back over your life. Select a surprising event to which you had an emotional reaction when you were informed about it. Can you remember where you were, and what you were doing, when you first learned about this event? If you can, you have a personal, firsthand example of what Brown and Kulik (1977) term a **flashbulb memory**—a vivid memory for what you were doing at the time of an emotion-provoking event.

Flashbulb memories tend to be very vivid and realistic. But are they accurate? Psychologists have begun to scrutinize them, and it turns out that they are often inaccurate (Neisser, 1991). In one study, students were asked, the day after the space shuttle *Challenger* exploded, how they had first heard this news. Three years later, the same individuals were asked to recall this information again. Most were sure that they could remember; but in fact, about one-third of their accounts were completely wrong. Flashbulb memories are a unique type of autobiographical memory. They may be vivid and real, but one should be cautious about assuming that they provide a precise and accurate account of a particular personal experience.

Distortion and Construction in Memory of Natural Events

A friend describes her "all-time" favorite movie to you. You come across it one night in the video store, take it out, and pop it into your VCR. As the movie unfolds, you find that the plot differs in a number of ways from the one your friend provided. You find the lead character less slow-witted and disaster-prone than your friend described, and the scene she considered the best in the movie takes place in a fast-food outlet, and not, as she related, in the lead's kitchen. What has happened?

One possibility is that your friend's description of the film has fallen prey to two basic types of errors that frequently affect memory in natural contexts. These are *distortion*—alterations in what is remembered and reported—and *construction*—the addition of information that was not actually provided, or, in some cases, the creation of "memories" of events or experiences that never actually took place.

DISTORTION AND THE INFLUENCE OF SCHEMAS We have all had experience with memory distortion. For example, when we look back on our own behavior in various situations, we often tend to perceive it in a favorable light; we remember saying or doing things we feel we *should* have said or done, even if we didn't actually say or do them. Similarly, when thinking about other people, we often remember them as closer to our stereotypes of the groups to which they belong than they actually are.

What accounts for memory distortions? In many cases, they seem to involve the operation of **schemas**—cognitive structures representing individuals' knowledge and assumptions about the world (Fiske & Taylor, 1991; Rumelhart, 1975). Schemas are developed through experience and act something like mental scaffolds; they provide basic frameworks for processing new information and relating it to existing knowledge. A schema can also be viewed as a packet of information consisting of a fixed core and a variable component. For example, your schema for buying something in a store has as its fixed aspect the exchange of money for some product or service. In addition, it allows room for variability with respect to the amount of funds involved, the specific item purchased, and so on.

Once schemas are formed, they exert strong effects on the way information is encoded, stored, and then retrieved. These effects, in turn, can lead to important errors or distortions in memory. Perhaps such effects are most apparent with respect to encoding. Current evidence suggests that when schemas are initially being formed—for example, when you are first learning about the activities, roles, and responsibilities of being a college or university student—information inconsistent with the newly formed schema is easier to notice and encode than information consistent with it. Such inconsistent information is surprising and thus seems more likely to become the focus of attention. In contrast, after the schema has been formed and is well developed, information consistent with it becomes easier to notice and hence recall (Stangor & Ruble, 1989; see Figure 6.8). It is the operation of schemas that, in part, accounts for the fact that in many cases, we are more likely to notice and remember information that supports our beliefs about the world than information that challenges them.

Do people living in different cultures develop different schemas? And do such differences influence their memory? For information on these issues, read **Perspectives on Diversity**, below.

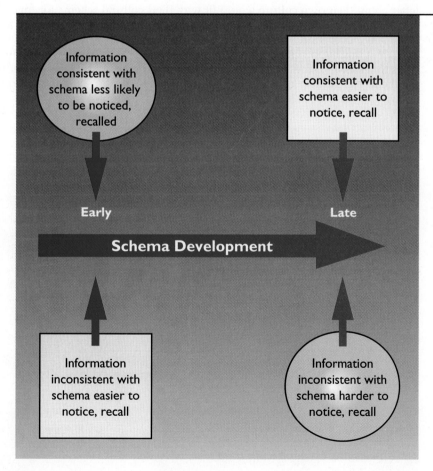

FIGURE 6.8

Schemas: How They Affect the Encoding of Information into Memory

When schemas are being formed, inconsistent information is easier to notice and encode than information that is consistent with the schemas. After schemas are well developed, however, the opposite is true.

Culture and Memory: Remembering What Fits with Our Cultural Schemas

Schemas play an important role in memory and in human cognition generally. These mental frameworks are acquired through experience and, once formed, strongly influence what aspects of the external world get our attention, what information gets entered into memory, and what is later retrieved from memory storage. Since schemas develop out of experience, it seems only reasonable to expect that they would reflect the cultures in which people live. People growing up in different cultures have different experiences in many areas of life, so their schemas for these areas, too, may differ. For example, people raised in Western cultures may have very different mental frameworks for courtship, work relationships, and entertainment than those raised in Asian or African cultures. And these contrasting schemas, in turn, may exert powerful effects on what people notice and remember in a given situation.

Direct evidence for the impact on memory of such culture-linked frameworks has been obtained in several studies (e.g, Shore, 1991). In one such investigation, Pritchard (1991) asked high school students in North America and in Palau (a small Pacific island nation) to read two letters written by a woman to her sister. In the letters the woman described events surrounding a typical funeral in each culture. Since funerals differ greatly in North America and Palau, Pritchard expected that participants would find the letter about their own culture more familiar than the one about the other culture. Moreover, since information in the letter about their own culture would fit with their cultural schema for funerals, it would be easier for the students to enter that information into memory and to recall it at a later time.

To test this hypothesis, Pritchard (1991) asked the participants from both cultures to tell everything they could remember about the letters shortly after reading them. The number of distortions in participants' accounts was also scored. As shown in Figure 6.9, the results provided clear support for the hypothesis that

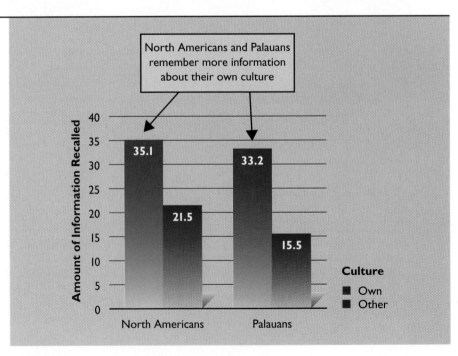

FIGURE 6.9

Culture and Memory

After reading letters containing information about funerals in two cultures, individuals from each culture remembered more information about their own culture than about the other one. These findings suggest that *cultural schemas* formed through experience with one's own culture can strongly influence what information is entered into long-term memory and later retrieved from it.
(Source: Based on data from Pritchard, 1991.)

North Americans and Palauans remember more information about their own culture participants would find it easier to remember information relating to their own culture than information relating to an unfamiliar culture.

These findings, and those of many related studies (e.g., Segall et al., 1990) indicate that cultural factors do indeed play an important role even in such basic psychological processes as memory. The culture in which we grow up can strongly shape the mental frameworks we use to understand the world around us, and hence many important aspects of our behavior.

MEMORY CONSTRUCTION Unfortunately, distortion is not the only type of error that can affect memory of everyday events. This type of memory is also affected by construction: our tendency to fill in the details when recalling natural events, or even to remember experiences we never actually had. This happens even to experts. Vincente and Brewer (1993) report a construction error that is commonly made in descriptions of the well-known studies of the memory of chess experts by de Groot. These studies were quite important, but could have been much more so if a particular control condition had been included. Information about the effects of this control condition was uncovered by later researchers. What Vincente and Brewer found is that many descriptions of the chess expert articles in the scientific literature mistakenly include the missing control condition as part of the original study. It is as if scientists, who are normally compulsively accurate in reporting details, are, at times like this, led into error by the importance of the study. Typically, important studies allow complete and definitive conclusions to be drawn. The missing control condition is thus conveniently added to the original study so that such conclusions can be made.

The addition of a missing control condition in the above example did not alter the conclusions that could be drawn about the memory abilities of chess experts. After all, the missing information about the required control condition had been provided by other researchers. There are times, however, when memory reconstruction can have devastating consequences. For example, in a widely publicized court case, two young women accused their father, Paul Ingram of Olympia, Washington, of having sexually abused them for many years when they were children. Very little confirming evidence was available for the women's stories, and Ingram at first denied the charges. Under repeated questioning by police and lawyers, however, he began to report "recovered memories" for these crimes. Were these memories accurate? Or did Ingram construct them in response to the repeated suggestion that he had committed the crimes? To find out, a trained psychologist, Richard Ofshe, made up a completely false story in which Ingram forced his son and daughter to have sex (Ofshe, 1992; Loftus, 1993). Ofshe then presented this story to Ingram, urging him to try to remember these events. At first Ingram denied any knowledge of them, but later he reported that he could remember them—indeed, he gradually developed detailed "memories" for events that were entirely fabricated!

This dramatically illustrates that under the power of suggestion, people may often construct memories of events that never took place (Loftus, 1993). This has been confirmed by many studies involving less traumatic events, such as people's remembering loud noises at night that never occurred (Weekes et al., 1992), or remembering that they voted in an election when they actually did not (Abelson, Loftus, & Greenwald, 1992). Unfortunately, young children seem to be especially susceptible to suggestions, readily constructing detailed memories of events that never took place when prompted by repeated questions from adults (Goleman, 1993). As you can see, this finding

MEMORY: OF THINGS REMEMBERED … AND FORGOTTEN

- Memory distortions arise for several reasons, including our tendency to perceive our own behavior in a favorable light, the influence of leading questions, misinformation from others, and the impact of schemas.

- Culture exerts strong effects on memory through the operation of cultural schemas.

- Memory construction can happen in response to suggestions from others, or when we fail to encode information about how and when information stored in memory was acquired.

- Eyewitness testimony is not as accurate or reliable as is widely believed.

has important implications for cases in which children are either victims or witnesses of crimes such as sexual abuse.

What accounts for the occurrence of memory construction? One possible answer involves processes at work during encoding. When we enter information into memory, we may store the information itself, but omit details about context—how and when the information was obtained. For example, as young children, we are often told at family gatherings about experiences and encounters that caused the family great amusement or distress. Even though we may not personally remember an event at the time of first telling, exposure to repeated tellings will contribute to the construction of a memory of it. If we do not encode the circumstances in which we acquired our knowledge about the event—family gatherings—we will tend to believe that we experienced the original event.

Whatever the precise mechanisms involved, it is clear that under appropriate conditions—repeated prompting or questioning—people may construct memories of events that never occurred or experiences they never had.

THE RESEARCH PROCESS

Eyewitness Testimony: How Accurate Is It? What Factors Affect It?

Memory distortion and construction are unsettling in any context, but in courts of law they can have truly disastrous consequences. **Eyewitness testimony**—evidence given by those people who actually witnessed a crime—plays an important role in many trials. At first glance, this makes a great deal of sense. After all, what better source of information about events could there be than people who were actually on the scene?

But are such accounts really accurate? There is little doubt that errors are made. Innocent people have been convicted of crimes they did not commit, and, conversely, people who are guilty of serious crimes have been wrongly cleared of the charges against them (Wells, 1993).

Two types of errors are thought to occur. One type arises from weaknesses in the lineup and photo identification procedures used by law enforcement officials. For example, officials may instill bias in witnesses by emphasizing that an offender is in the lineup, or by failing to inform them that a "not present" response is acceptable (Wells, 1993). The other type of error is assumed to result from memory changes that occur over time, especially from exposure to misleading information. Loftus best represents this position. She believes that memory can easily be modified, and she has reported a wide variety of laboratory studies

which show that the recollections of undergraduates witnessing such events as traffic accidents can be readily altered by exposure to misleading information (e.g., Loftus & Loftus, 1980). In her view, similar results ensue when witnesses are being interviewed by police and questioned in the courtroom. Thus, caution has to be exercised in accepting the claims of eyewitnesses (Christianson, Goodman, & Loftus, 1992).

Although Loftus makes a compelling case for the malleability of memory, there are those who have reservations about the degree to which laboratory research can be generalized to the real world. For example, researchers at the University of British Columbia have provided data suggesting that eyewitness testimony may not be as unreliable and vulnerable to change as Loftus believes (e.g., Yuille & Tollestrup, 1992).

The position of Yuille and his associates is that in the real world, (as opposed to the psychology laboratory), witnesses are not passive, detached observers, and their memories of what they observe will be different from those of participants in laboratory studies. Indeed, real-world witnesses do have a much greater degree of personal involvement than laboratory subjects. An examination of RCMP records by Yuille and his associates found that in the vast majority of

TRIAL WITNESS UNDER QUESTIONING

Eyewitness tesimony has played an important part at many trials. Unfortunately, growing evidence suggests that eyewitness testimony is less accurate than we think.

Enhancing the Accuracy of Eyewitness Testimony: Specific Techniques

One promising approach to increasing the accuracy of eyewitness testimony focuses on improving the procedures used to question witnesses (Geiselman et al., 1985). The results of this research indicate that a witness's accuracy improves substantially when procedures based on current scientific knowledge of memory are employed. Techniques that appear to be useful include asking witnesses to report everything—even partial information—and asking them to describe events from several different perspectives and in several different orders, not just the one in which the events actually occurred. Research on memory suggests that these techniques should enhance recall, and indeed, when they are used, witnesses' accuracy increases by almost 50 percent in some cases (Fisher & Geiselman, 1988).

A related procedure involves asking eyewitnesses to imagine themselves back at the scene and then to reconstruct as many details as possible (Malpass & Devine, 1981). This seems to provide witnesses with additional retrieval cues, thereby enhancing their memory. Finally, simply giving eyewitnesses repeated opportunities to recall what they observed can sometimes help, especially when the interval between the crime and the questioning is relatively brief (Roediger & Wheeler, 1993). Perhaps the most dramatic approach to increasing the accuracy of eyewitness testimony, however, involves the use of *hypnotism*.

Hypnotism: Can It Really Enhance the Eyewitness's Ability to Remember?

Chapter 4 discussed the relationship between hypnosis and memory. It has been suggested that people under hypnosis may be able to remember details and information that they could not recall in their normal state of consciousness. Is this actually the case? Some dramatic incidents seem to suggest that it is. For example, in 1976 a busload of children and their driver were kidnapped at gunpoint. The driver escaped and helped police rescue the children. Later, he tried but failed to remember the licence plate numbers of the kidnappers' vans. In an effort to improve his memory, the police arranged for him to be hypnotized. Under hypnosis he did manage to remember most of the digits, and this led to the arrest of the kidnappers (Kroger & Douce, 1979). More formal psychological studies have also demonstrated memory improvement with hypnosis. An analysis of Vancouver police files, undertaken by Yuille & Kim (1987), found that witnesses interviewed a second time with the help of hypnosis provided almost triple the amount of detail recorded during the first interview.

Do these incidents prove that hypnotism really works, and that it is an effective aid to eyewitness testimony? Unfortunately, there is one major problem in assessing the effect of hypnosis: an absence of appropriate control groups in which eyewitnesses were not

offenses involving robbery or sexual or nonsexual assault, the victim was the only witness—a very direct form of involvement. When witnesses other than the victim were present, they tended to be acquaintances of either the victim or the assailant, if not both. Even in cases of robbery, where the witness knew neither the assailant nor the victim, a sense of personal involvement may well have arisen through the feelings of threat and intimidation produced by the experience (Yuille & Tollestrup, 1992).

Field study assessments by Yuille and Tollestrup, and others (e.g., Fisher, Geiselman, & Amador, 1989), of the memories of witnesses to actual crimes support the view that such personal involvement does lead to the formation of memories that are qualitatively different from those created in a laboratory with uninvolved bystanders. The memories of witnesses to actual crimes are found by Yuille and Tollestrup to be accurate and detailed. Further, those memories appear to be highly durable.

Although Loftus and Yuille differ in their approach to eyewitness testimony, both would probably agree that steps should be taken to maximize the likelihood that witnesses utilize all available information in providing testimony about a crime. Can anything be done to enhance the accuracy of eyewitness testimony? Fortunately, yes.

hypnotized. Without this control, it is impossible to tell whether memory was enhanced by hypnosis or by factors unrelated to hypnosis, such as the way in which eyewitnesses were questioned, or instructions to them to "make a real effort" to remember. That such concerns are justified is clear from the assessment of the Vancouver interview data provided by Yuille and Kim. A second interview using hypnosis did indeed produce a large increase in the number of facts reported. Yuille and Kim found, however, that that second interview followed procedures advocated by Geiselman. As we already have noted, the Geiselman procedure can often by itself produce a dramatic improvement in recall. Thus, there is no way of knowing whether the very substantial increase in detail provided by the second interview was attributable to the use of hypnosis, to the Geiselman procedures, or to some third factor, such as increased levels of motivation produced by the fact that police were taking the trouble to conduct a second interview.

It could be that hypnosis improves memory, but only for dramatic events such as a kidnapping or robbery. This possibility has been tested in several studies in which participants watched highly realistic films of various crimes and were then questioned either under hypnosis or in their normal state (e.g., McEwan & Yuille, 1982). Again, the results were disappointing: No differences were found between the hypnotized and unhypnotized groups.

All in all, it seems that hypnosis is not an effective technique for improving the memory of eyewitnesses to crimes. It seems fair to conclude that hypnosis promises more than it delivers with respect to memory enhancement (Smith, 1983).

Alcohol and Eyewitness Memory: Drugs and Accuracy Don't Mix

While research on eyewitness testimony has generally failed to confirm the widespread belief in the benefits of hypnosis, it has confirmed another view held by many people: Alcohol reduces eyewitnesses' accuracy. A study by Yuille and Tollestrup (1990) indicates that even small amounts of alcohol can interfere with the accurate reporting of the details of a crime and increase the likelihood that witnesses will falsely identify an innocent person as the culprit. A review of Vancouver police files by Yuille and Tollestrup revealed that many eyewitnesses to crimes had consumed some alcohol at the time of the events on which they later reported. As noted earlier, alcohol seems to impair memory by interfering with the accurate encoding of information—its entry into memory—and eyewitnesses provide no exception to this general rule.

To conclude: Eyewitness testimony does not guarantee an unassailably accurate account of an event. The accuracy and durability of recall seems to be influenced by whether the witnesses are neutral bystanders or have a personal involvement in the events witnessed. Decisions made by witnesses viewing lineups can easily be biased as a result of inappropriate lineup compositions or inadequate instructions, or both. Techniques are available to increase the amount of detail recovered, but if alcohol or other drugs have been consumed, these procedures are of little help. A further problem is that there is no guarantee that additional information gathered through hypnosis, or by other techniques, will provide information significantly more useful than what is already available. Yuille and Kim observed that much of the additional information obtained on a second interview with hypnosis proved to be consistent with earlier information, but was rated by the hypnotist, and the Vancouver police, as being of little forensic value. In summary, many factors influence eyewitness testimony. Only a very careful examination of situation, circumstances, and interview procedures will establish how much weight to put on such testimony.

The Biological Bases of Memory: How the Brain Stores Knowledge

*L*et's begin with a simple but compelling assumption: When you commit information to memory, something must happen in your brain. Given that memories can persist for decades, it seems reasonable to suggest that this "something" involves relatively permanent changes within the brain. Where, precisely, are these changes located? And what kind of alterations do they involve? Questions such as these have fascinated—and frustrated—psychologists and other scientists for decades. Only recently have even partial answers begun to emerge.

Eyewitness Testimony: Information provided by witnesses to crimes or accidents.

Amnesia and Other Memory Disorders:
Keys to Understanding the Nature of Memory

The study of **amnesia**, or loss of memory, has added greatly to our understanding of the biological bases of memory. Amnesia is far from rare. Among human beings, it can stem from accidents that damage the brain, from drug abuse, or from operations performed to treat various medical disorders. Two major types exist. In **retrograde amnesia**, memory of events prior to the amnesia-inducing event is impaired. Individuals suffering from such amnesia may be unable to remember events from specific periods in their lives, such as events they experienced between the ages of eighteen and twenty-two. In **anterograde amnesia**, individuals cannot remember events that occur *after* the amnesia-inducing event. For example, if they meet someone for the first time after the onset of amnesia, they cannot remember this person the next day, or even a few minutes after being introduced.

ANTEROGRADE AMNESIA AND THE ROLE OF THE MEDIAL TEMPORAL LOBES Let's begin by considering a mystery. Two patients were admitted to the Montreal Neurological Institute in early 1950s because they were experiencing epileptic seizures that resisted conventional drug treatment. In an effort to control these seizures, an operation previously shown to be effective with other patients was performed by Dr. Wilder Penfield, a celebrated Canadian neurosurgeon. This procedure involved removal of part of the medial temporal lobe on one side of the patient's brain. Penfield was distressed to find that both patients developed a profound anterograde amnesia—they were quite unable to retain information about new experiences (Penfield & Milner, 1958). What went wrong?

The answer came when Penfield and Milner examined reports by an American surgeon. W.B. Scoville, indicating that two of his patients who had undergone a similar surgical procedure on both sides of the brain were unable to remember new information. Scoville's report, and other hints from the scientific literature about the relationship between the temporal lobes and memory, caused Penfield and Milner to wonder if the two Montreal patients had unsuspected damage in temporal lobe areas on the side of their brain untouched by surgery. This was found to be the case.

It seems obvious from these reports that the temporal lobes are significantly involved in the consolidation of memory. Without at least one functioning temporal lobe, information cannot be shifted from short-term to longer-term storage. More recent investigations have strengthened this conclusion and identified one structure in the temporal lobes—the hippocampus—as crucial for memory consolidation.

What is life like for a individual who has experienced destruction of the hippocampus in both temporal lobes? The most direct way to answer this question is to look at H.M.—one of the original two patients operated on by Scoville. The operation helped control H.M's seizures but had a devastating affect on his memory. This became obvious once he had recovered from surgery. He would meet and have a conversation with someone new, and moments after the meeting be quite unaware that either the meeting or the conversation had taken place. He would read the same magazine or do the same crossword puzzle repeatedly. He seemed to have no recollection of having ever seen a magazine or a puzzle once he turned away to attend to something else. Formal memory assessment tests confirmed that the surgical procedures had caused both retrograde and anterograde amnesia. H.M.'s retrograde amnesia was relatively minor. He could remember all of the past

Amnesia: *Loss of memory stemming from illness, accident, drug abuse, or other causes.*

Retrograde Amnesia: *The inability to recover events from long-term memory that occurred before an amnesia-inducing event.*

Anterograde Amnesia: *The inability to store in long-term memory information that occurs after an amnesia-inducing event.*

except for the most recent one or two years, which indicated that his long-term memory store was largely intact. His short-term memory seemed also to be intact; he had a normal digit span, and could hold information in short-term memory long enough to understand and answer questions. What he could not do was transfer information from short-term memory to long-term memory, where it could be preserved and accessed on demand. In short, he had an anterograde amnesia that would prevent him forever from leading a normal life. He became effectively suspended in time on that day when the surgical procedures rendered him unable to store new information about his own experiences or to record new happenings in the world at large. In an examination carried out by Milner, Corkin, and Teuber (1968), fourteen years after the surgery, H.M. was found to still have gross memory impairment. He still could not recognize neighbors or family friends who had entered his life after the surgery. Extended testing did indicate that he could acquire some procedural memory tasks involving motor skills and perceptual learning. However, H.M. is incapable of noticing or reporting this fact.

What, precisely, does the case of H.M. tell us about the biological bases of memory? Since it was portions of his temporal lobes that were removed, these findings suggest that these lobes—or structures within them—play a key role in our memory systems. In particular, the temporal lobes seem to be crucial in the **consolidation of memory**: the process of shifting new information from short-term to longer-term storage. Research has confirmed this conclusion and has identified one structure in the temporal lobes—the *hippocampus*—as crucial in this respect.

DECLARATIVE MEMORY AND THE HIPPOCAMPUS   Earlier in this chapter, a distinction was drawn between *semantic* and *episodic* memory on the one hand and *procedural* memory on the other. You should recall that both semantic memory and episodic memory involve our ability to recall information that we know—to bring it into consciousness and, if necessary, to describe it. Procedural memory, in contrast, is the kind of memory on which skillful behaviors—everything from riding a bike to playing golf—are based. While we can't put the information stored in this kind of memory into words, we know quite well that we possess it. Where does the hippocampus, a portion of the temporal lobes, fit into the picture? Converging lines of research conducted with humans and animals point to the conclusion that the hippocampus plays a key role in the first two kinds of memory, which are often grouped under the term *declarative memory* or **explicit memory**, since we can describe their contents verbally. However, the hippocampus does not seem to play a role with respect to the second type of memory, sometimes termed **implicit memory**. This latter memory system is related to other areas of the brain—specifically, the neocortex, striatum, and amygdala (Tulving & Schacter, 1990).

Many different forms of evidence offer support for this view of the potential role of the hippocampus in memory (Squire, 1991). Some of the most fascinating studies have focused on people suffering from amnesia. Many amnesics, it turns out, have experienced damage to the hippocampus. And their performance on tasks involving declarative or explicit memory seems to suffer as a result of these injuries. In contrast, their ability to perform some tasks involving implicit memory is not impaired (Graf & Schacter, 1985). Such effects are clearly illustrated in a study conducted by Knowlton, Ramus, and Squire (1992).

The study was conducted with two groups of participants. One group consisted of amnesic patients who had suffered damage to the hippocampus. The other group consisted of individuals whose memories were functioning normally. Procedures were identical for both groups. First, they were presented

Consolidation of memory:
The process of shifting new information from short-term to long-term storage.

Explicit (Declarative)
Memory: A memory system that permits us to express the information it contains verbally. It includes both semantic and episodic memory.

Implicit Memory: A memory system that stores information that we cannot express verbally; sometimes termed procedural memory.

with strings of letters that had been constructed according to artificial grammatical rules; these rules indicated that only certain letters could follow others, just as in English the letter *q* is always followed by the letter *u*, never by the letter *i*. Participants were not informed about the rules until after they had seen all the strings of letters. Then they were told about the rules and informed that they would see additional strings of letters. For each, they would try to judge whether it conformed or did not conform to the rules; some of the letter strings would conform, while others would not. After this, they were shown the grammatical letter strings again and asked to indicate whether they recognized them and whether the items were similar to the ones they had seen before. Knowlton and her colleagues reasoned that participants could acquire knowledge of the grammatical rules without being able to verbalize them; in other words, such knowledge would be stored in *implicit* memory. However, being able to recognize specific combinations of letters or to indicate that they were similar to ones previously seen would involve *explicit* memory—knowledge of specific letter strings rather than a sense of the underlying rules governing them. Thus, if the hippocampus played an important role in explicit but not in implicit memory, the amnesic individuals would do as well as the control participants on the classification task (deciding whether the letter strings met the grammatical rules). However, amnesics would do worse than the control group on the recognition and similarity tasks. As shown in Figure 6.10, these predictions were confirmed.

These findings, and those of many other studies (Squire & McKee, 1992), suggest that we possess at least two distinct memory systems, and that different portions of the brain play a key role in each. But what, precisely, are the functions of the hippocampus in this respect? Additional evidence indicates that the hippocampus somehow binds together distributed sites of activation in the neocortex with sites of activation in other regions of the brain, such as the medial temporal lobe. Such connections are needed for the formation of memories. When the hippocampus is damaged, these links cannot be formed.

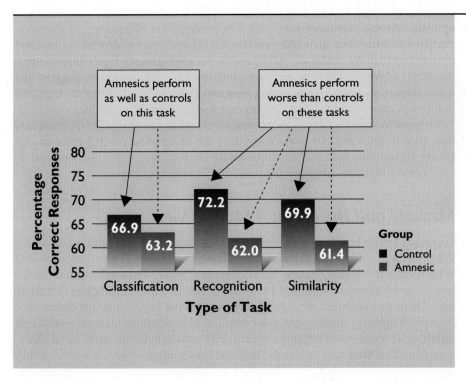

FIGURE 6.10

Role of the Hippocampus in Explicit Memory

Amnesic patients who had suffered damage to the hippocampus performed as well as control persons (no damage to the hippocampus) on a task involving *implicit memory*—determining whether letter strings met or did not meet "grammatical" rules. However, they did more poorly on tasks involving *explicit memory*—for example, distinguishing letter strings they had previously seen from ones they had not. These findings indicate that the hippocampus plays an important role in explicit memory, but not in implicit memory. (Source: Based on data from Knowlton, Ramus, & Squire, 1992.)

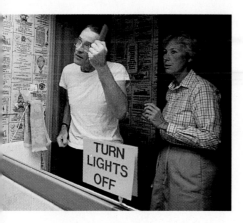

MEMORY FAILURE: ALZHEIMER'S DISEASE

Damage to specific neurons in the brain is implicated in Alzheimer's disease, one of the most tragic illnesses to affect older people.

The result is that "out of sight" does equal "out of mind"—no lasting storage of information brought to us by our senses can occur. Interestingly, the role of the hippocampus in the formation of explicit memories appears to be a temporary one. Later, after information has been stored and retrieved repeatedly, the hippocampus is no longer needed for it to remain in memory. The precise nature of the changes within the nervous system that produce this shift, however, remain to be identified.

AMNESIA AS A RESULT OF KORSAKOFF'S SYNDROME   Individuals who consume large amounts of alcohol for many years sometimes develop **Korsakoff's syndrome**. The many symptoms of Korsakoff's syndrome include sensory and motor problems as well as heart, liver, and gastrointestinal disorders. In addition, the syndrome is often accompanied by both anterograde amnesia and severe retrograde amnesia: Patients cannot remember events that took place even many years before the onset of their illness. Careful examination of these individuals' brains after death indicates that they have experienced extensive damage to portions of the diencephalon, especially to the thalamus and hypothalamus. This suggests that these portions of the brain play a key role in long-term memory.

THE AMNESIA OF ALZHEIMER'S DISEASE   One of the most tragic illnesses that can strike human beings in the closing decades of life is **Alzheimer's disease**. This illness, which afflicts some 5 percent of all people over sixty-five, begins with mild problems, such as increased difficulty in remembering names, phone numbers, or appointments. Gradually, patients become totally confused so that they are unable to perform even simple tasks like dressing or grooming themselves. They also experience an almost total loss of memory. Indeed, in the later stages patients may fail to recognize their spouse or children. Careful study of the brains of deceased Alzheimer's patients has revealed that in most cases they contain tiny bundles of *amyloid beta protein*, a substance not found in similar concentrations in normal brains. Growing evidence (Yankner et al., 1990) suggests that this substance damages neurons that project from nuclei in the basal forebrain to the hippocampus and cerebral cortex (Coyle, 1987). Since these neurons transmit information primarily by means of the neurotransmitter *acetylcholine*, it appears that this substance may play a key role in the functioning of memory. Further evidence that such acetylcholine-based systems are crucial is provided by the fact that the brains of Alzheimer's patients contain lower-than-normal amounts of acetylcholine. In addition, studies with animal subjects suggest that when the acetylcholine-transmitting neurons are destroyed, major dislocations in memory are indeed produced (Fibiger, Murray, & Phillips, 1983).

In sum, evidence obtained from the study of memory disorders indicates that specific regions and systems within the brain play central roles in our ability to transfer information from short-term to long-term storage and to retain it in long-term memory for prolonged periods of time.

Memory and the Brain: *A Modern View*

Korsakoff's Syndrome: An illness caused by long-term abuse of alcohol that often involves profound retrograde amnesia.

Alzheimer's Disease: An illness primarily afflicting individuals over the age of sixty-five and involving severe mental deterioration, including retrograde amnesia.

To return to the key questions: Where are memories stored within the brain? What changes within the brain underlie the long-term storage of information? With respect to the first of these questions, the answer seems to be that information is stored in several different locations. Existing evidence indicates that there are at least two different storage systems within the brain—one for declarative or explicit memory and the other for implicit or procedural memory—and that different structures and regions are primarily associated with each. In addition, it appears that the brain processes information simultaneously at several different locations rather than in a linear, step-by-step manner. If this processing actually occurs in several different locations at once, it seems reasonable to assume that representations of such information also exist in multiple places. So, again, where does the brain store specific memories? The most reasonable answer seems to be this: in multiple locations and in multiple forms.

Now for the second question: How, precisely, is such information actually stored? Apparently, through several subtle biochemical processes within the brain. It appears that the formation of long-term memories involves alterations in the rate of production or release of specific neurotransmitters. Such changes increase the ease with which neural information can move within the brain and may produce *localized neural circuits*. Evidence for the existence of such neural circuits or *neural networks* is provided by research in which previously learned conditioned responses are eliminated when microscopic areas of the brain are destroyed—areas that, presumably, contained the neural circuits formed during conditioning (Thompson, 1989). Long-term memory may also involve changes in the actual structure of neurons—changes that strengthen communication across specific synapses (Teyler & DeScenna, 1984). For example, there is some indication that after learning experiences, the shape of dendrites in specific neurons may be altered, and that these shifts may facilitate the neurons' responsiveness to neurotransmitters. Some of these changes may occur very quickly, while others may require considerable amounts of time. This, perhaps, is one reason why newly formed memories are subject to disruption for some period after they are formed (Squire & Spanis, 1984).

In sum, it appears that we are now entering an exciting period; armed with new and sophisticated research techniques, psychologists and other scientists may finally be able to unravel the biochemical code of memory. When they do, the potential benefits for people suffering from amnesia and other memory disorders will probably be immense.

MAKING PSYCHOLOGY PART OF YOUR LIFE

Improving Your Memory: Some Useful Steps

How good is your memory? If you are like most people, your answer is probably "Not good enough!" At one time or another, most of us have wished that we could improve our ability to retain facts and information. Fortunately, with a little work, almost anyone can learn to remember more information more accurately. Systematic research on memory, such as was described in this chapter, offers several useful suggestions for accomplishing this goal. Here are some you can readily put to use.

1. *Really think about what you want to remember* If you wish to enter information into long-term memory,

it is important to think about it: ask questions about it, consider its meaning, and examine its relationship to information you already know. Doing so will help make the new information part of your existing knowledge frameworks and will increase the chances of its entry into long-term memory. This kind of thinking calls for considerable cognitive work, but it's worth the effort because it will increase your retention.

2. *Pay attention to what you want to remember* Quick: Does the Queen's head face to the right or to the left on a loonie? On a quarter? All Canadians have

seen these images many, many times, yet the odds favor your misremembering. When students at Bishop's University in Quebec were asked this question, 71 percent picked the wrong direction (McKelvie & Aikins, 1993). Why does coin head orientation tend to be misremembered? The answer is simple: You haven't paid close attention to this information. While you have certainly paid close attention to the size and value of different Canadian coins, you have probably given little attention to the Queen's image. The point is that if you can't remember information such as this, to which you've been exposed on countless occasions, think how difficult it must be to remember other information to which you direct little attention. The moral is clear: If you want to remember something, you must first make it the center of your attention.

3. *Use visual imagery* You've probably heard the saying, "A picture is worth a thousand words." Where memory is concerned, this is sometimes true. Research indicates that it is often easier to remember information associated with vivid mental images—an approach that Paivio of the University of Western Ontario has explored since the 1960s (Paivio, 1986). If you wish to improve your memory, you can put this basic principle to use. In fact, imagery plays a central role in several well-known **mnemonics**—that is, strategies for improving memory. One of these, the *method of loci*, involves the following steps. Suppose you want to remember a series of points for a speech you will soon make. First, imagine walking through some familiar place, such as your own home. Then form a series of images in which each item you wish to remember is placed in a specific location. Perhaps the first point is, "Is the greenhouse effect a reality?" You might imagine approaching your house and finding an artist sitting on the front porch finishing a painting that portrays your house as having a large, steamy greenhouse containing tropical plants, on which is superimposed a large question mark. For the next point, "Some believe that the destruction of the rainforest in British Columbia is contributing to the greenhouse effect," you might imagine looking in the living room and seeing a large poster over the fireplace of protesters trying to block logging operations in Clayoquot Sound. You would continue in this fashion to lodge in different rooms of the house images connected with the various points you wish to make. When required to make the speech, you would imagine again approaching your house. The various images you formed should be available as you move toward and through the house, and this should allow you to remember the points in your speech.

4. *Give yourself extra retrieval cues* As we hope you remember, a key problem with long-term memory involves retrieving stored information. You can help yourself in this area through the use of retrieval cues. One type of cue is the *context* in which the information was first acquired. In other words, pause for a moment and try to remember the situations or surroundings in which you first entered the information into memory. Often, remembering the context will help you retrieve the information you seek. For example, maybe you are attempting to remember the name of a restaurant. Try as you may, you can't bring the name to mind. If you pause and think about the location of the restaurant, how you first heard about it, and what it looks like from the outside, the name may quickly follow.

5. *Develop your own shorthand codes* You may have learned the names of the nine planets by means of a simple procedure known as the first-letter technique, in which the first letter of each word in a simple phrase stands for an item you wish to remember. In the case of the planets, one such phrase is: "Mary's Violet Eyes Make John Stay Up Nights Pondering" (Mercury, Venus, Earth, Mars, Jupiter, Saturn, Uranus, Neptune, Pluto). This can be a very useful technique; indeed, more than half of first-year medical students report using it when studying anatomy (Gruneberg, 1978). If you need to remember lists of items, you can readily come up with your own sentences to represent them. And of course, the more meaningful or familiar a sentence is to you, the more helpful it will be.

6. *Develop your own cognitive scaffolds* One basic finding of research on memory is that organized information is much easier to remember than unorganized information. If you wish to retain a large array of facts, dates, or terms, it is very helpful to organize them in some manner. Organization provides a framework to which new information can be attached—a kind of mental scaffold. This is one reason why each chapter of this book begins with an outline and ends with a detailed summary. Together, they provide the "big picture"—an overview of the chapter's content. And this in turn can be very helpful to you in your studying.

There are additional techniques for enhancing your memory, but most are related to the ones already described. Whichever techniques you select, you will find that making them work does require some degree of effort. In memory training, as in any other effort at self-improvement, the old saying, "No pain, no gain," tends to hold true.

Mnemonics: Techniques for enhancing memory.

HUMAN MEMORY: THE INFORMATION PROCESSING APPROACH
 	
memory 228
encoding 229
storage 229
retrieval 229
information processing
  approach 229
selective attention 230
parallel distributed processing
  model 230
semantic memory 232
episodic memory 232
procedural memory 232
	• Several models of human memory indicate that we possess three distinct memory systems. One, sensory memory, represents sensory information present for very brief periods of time. Another, short-term memory, stores limited amounts of information for a few seconds. The third, long-term memory, retains huge amounts of information for long periods.
	• Evidence indicates that in at least some memory systems, information is processed in a parallel rather than in a step-by-step manner.
	• Several different types of information are stored in memory. Semantic memory holds general information about the world. Episodic memory holds information about experiences we have had in our own lives. Procedural memory holds nonverbal information that allows us to perform various motor tasks such as riding a bicycle or playing the piano.

SENSORY MEMORY: GATEWAY TO CONSCIOUSNESS sensory memory 234	• Sensory memory holds fleeting representations of our sensory experiences. These can be quite broad in scope, reflecting everything our senses tell us, but generally last less than one second.
SHORT-TERM MEMORY: THE WORKBENCH OF CONSCIOUSNESS short-term memory 235 serial positon curve 235 chunk 236	• Short-term or working memory retains information for a few seconds. Its existence is supported by the finding that words near the end of a list are remembered better than words near the middle, presumably because those near the end are still in short-term memory—the serial position curve. • Additional evidence for the distinction between short-term and long-term memory is the finding that people have more difficulty keeping words or letters that sound alike in short-term memory than retaining ones that do not.
LONG-TERM MEMORY: THE STOREHOUSE OF CONSCIOUSNESS long-term memory 237 tip-of-the-tongue phenomenon 237 elaborative rehearsal 238 levels of processing view 239 retrieval cues 240 context-dependent memory 241 state-dependent retrieval 241 encoding specificity principle 242	• Information moves from short-term memory to long-term memory through a process of elaborative rehearsal. • The levels of processing view suggests that the more cognitive effort we expend in processing information, the better we will remember it. • Retrieval cues are stimuli associated with information stored in long-term memory; they help us bring such information to mind.

FORGETTING FROM LONG-TERM MEMORY retroactive interference 243 proactive interference 243 repression 245 prospective memory 246	• Forgetting from long-term memory appears to result primarily from interference, not from the weakening of memories over time. • In retroactive interference, information being learned in the present interferes with information already in memory. In proactive interference, information already in memory interferes with the acquisition of new information. • Although there is widespread belief that traumatic memories may be repressed, there is little scientific evidence for it. Individuals who suddenly "remember" painful events from long ago may not be providing accurate descriptions of actual events. • Prospective memory is related to both motivation and the presence of retrieval cues.
MEMORY IN NATURAL CONTEXTS infantile amnesia 250 flashbulb memory 252 schemas 252 eyewitness testimony 258	• Autobiographical memory is memory for information about our own lives. Diary studies in which individuals keep detailed records of events in their lives indicate that some kinds of information are more useful to us than others. • Our inability to recall events from the first three years of life is often called infantile amnesia. This term is misleading, because memory does function during that period. We cannot remember specific events during this time primarily because we do not yet possess a well-defined self-concept. • Flashbulb memories—memories connected to dramatic events in our lives—are less accurate than we generally believe. • Memory distortions arise for several reasons, including our tendency to interpret our own behavior in a favorable light, the influence of leading questions from others, and the impact of schemas. • Culture exerts strong effects on memory through the operation of cultural schemas. People generally find it easier to remember information relating to their own culture than information relating to other cultures. • Memory construction can happen in response to suggestions from others, or when we fail to encode information about how and when information stored in memory was acquired. • Because of memory distortion and construction and other factors, eyewitness testimony is not as accurate or reliable as is widely believed. However, several techniques can assist eyewitnesses in remembering information about crimes they observed.
THE BIOLOGICAL BASES OF MEMORY: HOW THE BRAIN STORES KNOWLEDGE amnesia 259 retograde amnesia 259 anterograde amnesia 259 consolidation of memory 260 explicit memory 260 implicit memory 260 Korsakoff's syndrome 262 Alzheimer's disease 262 mnemonics 264	• The study of various memory disorders has provided important insights into the biological bases of memory. Retrograde amnesia involves loss of memory of events prior to the amnesia-inducing event; anterograde amnesia is memory loss for events that occur after this event. • Evidence is growing that the hippocampus plays a crucial role in implicit memory, while other portions of the brain are important for explicit or declarative memory. • Retrograde amnesia in Korsakoff's syndrome reflects damage to portions of the thalamus. Amnesia associated with Alzheimer's disease seems to result from damage to neurons that transmit information by means of the neurotransmitter acetylcholine.

CRITICAL THINKING QUESTIONS

APPRAISAL	At the present time, most psychologists accept the view that studying human memory from an information processing perspective is very useful. Do you agree? Or do you believe that this view omits important aspects of memory?
CONTROVERSY	The concept of *repressed memories* has long enjoyed widespread acceptance among psychologists and the general public. Yet there is little research evidence for the occurrence of such effects. What are your views on this issue? Is continued belief in *repression* justified? Or should we discard this concept as one that has little value?
MAKING PSYCHOLOGY PART OF YOUR LIFE	Knowing something about how memory operates is very useful from one obvious perspective: It can suggest ways for you to improve your memory. But this is not the only way in which you can benefit from such knowledge. Can you think of others? (Hint: What does your new knowledge about memory tell you about trusting your own memory, even in situations where you are confident that it is accurate?)

Cognition
Thinking, Deciding, Communicating

THINKING: FORMING CONCEPTS AND REASONING TO CONCLUSIONS 270
Basic Elements of Thought: Concepts, Propositions, Images
Reasoning: Transforming Information to Reach Conclusions
Animal Cognition: Do They Really Think?

MAKING DECISIONS: CHOOSING AMONG ALTERNATIVES 282
Heuristics: Using Quick—but Fallible—Rules of Thumb to Make Decisions
Framing in Decision Making
Escalation of Commitment: Getting Trapped in Bad Decisions

PROBLEM SOLVING AND CREATIVITY: FINDING PATHS TO DESIRED GOALS 289
Problem Solving: An Overview
Methods for Solving Problems: From Trial and Error to Heuristics
Factors That Interfere with Effective Problem Solving
Creativity: Innovative Problem Solving
Artificial Intelligence: Can Machines Really Think?

LANGUAGE: THE COMMUNICATION OF INFORMATION 298
Language: Its Basic Nature
The Development of Language
Langauge and Thought: Do We Think What We Say or Say What We Think?
Langauge in Other Species

SUMMARY AND REVIEW OF KEY POINTS 309

PERSPECTIVES ON DIVERSITY—WHEN CULTURE SHAPES REASONING—OR AT LEAST INFLUENCES ITS OUTCOMES 276

THE RESEARCH PROCESS—ANIMAL COGNITION: TALES OF INTELLIGENCE 280

KEY CONCEPT—FACTORS THAT INFLUENCE THE DECISION-MAKING PROCESS 285

THE POINT OF IT ALL—THE EDUCATION CRISIS IN NORTH AMERICA: PRACTICE MAY BE THE KEY 291

CANADIAN FOCUS—DO SOME KINDS OF LANGUAGE IMPAIRMENT RESULT FROM A GENETIC ABNORMALITY? 301

MAKING PSYCHOLOGY PART OF YOUR LIFE—MAKING BETTER DECISIONS 308

ARTIFICIAL-INTELLIGENCE SPECIALISTS TO GATHER HERE

THE GAZETTE (Montreal): JUNE 16, 1994

Can computers think for themselves? Not at present—but The Gazette tells about the 14th International Joint Conference on Artificial Intelligence, which is taking place at the Palais de Congres in Montreal in August 1995.

The 2,500 researchers attending the meeting will be from many countries and from most fields of science including psychology, biology, computer science, mathematics, logic, and linguistics.

Their goal is to combine their findings so that computers of the future will be able to think—for example, to make good decisions

with only partial information.

Artificial intelligence is now being used to speed up credit authorization, to support voice-activated word processing, and to enable video cameras to make adjustments as viewing conditions change.

Chapter 7 is mostly about real thought, but you will learn more about artificial thought as well.

269

*H*ave you ever wondered why some people are highly creative, whereas others are merely average? Will computers ever become as smart as people? Do animals think? These and related questions have to do with **cognition**—a general term used to describe various aspects of our higher mental processes. But creativity and thinking are only part of the picture where cognition is concerned. Have you ever agonized over an important decision, carefully weighing the advantages and disadvantages of potential alternatives? In all probability you have, perhaps in terms of selecting a college or university, choosing a major, or deciding between courses of action. To make the right decision you probably *thought* long and hard about the various alternatives; you tried to *reason* your way to a conclusion about their relative merits; and finally you made some sort of *decision*. We perform these activities many times each day, and in a variety of contexts. It is on these and related issues that we'll focus in the present chapter.

We'll begin our discussion by examining the nature of *thinking*, an activity that involves the manipulation of mental representations of various features of the external world. Thinking includes *reasoning*—mental activity through which we transform available information in order to reach conclusions. We'll also look at an intriguing question that would definitely *not* have been included in this book ten years ago: Do animals think? Next, we'll turn to *decision making*, the process of choosing between two or more alternatives on the basis of information about them. Here we'll explore different factors that influence the decision-making process. After that, we'll examine several aspects of *problem solving*, which typically involves processing information in various ways in order to move toward desired goals. Problem solving often calls for *creativity*—the formulation of new and sometimes unexpected perspectives and solutions. Finally, we'll examine an aspect of cognition that provides the basis for much of the activity occurring in each of the processes listed so far: *language*. It is through language that we can share the results of our own cognition with others and receive similar input from them. We'll also consider new evidence suggesting that other species may also possess several basic elements of language.

One additional point: As you'll soon see, our abilities to think, reason, make decisions, and use language are impressive in many respects. But they are far from perfect. As is true for memory, the cognitive activities are subject to many forms of error: When we think, reason, make decisions, solve problems, and use language, we do not always do so in ways that would appear completely rational to an outside observer (Hawkins & Hastie, 1990; Johnson-Laird, Byrne, & Tabossi, 1989). As we examine each aspect of cognition, we will draw attention to these potential sources of distortion, because understanding the nature of such errors can shed important light on the nature of the cognitive processes they affect (Smith & Kida, 1991).

Thinking: *Forming Concepts and Reasoning to Conclusions*

Cognition: *The mental activities associated with thought, knowledge, and memory.*

What are you thinking about right now? If you've answered the question, then it's safe to say that at least to some extent you are thinking about the words on this page. But perhaps you are also thinking about a snack, the movie you saw last night, the argument you had with a friend this morning … the list could be endless. At any given moment, consciousness contains a rapidly shifting pattern of diverse thoughts, impressions, and feelings. In order to try to understand this complex and ever-changing pattern, psychologists have often adopted two main strategies. First, they have focused on the basic elements of thought—on how, precisely, aspects of the external world are represented in our thinking. Second, they have sought to determine the manner in which we *reason*—how we attempt to process available information cognitively in order to reach specific conclusions.

Basic Elements of Thought: *Concepts, Propositions, Images*

What, precisely, does thinking involve? In other words, what are the basic elements of thought? While no conclusive answer currently exists, it appears that our thoughts consist largely of three basic components: *concepts, propositions,* and *images.*

CONCEPTS: CATEGORIES FOR UNDERSTANDING EXPERIENCE   What do apples, oranges, and cherries have in common? You probably have no difficulty in replying that they are all fruits. Now, how about a Nissan Pathfinder, an Air Canada jet, and an elevator? Perhaps it takes you a bit longer to answer, but soon you realize that they are all vehicles. Within each of these groups, the items look different from one another, yet in a sense you perceive them, and think about them, as similar at least in certain respects. The reason you find the task of answering these questions relatively simple is that you already possess well-developed concepts for both groups of items.

Concepts are mental categories for objects, events, experiences, or ideas that are similar to one another in one or more respects. Concepts play a central role in our task of understanding the world around us and representing it mentally. For example, imagine that in conversation a friend uses the term "Disk-Stack." You've never heard it before, so you ask what she means. When she replies, "It's new software for increasing the amount of information you can put on a hard drive," you're home free. You already have a concept for "software" and immediately place this new term in that category. Now you can think about it quite efficiently: You know that it probably comes on a disk, that its contents can be stored in a computer, and that it helps accomplish certain tasks. In this and countless other situations, concepts allow us to represent a lot of information about diverse objects, events, or ideas in a highly efficient manner.

ARTIFICIAL AND NATURAL CONCEPTS   Is a tomato a fruit or a vegetable? Many people would answer "vegetable." Botanists, however, classify tomatoes as a fruit, since they contain seeds and have a structure that is definitely more like that of apples and pears than potatoes or spinach. This fact illustrates the important distinction between what psychologists term artificial (or logical) and natural concepts. **Artificial concepts** are ones that can be clearly defined by a set of rules or properties. Thus, a tomato is a fruit because it possesses the properties established by botanists for this category. Similarly, as you learned in geometry, a figure can be considered a triangle only if it has three sides whose angles add to 180 degrees, and can be considered a square only if all four sides are of equal length and all four angles are ninety degrees. Such artificial concepts are very useful in many areas of mathematics and science.

In contrast, **natural concepts** have no fixed and readily specified set of defining features. They are fuzzy around the edges. Yet they more accurately reflect the state of the natural world, which rarely offers us the luxury of hard-and-fast, clearly defined concepts. For example, consider the following questions:

Concepts: Mental categories for objects or events that are similar to one another in certain respects.

Artificial Concepts: Concepts that can be clearly defined by a set of rules or properties.

Natural Concepts: Concepts that are not based on a precise set of attributes or properties, do not have clear-cut boundaries and are often defined by prototypes.

- Is chess a sport?
- Is a pickle a vegetable?
- Is a psychologist a scientist?
- Is someone who helps a terminally ill person commit suicide a murderer?

As you can readily see, these all relate to common concepts: sport, vegetable, science, crime. But what specific attributes are necessary for inclusion in each concept? If you find yourself puzzled, don't be surprised: The boundaries of natural concepts are somewhat indistinct.

Such natural concepts are often based on **prototypes**—the best or clearest examples (Rosch, 1975). Prototypes emerge from our experience with the external world; new items that might potentially fit within them are then compared with them. The more attributes new items share with an existing prototype, the more likely they are to be included within it. For example, consider the following natural concepts: *clothing, art.* For clothing, most people think of items like shirts, pants, or shoes. They are far less likely to mention wet suits, mink coats, or suits of armor. Similarly, for art, most people think of paintings, drawings, and sculptures. Fewer think of such artworks as laser shows, like the ones presented in large arenas on festive occasions, or of the kind of construction shown in the photo below.

In determining whether a specific item fits within a natural concept, then, we seem to adopt a *probabilistic* strategy. The more similar an object or event is to others already in the category, especially to the prototype for the category, the more likely we are to include the new item within the concept. In everyday situations, therefore, concept membership is not an all-or-nothing decision; rather, it is graded, and items are recognized as fitting within a category to a greater or lesser degree (Medin & Ross, 1992).

Prototypes: *The best or clearest examples of various objects or stimuli in the physical world.*

CONCEPTS: HOW THEY ARE REPRESENTED   That concepts exist is obvious. But how are they represented in consciousness? No firm answer to this question exists, but several possibilities have been suggested. First, concepts may be

PROTOTYPES AND NATURAL CONCEPTS

Prototypes are the best or clearest examples of concepts. For the concept *art*, which of the examples shown here is more prototypical?

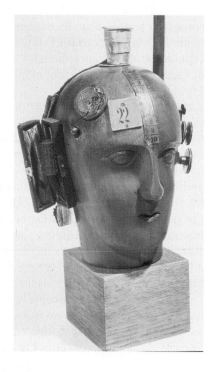

CHAPTER 7

represented in terms of their features or attributes. As natural concepts are formed, the attributes associated with them may be stored in memory. Then, when a new item is encountered, its attributes are compared with the ones already present. The closer the match, the more likely is the item to be included within the concept.

A second possibility is that natural concepts are represented, at least in part, through images. Paivio (1990) at the University of Western Ontario has long argued that knowledge of the world is conveyed to us through the various senses, and that our representations of the world retain the character or properties of the sensory systems in which they first come to us. To put it more simply, we have visual-like images in consciousness of objects and events we have experienced by sight; we have auditory images of voices, sounds, and music we have heard; we have haptic images of feelings that derive from the touching and manipulating of objects and materials. Although we have a variety of different nonverbal ways of conceptually representing objects and experiences, it is generally held that **visual images** play the most significant role in the representation of natural concepts. We will have more to say about the role of images—especially visual ones—later in this discussion.

Finally, it is important to note that concepts are closely related to *schemas*, cognitive frameworks that represent our knowledge of and assumptions about the world (refer to Chapter 6). Like schemas, natural concepts are acquired through experience and represent information about the world in an efficient summary form. However, schemas appear to be more complex than concepts, and to contain a broader range of information; also, they may include a number of distinct concepts. For example, each of us possesses a *self-schema*, a mental framework holding a wealth of information about our own traits, characteristics, and expectations. This framework, in turn, may contain many different concepts, such as intelligence, attractiveness, health, and so on. Some of these are natural concepts, so the possibility exists that natural concepts are represented, at least in part, through their links to schemas and other broad cognitive frameworks.

To summarize, concepts may be represented in the mind in several ways. Whatever their precise form, they certainly play an important role in thinking and in our efforts to make sense out of a complex and ever-changing external world.

PROPOSITIONS: RELATIONS BETWEEN CONCEPTS Thinking is not a passive process; it involves active manipulation of internal representations of the external world. As we have already seen, the representations that are mentally manipulated are often concepts. Frequently, thinking involves relating one concept to another, or one feature of a concept to the entire concept. Because we possess highly developed language skills, these cognitive actions take the form of **propositions**—sentences that can stand as separate assertions. For example, consider the following propositions:

- Politicians are often self-serving.
- This is a very interesting book.
- Frozen yogurt is not as sweet as ice cream.

Concepts play a key role in each: *politicians* and *self-serving* in the first; *book* and *interesting* in the second; *frozen yogurt*, *sweet*, and *ice cream* in the third. Moreover, each sentence indicates some kind of relationship between the concepts or between the concepts and one or more of their features. For example, for many people, *self-serving* is one feature of the concept *politician*. Research evidence indicates that much of our thinking involves the formulation and consideration of such propositions. Thus, propositions can be considered one of the basic elements of thought.

Visual Images: *Mental pictures or representations of objects or events.*

Propositions: *Sentences that relate one concept to another and can stand as separate assertions.*

IMAGES: MENTAL PICTURES OF THE WORLD   Look at the drawing in Figure 7.1. Now cover it up with a piece of paper and answer the following questions:

1. Was there a flag? If so, in what direction was it fluttering?

2. Was there a handle attached to the rudder?

3. Was there a porthole? On which side of the boat?

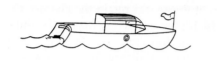

FIGURE 7.1

Mental Scanning of Visual Images

When shown a drawing such as this one and then asked questions about it, most people take longer to estimate the distance between the flag and the rudder than between the flag and the porthole.
(Source: Based on an illustration used by Kosslyn, 1980)

You probably answered all of these questions quite easily. But how? If you are like most people, you formed a visual image of the boat. Then, when asked about the flag, you focused on that part of your image. Next, you were asked to think about the rudder at the opposite end of the boat. Did you simply jump to that end of the boat or scan the entire image? Research findings indicate that you probably scanned the entire image: After being asked about some feature near the front of the boat, most people take longer to answer a question about a feature near the back than to respond concerning a feature somewhere in the middle (Kosslyn, 1980). Such findings suggest that once we form a mental image, we think about it by scanning it visually just as we would if it actually existed.

Images can be manipulated in much the same way as visual objects in the real world. This is nicely illustrated in an example provided by Paivio (1983). He tells how he once asked his young daughter to form a pictorial image of a capital N. She readily did so. He then asked her to tip it over onto its right side and tell him what it looked like. She immediately reported that it looked like a "Z." Could his daughter have provided the answer in any way other than by mentally rotating her image of the N? Paivio thinks not, and there is an enormous amount of literature on the rotation of mental images that supports his conclusion. (e.g., Shepard & Metzler, 1971).

Not everyone supports the role of imagery in thought processes as enthusiastically as Kosslyn and Paivio. For example, a colleague of Paivio's at the University of Western Ontario, Zenon Pylyshyn, has been especially critical of the notion that having an image is akin to having a picture in the head (Pylyshyn, 1973; 1981). Indeed, there are studies indicating that our use of visual images in thinking does not correspond precisely to actual vision. In one such study, participants were asked to imagine carrying either a cannonball or a balloon along a familiar route (Intons-Peterson & Roskos-Ewoldsen, 1988). As is usual in such studies, the time required for the subjects to complete their imaginary journey was carefully measured. The outcome expected was that the longer the imagined distance to be traversed, the more time would be required to complete the journey. However, it was found that even when the distance over which the two objects were carried was the same, it took the participants longer to complete their imaginary journey when carrying the heavy object. Such findings suggest that we don't simply "read" the visual images we generate; if we did, the participants in this study should have been able to move through the imagined route equally quickly in both conditions. The fact that they could not indicates that visual images are actually embedded in our knowledge about the world, and are interpreted in light of such knowledge rather than simply scanned.

Whatever the precise mechanisms of their use, mental images do seem to serve important purposes in thinking. People report using them for understanding verbal instructions, by converting the words into mental pictures of actions; for increasing motivation, by imagining successful performance; and for enhancing their own moods, by visualizing positive events or scenes (Kosslyn et at., 1991). Clearly, then, visual images constitute another basic element of thinking.

Reasoning: Transforming Information to Reach Conclusions

One task we often face in everyday life is **reasoning**: drawing conclusions from available information. More formally, reasoning involves cognitive transformations of appropriate information in order to reach specific conclusions (Galotti, 1989). How do we perform this task? And to what extent are we successful at it—in other words, how likely are the conclusions we reach to be accurate or valid?

FORMAL VERSUS EVERYDAY REASONING   First, it's important to draw a distinction between *formal reasoning* and what might be described as *everyday reasoning*. In formal reasoning, all the required information is supplied, the problem to be solved is straightforward, there is typically only one correct answer, and the reasoning we apply follows a specific method. One important type of formal reasoning is **syllogistic reasoning**—reasoning in which conclusions are based on two propositions called *premises*. For example, consider the following syllogism:

Premise: All people who love chocolate are extremely kind.

Premise: Saddam Hussein loves chocolate.

Conclusion: Therefore, Saddam Hussein is extremely kind.

Is the conclusion correct? According to the rules of formal reasoning, it is. But you may find it hard to accept—and the reason for the problem should be obvious. At least one of the premises is incorrect: There is no strong evidence that all people who love chocolate are extremely kind. This simple example illustrates an important point: Formal reasoning can provide a powerful tool for processing complex information, but *only* when its initial premises are correct.

In contrast to formal reasoning, *everyday reasoning* involves the kind of thinking we do in our daily lives: planning, making commitments, evaluating arguments. In such reasoning some of the premises are implicit, or unstated. Others may not be supplied at all. The problems involved often have several possible answers, which may vary in quality or effectiveness; and the problems themselves are not self-contained—they relate to other issues and questions of daily life. For example, imagine that you have a problem with your next-door neighbor. You and your neighbor share a driveway leading to your respective garages. It is narrow, so only one car at a time can pass. Lately, your neighbor has taken to parking her car midway down the driveway, next to her side door. This prevents you from putting your own car in your garage. You begin to reason about this situation in order to understand why your neighbor is doing this. One potential premise might be, "She has been quite ill lately"; a second might be, "People who are ill are weak and don't want to walk a lot." These could lead to the conclusion, "Although she is a nice person, she is too ill to be considerate." Other premises, however, are also possible: "She has been quite ill lately" coupled with "But she has gotten a lot better" and "People who look as healthy as she does don't mind walking." Your conclusion then might be quite different: "She is using her recent illness as an excuse for being irresponsible."

Reasoning: Cognitive activity that transforms information in order to reach specific conclusions.

Syllogistic Reasoning: A type of formal reasoning in which two premises are used as the basis for deriving logical conclusions.

Notice that in this situation, the premises are not specified for you, as in syllogisms; you must generate them for yourself. And many different premises are possible. The ones you choose will probably depend on many factors, including your recent experiences with other neighbors, with people who are ill, and so on. Finally, when you do reach a conclusion, it is not easy to determine whether it is correct or whether others, too, might be accurate.

Everyday reasoning, then, is far more complex and far less definite than formal syllogistic reasoning. Since it is the kind we usually perform, however, it is worthy of careful attention. This brings up an intriguing question: Do people from different cultural backgrounds reason in similar ways? As we'll see in **Perspectives on Diversity**, cultural factors *do* seem to play an important role.

PERSPECTIVES ON DIVERSITY

When Culture Shapes Reasoning—or at Least Influences Its Outcomes

Most people in Western cultures, where formal rules of logic are routinely taught in school, can solve simple syllogisms quite successfully. However, this is not necessarily true of individuals raised in other cultures. For example, in one study, Scribner (1977) presented people from cultures where most people could not read or write with syllogisms such as this one:

Premise: All people who own houses pay house tax.

Premise: Boima does not pay a house tax.

Conclusion: Does Boima own a house?

Participants had a great deal of difficulty in answering, mainly because they refused to accept the premises at face value. They said that they did not know the person named and so could not tell whether he really had no house, or he had a house but was avoiding paying taxes because he was related to the tax collector. It's important to realize that participants' inability (or unwillingness) to answer in no way implies that they were less intelligent than people from other cultures; it merely suggests that they were unfamiliar with the rules of the syllogistic game.

Such effects have also been observed in cultures where most people are quite familiar with rules of formal logic. Solso (1991) presented students at a Moscow university with the following syllogism:

Premise: Ivan and Boris always eat together.

Premise: Boris is eating.

Question: What is Ivan doing?

Surprisingly, few of the students answered correctly ("Ivan is eating too") immediately. Instead, many replied something like this: "How can I tell? I can't see him." This is precisely how many individuals from non-Western cultures replied when presented with the same type of situation (Cole & Scribner, 1974).

Why do participants in these studies answer this way? One explanation emphasizes the role of cultural factors in reasoning (Solso, 1991). Many cultures, it appears, view the laws of formal logic as less trustworthy or applicable than their own senses. Participants answer accordingly, by noting that they have no direct experience with the situation and so really can't answer intelligently. In short, cultural factors and beliefs can, and sometimes do, take precedence over formal rules of logic. What people say in such situations generally makes sense from the perspective of their own culture; ignoring this fact can lead to false conclusions about their abilities to reason clearly.

CULTURE AND REASONING

When researchers asked Moscow University students to complete syllogisms, few answered correctly. Why? One answer may be that Russian culture puts less trust in the laws of formal logic than Western cultures.

How good are we at reasoning? Unfortunately, not as good as you might guess. Several factors, working together, seem to reduce our ability to reason effectively.

REASONING ERRORS: THE ROLE OF EMOTION AND BELIEFS Growing evidence indicates that the way we feel—our current moods or emotions—can strongly affect various aspects of cognition (Forgas & Bower, 1988). So it is not surprising to learn that reasoning is often influenced by emotions and emotion-laden beliefs. For example, imagine that a person with deeply held convictions against the death penalty listens to a speech favoring capital punishment. Suppose that the arguments presented by the speaker contain premises the listener can't readily refute, and thus point to the conclusion that the death penalty is justified for the purpose of preventing further social evil. Yet the listener totally rejects this conclusion. Why? Because of his or her passionate beliefs and convictions against the death penalty, the listener may alter the meaning of the speaker's premises or "remember" things the speaker never really said. This, of course, serves to weaken the speaker's conclusion. Such effects can arise in many ways. Whatever your views on this particular issue, the general principle remains the same: When emotions or powerful beliefs come face-to-face with logical arguments, it is often the latter that give way. We'll consider the powerful effects of emotion again in Chapter 10.

THE OVERSIGHT BIAS: OVERLOOKING IMPORTANT INFORMATION In the last federal election, supporters of Kim Campbell advanced many reasons why she should be elected prime minister. She had extensive experience in Parliament; she had held several cabinet positions; she had brought twenty-six bills to the House; she was young and ambitious and had clear ideas about the direction the country should take; and because she was a woman, she was capable of adding a new dimension to Canadian political life. What her supporters tended to forget was that in the last few months before the election, she was prime minister and chief symbol for an extremely unpopular government—a fact that the electorate did not overlook. This example illustrates the **oversight bias**: Our assessment of what is important can cause us to overlook flaws and fail to see troublesome problems. Campbell's supporters perceived her qualifications for office to be of crucial importance. What they overlooked was the electorate's intention to punish anyone associated with the existing government.

Even experts, it seems, are prone to this type of oversight. In a recent study, Wilson and colleagues (1993) asked two groups of scientists to evaluate descriptions of several fictitious studies in terms of their scientific merit. All of the studies described contained obvious flaws. There were two versions of each study. Both versions were identical except that in one, the topic of the study was *important* (the effects of alcohol on cardiovascular disease); while in the other, the topic was relatively *unimportant* (the effects of alcohol on heartburn). As predicted by the oversight bias, the scientists rated descriptions of studies of important topics as having greater merit than descriptions of studies of unimportant topics—even though both were *equally* flawed (refer to Figure 7.2).

THE CONFIRMATION BIAS: SEARCHING FOR POSITIVE EVIDENCE To illustrate another source of error in reasoning, let's consider our anti-death penalty person once again. Suppose that over several weeks this individual encounters numerous magazine articles; some report evidence confirming the usefulness of the death penalty, while others report evidence indicating that it is ineffective in terms of deterring crime. As you can readily guess, he or she

Oversight Bias: The tendency to overlook flaws if the overall topic or issue is perceived as important.

FIGURE 7.2

The Oversight Bias: Overlooking the Unimportant

The oversight bias seems to affect experts, too. As shown in this figure, the perceived importance of the topic greatly affected scientists' evaluations of the rigor of the research. Scientists rated the important versions higher than the unimportant versions in terms of their scientific rigor—despite the fact that both versions were equally flawed.
(Source: Based on data from Wilson et al., 1993.)

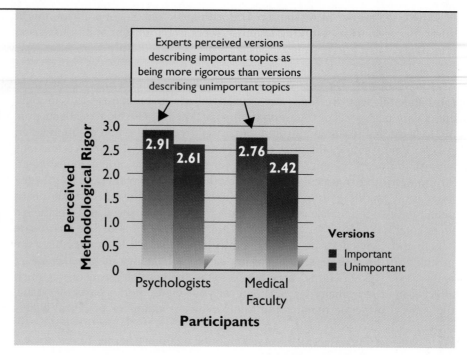

will probably remember more of the information that supports the anti-death penalty view. In fact, there is a good chance that this person will read only these articles, or will read these articles more carefully than the ones arguing in favor of capital punishment. To the extent that this happens, it demonstrates the **confirmation bias**—our strong tendency to test conclusions or hypotheses by examining only, or primarily, evidence that confirms our initial views (Baron, 1988; Klayman & Ha, 1987). Because of the confirmation bias, individuals often become firmly locked into their conclusions; while this bias operates, it prevents them from even considering information that might call their premises, and thus their conclusions, into question (see Figure 7.3).

Confirmation Bias: The tendency to pay attention primarily to information that confirms existing views or beliefs.

HINDSIGHT: THE "I KNEW IT ALL ALONG" EFFECT REVISITED   Have you ever heard the old saying "Hindsight is better than foresight"? What it means is that after specific events occur, we often have the impression that we could have or

FIGURE 7.3

The Confirmation Bias

The confirmation bias leads individuals to test conclusions or hypotheses by examining primarily—or only—evidence consistent with their initial views. As a result, those views may be maintained regardless of the weight of opposing evidence.

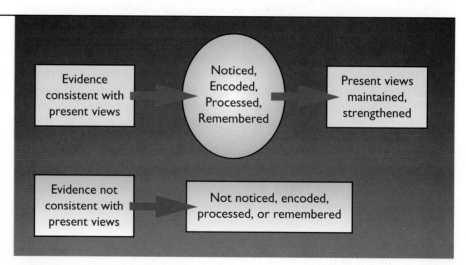

actually did predict them. This is known in psychology as the **hindsight effect**: the tendency to think that we knew some event was likely to occur even before we learned that it had in fact taken place (Hawkins & Hastie, 1990). A dramatic real-life illustration of this effect was provided by the launch of the Hubble space telescope in the spring of 1990. Shortly after the telescope reached orbit, it was discovered to have a serious defect. Within a few days of this discovery, several officials stated that they had known all along this might happen; in fact, the problem resulted from a failure to conduct certain tests of the telescope that they had personally recommended.

Were these individuals correct? Existing evidence on the hindsight effect suggests that this is highly doubtful. In many studies, conducted in widely different contexts, it has been found that learning that an event occurred causes individuals to assume that they could have predicted it more accurately than is actually the case (Fischoff, 1975; Mitchell, Russo, & Pennington, 1989).

Can anything be done to counteract the hindsight effect? There are several possibilities. For example, if individuals are asked to explain a reported outcome along with *other* possible outcomes that did *not* occur, they are better able to recall their actual views before learning of the event, and this reduces the hindsight effect (Davies, 1987; Slovic & Fischoff, 1977). Also, other people may reduce the hindsight effect by calling attention to the fact that others were surprised by the event and that it was indeed truly difficult to predict (Wasserman, Lempert, & Hastie, 1991). In sum, it does appear that we can combat our strong tendency to assume that we are better at predicting events than we actually are. And to the extent that we avoid tendencies to flawed thinking, our ability to reason effectively may be enhanced.

Animal Cognition: *Do They Really Think?*

That human beings possess cognitive abilities, such as the abilities to think, reason, and plan, is obvious. But what about other species? Do animals have similar abilities? Our discussions in this chapter have implied so far that cognitive processes are mainly a human attribute. After all, it is difficult for most of us to picture animals thinking, or performing other complex mental activities. For many years, this view prevailed among behavioral researchers as well. Several developments, however, have led scientists to reconsider their initial assumptions. For example, as discussed in Chapter 5, behavioral researchers throughout this century have encountered many instances of animal learning that cannot be explained solely through conditioning processes (e.g., Tolman & Honzik, 1930; Capaldi & Miller, 1988). Also, growing evidence suggests that animals do form complex mental representations of their environment—a cognitive activity that helps them adapt to changing conditions they often face in nature (Cook, 1993). In **The Research Process**, we'll see that animals can indeed display cognitive operations that are in many respects quite humanlike.

Research in Canada

Sara J. Shettleworth
University of Toronto

Hindsight Effect: The tendency to assume that we would have been better at predicting actual events than is really true.

Animal Cognition: Tales of Intelligence

To appreciate the sophistication of cognitive operations evident in nonhuman animals, let's consider an aspect of cognition with which most of us are familiar: categorization, or the formation of concepts. Most people learn to form categories at a very early age. For example, we learn that lions, tigers, and bears are animals, whereas football, soccer, and jogging are sports. Parents often teach their children to categorize various stimuli through games such as the "name game," in which they point to a picture and then ask their child, "What's that?" Not surprisingly, children quickly become proficient at categorizing a wide variety of stimuli. But do other animals possess similar abilities? Since animals do not speak, it is difficult to ask them directly.

To assess animals' categorizing abilities, Bhatt and his colleagues (1988) devised a "name game" for pigeons that did not require the use of language. Pigeons were asked to "name" examples of four distinct categories—cats, flowers, cars, and chairs—by pecking colored keys that corresponded to each of the four categories. The subjects viewed slides depicting examples of each of the four categories and received food reinforcement for their correct responses. The pigeons quickly learned to categorize these stimuli correctly—and subsequent testing with novel slides showed that they were able to extend their categorization abilities beyond the slides used during training. These results suggest that pigeons, like people, have the ability to behave conceptually.

Although some critics argue that these results may be the product of simple conditioning, additional research has shown that learning occurs faster and accuracy is higher when pigeons are asked to sort pictures into "human" categories than when they are asked to sort stimuli into arbitrary "pseudocategories" (Wasserman, Kiedinger, & Bhatt, 1988). In other words, pigeons, like their human counterparts, can categorize stimuli on the basis of physical similarity (Astley & Wasserman, 1992; Wasserman et al., 1988). But can pigeons and other animals categorize stimuli that differ in ways other than physical similarity? Researchers are just beginning to explore this possibility, as well as others (e.g., Terrace, 1993; Church, 1993).

For example, a cognitive ability that has been well established in humans—but not in nonhuman species—is the ability to mentally rotate visual forms (Shepard & Metzler, 1971). To test mental rotation, people first view a sample stimulus—say, the letter R. They are then shown two comparison stimuli—rotated versions of the same stimulus and of its mirror

image. Their task is to determine which of the comparison stimuli matches the sample. To do so, participants must first mentally rotate both stimuli to a normal position. The amount of time required to select the correct stimulus usually varies directly with the amount of mental rotation required.

To test whether baboons are also capable of mentally rotating visual stimuli, Vauclair, Fagot, and Hopkins (1993) developed a procedure appropriate to the abilities of baboons (refer to Figure 7.4). In their study, the subjects (baboons) first viewed a sample shape (such as the letter F) that was flashed briefly on a screen. Then two comparison shapes that were rotated 0, 60, 120, 180, 240, or 300 degrees were presented. One of the comparison shapes always matched the sample; the other comparison shape was its mirror image. The baboons' task was to use a joystick to select the comparison shapes that matched the original samples. Each correct response produced a small food reward.

The results showed that baboons were able mentally to rotate visual stimuli—an ability that some researchers had previously believed was beyond the capacity of nonhuman species. Moreover, the baboons' performance varied directly with the degree of rotation of the comparison stimuli—a finding that closely paralleled the performance of humans on the same task.

The results of these studies, as well as others, suggest that when appropriate methods are used, other animal species demonstrate cognitive abilities that are similar in many respects to those of humans. The question that has to be asked, however, is whether attempting to get other animals to perform humanlike cognitive operations is going to tell us much about important issues in human or animal cognition. A number of scientists think not. In **Canadian Perspective** we will consider the work of Sara Shettleworth of the University of Toronto, who thinks that a different, ecological, approach is required.

🍁 CANADIAN PERSPECTIVE

Should the Intelligence of Nonhuman Species Be Assessed by Their Ability to Perform Humanlike Cognitive Tasks?

Shettleworth (1993) distinguished between *anthropocentric* and *ecological* approaches to comparative cognition. As the name implies, an anthropocentric approach is human centered. According to Shettleworth, it involves singling out cognitive abilities that play an important role in the everyday life of humans and making comparisons to establish whether other organisms display

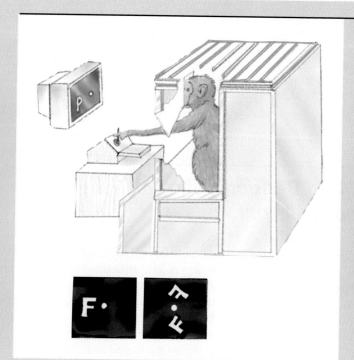

FIGURE 7.4

Animal Cognition: A Sample Test Environment

The upper portion of the figure shows the apparatus used to assess the baboon's ability to rotate visual stimuli mentally. Subjects were trained to use the joystick to manipulate stimuli displayed on a 30 centimeter color monitor. The bottom portion of the figure shows an example of a sample stimulus (left) and two comparison stimuli (right). Source: Vauclair, Fagot, & Hopkins, 1993.)

these cognitive skills. Shettleworth objects to this approach for a variety of reasons. For example, she rejects the implicit assumption that the highest-developed animal is the human animal and that the cognitive capabilities of other animals should be judged in terms of the degree to which they are able to mirror humanlike cognitive skills. Consider the pigeon and baboon studies we considered earlier. Clearly, a pigeon can perform conceptual classifications involving cars and chairs and flowers, and a baboon can mentally rotate simple shapes to match a standard. What is of interest to an advocate of the ecological approach, however, is whether either of these animals would ever use these sorts of cognitive skills in their natural habitat. It does seem unlikely. Thus, it can be argued that such studies tell us nothing about cognitive skills that are relevant to the nonhuman animals being studied.

Supporters of the ecological approach, such as Shettleworth, suggest that animal cognition studies should not be about how closely a nonhuman animal can emulate peculiarly human cognitive skills; rather, they should focus on the cognitive skills that allow these animals to deal effectively with the day-to-day problems of survival in their natural habitat. Animals certainly do possess distinctive cognitive abilities that allow them to cope effectively with environmental demands. Some display remarkable foraging strategies; some demonstrate extraordinary navigation skills; some are remarkably adept at hoarding and recovering food; and all are capable of discriminating their direct kin from the offspring of other members of their group. Advocates of the ecological approach

take the position that cognitive operations underlying these sorts of tasks are much more worth studying than seeing whether animals can perform humanlike cognitive tasks.

Proponents of the ecological approach are especially interested in determining whether some cognitive-type skills found in nonhuman animals reflect special evolutionary adaptations. For example, some birds possess rather amazing skills in hoarding and recovering food. Clark's nutcracker is particularly interesting in this respect. It buries piñon-nut seeds at as many as 6,000 different locations in the latter part of the summer and has been seen recovering these seeds as late as the next spring (Shettleworth, 1983). To do this, the nutcracker must have a vast spatial-memory capacity. Supporters of the ecological approach seek to determine for example, whether this bird's abilities reflect a special evolutionary adaptation that distinguishes it from other, closely related species, and to explain why and how any such differences developed.

What are we to conclude? Is Shettleworth correct? Some researchers think that advocates of the ecological approach go too far. Riley and Langley (1993) offer a spirited defense of more traditional approaches. They emphasize the difficulty of achieving the objectives advanced by supporters of the ecological approach and argue that direct comparisons between human and nonhuman animals on specific tasks can be useful. For example, a bowed serial-position curve has long been observed in human memory studies. It has been suggested that this effect is attributable to linguistic coding operations. The fact that this curve can be found in memory studies involving nonlinguistic animals helps to rule out this explanation.

Arguments such as those advanced by Riley and Langley are reasonable: Direct comparisons of humans and nonhuman animals on tasks can be use-ful. However, it is difficult to ignore the compelling logic of Shettleworth's contention that we should spend less time attempting to determine whether animals can perform human cognitive tasks, and more time studying the kinds of cognitive activities they perform in their natural environment.

Making Decisions: Choosing Among Alternatives

Reasoning is hard work; in fact, it's an activity many people try to avoid. In some respects, though, reasoning is less difficult than another cognitive task you perform many times each day: **decision making**. From the moment you wake up until you turn out the light at night, life presents a continuous series of choices. What to wear, what to eat for breakfast, whether to attend a class or meeting, whether to speed up so you can get through that yellow traffic light … the list of everyday decisions is endless. And at intervals we face much more important decisions: what school to attend, what job to accept, what house to buy, whether to continue or end a long-term relationship.

If you were a perfectly rational decision maker, you would make each of these choices in a cool, almost mathematical way. You would consider (1) the utility or value to you of the outcomes each alternative might yield and (2) the probability that such results would actually occur. Having taken these two factors into account, you would then make your decision on the basis of **expected utility**—the product of the value and the probability of each possible outcome. As you know from your own life, however, you don't usually pause to reason in such a systematic manner. Instead, you often make decisions informally, on the basis of hunches, intuition, or the opinions of others. And even if you did try to make decisions in a perfectly rational way, you would quickly find that the process isn't foolproof. For example, both the values you attach to various outcomes and your estimates concerning their probability might shift over time. Let's consider several factors that influence the decision-making process, making it less rational or effective than might otherwise be the case.

Decision Making: The process of choosing among various courses of action or alternatives.

Expected Utility: The product of the subjective value of an event and its predicted probability of occurrence.

Heuristics: Mental rules of thumb that permit us to make decisions and judgments in a rapid and efficient manner.

KEY POINTS

- Reasoning involves transforming available information in order to reach specific conclusions. Formal reasoning derives conclusions from specific premises. In contrast, everyday reasoning is more complex and less clear-cut.

- Cultural factors and beliefs often take precedence over formal Western rules of logic.

- Reasoning is subject to several forms of error and bias. These include emotion, the oversight bias, the confirmation bias, and the hindsight bias.

- Animals can perform complex cognitive tasks. Advocates of the ecological approach to comparative cognition think that attention should be focused on the cognitive skills an animal uses in its natural environment.

Heuristics: Using Quick— but Fallible—Rules of Thumb to Make Decisions

Where cognition is concerned, human beings follow the path of least resistance whenever possible. Since making decisions is hard work, it is only reasonable to expect people to take shortcuts in performing this activity, as demonstrated by Calvin in the cartoon on page 283. One group of cognitive shortcuts is known as the **heuristics**—rules of thumb that reduce the effort required, though they may not necessarily enhance the quality or accuracy of the decisions reached (Kahneman & Tversky, 1982). Heuristics are extracted from past experience and serve

HEURISTICS: QUICK BUT FALLIBLE DECISION TOOLS

Calvin recognizes that decision making is hard work. Like many people, Calvin may resort to heuristics—rules of thumb that reduce the amount of effort required—to help him make quicker, but not necessarily better, decisions.
(Source: Universal Press Syndicate, 1993.)

as simple guidelines for making reasonably good choices quickly and efficiently. We'll focus on the three heuristics that tend to be used most frequently.

AVAILABILITY: WHAT COMES TO MIND FIRST? Let's start with the **availability heuristic**: the tendency to make judgments about the frequency or likelihood of events in terms of how readily examples of them can be brought to mind. This shortcut tends to work fairly well, because the more readily we can bring events to mind, the more frequent they generally are; but it can lead us into error as well.

A good example of the availability heuristic in operation is provided by a study conducted by Tversky and Kahneman (1974). They presented participants with lists of names like the one in Table 7.1 and then asked them whether the lists contained more men's or women's names. Although the numbers of male and female names were equal, nearly 80 percent of the participants reported that women's names appeared more frequently. Why? Because the women named in the lists were more famous, so their names were more readily remembered and brought to mind.

The availability heuristic also influences many people to overestimate their chances of being a victim of a violent crime, being involved in an airplane crash, or winning the lottery. Because such events are given extensive coverage in the mass media, people can readily bring vivid examples of them to mind. They conclude that such outcomes are much more frequent than they actually are (Tyler & Cook, 1984).

REPRESENTATIVENESS: ASSUMING THAT WHAT'S TYPICAL IS ALSO LIKELY You have just met your next-door neighbor for the first time. On the basis of a brief

Availability Heuristic: A cognitive rule of thumb in which the importance or probability of various events is judged on the basis of how readily they come to mind.

TABLE 7.1

Margaret Atwood	Bruce Holliday	Peter Mitchell
Kim Campbell	Arthur Hutchinson	Allan Nevins
Monika Deol	Silken Laumann	Cliff Newman
Céline Dion	Margaret Laurence	Edward Palmer
Michael Drayton	Edward Lytton	Robert Porter
Erica Ehm	Jack Lindsay	Larry Schneider
Linda Evangelista	Elizabeth Manley	Henry Vaughan
Charles Fisher	Audrey McLaughlin	Pamela Wallin
Ron Fisher	Alannah Myles	

The Availability Heuristic in Operation

Does this list contain more men's or women's names? The answer may surprise you: The number of male and female names is about equal. Because of the *availability heuristic*, however, most people tend to guess that female names are more numerous. Since the women listed are more famous than the men, it is easier to bring their names to mind, and this leads to overestimates of their frequency in the list.

conversation, you determine that he is neat in his appearance, has a good vocabulary, seems very well-read, is somewhat shy, and dresses conservatively. Later, you realize that he never mentioned what he does for a living. Is he more likely to be a business executive, a dentist, a librarian, or a waiter? One quick way of making a guess is to compare him with your idea of typical members of each of these occupations. If you proceeded in this fashion, you might conclude that he is a librarian, because his traits seem to resemble those of your image of librarians (and especially your image of the prototypical librarian) more closely than those of your image of waiters, dentists, or executives. If you reasoned in this manner you would be using the **representativeness heuristic**. In other words, you would be making your decision on the basis of a relatively simple rule: The more closely an item—or event, or object, or person—resembles the most typical examples of some concept or category, the more likely it is to belong to that concept or category.

While making judgments or decisions on the basis of representativeness saves cognitive effort, it can also be a source of serious errors. In particular, use of this heuristic sometimes causes us to ignore forms of information that could potentially prove very helpful. The most important of these is information relating to *base rates*—the relative frequency of various items or events in the external world. Returning to your new neighbor, there are many more businessmen than male librarians. Thus, of the choices given, the most rational guess might be that your neighbor is a business executive. Yet because of the representativeness heuristic, you might well decide that he is a librarian and reach a false conclusion (Tversky & Kahneman, 1974).

ANCHORING-AND-ADJUSTMENT: REFERENCE POINTS THAT MAY LEAD US ASTRAY Once we gain something in the way of a steady income, most of us start to look around for our first car. We scan the newspaper ads zealously, and inevitably meet up with the ideal solution to our transportation problems. The question then becomes, "How much will it cost?" A totally rational person obtains this information from the *Red Book*, which lists the average prices paid for various used cars in recent months. Do most of us proceed in this fashion? Absolutely *not*. Given our strong tendency to follow the path of least resistance (and the fact that the *Red Book* is not readily available everywhere), we use the simpler approach of asking the seller the price of the car, and bargaining from there. At first glance, this may seem like a reasonable strategy, but it is not. If you adopt this tactic, you allow the seller to set a *reference point*—a figure from which your negotiations will proceed. If this price is close to the one in the *Red Book*, all well and good. If it is much higher, though, you may end up paying more for the car than it is really worth—as many of us often do.

In such cases, decisions are influenced by what is known as the **anchoring-and-adjustment heuristic**: a mental rule of thumb for reaching decisions by making adjustments in information that is already available. The basic problem with the anchoring-and-adjustment heuristic is that the adjustments are often insufficient in magnitude to offset the impact of the original reference point. In this case, the reference point was the original asking price. In other contexts, it might be a performance rating assigned to an employee, a grade given to a term paper, or a suggested asking price for a new home (Northcraft & Neale, 1987). See the **Key Concept** illustration on page 285 for an overview of the heuristics we have discussed.

Although the influence of heuristics appears to be quite strong, growing evidence indicates that it is often reduced in the case of experts working on tasks with which they are very familiar (Frederick & Libby, 1986; Smith & Kida, 1991). So, while the impact of such potential sources of error is strong, it is not irresistible; it can be reduced by expertise and experience.

Representativeness Heuristic: A mental rule of thumb suggesting that the more closely an event or object resembles typical examples of some concept or category, the more likely it is to belong to that concept or category.

Anchoring-and-Adjustment Heuristic: A cognitive rule of thumb for making decisions in which existing information is accepted as a reference point but then adjusted in light of various factors.

Factors That Influence the Decision-Making Process

HEURISTICS Rules of thumb extracted from past experience that serve as guidelines for making decisions quickly and efficiently—but not necessarily infallibly.

Availability Heuristic:
The tendency to make judgments about the frequency or likelihood of events in terms of how readily examples of them can be brought to mind.

Because lotto winners are given extensive media coverage, people can readily bring examples of them to mind. They falsely conclude that such outcomes are much more frequent than they really are.

Representativeness Heuristic:
A rule of thumb suggesting that the more closely an event or object resembles typical examples of some concept or category, the more likely it is to belong to that concept or category.

Because of the representativeness heuristic, you might be tempted to label these youths as gang members.

Anchoring-and-Adjustment Heuristic:
A rule of thumb in which existing information (the anchor) is accepted as a reference point but then adjusted—usually insufficiently—in light of various factors.

Familiarity with the anchoring-and-adjustment heuristic could save you a bundle—in this case, thousands of dollars when you're negotiating the price of a new home.

Framing in Decision Making

Imagine that a new, virulent strain of flu is on its way toward Canada and is expected to kill 600 people. Two plans for combating the disease exist. If plan A is adopted, 200 people will be saved. If plan B is adopted, the chances are one in three that all 600 will be saved, but two in three that no one will be saved. Which plan would you choose?

Now consider the same situation with the following changes. Again, there are two plans. If plan C is chosen, 400 people will definitely die; if plan D is chosen, the chances are one in three that no one will die, but two in three that all 600 will die. Which would you choose now?

If you are like most respondents to these scenarios, you probably chose plan A in the first example but plan D in the second example (Tversky & Kahneman, 1981). Why? Plan D is just another way of stating the outcomes of plan B, and plan C is just another way of stating the outcomes of plan A. Why, then, do you prefer plan A in the first example but plan D in the second? Because in the first example the emphasis is on *lives saved*, while in the second the emphasis is on *lives lost*. In other words, the two examples differ in what psychologists term **framing**—presentation of information about potential outcomes in terms of gains or in terms of losses. When the emphasis is on potential gains (lives saved), research indicates that most people are *risk averse*. They prefer avoiding unnecessary risks. Thus, most choose plan A. In contrast, when the emphasis is on potential losses (deaths), most people are *risk prone*; they prefer taking risks to accepting probable losses. As a result, most choose plan D.

Framing effects have been found to be quite general in scope. For example, negotiators tend to evaluate offers from their opponents more favorably, and to make more actual concessions, if they are urged to think about potential gains than if they are urged to think about potential losses that may result from such concessions (Neale & Bazerman, 1985).

Framing also seems to play a role in the consistency with which we make decisions. In one study, Schneider (1992) presented participants with several incidents similar to the flu example described above, and asked them to select among negatively and positively framed options. The results showed that participants were certain and consistent in their preferences when the options were framed as gains, but less certain and more inconsistent when the *same* options were framed as losses. Schneider offers the following explanation: The use of *negative* frames draws our attention to the unpleasant consequences of potential outcomes. This, in turn, heightens our awareness of conflicting goals that cannot be met regardless of which option we choose. Thus, we tend to vacillate between options when they are framed negatively. In contrast, *positive* frames tend to focus our attention on the desirable consequences of potential outcomes, thereby obscuring the presence of conflicting goals and the need to make tough trade-offs.

Finally, recent evidence suggests that the effects of framing also extend to the *amount* of information we have available to us and the *type of choice* we must make (Shafir, 1993). Imagine that you are in charge of making hiring decisions for your company. Two people have applied for a job. Both people are equally qualified, but person A's application contains more information than person B's—both positive and negative. What will you do? It depends on the type of choice you must make. If asked to *choose* one of the applicants, you will tend to focus on the amount of positive information present in each application. Because more positive information is contained on person A's application, it is likely you will choose this person. If, instead, you are asked to *reject* one of the applicants, you will tend to focus on potentially negative

Framing: *Presentation of information concerning potential outcomes in terms of gains or in terms of losses.*

CHAPTER 7

characteristics. On the basis of the amount of negative information available, it is likely you will reject person A, because person A's application also has more potentially negative features than person B's. In sum, the way in which information is framed can have major effects on our decisions.

Escalation of Commitment: Getting Trapped in Bad Decisions

Have you ever heard the phrase "throwing good money after bad"? It refers to the fact that in many situations, individuals who have made bad decisions—ones that yield negative consequences—tend to stick to those decisions even as the evidence for failure mounts. In fact, they may decide to commit additional time, effort, and resources to the failing course of action in order—they hope—to turn the situation around and snatch victory from the jaws of defeat. This tendency to become trapped in bad decisions in known as **escalation of commitment** and is all too common in many spheres of life. Escalation of commitment helps explain the tendencies of many investors to hold on to what are clearly bad investments, and it underlies situations in which people remain in troubled marriages or relationships long after these have begun to yield more pain than happiness (Brockner & Rubin, 1985; Staw & Ross, 1989). In these and many other situations, people do indeed seem to become trapped in bad decisions with no simple or easy means of getting out.

ESCALATION OF COMMITMENT: WHY DOES IT OCCUR?   Escalation of commitment is both real and widespread. But why, precisely, does it occur? Staw and Ross (1989) have suggested that it probably stems from several different factors. Early in the process, initial decisions are based primarily on what might be termed rational factors. People choose particular courses of action because they believe that these will yield favorable outcomes. When things go wrong and negative results occur, it is at first quite reasonable to continue. After all, temporary setbacks are common, and it is often necessary to increase one's effort or investment in order to attain a favorable outcome (Staw & Ross, 1987). In addition, there may be considerable costs associated with changing an initial decision before it has had a chance to succeed.

As negative outcomes continue to mount, however, other factors that can be described as primarily psychological in nature come into play. First, as indicated above, individuals feel responsible for the initial decision and realize that if they now back away from or reverse it, they will be admitting that they made a mistake. Growing evidence suggests that the unpleasant consequences of flawed decisions—including embarrassment and damage to one's self-image—can profoundly affect the quality of subsequent decisions (Larrick, 1993). Indeed, as negative results increase, individuals may experience a growing need to obtain *self-justification*—to justify both their previous judgments and the losses already endured.

Finally, in later phases of the process, external pressures stemming from other individuals or groups affected by the bad decision may come into play. For example, individuals who did not originally make the decision but have gone along with it may now block efforts to reverse it because they too have become committed to actions it implies. Similarly, within groups, political forces may emerge that tend to lock the decision in place. Figure 7.5 summarizes the escalation process and several factors that play a role in its emergence and persistence.

Can anything be done to counter these effects? Researchers have found that under several conditions, people are less likely to escalate their commit-

Escalation of Commitment: The tendency to become increasingly committed to bad decisions even as losses associated with them increase.

FIGURE 7.5

Escalation of Commitment: An Overview

Early in the escalation-of-commitment process, there may be a rational expectation of a positive outcome. As losses occur, however, people are reluctant to admit their errors. Later, external factors may strengthen tendencies to stick to the initial bad decision. However, other conditions may reduce the likelihood of escalation of commitment. (Source: Based on suggestions by Staw & Ross, 1989, and Garland & Newport, 1991.)

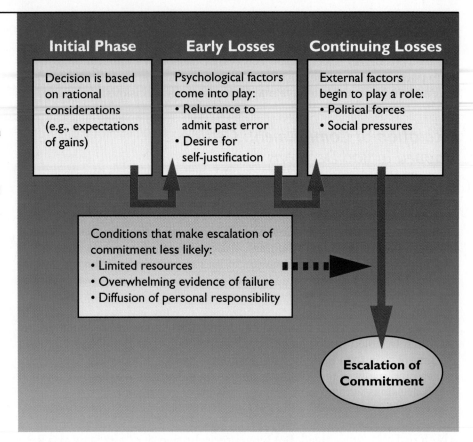

- We do not make all decisions on the basis of expected utility; rather, we often use heuristics, or mental rules of thumb.
- Heuristics include the availability heuristic, the representativeness heuristic, and the anchoring-and-adjustment heuristic.
- Decisions can be strongly affected by framing—the presentation of information about possible outcomes in terms of gains or losses.
- People are generally less certain and more inconsistent in their preferences when options are framed as losses.
- People often become trapped in bad decisions through escalation of commitment, an effect that derives from reluctance to admit past mistakes and a desire to justify past losses.

ment to a failed course of action (refer to Figure 7.5). First, people are likely to refrain from escalating commitment when available resources to commit to further action are limited and the evidence of failure is overwhelmingly obvious (Garland & Newport, 1991). Thus, an individual or a group can decide in advance that if losses reach certain limits, no further resources will be squandered. Second, escalation of commitment is unlikely to occur when people can *diffuse their responsibility* for being part of a poor decision (Whyte, 1991). In other words, the less we feel personally responsible for making a bad decision, the less we may be motivated to justify our mistake by investing additional time or money. Thus, a helpful strategy is to assign the tasks of making decisions and implementing them to different individuals. This allows the people who carry out decisions to be psychologically aloof from them. Together, these steps can help both individuals and groups to avoid getting trapped in costly spirals that magnify the harmful effects of poor decisions. (See Chapter 16 for more information on the effects of diffusion of responsibility.)

Problem Solving and Creativity: Finding Paths to Desired Goals

*I*magine that you are a parent whose son is attending university in another province. You've asked him to keep in touch by phone and mail, but long periods go by without a word. In fact, several weeks have now passed since you heard from him. You're a worrier, so you phone him repeatedly; all you get is his answering machine. What do you do? Several possibilities exist. You could call some of his friends and ask them to urge him to get in touch with you. You could try leaving a message that, you hope, will cause him to phone. Or—and here's the interesting one—you can try something like this: You write a letter to your son. In your letter, you allude to a really tantalizing or funny piece of family gossip, as if you thought your son knew about it. Have you solved your problem? In all probability, yes. Unless your son is truly unusual, he is very likely to pick up the phone and dial your number to learn the hot news.

While you may not have any children, there is little doubt that you have encountered situations that resemble this one in basic structure: You'd like to reach some goal, but there is no simple or direct way of doing so. Such situations involve **problem solving**—efforts to develop responses that permit us to attain desired goals. In this section we'll examine the nature of problem solving, techniques for enhancing its effectiveness, and factors that interfere with its

"THE CARD PLAYERS" BY PAUL CÉZANNE

How are problem-solving skills used during card games? The winner is the person who has successfully solved the problem set by the rules of the game. (Of course, luck may also play a role!)

successful execution. In addition, we'll analyze creativity—the ability to produce new and unusual solutions to various problems.

Problem Solving: An Overview

What does problem solving involve? Psychologists are not totally in agreement on this, but many believe that four aspects, as summarized in Figure 7.6, are central (Matlin, 1990).

First, we must *understand* the problem—figure out just what issues, obstacles, and goals are involved. In the example above, the immediate problem boils down to this: You want to find some way of inducing your son to contact you. But identifying the problems we face is not always so simple. For example, imagine that your car won't start. Why? Is it a bad battery? Bad ignition? Lack of fuel? Until you identify the problem, it is difficult to move ahead with its solution.

Second, we must *formulate potential solutions*. While this, too, might seem fairly simple, it is actually very complex. Solutions cannot arise out of a cognitive vacuum; they depend very heavily on the information at our disposal—information stored in long-term memory that can be retrieved (refer

> **Problem Solving:** *Efforts to develop or choose among various responses in order to attain desired goals.*

to Chapter 6). The more information available, the greater the number and the wider the scope of potential solutions we can generate—an issue we'll consider in greater detail in **The Point of It All**. Formulating a wide range of possible solutions is an extremely important step in effective problem solving. Yet even when abundant information is available, several tendencies and potential sources of bias can cause us to overlook useful solutions and get stuck on less productive ones.

Third, we must *evaluate* each alternative and the outcomes it will produce. Will a given solution actually work—bring us closer to the goal we want to achieve? Are there any serious obstacles to its use? Are there hidden costs that will make a potential solution less useful than it seems at first? These are considerations that must be made.

Finally, we must *try* potential solutions and evaluate them on the basis of the effects they produce. All too often, a potential solution is only partially effective: It brings us closer to where we want to be but doesn't solve the problem completely or finally. The tantalizing-letter strategy described earlier illustrates this point. Yes, it may induce a response from the erring child on this occasion. But it does not guarantee that he will write or phone more frequently in the future. So it constitutes only a partial solution to the problem. In this case it is easy to recognize that the solution is only a partial one. In many other situations, though, it is difficult to know how effective a potential solution will be until it is actually implemented. Thus, careful assessment of the effects of various solutions is another key step in the problem-solving process. In **The Point of It All**, we'll turn to a discussion of how educators have attempted to solve a problem of critical importance in North America.

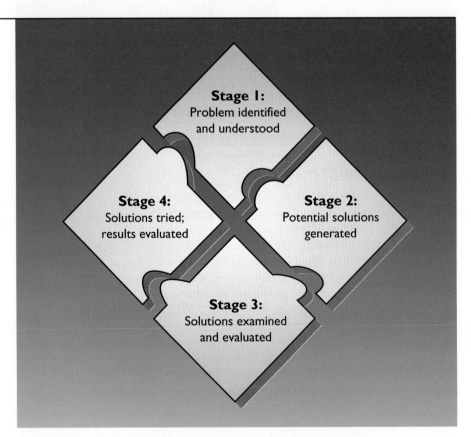

FIGURE 7.6

Problem Solving: An Overview

Effective problem solving involves four stages. First, the problem must be identified and understood. Next, potential solutions must be generated. Third, these must be examined and evaluated. Finally, solutions must be tried and then evaluated in terms of their successes.

Stage 1: Problem identified and understood

Stage 2: Potential solutions generated

Stage 3: Solutions examined and evaluated

Stage 4: Solutions tried; results evaluated

THE POINT OF IT ALL

The Education Crisis in North America: Practice May Be the Key

Unless you've been living in a cave, you've no doubt heard about the "education crisis" in North America. We are repeatedly told by the media that American and Canadian children perform worse on many knowledge tests—notably, mathematics tests—than their counterparts in other countries of the world. In a 1992 study, a large sample of grade 11 (or equivalent) students from Canada, the United States, Japan, and Taiwan had their math skills tested. The mean score of the Canadian students was half that of the Japanese students. The American students performed only slightly better than the Canadian students against their Japanese counterparts (Wood & Kakuchi, 1994). Why is this? There is no evidence to suggest that North American children are less intelligent. A more plausible explanation is that North American children lack important skills that are necessary for acquiring mathematical knowledge (Mayer, Tajika, & Stanley, 1991).

A recent comparison of American and Chinese students lends support to this conclusion. Geary, Fan, and Bow-Thomas (1992) asked first-graders in the United States and China to solve a series of simple arithmetic problems. Of particular interest to these researchers were the strategies the children used to solve the problems. As predicted, the Chinese children outperformed their American counterparts by a three-to-one margin in terms of the overall number of problems they solved correctly. More important, however, were differences observed between the two groups of children in terms of the problem-solving strategies they used and the efficiency with which they used them.

Children in the United States were more likely to solve the problems by counting on their fingers or counting verbally—both somewhat inefficient problem-solving techniques. The Chinese children relied on more advanced strategies. They retrieved most of the answers directly from memory, and when a backup strategy was needed, they "decomposed" the problem into a simpler form. When the American children used these strategies to solve problems—which was not often—they did so much less efficiently.

These results suggest that children need to acquire mathematical information, as well as basic concepts, by means of practice and drill. In doing so they may develop a solid foundation for acquiring more complex mathematical skills and concepts later on (Geary & Widaman, 1992).

These concerns have led a number of provinces to consider introducing standard testing of basic skills at specific age or grade levels. Some are also considering lengthening the school year so that more time can be spent teaching basic skills.

Methods for Solving Problems: From Trial and Error to Heuristics

Suppose that you are working on your friend's computer, trying to complete a term paper that is due tomorrow. The pressure is mounting. You decide to take a break and then realize—with panic—that you don't remember how to save, or put in memory, what you've written with this word processor. You think for a moment, then try hitting one of the keys, but nothing happens. You try another key—again, no result. You hit a third one, and the message FIND WHAT? appears on the screen. Now you decide to try a combination of keys. You are still trying, and still in a panic, when your friend arrives and rescues you.

This incident illustrates a problem-solving technique you have certainly used yourself—**trial and error**. Trial and error involves trying different responses until, perhaps, one works. Sometimes this is all you can do: You don't have enough information to adopt a more systematic approach. But this approach is not very efficient and offers no guarantee that you'll actually find a useful solution.

A second general approach to solving problems involves the use of **algorithms**. These are rules for a particular kind of problem that will, if followed, yield a solution. For example, imagine that you are supposed to meet a friend at a Chinese restaurant. Try as you may, you can't remember the name of the place. What can you do? One approach is to get out the Yellow Pages and see if this refreshes your memory. If it doesn't, you can try calling all the restaurants listed to ask if your friend made a reservation (which you know she was planning to do). Following this algorithm—"Call every restaurant in the book"—will eventually work; but it is time-consuming and inefficient. A much more effective way to solve many problems is by using an appropriate *heuristic*.

Heuristics, as you'll recall, are rules of thumb we often use to guide our cognition. With respect to problem solving, heuristics involve strategies suggested by prior experience—ones we have found useful in the past. These may or may not work in the present case, so a solution is not guaranteed. But what heuristics lack in terms of certainty they gain in efficiency: They often provide useful shortcuts. In the case of the Chinese restaurant search, you might begin by assuming that your friend probably chose a restaurant close to where she lives. This simple rule could eliminate many of the most distant restaurants and considerably simplify your task.

One heuristic we often employ is known as **means-ends analysis** (or subgoals analysis). This involves dividing the problem into a series of smaller pieces or subproblems. Each of these is then solved, and the distance between our original state and the goal is reduced in a step-by-step fashion.

Finally, we sometimes attempt to solve problems through the use of **analogy**—by applying techniques that worked in similar situations in the past. For example, imagine that while driving through an unfamiliar town, you are suddenly seized by an uncontrollable desire for a cup of Tim Horton coffee. You don't know your way around this town, but you know from past experience that many Tim Horton shops are located near busy entry and exit ramps to the Trans-Canada Highway. Applying this knowledge, you follow signs showing the way to the nearest link to the Trans-Canada. If you are then rewarded with a cup of coffee (with a bag of TimBits), you have solved the problem through analogy.

Factors That Interfere with Effective Problem Solving

Sometimes, despite our best efforts, we are unable to solve problems. In many cases our failure has obvious causes, such as lack of necessary information or experience. Similarly, as we'll soon see, we may lack internal frameworks that allow us to represent the problem situation fully and effectively. As a result, we don't know which variables or factors are most important, and we spend lots of time "wandering about," using an informal type of trial and error (Johnson, 1985). In other cases, though, difficulties in solving problems seem to stem from more subtle factors. Let's consider some of these now.

Trial and Error: A method of solving problems in which possible solutions are tried until one succeeds.

Algorithm: A rule that guarantees solution to a specific type of problem.

Means-Ends Analysis: A technique for solving problems in which the overall problem is divided into parts and efforts are made to solve each part in turn.

Analogy: A strategy for solving problems based on applying solutions that were previously successful with other problems similar in underlying structure.

FIGURE 7.7

Solving Complex Problems

How can you attach the candle to a wall so that it stands upright and burns normally, using only the objects shown here?

FUNCTIONAL FIXEDNESS: PRIOR USE VERSUS PRESENT SOLUTIONS Suppose you want to use the objects shown in Figure 7.7 to attach the candle to a wall so that it can stand upright and burn properly. What solution (or solutions) do you come up with? If you are like most people, you may mention using the tacks to nail the candle to the wall, or attaching it with melted wax (Duncker, 1945). While these techniques may work, they overlook a much more elegant solution: emptying the box of matches, attaching the box to the wall, and placing the candle on it (see Figure 7.8). Described this way, the solution probably sounds obvious. Then why don't most people think of it? The answer involves **functional fixedness**—a strong tendency to think of using objects only in ways they have been used before. Since most of us have never used an empty box as a candle holder, we don't think of its use in these terms and so fail to hit upon this solution. Interestingly, if the matchbox is shown empty, people are much more likely to use it as a candle holder (Weisberg & Suls, 1973); it doesn't take much to overcome such mental blind spots. But unless we can avoid functional fixedness, our ability to solve many problems can be seriously impaired.

Functional Fixedness: The tendency to think of using objects only as they have been used in the past.

Mental Set: The impact of past experience on present problem solving; specifically, the tendency to retain methods that were successful in the past even if better alternatives now exist.

MENTAL SET: STICKING TO THE TRIED-AND-TRUE Another factor that often gets in the way of effective problem solving is **mental set**. This is the tendency to stick with a familiar method of solving particular types of problems—one that has worked before. Since past solutions have in fact succeeded, this is certainly reasonable—at least up to a point. Difficulties arise, however, when this tendency causes us to overlook other, more efficient approaches. The powerful impact of mental set was first demonstrated by Luchins (1942) in what is now a classic study. Luchins presented study participants with the problems shown in Table 7.2, which involve using three jars of different sizes to measure amounts of water. If you work through the first two or three items, you will soon discover that you can solve them all by following this simple formula: Fill jar B, and from it fill jar A once and jar C twice. The amount of water then remaining is the desired amount.

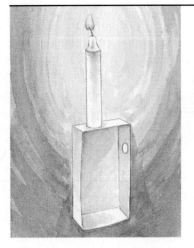

FIGURE 7.8

Functional Fixedness: How It Interferes With Problem Solving

Because of functional fixedness, surprisingly few people think of using the tacks to attach the box to the wall as a candle holder.

- Problem solving involves efforts to develop or choose among various responses in order to attain desired goals.

- Problems can be solved through trial and error or through the use of algorithms—rules that will, if followed, yield solutions in given situations.

- Heuristics are rules of thumb, suggested by our experience, that we often use to solve problems.

- Functional fixedness (the tendency to think of using objects only as they have been used before) and mental sets (tendencies to stick with familiar methods) can interfere with effective problem solving.

Because this formula works for all items, subjects in Luchin's study tended to stick with it for all seven problems. But look at item 6, which can be solved in a simpler way: Just fill jar A, then from it fill jar C. The amount remaining in jar A is precisely what's required (20 units). A simple solution also exists for item 7; see if you can figure it out. Do you think many of the subjects in Luchin's experiment noticed these simpler solutions? Absolutely not. When they reached item 6, almost all continued to use their old tried-and-true formula and overlooked the more efficient one.

Similar effects occur in many other contexts. For example, commuters often continue to take the same crowded roads to work each day because they have always done so; they don't even consider alternative routes that might seem less direct but are actually easier to travel. In these and many other situations, sliding into mental ruts can indeed prove costly.

Creativity: *Innovative Problem Solving*

After the battle of Marengo in 1805, at which he won a great victory, Napoleon asked his chef to prepare a special celebration dinner. Unfortunately, the poor chef had very little to work with—nothing but a chicken, some onions, mushrooms, tomatoes, and wine. What could he do? Drawing on his culinary expertise, he created a new dish that has now become a classic of French cooking: chicken Marengo.

Most people would say that the chef's solution to this problem showed **creativity**—cognitive activity that results in a new or novel way of viewing or solving a problem (Solso, 1991). Further, most people would agree that creativity is desirable; after all, it is from creativity that major inventions, scientific breakthroughs, and great works of music, literature, and art derive. While it is tempting to assume that creativity springs suddenly from flashes of inspiration or other heroic sources, psychologists who have studied it conclude that in fact creativity involves a series of specific steps.

First, creativity involves considerable *preparation*. A person who develops a creative solution to an important problem generally spends long periods of time immersed in the problem, gathering knowledge relevant to it, and working on it. As Thomas Edison once remarked, "Success is ninety-eight percent perspiration and only two percent inspiration."

Creativity: Cognitive activity resulting in new or novel ways of viewing or solving problems.

TABLE 7.2

Mental Set: Another Potential Deterrent to Problem Solving

How can you use three jars, A, B, and C, each capable of holding the amounts of liquid shown, to end up with one jar holding the exact amount listed in the right-hand column? See the text for two possible solutions.

	AMOUNT HELD BY EACH JAR			
PROBLEM	**JAR A**	**JAR B**	**JAR C**	**GOAL (AMOUNT OF WATER DESIRED)**
1	24	130	3	100
2	9	44	7	21
3	21	58	4	29
4	12	160	25	98
5	19	75	5	46
6	23	49	3	20
7	18	48	4	22

Second, creative solutions often emerge after a period of *incubation*—an interval during which the person stops working actively on the problem and turns to other matters. Incubation periods may provide people with an opportunity to recover from the fatigue generated by the intense preparation phase. And as noted in Chapter 4, during incubation additional work on the problem may be occurring even outside the realm of consciousness, such as during sleep.

Third, creativity does often involve a sudden *illumination* or insight. At such times, individuals report that they suddenly see—perhaps only in partially developed form—the first glimmer of a solution they have been seeking for months or even years. This is how James Watson and Francis Crick, the scientists who discovered the structure of the DNA molecule, described their experience; suddenly, they saw that it *must* be something like a double helix, with one strand intertwined with the other.

Illumination, however, is not the end of the process. Considerable *refinement* must often follow. The idea must be worked out, translated into testable form, and then actually tested. Only when mounting evidence indicates that it does work is the creative solution carried to its final conclusion.

Describing the creative process is certainly useful, but it does not address several key questions: What cognitive processes does creativity involve? Can these be encouraged? And how can creativity be assessed?

With respect to the first of these issues, research findings suggest that creativity often derives from divergent thinking. This is thinking that moves outward from conventional knowledge or wisdom down unexplored paths toward unconventional solutions. It is from such thinking that creative breakthroughs seem to derive. In contrast, **convergent thinking** applies existing knowledge and rules of logic to the task of narrowing the range of potential solutions and zeroing in on a single correct answer. While such thinking is productive in many situations, it does not appear to foster true creativity.

Second, and perhaps even more important from a practical point of view, how can creativity be encouraged? What can individuals and societies do to foster creativity? Decades of research on this question point to the following steps (Isen & Baron, 1991; Schank, 1988):

1. *Develop a broad and rich knowledge base* Solutions—even creative ones—do not emerge out of the air. Rather, they stem from the integration and combination of knowledge that is at the disposal of problem solvers. There seems to be no substitute for the hard work of the preparation stage described above.

2. *Foster independence* Creative people are willing to take risks, depart from the crowd, and strike out on their own. If we wish to encourage creativity, it is important that society tolerate such independence and perhaps even seek to encourage it. Some degree of conformity is necessary for most societies. But if pressures to go along with the crowd are too strong, creativity may suffer.

3. *Encourage the use of analogies* Many creative breakthroughs seem to involve the use of analogies—recognition of similarities between a new problem and an old one or between a new potential solution and one that has worked before. Fortunately, most people can develop this skill if given the opportunity. Thus, making the use of analogies part of school curricula may help foster creativity.

4. *Encourage curiosity* Creative people, it turns out, often have a high level of curiosity. They are interested in many different topics, they read widely, and they actively seek new experiences. These characteristics help expand and enrich their knowledge base—one of the key ingredients in creativity.

Divergent Thinking: Thinking that moves outside conventional solutions or knowledge in an effort to develop novel solutions to a problem.

Convergent Thinking: Thinking that applies existing knowledge and rules of logic so as to zero in on a single correct solution to a problem.

COGNITION: THINKING, DECIDING, COMMUNICATING

5. *Enhance positive affect* The last technique for encouraging creativity is in some ways the most unexpected, but it is based on a growing body of empirical reserach (Isen, 1987). Several studies concerned with the influence of *affect*, or mood, on cognition indicate that when people are in a positive mood, they are often more creative than when they are in a neutral or negative mood. In one study, for example, Isen, Daubman, and Nowicki (1987) asked participants to perform the candle task described earlier. Some participants had been put in a positive mood by viewing a comedy film; others had viewed a film that was not expected to influence their current mood in any manner—it was about basic issues in statistics. The results: 67 percent of those in a good mood correctly solved the problem, but only about 20 percent of those in a neutral mood did. Other findings in this and related investigations suggest that people in a good mood think more expansively and tend to see relationships between diverse stimuli more readily than those in a neutral or negative mood. Given such effects, it is not at all surprising that a good mood can enhance creativity.

MEASURING CREATIVITY Finally, how can creativity be measured or assessed? Panels of judges often attempt to assess creativity in everything from designs for buildings to poetry, high fashion, and even doctoral dissertations; yet there is no single agreed-upon psychological test for measuring creativity. One approach, developed by Guilford (1967), is based on the distinction between convergent and divergent thinking described earlier. In the divergence production test, people are asked to list the number of uses they can generate for common objects—for example, bricks. The more uses a person can list, and the more unusual these are, the higher the score. Thus, responses like "build a wall" or "make a chimney" are scored as lower in creativity than ones like, "Grind them up to make emergency face powder," or, "Give them to people going to work on Mars to use as shoes." The very strangeness of the unusual answers reflects thinking that breaks out of the ordinary cognitive channels most of us follow most of the time.

Artificial Intelligence: Can Machines Really Think?

Newspapers, magazines, television, and movies have defined the future of technology for us. We know that at some point—probably in the not too distant future—we will be able to talk to computers and receive an intelligent and intelligible answer back. Those of us who have survived more than one generation of "Star Trek" know that computers will ultimately have mental capacities on par with those that humans possess. We are at present somewhat short of this goal: Witness the difficulty a well-known computer company is having in getting its notebook computer to perform the relatively simple task of deciphering its owner's handwriting. Nevertheless, progress is being made, and every year we move closer to the goal of producing an intelligent computer. This goal is pursued by those who work in **artificial intelligence**—an interdisciplinary branch of research in which psychologists and other scientists study the capacity of computers to perform in a way that, in humans, would be described as intelligent. (We will examine the nature of intelligence in more detail in Chapter 11.)

How much intelligence do computers actually show? Actually, quite a lot. Modern computers perform at blinding speeds, often at a rate of millions of computations per second—a capability far beyond that of mere mortals. It is

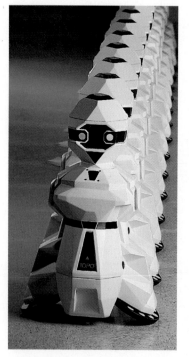

therefore not surprising that computers are more proficient than people at doing repetitive tasks requiring speed and accuracy. For example, with the help of various scanning devices, computers have been trained to perform important perceptual tasks, such as detecting flaws in many different products (Robotics Institute, 1984). Since computers are tireless and can make accurate judgments with amazing speed, they are better suited than humans for such tasks.

Computers can also be efficient problem solvers. For instance, they have been programmed to play chess very well—almost as well as the very best human players. As you might guess, they do this mainly by relying on great speed. Even ten years ago, chess-playing computers could scan 100,000 possible moves per second (Elmer-Dewitt, 1985); now, of course, they are considerably faster. This means that each time an opponent makes a move, the computer can rapidly consider all possible counters and their likely effects. And new programs allow computers to play chess the way expert humans do—on the basis of long-range strategies that take account of an opponent's style and apparent weaknesses.

However, as noted earlier, efforts to harness computers to human language have been somewhat mixed. This has caused artificial intelligence researchers to revise their initial predictions that development of speaking computers is "just around the corner." Nevertheless, some success has been achieved. For example, banks, credit unions, and credit card companies now use computerized voice recognition systems regularly to handle certain business transactions, such as customer calls to check account balances. More impressive are computers that can, to some extent, converse with their owners and carry out certain restricted sets of tasks such as reservation bookings. These complex machines possess large vocabularies, understand syntax well enough to allow them to follow very simple conversations, and know when to ask relevant questions if they do not understand or do not have enough information to act (Rensberger, 1993). In general, however, it has so far been frustratingly difficult to teach computers to grasp many of the subtleties of human speech. And many ordinary tasks that most people take for granted, such as shopping at the mall or understanding everyday conversations, exceed the capabilities of even the most powerful modern computers.

In response to all this, researchers have designed computers that imitate the way in which the brain—perhaps the most powerful computer in the universe—operates. Most computers process information in a sequential fashion; the brain processes the input from all of our senses simultaneously through a complex network of highly connected neurons. The new computer systems, called **neural networks**, consist of highly interconnected computational units that work together in parallel (Denning, 1992; Levine, 1991). The primary advantage of neural networks comes not from the individual units themselves but from the overall pattern that results when large numbers of these units are working together.

Such networks can readily learn to make discriminations. The high degree of interconnection among the units can be weakened or strengthened by special built-in algorithms that nudge the network toward a desired discriminative output (Rumelhart, Hinton, & Williams, 1986). Although research on neural networks is still in its infancy, this technology shows enormous promise, in its ability to produce intelligent behavior in machines and to provide insight into brain function.

Neural Networks: Computer systems modeled after the brain and made up of highly interconnected elementary computational units that work together in parallel.

KEY POINTS

- Creativity seems to involve several distinct aspects; careful preparation; incubation, or time away from the problem; flashes of illumination; and refinement of proposed solutions through testing.

- Creative breakthroughs seem to stem from divergent thinking—thinking that moves away from conventional knowledge or wisdom.

- Creativity can be encouraged by development of a rich knowledge base, independence, curiosity, and the use of analogies. It can also be increased by positive affect.

- Artificial intelligence is an interdisciplinary field concerned with the capacity of computers to demonstrate intelligent performance.

- Neural networks are structures consisting of large numbers of highly interconnected computational units working together in parallel, in imitation of the human brain.

For example, G. Hinton of the University of Toronto, who is one of the leading experts on network theory, has applied network analysis to a wide variety of problems in human perception, such as figure-ground differentiation, shape perception, and stereopsis (e.g., Kienker, Sejinowski, Hinton, & Schumacher, 1986; Hinton & Parsons, 1988). More recently, he has extended the reach of his neural modeling exercises to include clinical problems such as deep dyslexia (Hinton & Shallice, 1991).

Where does all this leave us with respect to artificial intelligence? Most psychologists who specialize in this field would readily admit that early predictions about the capacities of computers to show such characteristics as intention, understanding, and consciousness were greatly overstated (Levine, 1991; Searle, 1980). However, they note that computers are indeed exceptionally useful in the study of human cognition and can, in certain contexts, demonstrate performance that closely resembles that of intelligent human beings. You may not soon meet a robot who can speak with you in a fluent manner like the ones in films, but the chances are good that computers and other machines will continue to become more "intelligent" with the passage of time.

Language: The Communication of Information

At present, most scientists agree that what truly sets us apart from other species of animals is our use of **language**—our ability to use an extremely rich set of symbols, as well as rules for combining them, to communicate information. While the members of all species do communicate with one another in some manner, and while some may use certain features of language, the human ability to do so far exceeds that of any other organism on earth. In this final section we'll examine the nature of language and its relationship to other aspects of cognition.

Language: Its Basic Nature

Language uses symbols for communicating information. In order for a set of symbols to be viewed as a language, however, several additional criteria must be met.

First, information must actually be transmitted by the symbols: The words and sentences must carry *meaning.* Second, although the number of separate sounds or words in a language may be limited, it must be possible to combine these elements into an essentially infinite number of sentences. Finally, the meanings of these combinations must be independent of the settings in which they are used. In other words, sentences must be able to convey information about other places and other times. Only if all three of these criteria are met can the term *language* be applied to a system of communication. In actual use, language involves two major components: the *production* of speech, and its *comprehension.*

THE PRODUCTION OF SPEECH All spoken language consists of **phonemes**, a set of basic sounds; **morphemes**, the smallest units of speech that convey meaning; and **syntax**, rules about how these units can be combined into sentences.

Language: A system of symbols, plus rules for combining them, used to communicate information.

Phonemes: A set of sounds basic to a given language.

Morphemes: The smallest units of speech that convey meaning.

Syntax: Rules about how units of speech can be combined into sentences in a given language.

English has forty-six separate phonemes: the vowels, *a, e, i, o,* and *u;* consonants, such as *p, m, k,* and *d;* and blends of the two. Other languages have more or fewer basic sounds. Further, different languages often employ different groups of phonemes; sounds used in one may be absent in another.

English has about 100,000 morphemes. Some of these are words; others, such as the plural *s* or prefixes such as *un* or *sub,* are not. The number of English words is greater still—about 500,000. And the number of combinations of these words, or sentences, is for all practical purposes infinite.

SPEECH COMPREHENSION Have you ever listened to a conversation between two people speaking a foreign language you don't know? If so, you may recall that it seemed very confusing. In part, this confusion results from the fact that when you listen to a language you don't speak, you can't recognize the boundaries between words.

Even in our own language, not all speech is equally easy to interpret. For example, sentences containing *negatives* (not, no) are more difficult to understand than sentences without them (Clark & Chase, 1972). Also, ambiguous sentences—those with two or more possible meanings—are harder to understand than unambiguous sentences (Mistler-Lachman, 1975). Compare "Last night I saw a wolf in my pajamas" with "Last night I saw a wolf while wearing my pajamas." Clearly, the first is harder to understand than the second. Incidentally, such ambiguity is far from rare; newspaper headlines often show this characteristic. Does HOMELESS APPEAL TO MAYOR mean that homeless people are making an appeal to the mayor for help, or that the mayor finds homeless people personally attractive? The first possibility is much more likely, but from the structure of the sentence, it's really not possible to be completely certain.

SURFACE STRUCTURE AND DEEP STRUCTURE Suppose you run into one of your cousins on the street and he introduces you to his companion with the following statement: "Meet Stuart; he's my oldest friend." Does that mean that he is the oldest person your cousin has as a friend, or that your cousin has been friends with him longer than with anyone else? In all probability, you can tell from the context. If Stuart is about your cousin's age, you would conclude that your cousin has been friends with Stuart longer than anyone else. If, however, Stuart is much older than your cousin, you would conclude that the first meaning applies: He's the oldest person your cousin calls "friend."

This simple example illustrates one aspect of the difference between what linguists such as Noam Chomsky (1968) describe as the **surface structure** and **deep structure** of language. Surface structure refers to the actual words people use and what's readily apparent about them, whereas deep structure refers to the information that underlies a sentence and gives it meaning. Another way of seeing this distinction is by considering sentences that are grammatically correct but totally devoid of meaning. For example, consider the sentence, "Dark purple ideas eat angrily." It is perfectly correct in terms of grammar but has no meaning whatsoever. In view of such facts, Chomsky and others have argued that we can never understand the true nature of spoken language by focusing only on words and grammatical rules. Rather, we must search for underlying meaning and for the ways in which people translate, or transform, this into overt speech. While some psychologists question the validity of the distinction between surface and deep structure, most agree that it is useful to look beyond verbal behavior and rules of grammar and to examine the cognitive representations on which speech is based. In this sense, the distinction Chomsky proposed has been extremely useful.

Surface Structure: The actual words of which sentences consist.

Deep Structure: Information that underlies the form of a sentence and is crucial to its meaning.

The Development of Language

Throughout the first weeks of life, infants have only one major means of verbal communication: crying. Within a few short years, however, children progress rapidly to speaking whole sentences and acquire a vocabulary of hundreds or even thousands of words. Some of the milestones along this remarkable journey are summarized in Table 7.3. Although we'll consider other developmental issues in more detail in Chapter 8, this section will focus on two questions relating to the development of language: What mechanisms play a role in this process? And how, and at what ages, do children acquire various aspects of language skills?

THEORIES OF LANGUAGE DEVELOPMENT: SOME CONTRASTING VIEWS The *social learning view* suggests one mechanism for the rapid acquisition of language. This view proposes that speech is acquired through a combination of operant conditioning and imitation. Presumably, children are praised or otherwise rewarded by their parents for making sounds approximating those of their native language. Moreover, parents often model sounds, words, or sentences for them. This view contends that together, these basic forms of learning contribute to the rapid acquisition of language.

A sharply different view has been proposed by linguist Noam Chomsky (1968): the *innate mechanism view*. According to Chomsky, language acquisition is at least partly innate. Human beings, he contends, have a language acquisition device—a built-in neural system that provides them with an intuitive grasp of grammar. In other words, humans are prepared to acquire language and do so rapidly for this reason.

Finally, a *cognitive theory* offered by Slobin (1979) recognizes the importance of both innate mechanisms and learning. This theory suggests that children possess certain information-processing abilities or strategies that they use in acquiring language. These are termed *operating principles* and seem to be present, or to develop, very early in life. One such operating principle seems to be, "Pay attention to the ends of words"—children pay more attention to the ends than to the beginnings or middles of words. This makes sense, since in

A FIRST STEP TOWARD LANGUAGE DEVELOPMENT

Most children say their first spoken words by their first birthday. After this milestone their vocabulary grows rapidly.

TABLE 7.3		

Language Development: Some Milestones

Children develop language skills at an amazing pace. Please note: These approximate ages are only *averages*; individual children will often depart from them to a considerable degree.

AVERAGE AGE	LANGUAGE BEHAVIOR DEMONSTRATED BY CHILD
12 weeks	Smiles when talked to; makes cooing sounds
16 weeks	Turns head in response to human voice
20 weeks	Makes vowel and consonant sounds while cooing
6 months	Progresses from cooing to babbling that contains all sounds of human speech.
8 months	Repeats certain syllables (e.g., "ma-ma")
12 months	Understands some words; may say a few
18 months	Can produce up to fifty words
24 months	Has vocabulary of more than fifty words; uses some two-word phrases
30 months	Has vocabulary of several hundred words; uses phrases of three to five words
36 months	Has vocabulary of about a thousand words
48 months	Has mastered most basic elements of language

many languages suffixes carry important meanings. Another principle is, "Pay attention to the order of words." And indeed, word order in children's speech tends to reflect that of their parents. Since word order differs greatly from one language to another, this, too, is an important principle.

Which of these theories is correct? At present, all three theories seem to be at least partly correct. There is no question that innate factors are particularly important—language is learned much too readily, and too rapidly, to be explained in terms of operant conditioning or social reinforcement. In addition, there is evidence to suggest that there may be a *critical period* for language development during which children find it easiest to acquire various language components (Elliott, 1981). If for some reason children are not exposed to normal speech at this time, they find it increasingly difficult to master language (De Villiers & De Villiers, 1978). There is also evidence that, contrary to what the social-learning view suggests, parents do not directly praise or reward their children for correct syntax or grammar often enough to shape such skills through conditioning (Hirsch-Pasek, Treiman, & Schneiderman, 1984). Finally, there are certain linguistic deficits that seem very likely attributable to a genetic factor. One such example is provided in **Canadian Focus**.

CANADIAN FOCUS

Do Some Kinds of Language Impairment Result from a Genetic Abnormality?

Most of us skip past the various linguistic milestones detailed in Table 7.3 with effortless ease. Not so everyone. There are those who encounter many difficulties in moving down the road to linguistic maturity. One group of children who do not follow normal development are those with what is termed *specific language impairment*. These children, who appear otherwise perfectly normal, tend to be late in developing language; and when it does appear, they have difficulty in sounding words and persist in making certain kinds of grammatical errors. This disorder is extremely uncommon. In a 1990 study, M. Gopnik and M.B. Crago of McGill University presented evidence suggesting that some cases of this disorder may be linked to a genetic abnormality.

Gopnik and Crago examined a family in which 53 percent of the members were afflicted. The family was large, and extended over three generations. The oldest family member—the grandmother—had the disorder. Four of her five adult sons and daughters also had the disorder, as did some of the children of each of the four afflicted adults. The single son without the disorder had no children with the disorder. The distribution of the disorder within the family, and the fact that it afflicted males and females equally, lends credence to the view that genetic rather than social or environmental factors were involved. Besides, if social or environ-

mental factors were responsible, it would have to be explained how so many of those raised in similar environmental conditions could escape the problem.

When they tested the family members, Gopnik and Crago found no evidence of any general intellectual impairment. The impairment evidence was exclusively linguistic, and also quite selective in its effects. Difficulties were apparent in the use of suffixes required for pluralization and in the production of the past tense. Errors in pronoun use and the progressive verb form were also seen. For example, if they said to a younger family member with the disorder, "Every day he walks his dog," and asked him or her to complete the sentence, "Yesterday he ____ his dog," the subject had great difficulty adding the "-ed" to "walk-" to produce the appropriate past tense. In the case of plurals, the researchers frequently heard statements such as, "The boys won all five game." Errors reflecting misuse of the progressive, such as, "Mary is rest in the bedroom," were also common.

Especially interesting was that adults in the family with the disorder showed little evidence of many of these difficulties in casual conversation. Pluralization errors were noticeably absent with common words. Did this mean they had overcome their difficulty? It did not. If they were asked to produce the plural form of unfamiliar words, they were unable to do so. This was shown by their inability to pass the Wug test. In the Wug test, a drawing of an imaginary bird is presented to the person being tested, who is informed that the drawing is of a Wug. A drawing of two of these creatures is then presented to the subject, who is told, "Now there are two," and asked to finish the sentence, "Now there are two___." A four- or five-year-old child can pass this test. Adult members of the family with the language disorder were unable to do so.

How is it that adult members of this family can cope with familiar words? Gopnik (1990) suggests that they are quite aware of their difficulty, and their inability to use the pluralization rules the way the rest of us do. They mask their disability by learning, *as separate vocabulary items*, the singular and plural word forms of common words. Although laborious, it works—as long as they only encounter common words.

The fact that this peculiar linguistic disorder occurs within families does not prove it is genetically based. There is, however, other supporting evidence. Twin studies show that if one identical twin has the disorder, the probability is high that the other twin does also. A search for more conclusive evidence, in the form of a genetic marker, is being actively pursued.

Although there is strong support for the role of innate processes in language acquisition, this does not mean that conditioning, learning, and social reinforcement do not play an important role. Infants have to be exposed to an appropriate linguistic milieu. Also, interaction between children and caregivers is crucial in narrowing, or tuning, the phonetic distinctions made by young children, thus ensuring that their language development proceeds smoothly and uneventfully. Genetically determined innate processes are important, but they are in no sense wholly responsible for language acquisition.

Babbling: An early stage of speech development in which infants emit virtually all known sounds of human speech.

Universal Phonetic Sensitivity: The ability to discriminate the contrasts between speech sounds in any human language.

Phonological Development: Development of the ability to produce recognizable speech.

PHONOLOGICAL DEVELOPMENT: THE SPOKEN WORD At some point between three and six months, babies begin **babbling**. They begin doing this at about the same age in all parts of the world, and the babble sounds are much the same. It is a rich auditory blend, full of intonation variations and complex sound patterns. After about ten months, the worldwide similarity in the sounds of babbling begins to diminish. What is happening is that the babies are beginning to articulate linguistic variations that are peculiar to the language group of their caregivers. Because all languages of the world do not use the same set of phonemes, or speech sounds, the babbling of infants in different language groups becomes increasingly different.

The process whereby infants acquire the set of speech sounds they need to function within their linguistic community has been clarified in a series of studies by Werker at the University of British Columbia (e.g., Werker, 1989). Werker's studies suggest that at first, infants have **universal phonetic sensitivity**—that is, they seem to be able to discriminate the contrasts between speech sounds that are necessary for learning any human language. Although equipped with the ability to register speech sounds in any language, infants will capture and retain only speech sounds that are associated with the natural language (or languages) they are exposed to through caregivers. This period of plasticity is quite short. Studies in **phonological development** typically show a loss in universal phonetic sensitivity by the end of the first year. One such study, carried out by Werker, showed that children of exclusively English-speaking parents could easily discriminate phonetic contrasts required in both Hindi and English when first tested at six to eight months. Four months later they had retained this adeptness in contrast discrimination in English, but had lost it for Hindi. Although universal phonetic sensitivity is lost rapidly, once a phonetic contrast has been established, it may well be locked in forever. Werker reports that two English-speaking adults who were exposed to Hindi for only their first two years, and who acquired no more than a few words of the language, were later in life as capable as native Hindi speakers in discriminating phonetic contrasts in that language.

The period of universal phonetic sensitivity is an important adaptive device. It provides the newborn child with a way of adjusting rapidly to its linguistic community (of which there are a huge variety). The rather rapid decline in sensitivity to speech sounds of foreign languages does not mean that we cannot learn them; it *does* mean, as most of us can testify, that the learning process is much more difficult.

Once the phonetic contrasts required for a native language are in place, vocabulary growth is rapid. However, children do not always speak the words they learn with an adultlike clarity, even when they have heard them accurately. Many children apply **phonological strategies**—techniques for simplifying the pronunciation of many words. For example, they may delete unstressed syllables so that *banana* becomes *nana* or a name like *Melissa* becomes *Missy*. Pronunciation improves rapidly during the preschool years, but some refinements continue throughout childhood; for example, children learn to change the stressed syllable when words add endings (*prac*tical to practi*cal*ity, *hu*mid to hu*mid*ity)?

Research in Canada

Janet Werker
University of British Columbia

SEMANTIC DEVELOPMENT: THE ACQUISITION OF MEANING   By age six, most children have a vocabulary of more than 14,000 words. This means they add an average of about nine new words to their vocabulary each day—in part by asking their parents to name everything in sight (Clark, 1973). Some researchers suggest that children accomplish this feat through a process called **fast mapping**: they "map" a new word to an underlying concept after a single exposure. This is fast indeed; consider how many times you, as an adult, must encounter a word in a foreign language before you can enter it into your vocabulary.

Semantic development follows a predictable course. The first words acquired by children are *object words*, which apply to specific objects in the world. These are followed by *action words*, which describe specific activities. The way children use specific words does not always conform to adults' usage, however. Initially, they may use a noun such as *door* and a verb such as *open* to refer to the same action—opening the door. It is not until they are between two and two-and-a-half that most children begin to use *state words*—ones describing transient conditions such as *dirty, clean, hot,* or *cold*.

As children increase their vocabulary, they often demonstrate several interesting forms of error. First, they show *mismatches*, instances in which a new word is attached to an inappropriate concept. For example, they may relate the word *old* to something they want and *new* to something they dislike, as in "I want *old* candy, not *new* candy." In addition, they often show *underextensions*, in which a term is applied to a smaller range of objects or events than its true meaning calls for, or *overextensions*, in which a term is applied to a wider range than appropriate. An underextension might be the use of the word *apple* to refer only to red apples; an overextension might involve applying the word *car* to any and all vehicles. Finally, children often coin new words; they may refer to a hammer as a "hitter," for instance.

GRAMMATICAL DEVELOPMENT   Every language has **grammar**, a set of rules dictating how words can be combined into sentences. Children must learn to follow these rules, as well as to utter sounds that others can recognize as words. At first, grammar poses little problem, since early speech is *holophrastic*—that is, young children use single words to express complex meanings. Thus, "Eat!" may mean "I want to eat" or "Mommy is eating." By the time most children are two, they progress to telegraphic speech, omitting less important words. An example: "Daddy cookie" may mean "Give Daddy a cookie" or "Daddy, bring me some cookies."

Between two and three, most children begin to use simple sentences consisting of three words. *Mean utterance length*—the average length of the sentences

Phonological Strategies:
Simplifications used by young children to facilitate the task of producing recognizable speech.

Fast Mapping: A process through which children attach a new word to an underlying concept on the basis of a single encounter with it.

Semantic Development:
Development of understanding of the meaning of spoken or written language.

Grammar: Rules within a given language indicating how words can be combined into meaningful sentences.

COGNITION: THINKING, DECIDING, COMMUNICATING

KEY POINTS

- Language involves the ability to use a rich set of symbols, and the rules for combining these, to communicate information. It includes the abilities to produce and to comprehend speech.

- Language seems to involve more than mere spoken words and rules of grammar, or surface structure. The underlying meaning, or deep structure, is also important.

- Innate processes play an important role in language acquisition, but they cannot totally explain the development of language. Learning, social reinforcement, and various cognitive operations are also vital.

- Language acquisition involves phonological development, semantic development, and acquisition of grammar. During the initial phase of phonological development, the infant seems able to respond to the crucial speech sounds of any human language.

children use (Brown, 1973)—increases to about three or four words between the ages of three and six. More complex grammatical forms also appear at this time, involving the use of conjunctions such as *and*, and connected clauses—"Dad picked me up at school and we went for hamburgers." The use of increasingly complex forms in everyday speech continues throughout childhood and is not complete until early adolescence.

In sum, language development is a continuing feature of cognitive development throughout childhood. Given the complexity of language, and its central role in many aspects of cognition, this is far from surprising.

Language and Thought: Do We Think What We Say or Say What We Think?

Although we often have vivid mental images, most of our thinking seems to involve words. This fact raises an intriguing question: What is the precise relationship between language and thought? One possibility, known as the **linguistic relativity hypothesis**, suggests that language actually shapes or determines thought (Whorf, 1956). According to this view, people who speak different languages may actually perceive the world in different ways because their thinking is determined, at least in part, by the words available to them.

The opposing view is that thought shapes language—that language merely reflects the way we think and how our minds work. Which position is more accurate? Existing evidence seems to argue against the linguistic relativity approach (Miura & Okamoto, 1989). If this approach is correct, people who speak a language that has few words to describe colors should have greater difficulty in perceiving various colors than people who speak a language rich in color words. But research designed to test such possibilities has generally failed to support them. In one experiment, Rosch (1973) studied natives of New Guinea. Their language, Dani, has only two color names: *mola*, for bright, warm colors, and *mili*, for dark, cool ones. Rosch found that despite this fact, Dani speakers perceived colors in much the same manner as English speakers, whose language contains many color words.

So, while it may indeed be easier to express a particular idea or concept in one language than another, this in no way implies that our thoughts or perceptions are strongly shaped by language. On the contrary, basic aspects of human perception and thought seem to be very much the same around the world, regardless of spoken language.

Language in Other Species

Members of nonhuman species communicate with one another in many ways. Bees do a complex dance to indicate the distance to and direction of a food source; birds sing songs when seeking to attract a male; seagoing mammals in the wild, such as whales, communicate with one another through complex patterns of sounds. But what about language? Are we the only species capable of using this sophisticated means of communication? Until the 1970s there seemed little question about this. Early efforts to teach chimpanzees to speak failed miserably. For example, during the 1940s Keith and Cathy Hayes raised a chimp named Vicki from infancy in their home and

Linguistic Relativity Hypothesis: *The view that language shapes thought.*

provided her with intensive speech training; but she was able to utter only a few simple words such as "mama," "papa," and "cup."

These disappointing results were due in part to the fact that nonhuman primates (and other animals) lack the vocal control necessary for spoken language. But as we saw earlier, in our discussion of animal cognition, it is not always appropriate to ask animals to do what people do. The ability to speak is not essential for the use of language. For example, people who have lost the power of speech through accident or illness can still communicate by writing or sign language. The fact that chimps cannot learn to speak, then, does not rule out the possibility that they or other animals can learn to use some form of language.

Beatrice and Allen Gardner succeeded in teaching Washoe, a female chimp, to use and understand almost 200 words in American Sign Language (ASL), which is used by many deaf people (Gardner & Gardner, 1975). After several years of practice, Washoe learned to respond to simple questions, and to request actions such as tickling and objects such as food. She even learned to describe her mood with signs for such words as "hurt," "sorry," and "funny."

Research with gorillas has also yielded what some consider evidence for the ability to use language. Francine Patterson reported that Koko showed great flexibility in using signs, constructing original sentences, remembering and describing past events, and even creating her own signs for new objects and events. Thus, she termed zebras "white tigers." Interestingly, Koko learned to use language in complex and all-too-human ways, such as to bend the truth to her own advantage. In one incident, she jumped on a sink and pulled it out from the wall. When asked if she had caused this damage, she accused one of the researchers of being responsible.

In what may be the most surprising evidence of all, Irene Pepperberg has trained an African gray parrot named Alex to use speech in what appears to be a highly complex way (Stipp, 1990). Alex can name more than eighty objects and events, frequently requests things he wants ("I want shower"), and has been known to give directions to his human trainers. But does Alex really understand the words he uses? Professor Pepperberg believes that he does. On one occasion Alex was given an apple for the first time. He immediately labeled it "banerry," and he stuck with this word despite her best efforts to teach him "apple." Her explanation: Apples taste somewhat like bananas and look something like cherries, so Alex had chosen a word that from his perspective was quite appropriate.

ALEX: THE AFRICAN GRAY PARROT

Irene Pepperberg has trained an African gray parrot to use speech in apparently complex ways. But does Alex really understand the words he uses?

ARE WE THE ONLY SPECIES CAPABLE OF USING LANGUAGE? SOME RECENT FINDINGS Based on the evidence presented thus far, you may now be ready to conclude that members of these species can indeed use language. Note, however, that many psychologists have carefully examined the data reported in the studies described and take the position that the animals in these studies, while exhibiting impressive learning, are not really demonstrating the use of language (e.g., Terrace, 1985; Davidson & Hopson, 1988; Wallman, 1992). For instance, close examination of the procedures used to train and test the animals suggests that their trainers may often unintentionally provide subtle cues that help the animals respond correctly to questions. It also appears that in some cases, trainers may have wildly overinterpreted the animals' responses, reading complex meanings and intentions into relatively simple signs. Finally, it is still very unclear whether animals are capable of mastering several basic features of human language—for example, *syntax* (the rules by which words are arranged to form meaningful sentences) and *generativity* (the ability to combine a relatively limited number of words into unique combinations that convey a broad range of meaning).

COGNITION: THINKING, DECIDING, COMMUNICATING

Recent studies involving other species of animals, including bonobos (a rare type of chimpanzee) and dolphins, have begun to address these and related issues. For example, consider the language abilities demonstrated by a twelve-year-old bonobo named Kanzi (Linden, 1993). Psychologist Sue Savage-Rumbaugh first began studying bonobos in the 1980s. While attempting to teach Kanzi's mother to use an artificial language made up of abstract visual symbols, she noticed that Kanzi (then an infant) had learned several symbol-words just by watching. Intrigued by the possibilities raised by this, Savage-Rumbaugh and her colleagues continued to train Kanzi in this informal way—speaking to him throughout the day, while simultaneously pointing to the corresponding word symbols on portable language boards they carried with them. Kanzi quickly learned to combine the symbol-words to request tasty snacks and preferred activities, such as watching Tarzan movies.

Since then, Kanzi has demonstrated a grasp of grammatical concepts, and he now comprehends several hundred spoken words. In one experiment, Savage-Rumbaugh and her colleagues compared Kanzi and a two-year-old girl in terms of their ability to respond to commands expressed in spoken sentences (Savage-Rumbaugh et al., 1992). The sentences consisted of familiar words that were combined to produce commands that Kanzi and the little girl had never heard before. Surprisingly, Kanzi's progress in comprehending the novel commands paralleled the little girl's throughout most of the experiment, although her language abilities eventually surpassed Kanzi's (his ability topped out at the level of an average two-year-old child). More important, though, the use of strict control procedures ruled out the possibility that Kanzi was responding to subtle cues from his trainers—a criticism leveled against many early demonstrations of animal language. For instance, a one-way mirror prevented Kanzi from seeing who gave him the commands, and the people recording his responses wore headphones to prevent them from hearing the requests. Psychologists are now more willing to accept that Kanzi was responding solely to the requests.

But what about more complex features of language? Are animals capable of grasping these concepts, too? Psychologist Louis Herman believes they are. Herman and his colleagues taught a female dolphin named Akeakamai—or Ake for short—an artificial language in which sweeping hand gestures are the

LANGUAGE IN OTHER SPECIES: KANZI

Researcher Sue Savage-Rumbaugh has taught Kanzi, a chimp, to communicate using symbols on a special keyboard. Kanzi is unusual because he can also respond to spoken commands like, "Please bring me the flashlight."

words (Herman, Richards, Wolz, et al., 1984). Each gesture symbolizes either an *object* such as "Frisbee," an *action* such as "fetch," or a *description of position* such as "over" or "left." Ake has learned more than fifty of these gesture-words. Next, to test whether Ake was capable of comprehending complex features of language, the researchers established a set of rules governing word order and the grammatical function of each type of gesture. Herman and his colleagues have discovered that Ake comprehends word order and syntax in word sequences up to five gestures. For example, RIGHT BASKET LEFT FRISBEE instructs Ake to take the Frisbee on her left to the basket on her right. More impressively, though, when familiar gestures are rearranged to form novel commands—ones Ake has never seen before—she continues to respond correctly.

"Sorry, ma'am, but your neighbors have reported not seeing your husband in weeks. We just have a few questions, and then you can get back to your canning."

TALKING TO THE ANIMALS

Although nonhuman species have not yet demonstrated the ability to carry on conversations like this one, growing evidence suggests that some species of animals, including dolphins, comprehend several basic aspects of language. (Source: Universal Press Syndicate, Inc., 1993.)

Herman has continued to probe Ake's language comprehension through the use of *anomalous sentences*—sentences that are grammatically incorrect, use nonsense words, or make impossible requests, such as asking her to fetch an immovable object. These procedures are often used to test children's comprehension of language. In one instance, Herman and his colleagues issued a series of commands to Ake that consisted of either grammatically correct sequences or anomalous sequences (Herman, Kuczaj, & Holders, 1993). Interestingly, Ake was highly accurate in responding to requests that were grammatically correct and rarely refused to carry them out. In contrast, she refused nearly all of the anomalous requests, making no attempt to respond to them. It appeared as if Ake recognized that the requests were "silly," a response often observed in children who are presented with anomalous sentences. Although dolphins may be a long way from achieving the level of language proficiency illustrated in the above cartoon, it is clear that they are capable of comprehending features of language that go beyond the forms of behavior observed in the earlier studies of animal language.

Research with highly intelligent animals such as primates and dolphins is proceeding. To some, the findings suggest that language may not be a uniquely human possession, but rather a continuum of skills that different species exhibit to varying degrees. To others, the findings are much too anecdotal to be convincing (Gisiner & Schusterman, 1992; Wallman, 1992). The field of study is a fascinating one, however, and it can be argued the jury is still out. Further studies will undoubtedly shed additional light. In the meantime, the question of whether we'll ever "talk with the animals" remains open.

KEY POINTS

- According to the linguistic relativity hypothesis, language actually shapes or determines thought. Existing evidence does not offer strong support for this hypothesis.

- Growing evidence suggests that some species of animals, including bonobo chimpanzees and dolphins, may be capable of acquiring some very basic language-like skills.

Making Better Decisions

Have you ever made a bad decision—one that you later wished you could change? Unless you have led a charmed life, you probably have. And since decisions often have important consequences, such errors in judgment may prove quite costly. Given the vast complexity of the world and the diversity of options we often face, it is unlikely that anyone can provide you with a perfect system for making correct decisions. Nevertheless, here are some guidelines for increasing the chances that many of your decisions will be good ones—or at least as free from sources of error and bias as possible.

1. *Don't trust your own memory*, or *Beware of availability* When we make decisions, we can do so only on the basis of the information available to us. Be careful! The information that comes most readily to mind is not always the most useful or revealing (Kahneman & Tversky, 1982). When you face an important decision, therefore, jog your memory in several ways and, if time permits, consult written documents or sources before proceeding. As noted in Chapter 6, memory often plays tricks on us, and relying on a quick scan of it when making an important decision can be risky.

2. *Don't take situations at face value*, or *Question all anchors* In many decision-making situations the stage is set long before we come on the scene. The asking price for a house or car is set by the seller, the number of meetings for a committee has been determined by its chair, and so on. While you can't always change such givens, you should at least recognize them for what they are and question whether they make sense. If you don't raise such questions, you will probably accept these "anchors" implicitly and then offer only minor adjustments to them (Northcraft & Neale, 1987). This can be a mistake! It may lead you to decisions that work against your own best interests. So whenever and to whatever extent you can, question all proposed anchors.

3. *Remain flexible*, or *Don't fall in love with your own decisions* Making decisions is effortful, so once they are made we tend to heave a sigh of relief, and to stick with them through thick and thin. Then, before we know it, we may have too much invested to quit. In other words, we may become trapped in a situation where we ought to change our initial decision and cut our losses but where, instead, we continue down the path to ruin—or at least to negative outcomes (Brockner & Rubin, 1985). Don't let this happen! It's always difficult to admit a mistake, but doing so is often far better than sticking to a losing course of action.

4. *Consider all options*, or *Is half an orange always better than none?* When you make a decision, you must choose among the available options. But what, precisely, are they? Sometimes they are not all out on the table when you begin. Thus, a useful strategy is to start by gathering as much information as you can and then to use it to generate as many potential options as possible. Doing so can often suggest choices or courses of action that you did not consider at first. For example, suppose two cooks are both preparing dishes that require an orange, yet there is only one orange available. What do they do? The obvious answer: Cut it in half. But what if one needs only the juice and the other only the peel? Now a very different option exists: Give the juice to one cook and the peel to the other. This kind of integrative option is often not apparent at first glance, so only careful consideration will suggest it (Pruitt & Rubin, 1986). A good rule to follow, then, is this: Never assume that the options with which you start are the only ones available or the best that can be devised.

We make decisions every day, some relatively trivial (such as which brand to buy in the supermarket), some relatively important (such as which job offer to accept). How can you improve *your* decision-making skills?

CHAPTER 7

Summary and Review of Key Points

Thinking: Forming Concepts and Reasoning to Conclusions

cognition 270
concepts 271
artificial concepts 271
natural concepts 271
prototypes 272
visual images 273
propositions 273
reasoning 275
syllogistic reasoning 275
oversight bias 277
confirmation bias 278
hindsight effect 279

- Concepts are mental categories for objects, events, or experiences that are similar to one another in one or more respects.
- Artificial concepts can be clearly defined by a set of rules or properties. Natural concepts cannot; they are usually defined in terms of prototypes—the most typical category members.
- Propositions—sentences that can stand as separate assertions—are useful for relating one concept to another, or one feature of a concept to the entire concept. Images—mental pictures of the world—are a basic element of thinking.
- Reasoning involves transforming available information in order to reach specific conclusions. Formal reasoning derives conclusions from specific premises. In contrast, everyday reasoning is more complex and less clear-cut.
- Cultural factors and beliefs often take precedence over formal Western rules of logic.
- Reasoning is subject to several forms of error and bias. It can be distorted by emotion and belief; by a selective focus on certain sources of information, or oversight bias; by the tendency to focus primarily on evidence that confirms our beliefs, or confirmation bias; and by the tendency to assume that we could have predicted actual events more successfully than is really the case, or the hindsight effect.
- The ecological approach focuses on how animals solve cognitive problems that are important to their survival.

Making Decisions: Choosing Among Alternatives

decision making 282
expected utility 282
heuristics 282
availability heuristic 283
representativeness heuristic 284
anchoring-and-adjustment
  heuristic 284
framing 286
escalation of commitment 287

- We do not make all decisions on the basis of expected utility—the product of the probability and the subjective value of each possible outcome. Instead, we often use heuristics, or mental rules of thumb.
- The availability heuristic is our tendency to make judgments about the frequency or likelihood of various events in terms of how readily they can be brought to mind.
- The representativeness heuristic is the tendency to assume that the more closely an item resembles the most typical examples of some concept, the more likely it is to belong to that concept.
- The anchoring-and-adjustment heuristic is the tendency to reach decisions by making adjustments to reference points or existing information.
- Decisions can also be strongly affected by framing—the presentation of information about possible outcomes in terms of gains or losses. People are generally less certain and more inconsistent in their preferences when options are framed as losses.
- People often become trapped in bad decisions through escalation of commitment, an effect that derives from reluctance to admit past mistakes and a desire to justify past losses.

PROBLEM SOLVING AND CREATIVITY: FINDING PATHS TO DESIRED GOALS	• Problem solving involves efforts to develop or choose among various responses in order to attain desired goals. Problems can be solved through trial and error or through the use of algorithms—rules that will, if followed, yield solutions in given situations. • Heuristics are rules of thumb suggested by our experience that we often use to solve problems. • Both functional fixedness—the tendency to think of using objects only as they have been used before—and mental sets—tendencies to stick with familiar methods—can interfere with effective problem solving. • Creativity involves cognitive activity that results in new or novel ways of solving problems. Creativity seems to entail careful preparation, or hard work on the problem; incubation, or time away from the problem; flashes of illumination; and refinement of proposed solutions through testing. • Creative breakthroughs seem to stem from divergent thinking—thinking that moves away from conventional knowledge or wisdom. • Creativity can be encouraged by development of a rich knowledge base, independence, curiosity, and the use of analogies. It can also be increased by positive affect. • Artificial intelligence is an interdisciplinary field concerned with the capacity of computers to demonstrate intelligent performance. • The primary advantage of neural networks—highly interconnected elementary computational units—stems from the overall pattern created by large numbers of individual units working together in parallel.
problem solving 289 trial and error 292 algorithm 292 means-ends analysis 292 analogy 292 functional fixedness 293 mental set 293 creativity 294 divergent thinking 295 convergent thinking 295 artificial intelligence 296 neural networks 297	
LANGUAGE: THE COMMUNICATION OF INFORMATION	• Language involves the ability to use a rich set of symbols, plus rules for combining these, to communicate information. It includes the abilities to produce and to comprehend speech. • Language seems to involve more than mere spoken words and rules of grammar, or surface structure. The underlying meaning, or deep structure, is important also. • Language acquisition is heavily influenced by innate processes, but learning, social reinforcement, and various cognitive operations also play an important role. • Language acquisition involves phonological development—learning to produce speech; semantic development—learning to understand the meaning of words and sentences; and acquisition of grammar—the rules through which words can be combined into sentences in a given language. • According to the linguistic relativity hypothesis, language actually shapes or determines thought. Existing evidence does not offer strong support for this hypothesis. • Growing evidence suggests that some species of animals, including bonobo chimpanzees and dolphins, are capable of grasping some basic aspects of language such as word order and grammar.
language 298 phonemes 298 morphemes 298 syntax 298 surface structure 299 deep structure 299 babbling 302 universal phonetic sensitivity 302 phonological development 302 phonological strategies 303 fast mapping 303 semantic development 303 grammar 303 linguistic relativity hypothesis 304	

CRITICAL THINKING QUESTIONS

APPRAISAL	Throughout this chapter, we've seen that human thought processes are suboptimal in several important respects. For example, our reliance on heuristics often provides efficient but flawed decision making. And we often fall prey to biases that lead us astray in our ability to think and reason correctly. What can psychologists do to help people reduce or eliminate the effects of these errors from their thinking?
CONTROVERSY	Growing evidence suggests that animals are much "smarter" than psychologists initially believed. Indeed, the results of numerous studies demonstrate that animals are capable of grasping several important grammatical concepts that many believed were beyond their capabilities. Do you think it is possible that in the coming years scientists will discover a way to "talk with the animals"? If so, why? If not, why?
MAKING PSYCHOLOGY PART OF YOUR LIFE	Now that you understand the basic nature of cognitive processes and the many factors that affect them, can you think of ways in which you can use this knowledge to improve your problem-solving abilities? Name several specific steps you could take to become more proficient in this respect. How about creativity? Can you use the information in this chapter to enhance your own creativity?

*H*uman
Development I

The Childhood Years

PHYSICAL GROWTH AND DEVELOPMENT 315
The Prenatal Period
Prenatal Influences on Development:
  When Trouble Starts Early
Physical and Perceptual Development
During our Early Years: Infancy and
  Childhood

COGNITIVE DEVELOPMENT: CHANGES IN HOW
WE KNOW THE EXTERNAL WORLD ... AND
OURSELVES 323
Piaget's Theory: An Overview
Piaget's Theory: A Modern Assessment
Cognitive Development: An Information
  Processing Perspective
Moral Development: Reasoning About
  Right and Wrong

SOCIAL AND EMOTIONAL DEVELOPMENT:
FORMING RELATIONSHIPS WITH OTHERS 342
Emotional Development and
  Temperament
Attachment: The Beginnings of Love

GENDER: THE DEVELOPMENT OF GENDER
IDENTITY AND SEX-STEREOTYPED BEHAVIOR 350
Gender Identity: Some Contrasting Views
Sex-Stereotyped Beliefs and Behavior

SUMMARY AND REVIEW OF KEY POINTS 354

PERSPECTIVES ON DIVERSITY—MATERNAL
RESPONSIVENESS AND DIVERSITY 319

THE RESEARCH PROCESS—LULLABIES AND
GOOD NIGHT 322

THE RESEARCH PROCESS—BASIC METHODS
FOR STUDYING HUMAN DEVELOPMENT 324

THE POINT OF IT ALL—ATTENTION-DEFICIT
HYPERACTIVITY DISORDER: KIDS WHO REALLY
CAN'T SIT STILL 332

KEY CONCEPT—TWO VIEWS OF COGNITIVE
DEVELOPMENT 336

PERSPECTIVES ON DIVERSITY—MORAL
DEVELOPMENT: UNIVERSAL OR CULTURE-
RELATED? 341

CANADIAN FOCUS—IS DAY CARE A THREAT
TO SECURE ATTACHMENT? 347

MAKING PSYCHOLOGY PART OF YOUR
LIFE—BEING A SUCCESSFUL PARENT 353

HOW EARLY STIMULUS BOOSTS BRAIN POWER

The Toronto Star:
May 3, 1993

The Star in a two part series called "The Amazing Brain" explains how recent research using the most advanced technologies—MRI and EEG recordings, for example—has advanced our understanding of how early development takes place.

For example: "After birth, trillions of brain cell connections are established ... that govern ... vision, language and hearing ... The number of connections could easily go up or down by 25 percent or more, depending upon whether a child grows up in an enriched environment or in an impoverished one."

In Chapter 8 you will learn about human development from infancy through childhood. You will also find the latest news about how heredity and environment combine as behavior progresses through those early years of life.

RESEARCH IN DEVELOPMENTAL PSYCHOLOGY

Janet Werker at the University of British Columbia studies the development of language in infants and young children.

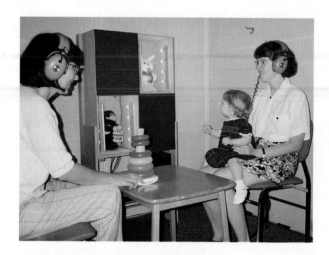

CHANGE IS BASIC TO HUMAN DEVELOPMENT: WE ARE ALL IN A CONTINUOUS STATE OF FLUX AS WE MOVE THROUGH LIFE'S JOURNEY.

Developmental Psychology: *The branch of psychology that studies all types of changes occurring throughout the life span.*

Physical growth and Development: *Physical changes in the size and structure of our bodies between conception and adulthood.*

Cognitive Development: *Changes in cognitive abilities and functioning occurring as individuals grow older.*

Social and Emotional Development: *Changes in emotional experiences and expressions, and in behaviors and attitudes toward others, occurring with age.*

Childhood: *The period between birth and adolescence.*

Change, it is often said, is the only constant. And where human beings are concerned, that is certainly true. Stop for a moment and think about the ways in which you've changed over the course of your life, or even during the past few years. You'll be struck by both the scope and the magnitude of these alterations. Some are obvious—you've grown in size and matured sexually. Others are less apparent—you've acquired a knowledge, learned to think in far more complex and sophisticated ways, formed a personal code of ethics, and developed a much deeper understanding of human relationships. Not all the changes we experience as we grow older are positive—of course—but in a very real sense, change is basic to human development.

The field of **developmental psychology** focuses on such changes. For example, psychologists are just beginning to integrate behavioral studies of child development with our understanding of how the nervous system develops—in particular the frontal lobes (Segalowitz & Rose-Krasnor, 1992). In this chapter and the next one, we will examine some of the major findings in developmental psychology and some new ones as well.

While the changes we experience throughout life are all related, developmental psychologists have found it helpful to categorize these shifts as follows: **physical growth and development**, **cognitive development**, and **social and emotional development**. These terms refer, respectively, to changes in the physical size and structure of our bodies; changes in our mental abilities and functions; and changes in our emotions and in our relationships with other people. In this chapter, we'll consider these as they occur during **childhood**—the years between birth and adolescence. In the next chapter we'll examine changes occurring during adolescence and in the adult years.

An additional topic to which we'll devote special attention is sex-role development, the process by which children learn that they belong to one of the two genders and acquire knowledge of the behaviors and attitudes their culture associates with feminine or masculine. We'll examine this process here, then return to some of its long-lasting effects in Chapter 11.

Physical Growth and Development

*F*rom a biological standpoint, you began when one of the millions of sperm released by your father during sexual intercourse fertilized an ovum deep within your mother's body. The product of this union was less than half a millimeter in diameter—smaller than the period at the end of this sentence. Yet packed within this tiny speck were the genetic blueprints (twenty-three chromosomes from each parent) that guided all your subsequent physical growth.

The Prenatal Period

After fertilization, the ovum moves through the female reproductive tract until it reaches the womb, or uterus. That trip takes several days, and meanwhile the ovum divides again and again. Ten to fourteen days after fertilization, the ovum becomes implanted in the wall of the uterus. For the next six weeks it is known as the embryo and develops very rapidly. By the third week a primitive heart has formed and begun to beat. By the fourth week the embryo is about half a centimeter long and the region of the head is visible. Rapid growth continues, so that by the end of the eighth week the embryo is about 2.5 centimeters long and a face, arms, and legs are present. By that time, too, all major internal organs have begun to form. Some of these, such as the sex glands, are already active. Also, the nervous system develops rapidly; simple reflexes begin to appear during the eighth or ninth week of life.

During the next seven months, the developing child—now known as the fetus—takes on an increasingly human form. The genitals take shape, so that the sex of the baby is recognizable externally by the twelfth week. Fingernails and toenails form, hair follicles appear, and eyelids develop that can already open and close. Physical growth is also impressive. By the end of the twelfth week the fetus is 7.6 centimeters long and weighs about 21 grams. By the twentieth week it is almost 25 centimeters long and weighs between 227 and 255 grams. By the twenty-fourth week all the neurons that will be present in the brain have been produced. The eyes are formed and are sensitive to light by the end of the twenty-sixth week.

During the last three months of pregnancy, the fetus gains about 250 grams each week and grows rapidly. By the seventh and eighth months, he or she appears to be virtually fully formed. However, if born prematurely at this time, there may still be difficulties in breathing, because the alveoli—the tiny air sacs within the lungs—are not yet fully formed. At birth, babies weigh more than 3.17 kilograms on average and are about 50.8 centimeters long.

Embryo: *The developing child during the second through the eighth week of prenatal development.*

Fetus: *The developing child during the last seven months of prenatal development.*

THE STAGES OF PRENATAL DEVELOPMENT

This series of photos illustrates prenatal development, from fertilization to the embryo at seven weeks and the fetus at twenty-two weeks.

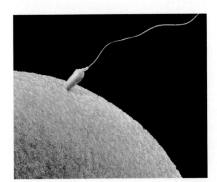 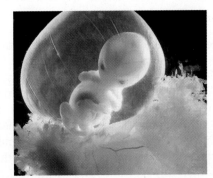 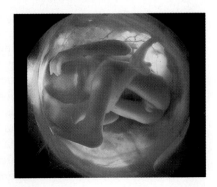

**Jean Piaget
(1892?–1980)**

Piaget was a Swiss psychologist renowned for his extensive work with children and his theories about cognitive development. Piaget's theories, still widely used today, focused on *how* people think, rather than on *what* they think.

Carol Gilligan

Gilligan is widely known for her work on gender differences. Some of her most fascinating research has focused on children's development of morality, and how girls and boys differ in their conceptions of relationships, caring, and justice.

PSYCHOLOGISTS OF NOTE

Cognitive abilities also take shape during the prenatal period. In an ingenious series of studies, DeCasper and his colleagues (e.g., DeCasper & Fifer, 1980; DeCasper & Spence, 1986) arranged for mothers-to-be to read *The Cat in the Hat* to their unborn children twice each day during the last six weeks of pregnancy. At the end of that period, the familiar story produced a slight decrease in fetal heart rate, while an unfamiliar one produced a slight increase. Because a decrease in heart rate is taken as a sign of increased attention, these findings suggest that the fetuses could indeed distinguish between familiar and unfamiliar stories.

Prenatal Influences on Development:
When Trouble Starts Early

Under ideal conditions, development during the prenatal period occurs in an orderly fashion and the newborn child is well equipped at birth to survive outside its mother's body. Unfortunately, however, conditions are not always ideal. Studies show that physical trauma, fear, or psychological stress may disrupt pregnancy both in humans and in animals; in the case of stress, this may result in an increase in the release of estrogens (de Catanzaro & MacNiven, 1992). Many other environmental factors can cause damage and interfere with normal patterns of growth. Such factors are known as **teratogens**; their impact can be significant (Fried & Watkinson, 1988, 1990).

Teratogens: Factors in the environment that can harm the developing fetus.

Harry Harlow
(1905–1981)

Harlow is best known for
his research on emotional
development. His studies
with baby rhesus monkeys
and wire surrogate "moth-
ers" showed that early
social deprivation is correlated with later socially
deviant behavior.

Joan E. Grusec

Joan Grusec studies ways
parents and children think
about and interact with
each other and the ways
children acquire self-
control and concern for
others. Grusec is at the
Department of Psychology
at the University of
Toronto.

PSYCHOLOGISTS OF NOTE

DISEASE DURING PREGNANCY   The blood supply of the fetus and that of its mother
come into close proximity in the **placenta**, the structure within the uterus that
holds, protects, and nourishes the growing child. As a result, disease-producing
organisms present in the mother's blood can sometimes infect the developing
child. Tragically, diseases that exert only relatively minor effects on mothers can
be very serious for the fetus. For example, rubella, or German measles, can
cause blindness, deafness, or heart disease in the fetus if the mother contracts
this illness during the first four weeks of pregnancy. Other diseases that can be
transmitted to the fetus and inflict serious damage include chicken pox, mumps,
tuberculosis, malaria, syphilis, and herpes (Samson, 1988).

Since the early 1980s, AIDS has been added to this list. At present, many
babies infected with AIDS are born each year. The prognosis for these
infants is poor. They often have a wide range of serious birth defects, including facial abnormalities such as a prominent, box-like forehead or a small
head, and widely spaced, diagonally oriented eyes (Novick, 1989). Typically,
babies born with AIDS do not survive for more than five to eight months
(Minkoff et al., 1987).

PRESCRIPTION AND OVER-THE-COUNTER DRUGS   The use of drugs by the mother can
also exert important effects on the developing fetus. Excessive use of aspirin, a
drug most people take without hesitation, can result in harm to the circulatory
system (Kelsey, 1969). Some evidence suggests that caffeine can slow fetal
growth and contribute to premature birth (Jacobson et al., 1984). Children born

*Placenta: A structure that sur-
rounds, protects, and nourishes
the developing fetus.*

to mothers who consume large amounts of caffeine show increased irritability and a higher than normal incidence of vomiting (Aaronson & MacNee, 1989).

ILLEGAL DRUGS   The abuse of heroin, cocaine, crack, and other illegal drugs is a fact of the 1990s. Growing evidence suggests that the use of such drugs by prospective mothers can be disastrous (Samuels & Samuels, 1986). Infants born to heroin-addicted mothers suffer from numerous problems, including physical malformations, respiratory disease, and premature birth. Thousands of babies addicted to cocaine or its derivatives are born in Canada each year (Reid, 1990), and these infants too suffer from a wide range of physical problems, including low birth weight, breathing difficulties, and physical defects (Chasnoff et al., 1989). Given that they are usually born to mothers who are also poor and malnourished, the outlook for these infants is bleak. Furthermore, women who smoke marijuana while pregnant put their infants at risk for lowered verbal and memory abilities later in childhood—for example, at forty-eight months (Fried & Watkinson, 1990).

THE FETAL ALCOHOL SYNDROME   Although consumption of alcohol is legal in most countries, the harm it produces can be devastating. Children born to mothers who use this drug heavily may have fetal alcohol syndrome, or FAS (Aaronson & MacNee, 1989). Full-blown FAS includes severely retarded growth, and one leg shorter than the other. There are distortions in the normal shape of the face, including widely spaced eyes, short eyelid openings, a small, upturned nose, and a thin upper lip. There is damage to the brain and the rest of the nervous system. Currently, fetal alcohol syndrome is the third-highest cause of childhood retardation.

Two ounces of alcohol a day taken very early in pregnancy can produce FAS-like facial features (Astley et al., 1992). Some infants show low body weight and size but no facial distortions; however, they suffer from other fetal alcohol effects such as attention deficits (Nanson & Hiscock, 1990) and mental retardation (Hoyseth & Jones, 1989). The prevalence of FAS in some areas of the Northwest Territories (one in every three infants born) has led some legislators there to propose laws that would impose penalties upon pregnant women who drink alcohol. Others argue strongly that prevention through public education is more likely to reduce the prevalence of FAS.

SMOKING   The proportion of adults who smoke is increasing in many parts of the world. Moreover, the proportion of women who smoke is rising even where the proportion of men who smoke is steady or decreasing. From the standpoint of fetal development, this is indeed unfortunate, for smoking by future mothers may have consequences for both the fetus and the newborn child. These include spontaneous abortion, low birth weight, and small birth size (Aaronson & MacNee, 1989). According to an American study, the single most reliable predictor of infant death is low birth weight. Moreover, smoking increases the concentration of carbon monoxide in the bloodstream of both mother and fetus. Increased carbon monoxide, in turn, displaces oxygen from red blood cells and may damage the central nervous system of the fetus (Nash & Persaud, 1988).

MATERNAL RESPONSIVENESS   The moment of childbirth represents an enormous change for both the fetus and the woman who has just given birth. There are biological and psychological factors that increase the mother's responsiveness to her newborn child, not only in humans but also in animals (Fleming & Corter, 1988). First, hormonal levels adjust to the early postpartum period. Specific changes follow that relate to caregiving. For example, new mothers are faced immediately after birth with a number of new odors: the infant's body, urine, and stool. An investigation of mothers' attraction to their newborns' odors, by Fleming (et al., 1993), found that new mothers were more positive about their infant's body odors than were other females—and fortunately so.

Sometimes, however, there are negative reactions. Most women have only informal training for motherhood. For some, low self-esteem and self-doubt about their ability to parent successfully may influence their mood. Postpartum depression may be the result (e.g., Olioff & Aboud, 1991). The mother's depressed mood may influence her ability to cope with even the minor stresses of everyday life, and alter her perceptions of her children and her emotional responses to their behavior (Krech & Johnston, 1992), although that may not reflect the quality of her marital relations (Whiffen & Gotlib, 1993).

Physical and Perceptual Development During Our Early Years: Infancy and Childhood

Physical growth is rapid during infancy. Assuming good nutrition, infants almost triple in weight (to 9 kilograms) and increase in body length by about one-third (to 71–74 centimeters) during the first year alone.

Newborns possess a number of simple reflexes at birth. They can follow a moving light with their eyes, suck on fingers or a nipple placed in their mouth, and turn their head in the direction of a touch on the cheek. In addition, they can grasp a finger placed in their palm and make stepping motions if held so that their feet barely touch a flat surface. In a study of infants during weeks 6 to 13 of the first year, Zelazo (et al., 1993) found that stepping increased if infants were given practice, which indicated that this neuromotor pattern could be changed with experience.

PERSPECTIVES ON DIVERSITY

Maternal Responsiveness and Diversity

In a 1992 study conducted in New York City, Paris, and Tokyo, Bornstein and colleagues observed mothers as they responded to the needs of their five-month-old children in their own homes. They observed the following responses: nurturing (feeding and comforting, for example), imitating (of the infant's babbling by the mother), extradyadic (occasions when the mother showed the infant something), and dyadic (affectionate interactions—kissing, tickling, peek-a-boo, and so on).

The study identified two kinds of maternal responses: those that were universal and were similar in all three settings, and those that were specific to a particular setting. For example, in all cases mothers encouraged their infants to explore the area around them, and in all cultures they imitated the happy sounds their own infants made. However, there were also some differences. For example, American mothers responded more often to their infants by showing them things in the environment and how they worked, and Japanese mothers were most responsive to eye contact between mother and infant. The conclusion here seems to be that all of the mothers in this study responded to their children in all categories of responding, but some of these responses were universal and some were more culture-specific.

Initially of course, their ability to move about and reach for objects is quite limited, but this changes quickly. Within a few months, infants can sit and then crawl. And as proud parents quickly learn, most infants are quite mobile by the time they are fifteen months old. Figure 8.1 summarizes several milestones of motor development. It is important to keep in mind that the approximate ages indicated are merely average values. Even large departures may be of little importance.

After the initial spurt of the first year, the rate of physical growth slows considerably; both boys and girls gain about 5 to 10 centimeters and 2 to 4 kilograms per year. The rate accelerates during adolescence, when both sexes experience a growth spurt lasting about two years.

LEARNING ABILITIES OF NEWBORNS What can newborn infants learn? Classical conditioning studies have found that newborn infants (only two hours old) readily learn to associate gentle stroking on the forehead with the taste of a sweet solution; after these two stimuli have been paired repeatedly, they will show sucking responses to the stroking (Granchrow, Steiner, & Daher, 1983). Moreover, even newborns show stimulus generalization (Tarquinio et al., 1991) and habituation (Zelazo et al., 1989). In contrast, until they are at least eight months old, human infants do not readily acquire conditioned fears. Remember Little Albert, discussed in Chapter 5, who acquired fear of a white rabbit (CS) after it was paired with a loud sound (UCS)? He was already eleven months old at the time the study was conducted. Why do infants not acquire conditioned fears earlier? Perhaps it is because doing so has little survival value for them: They lack the motor skills needed to escape from unpleasant events, so acquiring such fears would do them little good (Berk, 1993).

Turning to operant conditioning, there is considerable evidence that newborns can acquire new behaviors according to their consequences. For example,

FIGURE 8.1

Milestones of Motor Development

Some highlights of motor development. Note that the approximate ages shown here are only *averages*. Most children will depart from them to some extent; departures are of little importance unless they are extreme.
(Source: Frankenberg & Dodds, 1967.)

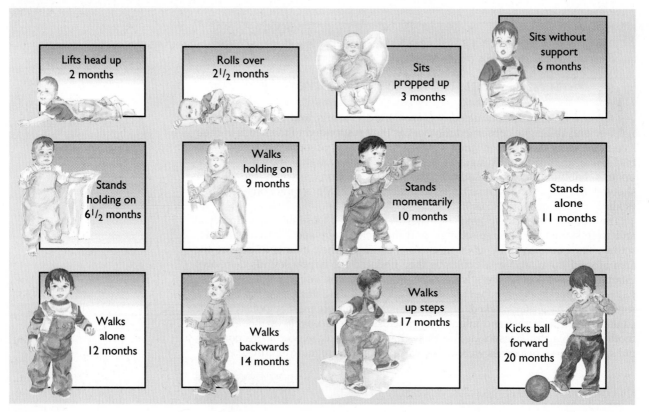

they readily learn to suck faster in order to see visual designs, or hear music and human voices (Rovee-Collier, 1987). And by the time they are two months old, they will move their heads against a pressure-sensitive pillow in order to produce movements of a mobile hung above their cribs (Pomerleau et al., 1992).

Newborns are capable of imitation. In a series of well-known studies, Meltzoff and his colleagues (Meltzoff & Moore, 1977, 1989) found that infants between 12 and 20 days of age could imitate facial gestures shown by an adult—for example, sticking out their tongue or opening their mouth. Indeed, in one well conducted study, infants tested only a few minutes after birth imitated two facial expressions: widened lips and pursed lips (Reissland, 1988).

Infants are able, at birth, to express pain through their cries and their facial expressions (Craig et al., 1988). These behaviors develop over the early months (Johnston et al., 1993).

PERCEPTUAL DEVELOPMENT   How do infants perceive the world around them? Of course infants cannot talk, so they cannot tell us in words what it is they perceive. Nevertheless, they can tell us in other ways—by changes in heart rate, sucking rate, and length of gaze. They show us that they perceive a stimulus by turning their head or eyes toward it rather than away. They show us their preferences by turning toward one stimulus and not another. They show us they are less interested in a stimulus by turning toward it less often, after it has been presented a number of times. These are some of the observable behaviors that tell researchers about the perceptual world of the not-yet-verbal infant. This is how we know that newborns can distinguish between different colors (Adams, 1987), odors (Balogh & Porter, 1986), tastes (Granchrow, Steiner, & Daher, 1983), and sounds (Morrongiello & Clifton, 1984).

The auditory systems of infants are functional before birth. In one experiment, conducted at Queen's University by Kisilevsky and her colleagues, a vibroacoustic instrument was placed on the pregnant woman's abdomen, over the fetus's head. The increase in heart rate and in movement indicated that the infants perceived in utero the vibration and the sound produced. After birth, infants as young as three days old detect sounds and turn toward them with their eyes and head. Furthermore, even in the dark, infants respond to illusions in sound localization—they reach out in the direction of the simulated sounds of toys, for example (Hillier et al., 1992)—although reaching for invisible sounds is not as well developed as reaching for visible targets (Stack et al., 1989).

Knowledge of how the auditory system localizes sound was used at the University of Western Ontario to design a sonar-sensory device that would

Barbara S. Kisilevsky
Queen's University

NEWBORNS IMITATING ADULT FACIAL EXPRESSIONS

Research by Dr. Nadja Reissland-Burghart has shown that newborns only a few minutes old can imitate facial expressions. Widened lips were modeled for the infant on the left, and pursed lips were modeled for the infant on the right.

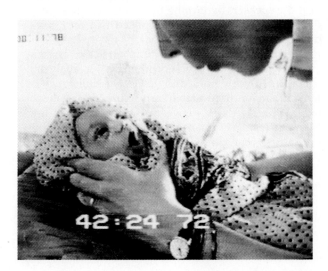

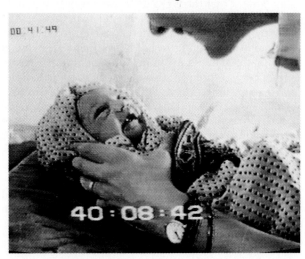

provide auditory information to blind infants and toddlers—to assist in their exploration of space, to guide their reaching for objects, and to help them avoid obstacles. The device was intended also to allow blind children of school age "to locate objects, perceive spatial layouts, and to identify surfaces and objects" (Humphrey et al., 1988). This is just one of many examples of basic research being applied to solve practical problems.

As you learned in Chapter 7, a great deal of attention has been paid to language development in infancy, and there have been important advances in our understanding of early infant perception of language. We now appreciate that exposure to language in infancy has significant consequences for language development in general (Juscyck, 1993). Infants are especially sensitive to sounds within the frequency range of normal human speech. Indeed, they can even distinguish between similar stimuli such as *ba* and *ga* (Eimas & Tarter, 1979). Very early in life, infants can discriminate among many more speech sounds than those in their native language (see Chapter 7; Werker, 1989).

Let us turn now to current knowledge about infants' visual abilities. At McMaster University, it has been found that as infants develop, their visual fields grow. Lewis and Maurer (1992) studied infants of ages one to six months and found that their visual fields expanded from the center out, and that their temporal visual fields developed faster than their nasal visual fields.

THE RESEARCH PROCESS

Lullabies and Good Night

We all know that infants like to listen to music, and from your own observations, you may know that infants babble in singsong and enjoy music—though not so much the tunes of Sloan, or the Tragically Hip, or the Grapes of Wrath. Rather, they prefer special kinds of songs we call lullabies. Remember "Hush little baby, don't say a word…"? Or "Kumbaya"? You probably had a favorite of your own. These special songs have been the focus of research at Erindale College of the University of Toronto. There, Sandra Trehub and her associates have found that there is a distinctive way that people across cultures sing to infants and that this way of singing is perceptually different when, for example, the mother is singing to her infant than when she is singing the same song but her infant is absent (Trehub et al., 1993). Moreover, this distinctive way of singing when the song is directed toward the infant is recognizable by other infants, even after the songs have been electronically filtered so that the words are removed. According to Trehub, this means there may be something in the tone of the singing—perhaps "musical prosody" that is analogous to the prosody of language—that makes the difference.

What else do infants know about music and musical structure? This question was asked by Annabel Cohen at Dalhousie University (Cohen et al., 1987). In the following study, they found that infants can tell whether the notes of a familiar melody are correct or not. Infants aged seven to eleven months, seated on their mothers' laps heard the same melody over and over again, but in different keys—the key of C, followed by the key of E, and so on. Occasionally, one note in the melody was wrong—that is, it was in the wrong key. Infants who turned toward the audio speaker on one of those trials were "rewarded" by the presentation of an illuminated, animated toy animal in a Plexiglas display case near the speaker. By turning more often on those trials than on correct ones, infants showed that they could distinguish the incorrect melodies.

Trehub's general observation (1987) was that "infants possess the prerequisite skills for analyzing complex auditory input, and that [those skills] may be musical universals available early in life." You will recognize the parallel between that conclusion and Werker's results of infant perception of speech sounds in the first year. Support for Trehub's idea has been provided by a recent study in which American infants were exposed to Indonesian music, which uses a different scale than Western European music. At an earlier age, American infants were better able to discriminate between Indonesian and American scales.

Infants have impressive abilities in form or pattern perception. In classic research on this topic, Fantz (1961) showed babies six months old a variety of visual patterns. By observing how long they fixated visually on each, he determined that the babies had a clear preference for patterned as opposed to plain targets (and to symmetrical rather than asymmetrical; Humphrey & Humphrey, 1989); and that they preferred the human face over all other stimuli tested. Subsequent research found that recognition of faces may develop even earlier. By two months of age, infants prefer faces with features in normal locations (Maurer & Barrera, 1981). By three months they can distinguish between their mother's face and that of a stranger, and distinguish one stranger's face from another (Barrera & Maurer, 1981). As babies grow older, they prefer increasingly complex patterns, such as a checkerboard containing many squares rather than one containing a smaller number of larger squares (Brennan, Ames, & Moore, 1966).

The ability to perceive depth also develops rapidly in the months immediately after birth. Early studies on depth perception used an apparatus known as the visual cliff (Gibson & Walk, 1960). As you can see from the photo, the patterned floor drops away on the deep side of the cliff. A transparent surface actually continues across this chasm, so that there is no actual drop, and no real danger. Yet human infants six or seven months old refuse to crawl across the deep side, thus indicating that they perceive depth by this time. Does this perceptual ability appear prior to this age? Since younger infants can't crawl across the cliff even if they want to, it is necessary to use other measures to find that out. Such research has been performed and indicates that depth perception may first appear when infants are about three months old (Fox et al., 1979; Yonas, Arterberry, & Granrud, 1987). Of course, these competencies in sensation and perception develop normally when environmental stimulation is provided, as experiments with animals have often shown (e.g., Timney, 1990). A great deal of what we know about the fundamentals of perceptual development has come from comparisons with animals (e.g., Mitchell, 1989).

In sum, shortly after birth, infants have sophisticated abilities to interpret complex sensory input. How do they then integrate this information into cognitive frameworks for understanding the world? That is the question we will consider next. The basic research methods used by psychologists to understand human development are described in **The Research Process**.

THE VISUAL CLIFF: STUDYING INFANT DEPTH PERCEPTION

Infants six or seven months old refuse to crawl out over the deep side of the visual cliff. This indicates that they can perceive depth.

Cognitive Development: *Changes in How We Know the External World ... and Ourselves*

Do children think, reason, and remember like adults? Until well into the twentieth century, it was widely assumed that any differences between the cognitive processes of children and adults were largely of degree: Adults could do more, but the way individuals thought was similar regardless of age.

These assumptions were challenged by the Swiss psychologist Jean Piaget. On the basis of careful observation of his own and many other children, Piaget

Basic Methods for Studying Human Development

That human beings, and especially children, change with the passage of time is obvious. But how can we map the course of development and identify the factors that affect it? Developmental psychologists use several different methods for this. We'll examine the most important ones here and consider the relative strengths and potential weaknesses of each.

Longitudinal Research: Studying the Same Individuals Across Time

Longitudinal research studies use the same individuals repeatedly over long intervals (see Figure 8.2). For example, researchers might identify two groups of children, one being cared for by their own mothers and the other in day care centers, and study them for several years to determine whether the groups differ in cognitive development—for example, in their language skills or their ability to solve problems.

Longitudinal research offers important advantages. First, since the same individuals are tested or observed repeatedly, individual variations in the course of development can be observed. Second, because the same individuals are studied over relatively long periods of time, it may be possible to draw conclusions about how specific events influence the course of development.

There are several potential disadvantages to longitudinal research, however. First, there may be subject attrition—the loss of some participants over the course of the project. In the case of day care, families may move, break up, or lose interest, the result being that their children are lost to the study. As well, the children who

---

FIGURE 8.2   Basic Methods of Studying Human Development

In the *longitudinal method*, the same individuals are studied across time. In the *cross-sectional method*, people of different ages are studied at one time.

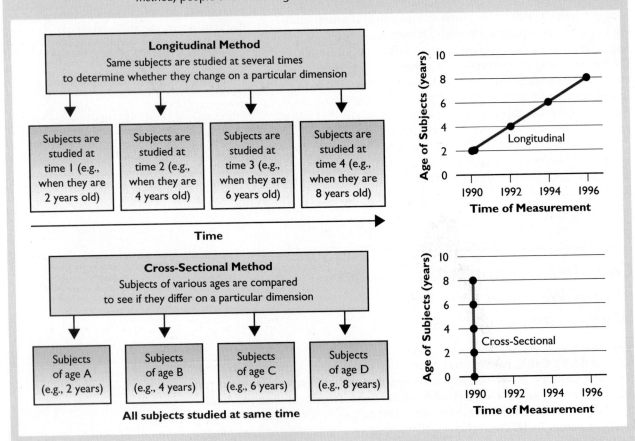

Longitudinal Method
Same subjects are studied at several times to determine whether they change on a particular dimension

| Subjects are studied at time 1 (e.g., when they are 2 years old) | Subjects are studied at time 2 (e.g., when they are 4 years old) | Subjects are studied at time 3 (e.g., when they are 6 years old) | Subjects are studied at time 4 (e.g., when they are 8 years old) |

Time

Cross-Sectional Method
Subjects of various ages are compared to see if they differ on a particular dimension

| Subjects of age A (e.g., 2 years) | Subjects of age B (e.g., 4 years) | Subjects of age C (e.g., 6 years) | Subjects of age D (e.g., 8 years) |

All subjects studied at same time

remain in the study may be different in important respects from those who withdrew. To the extent this is the case, any differences between the mother and day care groups may be a result of factors that do not involve being raised at home or in a day care center. Also, there may be practice effects. People who are tested or observed repeatedly may become familiar with the kinds of tasks used in the research. To the extent these effects occur, the results obtained may be invalid.

Cross-Sectional Research: Studying People of Different Ages at one Time

Now, consider another way of studying the mother/day care question. Instead of following the development of two groups of children for several years, we might instead compare children who are different ages right now. For example, we might study three-, four-, and five-year-olds who have been cared for by their mothers and compare them with three-, four-, and five-year-olds in day care centers, to determine (for each age) whether the two groups differ with respect to cognitive development. This is an example of **cross-sectional research**, in which people of different ages are studied at the same point in time (refer to Figure 8.2).

Cross-sectional research also offers several advantages. It can be conducted much more quickly than longitudinal research—in the time it takes to collect the data. And since participants are tested only once, practice effects are minimal.

Unfortunately, cross-sectional research also has several disadvantages. Perhaps the most important one has to do with **cohort effects**. These are differences between groups of individuals of different ages that derive not only from differences in age but also from the fact that the subjects were born at different times and so may have had different life experiences. These differences may be small among children who are currently three, four, and five years old. But suppose we are comparing people who are 65, 45, and 25 to find, for example, how sexual behavior varies over the life span. Individuals in these three groups certainly differ in age. But they also differ in terms of the times during which their life experiences were acquired.

As an illustration, assume that people who are 65 engage in a narrower range of sexual practices than those who are 25. Is this finding a result of age differences? Perhaps. But it may also be a result of the fact that the older individuals grew up at a time when society showed much less tolerance for many forms of sexual behavior. In this manner, cohort effects sometimes make it difficult to interpret correctly the findings of cross-sectional research.

Summing Up, and an Alternative Approach

Faced with the mixed advantages and disadvantages outlined above, developmental psychologists have devised an approach to research that maximizes the advantages of longitudinal and cross-sectional research while minimizing the disadvantages. In this third method, known as **longitudinal-sequential design**, several different ages are studied repeatedly over a period of years. In effect, the longitudinal and cross-sectional methods are combined. Since each sample of participants is studied over time, changes within each group can be attributed to development. But since several ages are studied, researchers can also assess the impact of cohort effects and cultural changes, by comparing, at the same age, people born in different years. This type of design permits both longitudinal and cross-sectional comparisons. If the results of both are the same, we can be quite confident about the validity of the findings. While the longitudinal-sequential design is still vulnerable to participant attrition, practice effects, and the like, it does offer means of untangling the influences of cultural change and individual development.

Critical Thinking Questions

1. In recent years, both divorce rates and family mobility (the rate at which families move from one geographic location to another) have increased. What are the implications of these changes for successful use of the longitudinal method of research?

2. Suppose that a cross-sectional study compared people of three age groups—55–60, 30–35, and 15–20—with respect to several cognitive abilities. Results indicated that the two older groups outperform the youngest group. How could these results be interpreted? What follow-up research could be conducted to help clarify the meaning of these results?

concluded that, in several important ways, children do not think or reason like adults. Their thought processes are different not only in degree but also in kind.

Piaget's theory of cognitive development contains many valuable insights (Case, 1993) and has generated much important research. However, many psychologists no longer accept his theory as complete. Furthermore, Piaget's theory has been seriously challenged by the information processing perspective we discussed in detail in Chapter 6 (Case, 1991). After considering Piaget's theory and modern assessments of it, we will consider the information processing approach to cognitive development.

Piaget's Theory: An Overview

Piaget's theory of cognitive development is a **stage theory**. It proposes that, in the development of our thinking, we move through an orderly and predictable series of steps. Stage theories have been applied to many other aspects of human behavior as well—notably to the development of personality (see Chapter 12). However, many psychologists currently question the ideas that (1) all human beings move through set stages; (2) they do so at certain ages; and (3) the order of this progress is unchanging (Flavell, 1985). Indeed, there is so much variability among people that there is some question about how valid stage theories are.

What is it that, in Piaget's view, underlies cognitive development? What keeps us advancing from stage to stage, to more and more complex thinking? According to Piaget, from birth on, as we interact with the world, we construct mental representations of it (Olson, 1993). This ongoing process is called **adaptation**. We adapt our past mental representations of the world to include our current experience. Adaption occurs in two ways. First, there is **assimilation**, which occurs when we incorporate new information into existing mental structures. For example, when infants encounter a new kind of toy—perhaps a jack-in-the-box—they try to treat it as they have other toys—perhaps shaking it like a rattle or banging it like a drum. When these old strategies do not work, **accommodation** must be made. Since existing structures cannot handle the new information being received, a new way to deal with the environment (in this case, turning a handle) must be devised.

For Piaget, it is the tension between assimilation and accommodation that results in adaptation, cognitive development, and ever more complex understanding of the world around us.

Now let's turn to the details of Piaget's stages of cognitive development.

THE SENSORIMOTOR STAGE: LEARNING TO REPRESENT THE WORLD INTERNALLY

The first of Piaget's stages lasts from birth until between 18 and 24 months. During this period—the **sensorimotor stage**—infants gradually learn there is a relationship between their actions and the external world. They discover that when they manipulate objects, there are consequences. In short, they acquire a basic idea about cause and effect. For example, they learn to perform movements that affect the physical world: pulling, striking, swinging, and rubbing. They learn to reach for objects while looking at them, and to open their mouths differently for a nipple or a spoon.

Throughout the sensorimotor period, infants know the world through motor activities (Bebko et al., 1992) and sensory impressions (Reid, 1989). They have not yet learned to use mental representations or images to represent objects or events. This results in some interesting contradictions. For example, if an object is hidden from view, four-month-olds will not attempt to search for it. Generally for these infants, it is "out of sight, out of mind." By eight or nine months of age, however, the situation changes. Infants of this age will search for the hidden object. They have developed **object permanence**—the understanding that objects continue to exist even after they are no longer seen. In contrast, object permanence in kittens appears much more rapidly (Dumas & Dore, 1989). Delays in the appearance of object permanence have been studied in special populations, such as children with defective limbs (McDonnell, 1988) and children who are visually impaired from birth (Bigelow, 1990). In blind children there are similarities in the development of object permanence, but also differences because of their special reliance on touch perception (Bigelow, 1986).

Longitudinal Research: Research in which the same individuals are studied across relatively substantial periods of time, such as years.

Cross-Sectional Research: Research comparing groups of individuals of different ages in order to determine how some aspect of behavior or cognition changes with age.

Cohort Effects: Differences between individuals of different ages stemming from the contrasting social or cultural conditions of the periods in which they grew up.

Longitudinal-Sequential Design: A research approach in which several groups of individuals of different ages are studied across time.

Stage Theory: Any theory proposing that all human beings move through an orderly and predictable series of changes.

Adaptation: In Piaget's theory of cognitive development, building mental representations of the world through interaction with it.

Assimilation: In Piaget's theory, the tendency to understand new information in terms of existing mental frameworks.

Accommodation: In Piaget's theory, the modification of existing mental frameworks to take account of new information.

Sensorimotor Stage: In Piaget's theory, the earliest stage of cognitive development.

Object Permanence: An understanding of the fact that objects continue to exist when they pass from view.

Preoperational Stage: In Piaget's theory, a stage of cognitive development during which children become capable of mental representations of the external world.

THE PREOPERATIONAL STAGE: GROWTH OF SYMBOLIC ACTIVITY Some time between the ages of 18 and 24 months, Piaget contends, children develop the ability to form mental representations of objects and events. At the same time, language develops, as does the beginning of thinking in words. These developments mark the end of the sensorimotor period and the start of the **preoperational stage**.

During this stage, which lasts until about age seven, children are capable of many feats they could not perform earlier. For example, they begin **make-believe play** (Weininger & Fitzgerald, 1988), enacting familiar routines, such as pretending to eat or go to sleep. In order to create play, they must represent these activities mentally and translate them into overt actions.

While the thinking of preoperational children is more advanced, Piaget emphasizes that children at this stage of cognitive development are still quite immature in several important respects. First, they are limited by **egocentrism**; that is, they have difficulty understanding that other people may perceive the world differently (Piaget, 1975). Consider the following demonstration (Flavell, 1973): Two-year-olds are shown that a card has a picture of a dog on one side and a cat on the other. The card is then placed between the child and the experimenter so that each can see only one side. Now the experimenter asks the child two questions: What do *you* see? and What do *I* see? Because of egocentric thought, many children say that the experimenter sees the same picture as they do. As we'll soon see, however, the results obtained in such demonstrations depend on which questions are asked. Under some conditions, even two-year-olds are capable of recognizing that what other people see may be quite different (Lempers, Flavell, & Flavell, 1977).

Children in the preoperational stage lack understanding of relational terms, such as *darker*, *larger*, and *harder*. Further, they lack seriation—the ability to arrange objects in order from large to small, for example. Finally, and perhaps most important, they lack **conservation**—the understanding that the physical attributes of an object remain unchanged even though their appearance has changed. For example, say a four-year-old is shown two identical lumps of clay. One lump is then flattened into a large pancake as the child watches. Asked whether the two lumps still contain the same amount of clay, the child may answer no (see Figure 8.3). Similar findings result when children of this age watch water from a tall, thin container being poured into a shorter but wider one. When asked whether a second tall container and the new shorter one contain the same amount of water, at this stage children again answer no.

MAKE-BELIEVE PLAY

When they engage in make-believe play, children demonstrate that they can represent everyday activities mentally. According to Piaget, they become capable of such behavior during the preoperational stage.

Make-Believe Play: Play in which children pretend to be engaging in various familiar activities, such as eating or going to sleep.

Egocentrism: The inability of young children to distinguish their own perspective from that of others.

Conservation: Principle that states that certain physical attributes of an object remain unchanged even though its outward appearance changes.

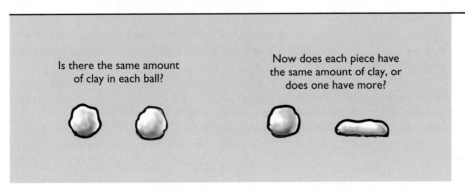

Is there the same amount of clay in each ball?

Now does each piece have the same amount of clay, or does one have more?

FIGURE 8.3

Lack of Understanding of Conservation During the Preoperational Stage

A four-year-old is shown two identical lumps of clay (left). Then one lump is flattened into a large pancake (right). Asked whether the two lumps still contain the same amount, the child may answer "no." Such behavior indicates that the child lacks understanding of the concept of *conservation.*

THE STAGE OF CONCRETE OPERATIONS: THE EMERGENCE OF LOGICAL THOUGHT By the time they are six or seven, most children have gained an understanding of conservation. According to Piaget, this marks the beginning of the third major stage of cognitive development—the stage of **concrete operations**.

During this stage, which lasts until about the age of eleven, many important cognitive skills emerge. Children gain an understanding of relational terms and seriation. They come to understand reversibility—the fact that many physical changes can be undone by reversing the original action. They also begin to make greater use of categories in describing and thinking about the physical world. Thus, if asked to sort various objects, four-year-olds will often do so in terms of color or size. Older children place objects in more complex categories, those which take account of several features at once. For example, they will categorize bananas, oranges, apples, and pineapples as fruits, despite major variations in color, shape, and size.

Finally, when children reach the stage of concrete operations, they begin to engage in logical thought. If asked, "Why did you and your mother go to the store?" they will reply, "Because my mother needed some milk." Younger children, in contrast, might say, "Because afterwards, we came home."

THE STAGE OF FORMAL OPERATIONS: DEALING WITH ABSTRACTIONS AS WELL AS REALITY At about the age of twelve, Piaget suggests, most children enter the final stage of cognitive development—the stage of **formal operations**. During this time, major features of adult thought appear. This may have to do with changes in frontal lobe function by this age (Segalowitz et al., 1992).

While children in the stage of concrete operations can think logically, they do so about concrete events and objects. In contrast, at the stage of formal operations, they can think abstractly. That is, they can deal not only with the real, or concrete, but also with possibilities—with potential events or relationships that do not exist but can be imagined. As a result, they become able to doubt, as studies by Bayers and Chandler at the University of Calgary have shown (1992).

During this final stage of cognitive development, children become capable of **hypothetico-deductive reasoning**. When faced with a problem, they can formulate a general theory that includes all possible factors. From this, they reason deductively to formulate specific hypotheses, which can then be tested by examining existing evidence (or acquiring new evidence). Individuals who reach the stage of formal operations use **propositional reasoning**. They assess the logical validity of verbal statements, even when those refer to possible events rather than to real events in the real world.

While thinking of young adolescents matches (approximately) that of adults, Piaget believed that it still falls short. Thus, young adolescents, often use their new reasoning to construct sweeping theories of religion, ethics, or politics. While this reasoning may be logical, the theories are often naive, because the individuals who construct them do not consider adequately the consequences in real life.

One final point: While people who have reached the stage of formal operations are capable of engaging in hypothetico-deductive reasoning, propositional thought, and other advanced forms of thinking, there is no guarantee that they will actually do so. On the contrary, even adults slip back (Kuhn, 1989). Having the capacity for logical thought, then, does not ensure that it will actually occur.

Piaget's Theory: *A Modern Assessment*

All theories in psychology are subject to rigorous scientific scrutiny. But theories like Piaget's need very careful assessment because of their sweeping assertions. This being the case, it is not surprising to learn that Piaget's ideas

Concrete Operations: *In Piaget's theory, a stage development occurring roughly between the ages of seven and eleven. It is at this stage that children become aware of the permanence of objects and the capacity for logical thought emerges.*

Formal Operations: *In Piaget's theory, the final stage of cognitive development during which individuals may acquire the capacity for deductive or propositional reasoning.*

Hypothetico-Deductive Reasoning: *In Piaget's theory, a type of reasoning first shown during the stage of formal operations. It involves formulating a general theory and deducing specific hypotheses from it.*

Propositional Reasoning; *In Piaget's theory, reasoning during the stage of formal operations, in which individuals can assess the validity of verbal assertions even when these refer to possibilities rather than to actual events.*

have been the focus of a large number of subsequent investigations (Flavell, 1982). The results suggest that his theory, although insightful in many respects, does not provide a completely accurate account of cognitive development. Piaget's theory is incorrect, or at least requires major revision, with respect to these three issues: (1) the ages at which infants and preschoolers reach the milestones of cognitive development; (2) how distinct the stages of cognitive development are; and (3) the role of language and the importance of social interaction with caregivers in cognitive growth.

THE CASE OF THE COMPETENT PRESCHOOLER There is reason to believe that Piaget seriously underestimated the cognitive abilities of infants and young children. For example, infants show a basic grasp of object permanence even at four-and-a-half months (Baillargeon, 1987). Similarly, children as young as three have some understanding of the concept of conservation—the fact that certain physical attributes of an object can remain unchanged even though the outward appearance of the object is altered (Cuneo, 1980)—and of symbolic thought (Bialystok, 1992).

DISCRETE STAGES IN COGNITIVE DEVELOPMENT: MYTH OR REALITY? Piaget proposed that cognitive development happens in discrete steps and that these are discontinuous: children must complete one before entering the next. Most research findings, however, indicate that cognitive changes occur in a gradual manner. Rarely does an ability that is entirely absent at one age make a sudden appearance. Developmental psychologists disagree about this basic aspect of Piaget's thought.

LANGUAGE AND THE SOCIAL CONTEXT OF COGNITIVE DEVELOPMENT Young children often talk to themselves as they go about their daily activities, giving themselves instructions about what to do next. Piaget called this egocentric speech and suggested that it was a sign of cognitive immaturity—an inability to take account of the perspective of others. The Soviet psychologist Vygotsky (1987) objected strongly, contending that **private speech** is not egocentric; on the contrary, he thought that it occurs when young children encounter obstacles and difficulties, and that it represents their efforts at self-guidance. Vygotsky felt that this early use of language helps young children reflect on their own behavior, and that it plays a key role in cognitive development. The results of many studies have confirmed his views (e.g., Bivens & Berk, 1990).

There is also support for Vygotsky's contention that social communication with caregivers plays a key role in cognitive growth. He taught that cognitive development is enhanced by parent-child interactions, and again, research findings offer support for this idea. For example, children whose parents encourage them to use more private speech are more successful when working alone (Behrend, Rosengren, & Perlmutter, 1992). Of course, verbal communication between adult and child is not the only means through which children's thinking develops. However, it does seem to play a more important role than Piaget believed, so Vygotsky's views pose another serious challenge to Piaget's theory.

In sum, there is now general agreement among developmental psychologists that Piaget's theory is not completely accurate (MacNamara & Austin, 1993; Siegel, 1993). It gives too little credit to the cognitive abilities of infants and young children, it overemphasizes the importance of discrete stages, and it underestimates the role of private speech and social interaction with caregivers. Despite these problems, however, the impact of Piaget's theory remains profound. It has forever altered our ideas about how children think and reason and has served as a framework for much research on cognitive development.

THE SOCIAL CONTEXT OF COGNITIVE DEVELOPMENT
According to Vygotsky (1987), children often learn in situations in which parents present them with cognitive tasks that are slightly too difficult for them to perform alone. The social interaction and dialogue that occur in such situations help children master new skills.

Private Speech: The instructions about what to do next that young children often give themselves as they perform various activities.

- According to Piaget, young children move through a series of discrete stages of cognitive development. In the sensorimotor stage, infants acquire a basic understanding of the links between their own behavior and the effects it produces; however, they lack object permanence.

- In the preoperational stage, babies form mental representations of the external world. However, they show egocentrism in their thinking.

- In the concrete operations stage, logical thought emerges. Finally, in the stage of formal operations, older children and adolescents can think logically, manipulate abstract concepts and ideas, and engage in propositional reasoning.

- Challenges to Piaget's theory have asserted that young children attain key cognitive milestones at much younger ages than Piaget suggested; that children generally do not seem to pass through discrete and discontinuous stages of cognitive development; and that Piaget underestimated the importance of language and social interactions.

Cognitive Development: An Information Processing Perspective

Whatever the ultimate validity of Piaget's theory, his views remain influential today. Nevertheless, during the past twenty years, an alternative perspective on cognitive development, the *information processing approach*, has emerged, and gained increasing support among psychologists. Psychologists who adopt this approach study children's capacities to process, store, retrieve, and actively manipulate information, and how these capacities change with age (Case, 1991).

Here is just one example. At Scarborough College of the University of Toronto, Nicholls and Kennedy (1992) studied the way in which people of all ages draw a cube. They had their subjects (about 1,700 in all—volunteers at the Ontario Science Centre and students at U of T) handle a small cube and then draw it on a blank piece of paper. The various results are shown in Figure 8.4. Until age five, children are satisfied that their single square (example 2) is the best representation of the cube. After age fourteen, the most common representation is the square with parallel oblique lines (example 6) to show depth. Between these two ages, various other kinds of drawings are made. According to Nicholls and Kennedy, these data say that, between ages 5 and 14, children may take different routes to the mature representation that is most commonly found later on.

FIGURE 8.4

Drawing Classification Categories

Top row, left to right: Enclosure (category 1), One-square (2), Fold-out (3), Two squares (4), Second Row: Drawings with frontal vertex shown by a Y-junction, and a vertex at the base shown by a T-junction (5), Square with obliques (6) Edge with obliques (7), Convergent square with obliques (8), Bottom row: Convergent edge with obliques (9), Dissection (10), and other (11).
(Source: Nichols & Kennedy, 1992.)

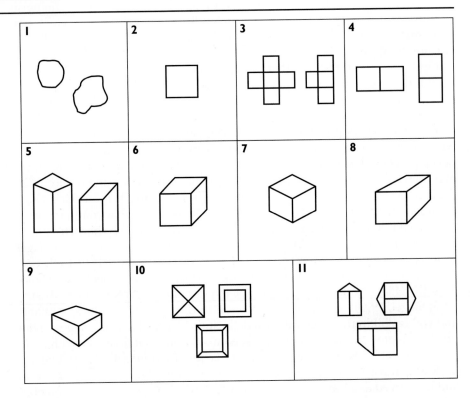

Because the information processing approach is supported by a rapidly growing body of scientific evidence, and because it is consistent with the growing emphasis on cognitive processes in all of modern psychology, it merits careful consideration.

John M. Kennedy
University of Toronto

SENSORY PROCESSING: EFFICIENCIES IN PERCEIVING THE EXTERNAL WORLD Earlier in this chapter, you learned that newborns possess considerable ability to perceive the world around them. As you can guess, that ability improves rapidly over the years. The information processing approach suggests that those improvements include an increasing ability to notice fine-grained and subtle features of the external world—that is, not only the difference between a human face and a jumbled pattern, but also the differences between individual faces. With cognitive growth also come sophisticated cognitive structures, or schemes, for interpreting new experiences. That newborns possess impressive abilities to form such frameworks is indicated by the findings of numerous studies (e.g., Langlois, Roggmann, & Reisser-Danner, 1990; Walton, Bower, & Bower, 1992).

For example, consider a study performed by Walton and Bower (1993). By sucking on a pacifier, infants only a few hours old (8 to 78 hours) could cause color images of women's faces to appear on a screen in front of them. Each face remained on the screen for the time the infants sucked on the pacifier. When they stopped for a second, however, another face was shown. Six different faces were shown one at a time. The first four were of individual women (two blondes and two brunettes). The fifth was a composite picture with features of the four already shown, while the sixth was a new composite, constructed from faces not seen before. Walton and Bower reasoned that, if the infants formed a cognitive representation of the faces they saw (a prototype), they would look longer at the first composite face, which was based on faces they had seen, because it would resemble their prototype, than at the second composite face, which was based on faces they had not seen. That is precisely what happened.

These findings, and those of related studies, indicate that newborns can form mental representations of the stimuli they are exposed to, and that they do so very rapidly (in Walton and Bower study, in less than a minute). Of course, as we grow older, our ability to form complex representations improves, which helps us make sense out of the more and more complex world around us.

ATTENTION: FROM UNFOCUSED SCANNING TO FOCUSED PLANFULNESS If you've ever observed very young children, you know that they are readily distracted. In other words, they seem unable to keep their attention exclusively on whatever they are currently doing. As children grow older, however, they acquire an increasing ability to concentrate; by the time they are about seven years old, they can tune out distractions such as music or other background noise (e.g., Higgins & Turnure, 1984). Since our information processing capacities have limits, this growing ability to focus on the most important aspects of a given situation, to the exclusion of others, offers important advantages.

In addition, as they grow older, children develop greater skill in *planning*, which is defined here as active decision making about where and how they will direct their attention. In a revealing study of this aspect of cognitive development, children aged three to five walked (one by one) with an experimenter through a familiar playground (Wellman, Somerville, & Haake, 1979). In each case, they stopped at eight locations; at the third stop, the experimenter took the child's picture. When they reached the seventh stop, however, the camera was missing and the child was asked to search for it. Three-year-olds went to the location where the picture had been taken, but then often gave up. Older preschoolers were more likely to start there, but then to search all of the locations in sequence. Thus, they showed evidence of planning with respect to their search. Later, children show even greater sophistication with respect to planning. By the time they are nine, for instance, they plan activities in detail, even searching for various shortcuts (Gauvain & Rogoff, 1989).

Unfortunately, not all children show such increases in the focus of their attention. See **The Point of It All** for a discussion of the difficulties faced—and caused—by such children.

THE POINT OF IT ALL

Attention-Deficit Hyperactivity Disorder: Kids Who Really Can't Sit Still

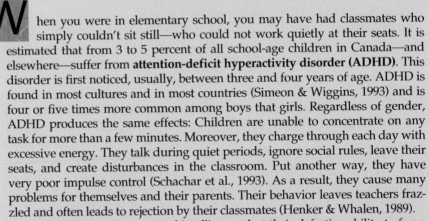

When you were in elementary school, you may have had classmates who simply couldn't sit still—who could not work quietly at their seats. It is estimated that from 3 to 5 percent of all school-age children in Canada—and elsewhere—suffer from **attention-deficit hyperactivity disorder (ADHD)**. This disorder is first noticed, usually, between three and four years of age. ADHD is found in most cultures and in most countries (Simeon & Wiggins, 1993) and is four or five times more common among boys that girls. Regardless of gender, ADHD produces the same effects: Children are unable to concentrate on any task for more than a few minutes. Moreover, they charge through each day with excessive energy. They talk during quiet periods, ignore social rules, leave their seats, and create disturbances in the classroom. Put another way, they have very poor impulse control (Schachar et al., 1993). As a result, they cause many problems for themselves and their parents. Their behavior leaves teachers frazzled and often leads to rejection by their classmates (Henker & Whalen, 1989).

ADHD children have normal intelligence, but their defective ability to focus their attention prevents them from performing well. They find it difficult to ignore irrelevant information (Landau, Milich, & Lorch, 1992), and they do poorly on tests requiring sustained attention. For example, when they retell a story, they organize their account poorly, omit information, and include details that are not accurate (Tannock et al., 1993). When they are tested for memory problems, they are low on all measures requiring verbal processing (Douglas & Benezra, 1990).

What are the causes of ADHD? First, heredity plays a role. For example, work at the Ottawa Board of Education has shown that identical twins are more likely to share the disorder than nonidentical twins, and adopted children with a hyperactive biological parent are more likely to show it than adopted children without such a parent (Alberts-Corush, Firestone & Goodman, 1986). The particular bad gene is thought to be one that carries instructions about the manufacture of thyroid-hormone receptors, and there are now diagnostic tests for newborns to assess thyroid hormone levels. But ADHD is also related to high levels of stress at home; and prenatal teratogens, such as alcohol and smoking, also seem to play a part.

Treatment methods are diverse. ADHD can be effectively treated with medication; Ritalin is the most common drug used. Hyperactive children also benefit from family intervention, and from therapy in which appropriate behavior is modeled for them (Blakemore et al., 1993; Barkley, 1990). Family therapy (Morris, 1993) and parent-training programs (Cousins & Weiss, 1993) are also important, because the unruly behavior of ADHD children often strains parents' patience to the breaking point, leading to punishment—which only increases the wild behavior. To conclude, there is help for ADHD children, their parents, and their teachers. If left untreated, ADHD children often develop into hyper, hostile, impulsive adults.

ATTENTION-DEFICIT HYPERACTIVITY DISORDER

Children with this disorder cannot focus their attention on any task for more than a few minutes. As a result, they quickly become bored and often disrupt classroom activities.

Attention-Deficit Hyperactivity Disorder: A psychological disorder in which children are unable to concentrate their attention on any task for more than a few minutes.

MEMORY: IMPROVING STRATEGIES, IMPROVING PERFORMANCE Memory improves in many ways as children mature (e.g., Cohen & Griffiths, 1987). With respect to *short-term memory*, there is the increasing use of rehearsal. At age five and six years, children are much less likely to repeat information to themselves as they try to memorize it. By the time children are eight years old, however, they engage in the simple forms of rehearsal. At ten or eleven, they combine various pieces of information and rehearse larger chunks (e.g., Kunzinger, 1985). Spontaneous rehearsals in short-term memory by deaf children between five and eight were studied by Bebko and colleagues at York University. They found that these children began using rehearsals in short-term memory several years later than hearing children.

Interestingly, even children as young as three try to improve their own short-term memory. When children of this age are given familiar toys and asked to remember as many as possible, they play with the toys less and spend more time naming them than children not asked to remember (Baker-Ward, Ornstein, & Holden, 1984). As they grow older, children make use of other techniques for retaining information in short-term memory, such as organization (e.g., Bjorklund & Muir, 1988).

The development of memory for source has also been the focus of some research. At Scarborough College, Gopnik and Graf (1988) studied the ability of three- to six-year-olds to remember how they had learned about the contents of a drawer—that is, whether they saw what was in the drawer, heard about it, or figured it out from a clue that they were given. Their memory for the source of the information improved considerably, particularly if a delay was imposed between learning about the contents of the drawer and being asked to remember how they had learned that information.

Memory development follows the expansion of knowledge, particularly domain-specific knowledge pertaining to particular areas of life and activity. As domain-specific knowledge increases, new information becomes more meaningful and familiar. As a result, it is processed more efficiently and entered more readily into long-term memory (e.g., Howe et al., 1989; Bjorklund, 1987).

Children also acquire increasingly sophisticated **scripts**—mental representations of expected sequences of events—as they grow older. This improves their episodic memory—that is, memory for the events in their own lives. Recent findings indicate that even those who lack the verbal skills to describe scripts—even children only one or two years old—can act out rudimentary scripts for various situations—for example, with toys (e.g., Bauer & Mandler, 1992). Children as young as three can give simple scripts for everyday activities. Four- and five-year-olds were observed in three day care centers in Montreal; by playing out pretend scripts, these children improved their social competence (Doyle & Connoly, 1989). Most relevant here, however, is the contribution that scripts make to children's episodic memories for events in their own lives. At Laval University, Loranger and his associates (1989) showed that students in grades 4, 6, 10, and 13 have scripts for entering and leaving the classroom, the roles of students and teachers, and various school activities, including recess time.

A good example of the expansion of knowledge as it relates to life experience is the recent work done by Dalhousie researchers McGrath and McAlpine (1993) about how children develop an understanding of pain (see Table 8.1).

McGrath and McAlpine list the various kinds of learning that contribute to children's understanding of pain: imitation (of a parent or sibling, perhaps); positive reinforcement (attention or contact comfort); and punishment (for crying, for example).

Scripts: *Mental representations of the sequence of events in a given situation.*

Research in Canada

Patrick J. McGrath and daughter Mika
Dalhousie University

TABLE 8.1

Developmental Sequence of Children's Understanding of Pain

0–3 months	No apparent understanding of pain; memory for pain likely but not conclusively demonstrated; responses appear reflexive and are perceptually dominated
3–6 months	Pain response supplemented by sadness and anger response
6—18 months	Developing fear of painful situations; words common for pain, e.g., owie, ouchie, boo-boo; localization of pain develops
18–24 months	Use of the word "hurt" to describe pain; beginning to use noncognitive coping strategies
36–60 months	Can give a gross indication of the intensity of the pain, and beginning to use more descriptive adjectives and attach emotional terms such as "sad" or "mad" to the pain
5–7 years	Can more clearly differentiate levels of pain intensity; beginning to use cognitive coping strategies
7–11 years	Can explain the value of pain

They also identify various areas in which development is seen: quality of emotional responding; kinds and accuracy of descriptions, particularly of pain location and its intensity; and ideas about what is going on when they hurt. Moreover, the ways that children cope with pain change over time, from reflexive responding to self-imposed relaxation. In that development, changes in memory, cognition, emotional control, and self-knowledge are all involved.

As they grow older, then, children's scripts become more complete and more sophisticated, with the result that their memory for everyday events improves. So in a sense, memory development throughout childhood reflects children's increasingly sophisticated strategies for retaining information, coupled with a growing knowledge base and all the benefits this new knowledge confers.

METACOGNITION: THINKING ABOUT—AND UNDERSTANDING—THINKING Another important aspect of cognitive development is **metacognition**: what we know about our own cognitive processes. For example, we are abe to think such thoughts as, "I'd better read this paragraph again; I didn't understand it the first time," or, "I'd better make a note of that information—it seems important, and I may want to use it later." Clearly, young children lack such insights in comparison to older children and adults. Yet they are not totally lacking metacognition. Three-year-olds understand that thinking about other things can hinder their performance on a task (Miller & Zalenski, 1982). Four-year-olds have beliefs about the effect that effort has on what they recall (O'Sullivan, 1993). And by the time they are four or five, most children realize that other people can hold false beliefs (Harris, 1991), and that their own memories are limited (Miller & Zalenski, 1982).

At Memorial University, O'Sullivan and Joy (1994) studied metacognition about reading problems. Students in grades 1, 3, 5, and 7 read about the reading problems of four imaginary children. They were given information about the ability of each child and how much effort he or she put into reading. The subjects then suggested the cause of each child's reading problem and recommended what could be done about it. Children at all these grade levels gave complex causal explanations for reading problems, but they were less able to suggest remedies that would clear up the difficulty.

Gradually, as they develop increasing understanding of how their own minds work, children acquire new and more sophisticated schemes for maximizing their efficiency. They combine various strategies for enhancing attention

Metacognition: Awareness and understanding of our own cognitive processes.

and memory, monitor their own progress toward chosen goals, and examine their own understanding of information and feedback as it is received. In short, they become increasingly capable of self-regulation of their own cognitive processes as well as of other aspects of their behavior.

COGNITIVE VARIABILITY AND COGNITIVE DEVELOPMENT All of the changes we have discussed with respect to attention, memory, and metacognition point to the scope of such cognitive change. But how precisely can we tell that these changes are happening? In the past, this basic issue received surprisingly little attention (Siegler, 1994). Recently, however, developmental psychologists have shown growing interest in this important issue (Siegler & Crowley, in press). Current findings point to a high degree of variability in children's thinking—a variability that often increases just before children discover new strategies for solving certain types of problems or develop new ways of thinking about the world (Siegler & Jenkins, 1989). In other words, there is a period of disequilibrium and then a period of consolidation (Walker & Taylor, 1991).

How does increased variability in thinking contribute to cognitive development? Perhaps by allowing us to discover what works and what doesn't work in a given situation. As one researcher puts it (Siegler, 1994, p. 4): "Variability of cognition and action allows us to discover a great deal about the environments toward which the thinking and action are directed." In other words, cognitive variability facilitates learning at a time of life when we are beginners with respect to various tasks. It is at that time, especially, that we can profit from variability in thinking. Of course, other mechanisms may also contribute to cognitive growth. However, focusing on the high levels of variability in young children's thought may advance our knowledge of this key question: When does such development actually take place?

To conclude: The information processing perspective suggests that cognitive development can best be understood as improvement in basic aspects of information processing—in the ways in which we perceive, attend, memorize, retrieve, and manipulate information. This is a very different view of cognitive development from Piaget's. However, in important respects, it is more in line with contemporary psychology. Thus, it seems likely that the information processing approach will continue to provide information about how we come to understand the world around us. See **Key Concepts** for a comparison of these two important perspectives on cognitive development.

KEY POINTS

- According to the information processing perspective, cognitive development involves the increasing ability to actively process, store, retrieve, and manipulate information.

- Infants can form prototypes—mental representations of external stimuli—within hours of birth. They rapidly acquire the ability to notice increasingly fine-grained features of the external world.

- Babies' abilities to focus their attention on tasks they are performing increase rapidly, as does planfulness—the capacity to decide actively where and how to direct attention.

- As they grow older, children acquire increasingly sophisticated strategies for enhancing their own domain-specific knowledge.

- Finally, they acquire metacognition—that is, an increasingly sophisticated understanding of their own cognitive processes.

Moral Development: *Reasoning About Right and Wrong*

Is it ever right to cheat on an exam? What about cheating on income taxes? Would it ever be right to lie to another person—for example, to tell someone that you like their new haircut when you really hate it? Is it okay to remove the pollution-control system from your car in order to improve its fuel efficiency? These are moral questions about what is right and what is wrong in a given situation. As adults, we realize that such matters are complex. Whether a given action is right or wrong may depend on many factors, including the specific circumstances involved, legal considerations, and our own personal code of ethics.

Two Views of Cognitive Development

Piaget's Theory

- There is tension between these drives: assimilation and accommodation.
- Cognitive development is an invariant movement through a fixed order of stages.
- New cognitive abilities appear at each stage:

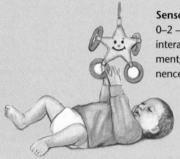

Sensorimotor stage
0–2 — The child begins to interact with the environment; the idea of permanence develops.

Concrete operational stage
7–11 or 12 — The child learns to appreciate such principles as conservation; logical thought emerges.

Preoperational stage
2–6 or 7 — The child begins to represent the world symbolically.

Formal operational stage
12–adulthood — The adolescent becomes capable of logical thought.

Information Processing Perspective

- Children's capacities to process information increase with age.
- Neither the rate nor the order of these changes is invariant.
- Improvements occur with respect to each capacity:

Attention
Children's ability to focus attention and make plans increases with age.

Memory
Children acquire increasing capacity and more sophisticated techniques for enhancing memory.

Sensory processing
The child gains in ability to notice subtle features of the external world.

Metacognition
As children grow, their capacity to regulate their own cognitive processes increases.

But how do children learn the difference between right and wrong? How do they acquire their values and their standards of behavior, and how do they reason about what is good and what is bad? We will examine current thinking on **moral development**, starting with the ideas of Grusec and Goodnow (1994) about how children acquire morals—that is, how they "internalize" values. Then we will examine the idea of Lawrence Kohlberg about how moral reasoning changes from early childhood on when right and wrong choices are not clear at all.

LEARNING THE DIFFERENCE BETWEEN RIGHT AND WRONG University of Toronto researcher Joan Grusec and Jacqueline Goodnow at Macquarie University in Sydney, Australia, have some new ideas about how society's values become incorporated into children's thinking. We all know that the goal of parental discipline is not only to pass on ideas of right and wrong from one generation to the next, but also to empower children to form their own moral codes as they mature and develop and as new situations arise. The requirements of effective discipline are presented as a flow chart in Figure 8.5 (Grusec & Goodnow, 1994).

The main points illustrated in this chart are these: In order for moral values to be acquired by children—that is, in order for *internalization* to occur—two conditions must be met. Both have to do with communication between parent and child. First, the child must listen accurately to what the parent means to say and perceive how important it is. Second, and equally necessary, the child must accept what is being said. Acceptance means three things: "The child must perceive the message as appropriate, the child must be motivated to comply ... and the child must feel that the message ... has been self-generated."

Moral Development: Changes in the capacity to reason about actions' rightness or wrongness that occur with age.

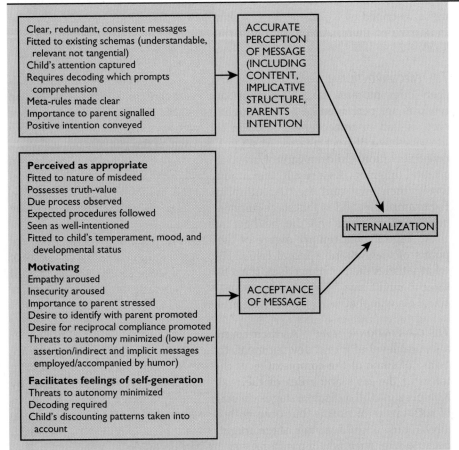

FIGURE 8.5

Features of Parental Discipline

For moral values to be acquired by children, they must listen accurately and accept what is being said.
(Source: Grusec & Goodnow, 1994.)

So accurate perception is necessary for communicating right and wrong; but so is acceptance of the parent's moral message by the child. Successful internalization also relies on the child seeing that message as appropriate, and on the child's self-esteem remaining intact. At the same time, Grusec and Goodnow emphasize that differences between parent and child should be tolerated when it promotes development of a set of values of the child's own.

A different but related focus of much research has been on this question: As we grow older and acquire more experience, how do we change in the reasoning we use to come to conclusions about right and wrong? The most influential view on this has been that of Lawrence Kohlberg (1984). Let's now consider his theory, and some of the evidence relating to it.

KOHLBERG'S STAGES OF MORAL UNDERSTANDING Building on earlier views proposed by Piaget, Kohlberg studied the moral development of boys and men. He suggested that there are three distinct levels of moral reasoning, each divided into two separate phases. In order to determine an individual's stage of moral development, Kohlberg presents an imaginary moral dilemma—that is, a scenario in which at least two different courses of action are possible. Participants then indicate what they would do and why. Note that according to Kohlberg, it is not the decision itself, but rather the explanation for the choice made with respect to right and wrong, that reveals the individual's stage of moral development.

One dilemma is this: A man's wife is ill with a special type of cancer. There is a drug that may save her, but it is very expensive. The pharmacist who discovered this medicine will sell it for $2,000, but the man has only $1,000. He asks the pharmacist to let him pay part of the cost now and the rest later, but the pharmacist refuses. Being desperate, the man steals the drug. Should he have done that? Why?

Let's consider, with reference to this example, the levels of moral development described by Kohlberg, and the kinds of explanations he feels would be indicative of them. An overview of these levels (or stages) is provided in Table 8.2.

THE PRECONVENTIONAL LEVEL At the first level of moral development, children judge morality largely in terms of consequences. Actions that lead to rewards are perceived as good or right; those that lead to punishments are seen as bad or unacceptable. Within the **preconventional level**, Kohlberg describes two distinct phases. At stage 1, known as the *punishment-and-obedience* orientation, children cannot grasp the existence of two points of view in a moral dilemma. As a result, they unquestioningly accept an adult perspective as their own, and use that authority as the basis for behaving morally. For example, a child at this stage might state, "The man should steal the drug because if he lets his wife die, he'll get in trouble."

At stage 2, children are aware of the fact that people can have different points of view about a moral issue. Thus, they judge morality in terms of what satisfies their own needs or what satisfies the needs of others. A child at stage 2 might say, "The man shouldn't steal the drug unless he's so crazy about his wife that he can't live without her."

THE CONVENTIONAL LEVEL As their cognitive abilities increase, children enter a second level of moral development, the **conventional level**. Now they are aware of some of the complexities of the social order and judge morality in terms of the laws and rules of their society. This level, too, is divided by Kohlberg into two distinct stages. In stage 3, people judge morality in terms of social rules or norms (but only with respect to people they know personally). Thus, a child at this stage might state, "It's O.K. to steal the drug, because your friends will not think you are bad if you do."

Preconventional Level (of morality): According to Kohlberg, the earliest stage of moral development, in which individuals judge morality in terms of the effects produced by various actions.

Conventional Level (of morality): According to Kohlberg, a stage of moral development during which individuals judge morality largely in terms of existing social norms or rules.

In stage 4, the *social-order-maintaining* orientation, judgments of morality include the perspective of third persons in general, not just of themselves or people they know. Moreover, such judgments are for all people, not only friends or relatives. For example, a child at stage 4 who argues for stealing the drug might state, "The man should steal the drug since that's what you do after you take a marriage vow to stand by your wife." Similarly, a child who argues against stealing the drug might say, "It's wrong to steal. If everybody did that, society couldn't exist."

THE POSTCONVENTIONAL LEVEL   Finally, in adolescence or early adulthood, many (though by no means all) individuals enter a third level known as the **postconventional level**, or principled level. At this stage, people judge morality in terms of abstract principles and values, rather than in terms of existing laws or rules of society. At stage 5, people realize that laws can sometimes be inconsistent with the rights of individuals or the interests of the majority, and that such laws should be changed. Individuals at this stage of moral development might reason as follows: "Although it is against the law to steal, stealing the drug is justified. In this case, that is because life is more important than property." Or if they argue for not stealing the drug, they might state, "There is a law against stealing, and it represents the will of the majority—how people have decided to live together in society. By living in that society, the man agrees to maintain its laws, so stealing the drug is a violation of this agreement."

Finally, in stage 6, individuals judge the morality of actions in terms of self-chosen ethical principles. Individuals who attain this highest level of moral development believe that certain obligations and values may transcend the laws of society in certain very specific situations. The rules they follow are abstract and ethical, not concrete (like the Ten Commandments) and are based on inner conscience rather than external sources of authority. Individuals at stage 6 might argue for stealing the drug as follows: "If the man doesn't steal the drug, he is putting property above human life; that makes no sense. People could live together without private property, but not without respect for human life." In contrast, if they argue for not stealing the drug, they might state, "If the man stole the drug he wouldn't be blamed by others, but he would probably blame himself, since he has violated his own standards of honesty and has furthered his own needs at the expense of another person."

EVIDENCE CONCERNING KOHLBERG'S THEORY   Do we really pass through the series of stages described by Kohlberg, and become increasingly sophisticated in our judgments of morality as we gain more experience? Many studies do support at least his broad outline. According to a review of many cross-sectional studies (with a total of more than 6,000 participants), moral maturity, as measured by Kohlberg's system, does increase with age (Pratt et al., 1988; Rest, 1986). Several longitudinal studies also find that as people grow older, increasing numbers of them enter higher levels of moral development (e.g., Colby et al., 1983). Also, in many different cultures, people do move through the stages described by Kohlberg.

However, such progress is more variable and less universal than Kohlberg assumed. Also, moral reasoning is strongly affected by environmental factors, such as level of formal education (Rest & Thomas, 1985, 1985), parents' child-rearing practices (Boyes & Allen, 1993; Walker & Taylor, 1991), and culture. For information on the effects of culture, see **Perspectives On Diversity**.

SEX DIFFERENCES IN MORAL DEVELOPMENT: IS KOHLBERG'S THEORY SEX-BIASED?
Perhaps the most controversial aspect of Kohlberg's theory was the early finding that females lag behind males in terms of level of moral reasoning.

Postconventional Level (of morality): According to Kohlberg, the final stage of moral development, in which individuals judge morality in terms of abstract principles.

TABLE 8.2

Kohlberg's Theory of
Moral Development: A
Summary
According to Kohlberg, we move
through three distinct levels of
moral development.

LEVEL/STAGE	DESCRIPTION
Preconventional level	
Stage 1: Punishment-and-obedience orientation	Morality judged in terms of consequences.
Stage 2: Naive hedonistic orientation	Morality judged in terms of what satisfies own needs or those of others.
Conventional level	
Stage 3: Good boy-good girl orientation	Morality judged in terms of adherence to social rules or norms with respect to personal acquaintances.
Stage 4: Social-order-maintaining orientation	Morality judged in terms of social rules or laws applied universally, not just to acquaintances.
Postconventional level	
Stage 5: Legalistic orientation	Morality judged in terms of human rights, which may transcend laws.
Stage 6: Universal ethical principle orientation	Morality judged in terms of self-chosen ethical principles.

Specifically, studies reported that girls attain stage 3 but progress no further, while boys move on to stages 4, 5, and 6 (Holstein, 1976). In reply, Gilligan (1982) argued that Kohlberg's theory is sex-biased. She pointed out that Kohlberg did not include females in his original research. Also, that within Kohlberg's theory, morality is judged solely on the ability to reason abstractly about moral dilemmas, and for this reason overlooks an equally plausible factor in moral judgments: concern for others. According to Gilligan, females move through several stages of moral development based on that factor. In other words, women's morality is based more on concerns for interpersonal approval and maintaining positive relationships, while men's morality includes abstract principles. Thus, at first women make moral judgments in terms of concrete commitments to specific people (stage 3). Later, they shift to an abstract understanding of care as a universal obligation, which is a form of postconventional reasoning. The idea here is that males and females are equal in terms of the complexity of their moral reasoning; but they have different priorities.

Does Kohlberg's theory underestimate the moral maturity of females? It must be noted that most later studies (e.g., Pratt et al., 1988) contradict the earlier results to which Gilligan had raised her objections: On both hypothetical dilemmas and everyday moral problems, females have scored as high as males (Walker & DeVries, 1985). Indeed, in some research, females scored higher. Moreover, when asked to recall personal moral conflicts they had actually experienced, males and females of various ages did not differ as to whether they described those in terms of concerns for impersonal rights, or in terms of caring for others and personal relationships (Walker, 1988). Thus, there is little reliable evidence that the two sexes judge morality on different sets of principles. Despite this confusion, Gilligan's contribution is important. She called attention to the fact that evaluating moral development solely in terms of rights and justice is not enough; concern for the welfare of others must also be taken into account (Galotti, Kozberg, & Farmer, 1991).

This general conclusion may not be quite complete. At Dalhousie University, Ozier and Morris (1987) identified a

- Kohlberg's theory of moral development suggests that all human beings move through a series of stages of moral reasoning: preconventional, conventional, and postconventional.

- Longitudinal research indicates that moral reasoning does increase with age. However, environmental factors, such as level of education, parents' child-rearing practices, and cultural traditions, influence its development.

- Contrary to initial findings, there is now no reason to believe that males and females attain different levels of moral development.

PERSPECTIVES ON DIVERSITY

Moral Development: Universal or Culture-Related?

In technologically advanced cultures, longitudinal research indicates that many individuals move through the stages outlined by Kohlberg. On the basis of those findings, Leroux (1986) has made some recommendations for training students in educational settings. But what about other cultures? Is the same progression seen? Growing evidence indicates that it is not. For example, in isolated peasant and tribal communities studied by Boyes and Walker (1988), few if any people reached stage 4. This finding does not reflect communication problems, because even in these cultures, the research participants understand the dilemmas presented to them and view the issues raised as important and familiar (Walker, 1988). Rather, the absence of stage 4 (and higher reasoning) relates to the absence of contact with formalized systems of government, law, and ethics. Experience with such systems seems to be necessary for the upper stages of moral reasoning.

Evidence for that conclusion was provided by a comparison of American children and kibbutz-raised Israeli children (Fuchs et al., 1986). Kibbutz-raised children scored higher on moral development than Americans from age thirteen on, and a higher proportion eventually reached stage 5. The explanation referred to the fact that children on kibbutzim participate regularly in the cooperative institutions of their society. For this reason, it might be expected that they would score higher in moral development than other children who do not have that experience.

Does Kohlberg's theory apply only to societies that emphasize institutionalized moral values and individual rights? India's society is as complex as ours but has different ideas about how to resolve moral issues. There, moral-reasoning interviews were conducted with middle-class people ranging in age from 11 to over 50 (Vasudev & Hummel, 1987). The religions of the participants included Hindu, Jain, and Sikh. All these religions emphasize nonviolence as a basic moral value, as well as the interrelatedness of all forms of life. Also, Indian cultural traditions emphasize collective solutions to moral dilemmas, rather than appeals to private conscience.

This study found that moral reasoning did increase with age. About 20 percent of adults gave postconventional responses. However, cultural factors also played an important role. Many participants were reluctant to select a solution to the problem of the man and the drug. Instead, they suggested the solution should be worked out in terms of the needs of the entire society, not of a single individual. Similar comments have also been obtained from Israeli and Chinese participants (Hwang, 1986).

What do these findings mean? On the one hand, it seems that Kohlberg's theory does indeed tap universal dimensions of moral reasoning—dimensions that exist in all cultures. On the other hand, what is right in one culture may be wrong in another, and vice versa, even when the people in both groups recognize the same complexities and issues in a given situation. Where morality is concerned, then, we must consider not only universal principles but also important culture-based factors.

CULTURAL INFLUENCES ON MORAL DEVELOPMENT

Children raised on Israeli kibbutzim, where a sense of community is emphasized, score higher on moral development than American children of the same ages. What underlying reasons might help explain this difference?

different methodological problem in Kohlberg's research. The dilemmas he used were all about moral choices of men. That is, the main figure in each dilemma was male (i.e., had a male name). In the Dalhousie study, male and female students were presented with the same dilemmas, but there were two versions of each—Kohlberg's original with a male name for the main figure, and one with a female name for the main figure. The results of this study (Sara Morris's honors thesis) were surprising. They showed that both males and females set higher moral standards for the behavior of members of their *own* sex and lower moral standards for members of the *opposite* sex.

Social and Emotional Development: *Forming Relationships with Others*

Cognitive development is a crucial aspect of human growth. Yet it does not occur in a social vacuum. As Chris Moore and Valerie Corkum (1994) suggest, there is development of some social understanding by the end of the first year of life. At the same time that infants and children are acquiring the capacities to think, reason, and use language, they are also gaining the basic experiences, skills, and emotions that permit them to form close relationships with others, and to interact effectively in a wide range of settings. How does such social and emotional development occur? What are its important milestones? It is on these and related questions that we'll focus next. (We'll postpone our consideration of personality development, and an influential theory proposed by Erikson, till Chapter 9.)

Emotional Development and Temperament

At what age do infants experience different emotions? They can't describe their subjective feelings in words, so to answer these questions, we study their facial expressions—that is, their outward signs of distinct emotions. Research on emotional development has documented that such expressions appear very soon after birth (Izard, 1992). Infants as young as two months express emotion—social smiling in response to human faces (but not to objects; Ellsworth et el., 1993). By the time they are three or four months old, they laugh (Sroufe & Waters, 1976). Other emotions, such as anger, sadness, and surprise, also appear very early and are easily recognized by adults.

Interestingly, some expressions appear and then change. For example, following medical inoculations, two-month-old infants express pain on their faces more frequently than anger (Izard, Hembree, & Huebner, 1987). A few months later, however, they show anger more often than pain, and this difference increases during the next year. These findings, and many others, underscore an important point: Emotional development and cognitive development occur simultaneously, and there are many connections between them. The finding that anger in response to painful experiences becomes increasingly common during the first eighteen months of life can be interpreted as the result of infants' growing ability to understand who or what has caused their discomfort. Before the age of seven months, infants cannot tell, but after this age, they can. Thus, the sharp rise in anger at that time.

Much research has been devoted to discovering the imitative abilities of infants in the first weeks after birth. As you already know, very young infants imitate the facial expressions of people—for example, an open mouth or a protruding tongue. Note, however, that they do not imitate those of objects. At York University, Legerstee (1990) had infants watch an adult mouth vowel sounds. The adults were actually silent; the sounds came from a tape recorder. Sometimes the sounds matched the vowel that was being mouthed, and sometimes there was a mismatch between the visual and the auditory information. At about four months, infants imitated only when the auditory and visual information indicated the same vowel sound. With respect also to their responses to speech, recent studies show that young infants do have a preference for infant-directed speech (i.e., baby talk, or talk that is directed to infants) over adult-directed speech. This is true in many cultures and languages, including those of Britain, France, Germany, Italy, Japan, Mandarin China, and the United States (Pegg et al., 1992). Why this should be the case is not clear, but baby talk may be effective because it grabs the attention of the infant or because it communicates positive emotion (McLeod, 1993).

As they grow older, babies also become increasingly able to comprehend the emotional expressions of others (Strayer, 1985). For example, at three months, they become upset when their mother's face remains immobile (Stack & Muir, 1990; Tronick, 1989). This happens even when the mother's expression is neutral. However, touching the infant (while keeping the face still) seems to reduce the distress (Stack & Muir, 1992). By eight or ten months, infants actively seek out information about other people's feelings and begin **social referencing**—that is, using the reactions of others to evaluate uncertain situations. Thus, after a fall, a one-year-old will look at the caregivers and, depending on their reactions, will cry or merely continue whatever he or she was doing (Walden & Ogan, 1988).

Finally, children improve in their ability to regulate their own emotional reactions. As infants, they have very little capacity to do this, but as preschoolers, they make an effort to understand and control their own internal states. For example, they may cover their eyes or ears to avoid stimuli they find disturbing, and they may talk to themselves to reduce anxiety (e.g., "Mommy said she'd be right back."). These abilities increase throughout the school years. By the time they are ten, most children can engage in fairly sophisticated strategies for regulating their own emotions; for example, they lower their expectations in order to minimize the threat of failure (Altshuler & Ruble, 1989). By the same age, children have learned how to regulate the emotions of others. Children between ages four and nine (volunteers at the Ontario Science Centre) were able to identify ways they could behave that would reduce the emotions of the parents—for example, the anger that occurs during an argument. Their choices were: "give ... a hug, play games ..., be very good, make ... a card or picture, smile ..." (Covell & Miles, 1992). Moreover, parents rated these as effective ways of doing just what the children intended.

As they grow older, then, children gain increasing ability to express emotions, regulate them, and recognize and even regulate the emotions of others. These are important changes and they lead to more and more complex social interactions during the early years of life.

TEMPERAMENT: INDIVIDUAL DIFFERENCES IN EMOTIONAL STYLE Do you know anyone who is almost always cheerful and upbeat—a true optimist? And what about the other extreme: Do you know someone who is reserved and usually irritable and gloomy? Psychologists refer to such stable individual differences in the quality and intensity of emotional reactions as **temperament**. There is growing evidence that these differences are present very early in life—perhaps even at birth (e.g., Kagan & Snidman, 1991). In fact, systematic research on temperament indicates that infants fit into one of four basic categories in this respect (Thomas & Chess, 1977). About 40 percent of infants are easy children. They quickly establish regular routines in infancy, are generally cheerful, and adapt easily to new experiences. In contrast, about 10 percent are difficult children. They are irregular in daily routines, are slow to accept new situations or experiences, and have many negative reactions, such as crying more than other infants. About 15 percent can be described as

Social Referencing: Using others' reactions to appraise an uncertain situation or experience.

Temperament: Stable individual differences in the quality of emotional reactions.

"slow to warm up" children. They are relatively inactive and apathetic and have mild negative reactions to many new situations or experiences. The remaining 35 percent cannot be readily classified under one of these headings. Obviously, parents of children in the first group have a much easier time dealing with their offspring than those in the latter categories.

How stable are such differences in temperament? Research findings are mixed. On the one hand, several studies have reported that attentiveness, activity level, and irritability are quite stable (Ruff et al., 1990). For example, Kagan, Snidman, and Arcus (1992), tested several hundred infants when the babies were four months old and, on the basis of those tests, put them into two categories: high-reactive or low-reactive. High-reactive infants showed fretting, crying, and a high level of motor activity when exposed to unfamiliar events (tape-recorded human voices, unpleasant tastes, moving mobiles). Low-reactive infants showed low motor activity and minimal crying. The researchers tested both groups again at fourteen months, by observing their reactions as they encountered unfamiliar rooms, people, toys, and procedures (e.g., placement of a blood pressure cuff on their arm, facial and vocal disapproval from the researcher, a request to test liquid from a dropper). Results indicated that 50 percent of the high-reactive children had a high level of fear, while only 10 percent of the low-reactive infants did. Similar results were obtained when the children were tested again at twenty-one months of age (see Figure 8.6). In related research (Kagan, Reznick, & Snidman, 1988), differences such as these were found to remain into middle childhood.

On the other hand, the long-term stability in various aspects of temperament may occur only for those who are relatively extreme on these dimensions (Kagan, Reznick, & Gibbons, 1989). So, although temperament may be influenced by genetic factors, and tends to be quite stable, it does not seem to be etched in stone. Rather, temperament may be changed by experience and by other factors, such as child-rearing practices (Otaki et al., 1986).

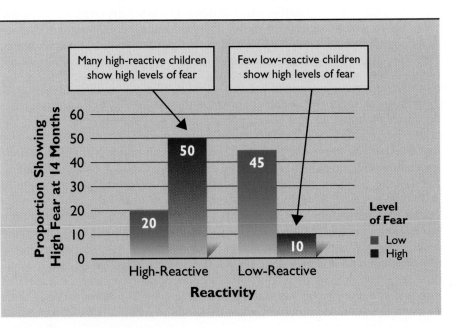

FIGURE 8.6

The Stability of Temperament

Four-month-olds who showed fretting, crying, and a high level of motor activity when exposed to unfamiliar events (high-reactive infants) were much more likely than infants who did not fret or cry (low-reactive infants) to show a high level of fear when tested again in unfamiliar situations at fourteen months. These findings suggest that some aspects of temperament are quite stable over time.
(Source: Based on data from Kagan, Snidman, & Arcus, 1992.)

Whatever the relative contributions of genetic and environmental factors to temperament, individual differences have important implications for social development. For example, a much higher proportion of difficult than easy children experience behavioral problems later in life (Chess & Thomas, 1984). They find it more difficult to adjust to school, to form friendships, and to get along with others. In addition, many high-reactive children demonstrate shyness as they grow older and enter an increasingly broad range of social situations. This can be a serious problem for them and may adversely influence many aspects of later social development (Kagan, Reznick, & Snidman, 1988).

Attachment: *The Beginnings of Love*

Do infants love their parents? They can't say so directly, but by the time they are six or seven months old, most are bonded emotionally to the people who care for them (Ainsworth, 1973; Lamb, 1977). Infants recognize their mothers, fathers, and other caregivers, smile at them more than at other people, seek them out, and protest when separated from them. This bond between infants and their caregivers is known as **attachment** and is, in an important sense, the first form of love we experience.

What are the origins of this initial form of love? One explanation emphasizes the role of learning. Caregivers provide for infants' needs, so caregivers are associated with many forms of reward. Thus, both operant conditioning and classical conditioning may play a role in the formation of attachment.

An alternative view of attachment is the **ethological theory**, first proposed by Bowlby (1969). According to this theory, infants are born with behaviors that elicit parental care and thus increase their chances of survival. These behaviors include sucking, clinging, crying, smiling, gazing at the caregiver's face, and (later) crawling after the caregiver. As infants emit these behaviors, they elicit attention and caring behavior from adults. Accordingly, this cycle lays the foundation for reciprocal bonds of attachment.

Either way, most often, if the infant's needs are attended reliably, and if the infant can count on a response when distressed, then a basis for trust is established by affectionate ties between the child and the significant others. Sometimes, however, bonding goes bad. If the child is mistreated and hurt—by rejection, neglect, or abuse, or a combination of these—the basis is laid for serious attachment problems. For example, the "unattached child" is self-destructive, deceitful and cruel to others, without friends, and unable to offer or accept affection. In adult life, this individual's psychopathic behavior may be a serious threat to the safety of others (Magid & McKelvey, 1993).

MEASURING ATTACHMENT: REACTIONS TO THE STRANGE SITUATION TEST How can the strength of attachment be measured? Mary Ainsworth and her colleagues (e.g., Ainsworth et al., 1978) observed babies in situations were fear and distress occurred. In such situations, children seek comfort from their caregiver; and the stronger their attachment, the greater their comfort in that person's presence—and the stronger their fear in his or her absence. In assessing attachment, researchers expose babies to the sequence of events shown in Table 8.3. The mother and baby are placed in an unfamiliar room, and a stranger enters. The mother departs and returns. As each event occurs, the baby's reactions are carefully noted. Do they cry when the mother leaves? How do they react to her when she returns? Do they appear confident in her presence, despite the presence of a stranger? These are the kinds of questions considered. (Note that most of this research has focused on the attachment between infants and their mothers. Presumably, the same procedures could be applied to fathers or any other caregivers.)

Attachment: *A strong affectional bond between infants and their caregivers.*

Ethological Theory: *(of attachment): A theory suggesting that infants are born with a set of behaviors that elicit parental care and so increase the infants' chances of survival.*

TABLE 8.3

EPISODE	PERSONS PRESENT	DURATION	EVENTS/PROCEDURES
1	Mother and baby	30 seconds	Experimenter brings mother and baby to room; leaves
2	Mother and baby	3 minutes	Baby plays; mother seated
3	Mother, baby, stranger	3 minutes	Stranger enters; talks to mother
4	Stranger and baby	3 minutes (or less)	Mother leaves room; stranger remains; offers comfort to the baby
5	Mother and baby	3 minutes (or more)	Mother returns, greets baby, offers comfort
6	Baby alone	3 minutes (or less)	Mother leaves room
7	Stranger and baby	3 minutes (or less)	Stranger enters room, offers comfort
8	Mother and baby	3 minutes	Mother returns; offers comfort

Sequence of Events in the Strange Situation

The *strange situation* is used to study infants' attachment to their mothers. Researchers carefully study the infants' reactions to each of the events described here so as to determine the strength and nature of their attachment bonds to their mothers.
(Source: Adapted from Ainsworth et al., 1978.)

Strange Situation Test: A procedure for studying attachment in which mothers leave their infants alone with a stranger for several minutes and then return.

Secure Attachment: A pattern of attachment in which infants actively seek contact with their mother and take comfort from her presence when they are reunited with her during Strange Situation Test.

Avoidant Attachment: A pattern of attachment in which infants don't cry when their mother leaves them alone during the Strange Situation Test.

Resistant Attachment: A pattern of attachment in which infants reject their mother and refuse to be comforted by her after she leaves them alone during the Strange Situation Test.

Disorganized or Disoriented Attachment: A pattern of attachment in which infants show contradictory reactions to their mother after being reunited with her during the Strange Situation Test.

This **Strange Situation Test**, as it is often called, has been used to study attachment in young children. The results reveal that most children show one of four different patterns of attachment to their caregiver. About 67 percent of middle-class babies show **secure attachment**. They may or may not cry on separation from their mothers, but if they do, it is because of her absence; they take little comfort from the presence of a stranger. When she returns, they actively seek contact with her, and crying is reduced at once. About 20 percent show **avoidant attachment**. They don't cry when their mother leaves, and they react to the stranger in much the same way as to their mother. When the mother returns, they typically avoid her or are slow to greet her. About 10 percent of American middle-class babies show a different pattern known as **resistant attachment**. Before separation, these infants seek contact with their mother. After she returns, however, they seem angry and they push her away. Many continue to cry, even after she picks them up and attempts to comfort them. Finally, about 5 percent of middle-class infants show **disorganized** or **disoriented attachment**. When reunited with their mothers, these babies show disorganized or even contradictory responses. They look away from the mother while being held by her, or approach her with a lack of emotion. They show a dazed facial expression and often adopt odd, frozen postures after being comforted.

Differences in patterns of attachment are significant, because these children differ in other respects as well. For example, those who are securely attached are more sociable, better at solving certain kinds of problems, and more flexible and persistent in many situations than children who are avoidantly or insecurely attached (Pastor, 1981). Moreover, securely attached children experience fewer behavioral problems during later childhood and late adolescence (Blain et al., 1993; Fagot & Kavanaugh, 1990). These patterns of attachment persist, and may even affect adult romantic relationships (Simpson, 1990; Vormbrock, 1993.)

Which factors determine the pattern of attachment shown by a child? Several seem to play a role. For example, children who experience maternal deprivation—for example, separation from their mother as a consequence of being placed for adoption—may not form secure attachments to any caregiver, and may later experience a wide range of behavioral problems, ranging from depression to an excessive desire for adult attention (e.g., Hodges &

Tizard, 1989). Animal studies have shown that maternal deprivation may predispose rats to increased alcohol consumption and susceptibility to stress as adults (Rockman et al., 1987). Moreover, infants who "fail to thrive" may also develop a relationship disorder with their caregivers (Benoit et al., 1989).

Quality of caregiving also plays a role. Maternal sensitivity is important to secure attachment of normal children (Pederson et al., 1990), and of children whose development occurs later than usual (Moran et al., 1992). When caregivers are sensitive to the needs and signals of children, infants are much more likely to form secure attachments (Isabella & Belsky, 1991). In contrast, avoidant infants tend to have mothers who are either intrusive or overstimulating—that is, who act without waiting for signals from their infants.

Here is a contemporary question that has important relevance to these findings: What do we know about attachment and infants in day care? Does placing children in day care centers interfere with their forming secure attachments to their parents? For information on this issue, see **Canadian Focus**.

CANADIAN FOCUS

Is Day Care a Threat to Secure Attachment?

In the 1990s, in most Canadian families of preschoolers, there is a single parent who works, or there are two parents who both work, and that work is usually full-time. Most often, the problem of how to care for a child while also earning a living is seen as that of the mother. However, the issue is becoming so common that it is now a matter for public policy. For example, a study conducted at the University of Guelph (Lero, 1992) found that at least one in every two very young Canadian children requires child care while the parents (or single parents) are at work.

The options available to parents vary. Often, grandparents are enlisted. Many senior citizens in Canada provide some kind of child care for relatives—some of it being full-time day care. Sometimes, neighbors or other relatives become caregivers.

Also, many infants and toddlers spend their days in full-time day care centers. For those who are able to obtain one of the 300,000 places available (for 3,000,000 children under age twelve), the economic cost can be significant. It ranges from $70 a week in Saint John, New Brunswick, to $134 a week in the Toronto suburbs—that is, from $3,600 to about $7,000 a year. Perhaps more important, the personal costs are serious. For example, studies at the University of British Columbia find that mothers who work outside the home feel guilty, although those who do not also fell uneasy—albeit in a different way (Hall, 1991).

Some private sector companies have begun to provide day care for their workers. For example, Chemex Labs in North Vancouver introduced on-site day care for its employees in late 1991. The result was positive, because the company was able to attract excellent new female employees, and the savings in reduced absenteeism helped reduce the program's costs. However, programs like this one are still not common in either the private or the public sector. In 1986, legislation was proposed to create a national day care system in Canada. It would have created 200,000 more places over seven years. That plan was scrapped because the $4 billion required was needed elsewhere. Since then, many working Canadians have asked whether the needs of children are a government priority.

One public project that has been initiated has a different purpose—to keep teen mothers in school. In 1993 there were said to be twenty-five child care centers in high schools across Canada—for example, in Fredericton and Etobicoke. These provided, in addition to care for infants, instruction in parenting in general, and in how to handle specific infant difficulties— for example, teething and diaper rashes. The success of this project has been important.

Let us now turn our attention to a different question: How do children raised in day care centers compare with those raised at home? More specifically, does being separated from the parents affect the child's ability to form secure attachments? One finding, by Belsky and Braungart (1991), has suggested that this might be the case. In that study, infants in day care centers showed slightly higher rates of insecure attachment in the strange situation than infants raised at home (34 percent versus 29 percent).

But is this higher rate of insecure attachment an effect of day care? The answer is no. More than two-thirds of infants of working mothers are securely attached (Thompson, 1988). Moreover, comparisons of young adolescents who took care of themselves after school with those who spent their after-school hours in the care of adults (Galambos & Maggs, 1991) found "that self-care adolescents who stayed in the home were not different on any variable studied from those adolescents in adult care." The variables these researchers looked at included coping ability, emotional tone, and impulse control—all of these taken to be measures of adolescent self-image—and several measures of interactions with peers.

The fact that most infants cared for in day care centers form secure attachments despite the absence of their parents—on most days—suggests that day care, in and of itself, does not interfere with attachment. The slightly higher rates of insecure attachment among infants in day care may stem from other factors that are quite distinct from day care itself. The parents of such children

may be stressed from full-time work and may not interact with their children as often or as well as those who do not work outside the home. Perhaps it is that factor, and not day care, that interferes with attachment.

Finally, much hinges on the quality of the day care infants receive. In a day care center with a large number of children and few adults, any one child may be ignored. Attachment, and other aspects of development, may indeed suffer as a result. But in centers where children receive high levels of social stimulation and attention from adults, those negative effects may not occur. In fact, under these conditions, children benefit much from the special care they receive.

In sum, existing evidence indicates that day care, in and of itself, is neither a definite plus nor a clear-cut minus where social development is concerned. What is more important is that the quality of care children receive both at home and in the day care center be good.

HARLOW'S STUDIES OF ATTACHMENT

Although the wire "mothers" used in Harlow's experiments provided the monkey babies with nourishment, the babies preferred the soft cloth "mothers" which provided contact comfort. What do these famous experiments demonstrate?

CONTACT COMFORT AND ATTACHMENT: THE SOFT TOUCH OF LOVE An additional factor that plays an important role in attachment is close physical contact between infants and their caregivers. In short, attachment rests partly on touching—that is, on the hugs, cuddles, and caresses babies receive from adults (Stack & Muir, 1992). The classic research that first established this fact was conducted by Harry Harlow and his colleagues.

When Harlow began his research, infant attachment was not on his mind. Rather, he was interested in the effects of brain damage on learning. Since he could not perform such tests with humans, he worked with rhesus monkeys. In order to prevent baby monkeys from catching various diseases, Harlow raised them in isolation, away from their mothers and each other. This practice led to a surprising observation. Many of the infants became quite attached to small scraps of cloth in their cages. They would hold tightly to these "security blankets" and protest strongly when they were removed for cleaning. This led Harlow to wonder about this special need for contact with soft materials.

In order to find out more about that, Harlow built the two artificial mothers shown in the photo on the left. As you can see, one consisted of bare wire while the other possessed a soft terrycloth cover; however, the infant monkeys could get milk only from the wire mother. According to the conditioning explanation of attachment, they should soon have developed a strong bond to this cold wire mother, which was the source of all their nourishment. In fact, this was not what happened. Instead, the infants spent almost all of their time clinging tightly to the soft, cloth-covered mother. Only when driven by pangs of hunger did they leave to obtain milk from the wire mother.

Additional and even more dramatic evidence that the infants formed strong bonds with the cloth mothers was obtained in further research (Harlow & Harlow, 1966), in which young monkeys were exposed to various forms of rejection by their artificial mothers. Some of the mothers blew them away with strong jets of air; others contained metal spikes that suddenly appeared from inside the cloth covering and pushed the infants away. However, none of these actions had any lasting effects on the infants' attachment. They waited until these periods of rejection were over and then clung to the cloth mother as tightly as before.

On the basis of these and related findings, Harlow concluded that a young monkey's attachment to its mother rests, at least in part, on her ability to satisfy its need for contact comfort. The satisfaction of other physical needs, such as for food, is not enough.

Do such effects occur among human infants as well? Some studies seem to suggest so. For example, two- and three-year-old children placed in a strange room play for longer periods of time without becoming distressed if their security blanket is present (Passman & Weisberg, 1975). In fact, they play almost as long as they do when their mother is in the room. These findings suggest that for blanket-attached children, the presence of this object provides comfort and reassurance similar to that provided by the mother. So human infants, too, may have a need for contact comfort, and the gentle hugs, caresses, and cuddles they obtain from their caregivers promote secure attachment (Stack & Muir, 1992).

FATHERS AND ATTACHMENT   Even though many mothers work at full-time jobs outside the home, most of them are still the primary caregivers for their children. Yet there can be little doubt that infants form strong attachments to their fathers, even though they often spend less time together. Careful study of patterns of parent-child interaction indicates that mothers spend more time providing physical care to their children, while fathers spend more time in playful interactions with them (Roopnarine et al., 1990). Further, mothers and fathers engage in different types of play with their offspring. Mothers provide toys, talk to infants, and initiate games such as peekaboo; fathers engage in more physical play, such as lifting, swinging, and bouncing their infants. These differences persist even when fathers are the primary caregivers; they still interact with their children in a more vigorously physical manner (Yogman, 1981).

Do fathers play a special role in children's development? A growing number of psychologists believe that they do (Kerig et al., 1993). For example, fathers discipline their children in accordance with established and specific rules, while mothers discipline them on a moment-by-moment basis. Also, fathers worry more about future success, while mothers worry more about the infant's welfare (Gibbs, 1993). Thus, children acquire somewhat different skills and information from their two parents. As one psychologist puts it (Shapiro, 1993): "Kids learn from their moms how to be aware of their emotional side. From dad, they learn how to live in society." Of course, these generalizations do not apply to all, or perhaps even to most, families. Yet there is growing concern in many quarters over the absence of fathers in a large number of families. In Canada, it is estimated that because of divorce, other single-parent situations, special demands of employment, and other factors, as many as half of all children spend part of their childhood without a father in residence. What effect does this have on their development? Evidence on this issue is just beginning to emerge (Phares & Compas, 1992). Not only mothers but also fathers are important to infants, but perhaps in different ways.

KEY POINTS

- Infants quickly form a strong emotional bond with their caregiver; this is known as attachment.

- The strength of attachment is often measured by the strange situation. Many factors, including maternal deprivation, family circumstances, and culture influence the strength of attachment.

- Placing infants in day care facilities does not necessarily interfere with the formation of secure attachment to parents.

- Contact comfort—close physical contact between infants and caregivers—also plays a role in the formation of attachment.

Gender: The Development of Gender Identity and Sex-Stereotyped Behavior

At least from birth, **gender**—the fact that we belong to one sex or the other—plays a crucial role in our lives. Consider that the first words spoken about newborns refer to their sex. From the moment that parents hear "It's a girl!" or "It's a boy!" they think about and behave toward their child in ways that differ. In this section we'll consider the important effects of gender on social development. First we will examine several views of how children acquire **gender identity**—the understanding that they belong to one gender or the other. Next, we'll turn to **sex-stereotyped behavior**—how children acquire the stereotyped beliefs and patterns of behavior that society associates with each sex.

Gender Identity: Some Contrasting Views

At what age does a child become aware of being a girl or a boy—of belonging to one of the two sexes? This process begins very early in life; by the time they are two, many children have learned to use *gender labels* appropriately. They refer to themselves as a boy or a girl, and they correctly label others as well. However, they are still uncertain about the implications of gender differences. When asked, "Could you ever become a daddy?" up until the age of about three-and-a-half, girls say yes. In the same way, little boys say they could become mothers. Between three-and-a-half and four-and-a-half, however, children begin to understand **gender constancy**—that is, the fact that gender is stable over time. Is this late development due to children's cognitive immaturity? Recent evidence suggests that perhaps there is another factor: a child's lack of knowledge about genital differences between the sexes. Children as young as three who are aware of genital differences show a grasp of gender constancy (Bem, 1989).

But how do children acquire gender identity? Several different theories have been proposed. According to social learning theory, observational learning and operant conditioning are involved. For example, through observational learning, children gradually match their behaviors to those of same-sex individuals, especially those of their parents. Moreover, such imitation is actively reinforced by adults.

As children become increasingly similar to their same-sex parent, they gradually recognize their similarities and conclude that they are "a girl like Mommy" or "a boy like Daddy." For example, at the University of Quebec at Montreal, Pomerleau and her associates (1990) gave this summary of their research findings. "Boys were provided with more sports equipment, tools and large and small vehicles. Girls had more dolls, fictional characters, child's furniture, and other toys for manipulation. They wear pink and multi-colored clothes more often, had more pink pacifiers and jewelry. Boys wore more blue, red, and white clothing and had more blue pacifiers." And they concluded, "It thus seems that very early in their development, girls and boys already experience environments that are dissimilar, which may affect the later development of specific abilities and preferred activities."

A more cognitive view of how children acquire gender identity has been proposed by Bem (1984). This approach, known as **gender schema theory**, focuses on the cognitive mechanisms underlying gender identity—that is, the

Gender: *An individual's membership in one of the two sexes.*

Gender Identity: *Children's understanding of the fact that they are male or female.*

Sex-Stereotyped Behavior: *Patterns of behavior associated by society with each sex.*

Gender Constancy: *Children's understanding that gender is stable over time.*

Gender Schema Theory: *A theory that children develop a cognitive framework, or schema, reflecting the beliefs of their society concerning the characteristics and roles of males and females: this gender schema then strongly affects the processing of new social information.*

development of gender schemas. These are cognitive structures for children's knowledge about males and females, based on instructions from their parents, observations of how males and females typically behave, and so on. Once a gender schema takes shape, it influences children's processing of a wide range of social information (Martin & Little, 1990). For example, children with a firmly established gender schema automatically categorize the behaviors consistent with their own gender schema more easily. In short, gender is a key concept for children, one they use in their thinking to make sense out of the social world.

This theory also argues that a child's self-concept becomes linked to the gender schema (Absi-Semaan, 1993). Thus, children come to view their own preferences, attitudes, and behaviors as acceptable, to the extent that these are consistent with what is specified by the gender schema. As Bem puts it (1981): "The gender schema becomes ... a standard or guide ... and self-esteem becomes its hostage."

Which of these theories is correct? At present, there is some evidence consistent with each. It seems likely that both social learning and cognitive processes are involved in the formation of gender identity. Together, these views provide a more complete picture of this process.

Sex-Stereotyped Beliefs and Behavior

At the same time that children acquire their identity, they also learn about their own society's view concerning gender. They acquire beliefs about the supposed characteristics of males and females (sex-role stereotypes or beliefs) and a basic understanding of how their society expects males and females to behave (sex-stereotyped behaviors). Such stereotypes are not neutral; in Western cultures, they attribute more admired characteristics to males. Thus, both boys and girls learn that males are (supposedly) independent, aggressive, dominant, and adventurous, while females are (again, supposedly) emotional, gentle, submissive, and passive (Deaux, 1993; Deaux & Lewis, 1986).

Research on gender-role stereotypes suggests that they increase in strength throughout childhood. For instance, when children are given adjectives typically attributed to males (tough, aggressive, dominant) and ones typically attributed to females (gentle, excitable, affectionate) and asked to assign these to a male or a female drawing, the proportion assigned in accordance with stereotypes increases with age (Best et al., 1977).

From 1979 to 1986, the Ottawa Board of Education implemented a seven-year plan to overcome sex-role stereotypes in elementary schools. An evaluation was done by Richer (1988) to determine whether progress had been made. He compared children's drawings made in grade one with those made in grade six, after the extensive program had been established, and found that males in grade six still drew themselves as bigger and more prominent than girls, and more often in competition with each other. On the basis of several findings like these, he concluded that instruction in school alone had not succeeded in changing children's ideas much.

As you might expect, stereotypes and beliefs about **gender roles** (or behaviors) differ greatly from one culture to another, and over time within a given culture. For example, in the United States, it has been found that African-American children often hold less stereotyped views of women than do white children (Bardwell, Cochran, & Walker, 1986), perhaps because they have been exposed more often to women as principal family wage earners and as heads of households. There has certainly been some change in gender stereotypes in many countries in recent decades. Yet such stereotypes continue to persist and to exert strong effects on developing children (e.g., Deaux, 1993).

BOYS AND GIRLS: CONTRASTING STYLES OF INTERACTION

Careful observation suggests that girls are often at a disadvantage when interacting with boys (Maccoby, 1990). They are more polite and restrained and, as a result, exert less influence on the group and its activities.

Gender Roles: Beliefs people hold about how they are expected to behave in many situations.

How do children acquire sex-stereotyped beliefs and behaviors? First, there are various environmental influences, such as family, teachers, and peers. All of these behave in ways that confirm the belief that boys and girls differ in important ways and that certain activities are appropriate for boys and others for girls (McGuire, 1988; Weisner & Wilson-Mitchell, 1990). Also, when they interact with peers, children prefer playmates whose behavior matches their own. Thus, they gradually come to spend more and more time interacting with same-sex peers. At age four, children spend three times as much time with same-sex peers as with opposite-sex peers; by the time they are six, this ratio has risen to eleven to one (Maccoby & Jacklin, 1987).

Observation of children's play supports these suggestions. Groups of boys engage in much more rough-and-tumble play than groups of girls. Also, for boys, maintaining status within the group seems to be much more important than for girls. As a result, when boys and girls do come together in mixed-sex groups, girls may be at a distinct disadvantage (Maccoby, 1990). Girls behave more politely than boys, waiting for a turn to speak—which may never come! And they often attempt to exert influence by polite requests rather than through demands or physical force, unlike boys, who have learned to assert their independence in order to maintain high status.

As Maccoby (1990) notes, such differences in style of social interaction are potentially important, especially during this current period of profound change, when many more women are moving into positions of power and authority. The outcome of that social change may not be quite what is expected. For example, at Laval University, Marguerite Lavallee and René Pelletier (1992) have found that women engaged in nontraditional jobs have different gender schema profiles than women working in traditional settings. Researchers at the University of Manitoba (Sztaba & Colwill, 1988) have found this to be true for women college students training for secretarial positions (which are classified as more traditionally female). These subjects scored higher on a self-assessment of femininity than did women training for management positions (which are classified as more male), who scored higher on masculinity scales.

A DIFFERENT POINT OF VIEW ABOUT THE ORIGINS OF SEX-STEREO-TYPED BEHAVIORS Recently, Lytton & Romney (1991) have challenged widely held assumptions about whether parents treat boys and girls differently. Their analysis of the results of 172 studies has led them to conclude that, in North America at least, there are few differences in how parents treat their male and female children. They have interpreted this result to mean that boys may respond differently than girls to similar treatment by their parents, as a result of biological differences, which may be genetic, or hormonal, or both. For example, it may be that there are gender-based differences in the responses to toys—differences that result in male children being more manipulative. Also, it may be that parents treat boys and girls similarly with respect to warmth, but that boys respond differently to that warmth. This is an intriguing idea, but further research is needed to test its validity.

MAKING PSYCHOLOGY PART OF YOUR LIFE

Being a Successful Parent

Do you plan to have children? That will be one of the most important decisions of your life, for having children is a choice that cannot be undone. In the 1990s, people may change their careers, their spouses, and virtually every aspect of their lives. But once you are a parent, you are a parent for life. Also, raising children is one of the most important jobs anyone can do. Given all this, you will want to know as much as possible about how to be an effective parent. Even though preparation for parenting is important to everyone, the emotional preparation of sons has often been neglected (Kaplan, 1986).

Psychology has much information to offer you. Here are some basic principles you can apply, if parenthood turns out to be in your future:

1. *Don't expect too much too early* Many first-time parents expect their children to beat the averages. They anticipate that their child will walk, talk, and do just about everything else ahead of what the charts suggest. And they are disappointed if it doesn't happen. Avoid such unrealistic expectations: They can mean unnecessary added stress for both you and your child. Most often, early development has little bearing on anything else.

2. *Don't assume that a child can reason like an adult* Well educated parents are often tempted to reason with their children as mini-adults. They are mystified when that approach fails. In fact, young children cannot think and reason like adults. Be ready to substitute other techniques when adult reasoning fails. Turn situations in which children are behaving in unacceptable ways into joint problem-solving projects—for example, by asking, "How can we fix this?" This is a question young children can understand. Trying to reason about abstract concepts (such as fairness, or consideration for others) too early is probably worse than useless, although that is not the case later on.

3. *Never let your children divide and conquer* Remember that young children do not yet have the cognitive capacity to decide what is right and what is wrong. As a result, they may exploit disagreements between their parents if they are rewarded by one or the other for doing so. Don't let this happen. Instead, establish as few rules as possible, but when establishing them, agree on them. A united team of parents is far more helpful to children than one that is divided.

4. *Remember that children are highly observant* Young children acquire a tremendous amount of information, and many behaviors, by observing adults. They are alert and adept at watching intently from the sidelines as important events take place. Many parents are shocked when their children repeat things they have overheard to friends or relatives—usually at the most embarrassing moment. And always remember to practice what you preach. If you say one thing but do another, your deeds will carry greater weight!

5. *Choose a day care center carefully* If both you and your spouse work, day care may be necessary. Indeed, it may be helpful. Choosing a specific center is a very important task. Before placing your child, find out who is in charge, what their credentials are, what tests the center has passed, and what specific programs and activities it provides. It is very important that its philosophy and child care techniques be similar to your own.

6. *Be consistent* If there's one think that causes children difficulty, it is inconsistency on the part of their parents and in the world in which they live. Children need to learn that their behaviors have dependable consequences. If you set a rule for your children, enforce it consistently. One of the surest ways to confuse your child is to enforce rules on some occasions but not on others. If you do want to bend a rule occasionally, be sure to make it clear how this is a special situation, and that at other times the standard rule will apply. It is not wise to punish children for infractions on some occasions and not on others. Consistency may be the hobgoblin of little minds, but that, in a sense, is what you are dealing with where children are concerned: minds—and consciences—in formation.

Parenting is a lifelong role, one of the most challenging yet rewarding experiences a person can have.

PHYSICAL GROWTH AND DEVELOPMENT	• Physical growth is rapid during the prenatal period. From a tiny speck, smaller than the period at the end of this sentence, the developing child increases to more than 3.15 kilograms and 50.8 centimeters at birth.

developmental psychology 314

physical growth and
  development 314

cognitive development 314

social and emotional
  development 314

childhood 314

embryo 315

fetus 315

teratogens 316

placenta 317

longitudinal research 324

cross-sectional research 325

cohort effects 325

longitudinal-sequential
  design 325

• Many environmental factors can adversely affect the developing fetus. These include diseases, drugs, alcohol, and smoking by the prospective mother. The precise time during pregnancy when these harmful agents make their effect can strongly determine the extent of the harm suffered by the fetus.

• Ingenious methods of research have revealed that newborns are capable of perceiving many aspects of the physical world. They can distinguish between different colors, sounds, and tastes, and they prefer certain patterns—for example, the human face. Also, they can perceive depth by the time they are two or three months old.

COGNITIVE DEVELOPMENT: CHANGES IN HOW WE KNOW THE EXTERNAL WORLD ... AND OURSELVES

stage theory 326

adaptation 326

assimilation 326

accommodation 326

sensorimotor stage 326

object permanence 326

preoperational stage 327

make-believe play 327

egocentrism 327

conservation 327

concrete operations 328

formal operations 328

hypothetico-deductive
  reasoning 328

propositional reasoning 328

private speech 329

attention-deficit hyperactivity
  disorder 332

scripts 333

metacognition 334

moral development 337

preconventional level 338

conventional level 338

postconventional level 339

• According to Piaget, young children do not think or reason like adults. They acquire adult cognition only after passing through a series of discrete stages of cognitive development. In the first—the sensorimotor stage—infants acquire basic understanding of the links between their own behavior and the effects it produces. In the second—the preoperational stage—babies can form mental representations of the external world; however, they show egocentrism in their thinking and are unable to understand that others perceive the world differently from themselves.

• In Piaget's third stage—concrete operations—children are capable of logical thought and show understanding of conservation and the reversibility of physical operations. Finally, in the stage of formal operations, older children and adolescents can think logically, manipulate abstract concepts in their mind, and engage in propositional reasoning.

• Piaget's theory has been challenged on several grounds. Young children attain key cognitive milestones much earlier than he proposed. Further, children generally do not seem to pass through discrete stages of cognitive development. Finally, Piaget underestimated the importance of language and social interactions in cognitive development.

• The information processing perspective provides a sharply different view of cognitive development. According to this approach, cognitive development involves the increasing ability to actively process, store, retrieve, and manipulate information.

• Infants can form prototypes—mental representations of external stimuli—within hours of birth. They rapidly acquire the ability to notice increasingly fine-grained features of the external world.

• Babies' ability to focus their attention on tasks they are performing increases rapidly, as does planfulness—the capacity to decide actively where and how to direct attention. As they grow older, children acquire increasingly sophisticated strategies for enhancing their own memory. They also expand their domain-specific knowledge, and acquire increasingly sophisticated understanding of their own cognitive processes—metacognition.

• Kohlberg's theory of moral development suggests that all human beings move through a series of stages of moral reasoning. At the preconventional level, morality is judged largely in terms of its consequences. At the conventional level, morality is judged in terms of laws and rules of society. At the postconventional level, morality is judged in terms of abstract principles and values.

	• Moral reasoning does increase with age, but environmental factors such as level of education, parents' child-rearing practices, and cultural tradition also play an important role. Contrary to initial findings, there is no evidence that males and females attain different levels of moral development or reasoning.
SOCIAL AND EMOTIONAL DEVELOPMENT: FORMING RELATIONSHIPS WITH OTHERS social referencing 343 temperament 343 attachment 345 ethological theory 345 Strange Situation Test 346 secure attachment 346 avoidant attachment 346 resistant attachment 346 disorganized or disoriented attachment 346	• Infants show a wide range of recognizable facial expressions. As they grow older, they also acquire an increasing ability to read the emotions of others and to regulate their own emotions. • Differences in temperament—consistent individual differences in quality and intensity of emotions—are present very early in life. Such differences are relatively stable, at least for people at the extremes of several dimensions of temperament. • Biological factors play a role in temperament, but it is also affected by external factors such as cultural and child-rearing practices. • Infants quickly form a strong emotional bond with their caregiver; this is known as attachment. Basic learning processes play a role in attachment, but the fact that infants are born with responses that elicit caregiving from adults appears to be even more crucial. Most infants form secure attachments to their caregivers, but others form insecure, avoidant, or disorganized attachments. • The strength of attachment can be measured by means of the strange situation. Placing infants in day care facilities does not necessarily interfere with the formation of secure attachment to parents. Contact comfort—close physical contact between infants and caregivers—also plays a role in the formation of attachment.
GENDER: THE DEVELOPMENT OF GENDER IDENTITY AND SEX-STEREOTYPED BEHAVIOR gender 30 gender identity 350 sex-stereotyped behavior 350 gender constancy 350 gender schema theory 350 gender roles 351	• Many children do not acquire an understanding of gender constancy—the fact that their sexual identity is stable—until they are least four. Such understanding may occur earlier, however, if children acquire knowledge of the physical differences between the sexes. • Children acquire gender identity through social learning and through development of gender schemes. Children also acquire sex-stereotyped beliefs about the supposed characteristics of males and females and how they are expected to behave. • Gender differences are acquired primarily through learning, but there is some indication that genetic factors such as hormonal differences between girls and boys may also influence this process.

CRITICAL THINKING QUESTIONS

APPRAISAL	Physical, cognitive, and emotional/social development obviously occur together, in a simultaneous manner. Given this fact, does it make sense to try to study each one separately?
CONTROVERSY	Growing evidence suggests that genetic factors, such as differences in hormonal levels, may play a role in the development of at least some differences in the behavior of boys and girls. These differences, in turn, may influence several aspects of their development. Do you think that these findings mean that efforts to ensure equal opportunities for women in all walks of life will run into obstacles that can't be overcome? If so, why? If not, why?
MAKING PSYCHOLOGY PART OF YOUR LIFE	Many parents worry about the impact on their children of television, movies, and other forms of the mass media. Do you think that such concerns are justified? And if so, how can you—when you are a parent—reduce these potential harmful effects on your own children? Should society play an active role in this respect, by regulating the content of television programs and movies?

Human Development II

Adolescence, Adulthood, and Aging

ADOLESCENCE: BETWEEN CHILD AND ADULT
358
Physical Development During Adolescence
Cognitive Development During
   Adolescence
Social and Emotional Development During
   Adolescence
Adolescence in the 1990s: A Generation at
   Risk

ADULTHOOD AND AGING 371
Contrasting Views of Adult Development:
   Internal Crises or External Life Events?
Physical Change During Our Adult Years
Cognitive Change During Adulthood
Social Change in Adulthood: Tasks and
   Stages of Adult Life
Crises of Adult Life
Gender and the Adult Years: How Men
   and Women Differ

AGING AND DEATH: THE END OF LIFE 389
Why Do We Die?
Theories of Aging: Contrasting Views
   about Why We Grow Old
Meeting Death: Facing the End of Life
Bereavement: Mourning the Death of
   Loved Ones

SUMMARY AND REVIEW OF KEY POINTS 395

CANADIAN FOCUS—PUBERTY AND GENDER
IDENTITY 360

KEY CONCEPT—ERIKSON'S EIGHT STAGES OF
PSYCHOLOGICAL DEVELOPMENT 366

THE POINT OF IT ALL—OVERCOMING THE
ODDS: ADOLESCENTS IN HIGH-RISK
ENVIRONMENTS 370

PERSPECTIVES ON DIVERSITY—
MENOPAUSE: THE ROLE OF CULTURAL FACTORS
375

THE RESEARCH PROCESS—AGE,
INTELLIGENCE, WISDOM, AND CREATIVITY:
CHANGE OR STABILITY ACROSS THE LIFE SPAN?
381

MAKING PSYCHOLOGY A PART OF
YOUR LIFE—PREPARING FOR TOMORROW'S
JOB MARKET TODAY 393

"GIVE US A PLACE WITHOUT DRUGS"

**The Yellowknife News/North:
August 1, 1994**

Each stage in life has its own challenges, but those facing adolescents seem most difficult. What can be done to help?

As reported in News/North, on July 9, 1994, five hundred residents of Iqaluit marched to protest against dealers who supply drugs and alcohol to local teens. Contrary to what you might expect, the response of at least one young person was "it's about time, Mom..." In addition to their march, parents are planning to make changes in the local recreation facilities to match the "kids'" needs for them.

In Chapter 9, you will learn more about the challenges of adolescence—and each age beyond that—and about the findings of researchers who study development over the entire lifespan.

Shinsho Nakajima
Dalhousie University

Do you think the younger Dr. Nakajima would be able to recognize his future self?

*I*magine that you are transported twenty-five years into the future, where you encounter … yourself! How will you look? Will you have the same personality traits, attitudes, beliefs, and feelings? Will this future self be … *you*? These are questions to which there are no simple answers, for as you learned in Chapter 8, change is a constant where human beings are concerned. Here is how Honus Wagner, a famous baseball player of the early twentieth century, put it: "Things ain't never gonna be the same again but we don't know *how* they ain't never gonna be the same again."

Wagner's insight into human behavior was apparently greater than his grasp of grammar. But his point still holds: People do change in many different ways through their adult years; but no, we can't be sure just how they will change and in which specific directions. Some of our central traits remain stable for years or even decades (Stein et al., 1991). Yet others change—so much that you might not recognize future versions of yourself.

One important reason for the uncertainty in predicting change during our adult years is this: While development during childhood is determined to an important extent by *maturation*—physical growth and change—development during adulthood derives primarily from life experience. True, we do change physically during our adult years, but this change is slower than during childhood (Briggs, 1990). Also, development during the decades after childhood is tied more closely to social and environmental factors. Since these factors are unique for each individual, the course of development, too, is highly variable. For example, while practically all children learn first to crawl, then to walk, and finally to run, not all adults experience a "midlife crisis."

But how, precisely, *do* we change during the years after childhood? Continuing the discussion of human development begun in Chapter 8, the present chapter will trace some of the changes individuals encounter during *adolescence*—the years between *puberty* (sexual maturity) and entry into adult status; and during *adulthood*—the remaining decades, which constitute the longest portion of our lives. As in Chapter 8, we'll consider changes during each of these periods under three headings: *physical, cognitive,* and *social* and *emotional.* And as *aging* and *death* are inevitable facts of life, those topics, too, will be part of our discussion.

DEVELOPMENT DURING ADULTHOOD DERIVES PRIMARILY FROM THE EFFECTS OF VARIED LIFE EXPERIENCE.

Adolescence: *Between Child and Adult*

*W*hen does childhood end and adulthood begin? Since development is a continuous process, there is no hard-and-fast answer to this question. Rather, every culture draws its own dividing line. In some primitive cultures, there are "rites of passage." The idea here is that the child must earn the right to leave childhood and become an adult. Young adolescents must successfully overcome challenges, which may involve instruction, isolation, pain, and other tests of endurance. In this tradition, "to become fulfilled members of their society, adolescents must understand when childhood ends, adulthood begins and what their culture expects of them" (Cohen, 1991). Many cultures mark this transition with special ceremonies. Individuals enter as children and a few hours or days later are counted as adults. In contrast, in many Western countries, the transition from child to adult takes place gradually, during a period known as **adolescence**, which lasts for several years. Here the rites of passage may include a driving test, a liquor ID, or a grad ball—hardly events that count as earning passage to adulthood. Some psychologists argue that this is part of the reason that adolescents in our culture go to such lengths to do adult things—they are trying to prove themselves worthy of that status.

The beginning of adolescence has usually been the onset of **puberty**, the sudden spurt in physical growth accompanied by sexual maturation. This period ends when individuals assume the responsibilities associated with adult life—live independently, work full-time, study away from home, and so on (Rice, 1992). Remember, though, that entry into adolescence, the length of this phase, and even whether adolescence is a distinct period are all matters that are culturally defined. In Canada and the United States, for instance, the idea that there is a separate period of adolescence did not attain widespread acceptance until well into the twentieth century. Before that time, children were called upon to work as soon as they were strong enough to do so, and they assumed adult roles and responsibilities very early. Thus, the definition of adolescence is largely a social one, determined by culture. Moreover, ideas concerning this phase of life can change greatly *within* a given culture over time.

Remarkable new evidence points to other social factors that contribute to the onset of puberty. Female prepubescent mice reach puberty earlier if an adult male is placed in their cage. This has been linked to pheromones released by the male and sensed by the young females (Vandenbergh, 1989). Studies of prepubescent male antelopes have found that in dangerous times or in time of scarce resources, puberty may be delayed. It may be that there is a hormonal mechanism at work that delays the young antelopes' conflict with adult males—a conflict that occurs naturally as the young start to develop secondary sexual characteristics of their own—horns, and so on.

A controversial extension of these ideas was made by Surbey (1990). Her research found that in families in which the father was absent (because of divorce or abandonment), the onset of puberty in young girls is accelerated. The hormonal basis for this, if there is any, has yet to be determined.

Physical Development During Adolescence

As was mentioned in Chapter 8, adolescence begins with a sudden increase in the rate of physical growth. While this *growth spurt* occurs for both sexes, it starts earlier for girls (at about age 10 or 11) than for boys (about age 12 or 13). Prior to this spurt, boys and girls are similar in average height; in early adolescent phases, girls are frequently taller than boys; eventually, men are several inches taller (on average) than women.

This growth spurt is just one aspect of puberty, the period of rapid change during which individuals reach sexual maturity and become capable of reproduction (Rice, 1992). During puberty the *gonads*, or sex glands, produce increased levels of sex hormones, and the external sex organs assume their adult form. Girls begin to *menstruate* and boys start to produce sperm. These

ADOLESCENCE IN HISTORICAL CONTEXT

Until recently, there was no recognition of adolescence as a distinct developmental phase in North America. At the turn of the century, for example, young people were expected to take on adult responsibilities and roles.

Adolescence: A period beginning with the onset of puberty and ending when individuals assume adult roles and responsibilities.

Puberty: The period of rapid change during which individuals reach sexual maturity and become capable of reproduction.

PUBERTY AND THE SPURT OF GROWTH

Girls tend to mature somewhat earlier than boys; they experience the growth spurt one or two years sooner.

are *primary sexual characteristics;* in addition, both sexes undergo many other changes in sexual maturity. Boys develop facial and chest hair, and their voices deepen; girls experience breast enlargement and a widening of their hips. Both sexes develop pubic hair.

There is great variability in the onset of sexual maturity. Most girls have begun to menstruate by the time they are 13; but for some this process does not start until 15 or 16, and for others it may commence as early as 7 or 8. Education about menstruation does have a positive effect upon attitudes toward this change (Kieren & Morse, 1992). Note that a higher percentage of body fat is associated with an earlier start to menstruation (Blade, 1993), while vigorous exercise tends to delay it (Stager, 1988). Most boys begin to produce sperm by the time they are 14 or 15, but for some the process may begin considerably earlier or later. As you undoubtedly know from your own experience, many adolescents find the rapid pace of these changes quite unsettling.

Facial features, too, change during puberty. Characteristics associated with childhood, such as large eyes, a high forehead, round cheeks, and a small chin, give way to a more adult appearance (Berry & McArthur, 1986). Recent studies indicate that individuals who retain childlike facial features—a *baby face*—are perceived as being weaker, more naive, and more submissive than those who do not retain such features. Interestingly, however, baby-faced people are also perceived as being more honest, warm, and sincere (Berry, 1991). A baby face is also related to attractiveness. Males generally find baby-faced females to be attractive (Berry & Zebrowitz-McArthur, 1988), but not vice versa.

There is some evidence that sex differences exist with respect to the effects of early sexual maturation. Early-maturing boys seem to have a definite edge over those who mature somewhat later. They are stronger and more athletic than their later-maturing counterparts, and so often excel in competitive sports. Partly as a result of these advantages, they tend to be more self-assured and popular and are often chosen for leadership roles (Blyth, Bulcroft, & Simmons, 1981). In contrast, early sexual maturation seems to confer fewer benefits on girls. Early-maturing girls are taller than their classmates—frequently taller than boys of their age—and their increased sexual attractiveness may invite envy from classmates and unwanted sexual advances from older people (Peterson, 1981). However the timing of puberty influences an adolescent's developing self-identity (and later social development), it is important not to overemphasize that event. We'll return to this topic in a later section.

CANADIAN FOCUS

Puberty and Gender Identity

Although in some ways, the age at which puberty occurs influences adolescents' developing self-identity and the way they are seen and treated by others—and thus, their later social development—the precise timing of puberty may not be as important as the comparison between early and late sexual maturity would have us believe. Other influences matter, including parents' and teachers' attitudes, media messages, and examples set within the family. Nancy Galambos at the University of Victoria, and others (Galambos et al., 1990), have studied changes in adolescents' gender identity between the ages of 11 and 13. In their research they have investigated adolescent gender intensification—the hypothesis that the "behavioral, attitudinal, and psychological differences between adolescent boys and girls increase with age." The data of an earlier longitudinal study of 200 adolescents were analyzed to determine how differences in gender intensified across grades 6, 7, and 8.

The adolescents in this study completed a gender role identity questionnaire. On a scale from 1 (almost never true) to 7 (almost always true), they rated themselves on ten adjectives commonly associated with masculinity (e.g., "self-reliant") and on ten others most often associated with femininity (e.g., "affectionate"). For each group, then, both an average masculinity rating and an average femininity rating could be calculated. The results indicated that, over the years, the ratings of feminine characteristics increased in intensity in a similar way for male and female adolescents. Both groups saw themselves as more and more affectionate, sympathetic, or cheerful, for example, as they progressed in age.

However, in their ratings of masculinity, the two sexes saw themselves differently. The ratings of male adolescents, for how assertive, competitive, and ambitious they saw themselves to be, intensified at a much faster rate than those of female adolescents. Galambos interpreted that result as reflecting the general social value placed upon the masculine characteristics, and the severe social pressure put on young male teens to conform to a gender identity—one that is particularly masculine.

The timing of puberty—that is, when puberty actually occurred—had no effect on gender intensification, which increased whether puberty had passed or not. Galambos interpreted that negative result as reflecting, perhaps, the fact that "the messages regarding sex roles that adolescents receive, observe, and incorporate into their self-concepts may be similar [as they move through puberty], regardless of their outward physical appearance." In other words, what matters to adolescents is their outward age—that is, how old they perceive themselves to be—rather than their chronological age or when they pass puberty (Galambos et al., 1995, submitted).

Mixed-Sex Interactions in Adolescence

In evolutionary theory, the purpose of each member of a species is to survive and procreate. The specific contribution animals make to the survival of their species is the genes they pass on to the next generation. The "mating game" is more or less the same with all animals. Among fish, birds, and many insects—bees, for example—there are standard courtship rituals that are genetically determined. An example: The three-spine stickleback is a small fish found in northern Europe. At breeding time, the male stakes out a territory and courts an appropriate female (one whose belly is already swollen with eggs) by turning his own belly bright red and doing a zigzig dance. If she accepts, she does so by the posture of her head and body. He then

leads her to the nest he has prepared and encourages her to enter it. Inside, he prods her to lay her eggs in the nest and then to leave. After that, he enters the nest himself and fertilizes the eggs she has laid.

While all of these behaviors are unlearned, their intent is perfectly clear. There is a complex communication taking place without any words at all. You will learn more about nonverbal communication between people in Chapter 16. Here, however, is a study about the verbal and nonverbal messages that adolescents use in face-to-face conversation. In this study, Kolaric and Galambos (1995) paired fifteen-year-old teens with partners of the same age but the opposite sex with whom they were not already acquainted. The researchers observed the verbal and nonverbal exchanges that took place as these pairs discussed three topics: changing the oil in a car (a "masculine" topic); babysitting (a "feminine" topic); and caring for a pet (a "gender neutral" topic).

The researchers tallied the following verbal behaviors: the frequency with which questions were asked; the frequency with which one partner interrupted the other; the frequency of statements that reflected self-doubt or uncertainty; the amount of time each member of the pair spoke. They also tallied these nonverbal behaviors: certain movements of the arm, hand, or fingers; touching of the head or face; the amount of time spent smiling; and the amount of time spent gazing at their partner. Also observed were other nonverbal displays: hair flips or hair brushes with the fingers; head tilts and chin strokes; and "coy" looks (defined as putting the head to the chin and looking up at the other person).

With respect to the frequency of many of these behaviors, the fifteen-year-olds in this study did not differ by sex. Indeed, they were very much alike in measures of speaking, questioning, gesturing, and touching the head or face, and in the duration of gazing, although the females did spend more time smiling. However, in display behaviors, there were a number of differences. The males stroked their chins more than the females, who flipped their hair more and gave the males more coy looks. Also, the male teens spoke more about oil changes, while the females spoke more about babysitting.

In view of the very clear differences in all of these behaviors *that have been found in adults*—for example, in mixed groups, adult men generally speak far more than women—how do we account for the findings of this study? That remains for future research, because the data available about these behaviors in adolescents are very scarce. It may well turn out that adolescent display behaviors occur in all human cultures, but that the particular displays we see within a culture are socially determined and acquired by adolescents by imitation of adults of a particular sex in a particular social circle.

Nancy L. Galambos
University of Victoria

ADOLESCENTS: A PROPENSITY FOR HIGH-RISK BEHAVIORS

Adolescents often engage in high-risk behaviors. Is this because they feel invulnerable to the potential risks of such actions? Recent evidence casts doubt on this widely held belief.

Adolescent Invulnerability: Adolescents' belief that they are immune from the potential harm of high-risk behaviors.

Cognitive Development During Adolescence

Do adolescents think and reason like adults? As we saw in Chapter 8, Piaget believed that in many respects they do. In the stage of *formal operations*, adolescents can assess the validity of verbal statements and reason deductively; they also show many other logical capabilities. Yet Piaget contended that adolescent thinking still differs from that of adults in several important respects. Adolescents use their newly found cognitive skills to construct sweeping theories about various aspects of life, but these theories seem naive, and reflect a lack of experience. Similarly, they show *egocentrism*, and they assume that everyone else thinks the way they do.

The idea that adolescents' thinking is different from that of adults is widely shared among theorists. For example, Elkind (1967) suggested that adolescents often go seriously astray when they try to take the perspective of another person. Although they understand that other people have ideas too, adolescents often assume that those ideas are the same as their own. Since their thoughts are focused upon themselves, it follows that the attention of other people must be as well. As a result, they act as though they have an imaginary audience. They try out different acts (grunge, punk, prep) and are painfully self-conscious—embarrassed by any apparent defect, such as parents, bad hair, zits, and so on. Also, they often believe that their feelings and thoughts are totally unique—that no one else on the planet shares their experiences. Elkind (1967) referred to this as the *personal fable*.

These ideas have captured the attention of psychologists (e.g., Lapsley, 1993), educators, and parents for decades. But are they correct? Does the thinking of adolescents actually differ appreciably from that of adults? Surprisingly, growing evidence suggests that such differences are smaller than everyday experiences—and several theories—suggest (Beyth-Marom et al., 1991). Perhaps the most intriguing research finding is that adolescents and adults think about *risk* in different ways.

ADOLESCENT INVULNERABILITY: DO ADOLESCENTS THINK DIFFERENTLY THAN ADULTS DO ABOUT RISK? Why is it that adolescents engage in lots of high-risk behaviors, ranging from unprotected sex to reckless driving? One explanation is that young people suffer from **adolescent invulnerability**—the belief that they are immune from the potential harm of high-risk behaviors (Baron & Brown, 1991). Is that explanation correct? Surprisingly, several studies (e.g., Fischoff, 1992; Quadrel, 1990) indicate that adolescents are no more likely than adults to view themselves as invulnerable to the negative outcomes of risky behavior.

A very clear illustration of this point is provided by a study conducted recently by Quadrel, Fischoff, and David (1993). Individuals in three groups—teenagers living in group homes for troubled teens, teenagers living at home with their parents, and the parents of those living at home—were asked to rate the probability that negative events would happen to them. These events included four that were judged to be easy to control (auto accident injury, alcohol dependency, unplanned pregnancy, mugging), and four judged to be difficult to control (sickness from air pollution, injury in an explosion, sickness from pesticides, and sickness from radiation). The results were clear: The teenagers did *not* rate themselves as more invulnerable than the adults—that is, as less likely to experience these negative events. In fact, the teens living at home with their parents had less confidence in their own invulnerability than did their parents! Adolescents and adults do not seem to differ greatly in the way they think about vulnerability.

Nevertheless, adolescents do engage in high-risk behaviors, some of which are very likely to cause them problems. There are many examples of these. They disregard rules at home by deliberately staying out very late at night; they disregard rules at school by skipping class; they disregard rules of society by drinking when they are not of age and by shoplifting items of little value (see Chapter 13); and they show a willingness to engage in unprotected sex, even when they understand the risk of AIDS and other sexually transmitted diseases (e.g., Fisher & Misovich, 1989; Netting, 1982).

In a recent report by Maggs and others (1995), it was maintained that these problem behaviors are not entirely negative. On the positive side, adolescents enjoy the risks involved and see them as a source of good feelings and good times, Also, "forbidden" behaviors are a way to make friends, blow off steam, and establish their independence. Through them, adolescents gain experience in making choices and in evaluating potential gains and losses. Even so, they may well have serious costs to relationships with parents and teachers. They are also dangerous, and hazardous to health, and put future opportunities at risk.

Maggs and colleagues studied adolescent beliefs about fun and risk, as well as their self-image and their relationships with peers. The results indicated clearly how important beliefs can be. When adolescents believe that problem behaviors are fun, the likelihood is high that they will take risks like those inherent in disobeying rules. Contrary to what might be expected, however, adolescents who engage increasingly in problem behaviors view *themselves* more and more negatively. The point to be made is this: The problem behaviors of young adolescents are unlikely to cease without a change in their beliefs and an improvement in their self-image.

KEY POINTS

- Puberty is a period of rapid change during which individuals reach sexual maturity and become capable of reproduction.

- Boys who undergo puberty early experience several advantages relative to those who mature later. For girls, the benefits of early maturity are offset by several negative factors.

- Growing evidence suggests that any differences between the thinking of adolescents and adults are smaller than was previously believed.

- Adolescents do not appear to differ from adults in terms of perceiving themselves as invulnerable to harm.

Social and Emotional Development During Adolescence

It would be surprising if the major physical and cognitive changes that occur during adolescence were not accompanied by equally extensive changes in social and emotional development. After all, as we'll see in detail in Chapter 16, our ability to think about others in complex ways can influence their reactions to us and our reactions to them. What, then, are some of the major social and emotional changes that occur during adolescence?

EMOTIONAL CHANGES: THE UPS AND DOWNS OF YOUTH   Common folklore suggests that adolescents are unpredictable creatures, prone to wide swings in mood and wild outbursts of emotion. Are these assertions true? To some degree, they are. In several studies, large numbers of teenagers wore beepers and were signaled at random times throughout an entire week. When signaled, they entered their thoughts and feelings in a diary. The results indicated frequent and large swings in mood—from the heights to the depths (Csikszentmihalyi & Larson, 1984). Moreover, these swings occurred very quickly, sometimes within only a few minutes. Older people also show shifts in mood, but theirs tend to be less frequent, slower, and smaller in magnitude. Some evidence supports, then, the view that adolescents (at least in Western nations) are more emotionally volatile than adults.

Other widely accepted ideas about adolescent emotionality, however, do not appear to be correct. For example, it is often assumed that adolescence is a

PHYSICAL CHANGE DURING ADOLESCENCE: SOMETIMES IT'S DISCONCERTING

The rapid pace of physical change sometimes makes adolescents feel like the character in this cartoon. (Source: Copyright 1990, Randy Glasbergen. Reprinted by permission.)

"You're a teenager now, Lester. Your body is changing in ways that are not always easy to understand."

ADOLESCENT FRIENDSHIPS

Friendships are an important aspect of adolescence. They can have either a positive influence, helping adolescents improve their social skills and giving them a sense of belonging, or a negative influence, encouraging undesirable attitudes and potentially harmful behaviors.

period of great stress and unhappiness. In fact, this does not appear to be the case. On the contrary, most teenagers report feeling quite happy and self-confident, *not* unhappy or distressed (Offer & Sabshin, 1984). Moreover, and again contrary to a prevailing stereotype about adolescence, most teenagers report that they enjoy relatively good relations with their parents. They *agree* with their basic values; on future plans, such as whether they should continue in school; and on many other issues (Bachman, 1987). There are, of course, points of friction: Teenagers often *disagree* with their parents about how they should spend their leisure time; how much money they should have or spend; and to some extent about sexual behavior, though this seems to be decreasing (Kelley & Byrne, 1992). Other variables are also important in determining adolescent-parent conflict. For example, within families where both parents are overloaded at work, and that causes stress, adolescent-parent conflict is highest. These are the times when there is the greatest potential for disagreement and disharmony. Also important, however, is the quality of the relationship that has been established between adolescents and their parents (Galambos et al., 1995, in press). By and large, however, the so-called *generation gap* is much narrower than many people have assumed (Galambos, 1992).

SOCIAL DEVELOPMENT: FRIENDSHIPS, THE QUEST FOR IDENTITY, AND SEXUALITY
While most adolescents report mainly positive relations with their parents (Galambos & Almeida, 1992), such family-based relationships are only part of their social development. *Friendships*, not only with members of one's own sex but also with members of the other sex, become increasingly important to personal adjustment (Claes, 1992).

Preteens have already developed ideas about what they should expect from friends at various activities—for example, on the telephone, at sports, and in school (Zarbatany et al., 1992). Also, conceptions about friendship are similar for socially accepted, rejected, and neglected children (Bichard et al., 1988). And along with sexual maturity, of course, comes the capacity for—and interest in—romantic and sexual relationships.

Friendships confer many obvious benefits: Within these relationships adolescents practice, and improve, a wide array of social skills (Berndt, 1992) and develop the capacity for *intimacy*—the capacity to share their innermost thoughts and feelings with another person.

While adolescents' growing and deepening friendships confer important benefits, the potential costs of such relationships should not be ignored. Many studies indicate that adolescents experience intense conflict with friends—conflict that can leave serious psychological scars. Newspapers have reported tragic cases of adolescents who have murdered their lovers or rivals—sometimes right in school. In addition, adolescents may acquire undesirable attitudes and self-destructive patterns of behavior from friends (Shantz & Hartup, 1993). For example, they may be influenced to smoke (Van Roosmalen & McDaniel, 1992), consume alcohol or other drugs (Hundleby & Mercer, 1987), or engage in multiple sexual relations just because members of their gang do so. As Berndt (1992) notes, however, influence among adolescent friends flows in both directions, so the potential negative effects of having "wild" or risk-taking friends should not be overemphasized.

Friendship also plays an important role in another key aspect of social development during adolescence—the quest for a *personal identity*. This process is a key element in an influential theory of psychosocial development proposed by Erik Erikson (1950, 1987).

ERIKSON'S EIGHT STAGES OF LIFE   Erikson's theory deals with development across the entire life span.

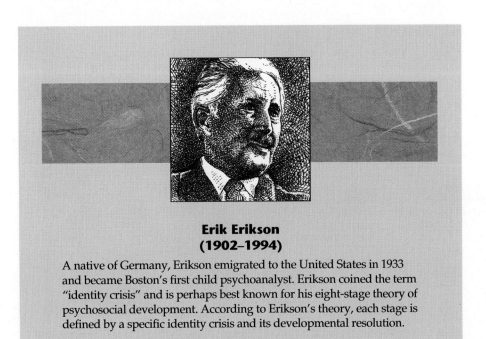

**Erik Erikson
(1902–1994)**

A native of Germany, Erikson emigrated to the United States in 1933 and became Boston's first child psychoanalyst. Erikson coined the term "identity crisis" and is perhaps best known for his eight-stage theory of psychosocial development. According to Erikson's theory, each stage is defined by a specific identity crisis and its developmental resolution.

PSYCHOLOGISTS OF NOTE

Like the one proposed by Piaget, Erikson's theory is a stage theory: It suggests that all human beings pass through specific stages or phases of development in a certain order. In contrast to Piaget's theory, however, Erikson's is concerned primarily with social rather than cognitive development. Erikson believed that each stage of life is marked by a specific crisis, struggle, or conflict. Only if individuals negotiate each of these hurdles successfully will they continue to develop normally.

The stages in Erikson's theory are summarized in the **Key Concept** feature on page 366. The first four occur during childhood; one takes place during adolescence; and the final three occur during our adult years. The first stage, which occurs during the first year of life, centers on the struggle between *trust and mistrust*. Infants trust others to satisfy their needs. If those needs are not met, they fail to develop trust in others and may remain suspicious and wary throughout life.

The second crisis occurs during the second year of life and involves *autonomy versus shame and doubt*. During this time, toddlers are learning to regulate their own bodies and to act in independent ways. If they succeed in these tasks, they develop a sense of autonomy. If they fail, or if they are labeled inadequate by their caregivers, they may experience shame, and doubt their ability to interact effectively with the external world.

The third stage takes place during the preschool years, between the ages of three and five. The conflict then involves *initiative versus guilt*. At this time, children acquire many new physical and mental skills.

Simultaneously, however, they must develop the capacity to control their impulses, some of which can lead to unacceptable behavior. If they strike the right balance between initiative and guilt, all is well. If initiative overwhelms guilt, children may become too unruly for their own good; if guilt overwhelms initiative, they may become too inhibited.

Erikson's Eight Stages of Psychosocial Development

CRISIS/PHASE	DESCRIPTION	
Trust versus mistrust	Infants learn either to trust the environment (if their needs are met) or to mistrust it (if their needs are not consistently met).	
Autonomy versus shame and doubt	Toddlers acquire self-confidence if they learn to regulate their own bodies and act independently. If they fail or are labeled as inadequate, they experience shame and doubt.	
Initiative versus guilt	Preschoolers (3–5 years old) acquire many new physical and mental skills but must also learn how to control their impulses. Unless a good balance is struck between skills and impulses, they may become either unruly or too inhibited.	
Industry versus inferiority	Children (6–11 years old) acquire many skills and competencies. If they take justified pride in these, they acquire high self-esteem. If, in contrast, they compare themselves unfavorably with others, they may develop low self-esteem.	
Identity versus role confusion	Adolescents must integrate various roles into a consistent self-identity. If they fail to do so, they may experience confusion over who they really are.	
Intimacy versus isolation	Young adults must develop the ability to form deep, intimate relationships with others. If they do not, they may become socially or emotionally isolated.	
Generativity versus self-absorption	During adulthood, individuals must take an active interest in helping and guiding younger people. If they do not, they may become preoccupied with selfish needs and desires.	
Integrity versus despair	In the closing decades of life, individuals ask whether their lives have had any meaning. If they can answer yes, they attain a sense of integrity. If they answer no, they may experience deep despair.	

The fourth and final stage of childhood occurs during the elementary school years, when children are between six and eleven or twelve years of age. This stage involves the struggle between *industry and inferiority*. During these years, children learn to make things and use tools, and acquire many of the skills necessary for adult life. Children who successfully acquire these skills develop their own sense of competence; those who do not may compare themselves unfavorably with others and suffer from low self-esteem.

Now we come to the adolescent years in Erikson's theory: the crisis of *identity versus role confusion*. At this time of life, individuals ask themselves, "Who am I?" "What am I *really* like?" "What do I want to become?" In other words, they seek to establish a clear *self-identity*—an understanding of their own unique traits and what really matters to them. These questions, of course, are asked at many points in life. According to Erikson, though, during adolescence it is crucial that these questions be answered effectively. If they aren't, individuals may drift along uncertain of who they are or what they wish to accomplish.

Adolescents adopt many different strategies to help themselves resolve their own personal identity crises. They try out many different roles—the good girl/boy, the rebel, the dutiful daughter/son, the athlete—and join many different social groups. They consider many possible *social selves*—different kinds of people they might potentially become (Markus & Nurius, 1986). Out of these experiences, they gradually piece together a cognitive framework for understanding themselves—a *self-schema*. Once formed, this framework remains fairly constant and serves as a guide to behavior in many different contexts.

The remaining three stages in Erikson's theory relate to crises we face as adults. Since we'll consider them in our later discussion of adult development, we won't examine them here. However, they are described in **Key Concept**.

HIGH-RISK ENVIRONMENTS

Despite the fact that millions of children around the world grow up in disadvantaged environments like this one in Sarajevo, most of them grow up to be productive, law-abiding members of society. Psychologists are attempting to identify the factors that help such children overcome these tremendous early disadvantages.

Adolescence in the 1990s: *A Generation at Risk*

During many periods of world history, adolescents have been at great risk of psychological and physical harm. Warfare, revolution, plague, invasion, and conquest by foreign powers—such events have torn the social fabric and crushed families in all corners of the world. In view of this, it is difficult to contend that today's adolescents face a more dangerous and threatening world than preceding generations. Yet in the 1990s they *do* seem to face new and uniquely disturbing challenges. Consider a few facts:

- Between 3,000 and 10,000 adolescents live on the streets of Toronto, the capital city of Canada's street youth, with no permanent address, no place to live, and nowhere to sleep.

- The Canadian child poverty rate is more than double that of several European countries, including Sweden and France.

- Young Canadians have the second-highest rate of death by homicide among fourteen industrialized nations surveyed by the United Nations Children's Fund.

- Canada has the third-highest rate of teen suicide, after Australia and Norway. The greatest risk is among males age 15 to 19 (Leenar & Lester, 1990).

- The number of "parasuicides"—incidents in which young Canadians deliberately cause injury to themselves, with or without the intent to end their life—is rising steadily.

KEY POINTS

- According to Erikson's theory, social development involves the resolution of a series of internal crises.

- For adolescents, the most important of these concerns is establishing a clear self-identity.

- Adolescents try out many roles and social selves before establishing a clear self-schema.

- More than 90 percent of Canadian teens have tried drinking alcohol, and one in every four has tried illegal drugs.

- The use of strength-enhancing drugs has gone well beyond football, hockey, and track stars. In 1991, 83,000 young Canadians had tried steroids.

In the 1990s adolescents face conditions unlike those encountered by any recent generation (Takanishi, 1993). Taking note of that fact, an influential journal *The American Psychologist* recently devoted an entire issue to the topic of adolescence, with special focus on the challenges faced by today's teens.

DIVORCED, PARENT-ABSENT, AND BLENDED FAMILIES   At present more than half of all marriages in Canada and other countries end in divorce. This means that many children and adolescents will spend at least part of their life in a different kind of family arrangement (Gross, 1986), and face special problems in adjustment (Addington, 1986). Like all adolescents, teens of divorced parents continue to need love, limits, emotional space, and access to adults (Levine, 1987; Norton & Moorman, 1987). Adolescents react to divorce with fear, anxiety, and feelings of insecurity about their future. Divorce can cause stress and psychological vulnerability, as well as hostility toward parents or siblings, or both (Kurtz & Derevensky, 1993). Further, many adolescents blame one or the other of the parents for the divorce: "What did she do to make Daddy leave?" "How can he desert us like this?" Some adolescents turn these feelings inward and blame themselves. They feel guilt—that *they* were responsible for the separation of their parents.

The effects of divorce on adolescent emotional well-being depend on many different factors, including the quality of the care they received before the divorce (Raphael et al., 1990) and the nature of the divorce—that is, whether it was amicable or filled with anger and resentment. Recent findings at the University of Quebec in Montreal (Tousignant et al., 1993) indicate that poor care by the father is the best predictor of adolescent suicidal behavior after divorce. Needless to say, the more negative the parents act toward each other, the more likely that emotional harm will be done to the adolescent. In addition, adolescents described as *academic underachievers*—those whose academic performance is below what their intelligence would predict—are more likely to come from divorced than two-parent homes (McCall, 1994).

"FATHER KNOWS BEST": A 1950S VIEW OF FAMILY

During the 1950s, American television shows painted a glowing picture of the joys of family life. Even then, few families could live up to this unrealistic image.

Blended Families: Families resulting from remarriage, consisting of biological parents, stepparents, and biological children of one or both spouses.

Adolescents living in *parent-absent* families face different problems. Many children are born to single mothers, and some of these children may not know their father at all. As in other families, there are some special risks associated with growing up in a parent-absent (typically *father-absent*) family. Research findings suggest that they include the following: increased risk for delinquent behaviors, reduced school performance (Bisnaire et al., 1990), and difficulties in forming meaningful relationships—including stable romantic ones—with members of the opposite sex (Eberhardt & Schill, 1984).

Is the happiest outcome for adolescents from single-parent families the remarriage of the remaining parent? When divorced or single parents marry, adolescents find themselves facing other problems. The resulting **blended families** of one biological parent, one stepparent, and perhaps siblings and step-siblings, creates new complications. Favoritism by parents toward biological children, rivalries with step-siblings, and friction with stepparents generate painful conflicts. These conflicts are intensified by the fact that most stepparents, having had experience with being a parent to their own children, expect the role of stepparent to be one they already know how to play. Imagine the shock—and anger—when their stepchildren make such comments as, "You're not my real mother/father; I don't have to listen to you!" Clearly, then, shifting patterns of birth, marriage, divorce, and remarriage create serious challenges for today's adolescents. Many children adjust well to their altered circumstances, and progress normally. Others suffer.

DYSFUNCTIONAL FAMILIES: THE INTIMATE ENEMY　During the 1950s, television painted a glowing picture of ideal family life. A caring, loving mother, a kind and wise father, considerate siblings—that was the image portrayed on the screen. Today, many teenagers find themselves in **dysfunctional families**—families that do not meet children's needs and that may do them serious harm (Amato, 1990; McKenry, Kotch, & Browne, 1991). From experience, Priest (1985) concluded that "most of such children suffer disabling emotional effects [of fear, anger, and grief] that they will carry over to adulthood and that adversely affect at least one more generation."

Some dysfunctional families are neglectful or engage in mistreatment of adolescents. Violence, family instability, poverty, and psychiatric disorders among members of the family are some of the factors in this (Ledingham & Crombie, 1988). For example, consider that some adolescents grow up in homes where one or both parents abuse alcohol, or other drugs, or both. These young people can only guess what normal parental behavior is like, since they see very little of it at home. Moreover, the physical abuse that some of the parents inflict on their children predicts violent behavior in adolescence (Truscott, 1992). Because their parents behave very differently under the influence of drugs, these adolescents experience high levels of uncertainty: What will happen when they return home from school? For some adolescents, family life includes physical, emotional, and verbal abuse. A strong predictor of child abuse is child neglect (Ney et al., 1993). A strong predictor of adult assault is adolescent assault of younger children (Stenson & Anderson, 1987).

For some teenagers, family life includes **sexual abuse**. Unfortunately, sexual abuse is far from rare (Kendall-Tackett, Williams, & Finkelhor, 1993); indeed, large numbers of children and adolescents are betrayed by adults they know every year. Common among adolescent victims of sexual abuse are depression, withdrawal, anxiety, psychiatric disorders, substance abuse, and physical complaints (Morrow & Sorrell, 1989). These harmful effects increase with the frequency and duration of the abuse; when the perpetrator is a close family member such as father, mother, or sibling; and when overt force is involved (Kendall-Tackett, 1991).

Has the incidence of sexual abuse increased in recent years? Or does the rise in complaints reflect greater attention to this problem on the part of society and greater willingness of victims to come forward? This is a difficult question to answer, but many experts feel that because of other changes in society, children and adolescents may be at greater risk for such abuse than was the case in the past. Whatever the ultimate conclusion, it is clear that mistreatment in general, and sexual abuse in particular, have serious consequences.

ADOLESCENT SEXUALITY　Recent surveys indicate that adolescents and college and university students are actually becoming more conservative about several aspects of sexual behavior; their parents, on the other hand, have become *less* conservative (Gerrard, 1986; Kelley & Byrne, 1992). The shift toward greater restraint among adolescents may reflect the growing—and justified—concern with *sexually transmitted diseases*. Many people in North America are now infected with illnesses such as *chlamydia*, *gonorrhea*, and *herpes*. And many others are carrying HIV, the virus that causes AIDS.

Dysfunctional Families: Families that do not meet the needs of children and in fact do them serious harm.

Sexual Abuse: Sexual contact or activities forced upon children or adolescents by other persons, usually adults.

Whatever the specific causes, it does appear that the gap between adolescents and their parents with respect to sexual behavior has narrowed in the 1990s. At Okanagan College, Netting (1992) conducted a study of the sexual behavior of students and the sexual choices that they make. Her students responded to questions in early 1990. She compared their responses with those of other students she had tested ten years earlier. Netting made a deliberate effort to sample widely and to include night students who were somewhat older. She found that students today make one of three choices with respect to sexual lifestyle: celibacy, monogamy, or free. There was a dramatic decrease in the free lifestyle between 1980 and 1990, for both male and female students—but not, however, because students knew AIDS victims or believed that the disease was relevant to them. In fact, one of them said, "I don't worry [about AIDS] because I live in Kelowna." Results were similar in a study done 5,000 kilometers to the east, in Montreal, by Maticka-Tyndale (1991).

Studies of another aspect of adolescent sexuality found that rates of single motherhood have increased substantially in recent decades. Also, more and more of these mothers are teenagers, some only 13 or 14 years old. Given the pressures placed on these mothers, who are themselves only adolescents, these statistics indicate a serious social problem. Prevention is of key importance here (Jaccard, 1992). Particularly critical is that the example of sexual responsibility be set early by members of the immediate family (Hornich et al., 1986).

That large numbers of adolescents are at risk for psychological or even physical harm is obvious. Yet despite the adverse conditions under when they are raised, many of these young people grow up to lead normal lives. How is this possible? This question is being investigated in much ongoing research. For information on this work and its early conclusions, see **The Point of It All.**

THE POINT OF IT ALL

Overcoming The Odds: Adolescents in High-Risk Environments

I magine what it must be like to grow up in an extremely impoverished environment. Or perhaps you did. These are some of the things you would face every day: severe economic hardship; schools where the teachers spend their time maintaining order and responding to violent behavior; and the only people with money in their pockets are engaged in drug dealing, prostitution, theft, and so on. What kind of person would you become? There seems every reason to predict that you would choose a lifestyle similar to the one you saw all around you. This does often happen. For example, child molesters often have a history of child abuse (Hilton, 1993), as do patients with some personality disorders (Links & Van Reekum, 1993). According to studies at the University of Victoria and the Addiction Research Foundation in Toronto, some children from disadvantaged backgrounds join the ranks of the homeless (McCarthy & Hagan, 1991, 1992; Smart & Walsh, 1993), roaming the streets, malls, arcades, and other public places, panhandling for a living, and becoming involved in theft, burglary, prostitution, and the drug trade.

But millions of other young people, despite their serious early disadvantages, grow into productive and well-adapted adults. They do legitimate and honorable work and are responsible spouses and parents. What determines which outcome will occur? Although systematic research has only just begun (Jessor, 1993), important conclusions have already begun to emerge.

First, it seems clear that many families adopt special strategies to protect their adolescents from the risks of living in high-risk neighborhoods (Furstenberg, in press). These strategies include negotiating with schools or police when their children get into trouble; seeking out resources from community-sponsored facilities; monitoring their children's behavior; providing support against drug use and other dangerous behaviors (modeled by friends and peers); and seeking out safer niches for their children, such as alternative schools when neighborhood schools become too dangerous.

Other research shows that parents often work with their children's teachers and schools to ensure a safe, healthy, and supportive classroom climate (Anson et al., 1991). In other words, home and school cooperate to ensure that positive behaviors are encouraged in both settings, and that the messages young people hear in one place are echoed in the other.

Adolescents are at the center of intersecting influences from family, schools, and neighborhoods. For this reason, maximum benefits are obtained when all three provide the same direction.

What else can we do to promote positive behaviors and prevent negative ones? At the University of New Brunswick, an effective program was designed by Hiew and MacDonald in 1986. Their idea was to provide preemployment skills training and group support to adolescents who were seeking part-time employment, on the assumption that socially skilled students would be more successful. The ratings done by local business managers indicated that preemployment skills training was important, but that group support contributed significantly as well. Also, according to Stenson and Anderson (1987), working at AYLA in Calgary, treatment of adolescents who commit acts of assault should begin as early in life as possible.

Again, research to identify the factors that help adolescents from disadvantaged backgrounds overcome their problems is very recent. However, it is clear that children raised in difficult environments are not doomed to failure and despair. Rather, studies point to a much more optimistic conclusion: Given half a chance, human beings can—and often do—rise above conditions that seem designed to stunt their growth and limit their options.

PROTECTING ADOLESCENTS AT RISK

These residents at Iqaluit, Northwest Territories, are protesting the sale of drugs to adolescents in their community. By combatting this problem, they hope to make their neighborhoods safer for teenagers.

Adulthood and Aging

If you live for an average number of years, you will spend more than 70 percent of your life as an adult. This section, therefore, will focus on key aspects of physical, cognitive, and social development during adulthood. Before we turn to specific changes, here are two different views of change that occurs during the adult years.

Contrasting View of Adult Development: *Internal Crises or External Life Events?*

What causes the changes that occur over the adult years? On the simplest level, it may be that we change primarily as a function of living. Small adjustments in response to the everyday events of life may, over time, accumulate. While that idea seems reasonable, there are other perspectives on adult development as well. These are called the *crisis* or *stage approach* and the *life-event* (or *timing of life events*) approach.

THE CRISIS APPROACH: ERIKSON'S THEORY REVISITED   You have already met the crisis-oriented theory of adult development, proposed by Erikson (1950, 1987). He taught that as people grow older, they confront new combinations of biological drives and societal demands. The biological drives reflect individual growth and physical change, while the societal demands reflect the expectations and requirements that society places on people at different ages. During adulthood, Erikson suggested, we encounter three major crises.

The first of these is the crisis of intimacy versus isolation. During late adolescence and early adulthood, individuals develop the ability to form deep, intimate relationships with others. This does not refer only to sexual intimacy; rather, it is the more general ability to form intense interpersonal attachments (Ratenberg et al., 1993). According to Erikson, people who fail live their lives in isolation—unable to form truly intimate, lasting relationships with others. The development of commitment at this stage determines how we contribute in later life to career, family, and society at large.

Erikson calls the second crisis of adult life the crisis of *generativity versus self-absorption:* the need for individuals to overcome selfish, self-centered concerns and to take an active interest in the next generation. For parents, such activities are focused on their children. After the children have grown, however, and for those who are not parents, the tendency toward generativity may involve being a *mentor* or guide for members of the younger generation, providing help and guidance to many young people—students, younger co-workers, nieces, nephews, and so on. Individuals who successfully resolve this crisis discover new meaning in life. People who do not resolve this crisis become absorbed in their own lives and deprive themselves of important growth and satisfaction.

Erikson called the last crisis of adult development *integrity versus despair*. As people reach the last decades of life, it is natural for them to look back and to ask, "Did my life have meaning? … Did my being here really matter?" If they feel that they have reached many of their goals and have made positive contributions to others and to society, they attain a sense of *integrity*. Otherwise, they may experience intense feelings of *despair*. Successful resolution of this final crisis can have important effects on how individuals come to terms with their own physical and psychological health during the late decades of life, with their own mortality, and with the inevitable fact of death.

In sum, according to Erikson and to others who view adult development in terms of discrete phases or stages, life-span development is a series of crises (or struggles) we face as we mature and grow older. It is the way we deal with these that determines the course of our future life.

LIFE-EVENT MODELS: CHANGE IN RESPONSE TO THE OCCURRENCE AND TIMING OF KEY EVENTS   Another perspective on adult development is offered by *life-events* or *timing-of-life-events* models. These models suggest that people change and develop in response to specific events in their lives, which may or may not be crises.

During childhood and even adolescence, such theories acknowledge, development does occur in accordance with a built-in *biological clock*. During our adult years, however, change occurs in response to important life events—one of which is of course graduation. Development then becomes tied much more closely to a *social clock* than to a biological one.

Most people expect certain life events to occur at specific times. For example, in Canada, graduation from university and leaving home are both expected to happen when people are in their twenties; the death of one's parents (Gee, 1991) is expected to come much later, as is grandmotherhood. If these events actually occur at times other than those which are usual, they are out of sync with society's clock, so people may be unprepared for the difference they make.

The points on the social clock include a number of other transitions: marriage, parenthood, retirement, and so on. However, there are certainly individual differences in these, and besides, our expectations may be flawed. For example, not nearly all adults are married; in 1992, only about six in ten Canadian adults were married or in common-law arrangements, and about 25 percent had never been married. Moreover, the average age of newly married Canadians, about twenty-seven years, is different from what most would estimate.

Several life-events models divide the marks on the social clock into two categories: events which occur at the "right time" and so are expected, or *normative*, and those which are unexpected or *non-normative* (Neugarten, 1979, 1987). Normative events include graduation from school, marriage, parenthood during the early adult years, and retirement in later life. Non-normative events include divorce, traumatic accidents, the sudden death of loved ones, and the unexpected loss of a long-term job or position. Normative events, although of crucial importance, are generally less stressful and less disruptive. Thus, the timing of life events is very important to development (Neugarten, 1987).

In sum, the two contrasting perspectives about development during our adult years hold, respectively, that (1) changes during adulthood occur in response to a series of internal conflicts or crises, and (2) they occur in response to the occurrence and timing of specific life events. These two perspectives are not complete; nor are they necessarily contradictory. Each adds to our understanding of the complex pattern of changes during the adult years.

Physical Change During Our Adult Years

Looking through a family photo album—one that spans several decades—can be a very revealing experience. There, with youthful faces that you may not recognize immediately, are your grandparents, parents, aunts, and uncles. When you compare their appearance in the photos with their appearance today, you can easily see the physical changes that happen during the adult years.

PHYSICAL CHANGE DURING EARLY ADULTHOOD   Physical growth is usually complete by the time people leave their teens; however, for some parts of the body, the aging process actually begins long before that time. For example, the lenses in our eyes begin to lose their flexibility by the time we are only 12 or 13 years old; and for some people, the tissues supporting the teeth may begin to recede even before they have attained full physical maturity. So aging, like growth, is a continuous process that starts early. Changes in the brain as a result of aging also occur. For one thing, as we get older, the brain gets slightly smaller, and so do some brain structures. Between the ages of 20 and 70, the corpus callosum (the bridge between the two hemispheres) shrinks in size, particularly in men (Witelson, 1991).

Muscular strength, reaction time, sensory acuity, and heart action and output are all at or near their peak through the mid-twenties. They then decline slowly—usually imperceptibly—through the mid-thirties. Many members of both sexes do gain weight during early adulthood, and some men undergo significant hair loss. Balding is now thought to be associated with a gene that is passed on from parents to children. When the particular gene is identified, it may be possible for scientists to develop a drug that blocks its action—for those men who do not understand how attractive balding can be. Other kinds of hair loss have different origins. For example, about 200,000 Canadians have a disorder in which the immune system begins to destroy healthy hair follicles and prevents them from regrowing. Note, however, that by and large, physical change is both slow and minimal during this period of life.

PHYSICAL CHANGES DURING MID-LIFE   By their forties, most people are aware that age-related changes are occurring within their bodies. *Cardiac output,* the amount of blood pumped by the heart, decreases noticeably, and the walls of the large arteries lose some flexibility. As a result, less oxygen can be delivered to working muscles within a given period of time. Those who exercise regularly become aware of some decline in this respect—they can't do quite as much as they once could. The performance of other major organ systems also declines—for example, there are difficulties with the digestion of food. Other changes are readily visible when middle-aged people look in the mirror: thinning and graying hair, bulges and wrinkles in place of the sleek torso and smooth skin of youth. There are huge individual differences in the rate at which such changes occur, however. Thus, wile some 40- and 50-year-olds closely match common stereotypes concerning middle age, most retain much of their youthful appearance and vigor during this period of life.

Among the most dramatic changes occurring during middle adulthood is the **climacteric**—a period of several years during which the functioning of the reproductive system changes greatly, along with various aspects of sexual maturity. While both sexes experience the climacteric, its effects are more obvious for females, most of whom experience **menopause**—the cessation of the menstrual cycle—in their late forties or early fifties. During menopause the ovaries stop producing estrogens, and many changes in the reproductive system occur: thinning of the vaginal walls, reduced secretion of the fluids that lubricate the vagina, and so on. Since females no longer release ova, pregnancy is no longer possible.

In the past, menopause was expected to be a stressful process for many women (Stewart et al., 1992). Now, however, it is recognized that cultural factors play an important role in reactions to menopause and its effects. See **Perspectives on Diversity** for a discussion of this issue.

For men, the climacteric involves reduced secretion of testosterone and reduced functioning of the *prostate gland,* which plays a role in semen formation. In many men the prostate gland becomes enlarged, and this may interfere not only with sexual functioning but with urination as well. Men may experience reduced sexual drive at this time of life. Although sperm production decreases, many men are still capable of fathering children.

PHYSICAL CHANGE

As these photos of a man at ages 4, 17, and 50 show, we all change tremendously in appearance over the course of our lives.

Menopause: The Role of Cultural Factors

"T he change of life"—that's the phrase that was often used to describe menopause, which is a natural aging process in women. Until recently, cultural stereotypes suggested that women undergoing menopause had these symptoms: hot flashes, wild swings of mood, depression, irritability, and headaches.

Is that picture of menopause correct? In other words, is that kind of menopause a biological event that is shared by all women around the world?

Information about the nature and extent of cultural factors has been provided by a well-known study conducted by Datan, Antonovsky, and Moaz (1984). These researchers took advantage of the fact that, in modern Israel, individuals who were raised in quite different cultures now live in a single society. Would women from these diverse cultural backgrounds experience menopause in the same way? To gather evidence on this question, the researchers interviewed middle-aged women (all Israeli) who had been raised in five distinct cultures. One group consisted of Moslem Arab women. The Jewish women in the other four groups had been reared in the following cultures: Central Europe, Turkey, Persia, and North Africa. These cultures differed in many respects.

Did the women in these groups have different experiences during menopause? Carefully conducted interviews revealed that they did. The women from the European and Arab cultures reported the least stress and the fewest adverse symptoms. For them, menopause was just another phase of life—one to be taken readily in one's stride. In contrast, women in the three cultures that were intermediate in terms of modernity or social change reported greater stress.

These findings, together with those of other researchers (Lonner & Malpass, 1994), indicate that cultural values and personal expectations do shape the experience of menopause. In this context as in many others, then, biology and psychology overlap; and cultural and social factors have much to tell us about a biological process.

Both the magnitude and the rate of aging are strongly influenced by individual lifestyle. Physical exercise, personal nutrition, and effective management of stress may be better predictors of physical vigor and health than biological age (Roskie, 1987). In other words, a fifty-year-old who exercises regularly, eats a balanced diet, avoids excessive stress, and doesn't smoke may show higher performance on a wide range of tests of physical fitness than a twenty-five-year-old who gets no exercise, lives on fast food, smokes heavily, and burns the candle at both ends.

The human body evolved to be used, to move us around—so that we could search for food and safety. (We are not naturally couch potatoes.) Our cells, bones, and muscles rely for their health on the biological processes that occur when we are active. Although most Canadians know that exercise is good for them (studies confirm this to be the case up to the age of ninety-six), most do not act on that knowledge. Perhaps it is because those who choose a sedentary lifestyle do not feel pain along the way. Even so, inactivity does increase the likelihood of health problems at all ages, and "participation" reduces it. Moreover, elderly people who engage in cognitively demanding activities not only do better on tests of cognitive ability, but also report better physical health (Hultsch et al., 1993). Clearly, the best advice for maintaining body and brain function over the whole life span continues to be, "Use it or lose it."

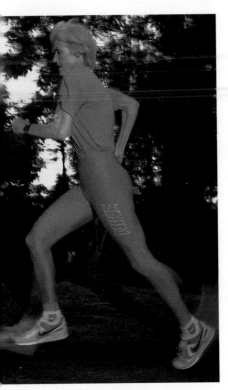

SLOWING THE PACE OF PHYSICAL CHANGE

Physical change during our adult years is a fact of life. By remaining fit, however, we can slow this process greatly and reduce many of its adverse effects.

Primary Aging: Aging due to the passage of time and, to some extent, inherited biological factors.

Secondary Aging: Aging due to the effects of disease and disuse, or abuse of our bodies.

A number of Canadian studies have looked for ways to improve exercise participation rates among elderly adults (e.g., Cousins & Gurgess, 1992; O'Brien & Vertinsky, 1991). The key may be to learn which type of motivation will work (Vallerand & O'Connor, 1989).

PHYSICAL CHANGES IN LATER LIFE Average life span in many countries is increasing. In Canada, for example, the proportion of the population sixty-five or older was 4 or 5 percent in 1900; it is now about 12 or 13 percent, and it will rise to almost 20 percent when the "baby boom" generation born during the 1950s and 1960s turns sixty-five. This trend gives sharp focus to the question of physical changes during the closing decades of life, for the nature and magnitude of these changes have important implications for Canada's health care system and therefore for the national economy as well.

What do we know from systematic research about physical changes in later life? First, the idea that in later life, people are generally frail, in poor health, and unable to take care of themselves is *false*. People in their sixties, seventies, and even eighties report excellent or good health and are not much more likely than middle-aged people to suffer from chronic *illnesses*—ones that are long-term, progressive, and incurable. Further, even in their seventies and eighties, many elderly do not receive hospital care during any given year (Thomas, 1992). In short, the picture of older people that emerges, at least in highly developed nations, is quite encouraging. There are indeed declines in physical functions and health as people age, but these are not nearly as prevalent as our stereotypes of old age would suggest.

One additional—and important—point: While many physical changes do occur with increasing age, it is crucial to distinguish between **primary aging** (i.e., changes caused by the passage of time and, perhaps, inherited biological factors) and **secondary aging** (i.e., changes due to disease and disuse or abuse of our bodies). Here are the consequences of primary aging.

There are several kinds of decrements in *sensory abilities*. As people age, and more so beyond mid-life, they gradually decline with respect to vision, hearing, smell, taste, and other senses. *Visual acuity*, as measured by the ability to read letters on a standard eye examination chart, drops off sharply after age seventy; many people experience these changes as slower *dark adaptation* and reduced ability to notice moving targets, such as cars on a highway (Long & Crambert, 1990). Cooper and colleagues (1993) tested adults aged 20 to 89 for discrimination of color (saturation, hue, and brightness). They found changes after age sixty, and suggested that this information be used when designing environments for senior citizens. Moreover, training in sensory discrimination may be helpful. A training program designed by Trudeau and colleagues (1990) was successful in improving the figure-ground discrimination of seventy-year-olds.

Similarly, auditory sensitivity decreases with age, especially among people who have worked in noisy environments (Corso, 1977). Declines also occur in ability to identify specific tastes and aromas, although this does not become noticeable until after seventy-five (Spence, 1989). There is also a gradual slowing of responses in general, so *reaction time* increases with age (Spirduso & Macrae, 1990). The abilities in this respect of drivers across the life span were tested by Kline and colleagues (1992). Their tests included five kinds of visual problems: unexpected vehicles, speed of vehicles, reading of signs, dim displays, and windshield difficulties. In each case, age was a factor in performance. However, there are wide individual differences; a particular seventy-year-old may still respond more quickly than a particular thirty-year-old. For example, typing skill is important in determining whether an age-related decrease in typing speed occurs. Bosman (1993) found that in order to compensate for the slowing that comes with age, older typists begin keystroke preparation of their fingers sooner.

These changes have important practical implications, especially with respect to driving, for which good vision and normal reaction times are essential. The perceptions younger and older drivers have of each other was the focus of a study by Nelson and colleagues (1992). They had younger (about nineteen years old) and older (about sixty-six years old) drivers rate their peers and each other on driving attitudes, driving courtesy and discourtesy, and safe and unsafe driving. Younger drivers rated their peers as overly aggressive and discourteous. Older drivers rated the younger ones as discourteous and unsafe. Younger drivers rated older ones as too cautious, too slow, and likely to cause accidents. Older drivers rated their peers as courteous, cautious, and aware of their limitations.

The two age groups were consistent in their views of the younger drivers, and differed in their evaluations of older ones. Additional evidence on this point is scarce. However, in his research, Harrell (1992) has found that drivers over the age of sixty-five are just as likely to stop for a pedestrian at a city crosswalk as younger ones.

The bottom line here is that some people in their seventies and eighties are a menace on the roads, but many are safe and competent drivers. Perhaps, then, for drivers above age 70 or 75 who wish to renew their licences, there might be a test of visual acuity, hearing, reaction time, and the ability to detect motion to identify those who are fully capable of safe driving. Further, such testing would not necessarily result in a "Yes, you can continue driving" or "No, you cannot…" decision. Rather, intermediate steps would be possible. For example, older drivers might be certified only for daytime driving. In that way, a balance would be struck between the rights of older drivers and the interests of safety.

KEY POINTS

- Stage theories such as Erikson's suggest that we move through distinct stages or crises.

- Life-event theories view adult development as tied to individuals' responses to important events in their lives.

- Physical change occurs relatively slowly during our early adult years but accelerates in middle adulthood.

- Both men and women experience changes in their reproductive systems during mid-life; these are known as the climacteric. Women undergo menopause at this time. Reactions to menopause appear to be strongly influenced by cultural factors.

- Many physical changes occur in later life, including declines in sensory abilities.

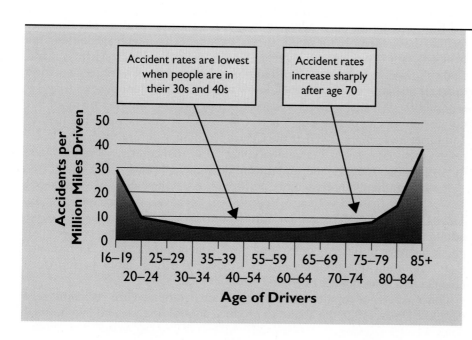

FIGURE 9.1

Age and Automobile Accidents

Older drivers—those above the age of seventy—have a higher rate of accidents than those in their thirties, forties, and fifties. Only drivers below the age of twenty experience higher accident rates.
(Source: Based on data from Cerrelli, 1989.)

Cognitive Change During Adulthood

What about *cognition*? Do adults change in this respect as well? And if so, how? Is there a decline or do more experience, a growing knowledge base, and ever-richer schemas lead to enhanced rather than reduced cognitive performance?

The variety of ways of investigating the relationship between aging and memory is remarkable. Data are provided by *clinical* cases in which elderly patients show memory loss as a symptom; and, of course, there are numerous *experimental* approaches to the study of memory (Webster & Cappeliez, 1993). Many animal studies look into the brain structures involved in different kinds of memory (e.g., Winocur, 1992); others examine the effects of radiation in outer space on the aging of the brain and on memory (Joseph, 1992). At the University of Victoria, Read (1987) studied how memory changes with age. The purpose of that program was to determine what is "normal" for the memory systems of *healthy* individuals.

AGING AND MEMORY   First, let's consider the impact of aging on different memory systems. Research on *short-term memory* indicates that older people are able to retain just as much information in this limited-capacity system (Poon & Fozard, 1980). However, when information in short-term memory must be processed—as, for example, when they solve *anagrams* (scrambled words)—older people sometimes perform more poorly (Babcock & Salthouse, 1990).

With respect to long-term memory, studies suggest that young people do have an edge with respect to *recall*, but not with respect to *recognition* (Hultsch & Dixon, 1990; Craik & McDown, 1987). When older people are expert in a specific area, even differences in recall tend to disappear (Charness, 1989). Why do young adults sometimes outperform older ones with respect to recall? One possibility is that older people experience an *encoding deficit*: When entering new information into memory, they are less likely than younger people to organize this information spontaneously in various ways. As we saw in Chapter 6, information that is organized is usually easier to remember later than information that is not organized. So all in all, it appears that as we age, our ability to enter new information into memory efficiently may decrease slightly, but that the capacity to bring information to mind once it has been stored remains largely unchanged (Zacks & Hasher, 1988).

As you have already learned, researchers in Canada have made substantial contributions to our understanding of how we remember. The findings include these: Memory for public (news) events declines with age, but not for personal (autobiographical) events (Howes & Katz, 1992). McIntyre and Craik showed that there were differences when people of various ages tried to recall the sources of facts they knew about Canada. Jennings and Jacoby reported in 1993 that aging is related to consciously controlled memory but not to automatic processing. Their conclusion is consistent with that of Tainturier and others (1989) at the Centre Hôpitalier in Montreal, who interpreted their data as "further evidence that ... normal aging ... does not interfere with passive, automatic, and unconscious mental processes."

Possibly influential on memory performance are the beliefs we hold about how memory changes with age (Ryan & See, 1993; Ryan, 1992; Hultsch et al., 1987). These beliefs are similar throughout life. Both younger and older adults have more positive opinions about memory in young people than about memory in older people. How these beliefs interact with performance is an important question, because it is possible that memory performance changes as a consequence of altered *beliefs about memory*.

Other aspects of cognitive behavior that are age-related are visual imagery (Craik & Dirkx, 1992), the ability to produce neutral images; and "verbosity," which is the term Arbuckle and Gold gave to the off-target stream of speech one sometimes finds in elderly people. Age-related increases in verbosity may reflect a decline in the ability to ignore thoughts that interfere with the meaningful flow of speech (Arbuckle & Gold, 1993).

Tannis Y. Arbuckle-Maag
Concordia University

The findings discussed so far derive primarily from experiments with relatively less meaningful information—pairs of unrelated words, nonsense syllables, anagrams, and the like. What about memory for more meaningful information—memory in everyday life? Here, findings suggest that old people often perform as well as young ones (May, Hasher & Stoltzfus, 1993). For example, in one revealing study, Sinnott (1986) asked individuals to recall information in *intentional memory*—that is, information that was meaningful to them and that they *wanted* to remember. This included the date of their next appointment, the hours during which the hospital cafeteria served dinner, and so on. In addition, participants were asked to remember information in *incidental memory*—that is, information that was less meaningful to them and that they had not intended to remember, such as the objects that were on the table while they worked on various tasks. Results indicated that younger adults outperformed older ones in terms of incidental memory, but not with respect to intentional memory. In terms of recalling information that was meaningful to them and that they intended to remember, older people did just as well as younger ones.

The connection between age-related memory changes and bidding in a game of bridge was the focus of a study by Charness (1987). Bidding in bridge requires the player to assess quickly the points (the honor cards) in a hand and the distribution (of all the cards) among the four suits. Elderly players were slower to assess a hand and to respond, and therefore to bid, but were not less accurate.

Doloris P. Gold
Concordia University

At Science World in Vancouver, Uttl and Graf (1993) used an exhibit on human memory for an experiment on *spatial memory*. They asked volunteers to indicate, on a floor plan of the exhibit, where certain items were located. They found that until the sixth decade of life, subjects of different ages were equally able to recall. After that, the data showed an age-related decline in spatial memory.

Other findings indicate that *prospective memory*—remembering to perform various actions—does decline with age for most people (Hultsch & Dixon, 1990; Dobbs & Rule, 1987). This does not appear to be true, however, for older adults who are high in verbal ability: Their prospective memory matches that of younger adults (Hartley, 1986). So in answer to the question, "Does memory decline with age?" we can reply this way: Some types of memory, such as recall of relatively meaningless information and prospective memory, may decline with age. However, many other types—especially recognition of meaningful information—show little change.

MEMORY, AGING, AND CIRCADIAN RHYTHMS: A METHODOLOGICAL POINT Do you remember the discussion of circadian rhythms in Chapter 4, and the distinction between morning people and night people? This difference is important in connection with the effects of aging on memory. For several biological reasons, as people get older, they tend to shift more and more toward being most alert and active early in the day. This means that if memory is tested in the afternoon, younger people may have a decided edge, since many of them are night people.

That this is actually the case was indicated by a study conducted by May, Hasher, and Stoltzfus (1993). These researchers asked two groups—old adults ages 66 to 78 and young adults ages 18 to 20—to perform a recognition task.

Testing occurred early in the day at eight or nine a.m., or later in the day, at four or five p.m. As you can see in Figure 9.2, during the afternoon, young adults performed significantly better than older ones. In the morning, however, this difference did not arise. These findings indicate that research designed to investigate memory should take age and circadian rhythms into account.

AGING AND PROBLEM SOLVING   As we saw in Chapter 7, we use our ability to solve problems throughout life. Does that ability change with age? Many studies indicate that, in general, people in their twenties and thirties outperform middle-aged and older people (Reese & Rodeheaver, 1985). Older people adopt less efficient problem-solving strategies—in *some* cases. For example, when shown pictures of common objects and asked to identify which one the experimenter has selected as a target, younger people ask questions that quickly narrow the field; in contrast, older people ask questions that eliminate only one picture at a time (Denney & Palmer, 1981). These differences in strategies do *not* hold true for more practical problems that people might encounter in their own lives (Cornelius & Caspi, 1987) or in applying practical knowledge (Labouvie-Vief & Hakim-Larson, 1989).

Research on problem-solving ability leads us to a more general question: What are the effects of age on intelligence? See **The Research Process** for a discussion of this important topic.

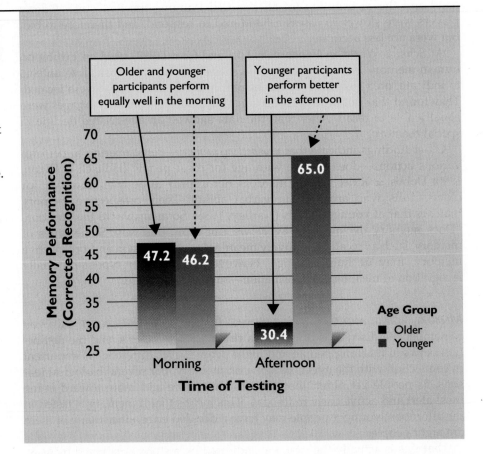

FIGURE 9.2

Circadian Rhythms and the Effects of Age on Memory

When tested in the morning—a time when they are operating at peak efficiency—people in their sixties and seventies performed as well as much younger people. However, when tested in the afternoon, older people were outperformed by younger ones. These findings demonstrate the importance of taking circadian rhythms into account when investigating the impact of aging on memory.
(Source: Based on data from May, Hasher, & Stoltzfus, 1993.)

THE RESEARCH PROCESS

Age, Intelligence, Wisdom, and Creativity: Change or Stability Across the Life Span?

Have you ever heard the old saying, "What goes up must come down"? Many psychologists once assumed that this saying applied to human intelligence. However, they were basing their conclusions on the results of cross-sectional research, in which the performances of people of different ages on standard tests of intelligence were compared. Because people who live at the same time but are of different ages may differ in other ways—in levels of education and health, for example—the conclusions drawn from cross-sectional studies may be incorrect. More recent research on aging and intelligence has often employed a *longitudinal* design—that is, the same people are tested again, after a certain period of time has passed. These studies show that instead of declining sharply with age, many intellectual abilities remain quite stable across the entire life span.

At the Centre for Research in Human Development at Corcordia University, Arbuckle and associates (e.g., Schwartzman et al., 1987) contacted men who had been World War II army recruits at the time their intelligence was first tested. About forty years later, they were retested, in either English or French. Their intelligence scores were about the same, indicating that intelligence as tested in this study remained stable over those decades. In a second series (Arbuckle et al., 1992), it was found that most age differences in memory could be accounted for by differences in intelligence test scores. When intelligence scores were equated statistically the only difference that was directly linked to age was in free recall, the memory task which makes the most demands on the individual's own strategy and initiative.

In another longitudinal study, Schaie and colleagues (Schaie, 1986, 1990, 1993) tested thousands of people, ranging in age from 25 to 81, at seven-year intervals. As shown in Figure 9.3, various components of intelligence (as measured by the Primary Mental Abilities Test, a standard test of intelligence) remain stable throughout adult life. A reliable average decline appears only when people are in their seventies (see Figure 9.3). Further, even at age eighty-one, fewer than half of the people show any changes over the preceding seven years. Only on speed of reasoning does there appear to be a consistent decline in performance. Since that may reflect increased reaction time, there is little if any indication of a general decrease in intelligence with age.

Such findings are not the whole story, because standardized intelligence tests may not capture all aspects of adult intelligence. The distinction between *crystallized* and *fluid intelligence* is especially relevant

FIGURE 9.3

Evidence for the Relative Stability of Intelligence Across the Life Span

Longitudinal research indicates that intelligence is stable across virtually the entire life span. Significant declines in components of intelligence measured by standardized tests of intelligence do not occur for most people until they are well into their seventies. (Scores for inductive reasoning, one important component of intelligence, are shown here.)
(Source: Based on data from Schaie, 1993.)

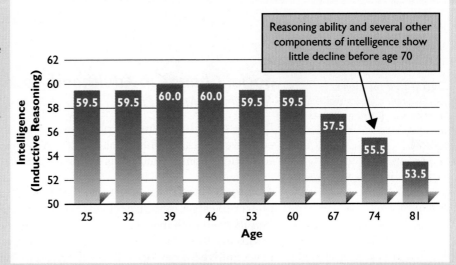

here. **Crystallized intelligence** refers to the aspects of intelligence that draw on previously learned information to make decisions or solve problems. Classroom tests, vocabulary tests, and many social situations require crystallized intelligence. In contrast, **fluid intelligence** includes the abilities to form concepts, to reason, and to identify similarities. Research shows that fluid intelligence increases into the early twenties and then gradually declines. In contrast, crystallized intelligence increases across the life span (Lerner, 1990; Willis & Nesselroade, 1990).

Wisdom and Creativity: Two Other Pieces of the Puzzle

Many cultures assume that as people grow older, they gain in wisdom—that is, in insight and judgment about many practical matters and life problems. In other words, whatever happens to reaction time, memory, or even fluid intelligence, individuals increase in value as a result of their accumulated wisdom.

Is there anything to such views? As yet, there is relatively little research evidence partly because it is difficult to design reliable measures of wisdom. However, several studies have been conducted in which researchers present young and older adults with complex problems and ask them to solve these out loud. Participants' reasoning is then judged (by others) for its wisdom (Thomas, 1992). To date, the results have been mixed, but it does appear that older people offer wiser solutions when the problems involve complex or unusual situations (Smith & Baltes, 1990).

Finally, does creativity change with age? Some cross-sectional research indicates that creativity, as measured by standard tasks, such as arriving at novel ways of using everyday objects, declines with age (Simonton, 1990). However, other research that focuses on the age at which scientists, authors, poets, painters, and architects make their creative contribution, points to somewhat different conclusions (e.g., Lehman, 1953; Abra, 1989; Simonton, 1990; Dudek & Hall, 1991). Apparently, the age of peak creativity varies greatly from one field to another. Mathematicians and physicists tend to make their major contributions while in their twenties or thirties; historians, philosophers, and psychologists make theirs when they are considerably older—in their forties and fifties (Horner, Rushton, & Vernon, 1986). Further, while the number of creative accomplishments may decrease with age, their *quality* remains high.

Where does all this leave us? An overall pattern of evidence suggests that few intellectual abilities decline sharply with age. Some do decrease—especially those which rely on speed of responding. But others remain quite stable over many years, and some may actually increase as individuals gain in experience.

Critical Thinking Questions:

1. Suppose that performance on standardized tests of intelligence decline with increasing age. Would this necessarily mean that intelligence decreases as people grow older?

2. Can you offer an explanation for why *crystallized* intelligence increases with age while *fluid* intelligence decreases with age?

3. Measuring *wisdom* is a difficult task. Can you think of ways in which scientists might assess this quality in order to determine whether it really increases with age?

4. People acquire new information throughout life. If that's so, then shouldn't *creativity*, which involves combining information into new patterns or ideas, also increase?

Crystallized Intelligence: Aspects of intelligence that draw on previously learned information to make decisions or solve problems.

Fluid Intelligence: Aspects of intelligence that involve forming concepts, reasoning, and identifying similarities.

Life Structure: In Levinson's theory of adult development, the underlying pattern or design of a person's life.

Social Change in Adulthood: *Tasks and Stages of Adult Life*

During our adult years we play many roles: student, lover, spouse, parent, employee, boss, grandparent. That is why many psychologists study adult social development and focus on the activities it involves.

LEVINSON'S STAGES OF ADULT LIFE   D.J. Levinson (1986) divides the entire human life span into distinct *eras*, each separated from the next by a *cross-era transition*—the change from one era to the next. An important feature of Levinson's theory is the concept of **life structure**—that is, the idea of an evolving cognitive framework which reflects an individual's views about the nature and meaning of his or her life at a particular time. Work and family are usually central to an individual's life structure, but it may have other features as well—for example, cultural or ethnic background, or important external events that provide a backdrop for life, such as economic boom or depression.

Levinson suggests that there are four major eras of life, each separated from the next by a transition period of about five years. These are summarized in Figure 9.4. As you can see, the first transition occurs between the *preadult era* and early adulthood, between the ages of 17 and 22, when financial and emotional independence are being established. Many people pass through this transition during their college or university years, others when they accept their first full-time job. In either case it involves establishing a separate residence and learning to live on one's own.

Once this initial transition is complete, individuals enter *early adulthood*. Two key components of life structure at this time are, in Levinson's terms, the **dream** and the **mentor**. The dream here refers to a vision of future accomplishments—what the individual hopes to achieve in the years ahead. Such dreams are important sources of motivation. Mentors are older and more experienced individuals who guide young adults. They share their own wisdom and expertise with their younger protégés, aiding them with their careers. Additional crucial events in early adulthood are choosing an occupation and establishing a lasting relationship with a special person—someone who is central to one's plan.

Dream: In Levinson's theory of adult development, a vision of future accomplishments.

Mentor: In Levinson's theory of adult development, an older and more experienced individual who helps to guide younger adults.

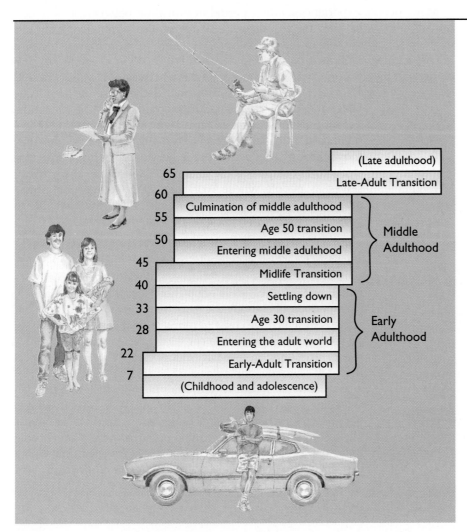

FIGURE 9.4

Levinson's Theory of Adult Development

According to Levinson (1986), individuals move through distinct *eras* of life, each separated from the next by a turbulent *cross-era* transition period. While this theory has received a great deal of attention, its validity remains open to discussion.

At about age thirty, Levinson contends, many people experience the *age thirty transition*. At this time, individuals realize that, if they remain on their present life course, they will soon have too much invested to change. Faced with that fact, they reappraise their initial choices and either make specific changes or decide that they have indeed selected the best course to follow.

Next, after the relative calm of the closing years of early adulthood, individuals move into another potentially turbulent transitional period—the **mid-life transition**. For most people, that happens sometime between the ages of 40 and 45. It is a time when many people must come to terms for the first time with their own mortality. Up until this period, most people view themselves as "still young"—older brothers or sisters to the twenty-year-olds around them. After age forty, however, this idea becomes increasingly difficult to retain, and most people come to view themselves, at last, as the older generation. Levinson's results suggest that this realization leads to a period of emotional turmoil. People take stock of where they have been, assess the success of their past choices, and consider the possibility of fulfilling their youthful dreams. Such reexamination leads to the formation of a new life structure—one that takes account of the individual's new position in life and may involve several new elements: change in career direction, divorce and remarriage, or a redefinition of the relationship with a life-partner. In this new life structure the individual perceives himself or herself as middle-aged, with all that implies.

Many people experience another period of transition between 50 and 55, a transition in which they modify their life structure once again—for example, by adopting a new role in their career or by coming to view themselves as a grandparent as well as a parent. However, this transition is often less dramatic than the next one, which occurs somewhere between the ages of 60 and 65. This **late adult transition** marks the close of the middle years and the start of late adulthood. During this transition, individuals must come to terms with their impending retirement and the major life changes this will bring. As they move through this period of readjustment, their life structure shifts to encompass these changes. They come to see themselves as people whose working career is over, or almost over, and who will now have much more time available to pursue hobbies and other leisure-related interests.

LEVINSON'S THEORY: A CRITIQUE In several respects, Levinson's portrayal of development during the adult years seems to match our intuitive ideas about how life proceeds. Relatively long periods of stability are punctuated by shorter, turbulent periods in which we come to terms with changes in our goals, perspective, and circumstances. However, Levinson based his theory primarily on extensive interviews with only forty participants—all men, and all ages 35 to 45. Critics argue that this is too small and too restricted a sample on which to base such sweeping generalizations (Wrightsman, 1988). Moreover, it is not known whether Levinson's suggestions apply to women as well as men. (We'll return to this point below.) In conclusion, then, at this point in time, Levinson's theory is an interesting description of social development during our adult years.

KEY POINTS

- Short-term memory does not decline with age, but recall of information from long-term memory does decline to a degree. Prospective memory, too, declines somewhat with age.

- There may be some decline in intelligence with age, but this decline is smaller and more limited in scope than was once widely believed. Some findings suggest that wisdom and creativity increase with age.

- A theory proposed by Levinson suggests that during our adult years we move through a number of distinct life eras. These are separated from each other by turbulent transition periods.

- Throughout life, we follow an underlying pattern or design that Levinson called the life structure; this constantly evolves as we move from one era to another.

Crises of Adult Life

Levinson's theory is a *stage theory* of adult development. According to stage theories, all people pass through a given series of eras and transitions. In contrast, other researchers focus on the major *events* of adult life, and how we are affected by these.

DIVORCE Divorce rates are at historically high levels. Between one-third and one-half of all first marriages end in divorce. Clearly, divorce is a major event for most people. Among the feelings most often experienced by divorced people are these: *anger*—relating to the conflict, the bitterness leading up to and surrounding the divorce, and the feelings of unfair treatment afterwards; *depression*—from the loss of contact with children and other family members, from the financial consequences of divorce, and from the loneliness that often follows; and *disequilibrium*—feelings of being lost, aimless, and adrift, resulting from physical relocation, severe disruption of established routines, and the many other changes that take place. Additional emotional experiences are insecurity, disillusionment, and helplessness (Forest, 1992). It is also true that some divorced people experience feelings of *relief*, because the intense conflict is behind them and they perceive an opportunity to begin a new, perhaps better, life (Tschann, Johnston, & Wallerstein, 1989).

Although the Supreme Court of Canada has ruled that the first consideration in custody arrangements is the best interests of the children, they nevertheless pay dearly when their parents' marriage is dissolved. Typically, they are dislodged and disrupted; sometimes they are even abducted during disputes over custody (Cole & Bradford, 1992). The severity of their reaction depends on a number of factors, including these: the personality of each parent; the adaptability of the child (Thiessen, 1993); the coping strategies of the mother (Krause & Long, 1993); whether the children have friends whose parents were divorced (Jenkins & Smith, 1993); and whether the father continues to relate to them afterwards.

In the movie *Mrs. Doubtfire*, Robin Williams played a father who was intensely involved in the lives of his children and who continued after the divorce to be an integral part of their lives. According to current research, however, that pattern is not typical. Although studies have confirmed that the "best interests" of children include an ongoing relationship with both parents, in Canada, Great Britain, and the United States, one out of every two divorced fathers disengages not only from the spouse, but also from the children when sole custody is awarded to the mother (Kruk, 1993, 1994).

In his investigation, Kruk studied both kinds of post-divorce fathers: those who were engaged with their children and those who had withdrawn. The remarkable finding of this research was that those fathers who were highly involved with their children *before* the divorce were the ones most likely to disengage themselves afterwards. And those fathers who had been more marginal participants in their children's lives became more involved with them. What can explain this contrary result? Kruk found that the fathers who had previously spent less time with the children now had formal responsibilities— for example, visitation on particular days or weekends—and dedicated themselves to their children at those times. The fathers who had been very involved had a very different experience: They lost a major component of their personal identity, they suffered because their children were absent from their lives, and they grieved intensely. As a result, by the time the transition period (divorce to one year later) was complete, they had disengaged. Kruk sets a challenge to mental health professionals—to continue to count fathers as part of the children's family, even when they are not given legal custody by the courts.

Grandparents are also adversely affected by divorce; often they are denied access to the grandchildren. The extent of this problem was made public in 1993, when an organization called GRAND (Grandparents Requesting Access and Dignity) submitted 5,000 signatures to the Canadian federal government in support of their rights to have access to their grandchildren.

WHAT ARE THE CAUSES OF DIVORCE? Long-term studies of couples who remain married and those who divorce provide revealing insights into this important question. Let's begin with couples who report being happy in their marriage. Studies indicate that people in these relationships agree with each other on aims, goals, and sex life; that they genuinely *like* their spouse, as a good friend; that they are committed to the relationship and want it to succeed; and that they share many positive experiences and are proud of their spouse's achievements (Lauer & Lauer, 1985). Happily married couples direct positive communication to their spouse: They express affection, approval, appreciation, and pleasure, just as they did during courtship (Bradbury & Fincham, 1992). In contrast, people who report being unhappy in their marriage often adopt a negative pattern of communication: They direct mainly criticisms toward their spouse, blame them for anything and everything that goes wrong, and rarely express positive feelings or approval (Miller, 1991).

Couples who divorce also differ from happy ones in many other ways. First, they have basic disagreements about goals, lifestyles, sex, and many other matters (Levinger, 1988). Second, they report high levels of boredom in their relationship. They feel that they are in a rut and don't enjoy doing things with their spouse (Bradbury & Fincham, 1992). Third, their spouse no longer fills their needs for affection, esteem, and approval (Cottrell, Eisenberg, & Speicher, et al., 1992).

Additional factors associated with divorce include low income, brief courtship, unrealistic expectations about the relationship, and pregnancy at the time of marriage (Kurdek, 1993). Perhaps the most surprising finding of all is that genetic factors may play a role in divorce. How could that be? Here is the reasoning behind that conclusion. That couples whose parents have been divorced are more likely to divorce is known (Glenn & Kramer, 1987). In general, however, this is assumed to be an adverse effect of growing up in a divorced home—perhaps the more direct factors are lower emotional stability and a lack of models of happy, long-term relationships.

However, McGue and Lykken (1992) compared the divorce rates of hundreds of monozygotic (identical) and dizygotic (nonidentical) twins whose parents were or were not divorced. If monozygotic twins were more likely to both divorce than dizygotic twins, that would be evidence for a genetic contribution to divorce. As shown in Figure 9.5, that is precisely what was found. Moreover, the same researchers also found that divorce was more likely if either the twins' own parents or their spouse's parents had been divorced. In probabilistic terms, in this study, if a monozygotic twin's sibling, parents, and spouse's parents were all divorced, the likelihood of the twin divorcing was about 77.5 percent. In contrast, if neither the sibling nor the parents or parents-in-law were divorced, the likelihood that the twin would divorce is 5.3 percent.

How can genetic factors influence divorce? McGue and Lykken suggest that people whose parents are divorced may inherit characteristics that make it difficult for them to maintain long-term relationships. These specific characteristics remain to be identified, so this is only one possible explanation. Moreover, this research does not deny at all that environmental factors are important predictors of divorce. Still, the findings suggest a new perspective on divorce that should be carefully considered in future research.

There is much that can be done to help individuals deal with the distress, conflict, and emotional upheaval that may occur in marriage, whether or not

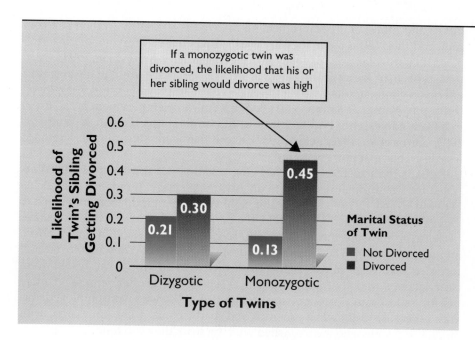

FIGURE 9.5

Evidence for the Role of Genetic Factors in Divorce

If a monozygotic twin was divorced, the likelihood that his or her twin would also be divorced was higher than if a dizygotic twin was divorced. These and other findings offer support for the view that genetic factors play some role in divorce, presumably through their influence on various aspects of personality. (Source: Based on findings from McGue & Lykken, 1992.)

it ends in divorce. One option is counseling that focuses clearly on the happy marital experiences of the past and makes connections between those happy experiences and future possibilities (Plechaty, 1988). Separation group therapy is beneficial to some participants (Addington, 1992), who may well find that their difficulties are not unique, but common to many other couples. Divorce mediation is an important service (Kruk, 1993), particularly when there are children involved. The reaction of friends and family, whether approving or disapproving, also makes a difference, particularly to post-divorce adjustment and remarriage after divorce (Huddleston & Hawkings, 1993). Many investigators recommend counseling prior to marriage—for example, premarital preparation (Tremblay, 1992).

UNEMPLOYMENT Work is central to our lives. When asked, "Who are you?" a large proportion of employed adults reply in terms of their job or occupation (Greenberg & Baron, 1993). "JOBS JOBS JOBS" was the political message that prevailed in the last federal election in Canada. Thus, it is not surprising that losing a job—or even the prospect of losing a job—is considered a crisis in adult life (Konovsky & Brockner, 1993). Unfortunately, getting laid off is an increasingly common experience for adults in the 1990s. In Canada, many companies have reduced the size of their work force; as a result, the term *downsizing* has taken on a frightening meaning. Increasing numbers of people are being laid off, and when it happens, it is harder for them to find other employment. The reasons why older job hunters have such difficulties were studied by Gibson and colleagues in 1992 at the University of Toronto. They found that there were false perceptions that hindered the older unemployed in their search for new employment. Three of these were that they were unqualified for today's work, that they were too costly to employ, and that they had difficulty fitting into a new workplace. These preconceived notions held by prospective employers need to be addressed by older job applicants if they are to succeed in finding new employment.

For the first time since the Great Depression of the 1930s, joblessness has fallen heavily on white-collar employees. Being unemployed is a new and devastating experience for people who formerly held excellent jobs and enjoyed numerous fringe benefits. Many of these newly unemployed are men in their forties and fifties; and because being employed is so central to their self-concept, and their self-esteem, they are crushed when their employment is terminated. In particular, they feel they no longer "matter" (Amundson, 1993).

As you may know from personal experience, there are equally negative effects on young adults who find themselves unemployed or underemployed (Empsom-Warner & Krahn, 1992). Indeed, full-time employment is the usual exit from adolescence and entrance to full adult status (Hagan & Wheaton, 1993; Cairns et al., 1992; Peters, 1987); and if that is missing, another, perhaps less desirable, exit must be found.

Perhaps the negative effects of being unemployed are most vividly illustrated by longitudinal research. In an Australian study, hundreds of students between 15 and 17 were followed for eight years after graduation (Winefield & Tiggemann, 1991). During this time, the participants completed questionnaires designed to measure their self-esteem, feelings of depression, negative affect, and general health. They also reported on whether they were employed and recorded their level of satisfaction with their current work. The results were clear: Unemployed youths reported lower self-esteem, greater depression, more negative affect, and poorer personal health than those who were employed; this was especially true when unemployed participants were compared with employed people who were satisfied with the work they had found.

These and other findings indicate that being unemployed can be stressful and disturbing and can threaten both physical and psychological health (and society as well). Programs for unemployed youths, high school and college or university dropouts, and social services recipients use current knowledge to assist those who cannot find work, or who are unprepared for employment (Wilgosh & Mueller, 1993). The problem is general, however. The steps one can take to overcome these difficulties are listed in **Making Psychology a Part of Your Life** at the end of this chapter.

Gender and the Adult Years: How Men and Women Differ

Before concluding this discussion of change during the adult years, it is important to consider another issue. Do women and men pass through the same phases of development and show the same patterns of change? Several researchers have studied how males and females differ in adult development.

The findings of this research (Baruch, 1984; Roberts & Newton, 1987) offer something of a mixed bag of results. On the one hand, in early adulthood, women do confront many of the same issues as men: They too tend to formulate a *dream* and choose an older and wiser *mentor*. However, there are important differences. First, *all* the men studied by Levinson possessed a dream, but it seems that all women did not. Some women have dreams centered on occupational roles and achievements, and others have dreams focused on relationships with others—for example, a dream of a happy marriage—while still others do not appear to have any well-defined dream. The largest number of women have *split dreams* that include a career and relationships in equal parts (Roberts & Newton, 1987).

Judging from available evidence, some men and women do seem to experience different patterns of change and growth during their adult years.

Aging and Death: The End of Life

Since ancient times, human beings have searched for the "Fountain of Youth"—some means of prolonging youth, and life, indefinitely. But alas, such dreams have remained only illusions. While life and health may be prolonged through proper diet, exercise, and control of stress, there appears to be no way to live forever. The challenge for elderly Canadians is "successful aging" (Butt & Beiser, 1987).

Normal aging is development in the later years—it is not a disease. Research has demonstrated that one key to successful aging is remaining active. O'Brien-Cousins at the University of Alberta studied aging women who had originally been "tomboys" and continued to be physically active, and compared them with others who were not. She took her study (of about 300 women aged 70 to 98) to support the conclusion that "fifty percent of aging [is] the result of inactivity, and that regular exercise prolongs life and contradicts several serious health hazards which arrive with age, for example heart disease and arthritis."

Health concerns, however, rank high among the concerns of aging individuals. While there are common health problems after age sixty-five that can be prevented, like falls, and depression, and bone deterioration (osteoporosis), and some cognitive changes (Hawranik, 1991), there are other health problems that are irreversible—senile dementia, for example.

Why Do We Die?

There are scientific, religious, and philosophical answers to that question. From the perspective of strict evolution, however, the reason is straightforward: Once an individual is past the peak age for mating, their contribution to survival of the species is complete. Why, then, do women live longer, on average, than men? Diamond (1990) has an answer: "These differences [in life expectancy] suggest that women put more energy into [biological] self-repair [to put in their extra years taking care of progeny], while men put more energy into fighting and swagger. [From the evolutionary point of view] it just isn't worth as much to repair a man as it is a woman." At least that is Diamond's idea of Mother Nature's rationale. Her real reason remains a matter of debate.

In this section, we'll consider several questions relating to the conclusion of life: (1) What, specifically, are the causes of aging and death? (2) How do terminally ill people react to their own impending death? (3) How do people cope with the loss of their loved ones?

Theories of Aging: Contrasting Views about Why We Grow Old

Many different views about the causes of aging have been proposed, but most fall under one of two major headings: **wear-and-tear theories** and **genetic theories**.

WEAR-AND-TEAR THEORIES OF AGING   These theories of aging suggest that we grow old because various organs of our bodies, or the cells of which they are composed, wear out. One such theory emphasizes the role of *free radicals*—atoms that are unstable because they have lost electrons. The thinking here is that these highly unstable particles are continuously produced by metabolism; and once formed, they react with other molecules in cells, producing damage. When this damage affects DNA, free radicals may interfere with cell

Wear-and-Tear Theories of Aging: *Theories suggesting that aging results from continuous use of cells and organs within our bodies.*

Genetic Theories of Aging: *Theories suggesting that aging results from genetic programming that regulates the aging process.*

maintenance and repair. The free-radicals theory proposes that this damage accumulates over time and results in the decline in biological function associated with aging. Other wear-and-tear theories focus on different mechanisms, but the outcome—cumulative damage to cells and organs—is similar.

The changes that brain cells undergo over time have been likened to a kind of biological "rust." At the University of Guelph, Janzen, along with Carney (et al., 1991), has developed a compound that counteracts the "bio-rust build-up" of oxidized proteins in gerbils' brains. This discovery may be the basis for future drugs that could be used in treating human disorders in which aging of the brain accelerates—for example, Alzheimer's disease (Eastwood et al., 1992).

Indirect evidence for wear-and-tear theories of aging is provided by individuals who repeatedly expose their bodies to harmful conditions and substances—for example, large doses of alcohol, various drugs, or harsh environments. Such individuals often show premature signs of aging, presumably because they have overburdened their capacity for internal repair.

GENETIC THEORIES OF AGING   A second group of theories attributes physical aging primarily to genetics. The thinking here is that every living organism contains a built-in biological clock that regulates the aging process. This clock may be located in all cells, or in special groups of cells within the brain. Whatever their location, these biological clocks limit the number of times various cells can reproduce. Once that number has been reached, no further cell division occurs, and a decline (leading to death) follows. Another genetic theory, *gene mutation theory*, suggests that genetic mutations interfere with normal cell functioning throughout life. When these mutations reach high enough levels, death results (Cristofalo, 1988).

Support for genetic theories is provided by the findings that certain cells do indeed divide only a set number of times before dying; that no environmental conditions seem capable of increasing numbers; and also, that members of a given species can live for only a limited amount of time, even under ideal conditions of nutrition and health.

Of the several different hypotheses proposed to account for physical aging and death, none is supported by sufficient evidence that it can be viewed as conclusive in nature. At present the best scientific guess is that aging is the result of several different biological processes and a complex interaction between environmental and genetic factors.

Meeting Death: *Facing the End of Life*

What does death mean? The answers to that question is most complex. To begin with, there are several kinds of death. *Physiological death* occurs when all physical processes that sustain life cease. *Brain death* is defined as a total absence of brain activity for at least ten minutes. *Cerebral death* means cessation of activity in the cerebral cortex. And *social death* refers to a process through which other people relinquish their relationships with the deceased (Thomas, 1992).

There are complex ethical issues connected with death, as became clear in the Supreme Court of Canada hearing in the case of Sue Rodriguez, who suffered from a terminal illness and was denied the legal right to end her own life. Should individuals have the right to die when they choose, perhaps by asking their doctor to "pull the plug" on life-sustaining medical apparatus? Should physicians strive to maintain life, even when there is no hope of recovery? In a study at the University of Toronto, it was found that out of every ten Canadians, about eight wished to have their wishes followed in such circumstances (Singer et al., 1993). In a living will, a person sets out the conditions (e.g., ongoing coma) under which they would choose to have life-sustaining treatment terminated. Since physicians are not likely to take on the responsibility (Kelner & Bourgeault, 1993; Family, 1992), the will may state who *can* decide (i.e., which family members or friends) when it should be done. The legality of living wills varies from province to province. These questions are only partly within the realm of science. They remind us of the many profound aspects of death—that it is both a biological and a social event.

People confronted with their own death are faced with several serious difficulties—for example, lack of control over their residence (home or hospital), poor memory, and loss of physical mobility (Chipperfield, 1993). What people think about death and about dying has been studied recently (e.g., de Vries et al., 1993), but perhaps the best known investigation of this subject was conducted by Elizabeth Kübler-Ross (1969), who studied the reactions of patients who had learned that they were terminally ill. On the basis of detailed interviews, she concluded that they pass through a series of five distinct stages.

The first stage is *denial*. In this phase, patients refuse to believe that the end is in sight. "No, it can't be true," they say. "I won't believe it." This stage is soon replaced by a second—*anger*. "Why me?" dying people ask. "It isn't fair." In the third stage, patients do what Kübler-Ross calls *bargaining*: They offer good behavior, prayer, or other changes in their lifestyle in exchange for the postponement of death. When it becomes apparent that their best offers (of a deal with death) have not been accepted, many dying people enter a stage of *depression*. This may occur also because they are growing weaker, or because medical efforts to help them, such as surgery, have failed.

According to Kübler-Ross, however, this is not the final stage in the process. Rather, many terminally ill people move from depression to *acceptance*. At this stage, dying individuals are no longer angry or depressed. Instead, they seem to accept their oncoming death with dignity, and they concentrate on putting their affairs in final order and taking leave of important people in their lives.

Different findings have been reported. For example, Aronoff and Spilka (1984–85) videotaped terminally ill patients at various points during their illness and examined their facial expressions for evidence of the five stages described by Kübler-Ross. They found an increase in sad expressions over time, but no evidence that these individuals became calmer or happier as death approached. Other researchers have found somewhat different patterns, such as expressions of hope throughout a terminal illness (Metzger, 1980) or of personal meaning in life (Cohen & Mount, 1992).

CAREGIVING AND CAREGIVERS   Terminal illness takes a profound toll upon those who care for those who are dying. These caregivers must make important decisions with respect to the extent of their responsibilities to the family member or friend who is now dying (e.g., Wolfson et al., 1993). They must make adjustments and accommodate demands; at the same time, they must not forget their own needs (Rosenthal et al., 1993). Patients develop "emotional silence" in order to survive. By the same token, caregivers suffer in silence to hide their pain; however, these silences can be understood (de Montigny, 1993).

Bereavement: *Mourning the Death of Loved Ones*

When people experience a loss, they grieve. We grieve friendships over, relationships ended, opportunities missed. However, the loss most intensely felt is bereavement—loss by death. As William Worden has put it: "When you lose your parent, you lose your past. When you lose your spouse, you lose

- Wear-and-tear theories of aging suggest that aging results from the fact that cells or organs within our bodies wear out with continued use.

- In contrast, genetic theories suggest that we possess a built-in biological clock that limits the length of our life.

- Research by Kübler-Ross suggests that human beings pass through five distinct stages when confronting their own death. However, these findings have not been confirmed and remain somewhat controversial.

- Bereavement involves several distinct phases, including shock; protest and yearning; disorganization and despair; and detachment, reorganization, and recovery.

your present. When you lose your child, you lose your future. When you lose your friend, you lose yourself." Freud taught that the outcome of loss is depression, but the emotional response is complex, as you will find below.

When mourning a loved one, most people experience the following reactions (Norris & Murrell, 1990). First comes *shock*, a feeling of numbness and unreality that lasts hours or even days. This is followed by *protest and yearning*, as the bereaved person objects to the loss and yearns for the deceased person. A third stage, *disorganization and despair*, may last a year or more. At this time, the mourning person may become apathetic and depressed (Hearty, 1989); life does not seem worth living without the deceased. For most people, this stage is followed by *detachment*, *reorganization*, and *recovery*, as the individual establishes new roles, regains a sense of purpose in life, and psychologically picks up the pieces. Even during this stage, however, painful bouts of grieving may recur on birthdays, anniversaries, and other occasions that remind the bereaved person of their loss. (Figure 9.6 summarizes the major stages of bereavement.)

Bereavement requires adjustments (Lehman et al., 1993; Tudiver et al., 1992). Adolescents who experience the death of a schoolmate, as a result of violence, drug overdose, or suicide, are in particular need of immediate attention, particularly since they may appear normal, yet be experiencing silent suffering. For adults, marital conflict may occur if the grieving partner withdraws and becomes angry without reason (Guttman, 1991); in these cases, therapy may be helpful (e.g., Piper & McCallum, 1991).

In sum, after a prolonged period of mourning, most people do recover and go on with their lives. Indeed, some researchers suggest that grief and mourning promote recovery because of the physiological events that occur during this process; these include changes in levels of a number of different neurohormones and neurotransmitters (Olders, 1989).

FIGURE 9.6

Major Stages of Bereavement

People undergoing *bereavement* seem to pass through the stages of mourning shown here.

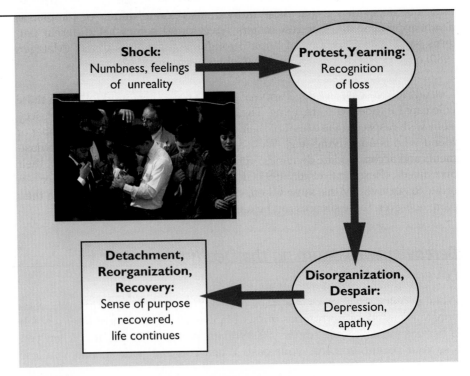

MAKING PSYCHOLOGY PART OF YOUR LIFE

Preparing for Tomorrow's Job Market Today

Faced with the uncertainties of today's and tomorrow's job market, are there any steps you can take to increase your chances of finding employment after graduation? Yes, there are. While they do not guarantee that you will get the job you want, they may give you an edge in an increasingly competitive economic climate (Meier, 1991).

1. *Choose a field with a future* Consider a career in a sector of the economy that promises to grow rapidly in the years ahead. What are these sectors? Like life in general, the job market changes constantly. Each month, Statistics Canada publishes the Help-Wanted Index, a survey of the help-wanted ads in twenty Canadian cities, to show the current job situation. This index measures the degree of change in the job market in various regions of the country. However, it does not tell how many people are looking for each particular job.

   By the way, information supplied by a federal database indicates that in 1993 there were 15,397 jobs in psychology across Canada. By 1999, there are expected to be 18,351 or more. That is a growth rate of at least 19 percent.

2. *Focus on small and medium-size companies* In the past, many graduates sought jobs with prestige companies—those with a big reputation and lots of glamor. In today's job market, this is not a good strategy, for these are precisely the companies that have announced plans to restructure and made the largest cutbacks. Moreover, while one out of every four Canadian workers is employed directly or indirectly by a government, that number is not increasing, because of budget restraints and hiring freezes. In the 1990s, a smaller company may be a better place to begin your career. For example, in the spring of 1993, Statistics Canada reported employment growth in firms with less than 200 employees, and employment decline in firms with more than that. So focus on smaller companies. They may not seem as exciting, but they may be a better place to launch your career.

3. *Be ready to travel to a new location* Job opportunities vary from place to place, and from time to time, in our country. For various reasons (the relative cost of office space being one of them), companies move from province to province, and jobs move from the downtown core of some big cities to smaller centers. In the spring of 1994, for example, there was a net growth in the number of jobs in British Columbia, but that growth took place outside the Lower Mainland, where there was a net decline in jobs and in population.

4. *Be ready to work for a foreign company* Multinational corporations that are expanding their operations are often the ones with the jobs. Working for a foreign company may mean that you must learn a new set of rules, because such companies often follow the home country's customary practices with respect to employees and to work. Given the continued movement toward an interconnected world economy, this is good experience and may open opportunities for you.

5. *Consider part-time or contract work as a way to get started* Full-time jobs with large corporations are becoming harder and harder to find, partly because large companies hire outsiders to do many jobs. Consider starting in this way because often people who are hired on a part-time or contract basis gain an important advantage. They may get the first shot at permanent full-time work when it comes available. Get as much varied experience, in as many kinds of job settings, as you can.

6. *Be prepared to study longer* After earning your first degree, you may need to take post-graduate classes in a specialty of one kind or another, or in a technical specialty, or take management training. Notwithstanding the horror stories we have all heard about Ph.D.s driving taxis and graduates on welfare, the fact is that education is the best predictor, by far, of whether or not you get a good job. When total employment is falling, the proportion of university graduates who find work increases steadily; this is true in every province. For example, in 1992, while the number of jobs for university graduates increased, the number for high school graduates declined, and the rate of unemployment of those with less than nine years of education was about 30 percent. The skills you gain in post-secondary education, in learning new material, in listening carefully, in organizing your thoughts, and in writing original reports will stand you in good stead throughout life, wherever your career path leads.

TABLE 9.1	JOB/CAREER	DESCRIPTION
Careers with a Future The careers listed here are among those expected to grow rapidly in the years ahead.	**Information Technology** Computer programmers	Develop new computer programs
	Systems analysts	Create computer applications for specific needs
	Telecommunications managers	Specialize in the transfer of information through telephones, modems, fax machines, voice mail
	Education and Training Employee trainers	Help people develop new skills needed to perform rapidly changing jobs
	Diversity managers	Help diverse groups of employees work together
	Health Care Nurse practitioners	Deal with a wide range of health problems
	Physical therapists	Specialize in rehabilitation of patients
	Occupational therapists	Specialize in retraining of patients for new jobs
	Business Management Fifty-plus marketing specialists	Promote and sell products aimed at people over fifty
	Employee leasing agents	Help companies "lease" employees for specific projects (as opposed to hiring permanent help)
	Managed care experts	Help organizations to obtain the best benefit plans for employees

ADOLESCENCE: BETWEEN CHILD AND ADULT adolescence 359 puberty 359 adolescent invulnerability 362 blended families 368 dysfunctional families 369 sexual abuse 369	• The most important feature of physical development during adolescence is *puberty*, a period of rapid change during which individuals reach sexual maturity and become capable of reproduction. • Boys who undergo puberty at a relatively early age experience several advantages relative to those who mature later. For girls, the benefits of early maturity are offset by several negative factors, including envy among classmates and unwanted sexual advances from older people. • Research findings indicate that differences between the thinking of adolescents and that of adults are smaller in magnitude and scope than was formerly assumed. For example, adolescents do not have a greater sense of invulnerability than adults. Nevertheless, they are still more likely than adults to engage in high-risk behavior. • According to Erikson's theory, social development involves the resolution of a series of internal crises. For adolescents the most important of these concerns is establishing a clear *self-identity*. Adolescents try out many roles and social selves before establishing a clear self-schema. • Today's adolescents face many conditions that threaten their psychological and physical well-being. Many grow up in single-parent families. Still others are raised in dysfunctional families, which do not meet their needs and in fact do serious harm. Some are exposed to maltreatment, including sexual abuse. • Large numbers of adolescents are sexually active. Negative consequences of this include teen pregnancies and the spread of AIDS and other sexually transmitted diseases.
ADULTHOOD AND AGING climacteric 374 menopause 374 primary aging 376 secondary aging 376 crystallized intelligence 382 fluid intelligence 382 life structure 382 dream 383 mentor 383 mid-life transition 384 late-adult transition 384	• *Stage theories* of adult development suggest that we move through distinct stages as adults. The most famous of these is a theory proposed by Erikson suggesting that we must resolve different crises as we move through various phases of life. In contrast, *life-event* theories view adult development as tied to individuals' responses to important events in their lives. • Physical change occurs slowly during our early adult years but accelerates in mid-life. Both men and women experience changes in their reproductive systems during mid-life; these are known collectively as the *climacteric*. This process may be more dramatic for women, who undergo *menopause* at this time. Reactions to menopause appear to be strongly influenced by cultural factors. • Many physical changes occur in later life, including declines in sensory abilities. • Short-term memory does not decline with age, but recall of information from long-term memory does decline somewhat. Prospective memory, too, declines somewhat with age. Performance on abstract problem-solving tasks declines with age, but performance in solving real-life problems increases. • There may be some declines in intelligence with age, but these are smaller and more limited in scope than was once widely believed. Some findings suggest that wisdom and creativity increase with age. • A theory proposed by Levinson suggests that during our adult years we move through a number of distinct *life eras*, which are separated from each other by turbulent *transition periods*. • Throughout life, we follow an underlying pattern or design that Levinson called the life structure; this constantly evolves as we move from one era to another. • Among major crises of adult life are divorce and unemployment. Happily married couples differ in many respects from couples who divorce. They show more agreement on goals, lifestyles, and sex, and the spouses communicate more praise and approval to each other. Divorce is also related to such factors as low income, lack of commitment, and boredom. Genetic factors, too, may play a role.

	• Job loss is an increasingly common experience for white-collar employees in many countries. Being unemployed can undermine an individual's psychological and physical well-being. • While men and women show many similarities in adult development, important differences between them seem to exist. Women often have split dreams that focus on both careers and relationships. Women who work outside the home appear to experience greater well-being than women who are not employed.
AGING AND DEATH: THE END OF LIFE wear-and-tear theories of aging 389 genetic theories of aging 389	• Wear-and-tear theories of aging suggest that aging results from continuous use of cells and organs within our bodies. In contrast, genetic theories suggest that we possess built-in biological clocks that limit the length of our lives. Research by Kübler-Ross suggests that human beings pass through five distinct stages when confronting their own death. However, ideas remain unconfirmed. • Bereavement involves several distinct phases, including shock; protest and yearning; disorganization and despair; and attachment, reorganization, and recovery.

CRITICAL THINKING QUESTIONS

APPRAISAL	People change in so many ways during the course of their adult lives that some psychologists are pessimistic about ever getting a firm handle on these changes; they doubt they'll ever be able to understand them fully. Do you agree? Or do you think that systematic study of adult development can yield conclusive scientific knowledge about this important process? Support your position.
CONTROVERSY	Growing evidence indicates that children from disadvantaged backgrounds in Canada and elsewhere are being placed at tremendous risk by the environments in which they live. This has led some people to recommend massive government programs to help these children. Do you think such programs are justified? How might they be designed? In what ways could they help?
MAKING PSYCHOLOGY PART OF YOUR LIFE	On the basis of what you've learned from this chapter, what steps could you take to enhance your own physical and psychological well-being, and, in this way, increase your own life span?

Motivation
and Emotion

MOTIVATION: THE ACTIVATION AND
PERSISTENCE OF BEHAVIOR 401
Theories of Motivation: Diverse Views of A
  Complex Process
Hunger: Regulating Our Caloric Intake
Sexual Motivation: The Most Intimate
  Motive
Aggressive Motivation: The Most
  Dangerous Motive
Achievement and Power: Two Complex
  Human Motives
Gender Differences in Achievement
  Motivation: Do They Really Exist?
Intrinsic Motivation: How (Sometimes) to
  Turn Play into Work

EMOTIONS: THEIR NATURE, EXPRESSION, AND
IMPACT 426
The Nature of Emotions: Some
  Contrasting Views
The Physiology of Emotion
The External Expression of Emotion:
  Outward Sings of Inner Feelings
Emotion and Cognition: How Feelings
  Shape Thoughts and Thoughts Shape
  Feelings

SUMMARY AND REVIEW OF KEY POINTS 440

CANADIAN FOCUS—SERIOUS EATING
DISORDERS: ANOREXIA NERVOSA AND BULIMIA
409

PERSPECTIVES ON DIVERSITY—THE ROLE
OF CULTURAL FACTORS IN AGGRESSION: THE
SOCIAL CONTEXT OF VIOLENCE 420

THE POINT OF IT ALL—TURNING WORK
INTO PLAY: INTRINSIC MOTIVATION IN THE
CLASSROOM 424

THE RESEARCH PROCESS—SUPPORT FOR
SCHACHTER AND SINGER 428

KEY CONCEPT—THREE MAJOR THEORIES OF
EMOTION 429

THE POINT OF IT ALL—CAN PHYSIOLOGICAL
REACTIONS BE USED TO DETECT LIES? 431

THE RESEARCH PROCESS—ARE PEOPLE IN
A GOOD MOOD EASIER TO INFLUENCE? EFFECTS
OF MOOD ON INFORMATION PROCESSING 436

MAKING PSYCHOLOGY PART OF YOUR
LIFE—GETTING MOTIVATED: SOME PRACTICAL
TECHNIQUES 439

HILL CLAIMS SEVERAL FAT TIRE RIDERS

**The Whitehorse Star Daily:
September 1, 1994.**

The Fat Tire Fever is a mountain bike race that takes place in Whitehorse every year. The course is 2.9 kilometers and begins with a long climb right at the start and a steep, sandy downhill right afterwards. As one competitor told The Whitehorse Star, "The billiard-ball sized rocks...can really throw you...you don't want to get going too fast."

This kind of race can be hazardous to the personal (and financial) well-being of the participants. Indeed, the winner of the Fat Tire Fever reported that he had not even finished the very first race of the season. He had serious wipe-out and he wrecked his bike.

Notwithstanding the billiard-ball-sized rocks, the difficulty, and the danger, men and women continued to toil through the season—to the finish line of the final race.

Why do human beings behave like this? What motivates us to persist in the face of these kinds of obstacles? What do we know about the emotion involved in winning...and in losing?

In Chapter 10 you will read about the answers that psychological research has found to the questions about human motivation and emotion.

THIS CHAPTER IS ABOUT THE "FEELING" SIDE OF LIFE—WHAT JAMES BROWN MEANS WHEN HE SINGS "I FEEL GOOD!"

*H*ere are some questions that psychologists working in motivation and emotion ask. Why do we continue to eat when we are no longer hungry? What makes some movies sexually arousing? What makes us think that someone is lying? Why do some people continue to work long hours, well after they have more money than the bank? Why do others try not to work at all? Why does the world seem beautiful when we are up, but bleak when we are having a down day? Do gray skies really clear up if we put on a happy face? These questions are about the "feeling" side of life—about, as psychologists would put it, the topics of motivation and emotion.

The term *motivation* refers to internal processes that activate, guide, and maintain our behavior. Motivation has to do with the goals we choose and the ways we achieve them. Understanding motivation often helps us to answer the question *why*—that is, to give reasons for our behavior and that of others. Clearly, motivation is relevant to several of the questions just raised—the differences between workaholics and shirkaholics, the nature of sexual arousal, and so on (Silver, Mitchell, & Gist, in press).

Emotion, in contrast, is about how we feel: happy or sad, afraid or angry, proud or ashamed. In psychology, emotion refers to an internal state composed of (1) physiological responses such as changes in blood pressure and heart rate; (2) subjective cognitive judgments—the feelings we describe as joy, anger, sorrow, sexual arousal, and so on; and (3) expressive reactions, such as changes in facial expression or posture. Emotions play a crucial role in all aspects of behavior. Moreover, they influence our perceptions—when we are in a good mood, we tend to see the world through rose-colored glasses (e.g., Forgas, 1991; Smith & Shafer, 1991).

This chapter will provide an overview of current knowledge about these two topics. First, we'll consider contrasting theories about the basic nature of motivation. Then we'll examine several important forms of motivation: *hunger, sexual motivation, aggression*, and motivation as it relates to *achievement* and *power*. After that we'll turn to *emotion*. Again, we'll begin by examining several theories; then we'll turn to the physiological bases of emotion, and consider the expression and communication of emotion—how emotional reactions are reflected in external behavior. Finally, we'll look at the complex relationship between emotion and cognition—how feelings shape thoughts and how thoughts shape feelings. Remember that motivation is what we ask about in the question, "Why did I do that?" And emotion is what we ask about in the question, "How do I feel?"

As with other aspects of our behavior, motivational and emotional states are biologically based—in the central and peripheral nervous systems. When those systems become damaged in some way, changes occur. The psychological disorders you will read about in Chapter 14 include such transformations. Moreover, current research finds that when the prefrontal lobes of the cerebral cortex are damaged, there are motivational and emotional consequences that may change the individual's personality and alter the "stable response patterns that define the individual as a unique self" (Stuss et al., 1992).

Motivation: *The Activation and Persistence of Behavior*

Consider the following events:

- A group of young women and men lower themselves into a dark cave to explore it. As they proceed, they must squeeze through openings barely large enough for their bodies, and avoid sudden drops where the cave floor plunges away into seemingly bottomless pits. They finally reemerge into the sunlight five days later, dirty and tired but happy.

- Employees of a large bank remain on strike for month after month, even though any settlement they ultimately obtain will not be enough to compensate them for the lost wages and benefits.

On the face of it, these actions are somewhat puzzling. Why would people risk life and limb exploring a cave, even though they can't hope to obtain any practical benefits by doing so? Why would people continue to strike even if there was nothing to be gained? One answers is this: Such actions occur because the individuals involved are *motivated* to perform them. In other words, they are responding to internal states that can't be directly observed but that activate, guide, and maintain overt behaviors. While there is general agreement on this basic point, there has been considerable *disagreement*, over the years, about the basic nature of **motivation**. Let's consider some of these contrasting perspectives.

MOTIVATION: A USEFUL CONCEPT FOR UNDERSTANDING BEHAVIOR

Why do people engage in risky behaviors? One answer involves motivation—an internal process that can't be directly observed but that activates, guides, and maintains overt behavior.

Theories of Motivation: *Diverse Views of a Complex Process*

In psychology, before there was *motivation* there was **instinct theory**. In other words, before psychologists attempted to explain human behavior in terms of motives, they explained it by reference to various **instincts**: innate patterns of behavior that are universal in a species, independent of experience, and elicited by specific stimuli or conditions. For a time, this approach was quite popular. William James (1890), one of the founders of American psychology, included *pugnacity* (or combativeness), *acquisitiveness* (or greed), *sympathy*, and *curiosity* on his list of basic human instincts. And Sigmund Freud suggested that many complex forms of behavior—from aggression to love—stem from inherited, biologically based instincts.

Do instincts really play a major role in human behavior? Most psychologists nowadays think not. This is because, in the past, in many cases, the fact of an instinct was inferred from the very behavior it was supposed to explain. For example, take the case of *aggression*, a form of behavior we'll consider soon in more detail. Why do human beings, in contrast to many other species, frequently attack others of their own kind? The answer provided by James, Freud, and many others was simple: It's because human beings possess a powerful aggressive instinct (Hanly, 1978). But how do we know that they possess this instinct? Because there is so much aggression. As I'm sure you can see, this is a circular argument in which an instinct is inferred from observations of behavior and then used to *explain* the occurrence of the same behavior (see Figure 10.1 for another example). As more and more psychologists recognized this basic flaw in the instinct approach, support for it waned. It was soon replaced by other perspectives on motivation.

Motivation: An inferred internal process that activates, guides, and maintains behavior over time.

Instinct Theory: A theory of motivation suggesting that many forms of behavior stem from innate urges or tendencies.

Instincts: Patterns of behavior assumed to be universal in a species.

FIGURE 10.1

The Concept of Instinct and Circular Reasoning

In the past it was suggested that people have a curiosity instinct. This instinct was inferred from the many instances in which people demonstrated natural curiosity. Then, in a dazzling display of circular reasoning, this supposed instinct was used to explain the occurrence of such behavior.

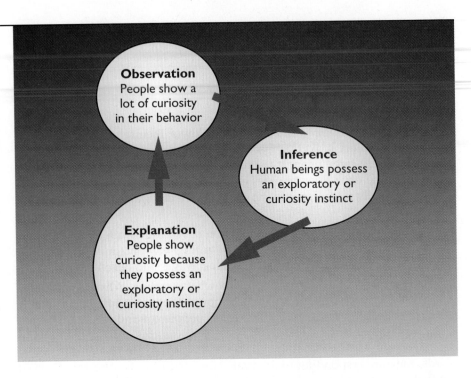

Observation
People show a lot of curiosity in their behavior

Inference
Human beings possess an exploratory or curiosity instinct

Explanation
People show curiosity because they possess an exploratory or curiosity instinct

Drive Theory: A theory of motivation suggesting that behavior is "pushed" from within by drives stemming from basic biological needs.

Homeostasis: A state of physiological balance within the body.

Arousal Theory: A theory of motivation suggesting that human beings seek an optimal level of arousal, not minimal levels of arousal.

DRIVE THEORY: MOTIVATION AND HOMEOSTASIS What do feelings like hunger, thirst, chill, and burn have in common? That's right … they're all unpleasant and we try to eliminate them. This is the basis for a second major approach to motivation: **drive theory**. According to drive theory, biological needs arising within our bodies create unpleasant states such as hunger, thirst, fatigue, and so on. In order to eliminate these feelings and restore a balanced physiological state (known as **homeostasis**) we engage in certain directed behaviors (see Figure 10.2). Behaviors that reduce the appropriate drive are strengthened and tend to be repeated. Those which fail to produce such effects are weakened and are less likely to be repeated when the drive is present again.

In its original form, drive theory focused primarily on biological needs and the aroused states, or drives, they produce. Soon, though, psychologists extended this model to other forms of behavior not so clearly tied to basic needs, including drives for stimulation, for status, and for wealth and power (Weiner, 1989).

Drive theory persisted in psychology for several decades; it has not been totally discarded even today. However, there is widespread agreement that this approach has several major drawbacks. The most important problem is this: Contrary to what drive theory seems to suggest, human beings often engage in actions that *increase* rather than reduce various drives. For example, people sometimes skip snacks and let their appetites increase in order to maximize their enjoyment of a special dinner. Similarly, some people watch or read erotic materials in order to increase their sexual excitement, even when they don't anticipate immediate gratification (Kelley & Byrne, 1992). In view of such evidence, most psychologists now believe that drive theory, by itself, does not provide a comprehensive framework for understanding human motivation.

AROUSAL THEORY: SEEKING OPTIMUM ACTIVATION When it became clear that people sometimes seek to increase rather than to decrease existing drives, an alternative theory of motivation known as **arousal theory** was formulated

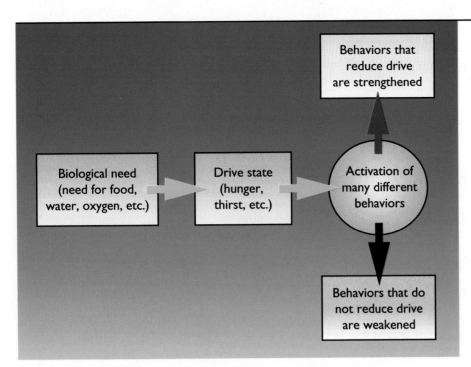

FIGURE 10.2

Drive Theory: An Overview

According to drive theory, biological needs lead to the arousal of appropriate *drives* that activate specific forms of behavior. Actions that satisfy (reduce) these drives are strengthened and tend to be repeated when the drive is again present. Behaviors that fail to satisfy the drives are weakened.

Behaviors that reduce drive are strengthened

Biological need (need for food, water, oxygen, etc.)

Drive state (hunger, thirst, etc.)

Activation of many different behaviors

Behaviors that do not reduce drive are weakened

(Geen, Beatty, & Arkin, 1984). This theory focuses on *arousal*, our general level of activation, which is reflected in physiological measures such as heart rate, blood pressure, muscle tension, and brain activity (Brehm & Self, 1989). Arousal varies throughout the day, from low levels during sleep to much higher ones when we are performing strenuous tasks. Arousal theory suggests that what we seek is *optimal arousal*—the level of arousal that is best suited to our own personal characteristics and whatever activity we are currently performing. So, for example, if you are listening to soothing music, a relatively low level of arousal will be optimal. If you are competing in a sports event, a much higher level will be best.

Many studies offer indirect support for arousal theory. For example, there *is* often a close link between arousal and performance (see Figure 10.3; Weiner, 1989). However, it is often difficult to determine in advance the optimal level of arousal for a given task or situation. Further, large individual differences exist with respect to preferred levels of arousal. At one extreme are individuals who prefer and seek high levels and therefore seek out situations that are exciting and/or risky (Coren & Mah, 1993). At the other are those who prefer much lower levels (Zuckerman, 1990). Thus, while the theory does provide useful insights into the nature of motivation, it also has important limitations.

EXPECTANCY THEORY: A COGNITIVE APPROACH   Why are you reading this book? It's probably not to reduce some biologically based drive. The chances are good that you are reading it because you expect that doing so will help you reach important goals: to gain useful and interesting knowledge, to get a higher grade on the next exam, to graduate from college or university. In short, your behavior is determined by your *expectancies*—that is, by your belief that your present actions will yield various outcomes in the future. This point provides the foundation for a third major theory of motivation, **expectancy theory**. This view suggests that motivation is not primarily a matter of being pushed by various urges; rather, it is more a question of being *pulled* by expectations of attaining desired outcomes. Such outcomes, known

Expectancy Theory: A theory of motivation suggesting that behavior is "pulled" by expectations of desirable outcomes.

FIGURE 10.3

Arousal and Performance

Across a wide range of tasks, performance increases as arousal rises to moderate levels. Beyond some point, however, optimal levels of arousal are exceeded, and performance begins to decline.

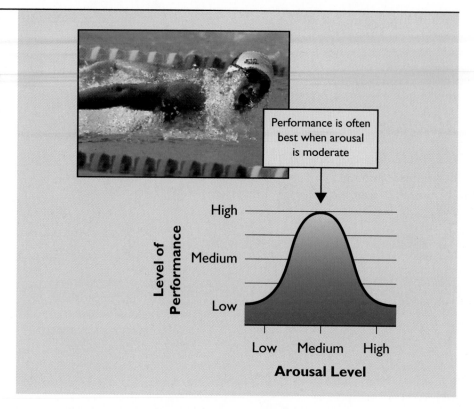

Performance is often best when arousal is moderate

as **incentives**, can be almost anything we have learned to value—money, status, power, and the admiration of others, to name just a few. In other words, while drive theory focuses mainly on the stick in the familiar carrot-and-stick notion, expectancy theory focuses more directly on the carrot. Why do people engage in complex, effortful, or even painful behaviors such as working long hours at the office, performing aerobic exercises, or studying long into the night? Expectancy theory answers this way: because they believe that doing so will yield outcomes they wish to attain.

Expectancy theory has been applied to many aspects of human motivation. For example, at the University of Windsor, Rogers and Brawley (1991) studied the expectancies of undergraduates as related to their motivation for participating in an exercise program. However, it is **work motivation**—the energy and effort we put out on the job—that has been found most central to our lives (Locke & Latham, 1990). Research indicates that people will work hard at their jobs when they believe that doing so will yield outcomes they desire, such as raises in pay, promotions, or increased status. (But that is only part of the story. We'll return to work motivation in more detail in Chapter 17, which discusses at length industrial–organizational psychology).

In short, expectancy theory suggests that our motivation to engage in various activities will be high when we expect that performing them will somehow pay off—that is, yield outcomes or results we desire.

Incentives: Rewards individuals seek to attain.

Work Motivation: Motivation to perform and complete various tasks.

MASLOW'S NEEDS HIERARCHY: RELATIONSHIPS AMONG MOTIVES Before concluding this discussion of contrasting perspectives on motivation, it is important to consider one additional question: Which specific motives influence behavior at any given time? One answer has been provided by Abraham Maslow

(1970), who proposed that different motives—or needs, as he called them—form a hierarchy. He also stipulated that those at the bottom of the hierarchy must be at least partly satisfied before those higher up can influence behavior. At the base of Maslow's **hierarchy of needs** are *physiological needs*, such as for food, water, oxygen, and sleep. One step above these are the *safety needs*, for feeling safe and secure in one's life. Above the safety needs are *social needs*, which include the need to have friends, to be loved and appreciated, and to belong—to fit into a network of social relationships.

Maslow describes physiological, safety, and social needs as *deficiency needs*: They are the basics and must be satisfied before higher levels of motivation, or *growth needs*, can emerge. Above the social needs in the hierarchy are *esteem needs*, which include the needs for self-respect, for the approval of others, and for success. Ambition and the need for achievement, to which we'll return in a later section, are also closely linked to esteem needs. Finally, at the top of the hierarchy are *self-actualization needs*, which include the need for self-fulfillment—the desire to become all one is capable of being. Self-actualization needs include concerns not only with one's selfish interests but also with issues that affect the well-being of others—of humanity. Figure 10.4 provides an overview of Maslow's theory.

These needs have been studied in a number of special Canadian populations: campers in three Canadian parks (Shin, 1993); perfectionists, who have difficulty achieving self-actualization (Flett et al.); public librarians in Ontario (Schell & Bonin, 1989); elderly adults in Quebec (Plouffe & Gravelle); and Ontario funeral directors (Schell & Zinger, 1985).

Maslow's theory is intuitively appealing, but is it accurate? Do needs exist in hierarchy, and must lower-level needs be met before higher-level ones can

Hierarchy of Needs: In Maslow's theory of motivation, an arrangement of needs from the most basic to those at the highest levels.

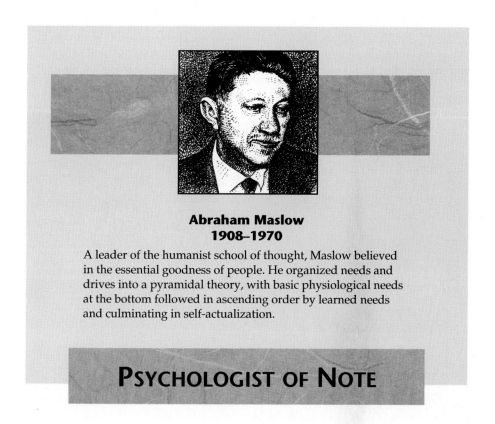

Abraham Maslow
1908–1970

A leader of the humanist school of thought, Maslow believed in the essential goodness of people. He organized needs and drives into a pyramidal theory, with basic physiological needs at the bottom followed in ascending order by learned needs and culminating in self-actualization.

PSYCHOLOGIST OF NOTE

- The concept of motivation is helpful in explaining behavior that can't readily be interpreted in terms of current conditions in a given situation.
- Drive theory proposes that motivation is basically a process in which various biological needs push (drive) us to actions designed to satisfy these needs.
- Arousal theory suggests that organisms seek optimal levels of arousal.
- Expectancy theory suggests that behavior is often motivated by expectancies concerning the outcomes that will result from specific actions.
- Maslow's theory suggests that needs exist in a hierarchy and that higher-level needs cannot be activated, or serve as sources of motivation, until lower-level needs have been satisfied.

Hunger Motivation: The motivation to obtain and consume food.

have a motivating effect? Research findings on these issues are mixed. Some results suggest that growth needs do come after lower-level deficiency needs (Betz, 1982). But other findings indicate that people sometimes seek to satisfy higher-order needs even when those lower in the hierarchy have not been met (Williams & Page, 1989). Moreover, several needs, and motivations relating to them, can sometimes be active at once (Greenberg & Baron, 1993). So, in sum, Maslow's needs hierarchy is best viewed as an interesting but largely unverified framework for organizing our thoughts about motivation.

Hunger: Regulating Our Caloric Intake

Mahatma Gandhi, one of the founders of modern India, once remarked, "Even God cannot speak to a hungry man except in terms of bread." By this he meant that when people are hungry, **hunger motivation**, the urge to obtain and consume food, takes precedence over all others. This view is consistent with Maslow's needs hierarchy. If you have ever gone without food for a day, you already know what a powerful source of motivation those strong and insistent feelings of hunger can be. This is known to the clients at the Daily Bread Food Bank in Toronto, at the Metro Food Bank in Dartmouth, Nova Scotia, and at similar services in many Canadian communities.

But where do such feelings come from? And how do we manage to regulate the amount of food we consume so that, for most people, body weight remains fairly stable even over long periods of time? These are some of the questions psychologists have addressed in their efforts to understand the nature of hunger motivation.

FIGURE 10.4

Maslow's Needs Hierarchy

According to Maslow (1970), needs exist in a hierarchy. Only when lower-order needs are satisfied can higher-order needs be activated.

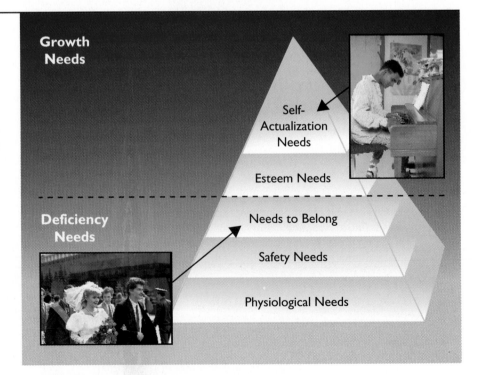

THE REGULATION OF EATING: A COMPLEX PROCESS   Consider the following: If you consume just twenty calories more than you need each day (less than the amount of a single small carrot), you will gain about two pounds a year—twenty pounds in a decade. How do people keep caloric input and output closely balanced and so avoid such outcomes? How do we maintain a stable body weight? The answer involves a complex system of regulatory mechanisms located in the hypothalamus, liver, and elsewhere. These systems contain special *detectors*, cells that respond to variations in the concentration of several nutrients in the blood. One type of detector responds to the amount of *glucose*, or blood sugar. Other detectors respond to levels of *protein*, and especially to certain amino acids. Finally, other detectors respond to lipids, or fats. Even if glucose levels are low, when the amount of protein or lipid circulating in the blood is high, we do not feel hungry.

Complex as all this seems, it is still only part of the story. Eating and hunger are also strongly affected by the smell and taste of food and by feedback produced by chewing and swallowing. The impact of these factors is well documented. For example, in one series of studies, volunteers wore special equipment fitted to their teeth that permitted the researchers to obtain records of their actual chewing (Stellar, 1985). Participants also reported on their feelings of hunger and on the tastiness of the foods they ate. At first, when they were very hungry, the volunteers chewed less and swallowed more often. As they satisfied their hunger, they reported that the foods were less and less tasty and they chewed more and swallowed less often; their rate of intake dropped. Tasty food is more satiating than bland (but nutritionally identical) versions of the same meal (Warwick et al., 1993).

The sight of food is also an important factor in eating. Foods that are attractive in appearance are hard to resist; many people eat more when food is presented attractively. Cultural factors also play a major role in determining what, when, and how much we eat. Would you happily munch on fried grasshoppers? Sea urchin? Octopus cooked in its own ink? How about snails or snake? Depending on the culture in which you have been raised, the thought of such items may induce hunger or nausea. These contrasting reactions suggest that although hunger does indeed stem from biological needs, it is strongly influenced by learning and experience, and by cognitive factors as well (Rodin, 1984). So even this seemingly basic form of motivation is more complex than you might at first suppose.

FACTORS IN OBESITY: DIFFERENCES IN THE LONG-TERM REGULATION OF BODY WEIGHT
People who weigh 28 kilograms (60 pounds) or more than they should for their height and body build have a condition known as **obesity**. In 1994 in Canada, about four in ten men, three in ten women, and two in ten children (6 to 11 years old) were obese. There is now convincing medical evidence that obesity is a health hazard. This level of excess weight has been linked to serious

Obesity: The state of being significantly overweight.

VISUAL CUES PAY AN IMPORTANT ROLE IN HUNGER
Even though you can't smell or taste the foods shown here, you would probably choose the one on the right as the more appetizing dish.

disorders such as high blood pressure, diabetes, and arthritis (Kolata, 1985). Also, employees who are significantly overweight miss more days of work than those who are not (Goode, 1990).

Why do some people weight so much more than they should? There are a number of different reasons. First, genetic factors may be involved—that is, some obese individuals may have inherited their condition. In all animals, body weight is carefully maintained at a stable level by powerful internal control systems. (That is why some people find it hard to lose weight—those control systems continue to increase weight back to its original level.) Also, individuals differ in their basal metabolic rate, which is a measure of the number of calories the human body burns when at rest. Individuals of the same age and weight performing the same activities differ greatly in this measure of metabolism; as a result, one person may be able to consume twice as many calories as another and still maintain a stable weight.

Researchers in Australia and the United States have reported different links between particular genes and obesity (Morris et al., 1993; Noble et al., 1994). Indeed, obesity may involve different genes in different people. In the Australian research, a single connection was found between genetic inheritance and obesity, although overeating and lack of exercise were also cited as important. The American study found a gene that was implicated in several different addictions (alcohol, nicotine, and cocaine), including the craving for sweets. Reportedly, the sugar rush that occurs when we consume sugar is linked to the neurotransmitter dopamine, which is important to feelings of happiness and satisfaction. Because of their genetic inheritance, obese people may have fewer dopamine receptors than normal. For them, it takes more dopamine to produce the same positive effects.

However, many people are seriously overweight for other reasons. What might those be? The fact is that learning plays an important role in eating behavior.

Many people acquire eating habits that are very likely to generate excess pounds. They learn to prefer high-calorie meals that are rich in protein and fats. Further, they learn to associate the act of eating with many different contexts and situations. If you feel a strong urge to snack every time you sit down in front of the television set or movie screen, you already know about this type of learning. The desire to eat can be classically conditioned (see Chapter 5); that is, cues associated with eating when we are hungry can acquire the capacity to prompt eating even when we are *not* hungry.

We also learn to eat by imitation. Goldman (et al., 1991) demonstrated that in an experiment with female undergraduate nondieters at the University of Toronto. In this study, the amount of food consumed was compared when subjects ate in the presence of another person, who ate either a little or a lot. The subjects' eating behavior followed the example set by their companion. In fact, the social pressure was so strong that even after not eating for twenty-four hours, these subjects ate very little. In a different study, male and female students ate a meal in the presence of an attractive male or female. The results showed that both men and women ate less than they would have otherwise. In both cases, the goal was to make a good impression, but for slightly different reasons. The men wanted to behave in a socially desirable manner; the women wanted to be socially desirable and appear feminine (Pliner & Chaiken, 1990).

A third factor that plays an important role in the regulation of weight among humans is stress. How do *you* react to stress—for example, to a big exam, a quarrel with a friend, a traffic ticket? If you are like most people, your appetite probably decreases at such times. That unpleasant feeling in the pit of your stomach makes eating unattractive, at least temporarily.

Overweight people, however, often have a different reaction—they tend to eat *more* during periods of stress.

Yet a fourth factor seems to contribute to unwanted weight gain. Overweight people respond more strongly to external cues relating to food (Rodin & Slochower, 1976). They report feeling hungrier in the presence of food-related cues—the sight or smell of foods—than others do; also, they find it harder to resist eating when tasty foods are available, even if they are not hungry (Rodin, 1984).

Taking all these factors together, it is not surprising that many people experience difficulties in regulating their own weight in the long term. There are simply too many variables (or conditions) that, together or separately, can overwhelm the exquisitely balanced—and extraordinarily complex—biological mechanisms that normally keep body weight stable.

Anorexia Nervosa: An eating disorder in which individuals starve themselves and often lose a dangerous amount of weight.

Bulimia: An eating disorder in which periods of binge eating alternate with periods of self-induced purging.

CANADIAN FOCUS

Serious Eating Disorders: Anorexia Nervosa and Bulimia

The gravest eating disorders are anorexia nervosa and bulimia. These afflictions are somewhat different, although they may coexist in the same person. They affect different age groups and different numbers of individuals, who react in distinct ways to some neurohormones (Vaccarino et al., 1993) or neurotransmitters (Goldbloom & Garfinkel, 1990). While over 90 percent of individuals suffering from eating disorders are female, at the Centre for Child and Adolescent Development in Edmonton it has been found that the number of males is rising, notably among athletes (Stoutjesdyk & Jevene, 1993) and compulsive exercisers.

In Canada, 1 percent of adolescent and young females suffer from **anorexia nervosa**. They literally starve themselves, often losing dangerous amounts of weight—reducing to less than 85 percent of the normal minimum for their height and age (Thompson, 1992). Such losses can be tragically serious. Estimates of death from the severe weight loss (and associated problems) range from 5 (Hsu, 1986) to 20 percent. In the 1970s, anorexia was fatal for singer Karen Carpenter.

Reports indicate that 1.5 percent of young women in their late teens or twenties suffer from **bulimia** (Hinz & Williamson, 1987). The percentage of men is higher than in anorexia. Bulimics are individuals who maintain normal or near-normal weight by drastic means. First, they engage in excessive or binge eating. Then they purge themselves by means of self-induced vomiting or laxative abuse. Fasting and excessive exercise may also be involved. Princess Diana is a bulimic who has made her eating disorder public.

Three more points will complete this brief survey of bulimia. Bulimics tend to be more preoccupied with their physical appearance than other people (e.g., Casper, 1990). Bulimics are lower in social self-confidence (and higher in social anxiety) than other people (e.g., Tobin et al., 1991). Finally, bulimics' reduced self-confidence and heightened social anxiety are linked to lower satisfaction with their own bodies (Striegel-Moore, Silberstein, & Rodin, 1993).

Why do so many young women deny themselves food in these ways? The suggested causes of eating disorders are varied and complex. First, and perhaps fundamental, is concern about appearance and the dissatisfaction many young women feel about their own bodies (Allgood-Merton & Lewinsohn, 1990). That dissatisfaction leads to a distorted self-image. In response to the relentless "thin is in" message put out by the fashion industry and the mass media, many young women conclude that they are fat, and therefore unattractive. After all, their bodies are much rounder than those of fashion models Linda, Monika, or Tricia, who have what is supposed to be the ideal female form. In this way, self-esteem becomes linked to what is said by the scale on which they weigh themselves. Also worth noting is the finding by researchers at the Toronto General Hospital, that one in four women with anorexia, bulimia, or anorexia with bulimia has suffered sexual abuse (DeGroot et al., 1992), with the resulting assault on self-esteem.

Distorted body image is characteristic of both anorexia and bulimia (e.g., Williamson, 1990; Thompson, 1992). For example, in one investigation (Williamson, Cubic, & Gleaves, 1993), both anorexics and bulimics were found to view themselves as further from their ideal than those who were not suffering from any eating disorder (see Figure 10.5). In fact, even at weights well below normal, they saw themselves as heavy. In a very recent series of experiments at the University of Guelph, Hundleby and colleagues (e.g., Hundleby et al., 1993) showed that female undergraduates who make errors in judging the size of their own bodies and their own body parts (but were not clinically anorexic or bulimic) also misjudge the sides of a blank card, the waist of an average person, the body of a life-sized figure, and three sizes of boxes. The idea here is that along with distorted body image, some people have a more general inability to make accurate judgments of reality.

Research in the United States has found that distorted thinking about their bodies is most characteristic of white female adolescents. Nicher and Parker (1994) found that 90 percent of the white teens they studied were unhappy with their weight; in contrast, the figure for African-American women was 30 percent. In fact, many men do not find extreme thinness in women attractive; on average, they prefer a woman whose body size is somewhat larger than the one selected by women as ideal (Fallon & Rozin, 1985).

Female competitive athletes in sports where appearance counts are especially at risk for these eating disorders (Davis, 1994). This is true not only for élite gymnasts, like Christy Henrich (who weighed sixty-one pounds when she died of anorexia and bulimia in August 1994), but also for figure skaters and others.

Research at York University has reported that appearance anxiety among young men is increasing (Davis et al., 1993). The hypermasculine stereotype of the ideal male body is different (Gillett & White, 1992); it includes exaggerated muscular development. For many young men, the purpose of bodybuilding is to increase feelings of self-worth.

Starvation changes the body's delicate neurochemical balance. Another biological reason for these eating disorders, and anorexia in particular, may be "reproductive suppression" (Anderson & Crawford, 1992). The idea here is that some females cope with the stresses of puberty by starving themselves, by which they are able to stop the development of secondary sex characteristics, including the onset of menstruation.

Eating disorders are deadly serious and difficult to treat. They trap young women in a vicious cycle from which they may escape—with professional help (Thompson, 1992). At eating disorder clinics across Canada, including those at the Douglas Hospital in Montreal, the Toronto Hospital, and St. Paul's Hospital in Vancouver, various forms of treatment are used (Garfinkel & Goldbloom), including nutrition programs, pharmacological intervention, and expressive therapies (Porter & Waisberg, 1992). All of these treatments may be helpful to some degree. More recently, hope has been pinned on injections of growth hormone releasing factor, which stimulates eating behavior when injected into the brains of animals (Vaccarino, 1990).

KEY POINTS

- Eating is regulated by complex biochemical systems within the body.

- Eating is also affected by the sight of food, feedback from chewing and swallowing, and cultural factors.

- Many factors contribute to obesity. These include eating habits, reactions to stress, basal metabolic rate, and responses to food-related cues.

- Anorexia nervosa and bulimia are two serious eating disorders.

- Both anorexics and bulimics are dissatisfied with their bodies and perceive their body size as larger than it actually is.

Does Thinness Equal Sex Appeal?

Many men do not find excessive thinness in women to be attractive. Yet many women believe that unless they are extremely thin, they will not be physically appealing.
(Source: CATHY copyright 1990 Cathy Guisewite. Reprinted with permission of UNIVERSAL PRESS SYNDICATE. All rights reserved.)

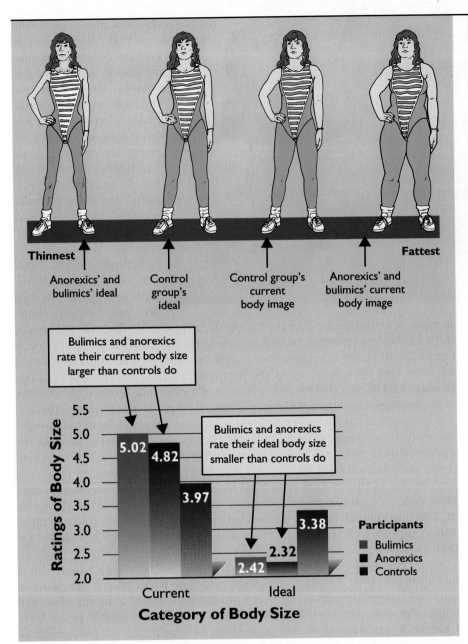

FIGURE 10.5

Dissatisfaction with One's Own Body: An Important Factor in Eating Disorders

As shown here, when actual body size was statistically controlled, both anorexics and bulimics viewed their current body size as larger than did controls, and both rated their ideal body size as smaller than did controls. (Source: Based on data from Williamson, Cubic, & Gleaves, 1993.)

Thinnest

Fattest

Anorexics' and bulimics' ideal

Control group's ideal

Control group's current body image

Anorexics' and bulimics' current body image

Bulimics and anorexics rate their current body size larger than controls do

Bulimics and anorexics rate their ideal body size smaller than controls do

Ratings of Body Size

5.02 4.82 3.97 2.42 2.32 3.38

Participants
- Bulimics
- Anorexics
- Controls

Current Ideal

Category of Body Size

Sexual Motivation: *The Most Intimate Motive*

Suppose that visitors from another planet arrived on earth and visited one of our cities. What would they see? That's right—it would be countless signs, billboards, and advertisements focused on two topics: food and sex. The space aliens might quickly conclude that human begins are obsessed with these two topics. Since we have already considered human behavior with respect to food in some detail, we'll now turn to **sexual motivation**, or the motivation to engage in sexual activity.

HORMONES AND SEXUAL BEHAVIOR: ACTIVATION AND DIFFERENTIATION As we saw in Chapter 9, at the onset of puberty there are rapid increases in the activity of the sex glands, or **gonads**. The hormones produced by the gonads affect the body in

Sexual Motivation: Motivation to engage in various forms of sexual activity.

Gonads: The primary sex glands.

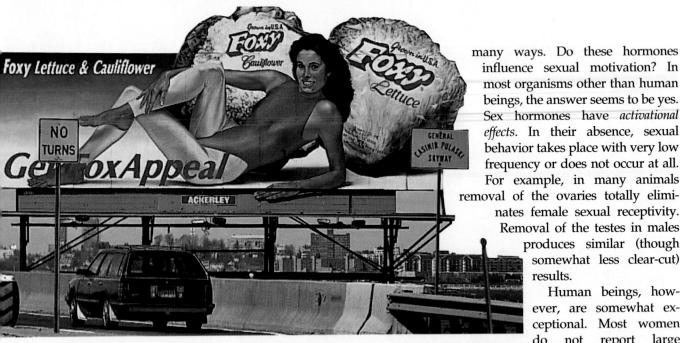

FOOD AND SEX: OBSESSIONS OF MODERN WESTERN SOCIETY?

Sights such as these might make visitors from different cultures believe that our society is obsessed with two things: food and sex.

many ways. Do these hormones influence sexual motivation? In most organisms other than human beings, the answer seems to be yes. Sex hormones have *activational effects*. In their absence, sexual behavior takes place with very low frequency or does not occur at all. For example, in many animals removal of the ovaries totally eliminates female sexual receptivity. Removal of the testes in males produces similar (though somewhat less clear-cut) results.

Human beings, however, are somewhat exceptional. Most women do not report large changes in sexual desire over the course of their monthly cycle, despite major shifts in the concentration of various sex hormones in their blood (Kelley & Byrne, 1992). Further, many women continue to engage in and enjoy sexual relations after *menopause*, when the hormonal output of their ovaries drops sharply. And in men there is little evidence of a clear link between blood levels of sex hormones such as *testosterone* and sexual responsiveness (Byrne, 1982).

That is not to say, however, that sex hormones play no role in human sexual motivation. Some women do experience peaks of sexual arousal in the middle of their cycle and again prior to menstruation (Harvey, 1987). Among some men testosterone levels are associated with differences in sexual arousal. For example, men with high levels of testosterone become aroused more quickly by erotic films than those with relatively low levels (Lange et al., 1980). In general, though, the link between sex hormones and sexual motivation appears to be far less clear-cut and less compelling for human beings than for many other species.

Other chemical substances in the body, however, may play a more direct and dramatic role. Recent findings suggest that when people are sexually attracted to another person, the brain produces increased amounts of several substances that are related to *amphetamines*. As you probably recall from Chapter 4, amphetamines are stimulants, so the increased production of amphetamine-like substances such as phenylethylamine (PEA) may account for the fact that many people describe strong sexual attraction—the first stage in falling in love—as a feeling that "sweeps them away." As one researcher puts it, "love is a natural high" (Walsh, 1993), one that confirms the words of the old song, "I get a kick out of you."

In sum, sex hormone levels do not seem to be as clearly linked to sexual motivation in humans as in other species; at the same time, there is some scientific evidence that other substances produced by our bodies do play an important role in sexual motivation, and even in romantic love. Does this mean that we will someday be able to produce pills that cause us to fall in (or out of) love? Probably not; because, as we'll now see, where human beings are concerned, cognitive factors—our own thoughts, fantasies, and memories—play a very powerful role in sexual motivation. There does, however, seem to be a biochemistry of love, and biochemical effects, too, deserve careful attention as we try to understand the nature of human sexual motivation.

HUMAN SEXUAL BEHAVIOR: SOME BASIC FACTS   Until the 1960s the only scientific information about human sexual motivation was that provided by surveys. The most famous of these were the *Kinsey Reports*, published in the 1940s and 1950s. These were based on interviews with more than 10,000 women and men and yielded many surprising facts. Half a century ago, most men and nearly half of all women reported having engaged in premarital sex (Kinsey, Pomeroy, & Martin, 1984; Kinsey et al., 1953). Further, many couples engaged in practices that society then considered objectionable, such as oral sex and a wide variety of sexual positions. If there was one basic theme in the Kinsey data, though, it was this: Where sexual behavior is concerned, individual differences are enormous. Some people said they remained celibate, while others engaged in sexual relations with a large number of partners. Some said they rarely experienced orgasm, but a few indicated that they experienced three or more orgasms every day.

PHEROMONES: A SOURCE OF SEXUAL ATTRACTION?
Some research findings suggest that pheromones—odorless substances produced by our bodies—may play a role in sexual attraction and arousal. Some colognes and perfumes supposedly have similar powers, but scientific research has not supported such claims.

Survey data such as those obtained by Kinsey and others are always open to question. First, who agrees to participate in a given survey? Many people refuse, and it is impossible to tell how the findings might change if *their* patterns of sexual behavior were included. Second, how accurate are self-reports? Do participants describe their sexual behavior and sexual motivation accurately? Or do they exaggerate, fail to provide some information, and generally seek to present themselves in a favorable light? Because of these complex issues, survey results are always somewhat in doubt.

Starting in the 1960s, however, direct and systematic observation of actual sexual activities began. The first and still the most famous project of this kind was conducted by Masters and Johnson in the mid-1960s. These researchers observed, filmed, and monitored the reactions of several hundred volunteers of both sexes as they engaged in sexual intercourse or masturbation. More than 10,000 cycles of arousal and satisfaction were studied. The results yielded important insights into the nature of human sexuality. Perhaps the clearest finding was that both men and women move through four distinct phases during sexual behavior.

First, there is the *excitement phase*. During this phase, many physiological changes indicative of growing sexual excitement occur. The penis and clitoris become enlarged, vaginal lubrication increases, and nipples may become erect in both sexes. If sexual stimulation persists, both women and men enter the *plateau phase*. The size of the penis increases still further, and the outer third of the vagina becomes engorged with blood, reducing its diameter. Muscle tension, respiration, heart rate, and blood pressure all rise to high levels.

After a variable period of direct stimulation, both men and women approach the *orgasmic phase*. This consists of several contractions of the muscles surrounding the genitals, along with intense sensations of pleasure. The pattern of contractions, including their timing and length, is virtually identical in women and men.

The most striking difference between the two sexes occurs during the final, *resolution phase*. For men, orgasm is followed by a reduction in sexual and physiological arousal. At that point, men enter a *refractory period* during which they cannot be sexually aroused or experience another orgasm. Among women, in contrast, two distinct patterns are possible. They, too, may experience a reduction in sexual and physiological arousal. Alternatively, if stimulation continues, they may experience additional orgasms.

The basic pattern just described seems to apply to all human beings. However, practically everything else seems to vary from one culture to another. Different cultures have widely different standards about such matters as the age at which sexual behavior should begin, the frequency with which it should occur, physical characteristics considered attractive or sexy, the particular positions and practices that are acceptable, the proper time and setting for sexual relations, the people who are appropriate partners, and the number of partners individuals should have at one time or in succession. So, to repeat: Where human sexuality is concerned, *variability* is definitely the central theme.

HUMAN SEXUAL BEHAVIOR: WHAT'S AROUSING AND WHY? Clearly, sexual motivation plays an important role in human behavior. But what, precisely, stimulates arousal? In certain respects, the same events or stimuli that produce such arousal in other species. First, direct physical contact—various forms of touching and foreplay—generates arousal. Second, human beings, like other organisms, can be sexually aroused by certain naturally occurring odors. For example, one study found that approximately 20 percent of men appear to be sexually stimulated by the scents of *copulins*, chemicals found in vaginal secretions (Hassett, 1978). More recently, some scientists have reported that odorless natural substances known as *pheromones* can produce attraction and arousal in both men and women (Blakeslee, 1993). On the basis of these findings, large perfume companies have added synthetic human pheromones to their products. Will wearing such perfumes make you more attractive to the opposite sex, as advertised? That is yet to be determined, and you probably should not count on it (Cain, 1988; Ehrlichman & Bastone, 1990; Galef, 1993).

One potential source of sexual motivation, however, does seem to set human beings apart from their species: real or imagined erotic stimuli and images. Unlike other species, human beings possess the capacity to generate their own sexual arousal on the basis of erotic fantasies or daydreams. And many people respond strongly to *erotic materials* containing either visual images or verbal descriptions of sexual behavior. Some sexual fantasies are less common than others. For example, Blanchard (1993) has studied 238 heterosexual men whose sexual fantasies are of themselves with female bodies, nude, in underwear or fully clothed; and Freund and Blanchard (1993) have studied men who imagined themselves as children. The purpose of studies like this is to understand better how these unusual sexual fantasies begin to influence conditions of sexual gratification.

Research findings indicate that many people can produce intense sexual arousal—and even orgasm—through internally generated sexual images (Money, 1985). Further, many report using sexual thoughts or images to enhance their pleasure during sexual intercourse or masturbation, or to speed up or delay the occurrence of orgasm (Davidson & Hoffman, 1986). In these and other ways, our impressive cognitive abilities can play a major role in sexual motivation.

Of course, external erotic stimuli, too, can produce such effects. Virtually every physiological reaction and behavior recorded by Masters and Johnson during actual sexual activity can occur in response to erotic movies, tapes, or written descriptions (Kelley & Byrne, 1992). Of course, not all people find all materials of this type equally exciting. Explicit erotic materials can be too explicit for some people's taste, so that exposure to them reduces rather than increases sexual motivation (Zillmann, 1984). However, given erotic stimuli that they *do* find attractive, most individuals can be sexually aroused in this indirect manner.

If the only effects produced by erotic materials were increases in sexual motivation and perhaps sexual behavior, there would be little reason to discuss them further. Unfortunately, however, growing evidence suggests that exposure to such materials produces other effects as well. First, repeated exposure to explicit erotica has been found to increase viewers' estimates of the frequency of several unusual sexual practices, including *sadomasochism* (sexual practices in which participants physically hurt one another), human–animal contact, and sex between adults and children (Zillmann & Bryant, 1984). Second, exposure to explicit erotic materials may reduce viewers' satisfaction with their own sex life and with their current sexual partner (e.g., Zillmann & Bryant, 1988). The link between explicit pornography and sexual dissatisfaction was the subject of *Not a Love Story*, produced by the National Film Board of Canada. The reality of the situation is that most women (and most men) do not measure up to the standards of eroticism set by pornographic videos, and that exposure may result in sexual dysfunction—in some men in particular.

GENDER DIFFERENCES IN SEXUAL JEALOUSY: A SOCIOBIOLOGICAL PERSPECTIVE

Some nonhuman species are monogamous—some seabirds, for example, mate for life (Jones & Hunter, 1993). Do these animals experience jealousy if they discover their mate with another member of the opposite sex? At present, we don't know. But we *do* know that **sexual jealousy**—aroused by a perceived threat to a valued sexual relationship—is very common among our own species (Salovey, 1991; White & Mullen, 1990). Indeed, in January 1994, the annual MacLean's/CTV poll showed that seven out of every ten Canadians agreed that extramarital sex is unacceptable. (In this, there were strong regional variations, from 55 percent of Quebeckers to 81 percent of Nova Scotians.)

As you undoubtedly know, both women and men experience sexual jealousy. Recent findings suggest, however, that the two sexes may differ. Specifically, it appears that men may experience more intense jealousy in response to *sexual* infidelity on the part of their partners, while women may experience more intense jealousy in response to *emotional* infidelity (Buss et al., 1992). Why should this be so? The field of *sociobiology* (or *evolutionary psychology*, as it is sometimes known; Buss, 1990) provides one potential answer.

According to sociobiology, men are upset by sexual infidelity for two reasons: A man can never be perfectly certain that he is the father of his children; and men invest a lot of energy and resources in caring for their mates and their offspring. If a man's partner engages in sexual relations with other males, he may be investing resources in another man's children! Emotional infidelity, as long as it doesn't result in actual sexual relations, is therefore less threatening, for obvious reasons.

What about women—why should they find emotional infidelity so disturbing? From a sociobiological perspective, the answer is as follows: Women know with certainty that they are the mothers of their children. However, throughout most of history, women raised their children with the assistance of men. Emotional infidelity threatens this support, for if a woman's mate falls in love with another, he may abandon her, leaving her without needed support. In contrast, sexual infidelity by the mate poses no threat in and of itself.

These are controversial hypotheses, and difficult to test scientifically. They are, however, consistent with the findings of several studies conducted by Buss and his colleagues (Buss et al., 1992). Male and female students were asked to indicate which would upset them more—learning that their romantic partner was forming a deep emotional attachment to another person, or that their partner was enjoying passionate sexual intercourse with that person. Results were clear: A large majority of the men (60 percent) reported greater distress of sexual infidelity, while a large majority of the women (83 percent) reported greater distress over emotional infidelity.

Sexual Jealousy: A negative state aroused by a perceived threat to one's sexual relationship with another person.

In a follow-up study, male and female participants were asked to imagine that their partner was either having sexual intercourse with another person or falling in love with another person. While the participants were imagining these scenes, the researchers rescored their physiological reactions: activity in a facial muscle involved in frowning, pulse rate, and electrodermal activity (electrical conductivity of the skin). Again, the results were clear. Males showed greater arousal and more signs of frowning when imagining sexual infidelity; females showed greater arousal and more frowning when imagining emotional infidelity (see Figure 10.6).

Studies have been done on the biological basis of these and other sex differences between males and females. For example, at McGill University in 1988, Sherwin reviewed studies of hormone replacement therapy in men and women. She reported that mini-changes in their levels of testosterone affected the sexual motivation of females.

Taken together, these findings and those of other studies (Buss, 1989) indicate that males and females differ with respect to the kinds of events that make them jealous. Men seem to find sexual infidelity more disturbing than emotional infidelity, while women show the opposite pattern. Are such differences really due to the factors sociobiology emphasizes—certainty of parenthood and covering one's investments? That is not yet known.

Homosexual (sexual orientation): A sexual orientation in which individuals prefer sexual relations with members of their own sex.

SEXUAL ORIENTATION Estimates vary, but about 2 percent of all adults are exclusively **homosexual**: They engage in sexual relations only with members of their own sex (Kelley & Byrne, 1992). Other people, perhaps another 2 or 3

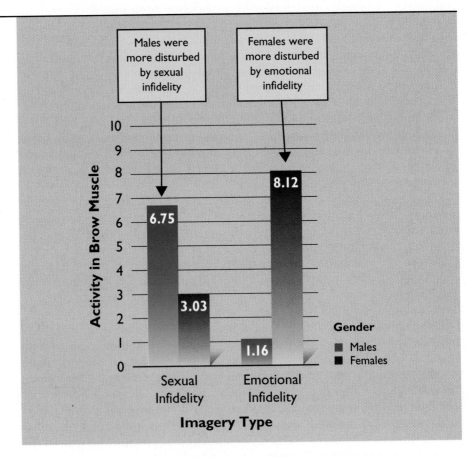

FIGURE 10.6

Gender Differences in Jealousy

Females were more disturbed by imagining scenes in which their romantic partner was falling in love with another person, while males were more disturbed by imagining scenes in which their partner engaged in sexual relations with another person.
(Source: Based on data from Buss et al., 1993.)

percent of each sex, are **bisexual**: They seek out and enjoy sexual contact with members of both sexes. The remainder of the population is **heterosexual** and engages in sexual relations only with members of the opposite sex.

In the past, homosexuals of both sexes often remained "in the closet," concealing their orientation from others. Since the early 1970s, they have made vigorous efforts to achieve equal treatment in many areas of life—employment, housing, military service, education, and so on—even as they openly avow their orientation. This has led to heightened interest in a basic question: Which factors influence or determine sexual orientation? In other words, why are some people exclusively homosexual while most others are exclusively heterosexual? Unfortunately, research findings to date have failed to yield any firm or definite answers. All of the most obvious possibilities appear to be false. Male homosexuals do not have lower levels of male sex hormones than heterosexuals (Gladue, 1991), and increasing their levels of male sex hormones does not alter their homosexual preferences (Money, 1980). Similarly, careful study of the family backgrounds of both male and female homosexuals has failed to yield any reliable differences between these groups and heterosexuals (Hammersmith, 1982).

Another theory is that homosexuality stems from experiences during puberty (Storms, 1981). According to this view, some individuals learn to associate their emerging sexual impulses with members of their own sex and so develop homosexual preferences. At present, however, direct evidence for such effects is lacking. On the contrary, many people who are homosexual report that they had sexual fantasies and thoughts about members of their own sex long before puberty.

This latter finding is consistent with yet another possible explanation of the origin of homosexuality: that genetic factors play an important role (Henry, 1993). Perhaps the most convincing evidence for this view is the finding that more male relatives of male homosexuals (than would be expected by chance) were also homosexual—but only on the *maternal* side of these families. Specifically, about 7.5 percent of the male cousins and uncles of the male homosexuals studied were homosexual, as opposed to about 2 percent in the general population. These findings suggest that a tendency toward homosexuality may be inherited and that it may be linked somehow to the X chromosome, which all children inherit from the mother (refer to Chapter 2). Further evidence for this conclusion is provided by additional research in which DNA samples were obtained from forty pairs of homosexual brothers. In thirty-three of the pairs, a portion of the X chromosome matched exactly (cited in Henry, 1993).

Not all people who inherit homosexual tendencies will become homosexual. On the contrary, environmental factors also play an important role. Still, the finding that homosexuality may be inherited is consistent with the experience of many homosexuals, who often feel that they knew they were "different" from most other people from a very early age. As one man recently put it (quoted in Henry, 1993): "I always believed that homosexuality was something I was born with. If homosexuality is genetic, there is nothing you can do about it. If there is more research like this in years to come, hopefully homosexuality will cease to be the issue it is today."

Bisexual (sexual orientation): A sexual orientation in which individuals seek sexual relations with members of both their own and the other sex.

Heterosexual (sexual orientation): A sexual orientation in which individuals engage in sexual relations only with members of the other sex.

KEY POINTS

- Sex hormones seem to play a relatively minor role in human sexual motivation. Other substances produced within the body may also play a role in sexual attraction and love.

- During sexual activity both males and females move through a series of distinct phases: excitement, plateau, orgasm, and resolution.

- In contrast to other species, humans can be sexually aroused by self-generated sexual fantasies and by exposure to erotic materials.

- Individuals differ in sexual orientation. Some are exclusively homosexual, others are bisexual, and the majority are exclusively heterosexual.

- Male homosexuals do not have lower testosterone levels than male heterosexuals, and homosexuals and heterosexuals do not appear to differ in terms of family background or early experiences.

- Recent evidence suggests that genetic factors may play a role in homosexuality.

Aggressive Motivation: *The most Dangerous Motive*

War. Murder. Rape. Child abuse. Consider the following statistics:

- In 1992, there were 307,491 cases of violent crime in Canada.

- A survey released in June 1994 revealed that from a sample of 10,000 Canadians, about one in every four had been the victim of at least one crime during the past year (Doob & Gartner, 1994).

- A report released in mid-August 1994 found violence in Canadian schools across the country. In some places, students arm themselves with weapons ranging from hunting knives and pocket knives to meat cleavers and machetes. Why do some students feel they must carry a weapon to school? The reasons they give vary, but include self-defense and intimidation of others.

- The incidence of violence in elementary schools is increasing, with more girls becoming involved.

- Twenty-five percent of Canadian sexual assault offenders are teenage males.

- In 1993, 55,300 restricted weapons, such as handguns and semiautomatic assault weapons, were registered for the first time.

- Between 1974 and 1993, the nature of sexual assault changed. The incidence is up, and assaults are becoming more violent, with greater physical force being used and more serious injury resulting.

- Twenty-five percent of the victims of violent crime in Canada are teens.

These facts suggest that **aggressive motivation**—the desire to inflict harm on others—plays an all-too-common role in human affairs (Baron & Richardson, 1994).

THE ROOTS OF AGGRESSION: INNATE TENDENCY OR EXTERNALLY ELICITED BEHAVIOR?

Is **aggression** an instinct? Is it an inherited and unavoidable human tendency as Freud believed? After witnessing World War I, he concluded, pessimistically, that human beings possess a powerful built-in tendency to harm others. Relevant to this point are Palmer's studies of ninety-five floor hockey games in Newfoundland. Palmer (1993) took an evolutionary point of view and observed that anger and aggression were most frequent at the age when men are also competing the most over potential mates. He also studied how humor was combined with aggressive behavior to maintain social relations among his players.

While Freud's view has been shared by many other scientists—for example, Konrad Lorenz, the famous *ethologist*—it is definitely *not* widely accepted by present-day psychologists (Berkowitz, 1990). Most believe that aggression, like many other forms of motivation, is elicited by a wide range of stimuli. In other words, it is often "pulled" from without rather than "pushed" from within ourselves. That is not to deny that aggression has biological and/or genetic roots. On the contrary—there is evidence to indicate that such factors do play a role in violent crime (Gladue, 1991). For example, men convicted of impulsive crimes of violence, such as murdering strangers, have lower than normal amounts of serotonin in their brains; in contrast, those convicted of cold-blooded and premeditated aggressive crimes show normal levels of serotonin (Toufexis, 1993). It may be that deficits in serotonin somehow interfere with the neural mechanisms that normally inhibit the expression of rage.

Aggressive Motivation: *The desire to inflict harm on others.*

Aggression: *Behavior directed toward the goal of harming another living being who wishes to avoid such treatment.*

An important cause of aggressive motivation is **frustration**—the thwarting or blocking of goal-directed behavior. People harm others when they have been prevented from obtaining what they want. The strongest statement of this view is the classic *frustration-aggression hypothesis*, which proposes that aggression always stems from frustration and that frustration always produces aggression. It is now clear that these assertions are far too general.

Aggression often stems from other causes, including (to name a few) direct provocation; unexpected annoyances (Ahmed, 1992); exposure to others behaving in an aggressive manner; the presence of weapons or other stimuli associated with aggression; sexually violent pornography and antiwoman attitudes (Demare et al., 1993); and the consumption of alcohol (Baron & Richardson, 1994). Also, frustration often produces depression or resignation rather than aggression against others. So frustration is only one of many factors that elicit aggression and seems to produce such effects only when it is unexpected (Ahmed & Mapletoft, 1989), unfair, or illegitimate (Berkowitz, 1989).

Studies at McGill University, the Alcohol Research Foundation in Toronto, and the Alberta Children's Hospital relate alcohol consumption and aggression (Pihl et al., 1993; Naranjo & Bremner, 1993; Murdoch et al., 1990). Alcohol is implicated in violent crime and in marital abuse. That does not tell us, however, how drinking may produce assaultive behavior. There are several different ways in which this may work. First, alcohol may disrupt the inhibition that controls aggressive behavior. Second, it may increase our sensitivity to pain, leading us to aggressive acts in our own defense. Third, it may reduce fear of injury. Fourth, it may narrow our attention, reduce our ability to plan, and limit the control that our past experience exerts on our present behavior. An overview of the many social, environmental, and personal factors that increase the likelihood of aggression is presented in Table 10.1. This table suggests that reducing the level of aggression in any given society is a complex and challenging task.

Frustration: The block of ongoing goal-directed behavior.

FACTOR	EFFECT ON AGGRESSION
High temperatures	Increase aggression
Audience	Increases aggression when this is a strong (dominant) tendency; decreases aggression if audience disapproves of this behavior
Exposure to aggressive models (others behaving aggressively)	Increases aggression
Heightened arousal	Increases aggression when arousal is interpreted as provocation or frustration
Alcohol	Increases aggression in large doses; reduces aggression in very small doses
Apologies, explanations for provocative actions	Reduce aggression if accepted as sincere
Humorous materials	Reduce aggression if they induce feelings of amusement
Signs of pain on part of victim	Increase aggression if aggressor is very angry; reduce aggression if anger is low
Type A behavior pattern	Increases aggression in many situations
Presence of weapons (not used in assault)	Increases aggression because of previous association with such behavior

TABLE 10.1

Factors Influencing Aggression

Reducing the level of aggression in any society is a difficult task. Even so, ways must be found.

Even so, ways must be found. Although more than 90 percent of Canadian children do not steal, lie, cheat, or cause others bodily harm, some do—and that proportion is rising. As one Canadian chief of police has stated: "Aggression is one thing kids do not grow out of." Aggression at a young age predicts later criminal behavior.

What about cultural factors? Do they too play a role with respect to the expression of aggressive motivation? For information on this topic, **see Perspectives on Diversity.**

PERSPECTIVES ON DIVERSITY

The Role of Cultural Factors in Aggression: The Social Context of Violence

D o cultures differ with respect to the expression of aggression? Figure 10.7 provides a partial answer. As you can see, murder is much more common in some industrialized nations than in others—for example, from 10 to 20 times more common in the United States than in some nations, by some estimates (Scott, 1992). What accounts for differences like those shown in Figure 10.7? The answer is complex, but the differences suggest that cultural variables exert powerful effects upon aggression. Let's take a brief look at several of these variables.

Aggression and Self-Perception: A Case in Point

In the Mexican state of Oaxaca, there are two Zapotec villages less than 7 kilometers apart. The two villages, which have existed for at least 450 years, are very similar in terms of language, religion, economics, and virtually every other aspect. Yet the murder rate in one is more than six times higher than in the other

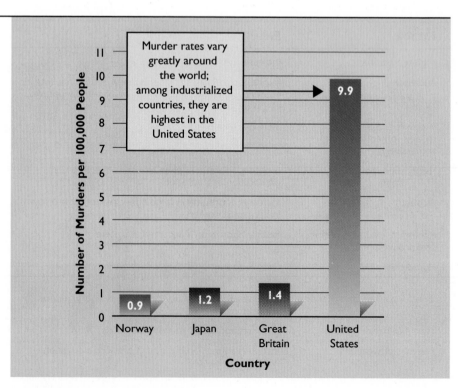

FIGURE 10.7

Cultural Differences in Aggression

As shown here, murders are much more frequent in the United States than in other industrialized nations. Differences such as these suggest that cultural factors play an important role in aggression. (Source: Based on data from Scott, 1992.)

Murder rates vary greatly around the world; among industrialized countries, they are highest in the United States

Number of Murders per 100,000 People

Norway	Japan	Great Britain	United States
0.9	1.2	1.4	9.9

Country

(Fry, 1990). What accounts for this difference? Careful comparison of the villages suggests that the key differences lie in contrasting *self-perceptions*. In the relatively nonviolent village, residents describe themselves as peaceful, kind, and respectful of the rights of others. In the more violent village, the people describe themselves as tough and aggressive and perceive overt acts of aggression, such as fistfights and spouse abuse, as proof of their vigor and strength. How did these contrasting views originate? The answer is lost in time, but one investigator (Scott, 1992) suggests that the two villages were probably founded by people with contrasting perspectives on aggression, and that the norms established then have persisted into the present, finding expression in the sharply contrasting rates of violence we now observe.

Culture and Reactions to Frustration

Culture influences when and how reactions to frustration are expressed. In many cultures aggressive behavior is strongly disapproved of, so people exposed to frustration are urged to show restraint. For example, in Sri Lanka, *quiet self-control* is highly valued (Spencer, 1990). As a result, people generally refrain from responding aggressively to provocations that would evoke strong retaliation in other cultures.

A clear illustration of the role of cultural factors is a study conducted in the United States by Kaufman, Gregory, and Stephan (1990). They examined the reactions of Hispanic and non-Hispanic students to one important type of frustration: belonging to an ethnic minority in school. Kaufman and his colleagues predicted that, because Hispanic culture strongly emphasizes being *simpatico*—being likable, easygoing, and fun to be with—Hispanic children would demonstrate increased moodiness but *not* increased aggression when in classrooms where they were an ethnic minority. In contrast, because Anglo culture is more accepting of overt aggression it was expected that Anglo children might demonstrate higher levels of aggression when they were an ethnic minority. That is precisely what was found. These findings illustrate the important role of culture in shaping the expression of aggression.

The Persistence of Cultural Differences in Aggression

One final point: Why do cultural differences in aggression persist? One answer lies in varied beliefs about the appropriateness of aggression and child-rearing practices. For example, a recent study by Osterwell and Nagano-Nakamura (1992) compared Japanese and Israeli mothers' views about aggression. The researchers found that Japanese mothers tend to view aggression as a natural part of their children's behavior, but believe that it should be expressed *within* the family, where it can be regulated and will do no serious harm. In contrast, Israeli mothers believe that aggression is mainly a response to external provocations, and feel that it should be expressed *outside* the family rather than within it. Such contrasting beliefs about aggression influence child-rearing practices in different cultures, and these practices help explain why cultural differences in many forms of aggression persist over time (Fraczek & Kirwil, 1992).

Achievement and Power: Two Complex Human Motives

Hunger, sex, and aggression: These are motives we share with many other forms of life. There are some motives, however, that, as far as we can tell, are unique to our own species. We'll focus on two that are often closely related: **achievement motivation** and **power motivation**. Achievement motivation is the desire to meet standards of excellence—to outperform others and accomplish difficult tasks (McClelland, 1961). Power motivation refers to the desire to be in charge, to have status and prestige and to influence others (Winter,

Achievement Motivation: The desire to accomplish difficult tasks and meet standards of excellence.

Power Motivation: Motivation to be in charge, have high status, and exert influence over others.

1973). These motives do not derive directly from basic biological factors, as do hunger, thirst, and, to some extent, sexuality. Yet they exert powerful effects upon behavior in many different circumstances. In Canada, such motivation has been studied in various groups: high school boys (Howe & Poole, 1992), nurses (Mecof & Wegener, 1992), élite professional hockey players (Davis, 1990), and children with learning disabilities (Durrant, 1993); also, in media reports of political speeches (Suedfeld et al., 1990).

ACHIEVEMENT MOTIVATION: THE QUEST FOR EXCELLENCE That individuals differ greatly in the desire for achievement is obvious. For some people, accomplishing difficult tasks and meeting high standards of excellence are extremely important. For others, just getting by is quite enough. How can differences in this motive be measured? What are the effects of these differences? These are issues that have received much attention in past research.

Achievement motivation and power motivation are measured by the same method. This technique, known as the **Thematic Apperception Test** (or TAT), involves a series of ambiguous pictures, such as an individual staring thoughtfully into space. Subjects are shown the pictures, one at a time, and asked to make up a story about each. The content of the stories is then evaluated by means of carefully developed keys; scores for achievement and power motivation are then calculated (McClelland, 1975). While the TAT continues to be used in its original form, Winter (1983) has also developed a technique for scoring these motives directly from any type of verbal material—books and speeches, for example.

EFFECTS OF ACHIEVEMENT AND POWER MOTIVATION Do individual differences in achievement and power motivation really matter? In other words, do people high and low in these motives have contrasting life experiences? Growing evidence suggests that they do. As you might expect, individuals high in achievement motivation tend to get higher grades in school, earn more rapid promotions, and attain greater success in running their own businesses than people who are low in such motivation (Andrews, 1967; Raynor, 1970). Perhaps more surprising is the fact that people who are high in achievement motivation prefer situations involving moderate levels of risk or difficulty to ones that are very low or very high on these dimensions (Atkinson & Litwin, 1960; Sorrentino et al., 1992).

Why would this be? In situations involving moderate risk or difficulty there is a good chance of success, but there is also a sense of challenge. In contrast, in situations that are very high in risk or difficulty, failure is likely—and high-achievement individuals dislike failure intensely. Moreover, situations that are very low in risk or difficulty fail to provide the challenge that people high in achievement motivation relish. Finally, elevated power motivation has been linked to marital violence. In their study at the University of British Columbia, Dutton and Strachan (1987) found that the need for power—as revealed by the Thematic Apperception Test—was characteristic of adult males who had assaulted their wives.

Thematic Apperception Test: A psychological test used to assess individual differences in several different motives, such as achievement motivation or power motivation.

Gender Differences in Achievement Motivation: *Do They Really Exist?*

Traditionally, concepts of femininity *seemed* incompatible with high levels of competence, success, and achievement motivation on the part of women. Horner (1970, 1972) found "fear of success" among young women. In

Horner's research, female undergraduates were asked to tell a story about Anne, a young woman who found herself at the top of her medical school class. Male undergraduates were given the same task with respect to a young man named John. Almost all the men wrote stories predicting a happy and successful life for the male character. In contrast, about two-thirds of the women wrote stories predicting serious problems for Anne. She was seen as having a future in which she would be rejected by others (especially men) and would be lonely and isolated. From these findings, Horner concluded that women did indeed fear success.

There is some doubt now about those results. Recent research indicates that what the women in Horner's studies feared was not success itself, but social rejection. The serious dispute about fear of success indicates the care that needs to be taken when making inferences about gender differences from experimental results.

Intrinsic Motivation: The desire to perform activities because they are rewarding in and of themselves.

Intrinsic Motivation: *How (Sometimes) to Turn Play into Work*

Individuals perform many activities simply because they find them enjoyable. Everything from bungee jumping to gourmet cooking fits within this category. Such activities may derive from **intrinsic motivation**; that is, we perform them primarily because of the pleasure they yield, not particularly because they lead to other, external rewards. But what happens if people are given external rewards for performing such activities—if, for example, they are paid for sipping vintage wines or for pursuing their favorite hobby? Some research findings suggest that they may then become *less* motivated to engage in the activities. Why is this so? Perhaps, on considering their own behavior, they conclude that they chose to perform the activities partly to obtain the external reward provided—that is, the payment. To that extent, they may view their own interest as less than they previously thought was the case. They may shift from explaining their behavior in terms of intrinsic motivation ("I did it because I enjoy it") to explaining it in terms of external rewards ("I did it because I was paid").

Many studies support this explanation. In such research, some participants are provided with extrinsic rewards for doing something they enjoy, while others are not. When subsequently given an opportunity to perform the task again, those who receive the external rewards are less motivated to do so (Deci, 1975; Lepper & Green, 1978). These results have important implications for anyone seeking to motivate others by means of rewards—parents, teachers, and managers, for example. (See **The Point of It All**.) The research suggests that if people already enjoy various activities, offering them rewards may lower their intrinsic motivation and, ultimately, produce the paradoxical effect of reducing rather than enhancing performance! At the University of Quebec in Montreal, Vallerand and his associates have developed, in both French and English, an Academic Motivation Scale that assesses an individual's intrinsic and extrinsic motivation. When college students who persisted to the end of a compulsory course

KEY POINTS

- Aggressive motivation involves the desire to inflict harm on others.

- Aggression does not stem primarily from frustration; rather, it occurs in reaction to a wide range of social, environmental, personal, and cultural factors.

- Achievement motivation is the desire to outperform others and accomplish difficult tasks. Power motivation is the desire to be in charge and to influence others.

- Contrary to initial findings, there appear to be no major differences between men and women with respect to achievement motivation.

- When individuals engage in activities because they find them pleasurable rather than to obtain external rewards, they are said to be intrinsically motivated to perform them.

- Extrinsic rewards can sometimes reduce intrinsic motivation. However, this is not always true if the rewards are perceived as a sign of recognition for good performance.

- Intrinsic motivation has important implications for education and can sometimes be used to enhance students' learning and performance.

Research in Canada

Robert J. Vallerand
University of Quebec at Montreal

were compared with those who dropped out, Vallerand and Bissonnette (1992) found that those who completed the course were more intrinsically motivated. A special Athletic Motivation Inventory has been designed; it was screened by David (1991) at the Calgary Flames Hockey Club.

Additional evidence suggests that intrinsic and extrinsic motivation are not necessarily incompatible (Rigby et al., 1992). In fact, Deci and his colleagues (e.g., Deci & Ryan, 1985) argue that what is crucial is the extent to which individuals perceive their behaviors to be *self-determined*. Intrinsically motivated behaviors are, by definition, self-determined. However, extrinsically motivated actions are not necessarily *non*-self-determined. If individuals find their actions consistent with their self-image, their preferences, and their values, they may view them as self-determined even though they yield extrinsic rewards. Only if such actions are perceived as not congruent with preferences or wishes—that is, as performed solely to gain external rewards—are rewards likely to reduce motivation.

If people perceive that they have a choice, in which external rewards will be received (Feehan & Enzle, 1991), and if external rewards are identified as recognition rather than as bribes (Rosenfield, Folger, & Adelman, 1980), and if the rewards provided are large and satisfying (Fiske & Taylor, 1991), intrinsic motivation may be enhanced (Ryan, 1982). In view of these facts, we can conclude that paying people for doing things they enjoy can sometimes reduce their intrinsic motivation—turn play into work. But that is not always the case. When external rewards are delivered with care and in accordance with the principles just described, they can enhance rather than reduce motivation and performance. For information on how psychologists are putting their knowledge about intrinsic motivation to practical use, see **The Point of It All**.

THE POINT OF IT ALL

Turning Work into Play: Intrinsic Motivation in the Classroom

It has often been contended that learning is—or at least should be—fun. A corollary of this belief is that when children enjoy activities occurring in their classes, they will become intrinsically motivated, and learning will be enhanced. Is this actually the case? Research performed recently by Lepper and his colleagues (Lepper & Cordova, 1992; Lepper & Hoddell, 1992) suggests that it is. Moreover, this research provides important insights into the specific procedures that teachers can use to enhance children's intrinsic motivation and therefore their subsequent learning.

The basic idea here is that children find tasks performed within a rich fantasy context to be intrinsically appealing. Thus, providing such a context for learning will increase their intrinsic motivation and their performance. To test this general prediction, Lepper and his associates have conducted a number of studies using computer-based educational games.

As an example of this research, consider a study conducted by Parker and Lepper (1992), in which children learned to use a computer graphics system either with fantasy or without. There were three versions of the fantasy condition. In one, students were encouraged to think of themselves as pirates in search of buried treasure. In another, they were detectives hunting down criminals; in a third, they were astronauts seeking out new planets. In the control condition, no fantasy was provided. In all four groups children performed identical activities: learning to draw lines connecting various objects, negotiating a passage through a series of mazes, and constructing simple geometric shapes. The researchers measured motivation to perform these tasks by asking the children to rate the appeal of the tasks. As predicted, the students rated the three fantasy games much higher than the unembellished one.

Learning was assessed by written tests of students' mastery of the graphics program. These were given immediately after the study or two weeks later. Again, results showed an impressive edge for the fantasy version, both for boys and for girls.

In follow-up research using a different type of game—one resembling the game Clue—Lepper and his co-workers obtained information on *why* the children learned more from the fantasy-rich games. Apparently, they used more efficient problem-solving strategies, and formulated hypotheses in a more systematic manner, when playing in a fantasy-rich context—where they were detectives, for example.

Perhaps most important of all, when children were offered extrinsic rewards (a prize from the experimenter's mystery box) for solving the puzzle, their performance dropped sharply. They used simpler problem-solving strategies, formulated hypotheses less systematically, and perceived themselves as less competent at the task.

The implications of these findings for classroom education seem clear (Lepper & Cordova, 1992): Under appropriate conditions, increasing students' intrinsic motivation can enhance their learning of important concepts and materials. Put somewhat differently, to the extent that teachers succeed in turning *work* into *play*, they may also substantially increase the learning and performance of their pupils. These data have implications for your own learning as well. For example, rather than relying on teachers to turn work into play, you might take a positive view of your own work and, as a result, do better.

Is there anything about the perceived motivation of the *teacher* that affects learning? That was the question studied at the University of Alberta by Wild, Enzle, and Hawkins (1992). In their experiment, undergraduates agreed to take a piano lesson. Some of the students were told that the teacher was paid $25 to a give the lesson (i.e., was extrinsically motivated); the other students were told that the teacher had volunteered to teach the lesson (i.e., was intrinsically motivated). The teacher had no knowledge of what information the student had been given and gave the same lesson to each one. The students who perceived the teacher as intrinsically motivated saw their teacher in a much more positive light. Moreover, they enjoyed their lesson more and were interested in taking more lessons. Furthermore, when left alone, these students spent more time trying out the piano than did the others. The implication of these data is clear: The kind of impression you have of your professors—in particular, of *why* they are doing what they do—can affect your own learning in many ways.

Emotions: *Their Nature,*
Expression, and Impact

Can you imagine life without emotions—without joy, anger, sorrow, or fear? Probably you cannot, for emotions are essential to our personal existence. Without them, we wouldn't really be ourselves.

But what are emotions? The closer we look, the more complex these reactions seem to be. Among scientists there is general agreement that emotions are the following: (1) physiological changes within our bodies—shifts in heart rate, blood pressure, and so on; (2) subjective cognitive states—the personal experiences we label as emotions; and (3) expressive behaviors—outward signs of these internal reactions (Izard, 1992; Zajonc & McIntosh, 1992). In the discussion that follows, we'll first look at several contrasting theories of emotion. Then we'll consider how emotions are expressed. Finally, we'll examine the complex interplay between emotions and cognition—how the way we feel influences the way we think, and vice versa.

"DAWN AND HER ALTER AGO"
BY MICHELLE PULEO

Can you imagine a life without emotions? Clearly, emotions are a key aspect of being human.

Emotions: *Reactions consisting of physiological reactions, subjective cognitive states, and expressive behaviors.*

Cannon-Bard Theory: *A theory of emotion suggesting that various emotion-provoking events simultaneously produce subjective reactions labeled as emotions and physiological arousal.*

James-Lange Theory: *A theory of emotion suggesting that emotion-provoking events produce various physiological reactions and that recognition of these is responsible for subjective emotional experiences.*

The Nature of Emotions: *Some Contrasting Views*

Among the many theories of emotion that have been proposed, three have been most influential. These are known, after the scientists who proposed them, as the *Cannon-Bard, James-Lange,* and *Schachter-Singer* theories.

The Cannon-Bard and James-Lange theories: Which comes first, action or feeling? Imagine that in one of your courses, you are required to make a class presentation. As you walk to the front of the room, your pulse begins to race, your mouth feels dry, and beads of perspiration form on your forehead. What is the basis for this reaction? Sharply contrasting answers are offered by the Cannon-Bard and James-Lange theories of emotion.

Let's begin with the **Cannon-Bard theory**, because it is consistent with our own informal observations of our emotions. This theory suggests that various emotion-provoking events induce *simultaneously* the subjective experiences we label as emotions and the physiological reactions that accompany them. Thus, the sight of the audience and of your professor (pen poised to evaluate your performance) causes you to experience a racing heart, a dry mouth, and other signs of physiological arousal, *and,* at the same time, to experience subjective feelings you label as fear. In other words, this situation stimulates various portions of your nervous system to produce both arousal, mediated by your *autonomic nervous system* (refer to Chapter 2) and subjective feelings, mediated in part by your *cerebral cortex.*

In contrast, the **James-Lange theory** offers a more surprising view of emotion. It suggests that subjective emotional experiences are actually the *result* of physiological changes within our bodies. In other words, you feel frightened when making your speech *because* you notice your heart is racing, your mouth is dry, and so on. As James himself put it in 1890, "We feel sorry because we cry, angry because we strike, and afraid because we tremble."

Which of these theories is closer to the truth? Until recent decades, most psychologists believed that the Cannon-Bard theory was more accurate. They reached this conclusion on the basis of several forms of evidence. First, surgical destruction of the sympathetic nervous system, which plays a key role in the types of physiological reactions James described, did not seem to eliminate emotional reactions (Cannon, Lewis, & Britton, 1927). Second, many, if not all, emotional states are accompanied by highly similar patterns of physiological activity. If that is the case, then such activity cannot be the basis for distinct emotional experiences such as anger, fear, joy, and sorrow.

More recently, though, certain aspects of the James-Lange approach have gained increasing acceptance. Research conducted with highly sensitive technology indicates that different emotions are indeed associated with different patterns of physiological activity (Levenson, 1992). For example, in several studies, participants were asked to recall experiences that evoked various emotions (e.g., Levenson et al., 1991). Careful measurement of processes regulated by the autonomic nervous system, such as heart rate and changes in skin conductance, indicated that some unpleasant emotions, such as anger, fear, and sadness, produce faster heart rate and larger increases in skin conductance than do pleasant ones such as happiness (Levenson, 1992). However, another negative emotion, disgust, slows heart rate down. These findings have been replicated with people in their seventies and eighties as well as with young children (Levenson et al., 1991), so they appear to be quite stable and general.

Additional support for the James-Lange theory of emotion is provided by studies of the **facial feedback hypothesis** (Laird, 1984; McCanne & Anderson, 1987). This hypothesis suggests that changes in our facial expressions sometimes produce shifts in our emotional experiences rather than merely mirroring them. In other words, as James would suggest, we feel happier when we smile, sadder when we frown, and so on. The results of several studies offer support for this idea (Ekman et al., 1990; McCanne & Anderson, 1987). So there may be substantial truth to the James-Lange theory (Zajonc, Murphy, & Inglehart, 1989). Subjective emotional experiences *do* often arise directly in response to specific external stimuli, as the Cannon-Bard view suggests. However, they can also be generated by changes in awareness of our own bodily states—even, it appears, by changes in our current facial expressions (Ekman, 1992).

SCHACHTER AND SINGER'S TWO-FACTOR THEORY   Strong emotions are a common part of daily life, but how do we tell them apart? How do we know that we are angry rather than frightened, sad rather than surprised? One potential answer is provided by a third theory of emotion. According to this view, known as the **Schachter-Singer theory** or the *two-factor theory*, emotion-provoking events produce increased arousal (Schachter & Singer, 1962). In response to feelings of arousal, we search the external environment in order to identify the causes of such feelings. The causes we then select play a key role in determining the label we place on our arousal, and so in determining the emotion we experience. If we feel aroused after a near-miss in traffic, we will probably label our emotion as "fear" or perhaps "anger." If, instead, we feel aroused in the presence of an attractive person, we may label our arousal as "attraction" or "love." In short, we perceive the emotion that external cues suggest we *should* be feeling. The theory is described as a two-factor view because it considers both the arousal and the cognitive appraisal we perform in our efforts to identify the causes of the arousal.

"I don't sing because I am happy. I am happy because I sing."

THE JAMES-LANGE THEORY IN OPERATION

The James-Lange theory suggests that the bird is correct: The subjective experiences we label as emotions are the result of changes within our body or our overt behavior.
(Source: Drawing by Frascino: © 1991 The New Yorker Magazine, Inc.)

Facial Feedback Hypothesis: A hypothesis indicating that facial expressions can influence as well as reflect emotional states.

Schachter-Singer Theory (two-factor theory): A theory of emotion suggesting that our subjective emotional states are determined, at least in part, by the cognitive labels we attach to feelings of arousal.

Support for Schachter and Singer

Many studies provide support for the Schachter-Singer theory. In 1974, Dutton and Aron at the University of British Columbia conducted an interesting field experiment on a suspension bridge over the deep Capilano Gorge in North Vancouver. The Capilano Bridge is very high and narrow, and it sways; it is said to be a "very scary" crossing. The male hikers met an attractive female research assistant either while crossing high above the rocky gorge or while on solid ground. Later, the men were asked to rate their attrac-tion to the assistant. As the Schachter-Singer theory predicts, those who met her on the swaying bridge, when arousal was high, found her more attractive and were more likely to actually call her for a date than those who met her on solid ground, when arousal was lower. Apparently, the male hikers interpreted their feelings of arousal on the bridge as attraction. (In her absence they might well have labeled it fear.) See the **Key Concept** page for an overview of the Cannon-Bard, James-Lange, and Schachter-Singer theories.

Opponent-Process Theory of Emotion: *A theory suggesting that an emotional reaction to a stimulus is followed automatically by an opposite reaction.*

OPPONENT-PROCESS THEORY: ACTION AND REACTION TO EMOTION Have you ever noticed that when you experience a strong emotional reaction, it is soon followed by the opposite reaction? Thus, elation is followed by a letdown, and anger is followed by calm, or even by regret over one's previous outbursts. This relationship is an important focus of the **opponent-process theory of emotion** (Solomon, 1982). The theory has two central assumptions: (1) emotional reactions to a stimulus are followed automatically by an opposite reaction; and (2) repeated exposure to a stimulus causes the initial reaction to weaken and the opponent process, or opposite reaction, to strengthen. So, for example, a politician who initially enjoys making speeches in public may experience a severe letdown after each speech is finished. With repeated experiences in delivering speeches, the pleasure she feels at addressing large crowds may weaken, while the letdown intensifies or occurs sooner after the speech is over. The result: She may gradually cut down on her public-speaking engagements.

Opponent-process theory provides important insights into drug addiction. For example, heroin users initially experience intense pleasure followed by unpleasant sensations of withdrawal. With repeated use of the drug, the pleasure becomes less intense, and unpleasant withdrawal reactions strengthen (Marlatt et al., 1988). In response, addicts begin to use the drug not for the pleasure it provides but to avoid the negative feelings that occur when they *don't* use it. In sum, according to opponent-process theory, emotional reactions often occur in action–reaction cycles, and many forms of behavior can be interpreted within this framework.

The Physiology of Emotion

As you may recall from Chapter 2, the physiological reactions that accompany emotions are regulated by the two parts of the *autonomic nervous system*. That is, activation of the *sympathetic*

KEY POINTS

- The Cannon-Bard theory of emotion suggests that emotion-provoking events simultaneously elicit physiological reactions and the subjective cognitive states we label as emotions.

- The James-Lange theory contends that emotion-provoking stimuli induce physiological reactions, and that these form the basis for the subjective cognitive states we label as emotions.

- The Schachter-Singer (two-factor) theory suggests that when we are aroused by emotion-provoking stimuli, we search the external stimuli for the causes of our feelings of arousal. The causes we select then determine the emotions we experience.

- According to opponent-process theory, strong emotional reactions are followed by opposite emotional reactions.

Three Major Theories of Emotion

Cannon-Bard Theory

- Emotion-provoking events or stimuli (e.g., watching or participating in an exciting sports event) stimulate the nervous system.

- The stimulation results in physiological reactions (e.g., faster pulse and higher blood pressure).

- Simultaneously, this stimulation also produces the subjective cognitive states we label emotions (e.g., anxiety, joy, anger).

James-Lange Theory

- Emotion-provoking events (e.g., watching or participating in an exciting sports event) produce physiological reactions (e.g., faster pulse, higher blood pressure, increased perspiration).

- Our awareness of these reactions results in the subjective cognitive states we label emotions (e.g., anger, joy, fear). That is, we feel frightened because we notice that our heart is racing, our mouth is dry, the palms of our hands are wet, and so on.

Schachter-Singer Two-Factor Theory

- Emotion-provoking events (e.g., watching or participating in an exciting sports event) produce increased arousal.

- In response to this state of increased arousal, we search the external environment to identify possible causes for it (especially in situations where several potential causes exist).

- The emotions we experience depend on the causes we choose.

Event

Exposure to emotion-provoking events is the starting point for all major theories of emotion.

Emotions

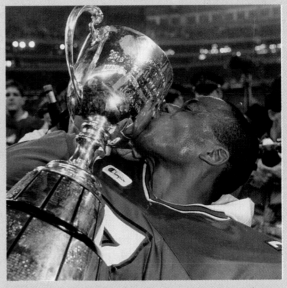

Athletes in an emotion-provoking situation such as a close, hard-fought game have little doubt about the causes of the arousal they experience. In many other situations, however, the causes of arousal will be far less obvious.

nervous system readies the body for vigorous activity, producing such reactions as increases in heart rate, blood pressure, and respiration. In contrast, activation of the *parasympathetic* nervous system influences activity related to restoration of the body's resources. For example, blood is diverted away from large muscles and to the digestive organs, and digestion itself is facilitated. As we saw earlier, research findings indicate that different emotions are associated with somewhat different patterns of physiological reactions; so the fact that emotions such as anger, joy, and disgust feel very different subjectively does appear to be mirrored, to some degree, in different biological reactions.

In addition, different emotions are related to specific patterns of activation in the cerebral cortex (Davidson, 1992). For more than a hundred years, medical reports have indicated that people who experience damage to the left hemisphere often develop deep depression, while those with damage to the right hemisphere show euphoria (Robinson et al., 1984). These cases suggest that positive feelings may be a result of activity in the left hemisphere, while negative ones arise in centers in the right hemisphere. Recent studies using recordings of electrical activity in the brain confirm this possibility. When watching films designed to elicit happiness or amusement, study participants generally show greater activation in the left than in the right cortex. In contrast, when watching films designed to elicit disgust, they show greater activation in the right cortex (Davidson, 1992; Tomarken, Davidson, & Henriques, 1990). Similar findings have been obtained with infants less than three days old: They show greater right-side activation in response to unpleasant tastes, greater left-side activation in response to pleasant ones (Davidson & Fox, 1988).

Large individual differences in these patterns exist. For example, depressed people show less left-frontal lobe activation than nondepressed people (Henriques & Davidson, 1991). Further, the inhibited children discussed in Chapter 8 (those who are shy and unwilling to approach new objects or situations) show less left-frontal lobe activation than uninhibited children (ones who are not shy, and who are willing to approach unfamiliar objects and people) (Davidson et al., 1991).

The cerebral hemispheres show some degree of specialization with respect to emotions. Positive feelings such as happiness are associated with greater activation in the left hemisphere, while negative ones such as sadness or disgust are associated with greater activation in the right hemisphere. So in brain activity as well as in heart rate and other bodily processes, there appears to be correspondence between our subjective emotional experiences and our physiological reactions. Mind and body are indeed one, or least intimately linked, as psychologists have long assumed. However, the task of deciphering the complex links between them can be accomplished only by continued research.

Can physiological differences among the emotions be put to practical use? For information on this topic, see **The Point of It All**.

The External Expression of Emotion: Outward Signs of Inner Feelings

Emotions are private. No one can truly share our subjective experiences. Yet we are able to recognize the presence of various emotions in others, and we are able to communicate our own feelings to them as well. How does that occur? As humans, of course, we have the option of telling our feelings in words (Storm & Storm, 1987). But how well do we understand what other people are telling us about their emotions? A study by Bortolotti and others (1993) at Laurentian University examined how well children (in grade 2 and grade 5) and university students understand statements about emotions of children.

THE POINT OF IT ALL

Can Physiological Reactions Be Used to Detect Lies?

R esearch findings indicate that heightened emotion is associated with physiological reactions and brain activity (Davidson, 1992; Levenson, 1992). That fact has been used in the design of technologies to detect when people are telling the truth and when they are not. The idea is that when they are lying, people's physiological reactions will be greater, and these can be measured. For example, suppose that we ask a crime suspect whether she is guilty. She answers no, and the needles on the polygraph show a large reaction. In contrast, when she is asked *control questions* such as "Is your name ..." (followed by her actual name), her reactions are much smaller. Since the reaction to the *relevant* question is greater, some investigators conclude that she is lying.

Are such conclusions warranted? Existing evidence is mixed. At the University of New Brunswick, Bradley and Rettinger (1992) gave different kinds of information about a "crime" to students and offered a cash reward for providing a polygraph recording that showed them innocent. They then recorded students' physiological responses to ten items on a questionnaire called the "Guilty Knowledge Test." Those students who had been assigned to the group that was guilty of the mock crime showed the highest responses; next highest were those who knew about the details of the crime but were not involved in it; lowest were those who did not have the information.

Lying need not necessarily be related to crime. Bradley and Cullen (1993) developed an interesting alternative. They had students record embarrassing incidents that had happened to them. Then, while being recorded by the polygraph, the students denied either their own reports or incidents that had happened to other people. When they were denying their own reports, they were lying, of course. When they denied incidents that had happened to others, they were telling the truth, because those incidents had not happened to them. These embarrassing incidents proved to be a useful alternative to mock crimes for studying the detection of deception with the polygraph.

It must be remembered that "lie detectors" measure only *arousal*, not necessarily whether people are telling the truth. People can and do influence their physiological reactions in many ways (Lykken, 1985). For example, they may tense their muscles or change their breathing. These actions and many others may change the pattern of recordings of the lie detector, though they may have no connection to the truth of what is being said. As Zajonc and McIntosh (1992) note, changes in physiological reactions mediated by the autonomic nervous system occur for many different reasons. Hence, attributing these changes solely, or even primarily, to lying could be quite a mistake. A critical issue here is that while the identification of the guilty is as high as 87 percent (e.g., Patrick & Iacono, 1989), the correct identification of innocent people may be only 56 percent—which is definitely not good enough! Nevertheless, polygraph testing has spread, and is used not only by law enforcement agents (sometimes as a threat to obtain a confession) but also by employers in selecting candidates for particular jobs.

Recognizing that the reliability of these results is a matter of dispute, in 1987 the Supreme Court of Canada decided that the outcome of polygraph testing is not admissible as evidence under Canadian law.

Of course, the polygraph is not the only way we humans have of telling whether others are attempting to deceive us. Nonverbal cues can also signal that someone is lying.

LIE DETECTORS: A RELIABLE MEASURE OF THE TRUTH?

Lie detectors measure changes in physiological reactions during questioning. The pattern of such changes reveals the truthfulness of the person's answers. However, growing evidence indicates that lie detectors are not reliable in determining truth.

They found that in general, statements about happiness and comfort are understood best, while those about anger and guilt are most poorly understood.

We also communicate emotion nonverbally. In daily conversation and on dates, we naturally show others whether we are interested in them (e.g., Fichten et al.). In deaf-parented families, "visual language" messages have a special part to play (Mallory et al., 1992). Some nonverbal messages involve objects. Reportedly, Queen Elizabeth always carries a purse, which she uses to send as many as twenty different signals to her guards when she needs assistance of some kind. The most revealing of nonverbal communications, however, involve **nonverbal cues**.

NONVERBAL CUES: THE BASIC CHANNELS   Research suggests that this kind of communication occurs through several basic *channels* or paths simultaneously. The most revealing of these are *facial expressions* (e.g., Coren & Russell, 1992), *eye contact, body movements and posture*, and *touching*.

UNMASKING THE FACE: FACIAL EXPRESSIONS AS GUIDES TO OTHERS' EMOTIONS
More than 2,000 years ago, the Roman orator Cicero stated: "The face is the image of the soul." By this he meant that feelings and emotions are often reflected in the face and can be read there from specific expressions. Modern research suggests that Cicero was correct in this belief: It *is* possible to learn much about others' current moods and feelings from their facial expressions. In fact, it appears that six different basic emotions are represented clearly, and from an early age, on the human face: anger, fear, sadness, disgust, happiness, and surprise (Ekman, 1992). It is the thinking of Kenneth Prkachin at the University of British Columbia (1992) that the expression of pain is universal as well. As in all scientific endeavor, the opinion with respect to the universality of basic emotions is not unanimous. In particular, the part that cultural factors play is a point of debate (Russell, 1994).

During development, changes occur in the perception of emotions in general (Stayer, 1993), and of facial expressions in particular. At the University of Lethbridge, these changes were studied by Kolb (et al., 1992) in children from 6 to 15 and in adults up to age 30. The findings indicated two ages at which increases in correct perception of facial expressions occurred—6 to 8 years, and 13 to 14 years. Kolb and his associates linked this to changes occurring in the development of the frontal lobes, which may take until age 14.

Of course, we are capable of showing many more than six different facial expressions. Emotions occur in many combinations—for example, anger along with fear, or surprise combined with happiness. Further, each emotion can vary greatly in intensity. Thus, while there are only a small number of basic themes in facial expressions, the number of variations on these themes is very large.

Until recently, it was widely assumed that basic facial expressions such as those for happiness, anger, or disgust are universal—that they are recognized as indicating specific emotions by people all over the world (e.g., Ekman & Friesen, 1975). However, a recent review of the evidence on this issue (Russell, 1994) suggests that the interpretation of facial expressions may be influenced also by cultural factors. In short, it appears that we must be cautious about assuming that a smile, for example, will be seen as a sign of happiness by people of all cultures of the world.

GAZES AND STARES: THE LANGUAGE OF THE EYES   Have you ever had a conversation with someone wearing dark glasses? If you have, you know that this can be an uncomfortable situation. When you can't see the other person's eyes, you can't tell how he or she is reacting. Ancient poets often described the

Nonverbal Cues: Outward signs of others' emotional states. Such cues involve facial expressions, eye contact, and body language.

eyes as "windows to the soul," and in one important sense they were right. We *do* often learn much about others' feelings from their eyes. For example, we interpret direct eye contact as a sign of liking or friendliness (Kleinke, 1986). In contrast, if others avoid eye contact with us, we may conclude that they are unfriendly, don't like us, or are shy (Zimbardo, 1977).

There is one important exception to this general rule. If another person gazes at us continuously and maintains this contact regardless of any actions we perform, he or she can be said to be *staring*. Most people attempt to minimize exposure to this particular kind of nonverbal cue if possible (Ellsworth & Carlsmith, 1973). Stares are often interpreted as a sign of anger or hostility, and may cause a great deal of anxiety and discomfort. Indeed, in one case it was clearly deemed sexual harassment; at one university, a professor was sanctioned for repeatedly leering at a female student.

BODY LANGUAGE: GESTURES, POSTURE, AND MOVEMENTS Try this simple demonstration: Recall an incident that made you angry—the angrier the better. Think about it for a minute. Now bring another incident to mind—one that made you feel sad—again, the sadder the better. Now, compare your behavior as you recalled the two events. Did you change your posture or move your hands, arms, or legs as your thoughts shifted from the first incident to the second? The chances are good that you did, for our current mood or emotion is often reflected in the posture, position, and movement of our body. Such nonverbal behaviors are termed **body language**, and they can provide several useful kinds of information about others' emotions.

First, frequent body movements—especially ones in which a particular part of the body does something to another, such as touching, scratching, or rubbing—suggest emotional arousal. The greater the frequency of such behavior, the higher a person's level of arousal or nervousness seems to be (Harrigan, 1987). The specific movements made, too, can be revealing. Consider the statements "He adopted a *threatening posture*" and "She greeted him with *open arms*." They indicate that different body orientations or postures are suggestive of particular emotional states (Rossberg & Poole, 1993).

Direct evidence is provided by research conducted by Aronoff, Woike, and Hyman (1992). These researchers first identified characters in classical ballet who played dangerous or threatening roles (the Angel of Death, Macbeth) or warm, appealing roles (Juliet, Romeo). Then they carefully examined samples of dancing by these characters in actual ballets to see the postures they used. Aronoff and his colleagues found that the threatening characters used diagonal poses three times as often as the friendly characters, and that the friendly characters adopted rounded poses almost four times as often as the threatening characters. These and related findings suggest that large-scale body movements or postures are an important source of information about emotions.

Finally, more specific information about others' feelings is often provided by **gestures** or *emblems*, body movements that have highly specific meaning in a given culture. For example, in several countries, holding the thumb up is a sign of approval. Similarly, holding the nose between the thumb and index finger is a sign of displeasure or disgust. Emblems vary greatly from culture to culture, but all human societies have signals of this type for greetings, departures, insults, and descriptions of various physical states—"I'm full," "I'm tired," and so on. In a study of bilingual nonverbal communication, Lacroix and Rioux (1978) found that there were differences in the gestures used by bilingual subjects when they gave short speeches in English and in French. However, other than the gestures they made, the nonverbal communication they used was the same, whichever official language they were speaking.

Body Language: *Nonverbal cues involving body posture or movement of body parts.*

Gestures: *Movements of various body parts that convey a specific meaning to others.*

BODY POSTURES AND EMOTIONS

Threatening characters in classical ballet adopt angular or diagonal poses such as the one on the left much more often than friendly characters do. In contrast, friendly characters adopt rounded poses such as the one on the right much more often than threatening characters do. These findings indicate that specific postures or movements can often be a useful guide to others' emotions.

TOUCHING: THE MOST INTIMATE NONVERBAL CUE Suppose that while you were talking with another person, he or she touched you briefly. What information would this convey? How would you react? The answer to both questions is, "It depends." Important factors include these: who does the touching (i.e., a friend or a stranger); which gender (e.g., Stoppard & Gruchy, 1992; Roese, et al., 1992); the nature of the touching (i.e., brief or prolonged, gentle or rough); and the context in which it takes place (i.e., a business or social setting, a doctor's office). Touch can suggest affection, sexual interest, dominance, caring, or even aggression. Despite these complexities, touching in a nonthreatening and appropriate manner can have positive effects (Alagna, Whitcher, & Fisher, 1979; Smith, Gier, & Willis, 1982). Consider, for example, the results of an ingenious study by Crusco and Wetzel (1984).

These investigators enlisted the aid of waitresses, who agreed to treat customers in one of three different ways when giving them their change: (1) they did not touch the customers in any manner, (2) they touched them briefly on the hand, (3) or they touched them for a longer period of time on the shoulder. The researcher assessed the effects of these treatments by examining the tips the customers left. Results were clear: Both a brief touch on the hand (about half a second) and a longer touch on the shoulder (one to one-and-a-half seconds) significantly increased tipping over the no-touch control condition. Assuming that tips increase when customers are in a positive mood, these findings are consistent with the view that touching in a nonthreatening and appropriate manner can have positive effects.

One final point about touching: Additional studies indicate that there are important *gender differences* in this area. In a field study, Hall and Veccia (1990) observed touching between thousands of people in many public settings, including shopping malls, hotel lobbies, and airports. Results indicated that overall, there was no difference between women and men in frequency of touching others. However, the investigators noted that among young people, men touched women more often than vice versa. This difference decreased with age, so that by middle age, women actually touched men more often than men touched women. More generally, women and men express hostility differently (Davidson, 1994). For example, when women become hostile, they cease speaking and draw their bodies away, while men show hostility by raising their voices and leaning forward.

What accounts for these age-related shifts? Hall and Veccia (1990) suggest that among younger people, especially teenagers, relationships are not yet well established and gender roles encourage visible gestures of possessiveness by males. As relationships "age," however, gender roles may require more gestures of possessiveness by females.

Communication of affective states also takes place in the tone of voice we use. As you learned in Chapter 2, this nonverbal aspect of speech is called *prosody*; reportedly, it is controlled by the right hemisphere (Lalande et al., 1992).

Here is one last question: How accurate are we at decoding nonverbal messages conveyed to us by others? Some research has delved into that question. The general finding is that our abilities are moderately good, although we are more confident than we should be. This makes us prone to making mistakes and easy to mislead. For example, our ability to tell facial expressions of genuine pain from suppressed or faked pain has been the focus of research at Simon Fraser University (e.g., Poole & Craig, 1992) and at the University of Waterloo, where undergraduates were able to tell "to a modest degree" deliberate from fake pain by the facial expressions they saw (Prkachin, 1992).

How competent are we at catching people in a lie? Moderately good, if all we are able to see is their face, and even better if we can observe their body as well (Ekman, 1985). People who have had special training in the detection of "microexpressions" (fleeting facial and body movements) which reveal lying, do relatively well.

DePaulo (1992) has uncovered an additional complexity, however. She studied the deliberate attempts by people who were lying to regulate their nonverbal behavior. Remarkably, their behaviors differed depending upon whether the person to whom they were lying was attractive or not.

Emotion and Cognition: *How Feelings Shape Thoughts and Thoughts Shape Feelings*

Earlier, we asked you to recall incidents that made you feel angry or sad. When you thought about these incidents, did your mood also change? Did recalling memories of these events influence the way you felt? The chances are good that it did, for in many instances, our thoughts seem to exert strong effects on our emotions. This relationship works in the other direction as well: Being in a happy mood often causes us to think happy thoughts, while feeling sad tends to bring negative memories and images to mind. In short, there appear to be important links between *emotion* and *cognition*—between the way we feel and the way we think (Schiff & Lamon, 1989). Let's take a brief look at some of the scientific evidence for the reality—and the importance—of these links (e.g., Forgas, 1991).

HOW AFFECT INFLUENCES COGNITION   Does **affect**, our current mood, influence the way we think, the way we perceive emotions in the face of uncertainty— that is, how we process information about ourselves or the external world? The findings of many different studies indicate that our current moods do indeed influence our judgments. A depressed mood much reduces our ability to judge the emotions of others (Persad & Polivy, 1993), and this may contribute to the persistence of depression.

Our moods, or *affective states* as they are often termed (Isen, 1987), strongly influence the way we understand ambiguous stimuli. In general, we perceive and evaluate these stimuli more favorably when we are in a good mood than when we are in a negative one (e.g., Fiske & Neuberg, 1990; Isen & Shalker, 1982). For example, when asked to interview applicants whose qualifications for a job are ambiguous, subjects assign higher ratings when in a positive mood (such as when they have just received favorable feedback or won a small prize) than when they are in a negative mood (when they have just received negative feedback) (Baron, 1987, 1993).

Positive and negative moods influence memory. In general, information consistent with our current mood is easier to remember (Forgas, 1991). Positive and negative affect have also been found to influence the way in which information is organized in memory. People experiencing positive affect seem to include a wider range of information within various memory categories than those in a neutral or negative mood (Isen & Daubman, 1984). People experiencing positive affect also provide more unusual associations to neutral words, and rate objects that are not very typical of a given category as more representative of it than people who are not in a positive mood. For example, they rate the word *elevator* as more typical of the category "vehicle" than people in a negative mood (Baron, Rea, & Daniels, 1992; Isen et al., 1985).

Moods often influence the decisions we make. In a sad mood, we make decisions more slowly. Would you be more likely to take risks in a good mood

KEY POINTS

- Research findings indicate that different emotions are associated with different physiological reactions and patterns of brain activity.
- Positive emotional reactions are associated with greater activation of the left cerebral hemisphere, while negative emotional reactions are associated with greater activation of the right cerebral hemisphere.
- Emotional states are communicated to others through a wide range of nonverbal cues, including facial expressions, eye contact, body language, and touching.

Affect: A person's current mood.

or in a bad mood? Informal observation suggests a good mood. Research findings, however, indicate that the issue is more complicated than that. People experiencing positive affect are indeed more likely to make risky decisions, but only when the potential losses involved are minor (or very unlikely to occur; Arkes, Herren, & Isen, 1988). They are actually *less* willing to take risks when potential losses are important (or likely to occur)—perhaps because they don't want to take a chance on reducing their current positive feelings.

Finally, people in a good mood are more creative than those in a bad mood. They are more successful in performing tasks involving creative problem-solving, such as coming up with novel uses for everyday objects, than people in a neutral mood (Isen, Daubman, & Nowicki, 1987).

Overall, then, it seems clear that emotions, or even relatively minor shifts in mood, can strongly influence important aspects of cognition. But what about our overall capacity to engage in cognitive tasks—to think clearly and rationally, for example? Does mood influence this as well? For some revealing—and thought-provoking!—information on this issue, see **The Research Process**.

THE RESEARCH PROCESS

Are People in a Good Mood Easier to Influence? Effects of Mood on Information Processing

People seeking to influence others—to change their attitudes—often follow a strategy that goes something like this: "Put them in a good mood first, then try to persuade them." You probably observe this strategy yourself, when salespeople compliment you or joke with you in an effort to put you in a good mood and soften you up for the pitch to follow. Is this strategy effective? An information-processing perspective suggests that it may work because (1) we have limited capacity to process new information, and (2) being in a good mood might absorb some of this capacity and so reduce our ability to defend ourselves against persuasion.

Evidence consistent with this reasoning was reported by Mackie and Worth (1989), who compared positive and neutral moods. In their study, male and female participants read a persuasive message on a computer screen that argued against their own views (whatever these were) concerning two issues: government control over gun sales and acid rain. Half the participants read these messages in a good mood (they learned that they had been chosen to receive a small cash prize); the remainder never received such a mood elevator. Within each of these two conditions, the positive mood and the neutral mood, half the participants received *strong* arguments in favor of a view different from their own, while the remainder received *weak* arguments. Finally, half were told that

they could look at the persuasive message for as long as they wished; the remainder learned that they could only read it through once.

After reading the messages, subjects reported their attitudes toward each issue. Mackie and Worth (1989) found that those in a positive mood were less able to engage in careful processing of the arguments they read, presumably because their mood used up part of their information-processing capacity. Thus, they were less successful in formulating counterarguments against the strong messages (and were influenced by them to a greater extent) under conditions where they had only limited time to read. On the basis of these and related findings, many psychologists have concluded that being in a good mood does indeed reduce our capacity to process incoming information (e.g., DeBono, 1992).

Motivational Effects of Positive Affect: Does Positive Affect Really Interfere with Our Ability to Process Information?

Mackie and Worth (1989) interpreted their findings as suggesting that people in a good mood are less *able* to process information than those in a neutral mood. While that interpretation is consistent with their results, there may be an alternative explanation: Perhaps people in a good mood are still able to process information as effectively, but they are less *motivated* to do so. They may be unwilling to engage in hard cognitive work that will interfere with their good mood; they may prefer to focus instead on pleasant activities that maintain mood.

To test this possibility, Smith and Shaffer (1991) conducted a series of studies. In the first of these, they asked two groups of students to listen to a brief message arguing in favor of comprehensive examinations for senior students. In the *high relevance* condition, these exams were to be introduced the following year, when the participants would still be on campus; in the *low relevance* condition, the message argued for starting the exams in five years, long after the participants would have graduated. Half the people in each group were put in a positive mood before hearing the message (by watching a video known to induce a good mood); the other half watched a video known to have little if any effect on mood.

After listening to one of these messages about examinations, participants rated their agreement with the message and listed all the thoughts they had while listening to it. Careful analysis showed that when issue relevance was low, those in a good mood remembered less of the message and generated fewer message-related thoughts (including counterarguments) than those in a neutral mood. When issue relevance was high, in contrast, these differences disappeared. Under these conditions, being in a good mood did *not* interfere with information processing (see Figure 10.8).

Taking available information into account (Bless et al., 1990; DeBono, 1992; Mackie & Worth, 1989; Smith & Shaffer, 1991), it appears that being in a good mood can indeed interfere with the processing of new information. However, such effects may stem from reduced motivation to engage in careful processing rather than from the fact that positive affect absorbs precious information-processing capacity. In short, perhaps people in a good mood are able to process information but, wishing to maintain their positive feelings, are less willing to do so.

Critical Thinking Questions:

1. Suppose that Mackie and Worth (1989) found that being in a good mood increased persuasion even when the arguments presented were weak. What would this imply concerning the effects of mood on information processing?

2. Have you ever had trouble concentrating on difficult tasks when you felt elated? If so, why do you think you experienced such problems? Do your subjective impressions seem consistent more with the reduced capacity or with the motivational interpretation discussed above?

3. Is it possible that being in a good mood increases persuadability both by absorbing information capacity and by reducing motivation? How could this possibility be tested?

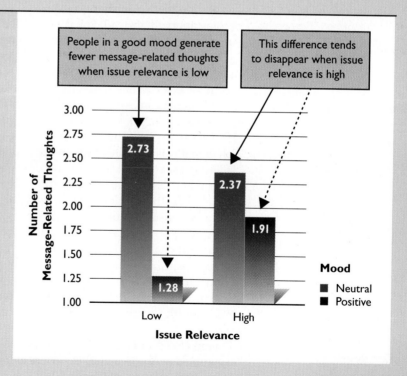

FIGURE 10.8

Positive Affect and Information Processing

When issue relevance was low, people in a good mood generated fewer thoughts related to a persuasive message than people in a neutral mood. However, when issue relevance was high, this difference tended to disappear. These findings suggest that people in a good mood are able to process information effectively, but are sometimes less motivated to do so than are people in a neutral mood.

People in a good mood generate fewer message-related thoughts when issue relevance is low

This difference tends to disappear when issue relevance is high

- We tend to remember information consistent with our moods more readily than information inconsistent with them.
- Positive and negative moods influence decision making, and positive moods can sometimes increase creativity.
- Positive affect may increase susceptibility to persuasion by reducing motivation to engage in careful information processing, thus preventing us from formulating counterarguments.
- Cognition influences affect in several ways. Activation of schemas that contain an affective component can strongly influence our current moods or emotions.
- Our interpretations of potentially emotion-provoking events can strongly influence our emotional reactions to them.
- Expectancies exert strong effects on emotional reactions, and may even alter memories of actual experiences.

HOW COGNITION INFLUENCES AFFECT Most research on the relationship between affect and cognition has focused on how feelings influence thought. However, there is also compelling evidence for the reverse—that cognition influences affect. We mentioned one aspect of this relationship in discussing the two-factor theory of emotion (Schachter & Singer, 1962). This is the theory which suggests that often we don't know our own emotions directly; rather, since our internal reactions are often somewhat ambiguous, we look outward—at our own behavior or other aspects of the external world—for clues about what we are feeling. In such cases, the emotions or feelings we experience are strongly determined by the interpretation or cognitive labels we select.

A second way in which cognition can influence emotions is through the activation of *schemas* containing a strong affective component. For example, if we label an individual as belonging to some group, that may also tell us how we *feel*. Activation of a strong racial, ethnic, or religious schema or *stereotype* may exert powerful effects on our current feelings or moods.

Is there a link between mood and negative thinking? At the University of Toronto, Schiff (et al., 1992) manipulated the mood of university students by having them contract the right (negative mood) or left (positive mood) side of their faces. The students were then tested for ethnic stereotypes. The results showed that mood did influence how negative the expressions of ethnic stereotypes were.

Third, our thoughts can often influence our reactions to emotion-provoking events by determining how we interpret or appraise those events. For example, imagine that you are standing in line outside a theater and a man bumps into you. How will you interpret his action? If you decide that he is trying to shove you, the chances are high that you will become angry. If, instead, you conclude that he merely tripped on the sidewalk, you probably won't experience such feelings or take defensive action.

Finally, consider the impact of *expectancies* on our emotional reactions. When individuals have expectations about how they will react to a new event or stimulus, these expectations shape their perceptions and feelings (e.g., Wilson et al., 1989). Thus, if you expect to dislike a new food, you probably will. If you expect to enjoy a film or a joke, the chances are good that you will. Moreover, expectations shape our later memories of how we felt about events. A dramatic illustration of that was the outcome of a study conducted by Wilson and Klaaren (1992).

These researchers told some people who had signed up to participate in an experiment that it was a lot of fun; others did not receive positive expectations. When the participants arrived for the study, half the people in each group watched a film under pleasant conditions (they sat in comfortable chairs). The others watched the same film under unpleasant conditions (they sat in hard chairs and were required to keep their chin on a headrest). Three to four weeks later, all participants were phoned and asked if they would be willing to be in the study once again. Results indicated that expectations played a key role in participants' responses. Those who had expected to enjoy the film were significantly more likely to volunteer again, *regardless of whether they had participated under pleasant or unpleasant conditions*. Wilson and Klaaren (1992) interpreted these findings as indicating that expectations may sometimes override actual experience; indeed, in an important sense, expectations may *become* our reality! In such cases, cognition is a more important determinant of our emotions than reality itself.

Getting Motivated: Some Practical Techniques

At one time or another, almost all of us feel that getting motivated to do the things we should do is difficult if not impossible. Are there any techniques you can use to help overcome this kind of *behavioral inertia*? As we'll see in Chapter 17, industrial/organizational psychologists have focused a great deal of attention on this question in the context of *work motivation*—the motivation to perform various tasks. The results of their research suggest that one technique is especially helpful: *goal setting*, or establishing specific levels of performance or achievement that individuals should strive to attain (Locke & Latham, 1990). You probably already use goal setting informally, but here are several guidelines that will help you maximize its benefits.

1. *Set specific goals* First, be careful to set very specific goals. This means indicating precisely what will be defined as adequate performance. For example, if you are preparing for an exam, don't set yourself the general goal of "reading all the material twice." Instead, decide how many pages you must read each day in order to be ready for the test. Then be sure to stick to this specific goal.

2. *Set challenging goals* Don't fall into the trap of setting your goals so low that meeting them is trivial. People seem to be motivated to a much greater extent by goals that are challenging than by ones that are too easy to attain. So set your goals high enough that they stretch your ability to reach them.

3. *Set attainable goals* But don't fall into the opposite trap—setting your goals so high that you can't possibly reach them. When this happens, it's easy to get discouraged and give up. The trick is to choose goals that are difficult enough to present a challenge but not so difficult that failure is guaranteed. Remember the discussion of achievement motivation? High achievers tend to prefer goals of moderate but not excessive difficulty; you should too.

4. *Reward yourself for reaching each goal* Often, people forget to reward themselves for reaching each goal: As soon as one goal is attained, they rush full steam ahead to the next one. This is a mistake! When choosing your goals, also identify rewards you will give yourself for reaching them. For example, in studying for a test, plan to give yourself a break—popcorn, or some other treat—after you finish each chapter. Doing so can be a big help in terms of keeping your momentum going.

5. *Become committed to your goals* Once you establish your goals, it's important that you accept them as *goals*—ones you are really committed to reaching. If you don't have such a commitment, it's too easy to change the goals, to ignore them, just to give up altogether. So be sure to adopt your goals as ones you are committed to reaching, as real standards for your behavior.

6. *Build feedback into the process* A final question you should ask yourself before you begin is this: "How will I know when I've reached each goal?" This sounds simple, but in some instances it's more complicated than it seems. For example, in writing a term paper, you can set a specific goal, such as, "I'll do five pages each night." In this case the feedback is obvious: You know you've reached the goal when you have a pile of five completed pages in front of you. But for other tasks you may have to turn to other people for feedback. For example, suppose that you've decided to work on getting along better with your roommate. How will you know when you've made real progress? One way is to set very specific goals, such as, "I won't get into arguments over the groceries, or over cleaning the apartment." But it may also be necessary to ask the roommate directly whether she or he perceives any changes in your behavior. The main point is that feedback is essential for goal setting to work, so be sure to build this kind of information into the process.

Industrial organization psychologists have studied techniques for helping people increase their motivation, in both their work and their personal lives.

Motivation: The Activation and Persistence of Behavior

motivation 401

instinct theory 401

instincts 401

drive theory 402

homeostasis 402

arousal theory 402

expectancy theory 403

incentives 404

work motivation 404

hierarchy of needs 405

hunger motivation 406

obesity 407

anorexia nervosa 409

bulimia 409

sexual motivation 411

gonads 411

sexual jealousy 415

homosexual 416

bisexual 417

heterosexual 417

aggressive motivation 418

aggression 418

frustration 419

achievement motivation 421

power motivation 421

Thematic Apperception Test
  (TAT) 422

intrinsic motivation 423

- The concept of motivation is helpful in explaining behavior that can't readily be interpreted in terms of current conditions in a given situation.
- Drive theory suggests that motivation is basically a process in which various biological needs push (drive) us to actions designed to satisfy these needs. Arousal theory suggests that organisms seek optimal levels of arousal, not minimal levels of arousal. Expectancy theory suggests that behavior is often motivated by expectancies concerning the outcomes that will result from specific actions.
- Maslow's needs hierarchy theory suggests that needs exist in a hierarchy and that higher-level needs cannot be activated, or serve as sources of motivation, until lower-level needs have been satisfied.
- Eating is regulated by complex biochemical systems within the body. Eating is also affected by the sight of food, feedback from chewing and swallowing, and cultural factors.
- Many variables contribute to obesity. These include eating habits, reactions to stress, basal metabolic rate, and responses to food-related cues.
- Anorexia nervosa and bulimia are two serious eating disorders. People suffering from anorexia starve themselves and experience extreme weight loss. People suffering from bulimia engage in binge eating followed by purging. Both anorexics and bulimics are dissatisfied with their bodies and perceive their body size as larger than it actually is.
- Sex hormones seem to play only a subtle and relatively minor role in human sexual motivation. However, other chemical compounds produced within the body may also play a role in sexual attraction and love. During sexual activity both males and females move through a series of distinct phases. In contrast to other species, humans can be sexually aroused by self-generated sexual fantasies and by exposure to erotic materials.
- Individuals differ in sexual orientation. Some are exclusively homosexual, others are bisexual, and the majority are exclusively heterosexual. Male homosexuals do not have lower testosterone levels than male heterosexuals, and homosexuals and heterosexuals do not seem to differ in terms of family background or early experiences. Recent evidence suggests that genetic factors may play a role in homosexuality.
- Aggressive motivation involves the desire to inflict harm on others. Contrary to popular belief, aggression does not stem primarily from frustration. Rather, it occurs in reaction to a wide range of social, environmental, and personal factors. Culture, too, influences its occurrence.
- Achievement motivation is the desire to meet standards of excellence: to outperform others and accomplish difficult tasks. Power motivation is the desire to be in charge and to influence others. Contrary to initial findings, women do not fear success. Women are equal to men with respect to achievement motivation.
- When individuals engage in activities because they find them pleasurable rather than to obtain external rewards, they are said to be intrinsically motivated to perform them. Extrinsic rewards can sometimes reduce intrinsic motivation, but this does not always occur if the rewards are perceived as a sign of recognition for good performance. Intrinsic motivation has important implications for education and can sometimes be used to enhance students' learning and performance.

EMOTIONS: THEIR NATURE, EXPRESSION, AND IMPACT

emotions 426
Cannon-Bard theory 426
James-Lange theory 426
facial feedback hypothesis 427
Schachter-Singer theory 427
opponent-process theory of
emotion 428
nonverbal cues 432
body language 433
gestures 433
affect 435

- The Cannon-Bard theory of emotion suggests that emotion-provoking stimuli simultaneously elicit physiological arousal and the subjective cognitive states we label as emotions.
- The James-Lange theory contends that emotion-provoking stimuli induce physiological reactions and that these form the basis for the subjective cognitive state we label as emotions.
- The Schachter-Singer theory, or two-factor theory, suggests that when we are aroused by emotion-provoking stimuli, we search the external stimuli for the causes of our feelings of arousal. The causes we select then determine the emotions we experience.
- According to opponent-process theory, strong emotional reactions are followed by opposite emotional reactions.
- Research findings indicate that different emotions are associated with different physiological reactions and patterns of brain activity. Positive emotional reactions are associated with greater activation of the left cerebral hemisphere, while negative emotional reactions are associated with greater activation of the right cerebral hemisphere.
- Emotional states are communicated to others through a wide range of nonverbal cues. These include facial expressions, eye contact, body language, and touching.
- People in a good mood evaluate ambiguous stimuli more favorably than those in a neutral mood. We tend to remember information consistent with our moods more easily than information inconsistent with them. Positive and negative affect also influence decision making. Positive affect can sometimes increase creativity.
- Positive affect may increase our susceptibility to persuasion by reducing our motivation to engage in careful information processing, thus preventing us from coming up with counterarguments.
- Cognition influences affect in several ways. Activation of schemas containing an affective component can strongly influence our current moods or emotions. Our interpretations of potentially emotion-provoking events can strongly influence our emotional reactions to them. Expectations exert strong effects on emotional reactions and may even alter memories of actual experiences.

CRITICAL THINKING QUESTIONS

APPRAISAL	In an ultimate sense, emotions are a private experience: No one can ever share them with us directly. Despite this fact, psychologists have attempted to investigate emotions scientifically. Do you think that a scientific understanding of emotions is possible? If so, why? If not, why?
CONTROVERSY	Not long ago, a large federal agency in the United States planned to fund research designed to study the possibility that aggressive tendencies are inherited. Vigorous objections to this plan were voiced by many political groups because these groups feared that the proposed research would yield findings very unfavorable to minority groups. In view of the protests, the plan was shelved. Do you think this was appropriate? Or should the research have been funded, no matter how unpopular its results might be?
MAKING PSYCHOLOGY PART OF YOUR LIFE	Now that you understand the basic nature of hunger motivation and the many factors that affect it, can you think of ways in which you can use this knowledge to regulate your own weight better? Describe at least three concrete steps you can take, based on the research findings discussed in this chapter, to help ensure that your own weight stays at desirable levels in the decades of life that lie ahead of you.

Individual Differences I
Intelligence and Gender

INTELLIGENCE: ITS NATURE AND
MEASUREMENT 444
Human Intelligence: Some Contrasting
    Views
Measuring Human Intelligence
Reliability and Validity: Basic Requirements
    for All Psychological Tests
Intelligence Testing and Public Policy: Are
    Intelligence Tests Fair?

HUMAN INTELLIGENCE: THE ROLE OF HEREDITY
AND THE ROLE OF ENVIRONMENT 463
Evidence for the Influence of Heredity
Evidence for the Influence of
    Environmental Factors
Environment, Heredity, and Intelligence:
    Summing Up

GENDER: HOW MALES AND FEMALES DIFFER 467
Gender Differences in Social Behavior
Mate Selection, Relationships, and
    Sexuality
Gender Differences in Psychological
    Adjustment
Cognitive Abilities
Gender Differences: A Note on Their
    Possible Origins

SUMMARY AND REVIEW OF KEY POINTS 486

CANADIAN FOCUS—STUDIES OF THE
SAVANT SYNDROME: ISLANDS OF SUPERIOR
FUNCTIONING IN A SEA OF GENERAL
IMPAIRMENT 446

THE POINT OF IT ALL—INDIVIDUAL TESTS OF
INTELLIGENCE: THEIR PRACTICAL USES 461

THE RESEARCH PROCESS—INTEGRATING THE
EVOLUTIONARY AND SOCIAL EXCHANGE MODELS
OF MATE PREFERENCES: TAKING ACCOUNT OF
OUR OWN "MARKET VALUE" 475

CANADIAN FOCUS—THE MONTREAL MASSACRE:
GENDER HATRED 483

MAKING PSYCHOLOGY PART OF YOUR LIFE—
MEASURING ATTITUDES TOWARD WOMEN: A
SHORT TEST FOR SEXISM 484

HOW [HUMANS] BECAME UPRIGHT, NAKED AND BRAINY

The Globe and Mail:
November 27, 1993

The subhead of a report in The
Globe and Mail *reads as
follows: "We owe our
coolheadedness and mighty
intellects to our ape forbears,
who took it into their heads to
walk upright."*

*The article tells about a
theory of one scientist who has
suggested that, when our
ancient ancestors (who lived
near the equator) stood up and
began to walk on two legs, they*
*succeeded in keeping
themselves 40 percent cooler.
There were several reasons for
that—one was the new distance
from the reflection of the sun's
rays by the earth, another was
the exposure to the cooling
breezes higher off the ground.*

*In time, they shed their fur
coats, and furthermore: "By
walking on two feet, humans
developed the animal world's
most powerful cooling system,
and that allowed us to acquire
larger brains." That is, the very*
*heat-sensitive brain—being now
much cooler—could evolve and
expand in a way that would not
have been possible at the higher
temperature at ground level.*

*Whether the prerequisite for
human intelligence was a new
cooling system for the brain is
not known, and perhaps not
knowable. Nevertheless, curiosity
about how human intelligence
evolved and how it works
continues to interest researchers,
as you will find out as you
proceed through Chapter 11.*

PEOPLE DIFFER FROM EACH OTHER IN COUNTLESS WAYS. HOWEVER, SOME OF THESE WAYS ARE MORE IMPORTANT THAN OTHERS.

*E*veryone is different. From a purely biological perspective this is hardly surprising: Human beings possess thousands of genes, and since half of these come from each parent, the number of different ways in which these genes can combine is astronomical—a figure in the hundreds of billions, at least. So, from the very start, we really *are* unique individuals. It's equally clear, however, that some of the dimensions of difference, or ways in which people differ from one another, are more important than others. It is for this reason that psychologists who study **individual differences**—the differences that distinguish individuals from one another—have generally focused on a relatively small number of key dimensions. In this chapter and the next one, we'll examine several of these dimensions. Chapter 12 will focus on individual differences relating to *personality*. Here, we'll begin our discussion of individual differences by focusing on two important topics: *intelligence* and *gender*.

The term *intelligence* refers primarily to individual differences in a wide range of cognitive abilities. Intelligence is obviously a very important aspect of individual distinctiveness. To acquaint you with what psychology has learned about intelligence during almost a century of careful study, we'll consider several topics: the nature of intelligence, how it is measured, and the potential contributions of heredity and environment to individual differences.

The term *gender*, defined in Chapter 8, refers in part to differences between males and females (Unger, in press). As we'll soon see, gender involves much more than differences related to the biological categories of *male* and *female* (Deaux, 1993). As Chapter 8 explained, *social factors*, such as a society's ideas about the characteristics of males and females, and about what is and is not appropriate behavior for each sex, also play a key role. This chapter's discussion of gender will focus primarily on the following question: What differences between males and females actually exist? Where possible, we will comment on current evidence about the possible origins of such differences.

Intelligence: *Its Nature and Measurement*

*I*n everyday life, we make judgments about other people—and ourselves—along many different dimensions: attractiveness, ambition, patience, charm, and energy, to name just a few. Among these, one of the most important is clearly **intelligence**, which is defined as the ability to think abstractly and learn readily from experience (Flynn, 1987). Why do we consider the dimension of intelligence to be so important? Partly because we believe it predicts many important aspects of behavior: how quickly people can master new information and tasks; how quickly they will understand and adapt to new situations; how successful they will be in school, in various kinds of training, and in life generally. As we'll soon see, these commonsense notions are correct, at least to a degree: The higher people score on various measures of intelligence, the better able they are to accomplish many different tasks (Ceci, 1991; Matarazzo, 1992). So, from this perspective, individual differences in intelligence are a very important topic, and worthy of careful study.

Psychologists have recognized this for many years. In fact, efforts to understand the nature of intelligence and to measure intelligence were among the first tasks addressed by the field of psychology. In this section we will consider several contrasting views of the nature of intelligence. Then we will turn to the question of how this important characteristic can be measured. In this

Individual Differences: *Differences between individuals that distinguish them from one another.*

Intelligence: *The ability to think abstractly and to learn readily from experience.*

context we'll consider some of the basic requirements of *any* tests designed to assess individual differences in *any* aspect of psychological function. Finally, we'll look at the evidence relating to the relative contributions to intelligence of environmental and genetic factors.

Human Intelligence: Some Contrasting Views

What is intelligence? Every person has his or her own definition, and psychologists, too, disagree about the question (e.g., Glazer, 1993; Sternberg, 1985). Most would define intelligence partly as the ability to think abstractly and to learn readily from experience, but beyond these basics, there is little consensus. Let's examine several contrasting views about the nature of intelligence to see how they differ.

INTELLIGENCE: UNIFIED OR MULTIFACETED? Is intelligence a single characteristic, or does it consist of several distinct parts? In the past, psychologists often disagreed sharply on this issue. In one camp were scientists who viewed intelligence as a general, unified capacity—as a single characteristic or dimension along which people vary. An early supporter of this view was Spearman (1927), who believed that performance on any cognitive task depended on a primary general factor, which he named *g*, and on one or more specific factors *s* relating to that particular task. Spearman based this view on the observation that people who score high or low on one kind of test of intelligence tend to score at a similar level on other tests as well.

In contrast, other experts believed that intelligence is actually composed of many separate mental abilities that operate more or less independently (Thurstone, 1938; Gardner, 1983; Guilford, 1967, 1985). For example, Thurstone's position was that intelligence is a composite of seven primary mental abilities. More recently, Gardner has argued that there are six distinct domains of intelligence: linguistic, musical, logical–mathematical, spatial, bodily–kinesthetic, and personal knowledge of both self and others. On what basis can it be claimed that a particular domain of intelligence exists as a unique entity? Gardner maintains that there has to be psychometric and experimental evidence available that makes it possible to define or specify the distinct nature of that domain. He requires also that there be evidence that a given intelligence can function at a normal level in the presence of mediocre or even subnormal levels of performance in other domains of intelligence. Finally, he suggests, it should be possible to show that other forms of intelligence can continue to function normally in the presence of a gross deficiency in the given intelligence. To illustrate, consider musical and spatial intelligence. There is psychometric and experimental evidence to specify the nature of these particular intellectual domains. Also, studies of brain-injured patients have shown that an individual can be impaired in musical or spatial–imaginal abilities and be otherwise unimpaired intellectually. The reverse is also true. In **Canadian Focus**, individual cases are described in which musical and spatial–imaginal functions are preserved even though intellectual function in other domains is severely impaired.

Not all views of intelligence divide sharply on the unified/multifaceted issue, however. One influential perspective, proposed by Cattell (1963, 1987), adopts a more integrated approach. According to Cattell, intelligence consists of two major components: *fluid intelligence* and *crystallized intelligence*. *Crystallized intelligence* includes those aspects of intelligence which involve drawing on previously learned information to make decisions or solve problems. Classroom tests, vocabulary tests, and many social situations involve crystallized intelligence. In contrast, *fluid intelligence* involves the abilities to form concepts, reason, and identify similarities. In short, fluid intelligence is more intuitive and is active in forming new mental structures rather than in making use of existing ones. Research focusing on these two types of intelligence suggests that fluid intelligence may peak in early adulthood, while crystallized intelligence increases across the life span (Lerner, 1990; Willis & Nesselroade, 1990).

Where does the pendulum of scientific opinion rest today? Somewhere in the middle. Today most psychologists believe that intelligence involves both a *general* ability to handle a wide range of cognitive tasks and problems and a number of more *specific* abilities. All of this being noted, modern thinking about the nature of intelligence has shifted from the unitary-versus-multifaceted issue and now tends to focus on very different questions relating to *information processing* and *culture*.

Savant Syndrome: Condition in which an individual is cognitively impaired but nevertheless demonstrates some normal or above-normal intellectual skills in one domain.

CANADIAN FOCUS

Studies of the Savant Syndrome: Islands of Superior Functioning in a Sea of General Impairment

The **savant syndrome** supports the notion of independent domains of intelligence. An individual with savant syndrome is impaired, sometimes grossly, but nevertheless demonstrates normal or above-normal skills in a particular intellectual domain. This syndrome is occasionally seen among the developmentally disabled. It is more commonly observed among those afflicted with early infantile autism. Slightly over 9 percent of individuals with autistic disabilities show some evidence of superior ability in a specific intellectual domain (Treffert, 1989). Most often, the level of special ability displayed is remarkable only in comparison with the deficiencies in other intellectual domains. In some cases, however, evidence of clearly superior abilities in a specific intellectual domain can be seen. Two cases have recently been reported by Canadian researchers.

The case of J.L., described by Charness, Clifton, and MacDonald (1988) of the University of Waterloo is particularly interesting. J.L. is profoundly impaired. Presently in his early forties, he has been institutionalized since the age of fifteen. He is blind and has experienced epileptic seizures since early childhood. He has very limited linguistic abilities. Communicating with him is extremely difficult. He often displays ecolalia—a tendency to simply repeat the words that are addressed to him. His cognitive abilities are so impaired that normal intelligence tests cannot be used to assess him. His ability to care for himself is very limited. He is unable to shave, comb his hair, or discriminate simple forms by touch. He can convey food

to his mouth but is reportedly unable to understand when the plate from which he is eating is empty.

Amid this intellectual wreckage, one single ability has been preserved and developed to a superior level. He has extraordinary musical skills. He is able to make absolute-pitch judgments. Although blind, and capable of using only one hand, he can perform skillfully on the piano, organ, melodica and harmonica. His musical repertoire is wide; he can engage in jazz improvisation; and he is very adept at reproducing musical pieces by ear. His melody and chord spans are held by Charness and colleagues to be comparable with those of a competent musician. In sum, J.L. has above-normal musical abilities yet is profoundly impaired in virtually every other intellectual domain.

A second case of savant skills has been reported by Mottron and Belleville (1988). The individual on whom they report, E.C., is not nearly as impaired as J.L. He is autistic and has many speech irregularities. Communication with him can be readily established, however, and he has reasonable social skills. Although unable to count, he can read in a slow and deliberate manner; he can also write, though only in a peculiar and exclusively phonetic fashion. He tends to interpret words very literally, and this makes it difficult for him to understand any form of humorous wordplay that involves variations in the meanings of words. Although he is in his mid-thirties, academic performance tests involving reading and classification operations suggest that, in these domains, he functions at the level of a six-year-old.

Like J.L., he has a single, remarkable skill, which lies in the domain of spatial–imaginal intelligence. He can produce highly detailed drawings of objects and landscapes, from imagination or from a model. He is quite accomplished. The objects he draws are very accurately detailed and appropriately placed. Their perspective is precisely rendered. Reportedly, these drawings are sought after and collected. His technique is unusual: Instead of starting with an overall sketch, he begins at a peripheral location and adds detail until the drawing is complete. His drawings are painstakingly executed and completed without error or correction. Interestingly, he can draw physical objects effortlessly but has problems drawing human and animal faces.

In E.C. and J.L. we see two individuals who have broad general intellectual impairment. What is unique about them is that, in spite of their general impairment, both have a domain of expertise in which they demonstrate abilities well above those displayed by the average person. Advocates of the view that there are multiple, relatively independent intellectual domains—such as Gardner—take this as strong evidence that there are multiple intelligences. Their argument is that, if there were only a single unitary intellectual process, all intellectual capacities should be impaired to a comparable degree, and there should be no isolated islands of ability. This argument is compelling, but it has to be admitted that it is not embraced by all workers in the field. For example, Charness and colleagues are more comfortable with the view that the abilities displayed by savants result from a massive amount of attention being focused on a single pursuit by individuals who lack the resources to be distracted by other concerns. Mottron and Belleville have a different interpretation: They speculate that the "spared" skill of a savant results from a fundamental impairment that affects that particular domain of skills less than other domains. Resolution of these issues must await future research.

THE INFORMATION PROCESSING APPROACH: BASIC COMPONENTS OF INTELLIGENT THOUGHT   As we've seen repeatedly in this book, psychologists have applied an *information processing perspective* to many aspects of human behavior—everything from the nature of memory through cognitive development to key aspects of motivation (see Chapters 6, 7, 8, and 10). It is not surprising, then, that this approach has also been applied in studies of the nature of intelligence. According to information processing perspective, to understand intelligence, we must understand the cognitive strategies used by individuals who score high or low on this dimension. In other words, we must define intelligence in terms of basic aspects of cognition (Das, 1992; Kirby & Das, 1990; Naglieri & Das, 1990; Matarazzo, 1992). This approach has already led to important new insights about intelligence.

For example, consider a theory proposed by Sternberg (1985, 1986). According to this theory, known as the **triarchic theory** of intelligence, there are actually three types of human intelligence (see Figure 11.1). The first, known as **componential intelligence**, emphasizes effectiveness in information processing. People who are high on this dimension are able to think critically and analytically. Thus, they usually excel on standard tests of academic potential and make excellent students. In contrast, the second type, **experiential intelligence**, emphasizes insight and the ability to formulate new ideas. People who are high on this dimension excel at zeroing in on what information is crucial in a given situation, and at combining seemingly unrelated facts. This is the kind of intelligence shown by many scientific geniuses and inventors, such as Einstein, Newton, and—some would say—Freud. Johannes Gutenberg, for example, inventor of the movable type that first made large-scale production of books possible, combined the mechanisms for producing playing cards, pressing wine, and minting coins into his invention (see Figure 11.2).

Finally, there is what Sternberg terms **contextual intelligence**. People who are high on this dimension are intelligent in a practical, adaptive sense. They quickly recognize what factors influence success on various tasks and are competent at both adapting to and shaping their environment. Successful people in many fields excel in this capacity.

Triarchic Theory: A theory suggesting that there are actually three distinct kinds of intelligence.

Componential Intelligence: The ability to think analytically.

Experiential Intelligence: The ability to formulate new ideas or to combine seemingly unrelated information.

Contextual Intelligence: The ability to adapt to a changing environment.

FIGURE 11.1

Sternberg's Triarchic Theory of Intelligence

According to Sternberg's triarchic theory, there are three distinct types of intelligence: componential, experiential, and contextual.

Componential Intelligence

- Ability to think abstractly and process information
- Tasks that can be used to measure the elements of componential intelligence are analogies, vocabulary, and syllogisms

Experiential Intelligence

- Ability to formulate new ideas and combine unrelated facts
- Examples include scientific creativity and diagnosing a problem with an automobile engine

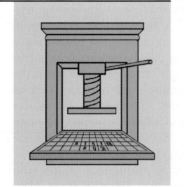

Contextual Intelligence

- Ability to adapt to a changing environment and to shape one's world to optimize opportunities
- Contextual intelligence deals with an individual's ability to prepare for problem solving in specific situations; for example, this Lapp herder in northern Scandinavia stuffs his boots with dried grasses for warmth

FIGURE 11.2

Experiential Intelligence in Operation

When he combined existing technology used in making playing cards, pressing wine, and minting coins to invent the printing press with movable type, Gutenberg was showing what Sternberg would term experiential intelligence.

Sternberg has expanded his triarchic theory to bridge the gap between intelligence and personality, the topic we'll consider in the next chapter (Sternberg, 1988, 1989). In this expanded view, known as *mental self-government*, Sternberg notes that in addition to the three types of intelligence described above, we must also consider *intellectual styles*—the ways in which the three types are actually used in solving the problems of everyday life. Whether or not Sternberg's theories are confirmed by future research, they are representative of a new approach to the study of intelligence that draws heavily on basic knowledge about cognition generally. Clearly, this is a promising new perspective.

THE NEUROSCIENCE APPROACH: INTELLIGENCE AND NEURAL EFFICIENCY Highly intelligent people are often described as being "fast thinkers," as responding rapidly to changing situations and new events. This everyday term suggests another possible perspective on intelligence—one emphasizing neural factors, such as more rapid or efficient processing of information by nerve cells within the brain. And in fact, such an approach has been given increasing attention by psychologists. A growing body of evidence suggests that intelligence may actually be closely linked to physiological processes, especially ones going on in the nervous system—in the brain in particular. A good description of the various approaches that have been taken in an attempt to develop "biological" measures of intellectual function has been provided by Philip Vernon of the University of Western Ontario (1991). As we have noted, the basic notion underlying this approach is that efficiency in neural functioning should be correlated with higher intelligence.

Three different techniques are currently being used to measure the neural efficiency of the physiological processes assumed to underlie intellectual operations. One technique involves recording, through electrodes attached to the surface of the skull, evoked potentials produced by neural activity in reaction to stimuli. Average evoked potential activity is then correlated with performance on intelligence tests. In one recent study, Reed and Jensen (1993) recorded evoked potential activity in the brains of 147 male volunteers who were presented with a visual stimulus. The average *latency*, or delay, with which this potential followed presentation of the visual stimulus was obtained for each volunteer; the latency was then divided by the length of the volunteer's head to obtain a measure of the speed with which nerve impulses were conducted in the visual system. These data were then correlated with the volunteers' scores on one written test of intelligence, the Raven Progressive Matrices (a test we will consider in a later section). As shown in Figure 11.3, the results were startling: The higher this measure of neural speed, the higher the participant's measured intelligence.

A second technique involves examining metabolic activity in the brain during cognitive tasks (e.g., Haier et al., in press). Again, the assumption is that if intelligence is related to efficient brain functioning, then the more intelligent people are, the less energy their brains should expend on various tasks. This prediction has been confirmed: The brains of individuals scoring highest on written measures of intellectual ability *do* expend less energy when these individuals perform complex cognitive tasks. The data in these studies have been gathered using the PET technique of brain imaging described in Chapter 2.

A third technique involves measuring nerve conduction velocity. Following the line of argument being pursued, it seems inevitable that efforts

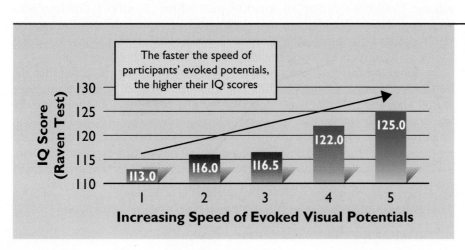

FIGURE 11.3

The Physiological Basis of Intelligence

The faster their nerve impulses in response to visual stimuli, the higher research participants scored on one test of intelligence. These findings, and many others, suggest that intelligence may rest in part on the efficiency with which individuals' brains process information.
(Source: Based on data from Reed & Jensen, 1993.)

are being made to see if the speed with which neural impulses are transmitted is correlated with intelligence scores. Experiments carried out by Vernon and Mori (1992) do provide evidence that neural transmission rates in peripheral nerve fibers are correlated with intelligence scores.

Some researchers doubt that efforts to measure neural efficiency are likely to contribute meaningfully to our basic understanding of intelligence. They take the position that the most that can be expected are relatively low-level correlations with various intellectual operations—with no gain in understanding the fundamental process of intelligence. Advocates of the neural efficiency approach, such as Vernon, reply that not so long ago, few believed that reaction-time measures or speed-of-processing research would tell us much about higher cognitive processing. In fact, these techniques have been shown to be extremely valuable. Vernon is optimistic that the neural efficiency measures will prove just as valuable in unraveling the complexity of intelligence.

Given that neural efficiency seems to be correlated with intelligence, it will come as no surprise that there is a link between brain structure and intelligence (Andreasen et al., 1993). Specifically, scores on standard measures of intelligence, such as the *Wechsler Adult Intelligence Scale* (to be discussed shortly), are related to the size of certain portions of the brain, including the left and right temporal lobes and the left and right hippocampus (Andreasen et al., 1993). Moreover, this is true even when participants' overall physical size is statistically controlled and so cannot play a role in these findings.

In sum, it appears that the improved methods now available for studying the brain and nervous system are beginning to establish the kinds of links between intelligence and physical structures that psychologists have long suspected to exist. Such research is very recent, and there is not yet enough of it to warrant firm conclusions. Still, it does appear that we are on the verge of establishing much firmer links between intelligence—a crucial aspect of mind—and body.

Measuring Human Intelligence

In 1904, when psychology was just emerging as an independent field, members of the Paris school board approached Alfred Binet with an interesting request: Could he develop an objective method for identifying children who were cognitively disabled, so that they could be removed from the regular classroom and given special education? Binet was already at work on related topics, so he agreed, enlisting the aid of his colleague, Theodore Simon.

In designing this test, Binet and Simon were guided by the belief that the items used should be ones children could answer without special training or study. They felt that this was important because the test should measure the ability to handle intellectual tasks—*not* specific knowledge acquired in school. Therefore, Binet and Simon decided to use items of two basic types: ones so new or unusual that none of the children would have prior exposure to them, and ones so familiar that almost all children would have encountered them in the past. For example, children were asked to perform the following tasks:

- Follow simple commands or imitate simple gestures.

- Name objects shown in pictures.

- Repeat a sentence of fifteen words.

- Tell how two common objects are different.
- Complete sentences begun by the examiner.

The first version of Binet and Simon's test was published in 1905 and contained thirty items. Much to the two authors' satisfaction, it was quite effective: With its aid, schools could readily identify children in need of special assistance. Encouraged by this success, Binet and Simon broadened the scope of their test to measure variations in intelligence among children of normal intelligence. This revised version, published in 1908, grouped items by age, with six items at each level between three and thirteen years. Items were placed at a particular age level if about 75 percent of children of that age could pass them correctly.

Binet's tests were soon revised and adapted for use in the United States by Lewis Terman, a psychologist at Stanford University. The **Stanford-Binet Test**, as it came to be known, gained rapid acceptance and was soon put to use in many settings. Over the years it has been revised several times; see Figure 11.4 for a description of the most recent version, published in 1986. One of the features of the Stanford-Binet that contributed to its popularity was that it yielded a single score assumed to reflect an individual's level of intelligence—the now famous IQ.

IQ: Its meaning then and now Originally, the letters **IQ** stood for *intelligence quotient*, and a "quotient" is precisely what such scores represent. To obtain an IQ, the examiner divides the student's mental age by his or her chronological age, then multiplies by 100. For this computation, mental age is

Stanford-Binet Test: *A popular test for measuring individual intelligence.*

IQ: *A numerical value that reflects the extent to which an individual's score on an intelligence test departs from the average for other people of the same age.*

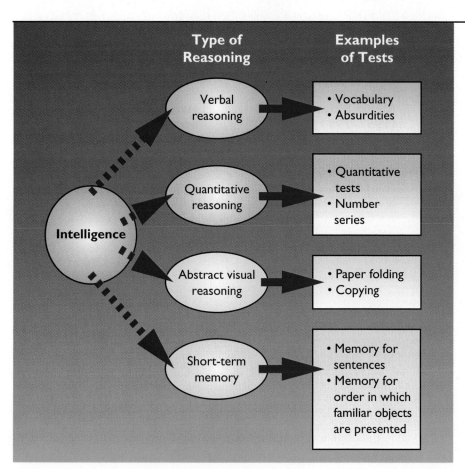

FIGURE 11.4

The Stanford-Binet Test

A recent version of the Stanford-Binet Test measures intelligence with a composite score made up of four scores for broad types of mental activity: verbal reasoning, quantitative reasoning, abstract visual reasoning, and short-term memory. Each of the scores is obtained through a series of subtests that measure specific mental abilities.

based on the number of items a person passes correctly on the test. Test takers are awarded two months for each correct item. If an individual's mental and chronological ages are equal, an IQ of 100 is obtained. Numbers above 100 indicate that the student's intellectual age is greater than his or her chronological age; in other words, the individual is more intelligent than typical students of this age. In contrast, numbers below 100 indicate that the individual is less intelligent than his or her peers.

Perhaps you can already see one obvious problem with this type of IQ score: At some point, mental growth levels off or stops, while chronological age continues to rise. As a result, IQ scores begin to decline after the early teen years! Partly because of this problem, IQ scores now have a different meaning. They simply reflect an individual's performance on an intellectual test relative to that of individuals of the same age.

THE WECHSLER SCALES   As noted above, the tests developed by Binet and later adapted by Terman and others remained popular for many years. They do, however, suffer from one major drawback: All are mainly verbal in content. As a result, they pay little attention to the fact that intelligence can be revealed in nonverbal activities as well. For example, an architect who visualizes a

**Alfred Binet
(1957–1911)**

In 1905, Binet developed the first intelligence test, known as the Binet-Simon Test. He developed the concept of mental age and based much of his early work on intelligence on his own daughters.

**Lewis Madison
Terman
(1877–1956)**

Terman translated and adapted the Binet-Simon intelligence test to create the Stanford-Binet Test. Terman's well-known studies of gifted children dispelled many misconceptions about such children.

PSYCHOLOGISTS OF NOTE

majestic design for a new building is obviously demonstrating intelligence. Yet no means of assessing such abilities was included in early versions of the Stanford-Binet Test.

To overcome this and other problems, David Wechsler devised a set of tests for both children and adults that included nonverbal, or *performance*, items as well as verbal ones, and that yielded separate scores for these two components of intelligence. The Wechsler tests are perhaps the most frequently used individual intelligence tests today. Table 11.1 presents an overview of the subtests that make up one of the Wechsler Scales, the Wechsler Adult Intelligence Scale–Revised (WAIS–R for short).

Wechsler believed that differences between scores on the various subtests could be used to diagnose serious mental disorders. Research on this possibility has yielded mixed results, however. Some findings suggest that a Verbal IQ significantly higher than a Performance IQ can indicate damage to the left brain hemisphere, while the opposite pattern can indicate damage to the right hemisphere (Aiken, 1991). But this is not always the case, and other evidence is usually required before conclusions can be reached about possible brain damage. Other findings indicate that patterns of scores on the Wechsler tests may be linked to various psychological disorders. For example, some research

Albert Sidney Beckham (1897–1964)

Beckham conducted research into the nature of intelligence and developed reports such as "Minimum Levels of Intelligence for Certain Occupations," which became a guide at institutions for training cognitively disabled people. In the 1920s Beckham established a psychological laboratory at Howard University, the first of its kind at a black institution of higher learning.

Sandra Scarr

Scarr is a developmental psychologist whose research on the impact of heredity and the environment on intelligence is widely known. Her adoption studies have provided strong evidence for the role of environment in intelligence scores.

TABLE 11.1

Subtests of the Wechsler Intelligence Scale

This widely used test of adult intelligence includes the subtests described here.

VERBAL TESTS	
TEST	**DESCRIPTION**
Information	Examinees are asked to answer general information questions, increasing in difficulty.
Digit span	Examinees are asked to repeat series of digits read out loud by the examiner.
Vocabulary	Examinees are asked to define thirty-five words.
Arithmetic	Examinees are asked to solve arithmetic problems.
Comprehension	Examinees are asked to answer questions requiring detailed answers; answers indicate their comprehension of the questions.
Similarities	Examinees indicate in what way two items are alike.

PERFORMANCE TESTS	
TEST	**DESCRIPTION**
Picture completion	Examinees indicate what part of each picture is missing.
Picture arrangement	Examinees arrange pictures to make a sensible story.
Block design	Examinees attempt to duplicate designs based on red and white blocks.
Object assembly	Examinees attempt to solve picture puzzles.
Digit symbol	Examinees fill in small boxes with coded symbols corresponding to a number above each box.

has found that chronic schizophrenics have higher Verbal than Performance IQs, while people suffering from a disorder known as the *antisocial personality disorder* (see Chapter 14)—a disorder marked by lack of conscience and by impulsive and often violent behavior—have higher Performance than Verbal IQs (Kunce, Ryan, & Eckelman, 1976). Once again, though, not all studies have confirmed such findings, so they must be interpreted with caution.

A Wechsler test for children, the *Wechsler Intelligence Scale for Children— Revised* (WISC–R), has also undergone development and modification. Here, too, efforts have been made to determine whether differences in scores on the various subtests indicate various kinds of disorders. Some of the results obtained in this research are intriguing. For example, echoing the findings with respect to the antisocial personality disorder mentioned above, it has been found that Performance IQ almost always exceeds Verbal IQ in children classified as *delinquent* (Hubble & Groff, 1982).

Patterns of scores on the subtests of the WISC are also sometimes used to identify children with various *learning disabilities*. Some findings indicate that children who score high on certain subtests, such as Picture Completion and Object Assembly, but lower on others, including Arithmetic, Information, and Vocabulary, are more likely to be suffering from learning disabilities than children with other patterns of scores (Aiken, 1991). Again, however, not all findings point to such conclusions, so the value of the WISC for this kind of diagnosis remains somewhat uncertain.

GROUP TESTS OF INTELLIGENCE Both the Stanford-Binet and the Wechsler Scales are *individual* tests of intelligence: They are designed for use with one person at a time. Obviously, it would be much more efficient if *group* tests could be administered to large numbers of people at once. The need for such tests was driven home at the start of World War I, when the armed forces in the United States suddenly faced the task of screening several million

THE WISC–R

Developed by David Wechsler, the WISC– R (a revised form of the WISC) is one of the most widely used intelligence tests for children.

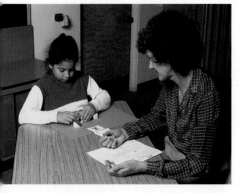

recruits. In response to this challenge, psychologists such as Arthur Otis developed two tests: *Army Alpha* for people who could read, and *Army Beta* for people who could not read or who did not speak English. These early group tests proved highly useful. For example, they were used to select candidates for officer training school.

In the succeeding decades many other group tests of intelligence were developed. Among the more popular of these are the *Otis tests,* such as the Otis-Lennon School Ability Test (Otis & Lennon, 1967); the *Henmon-Nelson Test* (Nelson, Lamke, & French, 1973); and the *Cognitive Abilities Test,* or CAT (Thorndike & Hagen, 1982). All are available in versions that can be administered to large groups. The advantages offered by such tests soon made them very popular, and they were put to routine use in many school systems during the 1940s and 1950s. As you probably already know, in the 1960s this practice became the focus of harsh criticism. There were many reasons why, including the suggestion that such tests were unfair in several respects to children from disadvantaged backgrounds—especially children from certain minority groups. We'll return to these objections below. Now, however, let's consider two other issues relating to the use of these, or any other, psychological tests: *reliability* and *validity.*

KEY POINTS

- The first individual test of intelligence was devised by Binet and Simon. This test yielded an IQ score, obtained by dividing children's mental age by their chronological age. Revised repeatedly over the years, this test is still in widespread use as the Stanford-Binet Test.

- Because intelligence can be demonstrated nonverbally as well as verbally, another widely used test of intelligence, the Wechsler Scales, obtains both a Performance and a Verbal IQ.

- Group tests of intelligence are highly efficient, but serious questions have been raised about their use with minority groups.

Reliability and Validity: Basic Requirements for All Psychological Tests

Suppose that in preparation for a summer at the beach, you decide to go on a diet in order to lose 5 kilograms. Your current weight is 60, and for two weeks you skip desserts and engage in vigorous exercise. Then you step on your bathroom scale to see how much progress you've made. To your shock, the needle reads 63; you've actually *gained* 3 kilos! How can this be? Perhaps you made a mistake. So you step back on the scale. Now it reads 61. Yet get off and step on again; now it reads 62. At this point you realize the truth: Your scale (thank goodness!) is *unreliable*—the numbers it shows change even though your weight, obviously, can't change from one second to the next.

This is a simple illustration of a very basic point. In order to be of any use, measuring devices must have high **reliability**—that is, they must yield the same result each time they are applied to the same quantity. If they don't, they are essentially useless. The same principle applies to psychological tests, whether they are designed to measure intelligence or any other characteristics. But how do we know whether and to what extent a test is reliable? In fact, several different methods exist for assessing a test's reliability.

INTERNAL CONSISTENCY: DO THE ITEMS ON A TEST MEASURE THE SAME THING? If we wish to develop a test that measures a single psychological characteristic such as intelligence, then it is important to establish that all the items actually measure this characteristic—that the test has what psychologists call *internal consistency.* One measure of the internal consistency of a test is known as **split-half reliability**. Checking for split-half reliability involves dividing the test into two equivalent parts, such as the first and second halves or odd- and even-numbered items, and then comparing people's scores on each. If the test really measures intelligence, the correlation between the scores on each half should be positive and high. If it is not, some of the items may be measuring different things, and the test may be unreliable in one important sense. There

Reliability: The extent to which any measuring device yields the same results when applied more than once to the same quantity.

Split-Half Reliability: The extent to which an individual attains equivalent scores on two halves of a psychological test.

are several statistical formulas for measuring internal consistency. The most widely used formula, *coefficient alpha*, simultaneously considers all of the possible ways of splitting into halves the items on a test. Since this is done by computer, the process is very efficient, and coefficient alpha has become one standard measure of tests' internal consistency.

CONSISTENCY ACROSS TIME: TEST-RETEST RELIABILITY A test that yields very different scores when taken by the same individuals at different times is of little value if the characteristics it supposedly measures are ones that are stable over time, such as intelligence. Thus, another type of reliability, **test-retest reliability**, is also important. Test evaluators can measure this by giving the test to the same group of people on more than one occasion and comparing the scores. The more similar these are, the higher the test's reliability.

One obvious problem with the test-retest method is that people's scores on the retest may increase simply because they have taken the test again—that is, because of *practice effects*. To reduce this problem, psychologists often use *alternate forms* of the same test—two different forms that cover the same material at the same level of difficulty. Figure 11.5 provides an overview of assessment procedures for both split-half and test-retest reliability.

Test-Retest Reliability: The extent to which a psychological test yields similar scores when taken by the same person on different occasions.

FIGURE 11.5

Reliability: A Basic Requirement of Psychological Tests

In order to be useful, psychological tests must be reliable. Two types of reliability are illustrated here: (A) split-half reliability (a type of internal consistency) and (B) test-retest reliability.

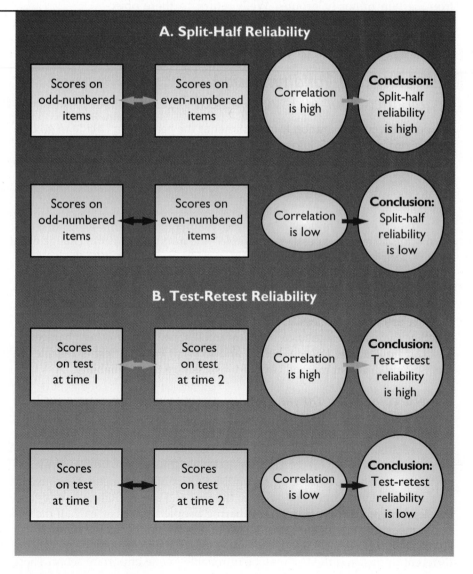

A. Split-Half Reliability

Scores on odd-numbered items ⟷ Scores on even-numbered items — Correlation is high ⟷ **Conclusion:** Split-half reliability is high

Scores on odd-numbered items ⟷ Scores on even-numbered items — Correlation is low ⟶ **Conclusion:** Split-half reliability is low

B. Test-Retest Reliability

Scores on test at time 1 ⟷ Scores on test at time 2 — Correlation is high ⟷ **Conclusion:** Test-retest reliability is high

Scores on test at time 1 ⟷ Scores on test at time 2 — Correlation is low ⟶ **Conclusion:** Test-retest reliability is low

VALIDITY: DO TESTS MEASURE WHAT THEY CLAIM TO MEASURE? On a recent visit to one of your local malls, you may have noticed a new type of machine outside one of the stores. A sign on the machine reads TEST YOUR SEX APPEAL and goes on to explain that after inserting a quarter and pushing some buttons, users will receive a score indicating their appeal to members of the opposite sex. Do you think a machine like this is really capable of measuring sex appeal? The answer is obvious: No! In all probability, it measures nothing at all except, perhaps, the user's willingness to believe silly claims. Psychologists say that such machines are low in **validity**, which is a device's ability to measure what it is supposed to measure.

The same principle applies to psychological tests: They too are useful only to the extent that they really measure the characteristics they claim to assess. Thus, an intelligence test is useful only to the extent that it really measures intelligence. How can we determine whether a test is valid? There are several methods. One of these to is to gauge **content validity**—that is, the extent to which the items on a test sample the behaviors we can reasonably assume are related to the characteristic in question. For example, if an intelligence test consists of measurements of the length of people's earlobes or the sharpness of their teeth, we can probably assume that it is low in content validity: These measurements do not seem to be related to what we mean by the term *intelligence*. If, instead, the test measures the breadth of a person's vocabulary or his or her ability to solve various kinds of puzzles, we will have more faith in the content validity of the items: They do seem to be related to various aspects of intelligence.

Another type of validity is known as **criterion-related validity** and is based on the following assumption: If a test actually measures what it claims to measure, then individuals attaining different scores on it should also differ in terms of their behavior. Specifically, they should differ in terms of some *criterion* or standard relating to the trait being measured. For example, we might expect that scores on an intelligence test would be related to the criterion of achievement in school, or to success in various occupations.

Two kinds of criterion-based validity that psychologists often measure are **predictive validity** and **concurrent validity**. To measure predictive validity, psychologists use scores on a test to predict *later* performance relative to some criterion. For example, scores on an intelligence test taken now are used to predict success in some kind of training program. To measure concurrent validity, psychologists relate scores on a test taken now to *present* performance on some criterion. Thus, we might relate scores on the test to students' current performance in school.

A third type of validity, **construct validity**, is a bit more complex. This type of validity has to do with the extent to which a test measures a psychological concept or variable that can't be assessed directly, but that plays an important role in psychological theory. Such validity can be established in several ways. For example, we can find out whether results on our test are consistent with results obtained on other obvious or well-established measures of the same *construct*—that is, the same variable or concept. Suppose we develop a test that we believe measures the tendency to take risks. If individuals who score high on our test also have more traffic accidents and are more likely to belong to skydiving or mountaineering clubs than those who score low on the test, we have some *convergent evidence* that the test really does measure something like risk-taking tendencies. See the **Key Concept** illustration on page 458 for an overview of different types of validity.

In sum, any psychological test is useful only to the extent that it is both reliable and valid—to the extent that the test yields consistent scores and that independent evidence confirms that it really does measure what it purports to measure. How do intelligence tests stack up in this respect? In terms of

Validity: *The extent to which tests actually measure what they claim to measure.*

Content Validity: *The extent to which the items on a test sample the skills or knowledge needed for achievement in a given field or task.*

Criterion-Related Validity: *A measure of the validity of any psychological test, determined by correlations between scores on the test and some standard of the characteristic the test supposedly assesses.*

Predictive Validity: *The relationship between scores on a test and later performance relative to some criterion.*

Concurrent Validity: *The relationship between test scores and current performance relative to some criterion.*

Construct Validity: *The extent to which a test measures a variable or concept described by a psychological theory.*

Major Types of Test Validity

Content Validity

The extent to which items on a test are related to the characteristics or behaviors we wish to measure.

For example, the flight simulator shown here tests many behaviors that pilots must demonstrate when actually flying a plane. Because of this close linkage between test components and real flight skills, the simulator may be said to possess high content validity.

Criterion-Based Validity

The extent to which test scores are related to some accepted measure of the characteristic or behavior we wish to measure.

For example, scores on some tests of *academic aptitude* (the ability to learn the kinds of skills taught in school) are related to grades and, ultimately, to graduation. The stronger this relationship, the greater is the criterion-related validity of such tests.

Construct Validity

The extent to which a psychological test measures a psychological variable that can't be assessed directly and has no simple or clear-cut criteria.

For example, scores on a test of the psychological variable *stress tolerance* may be related to several other possible indicators of tolerance for stress. People who score high on this test may be more likely to work in high-stress occupations such as emergency room medicine than are those who score low. And people who score low may be more likely to experience stress-related illnesses such as heart attacks.

reliability, the answer is "quite well." Widely used tests of intelligence do yield consistent scores and do possess internal consistency. The question of validity is much more controversial, especially where group tests of intelligence are concerned. The issue of validity leads us back to an issue raised earlier: Are intelligence tests suitable for use with individuals from all minority groups?

Intelligence Testing and Public Policy: Are Intelligence Tests Fair?

Objections to the widespread use of group tests of intelligence have touched on many different points. Perhaps the most important of these is the possibility that such tests are biased against certain groups. The basis for such concerns is obvious: In North America and elsewhere, people belonging to several minorities score lower than other people on group tests of intelligence (Weinberg, 1989). For example, native people, and members of other minority groups, often score lower on intelligence tests than North Americans of European ancestry (Aiken, 1991; Cohen et al., 1988; Darou, 1992). Further, it appears that these tests may be less *valid* when used with such groups; for example, these groups' scores on the tests are less successful in predicting future performance in school (Aiken, 1991; Darou, 1992). What factors are responsible for such differences? Many critics of group intelligence tests contend that the differences stem mainly from a strong **cultural bias** that is built into these tests. In other words, because the tests were developed by and for people belonging to a particular culture, individuals from other backgrounds may be at a disadvantage when taking them.

Are such concerns valid? Careful examination of the items used on intelligence tests suggests that they are. Many items assume that all children have had the opportunity to acquire certain kinds of information. Unfortunately, this is not always true for children from disadvantaged or minority backgrounds, who may never have had the chance to acquire the knowledge being tested. Thus, they cannot answer correctly, no matter how high their intelligence.

An example of this problem is provided by Darou in his description of his experiences with intelligence testing in northern Canada. His initial assumption was that a question such as, "Saw is to whine as snake is to __," which is used on a well-known test, would be culture-free on the grounds that it dealt with tools and animals. He rapidly discovered that Native Canadians in the Far North are unfamiliar with the hissing of snakes and have experience only with saws that do not whine. Other test items were found to be biased in the opposite direction. On certain tests requiring patterns to be discerned and reproduced, individuals with extensive hunting and navigational experience are so adept they are off-scale. On the basis of these and other experiences, Darou (p. 98) maintains that "virtually all intelligence tests lack validity with Native subjects."

A further issue, raised by Helms (1992), is that widely used intelligence tests may suffer from other forms of cultural bias that, while somewhat more subtle, are just as damaging for minority children. Such tests, Helms contends, incorporate unstated values that derive primarily from a *Eurocentric perspective*—that is, they implicitly accept European values as the standards against which everything is to be judged (Helms, 1989). For example, Helms contends, European cultures accept a *dualist* view—that is, the idea that answers are either right or wrong and that only logical thinking is to be valued. Children from European cultural backgrounds accept this value, so when they take intelligence tests, they look for the one correct answer on each item. According to Helms, children from other backgrounds may accept this value to a lesser degree, or may even accept other values that can interfere with their test performance. For instance, they may not assume that answers are right or

Cultural Bias: *Tendency of items on a test of intelligence to require specific cultural experience or knowledge.*

- In order to be useful, any psychological test must have high reliability: It must yield very similar scores when applied more than once to the same quantity. Reliability can be measured in terms of internal consistency—the extent to which all items on the test measure the same characteristic; and through test-retest reliability—the extent to which scores on a test are stable over time.

- In order to be useful, psychological tests must also be high in validity—the capacity to measure what they claim to measure.

- Types of validity include content validity, criterion-related validity, and construct validity.

- In North America and elsewhere, members of several minority groups score lower on standard intelligence tests than people of European descent. This appears to be due at least in part to the cultural bias of these tests.

- Efforts to construct culture-fair tests of intelligence have been only partly successful.

wrong, and they may spend time reasoning about the extent to which each possible answer is accurate. In other words, Helms suggests, subtle cultural factors may influence the tactics children use when taking intelligence tests, and these, in turn, may influence their scores.

In an effort to eliminate cultural bias from intelligence tests, some psychologists have attempted to design *culture-fair* tests. Such tests attempt to include only items to which all groups, regardless of background, have been exposed. Because many minority children are exposed to languages other than standard English, these tests tend to be nonverbal in nature. One of these—the **Raven Progressive Matrices Test** (Raven, 1977)—was referred to earlier, in our discussion of the biological bases of intelligence. This test consists of sixty matrices of varying difficulty, each containing a logical pattern or design with a missing part. Individuals select the item that completes the pattern from several different choices. Evidence indicates that the Raven test is a valid measure of general intelligence (Paul, 1985); however, it is not clear that it or any other supposedly culture-fair test fully addresses the sources of cultural bias described by Helms (1992) and others. Items from another such test, the *Culture-Fair Intelligence Test*, are shown in Figure 11.6. As you can see, it requires test takers to work with abstract figures or with relationships between various objects. Presumably, such items are less subject to cultural bias than verbal items; but again, this has not been clearly established.

Perhaps, ultimately, the solution to the problem of designing completely culture-fair tests of intelligence will involve the development of reliable *physiological measures*—ones that

FIGURE 11.6

Sample Items from One Culture-Fair Test of Intelligence

The Culture-Fair Intelligence Test includes items designed to be unaffected by specific cultural knowledge or experience. The items shown here are similar to those in one such test. Unfortunately, it has proved impossible to devise a test that is totally independent of culture-related factors.

(Source: Based on items from the Culture-Fair Intelligence Test, Institute for Personality and Ability Testing Inc. Copyright © 1949, 1960, by the Institute for Personality and Ability Testing Inc. All rights reserved. Reproduced by permission.)

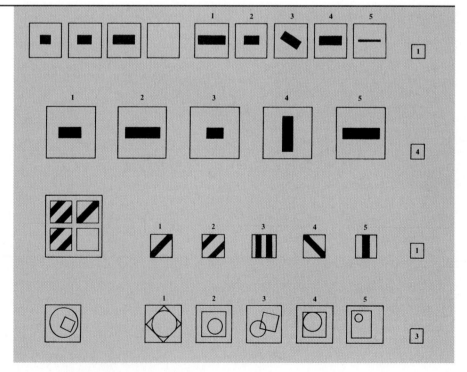

assess the speed and efficiency with which the human brain processes information (e.g., Matarazzo, 1992). Presumably, basic aspects of brain functioning are much the same for all human beings, so it may be possible to eliminate, or at least reduce, the impact of cultural bias through such measures. It has to be admitted, however, that at present this is merely a possibility; research relating brain structure and function to intelligence is too new and too fragmentary to permit any firm conclusions. But at least this research does offer one promising avenue for meeting a need on which all psychologists agree: the need for tests of intelligence that do not place *any* group at an unfair disadvantage.

What are the practical uses to which existing tests of intelligence are put? See **The Point of It All** for information on this.

THE POINT OF IT ALL

Individual Tests of Intelligence: Their Practical Uses

Individual tests of intelligence are costly: They must be administered one-on-one by a psychologist or other trained professional. Why, then, do they continue to be widely used? The answer is that these tests have several practical uses and provide benefits that offset their obvious costs. One use is to identify children at the extremes with respect to intelligence: those who suffer from some degree of cognitive disability and those who are intellectually gifted. Increasingly, testing is also being used to develop remedial programs (Das, 1992).

Cognitive disability is defined as considerably below-average intellectual functioning combined with varying degrees of difficulty in meeting the demands of everyday life (Aiken, 1991; Wielkiewicz & Calvert, 1989). As shown in Figure 11.7, people with a cognitive disability are typically described as belonging to one of four broad categories of cognitive dysfunction: mild, moderate, severe, or profound. An individual's level of disability is determined by at least two factors: test scores, *and* success in carrying out age-related activities of daily living.

In some cases, cognitive disability can be traced to genetic abnormalities such as **Down syndrome**, which is caused by the presence of an extra chromosome; an individual with Down syndrome usually has an IQ below 50. Cognitive disability can also result from environmental factors, such as infection, a toxic agent, trauma, a lack of oxygen during birth, inadequate nutrition, or use of drugs or alcohol by the mother during pregnancy. Most cases of mild intellectual impairment, where the IQ is between 50 and 70, cannot readily be traced to specific genetic or environmental causes.

Intelligence tests have also been used to identify the *intellectually gifted*—those whose intelligence is far above average (Terman, 1954; Goleman, 1980). The most comprehensive study of people with high IQs was begun by Lewis Terman in 1925. He followed the lives of 1,500 children with IQs of 130 or above to determine the relationship between high intelligence on the one hand, and occupational success and social adjustment on the other. As a group, the gifted children in Terman's study were tremendously successful: They earned more academic degrees, attained higher occupational status and salaries, experienced better personal and social adjustment, and were healthier than the average adult. You might be interested to learn that a recent comparison of the hundred most successful and the hundred least successful men in Terman's study by Pyryt (1993) of the University of Calgary found that the major discriminating

Raven Progressive Matrice: One popular "culture-free" test of intelligence.

Cognitive Disability Test: Intellectual functioning that is considerably below average.

Down Syndrome: A disorder caused by an extra chromosome and characterized by varying degrees of cognitive disability and physical disorders.

FIGURE 11.7

Degrees of Cognitive Impairment

Degree of cognitive impairment is often identified according to IQ scores on standard tests of intelligence. In general, an IQ score that falls below 70 suggests some level of cognitive impairment. IQ scores are not the only consideration, however; the individual's capacity to function adequately in everyday life is also important.

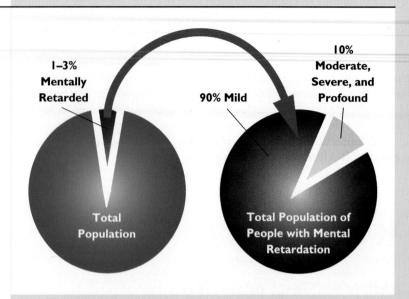

CLASSIFICATION	STANFORD-BINET IQ SCORE	WECHSLER IQ SCORE	PERCENTAGE OF MENTALLY HANDICAPPED	EDUCATION LEVEL POSSIBLE
Mild	52–68	55–69	90	Sixth grade
Moderate	36–51	40–54	6	Second to fourth grade
Severe	20–35	25–39	3	Limited speech
Profound	Below 20	Below 25	1	Unresponsive to training

factor separating the two groups was educational achievement. It would seem that attaining an advanced degree can pay off even if you are gifted.

Although intelligence tests are most commonly used to "sort" individuals on the basis of intellectual abilities, there are those, such as J.P. Das of the University of Alberta, who argue that intelligence tests should not be designed to rank individuals in terms of general ability, but rather to provide information about the basic cognitive mechanisms that underlie intelligent behavior. Tests based on his **PASS theory** of intelligence attempt to do exactly that. Das sees intelligent behavior as involving three interdependent components: attention, processing, and planning. The roles of attention and planning in intelligent behavior are straightforward; it is the operations involved in the processing of information that are complicated. Das presents evidence indicating that two operations are of critical importance in information processing: the ability to process information *simultaneously* and *sequentially*. By this, he means that it is necessary to have both a global overview of the pattern of incoming information and the ability to successively relate incoming information with information that has preceded it. This successive–simultaneous model seems to capture a fundamental aspect of information processing operations, and others besides Das and his associates have developed assessment devices based on it. For example, the popular Kaufman Assessment Battery for Children (Kaufman, 1983) measures successive and simultaneous information processing capacities. Das and his associates, of course, require that intelligence assessments also include measurement of planning and attention, and the Cognitive Assessment System that he has developed with Naglieri does just that (Kirby & Das, 1990; Naglieri & Das, 1990).

PASS Theory: Theory that intelligence involves the three interdependent components of attention, processing, and planning.

What is important about the approach advocated by Das and his associates is that it attempts to provide a direct assessment of cognitive functioning. If it turns out that such measurements can be made, it will be possible to use the deficiencies found in cognitive operations as a basis for developing remedial programs. This strategy has promise. Kirby and Das report they have employed it with some success in uncovering and addressing cognitive deficiencies in a reading disabled group.

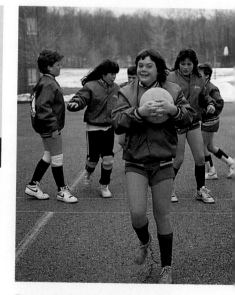

Human Intelligence: *The Role of Heredity and the Role of Environment*

*T*hat people differ in intelligence is obvious. Indeed, we rarely need test scores to remind us of this fact. The causes behind these differences, though, are less obvious. Are they largely a matter of heredity—differences in the genetic materials and codes we inherit from our parents? Or are they primarily the result of environmental factors—conditions favorable or unfavorable to intellectual growth? You probably know the answer: Both types of factors are involved. Human intelligence appears to be the product of an extremely complex interplay between genetic factors and environmental conditions (Plomin, 1989; Weinberg, 1989). Let's now review some of the evidence pointing to this conclusion.

Evidence for the Influence of Heredity

Several lines of research offer support for the view that heredity plays a significant role in human intelligence (see Figure 11.8). First, consider findings with respect to family relationship and measured IQ. If intelligence is indeed determined by heredity, we would expect that the more closely two individuals are related, the more similar their IQs will be. This prediction has generally been confirmed (Bouchard & McGue, 1981; Erlenmeyer-Kimling & Jarvik, 1963). For example, the IQs of identical twins raised together correlate almost +0.90, those of brothers and sisters about +0.50, and those of cousins about +0.15. (Remember: Higher correlations indicate stronger relationships between variables.)

Additional support for the impact of heredity upon intelligence is provided by studies involving adopted children. If intelligence is strongly affected by genetic factors, the IQs of adopted children should resemble those of their biological parents more closely than those of their adoptive parents. In short, the children should be more similar in IQ to the people from whom they received their genes than to the people who raised them. This prediction, too, has been confirmed. While the IQs of adopted children correlate about +0.40 to +0.50 with those of their biological parents, they correlate only about +0.10 to +0.20 with those of their adoptive parents (Jencks, 1972; Munsinger, 1978). Be aware, though, that not all studies have yielded such results. Further, in some investigations, the IQs of adopted children have been observed to become increasingly similar to those of their adoptive parents over time (Scarr & Weinberg, 1976). These findings indicate that environmental factors, too, play an important role.

DOWN SYNDROME: A GENETIC CAUSE OF MENTAL DISABILITY

One cause of cognitive impairment is Down syndrome, a genetic defect that occurs when the cells in the body have an extra copy (or trisomy) of chromosome 21.

HEREDITY AND INTELLIGENCE

Research has shown that the more closely two individuals are related, the more similar their IQ scores tend to be. But does this suggest that a person's environment has no effect on intelligence?

FIGURE 11.8

Correlations Between IQ Scores of Individuals in Varying Relationships

The closer the biological relationship of two individuals, the more similar their IQ scores—strong support for a genetic component to intelligence. (Source: Based on data from Bouchard & McGue, 1981; and Erlenmeyer-Kimling & Jarvis, 1963.)

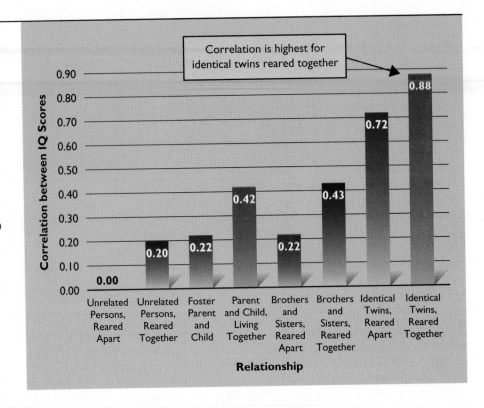

Correlation is highest for identical twins reared together

Relationship

IDENTICAL TWINS REARED APART

The IQ scores of identical twins separated at birth and raised in different home environments—such as the people shown here—are highly correlated. This finding provides evidence for the impact of genetic factors on intelligence.

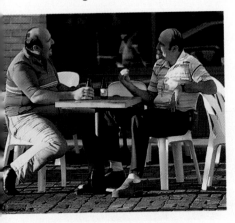

Perhaps the most intriguing evidence for the role of genetic factors in intelligence has been provided by Bouchard and his colleagues through a project called the *Minnesota Study of Twins Raised Apart* (Bouchard, 1987; Bouchard et al., 1990). In this research, Bouchard and his colleagues have tracked pairs of identical twins who were separated early in life and were raised in different homes. Since these people were exposed to different environmental conditions—in some cases, sharply contrasting ones—a high correlation between their IQs would suggest that heredity plays a key role in human intelligence. In fact, this is what has been found. The IQs of identical twins reared apart (in many cases, from the time they were only a few days old) correlate almost as highly as those of identical twins reared together. Moreover, such people are also amazingly similar in many other characteristics, such as physical appearance, preferences in dress, mannerisms, and even personality (see the photo on the left). Clearly, such findings suggest that heredity plays an important role in intelligence and in many other aspects of psychological functioning.

We have already considered another line of evidence that can be interpreted as evidence for the role of heredity in intelligence. This is the finding that various measures of the speed of neural conduction or efficiency in brain functioning are associated with scores on intelligence tests (Vernon, 1991; Reed & Jensen, 1993). One interpretation of these findings is that intelligent people have efficient brains: They can accomplish the same amount of cognitive work faster and with less physical effort. Since the physical structure of the brain, like that of other parts of the body, is strongly determined by genetic factors, it seems possible that intelligence, too, is shaped at least partly by such factors. Needless to add, such suggestions are mainly speculative at present. Additional evidence is needed before we can reach firm conclusions about the relationship between brain activity, the brain's physical structure, and intelligence.

Evidence for the Influence of Environmental Factors

Genetic factors are definitely not the total picture where human intelligence is concerned, however. Other findings point to the conclusion that environmental variables, too, are of great importance. One such finding is that in the late twentieth century, IQ scores have risen substantially around the world at all age levels (Flynn, 1987). Since it seems very unlikely that massive shifts in human heredity have occurred during these decades, this rise can be interpreted only as stemming from environmental factors—rising living standards, improved diets, and better educational opportunities for millions of human beings.

Second, studies of *environmental deprivation* and *environmental enrichment* offer support for the important role of environmental factors. With respect to deprivation, it has been found that intelligence can be reduced by the absence of certain forms of environmental stimulation early in life (Gottfried, 1984). In terms of enrichment, removing children from sterile, restricted environments and placing them in more favorable settings seems to enhance their intellectual growth. For example, in one of the first demonstrations of the beneficial impact of an enriched environment on IQ, Skeels (1938; 1966) removed thirteen children, all aged about two, from the impoverished orphanage in which they lived and placed them in the care of a group of cognitively impaired women living in an institution. After a few years, Skeels noted that the children's IQs had risen dramatically—on average, 29 points. Interestingly, Skeels also obtained IQ measures of children who had remained in the orphanage and found that the average IQ for this group had actually *decreased* by 26 points— presumably as a result of the impoverished environment at the orphanage. Twenty-five years later, the thirteen children who had experienced the enriched environment were all doing well; most had graduated from high school, found work, and married. In contrast, those in the original control group either remained institutionalized or were functioning poorly in society.

Third, some special programs designed to enrich the educational experiences of children from disadvantaged backgrounds have been found to produce substantial increases in IQ scores (Royce, Darlington, & Murray, 1983). Perhaps the most famous (and controversial) of these programs is Project Head Start, a program in the United States that provides special intellectual and social-skills training for young children from disadvantaged environments (Zigler & Berman, 1983). Evaluations of Project Head Start have yielded mixed results; children who participate in it do not demonstrate lasting gains in IQ (Haskins, 1989), but they do surpass nonparticipants in other important ways. For example, Head Start graduates are less likely than nonparticipants to fail in school or require remedial courses, and are more likely to exhibit positive self-esteem (McKey et al., 1985).

Fourth, evidence for the important impact of environmental factors on intelligence is also provided by kinship studies of the type described earlier. Such studies indicate that for a given degree of kinship, or family relationship, individuals raised in the same environment have more similar IQs than individuals raised apart, in different environments. For example, the IQs of brothers and sisters raised together correlate about +0.50, whereas those of brothers and sisters raised apart correlate about +0.45. Similarly, the IQs of unrelated people raised apart show virtually no correlation.

A fifth kind of evidence for the influence of environmental factors is provided by research on birth order and intelligence. Several studies report that first-borns tend to have higher IQs than second-borns, who tend to have higher IQs than third-borns, and so on (Zajonc & Markus, 1975). The differences are not large— only a few IQ points at most—but they do seem to be real. Why do such differences exist? One possibility is suggested by **confluence theory**, a theory proposed by Zajonc (1975, 1986). According to confluence theory, each individual's intellectual growth depends to an important degree upon the intellectual environment in which he or she develops. A first-born child benefits from the fact that for some period of time, until the birth of another child, he or she lives with two adults who provide a relatively advantaged intellectual environment (see Figure 11.9). A second-born child, in contrast, lives with two adults who divide their attention with another child; thus, the average level of his or her intellectual environment is somewhat diluted. Such effects become even stronger for third-borns, and continue to increase as the number of children in a family rises.

Regardless of whether Zajonc's interpretation proves accurate, the fact that first-borns tend to have higher IQs than later-borns cannot readily be explained in terms of heredity; the genes contributed by parents should remain fairly constant across the entire birth order. Thus, the impact of environmental factors is suggested once again.

Finally, the role of environmental factors in intelligence is evidenced by many studies indicating that the longer students remain in school, the higher their IQ scores tend to be (Ceci, 1991). While this finding could also be interpreted as suggesting that it is the more intelligent people who choose to remain in school, several facts point to the conclusion that staying in school may actually benefit intelligence. For example, it has been found that people who attend school regularly score higher on intelligence tests than people who attend irregularly, and that those who start school at an older-than-average age score lower than those who start at an average or early age. In addition, there is some indication that the worldwide increase in IQ scores referred to earlier stems at least in part from the increased years in school many people enjoy in many countries (Ceci, 1991).

Finally, a number of other environmental factors have been found to be related to IQ scores. These include nutrition, family background—for example, parents' education and income—and quality of education, to mention just a few (Bouchard & Segal, 1985). The measurable effects of such factors are small, but, again, they appear to be real.

Confluence Theory: A theory suggesting that IQ tends to decrease across the birth order within a family; first-borns tend to have a higher IQ than second-borns, and so on.

FIGURE 11.9

Birth Order and IQ: Confluence Theory

According to confluence theory, the intellectual environment in which children develop becomes less and less favorable as the number of previous children in the family increases. As a result, the IQ of first-borns is higher than that of second-borns; the IQ of second-borns is higher than that of third-borns, and so on. Research on confluence theory suggests that these differences are quite small but do seem to exist.

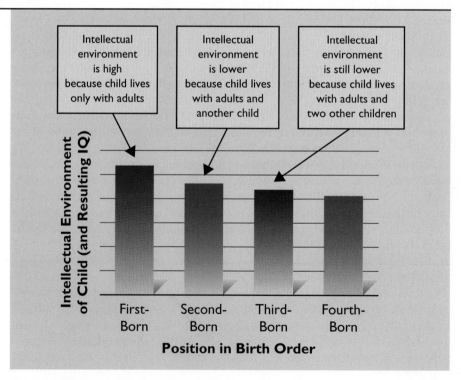

Environment, Heredity, and Intelligence: Summing Up

There is considerable evidence that both environmental and genetic factors play a role in intelligence. This is the view accepted by almost all psychologists, and there is little controversy about it. Greater disagreement continues to exist, however, concerning the *relative* contribution of each of these factors. Do environmental or genetic factors play a stronger role in shaping intelligence? Or are the two kinds of influences of roughly equal importance? To date, efforts to address this question have failed to yield a clear answer. However, growing evidence from the field of *behavioral genetics* does seem to point to the possibility that genetic factors are quite important—perhaps more important in some respects than environmental ones (Plomin, 1989).

As you can probably guess, many psychologists are made uneasy by the implications of this possibility (Herrnstein, 1973; Kamin, 1978). Being concerned with human welfare, psychologists would strongly prefer to be in a position to intervene—to help enhance the intellectual capacity of all human beings. Evidence favoring a genetic basis for intelligence might seem, at first glance, to rule out such helpful interventions. In fact, however, it does not. Genes do not *fix* or determine behavior; rather, genetic factors establish a range of possible responses to a given environment—a range referred to as *malleability* (Weinberg, 1989). Even if intelligence is strongly affected by genetic factors, therefore, it can still be influenced by environmental conditions. From this perspective, programs designed to enrich the intellectual environments of children from disadvantaged backgrounds may still produce beneficial results. Heredity, in short, should definitely *not* be viewed as a set of biological shackles, nor as an excuse for giving up on children who are at serious risk because of poverty, prejudice, or neglect.

> **Gender:** *All the attributes, behaviors, and expectancies associated with each sex in a given society.*

KEY POINT

- Intelligence is influenced by a complex interplay between environmental and genetic factors.

Gender: How Males and Females Differ

*A*t birth, hospital records designate a person as being either *female* or *male* on the basis of *biological* evidence. In only a few cases, where it is difficult to tell immediately whether a child is male or female, is this decision delayed (Berenbaum & Hines, 1992).

However, the term **gender** involves much more than biological sex. In Chapter 8 we saw that every society has preconceived notions of the traits supposedly possessed by males and females—what psychologists term *gender stereotypes* (Unger & Crawford, 1993). Further, all societies have more or less clearly defined *gender roles*—expectations concerning the roles people of each sex should fill and the ways in which they are supposed to behave (Deaux, 1993). In other words, each society has a set of ideas concerning the nature of *masculinity* and *femininity*; and as we'll see below, violating those expectations has a cost (Aubé & Koestner, 1992).

Because of the existence of gender stereotypes and gender roles, it is difficult to determine whether differences in the behavior of males and females stem from biological differences or from the self-fulfilling impact of these stereotypes and roles. This topic arose in Chapter 2, and we'll return to it again later in this chapter. For the moment, however, let's put aside the

GENDER ROLES BEGIN AT BIRTH

Infants are classified as male or female at birth. From this moment on, their sexual identity plays an important role in the way they are treated by society.

important issue of *why* females and males differ, and turn instead to the questions of *whether* and *how* they differ.

The first issue—do males and females differ in their behavior?—has an increasingly clear answer: Yes, they do. While these differences often vary in nature and magnitude from what commonly held gender stereotypes suggest, there *are* measurable differences between females and males in many respects (Feingold, 1992; Oliver & Hyde, 1993). What, precisely, are these differences? This is the issue on which we'll focus next.

Gender Differences in Social Behavior

Many of the traits attributed to females and males in gender stereotypes seem to relate to social behavior—for example, traits like *sensitivity* and *nurturance* on the part of females and *aggressiveness* and *dominance* on the part of males (Eagly, 1987; Friedman & Zebrowitz, 1992). Widely held stereotypes often exert powerful self-confirming effects on behavior; nevertheless, research findings do point to the existence of several differences in the social behavior of males and females. While these differences are quite small and subtle in nature, they do seem to exist.

EMOTIONAL EXPRESSION: SENDING AND RECEIVING NONVERBAL CUES Informal experience suggests that in many social situations, males seem surprised and bewildered by others' behavior: Often males don't expect the people with whom they interact to say or do what they do, and are at a loss to account for such actions after they occur. In contrast, females experience fewer surprises of this type; they seem to know what to expect from others. Are such differences real? A large body of research on the transmission and interpretation of *nonverbal cues* (refer to Chapter 10) suggests that they are (e.g., DePaulo, 1992). Nonverbal cues are subtle cues involving facial expressions, eye contact, body posture or movements, and so on. And females seem to be better than males at transmitting their own feelings to others through nonverbal cues, and also at understanding the nonverbal messages sent by others (e.g., DePaulo, 1992; Rosenthal & DePaulo, 1979). Since nonverbal cues often reveal much about others' reactions and emotional states, females' superior skills in these respects are very beneficial in many different social contexts (e.g., Hall & Veccia, 1990). So, in one sense at least, widely held beliefs about the existence of "feminine intuition"—females' superior ability to predict how others will behave or feel—seem to have a basis in fact.

Offsetting these potential benefits, however, is another gender difference with respect to emotional expression. Gender stereotypes suggest that females are more sensitive and caring than males, so females are expected to express positive emotions toward others to a greater extent than males. Interestingly, this difference does not apply to expressing positive emotions about *themselves* or their own accomplishments—it applies only with respect to expressions of positive emotion toward others (Stoppard & Gruchy, 1993).

Gender Differences in the Use of Nonverbal Cues

Females are better at both sending and receiving nonverbal cues than males.
(Source: © 1984 King Features Syndicate, Inc. World rights reserved. Reprinted with special permission of King Features Syndicate.)

In other words, females experience considerable pressure to express positive emotions to *others*—to act in ways consistent with gender stereotypes suggesting that they are kind, nurturant, and sensitive. In contrast, males experience less pressure of this kind and are also encouraged, to a greater degree than females, to express positive emotions about their own accomplishments. As you can see, this is one way in which gender stereotypes are self-confirming: They induce people to act in ways that confirm their accuracy.

SOCIAL INFLUENCE: ARE FEMALES MORE SUSCEPTIBLE, AND IF SO, WHEN? At one time in the past, it was widely assumed that females are more susceptible to various forms of *social influence*—efforts to change their attitudes or behavior—than males. As will be explained in detail in Chapter 16, however, research findings on this topic indicate that in fact there are no overall gender differences in this particular respect (e.g., Maupin & Fisher, 1989). This does not mean that there are *no* differences between females and males with respect to social influence. In fact, there is growing evidence that some differences of this type do exist (e.g., Graziano et al., 1993).

Perhaps the most important of these relates to reactions to feedback from others. Several studies indicate that women's evaluations of their own performance in achievement situations are more strongly influenced by such feedback than are men's self-evaluations (Eagly & Carli, 1981; Roberts, 1991). For instance, consider a study on this issue by Roberts and Nolen-Hoeksema (1990). They asked male and female students to deliver speeches on topics that were important to them. Then the students received prearranged positive or negative feedback about their speeches from audience members. Finally, both before and after receiving the feedback, the students rated their own performances. Results indicated that only the women changed these ratings in response to the feedback they received. If they received positive feedback, they raised their self-evaluations, while if they received negative feedback, they lowered them. In contrast, men did not change their self-evaluations in response to the feedback.

Why are females influenced to a greater extent than males by evaluative feedback? According to Roberts (1991), several factors may play a role. First, some women may perceive themselves as being less empowered than men and therefore weigh more heavily information about themselves that they obtain from others. Second, some studies indicate that females generally receive less evaluative attention in school and elsewhere than males (e.g., Minuchin & Shapiro, 1983). As a result, they may perceive evaluative feedback as informative more than males do, and so take it more seriously. Finally, and perhaps most important of all, males and females may approach achievement situations somewhat differently. Males tend to perceive such situations as competitive challenges. They view others as actual or potential competitors, and so they view feedback from others with skepticism and tend to ignore it—especially if it is negative! In contrast, females may approach achievement situations as opportunities to learn about their skills and abilities. Thus, they view others' evaluations as highly informative and pay careful attention to them (see Figure 11.10). To the extent these differences exist, it is not surprising that females' self-evaluations are influenced to a greater degree than males' self-evaluations by feedback from others. However, it's important to realize that at present there is little direct evidence concerning these interesting suggestions. They must be subjected to careful testing before they can be accepted with confidence.

LEADERSHIP: PERFORMANCE AND EVALUATIONS Do male and female leaders differ in their style of leadership? While there is a widespread belief that they

FIGURE 11.10

Evaluative Feedback: Contrasting Reactions Among Females and Males

Males tend to view situations in which they receive feedback on their performance as competitive ones. As a result, they view such feedback with skepticism. In contrast, females view such situations as learning opportunities and therefore pay greater attention to the feedback they receive. (Source: Based on suggestions by Roberts, 1993.)

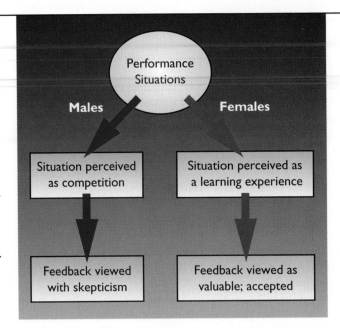

FEMALE LEADERS: OFTEN THEY ARE DOWN-RATED

Research suggests that female leaders often receive lower ratings than male leaders, even when their performance is the same. This finding is especially strong in situations where the raters are male, the female leaders adopt a "masculine leadership style," and most leaders in that particular setting are male.

do, systematic research on this issue suggests that in general, they actually do not (Korabick, Baril, & Watson, 1993; Powell, 1990). Female and male leaders appear to differ in a few respects, but these differences are smaller in magnitude and fewer in number than gender-role stereotypes suggest. Evidence pointing to these conclusions has been collected by Eagly and her colleagues in a series of careful reviews of existing research evidence—reviews employing the technique of *meta-analysis* described in Chapter 1.

The first of these reviews (Eagly & Johnson, 1990) examined more than 150 separate studies of leadership in which comparisons were made between female and male leaders. The researchers examined potential differences between male and female leaders with respect to two dimensions generally viewed as important aspects of leader behavior: (1) concern with good interpersonal relations (often termed *showing consideration*) versus concern with task performance (known as *initiating structure*); and (2) *participative* versus *autocratic* decision-making style. Gender-role stereotypes suggest that female leaders might show more concern with interpersonal relations and might tend to make decisions in a more participative manner than male leaders. Results, however, offered only weak support for such beliefs. With respect to the first dimension—interpersonal relations versus task orientation—there were few significant findings. For decision-making style, however, females did appear to adopt a more democratic or participative style than males. All in all, there were few differences between female and male leaders, and the differences that did emerge were smaller than suggested by gender stereotypes.

In a follow-up investigation, Eagly and her colleagues (Eagly, Makhijani, & Klonsky, 1992) focused on a related issue: Are female and male leaders evaluated differently by others? Because serving as a leader is in some respects contrary to the gender stereotype for females, the researchers predicted that female leaders might receive lower ratings than male leaders, even when their performance was identical. Moreover, Eagly and her co-workers also expected that such down-rating of female leaders would be greater among male evaluators than among female evaluators, and would be more likely to occur in fields that were male-dominated and in situations where the female leaders adopted a directive, autocratic style of leadership—a traditionally "masculine" leadership style. A meta-analytic review of more than sixty different studies provided support for all of these predictions. Overall, the tendency for female leaders to be rated lower than male leaders was significant, but quite small in magnitude. This is an encouraging finding, suggesting, perhaps, that bias against female leaders is decreasing. However, the down-rating of female leaders was stronger when they adopted a style of leadership viewed as stereotypically masculine (autocratic, directive), when the evaluators were male, and when the women occupied leadership roles in fields where most leaders were males.

Stereotypes about gender-appropriate behavior are firmly entrenched. Adopting a leadership style perceived to be incongruent with gender can have costs for both females and males. K. Korabik, of the University of Guelph, and her colleagues report that women are viewed as being less effective than men when they adopt a very directive style, and that men are deemed less effective than women when they adopt an accommodating or obliging management style (Korabik, Baril, & Watson, 1993).

AGGRESSION: WHAT KIND AND HOW MUCH?   Are males more aggressive than females? Gender stereotypes endorse this view, and crime statistics seem to support the stereotype: Males are much more likely than females to be arrested and convicted for violent acts. Does this mean that large differences actually exist between males and females with respect to overt aggression? Once again, systematic research provides a mixed answer. On the one hand, males do seem to be more likely both to instigate aggression and to be its target (e.g., Baron & Richardson, 1994; Bogard, 1990; Harris, 1992). On the other hand, on closer inspection, the size of the difference appears to be relatively small. Further, the tendency for males to engage in aggressive actions more frequently than females is greater for *physical* forms of aggression (hitting, kicking, use of weapons) than for other forms of aggression (yelling at people, treating them in a condescending manner) (Harris, 1992). In fact, recent findings indicate that females may actually be *more* likely than males to engage in various *indirect* forms of aggression, such as spreading rumors about another person, rejecting someone as a friend, or ignoring or avoiding a target person (Lagerspetz, Bjorkqvist, & Peitonen, 1988). Precisely such effects have been found by Lagerspetz and her associates in a series of revealing studies.

In one of these investigations (Bjorkqvist, Lagerspetz, & Kaukiainen, 1992), boys and girls in three age groups—8, 11, and 15 years old—were asked to indicate how other members of their class in school reacted when they became angry. Responses were then divided into three categories: *direct aggression* (classmate kicks or strikes others, uses profanity, pushes or shoves); *indirect aggression* (gossips, says "I'm not your friend," shuns the target person); or *withdrawal* (goes away, sulks). The researchers predicted that girls would be more likely than boys to use indirect aggression or withdrawal at all ages, but that such differences would strengthen with increasing age, as the cognitive skills needed for use of indirect forms of aggression developed. As shown in Figure 11.11, this is precisely what was found. At all ages, boys were more likely to use direct forms of aggression than girls. Similarly, at all ages, girls were more likely to use indirect forms of aggression, although this difference was smallest among eight-year-olds and largest among the older children.

Given that females are generally smaller in size and physical strength than males, it is not surprising that they make greater use of indirect rather than

FIGURE 11.11

Gender Differences in the Use of Indirect Aggression

While boys show more direct aggression than girls, girls show more indirect aggression against others. This difference increases with age and girls' growing cognitive skills.

(Source: Based on data from Bjorkqvist, Lagarspetz, & Kaukiainen, 1992.)

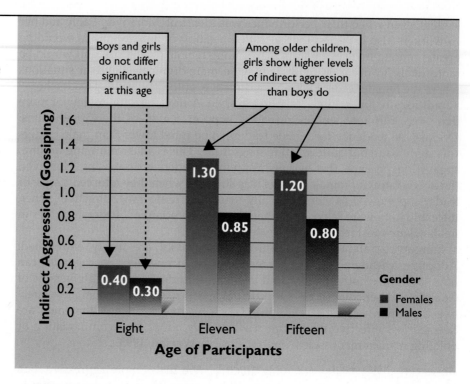

direct modes of aggression. However, as with many other gender differences, this difference probably stems in large part from an inappropriate gender stereotype suggesting that males should always be tough and aggressive while females should be nurturant and forgiving. A number of studies suggest that what really controls the expression of aggression by females is how a given situation is assessed, and how appropriate the social prohibitions against women expressing aggression are deemed to be in that situation.

The influence of these factors has been detailed in a number of studies. For example, Towson and Zanna (1982) at the University of Waterloo examined how males and females reacted to a vignette describing the frustration of an activity. Males endorsed a higher level of aggression than females when the frustrated activity was perceived to be "masculine" in significance and importance. Females considered a level of aggression equivalent to that of males as acceptable when the frustrated activity was "feminine" in significance and importance. Clearly, males and females define situations in gender-specific ways, and the acceptability of an aggressive response in females can equal that of males if the situation is assessed as being gender-relevant and important. Lightdale and Prentice (1994) also found that females were *not* less aggressive than males under conditions where they were made to feel *deindividuated*—that is, anonymous and unaccountable for their actions. Under these conditions, Lightdale and Prentice reasoned, the influence of social conventions about appropriate feminine behavior should be weakened, and differences between males and females should tend to disappear. This is precisely what was found. It seems reasonable to conclude that females are not inherently less aggressive than males. If the given circumstances are gender-relevant and important, and the influence of social prohibitions can be lessened, they can be just as aggressive as males.

FRIENDSHIPS: ARE FEMALE FRIENDSHIPS MORE INTENSE—AND BENEFICIAL? When do you seek the company of your close friends? When you want to engage in some activity you and your friends enjoy, or when you feel the need to share your inner feelings and thoughts or to ask for emotional support? While people of both sexes seek contact with their friends for all these reasons, there appear to be some interesting gender differences in this respect. Males more often hang out with friends in order to participate in shared activities, while females more frequently spend time with friends to discuss feelings and thoughts and to obtain social support (Barth & Kinder, 1988). Moreover, although females and males report having about the same number of close friends, females report greater satisfaction with these friendships (Reis, Senchak, & Solomon, 1985). A recent Montreal study of adolescent males and females confirms that females feel more strongly attached to their friends. They also view their friendships as more intimate, and they expect more from a friendship than males (Claes, 1992).

Finally, close friendships seem to be more beneficial for females than for males, at least with respect to reducing unhappiness and raising self-esteem. In a study focusing on these differences, Elkins and Peterson (1993) asked male and female students to describe their relationships with their actual best friends, and with what would be their *ideal* best friends. In addition, participants completed measures of their current self-esteem and of the extent to which they were feeling depressed. These two scales were combined in a single measure of current *dysphoria*—a rough index of unhappiness. Results indicated that in general, females were more satisfied with their actual friendships than males. In addition, for both females and males, the greater the disparity between actual and ideal friendships, the greater the unhappiness reported. This suggests that both sexes rely on close friendships for emotional and social support. However, since females report greater satisfaction with their current friendships, they appear more likely to derive more gratification from such benefits than males. In any case, male and female friendships do seem to differ in some respects; and, once again, these differences are relatively consistent with gender stereotypes and gender roles.

KEY POINTS

- The term *gender* refers to more than biological sex; it includes references to gender stereotypes and gender roles.

- Females are better than males at both sending and reading various nonverbal cues. However, they experience greater social pressure to express positive emotions toward others.

- There are no overall differences between males and females with respect to susceptibility to social influence. However, females are often influenced more than males by evaluative feedback about their performance.

- Female and male leaders do not appear to differ greatly in terms of style or performance. Female leaders often receive lower evaluations than male leaders, especially if they engage in what are viewed to be gender-incongruent managerial styles. Males can also be evaluated less favorably for the same reason.

- Males engage in acts of direct physical aggression more often than females. However, females engage in more acts of indirect aggression. A critical factor influencing aggressiveness in females is how the situation is evaluated.

Mate Selection, Relationships, and Sexuality

"Female, 30, smart, pretty, sensuous, lots to offer, seeks wealthy man to show me life of luxury and love."

"Single white female, 22, athletic, blonde, blue eyes, university graduate, seeks single white male who is honest, romantic, spontaneous, to have fun and build relationship."

"Single white male, scientific professional; successful, fit, handsome, witty, but lonely. Looking for single/divorced woman to marry. I'm tired of the single life."

"Male, 40, fit, attractive, professional; caring, funny, looking for attractive female 30's, for fun, good conversation, quiet times, romance."

These are actual "personal" ads from the "Getting Together" column of a local newspaper. If you read these and other personals carefully, an interesting pattern emerges: Females and males seem to be seeing—and offering— somewhat different packages of traits. Many such ads placed by females indicate that the person advertising is young and physically attractive and is seeking a partner who has wealth or high status *and* who is interested in a serious relationship. In contrast, many ads placed by males indicate that the advertiser *has* high status (education, wealth, professional standing) and is seeking a partner who is young and attractive. In addition, such ads also frequently indicate that the men who have placed them are sincere and reliable and are also searching for a stable relationship.

All in all, then, an analysis of these ads points to two conclusions: (1) There are interesting differences in what females and males seek in potential mates; and (2) both sexes seem to be well aware of these differences! Ads in personal columns, of course, do not provide a very strong basis for reaching conclusions about gender differences. However, a substantial body of research evidence indicates that the patterns appearing in the personals may be quite real (Feingold, 1992). Why would this be the case? Why, in short, would males tend to seek youth and physical beauty in potential partners while females tend to seek high status, ambition, intelligence, and such traits as sincerity?

One theory, favored by evolutionary *psychologists* and *sociobiologists*, suggests that the answer lies in biological differences relating to reproduction. This view, known as the **parental investment model** (Trivers, 1985), contends that for men the investment of time and effort in producing offspring is relatively small: Each man can father numerous children with many different women. Thus, in choosing potential mates, men need only seek ones who are capable of reproducing—women who possess youth, physical attractiveness, and other outward signs of good health and vigor. In contrast, for women, the investment of time and energy in each child is very large. Therefore, it is reasonable for women to seek potential mates who can help share the burden of raising these children; and males with high status, ambition, and intelligence fill the bill. In addition, since it's important that potential mates remain on the scene for many years, women should also favor men who are sincere, honest, and willing to form long-term relationships.

Some research findings are consistent with predictions derived from this theory. For example, in a recent meta-analysis of the findings of several dozen studies on the characteristics sought in potential mates by females and males, Feingold (1992a) found that in selecting potential mates, females did give greater weight than males to success (as indexed by socioeconomic status), ambition, and intelligence. This was true both in studies using questionnaires and in ones that analyzed the contents of personal ads such as the ones above. Further, when Feingold examined the results of studies conducted several decades ago, similar results were obtained: In the 1940s and 1950s, too, females assigned greater weight to status, intelligence, ambition, and character, while males assigned greater weight to physical attractiveness (Hill, 1945; McGinnis, 1958). Finally, and perhaps most impressive of all, similar findings have been found around the world, in samples drawn from thirty-three different countries (Buss et al., 1990). In sum, there do appear to be reliable, and quite general, differences in the weights attached by females and males to various factors in their choices of romantic partners or potential mates. However, while these results are consistent with the parental investment model, they can also be explained in terms of social factors. See **The Research Process** for a discussion of this issue.

Now for another fascinating question: Does the fact that males attach greater importance to physical attractiveness indicate that females are uninfluenced by this factor? Research conducted by Graziano and his colleagues (1993) indicates that this is definitely not the case. On the contrary, women seem to be just as sensitive to differences along this dimension as men. However, it also appears that for females, making judgments about others' physical attractiveness may involve more complex processes than is true for men. For example, in

Parental Investment Model:
The view that males and females adopt contrasting strategies of mate selection because they invest different amounts of resources in their offspring.

one study (Graziano et al., 1993), female and male students looked at photos of men and women previously rated as being average in attractiveness, and rated the attractiveness of the individuals shown. Before doing so, the students also received prearranged information indicating that members of their own sex had rated some of the people in the photos as either very attractive or very unattractive. (For some photos, there were no ratings.) Results indicated that females were strongly influenced by the bogus ratings: Their ratings were higher when other people had supposedly rated the photo subjects as attractive, and lower when others had supposedly rated the photo subjects as unattractive. These effects were *not* found for males.

Graziano and his colleagues (1993) interpret these findings as suggesting that males' ratings of physical attractiveness are relatively automatic. They occur without much thought or attention to social information. For females, this process is more complex: Females take several factors into account when judging attractiveness, including others' opinions. In sum, both sexes are influenced by and sensitive to physical beauty, but the factors affecting their judgments of attractiveness may be somewhat different (see Figure 11.12).

Matching Hypothesis: The hypothesis that individuals seek romantic partners whose assets are at least equal to their own level of desirability.

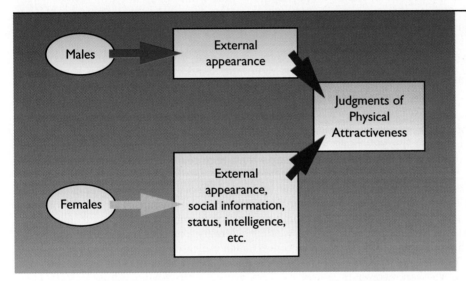

FIGURE 11.12

How Females and Males Judge Attractiveness

Among males, judgments of physical attractiveness appear to be relatively automatic; they are based largely on outward appearance. For females, in contrast, judgments of outward attractiveness are more complex and involve attention to social information and other characteristics aside from physical appearance. (Source: Based on suggestions by Graziano et al., 1993.)

THE RESEARCH PROCESS

Integrating the Evolutionary and Social Exchange Models of Mate Preferences: Taking Account of Our Own "Market Value"

Long before the field of evolutionary psychology emerged, social psychologists noticed an interesting phenomenon: Romantic partners are often quite similar in physical attractiveness. Highly attractive people have highly attractive partners, average people have average ones, and so on. This led to formulation of the **matching hypothesis**—the suggestion that people tend to choose romantic partners who are

similar to themselves in attractiveness (Berscheid et al., 1971; Kalick & Hamilton, 1986). Many studies provided support for this view (Forgas, 1993), but it soon became apparent that physical attractiveness is only one of the factors that may be involved in determining our "exchange value" in the romantic marketplace. Thus, the matching hypothesis was soon expanded to suggest that people match on their *overall personal appeal*—not just on physical beauty. Factors such as wealth, education, status, and charm all play a role, and the general rule is this: The more of these desirable characteristics an individual possesses, the more desirable the partners she or he can obtain (Hatfield & Rapson, 1993). This is why, for example, older males who possess wealth and status often seek, and attract, younger females—a fairly common pattern throughout the world (Kenrick & Keefe, 1992). The older males are trading high status and wealth for the youth and physical charms of their partners. Needless to add, older, high-status females can follow the same strategy, exchanging *their* desirable social characteristics for the physical attractiveness of younger males.

In short, the matching hypothesis and related ideas about *social exchange*—what we bring to a relationship and what we receive from it—offer an alternative interpretation for the tendency of males and females to emphasize different factors in the process of mate selection. According to this model, both sexes seek to obtain the best possible bargain in romantic partners, but at the same time, the two sexes bring somewhat different personal assets to the table.

Integrating the Evolutionary and Social Exchange Perspectives

At first glance, the social exchange and evolutionary perspectives on mate selection might seem to be incompatible. The matching perspective suggests that males and females both follow the same strategy with respect to mate selection: Try to get a partner at least as desirable as oneself. In contrast, the evolutionary perspective suggests that males and females may adopt contrasting approaches, and will attach different values to various characteristics such as physical beauty. However, Kenrick and his colleagues (Kenrick et al., 1993) have pointed out that the two perspectives may actually be *complementary* rather than incompatible. They reason as follows.

First, it makes good sense, from an evolutionary perspective, for *both* males and females to be aware of their relative desirability and to seek to obtain partners who are at or slightly above their own level. After all, if people don't take account of their own level of desirability, they may waste lots of time and energy competing for mates they can't reasonably expect to obtain. So social exchange theory helps to expand evolutionary theory by calling attention to the importance of *self-appraisal*—accurate knowledge of one's own desirability.

Second, and conversely, evolutionary theory helps to expand social exchange theory by noting that males and females may differ in their tendency to seek such matching, depending on the nature of the relationship. In long-term relationships such as marriage, both females and males should be concerned with obtaining a mate whose desirability at least equals their own. In short-term flings or one-night stands,

however, females may retain higher minimum standards than males, since (in an evolutionary sense) they invest so much more in a potential offspring.

Integrating these two theories, then, leads to an interesting prediction that would not be generated by either theory alone: For females, the relationship between their self-appraisals of their own desirability and the *minimum standards* they require for potential partners will be relatively strong for both long-term and short-term relationships. For males, however, this link will be stronger for long-term than for short-term relationships. To test this prediction, Kenrick and his colleagues (1993) conducted research in which they asked female and male students to indicate the minimum standards they would require for entering into five different relationships with another person: a single date, steady dating, sexual relations, marriage, or a one-night stand. The students rated the minimum they would require from potential partners in terms of attractiveness, status, agreeableness, intellect, and several other dimensions. In addition, participants rated themselves on the same dimensions.

Results indicated, first, that women required higher minimum standards than men for entering *all* of the relationships. This is consistent with evolutionary theory, which emphasizes the large investment females make in each of their children. Second, as expected, the correlations between females' self-appraisals of their own desirability and the minimum standards they required for potential partners were high across all five relationships. Third, as predicted by the integrated theory, these correlations differed for males across the relationships. The correlation was as high as that for women with respect to marriage, but was considerably *lower* for a one-night stand. In that context, men indicated that they would not necessarily try to get a partner at least as desirable as themselves: They would settle for just about anyone (see Figure 11.13).

These results suggest that the evolutionary and social exchange perspectives truly are complementary. Evolutionary theorists have often ignored the impact of different relationship levels, while exchange theories have generally overlooked differences in the selection strategies employed by females and males. By combining these perspectives, we can obtain a fuller and richer picture of how, and why, people go about selecting everything from casual romantic partners to lifelong mates.

Critical Thinking Questions:

1. If people seek romantic partners at least equal to themselves in attractiveness, do you think that the degree of similarity on this dimension will increase as relationships become more serious?

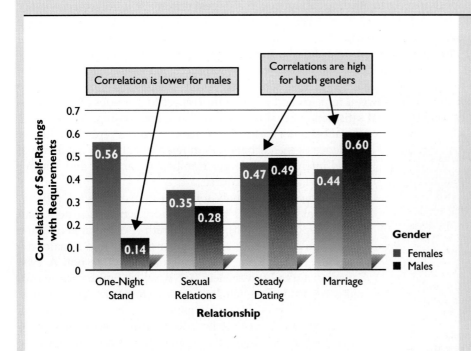

Correlation is lower for males

Correlations are high for both genders

Gender
■ Females
■ Males

One-Night Stand · Sexual Relations · Steady Dating · Marriage

Relationship

Correlation of Self-Ratings with Requirements

FIGURE 11.13

Matching One's Own Assets in Romantic Relationships: Some Gender Differences

Males and females show equal degrees of matching with respect to long-term relationships such as marriage, but different degrees of matching for one-night stands. For one-night stands, males show lower tendencies toward matching than females. That is, more attractive males don't necessarily seek more attractive partners; rather, males seem willing to accept a wide range of partners in this context. (Source: Based on data from Kenrick et al., 1993.)

2. Suppose that one member of a couple becomes more desirable over time—earns an advanced degree or inherits great wealth, for example. Will this threaten the stability of their relationship?

3. The participants in Kenrick and colleagues' (1993) research were university students. Do you think similar findings would be obtained with older participants? If so, why? If not, why not?

4. Suppose you went to bars and observed the couples who met for the first time and then left together. Would you predict major differences in physical attractiveness between the females and the males in the couples, or would they generally be similar in this respect?

SEXUALITY: ATTITUDES AND BEHAVIORS If there is one area of behavior where cultural beliefs suggest the existence of large differences between females and males, it is with respect to sexuality. Sexual attitudes and behaviors vary from culture to culture, but in North America and many countries of the world, it has long been, and to some extent still is, assumed that males are more permissive than females in their attitudes about sex, as well as more interested in varied forms of sexual behavior. Moreover, elements of the *double standard*, which traditionally permitted or even encouraged premarital sexual experience for males but forbade such experiences for females, persist. It's important to bear in mind that attitudes about sex are a very personal matter and are often strongly affected by religious and moral principles outside the realm of science. However, psychologists have attempted to determine whether females and males actually *do* differ in their attitudes about sex and in their actual sexual practices. These are the questions on which we'll focus here.

Research on these differences has been done for decades (Kelley & Byrne, 1992). Perhaps the most revealing recent evidence has been provided by Oliver and Hyde (1993). These researchers conducted an extensive meta-analysis of almost 200 studies that compared the sexual attitudes and behavior of females and males. Results indicated that several notable differences do indeed exist.

With respect to attitudes about sex, the largest difference involved acceptance of casual premarital sex: Males reported much more permissive attitudes about such actions then females. In addition, males also reported more permissive attitudes about extramarital sex, and greater sexual permissiveness generally—more positive views about having many different partners, belief that extensive sexual experience is acceptable, and so on. Interestingly, there were *no* differences between females and males with respect to attitudes about homosexuality, sexual satisfaction, masturbation, oral sex, and kissing. As for actual sexual behavior (rather than attitude), males reported a higher incidence of masturbation than females, a higher incidence of sexual intercourse, a larger number of partners, and a lower age of first sexual intercourse.

An interesting anomaly found in the sexual survey literature is that males tend to report more female partners than women report male partners. As Smith (1992) points out, in a population of fixed size, the number of male and female sexual partners should be roughly equal. They are not. A 1988 Canadian survey by Ornstein (1989), which Smith cites, shows males reporting 3.61 female partners, and females reporting 1.17 male partners. A similar pattern can be seen in surveys conducted in other countries. How is this discrepancy to be explained? Smith argues that gender differences in reporting biases account for the difference: Men tend to exaggerate sexual encounters, and women tend to play them down.

Although there is evidence that differences in male and female attitudes and behaviors with respect to sexual matters have diminished over the years, reporting discrepancies in sexual surveys such as those described above suggest that gender differences with regard to what is acceptable sexual practice remain firmly entrenched. It is unlikely these differences will vanish in the near future.

KEY POINTS

- Females and males differ to some extent in the characteristics they seek in potential mates. Females often seek high status, ambition, and intelligence in romantic partners, while males tend to emphasize youth and physical attractiveness.

- Both parental investment theory and social exchange theory help to explain these differences.

- Females and males differ to some extent with respect to their sexual attitudes and sexual behavior. Males are more accepting of casual sexual encounters and express more permissive attitudes toward extramarital sex.

- Males report a higher incidence of masturbation and greater incidence of intercourse. Both sexes misrepresent the number of their sexual partners.

Gender Differences in Psychological Adjustment

Gender stereotypes suggest that females are more emotional than males and experience wider swings in mood, but in fact there is very little evidence for the validity of such views (Strickland, 1992). On the other hand, there *are* sizable differences between females and males with respect to one important psychological disorder, *depression*. Around the world, females are more than twice as likely as males to suffer from some forms of depression (Nolen-Hoeksema, 1990). They are much more likely to experience such symptoms as persistent feelings of sadness; loss of energy; and reduced pleasure in activities that are normally quite enjoyable, such as eating and sex. Why is this the case? Biological factors may play some role. For example, use of oral contraceptives seems to cause depression in some women, and menopause brings feelings of depression for a small percentage of them (Stanton & Dunkel-Schetter, 1991). However, as noted recently by Strickland (1992), psychological and cultural factors probably play a much stronger role.

First, as Chapter 14 will explain in more detail, depression often involves feelings of *helplessness*—the sense that one cannot change unpleasant or stressful life situations. Because of their lower power, status, and income, females seem especially at risk for experiencing such feelings. Second, sexual and physical violence against women has risen to truly alarming levels in

North America. Brickman (1992) cites a study by Linda MacLeod (1989) indicating that 56 percent of Canadian women are afraid to venture out in their own neighborhoods once darkness sets in. Brickman and Briere (1984) found that one in five women in a Winnipeg sample had been assaulted sexually at some point in life. The burden of constantly worrying about personal safety is a heavy one for many women—especially those living in poverty—and may contribute to the high incidence of depression among them (Strickland, 1992). Third, females experience *sexual harassment* and discrimination based on gender much more often than males. These factors, too, may contribute to their greater tendency to experience depression. In fact, it is reasonable to ask: Wouldn't males, too, be at increased risk for depression if they experienced the dangers, restrictions, and limitations many societies have placed, and continue to place, upon females? (Females are also more likely than males to experience serious *eating disorders*; see Chapters 10 and 14.)

Another problem of adjustment faced by at least some females has important implications for careers in the industrialized West: the greater tendency of females to experience **mathematics anxiety**. Many girls grow up believing that they do not have the ability to understand mathematics. A Carleton University study found that women who were just as competent and well prepared as men tended to avoid majors requiring even modest amounts of mathematical skills (LeFevre, Kulak, & Heymans, 1992). Why do women avoid mathematics? Flessati & Jamieson (1991) of Lakehead University suggest two reasons. Although both men and women experience math anxiety, women are much more concerned about the presence of such feelings. Also, women appear to be much more self-critical of their performance. As a consequence, women are much less likely to enter mathematics courses or math-related subjects. This can restrict their career goals in important ways (Chipman, Brush, & Wilson, 1985).

At this point it should be pointed out that females are not the only victims of rigid gender stereotypes and roles: Growing evidence indicates that males, too, are adversely affected. Let's review some of the evidence relating to these effects. First, however, we should clarify one important fact: Gender identity is *not* a single dimension, with *masculine* at one end and *feminine* at the other. Rather, masculinity and femininity are better viewed as two independent dimensions, along which individuals vary. Thus, a given person can be anywhere from high to low in femininity and, at the same time, anywhere from high to low in masculinity (Bem, 1974; Spence, Helmreich, & Stapp, 1975). In fact, recent evidence suggests that the picture may be even more complex than this, and that individuals can accept some aspects of their society's gender stereotype while rejecting others. Thus, gender may actually involve a multiplicity of dimensions instead of only one or two.

Much research on gender stereotyping has focused on the question of whether people who are clearly *sex-typed*—that is, males who score high on masculinity and low on femininity, and females who score high on femininity and low on masculinity—are more or less well adjusted than those who are **androgynous**—relatively high on both dimensions. While the findings of such research are not conclusive, they generally indicate that androgynous individuals enjoy some advantages. They appear to be happier, better adjusted, and more adaptable than those who are strongly and traditionally sex-typed (Major, Carnevale, & Deaux, 1981; Rosenzweig & Darley, 1989).

There appears to be one important exception to this pattern, however: Males who score relatively high on femininity tend to show *lower* adjustment than those who score low on femininity (Aubé & Koestner, 1992). Why would this be so? One possibility may involve the fact that males generally hold more traditional gender stereotypes than females (Orlofsy & O'Heron, 1987). Thus, they experience considerable stress when they find that their interests

Mathematics Anxiety: *Fear on the part of individuals that they cannot master the concepts or operations of mathematics.*

Androgynous: *High in both femininity and masculinity.*

and behaviors don't match the masculine stereotype. Another possibility, noted by Aubé and Koestner (1992, p. 491) is that while recent changes in many societies have made it more acceptable for females to show interests and characteristics generally attributed to males, corresponding opportunities have not developed for males. In other words, males are still expected to show traditionally masculine characteristics, and there is little acceptance of males who evidence traditionally feminine interests or traits. Further research is needed to investigate these and other possibilities. Regardless of the outcome of such studies, one conclusion seems clear: Males who demonstrate interests or behaviors viewed by their society as being *feminine* are at considerably greater risk for maladjustment than females who demonstrate interests or behaviors viewed as being *masculine*.

Cognitive Abilities

It is widely assumed that females have higher verbal abilities than males and that males surpass females in mathematics and in tasks that involve *spatial relations*—the movement of objects in space, or visualization of such movements. Do these cognitive differences actually exist? Research on this question has continued for several decades, and there is now an extensive body of evidence on which to base conclusions. Meta-analyses of these data indicate that while some differences do appear to exist between females and males with respect to various cognitive abilities, such differences are generally smaller than gender stereotypes suggest (Feingold, 1992b; Hyde & Linn, 1988; Hyde, Fennema, & Lamon, 1990). In addition, in recent years there has been a tendency for these differences to decrease in magnitude, especially among adolescents (Feingold, 1992b). Finally, the differences that occur seem to appear among young children, then to decrease or totally vanish during adolescence. Some differences in certain cognitive abilities seem to be present among adults; but, as noted by Feingold (1992b, p. 109), this finding may be due to the fact that adults in many of these studies were born before the 1960s, at a time when gender stereotypes were much stronger than has been true since the advent of the women's movement. Thus, it seems possible that even these remaining differences will decrease or disappear in the future. A summary of research evidence concerning differences in cognitive abilities between males and females is presented in Table 11.2.

TABLE 11.2

Gender Differences in Cognitive Abilities

Differences between males and females appear to be relatively small in most cases; differences also tend to increase with age. (Source: Based on data from Feingold, 1992.)

COGNITIVE ABILITY	GENDER DIFFERENCES
Vocabulary	No appreciable difference.
Reading	Girls score higher than boys, but this difference disappears with adolescence.
Spelling	Girls score higher than boys.
General information	Males score higher at all ages.
Mathematics	Girls outperform boys in the first two years of high school; this difference disappears by the time they are seniors.
Spatial visualization	Boys score slightly higher than girls, and this difference persists throughout adolescence.
Perceptual speed	Females score higher than males of all ages.
Memory	No difference between males and females.

Gender Differences: A Note on Their Possible Origins

Throughout this discussion we have emphasized the role of cultural and social factors in differences between males and females. This emphasis is consistent with the views of most psychologists, who firmly believe that such differences arise in large measure from contrasting socialization practices for girls and boys, and from the pervasive influence of gender stereotypes and gender roles (Etaugh & Liss, 1992; Stoppard & Gruchy, 1993). How powerful are these influences? They are *very* powerful indeed, as illustrated in the research conducted by Etaugh and Liss (1992).

In this study, children of various ages—kindergarten, third grade, sixth grade, and eighth grade—were asked questions about their toy preferences ("What do you want for Christmas?"), the identity of their friends ("What are the names of your friends?"), the chores they were assigned at home, and their career choices. Results clearly illustrated the powerful role of parents and friends with respect to sex-typing. First, as expected, boys requested "male" types of toys while girls asked for "female" toys; and, as shown in Figure 11.14, this, by and large, is what they received. Similarly, boys reported having more male friends and girls having more female friends. Moreover, those who asked for the toys favored by their own sex played most with same-sex friends. As for household chores, more than half the girls had kitchen-related tasks as opposed to only 29 percent of the boys, while boys were more likely to take out the garbage or have no chores. Finally, children who did yard work and took out the garbage were more likely to express interest in occupations that in the past have been viewed as male (e.g., police officer or lawyer) than those who did not perform such chores.

Together, these finding present a picture of a socialization process in which parents behave differently toward girls than boys. This differential treatment is reflected in the children's behavior and influences many aspects of their lives, including preferences for sex-typed toys, choice of friends, and even career aspirations. It is on the basis of such evidence that many psychologists emphasize the role of social and cultural factors in gender differences.

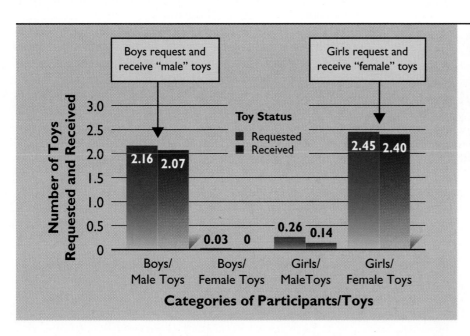

FIGURE 11.14

Sex Typing in Action

As shown here, boys and girls generally requested toys traditionally viewed as appropriate for their gender, and generally received these toys from parents. (Source: Based on data from Etaugh & Liss, 1992.)

THE POTENTIAL ROLE OF BIOLOGICAL FACTORS   Yet social and cultural factors are not the entire story. Growing evidence suggests that *biological factors*, too, may play some role in these differences. This does not in any way imply that differences between females and males are predetermined or unmodifiable—far from it. It simply indicates that there may be biological factors that tend to predispose females and males toward somewhat different patterns of behavior in some situations. Clearly, such biological dispositions can be altered or even reversed by experience or by social and cultural factors. But some evidence indicates that they do exist.

We have already considered this issue in Chapter 2, where we saw that there may be subtle differences between the brains of females and males (Berenbaum & Hines, 1992; Law, Pellegrino, & Hunt, 1993). For example, some evidence suggests that the structure of the *corpus callosum*, a broad band of neurons that connects the two hemispheres of the brain, may differ in females and males. Moreover, these differences may be related to subtle differences in cognitive abilities between the sexes, such as higher verbal fluency among females. Additional evidence for the role of biological factors in gender differences comes from studies of individuals who have experienced damage to one cerebral hemisphere (Kaufman, 1990). In these studies, males and females seem to show somewhat different effects from such damage. For example, in one study (Turkheimer & Farace, 1992), damage to the *left* hemisphere produced deficits in verbal aspects of intelligence in both males and females. However, reductions in other nonverbal aspects of intelligence, such as the ability to complete missing parts of pictures, were larger in females than in males. In contrast, damage to the *right* hemisphere, which generated deficits in nonverbal aspects of intelligence for both sexes, produced larger deficits in *verbal* aspects of intelligence among females. Since in most people the left hemisphere plays a dominant role in regulating verbal abilities and the right hemisphere in nonverbal abilities, these findings suggest that damage to a given cerebral hemisphere produces larger deficits in the cognitive functions *for which that hemisphere is nondominant* among females than among males (see Figure 11.15). This conclusion, in turn, is consistent with the view that females show higher levels of *bilateral processing* than males; that is, females, more than males, process incoming information in both hemispheres of the brain.

Other evidence could be cited here, but the main point is probably clear: There do appear to be subtle differences between the brains of females and males, and these differences may influence some aspects of cognitive functioning and overt behavior. So in this sense at least, biological factors may contribute to gender differences. But keep firmly in mind the fact that biology is only one of many different factors affecting behavior, and is *not* irresistible or unmodifiable. Indeed, where complex forms of behavior such as leadership, mate selection, psychological adjustment, and aggression are concerned, biological tendencies are almost certainly outweighed by social and situational variables.

KEY POINTS

- Females are more likely than males to suffer from *depression* and eating disorders. In addition, they experience higher levels of math anxiety.

- With the exception of males who are high in femininity, androgynous individuals show better adjustment than those who are traditionally sex-typed.

- Strong evidence indicates that contrasting socialization practices for girls and for boys, along with gender stereotypes and gender roles, are largely responsible for most gender differences.

- However, some evidence indicates that biological factors also play some role.

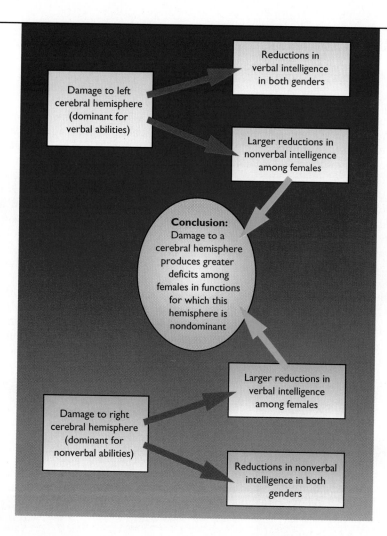

FIGURE 11.15

Contrasting Effects of Brain Damage Among Females and Males

Damage to the left cerebral hemisphere produces deficits in verbal intelligence for both males and females. However, reductions in other aspects of intelligence are larger for females. Further damage to the right hemisphere produces larger deficits in verbal intelligence among females. Together, these findings suggest that females show higher levels of bilateral processing than males. (Source: Based on findings reported by Turkheimer & Farace, 1992.)

Within the figure:

Damage to left cerebral hemisphere (dominant for verbal abilities)

Reductions in verbal intelligence in both genders

Larger reductions in nonverbal intelligence among females

Conclusion: Damage to a cerebral hemisphere produces greater deficits among females in functions for which this hemisphere is nondominant

Larger reductions in verbal intelligence among females

Damage to right cerebral hemisphere (dominant for nonverbal abilities)

Reductions in nonverbal intelligence in both genders

CANADIAN FOCUS

The Montreal Massacre: Gender Hatred

In December 1989 Marc Lepine roamed the halls of L'École Polytechnique in Montreal looking for victims. Not just any victims—only female victims. He entered a classroom brandishing a semi-automatic weapon and separated the men from the women. He told the men to leave. He then lined up the ten remaining women along the wall and gunned them down, shouting, "You're all a bunch of feminists, and I hate feminists!" He then went in pursuit of other female students. He killed a total of fourteen women before he killed himself (Came, Burke, Ferzoco, O'Farrell, & Wallace, 1989).

How does one understand or explain such an act? In an analysis of possible explanations of the Montreal massacre, Kafer, Hodkin, Furrow, and Landry (1993) note that the media focused on two explanations. One assumes that we live in a profoundly sexist society, and that acts of a person like Marc Lepine are an expression of the violent antagonism men harbor against women. The other explanation is that in any society there are misfits and madpeople who commit unpredictable acts of extreme violence. Implicit in this explanation is the notion that women just happened to be the target of this misfit's violence.

Single-factor explanations are appealing in that they are both simple and straightforward, but the behavior they are called upon to explain in this case is not simple and straightforward. As Boyanowski

(1991) points out, Lepine attributed all his failures in life to a single cause—women—and it is a mistake to follow his logic and attempt to account for his behavior in terms of a single cause.

According to the Kafer et al. study, most people agree with Boyanowski. That study sampled the opinion of students at Dalhousie, Mount Saint Vincent, and the Technical University of Nova Scotia. Those interviewed saw many interacting factors as responsible for Lepine's murderous aggression. For most, neither the sexism explanation nor the unpredictable-violence explanation was seen as tenable on its own. Rather, they were seen as valid *in combination* with many other factors, such as violence on television, the portrayal of women as victims in horror movies, a prevailing high tolerance for violence, and the fact that the victims were entering a "male" profession.

There is merit in avoiding simplistic interpretations of complicated activities, and it seems likely that a host of interacting factors molded Lepine into the killer he became. Even so, all the explanations consid-ered so far remain unsatisfactory. Somehow, seeing Lepine's behavior as rising from many factors diminishes the horror of what he did. It dilutes his responsibility as an individual for his behavior, and this is a mistake. Perhaps the best way to try to understand the Montreal massacre is to ask a simple question: Why do men in general aggress against women?

This is the approach taken by Brickman (1992) in her consideration of the Montreal massacre. The conclusions she draws are disturbing. She maintains that men aggress against women because it is rewarding. It can relieve sexual urges, release tension, and reduce anger. Normally, she holds, much of this aggression is carried out in private, unseen and unreported. It is, as she says, "socially invisible," and because it is invisible, men as a group escape censure. She makes the discomforting but defensible argument that even when the violence becomes visible, as in the Montreal massacre, a man can benefit. At the expense of his female victims, Lepine gained attention and enduring notoriety that he would have otherwise never had.

Research in Canada

Rudy Kafer
Mount Saint Vincent University

Barbara Hodkin
Mount Saint Vincent University

David Furrow
Mount Saint Vincent University

Trudy Landry
Mount Saint Vincent University

MAKING PSYCHOLOGY PART OF YOUR LIFE

Measuring Attitudes Toward Women: A Short Test for Sexism

Overt discrimination against females has decreased in recent years in many countries, partly because of growing awareness of this problem and partly as a result of legislation making discrimination illegal. Even now, however, people continue to hold divergent views concerning what is and is not appropriate behavior and career activity for women. Some people retain traditional views; others reject these entirely; and, of course, many people fall somewhere in between. Where do *you* fall in this dimension? To find out, answer the questions below, according to the instructions provided.

Instructions: The statements below describe attitudes toward the role of women in society. There are no right or wrong answers, only opinions. Express your feeling about each statement by indicating whether you (A) agree strongly, (B) agree mildly, (C) disagree mildly, or (D) disagree strongly.

___ 1. Swearing and obscenity are more repulsive in the speech of a woman than in that of a man.

___ 2. Women should take increasing responsibility for leadership in solving the intellectual and social problems of the day.

___ 3. Both husband and wife should be allowed the same grounds for divorce.

___ 4. Telling dirty jokes should be mostly a masculine prerogative.

___ 5. Intoxication in a woman is worse than intoxication in a man.

___ 6. Under modern economic conditions, with women being active outside the home, men should share in the household tasks such as washinig dishes and doing the laundry.

___ 7. It is insulting to women to have the "obey" clause in the marriage service.

___ 8. There should be a strict merit system in job appointment and promotion without regard to sex.

___ 9. A woman should be as free as a man to propose marriage.

___ 10. Women should worry less about their rights and more about becoming good wives and mothers.

___ 11. Women earning as much as their dates should bear equally the expense when they go out together.

___ 12. Women should assume their rightful place in business and all the professions along with men.

___ 13. A woman should not expect to go to exactly the same places or to have quite the same freedom of action as a man.

___ 14. Sons in a family should be given more encouragement to go to university than daughters.

___ 15. It is ridiculous for a woman to run a locomotive and for a man to darn socks.

___ 16. In general, the father should have greater authority than the mother in the bringing up of children.

___ 17. Women should be encouraged not to become sexually intimate with anyone before marriage, even with their fiancés.

___ 18. The law should not favor the husband over the wife in the disposal of family property or income.

___ 19. Women should be concerned with their duties of childbearing and house tending, rather than with desires for a professional or business career.

___ 20. The intellectual leadership of a community should be largely in the hands of men.

___ 21. Economic and social freedom are worth far more to women than acceptance of the ideal of femininity that has been set up by men.

___ 22. On the average, women should be regarded as less capable of contributing to economic production than are men.

___ 23. There are many jobs in which men should be given preference over women in being hired or promoted.

___ 24. Women should be given equal opportunity with men for apprenticeship in various trades.

___ 25. The modern girl is entitled to the same freedom from regulation and control that is given to the modern boy.

After you have finished, enter a score for each item as follows:

Items 1, 4, 5, 10, 13, 14, 15, 16, 17, 19, 20, 22, and 23:
A = 0   B = 1   C = 2   D = 3
Items 2, 3, 6, 7, 8, 9, 11, 12, 18, 21, 24, and 25:
A = 3   B = 2   C = 1   D = 0

Finally, obtain your score on the scale by adding the scores from the two sets of items listed above. The higher this number, the more nontraditional are your views.

You may find it interesting to know that when this scale, the *Attitudes Toward Women Scale* (Spence & Helmreich, 1972), was given to a large group of university students (241 females, 286 males), in the 1980s, the average scores were as follows: males = 44.80; females = 50.26. Thus, as we saw earlier in this chapter, females held less traditional views than males. When the scale was given to 292 mothers and 232 fathers, the average scores were as follows: fathers = 39.22; mothers = 41.86. Mothers were less traditional than fathers, but both sets of parents were more traditional in their beliefs than university students. These findings were obtained more than ten years ago, so you might find it interesting to give the scale to your own parents or to several friends. How do their scores compare?

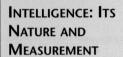
INTELLIGENCE: ITS NATURE AND MEASUREMENT

individual differences 444

intelligence 444

Savant syndrome 446

triarchic theory 447

componential intelligence 447

experiential intelligence 447

contextual intelligence 447

Stanford-Binet Test 451

IQ 451

reliability 455

split-half reliability 455

test-retest reliability 456

validity 457

content validity 457

criterion-related validity 457

predictive validity 457

concurrent validity 457

construct validity 457

cultural bias 459

Raven Progressive Matrices and Test 461

cognitive disability 461

Down syndrome 461

PASS theory 462

- Psychologists generally agree that intelligence involves the ability to think abstractly and to learn from experience.
- In the past, psychologists disagreed over whether intelligence was unitary or multifaceted in nature; today, most believe that intelligence involves both a general capacity to solve many types of problems and several specific abilities.
- In recent years, many researchers have adopted an information processing approach to intelligence. Sternberg's triarchic theory of intelligence and Das's PASS theory are two examples of this newer approach. Additional research indicates that people scoring high on intelligence tests show signs of faster rates of neural conduction and greater metabolic efficiency in their brains than people scoring lower on such tests.
- The first individual test of intelligence was devised by Binet and Simon. This test yielded an IQ score, obtained by dividing the child subject's mental age by his or her chronological age. Revised repeatedly over the years, this test is still in widespread use as the Stanford-Binet Test. Because intelligence can be demonstrated nonverbally as well as verbally, another widely used test of intelligence, the Wechsler Scales, obtains both a Performance and a Verbal IQ. Group tests of intelligence are highly efficient, but serious questions have been raised about their use with minority groups.
- In order to be useful, any psychological test must have high reliability—that is, it must yield very similar scores when applied more than once to the same quantity. Reliability can be measured in terms of internal consistency (the extent to which all items on the test measure the same characteristic), and through test-retest reliability (the extent to which scores on a test are stable over time).
- In order to be useful, psychological tests must also be high in validity—the capacity to measure what they claim to measure. Types of validity include content validity, criterion-related validity, and construct validity.
- In North America and elsewhere, members of several minority groups score lower on standard intelligence tests than people of European descent. This appears to be due at least in part to the cultural bias of these tests. Efforts to construct culture-fair tests of intelligence have been only partly successful.

HUMAN INTELLIGENCE: THE ROLE OF HEREDITY AND THE ROLE OF ENVIRONMENT

confluence theory 466

- Intelligence is influenced by a complex interplay between environmental and genetic factors.

GENDER: HOW MALES AND FEMALES DIFFER gender 467 parental investment model 474 matching hypothesis 475 mathematics anxiety 479 androgynous 479	• The term *gender* refers to more than biological sex; it includes references to gender stereotypes and gender roles. • Females are better than males at both sending and reading various nonverbal cues. However, they experience greater social pressure to express positive emotions toward others. • There are no overall differences between males and females with respect to susceptibility to social influence, but females are often influenced to a greater extent than males by evaluative feedback about their performance. • Female and male leaders do not appear to differ greatly in terms of style or performance. Female leaders often receive lower evaluations than male leaders, especially if they engage in what are viewed to be gender-incongruent managerial styles. Males can also be evaluated less favorably if they are perceived to adopt a gender-incongruent management style. • Males engage in acts of direct physical aggression more often than females. However, females engage in more acts of indirect aggression. A critical factor influencing aggressiveness in females is how the situation is evaluated. • Females and males differ to some extent in the characteristics they seek in potential mates. Females often seek high status, ambition, and intelligence in romantic partners, while males tend to emphasize youth and physical attractiveness. Both parental investment theory and social exchange theory help to explain these differences. • Females and males differ to some extent with respect to their sexual attitudes and sexual behavior. Males are more accepting of casual sexual encounters and express more permissive attitudes toward extramarital sex. Males report a higher incidence of masturbation, a greater incidence of intercourse, and more partners. Both sexes misrepresent the number of their sexual partners. • Females are more likely than males to suffer from depression and eating disorders. In addition, they experience higher levels of math anxiety. With the exception of males who are high in femininity, androgynous people show better adjustment than those who are traditionally sex-typed. • Strong evidence indicates that contrasting socialization practices for girls and for boys, as well as gender stereotypes and gender roles, are largely responsible for most gender differences. However, some evidence indicates that biological factors also play some role.

CRITICAL THINKING QUESTIONS

APPRAISAL	Human beings differ in an almost limitless number of ways. Do you agree that differences relating to gender and intelligence are among the most important? If so, why? If not, why?
CONTROVERSY	Suppose that at some future time, highly reliable measures of intelligence based on physiological functioning are developed. Do you think that such measures should replace standard tests of intelligence? What advantages would they offer? Would such measures be entirely culture-free, or can you think of subtle ways in which cultural differences might influence performance on even *these* tests?
MAKING PSYCHOLOGY PART OF YOUR LIFE	Now that you understand some of the basic requirements of all psychological tests, do you think you will be more skeptical of the kinds of questionnaires that are published in many magazines and claim to measure various psychological traits? I hope so! Why should you approach such quizzes with caution? Under what circumstances could you view them as useful or informative?

Individual Differences II
Personality—Consistency in the
Behavior of Individuals

THE PSYCHOANALYTIC APPROACH: MESSAGES FROM THE UNCONSCIOUS 491
Freud the Person: A Life in Summary
Freud's Theory of Personality
Research Evidence Concerning Freud's Theory: Freudian Slips
Freud's Theory: An Overall Evaluation

OTHER PSYCHOANALYTIC VIEWS: FREUD'S DISCIPLES ... AND DISSENTERS 500
Jung: The Collective Unconscious
Horney: The Importance of Social and Cultural Factors
Adler: Striving for Superiority
The Neo-Freudians: An Evaluation

HUMANISTIC THEORIES: EMPHASIS ON GROWTH 505
Rogers's Self Theory: Becoming a Fully Functioning Person
Maslow and the Study of Self-Actualizing People
Humanistic Theories: An Evaluation

TRAIT THEORIES: SEEKING THE KEY DIMENSIONS OF PERSONALITY 510
Allport's Central, Secondary, and Cardinal Traits
Cattell's Surface and Source Traits
Five Robust Factors: A Modern Framework
Trait Theories: An Evaluation

LEARNING APPROACHES TO PERSONALITY 514
Social Cognitive Theory: Reciprocal Causality in Human Behavior
Evaluation of the Learning Approach

KEY ASPECTS OF PERSONALITY: A SAMPLE OF RECENT RESEARCH 517
Aspects of the Self: Self-Perception, Self-Esteem, and Self-Monitoring
Sensation Seeking: The Desire for Stimulation

SUMMARY AND REVIEW OF KEY POINTS 527

CANADIAN FOCUS—CULTURAL VARIATIONS IN LOVE AND INTIMACY 499

THE RESEARCH PROCESS—SELF-DISCLOSURE: THE POTENTIAL BENEFITS OF REVEALING OURSELVES TO OTHERS 508

THE POINT OF IT ALL—THE ATLAS PERSONALITY 516

KEY CONCEPT—MAJOR THEORIES OF PERSONALITY: AN OVERVIEW 518

CANADIAN FOCUS—THE ROLE OF PERSONALITY FACTORS IN ADJUSTING TO LIFE IN A NEW CULTURE 524

MAKING PSYCHOLOGY PART OF YOUR LIFE—HOW ACCURATE IS YOUR SELF-CONCEPT? 526

UBC STUDY MAY REVEAL EXTENT TO WHICH GENES DETERMINE PERSONALITY

The Vancouver Sun: January 24, 1992

Are our personalities genetically determined? Do we inherit how orderly, anxious, or impulsive we are? How can we find out? And why would we care?

Current research as reported here in the Vancouver Sun, relies upon data collected from genetically identical twins who are reared in different environments. The hypothesis is that similarities in the personalities of these very special pairs of people are the result of their common inheritance.

According to a UBC researcher: "[If] we learn that social avoidance [for example] is a learned trait, it means [that to change that behavior] we teach people social skills. If it's a genetic trait, it might mean we would have to alter [child rearing practices and] educational systems to take that into account."

In Chapter 12 you will study different theories about why each of us has a unique personality, and what we have in common with other people whose personalities are something like our own.

WE EXPECT OTHERS TO DEMONSTRATE CONSISTENCY IN THEIR BEHAVIOR ACROSS DIFFERENT SITUATIONS AND OVER LONG PERIODS OF TIME.

Personality: Individuals' unique and relatively stable patterns of behavior, thoughts, and feelings.

PERSONALITY: CONSISTENCY IN THE BEHAVIOR OF INDIVIDUALS

We generally assume that people show consistency in at least some aspects of their behavior across time and in a wide range of contexts.
(Source: ZIGGY copyright 1982 ZIGGY AND FRIENDS, INC. Dist. by UNIVERSAL PRESS SYNDICATE. Reprinted with permission. All rights reserved.)

ZIGGY   By Tom Wilson

© 1982 Universal Press Syndicate   2/26   Tom Wilson

According to one old saying, variety is the spice of life. Whether that's true or not, there's no doubt that the people around us provide us with plenty of variety: They differ tremendously in their behavior, their preferences, their outlook on life, and their emotional volatility, and in a thousand and one other ways too. We considered several important aspects of individual differences in Chapter 11. Here, we will continue to explore this important topic by focusing on another key aspect of it: *personality*.

Personality can be defined as an individual's unique and relatively stable patterns of behavior, thoughts, and emotions (Burger, 1990; Carver & Scheier, 1992; Wallace, 1993).In daily life, we generally act as though personality is a fact. We expect others to demonstrate consistency in their behavior across different situations and over long periods of time. Once we conclude that a person possesses certain traits—that he or she is, for example, *friendly, sloppy,* and *generous*—we expect that person to behave in ways consistent with these traits in many situations. This raises an intriguing question: Does such consistency really exist? Some psychologists have argued that it does not—that behavior is largely determined by external factors rather than by stable traits or dispositions (Mischel, 1977, 1985). According to these critics of the concept of personality, individuals actually behave very differently in different situations; our perception that they act consistently is largely an error stemming from our desire to simplify the task of predicting their actions (Kunda & Nisbett, 1986; Reeder, Fletcher, & Furman, 1989.)

While these are intriguing arguments, the weight of existing evidence suggests that personality, defined in terms of stable behavioral tendencies, is indeed real. Long-term studies indicate that people *do* show a fair amount of consistency with respect to many aspects of behavior (e.g., Woodall & Matthews, 1993). In other words, if someone tends to be *friendly, sloppy,* and *generous* today, the chances are quite good that he or she will also be *friendly, sloppy,* and *generous* tomorrow, next month, next year, and even ten years from today. Indeed, several recent studies indicate that personality traits measured in childhood are often good predictors of adult behavior as many as fifty years later (e.g., Friedman et al., 1993).

It is important to be aware, however, that such consistency over long periods of time does *not* exist for all traits and for all people (Baumeister & Tice, 1988; Tice, 1989). In fact, the extent to which people show such consistency across time and situations may itself be an important aspect of personality—one known as *self-monitoring* (Koestner, Bernieri, & Zuckerman, 1992). We will examine self-monitoring in a later section. Also, the existence of stable traits in no way implies that situational factors are unimportant in determining behavior; on the contrary, most psychologists now agree that both traits *and* situations are important. In other words, behavior in a given context is often a function of both internal factors—those which people bring with them to a situation—*and* external ones. Further, there are many instances in which situational factors overwhelm dispositions or strongly influence their expression. For instance, even people with wild tempers tend to behave politely when stopped for speeding by a Mountie. In summary, behavior is generally influenced by both situational and internal factors; and among the internal factors, the stable tendencies included in the concept of personality appear to be quite important.

In the remainder of this chapter, we will assume that personality does indeed exist and that it can exert important effects upon behavior. But what, precisely, is the nature of personality? How do individual differences in it arise? And which personal dispositions or traits are the most important? In order to provide you with an overview of psychology's insights concerning these issues, we will proceed as follows.

First, we will survey several *theories of personality*—theoretical frameworks, many of them grand and sweeping in nature, designed to explain the origins and nature of personality. Few of these frameworks are currently accepted as wholly adequate but as a group they have called attention to important issues and so are worthy of our attention. Each theory will first be described; some research evidence relating to it will then be presented; finally, the theory's current status in psychology will be evaluated. After this, we will focus on the nature and impact of several specific *personality traits*—that is, on key dimensions along which individuals differ in consistent, stable ways (Wallace, 1993).

The Psychoanalytic Approach: Messages From the Unconscious

When asked to name the three people who exerted the greatest influence on intellectual developments during the twentieth century, many historians reply without hesitation: Albert Einstein, Karl Marx, and Sigmund Freud. By this measure, a psychologist—or at least someone who operated as a psychologist for much of his career—is one of the key figures of modern history. Why is Freud's impact considered to be so profound? The answer is found largely in his theories, which focus on personality and on other important topics, such as the root causes of psychological disorders. Before turning to his theories, it seems appropriate to spend a moment or two on Freud's background—on *his* personality, if you will.

Freud the Person: A Life in Summary

Freud was born in what is now part of the Czech Republic. When he was four years old, his family moved to Vienna, and he spent almost his entire life in that city. As a young man, Freud was highly ambitious, and he decided to make a name for himself as a medical researcher. He became discouraged with his prospects, however, and soon after receiving his medical degree he entered private practice. It was at this time that he formulated his theories of human personality and psychological disorders.

Freud's mother was his father's second wife, and she was much younger than her husband. In fact, she was only twenty-one when Freud was born. Although she had other additional children, Sigmund was always his mother's favorite. Among the Freud children only Sigmund had his own room, and when his sister's piano practice disturbed his studies, her lessons were stopped and the piano sold. Freud's relationship with his father, in contrast, was cold and distant. Indeed, he even arrived late at his father's funeral and missed most of the service. At the age of twenty-six Freud married Martha Bernays. The marriage was a happy one and produced six children. Freud had a powerful personality, and as he developed his controversial theories, he attracted many followers. In many cases these people began as ardent supporters but came to question some aspects of his work. Freud was intolerant of such criticism, and this often led to angry breaks with once-cherished students. One disciple, however, never broke with his views: his daughter Anna, who became a famous psychoanalyst in her own right.

Freud loved antiques and collected them throughout his life. His collection filled the walls and shelves of his office and even the top of his desk. Each morning the first thing he did was reach over and affectionately pat one or more of his stone sculptures. Freud recognized that there was a connection between his hobby and his work; he told many of his patients that his search for hidden memories in their unconscious minds was similar to the excavation of a buried ancient city. Freud smoked heavily (he was often photographed with a large cigar in his hand). He eventually contracted oral cancer, which caused him great pain, and starting in 1923 he underwent many operations for this disease. These interfered with his speech and finally ended his career as a public speaker.

Like many people of Jewish descent, Freud found it necessary to flee the Nazis, and in 1938 he left Vienna for England. He died there of throat cancer the following year. Many biographies of Freud have been written, and several draw connections between his theories and his personal experiences—for example, his close relationship with his mother and distant relationship with his father. Whether such links actually exist remains open to debate. What is certain, however, is that this complex, brilliant, and domineering man changed Western ideas about human behavior and personality in a lasting way.

Freud's Theory of Personality

SIGMUND FREUD

Freud is clearly a major figure in the history of psychology. His theories of personality had a profound effect on intellectual thought for many decades.

As noted earlier, Freud entered private practice soon after obtaining his medical degree. A turning point in his early career came when he won a research grant to travel to Paris in order to observe the work of Jean-Martin Charcot, who was then using hypnosis to treat several types of mental disorders. When Freud returned to Vienna, he worked with Joseph Breuer, a colleague who was using hypnosis in the treatment of *hysteria*, a condition in which individuals experience physical symptoms—such as blindness, deafness, or paralysis of arms or legs—for which there seems to be no underlying physical cause. Out of these experiences, and out of his growing clinical practice, Freud gradually developed his theories of human personality and mental illness. His ideas were complex and touched on many different issues. With respect to personality, however, four aspects of his work are central: levels of consciousness, the structure of personality, anxiety and defense mechanisms, and psychosexual stages of development.

LEVELS OF CONSCIOUSNESS: BENEATH THE ICEBERG'S TIP Freud saw himself as a scientist, and he was well aware of research on thresholds for sensory experience (refer to Chapter 3). He applied some of these ideas to the task of understanding the human mind and reached the startling conclusion that most of the mind lies below the surface—in other words, below the threshold of conscious experience. Above this threshold is the realm of the *conscious*, which includes our current thoughts—that is, whatever we are thinking about or experiencing at a given moment. Beneath the conscious realm is the much larger *preconscious*, which contains memories that are not part of current thoughts but can readily be brought to mind if the need arises. Finally, beneath the preconscious, and forming the bulk of the human mind, is the *unconscious*—those thoughts, desires, and impulses of which we remain largely unaware (refer to Figure 12.1). Freud believed that although some of this material had always been unconscious, much of it was once conscious but had been actively *repressed*—that is, driven from consciousness because it provoked too much anxiety. For example, according to Freud, shameful experiences or unacceptable sexual or aggressive urges are often driven deep within the unconscious. The fact that we are not aware of the unconscious, however, in no way prevents it from affecting our behavior. Indeed, Freud believed that many of the symptoms experienced by his patients were disguised and indirect reflections of repressed thoughts and desires. This is why one major goal of **psychoanalysis**—the method of treating psychological disorders devised by Freud—is to bring repressed material back into consciousness. Presumably, once this material is made conscious, it can be dealt with more effectively, and important causes of mental illness may be eliminated.

Psychoanalysis: A method of therapy based on Freud's theory of personality, in which the therapist attempts to bring repressed unconscious material into consciousness.

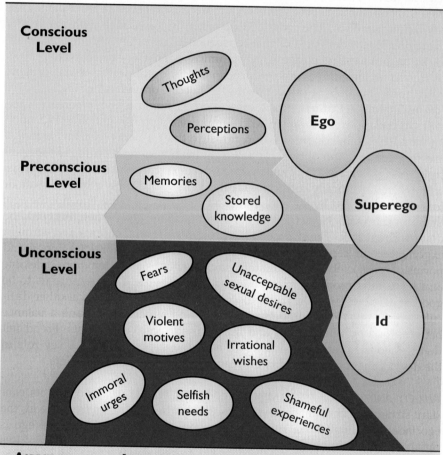

FIGURE 12.1

Freud's Views About Levels of Consciousness and Structures of Personality

Freud believed that the human mind has three distinct levels of consciousness: the *unconscious*, the *preconscious*, and the *conscious*. He also believed that personality involves three important structures: the *ego*, the *superego*, and the *id*, which serve different but related functions and operate at different levels of consciousness.

ASPECT OF PERSONALITY	LEVEL OF CONSCIOUSNESS	DESCRIPTION & FUNCTION
Ego	Mostly conscious	Mediates between id impulses and superego inhibitions; reality principle; rational
Superego	All levels, but mostly preconscious	Ideas and morals; conscience; incorporated from parents
Id	Unconscious	Basic impulses (sex and aggression); pleasure principle; seeks immediate gratification; irrational, impulsive

THE STRUCTURE OF PERSONALITY: ID, EGO, AND SUPEREGO Do you know the story of Dr. Jekyll and Mr. Hyde? If so, you already have a basic idea of some of the key structures of personality described by Freud. He suggested that personality consists largely of three parts: the *id*, the *ego*, and the *superego* (refer to Figure 12.1). As we'll soon see, these correspond, roughly, to *desire*, *reason*, and *conscience*.

The **id**, or desire, consists of all our primitive, innate urges. These include various bodily needs, sexual desire, and aggressive impulses. In this scheme of things, the id is totally unconscious and operates in accordance with what Freud termed the **pleasure principle:** It wants immediate, total gratification and is not capable of considering the potential costs of seeking this goal. In short, the id is the Mr. Hyde of our personality—although, in contrast to this literary character, it is not necessarily evil.

The world offers few means for instant pleasure, and attempting to gratify many of our innate urges would soon get us into serious trouble. It is for these reasons that the second structure of personality, the **ego**, develops. The ego's task is to hold the id in check until conditions exist that are appropriate for satisfying its impulses. Thus, the ego operates in accordance with the **reality principle:** It considers the external consequences of actions and directs behavior so as to maximize pleasure *and* minimize pain. The ego is partly but not entirely conscious; thus, some of its actions—for example, its eternal struggle with the id—are outside our conscious knowledge or understanding.

The final aspect of personality described by Freud is the **superego**. It too seeks to control satisfaction of the id's impulses, permitting their gratification only under certain conditions. In contrast to the ego, however, the superego is concerned with morality: It can tell right from wrong according to the principles of a given society. The superego permits gratification of id impulses only when it is morally correct to gratify them—not simply when it is safe or feasible, as required by the ego. In this scheme, it is the superego, not the ego, that prevents a stockbroker from defrauding clients even when this could be done without risk. The superego is acquired from our parents and through experience and represents our internalization of the moral teachings and norms of our society. Unfortunately, such teachings are often quite inflexible and leave little room for gratifying our basic desires. They require us to be good at all times, like Dr. Jekyll. Because of this, the ego faces another difficult task: It must mediate between the id and superego, striking a balance between our primitive urges and our learned moral constraints. Freud felt that this constant struggle among id, ego, and superego plays a key role in the development of personality and in many psychological disorders.

ANXIETY AND DEFENSE MECHANISMS: SELF-PROTECTION BY THE EGO In its constant struggle to prevent the outbreak of unbridled impulses from the id, the ego faces a difficult task. Yet for most people, most of the time, the ego is capable of performing this crucial function. Sometimes, though, id impulses grow so strong that they threaten to get out of control. For example, consider the case of a middle-aged widow who finds herself strongly attracted to her daughter's boyfriend. She hasn't had a romantic attachment in years, so her sexual desire quickly rises to powerful levels. What happens next? According to Freud, when her ego senses that unacceptable impulses are about to get out of hand, it experiences **anxiety**—unpleasant feelings of nervousness, tension, or worry. These feelings arise because the unacceptable impulses are getting closer and closer to consciousness, as well as closer and closer to the limits of the ego for holding them in check.

At this point, Freud contends, the ego may resort to one of several different **defense mechanisms**. These are all designed to keep unacceptable

---

Id: *In Freud's theory, the portion of personality concerned with immediate gratification of primitive needs.*

Pleasure Principle: *The principle on which the id operates, according to which immediate pleasure is the sole motivation for behavior.*

Ego: *In Freud's theory, the part of personality that takes rational account of external reality in the expression of instinctive sexual and aggressive urges.*

Reality Principle: *The principle on which the ego operates, according to which the external consequences of behavior are considered in the regulation of expression of impulses from the id.*

Superego: *According to Freud, the portion of human personality representing the conscience.*

Anxiety: *In Freudian theory, unpleasant feelings of tension or worry experienced by individuals in reaction to unacceptable wishes or impulses.*

Defense Mechanisms: *Techniques used by the ego to keep threatening and unacceptable material out of consciousness and so to reduce anxiety.*

impulses from the id out of consciousness and so prevent their open expression. Defense mechanisms take many different forms. For example, in **sublimation**, the unacceptable impulse is channeled into some socially acceptable action. Instead of making love to the young man, as Freud would say she really wants to do, the widow may "adopt" him as a son and provide financial support for his education. Another mechanism, known as **reaction formation**, consists of efforts to hide from the threatening impulse by behaving in a manner directly opposite to it. For example, the widow might convince herself that she intensely dislikes the young man and urge her daughter to stop seeing him. Table 12.1 describes additional defense mechanisms. While they differ greatly in specific form, all serve to reduce anxiety by keeping unacceptable urges and impulses from breaking into consciousness.

PSYCHOSEXUAL STAGES OF DEVELOPMENT   Now we come to what is perhaps the most controversial aspect of Freud's theory of personality. Many people find Freud's ideas about levels of consciousness to be quite reasonable; after all, as we saw in Chapter 4, we do seem to move through distinct levels of consciousness during the course of a single day. Similarly, many find appealing the idea that distinct aspects of personality reflect primitive urges and conscience, and the mediation between these forces. When we turn to Freud's ideas about the formation of personality, however, the situation changes radically. Even a hundred years after he proposed them, Freud's views on this issue offend some people and seem totally absurd to others. These views can be grouped under the heading **psychosexual stages of development**: innately determined stages of sexual development through which, presumably, we all pass.

To understand Freud's ideas concerning psychosexual development, we must first grasp his concepts of *libido* and *fixation*. According to Freud, the **libido** is the instinctual life force that energizes the id. Release of libido is closely related to pleasure, but the focus of such pleasure—the expression of libido—changes as we move through discrete stages of development. As we move through these stages, and obtain different kinds of pleasure in them, we leave behind small amounts of our libido. If an excessive amount of energy is tied to a particular stage, **fixation** is said to result. This can stem from either too

Sublimation: A defense mechanism in which threatening unconscious impulses are channeled into socially acceptable forms of behavior.

Reaction Formation: A defense mechanism in which people act in a manner directly opposite to their unconscious wishes.

Psychosexual Stages of Development: According to Freud, an innate sequence of stages through which all human beings pass. At each stage, pleasure is focused on a different region of the body.

Libido: According to Freud, the psychic energy that powers all mental activity.

Fixation: Excessive investment of psychic energy in a particular stage of psychosexual development, which results in various types of psychological disorders.

DEFENSE MECHANISM	ITS BASIC NATURE	EXAMPLE
Repression	"Forgetting"—or pushing from consciousness into unconsciousness—unacceptable thoughts and impulses.	A woman fails to recognize her attraction to her handsome new son-in-law.
Rationalization	Conjuring up socially acceptable reasons for thoughts or actions based on unacceptable motives.	A young woman explains that she ate an entire chocolate cake so that it wouldn't spoil in the summer heat.
Displacement	Redirection of an emotional response from a dangerous object to a safe one.	Anger is redirected from one's boss to one's child.
Projection	Transfer to others of unacceptable motives or impulses	A man sexually attracted to a neighbor perceives the neighbor as being sexually attracted to him.
Regression	Responding to a threatening situation in a way appropriate to an earlier age or level of development.	A student asks a professor to raise his grade; when she refuses, the student throws a temper tantrum.

TABLE 12.1

Defense Mechanisms: Reactions to Anxiety

According to Freud, when the ego feels that it may be unable to control impulses from the id, it experiences anxiety. To reduce such feelings, the ego employs various *defense mechanisms*, such as the ones described here.

FREUD'S ANAL STAGE OF DEVELOPMENT

Freud believed that fixation during the anal stage, resulting from traumatic toilet-training experiences, could lead to an excessive need for order and a stubborn personality in adults.

Oral Stage: In Freud's theory, a stage of psychosexual development during which pleasure is centered in the region of the mouth.

Anal Stage: In Freud's theory, a psychosexual stage of development in which pleasure is focused primarily on the anal zone.

KEY POINTS

- According to Freud, three distinct levels of consciousness exist: the conscious, preconscious, and unconscious.

- Freud contended that personality consists of three basic parts: id, ego, and superego. These correspond roughly to desire, reason, and conscience.

- According to Freud, all human beings move through a series of psychosexual stages, during which the id's search for pleasure is focused on different regions of the body.

- Too much or too little gratification at any of these stages can result in fixation and later in psychological disorders.

little or too much gratification during this stage, and in either case the result is harmful. Since the individual has left too much "psychic energy" behind, less is available for full adult development. The outcome may be an adult personality reflecting the stage or stages at which fixation has occurred. To put it another way, if too much energy is drained away by fixation at earlier stages of development, the amount remaining may be insufficient to power movement to full adult development. In such cases an individual may develop an immature personality and so be subject to several forms of psychological disorder.

Now back to the actual stages themselves. According to Freud, as we grow and develop, different parts of the body serve as the focus of the constant quest for pleasure. In the initial **oral stage**, lasting until we are about eighteen months old, we seek pleasure primarily through the mouth. If too much or too little gratification occurs during this stage, an individual may become *fixated* at it. Too little gratification results in a personality that is overly dependent on others; too much, especially after the child has developed some teeth, results in a personality that is excessively hostile, especially through verbal sarcasm and similar "biting" forms of behavior.

The next stage occurs in response to parents' efforts to toilet train their children. During the **anal stage**, the process of elimination becomes the primary focus of pleasure. Fixation at this stage, stemming from traumatic toilet-training experiences, may result in individuals who are excessively orderly and stubborn or, alternatively, excessively generous and undisciplined.

At about age four, the genitals become the primary source of pleasure, and children enter the **phallic stage**. Freud speculated that at this time we fantasize about sexual relations with our opposite-sex parent—a phenomenon he termed the **Oedipus complex**. (Oedipus was a character in ancient Greek literature who unknowingly killed his father and then married his mother. When he discovered the true nature of his monstrous acts, he blinded himself.) Fear of punishment for such desires then enters the picture. Among boys, the feared punishment is castration, leading to *castration anxiety*; among girls, the feared punishment is loss of love. In both cases, these fears bring about resolution of the Oedipus complex and identification with the same-sex parent. This, in turn, stimulates development of the superego. Because fear of castration is more vivid and threatening than fear of loss of love, Freud contended that resolution of the Oedipus complex is more complete in boys than in girls. This is why he theorized that the superego is stronger in males than in females.

Even more controversial is Freud's suggestion that little girls experience *penis envy*: feelings of envy upon seeing the male organ and realizing that they do not possess one. Freud suggested that girls, when confronted with this realization, experience strong feelings of inferiority and jealousy—feelings they may carry with them in disguised form even in adult life. As you can readily guess, these ideas now are strongly rejected by virtually all psychologists.

After resolution of the Oedipus conflict, children enter the **latency stage**, in which they remain until the onset of puberty. During the latency period, Freud contended, sexual urges are largely repressed. After puberty, we enter the final, **genital stage**. During this stage pleasure is again focused on the genitals. Now, however, lust is blended with affection, and we become capable of adult love in its fullest meaning. Please remember this: Progression to the genital stage is possible only if serious fixation has *not* occurred at the earlier stages of development. If such fixation has occurred, the normal pattern of development is blocked, and various forms of psychological disorders result. Figure 12.2 summarizes the various stages of psychosexual development.

Research Evidence Concerning Freud's Theory: *Freudian Slips*

Freud's theory of personality is filled with provocative ideas and suggestions. Moreover, there can be little doubt that it is now part of our general culture. It is equally clear, however, that many of the ideas and concepts introduced by Freud are difficult to assess through empirical research. This is one of the key criticisms of his theory. Yet over the years, many investigators have developed ingenious ways of testing some of Freud's ideas and hypotheses (Deckers & Carr, 1986; Hall, 1984). For example, researchers have attempted to study what have come to be known as **Freudian slips**—occasions on which we say something quite different from our intended meaning. Consider the following examples:

Guest to hostess: "The food is really inedible ... I mean incredible!"

Sales clerk to customer: "You can't get a better deal everywhere ... I mean anywhere!"

Are these merely slips of the tongue? Perhaps. But according to Freud, these slips may also reflect hidden, unconscious thoughts. That is why they are called *Freudian slips*. This intriguing suggestion has been subjected to careful empirical testing. For example, in one study (Motley & Camden, 1985), male students were asked to complete innocent-sounding sentences. Half performed this task in the presence of a male experimenter; half performed the

Phallic Stage: In Freud's theory, a psychosexual stage of development during which pleasure is centered in the genital region. It is during this stage that the Oedipus complex develops.

Oedipus Complex: In Freud's theory, a crisis of psychosexual development in which children must give up their sexual attraction for their opposite-sex parent.

Latency Stage: In Freud's theory, the psychosexual stage of development that follows resolution of the Oedipus complex. During this stage, sexual desires are relatively weak.

Genital Stage: In Freud's theory, the final psychosexual stage of development—one in which individuals acquire the adult capacity to combine lust with affection.

Freudian Slips: Statements that seem to be simple errors in speech, but which in fact reveal unconscious thoughts or impulses.

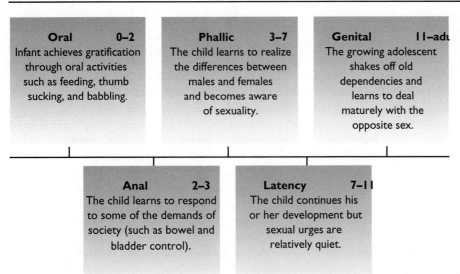

FIGURE 12.2

Psychosexual Stages of Development: Freud's View

According to Freud, all human beings pass through a series of discrete *psychosexual stages of development*. At each stage, pleasure is fixated on a particular part of the body. Too much or too little gratification at any stage can result in *fixation* and lead to psychological disorders.

Oral 0–2	Phallic 3–7	Genital 11–adu
Infant achieves gratification through oral activities such as feeding, thumb sucking, and babbling.	The child learns to realize the differences between males and females and becomes aware of sexuality.	The growing adolescent shakes off old dependencies and learns to deal maturely with the opposite sex.

Anal 2–3	Latency 7–11
The child learns to respond to some of the demands of society (such as bowel and bladder control).	The child continues his or her development but sexual urges are relatively quiet.

same task in the presence of an attractive and seductively clad female experimenter. Results indicated that the participants made more slips of the tongue with a sexual connotation in the presence of the female experimenter. For example, when asked to complete the sentence, "With the telescope, the details of the distant landscape were easy to …", they were more likely to say "make out" in the presence of the female. Similarly, they were more likely to complete the sentence, "The lid won't stay on regardless of how much I …" with the words "screw it." In a sense, these *were* slips of the tongue, because many of the students found their own words, once uttered, to be embarrassing.

At first glance, these studies seem to support Freud's contention that slips of the tongue are revealing of unconscious motives or desires—although in the above examples, it seems more likely that the desires were quite conscious! However, other interpretations also exist. For instance, in the presence of the strong sex-related cues provided by the attractive experimenter, activation of sex-related words may have been stronger than the activation of other, more neutral words. Thus, it is not surprising that the sex-related words were selected more frequently by subjects. Unfortunately, similar ambiguity with respect to interpretation is present in many other studies designed to test various aspects of Freud's theory (e.g., Dworkin & Efran, 1967; Zillmann, 1988).

Freud's Theory: *An Overall Evaluation*

Research in Canada

Karen K. Dion
University of Toronto

Kenneth L. Dion
University of Toronto

As noted earlier, Freud's place in history seems assured: His ideas and writings have had a profound impact on the twentieth century. But what about his theory of personality? Is it currently accepted by most psychologists? As you can probably guess from earlier comments, the answer is *definitely not*. The reasons why are also clear. First, as many critics have noted, Freud's theory is really not a theory at all, at least in the scientific sense of the term. Several of the concepts it contains cannot be measured, even indirectly. How, for example, does one go about observing an id, a fixation, or the psychic energy contained in the libido? Similarly, the theory offers few if any testable hypotheses about human behavior. As you will recall from Chapter 1, a theory that cannot be tested is of limited value.

Second, as we have already seen, several of Freud's proposals are not consistent with the findings of modern research. For example, he believed that dreams reflect unconscious urges and desires. As Chapter 4 explained, there is little evidence for this view.

Third, in constructing his theory, Freud relied heavily on a small number of case studies—no more than a dozen at most. Almost all of these individuals came from wealthy backgrounds and lived in a large and sophisticated city in a single culture. Thus, they were hardly representative of human beings generally. (See **Canadian Focus** for more information on this point.) Moreover, Freud indicated that he accepted for study and treatment only patients he viewed as particularly good candidates for successful therapy, and he himself recorded and later analyzed all of the information about these cases. Thus, there were many opportunities for unconscious forms of bias to enter the process through which he constructed his theories.

Finally, and perhaps most important of all, Freud's theories contain so many different concepts that they can explain virtually any pattern of behavior in an after-the-fact manner. Imagine, for example, that someone suffering from an "anal" personality is very messy rather than neat, as the theory would initially predict. Freudian psychoanalytic theory is not at a loss: It might suggest that the person's messiness is a defense reaction against anxiety stemming from the need to be neat. In short, no matter what pattern of behavior is demonstrated,

Freudian concepts can "explain" them. As you can see, this leaves little room for disconfirmation, and thus for testing the theory adequately.

For these and other reasons, Freud's theory of personality is not accepted as accurate by most present-day psychologists. Yet, having said this, it should be noted that several of Freud's ideas and insights—especially his ideas about levels of consciousness and about the importance of anxiety in various psychological disorders—*have* contributed to our understanding of human behavior in general and of personality in particular. There can be no doubt that he has had a major and lasting impact upon psychology and upon the overall intellectual heritage of the twentieth century.

❦ CANADIAN FOCUS

Cultural Variations in Love and Intimacy

According to Freud, all human beings pass through a fixed series of stages with respect to sexuality—stages of psychosexual development. If this is true, then we should expect human beings all over the world, even in sharply divergent cultures, to express love and intimacy in similar ways. After all, if Freud's theory is correct, then all human beings move through the same stages of development and, ultimately, attain the same final stage.

In fact, this is definitely not the case. On the contrary, ideas about love and intimacy, and the overt forms these ideas take, vary greatly between cultures. An account of this is provided by two researchers from the University of Toronto.

Dion and Dion (1993) contend that cultures differ along what can be termed an individualist/collectivist dimension. Some societies are extremely individualistic; others are the opposite (Hofstede, 1980).

In individualist societies, individual self-achievement and self-satisfaction are highly prized. Individuals within such societies are viewed as free and independent agents, and there is general acceptance of the idea that each individual should strive to reach the highest possible level of self-fulfillment. Self-interest and self-development take precedence over obligations and responsibilities. As you might expect, Canada and the United States exemplify individualistic cultures.

In collectivist societies, the emphasis is on a network of dependent relationships binding each individual to his or her family or social group. The family or social group provides a station or position for the individual within the culture. It protects, supports, and encourages the individual's advancement. In return, the individual recognizes his or her responsibility for ensuring the continued well-being of the group or family. Single-minded pursuit of goals or objectives

LOVE IN DIFFERENT CULTURES

Research suggests that love and intimacy are expressed in sharply different ways in various cultures. These findings appear to contradict Freud's belief that all human beings pass through the same stages of psychosexual development.

designed exclusively for self-satisfaction is frowned upon. In undertaking any course of action, the individual must always consider the consequences, costs, and benefits for the family or group. Collectivist cultural attitudes are found in China, India, and Japan.

How does cultural individualism and collectivism influence love and intimacy? The argument advanced by Dion and Dion is straightforward. Romantic love is fundamentally an exercise in self-fulfillment. In individualist societies, experience with love and intimacy is viewed as essential for full self-development. The intimate acts of self-disclosure that take place between partners in romantic pursuits are seen as providing insight into needs, feelings, and objectives that contribute to full self-realization. Also, more than anything else, romantic love is about the individual freedom to enter into relationships that offer the greatest opportunity for self-fulfillment without first having to weigh the possible reactions of others. Such a self-fulfilling process can only occur in a fundamentally individualistic society.

In a collectivist society, love and intimacy are not seen to be principally concerned with satisfying individual needs. The feelings and views of others have to be considered when a love or marriage relationship is entered into. Because of the deep interactive dependency an individual has with the group or family, the degree to which a prospective partner will fit into this relationship has to be carefully weighed. This is not to say that deeply affectionate relationships fail to develop in collectivist societies. What is different in such societies is that love and intimacy are not as self-centered as is the case in individualistic societies. There is evidence to support this conclusion. Ting-Toomey (1991) surveyed university students in a number of countries about the quality of intimacy experienced in relationships. Students in North America reported deeper feelings of self-involvement in intimate empathetic interactions with romantic partners than did students in Japan.

Although romantic love and intimacy flourish in individualistic societies, excessive individualism can change the character of the romantic experience. Love relationships can become competitive games where the object is to gain the most and give the least. Should the game cease to be sufficiently rewarding, it is abandoned. Dion and Dion (1991) claim that such considerations may play an important role in the high divorce rate in Canada and the United States.

It is quite clear that there are indeed important cultural differences both in ideas about love and intimacy and in their overt expression. To the extent such differences exist, any theory (e.g., Freud's) which assumes that all human beings move through an identical series of psychosexual stages must be called into question. Where the study of personality is concerned, wearing cultural blinders can severely limit our understanding of important aspects of human behavior.

Other Psychoanalytic Views: Freud's Disciples … and Dissenters

Whatever else Freud was, he was an intellectual magnet. Over several decades, he attracted as students or colleagues many brilliant and creative people. Most of them began by accepting his views. Later, however, they often disagreed with some of his key assumptions. For example, while many **neo-Freudians** accepted the importance of the unconscious, they objected to Freud's contention that personality is fully formed during the first years of life and to his emphasis on instinctual rather than social influences on personality. As mentioned earlier, these disagreements sometimes led to angry breaks between Freud and his followers; the master, it seems, was unwilling to accept even slight deviations from what he defined as the only true path to greater knowledge. An excellent account of the politics of psychoanalysis is provided by Phyllis Grosskurth of the University of Toronto (Grosskurth, 1991). Let's consider some of the intriguing views proposed by these one-time protégés of Freud.

Neo-Freudians: Personality theorists who accepted basic portions of Freud's theory but rejected or modified other portions.

Jung: The Collective Unconscious

Perhaps the most bitter of all the defections from Freud's inner circle was the departure of Carl Jung. Freud viewed Jung as his heir apparent and was deeply upset when his former disciple broke with him. Jung shared Freud's views concerning the importance of the unconscious; he contended, however, that Freud had overlooked another part of this aspect of personality—the **collective unconscious**. According to Jung, the material in the collective unconscious is shared by all human beings as part of our biological heritage. Of what does the collective unconscious consist? For one thing, it includes **archetypes**—images that predispose us to perceive the external world in certain ways. Included among the archetypes we all share, Jung maintained, are these: *mother, father, wise old man, the sun, the moon, God, death*, and *the hero*. It is because of these shared innate images, Jung contended, that the folklore of many different cultures often contains similar figures and themes.

Two especially important archetypes in Jung's theory are known as the animus and the anima. The **animus** is the masculine side of females, while the **anima** is the feminine side of males. Jung believed that in looking for a mate, we search for the person onto whom we can best project these hidden sides of ourselves. When there is a good match between such projections and another person, attraction occurs.

Another aspect of Jung's theory is that we are all born with innate tendencies to be concerned primarily either with ourselves or with the outside world. Jung labeled people in the first category **introverts** and described them as hesitant and cautious; they do not make friends easily and prefer to observe the world rather than become involved in it. He labeled people in the second category **extroverts**. Such individuals are open and confident, make friends readily, enjoy high levels of stimulation, and take part in a wide range of activities. While many aspects of Jung's theory have been rejected by psychologists, the dimension of *introversion–extroversion* seems to be a basic one and continues to be the subject of a considerable amount of research (Eysenck & Eysenck, 1985).

Horney: The Importance of Social and Cultural Factors

Why do men and women differ to some extent in some aspects of their behavior? Almost all modern psychologists would answer that it is largely because of contrasting experiences during childhood, exposure to different kinds of social models, and so on. Freud, as you already know, held a sharply different view. In many of his writings, he attributed behavioral differences between men and women to innate factors—for example, to anatomical differences between the sexes and the resulting *penis envy* that he believed all females experience.

Karen Horney, one of the few women in the early psychoanalytic movement, disagreed strongly. She contended that differences between males and females were largely the result of social factors, *not* innate inferiority on the part of females. In fact, Horney (1967) countered Freud's concept of penis envy with one of her own: *womb envy*—males' envy of women's ability to bear and nurse children. Her point was not that males are inferior to females. Rather, she wished to emphasize the fact that each sex has attributes admired by the other and that neither should be viewed as superior *or* inferior.

Collective Unconscious: *In Jung's theory, a portion of the unconscious shared by all human beings.*

Archetypes: *According to Jung, inherited images in the collective unconscious that shape our perceptions of the external world.*

Animus: *According to Jung, the archetype representing the masculine side of females.*

Anima: *According to Jung, the archetype representing the feminine side of males.*

Introverts: *Individuals who are quiet, cautious, and reclusive, and who generally inhibit expression of their impulses and feelings.*

Extroverts: *Individuals who are talkative and sociable, and who often give free reign to their impulses and feelings.*

ARCHETYPES: A KEY CONCEPT IN JUNG'S THEORY OF PERSONALITY

According to Jung, all human beings possess archetypes—shared images of figures such as heros. What other archetypes can you think of?

Sigmund Freud (1856–1939)

For many, Freud is the best-known figure in all of psychology. His theory of personality focuses on three main concepts: the id, ego, and superego. Freud believed that psychological problems are the result of early life experiences. Freud's psychoanalytic approach to therapy is still in use today, mainly among psychiatrists.

Carl Jung (1875–1961)

Jung is best known for his theories about the *collective unconscious*—accumulated awareness of the experience of past generations and civilizations.

PSYCHOLOGISTS OF NOTE

While well-reasoned objections to some of Freud's negative ideas about women constitute an important part of her contribution, Horney focused on other issues as well. She believed strongly that psychological disorders stem not from the fixation of psychic energy, as Freud saw it, but rather from disturbed interpersonal relationships experienced during childhood. In particular, she contended that parents often generate feelings of isolation and helplessness in their children—feelings that interfere with healthy development. Unfortunately, parents can produce such outcomes in many different ways—by being too dominant; by showing indifference; by providing too much approval and admiration, or by providing too little. The list of ways is a long one. In such circumstances, individuals do not develop adequately and may adopt several ineffective styles of interacting with others.

Horney described one of these styles as *moving toward people*. This pattern involves compulsively seeking affection and acceptance from others. People who show it need desperately to be liked and loved but are often unable to return true affection to those who fulfill these needs. Another pattern is termed *moving against people*. Individuals who show this approach assume that all others are hostile and that it is appropriate to manipulate and take advantage of them in any way they can. A third pattern, *moving away from people*, centers on striving for independence and privacy. People who show this pattern form few friendships and prefer privacy and isolation to social

**Karen D. Horney
(1885–1952)**

Horney was trained in Freudian psychoanalysis at the Berlin Psychological Institute. Highly critical of Freud's theory and his ideas about female sexuality, Horney split from strict Freudian ideas. She emphasized the importance of social and environmental conditions in the development of personality.

**Alfred Adler
(1870–1937)**

Adler disagreed with many of Freud's basic beliefs, especially the idea that sexual impulses are the source of personality development. Adler maintained that we are driven by the need to compensate for feelings of inferiority and to strive for superiority in our lives.

contacts. To summarize, people with these three patterns seem to go through life asking, respectively, the following questions: "Will he/she like me?" "Can he/she be useful to me?" "Will he/she interfere with me or leave me alone?" Needless to say, all of these patterns are ineffective and lead to considerable unhappiness. Only if people can overcome them through appropriate therapy can they recover from the damage produced by their early experiences with disturbed interpersonal relations.

Adler: *Striving for Superiority*

Do the views of these personality theorists reflect their own life experiences? This possibility was raised when Freud' early life was described. If there is a theorist for whom these potential links seem even stronger, it is Alfred Adler. Like Freud, Adler lived in or near Vienna. Unlike Freud, he was a pampered and sickly child. He suffered from a series of childhood illnesses that made him feel weak and awkward, especially in comparison with his strong and healthy older brother. Indeed, Adler recalled an incident in which a physician informed his father, "Your boy is lost." (He was suffering from pneumonia at the time.) In later childhood Adler worked very hard to overcome his physical disabilities. In this, he was so successful that he rose to leadership among his friends.

These early experiences had a profound impact upon Adler and led him to formulate a theory in which feelings of inferiority play a central role. According to Adler, we are motivated by feelings of inferiority, which stem initially from our small size and physical weakness during early childhood. We try to overcome these feelings through **striving for superiority**. In other words, we engage in *compensation* by striving to overcome real or imagined inferiorities by developing our abilities. If we succeed, healthy development may follow. If we overcompensate, however, we may conceal our feelings of inferiority even from ourselves, and so develop a distorted self-image.

Like several other neo-Freudians, Adler emphasized the importance of social factors in personality development. For example, he felt that birth order was an important variable: Only children are spoiled by too much parental attention, while firstborns are "dethroned" by a second child. Second-borns, Adler felt, are often competitive, since they have to struggle to catch up with an older sibling. The *family constellation*—a child's early perceptions of the family's dynamics—is also important. Later, we develop a distinctive *style of life*, in which our emotions, thoughts, and actions are directed toward the achievement of life goals we have formulated out of our strivings to overcome feelings of inferiority. In contrast to Freud, Adler believed that personality development is driven by forces other than sexual impulses, and that in order to understand adult personality, we must focus on these diverse factors.

The Neo-Freudians: *An Evaluation*

Several neo-Freudians paid a high price for their objections to features of Freud's theory: They were driven out of the group for dissenting. Was this high personal cost justified by the magnitude of their contributions? This is a difficult question to answer, but some modern psychologists would answer yes.

The theories proposed by the neo-Freudians are subject to some of the same criticisms as are applied to Freud's views. For example, they are not based on the kind of hard data that science requires; they are difficult if not impossible to test through actual research. And since these theories were often derived from case studies from the neo-Freudians' own clinical practice, they are subject to the same potential types of bias as Freud's original theories.

But—and this is an important point—the theories proposed by some neo-Freudians have served as a kind of bridge between the psychoanalytic approach and later, modern theories of personality. In particular, two of the neo-Freudians' ideas—that the ego is the most important aspect of personality, and that human relationships are a key part of life and strongly affect personality—are very similar to those of *humanistic theorists*, a group to which we will turn in the next section. Don't misunderstand: The neo-Freudians themselves did not seek to build bridges to modern psychology. Most had been trained in medicine and focused their attention on Freud's theories, not on the research and thinking of academic psychologists (Carver & Scheier, 1992). However, there was some degree of contact between these two groups of scholars, and it seems possible that the neo-Freudians contributed to the advancement of personality theory in this manner. So in a sense, the intellectual (and sometimes personal) battles waged by the neo-Freudians were not in vain. They never toppled the edifice erected by Freud, but they did help connect it to important developments that followed.

Striving for Superiority: Attempting to overcome feelings of inferiority. According to Adler, this is the primary motive for human behavior.

KEY POINTS

- Jung believed that all human beings share a collective unconscious: shared memories and images that strongly shape our perceptions of the world and our behavior.

- Horney rejected Freud's suggestion that females experience penis envy; she also contended that many psychological disorders stem largely from social factors rather than from fixation.

- Alder believed that human beings experience strong feelings of inferiority during early life. They strive to overcome these through compensation. He also believed that social factors play an important role in shaping adult personality.

Humanistic Theories: Emphasis on Growth

*I*d versus ego, Jekyll versus Hyde—on the whole, psychoanalytic theories of personality take a dim view of human nature. They contend that we must struggle constantly to control our own brutish impulses if we are to function as healthy, rational adults. Is this picture accurate? Many psychologists contend that it is not. They believe that human strivings for growth, dignity, and self-determination are just as strong as, if not stronger than, the more primitive motives Freud emphasized. Several modern theories of personality, because of their more optimistic conclusions regarding human nature, are known collectively as **humanistic theories** (Rogers, 1977, 1982; Maslow, 1970). These theories differ greatly in the concepts they employ and the aspects of personality on which they focus. However, they all share the following characteristics:

First, they emphasize the importance of *personal responsibility*. Each of us, these theories contend, is largely responsible for what happens to us. Our fate is mostly in our own hands; we are not at the mercy of dark forces within our personalities that leave us little choice but to act in certain ways. Second, while these theories don't deny the importance of past experience, they generally focus on the present. True, we may be influenced by traumatic early experiences. Yet these do not have to shape our entire adult lives, and our capacity to overcome them and to go on from there is both real and potent.

Third, humanistic theories emphasize the importance of *personal growth*. Such theories suggest that people are not content with merely having their current needs met. They wish to continue their development and to progress toward the goal of becoming the best they can be. Only when obstacles interfere with such growth is the process interrupted. A key goal of therapy, therefore, should be to help remove obstacles so that natural growth processes can continue. As examples of humanistic theories, we will now consider the influential views proposed by Carl Rogers and Abraham Maslow.

Rogers's Self Theory: Becoming a Fully Functioning Person

Carl Rogers planned to become a minister, but after exposure to several courses in psychology, he changed his mind. He decided, instead, to focus on efforts to understand the nature of human personality—and why it sometimes goes off the track. The theory Rogers formulated played an important role in the emergence of humanistic psychology and remains influential today.

One central assumption of Rogers's theory was this: Left to their own devices, human beings show many positive characteristics and move, over the course of their lives, toward becoming **fully functioning persons**. What are such individuals like? Rogers suggests that they are people who strive to experience life to the fullest, who live in the here and now, and who trust their own feelings. They are sensitive to the needs and rights of others, but they do not allow society's standards to shape their feelings or actions to an excessive degree. "If it feels like the right thing to do," such people reason, "then I should do it." Fully functioning people aren't saints; they can—and do—lose their tempers and act in ways they later regret. But throughout life, their actions become increasingly dominated by constructive impulses. They are in close touch with their own values and feelings and experience life more deeply than most other people.

Humanistic Theories: Theories of personal emphasizing personal responsibility and innate tendencies towards personal growth.

Fully Functioning Persons: In Rogers's theory, psychologically healthy persons who enjoy life to the fullest.

If all human beings possess the capacity to become fully functioning individuals, why don't they all succeed? Why, in short, aren't we surrounded by models of health and happy adjustment? The answer, Rogers contends, lies in the anxiety generated when life experiences are inconsistent with our ideas about ourselves—in short, when a gap develops between our **self-concept** (our beliefs and knowledge about ourselves) and reality, or our perceptions of it. For example, imagine an individual who believes that she is very likable and that she makes friends easily. One day she happens to overhear a conversation between two other people who describe her as moody, difficult to get along with, and definitely not very likable. She is crushed; here is information that is highly inconsistent with her self-concept. As a result of this experience, anxiety occurs, and she adopts one or more psychological defenses to reduce it. The most common of these is *distortion*—for example, the woman convinces herself that the people discussing her do not really know her very well or that they have misinterpreted her behavior. Another defense process is *denial*. Here, the woman may refuse to admit to herself that she heard the conversation or that she understood what the other people were saying.

In the short run, such maneuvers are successful: They help reduce anxiety. Ultimately, however, they produce sizable gaps between an individual's self-concept and reality. The larger such gaps, Rogers contends, the greater the individual's maladjustment and personal unhappiness (refer to Figure 12.3).

Rogers suggests that most people grow up in an atmosphere of *conditional positive regard*. They learn that others, such as their parents, will approve of them only when they behave in certain ways and express certain feelings. As a result, they are forced to deny the existence of various impulses and feelings. The all-too-common result is a badly distorted self-concept.

How can a distorted self-concept be repaired—that is, brought more closely into alignment with reality? Rogers suggests that therapists can help by placing individuals in an atmosphere of **unconditional positive regard**—a setting in which they realize that they will be accepted by another person *no matter what they say or do*. Such conditions are provided by *client-centered therapy*, a form of therapy developed by Rogers and his colleagues. We will consider client-centered therapy in detail in Chapter 15. Here, it will simply be noted that such therapy does seem to be effective in helping at least some people attain enhanced levels of personal happiness and adjustment.

Self-Concept: All the information and beliefs individuals have about their own characteristics and themselves.

Unconditional Positive Regard: *In Rogers's theory, communicating to others that they will be respected or loved regardless of what they say or do.*

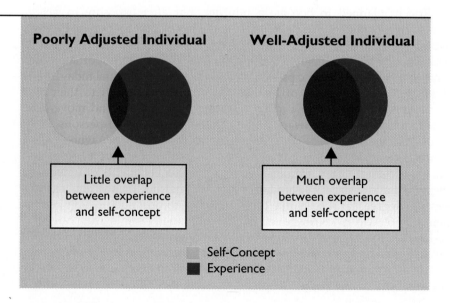

FIGURE 12.3

Rogers's View of Adjustment

According to Rogers, the larger the gap between an individual's self-concept and reality, the poorer this person's psychological adjustment.

Poorly Adjusted Individual

Well-Adjusted Individual

Little overlap between experience and self-concept

Much overlap between experience and self-concept

Self-Concept
Experience

Maslow and the Study of Self-Actualizing People

Another influential humanistic theory of personality was proposed by Abraham Maslow (1970). We encountered some of Maslow's theory—his concept of a *needs hierarchy*—in Chapter 10. As you may recall, this concept suggests that human needs exist in a pyramidal hierarchy, with *physiological needs* at the bottom, then *safety needs, belongingness needs, esteem needs*, and finally, at the top, *self-actualization needs*. According to Maslow, lower-order needs in this hierarchy must be satisfied before we can turn to more complex, higher-order needs. Thus, our basic biological needs must be at least partially met before we can concern ourselves about belonging to social networks or enhancing our self-esteem.

The needs hierarchy, however, is only part of Maslow's theory of personality. Maslow also devoted much attention to the study of people who, in his terms, are *psychologically healthy*—who have attained high levels of **self-actualization**, that is, reached their own fullest true potential. What are such people like? In essence, they are very similar to the fully functioning individuals described by Rogers. Self-actualized people accept themselves for what they are; they recognize their shortcomings as well as their strengths. Being in touch with their own personalities, they are less conformist or inhibited than most of us. Self-actualized people are well aware of the rules imposed by society but feel greater freedom to ignore them than is typical. Two additional characteristics of self-actualized people are also worthy of note. First, unlike most of us, they seem to retain their childhood wonder and amazement with the world. For them, life continues to be an exciting adventure rather than a humdrum routine. And second and finally, self-actualized people sometimes experience what Maslow describes as **peak experiences**—powerful feelings of unity with the universe and tremendous waves of power and wonder. Such experiences appear to be linked to personal growth, for after them individuals report feeling more spontaneous, more appreciative of life, and less concerned with the problems of everyday life. Examples of people Maslow describes as fully self-actualized are Thomas Jefferson, Albert Einstein, and Albert Schweitzer.

Humanistic Theories: An Evaluation

Humanistic theories of personality hit psychology like a cyclone in the 1960s and 1970s. Many psychologists quickly adopted them as a framework for understanding personality and as a basis for new forms of psychotherapy. Like all storms, however, their impact first rose to a peak and then gradually diminished. Have these theories left a lasting impact? Definitely. Many of the ideas first proposed by Rogers, Maslow, and other supporters of the humanistic perspective have entered the mainstream of psychology. For example, interest in the *self* as a central concept of personality has persisted and even spilled over into several other branches of the field (e.g., Baumeister, Heatherton, & Tice, 1993). Similarly, the contention that behavior stems more from positive forces, such as tendencies toward personal growth, than from primitive sexual and aggressive urges has done much to restore a sense of balance to current views of personality. And the importance of maintaining close contact with one's own feelings, emphasized in several humanistic theories, is seen as a positive development by many psychologists.

RICK HANSEN: AN EXAMPLE OF SELF-ACTUALIZATION

According to Maslow, only a few people become fully self-actualized. Rick Hansen could be one example. Can you think of others?

KEY POINTS

- Humanistic theories suggest that human beings strive for personal development and growth, not merely the satisfaction of biological needs.

- According to Rogers, all human beings possess the capacity to become fully functioning individuals. Often, they do not reach this stage because their distorted self-concept interferes with personal growth.

- Maslow suggests that when lower-level needs are met, human beings strive to attain self-actualization—to become the best people they can be.

Self-Actualization: A stage of personal development in which individuals reach their maximum potential.

Peak Experiences: In Maslow's theory, intense emotional experiences during which individuals feel at one with the universe.

But humanistic theories have also been subject to strong criticism. Many psychologists are uncomfortable with the strong emphasis these theories place on personal responsibility or *free will*. As you may recall, humanistic theories propose that individuals are responsible for their own actions and can readily change these if they wish to do so. To an extent, this is true. Yet this notion conflicts with *determinism*, which is the idea that behavior is determined by numerous factors and can be predicted from them. And determinism is one of the cornerstones of modern scientific psychology.

Second, many key concepts of humanistic theories are loosely defined. What, precisely, is self-actualization? A peak experience? A fully functioning person? Until such terms are clearly defined, it is difficult to know exactly what they mean and to conduct systematic research designed to test their validity.

Third, humanistic theorists have been criticized for making naive or overly optimistic assumptions about human nature. Are people really basically good? Many psychologists would answer that they are neither bad nor good. Rather, their behavior is a product of past experience, current situation, and many other factors. Assuming that people are innately good, therefore, is as untenable as assuming that they are filled with innate destructive impulses.

Self-Disclosure: *The act of revealing intimate information about oneself to another person.*

Despite these criticisms, the impact of humanistic theories has persisted. One reason is that in contrast to the psychoanalytic approach, such theories have stimulated a considerable amount of research. One line of research related to, if not always stimulated by, humanistic theories of personality is described in **The Research Process**.

THE RESEARCH PROCESS

Self-Disclosure: The Potential Benefits of Revealing Ourselves to Others

The *self-concept* plays a crucial role in several humanistic theories. Rogers (1977, 1982) suggested that it is distortions in the self-concept that block natural growth and are ultimately responsible for many forms of psychological disorder. One idea that follows logically from such suggestions is that **self-disclosure**—the process of revealing information about oneself to another person—can yield important benefits. Engaging in self-disclosure can increase the extent to which we understand ourselves. Such understanding, in turn, can help us to close gaps between our self-concept and external reality (Jourard, 1971). Does self-disclosure actually yield positive effects? Before considering the research evidence, let's focus briefly on when and how self-disclosure usually occurs.

Self-Disclosure: The Stranger-on-the-Bus Effect and Other Basic Patterns

You have probably had the experience of sitting beside someone—perhaps on a long bus ride or a cross-country flight—who begins a casual conversation and within a short time tells you intimate details about his or her life that you would prefer not to know about. Psychologists refer to this kind of incident, in which strangers engage in high levels of self-disclosure, as the *stranger-on-the-bus effect*. What makes it so interesting is that this kind of incident violates basic rules concerning when and how self-disclosure should take place. Such rules suggest that self-disclosure should be a gradual process (Altman & Taylor, 1973), increasing only as two people get to know each other better; and that it should be *reciprocal* in nature (e.g., Davis & Franzoi, 1986). Why, then, does the stranger-on-the-bus effect occur? Probably because in such situations the people involved realize that they'll never see each other again. Thus, they can act on their strong desire to "get it off their chest"—and with few, if any, consequences. If nothing else, the stranger-on-the-bus phenomenon indicates both our strong desire to bare our souls to others and our informal realization that doing so can have beneficial effects.

Individual Differences in Self-Disclosure: The Roles of Gender and Social Anxiety

As you probably know from your own experience, there are large individual differences in the tendency to engage in self-disclosure. Some people readily reveal personal information, while others are very reluctant to do so. Are there any factors that predict whether a specific person will be relatively high or low in self-disclosure? Research findings indicate that there are.

First, there appear to be small but relatively consistent gender differences in self-disclosure (Hosman, 1986). One meta-analysis covering almost 25,000 participants (Dindia & Allen, 1992) found that females engaged in slightly more self-disclosure than males. The word *slightly* should be emphasized here—the differences were far from large.

However, there is some evidence to suggest that men and women have different comfort levels with respect to reciprocal self-disclosure. An examination of dating behavior at the University of Guelph by Millar and Millar (1988), in which undergraduates monitored disclosure interactions over a two-week period, found that men were discomfited if they discerned themselves engaging in more self-disclosure than their dating partner; women felt exactly the opposite.

Another factor that plays an important role in such behavior is *social anxiety*, or *shyness*. The results of several studies indicate that socially anxious people do not show the usual reciprocity in self-disclosure. On the contrary, they engage in low to moderate levels of self-disclosure regardless of what others do (Arkin, Lake, & Baumgardner, 1986). Such effects are clearly illustrated by a study conducted recently at the University of British Columbia by Meleshko and Alden (1993). These researchers arranged for participants who were low and high in social anxiety to encounter an assistant who, during a brief interaction, demonstrated either a low or a high level of self-disclosure. As predicted, participants who were high in social anxiety did not reciprocate the assistant's behavior; they showed a moderate level of self-disclosure in both conditions. In contrast, participants low in social anxiety did engage in reciprocation: They echoed the assistant's behavior with relatively low or high levels of self-disclosure. In sum, individual differences in the tendency to engage in self-disclosure seem to be related to factors such as gender and social anxiety.

Self-Disclosure, Adjustment, and Health

Now, back to the question with which we began: Does self-disclosure confer real benefits on the people who engage in it? Growing evidence suggests that it does. In fact, there are indications that self-disclosure can be beneficial to physical as well as psychological health (Pennebaker, 1990; Pennebaker, Hughes, & O'Heeron, 1987). For example, Pennebaker, Kiecolt-Glaser, and Glaser (1988) asked students to write for about twenty minutes each day about one of two topics: their deepest thoughts and feelings concerning some traumatic event they had experienced; or their thoughts and feelings about something superficial (for instance, the decor of their living rooms). Among the traumatic events disclosed by the students were instances of rape, child abuse, intense family conflict, and the death of loved ones. Participants gave blood samples before they started writing, after the last writing session, and six weeks later. Analysis of these blood samples indicated increased functioning of the immune system among those who wrote about traumatic events, both at the end of the study and six weeks later. In addition, those who wrote about traumatic events subsequently made fewer visits to the campus health center for illness than those who wrote about trivial topics. Finally, and perhaps most revealing, those who indicated that they had revealed things in their essays that they had previously held back from others experienced the greatest improvement in immune function. That is, they benefited most from disclosing their upsetting experiences. Needless to say, such results must be replicated before they can be accepted with a high degree of confidence. Still, these and other findings indicate that self-disclosure, at least under some conditions, can be beneficial in several different ways. This

SELF-DISCLOSURE

Research shows that women engage in slightly more self-disclosure than men, especially when interacting with other women.

is what is suggested by humanistic theories of personality. It should also be pointed out that the benefits of self-disclosure are not confined to the individual. The presence of an ongoing pattern of reciprocal self-disclosure appears to be crucial to the continuation of any intimate social relationship. Many partner therapies concentrate on techniques that develop meaningful reciprocal self-disclosure (e.g., Russell, 1990; Waring, Stalker, Carver, & Gitta, 1991).

Critical Thinking Questions:

1. Can you think of other possible reasons why females engage in more self-disclosure than males, aside from prevailing gender roles or norms?

2. Do you think that the reluctance of shy individuals to reciprocate self-disclosure from others has any negative effects on their social interactions? For example, could this tendency reduce others' liking for them?

3. Engaging in self-disclosure (under appropriate circumstances and to appropriate people) seems to have important potential benefits. Why, then, are so many people so reluctant to engage in self-disclosure?

4. It has been suggested that many people seek religious confession or psychotherapy, or keep a personal diary, in order to gain the benefits of self-disclosure. Do you think this is true? If so, why? If not, why not?

Trait Theories: Seeking the Key Dimensions of Personality

When we describe other people, we often do so in terms of specific **personality traits**—stable dimensions of personality along which people may vary. This strong tendency to think about others in terms of specific characteristics is reflected in **trait theories** of personality. Such theories focus on the task of identifying key dimensions of personality—that is, the most important ways in which people differ. The basic idea behind this approach is this: Once we know *how* people differ, we can measure how *much* they differ and then go on to relate such differences to behavior in a wide range of settings.

Unfortunately, this task sounds easier than it actually is. Human beings differ in an almost countless number of ways. How can we determine which of these are most important and, perhaps, most stable? The scope of the problem was first suggested in a famous study conducted by Allport and Odbert (1936). By consulting a standard dictionary, these researchers identified fully 17,953 English words that referred to specific traits. Even when words with similar meanings were combined, 171 distinct traits remained. How can we hope to deal with this multitude of traits? One solution is to search for *clusters*—groups of traits that seem to go together. We will now examine some theories that have adopted this approach. Then we will turn to recent evidence suggesting that in the final analysis, the number of key traits or dimensions we must consider is actually relatively small.

Personality Traits: Specific dimensions along which individuals' personalities differ in consistent, stable ways.

Trait Theories: Theories of personality that focus on identifying the key dimensions along which people differ.

Allport's Central, Secondary, and Cardinal Traits

If you have a successful older sister or brother, you can empathize with Gordon Allport: He grew up in the long shadow of his brother Floyd. By the time Gordon entered Harvard as a freshman, his brother was already a graduate student. Later, Gordon actually took a course from his older brother, something few universities would permit today. But the two brothers chose different specialties in psychology: Floyd became a well-known social psychologist, while Gordon chose the study of personality.

Allport concluded that personality traits can be divided into several major categories. Of least importance are **secondary traits**, which exert relatively weak effects on behavior. More important are **central traits**: the five to ten traits that together best account for the uniqueness of an individual's personality. Finally, Allport noted that a few people are dominated by a single all-important **cardinal trait**. A few examples of such individuals and the cardinal traits that seem to have driven their personalities are Alexander the Great (ambition), Machiavelli (lust for power), and Don Juan (just plain lust).

Perhaps an even more important aspect of Allport's theory of personality is his concept of **functional autonomy** (Allport, 1965). This is the idea that patterns of behavior that are initially acquired under one set of circumstances, and that satisfy one set of motives, may later be performed for very different reasons or motives. For example, a child may at first learn to read because this pleases his teachers and parents and because failure to do so is punished. Later in life, however, the same person may read because he has come to enjoy this activity in and of itself. Notice how this contrasts with Freud's view that the roots of adult personality are planted firmly in the soil of childhood—that, as Freud himself put it, "The child is the father of the man." For Allport, such connections are not necessarily present. On the contrary, our adult behavior may spring from roots entirely different from those which gave rise to our childhood behavior.

Cattell's Surface and Source Traits

Another well-known advocate of the trait approach is Raymond Cattell. He and his colleagues have focused firmly on the task described earlier: identifying the basic dimensions of personality. Instead of beginning with hunches or insights, however, Cattell has followed a very different approach. In the course of his extensive research, literally thousands of individuals have been measured for individual differences on hundreds of traits. These responses have then been subjected to a statistical procedure known as *factor analysis*. This technique has revealed patterns in the extent to which various traits are correlated. In doing so, it has helped identify important clusters of traits. As such clusters are identified, Cattell reasons, the number of key traits in human personality will be reduced until we are left with those which are truly central.

Using this approach, Cattell and his associates (e.g., Cattell & Dreger, 1977) have identified sixteen basic **source traits**—ones he believes underlie differences in many other, less important surface traits. It is not yet clear whether this is actually the case, but at least the list Cattell proposes is more manageable in length than previous ones (refer to Table 12.2).

Five Robust Factors: *A Modern Framework*

The discussion of trait theories began with what seemed to be a fairly straightforward question: What are the key traits or dimensions of human personality? By now you realize that this issue is more complex than it seems. Fortunately, however, this is one instance where we do *not* have to leave matters dangling.

In a recent review of personality theory, Wiggins & Pincus (1992) of the University of British Columbia note a resurgence of interest in trait theory.

Secondary Traits: According to Allport, traits that exert relatively specific and weak effects upon behavior.

Central Traits: According to Allport, the five or ten traits that best describe an individual's personality.

Cardinal Trait: According to Allport, a single trait that dominates an individual's entire personality.

Functional Autonomy: In Allport's theory, maintenance of patterns of behavior by motives other than the ones originally responsible for the behavior's occurrence.

Source Traits: According to Cattell, key dimensions of personality that underlie many other traits.

TABLE 12.2

END POINTS ON SIXTEEN DIMENSIONS OF PERSONALITY

Cattell's Sixteen Basic Dimensions of Personality

According to Cattell, the sixteen *source traits* shown here underlie many other, less crucial *surface traits*. The two columns in the table list the extremes or end points for each trait (dimension). Cattell suggests that these traits are the most important or basic ones.
(Source: Adapted from the *Sixteen Personality Factor Questionnaire,* Cattell and the Institute for Personality and Ability Training, 1983).

Cool, reserved	Warm, easygoing
Concrete thinking	Abstract thinking
Easily upset	Calm and stable
Not assertive	Dominant
Sober, serious	Happy-go-lucky
Expedient	Conscientious
Shy, timid	Venturesome
Tough-minded	Tender-minded
Trusting	Suspicious
Practical	Imaginative
Forthright	Shrewd
Self-assured	Apprehensive
Conservative	Experimenting
Group-oriented	Self-sufficient
Undisciplined	Self-disciplined
Relaxed	Tense, driven

Extroversion: One of the "big five" dimensions of personality; a dimension ranging from sociable, talkative, fun-loving at one end to sober, reserved, and cautious at the other.

Agreeableness: One of the "big five" dimensions of personality; a dimension ranging from good-natured, cooperative, trusting at one end to irritable, suspicious, uncooperative at the other.

Conscientiousness: One of the "big five" dimensions of personality; a dimension ranging from well-organized, careful, responsible at one to disorganized, careless, unscrupulous at the other.

Emotional Stability: One of the "big five" dimensions of personality; a dimension ranging from poised, calm, composed at one end through nervous, anxious, excitable at the other.

Openness to Experience: One of the "big five" dimensions of personality; a dimension ranging from imaginative, sensitive, intellectual at one end to down-to-earth, insensitive, crude at the other.

One consequence has been a growing consensus that there may be only five key or central dimensions of personality (Digman, 1990; McCrae, 1989; Costa & McCrae, 1994). These are sometimes labeled the five robust dimensions:

1. **Extroversion** A dimension ranging from sociable, talkative, fun-loving, affectionate, and adventurous at one end to retiring, sober, reserved, silent, and cautious at the other.

2. **Agreeableness** A dimension ranging from good-natured, gentle, cooperative, trusting, and helpful at one end to irritable, ruthless, suspicious, uncooperative, and headstrong at the other.

3. **Conscientiousness** A dimension ranging from well-organized, careful, self-disciplined, responsible, and scrupulous at one end to disorganized, careless, weak-willed, and unscrupulous at the other.

4. **Emotional stability** A dimension ranging from poised, calm, composed, and not hypochondriacal at one end to nervous, anxious, excitable, and hypochondriacal at the other.

5. **Openness to experience** A dimension ranging from sensitive, intellectual, polished, and imaginative at one end to down-to-earth, insensitive, narrow, crude, and simple at the other.

How basic, and therefore important, are the "big five" robust dimensions? Many researchers believe that the answer is clear: *very basic.* This is indicated, in part, by the fact that most people, in many different cultures, refer to these dimensions when describing themselves (Funder & Colvin, 1991). In addition, three dimensions are readily apparent to total strangers, even in a very brief meeting (Watson, 1989). Compelling evidence for this latter conclusion is provided by an important study conducted recently by Funder and Sneed (1993).

These researchers videotaped pairs of unacquainted students as they interacted with each other for the first time. The researchers coded sixty-two different behaviors, such as "has high enthusiasm and energy level," "says or does interesting things," "shows lack of interest in the interaction," "appears relaxed and comfortable," "expresses hostility," "speaks fluently." A second group of participants then rated each of these behaviors for its usefulness in determining where others stood on each of the "big five" personality dimensions—conscientiousness, extroversion, agreeableness, and so on. Finally, two people very familiar with each participant described each participant's personality. On the basis of these descriptions, a rating of each participant for each of the big five dimensions was obtained.

With all these data in hand, Funder and Sneed (1993) could address two questions: First, are the behaviors people believe are important in rating others' personalities the ones we actually use in judging them? And second, are these behaviors actually useful in making such judgments accurately? The answer to both questions was a clear *yes*. When they made judgments about others' personalities, strangers did tend to use the behaviors identified by participants as useful. And these behaviors were indeed useful, in that they were closely related to the descriptions provided by those who knew the subjects well. This was especially true for three of the big five dimensions— extroversion, agreeableness, and conscientiousness—although it was less true for emotional stability and did not seem to hold for openness. In sum, where people stand on several of the big five dimensions is readily apparent in their behavior; even on the basis of very brief meetings, we can make fairly accurate judgments about their standing on each of these dimensions.

JOHN CANDY: AN EXAMPLE OF EXTROVERSION

According to the five-factor theory of personality, there are only five key dimensions that make up personality, and extroversion is one of them. How would you describe yourself on each trait?

Trait Theories: *An Evaluation*

In the 1990s, most research on personality has reflected the trait approach. Instead of seeking to propose and test grand theories such as the ones offered by Freud, Jung, and Rogers, most personality psychologists currently direct their efforts to the task of understanding specific traits—ones that appear to exert important effects upon behavior in key areas of life (Ball & Zuckerman, 1992; Friedman et al., 1993). This trend is due both to the success of the trait approach and to the obvious shortcomings of the grand theories described in earlier sections of this chapter.

This is not to imply that the trait approach is perfect, however. On the contrary, it, too, can be criticized in several respects. First, it is largely descriptive in nature. It seeks to describe the key dimensions of personality but does not attempt to determine how various traits develop or how they influence behavior. Thus, in a sense, the trait approach has not generated fully developed theories of personality in the way that other approaches have. Second, despite several decades of careful research, there is still no final agreement about which traits are most important and constitute the basic dimensions of personality. The five robust factors described earlier come closest to this goal, but acceptance of these is by no means universal, and they have not emerged as separate and distinct aspects of personality in all research studies (Church & Burke, 1994; Waller & Ben-Porath, 1987).

As you can readily see, these criticisms relate primarily to what the trait approach has not yet accomplished rather than to its findings or proposals. All in all, we can conclude that the trait approach is very useful to personality studies. It is also worth emphasizing that this approach is very broadly applicable. It not only provides a basis for understanding how humans differ from one another; it can also be applied to differences found within other

KEY POINTS

- Allport suggested that human beings possess a small number of central traits that account for much of their uniqueness.
- Cattell has identified sixteen source traits that he believes underlie differences between individuals on many specific dimensions.
- Research findings point to the conclusion that there are only five basic dimensions of personality: extroversion, agreeableness, conscientiousness, emotional stability, and openness to experience.

species. An example of the application of trait theory to animal behavior is furnished by Jennifer Mather of the University of Lethbridge and her colleague Roland Anderson of the Seattle Aquarium. Mather and Anderson (1993) undertook a trait analysis of octopus behavior. Three major dimensions of temperament, or personality, on which individual octopuses differed—activity, reactivity, and avoidance—were found to account for a substantial portion of octopus behavior. Activity refers to the degree to which an octopus is alert and interactively responsive to stimulation. Reactivity refers to whether it is anxious or calm in various situations. Avoidance refers to whether it tends to withdraw or display boldness in its interactions with the world. Other applications of trait theory to animals have looked at fish (Huntingford, 1976) and monkeys (Stevenson-Hinde, Stillwell-Barnes, & Zunz, 1980).

There is much to be said in favor of an interpretive framework that can span species differences the way trait theory can. Using this approach to gain insight into how people or animals differ seems to be a useful approach to understanding the uniqueness and consistency of key aspects of both human and animal behavior.

Learning Approaches to Personality

Whatever their focus, all personality theories must ultimately come to grips with two basic questions: What accounts for the *uniqueness* of human behavior? And what underlies its *consistency*? Freud's answer focused almost entirely on internal factors—hidden conflicts between the id, ego, and super-ego and the active struggle to keep unacceptable impulses out of consciousness. At the other end of the continuum are approaches to personality that emphasize the role of learning and experience.

While such views were not at first presented as formal theories of personality, they are often described as *learning theories of personality* to distinguish them from other perspectives (Bandura, 1986; Rotter, 1982; Skinner, 1974).

How can a learning perspective account for the uniqueness and consistency of human behavior? Very readily. Uniqueness, the learning approach contends, merely reflects the fact that we have all experienced distinctive life (and learning) experiences. Similarly, the learning approach can explain consistency in behavior over time and across situations simply by noting that responses, associations, and habits acquired through learning tend to persist. Also, since people often find themselves in situations very similar to the ones in which they acquired these tendencies, their behavior, too, tends to remain quite stable.

Early learning-oriented views of personality demonstrated another important characteristic. In general, learning theorists denied the importance of considering virtually *any* internal causes of behavior, such as motives, traits, intentions, and goals (Skinner, 1974). According to these theorists, the only things that mattered were external conditions determining patterns of reinforcement; recall the discussion of this topic in Chapter 5. At present, few psychologists agree with this position: Most now believe that internal factors play a crucial role in behavior. Moreover, several theorists contend that these internal factors must be carefully considered if we are ever to understand both uniqueness and consistency in human behavior. As an example of this approach, which more accurately reflects the flavor of modern psychology, we will now consider the *social cognitive theory* proposed by Bandura (1986).

Social Cognitive Theory: Reciprocal Causality in Human Behavior

In his **social cognitive theory**, Albert Bandura notes that people do indeed acquire many forms of behavior through basic processes of learning—operant conditioning and classical conditioning. He adds, however, that a third form—observational learning, described in Chapter 5—is of special importance. In observational learning, individuals acquire both information and new forms of behavior through observing others (Bandura, 1977). Such learning plays a role in a very wide range of human activities, from aggression (which can be acquired by observing violent models in daily life or in the media) to task performance (which can often be acquired from watching other people at work or from instructional videotapes and manuals).

Bandura also calls attention to the fact that learning is far from the entire story where human behavior and personality are concerned. Many cognitive factors also play a role. Unlike many other animals, Bandura notes, human beings do not respond passively or automatically to the external conditions around them. Instead, they plan, form expectancies, set goals, imagine various outcomes, and so on. In short, people's actions are often strongly determined by a wide range of factors that were totally ignored both by early behaviorists and by early learning theories of personality.

In addition, Bandura (1986) notes, human beings often demonstrate an impressive capacity for the *self-regulation* of their own behavior. While people may often respond to external factors such as positive reinforcement and punishment, they sometimes choose to ignore these and to operate in terms of internal standards and values. We set our own goals, and we often provide our own rewards when we reach them—a process known as **self-reinforcement**. These rewards range from a self-applied pat on the back to more generalized feelings of personal accomplishment. For example, consider the hundreds of amateur runners who participate in marathons. Few believe that they have any chance of winning and obtaining the external reinforcements offered—status, fame, cash prizes. Why, then, do they run? It is because, Bandura would contend, they have *self-determined goals,* such as finishing the race or merely going as far as they can. Meeting these goals is sufficient to initiate what is obviously very effortful behavior.

Another important concept in Bandura's theory is **self-efficacy**—an individual's sense of his or her ability to carry out a desired action (Bandura, 1986). The higher a person's feelings of self-efficacy, the better that person tends to do at a wide range of tasks. Such success, of course, can ultimately lead to more generalized positive feelings about oneself. We'll return to such feelings (often termed *self-esteem*) below.

Other learning-oriented approaches to personality share a similar perspective. For example, the *social learning theory* proposed by Julian Rotter (1954, 1982) suggests that the likelihood that a given behavior will occur in a specific situation is a function of the individual's *expectancies* concerning the outcomes the behavior will produce and the *reinforcement value* that individual attaches to such outcomes—the degree to which one reinforcer is preferred over another.

Also according to Rotter, on the basis of their experience, individuals form generalized expectancies concerning the extent to which their own actions determine the outcomes

Social Cognitive Theory: A theory of behavior suggesting that human behavior is influenced by many cognitive factors as well as by reinforcement contingencies, and that human beings have an impressive capacity to regulate their own actions.

Self-Reinforcement: The delivery of rewards to oneself for reaching one's self-set goals.

Self-Efficacy: Individuals' expectations concerning their ability to perform various tasks.

TV AND VIOLENCE

According to Bandura, children learn that aggression is acceptable—and sometimes even admirable—through watching violent models on television.

- Learning approaches to personality suggest that personality is strongly influenced by basic forms of learning. Early learning theories of this type denied the importance of internal factors such as goals and expectancies.

- More modern learning approaches, such as Bandura's social cognitive theory, assume that behavior is influenced by cognitive factors and personal dispositions as well as by reinforcement contingencies and the social and physical environment.

- Rotter's social learning approach calls attention to the importance of generalized expectancies concerning the internal or external control of outcomes.

Internals: In Rotter's terms, individuals who believe that they exert considerable control over the outcomes they experience.

Externals: In Rotter's terms, individuals who believe that they have little control over the outcomes they experience.

they experience. Rotter calls people who strongly believe that they shape their own destinies **internals**; those who believe their outcomes are largely the result of forces outside their control, he calls **externals**. As you can probably guess, internals are often happier and better adjusted. Note again how in this theory, internal factors such as subjective estimates concerning the likelihood of various outcomes, subjective reactions to these, and generalized expectancies of personal control play an important role in behavior. Certainly, such contentions contrast very sharply with the view, stated in early learning approaches to personality, that only external reinforcements need to be taken into account.

Evaluation of the Learning Approach

Do all human beings confront an Oedipus conflict? Are peak experiences real, and do they really constitute a sign of growing self-actualization? Considerable controversy exists with respect to these and many other aspects of psychoanalytic and humanistic theories of personality. In contrast, virtually all psychologists agree that behaviors are acquired and modified through basic processes of learning. Moreover, in the 1990s, after the "cognitive revolution" of the 1970s and 1980s (see Chapters 6 and 7), there is general agreement about the importance of cognitive factors in human behavior. Thus, a key strength of the learning approach is obvious: It is based on widely accepted principles in psychology, principles for which there is an impressive amount of evidence.

Another positive feature of this framework for understanding personality lies in the fact that it has been put to effective, practical use in modifying maladaptive behaviors. Learning theory has proved quite useful in treating a wide range of psychological disorders (Sherman, 1990).

An illustration of how the kinds of learning experiences one has early in life can permanently influence personality is provided in **The Point of It All**, which explains how a very unusual form of personality can develop if children are required to learn how to cope with responsibilities normally assumed by parents.

THE POINT OF IT ALL

The Atlas Personality

Children are commonly required to assume responsibilities for various household chores and to help look after younger siblings. In some families, however, the responsibilities the child assumes go far beyond these reasonable limits. Two researchers at St. Michael's Hospital in Toronto have outlined some of the consequences of this. Vogel and Savva (1993) focus on children who find themselves in troubled and chaotic family settings, where one or both parents are incapable of managing their own lives and family responsibilities. Often, one of the children gradually assumes more and more responsibility for managing both the household and the parents. This child tends to develop what Vogel and Savva term an *Atlas personality*. This term refers to the Greek god Atlas, who in Greek mythology was sentenced to bear the burden of supporting the heavens on his shoulders. The child, in effect, is sentenced to support the family on his or her shoulders.

Typically, the parents are incapable of providing direction, control, or support. The child has to learn to anticipate and deal with recurrent destructive encounters and with the often erratic emotional excesses and demands made by the parents. Often the child is forced to learn how to mediate disputes between the parents, and between parents and other family members, all the while endeavoring to conceal from the community the disorder with the household. Instead of being sheltered and protected and nourished, these children have to provide shelter, protection, and nourishment for others.

Consider one of the cases detailed by Vogel and Savva. The mother was described as immature, unstable, unable to deal with stress, and given to emotional excess. The father was described as reclusive and impulsive, often lashing out in rage at family members. The child growing up in this setting assumed primary responsibility for household management and meal preparation. She was required to deal at a very young age with crises, such as her brother's attempt to run away from home and her father's disposition for violence. As she grew older she had to find a way of preventing the father's assaultive behavior, which was increasingly directed against her brother. When the father died, the mother refused to accept any responsibility for the brother, and it fell to the girl to stand in for the mother.

What children learn in such an environment is to focus their concern on the welfare of others and to ignore or deny their own personal needs. When these children become adults, they continue to display the same excessive sensitivity and concern for the needs and welfare of others. What they do not learn is how to recognize and address their own needs. In later life, they tend to be chronically depressed and continually anxious for reasons that are not clear to them. Their focus on the needs of others is so extreme that even in therapy, they display an extraordinary concern for the well-being of the therapist. In group therapy settings, Vogel and Savva report, they often intrude to protect and defend individuals they think are not being given fair treatment. These people provide a sad example of what can happen when children are assigned responsibilities beyond those that are reasonable for their age. They also illustrate clearly how coping and life management practices learned within the family setting can permanently shape one's personality.

Criticism of the learning theory approach focuses mainly on various features of early learning theories rather than on the newer and more sophisticated theories proposed by Bandura (1986) and others. The early behaviorist theories generally ignored the role of cognitive factors in human behavior and often assumed that principles uncovered in research with animals would transfer readily to human beings. These views ignored the human capacity for self-regulation of behavior and the important fact that cognitive factors such as beliefs and expectancies may often be more important determinants of overt actions than reinforcement contingencies.

Clearly, these criticisms do not apply to new learning approaches such as social cognitive theory. In fact, it is fair to state that these social cognitive theories of personality are more in tune than any others with modern psychology's eclectic approach. As such, they are certain to play an important role in continuing efforts to understand many aspects of personality. See **Key Concept** on page 518 for an overview of several major theories of personality discussed in this chapter.

Key Aspects of Personality: A Sample of Recent Research

*I*n recent decades, efforts to understand personality have undergone a major shift. Instead of trying to construct grand theories, psychologists have concentrated on identifying and investigating key aspects of personality. One idea behind this approach is that a fuller understanding of personality will gradually emerge from knowledge about these factors and the ways in which they interact. Reflecting this modern approach, let us now look at modern research findings concerning several intriguing aspects of personality.

Major Theories of Personality: An Overview

Theory/Major Advocate	Major Focus	Key Concepts
Psychoanalytic  Freud	Levels of consciousness	Conscious, preconscious, unconscious
	States of psychosexual development	Oral, anal, phallic, latency, genital
	Anxiety and Defense Mechanisms	Repression, rationalization, displacement, projection, regression 
Humanistic Theories  Rogers	Personal growth, personal responsibility, the present rather than the past	Self-concept, self-actualization  Maslow
Trait Theories  Recent finding indicate that individual differences in shyness—one aspect of temperament—are present shortly after birth and tend to persist through life.	Stable dimensions of personality along which people vary	Cardinal traits, central traits, surface and source traits
		The big five dimensions of personality  Even if you had just met him briefly, it would be apparent to you that John Candy rated high on extroversion—one of the "big five" dimensions of personality.
Learning Approaches	Role of basic learning processes in uniqueness and stability of individual behavior	Operant conditioning, observational learning 
	Self-regulation of behavior	Self-efficacy
		Internal versus external locus of control

Aspects of the Self: *Self-Perception, Self-Esteem, and Self-Monitoring*

Many theorists have suggested that in several respects, *self-concept*—our beliefs and knowledge about ourselves—plays a crucial role in personality (Benesch & Page, 1989). Reflecting this, much current research on personality is concerned with investigating various aspects of the self. Here, we'll focus on three such aspects: self-perception, self-esteem, and self-monitoring.

SELF-PERCEPTION: KNOWING YOUR OWN PERSONALITY Is there something special about self-perception that sets it apart from the perception of others? The fact of the matter is that we do seem to accord ourselves a special status. A series of experiments undertaken by Sande, of the University of Manitoba, and his colleagues required undergraduates to make judgments about the personality traits they possessed and about the personality traits they would attribute to others of the same age and sex (Sande, Goethals, & Radloff 1988). Participants consistently judged themselves to have a wider variety of traits and to be more complex and less predictable than casual acquaintances. Why should this be so? Sande and colleagues suggest this as a major reason: As individuals, we have a long history of personal experience to draw upon when it comes to assessing our own behavior. Because we are aware how wide and varied our behavior has been in different situations, we are inclined to conclude that our personality is more complex and multifaceted than that of people whose behavior we have observed in only a limited number of situations. Extra credence is lent to this interpretation by this fact: When we are asked to make comparative personality judgments about the traits of people who are close to us, and whose inner thought processes we are familiar with, we judge those people to have a more complex constellation of personality traits than do casual acquaintances.

Whether all of this has significant behavioral consequences remains to be determined. In the interim, it is probably wise to resist our tendencies to underestimate the personality complexities of causal acquaintances.

SELF-ESTEEM: SOME EFFECTS OF FEELING GOOD—OR BAD—ABOUT OURSELVES How do you feel about yourself? Generally good? Generally bad? Most people tend to hold relatively a favorable view of themselves; they realize that they aren't perfect, but in general they conclude that their good points outweigh their bad ones. Large individual differences exist with respect to such self-evaluation, however, so one important aspect of the self is **self-esteem**: the extent to which our self-evaluations are favorable or not (Campbell, 1990; Epstein, 1983).

As you can probably guess, self-esteem is related to many forms of behavior. Higher levels of self-esteem in early adolescence are associated with more mature personality functions and greater adaptivity (Marton, Golombek, Stein, & Korenblum, 1988). Adults who are high in self-esteem tend to report fewer negative emotions and less depression than those who are low in self-esteem (Straumann & Higgins, 1988). It is also found that people high in self-esteem are better able to handle stress and experience fewer negative health effects when exposed to it (Brown & McGill, 1989).

Findings reported recently by Straumann, Lemieux, and Coe (1993) help explain why this may be so. They induced anxious, depressed, or control participants to think about themselves by asking them to consider questions about various traits—for example, "Is it important for you to be … ?" "Would your parents say that they want you to be … ?" Participants' answers to other questions were used to measure the gap between their ideal and actual selves. As expected, this gap was larger for depressed and anxious participants

Self-Esteem: The extent to which individuals have positive or negative feelings about themselves and their own worth.

than for controls. In addition, both anxious and depressed participants—who, presumably, were lower in self-esteem than controls—showed signs of reduced immune efficiency when they thought about themselves: Activity in their immune system's natural "killer cells" decreased. The controls, who presumably had higher self-esteem, did not experience such effects. These findings are consistent with the view that low self-esteem, or states linked to it, can reduce the effectiveness of the immune system, thus placing low-self-esteem individuals at increased risk for many illnesses.

Other findings indicate that people high in self-esteem, as compared with those who are low in self-esteem, are less susceptible to influence (Wylie, 1974) and more confident of achieving their goals (Wells & Marwell, 1976). They are also more effective in social situations—that is, they make more favorable impressions on others (Baron & Byrne, 1994).

Finally, people low and high in self-esteem also differ with respect to clarity of self-concept. Those low in self-esteem report less confidence in their judgments when asked to rate themselves on various traits; they also show less tendency to report the same ratings over time than do people with high self-esteem (Campbell, 1990). In addition, people low in self-esteem show less consistency in their self-ratings. When asked to rate the extent to which adjectives that are opposite in meaning describe them, they are more likely than people with high self-esteem to say that both opposite adjectives apply (Campbell, 1990). Together, these findings suggest that people low in self-esteem have self-concepts that are less clear or well-developed than those of people high in self-esteem (Conway & Giannopoulos, 1993). This uncertainty has been found to be negatively related to resistance to stress: People who have a less clear-cut self-concept are more vulnerable to the harmful effects of stress (Brown & Smart, 1989). This interesting finding has important applications to health. We will discuss individual differences in resistance to stress in Chapter 13.

Looking back over these diverse findings, it is easy to conclude that high self-esteem is desirable, while low self-esteem is undesirable and perhaps even dangerous to one's health. In general, these conclusions are true. But recent findings indicate that high self-esteem, too, can sometimes have its costs. People high in self-esteem may sometimes suffer from *overconfidence*—that is, unrealistically optimistic expectations. For example, they may set unrealistic goals or commit themselves to doing more than they can actually accomplish (Vallone et al., 1990). Direct evidence for these effects is provided by research carried out by Baumeister, Heatherton, and Tice (1993).

These investigators reasoned that under normal conditions, people high in self-esteem have an edge over those who are low in self-esteem with respect to performing many tasks, because they have more complete and consistent self-knowledge and can do a better job of choosing the most desirable goals—ones that are challenging but within their reach. However, the situation changes radically when people with high self-esteem are exposed to threats to their ego from negative feedback. Under these conditions, they may become unduly concerned with protecting their favorable self-concept, and this may interfere with their performance. In contrast, people low in self-esteem do not react as strongly to ego threats and so should suffer smaller decrements in performance in a negative-feedback situation.

To test these predictions, Baumeister and his colleagues (1993) had high- and low-self-esteem participants play a computer game in which they navigated an airplane through an obstacle course. Before playing the game, participants worked on another task: coming up with as many uses as possible for a doughnut. Some were told that they did very well on this task and were highly creative, while others received negative feedback. While playing the computer game, participants were told that they must bet on the outcome.

They had to bet at least 25 cents of the three-dollar payment they received, but they could bet anything up to the full amount. If they met a criterion based on their doughnut performance, they would receive triple their bet; if they failed to meet it, they would lose the entire bet. Baumeister and his colleagues predicted that after receiving failure feedback (an ego threat), participants with high self-esteem would be more likely to make inappropriate bets and would actually do worse than those low in self-esteem. After receiving success feedback, however, they would do better than low-self-esteem participants. As shown in Figure 12.4, this is precisely what happened.

So high self-esteem is generally but not always a plus. Under most conditions, people with high self-esteem are better at regulating their own behavior than people with low self-esteem. As a result, they may well set themselves up for confirmation of their favorable self-concept: One success, stemming from wisely chosen goals, follows another. When their ego is threatened, however, such people may focus on the task of protecting or restoring their self-esteem, and in doing so slip into ineffective, self-defeating strategies. In contrast, people with low self-esteem are accustomed to being "kicked around" in life and may not suffer equal decrements in performance. In such situations, then, self-esteem may fail to confer the kinds of benefits with which it is usually associated.

SELF-MONITORING: PUBLIC APPEARANCE AND PRIVATE REALITY Respond to each of the following statements with *true* or *false*:

- When I am uncertain how to act in social situations, I look to the behavior of others for cues.

- In different situations and with different people, I often act like very different people.

- My behavior is usually an expression of my true inner feelings, attitudes, and beliefs.

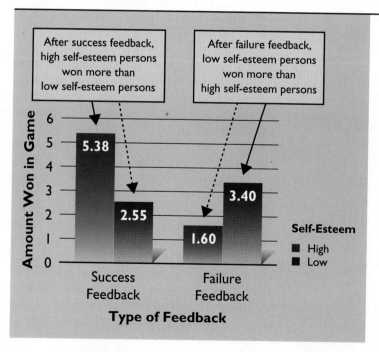

FIGURE 12.4

When High Self-Esteem Can Hurt

When they received feedback indicating they had failed at a preliminary task, individuals high in self-esteem actually did worse in terms of making appropriate bets, and so won less money, than those who were low in self-esteem. In contrast, when both groups received feedback indicating they had succeeded, those high in self-esteem did better than those low in self-esteem. These findings indicate that in situations involving ego threat, high self-esteem can actually interfere with performance. (Source: Based on data from Baumeister, Heatherton, & Tice, 1993.)

- I would not change my opinions or the way I do things to please someone else or to win their favor.

If you answered *true* to the first two statements but *false* to the remaining two, you may well be high in another interesting dimension of personality. In contrast, if you answered *false* to the first two and *true* to the others, you may well be relatively low on this dimension. This trait, **self-monitoring**, relates mainly to the ability to adapt one's behavior to the demands of a current social situation. People high in self-monitoring are social chameleons—they can change their behavior to match the current situation. (Chameleons are small lizards capable of altering their skin color to match different backgrounds.) If high self-monitors find themselves among beer-drinking construction workers, they roll up their sleeves and swig some beer. If, instead, they find themselves among wine connoisseurs, they roll *down* their sleeves and sip with the best of them. In short, they adjust what they say and what they do to the current situation in order to make a positive impression on others (Snyder, 1987; Snyder & Gangestad, 1986). In contrast, low self-monitors tend to show a higher degree of consistency: They act much the same across a wide range of situations.

Self-monitoring involves several other factors, such as the ability to control and modify one's own behavior, or skill in what might be termed *acting*; sensitivity to the expressive behaviors of others (Lennox & Wolfe, 1984); willingness to serve as the center of attention; and concern with being liked by others (Briggs & Cheek, 1988). High self-monitors exceed low self-monitors on all of these dimensions.

Self-monitoring plays a role in many different aspects of behavior. First, consider choice of friends. Low self-monitors are often closely attuned to their own attitudes and values. Thus, it seems reasonable to expect that they will often like others who resemble themselves in various ways—people who share their views and beliefs. In contrast, high self-monitors realize that they often act differently in different situations. As a result, they may like and choose as friends others who share their preferences for specific activities—people who enjoy doing the same things (Jamiesen, Lydon, & Zanna, 1987).

Given the character of high-self monitors, and their ability to adapt readily to different situations, it will probably not surprise you that they often become leaders in group situations. High self-monitors are adept at reading social cues to determine the acceptability of leadership behavior and the behavior that is most appropriate for achieving leadership.

Studies carried out by researchers at Sir Wilfred Laurier University and the University of Guelph indicate that this is especially true if the task or responsibilities of a situation require group effort and consensus (Ellis, 1988; Crownshaw & Ellis, 1991). Consonant with these findings is evidence reported by Kirchmeyer (1990) of the University of Lethbridge that in the business world the domain of office politics tends to be dominated by highly self-monitoring men and women.

Finally, high self-monitors are much better than low self-monitors at certain kinds of social deception. For example, they are better at managing their own nonverbal cues to conceal their true reactions (Friedman & Miller-Herringer, 1991). They have to be—an person considered to be displaying a high level of self-monitoring activity in social interactions may be viewed as lacking in sincerity. This was borne out in a study made by Jiujias and Horvarth (1991) at Acadia University. An individual engaged in a social interaction was

Self-Monitoring: A personality trait involving sensitivity to social situations and an ability to adapt one's behavior to the demands of those situations in order to make favorable impressions upon others.

Sensation Seeking: A trait relating to the extent to which individuals seek and enjoy high levels of stimulation.

KEY POINTS

- People high in self-esteem are generally happier, healthier, and more successful at many tasks than those who are low in self-esteem. They also have a more consistent and well-developed self-concept.

- High self-esteem is not always beneficial, however. Under conditions of ego threat, people high in self-esteem may experience larger decrements in performance than those who are low in self-esteem.

- High self-monitors are better at reading others and at making favorable impressions. In contrast, low self-monitors show more consistent behavior across situations.

- High self-monitors are more successful at social deception, partly because they are better at regulating their own expressive behavior.

less well liked when she was deemed to be engaging in a high level of self-monitoring than when she was deemed to be engaging in a low level of self-monitoring. Without question, there are many times when it is important to engage in self-monitoring and not to betray one's true feelings. Athletes aren't supposed to gloat openly after defeating their opponents, and therapists are supposed to refrain from acting like the character in the cartoon on the right—no matter what their patients say.

"Why, you swine!"

Sensation Seeking: The Desire for Stimulation

Most of us know people who seem to seek out excitement. Psychologists describe this activity as **sensation seeking**—acting on the desire for new, exciting experiences (Zuckerman, 1990). Sensation seeking is an aspect of personality that has received increasing attention from psychologists. Research indicates that high sensation-seekers drive faster (Zuckerman & Neeb, 1980); and are more likely to engage in substance abuse (Teichman, Barnea, & Rahav, 1989), more likely to get into trouble with the law while teenagers (Hamilton, 1983), and more likely to engage in high-risk sports such as skydiving (Humbaugh & Garrett, 1974). In short, they often lead lives in which they actively seek thrills and adventure wherever and however they can find them.

What accounts for this preference for dangerous behaviors and for the high levels of arousal they produce? Zuckerman (1984, 1990), the psychologist who first called attention to this aspect of personality, believes that it has important roots in biological processes. High sensation-seekers, he suggests, are people whose nervous systems operate best at high levels of arousal. The optimal level of arousal is much higher for them than for other people, so they seek situations and activities that will create this level.

Considerable evidence supports this. First, high sensation-seekers show stronger *orienting response* to the initial presentation of an unfamiliar auditory or visual stimulus (Zuckerman, Simons, & Como, 1988). In other words, they seem to pay more attention to such stimuli than do other people. Second, high sensation-seekers show greater ability to ignore irrelevant information (Martin, 1986). In sum, they are better able than low sensation-seekers to zero in on new stimuli and give them their full attention. Such effects are clearly illustrated in a study conducted by Ball and Zuckerman (1992). These researchers asked high and low sensation-seekers to perform a *shadowing* task. Different lists of words were presented simultaneously to each ear. They were to repeat out loud only the words they heard in one ear. It was found that high sensation-seekers made fewer errors than low sensation-seekers. Moreover, their performance improved more quickly than that of low sensation-seekers; this indicated that they could focus their attention more quickly.

Additional evidence for the view that sensation seeking is closely related to biological processes comes from research on patients undergoing treatment for pain. High sensation-seekers had lower levels of *endorphins*—substances produced within our brains that act somewhat like opiates—than low sensation-seekers (Johansson et al., 1979). Since endorphins are released by the body after painful experiences, one interpretation of

HIGH-RISK SPORTS: A FAVORITE PASTIME OF HIGH SENSATION-SEEKERS

People who rate high in sensation seeking are attracted to activities like white-water kayaking.

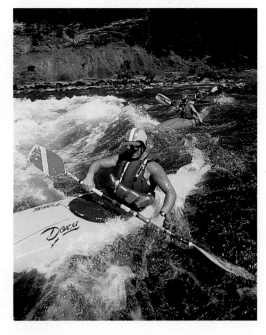

these findings is that the bodies of high sensation-seekers work less hard to counteract pain—one source of high arousal and stimulation.

Whatever the precise basis for high sensation-seeking, it is clear that people demonstrating this characteristic often engage in behaviors that expose them to danger. Does high sensation-seeking always have negative implications for personal health or safety? There are some grounds for predicting that this may not be true. It seems possible, for example, that people high in sensation-seeking may be better able to tolerate the emotional arousal produced by stressful life events. After all, their nervous systems operate best under high arousal, so they may be able to cope with stress more effectively than can people who are low in sensation seeking. Research by Smith, Ptacek, and Smoll (1992) provides support for this prediction. These psychologists found that high school athletes high in sensation seeking were actually *less* likely than athletes who were low in sensation seeking to experience injuries following stress (such as strong criticism from coaches). One interpretation of these findings is that the high sensation-seekers were indeed better able to cope with stress than the low sensation-seekers and so had fewer injuries.

As is true for other aspects of personality, therefore, the effects of high sensation-seeking are neither uniformly negative nor uniformly positive. In many cases, being high on this dimension does appear to have negative implications for one's health and well-being; but this is not always the case. In fact, in one area of life—participation in sports—being high in sensation seeking may confer important benefits.

Can knowledge about personality be put to practical use? For information on this, see **Canadian Focus**.

KEY POINTS

- High sensation-seekers prefer higher levels of arousal than low sensation-seekers.
- High sensation-seekers show stronger orientation responses and are better able to focus their attention on new stimuli.
- High sensation-seekers are also better able to withstand the effects of stress than low sensation-seekers, and so experience fewer accidents in athletics following exposure to high levels of stress.

☀ CANADIAN FOCUS

The Role of Personality Factors in Adjusting to Life in a New Culture

Moving to a new country as a student to undertake a program of study, or as an immigrant to take up permanent residence, can be stressful. For example, Asian students, who have a very different cultural background, often find university in Canada to be very stressful. Evidence of this has been provided by Chataway and Berry (1989). Similar findings were reported in an extensive study by Kathryn Mickel of York University (Bowen, 1986), which involved a variety of Canadian universities. The stress experienced by newcomers reflects not only difficulties in adjusting to a new country, but also the effects of the prejudice and discrimination often encountered. The resulting pressure can affect both the mental and the physical health of newcomers (Chataway & Berry, 1989; Dion & Giordano, 1990).

In an effort to understand what personality characteristics would serve to cushion newcomers against the effects of acculturation and discrimination, Dion, Dion, and Pak (1992) studied a large number of volunteers from Toronto's Chinese community. These people filled out an extensive questionnaire that probed for information about personality characteristics and health-related problems of a psychological nature (e.g., sleep difficulties, headaches, worries, and mood disturbances). Information was also requested about the amount of readjustment that participants had to undergo in coping with a wide variety of life events, and the degree of satisfaction felt regarding these readjustments.

As expected, health-related problems of a psychological nature were found to increase with adjustment difficulties and with perceived (and experienced) discrimination. Interestingly, the degree to which health problems were experienced depended on personality factors, two of which were found to be important: self-esteem, which as pointed out earlier influences stress tolerance and health; and the individual's perceived sense of personal control. A high level of self-esteem together with a strong sense of personal control was found to be effective in cushioning participants from physical and psychological problems associated with stress.

This does not mean that an exaggerated sense of confidence and an unrealistic conviction of personal control will facilitate coping with a new culture. Dion, Dion, and Pak emphasize that there must be a genuine basis for both high self-esteem and feelings of personal control. The individuals in their study who reported these did have higher educational levels, better English, and greater professional experience.

What conclusions can be drawn? It seems clear that individuals entering a different culture with a substantial measure of self-confidence and a strong sense of personal control will be more able to cope with the stress produced by acculturation and discrimination than those who are lacking in these attributes.

MAKING PSYCHOLOGY PART OF YOUR LIFE

How Accurate Is Your Self-Concept?

Self-knowledge is a useful thing; the better we understand ourselves, the better the choices we can make in many contexts and the more accurately we can predict our reactions to many events or situations. In addition, several theories of personality suggest that the more accurate our self-concept, the happier and better adjusted we will be (Maslow, 1970; Rogers, 1982). How well do you know yourself? Follow these procedures and find out:

First, make about ten copies of the questionnaire below. Next, complete one copy yourself. Then give copies (blank, of course, except for your name in the space for it) to several people who know you well—good friends, family members, romantic partners. Try to have at least five to ten people provide ratings. Finally, average their ratings on each dimension and then compare these averages with your own ratings. The larger the differences, the less accurate your self-concept. Do you find any dimensions on which your perceptions of yourself are sharply different from those of others—showing scale differences of one point or more? If so, consider why these differences exist. The insight you gain into your own traits may prove very valuable.

Rate _____ on each of the dimensions below. Circle one number to indicate where he/she falls on this dimension (4 is the middle of the scale).

1. Cautious   Adventurous
       1   2   3   4   5   6   7

2. Insensitive   Sensitive
       1   2   3   4   5   6   7

3. Calm   Anxious
       1   2   3   4   5   6   7

4. Cooperative   Uncooperative
       1   2   3   4   5   6   7

5. Irresponsible   Responsible
       1   2   3   4   5   6   7

6. Composed   Excitable
       1   2   3   4   5   6   7

7. Social   Shy
       1   2   3   4   5   6   7

8. Suspicious   Trusting
       1   2   3   4   5   6   7

9. Imaginative   Down-to-earth
       1   2   3   4   5   6   7

10. Careless   Careful
       1   2   3   4   5   6   7

Note: Items on this scale relate to four of the five robust factors of personality described earlier in this chapter as follows: extroversion (items 1 and 7); agreeableness (4 and 8); conscientiousness (5 and 10); openness to experience (2, 7, and 9).

How well do you know yourself? Awareness of our own thoughts, feelings, and abilities can help us become happier and better adjusted.

SUMMARY AND REVIEW OF KEY POINTS

THE PSYCHOANALYTIC APPROACH: MESSAGES FROM THE UNCONSCIOUS

personality 490
psychoanalysis 493
id 494
pleasure principle 494
ego 494
reality principle 494
superego 494
anxiety 494
defense mechanisms 494
sublimation 495
reaction formation 495
psychosexual stages of development 495
libido 495
fixation 495
oral stage 496
anal stage 496
phallic stage 497
Oedipus complex 497
latency stage 497
genital stage 497
Freudian slips 497

- Personality consists of the unique and stable patterns of behavior, thoughts, and emotions shown by individuals. Behavior is influenced by both situational factors and personal dispositions. Such dispositions do appear to be relatively stable over time and across situations.
- According to Freud, three distinct levels of consciousness exist: the conscious, preconscious, and unconscious. Freud contended that personality consists of three basic parts: id, ego, and superego, which correspond roughly to desire, reason, and conscience.
- Freud believed that all human beings move through a series of psychosexual stages during which the id's search for pleasure is focused on different regions of the body. Too much or too little gratification at any of these stages can result in fixation and later in psychological disorders.

OTHER PSYCHOANALYTIC VIEWS: FREUD'S DISCIPLES ... AND DISSENTERS

neo-Freudians 500
collective unconscious 501
archetypes 501
animus 501
anima 501
introverts 501
extroverts 501
striving for superiority 504

- Jung believed that all human beings share a collective unconscious: memories and images that strongly influence our perceptions of the world and our behavior.
- Horney rejected Freud's suggestion that females experience penis envy. She contended that many psychological disorders stem from social factors rather than from fixation at various stages of psychosexual development.
- Adler believed that human beings experience strong feelings of inferiority during early life and must struggle to overcome these through compensation. He also emphasized the influence of social factors such as birth order and family constellation in the formation of adult personality.

HUMANISTIC THEORIES: EMPHASIS ON GROWTH humanistic theories 505 fully functioning persons 505 self-concept 506 unconditional positive regard 506 self-actualization 507 peak experiences 507 self-disclosure 508	• Humanistic theories of personality take a much more optimistic view of human nature than psychoanalytic theory. They suggest that human beings strive for personal development and growth, not merely the satisfaction of biological needs. • According to Rogers, all human beings possess the capacity to become fully functioning individuals. Often, they do not reach this stage because distorted self-concepts interfere with personal growth. • Maslow suggests that when lower-level needs are met, human beings strive to attain self-actualization—to become the best people they can be. • Self-disclosure—revealing our inner thoughts to others—can have beneficial effects on our health and well-being.
TRAIT THEORIES: SEEKING THE KEY DIMENSIONS OF PERSONALITY personality traits 510 trait theories 510 secondary traits 511 central traits 511 cardinal traits 511 functional autonomy 511 source traits 511 extroversion 512 agreeableness 512 conscientiousness 512 emotional stability 512 openess to experience 512	• Allport suggested that human beings possess a small number of central traits that account for much of their uniqueness as individuals. Cattell has identified sixteen source traits that, he believes, underlie differences between individuals on many specific dimensions. • Research findings point to the conclusion that there are only five basic dimensions of personality: extroversion, agreeableness, conscientiousness, emotional stability, and openness to experience.
LEARNING APPROACHES TO PERSONALITY social cognitive theory 515 self-reinforcement 515 self-efficacy 515 internals 516 externals 516	• Learning approaches to personality suggest that personality is strongly influenced by learning and experience. Early learning theories denied the importance of internal factors such as goals and expectancies. • More modern learning approaches, such as Bandura's social cognitive theory, assume that behavior is influenced by cognitive factors and personal dispositions as well as by reinforcement contingencies and the social and physical environment. Rotter's social learning approach calls attention to the importance of generalized expectancies concerning the internal or external control of outcomes.

| KEY ASPECTS OF PERSONALITY: A SAMPLE OF RECENT RESEARCH

self-esteem 519
self-monitoring 522
sensation seeking 522 | • People high in self-esteem are generally happier, healthier, and more successful at many tasks than those low in self-esteem. They also have more consistent and well-developed self-concepts. However, high self-esteem is not always beneficial. Under conditions involving ego threat, people high in self-esteem may experience larger decrements in performance than those low in self-esteem.
• High self-monitors are better at reading others and better at making favorable impressions on them. Low self-monitors, in contrast, show more consistent behavior across situations. High self-monitors are more successful at social deception than low self-monitors, partly because they are better at regulating their own expressive behavior.
• High sensation-seekers like higher levels of arousal than low sensation-seekers. They show stronger orientation responses and are better able focus their attention on new stimuli. High sensation-seekers are also better able to handle stressful life events; thus, athletes high in sensation seeking experience fewer injuries following exposure to high levels of stress than athletes low in sensation seeking. |

CRITICAL THINKING QUESTIONS

APPRAISAL	People differ from one another in many different ways. In fact, some would say that they differ in so many ways that it is impossible ever to obtain a solid scientific understanding of personality. Do you agree or disagree? Why?
CONTROVERSY	Growing evidence indicates that some aspects of personality, just like some aspects of physical appearance, are influenced by genetic factors. Does this mean that personality, like eye color or height, is predetermined and can't be changed? If genetic factors do play a role, do you think that personality remains open to change throughout life?
MAKING PSYCHOLOGY PART OF YOUR LIFE	Different jobs or careers seem to require different traits. For example, a timid, shy person would probably not be successful as an emergency-room physician or as a politician. What kinds of jobs or careers do you think might provide a good match to *your* personality? Why? Do you think that taking careful account of your own traits and dispositions might help you choose the right career?

Health Psychology
Health, Stress, and Coping

HEALTH PSYCHOLOGY: AN OVERVIEW 532

STRESS: ITS CAUSES, EFFECTS, AND CONTROL 534
Stress: Its Basic Nature
Stress: Some Major Causes
Stress: Some Major Effects

UNDERSTANDING AND COMMUNICATING OUR HEALTH NEEDS 550
Symptom Perception: How Do We Know When We're Ill?
Health Beliefs: When Do We Seek Medical Advice?
Doctor-Patient Interactions: Why Can't We Talk to Our Doctors?

BEHAVIORAL AND PSYCHOLOGICAL CORRELATES OF ILLNESS: COGNITION AND HEALTH 553
Risky for You and Everyone Around You
Diet and Nutrition: What You Eat May Save Your Life
Alcohol Consumption: Here's to Your Health
Emotions: Mood and Health
AIDS: The New War on Public Health

PROMOTING WELLNESS: DEVELOPING A HEALTHIER LIFESTYLE 565
Primary Prevention: Decreasing the Risks of Illness and Injury
Secondary Prevention: Early Detection of Disease and Illness

SUMMARY AND REVIEW OF KEY POINTS 571

KEY CONCEPT—TWO SIDES OF STRESS 538

THE POINT OF IT ALL—PUTTING PSYCHOLOGY TO WORK: REDUCING STRESS IN THE WORKPLACE 544

PERSPECTIVES ON DIVERSITY—GLOBAL EQUALITY: SUSCEPTIBILITY TO THE ADVERSE EFFECTS OF SMOKING 556

THE RESEARCH PROCESS—CHANGING RISKY BEHAVIORS: AN OUNCE OF PREVENTION IS THE ONLY KNOWN CURE 563

MAKING PSYCHOLOGY PART OF YOUR LIFE— MANAGING STRESS: SOME USEFUL TACTICS 569

BATHURST RESIDENTS TO HELP MARK WORLD AIDS DAY

The Times–Transcript (Moncton, New Brunswick): November 29, 1994

The World Health Organization theme for 1994 was AIDS and the Family: Families Take Care. All across Canada, communities marked the occasion in a variety of ways—in an effort to promote awareness and prevention.

The Times–Transcript reported that in Bathurst, New Brunswick on December 1, there was an "informal dialogue about HIV/AIDS and its impact on the individual, the community and the family." The topics varied from the challenges of HIV/AIDS to sexuality and safe sex practices.

Chapter 13 is about psychology and health. Here you will find out that, as in the case of HIV/AIDS prevention, maintaining good health requires modifying the ways in which we behave—and that is where psychology can help.

INDIVIDUAL DIFFERENCES IN REACTION TO STRESS AND ILLNESS

It is often difficult to predict how people will react to bad news, such as learning that a family member or friend has a life-threatening illness. Sometimes the stress caused by these events can even lead to the development of physical illness.

Imagine that you've been granted three wishes. How would you use them? Would you request fame and power? Immense wealth? Irresistible charm or beauty? Obviously, the possibilities are endless. But what about good health—would that be among your choices? For many people, especially young people, the answer is probably no. In one sense, this is somewhat surprising, for without good health it would be impossible for you to enjoy the benefits you gained from your other wishes.

Fortunately, over the past several decades, we have become increasingly aware of the importance of good health and the value of taking active steps to ensure it. Thus, we eat healthier foods, refrain from smoking, drink alcohol only in moderation, and engage in regular physical exercise. Psychologists, too, have become increasingly interested in the issue of personal health and have made it the focus of a growing volume of research. This seems appropriate—after all, mental health has always been a central topic in psychology, and it is clear that mental and physical health are intimately linked.

In this chapter we'll explore important ways in which our increasing knowledge of psychological principles can be applied to promote health and wellness. We'll begin by considering the exciting new branch of psychology known as *health psychology*. The primary aim of health psychology is to determine how psychological variables and health are related (Gatchel, Baum, & Krantz, 1989; Matarazzo, 1980). Then we'll consider the nature of *stress*, a major health-related problem in the hectic 1990s. We'll focus both on the causes of stress and on some of its major effects—how it influences health and performance. In addition, we'll examine the short- and long-term effects of *environmental stressors*, which can arise from many things—civil war (the carnage in Rwanda), famine (in Ethiopia), a nuclear accident (at Chernobyl), a volcanic eruption (on Mount St. Helens). In Canada, we have had our own disasters, the worst of which was the Halifax Explosion of 1917, which took 1600 lives. More recently, there have been the wreck of the *Edmund Fitzgerald*, the bombing of Air India 007 over the North Atlantic, the Montreal massacre (which so shocked us all), and the Westray and Yellowknife mine explosions. After that, we'll consider how some of our *beliefs and attitudes* influence the way we interpret certain health symptoms and affect our willingness to seek necessary medical assistance. We'll also look at *behaviors* that can directly affect our risk of contracting certain lifestyle-related illnesses, such as cancer, heart disease, and AIDS. Finally, we'll consider the various ways that psychologists work to promote personal health by encouraging healthy lifestyles.

Health Psychology: *An Overview*

*H*ealth **psychology**, the branch of psychology that studies the relationship between psychological variables and health, takes the position that both the mind and the body determine health and illness (Feuerstein, Labbe, & Kuczmierczyk, 1986). Health psychologists assume that beliefs, attitudes, and behaviors contribute significantly to the onset or prevention of illness (Engel, 1980). Research in health psychology has examined a wide range of topics—for example, how to manage low back pain (e.g., Chenard et al., 1991), dental anxiety (Liddell & Locker, 1993), and maternal stress (Krech & Johnston, 1992). Canada is one of the few countries that have specific training programs in this specialty. A closely related field, behavioral medicine, combines biomedical with behavioral science to study not only how disease can be treated, but also how it can be prevented (Epstein, 1992).

Health Psychology: The study of the relation between psychological variables and health; reflects the view that both mind and body are important determinants of health and illness.

Health psychology and behavioral medicine have experienced tremendous growth since their beginnings in the early 1970s. Perhaps the most fundamental reason for the increased interest in this subfield is the dramatic shift in the leading causes of death, everywhere in the world, during this century. In 1900, many of the leading causes of death could be traced to infectious diseases such as influenza, pneumonia, tuberculosis, and diphtheria (see Figure 13.1). But because of advances in medical technology and a greater focus on prevention, deaths from such diseases have become far rarer. Most of the remaining leading causes of premature death can be attributed to individual **lifestyle**—that is, the overall pattern of decisions and behaviors that determines each individual's health and quality of life (Lalonde, 1974). Indeed, in the United States, more than half of all premature deaths (i.e., those that occur before sixty-five) result from unwise lifestyle choices (Burton, 1990). Many people would live longer if they ate healthier foods, reduced their alcohol consumption, practiced safe sex, quit smoking, and exercised regularly.

Lifestyle: In the context of health psychology, the overall pattern of decisions and behaviors that determine health and quality of life.

Leading Causes of Death

The top ten causes of death in 1900 (left) and in 1988 (right).
(Source: Based on data from Wiley & Camacho, 1980, and the National Center for Health Statistics, 1988.)

FIGURE 13.1

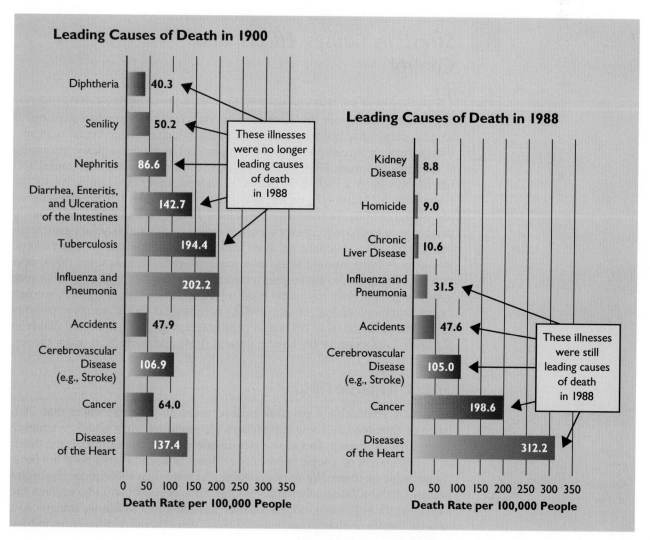

- The primary aim of health psychology is to determine important relationships between psychological variables and health.

- A related field, behavioral medicine, combines behavioral and biomedical science to prevent and treat disorders.

- Many of today's leading causes of premature death can be attributed to individual lifestyles.

On the brighter side, it is encouraging that during the 1980s, relatively fewer people were dying from lifestyle-related diseases (the exception to this: deaths from smoking). Now, more than ever, health psychologists must strive to learn how people can eliminate behaviors that lead to illness, and adopt behaviors that keep them well.

In a classic research project conducted in Alameda County, California (Wiley & Camacho, 1980), adult participants were asked, over a ten-year period, whether they followed certain healthy practices, including sleeping seven to eight hours each night, eating breakfast regularly, refraining from smoking, drinking alcohol in moderation or not at all, maintaining their weight within normal limits, and exercising regularly. Participants who reported practicing all or most of these behaviors were much less likely to die (during the study period) than those who practiced few or none of these behaviors. Although these results are based on correlations and are therefore not conclusive, they may reflect a casual relationship between lifestyle and life span.

The rapid development of health psychology and behavioral medicine began with the finding that stress can have adverse effects on physical health. Let's turn now to the nature and causes of stress.

Stress: Its Causes, Effects, and Control

*H*ave you ever felt that you were right at the edge of being overwhelmed by negative events in your life? Or felt so overwhelmed that you just gave up? If so, you are already quite familiar with stress, which is our response to events that disrupt, or threaten to disrupt, our physical or psychological functioning (Lazarus & Folkman, 1984; Taylor, 1991). Unfortunately, stress is natural and has always been a fact of human life. Indeed, in 1973, Hans Selye at the University of Montreal argued that "complete freedom from stress is … incompatible with the maintenance of life." Partly for that reason, and partly because it has negative effects on both physical health and psychological well-being, stress has become an important topic of research in psychology. Researchers have studied stress in squash players (Kerr & Cox, 1991), new parents (Earle, 1993), dual-earner couples (Galambos & Walters, 1992), care givers of people with traumatic head injury (Graffi & Minnes, 1989), women in management (Long et al., 1992), partners of heart surgery patients (Crossman & Eyjolfsson, 1991), and people at risk of dying suddenly (Baker et al., 1991). Let's examine the basic nature of stress and some of its major causes.

Stress: Its Basic Nature

Stress *: The process that occurs in us in response to events that disrupt, or threaten to disrupt, our physical or psychological functioning.*

Stressors *: Events or situations in our environment that cause stress.*

Stress is a physical and psychological response to life experiences that challenge or threaten us. These experiences (or **stressors**) vary widely—a raging forest fire is a stressor, and so is a vicious snowstorm; but so, also, is the death of a grandparent or a separation from a friend. Stressful events need not be as catastrophic as these. We may experience stress when there is an important hockey or chess game, when a telephone bill is beyond the budget, when the line-up at the registrar's office is taking "just too long," when we transfer to a new university or change our major subject. Also, there are differences in how individuals react to stress. Some people will interpret a particular situation as stressful; others will simply take it in stride. For example, Irving-Neto and Verny (1992) found that maternal stress during pregnancy was related to various personality traits. Also, a particular person may react quite differently to the same stressor at different points in time.

STRESSORS: THE ACTIVATORS OF STRESS What are stressors? Although we normally think of stress as stemming from negative events in our lives, positive events such as graduating or receiving as job promotion can also produce stress (Brown & McGill, 1989). There is a wide range of events that can produce stress, but all of them share several characteristics: (1) they are so intense in some respect that they produce a state of overload—we can no longer adapt to them; (2) they evoke incompatible tendencies in us, such as tendencies both to approach and to avoid some object or activity; (3) they are uncontrollable—that is, beyond our limits of control. A great deal of evidence suggests that when people can predict, control, or terminate an aversive event or situation, they perceive it to be less stressful than when they feel less in control (Karasek & Theorell, 1990; Rodin & Salovey, 1989).

PHYSIOLOGICAL RESPONSES TO STRESSORS When exposed to stressors in our environment, we generally experience many physiological reactions. If you've ever been caught off-guard by a car that appears out of nowhere, you are probably familiar with some common physical reactions to stress. Initially, your blood pressure soars, your pulse races, and you may even begin to sweat. As you saw in Chapter 2, it is the sympathetic nervous system that prepares our bodies for "fight or flight"—that is, for immediate action. Usually these responses are brief, and we soon return to normal levels. When we are exposed to stress chronically, however, there follows a longer sequence of responses activated by our efforts to adjust to the stressor. This sequence, which Selye called the **general adaptation syndrome** (**GAS**), has three stages. As shown in Figure 13.2, the first is the alarm stage, in which the body prepares itself for immediate action; arousal of the sympathetic nervous system releases hormones that help prepare our body to meet threats or dangers (Selye, 1976). If stress is prolonged, the resistance stage begins. During this second stage, arousal is lower than during the alarm stage, but our bodies continue to draw on internal resources at an above-normal rate in order to cope effectively with the stressor. Continued exposure to the same stressor, or the appearance of additional stressors, drains the body of its resources and leads to the third stage, exhaustion. During this stage our capacity to resist is depleted, and our susceptibility to illness increases. In severe cases of prolonged physical stress, the result may be death.

COGNITIVE APPRAISAL OF OUR STRESSOR Selye's general adaptation syndrome provides a framework for understanding our physiological responses to stressful events and suggests at least one reasonable explanation for the relationship between stress and illness. Indeed, chronic stress can reduce an individual's resistance to disease. However, Selye's model did not originally recognize the impact of cognitive processes, the importance of which is made clear by this fact: When confronted with the same potentially stressful situation, some people experience stress, while others do not. That is because their cognitive appraisals differ (Figure 13.3). In simple terms, stress occurs only to the extent that the individuals involved perceive the situation as threatening to them (primary appraisal) and believe they will be unable to cope with its dangers or demands (secondary appraisal) (Croyle, 1992; Lazarus & Folkman, 1984).

General Adaptation Syndrome (GAS): A profile of how organisms respond to stress: three-phases (1) alarm of mobilization, (2) resistance, and (3) exhaustion.

HEALTH, STRESS, AND COPING

FIGURE 13.2

Selye's General Adaptation Syndrome

According to Hans Selye (shown here), the body's reaction to prolonged stress progresses through three stages: alarm, resistance, and, finally, exhaustion. Seyle was the Director of the Institute of Experimental Medicine and Surgery at the University of Montreal.

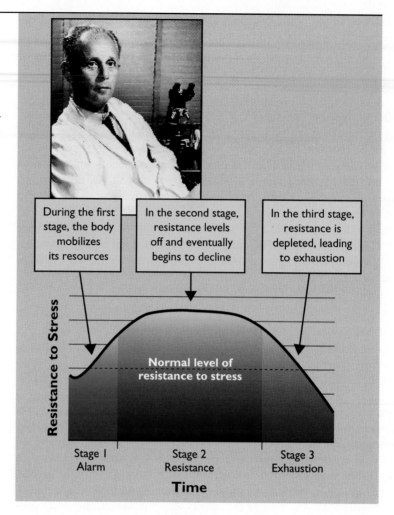

During the first stage, the body mobilizes its resources

In the second stage, resistance levels off and eventually begins to decline

In the third stage, resistance is depleted, leading to exhaustion

Resistance to Stress

Normal level of resistance to stress

Stage 1
Alarm

Stage 2
Resistance

Stage 3
Exhaustion

Time

An example will illustrate this point. Let's consider a recent study of cognitive appraisal by Tomaka and colleagues (1993). Participants in this study were initially told that the researchers were interested in measuring their physiological responses (heart rate, pulse) while they performed a mental task: counting backward from the number 2,737 by sevens—that is, 2,730, 2,723, 2,716, and so on. The participants were instructed to count as quickly and as accurately as possible. Just before they began, the researchers assessed participants' primary and secondary appraisals of the task. They assessed primary appraisals by asking them, "How threatening do you expect the upcoming task to be?" They assessed secondary appraisals by asking, "How able are you to cope with this task?" The researchers predicted that the participants who felt they could not successfully perform the task would perceive it as threatening and would therefore experience stress. They also reasoned that those who were more confident in their abilities might perceive the task as a challenge. Participants in the challenge group actually had greater physiological arousal, but participants in the threat group reported feeling greater stress. Moreover, the challenge group scored higher on both perceived and actual measures of performance. The **Key Concept** illustration on page 538 provides an overview of both the physical and cognitive aspects of stress.

Additional research suggests that other cognitive factors also play a role in our interpretation of potentially stressful events—for example, the reactions of those around us, and the extent of our experience in similar situations (Mendolia & Kleck, 1993; Tomaka et al., 1993). In one study, researchers wondered whether

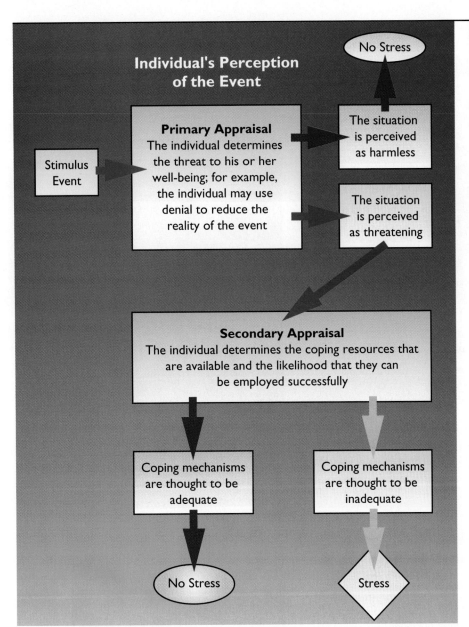

FIGURE 13.3

Stress: The Role of Cognitive Appraisals

The amount of stress you experience depends in part on your cognitive appraisals of it—the extent to which you perceive a situation as threatening and perceive that you will be unable to cope with it.
(Source: Based on data from Hingson et al., 1990.)

Individual's Perception of the Event

No Stress

Primary Appraisal
The individual determines the threat to his or her well-being; for example, the individual may use denial to reduce the reality of the event

Stimulus Event

The situation is perceived as harmless

The situation is perceived as threatening

Secondary Appraisal
The individual determines the coping resources that are available and the likelihood that they can be employed successfully

Coping mechanisms are thought to be adequate

Coping mechanisms are thought to be inadequate

No Stress

Stress

there was a relationship between sense of humor and stress. First, they assessed the sense of humor of forty-four female students. Then they obtained those students' cognitive appraisals and reappraisals of an academic exam. The subjects with the highest sense of humor rated the exam as a positive challenge (perhaps they thought it was funny), while those with the lowest sense of humor held a negative view (Kuiper et al., 1993). In another study, researchers investigated cognitive appraisal and stress in a parachute-training situation. They found that for aspiring parachutists, a higher appraisal of danger went along with a greater physiological reaction (Endler et al., 1992). These results, and the results of related research, provide evidence for the important role of cognitive and social processes in shaping our response to the stressors in our environment. We'll turn next to some of the causes of stress.

KEY POINTS

- Stress is the process that occurs in us in response to situations or events (stressors) that disrupt, or threaten to disrupt, our physical or psychological functioning.

- The GAS model of our physiological reactions to stressors includes three stages: alarm, resistance, and exhaustion.

- Cognitive appraisals play an important role in determining whether an event will be interpreted as stressful or as a challenge.

Two Sides of Stress

The Physical Side of Stress

Selye's *GAS model* provides a framework for understanding how stress affects us physically.

Stage One
During the *alarm stage* the body prepares itself for immediate action (increased heart rate, blood pressure, and energy consumption).

Stage Two
During the *resistance stage* the body draws on resources at an above-normal rate to cope with a prolonged stressor.

Stage Three
During the *exhaustion stage* the body's capacity to cope with stress is depleted and susceptibility to illness increases dramatically.

After finishing a race, long-distance runners may find themselves in the exhaustion stage of Seyle's GAS model: They have totally drained their body's capacity to cope with stress.

The Cognitive Side of Stress

The *cognitive appraisal model* illustrates how our interpretations of potentially stressful events—such as the one depicted in the photo below—greatly affect our reactions to them.

Primary appraisal addresses the following question: How threatening is a potentially stressful event?
Event not perceived as threatening—no stress.
Event perceived as threatening—leads to a secondary appraisal of the situation.

Secondary appraisal addresses the following question: Given that an event is viewed as a threat, do we have the resources to cope with it effectively?
If the answer is yes, the couple does not experience stress.
If the answer is no, the couple experiences stress.

If we interpret an event, such as news conveyed in a letter, as threatening, it will tend to be more stressful than if we interpret the same event as nonthreatening.

Stress: Some Major Causes

Which factors contribute to stress? The list is a long one, but among the most common factors are major life events, such as the death of a loved one or a painful divorce; the all-too-frequent minor hassles of everyday life; conditions and events relating to one's job or career; and certain aspects of the environment.

With respect to divorce, Statistics Canada has reported that in 1991, for every ten marriages that took place there were four divorces. On average, those divorcing couples (about 80,000 in total) had been married for over twelve years. If we were to include separation as it pertains to premarital break-up, and separated couples where the individuals part without obtaining a divorce, the figure would be much higher. Stress is always a major consequence when a stable relationship dissolves, not only for the divorcing couple but also for their children, the two sets of in-laws, and many others; and the effect upon the health of all of those people is a major concern (Rae-Grant & Robson, 1988). Divorce mediation and divorce-adjustment counseling use psychological principles to alleviate the stress that occurs when couples decide to part company. Both services are often available.

STRESSFUL LIFE EVENTS   The death of a spouse, an injury to a child, war, failure in school or at work, an unplanned pregnancy—unless we lead truly charmed lives, most of us experience traumatic changes at some time or other. What are their effects on us? This question was first investigated by Holmes and Rahe (1967), who asked a large number of people to assign arbitrary points (to a maximum of one hundred) to various life events according to how much readjustment each had required. They reasoned that the greater the number of points assigned to a given event, the more stressful it was for those experiencing it.

As you can see from Table 13.1, participants in this study assigned the greatest number of points to such serious events as the death of a spouse, divorce, or marital separation. In contrast, they assigned much smaller values to such events as a change in residence, a vacation, or a minor violation of the law (such as a parking ticket).

Holmes and Rahe then related the total number of points accumulated by individuals during a single year to changes in their personal health. The results were dramatic and did much to stir psychologists' interest in the effects of stress. The greater the number of "stress points" people accumulated, the greater was their likelihood of becoming seriously ill. Recently, Cohen, Tyrrell, and Smith (1993) asked volunteers to report all the significant stressful events of the previous twelve months. Then they gave out two kinds of nose drops. The experimental subjects got drops containing a virus known to cause the common cold. The control group received uncontaminated nose drops. The results showed that psychological stress increased susceptibility to the virus. That is, of the subjects who got the cold virus, those who perceived themselves to be under greater stress were more likely to become ill. Of course, it is not the stress itself that puts health at risk; rather, it is the effect of stress on the body's ability to combat the virus. There are a number of ideas about just what that effect is. It is likely that the immune system is involved, but the exact nature of the cell changes is not yet understood (Adamec, 1991). Also, other neurochemicals participate, as has been demonstrated in animals suffering from maternal stress (e.g., Peters, 1990).

The picture is complicated, however, by a finding that major life crises, like death or divorce or having a child, may actually bring relief from stress, if the stress that preceded the crisis was high (Wheaton, 1990).

TABLE 13.1	RANK	LIFE EVENT	LIFE CHANGE UNIT VALUE
	1	Death of spouse	100
	2	Divorce	73
	3	Marital separation	65
Life Events, Stress, and Personal Health	4	Jail term	63
	5	Death of close family member	63
When individuals experience stressful life events, such as those near the top of this list, their health often suffers. The greater the number of points for each event, the more stressful it is perceived as being.	6	Personal injury or illness	53
	7	Marriage	50
	8	Getting fired at work	47
	9	Marital reconciliation	45
	10	Retirement	45
	11	Change in health of family member	44
(Source: Based on data from Holmes & Masuda, 1974.)	12	Pregnancy	40
	13	Sex difficulties	39
	14	Gain of new family member	39
	15	Business readjustment	39
	16	Change in financial state	38
	17	Death of close friend	37
	18	Change to different line of work	36
	19	Change in number of arguments with spouse	35
	20	Taking out mortgage for a major purchase (e.g., a home)	31
	21	Foreclosure of mortgage or loan	30
	22	Change in responsibilities at work	29
	23	Son or daughter leaving home	29
	24	Trouble with in-laws	29
	25	Outstanding personal achievement	28
	26	Wife beginning or stopping work	26
	27	Beginning or ending school	26
	28	Change in living conditions	25
	29	Revision of personal habits	24
	30	Trouble with boss	23
	31	Change in work hours or conditions	20
	32	Change in residence	20
	33	Change in schools	20
	34	Change in recreation	19
	35	Change in church activities	18
	36	Change in social activities	18
	37	Taking out a loan for a lesser purchase (e.g., car or television)	17
	38	Change in sleeping habits	15
	39	Change in number of family get-togethers	15
	40	Change in eating habits	15
	41	Vacation	13
	42	Christmas	12
	43	Minor violation of the law	11

The picture is complicated still further by an unexpected relationship between income bracket and stress. When you ask people what causes them to worry, financial considerations are reported high on the list. However, worries about money are not related, in any simple manner, to the amount of money you have or earn. For example, a Canadian survey showed that people earning more than $100,000 were most likely to report frequent stress (66 percent of them did). Add this to your list of instances when perception is more relevant than reality.

The picture is complicated even more by large differences in the ability to withstand the impact of stress (Oullette-Kobasa & Puccetti, 1983). Some people suffer ill effects after exposure to a few mildly stressful events; others remain healthy even after prolonged exposure to high levels of stress. They are described as being stress-resistant or hardy. In general, the greater the number of stressful life events experienced by an individual, the greater the likelihood that the person's subsequent health will be adversely affected (Rowlison & Felner, 1988).

DAILY HASSLES AS A SOURCE OF STRESS

Many everyday hassles are stressful. Would you experience stress in the situation shown here?

THE HASSLES OF DAILY LIFE Certain catastrophic events are clearly stressful but—fortunately—occur fairly infrequently. Does this mean that people's lives are generally calm? Hardly. As you know, daily life is filled with countless minor sources of stress that seem to make up for their relatively low intensity by their much higher frequency. That such daily hassles are an important cause of stress is suggested by several studies by Lazarus and his colleagues (e.g., Kanner et al., 1981; Lazarus et al., 1985). These researchers have developed a Hassles Scale on which individuals indicate the extent to which they have been "hassled" by common events during the past month. The individual items on this scale deal with a wide range of everyday events, such as having too many things to do at once, dealing with delays, and owing money. A special paper-and-pencil scale, the Inventory of College Students' Recent Life Experiences, has been developed and tested by Kohn and colleagues at York University. "Hassles" may seem relatively minor when compared with the life experiences studied by Holmes and Rahe (1967), but they are very important.

Daily hassles also affect physical health, as indicated by a study conducted by Williams, Zyzanksi, and Wright (1992). These researchers asked Navajo tribespeople at an Indian Health Service facility in the United States about major events in their lives during the preceding six months and applied culturally relevant measures of daily irritation or satisfaction. Two years later, the researchers reviewed each participant's medical chart to determine the number of inpatient admissions and outpatient visits. Consistent with the researcher' predictions, the participants' daily hassles scores predicted how frequently they used inpatient and outpatient services. Of course, major life crises were also relevant to these outcomes. However, Malla and Norman (1992) found that scores on the Hassles Scale were more closely related to perceived stress than to major life events; Landreville and Vezina (1992) found the same thing when they studied 200 seniors. Similarly, DeLongis and colleagues (1988) found that daily stress predicted later health problems, which included not only headaches, backaches, sore throat, and flu, but also negative mood (for participants with poor social support and low self-esteem). Other personality characteristics have been related to perceived stress as well. For example, Hewitt and Flett (1993) found that perfectionism and perceived stress combined to produce depression.

These results, and those of previous studies, suggest this possibility: Major life events can indeed negatively affect health; but for many people, the more minor hassles of everyday life—perhaps because of their frequent, repetitive nature—may actually be even more important in this respect.

ENVIRONMENTAL SOURCES OF STRESS   Have you ever experienced a terrifying storm, such as the series of brutal tornadoes that ripped through the east end of Edmonton in 1987, leaving twenty-seven dead? Have you lived through a killer blizzard, such as the one that hit eastern Canada on March 13, 1993, leaving devastation in its path (and Ottawa with the most accumulated snow on the ground, 135 centimeters, ever)? Even if you haven't, you can no doubt appreciate that natural and human disasters are highly stressful. Commonly reported psychological problems that follow large-scale disasters include nightmares and flashbacks, distress at exposure to reminders of the event, irritability, difficulty concentrating, and a general unresponsiveness (Lindy, Green, & Grace, 1987). When severe, these problems are often referred to as **post-traumatic stress disorder**.

Do large-scale natural disasters produce lasting psychological effects? The most common finding is mild, transient distress that subsides soon after the visible effects of the disaster are no longer apparent (Bravo et al., 1990). Recent evidence suggests that there may be indirect effects of natural disasters—most importantly, deterioration in social support from friends, family, and community (Kaniasty & Norris, 1993; Norris & Uhl, 1993). Unfortunately, large-scale disasters often affect entire communities. As a result, important sources of social support are missing that would otherwise have helped alleviate stress.

Human-produced disasters, such as the meltdown of the Chernobyl nuclear reactor in the ex-Soviet Union, can exert similar effects. In some respects, the psychological trauma that results from human-produced disasters can be more dramatic and long-lasting (Baum & Fleming, 1993). Why should that be so? One important factor is perceived loss of control. If a natural disaster strikes—a hurricane, or earthquake, or tornado—we do not expect to have control, although there are obviously precautions that we could take, and sometimes do not (Lehman & Taylor, 1987). However, when a disaster occurs as a result of human actions—for example, in cases of violence against our person (as in sexual assault; Moscarello, 1991); or when we breathe in office fumes (Schmidt & Gifford, 1989) or machinery exhaust (Schell et al., 1992); or when our assumptions about our personal safety are violated—the perception is often planted in us that we no longer have the control over our lives we should rightfully have.

A second difference has to do with the consequences of each type of disaster. Natural disasters tend to be clearly marked and limited in time. In contrast, human-produced disasters—such as the contamination of groundwater with toxic chemicals—may affect us forever. Exposure to toxic chemicals like pesticides may increase the risk of cancer or genetic damage (Vaughan, 1993). Also, the uncertainty regarding these consequences can produce chronic stress-related problems. Consider what happened when the nuclear reactor at Three Mile Island in Pennsylvania released small amounts of radioactive gas into the environment in March 1979. Years later, the effects on health were still obvious (Gatchel, Schaeffer, & Baum, 1985). Similar outcomes have been observed for accidents involving toxic chemicals (Baum & Fleming, 1993).

POST-TRAUMATIC STRESS AND THE CHILDREN OF CHERNOBYL

The psychological trauma that results from human-produced disasters can be more devastating than trauma resulting from natural causes.

Perception of control as related to stress has been studied in more ordinary contexts as well. For example, DasGupta (1992) had thirty students in introductory psychology classes at the University of Toronto submit questions for a test they were going to have. Some students were told that their questions would be used to set the test; others were told that making up the questions would provide a review for them. The former group rated their control as higher and reported fewer stress symptoms.

Key Points

- Stressors can be major life events, such as the death of a spouse, or daily minor hassles.
- Survivors of devastating natural and human-produced events often experience severe psychological problems, termed post-traumatic stress disorder.
- Among sources of work-related stress are work overload and underload, role conflict, and performance appraisals.

Work-Related Stress Most adults spend more time at work than almost anywhere else, and research has shown that working (i.e., making a living) is a major source of stress. Some of the work-related stress factors are obvious—for example, discrimination, harassment, or overload. Too much to do in too short a time is stressful, but so is too little. Work underload produces intense feelings of boredom, which can also be very stressful.

Other sources of work-related stress are less apparent. One of these is role conflict, which arises when the worker faces conflicting demands or expectations from different groups of people. For example, consider the dilemma of many first-line managers. Their subordinates often expect them to improve their work assignments, pay, and conditions. In contrast, the managers' own bosses often expect them to do the opposite—perhaps to convince employees to work harder for fewer rewards. The result: role conflict and stress for the new managers.

Like examinations, performance appraisals (i.e., the procedures used to evaluate employees' job performance) may generate intense stress. If employees perceive these appraisals as fair, employee stress tends to be low; if they're seen as arbitrary or unfair, stress is almost certain to be high. The perception that rewards such as raises, promotions, or bonuses are being distributed in an unjust manner causes stress.

Work-related issues are of special interest to experts in industrial/organizational psychology. You will learn more about this subfield in Chapter 17. Additional factors that have been found to contribute to stress at work are summarized in Figure 13.4. Examine them carefully, for you are certain to encounter several in your own career, and recognizing sources of stress is a giant step toward dealing with stress successfully. For more information on what can be done to combat the effects of stress in the workplace, see **The Point of It All**.

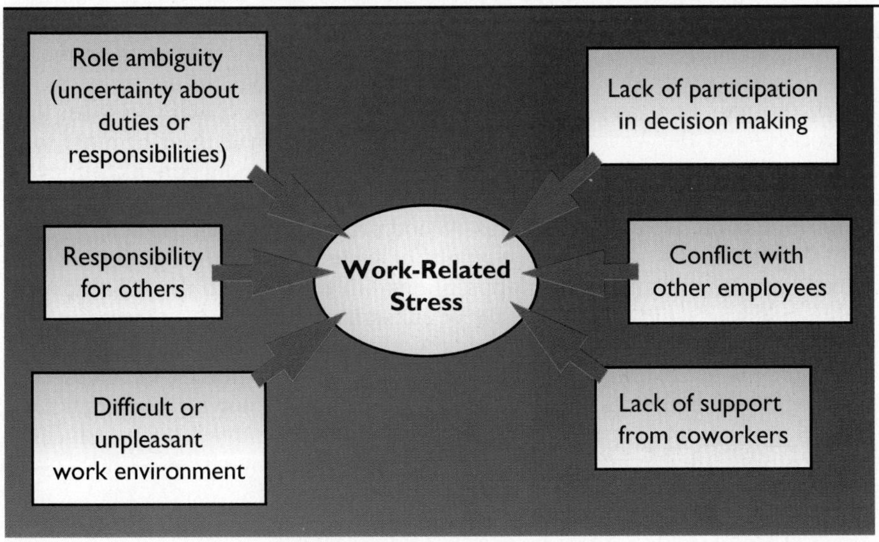
Role ambiguity (uncertainty about duties or responsibilities)
Lack of participation in decision making
Responsibility for others
Work-Related Stress
Conflict with other employees
Difficult or unpleasant work environment
Lack of support from coworkers

Figure 13.4

Sources of Work-Related Stress

Many factors contribute to stress at work. Several of the most important are summarized here.

Putting Psychology to Work: Reducing Stress in the Workplace

Many aspects of work are potential sources of stress. Moreover, a stressful working environment can lead to psychological and physical problems or worsen existing problems. Can anything be done to reduce these effects? Fortunately, yes.

First, employers can reduce workplace stress by considering the **person-environment (P-E) fit** (Edwards & Harrison, 1993). When there is a "misfit" between the strengths of the employee and the demands of the job, negative outcomes may follow, including psychological disturbances, job dissatisfaction, and increases in stress and stress-related illnesses (Harrison, 1985). For example, consider the potential negative outcomes that might result from placing someone with a low tolerance for anxiety into high-pressure work, or assigning someone who requires variety and challenge to a simple repetitive task. An employer can minimize the potential for P-E misfits—and thereby reduce the likelihood of stressful situations—by hiring workers with characteristics that closely match the demands of the job (Landsbergis et al., 1992).

Second, research suggests that the amount and availability of social support, both on and off the job, is crucial to the control of workplace stress (Cohen & Wills, 1985). It is not possible to eliminate all potential sources of workplace stress, nor is it possible to arrange a perfect P-E fit for every worker. However, the availability of social support apparently can serve as a buffer against stressful events at work (Landsbergis et al., 1992).

Third, companies can educate workers on how to cope with workplace stress and how to change unhealthy practices that can intensify the effects of stress (Maturi, 1992). The most effective programs are those that are designed to meet the specific needs of individuals and are comprehensive and long-term in their focus. For example, Gregg and his colleagues (1990) interviewed more than 7,800 employees in four manufacturing plants. There were substantial health risks among these workers: 19 percent had high blood pressure, 34 percent were obese, and 44 percent were smokers. In two of the plants, wellness counselors contacted employees identified as having one or more health risks and designed individualized wellness programs specific to their needs. Over a three-year period, the counselors met with each of the workers periodically to assess their progress, made changes to their programs as needed, and served as a support system to try to keep them motivated to stay with the program. As shown in Figure 13.5, the effectiveness of the wellness program closely mirrored the amount of contact between the workers and the wellness counselors. Workers who had three or more follow-up contacts with a counselor showed the greatest reduction in their level of health risk; those who had no follow-up contacts actually increased their health risk on two of the measures—blood pressure and weight gain.

The point of it all is that the results of systematic psychological research can have important practical applications—in this case, to the reduction of the potentially devastating effects of stress in the workplace. Research has found other strategies for minimizing workplace stress—for example, setting reasonable goals, attainable standards, and realistic deadlines; making technology and machines "people friendly"; managing time and organizing work appropriately; providing feedback (Sandell & Sullivan, 1992); reducing ambiguity; improving industrial relations (Kelloway et al., 1993); and improving relations among people who work together.

Person-Environment (P-E) Fit: The approach suggests that a misfit between a person and his or her work environment may produce stress.

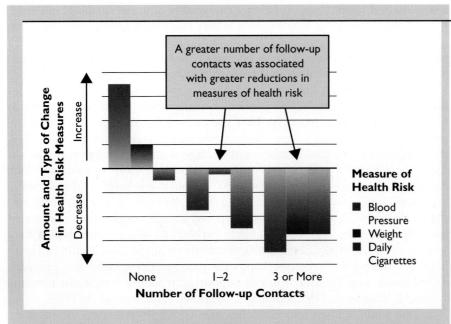

A greater number of follow-up contacts was associated with greater reductions in measures of health risk

Measure of Health Risk
- Blood Pressure
- Weight
- Daily Cigarettes

FIGURE 13.5

Reducing Workplace Health Risks: The Beneficial Effects of Wellness Programs

The greatest reductions in health risk were observed among participants having three or more follow-up contacts with their wellness counselors. In contrast, participants who had no contact with their counselors actually worsened on some measures of health risk.
(Source: Based on data from Gregg et al., 1990.)

The cost of ignoring stress in the workplace is staggering—for example, in the United Kingdom, 30 million working days a year are lost to stress. For this reason, a number of stress management programs have been introduced. The International Labor Organization is presently conducting a study of twenty stress prevention programs in nine different countries (List, 1993). For eighteen years, the University of Ottawa has been assessing the fitness of over 5,000 federal public servants. This program involves taking measures of resting and exercise heart rate and blood pressure, upper body strength, muscular endurance, body function, and blood tests. The results of the tests are reported to each participant, and during those sessions, efforts are made to raise awareness of stress and to influence attitudes and identify healthier behaviors. As psychologists continue to refine their techniques they will no doubt discover additional ways to help workers cope more effectively with the stressors they encounter at work.

Stress: Some Major Effects

By now you should understand that stress stems from many different sources and exerts profound effects on those who experience it. What is sometimes difficult to grasp, however, is just how far-reaching these effects can be.

Stress and health: The silent killer   According to medical experts, the link between stress and personal health is very strong indeed (Kiecolt-Glaser & Glaser, 1992). In fact, some authorities estimate that stress plays some role in 50 to 70 percent of all physical illness (Frese, 1985). Included in these percentages are some of the most serious and life-threatening ailments known to medical science. Stress has been implicated in heart disease, high blood pressure, hardening of the arteries, ulcers, and even diabetes.

How does stress produce such effects? The mechanisms involved have yet to be determined precisely, but the general idea is this: By draining our resources and keeping us off balance physiologically, stress upsets our complex internal chemistry. In particular, it may interfere with efficient operation of our immune system—the elaborate internal mechanism through which our bodies recognize and destroy potentially harmful substances and intruders, such as bacteria, viruses, and cancerous cells.

Here is more about that process. Foreign substances that enter our bodies are known as antigens. When they enter, some white blood cells, known as lymphocytes, begin to multiply. They then attack the antigens, often destroying them by engulfing them. Other white blood cells produce antibodies, chemical substances that combine with antigens and neutralize them. When functioning normally, the immune system is nothing short of amazing: Each day it removes or destroys many potential threats to our health and well-being.

Unfortunately, prolonged exposure to stress disrupts this system. For example, in studies with animals, subjects exposed to inescapable shocks produced fewer lymphocytes relative to subjects exposed to shocks from which they could escape (Ader & Cohen, 1984). A variety of stressors, including disruptions in interpersonal relations, family discord, loneliness, academic pressure, daily hassles, and the lack of social support, can interfere with our immune systems (Cohen et al., 1992; Jemmott & Magloire, 1988; Levy et al., 1989).

In one study, Cohen and his colleagues (1992) investigated the immune systems of monkeys. The monkeys were randomly assigned to stable or unstable social conditions for a twenty-six-month period. Some monkeys remained with the same group for the entire study period; others were frequently reassigned to different social circles. The researchers observed and assessed the amount of time each monkey spent in various forms of social interaction, including affiliative behaviors such as grooming and passive physical contact with other group members. It was found that social support served as a stress buffer.

Here are some human examples. The immune systems of divorced or recently separated individuals were compared with those of happily married couples. This study found that poorer immune function was associated with marriage disruption (Kiecolt-Glaser et al., 1987, 1988). Also, there are approaches to dealing with stress that allow for the maintaining of normal immune efficiency. Optimism, regular exercise, and feelings of control are all beneficial in this regard (Taylor, 1991). These findings are both unsettling and encouraging: They suggest that a complex, high-stress lifestyle has a serious cost, in that it undermines the individual's ability to resist many serious illnesses; also, that reductions in stress may be of major benefit to a person's overall health.

STRESS AND TASK PERFORMANCE Psychologists once believed that stress actually improved performance on a wide range of tasks. They theorized that the relationship between stress and task performance was an inverted U—that is, as stress increased, performance improved, presumably because it aroused and energized the individual. Beyond some point, though, stress became distracting, and performance actually deteriorated.

That *was* the theory. Not any more. We now know that even low or moderate levels of stress may interfere with performance (Motowidlo, Packard, & Manning, 1986; Steers, 1984). There are several reasons why. First, people experiencing stress may focus on their unpleasant feelings and emotions rather than on the task at hand. Second, prolonged or repeated stress may harm health, and this may interfere with effective performance. Finally, how well we do under stress depends greatly on the complexity of the task; the more complex it is, the more stress interferes with performance (Berlyne, 1967). Are the tasks performed by today's working people more complex than those of the past? Many observers believe so (Mitchell & Larson, 1987).

For that reason, even relatively low levels of stress may interfere with performance in today's complex work world.

All these factors help explain why stress, even at fairly moderate levels, may interfere with many types of performance. However, this is not always the case. People sometimes do rise to the occasion and turn in extraordinary performances at times when stress is intense. How that happens remains an important question for psychological research.

Burnout: When stress consumes Most jobs involve at least some stress. Yet somehow the people performing them manage to cope: They continue to function despite their daily encounters with various stressors. Some individuals, though, are not so lucky. Over time, they are ground down (or out) by repeated encounters with stress. These individuals are said to be suffering from burnout, and they show several distinctive characteristics (Maslach, 1982; Pines & Aronson, 1988).

First, victims of burnout often suffer from exhaustion, both physical and emotional. They have low energy and always feel tired. In addition, they report many signs of physical strain, such as frequent headaches, nausea, poor sleep, and changes in eating habits. Burnout may also be associated with risk for cardiovascular disease and electrocardiogram irregularities (Melamed, Kushnir, & Shirom, 1992). Burnout victims experience emotional exhaustion. Depression, feelings of hopelessness, and feelings of being trapped in one's job are all part of this, and their end result is that employees are no longer able to maintain relationships with other people. Second, burnout victims show depersonalization. They are cynical and negative and care nothing about the people with whom (and for whom) they work. Third, burnout victims denigrate themselves. They lose their sense of accomplishment and their personal confidence. To put it simply, they come to view the world around them, and themselves, through dark-gray rather than rose-colored glasses. Finally, burnout victims often report feelings of low personal accomplishment (Maslach & Jackson, 1984)—feelings that they haven't been able to accomplish much in the past and probably won't succeed in the future, either. Studies conducted in work settings (Lee, & Ashforth, 1990) show this to be an accurate description of burnout.

Burnout is by no means limited to high-powered executives in the express lane. In fact, it has been studied in many populations: vocational rehabilitation counselors (Day & Chambers, 1991); elementary, intermediate, secondary, and university teachers (Byrne, 1993); RCMP officers (Stearns & Moore, 1993); supervisors and managers in a public welfare system (Lee & Ashforth, 1993); male and female physicians across Canada (Garside, 1993); computer company employees (Evans & Fischer, 1993); occupational therapists (Pranger & Brown, 1992); and nurses and nursing assistants (Ogus, 1992; Chappell & Novak, 1992; Leiter & Maslach, 1988).

For example, several hundred employees of a telecommunications corporation in Atlantic Canada each completed a burnout inventory and provided several other kinds of information. A number of findings emerged about men and women in management and nonmanagement positions. It was found that in getting the job done, female managers were more sensitive to their staff, while male managers were more sensitive to the pressures from their superiors. The men in this study were more likely to experience emotional exhaustion if they were managers, while the women who were most prone to this were nonmanagers. With respect to the psychological environment at work, women placed more importance on their relationship with others, while control was important to men (Pretty, McCarthy, & Catano, 1992). See Figure 13.6 for a summary of this study's findings.

FIGURE 13.6

Burnout: An Overview

Individuals exposed to high levels of work-related stress over long periods of time may suffer from *burnout*. This state involves *physical, emotional,* and *mental* (or *attitudinal*) exhaustion, as well as feelings of low personal accomplishment.

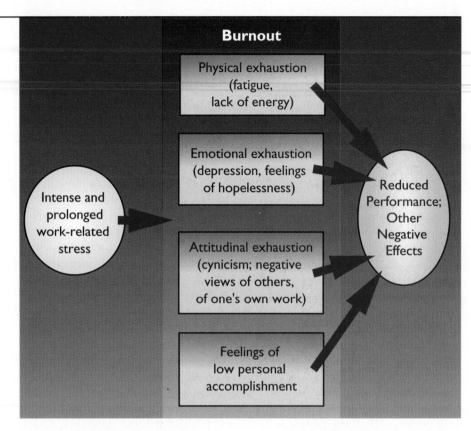

What are the causes of burnout? The first is prolonged exposure to stress—but other factors, too, play a role. The perception that our efforts are useless, ineffective, or unappreciated contributes much to burnout (Jackson, Schwab, & Schuler, 1986). Obstacles to promotion, inflexible rules, and feelings of lesser personal accomplishment lead individuals to feel that they are trapped in an unfair system; as a result, they may develop a negative view of their work (Gaines & Jermier, 1983). Personal factors also play a role. People with satisfying lives outside the work setting—for example, those who have stable relationships—are less likely to experience burnout.

Whatever its precise causes, once burnout develops, its victims change jobs or withdraw psychologically, marking time until retirement. Fortunately, recovery from the physical and psychological exhaustion of burnout is possible. If ongoing stress is reduced, and if individuals gain added support from friends and co-workers, and if they cultivate hobbies and other outside interests, some regain positive attitudes and high levels of productivity.

INDIVIDUAL DIFFERENCES: OPTIMISM, PESSIMISM, AND HARDINESS While some people suffer ill effects from even mild levels of stress, others are able to function effectively even in the face of intense, ongoing stress. How are these people different?

One answer involves the familiar dimension of optimism-pessimism. Optimists are people who expect good outcomes—that is, they see the glass as half-full; pessimists are those who expect bad outcomes—they see it as half-empty. Some evidence indicates that optimists are much more stress-resistant

STRATEGIES PREFERRED BY OPTIMISTS	DESCRIPTION
Problem-focused coping	Making specific plans for dealing with the source of stress; implementing such plans
Suppressing competing activities	Refraining from other activities until the problem is solved and stress is reduced
Seeking social support	Obtaining the advice of others; talking the problem over with others

STRATEGIES PREFERRED BY PESSIMISTS	DESCRIPTION
Denial/distancing	Ignoring the problem or source of stress; refusing to believe that it exists or is important
Disengagement from the goal	Giving up on reaching the goal that is being blocked by stress
Focusing on the expression of feelings	Letting off steam instead of working on the problem directly

TABLE 13.2

Optimists and Pessimists: Contrasting Strategies for Coping with Stress

Optimists and pessimists employ different strategies in coping with stress. The strategies used by optimists seem to be more effective than those used by pessimists.

than pessimists (Scheier & Carver, 1988). For example, optimists are much less likely to report physical illnesses and symptoms during highly stressful periods such as final exams. Why is this the case? Briefly, optimists and pessimists adopt different tactics for coping with stress (Scheier & Carver, 1992). Optimists' coping is problem-focused coping: making and carrying out specific plans for dealing with sources of stress. They also seek out social support—the advice and help of others (Carver et al., 1993). In contrast, pessimists adopt different strategies, such as giving up the goal or denying the stress (Scheier, Weintraub, & Carver, 1986). Table 13.2 presents a summary of the different strategies adopted by optimists and pessimists.

Another characteristic that distinguishes stress-resistant people from those who are more susceptible to it is **hardiness** (Kobasa, 1979). Hardy individuals are relatively stress-resistant and seem to differ from others in three respects. First, they show higher levels of commitment—deeper involvement in whatever they do and stronger tendencies to perceive such activities as worth doing. Second, they tend to view change as a challenge—an opportunity for growth and development—rather than as a threat or a burden. Third, they have a stronger sense of control over events in their lives and over the outcomes they experience. Hardy people generally report better health, even when they encounter major stressful life changes (Oullette-Kobasa & Puccetti, 1983).

These and other findings indicate that individuals differ greatly in terms of their ability to deal with stress. Understanding the reasons for these differences can be of considerable practical value. We'll discuss various techniques for coping with stress in **Making Psychology Part of Your Life**.

Hardiness: A personality style characterized by high levels of commitment, a view of change as an opportunity for growth, and a strong sense of being in control.

KEY POINTS

- Stress may play a role in 50 to 70 percent of all physical illness, primarily through its effect on our immune system.

- Even relatively low levels of stress may interfere with task performance. Prolonged exposure to high levels of stress may cause burnout.

- Individual differences in optimism and hardiness help explain the ability of some people to cope with stress better than others.

- Hardy individuals show high levels of commitment, view change as an opportunity for growth, and have a sense of control over events in their lives.

Understanding and Communicating Our Health Needs

*T*here is no doubt that modern medicine has provided us with the means to alleviate many diseases and illnesses that were considered incurable until this century. Yet all that does not ensure that we will seek proper treatment when we need it, or that we possess the knowledge or skills necessary to realize when help is required. Moreover, because of the beliefs and attitudes we often hold, it's often hard for health professionals to convince us to comply with good, healthy advice.

In an Australian study, people were asked to identify the lifestyle or behavior patterns responsible for health problems in their country (Hetzel & McMichael, 1987). The most frequently cited examples were alcohol and drug abuse, poor diet, lack of exercise, and smoking—a clear indication that respondents were aware of the health risks associated with these behaviors. Similarly, when asked to name the changes that would most likely improve their own future health, the respondents cited better diet, more exercise, stopping or reducing smoking, reducing alcohol consumption, and coping better with their worries—again proof that they knew what they were supposed to do to improve their health. Yet when they were asked why they didn't change the behaviors most essential to their own good health, their answers included "laziness," "lack of time," "not worthwhile," "too difficult or expensive," or "lack of social support." Sufficient motivation to change was simply not there. Here is an important role for health psychologists: Beyond helping people understand their health needs and the risks of specific healthy behaviors, it is paramount for them to identify techniques to reduce or eliminate unhealthy behaviors, and to promote the adoption of healthier lifestyles.

Symptom Perception: How Do We Know When We're Ill?

As you discovered in Chapter 3, we all experience the steady beating of our heart or the rush of air flowing in and out of our lungs as we breathe. Certain other sensations—like irregularities in our heartbeat, tiny aches and pains, a slight queasiness in our stomach, or a backache—are often named as symptoms, because they may reflect an underlying medical problem. The question is, which factors determine how people define symptoms?

There are individual differences in the attention we pay to our bodies, and certain situational factors that influence our attention (Taylor, 1991). Those who focus their attention on themselves tend to notice symptoms more quickly than those who focus on the external environment. People who have interesting work and who live with others are less likely to notice symptoms than less active people who have boring jobs or who live alone, or both (Pennebaker, 1983). In other words, we are less likely to notice symptoms when our attention is distracted. Situational factors, such as our mood, can also determine the direction of our attention and whether we notice symptoms. People who are in a good mood report fewer symptoms and rate themselves as more healthy than people who are in a bad mood (Salovey & Birnbaum, 1989).

Also, psychological factors determine how we interpret symptoms. For example, we often interpret our current symptoms by comparing them with those we have experienced in the past. We recognize a runny nose, watery

550   CHAPTER 13

eyes, and tiredness as symptoms of the onset of a cold. In these instances, our experience, or the experience of others, tells us that the underlying illness is probably not fatal and that the treatment of choice may include lots of rest, plenty of water, and staying dry and warm. Finally, expectations are important. We focus on symptoms we are expecting and ignore those we are not expecting. After you visit a sick friend, a barely noticeable tickle in your throat may lead you to believe you are catching her cold.

Health Beliefs: When Do We Seek Medical Advice?

How do we decide that a symptom is severe enough to require medical attention? When do we actually go to a doctor, clinic, or emergency room? Surprisingly, some evidence suggests that people do not seek help even when they know that something is seriously wrong (Locke & Slaby, 1982). Why is that so?

The **health-belief model** was initially developed to explain why people don't use medical screening services. As shown in Figure 13.7, our willingness to seek medical help depends on two factors: the extent to which we perceive a threat to our health, and the extent to which we believe a particular action will effectively reduce that threat (Rosenstock, 1974). For example, we may decide to stop smoking if we value our health, if we feel that our smoking might lead to fatal lung cancer, and if we don't like what we hear about death from lung cancer (refer again to Figure 13.7).

Beliefs are also important. Whether, for example, a smoker concerned about developing cancer will actually quit depends on two beliefs: that giving up smoking will reduce the risk of cancer, and that the benefits in doing so will outweigh the immediate pleasures of smoking.

The health-belief model helps explain why people who have never experienced a serious illness or injury often fail to engage in actions that would prevent illness or injury, such as using sunscreen outdoors or wearing a condom during sexual intercourse (Taylor & Brown, 1988). They don't engage in such preventive actions because they believe that the likelihood of illness (or injury) is low—so why bother? (See the discussion of adolescent invulnerability in Chapter 9.)

Health Belief Model: A theory predicting that whether a person practices a particular health behavior depends on the degree to which the person believes in a personal health threat and believes that practicing the behavior will reduce that threat.

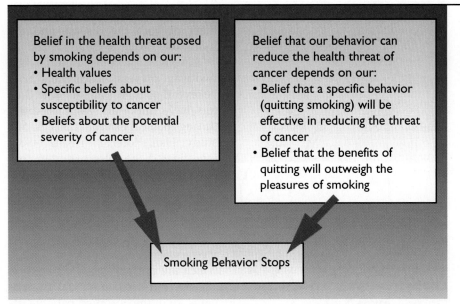

FIGURE 13.7

The Health Belief Model

The health belief model suggests that whether a person practices a particular health behavior depends on the degree to which he or she believes in a personal health threat—and believes that practicing the behavior will reduce that threat. Each of these beliefs is influenced by additional variables. Here, the health belief model is applied to smoking.

Belief in the health threat posed by smoking depends on our:
• Health values
• Specific beliefs about susceptibility to cancer
• Beliefs about the potential severity of cancer

Belief that our behavior can reduce the health threat of cancer depends on our:
• Belief that a specific behavior (quitting smoking) will be effective in reducing the threat of cancer
• Belief that the benefits of quitting will outweigh the pleasures of smoking

Smoking Behavior Stops

If people believe that their actions will not make a difference, they will be less likely to seek help or engage in healthy behaviors. For example, suppose you are overweight and have a family history of high blood pressure. If you believe that nothing can reduce your inherited susceptibility to heart attacks, you may refuse a recommended diet and exercise program, even after you experience symptoms.

Doctor-Patient Interactions: Why Can't We Talk to Our Doctors?

Imagine the following situation: You are waiting in a crowded doctor's office. It's already forty-five minutes beyond your scheduled appointment time, and you are growing more impatient by the minute. Just before you reach the end of your rope, the nurse finally calls your name. Relieved, you swallow the choice words you've been saving. But then, adding insult to injury, she says, "Please be seated, I'll be right back," and leaves! Fully twenty minutes pass. Then, after a rapid succession of questions, pokes, and prods, the doctor scribbles a prescription onto a piece of paper and says, "Take two of these four times a day, and call my office in a week if you have further problems."

Such ineffective doctor-patient interactions cause vast frustration. Indeed, research has repeatedly documented communication problems between physicians and their patients (Roter & Ewart, 1992; Waitzkin, 1984). It is only since the 1970s that researchers have systematically examined the doctor-patient communication process (Roter & Hall, 1989).

For example, Duffy, Hamerman, and Cohen (1980) identified ten vital communication skills and then observed how often doctors applied these skills during actual medical examinations. The communications most frequently observed related to the "mechanics" of patients' illnesses, such as examination, and to explanations of the prescribed medication and therapy. The communications observed least often were the psychosocial ones, such as what their patients knew about their illness and how they felt about being ill.

Results like these have suggested that it is important for physicians to receive training in communication skills as part of their medical education. In other words, physicians need not only technical skills, but also people skills (Pelsser, 1991). Indeed, growing evidence suggests that rapport and the quality of information communicated are critical factors in successful treatment of both the disease and the individual (Roter & Ewart, 1992).

Also, because communication is a two-way process, researchers now believe that both patients and doctors have important responsibilities during medical examinations. In one study, Hall, Roter, and Katz (1987) investigated the information-giving, question-asking, social talk, positive talk, negative talk, and partnership-building behaviors of both physicians and patients. The results showed that both physicians and their patients have important roles, which are not only task-focused but also have a socioemotional component. All of the observed patient out-

DOCTOR-PATIENT INTERACTIONS: COMMUNICATION IS THE KEY

Both physicians and their patients play an important role in the communication process. (Source: CLOSE TO HOME © Copyright 1993 John McPherson. Reprinted with permission of UNIVERSAL PRESS SYNDICATE. ALL RIGHTS RESERVED.)

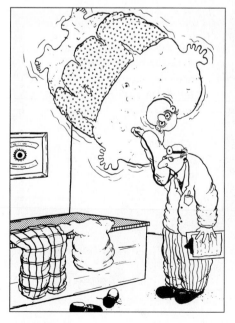

comes—satisfaction, recall of important medical information, and compliance—were strongly related to the amount of information given by the doctor during the medical encounter. This was particularly true when the interaction included positive social conversation.

In order to be effective in treating patients and promoting wellness, doctors, nurses, and other health professionals need to know how to get their message across—how to communicate effectively with the people who come to them for help. The important benefits include increased patient satisfaction and improved quality of diagnostic information (Macguire, Fairburn, & Fletcher, 1986).

Behavioral and Psychological Correlates of Illness: Cognition and Health

Consider this surprising chain of events. During the 1950s a terminally ill cancer patient learned of an experimental anticancer drug. Though the odds were slim, he took the drug, hoping it would result in a cure. Amazingly, the patient's cancer went into remission and he was able to leave the hospital, and even to return to work. Then a curious thing happened: Researchers found that the anticancer drug he had taken was ineffective as a cancer treatment. When the patient learned that, his cancer returned. Understandably concerned, his doctor promised him new treatment—an improved and purer drug. The patient made a second recovery, even though the new drug was a placebo. Unfortunately, a few months later, he learned that the new drug was of no value. Within a few days, he died (Levy, 1990).

Although one should be skeptical about miraculous remissions or cures for **cancer**—an illness in which abnormal cells proliferate till they overwhelm normal ones—psychological variables do interact in important ways with physical conditions to determine cancer's progression. In other words, aspects of our behavior, perceptions, and personality contribute to the disease process.

In individuals from families with high cancer rates, the efficiency of the body's natural killer cells—those designed specifically for the surveillance and destruction of cancerous tumor cells—is diminished (Kiecolt-Glaser & Glaser, 1992). In most cases, however, whether we actually develop a cancer or other disease depends on **risk factors**—aspects of our lifestyle that affect our chances of developing or contracting a particular disease, within the limits established by our genes (Canadian Cancer Society, 1994).

Risk factors are the behaviors that increase our exposure to **carcinogens**—that is, to cancer-producing agents in our environment. To some extent, tobacco and the smoke it produces, chemicals in the food that we eat and in the air that we breathe, alcohol in the beverages we drink, and radiation from overexposure to the sun are carcinogenic. Because of concerns about exposure to such substances, in 1994, consumers in the United States protested about milk from cows that had been fed large amounts of growth hormones: The protesters didn't want these substances in their milk.

Several behavioral risk factors that may contribute to the development of disease have been the focus of psychological research. Here is what we know about some of them.

Cancer: A group of illnesses in which abnormal cells are formed that are able to proliferate, invade, and overwhelm normal tissues and to spread to distant sites in the body.

Risk Factors: Aspects of our environment or behavior that influence our chances of developing or contracting a disease, within the limits set by our genetic structure.

Carcinogens: Cancer-producing agents.

Risky for You and Everyone Around You

Cigarette smoking is addictive and it is dangerous to your health. It causes 90 percent of all cases of lung cancer in Canada, and it is the leading cause of several other types, including cancer of the larynx, the bladder, and the cervix. It also causes diseases of the heart and the blood vessels (**cardiovascular disease**). Tobacco kills 35,000 Canadians every year, according to Health

Cardiovascular Disease: *All diseases of the heart and blood vessels.*

FIGURE 13.8

When Smokers Quit

Within 20 minutes of smoking that last cigarette, the body begins a series of changes that continues for years. All benefits are lost by smoking just one cigarette a day, according to the Cancer Societies of the United States and Canada.
(Source: American Cancer Society, Washington Division, Inc.)

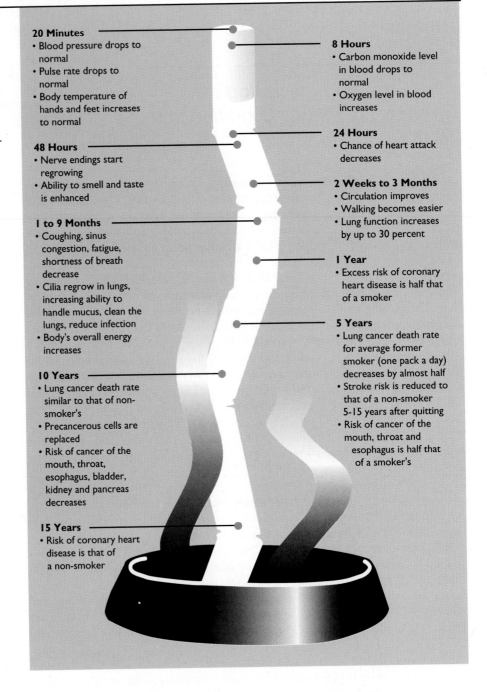

20 Minutes
• Blood pressure drops to normal
• Pulse rate drops to normal
• Body temperature of hands and feet increases to normal

48 Hours
• Nerve endings start regrowing
• Ability to smell and taste is enhanced

1 to 9 Months
• Coughing, sinus congestion, fatigue, shortness of breath decrease
• Cilia regrow in lungs, increasing ability to handle mucus, clean the lungs, reduce infection
• Body's overall energy increases

10 Years
• Lung cancer death rate similar to that of non-smoker's
• Precancerous cells are replaced
• Risk of cancer of the mouth, throat, esophagus, bladder, kidney and pancreas decreases

15 Years
• Risk of coronary heart disease is that of a non-smoker

8 Hours
• Carbon monoxide level in blood drops to normal
• Oxygen level in blood increases

24 Hours
• Chance of heart attack decreases

2 Weeks to 3 Months
• Circulation improves
• Walking becomes easier
• Lung function increases by up to 30 percent

1 Year
• Excess risk of coronary heart disease is half that of a smoker

5 Years
• Lung cancer death rate for average former smoker (one pack a day) decreases by almost half
• Stroke risk is reduced to that of a non-smoker 5-15 years after quitting
• Risk of cancer of the mouth, throat and esophagus is half that of a smoker's

and Welfare Canada. While many cancers have decreased over the past twenty-five years, there has been a fourfold rise in the number of deaths from lung cancer in women.

Not surprisingly, the vast majority of Canadians (including many who smoke) disapprove. In recent years, smoking has been banned on all airplanes, in all federal and provincial government buildings, and in most other public places, such as the Skydome. Moreover, smoking is expensive. In spite of the recent removal of some taxes, a pack-a-day habit still costs a smoker in Nova Scotia about $1,600 a year.

Despite the health risk (which is known to most children by seven years of age; Bhatia et al., 1993), the almost universal disapproval, the real inconvenience, and the significant cost, about one in every four Canadian adults continues to smoke cigarettes. In Ontario high schools, at least the same proportion of students smoked cigarettes every day (Adlef, Smart, & Walsh, 1993). Among members of the Canadian Navy between the ages of 17 and 19, the figure is one in two (likely because cigarettes are 75 percent cheaper for the Canadian Forces). In Ontario, 9.4 percent of grade seven students are smokers, and that figure is 54 percent higher than it was in 1991.

Why do people smoke? There are genetic, psychosocial, and cognitive reasons. Some people may be biologically predisposed to **nicotine** addiction. Individual differences in the reaction to nicotine are taken as evidence that our genes play a role in determining which people will become smokers (Pomerleau & Pomerleau, 1984). Also, nicotine enhances the availability of certain neurotransmitter substances, such as acetylcholine, norepinephrine, dopamine, and endogenous opioids. As you may recall from Chapter 2, these substances influence memory, attention, performance, pleasure, tension, anxiety, appetite, and pain, and can be pleasurable for some people.

Psychosocial factors also play a role in establishing smoking behavior, especially among young people. Adolescents may be more likely to smoke if their parents or other role models smoke, or if they experience peer pressure to do so (Millar & Hunter, 1990), or if their brothers or sisters do (Santi et al., 1990–91). The example set by smoking parents and peers is especially relevant to young people. When asked to give reasons why they smoke, students in Australia cited "image" and "friends" (Stanton et al., 1993). The irony is that, at least among university students, quite the opposite is the case. Dermer and Jacobsen (1986) studied the effects of cigarette smoking on first impressions made by average-looking other students. They found that nonsmokers made a better impression, even upon students who were smokers themselves. (Of course, you cannot tell smokers from nonsmokers by examining faces. In this experiment, the impression that a person smoked was given by including a cigarette package on the desk in the photo.)

Finally, there are cognitive factors. Smokers believe that smoking allows them to stay alert and handle stress, even though there is no clear evidence in support of those ideas (West, 1993). Most smokers recognize that smoking is harmful to their health, yet many continue to smoke. Their beliefs and their actions are out of synch. That is, they think that they, personally, are exempt from the harmful consequences of smoking.

Chapman and colleagues (1993) found that smokers also believed that "most people smoke," and that "medical evidence that smoking causes cancer is not convincing." As shown in Figure 13.9, smokers were more likely to agree with these beliefs than ex-smokers. These results suggest that helping smokers quit ought to involve consciously correcting their erroneous beliefs (Sadava & Weithe, 1985).

Nicotine: The addictive substance in tobacco.

FIGURE 13.9

The Role of Self-Exempting Beliefs in Smoking

As predicted, smokers were more likely to agree with *self-exempting beliefs* than ex-smokers. These data help explain why smokers continue to smoke, even when they are aware of the danger of doing so. These results also illustrate the important role of cognitive processes in determining health-related behaviors, including smoking.
(Source: Based on data from Chapman et al., 1993.)

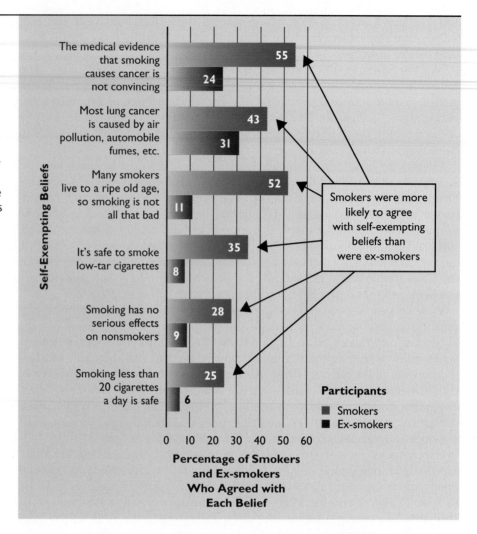

PERSPECTIVES ON DIVERSITY

Global Equality: Susceptibility to the Adverse Effects of Smoking

There are many ways in which people from around the globe differ, but one way in which they appear to be the same is this: Smoking is dangerous to everyone's health. This is an important point, since recent assessments of the prevalence of smoking show that the number of smokers worldwide—and hence the incidence of lung and other forms of cancer—is continuing to climb (LaVecchia et al., 1992, 1993). The number of deaths from lung cancer in Japan is now about nine times what it was in 1950. It is predicted that comparable increases among men in Eastern Europe will soon be the highest ever (Boyle, 1993).

In many parts of the world, the percentage of deaths attributable to smoking has been higher for men than for women (Pet et al., 1992; see Figure 13.10). However, this difference is diminishing. It is expected that there will be a swift rise in smoking-related deaths among women, for the simple reason that the number of women who smoke cigarettes is climbing rapidly (Boyle, 1993). In a British study of students in secondary school (junior high in Canada), one of the risk factors for smoking was "being a girl" (Goddard, 1992).

Smoking may also be dangerous to other people's health. Studies in various

Passive smoking: Inhaling other people's cigarette smoke.

countries confirm this. An English survey reported that in various European countries (including Germany, France, and Poland), tobacco-smoke pollution kills almost 140,000 people every year, through cancer and heart disease. The effect of passive smoke is commonly known. In the United States, 90 percent of adults polled did recognize that secondhand smoke can be hazardous to one's health. Indeed, cigarette smoke consists of about 4,000 chemicals, of which forty-three have been linked to cancer. Inhaling secondhand smoke—that is, **passive smoking**—can increase the incidence of respiratory disease and cardiovascular disease for smokers' family members and co-workers. Passive smoking also adversely affects children. It causes more frequent and more severe attacks of asthma and may even produce brain tumors (Chilmonczyk et al., 1993; Gold et al., 1993). An American investigation has confirmed ear and lung infections and worsened asthma; an Irish study has confirmed sudden infant death syndrome (crib death); and a British report has confirmed meningitis and cystic fibrosis, as other diseases for which children who breathe smoke passively are at risk. Further evidence shows that adolescents regularly exposed to their parents' smoking perform more poorly on tests.

These findings, and others, suggest that smoking is indeed the great equalizer. As smoking rates continue to soar around the world, death rates increase not only for smokers but also for those who happen to be around them.

SMOKING: NO CULTURAL BOUNDARIES

The adverse effects of smoking are seen worldwide. In Japan, deaths from lung cancer have increased tenfold since 1950.

Percentage of Deaths Attributed to Smoking for Men and Women Around the World

FIGURE 13.10

The percentage of deaths attributed to smoking is increasing in many parts of the world for men and women. The increase in the percentage of deaths due to smoking is increasing at an alarming rate for American women.
(Source: Based on data from Peto et al., 1992.)

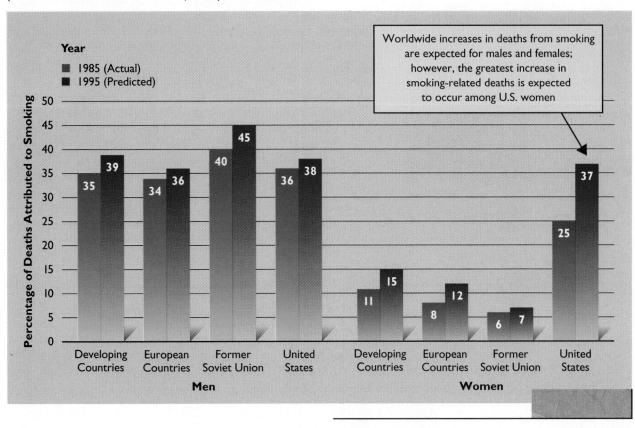

Diet and Nutrition: *What You Eat May Save Your Life*

We are the foods we eat. When we make wise choices—for example, foods rich in vitamin A (carrots, spinach, cantaloupe)—proper cell division is supported and the destruction of healthy cells by carcinogens is inhibited (Willet & MacMahon, 1984). Broccoli and cauliflower may reduce the risk of cancer by discouraging tumor growth. When we make poor choices, we put ourselves at risk for disease. Growing evidence implicates dietary fat and cholesterol in this. One major cause of heart disease is arteriosclerosis (also known as hardening of the arteries), which is caused by a buildup of cholesterol and other substances on arterial walls, which in turn narrows the blood vessels.

Dramatic increases in breast cancer rates around the world have led to large-scale multicultural studies to determine the cause. For psychologists, the challenge here is to discover how to help high-risk individuals make long-term changes in their eating habits. That has turned out to be very difficult. Measures taken to change the way we eat—for example, mass media campaigns—are often effective initially, but not in the long run. One factor that does contribute to change is the active involvement of the person's family in designing and implementing programs that promote healthful changes in behavior.

KEY POINTS

- Cancer is a group of diseases characterized by a loss of some cells' ability to function normally. Cancerous cells multiply rapidly, generating tumors.
- Individual differences in people's reaction to nicotine, the addictive substance in tobacco, help determine who will become a smoker.
- Both smoking and passive smoking are implicated in many cancers, in cardiovascular disease, and in sickness among children.
- Poor diet can raise our risk of cancer of the colon and rectum, breast cancer, and cardiovascular disease.
- Heavy drinking can cause diseases of the stomach, liver, and intestines, and impair mental and sexual functioning. It can also result in fetal alcohol syndrome.

Alcohol Consumption: *Here's to Your Health*

Although strong evidence suggests that biological and genetic factors contribute to alcoholism and problem drinking (Reid & Carpenter, 1990), psychosocial factors, including stress, environmental cues, and social pressure from peers, also determine drinking behavior. And while current "wisdom" has it that a daily glass of red wine may have health benefits, more alcohol can be harmful and lead to a variety of social and physical disorders. The consequences of drinking can include stomach disease, cirrhosis of the liver, cancer, impaired sexual functioning, cognitive impairment, and, as we saw in Chapter 8, fetal alcohol syndrome, which occurs in children of mothers who are heavy drinkers and results in developmental handicaps and physical abnormalities. Also, drinking an average of 1.5 or more beers every day has been linked to subsequent development of colon and rectum cancer (Pollack, Nomura, Heilbrun, Stemmermann, & Green, 1984). Alcohol interacts with smoke to increase cancer risk (Sobel et al., 1990; Grobe & Campbell). Drinkers of alcohol who smoke heavily have a twenty-two times greater risk of developing cancer than individuals who neither smoke nor drink. (Rothman et al., 1980).

Emotions: *Mood and Health*

Have you ever had to hold your temper or swallow your tears when the need to express yourself was intense? Or are you the kind of person who just lets it all out? Individuals who routinely cope with stress by keeping their negative emotions to themselves are likely to experience a suppression of their immune systems. This in turn creates a biological vulnerability, which may lead to the aggravation of disease (such as cancer) when the individual is exposed to environmental stress (Levy et al., 1985). By the same token, it may be possible to enhance immune function through classical conditioning, exercise, and confidence building (Kiecolt-Glaser & Glaser, 1992). And patients who demonstrate positive affect—especially joy, well-being, and happiness—increase the likelihood that they will recover (Levy et al., 1988).

Open expression of negative feelings and a willingness to fight illness have been connected to heightened immune function, decreased recurrence rates, and increased survival time, even among patients at advanced stages of cancer. For example, combative individuals—those who express anger about getting cancer and hostility toward their doctors and family members—often live longer than patients who passively accept their fate and quietly undergo treatment (Levy, 1990).

Emotion plays a role in cardiovascular disease, which is Canada's top killer and is a factor in about 40 percent of all deaths. Several factors put people at risk for heart disease (and stroke); these include smoking, obesity, high blood pressure, high **serum cholesterol** levels, and the use of oral contraceptives. Here is one example: Prolonged **hypertension** (also referred to as high blood pressure) may result in extensive damage to the entire circulatory system. In fact, about 30 percent of deaths from cardiovascular disease each year are attributable to hypertension. In order to see the connection here, you must understand that blood vessels are not simply hollow tubes through which blood circulates. Rather, their walls are made of regulated and responsive tissue and have many functions—for example, they dilate or constrict as appropriate. Very recently, renegade cells have been found in the blood vessel walls of patients with heart disease. These cells may actually cause the heart disease, and cause it to return after surgery. Heightened emotion also affects blood pressure (Krakoff et al., 1985). In addition, anxiety and hostility can increase general arousal and facilitate the release of catecholamines—a class of neurotransmitters that plays an important role in the sympathetic nervous system. The release of epinephrine (which is one powerful catecholamine) has the effect of boosting our overall readiness to act, including our blood pressure. Although the effects of emotional stressors are usually brief, anxiety, hostility, and anger may indicate a predisposition to hypertension (Rosenman, 1988). Not surprisingly, the strongest relationships between emotions and blood pressure have been found for unexpressed anger and hostility.

Why do some young adults who are nonsmokers and who seem to be doing everything right, as far as exercise and diet are concerned, suffer heart disease even before they are forty years of age? Scientists in Western Australia have recently isolated a gene which may predict this pattern. That heredity may play a role here is confirmed also by the fact that many children of hypertensive parents are also hypertensive. Why, then, would some of these children not have this trait? Miller (1992) may have found an answer by showing that some sons of hypertensive parents respond to stress (e.g., from the pain of electric shock while playing a video game) less emotionally than others.

PERSONALITY AND HEALTH: TYPE A BEHAVIOR PATTERN Think about the people you know. Can you name one person who always seems to be in a hurry, is extremely competitive, and is often hostile and irritable? Now, can you name another person who shows the opposite pattern? Someone who is relaxed, relatively uncompetitive, and easygoing? If you can, you now have in mind two people who show Type A and Type B behavior patterns, respectively.

Interest in the **Type A behavior pattern** was first stimulated by medical research. Several physicians (Jenkins, Zyzanski, & Rosenman, 1979, and their

Serum Cholesterol: The amount of cholesterol in our blood.

Hypertension: High blood pressure, a condition in which the pressure within the blood vessels is abnormally high.

Type A Behavior Pattern: A cluster of traits such as competitiveness, aggressiveness, urgency, and hostility; related to important aspects of health, social behavior, and task performance.

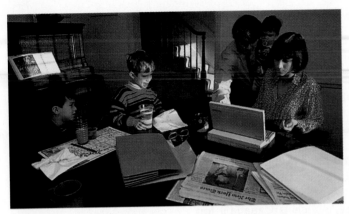

colleagues) noticed that many heart attack patients seemed to share certain personality traits (refer to Chapter 12). Individuals who tend to be competitive, aggressive, hostile, and impatient are displaying a pattern of behaviors termed Type A. They are likely to be hard workers and often seek out the most challenging and stressful work conditions. Often, their efforts are rewarded with additional work from their superiors and co-workers (Feather & Volkmer, 1988). Some researchers now believe that certain aspects of the Type A pattern are related to increased risk of heart disease, and that those Type A individuals who fail to express their emotions—especially anger, cynicism, and hostility—and who ignore early symptoms of cardiovascular disease, are at risk (Matthews, 1988). A particular type of hostility—cynical hostility, which is characterized by suspiciousness, resentment, anger, antagonism, and distrust of others—may be especially detrimental.

TYPE A BEHAVIOR PATTERNS AND HEALTH PROBLEMS

Type A people tend to be always in a hurry, competitive, aggressive, hostile, and impatient. They are more than twice as likely as Type B people to have coronary problems. Research shows that one aspect of Type A behavior—*cynical hostility*—may be particularly detrimental.

How can a Type A profile promote heart disease? First, the emotional reactions among Type A individuals may result in constriction of peripheral blood flow, higher blood pressure, and increased pulse rate (Lyness, 1993). All of these changes lead to cardiovascular disease (Contrada, 1989). Next, the emotional responses of Type A individuals reflect increased hormone levels in the bloodstream—in particular, increased levels of adrenaline and noradrenaline, which are both catecholamines. Here they act as hormones and these increased hormone levels may lead to greater fatty deposits on the walls of blood vessels and ultimately to heart disease (Dembrowski & Williams, 1989). Also, Type A individuals appear to evaluate themselves negatively, and this may be an important factor in explaining their maladaptive behavior patterns (Yuen & Kuiper, 1992).

Yet there may also be some health benefits to being Type A. In a thirteen-year longitudinal study of Type A and Type B men, researchers found that although the Type A subjects had significantly more heart attacks than Type B subjects, they were more likely to survive those heart attacks (Ragland & Brand, 1988). It appears that the personality features that drove them to a heart attack may encompass behaviors that increase adherence to treatment. Type A individuals may possess the personal characteristics—such as perfectionism (Hewitt & Flett, 1993)—that are required for success in a treatment regimen.

Other differences between these two types of personalities have been found. At York University, Esther Greenglass has reviewed the components of Type A behavior in both women and men (1990). In one study, she investigated the coping strategies of Type A and Type B women and men, all of whom were first-line supervisors at government social service offices. These supervisors completed a psychological inventory that covered four ways of dealing with stress: focusing on the problem; handling emotions; resolving potential problems; and dealing with general conditions of life. Here is one difference that she found: Type B supervisors were more likely to cope with job stress by using social support, while the Type A supervisors were more likely to focus on problems. Another study found that in this respect, Type A men and women were similar to each other, as were Type B men and women (Greenglass, 1988).

Research in Canada

Esther R. Greenglass
York University

How can Type A individuals be treated before they develop cardiovascular problems? That question was asked by Roskies (1988), who found that stress management training was the most effective of the programs she compared.

AIDS: The New War for Public Health

Acquired immune deficiency syndrome—AIDS—is a contagious and potentially fatal disease caused by the human immunodeficiency virus (HIV). HIV destroys blood cells that make the human body immune to foreign invaders. More specifically, it disables certain white blood cells—for example, the T-helper cells—that normally coordinate the work of the immune system. This leaves people susceptible to the serious diseases that are the actual cause of death for people with AIDS (Weiss, 1993).

Like the song says, this is a dangerous time for lovers. At least it can be, because HIV is sexually transmitted—most often during sexual intercourse, in the semen or vaginal fluids of HIV carriers. It can also be spread by sharing syringes or through blood transfusions. Also, one of every four pregnant women infected with HIV transmits the virus to her fetus.

The HIV virus is believed to have spread from monkeys to humans about 900 years ago. That is how long it must have taken for the monkey virus to evolve into the human virus of today. Robert C. Gallo (1990), a pioneer in AIDS research at the National Cancer Institute in the United States, reasons that until the 1950s, the AIDS virus was probably isolated in small pockets of central Africa. The migration from rural to urban communities, the appearance of the passenger jet in the 1960s, and the global use of blood products are all responsible for the rapid spread of the disease. As Gallo writes: "As a result, a virus that might once have remained relatively rare and isolated became common and global." In 1993, according to the World Health Organization, there were over 13 million infected individuals (refer to Figure 13.11), and by 1994 that figure had risen to 17 million.

It was not until 1984 that the HIV virus that causes AIDS was isolated. Since then, an antibody test has been developed to detect its presence. AIDS researchers in Ontario have established the HIV Ontario Observational Database (HOOD) to track the natural history and epidemiology of HIV and AIDS in that province, and Health Canada monitors carefully the cases of

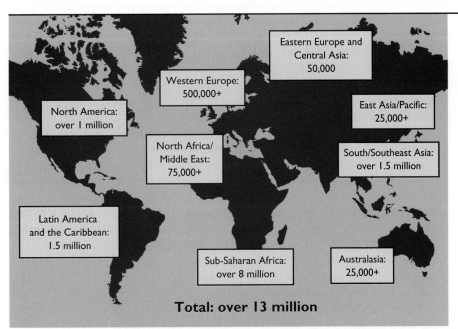

Eastern Europe and Central Asia: 50,000

Western Europe: 500,000+

North America: over 1 million

East Asia/Pacific: 25,000+

North Africa/Middle East: 75,000+

South/Southeast Asia: over 1.5 million

Latin America and the Caribbean: 1.5 million

Sub-Saharan Africa: over 8 million

Australasia: 25,000+

Total: over 13 million

FIGURE 13.11

Estimated Distributions of HIV Infections Worldwide

The World Health Organization estimates that as of mid-1993, more than 13 million people have become infected with HIV. (Source: Based on suggestions by Merson, 1993.)

AIDS reported by physicians. Together, these efforts have provided important information for disease control. For example, by determining the prevalence of HIV-infected pregnant women (1 in every 900), researchers in Newfoundland have identified a cluster of twenty-five individuals in one transmission chain.

Since 1981, researchers have uncovered a number of facts about AIDS. First, the incubation period—the time it takes for the disease to develop from HIV—may be as long as ten years, or even more (Bachetti, 1990). This means that the disease can be spread without either partner being aware. This is one reason why the incidence of AIDS has increased rapidly.

Although researchers at first believed that AIDS was a disease of homosexuals and intravenous drug users, we now know that anyone engaging in certain sexual activities is at risk for contracting HIV. It is transmission through heterosexual intercourse that is increasing HIV in Africa, Asia, and the Indian subcontinent. It is expected that 110 million people in these regions will be carrying HIV by the year 2000 (Mann, 1992).

According to the Canadian Public Health Association, there are five key factors in HIV transmission. First, there must be a source of HIV—that is, an HIV-infected individual. Second, there must be a means of transmission—most commonly, certain kinds of sexual activity. Third, the host individual must be susceptible to infection (which almost all human beings are). Fourth, there must be an point of entry to the blood stream of the host, such as a break in the skin. Finally, there must be a sufficient concentration of HIV in the body fluids that are exchanged.

According to Health Canada, 9,511 cases of AIDS (94 percent of them male) had been reported in this country as of March 1994, and 6,534 (almost 80 percent) of those people had already died. Many people believe, however, that those figures underestimate the incidence of AIDS by at least one-third. Furthermore, as many as 25,000 cases of HIV have been identified. Most but not all people infected with HIV will eventually develop AIDS; only 5 percent remain symptom-free after fifteen years.

In 1994, in Yokohama, Japan, at the Fifth International Conference on AIDS, most scientists were at best cautiously hopeful that an effective drug treatment for AIDS would be developed. That same year, Canada and eight other countries began an international trial of AZT, a drug currently used to treat people infected with HIV. New data suggest that its benefits are questionable, possibly because HIV mutates quickly into new forms that are resistant to the drug (Cohen, 1993). HIV-infected individuals receiving AZT may not live any longer than those who are receiving a placebo. Even so, the drug may make them feel better. Also, the risk that a pregnant carrier will infect her developing fetus may be reduced by this drug.

In their urgent quest for an effective vaccine, researchers have studied the two responses of the human immune system to bacterial and viral intruders. The slower response is the one that produces antibodies which, according to Caldwell (1994), "seek out bacteria and viruses traveling in the bloodstream, marking them for destruction by an arsenal of biochemical weapons." The faster response, called the cell-mediated system, involves an immediate response that destroys intruders. This latter defense has been less studied, but hope for an effective drug may be shifting to this strong, cell-mediated reaction.

There are a tiny number of individuals who engage in sexual activities with HIV-infected partners without seeming to contract HIV. These few cases have been of great interest to scientists such as Frank Plummer of the University of Manitoba. Plummer's interest lies in the differences between those who do and those who do not become infected. He and his research team identified a group of about thirty female prostitutes in a poor slum in

Pumwani, Kenya. These women have had unprotected sex with hundreds (perhaps thousands) of HIV-positive men. They have contracted other sexually transmitted diseases such as syphilis and gonorrhea, yet amazingly, they show no trace of HIV (Purvis, 1993). Plummer and his co-workers believe that the immune systems of these women mount an extraordinary defense against the virus. For that reason, they are a source of important information for scientists seeking an effective vaccine against HIV. If it could be determined how their immune systems are different, such a vaccine, and effective treatments, might be found.

Another small group of extraordinary cases was discovered in a hospice for AIDS babies in Nairobi, Kenya. There, forty-four HIV-infected children are thriving; some have survived as long as six years. Since HIV-infected infants are expected to live for an average of eight or nine months, these children are far out of the ordinary. At present, however, why they are is a mystery.

The spread of AIDS has a strong behavioral component. For more about this, see **The Research Process**.

THE RESEARCH PROCESS

Changing Risky Behaviors: An Ounce of Prevention Is the Only Known Cure

Why are psychologists so interested in AIDS? Primarily because HIV is spread as a result of particular behaviors. An individual can be infected only if the virus is introduced into the bloodstream, and that can only happen as a result of unprotected sexual intercourse or the "swapping" of infected blood or blood products. Efforts to develop an effective vaccine or therapeutic treatments for HIV have not yet borne results; at present, the only effective means to combat the spread of AIDS is to modify people's beliefs and attitudes so that they practice safe sex and use clean needles.

In the past decade, behavioral scientists doing research on the psychology of AIDS have made the remarkable finding that many people who don't use condoms belong to the groups at greatest risk for contracting or transmitting AIDS: homosexuals and intravenous drug users. In his 1992 study of students at ten colleges and universities across Canada, Charles Hobart found this paradox: Those "who knew the most AIDS victims and so were most aware of the spread of the disease and rated the seriousness of the AIDS threat most highly ... rated sex with briefly known partners as least risky and ... were least inclined to use condoms with passing acquaintances."

Why do people not practice safe sex? One explanation focuses on social norms—the unspoken rules that tell us how to act in social situations. For example, the more closely a homosexual man was involved in a social network that supported the use of condoms to prevent the spread of HIV, the more likely he was to use condoms (Fisher & Misovich, 1989). Other studies have revealed how people go about deciding to get tested for HIV (Myers et al., 1993).

Beliefs also do much to explain why some groups of people engage in high-risk behaviors. Hingson and his colleagues (1990) assessed whether beliefs about AIDS and condom use were related to the frequency of unprotected sex among adolescents. Those who believed that they were highly susceptible to AIDS, and that there is no cure for AIDS, and that condoms are effective in preventing AIDS, were more likely to report that they used condoms consistently. The results of these and related studies provide valuable information, which researchers have now begun using to develop ways to alter the behaviors of people at risk for contracting HIV.

AIDS prevention begins with educating people about the disease and about the behaviors that lead to HIV infection. This process takes place in various locations: for example, in school (Smith et al., 1993) and at home (Verby & Herold, 1992). Is education enough to change behavior? The data say it isn't, especially in groups at risk for contracting HIV (Fisher & Fisher, 1992). Indeed, in an investigation in nine dating bars in Ontario (Herold & Mewhinney, 1993), many of the participating men and women had not used a condom during their last sexual encounter, even though they were concerned about AIDS (women more so than men).

Researchers now recognize that developing an effective AIDS-prevention program is a complicated business; techniques that are effective for one group may not succeed with another. Thus, each group must be approached on its own terms. For each group's members, current knowledge about reducing the risk of AIDS must be assessed, along with motivation to reduce the risk of AIDS and current behavioral skills in practicing safe sex—such as the ability to be appropriately assertive about the use of a condom (Fisher & Fisher, 1992; and refer to Figure 13.12).

Although scientists have greatly advanced our understanding of the virus that causes AIDS, there is still no cure in sight. For this reason, the role of psychologists in designing effective programs to change risky behaviors that will prevent the spread of HIV is of paramount importance.

Psychological Help for People Who Are HIV-Positive or Have AIDS

The welfare of individuals already infected with HIV or suffering from AIDS is important to psychologists as well. These people have serious psychological, social, and psychiatric needs (Chuang et al., 1992). In particular, they suffer from heightened stress (Chuang et al., 1989). Programs for special populations—gay and bisexual men, for example—have been designed, evaluated, and compared (Tudiver et al., 1992). In some cases, marital therapy is helpful, to assist both partners in accepting bisexuality, as well as any infidelities that occurred (Myers, 1991).

With respect to physicians, nurses, and others dealing with AIDS patients, occupational stress may result in AIDS-related burnout (Garside, 1993; Taerk et al., 1993). In some cases this results from fear of contagion (Gallop et al., 1992), in others from homophobia, sexism, and a lack of understanding of high-risk behaviors (Whyte, 1992). Sometimes these attitudes and beliefs are given "moral meanings" by the media (Clark, 1992). For example, at the University of British Columbia, Boshier (1992) listed topics emphasized by the media in connection with HIV and AIDS: for example, the gay plague, the innocent victim, the heterosexual at risk. Whatever the source of their stress, however, the professionals who are dedicated to caring for these patients require preventative and supportive programs as well (Gallop et al., 1992).

Critical Thinking Questions:

1. Psychologists have shown how social norms and beliefs influence the occurrence of risky behaviors. Can you think of ways this knowledge can be applied to change risky sexual practices?

2. Researchers have developed AIDS-prevention programs for high-risk groups, such as homosexuals and intravenous drug users. Can you think of ways to convince heterosexuals that they too are at risk for AIDS?

3. If you were in charge of the federal government's campaign to prevent AIDS, what would your design for an effective AIDS-prevention program include?

FIGURE 13.12

AIDS-Preventive Behaviors: A Model

Growing evidence suggests that prevention programs are more effective when they are tailored to meet the needs of specific target groups and when they provide people with knowledge, motivation, and behavioral skills.
(Source: Based on Fisher & Fisher, 1992.)

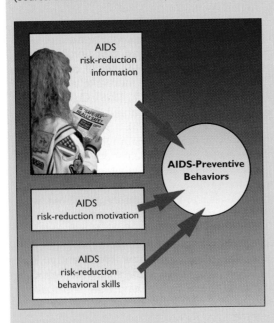

Promoting Wellness: *Developing a Healthier Lifestyle*

*H*ave you ever wondered why some people live to be more than one hundred? Several factors may play a role in this. One of these is diet: Long-lived individuals often eat more grains, leafy green and root vegetables, fresh milk, and fresh fruits, and eat low to moderate amounts of meat and animal fat. In addition, they maintain a low to moderate daily caloric intake (1,200 to 3,000 calories) and consume only moderate amounts of alcohol (Pelletier, 1986). Regular physical activity throughout life—working outdoors and walking often—is perhaps the most important factor contributing to longevity and good health. Additional factors that may contribute to an extended life span are continued sexual activity and continued involvement in family and community affairs (Reminder: Chapter 9 discusses many issues relevant to lifestyles of older adults.)

So, while genetic factors definitely play a role in determining life span, we also know that people may be able to extend their lives significantly by choosing a healthy lifestyle and maintaining it throughout life.

On the basis of these and similar findings, a growing number of health psychologists are focusing on **prevention strategies**—on techniques designed to reduce the occurrence of illness and other physical and psychological problems. Primary prevention is considered the optimal approach. Its goal is to reduce or eliminate altogether the incidence of preventable illness and injury. It usually involves one or more of the following components: educating people about the relationship between their behaviors and their health, providing skills and motivation to practice healthy behaviors, and directly modifying poor health practices through intervention. Secondary prevention focuses on early detection of illness. This involves individuals learning about their health status through medical tests that screen for the presence of disease. Screening for certain diseases is traditionally carried out by health professionals and often requires sophisticated medical tests; however, there are some methods of self-examination, especially for early detection of breast and testicular cancer.

Primary Prevention: *Decreasing the Risks of Illness and Injury*

In most instances, our initial attempts to change our unhealthy behaviors are unsuccessful. Although many smokers try, nicotine addiction is really difficult to overcome. For example, in the study of Ontario high school students, smokers were asked about their attempts to quit. Over half had tried to stop at least once in the twelve months prior to the survey. Of those, one-third had tried once, one-third twice, and one-third three or more times. And out of every two smokers who tried to stop, only one was able to stop for more than one week. Why is it so hard to quit smoking?

First, there are reminders—cues in the environment to light up now. Smoking is an integral part of a person's life; it goes together with a cup of coffee or with friends. Second, there are the difficulties of withdrawal: physiological cravings, headache, and sleeplessness. There is also weight gain and emotional distress. Next, there is the ordinary stress of everyday life. Smokers often relapse after encountering difficulties unrelated to smoking. Motivation and social support are both necessary. There are other factors besides these; for example, at the Clarke Institute of Psychiatry in Toronto,

Prevention strategies: Techniques designed to reduce the occurrence of physical and psychological problems.

Devins (1992) found that what was important in abstaining from cigarettes was whether the smoker had confidence in his or her ability to quit, and whether he or she expected success or failure.

Typically, we become aware of the need to change behaviors; we initiate change; we experience a series of failed attempts to change these behaviors; and sometimes—only sometimes—we succeed. The nature of this process indicates that we need help—a variety of intervention programs to meet our varied needs and purposes.

HEALTH PROMOTION AND THE MASS MEDIA: MARKETING HEALTHY LIFESTYLES IN THE COMMUNITY We often receive health warnings and information about disease. Recently, Canada's Tobacco Products Control Act was changed to require strong health warnings on cigarette packages. Two examples of these are "Smoking can kill you" and "Tobacco smoke can harm your children." The new messages must be displayed prominently—in fact, they must cover 25 percent or more of the surface of the package. Every effort is being made to bring to the attention of those involved, the health risks of their behavior.

In addition to the well-being of the individuals addicted to nicotine, there is the enormous cost to the economy of the diseases caused by smoking. Numerous health organizations use television commercials, newspaper articles, and magazine and radio ads to warn us about smoking (and about other unhealthy behaviors, such as unprotected sex, and alcohol and drug abuse; and their associated risks, which include cancer, heart disease, and AIDS).

Can the mass media campaigns alone produce widespread changes in behavior? There is some doubt about that (Meyer, Maccoby, & Farquhar, 1980). On the one hand, there has been some success. For example, Blashko and Paterson (1990) did the following. First, on five consecutive occasions, an open-line radio station featured experts on heart disease. Then, after six months, they interviewed by telephone listeners who had filled out a questionnaire. The researchers learned that, overall, half of the participants had changed to a more healthy way of living. Moreover, 66 percent had been checked for high blood pressure and 25 percent for diabetes.

On the other hand, there is evidence that, by itself, television is not very effective in promoting health. Why is that? First, on television, we see many messages that are contradictory. For example, unhealthy habits are often depicted as cool, and this directly counters messages that promote healthier practices. Even more perplexing is that fast food chains now use health messages to promote their less-than-ideal products. A second reason is that television offers a degree of information overload that is not helpful. The difference between fat-free, low-fat, sugar-free, and lite-anything as offered on television commercials is not immediately apparent, especially when there are two dozen ingredients listed on a package—with no additional explanation. For example, two tubs of frozen yoghurt of the same size and brand were purchased yesterday in a supermarket in Halifax. The tub that was labelled low-fat had more fat content than the tub that had no such information attached.

Third, those who produce material for the mass media sometimes misunderstand their target audience. The recent Break Free antismoking campaign conducted by our federal government is a case in point. Ottawa spent $8 million to produce ads intended to influence teens against smoking. You may have seen some of these on one of your local channels. However, the campaign had no effect on smoking habits. Why not? For one thing, some teens called the commercials annoying, stupid, ineffective, irritating, and unreal. Others felt that they had been depicted as "gullible, ill-informed and naive." Perhaps the age range of the target audience (11 to 17) was too large for any other outcome to be expected. The person in charge of the campaign defended it by maintaining that "advertising does not change behavior"—which is exactly the point being made here. In Chapter 17 you will read more about the psychological principles involved in influencing other people to behave differently.

Media campaigns do succeed, however, when they are combined with other efforts. For example, in the United States, the Stanford Heart Disease Prevention Project combined a media campaign and a program designed to change health-related behaviors (Farquhar, Maccoby, & Solomon, 1984). Three communities were chosen for the study. One community received an intense media campaign focusing on the risk factors associated with heart disease; a second group received the same media campaign as well as a personal instruction program to modify the health habits of people in high-risk groups; a third community served as a control group. The media campaign alone produced modest changes in health behavior; the program that included both a media campaign and behavior therapy was still more effective. Another successful American program, which used a combination of mass media, community antismoking programs, and physician intervention—termed the Quit for Life Project—reduced smoking in two major cities by 6.5 percent over a four-year period (Pierce et al., 1990).

In the 1980s and the 1990s, the mass media have done much to draw attention to AIDS and the AIDS crisis. That publicity may explain, in part, the dramatic increase in sales of condoms between 1984 and 1988 (Moran et al., 1990). Of course, an individual's beliefs do much to determine how effective an ad campaign will be. For example, ads about AIDS are most effective with individuals who are already very afraid of contracting AIDS; the same ads are less effective among those who have little fear of AIDS (Struckman-Johnson et al, 1990).

THE WORK OF STAYING HEALTHY: EXERCISING THE COUCH POTATO   It is now widely accepted that exercise has an important impact on health. An active lifestyle reduces the risk of many illnesses that lead to premature death. Exercise also contributes much to the rehabilitation of those who have been ill or injured.

Despite the great benefit and the low cost, only one in five of us does enough physical activity. Why do we not do what we know is good for us? Psychological theory suggests a number of reasons, these among them—we are held back by our beliefs about our ability to succeed, our attitudes toward trying, and our feelings of threat or challenge regarding the physical activity (Crocker, 1993).

Research also indicates that exercise can have a significant impact on our psychological well-being. For example, it may improve our self-concept, alleviate feelings of depression, and reduce anxiety (Dubbert, 1992). These effects are particularly apparent just after a workout, but there may also be some benefits long afterwards. There are changes in mood following exercise, which may result from socializing and being involved with others (Plante & Rodin, 1990). Mood may also improve because exercise affects our confidence in our ability to execute a particular behavior (that is, our self-efficacy)—for example, to run a mile or complete an aerobics workout (Rodin & Plante, 1989).

So how do we get you off the couch? Psychological principles dictate that to succeed at an exercise regimen, you must arrange your life so that your new activities are supported and competing behaviors are

MOTIVATING THE COUCH POTATO

Evidence suggests that regular and vigorous exercise reduces the risk of coronary disease.

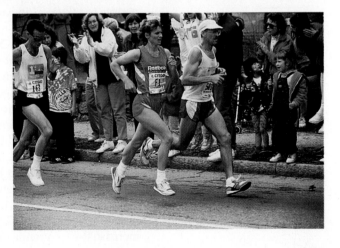

unlikely. First, it is important for you to identify effective cues that will become a signal to exercise. Working out in the same location, doing a consistent warm-up, and recording and posting the results are all helpful in this regard.

Second, arrange a regular time that minimizes the likelihood of competing demands—a time at which you would probably not be doing much of anything. For example, if you tend to work best late in the day, arrange to exercise in the morning. Third, to maintain your new activities, provide yourself with pleasurable consequences. Reward yourself, and avoid potential sources of punishment, such as sore muscles, fatigue, and injury.

Fourth, choose an exercise that you enjoy. As in life generally, there is no such thing as the only correct choice. There are lots of options here—an exercise for almost every letter of the alphabet, from aerobics to walking. According to Wankel (1993), the more you enjoy a physical activity, the more useful it is for countering stress.

The exercise trend of the 1990s is strength training with free weights. The cost can be minimal if you use cans of fruit of increasing sizes for resistance. Reportedly, strength training can have positive effects on your stamina, energy, and confidence, on your tennis and swimming, on your cholesterol levels and bone strength, and on your weight. The goal of strength training is to become fit by exercising different muscle groups. After you have established a routine, which should begin with stretching and end with a cooldown period, the full workout may take as little as thirty minutes (although an hour is more like it for most of us).

Fifth, let your motives for engaging in physical activity center upon fitness and health rather than appearance or pec size. Gauvin (1990) studied autonomous exercisers, sedentary people, fitness program dropouts, and fitness program enrollees. She found that autonomous exercisers gave fitness and health as their primary motivation. Finally, find some social encouragement (not competition); the other people in your life are an important resource in maintaining an exercise program.

Secondary Prevention: *Early Detection of Disease and Illness*

When is the last time you had your blood pressure taken? If you are like most people, procedures for early detection of the "silent killers"—high blood pressure, high blood cholesterol, and several types of cancer—are furthest from your mind. Yet identifying these conditions at an early stage can make an enormous difference—in some cases the difference between life and death. For that reason, psychological strategies are being developed to motivate people to take part in early detection programs.

SCREENING FOR DISEASE: SEEKING INFORMATION ABOUT OUR HEALTH STATUS   Early detection and treatment of an illness is more effective than later detection and treatment; that is the foundation of health. Widespread use of available screening procedures could decrease the incidence of cardiovascular disease; it could also significantly reduce the number of deaths from cervical, colon, and prostate cancer. For example, it is estimated that 10 to 20 percent of cervical cancers could be prevented by widespread Pap testing (Rothenberg et al., 1987).

Many companies, universities, community groups, and hospitals have screening programs to test for high blood pressure and serum cholesterol. Unfortunately, many employees either do not take advantage of screening programs at all, or fail to get screened regularly. They either forget, or forget how long it has been. Reminders from physicians and local ad campaigns do increase the frequency of screening visits (Mitchell, 1988).

DETECTING THE EARLY SIGNS OF ILLNESS Whether we take preventative measures depends, generally, on the perceived severity of the possible illness, our perceived vulnerability to disease, and our beliefs about what those people close to us think about screening (Henna & Knolls, 1990).

As is understood widely, self-examination is imperative for the early detection of breast cancer and skin cancer. However, testicular cancer—which, although quite rare, is the most common kind found in males between 15 and 35—is less well-known. It is easily treated if caught early (Dahl, 1985). Self-examination once a month, for a hard bit right at the surface, is recommended. (Goldenring & Putrell, 1984; Steffen, 1990).

For women over fifty, for breast cancers that are detected early through secondary prevention programs (such as self-examination, clinical breast examination, and mammography), there is an 85 to 90 percent chance of full recovery.

Lying in the sun is bad for your health, unless you use proper sunscreen. In the United States, for example, each year there are about 400,000 cases of skin cancer, and about 6,000 people die of melanoma (the deadliest form of it). What do we know about those who continue to tan seriously without taking proper precautions? That they know little about skin cancer, have friends who admire a dark tan, are more relaxed than others, and tend to take more risks (Keesling & Friedman, 1987). In addition to increasing awareness of skin cancers and dealing with erroneous beliefs, health psychologists design programs that motivate people to perform self-exams and to take steps to prevent this disease.

MAKING PSYCHOLOGY PART OF YOUR LIFE

Managing Stress—Some Useful Tactics

Stress is a fact of life. But we can use psychological principles to lessen its harmful effects (Carver, Scheier, & Weintraub, 1989; Folkman et al., 1986). Let's consider several of these techniques, dividing them into three major categories: physiological, cognitive, and behavioral.

Physiological Coping Techniques

Common physiological responses to stress include tense muscles, racing pulse, pounding heart, dry mouth, queasy stomach, and sweating. But several coping techniques can be effective. One of the best is progressive relaxation (Jacobson, 1938). To use this technique, begin by alternately flexing and relaxing your muscles to appreciate the difference between relaxed and tense muscles. Then shake out your arms and let them flop by your sides. Then relax your shoulders by slowly rolling them up and down. Now, relax your neck. Step by step,

you extend this process until your body is completely relaxed from head to toe. Control breathing is also important. (When you are tense, you tend to take in relatively short, shallow breaths. As your body slows down during relaxation, you will notice that you begin to take deeper, longer breaths.) Relaxation procedures are effective in reducing emotional as well as physical tension. A related technique that is often effective for achieving a relaxed state is meditation, which you learned about in Chapter 4.

Physical exercise is absolutely essential for dealing with stress. Any anxiety and hostility you felt before exercise will be reduced (Szabo et al., 1993).

The current wisdom, arrived at by taking many studies together, is that you do not have to train to run a marathon in order to live to a ripe old age. Almost any reasonable program will have a similar effect. At the University of Waterloo, for example,

TABLE 13.3	BASIC PRINCIPLES OF TIME MANAGEMENT

GETTING THE MOST OUT OF YOUR DAY: PSYCHOLOGY IN ACTION

One behavioral coping strategy is time management. Here are some tips to help you get the most out of your day.

1. Each day, make a list of things you want to accomplish.

2. Prioritize your list. Plan to do the toughest things first and save the easier tasks for later in the day when you are low on energy.

3. Arrange your work schedule to take best advantage of those hours when you work best.

4. Always set aside a block of time when you can work without any interruptions.

5. Be flexible about changes in your schedule so that you can handle unexpected events.

6. Plan for some leisure activity during your day—everybody needs a break.

7. Set aside some times each day or week in which you always do some planned leisure activity.

Ebbesen and colleagues (1992) found that for men who were relatively inactive, one or two hours of minimal exercise reduced the response of blood pressure to stress. One caution, however: Going from the couch directly to a heavy workout is unwise. As in all things, gradually increasing the time and energy spent is the proper way to proceed.

Behavioral Coping Techniques

We all behave in ways that increase stress. We load ourselves with too many responsibilities; or we procrastinate. It all adds up to stress. There are plenty of steps we can take to reduce the stress in our lives. One method is time management—that is, arranging our affairs so that time works for us instead of against us. A well-planned schedule, if we stick to it, can help us use our time more efficiently and eliminate wasteful behaviors. An important but often ignored principle is that work time and play time should be in balance. Table 13.3 offers several tips to help you get the most out of your day.

Cognitive Coping Techniques

We don't always have control over all the stressors in our lives. We can, however, gain some control over our reactions to them. In other words, there are different ways of thinking about a stressful situation, some of which are much more stress-inducing than others. The process of replacing negative appraisals of stressors with more positive ones is called *cognitive restructuring* (Meichenbaum, 1977). When applied to athletic competition—for example, to male and female gymnasts (Kerr & Leith, 1993)—emphasis is placed not only on perfor-

mance skills and mental rehearsal, but also on stress management and control of anxiety. That emphasis is vital, because stress is related to the incidence of athletic injuries—for example, among élite female gymnasts (Kerr & Minden, 1988). To use this technique yourself, begin by monitoring what you say to yourself during periods of stress. Modify your thoughts by thinking otherwise. For example, try to discover something humorous about the situation, or imagine creative ways to eliminate stress. Also, as mentioned earlier, social support is important. Other people—family, friends, associates—can help us restructure stressors (Bruhn & Phillips, 1987) so that we perceive stressful events as less threatening (and more under our control). Since cognitive appraisal plays a crucial role in the way we interpret stressors, it is helpful to be in contact with people who can suggest alternative strategies for dealing with sources of stress (Costanza, Derlega, & Winstead, 1988).

Research shows that there are a number of steps you can take to help reduce stress, including relaxation, time management, and cognitive restructuring.

HEALTH PSYCHOLOGY: AN OVERVIEW health psychology 532 lifestyle 533	• The primary aim of health psychology is to determine important relationships between psychological variables and health. • A related field, behavioral medicine, combines behavioral and biomedical science knowledge to prevent and treat disorders. • Many of today's leading causes of premature death can be attributed to people's lifestyles.
STRESS: ITS CAUSES, EFFECTS, AND CONTROL stress 534 stressors 534 general adaptation syndrome (GAS) 535 post-traumatic stress disorder 542 person-environment (P-E) fit 544 hardiness 549	• Stress is the process that occurs in us in response to situations or events (stressors) that disrupt, or threaten to disrupt, our physical or psychological functioning. • Selye's general adaptation syndrome (GAS) model helps describe our physiological reactions to stressors. It includes three stages: alarm, resistance, and exhaustion. • Cognitive appraisals play an important role in determining whether an event will be interpreted as stressful or as a challenge. • Stressors can be major life events, such as the death of a spouse, or daily hassles—minor irritations of everyday life. • Unusually stressful natural and human-produced disasters can often produce severe psychological problems, which are termed post-traumatic stress disorders. • Among sources of work-related stress are work overload, role conflict, and performance appraisals. • Stress may play a role in 50 to 70 percent of all physical illness, primarily through its effect on our immune system. Even relatively low levels of stress may interfere with task performance. • People who experience prolonged exposure to high levels of stress may experience burnout. • Two personal characteristics that influence reactions to stress are optimism and hardiness. Optimists adopt more effective tactics for dealing with their stressors than pessimists. Hardy individuals show high levels of commitment, view change as an opportunity for growth, and have a sense of control over events in their lives.
UNDERSTANDING AND COMMUNICATING OUR HEALTH NEEDS health belief mode 551	• Symptoms, or sensations such as irregularities in our heartbeat, are useful because they may reflect an underlying medical problem. • The health-belief model suggests that our willingness to make lifestyle changes or seek medical help depends on our beliefs about our susceptibility to an illness, the severity of the illness, and the effectiveness of taking steps to deal with it. • Doctors are often more effective in handling technical information than psychosocial concerns. Interventions designed to improve doctor–patient communication have a beneficial impact on patient satisfaction and the accuracy of diagnosis.

| BEHAVIORAL AND PSYCHOLOGICAL CORRELATES OF ILLNESS: COGNITION AND HEALTH

cancer 533
risk factors 533
carcinogens 533
cardiovascular disease 554
nicotine 555
passive smoking 556
serum cholesterol 559
hypertension 559
Type A behavior pattern 559 | • Cancer is actually a group of diseases characterized by cells' loss of ability to function normally. These cells typically multiply rapidly, generating tumors.
• Individual differences in people's reaction to nicotine, the addictive substance in tobacco, help determine who will become a smoker.
• Both smoking and passive smoking are implicated in many cancers, in cardiovascular diseases, and in sickness among children.
• Poor diet can raise our risks of cancer of the colon and rectum, breast cancer, and cardiovascular disease.
• Heavy drinking can cause diseases of the stomach, liver, and intestines. It can also impair mental and sexual functioning and result in fetal alcohol syndrome.
• Inadequate emotional expression can result in cancer progressing more rapidly. Emotions also affect blood pressure.
• People who tend to be competitive, aggressive, hostile, and impatient are displaying a pattern of behaviors termed Type A. In particular, a pattern of cynical hostility puts Type A people at risk for heart attack.
• Acquired immune deficiency syndrome (AIDS) is a reduction in the immune system's ability to defend itself against foreign matter. AIDS is transmitted primarily through unprotected sex and infected blood. |
| PROMOTING WELLNESS: DEVELOPING A HEALTHIER LIFESTYLE

prevention strategies 565 | • The mass media, in combination with other health promotion programs, can be an effective tool for promoting behavior changes.
• Regular and vigorous exercise promotes both physical and psychological health. Starting and maintaining an exercise habit requires participants to arrange their environment in a way that supports the desired exercise behavior and weakens competing behaviors.
• Primary prevention involves the following: educating people about the relationship between behavior and health; promoting healthy behaviors; and directly modifying poor health practices.
• Secondary prevention strategies emphasize early detection to decrease the severity of illness that is already present. |

CRITICAL THINKING QUESTIONS

APPRAISAL	Throughout this chapter we've seen that lifestyle factors—what we choose to eat, drink, or smoke, and whether we choose to exercise regularly—greatly influence our health. If one can achieve good health simply by changing one's own behaviors, then why aren't more people doing so?
CONTROVERSY	The number of people infected with HIV throughout the world is increasing at an alarming rate. Since it is clear that many infections result from unprotected sex with an infected person, behavioral researchers have developed interventions that effectively promote the use of condoms—particularly among high-risk populations. Others argue, however, that these interventions simply promote promiscuity and thereby worsen the problem. Which perspective is correct? What are your views on this issue?
MAKING PSYCHOLOGY PART OF YOUR LIFE	Now that you know something about the many practices that can improve our physical and psychological health, will you be more likely to follow these practices yourself? If so, why? If not, then why not?

Psychological Disorders
Their Nature and Causes

CHANGING CONCEPTIONS OF
PSYCHOLOGICAL DISORDERS: A BRIEF
HISTORICAL PERSPECTIVE 577
From Demons to Disease: Changing
  Concepts of Abnormal Behavior
The Biological/Medical Perspective:
  Psychological Disorders as Disease
The Psychodynamic Perspective:
  Desires, Anxieties, and Defenses
The Modern Psychological Approach:
  Recognizing the Multiple Roots of
  Abnormal Behavior

IDENTIFYING PSYCHOLOGICAL DISORDERS:
THE DSM-IV 580

MOOD DISORDERS: THE DOWNS AND UPS
OF LIFE 587
Depressive Disorders: Probing the
  Depths of Despair
Bipolar Disorders: Riding the Emotional
  Roller Coaster
The Causes of Depression: Its Biological
  and Psychological Roots
Suicide: When Life Becomes Unbearable
Why Suicide? A Host of Contributing
  Factors

ANXIETY DISORDERS: WHEN DREAD
DEBILITATES 592
Panic Attack: The Body Signals
  "Danger!" But Is It Real?
Phobias: Fear That Is Focused
Obsessive-Compulsive Disorder:
  Behaviors and Thoughts Outside
  One's Control
Post-Traumatic Stress Disorder
Anxiety: The Role of Subliminal
  Processing

SOMATOFORM DISORDERS: PHYSICAL
SYMPTOMS WITHOUT PHYSICAL CAUSES 596

DISSOCIATIVE DISORDERS: WHEN MEMORY
FAILS 597

SEXUAL AND GENDER IDENTITY DISORDERS
600
Sexual Dysfunctions: Disturbances in
  Desire and Arousal
Paraphilias: Disturbances in Sexual
  Object or Behavior
Gender Identity Disorders

EATING DISORDERS 602

PERSONALITY DISORDERS: TRAITS THAT
PROVE COSTLY 603
Paranoid and Schizoid Personality
  Disorders: Cut Off from Human
  Contact
The Antisocial Personality Disorder

SCHIZOPHRENIA: OUT OF TOUCH WITH
REALITY 607
The Basic Nature of Schizophrenia
Subtypes of Schizophrenia
The Origins of Schizophrenia

SUMMARY AND REVIEW OF KEY POINTS 615

KEY CONCEPT—CONTRASTING
PERSPECTIVES ON ABNORMAL BEHAVIOR
581

PERSPECTIVES ON DIVERSITY—
TAKING ACCOUNT OF CULTURAL FACTORS IN
PSYCHOLOGICAL DISORDERS: IMPROVEMENTS
IN THE DSM-IV 584

CANADIAN FOCUS—ASSESSING THE
PREVALENCE OF PSYCHOLOGICAL DISORDERS
IN CANADA 585

THE POINT OF IT ALL—DISSOCIATIVE
IDENTITY DISORDER: MULTIPLE
PERSONALITIES IN A SINGLE BODY? 598

CANADIAN PERSPECTIVES—THE CAUSE
AND CHARACTER OF DISSOCIATIVE IDENTITY
DISORDER 599

THE RESEARCH PROCESS—THE
ANTISOCIAL PERSONALITY DISORDER:
ANOMALOUS EMOTIONAL REACTIVITY, AND
IRREGULARITIES IN ALLOCATION OF
ATTENTION AND LEARNING 605

MAKING PSYCHOLOGY PART OF
YOUR LIFE—PREVENTING SUICIDE: SOME
BASIC STEPS 614

14

MULTIPLE PERSONALITIES: THE REALITY ESCAPE

**The Calgary Herald:
January 27, 1994**

For some unfortunate people, early childhood was a time when they were repeatedly and violently abused.

As the Herald recounts, the psychological consequence of that trauma may be the dissociation of their personality into a system of several different ones. That is Multiple Personality Disorder. In one individual, there may be personalities with different traits, which may include different handwriting, different intellectual abilities, and different political and religious views.

How does MPD develop? Here is the recollection of one patient: "A part of me handled the loving mother and another part of me handled the abusive mother, because if you put it all together you wouldn't have a mind left."

Two Calgary psychologists who have dealt with 80 individuals with MPD find that "Dissociation is an intellectual skill to cope with the trauma…" suffered in the early years of life. They also find that MPD is often misdiagnosed. The result is that many cases remain untreated, confused, and "end up in jail or in mental hospitals."

MPD is only one of the several serious psychological disorders you will study as you proceed through Chapter 14 of your introduction to psychology.

THERE APPEAR TO BE
NO SIMPLE WAYS OF
DISTINGUISHING
ABNORMAL BEHAVIOR
FROM NORMAL
BEHAVIOR. THE TWO
LIE ON A CONTINUUM.

Psychological Disorders: *Behaviors or thoughts that are unusual in a given society, that are maladaptive, and that cause the people who experience them considerable distress.*

PSYCHOLOGICAL DISORDERS: ATYPICAL AND MALADAPTIVE

Is the homeless man shown here suffering from a psychological disorder? We can't be sure without careful diagnosis, but his behavior certainly meets some of the key criteria defining such disorders.

*T*hink back over all the people you have known. Can you remember ones who experienced any of the following problems?

- Wild swings in mood, from deep despair to the heights of elation.

- Excessive dependence on alcohol, tranquilizers, or other drugs.

- Intense and seemingly unjustifiable fear of certain situations, such as being in a crowd, being alone, or traveling by airplane.

- Unusual preoccupation with illness, health, and various (perhaps largely imaginary) symptoms.

- Tremendous concern about being overweight, coupled with a near-starvation diet and an emaciated body.

If you *haven't* known people who experienced one or more of these problems, then you have certainly led a charmed life, for disorders like these are experienced by many millions of people in every corner of the earth every year. It is on these and other **psychological disorders**—maladaptive patterns of behavior and thought that cause the people who experience them considerable distress—that we will focus in this chapter.

But, what, precisely, are such disorders? What they involve has just been suggested, but only in the broadest terms. In fact, psychologists and other professionals concerned with psychological disorders have debated this question for decades, for there appear to be no simple ways of distinguishing *abnormal* from *normal* behavior. The two lie on a continuum, with one often shading into the other. Most psychologists agree, however, that psychological disorders (and, by extension, all forms of behavior described as "abnormal") often share some, if not all, of the following features.

First, these disorders usually generate *distress*—anxiety, internal conflict, depression, confusion, and other negative feelings—in the people who experience them. Second, psychological disorders involve patterns of behavior or thought that are judged to be unusual or *atypical*. People with these disorders don't behave or think like most others in their society, and this fact is noticed—often with discomfort—by the people around them. Third, psychological disorders involve behaviors that are *maladaptive*—that interfere with the individual's ability to function normally and meet the demands of daily life. People suffering from such disorders find it difficult to carry out their work, to interact with friends or strangers, to meet family obligations, and to accomplish the countless small tasks of daily life.

Finally, psychological disorders are associated with behavior that is evaluated negatively by the members of a particular society. In other words, those who suffer from such disorders often behave in ways that are viewed as objectionable or unacceptable by the people around them. Of course, ideas about what forms of behavior are acceptable and what forms are not can and often do vary between cultures, and can also change greatly within the same culture over time.

For example, in the early 1960s on a university campus, a young man who pierced his ears and wore two or more earrings would have been viewed as strange indeed. Today, such adornments hardly receive a second glance on most campuses; what might have been labeled as weird or abnormal in the 1960s is nothing out of the ordinary today.

Taking these points into account, we can define psychological disorders as *patterns of behavior and thought that are atypical, that are viewed as undesirable or unacceptable within a given culture, that are maladaptive, and that usually (although not always) cause the people who demonstrate them considerable distress.*

As we have observed, these problems are far from rare. In fact, some recent surveys indicate that perhaps as many as half of all people experience a psychological disorder at some point during their lives (Kessler, 1994; Robins & Regier, 1991). Fortunately, this need not be cause for alarm; as we will see in Chapter 15, many effective techniques exist for helping people with such difficulties.

In this chapter, we'll consider a number of different psychological disorders. Before turning to them, however, it's essential to complete two preliminary tasks. First, we'll review contrasting perspectives on the nature of psychological disorders and indicate how views concerning them have changed over the centuries. Second, we'll examine a widely used system for diagnosing various psychological disorders—the *DSM-IV*. After that, we'll turn to the disorders themselves, and consider both the symptoms they produce and potential reasons why they occur.

Trephining: An ancient surgical procedure in which holes are cut into the skull.

Changing Conceptions of Psychological Disorders: *A Brief Historical Perspective*

*A*re psychological disorders a product of the stress and turmoil of modern life? Existing evidence suggests that these disorders in fact existed long before the dawn of civilization. Stone Age skulls containing neatly drilled holes have been uncovered by archaeologists in Europe and South America. It may be that these operations, known as **trephining**, were performed to permit the escape of evil spirits that—so it was believed—were causing the sufferers to behave in bizarre ways (Maher & Maher, 1985). However, it is also possible that such operations were performed simply to treat various types of head injuries. The fact that most skulls showing trephining are those of adult males—the members of early societies most likely to be injured in an accident or wounded during warfare—suggests that this less colorful interpretation may be more correct. Still, there is indirect evidence that psychological disorders existed even in the distant past, and that people in primitive societies attempted to deal with these problems as best they could.

From Demons to Disease: *Changing Concepts of Abnormal Behavior*

While the precise meaning of the holes in ancient skulls is open to interpretation, the earliest written descriptions of psychological disorders are clear as to what people saw as causing these maladies: They lay the blame squarely on supernatural forces. In societies ranging from China to ancient Babylon, possession by demons or evil spirits was the explanation commonly accepted for bizarre forms of behavior and thought. This view of abnormal behavior persisted for many centuries. However, the ancient Greeks developed a radically different point of view—that mental disorders stemmed primarily from *natural* causes. Several centuries before the birth of Christ, Hippocrates, a famous physician, suggested that all forms of disease, including mental illness, derived from natural causes. In this vein, he attributed psychological disorders to such factors as brain damage, heredity, or imbalances within the body.

TREPHINING: EARLY TREATMENT FOR PSYCHOLOGICAL DISORDERS?

Stone Age skulls with neatly drilled holes may provide an example of early psychological treatment, or they may be the result of medical procedures for treating various types of injuries.

This view of abnormal behavior was maintained in Western societies until the fall of the Roman Empire. Then it was replaced once again by the idea that abnormal patterns of behavior had supernatural causes such as demonic possession or witchcraft. While there is some indication that abnormal behavior was sometimes seen as stemming from more ordinary factors, such as injuries to the head or the effects of high fevers, acceptance of the view that it was often caused by supernatural forces persisted into the fifteenth and sixteenth centuries. Indeed, even during the Renaissance, a period of dazzling advances in European art, music, and science, the supernatural theory persisted. It was during the fifteenth and sixteenth centuries—the heart of the Renaissance—that more than 100,000 people in Europe were convicted of being witches and executed for their "crimes" (Deutsch, 1949). Some of these executions were probably carried out for political or economic reasons; even so, it appears that many of the victims were individuals whose only crime was bizarre or unusual behavior stemming from psychological problems.

Gradually, however, the scientific approach first established by the Greeks reemerged. This led many scholars and physicians to search for natural causes of abnormal behavior. The result was a shift toward the idea that psychological disorders are a form of illness or disease—a perspective that remains highly influential today.

The Biological/Medical Perspective:
Psychological Disorders as Disease

Prior to the eighteenth century, people suffering from mental disorders were often subjected to harsh "treatment." Patients in so-called mental hospitals were shackled to walls in dark, unlighted cells, which they were never permitted to leave. Sanitation was primitive or nonexistent, and little if any attention was paid to diet.

But change would eventually come. Disturbed by these conditions, Jean-Baptiste Pussin, superintendent of a large hospital in Paris, established new and more humane rules for the treatment of those in his care. No beatings were allowed, and patients who had been chained for years were freed from their shackles in the hope that they would become more manageable. Because many did respond favorably to this improved treatment, the reforms were continued by Philippe Pinel, who became chief physician of the hospital's ward for the mentally ill in 1793. Like Pussin, Pinel believed that psychologically disturbed people were suffering from a form of illness, and that moving them from dungeons to bright, sunny rooms and treating them with kindness rather than violence would help them recover. The results were impressive: Many patients (those, we must assume, who were less seriously disturbed) improved rapidly under this new treatment. Indeed, many recovered to the point where they could be released—some after decades of confinement.

Similar actions by enlightened physicians in other countries produced similar encouraging results. As a result, the view that abnormal behavior is the result of *mental illness* gradually gained hold and became, at least in Western nations, the dominant approach. This **medical perspective** remains highly influential today. Indeed, it is the basis for the field of **psychiatry**, a branch of modern medicine specializing in the treatment of psychological disorders.

HUMANE TREATMENT OF PEOPLE WITH PSYCHOLOGICAL DISORDERS

Until the eighteenth century, people suffering from psychological disorders were subject to harsh conditions. Philippe Pinel introduced more humane procedures in a large Paris hospital, with very positive results.

Within psychology, there is less emphasis on abnormal behavior as a disease and more on the potential *biological* or *biochemical bases* of such disorders (e.g., Cromwell, 1992; Heinrichs, 1993). Growing evidence suggests that changes in the structure or functioning of the brain may play an important role in several forms of abnormal behavior (Raz, 1993). Further, it appears that the tendency to develop a psychological disorder may in some cases be inherited (Faraone, Kremen, & Tsuang, 1990). Thus, while many psychologists prefer to avoid describing abnormal behavior in strictly medical terms—as some form of disease requiring treatment—they do accept the view that psychological disorders often have biological causes.

The Psychodynamic Perspective:
Desires, Anxieties, and Defenses

A very different perspective on abnormal behavior was offered by Freud and several other important figures in the history of psychology. According to this *psychodynamic perspective*, which Chapter 12 discussed in detail, many mental disorders can be traced to unconscious urges or impulses and to the struggle over their expression that takes place in the hidden depths of human personality. Remember that in Freud's theory, the *id* (repository of our primitive desires) demands instant gratification, while the *superego* (conscience) denies it. The *ego* (consciousness) must strive to maintain a balance between these forces. According to Freud, mental disorders arise when the ego, sensing that it may soon be overwhelmed by the id, experiences *anxiety*. To cope with this anxiety, the ego employs different *defense mechanisms*, as described in Chapter 12. These serve to disguise the nature of the unacceptable impulses and so reduce the anxiety experienced by the ego; but they may also generate maladaptive behavior.

While few psychologists currently accept Freud's views about the origins of psychological disorders, his suggestion that unconscious thoughts or impulses can play a role in abnormal behavior remains influential. In this respect, the psychodynamic perspective has contributed to our modern understanding of abnormal behavior.

The Modern Psychological Approach:
Recognizing the Multiple Roots of Abnormal Behavior

The term "mental illness" makes some psychologists uneasy. Why? Because it implies acceptance of the medical model described above. To call an individual "mentally ill" implies that his or her problems constitute a disease that can be cured through appropriate medical treatment. In one respect, this view makes sense: As has been already noted, many psychological problems do seem to have an important biological component. In another sense, though, the medical perspective is somewhat misleading. Decades of research suggest that full understanding of many psychological disorders requires careful attention to *psychological* processes such as learning, perception, and cognition, as well as recognition of the complex interplay between

CULTURAL FACTORS AND ABNORMAL BEHAVIOR

Normal behavior in one culture may be considered quite abnormal in another. The Ashura ritual, practiced in the Middle East, involves self-flagellation, a behavior that many cultures would consider abnormal.

- Ideas concerning the nature of abnormal behavior have changed greatly over the centuries. Until well into the eighteenth century, psychological disorders were seen as largely the result of supernatural forces.

- The supernatural approach was replaced by the medical model, which sees psychological disorders as forms of mental illness.

- Psychologists recognize the importance of biological factors in many forms of abnormal behavior, but they also emphasize the importance of psychological processes such as cognition and learning, and the impact of sociocultural factors.

environment and heredity that seems to affect all forms of behavior.

For example, consider what is perhaps the most common form of psychological disorder—*depression*, which involves intense sadness, lack of energy, and feelings of hopelessness and despair. What are the roots of this complex problem? Existing evidence suggests that biochemical and genetic factors probably play an important role (Henriques & Davidson, 1990). But so, too, do cognitive and social factors. As we'll see later in this chapter, depressed people seem to process information about the external world in a different way than nondepressed people; they are, for example, much more likely to notice negative information (Segall, 1988) and to hold unfavorable perceptions of themselves and others (Gara et al., 1993). Awareness of these factors adds appreciably to our understanding of the nature of depression and also suggests effective new ways of treating it.

Finally, most psychologists also attach considerable importance to *social* or *cultural factors* in their efforts to understand abnormal behavior. Some disorders—especially those that are quite severe—appear to be universal, occurring in all or at least most cultures (Al-Issa, 1982). Other disorders, however, vary greatly across cultures in terms of their frequency, severity, and precise form. For example, depression appears to be more common in Western nations than in Asian ones (Kleinman, 1986). Moreover, some disorders seem to be restricted to specific cultures, occurring only within them. In isolated rural areas of Japan, for instance, some individuals suffer from a disorder known as *kitsunet-suki*—the belief that they are possessed by foxes; this specific problem is largely unknown elsewhere. While the role of biological factors should not be overlooked in these disorders, it seems likely that cultural beliefs, values, and conditions play a key role in their occurrence and specific form.

In sum, the modern psychological perspective on abnormal behavior suggests that such behavior can best be understood in terms of complex and often subtle interactions between biological, psychological, and sociocultural factors (see Figure 14.1). This perspective is certainly more complex than the one which views such disorders as biologically produced. However, as we'll discover later in this chapter, it is probably also considerably more accurate. See **Key Concept** for an overview of contrasting perspectives on abnormal behavior.

Identifying Psychological Disorders: The DSM-IV

No physician would attempt to treat a common cold through surgery or internal injuries with a Band-Aid. The first and often most crucial step in medical practice is *diagnosis*—identifying the nature of the problem that brought the patient to the doctor in the first place. Even if we do not view psychological disorders as medical illnesses, the need to identify these problems in a clear and reliable manner remains. Without an agreed-upon system of *classification*, different psychologists or psychiatrists might refer to the same disorder with different terms, or use the same term to describe very different problems (Millon, 1991).

Contrasting Perspectives on Abnormal Behavior

Supernatural View

Abnormal behavior stems from supernatural causes—possession by demons, evil spirits, goddesses, or gods.

Some evidence indicates that many of the persons burned at the stake during the fifteenth and sixteenth centuries because they were thought to be witches were actually suffering from psychological disorders.

Psychodynamic View

Abnormal behavior stems from hidden inner forces—that is, conflict between unconscious impulses and aspects of personality that restrain them.

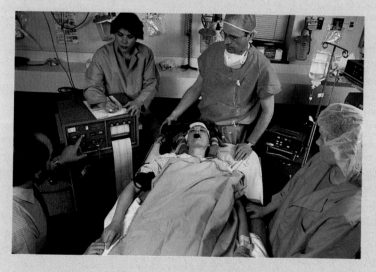

Medical Model

Abnormal behavior is a treatable disease that, like other diseases, has biological causes.

Electroconvulsive therapy, which involves the delivery of electric shocks to the patient's head, reflects the view that psychological disorders stem primarily from biological causes.

Modern Psychological View

Abnormal behavior has multiple causes. These include *psychological* factors such as learning, perception, and cognition; *sociocultural* factors; and *biological* factors.

FIGURE 14.1

Abnormal Behavior: A Psychological Perspective

Psychologists believe that in order to understand the nature and origins of abnormal behavior, we must take careful account of biological, psychological, and sociocultural factors.

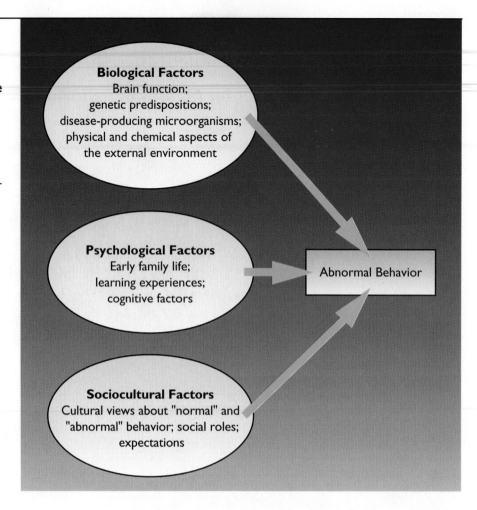

Biological Factors
Brain function; genetic predispositions; disease-producing microorganisms; physical and chemical aspects of the external environment

Psychological Factors
Early family life; learning experiences; cognitive factors

Abnormal Behavior

Sociocultural Factors
Cultural views about "normal" and "abnormal" behavior; social roles; expectations

Diagnostic and Statistical Manual of Mental Disorders-IV (DSM-IV): The latest version of a manual widely used for diagnosing various psychological disorders.

Recognizing this, the American Psychiatric Association has for many years published guides for diagnosing mental disorders. These guides or manuals are mainly *descriptive* in nature; they are designed to help practitioners recognize and correctly identify (diagnose) specific disorders. The most recent edition of this guide, from 1993, is the **Diagnostic and Statistical Manual of Mental Disorders** (**DSM-IV** for short). The major diagnostic categories of DSM-IV are shown in Table 14.1. Within the manual itself, literally hundreds of specific disorders are described. These descriptions focus on observable features and include *diagnostic features*—symptoms that must be present before an individual may be diagnosed as suffering from a particular problem. In addition, the manual includes information on *associated features and disorders*—clinical features that are frequently associated with the disorder but are not considered essential to its diagnosis; on *associated laboratory findings and physical examination signs*—biological factors associated with the condition; and on *age-related, culture-related*, and *gender-related features*—variations within each disorder that may be related to age, cultural, and gender factors.

Another important feature of the DSM-IV is that it classifies disorders along five *axes* rather than merely assigning them to particular categories. Axis I relates to the major disorders themselves. Axis II relates to what are known as *personality disorders*—maladaptive aspects of personality that exert a powerful effect on individual behavior. (We'll return to these disorders in a later section.) A third axis pertains to general medical conditions relevant to each disorder, while a fourth axis considers psychosocial and environmental

DIAGNOSTIC CATEGORY	EXAMPLES
Disorders usually first diagnosed in infancy, childhood, or adolescence	Cognitive impairment, learning disorders, disruptive behavior
Delerium, dementia, and other cognitive disorders	Disturbance of consciousness
Mental disorders due to a general medical condition	Delerium due to a high fever
Substance-related disorders	Alcohol dependence, amphetamine dependence, cocaine-use disorders
Schizophrenia and other psychotic disorders	Schizophrenia, delusional disorder
Mood disorders	Depression, bipolar disorders
Anxiety disorders	Panic attacks, agoraphobia
Somatoform disorders	Somatization disorder, conversion disorder
Factitious disorders	Intentional feigning of symptoms
Dissociative disorders	Dissociative amnesia, dissociative fugue, dissociative identity disorder (multiple personality disorder)
Sexual and gender identity disorders	Sexual desire disorders, sexual arousal disorders, paraphilias
Eating disorders	Anorexia nervosa, bulimia nervosa
Sleep disorders	Primary insomnia, nightmare disorder
Impulse control disorders not elsewhere classified	Intermittent explosive disorder, kleptomania, pathological gambling
Adjustment disorder	Development of emotional or behavioral symptoms in response to an identifiable stressor
Personality disorders	Paranoid personality disorder, schizoid personality disorder, antisocial personality disorder
Other conditions that may be a focus of clinical attention	Medication-induced movement disorders, problems related to abuse or neglect

TABLE 14.1

Major Diagnostic Categories of the DSM-IV

The DSM-IV classifies psychological disorders according to the categories listed here.

problems that may affect the diagnosis, treatment, or prognosis of various disorders. Finally, a fifth axis relates to assessing current functioning on a global basis. By evaluating people along these various axes, the DSM-IV offers a fuller and more sophisticated picture of the individual's current psychological condition than did earlier systems of diagnosis.

The DSM-IV differs from earlier versions in several important respects. Perhaps most important, it is the first version to which psychologists have had major input (Barlow, 1991). Partly as a result of this, and partly as a result of changes within psychiatry, strenuous efforts were made to base the DSM-IV more firmly than ever on empirical evidence concerning the nature and prevalence of psychological disorders. The task force of psychiatrists, psychologists, and other professionals who worked on this new version relied heavily on published studies and the reanalysis of existing data when refining descriptions of each disorder. The task force also conducted special field trials in which they compared new descriptions and categories with existing ones to determine if the proposed changes would indeed improve the reliability of diagnosis—that is, the consistency with which specific disorders could be identified. On the basis of these procedures, many changes were made in the DSM-IV—changes intended to help psychiatrists and psychologists accurately recognize a wide range of psychological disorders and thereby treat them effectively.

Additional changes in the DSM-IV reflect efforts to take fuller account of possible cultural factors in psychological disorders. Information on these changes is presented in **Perspectives on Diversity**.

One final important point: The DSM-IV merely describes various disorders; it makes no attempt to explain them. This is deliberate, for the DSM-IV is designed to be neutral with respect to theories about the origins of psychological disorders. But since psychology, as a science, seeks *explanation*, not simply description, many psychologists view this aspect of the DSM-IV as a shortcoming that limits its value.

PERSPECTIVES ON DIVERSITY

Taking Account of Cultural Factors in Psychological Disorders: Improvements in the DSM-IV

There is little doubt that some psychological disorders take much the same form throughout the world. Depressed people, for example, demonstrate negative moods, lack of energy, and feelings of hopelessness no matter where they happen to live and regardless of the specific cultural group to which they belong. But in many cases, cultural factors *are* reflected in psychological disorders in important ways. The specific symptoms shown by individuals, the terms in which they describe their discomfort, and even the frequency of various types of disorders can differ appreciably from one culture to another. This is an important point, because the DSM-IV, like earlier versions of the DSM, will be used all over the world, and with people from highly diverse backgrounds and societies (Maser, Kaelber, & Weise, 1991). It is crucial that professionals using the DSM be aware of and sensitive to these cultural differences.

The DSM-IV attempts to foster this crucial awareness in several different ways. First, for each description of each disorder, there is a new section that focuses on *culturally related features*. Culturally specific symptoms, ways of describing distress, and similar information are included whenever available. This information is designed to help professionals recognize the many ways in which an individual's culture can influence the forms that psychological disorders take.

Second, certain disorders that seem to appear only in specific cultures are described where relevant. For example, *kitsunetsuki* (see above) is included in the section describing the psychological disorders to which it seems to be related. Third, a new appendix describes culture-bound disorders. As stated by the task force charged with developing the DSM-IV: "It is hoped that these new features will increase sensitivity to variations in how mental disorders present in different cultures and will reduce the possible effect of unintended bias stemming from the clinician's own cultural background."

This is a valuable goal, because some evidence suggests that a psychologist's or psychiatrist's cultural background *can* sometimes influence clinical judgment. In the past, most research designed to uncover *clinical bias* focused on *overpathologizing*—the tendency to perceive women, blacks, and people from other disadvantaged groups as being more disturbed than they actually are. Such research yielded little evidence for this type of bias (e.g., Abramowitz & Murray, 1983). However, more recent research has examined clinical diagnoses for signs of an opposite form of bias—a tendency to diagnosis members of nonmale, nonwhite groups as being *less* disturbed than they actually are. For example, depression may be perceived as more "normal" among women than among men, and drug abuse may be perceived as more "normal" among blacks than among whites, with the result that these disorders (depression and substance abuse) are perceived as less serious than they actually are, or are less likely to be recognized when they do in fact exist.

In recent research applying this broadened definition of clinical bias, Lopez (1989) has found considerable evidence for its existence. These findings suggest that important clinical judgments are sometimes influenced by culture gaps between psychologists or psychiatrists and the people they seek to help. Certainly, such effects don't often arise from overt prejudice or bias on the part of clinicians; rather, they probably stem from the influence of unconscious assumptions, or the kinds of errors in memory and judgment we encountered in Chapters 6 and 7. Whatever their origins, culture-related errors in the diagnosis of psychological disorders can harm people belonging to disadvantaged groups—people who need all the help they can get. Thus, efforts to increase cultural sensitivity in the DSM-IV, and in diagnostic procedures generally, seem to be necessary as well as timely.

CULTURE AND THE DIAGNOSIS OF PSYCHOLOGICAL DISORDERS

Clinical judgments about psychological disorders can be influenced by cultural factors, including differences in ethnic background between therapists and clients. Such factors are given increased attention in the DSM–IV.

CANADIAN FOCUS

Assessing the Prevalence of Psychological Disorders in Canada

How common are psychiatric disorders? For some insight into this, consider the Stirling County study from the late 1950s (Leighton, 1959). The objective of this pioneering study was to examine the impact of social and cultural factors on the mental health of 20,000 inhabitants of a 2500-square-kilometer area of largely rural Nova Scotia. The initial approach involved a procedure termed *total case finding*. The investigators assumed that psychological disorders would be limited in number, and that it would be possible to obtain information about virtually every individual in the community suffering some form of psychological disorder. Sensibly enough, they began with an examination of mental and general hospital records, county homes, and poorhouses. Information from these sources was then supplemented, as in traditional anthropology, with information from informants such as teachers, community leaders, and general practitioners.

The deficiencies of the approach rapidly became clear. Institutional records were often lacking in necessary detail. Much more problematical was the *incorrect* assumption that only a relatively modest number of psychological disorders would be encountered. In fact, many more cases than anticipated were encountered; further, the investigators suspected that many more individuals in the community might be experiencing difficulties and not seeking assistance. These individuals would have no medical records and might well escape the attention of the various mental health informants. To try to find these people, health assessment questionnaires were developed and administered to a representative sample of the population.

In the end, researchers had to base their conclusions on information from a variety of interlaced sources, including mental and general hospital records, questionnaire assessments, and the treatment records of local physicians, which were examined by psychiatrists, who then made diagnostic assignments. What was concluded? That approximately 20 percent of the population experience some form of psychological disability meriting attention (Murphy, 1980).

More recent efforts to assess the prevalence of psychological disorders rely exclusively on questionnaires and other surveys, the data from which can be analyzed and classified by computer. A good example of this approach is a study by Bland, Newman, & Orn (1988), which looked into the prevalence of psychological disorders in the city of Edmonton. In this study, 3,258 households in the Edmonton area were sampled, with a single family member examined in each household. The Diagnostic Interview Schedule was used for assessment purposes. This is a highly structured procedure that provides the interviewer with a set of specific questions to be asked and follow-up questions to be pursued. The assessment focused on the prevalence of psychological disorders during the six-month period preceding the interview.

Bland and colleagues found that about 17 percent of Edmontonians had experienced some form of psychological disorder over the preceding six months. Interesting differences in the prevalence of the various disorders were also uncovered. A graphic representation of this study's findings is shown in Figure 14.2. (Note that a number of the individual disorders reported have been clustered to form more general categories.) As can be seen, the most common general categories of disorders are anxiety disorders (phobias, panic reaction, obsessive-compulsive disorders), mood disorders (manic episodes, major depressions), and substance abuse disorders (drug and alcohol). Clearly, there are significant male/female differences. Substance abuse disorders are much more common among males, as are symptoms indicating antisocial disorders; anxiety disorders and mood disorders are much more common among females. Students with a discerning eye may wonder why the sum of the individual percentages for the various disorders shown on the graph sum to over 40 percent when it is claimed that only 17 percent of individuals in the population had a psychological disorder. The answer is that individuals can, and very often do, have symptoms indicating the presence of *more than one disorder*.

The 17 percent prevalence rate reported by the Bland study is slightly lower than was reported in the Stirling County study, but given the differences in approach, the discrepancy is not large. The Bland results correspond reasonably closely to those reported in other North American studies, as do the differences reported in the relative frequency of the various psychological disorders.

One final point merits attention. The prevalence rates described by Bland are *period prevalence* rates. They refer to the prevalence of disorders over the previous six-month period. If *lifetime prevalence* rates are examined—that is, the occurrence of a disorder during any period of life up to the date of the study—the rates are substantially higher. Bland, Orn, & Newman (1988) report that approximately 34 percent of the Edmontonians sampled had had an experience with one or more psychological disorders at some point in their lives.

What this brief consideration of the prevalence of disorders shows is that psychological disorders are not rare curiosities; rather, they occur in the general population far more often than most people realize.

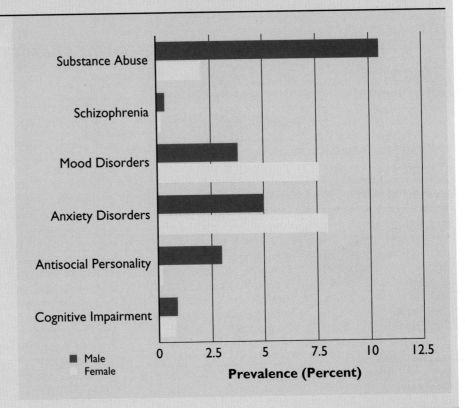

FIGURE 14.2

Prevalence of Mental Disorders in a Large Canadian Urban Center

Disorders involving mood, anxiety, and substance abuse are the most common in this Canadian city.
(Source: Based on a survey of Edmonton, Alberta, reported by Bland, Newman, & Orn, 1988.)

DESCRIBING PSYCHOLOGICAL DISORDERS: AN EXPLANATORY NOTE We will now consider individual psychological disorders. As mentioned earlier, the DSM-IV lists and describes literally hundreds of different disorders. All of these are important, but space limitations make it impossible to cover all of them here. Instead, therefore, we'll focus on those disorders which are most common and which for that reason have received the most attention from psychologists.

Mood Disorders: The Downs and Ups of Life

Everyone experiences swings in mood or emotional state—these are a normal part of life. For most individuals, extreme moods are short-lived; most of the time, people find themselves somewhere in between feelings of elation and sadness or despair. However, in contrast to this typical pattern, some people experience disturbances in mood that are both extreme and prolonged. Their highs are higher, their lows are lower, and the periods they spend at these emotional heights and depths are lengthy. Such people are described as suffering from **mood disorders**, which the DSM-IV describes under two major categories: depressive disorders and bipolar disorders. As shown in **Canadian Focus**, mood disorders are among the most common disorders people experience.

Depressive Disorders: Probing the Depths of Despair

None of us leads a perfect life; we all experience some events that make us feel sad or disappointed. An unexpectedly poor grade, breaking up with one's lover or spouse, failure to get a promotion or a raise—these and countless other events tip our emotional balance toward sadness. When do such reactions constitute depression? Most psychologists agree that several criteria are useful for making this decision. First, people suffering from **depression** experience truly profound unhappiness, and they experience it much of the time.

Second, people experiencing depression report that they have lost interest in all the usual pleasures of life. Eating, sex, sports, hobbies—all fail to provide the enjoyment and satisfaction people expect and, usually, derive from them. Third, people suffering from depression experience a major loss of energy. Everything becomes an effort, and feelings of exhaustion are common. Additional symptoms of depression include loss of appetite, followed by loss of weight; disturbances of sleep; difficulties in thinking (depressed people are indecisive and find that they cannot think, concentrate, or remember); recurrent thoughts of death; feelings of worthlessness or excessive guilt; and frequent feelings of agitation. As one depressed person described it—

> I began not to be able to manage ... the kinds of things I really had always been able to do easily, such as cook, wash, take care of the children, play games ... Another thing that was frightening to me was that I couldn't read any more. And if awakened early, I sometimes would lie in bed two hours trying to make myself get up ... Then when I did, I felt that I couldn't get dressed. And whatever the next step was, I felt I couldn't do that either. [Educational Broadcasting Corporation, 1975]

Mood Disorders: *Psychological disorders involving intense and prolonged mood shifts.*

Depression: *A psychological disorder involving intense feelings of sadness, lack of energy, and feelings of hopelessness and despair.*

When individuals experience five or more of these symptoms at once, they are classified by the DSM-IV as showing a *major depressive episode*. Unfortunately, depression is all too common. It is by far the most frequent type of psychological disorder, although, for reasons that are not yet entirely clear, it is considerably more common among women than among men (Nolen-Hoeksema, 1987).

Bipolar Disorders: *Riding the Emotional Roller Coaster*

If depression is the emotional black hole of life, then **bipolar disorder** is its emotional roller coaster. People suffering from bipolar disorder experience wide swings in mood. They move, over varying periods of time, between deep depression and an emotional state known as *mania*, in which they are extremely excited, elated, and energetic. During manic periods, these people speak rapidly, show a sharply decreased need for sleep, jump from one idea or activity to another, and show excessive involvement in pleasurable activities that have a high potential for painful consequences; for example, they may engage in uncontrolled buying sprees or make extremely risky investments. Clearly, bipolar disorders are very disruptive not only to the individuals who experience them but also to the people in their lives.

The Causes of Depression: *Its Biological and Psychological Roots*

Depression and other mood disorders tend to run in families (Egeland et al., 1987). Thus, if one identical twin experiences depression, the other has a substantial (perhaps as much as 40 percent) chance of developing a similar disorder. In contrast, among nonidentical twins, who don't share all of the same genes, this figure drops to 20 percent (Kolata, 1986).

Other findings suggest that mood disorders may involve abnormalities in brain biochemistry. For example, it has been found that levels of two neurotransmitters, *norepinephrine* and *serotonin*, are lower in the brains of depressed people than in those of nondepressed people. Similarly, levels of these substances are higher in the brains of people demonstrating mania. Further, when people who have recovered from depression undergo procedures that reduce the levels of serotonin in their brains, their depressive symptoms return within twenty-four hours (Delgado et al., 1990). Finally, drugs that produce depression as a side effect—such as reserpine, used in the treatment of high blood pressure—tend to reduce concentrations of norepinephrine; while drugs that counter depression act to increase brain levels of norephinephrine (Whybrow et al., 1984).

Unfortunately, this relatively neat picture is complicated by the following facts: Not all people suffering from depression show reduced levels of norepinephrine or serotonin; and not all those who demonstrate mania have increased levels of these neurotransmitters. In addition, drugs used to treat both types of disorders do much else besides change the presence or activity of these neurotransmitters. So, while it is clear at this time that biological factors play a role in depression, the precise nature of these factors remains to be determined.

While growing evidence indicates that depression involves subtle changes in biochemical processes, additional findings point to the importance of psychological mechanisms in this disorder. One of these is known as **learned helplessness** (Seligman, 1975; and see Chapter 5). When individuals are exposed to situations in which they cannot control their own outcomes, they often develop negative expectancies: They conclude that nothing they do really matters and

Bipolar Disorder: A mood disorder involving swings between depression and mania.

Learned Helplessness: Feelings of helplessness that develop after exposure to situations in which nothing individuals do affects their outcomes. Learned helplessness appears to play a role in the occurrence of depression.

that no actions on their part will permit them to avoid unpleasant outcomes. It is a short step from such beliefs to serious feelings of depression.

An important addition to the learned-helplessness view of depression concerns the causes to which people attribute their lack of control (Abramson, Seligman, & Teasdale, 1978; Alloy et al., 1988). According to this modified theory, sometimes known as the *hopelessness model*, depression is related not only to the belief that one cannot influence one's outcomes, but also to the depressed person's tendency to attribute unfavorable events to stable internal causes. In other words, when negative events happen to depressed people, they take the blame for their occurrence; they attribute the events to their own lasting innate shortcomings, such as laziness, poor judgment, lack of intelligence, and so on (Seligman et al., 1988).

Another factor that appears to play a crucial role in depression is the negative views that depressed people seem to hold about themselves (Beck, 1976; Beck et al., 1979). Individuals suffering from depression seem to possess negative **self-schemas**—negative conceptions of their own characteristics, abilities, and behavior. As a result of negative self-schemas, depressed people tend to be exquisitely sensitive to negative information about themselves—for example, to negative feedback from others (Bradley & Mathews, 1983). This, in turn, often leads them excessively to seek reassurance from others that these people "truly care" about them. As you can readily guess, these repeated requests for reassurance can be annoying, and so tend to backfire. Ultimately, they lead to increased *rejection* by others—precisely the outcome depressed people want to avoid (Joiner, Alfano, & Metalsky, 1993).

In addition to holding negative views about themselves, depressed people often seem to hold negative views about others. This is illustrated very clearly in a study conducted recently by Gara and his colleagues (1993). In this investigation, both depressed and nondepressed people were asked to describe nine people in their lives: mother, father, a significant other, three other people important to them, and three acquaintances who were less important. Then participants were asked to describe ten different aspects of their self-image: "Me as I actually am," "How I am with my father," "How I am with my mother," and so on, for the nine individuals they described earlier. Finally, they were asked to rate themselves and each of the nine individuals in terms of attributes they mentioned in their descriptions.

On the basis of this information, Gara and his colleagues constructed measures of the extent to which people described themselves and others in positive or negative terms. It was predicted that the depressed people would describe both themselves and others more negatively than the nondepressed people. As you can see in Figure 14.3, this is precisely what occurred.

Finally, depressed people are prone to several types of faulty or distorted thinking (Persad & Polivy, 1993). For example, they tend to dwell on and amplify the importance of negative events while ignoring or minimizing the importance of positive outcomes. As a result, they often show better memory for failures and other unpleasant events than for successes or other ego-boosting experiences (Kuiper, Olinger, & MacDonald, 1987). In sum, several psychological mechanisms and tendencies seem to play a key role in depression.

Suicide: *When Life Becomes Unbearable*

Hopelessness, despair, negative views about oneself and others—these are some of the hallmarks of depression. Given such symptoms, it is not surprising that many people suffering from this disorder seek a drastic solution to their problems—**suicide**. Suicide rates have been increasing since the middle of the century. Strachan, Johansen, Nair, & Nargundkar (1990) report that several

Self-Schemas: Cognitive frameworks that serve to organize information about the self.

Suicide: The act of taking one's own life.

million people in the world attempt suicide every year, and that more than a thousand a day succeed at it. Canada has not escaped this trend. In Figure 14.4, Canadian suicide rates are shown separately for males and females over a forty-year period. When we examine this figure, it is clear that the increase in the suicide rate that has occurred since 1951 is almost exclusively attributable

FIGURE 14.3

Depression: Negative Views of the Social World

Depressed people reported more negative views of themselves and of other people in their lives than did nondepressed people. (Source: Based on data from Gara et al., 1993.)

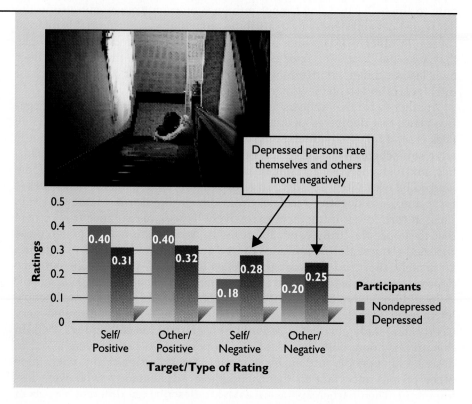

FIGURE 14.4

Canadian Suicide Rates as a Function of Sex from 1951 to 1991

The overall suicide rate increased during this period. The increase is almost entirely attributable to an increase in the suicide rate of young males. The female suicide rate was relatively unchanged. (Source: Statistics Canada).

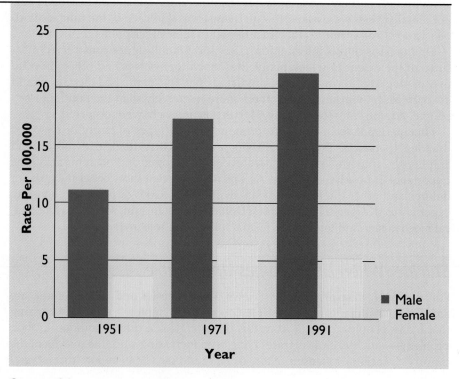

to growth in suicide among males. The female suicide rate has remained roughly stable. The shift in the male suicide rate is mainly attributable to a large increase in the frequency with which young males elect to commit suicide. Leenaars & Lester (1990) report that teenage boys have a suicide rate five times that of teenage girls. In fact, for males in the 15–24 age group, suicide is now the second-leading cause of death (Thibault, 1992). Without question, distressingly large numbers of young people consider suicide. In a large Ontario study it was found that 5 to 10 percent of boys and 10 to 20 percent of girls between 12 and 16 had either thought about or attempted suicide over the six-month period assessed by the study (Joffe, Offord, & Boyle, 1988).

You may be puzzled by the fact that the Ontario findings indicate that more girls than boys seem to contemplate or attempt suicide. Why should the suicide rate for the latter be so much higher, if the former contemplate or attempt suicide more often? The answer is that women are much more likely to think about and attempt suicide than men, but for men an attempt is much more likely to end in death. Men use more lethal devices: They resort to guns or hanging, whereas women tend to use less certain methods, such as a sleeping pill overdose or slashing their wrists.

Why Suicide? *A Host of Contributing Factors*

Many factors influence the likelihood of suicide. Psychological disorders play a role; depression and substance abuse (especially alcohol abuse) are also commonly linked with suicide. Dyck, Bland, Newman, & Orn (1988) found in an Edmonton survey that about half of those who had attempted suicide had previously suffered a major depression or alcohol dependency. He found also that environmental stressors such as unemployment, and exposure to ongoing family violence, increase the likelihood of suicide.

Location can be a significant factor. Suicide rates are higher in the North and in other isolated areas of Canada (Aldridge & Kimberly, 1991). Some native communities have intolerably high suicide rates. The suicide rate among native people in British Columbia is estimated to be 1.5 times that found among non-native people (Cooper, Corrado, Karlberg, & Adams, 1992). More shocking are figures provided by Aldridge & Kimberly indicating a suicide rate in Labrador that is about 3.5 times the Newfoundland average. In assessing these numbers, it is important not to lose sight of one important fact: High suicide rates are not observed in *all* native communities; rather, rates depend on conditions within the specific community. For example, the high suicide rates in Labrador are confined to that one-quarter of the community living in isolated settlements on the north shore, such as Davis Inlet. During the ten-year period assessed in the Aldridge-Kimberly study, no suicides were reported among the three-quarters of the native people living in the remaining area of Labrador. Similarly, studies in British Columbia indicate that high suicide rates are evident only in certain communities.

What is it about some communities that contributes to a high suicide rate? In some cases, one does not have to look

KEY POINTS

- People suffering from depression experience negative moods, reduced energy, feelings of hopelessness, a loss of interest in previously satisfying activities, difficulties in sleeping, and recurrent thoughts of death.

- In bipolar disorders, individuals ride an emotional roller coaster between states of mania (elation) and deep depression.

- Genetic factors seem to play a role in the occurrence of mood disorders.

- Disturbances in brain activity and biochemistry also seem to play a role in depression.

- Psychological factors are involved in the occurrence of mood disorders. These include feelings of helplessness, tendencies to attribute negative outcomes to internal causes, and negative perceptions of both oneself and others.

- Suicide rates have been increasing since the middle of the century. Suicide is a major cause of death among young people, especially teenage males.

- Suicide rates are especially high in the north and in other isolated areas. They are inexcusably high in some aboriginal communities, where the traditional lifestyle has vanished and no meaningful alternative has been established.

- People contemplating suicide frequently seem to show less concern over certain aspects of death than people who are not at high risk for suicide.

- Suicide may involve efforts by individuals to escape from a self they find inadequate and intolerable.

far to understand the high suicide rates. In Davis Inlet, for example, conditions within the community are described as appalling. The traditional lifestyle has been destroyed; no meaningful alternative lifestyle has been established; there is almost no possibility of employment; the proportion of young people in the community is extremely large (40 percent are under fifteen years of age); and there is widespread substance abuse. In those areas of British Columbia associated with high suicide rates, these factors are typically found: crowding, few elders, many single-parent and low-income families, and large households with many children living at home (Cooper et al.).

Various environmental conditions and stresses contribute to suicide; at the same time, suicides still occur in disconcertingly large numbers among young men and women who are not exposed to those conditions and stresses. What can be said about the psychological states that characterize an individual contemplating suicide? Baumeister (1990) suggests that suicide is the result of efforts by individuals to escape themselves—or, more accurately, to escape from awareness of their own faults and shortcomings.

When we contemplate our own death, we experience a variety of fears: fear of loss of self-fulfillment (it will bring an end to our plans); fear of self-annihilation (we will be forgotten by others); fear of consequences to our family; and a general fear of the unknown. Recent findings indicate that people who have actually attempted suicide report roughly equal fear of each of these outcomes (Orbach et al., 1993). In contrast, individuals who have not attempted suicide report contrasting levels of fear for these components: They are most frightened of loss of self-fulfillment and of the unknown, and least frightened about loss of social identity.

Anxiety Disorders: *When Dread Debilitates*

At one time or another we all experience **anxiety**—increased arousal accompanied by generalized feelings of fear or apprehension. If these feelings become very intense and persist for long periods of time, they can produce harmful effects. Such **anxiety disorders** take several different forms.

Panic Attack: *The Body Signals "Danger!" But Is It Real?*

Have you ever experienced *panic*—very high levels of physical arousal coupled with an intense fear of losing control? If you have, don't worry: Almost everyone has had this experience at some time or other. But people who suffer from a psychological condition known as **panic attack disorder** experience these reactions often, and sometimes without any specific triggering event. Such attacks can involve all or several of the following symptoms: a pounding heart, chest pains, nausea, dizziness, trembling or shaking, fear of losing control or going crazy, chills, hot flashes, or numbness. Consider the following case history—

Sally experienced her first panic attack out of the blue three weeks after completing her third year of university. She had just finished a job interview and was meeting some friends for dinner. In the restaurant, she began to feel dizzy. Within a few seconds, her heart was pounding and

Anxiety: Increased arousal accompanied by generalized feelings of fear or apprehension.

Anxiety Disorders: Psychological disorders centering on the occurrence of anxiety and including generalized anxiety, phobias, and obsessive-compulsive disorders

Panic Attack Disorder: Relatively brief periods during which individuals experience unbearably intense anxiety.

she was feeling breathless—as though she might pass out. Sally experienced a similar episode a week later while at a movie ... Her attacks became more and more frequent. Before long, she was having several attacks each week. In addition, she constantly worried about having attacks. She began to avoid exercise and other activities that produced physical sensations. She avoided driving, shopping in large stores, and eating in all restaurants. Some weeks she avoided leaving the house completely. Sally stopped looking for work, fearing that she would be unable to stay at her job in the event of a panic attack ... [Barlow, 1992, p. 79]

For some people, like Sally, panic attacks occur out of the blue, without any apparent cause. For others, they are linked with specific situations. In that case, panic disorder is associated with **agoraphobia**—intense fear of specific situations in which, individuals fear, they will experience panic attacks. Common patterns for agoraphobia include fear of being in a crowd, of standing in a line, of being on a bridge, of traveling in a bus, train, or car, or of merely leaving home.

What causes panic attacks? Existing evidence indicates that both biological factors and conditioning play a role (Barlow, 1988, 1992; Clark, 1988). For example, some people have a tendency to view their own emotions as unpredictable and uncontrollable. As a result, when they experience panic, they also experience anxiety that the panic will be repeated. This anxiety in itself may lead to additional panic attacks. The result: A vicious circle is established—panic ... anxiety ... panic ... anxiety ... A recent University of Windsor study shows that women are more prone to panic attacks than men, and that many people who experience them resort to drugs, especially alcohol, in an attempt to self-medicate their problem—a practice that can lead to drug dependency (Malan, Norton, & Cox, 1993).

MUNCH'S "THE SCREAM"
This famous painting seems to evoke the feelings associated with panic attack disorder.

Phobias: *Fear That Is Focused*

Most people express some fear of snakes, heights, violent storms, and buzzing insects such as bees or wasps. Since all of these can pose real threats to our safety, such reactions are adaptive, up to a point. Some people, though, experience intense anxiety when in the presence of these objects or even when they merely think about them. These *phobias* can be so strong that they interfere with everyday activities. Those who suffer from animal phobias may avoid visiting friends who own dogs, or may cross the street to avoid passing a person taking a pet for a walk. Similarly, those with *social phobias* may avoid a wide range of social situations in which they fear they will be exposed to and scrutinized by unfamiliar people.

What accounts for such strong and irrational fears? One possibility involves the process of *classical conditioning*, described in Chapter 5. Through this kind of learning, stimuli that could not initially elicit strong emotional reactions often come to do so. For example, consider the case of an individual who has a snake phobia. Perhaps as a child he witnessed one of his playmates actually being bitten by a snake. Although he himself experienced no harm, he reacted to the intense fear of his friend with strong arousal. The snake, a stimulus that was previously fairly neutral, had come, through classical conditioning, to evoke a similar reaction. (As you can readily see, observational learning also played a role in this example.) As we saw in Chapter 5, classical conditioning is especially likely to occur with respect to certain stimuli—ones for which we are biologically *prepared* to acquire associations. This is why phobias directed toward pencils, rabbits, or palm trees are virtually nonexistent, while those toward snakes or spiders are much more common.

Agoraphobia: Fear of losing control and experiencing a panic attack in specific situations, such as in open places, in a crowd, or on an airplane.

Obsessive-Compulsive Disorder: Behaviors and Thoughts Outside One's Control

Have you ever left your home, gotten halfway down the street, and then returned to see if you had really locked the door or turned off the stove? Most of us have had such experiences, which are completely normal. But for some people, these anxieties are so intense that they become trapped in repetitious behaviors known as *compulsions* that they seem unable to prevent, or in recurrent modes of thought called *obsessions*. Consider the following description of a person suffering from an **obsessive-compulsive disorder** of this kind:

> When George wakes in the morning ... he feels that his hands are contaminated so he cannot touch his clothing. He won't wash in the bathroom because he feels that the carpet is contaminated ... I have to dress him, having first cleaned his shoes and got out a clean shirt, underclothes, socks and trousers. He holds his hands above his head ... to make sure that he doesn't contaminate the outside of his clothing. Any error or mishap and he will have to have clean clothes ... George then goes downstairs, washes his hands in the kitchen and thereafter spends about twenty minutes in the toilet ... Basically he has to be completely sure that there is no contamination around because if he is not then he will start to worry about it later on. [Rachman & Hodgson, 1980, pp. 66–67]

What is the cause of such reactions? We all have repetitious thoughts occasionally. For example, after watching a film containing disturbing scenes of violence, we may find ourselves thinking about these over and over again. Most of us soon manage to distract ourselves from these unpleasant thoughts. But individuals who develop an obsessive-compulsive disorder are unable to do this. They are made anxious by their obsessional thoughts, yet they can't dismiss them readily from mind. As a result, they become even more anxious, and the cycle builds. Only by performing specific actions can they ensure their "safety" and reduce this anxiety. Therefore, they engage in complex repetitive rituals that can gradually grow to fill most of their day. Since these rituals reduce anxiety, the tendency to perform them grows stronger. Unless they receive effective outside help, people suffering from obsessive-compulsive disorders have little chance of escaping from their anxiety-ridden prisons.

Post-Traumatic Stress Disorder

We live in civilized times, protected by laws, safety regulations, and security devices of all kinds, but things nevertheless at times still go terrifyingly wrong. We hear reports on the news of people being abducted at gunpoint in parking garages, or terrified by intruders in their homes, or witnessing truly shocking events. Two recent examples of the latter: the recent killing of a

Obsessive-Compulsive Disorder: Anxiety disorder in which an individual is unable to stop thinking the same thoughts or performing the same ritualistic behaviors.

AN EXAMPLE OF COMPULSIVE BEHAVIOR

Like Ernie, people suffering from compulsions cannot stop themselves from engaging in certain behaviors.
(Source: FRANK & ERNEST reprinted by permission of NEA, Inc.)

FRANK and ERNEST

By Bob Thaves

ERNIE, THE COMPULSIVE SHOPPER CLUB WANTS YOU FOR A MEMBER.

I'LL BUY THAT!

THAVES 7-27
© 1987 by NEA, Inc.

young customer in a Toronto restaurant during a holdup, and the killing of fourteen young women by a gunman at l'École Polytechnique in Montreal. Such experiences are described as *traumatic* by psychologists because they are extraordinary in nature—and extraordinarily disturbing. It is not surprising, then, that some people exposed to them experience *post-traumatic stress disorder*, in which people persistently reexperience a traumatic event in their thoughts or dreams, persistently avoid stimuli linked with the trauma (places, people, thoughts), and persistently experience symptoms of increased arousal, such as difficulty falling asleep, irritability, and difficulty in concentrating (see Chapter 13).

Post-traumatic stress disorder can stem from a wide range of traumatic events—natural disasters, accidents, assaults such as rape, or even the horrors experienced during military peace-keeping exercises. For example, Canadian peacekeepers in the former Yugoslavia experienced events such as a mock execution by drunken soldiers, and witnessed the explosion of a mortar round among children being given candy. This has led to claims that at least one in ten of these peacekeepers may be suffering post-traumatic stress reactions from their tour of duty (Carbonneau, 1994). Often those who survive atrocities or natural disasters develop a sense of intense guilt. The fact that they have survived while those they loved have died weighs heavily on their conscience. Post-traumatic stress disorder can be an especially painful condition.

Anxiety: *The Role of Subliminal Processing*

For people suffering from anxiety disorders, the world is often a threatening place. They perceive danger everywhere, in contexts and actions that most people view as quite harmless. What accounts for this distorted view of the physical and social environment? One answer seems to involve a tendency on the part of anxious people to direct a larger-than-usual portion of their information-processing capacity to anxiety-relevant information. In other words, they "see" danger everywhere because, in a sense, they actively search for it (Mathews, 1990). Many studies offer support for this view, indicating that people suffering from anxiety disorders are indeed more likely to notice and process information relating to their anxieties (Martin, Williams, & Clark, 1991). And at least one recent investigation, conducted by Mogg and her colleagues (Mogg et al., 1993), suggests that anxious people are more sensitive than others to stimuli relevant to their anxiety even *before* such information has entered conscious awareness—that is, even when it is presented *subliminally*.

To test this possibility, Mogg and her co-workers asked three groups of participants—anxious people, depressed people, and normal controls—to perform a color-naming task. Briefly, they asked the participants to name the colors of patches on which words appeared while ignoring the words themselves. In one condition (*subliminal*), the words were shown so briefly that they could not be recognized; indeed, exposure was so brief (14 milliseconds) that participants could not even tell whether a word had been presented. In another (*supraliminal*) condition, in contrast, the words were shown until participants named the color of the background. Some of the words shown were related to anxiety (such as

NATURAL DISASTERS: ONE CASE OF POST-TRAUMATIC STRESS DISORDER

When individuals live through natural disasters they sometimes develop post-traumatic stress disorder.

KEY POINTS

- Anxiety disorders involve increased arousal accompanied by generalized feelings of fear or apprehension.

- Panic attacks involve symptoms of arousal coupled with intense fear—often of losing control in some specific situation. Both biological factors and several kinds of learning seem to play a role in their occurrence.

- Phobias are excessive fears focused on specific objects or situations. Obsessive-compulsive disorder involves repetitious thoughts or actions individuals seem powerless to prevent.

- People suffering from anxiety disorders seem to direct more of their information-processing capacity to anxiety-related stimuli.

"embarrassed," "candor"), while others were related to depression (such as "misery," "discouraged"). The others were either neutral ("carpet," "domestic") or positive ("adorable," "bliss").

Mogg and her associates reasoned that if anxious people automatically devote more of their information-processing capacity to anxiety-related words, then anxious participants would respond more slowly than the depressed or control participants on trials when these words were presented. In contrast, neither depressed nor controls would show such effects. This is precisely what happened (see Figure 14.5). Anxious people responded more slowly to both kinds of negative words—both anxiety-related and depression-related—than the other two groups. Moreover, this was true in both the subliminal and the supraliminal condition.

These findings, and those of related studies (e.g., Williams et al., 1988), indicate that people suffering from anxiety disorder do indeed direct more of their information-processing resources toward threatening information, even before such information enters conscious awareness. To the extent this is true, it may be difficult to eliminate anxiety through forms of therapy focused on conscious thoughts and reactions. Rather, the underlying tendency to notice threatening information must also be overcome.

Somatoform Disorders: *Physical Symptoms Without Physical Causes*

Somatoform Disorders:
Category of disorders in which psychological conflicts or other problems take on a physical form.

Several of Freud's early cases, ones which played an important role in his developing theory of personality, involved the following puzzling situation. An individual would show some physical symptom, such as deafness, or paralysis of some part of the body; yet careful examination would reveal no underlying physical causes for the problem. Such disorders are known as **somatoform**

FIGURE 14.5

Subliminal Processing and Anxiety

People suffering from anxiety disorders responded more slowly on a color-naming task when exposed to anxiety-related words. Moreover, this was true even when these words were presented so briefly that the participants could not tell whether words were present. These findings suggest that anxious individuals direct more of their information-processing resources toward threatening information than do other individuals. Moreover, they seem to do so in a rapid, automatic manner. (Source: Based on data from Mogg et al., 1993.)

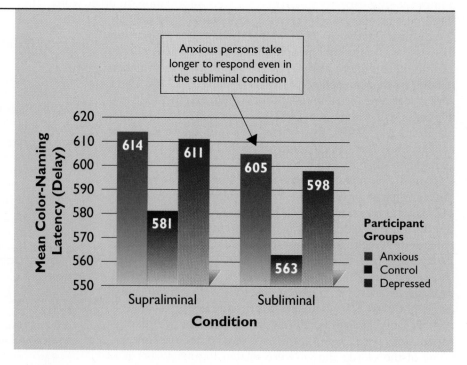

disorders—disorders in which psychological conflicts or other problems take on a *somatic*, or physical, form. The DSM-IV recognizes several distinct somatoform disorders.

One of these is known as **somatization disorder**, a condition in which individuals report physical complaints and symptoms that may include aches and pains, problems with their digestive system, and sexual problems (such as sexual indifference or irregular menstruation). Another is **hypochondriasis**—preoccupation with fears of disease. Such people do not actually have the diseases they fear; even so, they persist in worrying about them despite repeated assurances by their doctors that they are healthy. It is important to note that hypochondriacs are not simply faking; they feel the pain and discomfort they report and are truly afraid that they are about to fall ill.

Another somatoform disorder is known as **conversion disorder**. In hypochondria, there are no apparent physical disabilities—just the feeling that they will develop. In conversion disorders, however, there are actual impairments. Individuals suffering from such disorders may experience blindness, deafness, paralysis, or loss of sensation in various body parts. Yet while these disabilities are quite real to the people experiencing them, there is no underlying medical condition that would produce them.

What is the origin of somatoform disorders? Freud suggested that people experiencing unacceptable impulses or conflicts converted these into various symptoms. By doing so, they reduced the anxiety generated by the impulses, and at the same time gained much sympathy and attention. A behavioral interpretation of these disorders, in contrast, emphasizes the rewards individuals often obtain by adopting the *sick person role*. Being ill elicits sympathy and caring from others, and for some people these benefits seem to have an irresistible charm. A third interpretation emphasizes cognitive factors, suggesting that individuals who experience somatoform disorders have a tendency to focus excessively on normal bodily sensations and to misinterpret them, attributing them to various serious conditions (Barsky & Wyshak, 1989). Thus, for example, when these people experience increased heart rate, they interpret this as "I'm having a heart attack" rather than as "I'm excited or nervous," the kind of interpretation most people would adopt. Whatever their origins, somatoform disorders appear to be quite common. It has been estimated that as many as 20 percent of all patients admitted to hospitals may be suffering from symptoms produced by somatoform conditions (Jones, 1980).

Dissociative Disorders: When Memory Fails

Have you ever awakened during the night and, just for a moment, been uncertain about where you were? Such temporary disruptions in our normal cognitive functioning are far from rare; many people experience them from time to time as a result of fatigue, illness, or the use of alcohol or other drugs. Some individuals, however, undergo much more profound and lengthy losses of identity or memory. These are known as **dissociative disorders**, which, like several other psychological disorders, can take several different forms.

In Chapter 6, we saw that *amnesia*—loss of memory—can sometimes be produced by illness or by injury to the brain. Sometimes, however, amnesia

Somatization Disorder: A psychological condition in which individuals report physical complaints and symptoms, including aches and pains, problems with their digestive systems, and sexual problems such as sexual indifference or irregular menstruation.

Hypochondriasis: A psychological disorder in which individuals convert anxiety into chronic preoccupations with their health and bodily functions.

Conversion Disorder: Psychological disorder in which individuals experience real motor or sensory symptoms for which there is no known organic cause.

Dissociative Disorders: Psychological disorders in which individuals experience profound and lengthy losses of identity or memory.

seems to occur in the absence of any clear-cut physical cause. This **dissociative amnesia** appears to stem from the active motivation to forget. After experiencing some traumatic event, violating their own standards, or undergoing intense stress, individuals sometimes go blank with respect to these events and cannot recall them. Such amnesia can involve all events within a particular period of time (*localized amnesia*) or only some events occurring during this period (*selective amnesia*). Alternatively, it can erase memories for a person's entire life prior to a specific date (*generalized amnesia*). While individuals suffering from such disorders truly cannot remember past events, many aspects of their behavior remain intact: habits, tastes, previously learned skills. Musicians can continue to play their instruments, computer programmers can still operate computers, and beauticians can still give permanents; they may not remember that they once earned a living through such activities, however.

A second type of dissociative disorder is known as **dissociative fugue**. This is a sudden and extreme disturbance of memory in which individuals wander off, adopt a new identity, and are unable to recall their own past. Newspapers sometimes report accounts of individuals who simply vanish one day, only to reappear years later in a new location living a new life—often with a new spouse and family.

Such reactions can truly be described as *dissociative* in nature, for they seem to represent disorders in which some portion of memory is split off, or dissociated, from conscious awareness. See **The Point of It All** for discussion of another form of dissociative disorder.

Dissociative Amnesia:
Amnesia for which there is no organic cause.

Dissociative Fugue: *Form of dissociative amnesia in which individuals forget their identity and virtually all of their past lives.*

Dissociative Identity Disorder: *Multiple personality disorder, in which a single individual seems to possess more than one personality.*

MULTIPLE PERSONALITY: REAL OR FRAUD?

William Milligan, a convicted rapist, appeared to possess more than ten distinct personalities, including the one whose writing appears here. Although many cases of multiple personality (now termed dissociative identity disorder) are faked, others do appear to represent genuine psychological disorders.

THE POINT OF IT ALL

Dissociative Identity Disorder: Multiple Personalities in a Single Body?

Perhaps the most dramatic form of dissociative disorder is **dissociative identity disorder**, a condition labeled *multiple personality disorder* in earlier versions of the DSM. In this rare disorder, a single person seems to possess two, three, or even many more distinct personalities. Some of these personalities are dominant and alternately take control of the person's behavior. In addition, people suffering from this type of dissociative disorder report selective amnesia: Information retained by one personality is not necessarily available to the others.

A collection of case histories by Ross (1994) provides a number of interesting accounts of patients with dissociative identity disorders. An illustrative example is the case of Jenny Z. Initial consultation was occasioned by the fact that she was experiencing blank periods. She reported that she had returned from a three-day trip to Vancouver but could remember nothing that had transpired during those three days. There were other problems—for example, a joint bank account that she held with her boyfriend had been emptied, and some of the money had been spent on music recordings and a mirror that she had no recollection of purchasing. An explanation for these puzzling events became apparent during the course of treatment. Jenny was found to have a dissociative identity disorder, and a second personality. It was the second personality, named Sally, who was in control during the periods for which Jenny had no recollection, and who had removed, and spent, the money in the joint account. The two personalities were very different. Jenny was quiet, accommodating, indecisive, and lacking in self-confidence. Sally, on the other hand, was sarcastic, aggressive, extremely confident, and prone to impulsive behavior. Sally seemed to be quite aware of Jenny's activities and was disdainful of her many deficiencies. Jenny was initially unaware of Sally's existence, and amnesic for the periods during which Sally was in control. As therapy progressed, five other personalities surfaced. Eventually Ross was able to integrate the personalities into a single unified self. At last report, Jenny was much improved.

Dissociative identity disorders can produce interesting dilemmas. Some years ago, a multiple-personality patient accused a man she had dated, Mark Peterson, of rape. She claimed that only one of her personalities had given consent. Another had watched the event, and still another went to the police to report the assault. Peterson was convicted under a law that makes having sexual intercourse with a mental patient equivalent to rape (Kihlstrom Tataryn, & Hoyt, 1993).

These and other striking cases of dissociative identity disorder raise an intriguing question: Is multiple personality genuine—a real form of psychological disorder? Or are people like Jenny Z merely clever fakers? No final answer to this question currently exists. Some evidence, however, suggests that there is more to multiple personality than simple faking: Individuals showing this disorder sometimes demonstrate distinctive patterns of brain activity for each of their supposedly separate personalities (Kaplan & Sadock, 1991). In addition, each personality often scores differently on standardized personality tests (Kaplan & Sadock, 1991). Even the need for eyeglasses, or being right- or left-handed, may vary among different personalities. Finally, as will be shown next, there is a marked similarity from case to case in the background experiences that seem to lead to the disorder, and in the types of personality characteristics manifested by the alternative selves created.

🍁 CANADIAN FOCUS

The Cause and Character of Dissociative Identity Disorder

In addition to providing an engaging collection of case histories of patients with dissociative identity disorder, Collin Ross, with his associates at the University of Manitoba, has carried out some very interesting research on dissociative processes. In this section we will consider what these studies tell us about the cause and character of this disorder.

One of these studies was designed to build on earlier work by Putnam indicating that people with dissociative identity disorder typically have a history of childhood abuse (Putnam et al., 1986). The Ross study (1991) sought to flesh out existing accounts and provide a fuller description of the nature and scope of the abuse experienced. The backgrounds of over 100 patients with the disorder in two Canadian and two American centers were examined. It was found that abuse was reported by an overwhelming number of the patients: 95 percent experienced either sexual or physical abuse, or both, during childhood. The extent of the abuse reported was surprising. There was little report of single instances of abuse, or intermittent abuse; rather, reports chronicled sustained abuse over long periods of time. On average, physical abuse was carried on over a twelve-year period and sexual abuse over a fourteen-year period. Typically, abuse began early in life. More than 50 percent of the patients reported experiencing abuse before the age of five, whereas only 6 percent reported abuse beginning after the age of ten. The evidence seems overwhelming that a long period of physical and sexual abuse commencing early in life is characteristic of those with an identity disorder.

In a further study, Ross, Norton, and Wozney (1989) sent out questionnaires to Canadian psychiatrists and to members of an international society focusing on the study of identity disorders. These requested data about recently diagnosed patients with the goal of developing a character profile of the disorder.

The portrait of an average patient that emerged from the analysis of the over 200 responses obtained was of an individual having, at the time of first diagnosis, an average of 3.5 alternative selves. These personalities were complex and distinct, and only one personality was dominant at a given time. Typically, more selves emerged during the course of treatment. On average, 17.5 personalities had become apparent in these patients by the time the data were reported to Ross and his associates. Certain key personality types appeared repeatedly. In over 80 percent of the patients, a protector personality, a child personality, and a persecutor personality were reported. Eighty-eight percent of the patients in the sample were women, most of them in their early thirties.

What general conclusions can be drawn about the disorder? First, that it seems to grow out of a background of early and sustained physical and sexual abuse. Patients develop a habit of detaching themselves from the abuse being experienced by assuming the guise of another personality or self. This allows them to stand apart from the situation—the abuse is held to be experienced by another separate self, who is walled off by amnesia from other selves within the system. This process of dissociation may provide a way of coping with sustained abuse, but it leads, inevitably, to a progressive fragmentation of the personality into multiple selves, with each individual self being specialized to function in a different type of situation. For example, a protector personality becomes dominant in times of threat, and often a child personality, experienced in absorbing pain, dominates when pain and suffering is experienced. Most often, each specialty personality is amnesic with respect to the activities of the others.

Life is a complicated and disorganized experience for individuals with an identity disorder. Because they have many alternative selves, and because there is rampant amnesia among the selves with respect to one another's behavior, these people have great difficulty dealing with the world in any consistent way. To family, friends, and co-workers, these individuals appear erratic; also, they often seem to be lying, because of amnesia relating to the personalities they show and to the activities others have watched them perform.

At present we have only a skeletal outline of what is proving to be a very complicated disorder. It is a perplexing and puzzling disorder both for the person diagnosed and for those who interact with the person. Additional complications are provided by the fact that some individuals resort to fraud and deception in seeking such a diagnosis to escape the consequences of their actions. Without question, the dissociative identity disorder is one of the most bizarre forms of psychological disorder studied—and treated—by psychologists.

Sexual and Gender Identity Disorders

As we saw in Chapter 12, Freud believed that many psychological disorders can be traced to disturbances in *psychosexual development*—our progression through a series of stages in which our quest for pleasure is centered on different parts of the body and different activities. While this theory is not currently accepted by most psychologists, there is little doubt that problems relating to sexuality and gender identity constitute an important group of psychological disorders. Several of these are considered below.

Sexual Dysfunctions: *Disturbances in Desire and Arousal*

Sexual dysfunctions include disturbances in sexual desire, sexual arousal, or the ability to attain orgasm. These problems are classified according to when they occur in the normal pattern of sexual activity (see Chapter 10). **Sexual desire disorders** involve a lack of interest in sex or an active aversion to sexual activities. Individuals suffering from these disorders report that they rarely have the sexual fantasies most people generate, that they avoid all or almost all sexual activity, and that these reactions cause them considerable distress.

In contrast, **sexual arousal disorders** involve the inability to attain or maintain an erection (men) or the absence of vaginal swelling and lubrication (women). *Orgasm disorders* involve the delay or absence of orgasm in both sexes, and may also include *premature ejaculation* (reaching orgasm too quickly) in men.

Paraphilias: *Disturbances in Sexual Object or Behavior*

What is sexually arousing? For most people, the answer has to do with the sight or touch of another human being—one they find sexually attractive. But human beings may also be aroused by other stimuli. Many men report that they find certain types of women's lingerie arousing. Similarly, members of both sexes are sometimes aroused by specific aromas—perfumes or other scents that they associate with past enjoyable sexual experiences (Levine & McBurney, 1982). Still others find that either inflicting or receiving some slight pain increases their arousal and sexual pleasure. Do these reactions constitute sexual disorders? According to most psychologists, they do not. A disorder is indicated only when unusual or bizarre imagery or acts are *necessary* for sexual arousal. In other words, **paraphilias** (from the Greek *para*, meaning "amiss," and *philia*, meaning "love") exist only when unusual images, acts, or objects are required for sexual arousal and performance.

Several types of paraphilias exist. In *fetishes*, individuals become aroused exclusively by inanimate objects. Often these are articles of clothing, such as shoes or underwear; in more unusual cases they can involve human waste, dirt, animals, or even dead bodies. *Frotteurism*, another paraphilia, involves fantasies and urges focused on touching or rubbing against a nonconsenting person. The touching, not the coercive nature of the act, is what people with this disorder find sexually arousing. Perhaps more disturbing is *pedophilia*, in which individuals experience sexual urges and fantasies involving sexual activity with children, generally ones younger than thirteen. When these urges are translated into overt activity, the effects on the young victims can, of course, be devastating. Two other paraphilias are *sexual sadism* and *sexual masochism*. In the former, individuals become sexually aroused by inflicting pain or humiliation on others. In the latter, they are aroused by receiving such treatment. Other paraphilias are listed in Table 14.2.

Gender Identity Disorders

Have you ever read about a man who altered his gender to become a woman, or vice versa? Such individuals suffer from **gender identity disorder**—they feel, often from an early age, that they were born with the wrong sexual identity. They are often displeased with their own bodies and seek—again, often from an early age—medical treatment to alter their primary and secondary

Sexual Desire Disorders:
Psychological disorders involving a lack of interest in sex or active aversion to sexual activities.

Sexual Arousal Disorders:
Psychological disorders involving inability to attain an erection (males) or absence of vaginal swelling and lubrication (females).

Paraphilias: Sexual disorders involving choices of inappropriate sexual objects, such as young children, or the inability to experience arousal except in the presence of specific objects or fantasies.

TABLE 14.2

PARAPHILIA	DESCRIPTION/SYMPTOMS
Exhibitionism	Sexual urges or arousing fantasies involving exposure of one's genitals to an unsuspecting stranger
Voyeurism	Recurrent sexual urges or arousing fantasies involving the act of observing an unsuspecting person who is naked, disrobing, or engaging in sexual activity
Transvestic fetishism	Intense sexual urges and arousing fantasies involving cross-dressing (dressing in the clothing of the other sex)
Other paraphilias	Telephone scatologia (lewdness) Necrophilia (sexual arousal to corpses) Zoophilia (sexual contact with or fantasies concerning animals)

Paraphilias

Paraphilias—disorders in which unusual or bizarre imagery or acts are necessary for sexual arousal—take many different forms. A few are listed here.

KEY POINTS

- Sexual disorders involve disturbances in sexual desire, sexual arousal, or the ability to attain orgasm. Paraphilias are disturbances in which unusual imagery or acts are necessary for sexual arousal.

- People suffering from gender identity disorder feel that they were born with the wrong sexual identity and seek to change this identity through medical treatment or other means.

sex characteristics. In the past there was little that medicine could do to satisfy these wishes. However, advances in surgical techniques have now made it possible for these people to undergo *sex-change operations*, in which their sexual organs are altered to approximate those of the other sex. Before their operations, these individuals receive extended counseling, learning the mannerisms of the other gender—how to wear its clothes, and so on. Only then are the actual operations performed. Several thousand individuals have undergone these procedures, and existing evidence indicates that most report being satisfied with the results and happier than they were before (Green & Fleming, 1990). However, follow-up studies suggest that some people who undergo the operations experience regrets and continued unhappiness, sometimes to the point that they commit suicide or experience serious psychological disorders (Abramowitz, 1986). So it appears that sex-change operations have a serious potential downside that should be carefully considered.

Eating Disorders

Eating Disorders: *Serious disturbances in eating habits or patterns that pose a threat to individuals' physical health and well-being.*

KEY POINTS

- Eating disorders include anorexia nervosa and bulimia.

- Both anorexia nervosa and bulimia stem in part from dissatisfaction with one's appearance. In addition, bulimia involves actual reductions in taste sensitivity that make it easier for bulimics to continue their binge-purge cycles.

In our discussion of motivation (Chapter 10), we encountered two serious **eating disorders**: *anorexia nervosa* and *bulimia*. These disorders are very common at the present time and adversely affect the health and well-being of millions of young people. For these reasons, it seems important to return to these disorders now and to expand somewhat on the earlier discussion.

As you will recall, anorexia nervosa is a disorder in which individuals, intensely fearful of being or becoming "fat," literally starve themselves, failing to maintain a normal body weight. Bulimia involves episodes of binge eating followed by various forms of compensatory behavior designed to avoid weight gain—for example, self-induced vomiting or overuse of laxatives. You may recall from Chapter 10 that both of these eating disorders are much more common among young women than among young men (Hinsz & Williamson, 1987). Both disorders seem to stem at least in part from dissatisfaction with personal appearance and efforts to match the "thin is in" model that is held up by the mass media (Thompson, 1992; Williamson, Cubic, & Gleaves, 1993).

While both of these disorders are disturbing, bulimia is perhaps the more puzzling of the two. Typical bulimics report purging about twelve times per week. How can people with this disorder stand the repeated binge–purge cycles that they adopt as a basic aspect of their daily lives? One possibility is that as a result of their repeated purging, bulimics experience reduced taste sensitivity (Ramirez & Bartoshuk, 1987). This, in turn, makes vomiting less unpleasant, or at least more bearable. In fact, research by Rodin and her colleagues (1990) offers support for this reasoning: Individuals suffering from bulimia do indeed show reduced taste sensitivity.

The research on bulimia, then, suggests that it is even more complex than was at first assumed. Social pressures to be slim may indeed contribute to its initiation, but once it is established, shifts in the sense of taste may strengthen its occurrence and permit it to continue. One implication of these findings seems clear: Effective treatment for bulimia must include attention to sensory factors as well as to strong cultural pressures to be, and remain, slim.

Anorexia Nervosa

People who suffer from anorexia nervosa often starve themselves to the point where their health is seriously endangered. What societal factors play a role in this disorder?

Personality Disorders: *Traits That Prove Costly*

Have you ever known someone who was highly suspicious and mistrustful of others in virtually all situations? Someone who had no close friends and was a true loner in all respects? Someone who showed a strong need to be taken care of by others, coupled with a dependent, clinging approach to relationships? If you have, you may have already met people with **personality disorders**. These people possess specific personality traits (recall our discussion of traits in Chapter 12) that are inflexible and maladaptive and cause them major difficulties in many respects. Personality disorders, in other words, are long-standing habits of thought and behavior that color an individual's whole life, and also impair it by making the person unhappy, or by interfering with his or her functioning, or both. More formally, personality disorders can be defined as extreme personality variations associated with the failure to achieve the universal tasks of establishing a personal identity, forming attachments to others, experiencing intimacy with them, and seeking affiliation (Livesley et al., 1994). Many personality disorders exist; however, the DSM-IV combines these into several main categories, so we'll do the same here.

Paranoid and Schizoid Personality Disorders: *Cut Off from Human Contact*

From time to time, we all feel as though others are out to get us and that they can't be trusted. For people suffering from **paranoid personality disorder**, however, these feelings are pervasive. They suspect that virtually everyone around them is trying to deceive or take advantage of them in some way. Consistent with this tendency, they perceive hidden, threatening meanings in ordinary remarks and bear strong grudges for these imaginary slights or injuries.

A related pattern is shown by people suffering from **schizoid personality disorder**. They are truly detached from the social world, showing little interest in friendships, love affairs, or any other intimate contact with other people. They are indifferent to praise and criticism and often show emotional coldness and detachment. In short, contact with other individuals is of little interest to them, and they often tend to perceive the people around them as mere nuisances, obstacles to the goals they wish to reach—without others' help, of course!

Personality Disorders: Extreme personality variation associated with the failure to achieve the universal tasks of establishing a personal identity, forming attachments to others, experiencing intimacy with them, and seeking affiliation.

Paranoid Personality Disorder: A psychological disorder in which individuals feel that others are out to get them and cannot be trusted.

Schizoid Personality Disorder: A personality disorder in which individuals become almost totally detached from the social world.

The Antisocial Personality Disorder

The personality disorder that has received by far the most attention is **antisocial personality disorder**. Individuals with this disorder show an almost total disregard for the rights and well-being of others. In addition, they demonstrate several characteristics that make them dangerous to others. Rules and regulations are not for them, so they often have a history of antisocial behavior: delinquency, theft, vandalism, lying, drug abuse, and the like. They are often irritable and aggressive, highly impulsive, seemingly fearless in the face of danger, and highly deceitful—they will lie to anyone, anytime, if they perceive this as advantageous. And after performing actions that harm others, they typically show no remorse.

The impulsiveness shown by these individuals, coupled with several of their other traits, often lends a random, seemingly purposeless character to their antisocial behavior. Thus, the crimes committed by people with this disorder often seem to lack any rational purpose or goal. For example, consider the following chilling statement by Gary Gilmore, a convicted multiple murderer:

> I pulled up near a gas station I told the service station guy to give me all his money. I then took him to the bathroom and told him to kneel down and then I shot him in the head twice. The guy didn't give me any trouble but I just felt like I had to do it.

Why did Gilmore kill this innocent victim? He had no idea—and he didn't care. Because of their almost total lack of feelings of responsibility, individuals showing antisocial personality disorder engage unhesitatingly in actions other people only daydream about: They walk off jobs if they get bored, readily desert spouses and children, and simply disappear when debts mount. For these people, the term *obligation* has little if any meaning. Little wonder, then, that they often become petty thieves, confidence artists, pimps, drug pushers, and prostitutes.

What are the origins of this pattern? What factors lead some individuals to develop this disturbing collection of traits? This is a complex issue, and existing evidence suggests that many factors probably play a role. From a behavioral perspective, such people may learn as children, through exposure to violent models, that impulsive, aggressive behavior is appropriate—after all, the adults and older children they see around them regularly engage in such actions. As noted in our discussion of aggression (see Chapter 10), such **modeling** influences can exert powerful effects upon behavior (Bandura, 1986).

Cognitive factors, too, may play a role. People who show the antisocial personality disorder may fail to acquire the kinds of *schemas*, or cognitive frameworks, that other people employ to regulate their own behavior—for example, schemas relating to impulse control, a sense of responsibility, and the reciprocal nature of human relationships.

Perhaps the most intriguing possibility, however, is that antisocial personality disorder derives at least in part from physiological abnormalities. See **The Research Process** for a discussion of evidence relating to this suggestion. Also, see Table 14.3 for a description of several other personality disorders.

PERSONALITY DISORDER	DESCRIPTION
Borderline personality disorder	Instability in interpersonal relationships, self-image, and moods. Relationships often alternate between idealization and devaluation of others.
Histrionic personality disorder	Excessive emotionality and attention seeking, beginning in early adulthood. Discomfort when not center of attention; inappropriate seductive or provocative behavior; exaggerated expression of emotion.
Narcissistic personality disorder	Grandiosity in fantasy and behavior, coupled with need for admiration and lack of empathy. A grandiose sense of self-importance and preoccupation with fantasies of unlimited success, brilliance, or beauty.
Avoidant personality disorder	Social inhibition, feelings of inadequacy and hypersensitivity to negative evaluation. Unwillingness to get involved with people in new interpersonal situations.
Dependent personality disorder	Excessive need to be taken care of, leading to submissive and clinging behavior and fears of separation. Difficulty expressing disagreement with others; feeling of discomfort and helplessness when alone.

TABLE 14.3

Personality Disorders

As shown here, personality disorders take a wide range of different forms.

THE RESEARCH PROCESS

The Antisocial Personality Disorder: Anomalous Emotional Reactivity, and Irregularities in Allocation of Attention and Learning

"Fearless" and "impulsive" are two terms often used to describe people showing antisocial personality disorder. People with this condition engage in forms of behavior that most of the rest of us would avoid, and show little anxiety and fear in these situations. An unemotional detachment is a central hallmark of their behavior. This combination of traits has led some researchers to wonder whether individuals with this disorder differ from the rest of us in terms of the way in which their nervous system functions, and the way in which they process information. In exploring this prospect, much research has focused on possible differences in emotional reactivity.

The Antisocial Personality Disorder and Emotional Reactivity

Individuals with antisocial personality disorders are not merely impulsive and fearless—they are characteristically emotionally indifferent as well. They have little if any feeling or empathy for others and seem incapable of forming strong emotional ties. Are they really less emotionally reactive than other people? Some evidence indicates that this may be so (Ogloff & Wong, 1990).

Perhaps the clearest evidence pointing to this conclusion is that provided by Patrick, Bradley, and Lang (1993). These researchers asked three groups of prisoners—ones clearly suffering from antisocial personality disorder, ones showing some aspects of this disorder, and ones not showing the disorder—to view a series of slides. These slides were either pleasant (opposite-sex nudes, food), unpleasant (aimed guns, snakes), or neutral (household objects, neutral faces) in content. As the slides were presented, sudden bursts of loud noise would occur at intervals without warning. Measures of the strength of participants' *startle response* to these bursts were recorded, as well as the movements in their facial muscles relating to overt signs of displeasure (such as frowning). The researchers were aware that previous research on members of the general population had showed the magnitude of the startle response to be larger in the presence of unpleasant than of pleasant slides. They reasoned, therefore, that if individuals with an antisocial personality disorder have diminished emotional reactivity, they probably would *not* show larger startle reactions, or exaggerated facial muscle movement, when the bursts of noise occurred together with unpleasant slides. This is just what occurred. The group of prisoners highest in antisocial personality disorder did *not* show larger startle responses in the presence of the unpleasant than the pleasant slides; the other two groups did (see Figure 14.6). A similar pattern was found for movements of facial muscles. The antisocial prisoners did *not* show larger muscle movements in the presence of the unpleasant than the pleasant slides.

It is not only differences in emotional reactivity that distinguish individuals with an antisocial personality disorders from others. These individuals seem also to be unable to learn from experience the way others do. In particular, they seem to have a great deal of difficulty learning to avoid behaviors that get them into trouble. A second line of inquiry into differences between antisocial personalities and others has focused on differences in the way in which they process information and learn from experience.

The Antisocial Personality and Problems in Learning and Attention

A simple demonstration of a way in which those who have an antisocial personality disorder differ from others in processing information and learning is provided in an early study by Lykken (1957). Lykken asked three groups of participants—college students, prisoners with antisocial personality disorder, and prisoners without it—to perform a problem-solving task. The participants indicated their answers to each problem by pushing levers on a board. For each problem there were three wrong answers; one of these led to a mild electric shock, while the other two responses

simply turned on a red light. All three groups performed at a similar level, but the antisocial prisoners were less effective than the other two groups in avoiding errors that produced electric shocks. This finding suggests that the antisocial prisoners were little concerned with whether they received an electric shock or a red light. Other findings point to similar conclusions: In several studies, individuals with the antisocial personality disorder show poorer performance than normal controls in learning to inhibit punished responses (e.g., Newman, Widom, & Nathan, 1985).

Of course, the interesting question is *why* those with an antisocial personality disorder appear to have difficulty inhibiting responses that have negative consequences. One possibility, being explored actively by R.D. Hare and his associates at the University of British Columbia, is that those with the disorder allocate attention in a very different way than those who are not so afflicted. Essentially, the argument is that individuals with an antisocial personality disorder engage in what is termed "overfocusing" of attention. It is argued that when these individuals focus attention on a desired course of behavior, or objective, they do so in a way that "blocks off" or excludes from consideration any negative or opposing information or argument. This process would explain why they have such difficulty in learning to avoid punishing responses: The disposition to overfocus attention blocks off or masks consideration of potential punishing responses. Much more research is required, but this approach already has some support (Harpur & Hare, 1990).

Overall, these results indicate that people with an antisocial personality disorder differ from others in a

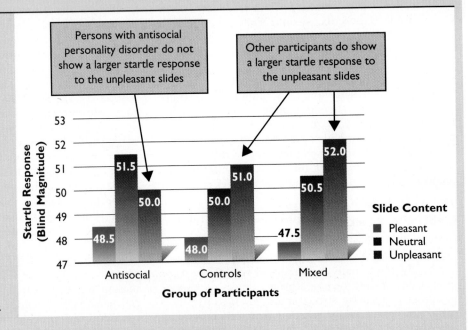

FIGURE 14.6

Reduced Emotionality and the Antisocial Personality

Research participants suffering from the antisocial personality disorder did not show larger startle reactions to unpleasant slides paired with bursts of noise than they did to neutral or pleasant slides. In contrast, other individuals showed larger reactions to unpleasant slides. These findings suggest that people with the antisocial personality disorder experience reduced emotional reactions to negative stimuli.
(Source: Based on data from Patrick, Bradley, & Lang, 1993.)

Persons with antisocial personality disorder do not show a larger startle response to the unpleasant slides

Other participants do show a larger startle response to the unpleasant slides

Startle Response (Blind Magnitude)

Antisocial: 48.5, 51.5, 50.0
Controls: 50.0, 48.0, 51.0
Mixed: 47.5, 50.5, 52.0

Slide Content
- Pleasant
- Neutral
- Unpleasant

Group of Participants

number of ways. They appear to be less emotionally reactive. They also appear to have difficulty in inhibiting responses that lead to punishment, perhaps because of a disposition to overfocus on desired objectives, thereby blocking out information about stimuli that signify negative consequences.

Critical Thinking Questions:

1. People with the antisocial personality disorder are not the only individuals to show low levels of fear: Test pilots, firefighters, and military heroes also show this characteristic. Does this imply that they too, are abnormal in some respect? Or are there other possible explanations for the fearless behavior of these people?

2. All of the participants in the study conducted by Patrick and his colleagues were prisoners. Should a group of normal control participants have been included?

3. It is suggested that individuals having an antisocial personality disorder tend to overfocus on desired goals or objectives, and to block off, or exclude, other information that might be relevant in determining how they should respond to a situation. Would such an arrangement always be disadvantageous, or are there times when this disposition might be useful?

4. Assuming that people with antisocial personality disorder do often experience lower levels of emotional arousal than others, what does this suggest in terms of treating this disorder?

Schizophrenia: Out of Touch with Reality

All of the disorders we've considered cause distress for the people who experience them. Yet for the most part these people *can* continue with their lives. Like people loaded down with lead weights, they toil and suffer, but generally *can* struggle on somehow. Individuals afflicted with *schizophrenia* face a different situation. They are so disturbed that they usually cannot live ordinary lives. Indeed, in many cases, they must be removed from society, at least temporarily, for their own protection as well as to undergo treatment. The term **schizophrenia** means "split mind," and modern definitions of this disorder reflect this meaning: All agree that it is a very serious disorder involving profound distortions of thought, perception, and affect (mood).

What is the precise nature of schizophrenia? What are its major causes? These are the questions we'll now examine.

The Basic Nature of Schizophrenia

Schizophrenia involves severe disruptions in virtually all aspects of psychological functioning. As noted recently by Heinrichs (1993), schizophrenia depletes the mind's resources, just as severe brain damage depletes these resources. But while people suffering from brain damage experience a world that is stripped of its meaning in many respects, those suffering from schizophrenia experience a world that has become, in Heinrich's words:

> excessively, terrifyingly rich in semantic possibilities. Instead of an inability to interpret experience, schizophrenia yields spurious experience in the form of hallucinations, or leads to ... unwarranted interpretations of experience in the form of delusions. Instead of an inability to reason, schizophrenia produces a reasoning that is so cryptic and obscure, it strikes the observer as incoherent.

Schizophrenia: *A group of serious psychological disorders characterized by severe distortions in thought and language, perceptions, and emotion.*

Let's look more closely at the major symptoms of this serious disorder. But first, one additional point: Although we will discuss schizophrenia as though it is a single disorder, it's important to note that many experts believe it may actually involve several different and distinct disturbances (Bellack, 1994; Heinrichs, 1993). Please keep this point in mind when we discuss the potential causes of schizophrenia.

DISTURBANCES OF THOUGHT AND LANGUAGE   First, and perhaps foremost, schizophrenics do not think or speak like others. Their words jump about in a fragmented and disorganized manner. There is a loosening of associations, so that one idea does not follow logically from another; indeed, ideas often seem totally unconnected. In addition, schizophrenics often create words of their own—neologisms such as "littlehood" for childhood, or "crimery" for bad actions. Indeed, in extreme cases, their words seem to be totally jumbled into what psychologists term a *word salad*.

These problems, and several others, seem to stem from a breakdown in the capacity for *selective attention*. Normally we can focus our attention on certain stimuli while largely ignoring others. This is not true for schizophrenics, who are easily distracted by anything and everything. Even the sound of their own words may disrupt their train of thought and send them wandering off into a mysterious world of their own creation.

Schizophrenics also frequently suffer from **delusions**—firmly held beliefs that have no basis in reality. Such delusions can take many different forms. One common type is *delusions of persecution*—the belief that one is being plotted against, spied upon, threatened, or otherwise mistreated. For example, Leopold Bellak (1994), who has studied schizophrenia for more than fifty years, describes a female patient who would shout "Here comes Bellak, the Russian spy!" from her window every morning as he approached the hospital building. Another common type is *delusions of grandeur*—the belief that one is extremely famous, important, or powerful. People suffering from such delusions may claim that they are the prime minister, a famous movie or rock star, or even Jesus, Mohammed, or Buddha. Finally, schizophrenics also sometimes suffer from *delusions of control*—the belief that other people, evil forces, or perhaps even beings from another planet are controlling their thoughts, actions, or feelings, often by means of electronic devices implanted in or aimed at their brain. As you can see, schizophrenics' ties to reality are tenuous at best, and may seem almost nonexistent in some cases.

DISTURBANCES OF PERCEPTION   Schizophrenics also show many signs of disturbed perceptions. Simply put, they do not perceive the world in the same way as other people do. Many experience **hallucinations** (see Chapter 4), which are vivid sensory experiences that have no basis in physical reality. The most common types of hallucinations are auditory. Schizophrenics "hear" voices, music, or other sounds that aren't present. Visual hallucinations are also quite frequent, and, again, these experiences can be quite intense. Hallucinations of smells and tastes are sometimes also reported.

In addition, schizophrenics often experience deficits with respect to *social perception*—their ability to recognize the emotions of others (Morrison, Bellack, & Mueser, 1988). For example, they are less successful than normal people in identifying the facial expressions of others, or in recognizing emotions from a speaker's tone of voice (Kerr & Neale, 1993). However, since schizophrenics are also less successful than normal people in recognizing nonsense syllables and in recognizing faces generally, it appears that their difficulties in social perception reflect more general deficits in perception.

DISTURBANCES OF EMOTION OR MOOD A third key symptom of schizophrenia involves inappropriate or unusual emotional reactions. Some schizophrenics show almost no emotion at all: They remain impassive in the face of events that evoke strong reactions from others. Others do show emotion, but their reactions are inappropriate. They may giggle when describing a painful childhood experience or when receiving tragic news. In sum, schizophrenics' disturbed patterns of thought, perception, and emotion weaken their grip on reality, and virtually ensure that they will live in a private world largely of their own creation.

DISTURBANCES OF MOTOR BEHAVIOR A fourth symptom of schizophrenia involves unusual actions. These can take an incredible range of forms, as the following description of a hospital ward for schizophrenics suggests:

> Lou stands hour after hour … just rubbing the palm of his hand around the top of his head. Jerry spends his days rubbing his hand against his stomach and running around a post … Helen paces back and forth … mumbling about enemies who are coming to get her, while Vic grimaces and giggles over in the corner … Nick tears up magazines, puts bits of paper in his mouth, and then spits them out … Bill sits immobile for hours, staring at the floor. [Hagen,1993]

POSITIVE AND NEGATIVE SYMPTOMS As you can readily see, schizophrenia is a complex disorder. Are there any underlying dimensions to it that can help us make sense of the vast range of diverse symptoms? One approach that has proved useful, and that has provided insights into the nature of this disorder, divides symptoms into two types. *Positive symptoms* involve the presence of something that is normally absent, such as hallucinations and delusions. *Negative symptoms* involve the absence of something that is normally present and include withdrawal, apathy, absence of emotion, and so on. (These two groups are sometimes referred to as *Type I* and *Type II* schizophrenia, respectively.) Patients with negative symptoms generally have a poorer prognosis: They remain hospitalized longer and are less likely to recover than patients with positive symptoms (Fenton & McGlashan, 1991). In addition, patients with positive and negative symptoms appear to experience different kinds of cognitive deficits. Those with negative symptoms do worse on tests that measure visual and spatial skills; for example, they have more difficulty in recognizing visual stimuli. In contrast, patients with positive symptoms do worse on tests of short-term memory (Braff, 1989). These findings, as well as many others, indicate that there may be two distinct types of schizophrenia; in fact, many experts believe there may be several types (Heinrichs, 1993).

Subtypes of Schizophrenia

Although all schizophrenics show some of the symptoms outlined above, the overall pattern of these problems varies greatly. Largely on the basis of such differences, schizophrenia can be divided into several subtypes.

PARANOID TYPE As its name suggests, people in this category have delusions of persecution—they see plots to harm them everywhere. These delusions are sometimes coupled with delusions of grandeur. Thus, they may claim that they possess tremendous power or wisdom, or maintain that they are a famous figure from history such as Napoleon and are being persecuted by dangerous enemies.

DISORGANIZED TYPE   People suffering from this type of schizophrenia show disorganized speech, disorganized behavior, and flat or inappropriate affect. They are the ones most likely to use neologisms and to show word salad. They sometimes have hallucinations or delusions, but these tend to be fuzzy or poorly developed. More common for this type are fits of giggling, making faces, and other childlike behavior.

CATATONIC SCHIZOPHRENIA   In some respects this is the most bizarre form of all. People suffering from *catatonic schizophrenia* show marked disturbances in motor behavior. Many alternate between total immobility—they sit for days or even weeks frozen in a single posture—and wild, excited activity. In the latter state they sometimes engage in violent behavior, so this condition can be quite dangerous. When immobile, some catatonic schizophrenics show *waxy flexibility*. Their limbs can be moved and remain in the position in which they are arranged. Yet those who suffer from this form of schizophrenia also seem to be aware of the world around them. Sometimes they do not merely refuse requests—they do the opposite.

The Origins of Schizophrenia

Schizophrenia is certainly one the most bizarre and troubling psychological disorders. It is not a common disorder, being found in less than 1 percent of the Canadian population (Bland, Orn, & Newman, 1988). This should not lead you to conclude that it is inconsequential. A better assessment of its significance is gained when you consider that schizophrenia is the leading cause of hospitalization in psychiatric hospitals, as well as the third-ranked mental disorder leading to hospitalization in general hospitals (Riley, 1992).

GENETIC FACTORS   Schizophrenia, like several other psychological disorders, tends to run in families. The closer the family relationship between two individuals, the higher the likelihood that if one develops schizophrenia, the other will also (Nicole & Gottesman, 1983; and see Figure 14.7).

CATATONIC SCHIZOPHRENIA

People who suffer from catatonic schizophrenia may remain totally immobile, frozen in a single posture, for long periods of time.

FIGURE 14.7

Family Relationship and Schizophrenia

The more closely two individuals are related, the greater the likelihood that if one develops schizophrenia, the other will too. This finding suggests that genetic factors play a role in the occurrence of schizophrenia.

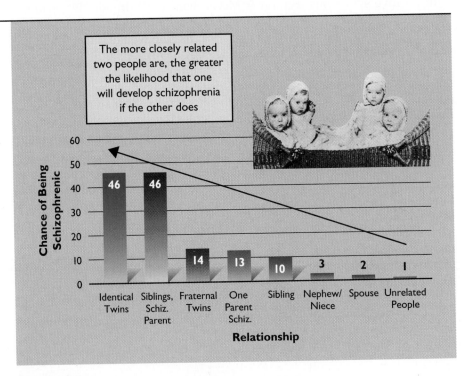

The more closely related two people are, the greater the likelihood that one will develop schizophrenia if the other does

Chance of Being Schizophrenic

Relationship	Value
Identical Twins	46
Siblings, Schiz. Parent	46
Fraternal Twins	14
One Parent Schiz.	13
Sibling	10
Nephew/Niece	3
Spouse	2
Unrelated People	1

Evidence suggesting that genetic factors play a role in schizophrenia is provided by studies of twins (Kendler & Robinette, 1983). For example, researchers have studied the children of twin pairs in which one twin is schizophrenic and the other is not. Clearly, being raised by a schizophrenic parent is very different from being raised by a nonschizophrenic parent. Thus, if the cousins show similar rates of schizophrenia despite this difference, strong evidence for the role of genetic factors has been obtained. In fact, this is just what such studies have shown (Gottesman & Bertelsen, 1989). The rates of schizophrenia among children raised by the schizophrenic and nonschizophrenic twins were 16.8 and 17.4 percent, respectively. These and other large-scale studies of twins and families (e.g, Kety, 1988) provide convincing evidence for the importance of genetic factors in schizophrenia.

At this point, it should be emphasized that what is inherited with respect to schizophrenia is not the disorder itself, but rather a predisposition (a *diathesis*) to develop it in conditions of high environmental stress. In other words, an individual who is at high risk for developing schizophrenia because of genetic factors may not develop it if the environment in which he or she lives is relatively supportive and benign. Only when a genetically inherited predisposition is coupled with stressful conditions does schizophrenia develop. This **diathesis-stress model** is widely accepted by researchers investigating the nature of schizophrenia.

FAMILY FACTORS As we have already seen, the fact that schizophrenia seems to run in families provides evidence for the role of genetic factors. It also raises the possibility that some families create a social environment that places the children at risk—that increases the likelihood of them developing schizophrenia. What is such an environment like? Research findings provide some intriguing answers.

First, it appears that in these families, children are exposed either to high levels of conflict between the parents (*schismatic families*) or to a situation in which all power rests with one parent and calm prevails for this reason (*skewed families*; Arieti, 1974). Apparently, for at least some children, both conditions are disturbing and increase the risk of their developing schizophrenia.

Second, in families with a greater than expected incidence of schizophrenia, the patterns of communication are confusing and upsetting to children. Several studies indicate that the families of schizophrenics express high levels of criticism and emotional overinvolvement toward the children (e.g., Miklowitz et al., 1989). In short, family members appear to be very concerned with the patient's well-being but at the same time are highly critical of them—often for their illness!

COGNITIVE FACTORS Earlier, we saw that schizophrenics are less accurate than normal people in judging the emotions of others (Kerr & Neale, 1993). Actually, this is just one piece of a larger pattern suggesting that schizophrenia involves—and may partly stem from—deficits in cognitive functioning. First, schizophrenics—especially those with positive symptoms (Type I schizophrenia)—show a reduced ability to ignore irrelevant or distracting stimuli (e.g., Braff & Geyer, 1990; Elkins, Cromwell, & Asarnow, 1992). For example, in one study (Grillon et al., 1990), schizophrenics were asked to press a button whenever they heard a tone of a specific frequency. On some trials, a tone of a different frequency was also sounded. This distracting stimulus reduced the performance of schizophrenics more than the performance of controls. In addition, the schizophrenics showed larger brain waves in response to the distracting stimulus than did controls.

In contrast, schizophrenics suffering from negative symptoms (Type II schizophrenia) seem to show opposite problems: They are *under*attentive to

Diathesis-Stress Model: A model of schizophrenia suggesting that persons with inherited dispositions to develop this disorder do so only when subjected to stressful environmental conditions.

external stimuli. For example, they often show weaker-than-normal *orienting responses*—physiological reactions indicative of attention—when unfamiliar stimuli are presented (Bernstein, 1987). Similarly, when shown one stimulus and then another similar (distracting or masking) stimulus, schizophrenics require a larger interval between the two before they can process the initial stimulus (Asarnow, Granholm, & Sherman, 1991). One interpretation of these findings is that schizophrenics are not paying as much attention to the first stimulus as are normal controls (Elkins, Cromwell, & Asarnow, 1992).

In sum, it appears that schizophrenics experience several kinds of cognitive deficits. Moreover, the precise pattern of these deficits seems to vary with their symptoms, and especially with whether these are positive or negative.

BIOCHEMICAL FACTORS   Consider the following observations:

- Large doses of amphetamines produce patterns of behavior highly similar, in some respects, to those observed in some types of schizophrenia—for example, delusions of persecution and hallucinations.

- Amphetamines seem to produce these effects by increasing levels of, or sensitivity to, the neurotransmitter dopamine.

- Drugs effective in treating schizophrenia, such as the phenothiazines, block the brain's receptor sites for dopamine (e.g., Farde et al., 1988).

When these observations are combined, it seems reasonable to suggest that schizophrenia may stem, at least in part, from excess activity in those parts of the brain that use dopamine as a neurotransmitter. This is the **dopamine hypothesis** of schizophrenia.

Evidence for this hypothesis is provided by the finding that the brains of deceased schizophrenics show increased brain dopamine and a higher-than-normal number of dopamine receptors (Mackay et al., 1982). Further, PET scans of the brains of living schizophrenics have sometimes (though not always) indicated an increased number of dopamine receptors in the limbic system (Wong et al., 1986). Such findings seem to apply primarily to schizophrenics with Type I schizophrenia.

Although the above evidence supports the dopamine hypothesis, not all findings are consistent with it. For example, schizophrenics who show improvement after taking dopamine-blocking drugs improve gradually over a period of about six weeks—but not immediately. Yet it takes only a few hours for these drugs to block dopamine receptors within the brain. If schizophrenia results solely from dopamine-stimulated activity, the effects of these drugs should be visible very quickly (Pickar, 1988). Similarly, antipsychotic drugs that block the activity of dopamine relieve the symptoms of many serious psychological disorders, not just schizophrenia. These findings suggest that while the dopamine hypothesis may provide important insights into the biochemical nature of schizophrenia, it by no means offers a complete picture of the biochemical imbalances that contribute to this disorder.

BRAIN STRUCTURE   Finally, growing evidence suggests that schizophrenia may also stem from subtle but important damage to various portions of the brain. In particular, it appears that among schizophrenics, brain *ventricles*—cavities within the brain containing cerebrospinal fluid—are enlarged relative to those of people not suffering from this disorder (Raz & Raz, 1990). Moreover, the longer individuals have been hospitalized for schizophrenia, and therefore the more serious their condition, the greater the degree of ventricular enlargement. Such enlargement, which may stem from damage to or atrophy of brain tissue in adjoining areas, seems to be quite general, involving

Dopamine Hypothesis: The hypothesis that schizophrenia is associated with excess activity in those parts of the brain in which dopamine is the primary neurotransmitter.

many areas of the brain. For example, in one recent study, Raz (1993) examined ventricles in many different regions of the brains of schizophrenics and normal volunteers. She found that ventricles of schizophrenics were enlarged in almost all of the regions studied.

Additional evidence suggests that it is damage in the frontal lobes and in certain subcortical regions (temporal limbic structures) that may be most closely linked to the symptoms of schizophrenia (e.g., Barta et al., 1990; Jernigan et al., 1991). Once again, however, the pattern may be different for people with Type I and Type II schizophrenia; definite conclusions are not yet possible.

In sum, it appears that genetic factors, certain types of home environments, and brain structure and function may all be related to the occurrence of schizophrenia. It remains for future research to determine the precise manner in which such factors combine to place specific individuals at risk for the development of this serious psychological disorder.

MAKING PSYCHOLOGY PART OF YOUR LIFE

Preventing Suicide: Some Basic Steps

When terminally ill people choose to end their life rather than endure continued pain and suffering, their actions are understandable, even if we disapprove of them on moral or religious grounds. But when young people, whose lives have just begun, follow the same route, nearly everyone agrees that the death is tragic. Preventing these suicides is *crucial*. Is there anything you as an individual can do to help prevent suicide by others? Research findings suggest that there is.

1. *Take all suicide threats seriously* One common myth about suicide is that people who threaten to kill themselves really won't; only those who tell no one about their plans will actually commit this act. *This is untrue!* Approximately 70 percent of all suicides communicate their intentions to others within a few months of their death. Thus, whenever someone talks about suicide, you should take it seriously.

2. *If someone mentions suicide, don't be afraid to discuss it* Another common myth about suicide, and a dangerous one, is that one should never discuss suicide with another person—that this will only increase the person's suicidal tendencies. This belief, too, is false. Encouraging people to talk gets these thoughts out into the open and can be helpful. It lets these people know that you are interested and allows you to gather information you can pass on to counselors and others. So don't be afraid to discuss this matter with potential suicides if it arises.

3. *Recognize the danger signs* These include statements by someone that he or she has no strong or compelling reasons for living; agitation or excitement followed by a period of calm resignation; sudden efforts to give valued possessions away to others; direct statements such as, "I don't want to be a burden any more," or "I don't really want to go on living"; and revival from a deeply depressed state. If you observe these changes in others, along with other indications that they are contemplating suicide, the situation may well be serious.

4. *Discourage others from blaming themselves for failing to meet unrealistic standards* Many people who attempt suicide do so because they feel that they have fallen far short of their own expectations and standards. Unfortunately, in many cases, these are unrealistically high—so high that almost no one could hope to attain them. If you hear someone you know criticizing himself or herself for such "failure," try to intervene by pointing out that these standards are exceptionally high, and by calling attention to the person's successes and good points. This may help break a downward cycle that can ultimately lead to thoughts of suicide.

5. *If a friend or family member shows the danger signs described above, don't leave him or her alone* With rare exceptions, suicide is a solitary act. So if you are concerned that someone you know is seriously contemplating such an action, don't leave him or her alone. If you can't stay with the person, get others to help or bring the person with you.

6. *Most important of all: Get help!* Perhaps the most important point to keep in mind is this: Determining whether someone is at risk for suicide is a complex judgment—one that is difficult even for trained experts. Thus, you should definitely *not* try to make this judgment for yourself. Rather, if you have even the slightest concern that someone you know is seriously thinking of suicide, *seek professional help*. Call a local suicide hot line; or discuss your concerns with a physician, psychologist, counselor, or member of the clergy. And, if possible, try to get the person to seek help from one or more of these sources. Don't be afraid of overreacting. In signal-detection theory terms, this is one of those cases where a miss (failing to notice suicidal tendencies when they are present) is *much* worse than a false alarm (concluding that suicidal tendencies are present when in fact they are not).

SUICIDE IN CANADA

SUICIDE INFORMATION & EDUCATION CENTRE

SUMMARY AND REVIEW OF KEY POINTS

CHANGING CONCEPTIONS OF PSYCHOLOGICAL DISORDERS: A BRIEF HISTORICAL PERSPECTIVE psychological disorders 576 trephining 577 medical perspective 578 psychiatry 578	• Ideas concerning the nature of abnormal behavior have changed greatly over the centuries. It was viewed as the result of supernatural forces until well into the eighteenth century. This view has been replaced by the medical model, which sees psychological disorders as forms of mental illness. Psychologists recognize the importance of biological factors in many forms of abnormal behavior, but they also emphasize the key role of psychological processes such as cognition and learning, and the impact of sociocultural factors.
IDENTIFYING PSYCHOLOGICAL DISORDERS: THE DSM-IV Diagnostic and Statistical Manual of Mental Disorders (DSM-IV) 582	• In order to improve the accuracy with which psychological disorders are diagnosed, many mental health professionals use the Diagnostic and Statistical Manual of Mental Disorders. The newest version of this manual, DSM-IV, is improved over earlier versions in several respects—for example, it is based more firmly in published research. • The DSM-IV provides descriptions of a wide range of psychological disorders and associated conditions. It uses a multiaxis approach, in which disorders are classified along five different axes. • In contrast to earlier versions, the DSM-IV pays more attention to the impact of cultural factors on psychological disorders.
MOOD DISORDERS: THE DOWNS AND UPS OF LIFE mood disorders 587 depression 587 bipolar disorder 588 learned helplessness 588 self-schemas 589 suicide 589	• People suffering from depression—one important form of mood disorder—experience negative moods, reduced energy, feelings of hopelessness, loss of interest in previously satisfying activities, difficulties in sleeping, and recurrent thoughts of death. Depression is more common among women than among men. In bipolar disorders, individuals experience wide swings of mood from mania (elation) to deep depression. • Mood disorders tend to run in families; thus, genetic factors play a role in their occurrence. Depression also seems to involve disturbances in brain activity and biochemistry. Psychological factors such as learned helplessness, tendencies to attribute negative outcomes to internal causes, and negative perceptions of oneself and others are also involved. • Suicide is a major cause of death among young people. People contemplating suicide or who have attempted it seem to show less concern over certain aspects of death than those not at high risk for suicide. Suicide is caused by many factors, including efforts by individuals to escape from a self they find inadequate and intolerable.
ANXIETY DISORDERS: WHEN DREAD DEBILITATES anxiety 592 anxiety disorders 592 panic attack disorder 592 agoraphobia 593 obsessive-compulsive disorder 594	• Anxiety disorders involve increased arousal accompanied by generalized feelings of fear or apprehension. Panic attacks involve symptoms of arousal coupled with intense fear—often of losing control in some specific situation. Both biological factors and learning seem to play a role in their occurrence. • Phobias are excessive fears focused on specific objects or situations. Obsessive-compulsive disorder involves repetitious thoughts or actions that individuals seem unable to control. • People suffering from anxiety disorders seem to direct more of their information-processing capacity to anxiety-related stimuli.

SOMATOFORM DISORDERS: PHYSICAL SYMPTOMS WITHOUT PHYSICAL CAUSES somatoform disorders 596 somatization disorder 597 hypochondriasis 597 conversion disorder 597	• In somatoform disorders, psychological problems find expression in physical symptoms for which there are no apparent biological causes. In somatization disorder, individuals experience physical complaints for which there is no apparent physical basis. Hypochondriasis, another type of somatoform disorder, involves preoccupation with fears of disease. • In conversion disorders, individuals suffer actual impairments in physical functioning, such as blindness, deafness, or loss of sensation. • Somatoform disorders may be explained by the rewards of the sick person role as well as by tendencies to attribute normal body sensations to serious causes.
DISSOCIATIVE DISORDERS: WHEN MEMORY FAILS dissociative disorders 597 dissociative amnesia 598 dissociative fugue 598 dissociative identity disorder 598	• Dissociative disorders involve profound losses of memory or identity. In dissociative amnesia, individuals are unable to remember various events, especially ones they found traumatic or disturbing. • In dissociative identity disorder (multiple personality), individuals seem to possess several distinct personalities, which alternate in controlling their behavior. There is evidence to indicate that such disorders are real—at least in some instances.
SEXUAL AND GENDER IDENTITY DISORDERS sexual desire disorders 601 sexual arousal disorders 601 paraphilias 601	• Sexual dysfunctions involve disturbances in sexual desire, sexual arousal, or the ability to attain orgasm. Paraphilias are disturbances in which unusual imagery or acts are necessary for sexual arousal. • People suffering from gender identity disorder feel that they were born with the wrong sexual identity and seek to change this identity through medical treatment or other means.
EATING DISORDERS eating disorders 602	• Eating disorders are common among young people, especially young women. People suffering from anorexia nervosa are afraid of being or becoming "fat"; consequently, they starve themselves and experience dangerous weight loss. • People suffering from bulimia engage in repeated cycles of binge eating and purging. Both anorexia nervosa and bulimia stem in part from dissatisfaction with one's appearance. In addition, bulimia involves reductions in taste sensitivity.
PERSONALITY DISORDERS: TRAITS THAT PROVE COSTLY personality disorders 603 paranoid personality disorder 603 schizoid personality disorder 603 antisocial personality disorder 604 modeling 604	• Personality disorders involve traits that are inflexible and maladaptive and cause those who suffer them serious difficulties. The paranoid personality disorder involves pervasive mistrust of others. The schizoid personality disorder involves a pattern of total isolation from others. • People with the antisocial personality disorder show total disregard for the rights of others, coupled with reckless behavior, fearlessness, and an inability to form close relationships. Research findings suggest that this disorder may stem both from early learning experiences and from biological factors such as reduced emotional reactions to threatening stimuli.

SCHIZOPHRENIA: OUT OF TOUCH WITH REALITY	• Schizophrenia is a very serious psychological disorder involving severe disturbances in thought, perception, affect, and motor behavior. Several distinct types of schizophrenia exist, including paranoid, disorganized, and catatonic. Schizophrenics can be divided into those showing positive symptoms (reactions that are not present in normal people) and those showing negative symptoms (the absence of normal reactions).
schizophrenia 607 delusions 608 hallucinations 608 diathesis-stress model 611 dopamine hypothesis 612	• Schizophrenia has complex origins involving genetic factors, certain aspects of family structure, and biochemical factors. In addition, schizophrenics suffer from deficits in cognitive functioning. Schizophrenia may also be related to damage in several regions of the brain.

CRITICAL THINKING QUESTIONS

APPRAISAL	Psychologists generally agree that only behavior that is atypical and evaluated negatively in a given society should be labeled as "abnormal." This implies that there are no absolutes in distinguishing between abnormal and normal behavior. As long as a behavior is viewed as acceptable within a culture, it will be described as "normal." Do you agree with this perspective? If not, why?
CONTROVERSY	Growing evidence indicates that genetic factors can predispose individuals to develop certain forms of psychological disorder. In other words, some persons are at "high risk" in this respect. This evidence leads to the suggestion that perhaps we should invest resources in identifying those individuals and taking steps to prevent their inherited dispositions from developing into serious psychological disorders. In order to do so, it would first be necessary to gather information on the genetic background of many people. Do you think that doing so is justified? Or should this kind of information be viewed as too private to allow for such projects?
MAKING PSYCHOLOGY PART OF YOUR LIFE	Near the beginning of this chapter we noted noted that many psychologists are uneasy with the term "mental illness." Now that you know much more about the many causes of psychological disorders, we hope you can appreciate more fully why this is so. Such disorders are not simply "diseases" in the classic sense of this word; they involve much more than the ravages of harmful microorganisms. In view of this fact—and it certainly is a fact—will you think differently about people who are suffering from such disorders than you did before you read this chapter? And do you think that your greater understanding of the many causes of psychological disorders will change your reactions to those who are experiencing these problems, perhaps increasing your level of sympathy for them?

Therapy
Diminishing the Pain of Psychological Disorders

PSYCHOTHERAPIES: PSYCHOLOGICAL APPROACHES
TO PSYCHOLOGICAL DISORDERS 620
Psychodynamic Therapies: From
   Repression to Insight
Humanistic Therapies: Emphasizing the
   Positive
Behavior Therapies: Psychological
   Disorders and Faulty Learning
Cognitive Therapies: Changing Disordered
   Thought
Cognitive Therapy: How to Manage the
   Linkage Between Thought and Emotions

GROUP THERAPIES: WORKING WITH OTHERS TO
SOLVE PERSONAL PROBLEMS 633
Psychodynamic Group Therapies
Behavioral Group Therapies
Humanistic Group Therapies
Self-Help Groups: Help from Our Peers

THERAPIES FOCUSED ON INTERPERSONAL
RELATIONS: MARITAL AND FAMILY THERAPY 637
Marital Therapy: When Spouses Become
   the Intimate Enemy
Family Therapy: Changing Environments
   That Harm

PSYCHOTHERAPY: SOME CURRENT ISSUES 639
Does Psychotherapy Really Work? An
   Optimistic Conclusion
Are Some Forms of Therapy More
   Successful Than Others? Solving a
   Persistent Puzzle

BIOLOGICALLY BASED THERAPIES 645
Early Forms of Biological Therapy
Electroconvulsive Therapy
Psychosurgery
Drug Therapy: The Pharmacological
   Revolution

THE SETTING FOR MAJOR THERAPY 650
Treatment Locations: The Shift from
   Hospitals to the Community
Community Services: What Are They? And
   Why Are They Needed?
Prevention: Heading Off Trouble Before It
   Begins—or Becomes Serious

SUMMARY AND REVIEW OF KEY POINTS 655

CANADIAN FOCUS—COPING WITH ANXIETY:
MEICHENBAUM'S STRESS INOCULATION TRAINING
PROGRAM 632

THE RESEARCH PROCESS—SUBLIMINAL
SELF-HELP AUDIOTAPES: DO THEY DELIVER
WHAT THEY PROMISE? 635

KEY CONCEPT—MAJOR FORMS OF
PSYCHOTHERAPY 640

CANADIAN FOCUS—ADDRESSING MENTAL
HEALTH PROBLEMS IN CANADA'S NORTH 643

MAKING PSYCHOLOGY PART OF YOUR
LIFE—HOW TO CHOOSE A THERAPIST: A
CONSUMER'S GUIDE 653

NO QUICK FIXES IN TREATMENT OF PSYCHOLOGICAL PROBLEMS

*The Vancouver Sun:
March 21, 1992*

This feature explored the reasons people hesitate before seeking assistance with psychological problems. According to the Sun, people may feel they should be able to deal with psychological problems themselves: only "crazy" people get help. They may not "understand that their 'talking cure,' to use Sigmund

Freud's phrase, can be a powerful healing process."

Many professionals are trained to treat psychological difficulties. Those include psychiatrists who may prescribe medications, such as anti-depressants. Other psychologists specialize in psychotherapy.

As the author of this column wrote: "I often recognize that medications are not required ...

but expert counselling is. In such a situation, I would prefer to send patients to psychologists who...are better suited by preparation and approach to deal with emotional problems."

In Chapter 15 you will find that psychological disorders are treated in a variety of ways such as psychotherapy, psychosurgery, and psychotherapeutic drugs.

THERE IS A LOT OF
PAIN IN LIFE—MORE
THAN ENOUGH
PSYCHOLOGICAL
DISCOMFORT TO GO
AROUND.

"*I* beg your pardon, I never promised you a rose garden." So starts a popular old song. Life is good, the lyrics suggest, but it's definitely no Eden free of problems. A few statistics help to drive this point home:

- More than half of all college and university students report that they have thought about suicide at least once (Meehan et al., 1992), and about 10 percent of adolescents indicate that they have actually attempted suicide (Shaffer et al., 1991).

- About 10 percent of adults suffer from depression or related disorders at any given time (Strickland, 1992); almost half report that they have experienced a major depressive episode at some time in their life (Kessler et al., 1994).

- More than six million North Americans are currently involved in various kinds of self-help groups—groups focused on problems ranging from alcoholism and drug abuse to stuttering and the trauma of losing one's spouse.

Yes, there is a lot of pain in life—more than enough to go around. But there are also many effective techniques for alleviating such discomfort. Many procedures for treating various psychological disorders exist. To acquaint you with the most important of these, this chapter will proceed as follows.

We'll begin with **psychotherapies**—procedures in which a trained person establishes a professional relationship with the patient in order to remove or modify existing symptoms, change disturbed patterns of behavior, and promote personal growth and development (Wolberg, 1977). As you'll soon see, many forms of psychotherapy exist, ranging from *psychoanalysis*, the famous procedures devised by Freud, to modern procedures founded on basic principles of learning and cognition. Then we'll explore several forms of therapy that involve several people rather than a single individual—*group therapies*. After that, we'll consider therapies focused on interpersonal relations—*marital* and *family therapy*. We'll then turn to some basic questions about all these approaches: Are they successful in alleviating psychological disorders? And if they are, are some more helpful than others? We'll also examine several *biologically based therapies*—efforts to deal with psychological disorders through biological means. Finally, we'll look at various *settings* for therapy. These range from large institutions providing full-time care, to community health centers where individuals receive treatment on a part-time outpatient basis.

Psychotherapies: Psychological Approaches to Psychological Disorders

*S*ay the word *psychotherapy* and many people quickly conjure up the following image: A "patient" lies on a couch in a dimly lit room while a therapist sits in the background. The therapist urges the patient to reveal the deepest secrets of his or her mind—hidden urges, frustrated desires, traumatic early experiences. As these painful revelations are brought to the surface, the patient, suffering much emotional turmoil, moves toward psychological health.

This popular image, however, has little to do with many modern forms of psychotherapy. In fact, it applies primarily to only one type, an approach developed by Freud that is now rarely used by psychologists (although it is

Psychotherapies: *Procedures designed to eliminate or modify psychological disorders through the establishment of a special relationship between a client and a trained therapist.*

FIRST OFF, IT'S ALL RIGHT TO PUT YOUR FEET ON THE COUCH.

THAVES 4-23

PSYCHOTHERAPY AS MANY PEOPLE SEE IT

This is the kind of scene many people imagine when they hear the term *psychotherapy*. (Source: FRANK & ERNEST reprinted by permission of NEA, Inc.)

still used by some psychiatrists). Psychotherapy, as it is currently practiced by psychologists and other professionals, actually takes place in many different settings, employs a tremendously varied range of procedures, and can be carried out with groups as well as with individuals.

What do these diverse procedures have in common? Most psychologists agree that two features are crucial: (1) establishment of a special relationship, sometimes known as the **therapeutic alliance**, between the person experiencing psychological distress and the trained therapist—a relationship in which the distressed person feels free to reveal important and often embarrassing facts and has confidence in the therapist's genuine desire to help; and (2) efforts by the therapist to bring about beneficial changes in the client's behavior, feelings, or thoughts. In short, whatever form it takes, psychotherapy strives to place disturbed individuals in an environment in which they feel free to confide in another human being who is specially trained to help them change in beneficial ways. Let's take a closer look at several important forms of psychotherapy.

Psychodynamic Therapies: From Repression to Insight

Psychodynamic therapies are based on the assumption that abnormal behavior stems primarily from the complex inner workings of personality. More specifically, psychological disorders occur because something has gone seriously wrong with the balance of these hidden inner forces. Several forms of therapy are based on these assumptions. The most famous is psychoanalysis, the approach developed by Sigmund Freud.

PSYCHOANALYSIS If Freud had known how many movies, television shows, and even cartoons would be based upon his method of psychotherapy, it seems just possible that he might have changed it in several respects. He was a serious person who viewed himself as essentially scientific in orientation, and he would probably have found popular representations of his work thoroughly distasteful. But, as is often the case, there is a grain of truth in media representations of psychoanalysis: Freud *did* use a couch, and he *did* employ several other techniques that have become part and parcel of our culture's conception of psychotherapy.

In order to understand Freud's methods, let's begin by briefly reviewing the reasoning that lay behind them. As you may recall from Chapter 12, Freud believed that personality consists of three major parts—the *id*, *ego*, and *superego*, which correspond roughly to desire, reason, and conscience. Freud suggested that psychological disorders stem from the fact that many impulses of the id are unacceptable to the ego or superego and are therefore *repressed*—driven into the depths of the unconscious. There they persist, and individuals must devote a considerable portion of their psychic energy to keeping them in check

Therapeutic Alliance: The special relationship between therapist and client that contributes to the effectiveness of many forms of psychotherapy.

Psychodynamic Therapies: Therapies based on the assumption that psychological disorders stem primarily from hidden inner conflicts with repressed urges and impulses.

FREUD'S FAMOUS COUCH

This scene of Freud's London office, which he opened after fleeing Nazi persecution in Vienna, shows the famous couch.

Free Association: A key procedure in psychoanalysis in which individuals spontaneously report all thoughts to the therapist.

Resistance: Efforts by individuals undergoing psychoanalysis to prevent repressed impulses or conflicts from entering consciousness.

and out of conscious experience—and to various *defense mechanisms* that protect the ego from feelings of anxiety. In short, Freud believed that hidden conflicts among the basic components of personality, if left unresolved, interfere with normal psychosexual development and so cause psychological disorders.

How can such problems be relieved? Freud felt that the crucial task is for people to overcome repression and come face to face with their hidden feelings and impulses. Having gained such insight into their inner conflicts, they experience a release of emotion known as *abreaction*. Their energies having been at last freed from the task of repression, patients can direct these into healthy growth. Figure 15.1 summarizes these suggestions.

These ideas concerning the causes and cure of mental illness are reflected in the specific procedures used in psychoanalysis. As popular images suggest, the patient undergoing psychoanalysis lies on a couch in a partly darkened room and engages in **free association**. This involves reporting everything that passes through his or her mind, no matter how trivial it may appear to be. Freud believed that the repressed impulses and inner conflicts present in the unconscious would ultimately be revealed by these mental wanderings, at least to the trained ear of the analyst. As we saw in Chapter 4, he felt that dreams were especially useful in this respect, since they often represented inner conflicts and hidden impulses in disguised form. As psychoanalysis progresses and the analyst gains an understanding of the patient's problems, he or she asks questions and offers suggestions designed to enhance the patient's awareness of inner conflicts. It is through this process of *interpretation* that the patient finally gains increased insight.

During the course of psychoanalysis, Freud reported, several intriguing phenomena often occur. The first of these is **resistance**—the patient's refusal to report certain thoughts, motives, and experiences, or overt rejection of the analyst's interpretations (Strean, 1985). Presumably, resistance occurs because of the patient's desire to avoid the anxiety produced as threatening or painful thoughts come closer and closer to consciousness.

FIGURE 15.1

Psychoanalysis: An Overview of Its Major Goals

According to Freud's theory, psychotherapists can overcome psychological disorders by helping individuals gain insight into their hidden inner conflicts. Once such insight is obtained, presumably, it will no longer be necessary to devote "psychic energies" to repressing unacceptable impulses, and the disorders caused by these conflicts and their repression will disappear.

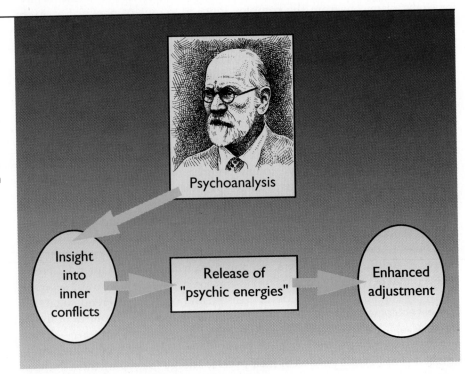

Another aspect of psychoanalysis is **transference**—intense emotional feelings of love or hate toward the analyst on the part of the patient. Often, patients react toward their analyst as they did to an earlier crucial person in their life—for example, one of their parents. Freud believed that the transference relationship can be an important tool for helping individuals work through conflicts regarding their parents, this time in a setting where the harm done by undesirable early relationships can be effectively countered. As the patient's insight increases, transference gradually decreases and ultimately fades away.

PSYCHOANALYSIS: AN EVALUATION   Psychoanalysis is probably the best-known form of psychotherapy. As noted by Hornstein (1992), early efforts by psychologists to ignore it (through the 1920s) and later to discredit it (in the 1930s and 1940s) largely failed. Psychoanalysis gained a firm grip on the public consciousness and refused to vanish, no matter how fervently psychologists trying to build a scientific field wished it to do so. Indeed, one of the founders of experimental psychology—Edwin Boring—chose to undergo psychoanalysis when he experienced deep depression. To protect his reputation at the time (1934), Boring claimed that he was studying the relationship between psychology and psychoanalysis; in reality, though, he hoped the treatment would benefit him (Hornstein, 1992). He was bitterly disappointed in this hope. After ten months, during which he saw his analyst four times a week, he concluded that the therapy had failed—he was no better off than before he entered treatment.

Unfortunately, Boring's experience seems to be typical; in general, the effectiveness of classical psychoanalysis has failed to match its fame. In the form proposed by Freud, it suffers from several major drawbacks that lessen its value. First, psychoanalysis is a costly and time-consuming process. Several years and large amounts of money are usually required for its completion. Second, it is based largely on Freud's theories of personality and psychosexual development. As was explained in Chapter 12, these theories are provocative but difficult to test scientifically. Third, Freud designed psychoanalysis for use with educated people who already possess high verbal skills. This limits the usefulness of psychoanalysis to what some have described as YAVIS patients—young, attractive, verbal, intelligent, and successful (Schofield, 1964). Other people, including many who may be desperately in need of psychological assistance, are left largely out in the cold (Snowden & Cheung, 1990). Finally, and perhaps most important, psychoanalysis has often adopted the posture of a closed logical system. Critics who raise questions about its validity or effectiveness are described as suffering from resistance and as showing severe psychological problems that prevent them from recognizing the obvious value of psychoanalysis! So, in sum, psychoanalysis has not turned out to be the major breakthrough that Freud predicted. While it may help some individuals gain insights into their own personalities, it does not appear to be practical or highly effective in treating a wide range of psychological disorders.

BEYOND PSYCHOANALYSIS: PSYCHODYNAMIC THERAPY TODAY   Because of such problems, classical psychoanalysis is a relatively rare type of therapy today. However, modified versions introduced by Freud's students and disciples, including the neo-Freudians we discussed in Chapter 12, are in more common use. These modified forms of psychodynamic therapy are usually briefer than classical psychoanalysis, requiring months rather than many years of treatment (Strupp & Binder, 1984); also, they focus less on the past than on the patient's present life and personal relationships. A couch is seldom used; instead, client and therapist sit face to face. And the therapist plays a more active role than in classical psychoanalysis, directing and advising rather than merely listening most of the time. Modern forms of psychodynamic therapy put less emphasis on the role of unconscious inner conflicts and devote more attention to current

Transference: Strong positive or negative feelings toward the therapist on the part of individuals undergoing psychoanalysis.

- Psychotherapy involves establishment of a special relationship between a trained professional and a distressed person, and efforts by the therapist to bring about beneficial changes in the client's behavior, feelings, or thoughts.
- Psychodynamic therapies such as psychoanalysis are based on the view that psychological disorders stem largely from hidden conflicts.
- Classical Freudian psychoanalysis is very famous, but there is little evidence that it is effective.
- Modern psychodynamic therapies focus more on patients' current problems than on their past histories.

ego functioning—how the ego acts as a controlling agent in the individual's life. In addition, social factors in the environment in which clients live are considered, and efforts are made to change these in beneficial ways. Despite these differences, however, the basic goal remains the same: helping patients gain insight into their hidden motives and conflicts.

Humanistic Therapies:
Emphasizing the Positive

Freud was something of a pessimist about basic human nature. He felt that we must constantly struggle with primitive impulses from the id. As we saw in Chapter 12, many psychologists reject this view. They contend that people are basically good and that our strivings for growth, dignity, and self-control are just as strong as—if not stronger than—the powerful aggressive and sexual urges Freud described. According to these *humanistic* psychologists, psychological disorders do not stem from unresolved inner conflicts. Rather, they arise because the environment somehow interferes with personal growth and fulfillment.

These views, of course, lead to forms of psychotherapy that are very different, both in purpose and procedure, from those developed by Freud. **Humanistic therapies** focus on the task of helping *clients* (note that humanistic therapists dislike the term "patient") to become more truly themselves—to find meaning in their lives and to live in ways consistent with their own inner values and traits. Unlike psychoanalysts, humanistic therapists believe that the client, not the therapist, must take essential responsibility for the success of therapy. The therapist is primarily a guide and facilitator, *not* the one who runs the show. Let's take a closer look at several major types of humanistic therapy.

PERSON-CENTERED THERAPY: THE BENEFITS OF BEING ACCEPTED Perhaps the most influential humanistic approach is the **client-centered therapy** developed by Carl Rogers (1970, 1980). Rogers strongly rejected Freud's view that psychological disorders stem from conflicts over the expression of primitive, instinctive urges. On the contrary, he argued that such problems arise primarily out of a distorted *self-concept*. According to Rogers, individuals often acquire unrealistic **conditions of worth** early in life. That is, they learn that they must be something other than what they really are in order to be loved and accepted. For example, they come to believe that they will be rejected by their parents if they harbor hostility toward their siblings. In response to such beliefs, people refuse to recognize large portions of their experience and emotions—any portions that violate their implicitly accepted conditions of worth. This in turn interferes with normal development of the self and results in various forms of maladjustment.

Humanistic Therapies: Forms of psychotherapy based on the assumption that psychological disorders stem from environmental conditions that block normal growth and development.

Client-Centered Therapy: A form of psychotherapy that concentrates on eliminating irrational conditions of worth—conditions people believe they must meet in order to be loved or accepted.

Conditions of Worth: In Roger's theory, individuals' beliefs that they must meet certain unrealistic conditions in order to be loved or accepted.

Person-centered therapy, as explained in Chapter 12, focuses on eliminating these unrealistic conditions of worth by creating a psychological climate in which clients feel valued as individuals. Person-centered therapists offer *unconditional acceptance,* or *unconditional positive regard,* of the client and his or her feelings; a high level of *empathetic understanding;* and accurate reflection of the client's feelings and perceptions. In the context of this warm, caring relationship, and freed from the threat of rejection, individuals can come to understand their own feelings and accept even previously unwanted aspects of their own personalities. As a result, they come to see themselves as unique human beings with many desirable characteristics. To the extent such changes occur, Rogers suggests, many psychological disorders disappear and individuals can resume their normal progress toward self-fulfillment (see Figure 15.2).

Gestalt therapy: Becoming whole   The theme of faulty or incomplete self-awareness so prominent in client-centered therapy is echoed in a second humanistic approach, **Gestalt therapy** (Perls, 1969). As noted in Chapter 3, the German word *gestalt* means "whole," and this word captures the essence of Gestalt therapy. According to Perls (1969), originator of this form of psychotherapy, individuals often experience difficulties because key aspects of their emotions are not acknowledged in consciousness. In short, they have, in a sense, psychologically disowned parts of their own being. They must recapture these before they can attain an accurate and complete self-concept.

How can progress toward this goal be achieved? Gestalt therapists use many different tactics. They may directly challenge their clients to give up their "phony games" and see themselves accurately. They may ask them to portray unresolved conflicts—a process referred to as *taking care of unfinished business*. In this process, clients are urged to reexperience their emotions vividly—to scream, swear, or weep as the need arises. Presumably, once such feelings are recognized and released, the unfinished business will be completed and the client will become whole once again.

Some of the techniques Gestalt therapists have developed for helping individuals recognize their own feelings are quite ingenious. For example, in the *two-chair exercise*, clients move back and forth between two chairs. While sitting in one they play themselves, while sitting in the other they assume the role of some important person in their life—wife, husband, mother, father. The ultimate goal, of course, is to increase their awareness of their feelings toward, and relations with, these important individuals in their life.

Humanistic psychotherapy: An overview   While humanistic psychotherapies differ in many respects, all share a basic orientation: All reject the view, so powerfully promoted by Freud, that psychological disorders stem from repressed urges and hidden conflicts and that a therapist's key task is to force unwilling patients to gain insight into these conflicts. Further, all assume that

Gestalt Therapy: A form of humanistic psychotherapy designed to increase individuals' awareness and understanding of their own feelings.

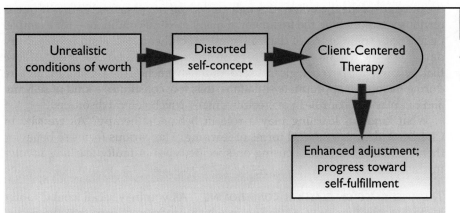

Figure 15.2

The Nature of Client-Centered Therapy

KEY POINTS

- Humanistic therapies assume that psychological disorders stem from the environment's interference with personal growth.
- Rogers's client-centered therapy focuses on eliminating unrealistic conditions of worth in a therapeutic environment of unconditional positive regard.
- Gestalt therapy focuses on helping clients acknowledge disowned parts of their own personality and feelings.
- Humanistic approaches have been criticized for being vague, but several of their concepts have been validated in ongoing research.

human beings have the capacity to reflect upon their own problems, to control their own behavior, and to make choices that will lead them toward more satisfying, fulfilling lives. And finally, all suggest that gaps in self-concept—flaws in our understanding of ourselves, our feelings, and our experiences—lie at the heart of much psychological distress.

Humanistic therapies have been criticized for their lack of a unified theoretical base and for being vague about precisely what is supposed to happen between client and therapist. They have, however, helped to alter the dismal picture of human nature painted by Freud by calling attention to our capacity for growth and self-fulfillment. Some of the central assumptions underlying humanistic approaches have been subjected to direct empirical testing. For example, Rogers's view that the gap between an individual's self-image and his or her "ideal self" plays a crucial role in maladjustment has been investigated and often confirmed in many studies (e.g., Bootzin, Acocella, & Alloy, 1993). Also, research findings tend to confirm that the therapist's personal warmth and ability to express empathy are predictive of the therapy's success. This is just what Rogers's theory suggested (e.g., Beutler, Crago, & Arizmendi, 1986). In these respects, then, humanistic therapies have made important and lasting contributions.

Behavior Therapies: *Psychological Disorders and Faulty Learning*

Psychodynamic and humanistic therapies differ in many important ways; however, both place considerable emphasis on early events in clients' lives as a key source of current disturbances. In contrast, **behavior therapies** focus primarily on present behavior. These therapies are based on the belief that many psychological disorders stem from faulty learning. Either the individuals involved have failed to acquire the skills and behaviors they need for coping with the problems of daily life, or they have acquired *maladaptive* habits and reactions—ones that cause them considerable distress. Within this context, the key task for therapy is to change current behavior: to provide clients with the skills they need, or to alter learned patterns of behavior that are causing them distress.

In addition, behavior therapy often seeks to provide individuals with behaviors and strategies they can use to overcome their problems when they are not in the presence of the therapist—through guided *self-care* (Marks, 1994). Self-care is obviously important in the treatment of many medical conditions—for example, people with some forms of diabetes must inject themselves with insulin every day or face the real threat of death. Similarly, many behavior therapists believe that people with psychological disorders must practice the skills they acquire during therapy in appropriate situations; this, too, constitutes a kind of self-care and can play a major role in overcoming many psychological disorders.

What kinds of learning play a role in behavior therapy? As we saw in Chapter 5, there are several forms of learning. The various forms of behavior therapy reflect this fact, focusing on specific types of faulty learning involving these basic processes.

THERAPIES BASED ON CLASSICAL CONDITIONING As you may recall from Chapter 5, *classical conditioning* is a process in which organisms learn that the occurrence of one stimulus will soon be followed by the occurrence of another. As a result, reactions that are at first elicited only by the second stimulus gradually come to be evoked by the first as well. (One example: your salivation to the beep of a microwave oven into which you've placed a container of popcorn.)

Behavior Therapies: Forms of psychotherapy that focus on changing maladaptive patterns of behavior through the use of basic principles of learning.

What does classical conditioning have to do with psychological disorders? According to behavior therapists, quite a lot. Experts in behavior therapy, such as Rachman at the University of British Columbia, suggest that some *phobias* can be acquired through conditioning (Rachman, 1991). That is, stimuli associated with real dangers may acquire the capacity to evoke the intense fear reactions that at first were elicited only by the actual dangers. However phobias are acquired, individuals with phobias experience intense fears of objects and situations that really pose no threat to their well-being, and avoid exposure to these objects or situations. In order to reduce such fears, behavior therapists sometimes employ a technique known as *flooding* (refer to Chapter 5). This involves prolonged exposure to the feared stimulus, or to a mental representation of it, under conditions where the person suffering from the phobia can't avoid the stimulus. Under these conditions, *extinction* of fear can occur, so that the phobia fades away (Levis, 1985).

Another technique based at least in part on principles of classical conditioning is known as **systematic desensitization**. In systematic desensitization, which is also used to treat various phobias, individuals first learn to how to induce a relaxed state in their own body—often by learning how to relax their muscles. Then, while in a relaxed state, they are exposed to the stimuli that elicit anxiety. Since they are now experiencing relaxation, the conditioned link between these stimuli and anxiety is weakened, and extinction of anxiety reactions can occur.

A third behavioral technique based on principles of classical conditioning is known as *aversion therapy* (Lovaas, 1977). Here, stimuli that have previously been associated with positive feelings, are associated instead with negative feelings. For example, consider the case of a man who is sexually aroused by young children and finds it difficult to resist making advances to them. How can such a person be helped—assuming that he *wants* to change? One possibility is as follows. The therapist shows the man color slides of attractive children, precisely the kind he finds arousing. A few seconds after each slide appears, the man receives a harmless but painful electric shock. As the process continues, the man's emotional reactions to these stimuli change. Initially his feelings are positive; but as the slides of the children are paired over and over again with shocks, his feelings begin to take on a distinctly negative tone. After all, the slides are now signals for the occurrence of a very unpleasant event.

If such treatment is successful, as it has been in several studies (Bucher & Lovaas, 1968), the man may find that he is no longer sexually excited by children and can seek more appropriate sexual partners. Many psychologists find delivering unpleasant stimuli to clients unacceptable, however, and so an alternative procedure known as *covert desensitization* has gained increasing use. In this procedure, clients are merely asked to imagine aversive stimuli; they never actually receive them. Research suggests that this technique can often prove highly effective (e.g., Cautela, 1985).

THERAPIES BASED ON OPERANT CONDITIONING Behavior is often shaped by the consequences it produces; actions are repeated if they yield positive outcomes, or if they permit individuals to avoid or escape from negative ones. In contrast, actions that lead to negative results are suppressed. These basic principles are applied in several forms of therapy based on *operant conditioning*. These differ considerably in specific procedures, but all incorporate the following basic steps: (1) clear identification of undesirable or maladaptive behaviors currently shown by individuals; (2) identification of events that reinforce and so maintain such responses; and (3) efforts to change the environment so that these maladaptive behaviors no longer receive reinforcement.

Several techniques incorporate these principles. One is based on the principle of *shaping* discussed in Chapter 5. This involves helping individuals acquire desired responses not currently in their repertoire by offering them reinforce-

Systematic Desensitization: A form of behavior therapy in which individuals imagine scenes or events that are increasingly anxiety-provoking and at the same time engage in procedures that induce feelings of relaxation.

Research in Canada

Stanley J. Rachman
University of British Columbia

SYSTEMATIC DESENSITIZATION: USING THE PRINCIPLES OF CLASSICAL CONDITIONING

After learning how to induce relaxation, this client, who has a fear of airplanes, is gradually exposed to stimuli that make her anxious.

MODELING: CHANGING BEHAVIOR THROUGH OBSERVING OTHERS

Seeing other people act in various ways can strongly influence our behavior.

ment for responses that more and more closely resemble the desired ones. A clear illustration of this procedure is provided by the following actual case:

> A three-year-old ... boy lacked normal verbal and social behavior. He did not eat properly, engaged in self-destructive behavior such as banging his head and scratching his face, and manifested ungovernable tantrums. He had recently had a cataract operation, and required glasses ... He refused to wear his glasses and broke pair after pair. The technique of shaping was decided upon to counteract the problem of glasses. Initially, the boy was trained to expect a bit of candy or fruit at the sound of a toy noise-maker. Then training was begun with empty eyeglass frames. First the boy was reinforced with candy or fruit for picking them up, then for holding them, then for carrying them around, then for bringing the frames closer to the eyes, and then for putting the empty frames on his head ... Through successive approximation, the boy ... learned to wear his glasses up to twelve hours a day. [Wolf, Risley, & Mees, 1964]

Operant principles have also been used in hospital settings, where a large degree of control over patients' reinforcements is possible (Kazdin, 1982). Several projects have involved the establishment of **token economies**—systems under which patients earn tokens that they can exchange for various rewards, such as television-watching privileges, candy, or trips to town. These tokens are awarded for various forms of adaptive behavior that will help the patients function effectively after leaving the hospital. Thus, keeping one's room neat, participating in group meetings or therapy sessions, coming to meals on time, and eating neatly all yield tokens. The results of such programs have been impressive. When individuals learn that they can acquire various rewards by behaving in certain adaptive ways, they often do so, with important benefits to them as well as to hospital staff (Paul, 1982; Paul & Lentz, 1977).

Another technique based on principles of operant conditioning involves decreasing the probability of an undesirable response by increasing the likelihood of another response that is *incompatible* with it. For example, people suffering from insomnia can learn various techniques for inducing relaxation, a state incompatible with feeling tense and wide awake; this can help them to get to sleep (e.g., Borkovec, 1982). Similarly, people trying to quit smoking can learn to pop a piece of gum in their mouth whenever the craving for a cigarette arises. Since gum chewing is clearly incompatible with smoking, this response may help them avoid slipping back into smoking unintentionally—the kind of *absent-minded transgression* we encountered in Chapter 4.

MODELING: BENEFITING FROM EXPOSURE TO OTHERS   Chapter 5 explained how we sometimes acquire new forms of behavior through observational learning—observing the actions and outcomes of others (Bandura, 1977, 1986). This is not the only way that we are affected by exposure to others' behavior, however. Seeing other people act in various ways can weaken or strengthen our tendencies to perform actions already at our disposal. For example, a motorist driving at 80 kilometers an hour in an 80 kph zone may soon speed up to 100 kph if she notices that everyone else is passing her. In this case, her restraints against engaging in a prohibited behavior are weakened when she sees others break the prohibition. Conversely, a student talking to a friend in class may quickly fall silent if he notices that everyone else is quiet and listening carefully to the instructor. In this case, restraints are strengthened by exposure to the actions of others. Even emotional reactions can be intensified or reduced when we observe outward signs of emotion—or their absence—in others (Izard, 1992). The process through which exposure to others affects behavior is known as *modeling*, and the effects it produces are varied and far-ranging.

Token Economies: Forms of behavior therapy based on operant conditioning, in which hospitalized patients earn tokens they can exchange for valued rewards when they behave in ways the hospital staff consider to be desirable.

A substantial body of evidence indicates that modeling principles can be used effectively in treating several different psychological disorders. Modeling has been used to change a wide range of maladaptive behaviors—for example, sexual dysfunctions (Kelley & Byrne, 1992) and the inability to control one's temper (Bandura, 1986). Perhaps the most impressive application of modeling, however, has been in efforts to alleviate various phobias (Bandura, Adams, & Beyer, 1977; Bandura, 1986). Many carefully conducted studies indicate that individuals who experience intense fear of relatively harmless objects can be helped to overcome these fears through exposure to appropriate fearless social models (Bandura, Blanchard, & Ritter, 1969).

Modeling techniques have also been very successful in modifying the behavior of highly aggressive children and adolescents (Schneider & Byrne, 1987). These young people often behave aggressively because they are lacking in basic social skills: They don't know how to ask for what they want in a nonaggressive manner, how to refuse a request without angering the requester, and so on. The results of many studies indicate that modeling can be used to teach such skills quickly and efficiently (Schneider, 1991). A dramatic illustration is provided by a study conducted recently by Bienert and Schneider (1993).

These researchers exposed highly aggressive sixth-graders to social skills training aimed specifically at teaching them how to deal with feelings of anger, stay out of fights, and respond nonaggressively to teasing. The children watched videotapes in which models showed both effective and ineffective actions; they also read passages in which other children coped successfully or unsuccessfully with problem situations. After only ten one-hour sessions, participants showed significantly lower levels of aggression and significant improvements in the ratings they received from peers and teachers. In contrast, a control group of highly aggressive children who were *not* exposed to the modeling procedures showed no improvements in these respects. Further, the benefits of the modeling procedures were still visible one year later, when the children moved to junior high school. Findings such as these indicate that modeling can indeed help individuals deal with a wide range of psychological problems.

INADEQUATE SOCIAL SKILLS: ONE CAUSE OF AGGRESSION

Highly aggressive children are often lacking in basic social skills. When they learn appropriate social skills through modeling therapy, their tendency to behave aggressively toward others often decreases.

Cognitive Therapies: *Changing Disordered Thought*

A central theme in modern psychology, and one that has been emphasized at several points in this book, is this: Cognitive processes exert powerful effects on emotions and behavior. In other words, what we *think* strongly affects how we *feel* and what we *do*. This principle forms the foundation for another major approach to psychotherapy: **cognitive therapy**. The basic idea behind cognitive therapy is that many psychological disorders stem from faulty or distorted modes of thought. Change these, it is reasoned, and the disorders, too, can be alleviated. We'll now consider several popular forms of cognitive therapy.

RATIONAL–EMOTIVE THERAPY: OVERCOMING IRRATIONAL BELIEFS Examine the list of beliefs or assumptions below:

- Everyone who meets me should like me.
- I should be perfect (or darn near perfect) at everything I do.
- Because something once affected my life, it will always affect it.

> **KEY POINTS**
>
> - Behavior therapies assume that psychological disorders stem from faulty learning.
> - Behavior therapies may be based on principles of classical conditioning, operant conditioning, or modeling.
> - Behavior therapies based on operant conditioning attempt to help individuals develop adaptive behaviors by offering positive reinforcement for these actions, or by helping them acquire responses that are incompatible with undesirable behaviors.

> *Cognitive Therapy: Psychotherapy that concentrates on altering faulty or distorted modes of thought so as to alleviate psychological disorders.*

- It is unbearable and horrible when things are not the way I would like them to be.

- It is impossible to control my emotions, and I can't help feeling the way I do about certain things.

Be honest: Do assumptions like these ever underlie your own thinking? You may be inclined to think that they do not, but Albert Ellis (1987), originator of one influential form of cognitive therapy, believes that thoughts like these are extremely common. Most of us do want to be liked by everyone, and believe that we should be much closer to that elusive goal of perfection than we think we are.

Ellis contends that such *irrational thoughts* lie behind many psychological disorders, and suggests that there are compelling reasons for having such thoughts. Most people, he reasons, have a strong desire for success, love, and a safe, comfortable existence. Life, however, often fails to gratify these desires. Irrational thinking, then, is a harmful but understandable reaction to the unavoidable disappointments and frustrations of life.

Ellis asserts that while such irrational beliefs take many different forms, most center on the tendency to escalate reasonable desires into "musts," as in "I *must* be loved by everyone," or "I *must* experience continuous success to be happy." Closely linked to such ideas is what Ellis describes as the tendency to *awfulize* or *catastrophize*—that is, to believe that if certain events occur or fail to occur, it will be a calamity of unbearable proportions from which one can never hope to recover. Here are two examples: "If I don't get that promotion, *my career will be completely over*," and "If I can't get into that course, *my semester will be totally ruined*."

Ellis maintains that people are often their own worst enemies. They cause their own disturbances by worrying about their inability to reach impossible goals and by convincing themselves that they simply cannot tolerate the normal frustrations and disappointments of life. To make matters worse, once such thoughts take hold, negative feelings and maladaptive behaviors soon follow; as Ellis puts it, irrational ideas create disruptive feelings and behavior, which then serve to sustain and even intensify the irrational beliefs (see Figure 15.3).

How can this self-defeating cycle be broken? Ellis suggests that the answer involves forcing disturbed individuals to recognize the irrationality of their views. **Rational–emotive therapy** (RET) is designed to do this. In this procedure, the therapist first attempts to identify irrational thoughts and then tries to persuade clients to recognize them for what they are—badly distorted views of reality. For example, imagine that a therapist practicing RET is confronted with a client who says, "I just had an important business proposal rejected. It's so depressing. All that work down the tubes. I *can't stand it* when that happens!" The therapist might reply, "So you had a proposal rejected. Have not proposals by others been rejected? Why do you think your business associates have to love and support everything you do, or that you have to be perfect?" The objective of such comments by the therapist is to help the client to recognize that many of the assumptions they are making are irrational, and that they interfere with adjustments and accommodations that make life manageable.

BECK'S COGNITIVE BEHAVIOR THERAPY FOR DEPRESSION   The discussion of depression in Chapter 14 noted that this common and serious psychological disorder has an important cognitive component: It stems, at least in part, from distorted and often self-defeating modes of thought. Recognizing this important fact, Beck and his colleagues (Beck, 1985) have devised a **cognitive behavior therapy** for alleviating this problem. Like Ellis, Beck assumes that depressed individuals' problems result from illogical thinking about themselves, the external world, and the future. Moreover, he contends, these illogical ideas and tendencies are

Rational-Emotive Therapy: *A cognitive therapy that focuses on changing irrational beliefs.*

Cognitive Behavior Therapy: *A form of psychotherapy designed to overcome depression by changing self-defeating patterns of thought.*

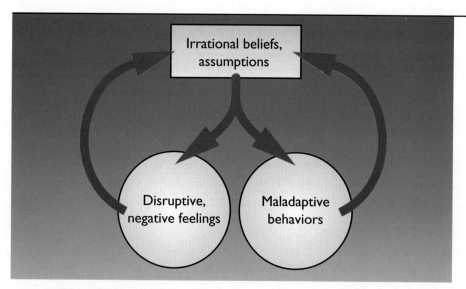

FIGURE 15.3

Rational-Emotive Therapy

According to Ellis, many psychological disorders stem from irrational thoughts. These create disruptive feelings and maladaptive behaviors, which in turn sometimes trap people in a vicious circle. Rational-emotive therapy seeks to break this cycle.

often maintained in the face of evidence that contradicts them. In an important sense, then, they are both self-defeating and self-fulfilling. What are the cognitive tendencies that foster depression? Among the most important are these:

- A tendency to overgeneralize on the basis of limited information—for example, to see oneself as totally worthless because of one or a few setbacks.

- A tendency to explain away any positive occurrences by interpreting them as exceptions to the general rule of failure and incompetence.

- A tendency toward selective perception—especially, to perceive the world as a dangerous, threatening place.

- A tendency to magnify the importance of undesirable events—to perceive them as the end of the world, and unchangeable.

- A tendency to engage in absolutistic, all-or-none thinking—for example, to interpret a mild rejection as final proof of one's undesirability.

How can such tendencies be altered? In contrast to rational-emotive therapy, Beck's cognitive behavior therapy does not attempt to disprove them. Rather, the therapist and client work together to identify the individual's assumptions, beliefs, and expectations and to formulate ways of testing them. For example, if a client voices the belief that she is a total failure, the therapist may suggest that this assumption should be evaluated. Together, the client and therapist then determine ways to test the assumption's accuracy. These tests are designed to provide the client with success experiences, thereby refuting her negative views, helping her toward enhanced self-esteem, and alleviating her depression.

Considerable evidence suggests that these procedures are highly effective in overcoming depression and helping depressed individuals return to healthy, active lives (Clark, Beck, & Brown, 1989; Robinson, Berman, & Neimeyer, 1990). So there seems to be a grain of truth to the old belief that the problems experienced by many depressed individuals are "all in the mind." Depression often *does* seem to stem from maladaptive patterns of thought. For this reason, forms of therapy that focus on changing these aspects of cognition are often highly effective.

KEY POINTS

- Cognitive therapies assume that psychological disorders stem from irrational thought. Rational-emotive therapy focuses on inducing individuals to recognize and reject irrational thoughts and assumptions.

- Cognitive behavior therapy for depression seeks to eliminate irrational and self-defeating modes of thought.

- Stress inoculation training is a technique for managing anxiety. The objectives of the training are these: to make clients understand that, to deal with anxiety, they have to develop control over emotions and attendant thoughts, imaginings, and expectations; and to aid them in developing the coping skills to achieve this goal.

Cognitive Therapy: How to Manage the Linkage Between Thought and Emotions

Both forms of cognitive therapy we have considered so far emphasize changing irrational and illogical thoughts. What merits further attention is the linkage between thoughts and emotions. Beck has emphasized inappropriate and negative conceptualizations as determinants of depression. However, cognitive structures, or entrenched thought patterns, can contribute not only to depression, but also to anxiety, which can be crippling in many situations. In **Canadian Focus**, we will outline a widely used anxiety management program. It illustrates the importance of cognitive factors, and cognitive restructuring, in anxiety control.

CANADIAN FOCUS

Coping with Anxiety: Meichenbaum's Stress Inoculation Training Program

The Stress Inoculation Training Program, developed by Donald Meichenbaum of the University of Waterloo, has proved valuable in dealing with a host of problems that are often encountered in academic and other settings—for example, test anxiety, social anxiety, panic and generalized anxiety disorders, and even anger management (e.g., Meichenbaum & Deffenbacher, 1988). There are three stages to the program.

In the first stage, the primary objective is for clients to acquire an understanding of the nature of anxiety and how it is generated. They learn that anxiety involves an exaggerated emotional reaction, in conjunction with troublesome thoughts, imaginings, and expectations. The client and therapist work together to establish as accurately as possible the situations and circumstances that generate anxiety, as well as the accompanying thoughts, and expectations. Commonly, the therapist assigns self-monitoring exercises so that the client can gain the fullest possible understanding of these matters. During this assessment, clients begin to understand that to deal with their anxiety, they will have to develop some control over their emotions and the thoughts, imaginings, and expectations that accompany them.

In the second stage, clients develops skills that will allow them to gain control over their emotional reactions, and over the inappropriate thoughts and expectations that attend those reactions. They learn emotion management skills, such as relaxation procedures and breathing exercises, that help regulate physiological arousal. At the same time, the therapist leads the client through cognitive restructuring exercises. The purpose of these is to increase the client's self-awareness of negative (and inappropriate) thoughts and expectations. The emphasis here is on changing self-concepts of inadequacy or incompetence. Together, the therapist and client systematically develop ways of dealing with problem situations and experiences, and for withdrawing or escaping if the difficulties in particular circumstances seem overwhelming. Exercises and role-playing techniques are used to increase the client's confidence. The overall goal is to change the ways clients think about anxiety, so that they stop seeing themselves as the helpless victims of events, and start seeing themselves as controlling and effectively managing their interactions with the world.

The third stage involves encouraging and supporting the application of coping responses that have been learned so far to everyday situations. Clients are encouraged to imagine specific situations and circumstances that provoke anxiety as vividly as possible, and to employ the various relaxation and cognitive coping skills they have acquired to alleviate the anxiety that is generated. To ensure that the client practices coping skills, the therapist assigns homework involving application of these skills in daily situations. The results of the homework exercises are discussed and evaluated, and modifications are suggested and applied. Most important of all, the client's progress is carefully monitored over a long period of time to ensure that any setbacks that occur are not viewed as defeats, but as challenges that can be readily overcome.

Stress inoculation training is a flexible and widely applicable technique for dealing with a host of difficulties that generate unmanageable anxiety. It is important to realize that most practicing psychotherapists do not spend all of their time dealing with major incapacitating disorders. They are consulted most frequently by individuals who are having problems coping with particular situations, tasks, and experiences that occur in everyday life. It is necessary that therapists have techniques available that can be readily applied to these various situations and circumstances. Stress inoculation training is one such technique.

Group Therapies: Working with Others to Solve Personal Problems

*A*ll of the therapies we have considered so far are conducted on a one-on-one basis—that is, one therapist works with one client. However, this is not the only approach to helping individuals deal with psychological problems. In recent decades, **group therapies**, in which treatment takes place in groups, have grown tremendously in popularity. We'll now examine several important types of group therapy, beginning with those which are closely linked to the individual therapies we considered earlier.

Research in Canada

Donald H. Meichenbaum
University of Waterloo

Psychodynamic Group Therapies

The techniques Freud developed for individual therapy have been modified for use in group settings. Perhaps the most popular form of psychodynamic group therapy is **psychodrama**, in which group members act out their problems in front of other group members, often on an actual stage. Psychodrama also involves such techniques as *role reversal*, in which group members switch parts, and *mirroring*, in which they portray one another on the stage. In each case the goal is to show clients how they actually behave and to help them understand *why* they behave that way—what hidden inner conflicts lie behind their overt actions (Olsson, 1989). While psychodrama is highly appealing to many people, it is subject to the same criticisms as all psychodynamic therapies, and its potential benefits may be somewhat overstated by its often ardent supporters.

Behavioral Group Therapies

In contrast, there is very compelling evidence for the effectiveness of *behavioral group therapies*—group approaches in which basic principles of learning are applied to solve specific behavioral problems. Such therapies have been especially successful in teaching individuals basic *social skills* and in helping them learn how to stand up for their own rights. In *assertiveness training*, for example, individuals practice such skills as expressing their feelings: verbally communicating their reactions to others, demonstrating their emotions nonverbally, expressing disagreement with others, and accepting praise by agreeing with it. By practicing these skills with and in front of other group members, people can often achieve major gains quite rapidly. In many cases, the therapist first models the appropriate behavior and then provides group members with opportunities to practice these actions. During therapy sessions, individuals also learn that no catastrophe will follow if they don't do it "right"—the other participants and the therapist are there to help them, not to damage their egos. This too is an important advantage.

Group Therapies: *Therapies conducted with groups of clients.*

Psychodrama: *A form of psychodynamic group therapy in which people act out their problems in front of fellow members.*

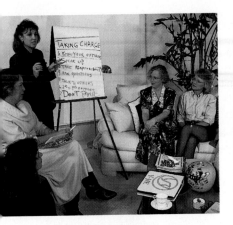

Members of self-help groups meet to discuss shared problems and find ways of coping with them.

Humanistic Group Therapies

Psychologists who practice humanistic therapies have been by far the most enthusiastic about the potential benefits of adapting their therapeutic techniques to group settings. Indeed, interest in group therapy originated among humanistic therapists, who developed two forms of such therapy—**encounter groups** and **sensitivity-training groups**. Both of these techniques focus on the goals of personal growth, increased understanding of one's own behavior, and increased openness and honesty in personal relationships. In both, group members are encouraged to talk about the problems they encounter in their lives. The reactions they elicit from other group members are crucial in helping them understand their own responses to these problems. The major difference between encounter groups and sensitivity-training groups is that encounter groups carry the goal of open exchange of views to a greater extreme—members in these groups are encouraged to yell, cry, touch each other, and generally "let it all hang out." Sensitivity-training groups are somewhat more subdued.

Humanistic group therapies use several ingenious warm-up exercises to start the process of open exchange of views. In one warm-up, for example, participants are blindfolded and wander around the room communicating only by touch. These procedures are designed to help members realize that normal restraints and rules don't operate in the group setting: that they are free to say and do almost anything—and so to come face to face with their own distorted self-concepts and perceptions.

Do such groups actually produce beneficial changes? Many people who have participated in them attest that they do, but most research on this issue has been relatively informal in nature, so it is hard to reach firm conclusions (Kaplan, 1982). In any case, literally millions of people have participated in such groups. Their sheer popularity may indicate that they are meeting a real need of some kind.

Self-Help Groups: *Help from Our Peers*

When we are anxious, upset, or otherwise troubled, we often seek comfort and support from others. Long before there were psychologists or psychiatrists, people sought informal help with their personal difficulties from family, friends, or clergy. This natural tendency has taken a new form in **self-help groups** (Christensen & Jacobson, 1994). These are groups of individuals experiencing the same kinds of problems who meet to help each other in their efforts to cope with their difficulties. Self-help groups are a very common fact of life in the 1990s. What kinds of problems do these groups address? Almost everything you can imagine—and then some. Self-help groups have been formed to help their members cope with alcoholism (Alcoholics Anonymous is perhaps the most famous of all self-help groups), the death of a spouse, rape, AIDS, childhood sexual abuse, being a single parent, divorce, stuttering, abusive spouses, breast cancer … the list is almost endless.

A guiding principle behind these groups is that people who share a problem have a unique understanding of it and can offer one another a level of empathy that no one else can provide. Do self-help groups succeed? Few scientific studies of the impact of such groups have yet been conducted, but there is some indication that they can yield important benefits (Christensen & Jacobson, 1994; Stuart, 1977). In any case, these groups do provide their members with emotional support and help them make new friends. Given the frequency with which many people relocate, this in itself can be beneficial.

Can people help solve their own psychological problems through the use of self-help audiotapes? See **The Research Process**.

Encounter Groups: A form of group therapy in which people are urged to tell other group members exactly how they feel; designed to foster personal growth through increased understanding of one's own behavior and increased honesty and openness in personal relations.

Sensitivity-Training Groups: A form of group therapy designed to foster personal growth similar to encounter groups, but tending to be more subdued.

Self-Help Groups: Groups of individuals experiencing the same kinds of difficulties that meet to discuss their shared problem and find solutions to it.

THE RESEARCH PROCESS

Subliminal Self-Help Audiotapes: Do They Deliver What They Promise?

elf-help—efforts by individuals to cope with their own problems, psychological or otherwise—is big business in the 1990s. Visit any large bookstore and you will see shelves overflowing with books promising to help purchasers improve their personality, their mental capacity, their energy level, and even their love life. And right next to these books, in many cases, is a large display of audiotapes designed to accomplish similar purposes. Perhaps the most intriguing—and controversial—of these tapes are the ones that incorporate *subliminal messages* as a means of inducing desired changes. Such messages are presented so briefly or at such low volume that listeners cannot report that they have heard them; in other words, they are below the sensory threshold for conscious awareness (see Chapter 3). Yet these tapes claim that their messages can produce important changes in behavior, presumably because people process them at some level,

Are such claims valid? Or are subliminal self-help tapes a waste of time and money? This question was touched on in Chapter 3, but let's examine it in more detail here. First, as noted in that earlier discussion, some research findings indicate that stimuli that are below the threshold for conscious awareness—ones we can't report having seen or heard—can sometimes influence our behavior (e.g., Niedenthal, 1990). Recent and convincing evidence for this conclusion is provided by a series of carefully conducted investigations by Krosnick and his colleagues (Betz & Krosnick, 1993; Krosnick et al., 1992).

These studies were designed to examine the possible effects of subliminal stimuli on attitudes. Results indicate that such effects do seem to occur. In one study, for example, university students saw photos of a stranger engaged in routine daily activities: walking into her apartment, shopping in a grocery store, sitting in a restaurant. Each photo was shown for two seconds. Immediately before these photos were presented, participants—in two groups—had been exposed to photos previously shown to produce either positive feelings (such as photos of people playing cards and laughing) or negative feelings (such as photos of open-heart surgery). These affect-inducing photos were shown so briefly (less than 0.10 second) that participants could not even tell whether they were words or photos. That is, the stimuli were presented *subliminally*—below the threshold for conscious awareness of their contents. After viewing these stimuli, participants were asked to indicate their attitudes toward the stranger shown in the photos and to rate her on a variety of trait dimensions (unfriendly–friendly, cruel–kind, and so on). Questioning of participants indicated that they could not guess the purpose of the study; yet their attitudes *were* influenced by the affect-inducing slides. Participants exposed to the scenes inducing positive affect reported more positive attitudes and rated the target person higher on trait dimensions (see Figure 15.4).

Subliminal Stimuli and Self-Help Tapes

The finding that subliminal stimuli can sometimes influence attitudes is interesting, but it does not necessarily mean that self-help tapes containing subliminal messages are effective in producing their stated goals. Is there any direct evidence on this issue? Yes, there is. A very careful study conducted by Greenwald and his colleagues (1991) tested the effectiveness of self-help audiotapes in a rigorous *double-blind* experimental design. In double-blind designs, neither the experimenter nor the participants have any knowledge of the condition to which participants have been assigned. Thus, the potential role of *demand characteristics* and other factors that can generate spurious results is greatly reduced. Let's take a closer look at this study.

Hundreds of volunteers were given self-help tapes purported either to improve their memory or to enhance their self-esteem. When played, these tapes seemed to contain only music or recorded nature sounds, but in fact they also presented subliminal messages designed to improve memory or boost self-esteem. Measures of participants' memory and self-esteem were collected twice: the first time before they received the tapes and a second time after they had listened to them for one month. Some of the tapes were labeled accurately; participants who received them knew they were receiving tapes that were supposed to enhance memory or self-esteem. Other tapes, however, were cross-labeled—self-esteem tapes were labeled "Memory Improvement," and memory tapes were labeled "Self-Esteem Enhancement."

If the tapes were actually capable of accomplishing their stated purposes, these effects should have occurred regardless of the label. For example, people receiving the memory tapes should have showed higher memory scores than those receiving the self-esteem tapes, *regardless of the labels on the tapes*. But results failed to confirm these predictions. Self-esteem increased for

FIGURE 15.4

Evidence for the Effects of Subliminal Stimuli on Attitudes

Participants were exposed briefly to affect-inducing photos. Then they saw scenes of a stranger engaged in routine activities such as shopping in a grocery store and sitting in a restaurant. Although the affect-inducing photos were shown so briefly that participants could not report their contents, these photos influenced their ratings of the stranger. Those who saw photos that induced positive affect rated her higher than those who saw photos that induced negative affect. (Source: Based on data from Krosnick et al., 1992.)

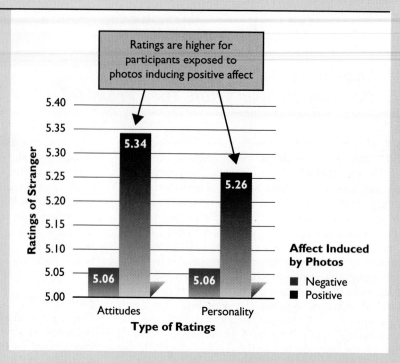

Ratings are higher for participants exposed to photos inducing positive affect

individuals who were told they had received self-esteem tapes, and memory increased for those who were told they had received memory-improving tapes, regardless of the actual tape content. So the only result was a general *placebo effect*: Merely being in the study and *expecting* positive effects increased participants' motivation and hence their performance.

In sum, there is no firm evidence that subliminal self-help tapes are of any benefit. While some findings do suggest that subliminal stimuli can influence our behavior in subtle ways, these effects aren't strong enough—at least in the subliminal tapes now available—to change important aspects of behavior. Our recommendation? Save your money!

KEY POINTS

- Psychodynamic group therapies such as psychodrama are designed to help individuals bring inner conflicts to the surface.

- Behavioral group therapies focus on changing specific aspects of behavior, such as assertiveness or social skills.

- Humanistic group therapies focus on enhancing personal growth and improving self-knowledge.

- Self-help groups consist of individuals who share a problem and who meet to help each other in their efforts to cope with this problem.

- There is evidence that subliminal stimuli can effect our moods and our attitudes, but careful tests provide no support for the effectiveness of subliminal self-help tapes.

Critical Thinking Questions:

1. Krosnick and his colleagues suggest that participants in studies of subliminal stimuli could not guess the real purpose, so demand characteristics did not influence the results. Do you think it's possible that participants really *did* figure out the purpose of the studies but were reluctant to admit this to the researchers? If it is, how could this have affected the results?

2. Participants in the Krosnick research could not recognize the positive and negative photos they saw; yet these influenced their attitudes toward a stranger. How could such effects occur? What mechanisms could possibly produce such results?

3. Suppose that subliminal self-help tapes had no labels at all. What would occur? Why?

4. What if tapes were labeled as containing subliminal self-help messages but actually contained none? Would the same findings as reported above be obtained? If so, why? If not, why?

Therapies Focused on Interpersonal Relations: Marital and Family Therapy

*T*he therapies we have considered so far differ greatly in many respects, yet in one sense they are all related: They search for the roots of psychological disorders in processes operating within individuals. Another group of therapies adopts a sharply different perspective. According to practitioners of this *interpersonal* approach, disturbed or maladaptive interpersonal relationships lie at the heart of many psychological disorders (Gurman, Kniskern, & Pinsof, 1986). In other words, individuals experience personal difficulties because their relationships with others are ineffective or unsatisfying—or worse. Several forms of therapy based on this idea are described below.

Marital Therapy: When Spouses Become the Intimate Enemy

Keeping people who are poorly matched in a joyless marriage is certainly not a useful goal or one likely to promote favorable psychological adjustment. However, growing evidence indicates that in many cases the downward spiral that characterizes a failing marriage can be stopped, and even reversed, if intervention occurs early enough in the process (Hendrick, 1989). Then the pain to both spouse and children can be reduced. What are the goals of **marital therapy**, or *couple therapy*? These are closely linked to the factors that tend to disrupt intimate relationships.

First, it appears that many couples get into serious difficulties largely because of a lack of appropriate *communication skills*. A happy couple, married or otherwise, tends to keep the channels of communication open. The partners talk to each other more often and more easily, sharing feelings, concerns, goals, and plans. They provide each other with more positive (and less negative) feedback than unhappy partners (Lauer & Lauer, 1985). They have more problem-solving sessions in which they discuss how to deal with difficulties in their relationship and get along better (Margolin & Wampold, 1981). An important task for couple therapy, then, is to improve the communication skills of both partners. The therapist works to foster such improvements in many different ways—for example, by having each partner play the role of the other person so that both can see the relationship in the other's eyes, and by having couples watch videotapes of their interactions. The latter procedure often leads to remarkable insights into just how poorly the partners have been communicating.

A second problem demonstrated by poorly adjusted couples involves *attributions*—the explanations each partner offers for the other's behavior. Unhappy couples tend to explain each other's behavior in unflattering terms (Brehm, 1992; Holtzworth-Munroe & Jacobson, 1985). For example, they explain negative actions by their spouse, such as coming home late or failing to do agreed-upon chores, as stemming from *internal* causes such as stable traits: "She's just irresponsible," or "He's just lazy." In contrast, happy couples, faced with the same behaviors, give the partner an out, assuming that some external factor beyond his or her control is to blame: "She must have missed the train," or "He's been so busy, he couldn't get to the chores." Couple therapy, therefore, is often directed toward helping both partners to recognize and change these destructive attributional patterns.

Marital Therapy:
Psychotherapy that attempts to improve relations and understanding in couples.

FAMILY THERAPY

Family therapy is based on the view that many psychological disorders stem from disturbed interpersonal relations among family members.

In sum, various forms of couple therapy focus on the task of arming couples with the basic social skills they need to live together in a more harmonious manner. As a result of such training, a couple's interpersonal relationships can improve dramatically, and the overall adjustment—and happiness—of both partners may be substantially improved.

Family Therapy: Changing Environments That Harm

Let's begin with a disturbing fact: When individuals who have been hospitalized for the treatment of serious psychological disorders and who have shown marked improvement finally return home, they often experience a relapse. All the gains they have made through individual therapy seem quickly to vanish (Carson, Butcher, & Coleman, 1988). This fact points to an important conclusion: The problems experienced by such people can be traced, at least in part, to their families—or more specifically, to disturbed patterns of interaction among family members (Hazelrigg, Cooper, & Borduin, 1987). To the extent this is true, attempting to help one member of a family makes little sense. Once he or she is back in the same disordered home environment, any benefits of therapy may be very short-lived. In one respect, returning these people to their families is akin to throwing a person who has just been saved from drowning back into deep, icy waters (Goldenberg & Goldenberg, 1985).

Recognition of this has spurred the development of several types of therapies designed to change the relationships among family members in constructive ways. One type of **family therapy** takes the *communications approach* (e.g., Selvini-Palazzoli et al., 1978). It focuses on the fact that family members often send each other contradictory messages: "I forgive you—but don't touch me!" "I don't care if you win; just do your best—but don't expect any hugs if you lose!" The primary goal is to help members of the family to recognize and change these conflicted messages.

Another type of family therapy is known as *structural family therapy*. Here, it is assumed that relationships *between* family members are more important in producing psychological disorders than aspects of personality or other factors operating largely *within* individuals (Minuchin & Fishman, 1981). Careful analysis of patterns of interaction within families often reveals key causes of distress. In one common pattern, a mother and child form a close relationship or *subsystem* within the family that all but excludes the father. This, in turn, may strain the relationship between the two parents to the point where the child, sensing conflict, develops various symptoms, such as disruptive behavior at school, or illness that has no apparent physical cause. Another frequent pattern is one in which hostility between the parents is reflected in rivalry between siblings, who take sides in each dispute and may, as a result, bear most of the distress produced.

How can such destructive patterns be changed? In structural family therapy, the therapist may interact with the family almost as an insider and so gain insight into repeated patterns occurring within it. The therapist tries to determine who dominates the power structure, who gets blamed when things go wrong, who usually tries to patch things up, and so on. Then, armed with this information, the therapist employs a wide range of techniques to facilitate positive change. In many cases, this involves efforts to alter specific behaviors (Gurman, Kniskern, & Pinsof, 1986). In others, the therapist may use modeling procedures to demonstrate more effective means of interacting. And in still other cases, the therapist tries to induce family members to recognize distorted thinking about one another or unfavorable patterns of attributions (Duck & Barnes, 1992).

Family Therapy: A form of psychotherapy that focuses on changing interactions or relations among family members.

of patients with a wide range of psychological disorders improve after therapy, but that *about the same proportion of people receiving no treatment also improve*. This was a disturbing conclusion for psychologists, and it quickly led to a great deal of soul-searching—and research—within the field. After all, if the same proportion of people recover from psychological disorders with and without therapy, why bother?

Fortunately, the findings of subsequent studies pointed to a very different conclusion: Contrary to what Eysenck suggested, psychotherapy *is* helpful (Bergin & Lambert, 1978; Clum & Bowers, 1990; Shapiro & Shapiro, 1982). Apparently, Eysenck had overestimated the proportion of people who recover spontaneously without any therapy. And he also underestimated the proportion who improve as a result of therapy. For example, in a major review of evidence on this issue, Smith, Glass, and Miller (1980) found that in almost 500 separate studies, the average person receiving therapy showed fewer symptoms or difficulties than 80 percent of those who had not yet received therapy (i.e., who were still on the waiting lists for such help). These findings have been confirmed over and over again in more recent reviews conducted with increasingly sophisticated procedures such as meta-analysis (e.g., Elkin et al., 1989).

Additional support for the effectiveness of therapy is provided by studies indicating that the more treatment individuals receive, the more improvement they show. In other words, as therapy progresses, people receiving it continue to improve and show fewer symptoms and less and less distress (Howard, et al., 1986; Orlinsky & Howard, 1987).

Such effects are not limited to therapy conducted with adults. Recent reviews indicate that therapy is also successful with children and adolescents (e.g., Kazdin, 1993; Weisz et al., 1992). Again, these reviews indicate that young people receiving therapy show greater improvement than most who do not receive treatment. Indeed, the average young person receiving therapy tends to score better, on various measures, than 70 to 80 percent of those not receiving therapy.

Finally, additional studies have compared the effectiveness of psychotherapy with that of drug therapy, which we'll consider in the next section. Results indicate that certain forms of psychotherapy are at least as effective as drug therapy and may be superior to it in some respects. For example, in a review of existing evidence, Hollon, Shelton, and Loosen (1991) found that these two forms of treatment were about equally effective in alleviating the symptoms of depression. However, cognitive therapy appeared to be superior to drug therapy in terms of rates of relapse. Fewer people who received cognitive therapy relapsed into depression, and cognitive therapy alone was about as effective in this respect as a combination of both drug and cognitive therapy (see Figure 15.5).

One note of caution: Many of these findings are based on the results of carefully controlled studies in which participants voluntarily entered treatment, in which efforts were focused on dealing with specific problems, and in which therapists were trained in using certain techniques immediately before therapy was administered. As noted by Weisz, Weisz, and Donenberg (1992), these conditions tend to load the dice in favor of positive outcomes for the types of therapy studied, and it is not clear whether similar positive outcomes would be obtained under more normal clinical conditions. However, even in the face of such concerns, existing evidence seems to suggest that psychotherapy really does work. It is certainly not equally effective for all people or for all disorders, and it does not necessarily totally eliminate various psychological problems (Robinson, Berman, & Neimeyer, 1990); but overall, it is considerably better than hoping that these problems will go away by themselves.

FIGURE 15.5

Cognitive Therapy and Drug Therapy: Which Is More Effective?

Cognitive therapy and drug therapy for depression seem to be about equally effective in alleviating the symptoms of this disorder. However, as shown here, cognitive therapy appears to be superior to drug therapy in terms of preventing future reappearance of depression.
(Source: Based on data reported by Hollon, Shelton, & Loosen, 1991.)

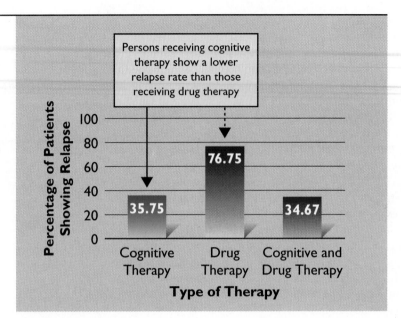

Persons receiving cognitive therapy show a lower relapse rate than those receiving drug therapy

Percentage of Patients Showing Relapse

Cognitive Therapy — 35.75
Drug Therapy — 76.75
Cognitive and Drug Therapy — 34.67

Type of Therapy

Are Some Forms of Therapy More Successful Than Others? Solving a Persistent Puzzle

The procedures used in various forms of therapy differ sharply. It seems only reasonable, then, to expect that some types of therapy will be more effective than others. But brace yourself for a surprise: Comparisons among therapies have generally yielded inconclusive results. Despite their contrasting procedures, all therapies seem to yield roughly equivalent benefits (Hollon, DeRubeis, & Evans, 1987; Hollon, Shelton, & Loosen, 1991; Kiesler, 1985; Luborsky, Singer, & Luborsky, 1975). How can therapies employing sharply different procedures yield similar results? Here are two possibilities.

DIFFERENCES AMONG VARIOUS THERAPIES EXIST, BUT WE HAVE TO SEARCH FOR THEM IN THE RIGHT PLACES   First, it is possible that some forms of therapy *are* more effective than others, but only with respect to certain types of disorders. As Kiesler (1966) put it, in comparing various psychotherapies we should not ask, "Which is better?" Rather, we should inquire, "What type of treatment by what type of therapist is most effective in dealing with what specific problems among specific individuals?" In short, it would be surprising if one type of psychotherapy was superior to others in all cases. It is much more likely that some types will prove to be more useful in dealing with certain types of psychological disorders and when administered by certain therapists. Many psychologists accept this view, although they realize that from a practical perspective, comparing the success of many types of therapy in overcoming a wide range of psychological disorders is a huge task (Stiles, Shapiro, & Elliott, 1986).

VARIOUS TYPES OF PSYCHOTHERAPY YIELD EQUIVALENT BENEFITS BECAUSE THEY HAVE A COMMON CORE   Another possibility is that while various forms of therapy do differ in rationale and procedures, these differences, from a practical point of view, are relatively unimportant. Under the surface, all share common, crucial features, and it is this shared core that accounts for their similar effectiveness. What is this common nucleus? It may consist of several key features.

First, all major forms of psychotherapy provide troubled individuals with a special type of setting—one in which they interact closely, usually one-on-one, with a highly trained, empathetic professional. For many clients this exposure to another person who seems to understand their problems and genuinely to care about them may be a unique experience, or at least one they have rarely encountered. The experience is very reassuring and may play an important role in many forms of therapy.

Second, every form of therapy provides individuals with an explanation for their problems. No longer do these seem to be mysterious and, perhaps, the result of hidden character flaws. As therapists explain, psychological disturbances stem from understandable causes, many of which lie outside the individual. This is something of a revelation to many people who have sought in vain for a clue as to the origins of their difficulties.

Third, all forms of therapy specify actions that individuals can take to cope more effectively with their problems. No longer must they merely suffer silently or wring their hands in despair. Rather, they are now actively involved in doing specific things that the therapist indicates will help.

Fourth, as was mentioned at the start of this chapter, all forms of therapy involve clients in what has been termed the *therapeutic alliance*—a partnership in which powerful emotional bonds are forged between client and therapist, and in which both work to solve the client's problems.

When all of these points are combined, the themes of *hope* and *personal control* seem to emerge very strongly. Perhaps diverse forms of therapy succeed because all provide people with increased hope about the future as well as a sense of heightened personal control. At least individuals in therapy have taken their fate into their own hands and are doing something constructive about it. To the extent this is the case, it is readily apparent why therapies that seem so different on the surface can all be effective. All cast a bright, comforting light into the emotional darkness of troubled people and in this manner help bring about positive change.

While many forms of therapy appear to be effective, it is important to note that all were first developed for use with white, middle-class city dwellers. Is psychotherapy also effective for other groups? And if not, how must therapeutic methods be altered to encompass cultural and geographic diversity? For a discussion of these issues, see **Canadian Focus**.

> ### KEY POINTS
>
> - Growing evidence indicates that psychotherapy is effective. Surprisingly, however, there is little evidence that one type of therapy is more effective than another. This may be because all forms of therapy share certain crucial features.
> - There is a need to consider multicultural issues in assessing the effectiveness of psychotherapy.

CANADIAN FOCUS

Addressing Mental Health Problems in Canada's North

In most of Canada, diagnosis and treatment for psychological problems is available on demand. What about in Canada's Far North? Northern communities are a long way from Canada's urban centers, where most psychological services are located. Also, these communities are small and far apart. How are psychological services provided to these?

The Clarke Institute in Toronto provides a consulting service for the Baffin Regional Health Board in the Northwest Territories (Abbey, Hood, Young, & Malcolmson, 1993; Young, Hood, Abbey, & Malcolmson, 1993). By examining this program, we can get some idea of the mental health problems facing Canada's northern people, and how they can be addressed.

Health workers from the Clarke Institute visit the Baffin Island area of the Eastern Arctic on average eight times a year. The area consists of thirteen scattered communities with a total population of about 10,000. Consultants interview and provide diagnostic and treatment recommendations for those who are referred to them by health workers in the community, or who seek assistance independently. Because four-fifths of the population are Inuit, Inuktitut-speaking interpreters are available to help bridge any cultural gaps.

Are psychological disturbances common in the North? Young and colleagues report that between 1986 and 1989, about 6 percent of the population either sought an interview or were referred for one. Any effort to compare this 6 percent figure with the actual prevalence of disorders (see Chapter 14) would be doomed. There is no way of estimating how many individuals are experiencing difficulties but were passed over or refused to participate in the consultative process. All that can be said is that referral rates for mental disorders in the North seem to be modest relative to other Canadian areas.

A few types of disorders dominate the referrals. First, there are serious disabilities involving schizophrenia and personality and affective disorders. Second, there are stress-induced disorders resulting from family and relationship conflicts, sociocultural conflicts, and traumatic experiences. Third, there are disorders associated with substance abuse. The first two categories are about equal in size and account for the largest number of consultations. Substance abuse as a distinct disorder was less common, but was found to be a pervasive compounding problem in up to one-quarter of the cases considered and is a major source of concern. The most common reason for consultation was depression followed by attempted suicide, or suicidal thoughts.

Does the North differ from southern Canada in the pattern of disorders observed? Some disorder patterns are similar. As in southern areas, women are more likely to seek help without referral, and depression is twice as common in women. One major difference is the infrequency of anxiety-based disorders. These are among the most common in the south, but not in the North. Another difference is in the high rates of suicide and suicidal thoughts—in some locations these are three to five times those found in the south. Also, the procedures used by women who attempt suicide are no less lethal than those used by men.

Treatment in the North is generally carried out at the community level. Hospitalization is not common unless there is clear evidence of an acute psychosis or affective disorder that involves a high suicide risk. Drug therapy is monitored by local health workers. Wherever possible, nondrug treatment is used. Because the number of trained professional therapists is obviously limited, there is a heavy reliance on community resources for counseling and support. Elders and other local volunteers have been pressed into service, and it is claimed that these "generic" therapies are very effective (Young et al., 1993).

It seems clear that local community organizations are going to become even more prominent in helping residents cope with stress in the rapidly changing North. Other community initiatives besides peer counseling are beginning to appear. For example, a theater production has been used to focus awareness on spousal abuse, and the first safe house for battered women—Nataraq's Place—has opened in the Eastern Arctic (Abbey et al., 1993).

It is important that all forms of psychotherapy, as well as other intervention techniques, be conducted against a backdrop of awareness of cultural differences. If important ethnic and cultural differences are overlooked, much effort may be wasted, and even dedicated, talented therapists may fail to accomplish their goals.

THERAPY IN DIVERSE CULTURAL AND GEOGRAPHICAL CONTEXTS:

Local community organizations are becoming an effective means of dealing with mental health problems in Canada's far North.

Biologically Based Therapies

Mind and body are intimately linked, so in one sense everything we think, remember, feel, or do reflects activity in the central nervous system. This basic fact has led some researchers to conclude that all psychological disorders ultimately have biological causes, or at least involve biological factors. In this section we'll consider forms of therapy deriving from this belief—approaches generally known as **biologically based therapies**.

Early Forms of Biological Therapy

At one time, people were willing to try almost anything—trephining, beatings, restraining devices—to free individuals who were suffering from psychological disorders from the evil influences that were believed to cause bizarre behavior. It is somewhat more unsettling to realize that crude efforts at biological intervention continued even into the present century. The device shown in the accompanying photo was often used by physicians in the late nineteenth and early twentieth centuries. The physician would apply the electrodes to various portions of a patient's anatomy in an effort to counter anxiety, depression, and many other psychological disorders. Needless to say, these efforts were largely ineffective.

Electroconvulsive Therapy

The idea of using electric shock to treat psychological problems did not disappear in the twentieth century; it merely reentered psychiatry in another form. In the 1930s, many physicians believed that schizophrenics rarely had epileptic seizures. This observation, it turned out, was false. However, it led a Hungarian psychiatrist, Von Meduna, to suggest that inducing such seizures artificially might be an effective means of treating this serious disorder. At first, psychiatrists produced convulsions by the injection of drugs such as camphor; however, after observing the use of shock to render animals unconscious in slaughterhouses, two Italian physicians, Cerletti and Bini, proposed using powerful electric shocks instead (Bini, 1938). This procedure, known as **electroconvulsive therapy** (ECT), became quite common; even today, it is widely used in North America. It involves placing electrodes on the patient's temples and delivering shocks of 70 to 130 volts for brief intervals (less than one second). These are continued until the patient has a seizure, involving bodywide muscle contractions lasting at least thirty seconds. In order to prevent broken bones and other injuries, a muscle relaxant and a mild anesthetic are administered before the start of the shocks. Patients typically receive three treatments a week for several weeks.

ECT is most commonly used as a treatment for severe depression. It is customarily employed when drug treatments prove ineffective or cannot be utilized. Because it works more rapidly than drugs, it may be the treatment of first choice if the depression is severe and the patient has a suicidal disposition (Endler & Persad, 1988).

Although ECT is widely employed, its use remains controversial. Many are convinced that applying an electric current to induce a coma must be injurious to the brain. For example, Breggin (1979) is certain it does cause harm and has called for its elimination as a form of therapy. Others are just as strongly convinced of its value and safety. The latest position paper of the Canadian Psychiatric Association on ECT concludes that, if properly used, ECT is a "safe and effective treatment" and recommends its continued use as a therapeutic

EARLY BIOLOGICAL THERAPY

Electrical devices such as this one were widely used by physicians in the late nineteenth century to "treat" many psychological disorders.

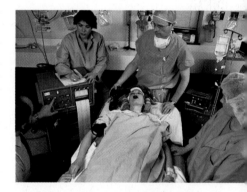

ELECTROCONVULSIVE THERAPY TODAY

In electroconvulsive therapy, a mild electric current passes through the brain for less than a second, causing a brief seizure.

Biologically Based Therapies:
Forms of therapy that attempt to reduce psychological disorders through biological means such as drug therapy or surgery.

Electroconvulsive Therapy (ECT): A treatment for depression in which patients receive powerful electric shocks to the head.

procedure (Enns & Reiss, 1992). Also supportive is a recent review of the history and use of ECT by Endler and Persad (1988). Endler, a prominent Canadian professor of psychology at York University, provides an interesting personal account of own his experience with depression in his book *Holiday of Darkness*, which is well worth reading. Although he had a strong initial bias against the use of ECT, he credits the procedure with lifting his depression.

It is safe to conclude that the controversy over the use of ECT is likely to continue. Given the character of the procedure, and the absence of any real understanding as to why it works, a degree of caution is necessary. The advantages and disadvantages of ECT—and of alternative drug therapies—should be weighed carefully before consent is given for use.

Psychosurgery

In 1935 a Portuguese psychiatrist, Egas Moniz, attempted to reduce aggressive behavior in psychotic patients by severing neural connections between the prefrontal lobes and the remainder of the brain. The operation, known as prefrontal lobotomy, seemed to be successful—aggressive behavior by unmanageable patients did decrease. Moniz received the 1949 Nobel Prize in Medicine for his work—but, in one of those strange twists of history, he was later shot by one of his lobotomized patients!

Encouraged by Moniz's findings, psychiatrists all over the world rushed to treat a wide range of disorders through various forms of **psychosurgery**—brain operations designed to change abnormal behavior. Tens of thousands of patients were subjected to prefrontal lobotomies and related operations. Unfortunately, it soon became apparent that results were not always positive. While some forms of objectionable or dangerous behavior did decrease, serious side effects sometimes occurred. Some patients became highly excitable and impulsive; others slipped into profound apathy and a total absence of emotion. A few became living vegetables, requiring permanent care after the operation.

In view of these harmful outcomes, most physicians stopped performing prefrontal lobotomies. Totally banned in the Soviet Union as early as 1951, prefrontal lobotomies had all but faded from the scene worldwide by the 1960s. In part, this dramatic decline reflected the development of drugs for treating psychoses—substances we'll consider in detail below. Today, psychosurgery, when it is performed, takes a much more limited form than prefrontal lobotomy. Instead of cutting connections between whole areas of the brain, modern-day brain surgery focuses on destroying tiny areas or on interrupting specific neural circuits.

While such operations sometimes seem to be effective in treating depression and uncontrollable aggression, even this limited type of psychosurgery raises important ethical questions. Is it right to destroy healthy tissue in a person's brain in the hopes that this will relieve symptoms of psychological disorder? And since the benefits are uncertain, should such irreversible procedures be permitted? These and related issues have led many to view psychosurgery as a very drastic form of treatment—something to be tried only when everything else has failed. For these reasons, only a small number of such operations are now performed in North America each year, and psychosurgery is no longer an important form of treatment for psychological disorders.

Drug Therapy: The Pharmacological Revolution

Psychosurgery: Efforts to alleviate psychological disorders by surgical means.

In the 1950s and early 1960s a remarkable change began to occur in the mental health field. The number of full-time resident patients in psychiatric hospitals in Canada and the United States began to fall; within twenty years, it

646

had declined by more than two-thirds. Were North Americans achieving mental health at a dizzying pace? Absolutely not. What happened in those years was something many describe as a *pharmacological revolution:* A great number of drugs effective in treating many serious psychological disorders were developed and put to use. So successful was **drug therapy** in reducing major symptoms that hundreds of thousands of individuals who had previously been hospitalized for their own safety (and that of others) could now be treated as outpatients. What are these wonder drugs, and how do they produce their positive effects? It is to these questions that we turn next.

ANTIPSYCHOTIC DRUGS If you had visited the wards of a psychiatric hospital for seriously disturbed people before about 1955, you would have had some very unsettling experiences. You would have observed some distressed patients confined in rooms with padded walls and floors, and at some point in your visit you would likely have heard a patient rattling the protective mesh on his or her window and screaming. You would have visited locked wards where personnel would instruct you on entering that it was advisable to always keep your back close to a wall. If you had returned a few years later, however, you would have observed a dramatic change: peace, relative tranquillity, and many patients now capable of direct, sensible communication. What accounted for this startling change? The answer involves the development of *antipsychotic drugs,* sometimes known as *major tranquilizers.* The first of these was *reserpine,* which as early as the 1950s was found to exert a calming effect on mental patients. But reserpine also produced harmful side effects such as low blood pressure and, in some patients, severe depression. Thus, its usefulness was quite restricted.

Much more effective relief of psychotic symptoms was provided by a family of drugs known as *phenothiazines.* The antipsychotic effects of these drugs were discovered by accident. Phenothiazine is also found in antihistamines—drugs widely used to relieve the symptoms of colds and allergies. As antihistamines came into widespread use for colds, it was found that they also had tranquilizing effects. This led chemists to examine other phenothiazines; and in 1950 a new derivative called *chlorpromazine* (trade name Thorazine) was produced. It was an immediate success, and within a few months had been given to almost two million patients. Chlorpromazine was soon followed by many other related drugs in the same chemical family. (Today there are also some antipsychotic drugs that are not phenothiazines.)

Antipsychotic drugs relieve a wide range of symptoms, including hallucinations, thought disorders, anxiety, and extreme hostility. The overall result is nothing short of amazing. Patients who are almost totally out of touch with reality and must be given custodial care can, after receiving the drugs, communicate with others and care for themselves. Perhaps even more important, they improve to the point where they become candidates for various forms of psychotherapy. The scope of the changes produced is perhaps best summarized by the following statistic: In the mid-1950s, 70 percent of all individuals diagnosed as suffering from schizophrenia spent most of their lives in mental hospitals. The present figure is less than 5 percent.

How do the antipsychotics produce such remarkable effects? Current evidence suggests that they block dopamine receptors in the brain. As noted in Chapter 14, the presence of an excess of this neurotransmitter, or increased sensitivity to it, may play a role in the development of schizophrenia. Whatever the precise mechanisms involved, there can be little doubt that the development of antipsychotic drugs has helped transform many previously hopeless patients into ones who are responsive to psychotherapy.

THE PHARMACOLOGICAL REVOLUTION

Drugs effective in treating a wide range of psychological disorders were developed during the 1950s and 1960s. As a result, the number of full-time patients in psychiatric hospitals decreased dramatically.

Drug Therapy: Efforts to treat psychological disorders through administration of appropriate drugs.

The use of these drugs, however, is not without drawbacks. They often produce fatigue and apathy as well as calming effects. And after receiving antipsychotic drugs for prolonged periods of time, many patients develop a side effect called **tardive dyskinesia:** loss of motor control, especially in the face. As a result, they experience involuntary muscle movements of the tongue, lips, and jaw. These motor reactions produce difficulties with speech and sometimes result in bizarre facial expressions. In order to avoid such side effects, many psychiatrists no longer place patients on maintenance doses of the drug. Rather, they employ *target dosing*—that is, they administer drugs only when serious symptoms appear and discontinue them when the symptoms are eliminated. One new antipsychotic drug, *clozapine*, seems to work without producing tardive dyskinesia. It is very expensive, however, and this limits its potential use.

While the antipsychotic drugs are of great value, they do not provide a total answer to schizophrenia and other serious psychological disorders. True, the most bizarre symptoms of schizophrenia decrease under medication. However, this does not usually result in an individual who can return to normal life. People on antipsychotic drug therapy often remain somewhat withdrawn and show relatively slow reactions and reduced levels of affect. And more serious symptoms often reappear if the drug therapy is stopped. In short, antipsychotic drugs seem to relieve the major symptoms of schizophrenia but don't deal with the underlying causes. For these reasons, it is imperative that people receiving drug therapy also receive other forms of psychotherapy, counseling, and community support—otherwise, the probability of relapse is high.

ANTIDEPRESSANT DRUGS Shortly after the development of chlorpromazine, drugs effective in reducing depression also made their appearance. There are two basic types of such compounds: the *tricyclics* and the *monoamine oxidase inhibitors* (MAO inhibitors). Both seem to exert their antidepressant effects by increasing the concentration of certain neurotransmitters—primarily serotonin and norepinephrine—in the synaptic gap. It appears, however, that there may be several different types of depression and that antidepressant drugs may exert their effects through a wide range of biochemical mechanisms. While these drugs influence neurotransmitter concentrations very quickly, their antidepressant effects often take several days or longer to appear. This suggests that the biochemical mechanisms underlying depression are complex, to say the least.

Both tricyclics and MAO inhibitors produce potentially dangerous side effects. For tricyclics, these include drowsiness, irregularity in heartbeat, blurred vision, and constipation. For MAO inhibitors, the most important side effect is *hypertension*—a rise in blood pressure above normal levels. In some cases MAO inhibitors can trigger a *hypertensive crisis* involving severe headache, intracranial bleeding, and even death. Because of such side effects, MAO inhibitors are used less frequently than tricyclics in the treatment of depression.

Because both tricyclics and MAO inhibitors show delayed action, and because both have potentially serious side effects, several other, even more effective drugs have been developed. Of these, *fluoxetine* (Prozac) is perhaps the most widely used. This drug, which seems to operate by blocking the reuptake of serotonin, has fewer and milder side effects than older antidepressants. Yet it matches or exceeds tricyclics in terms of countering depression. For these reasons, over 20,000 Canadians take Prozac (Nichols, 1994), and it is now the most widely prescribed antidepressant in the United States (Grilly, 1989). Prozac has been the subject of controversy, however, because a

Tardive Dyskinesia: A side effect of prolonged exposure to antipsychotic drugs in which individuals experience involuntary muscular movements, especially of the face.

small number of patients experience dangerous side effects from it: They become manic, hyperactive, or even dangerously violent (Angier, 1990). A newer drug, Zoloft, seems less likely to produce such effects.

One final point: While drugs *are* often effective in treating depression, research suggests that they are not necessarily more effective than several forms of psychotherapy, especially cognitive–behavioral and cognitive therapies (Robinson, Berman, & Neimeyer, 1990). Since psychotherapy does not involve the potential dangers found in drug therapy, it appears to be the more conservative form of treatment.

ANTIANXIETY DRUGS Alcohol, a substance used by many people to combat anxiety, has been available for thousands of years. As you probably already know, however, it has important negative side effects. Synthetic drugs with antianxiety effects—sometimes known as *minor tranquilizers*—have been manufactured for several decades. The most widely prescribed at present are the *benzodiazepines.* This group includes Valium, Ativan, Xanax, and Librium. In 1989, more than 52 million prescriptions for these drugs were written in North America (Shader, Greenblatt, & Balter, 1991). Another widely used antianxiety drug is *propanediol* (meprobamate); this drug seems to exert antianxiety effects mainly by reducing muscular tension. Yet another drug that has recently attained favor among physicians in treating mild anxiety is BuSpar.

The most common use for antianxiety drugs, at least ostensibly, is as an aid to sleep. At first glance, they seem safer for this purpose than *barbiturates,* since they are less addicting. However, substances deriving from the benzodiazepines remain in the body for longer periods of time than those from barbiturates and can accumulate until they reach toxic levels. Thus, long-term use of these antianxiety drugs can be quite dangerous. In addition, when they are taken with alcohol, their effects may be magnified; this is definitely a combination to avoid. The benzodiazepines seem to produce their effects by chemically binding to receptors at synapses, thus blocking neural transmission. Common side effects of these antianxiety drugs include fatigue, drowsiness, and impaired motor coordination, so people taking them should avoid driving or operating power tools.

LITHIUM AND MOOD DISORDERS In the late 1940s, findings were reported indicating that compounds of lithium, such as lithium carbonate, could be effective in treating *manic disorders.* For more than twenty years this evidence was largely ignored, mainly because researchers could not conceive of any mechanisms through which this simple substance could produce these changes. Now, however, it seems clear that lithium *is* indeed helpful in treating manic disorders. About 60 to 80 percent of manic states can be quickly brought to a close by administration of lithium (Campbell, Perry, & Green, 1984). It can sometimes terminate depressive episodes, especially in individuals with bipolar disorder. Lithium can be quite dangerous: Excessive doses can cause convulsions, delirium, and even death—and for many patients the effective dose is close to the overdose level. Thus, it is crucial that blood levels of lithium be closely monitored in people who take it. Another problem is that after people have taken the drug for two or more years, manic episodes occur again when it is discontinued. Since it *is* effective in diminishing wild mood swings, however, lithium continues in widespread use.

KEY POINTS

- Electroconvulsive therapy, used to treat depression, involves the delivery of strong shocks to the brain.
- Antipsychotic drugs reduce a wide range of symptoms, including hallucinations and extreme hostility.
- Antidepressant drugs are highly effective in countering depression.
- Antianxiety drugs are widely prescribed and may be effective, but are habit-forming and often produce side effects.
- Lithium is effective in countering manic disorders.

The Setting for Major Therapy

*T*herapeutic treatments for the less serious mental disorders are available in a host of different settings. In the case of major, incapacitating disorders, this has not always been the case. The time has come to look at where treatment is carried out, and to give some consideration to significant changes that have occurred over the years.

Treatment Locations: The Shift from Hospitals to the Community

The first specialized treatment facilities for those with serious mental disorders emerged in the 1800s. Large mental hospitals dedicated exclusively to the treatment of mental illness were built in the various provinces. These hospitals continued as primary treatment centers until well into the middle of the twentieth century. The prevailing practice was to treat mental disorders as if they were akin to physical diseases requiring hospital care and treatment. Unfortunately, few effective treatment programs were available for those with serious disorders. Before the 1950s the only therapies for the truly disturbed were electroconvulsive shock therapy, insulin therapy (inducing a comatose state by lowering blood sugar levels), and psychosurgery. As a result, these institutions were largely custodial in character—often no more than places to hide the disturbed from the public eye—and were often overcrowded and understaffed.

As already mentioned, in the 1950s and early 1960s the winds of change swept through the field of mental health. The development of effective drug therapies allowed, for the first time, a large measure of control over the troubling symptoms exhibited by the seriously disturbed. Many patients no longer required custodial care. Those who made mental health policy saw this as the end of the need for large mental hospitals and began a process of *deinstitutionalization*.

The process of deinstitutionalization was accelerated by federal–provincial funding arrangements associated with the introduction of universal health coverage in Canada. The federal government agreed to match provincial health expenditures to ensure universal coverage, but it would not enter into a cost-sharing arrangement for provincial mental hospitals (Rochefort, 1992). Provinces dealt with this problem by adding psychiatric units, and in many cases a variety of community service functions, to general hospitals for which joint funding was available. As would be expected, the number of resident patients in provincial hospitals dropped precipitously. There were 57,000 patients in Canadian mental hospitals in the early 1960s. By the early 1970s the patient population had dropped to 13,000 (Rochefort & Portz, 1993).

Has this change been beneficial? Yes, in the sense that it has ended the separation of those with mental disorders from those with other disorders. There have been costs, however, the heaviest of which have been borne by those with enduring serious mental disabilities. For many of these individuals, life follows a pattern of admissions to, and releases from, treatment centers. When their symptoms become pronounced, the seriously disabled are admitted to the psychiatric wards of general hospitals, where they are placed on a drug regimen. When the drugs have made their influence felt, and the symptoms have abated, these people are released back into the community. On release, all too often, they have no place to go and no likelihood of employment. The result is that they join the ranks of the homeless. In these conditions, the symptoms almost inevitably return. Once more, they are readmitted to a treatment center, and the cycle begins again. A substantial portion of the homeless street people who can be seen in any large Canadian city have had experience with the mental health system. A survey of the homeless carried out in Toronto in 1986 revealed that 43 percent had been hospitalized because of a psychiatric disorder within the previous three years (Wasylenki, Goering, Lemire, Lindsey, & Lancee, 1993). Estimates suggest as many as 44 percent of the 15,000 homeless people in Montreal have a history of mental illness (Dunn, 1991). Is there any way to break the **revolving door** pattern of hospitalization, admission, and release? One way is to provide a system of community support services.

Community Services: *What Are They?* *And Why Are They Needed?*

Patients who have been hospitalized because of a severe mental disorder need support on their release from a hospital setting. They need help in finding accommodation, as well as continuing case management to ensure that their prescribed drug programs are followed and continue to be effective. They need counseling and assistance in obtaining financial support and, if feasible, employment. Unfortunately, few urban centers have adequate community support systems. In a examination of the Canadian mental health care system, Rochefort observes that a "prime deficiency lies in therapeutic and community support services for chronic mentally ill persons, as one report after another from across Canada has documented" (Rochefort, 1992, p. 1087). A much-hospitalized, self-described "psychiatric survivor" of Canada's mental health system stated the problem clearly to a newspaper reporter: "We need income. We need housing. We need the dignity that goes with work." The same person pointed out that satisfaction of these needs "doesn't come from medication and it doesn't come from an institution" (Mittelstaetd, 1993).

All is not gloom and doom, however. A good example of what can be provided in the way of services can be seen in the work of the Greater Vancouver Mental Health Service Society. This is a decentralized, community-based organization employing multidisciplinary teams to work with both the patients and their families. It provides continuing treatment for clients and counseling services for family members. It offers housing assistance, money management advice, and employment services. It can also respond to emergencies (Sladen-Dew, Bigelow, Buckley, & Bornemann, 1993). Does this make a difference? It certainly does. The institutional readmission rate in Ontario hospitals is about 66 percent; in the Vancouver area it is down to 15 to 20 percent (Mittelstaetd, 1993).

Prevention: *Heading Off Trouble Before It Begins—or Becomes Serious*

Therapies, whatever their nature, are designed to correct or repair damage that has already occurred: They swing into action *after* individuals have begun to experience psychological disorders. A different approach to psychological problems is *prevention*. When psychologists use this term, they are referring to one of three goals: **primary prevention**, or preventing disorders from developing; **secondary prevention**, or early detection and treatment so that minor disorders do not become major; and **tertiary prevention**, or efforts to minimize the harm done to the individual and to society. In an important sense, prevention is where a considerable part of the action promises to be in the mental health field in the years ahead. A wide variety of programs are

INSTITUTION FOR TREATING PSYCHOLOGICAL DISORDERS

Large provincial institutions for treating psychological disorders were placed far from urban areas and operated on limited budgets. As a result, they were often able to provide only custodial care to patients.

Revolving Door: An ineffective cycle of psychological treament consisting of hospitalization, admission to treatment centers, and release.

Primary Prevention: Prevention techniques aimed at preventing the occurrence of psychological disorders.

Secondary Prevention: Techniques that focus on early detection of psychological disorders so that minor disturbances will not develop into major ones.

Tertiary Prevention: Techniques designed to minimize the harm done by psychological disorders.

- Large provincial institutions often provided only custodial care for psychologically disturbed people.

- As effective drug therapies became available, these institutions discharged large numbers of patients, some of whom have received further treatment in community mental health centers.

- In recent years, more attention has been focused on prevention of psychological disorders.

now under way to help prevent many serious psychological disorders and social problems. The scope of these efforts is extremely broad, as is the range of problems they address (e.g., Berman & Jobes, 1991). As an example of such work, let's look at recent efforts aimed at preventing child abuse.

CHILD ABUSE Each year many thousands of children are physically abused by their parents. Can anything be done to reduce this tragedy? Growing evidence provides a mildly encouraging answer. Conditions associated with child abuse by parents have been identified (see Table 15.1), and programs designed to help counter the effects of these conditions—and so to reduce the incidence of child abuse—have been devised and tested (e.g., Wolfe, Sandler, & Kaufman, 1981). The results obtained have been encouraging.

Consider, for example, a project involving 400 pregnant women who, because of a cluster of factors such as those shown in Table 15.1, were at risk for inflicting child abuse. One group received free transportation to medical appointments. A second received nine visits to the home by a nurse during pregnancy in addition to the free transportation. Women in a third group also received regular visits by a nurse—however, these visits extended to the child's second birthday. Moreover, during these visits, the nurse provided health consultations and information about parenting. Finally, women in a control group received none of these benefits. Results were clear: 19 percent of those in the control group abused or neglected their children within the first two years of life. In contrast, only 4 percent of those receiving the maximum intervention showed such behavior. (The other two groups were in between.) These findings, and similar results in other research, indicate that appropriate preventive programs can substantially reduce the incidence of child abuse. Given the damaging effects of child abuse on later development, it seems clear that such programs may be worth their weight in gold.

TABLE 15.1

Factors Related to Child Abuse

The greater the extent to which a parent experiences the conditions shown here, the greater the likelihood that the parent will abuse his or her children. (Source: Based on data from Nietzel & Himelein, 1986.)

PARENT'S HISTORY	CURRENT FAMILY SITUATION	PARENT'S APPROACH TO CHILD REARING
Experience of abuse or neglect	Social isolation	Infrequent praise
Lack of affection from own parents	Marital discord	Strict demands
Large family	Parental retardation or illiteracy	Low level of supervision
Teenage marriage	Stressful living conditions	Early toilet training; disagreements with partner over child-rearing practices.

How to Choose a Therapist: A Consumer's Guide

The odds are quite high that at some point during your life, you or someone very close to you will experience a psychological disorder. Depression, phobias, and anxiety are all very common. If there's one point this chapter should have made clear by now, it is this: Effective help is available. When psychological problems occur, don't hesitate to seek assistance. But how should you go about obtaining such help—that is, choosing a therapist? Here are some basic pointers.

1. *Where to go first* The first question—how to start the process—is perhaps the trickiest. While you are a student, this task is fairly simple. Virtually every college and university has a department of psychology and a student health center, and in these locations you are almost certain to find someone who can direct you to valuable sources of help—clinics, individual practitioners, referral services, and so on. So don't be shy. If you feel that you or someone close to you needs help, make an appointment to see someone.

But what if you are no longer a student and have no contact with a university campus? Can you still phone and ask for help from the nearest department of psychology? Absolutely. Psychology, after all, has a dual nature: It is both a branch of science and a helping profession. So the fact that you are not a student should not prevent you from asking for assistance in locating a therapist.

If for some reason this is not practical, there are other routes you can follow. First, you can ask your physician or a member of the clergy to direct you to the help you need. Both will almost certainly know someone you can contact in this regard. If have no local physician and don't know any clergy, you can contact your local Mental Health Association. This organization will be listed in the phone book and be able to direct you to the help you need. In short, there are several ways to proceed. Not knowing where to begin is definitely *not* a good excuse for delay.

2. *Choosing a therapist* Let's assume that by following one of the routes outlined above, you have obtained the names of several different therapists. How can you choose among them? Several guidelines are useful.

First, always check for credentials. Therapists should generally be trained professionals. Before you consult one, be sure that this person has a Ph.D. in psychology, an M.D. with a residency in psychiatry, or other equivalent training. While such credentials don't guarantee that the therapist can help you, they are an important step in this direction.

Second, try to find out something about the kinds of disorders in which each therapist specializes. Most will readily give you this information. What you are looking for is a good match between your needs and the therapist's special competence.

Third, it is often helpful to know something about a therapist's preferred techniques of therapy. Most psychologists are quite eclectic: They use a wide variety of treatment procedures and tailor these to the needs of individual clients. Still, many therapists are most familiar with, and most highly trained in, the use of specific procedures. If you are uncomfortable with the particular type of therapy favored by a given therapist, then by all means look elsewhere.

3. *Signs of progress: How long should therapy take?* If therapy is going well, both you and the therapist will know it. You'll be able to see the beneficial changes in your behavior, your thoughts, and your feelings. But what if it is not going well? When and how should you decide to go elsewhere? This is a difficult decision, but a rough rule of thumb is this: If you have been visiting a therapist regularly (once a week or more) for three months and see no change, it may be time to ask the therapist whether he or she is satisfied with your progress. Most forms of therapy practiced by psychologists at present are relatively short-term: They are designed to produce results relatively quickly. If several months have passed and your distress has not decreased, it is probably time to raise this issue with your therapist. In fact, it is a good idea to ask about the length of treatment when you first begin. Given the fact that all individuals differ, length of treatment is hard to predict. Still, an experienced therapist should have a general idea of how long therapy should take and will gladly share this information with you.

4. *Danger: When to quit* Therapy is designed to help—to relieve the distress of psychological disorders. Unfortunately, there are instances in which it can actually hurt. Estimates indicate that negative effects may occur as often as 10 percent of the time (Lambert, Shapiro, & Bergin, 1986). How can you tell that you are in danger of a negative outcome? Several basic points can help.

First, and most obvious, if you or the people around you notice that you are actually becoming more distressed—more depressed, more anxious, more nervous—you should take a step back and ask yourself whether you are satisfied with what is happening. It may be that these trends are only temporary. Still, signs that things are actually getting worse are certainly grounds for concern, and you should raise this issue with your therapist.

Second, never, in any circumstances, should you agree to perform activities during therapy that run counter to your own moral or ethical principles. A very large majority of therapists adopt extremely high standards and would never dream of making such requests. Sad to relate, however, there are a few who will take advantage of the therapeutic relationship to exploit their patients. The most common forms of this exploitation are sexual in nature. Unprincipled therapists may suggest that their clients engage in sexual relations with them as part of their "treatment." *This is never appropriate and is strongly censured by all professional associations.* So if your therapist makes such suggestions, that's the time to leave.

Third, beware of exaggerated claims. If a therapist guarantees to remake your life, convert you into a powerhouse of human energy, or ensure your total happiness, be cautious. This is probably a sign that you are dealing with an unprincipled—and probably poorly trained—individual. Again, beat a hasty retreat.

How would you seek help for psychological problems if you needed to?

All of these suggestions are merely guidelines you can follow in order to be a sophisticated consumer of psychological services. There may be cases, for example, in which therapy requires considerably longer than the several months noted above; in which the therapist has valid reasons for being reluctant to discuss the procedures he or she will use; or in which someone without full credentials can be exceptionally helpful. These guidelines, however, should help you avoid some of the pitfalls that exist with respect to finding a competent, caring therapist. Remember: Effective help is definitely out there if you take the trouble to look for it.

SUMMARY AND REVIEW OF KEY POINTS

PSYCHOTHERAPIES: PSYCHOLOGICAL APPROACHES TO PSYCHOLOGICAL DISORDERS

psychotherapies 620
therapeutic alliance 621
psychodynamic therapies 621
free association 622
resistance 622
transference 623
humanistic therapies 624
client-centered therapy 624
conditions of worth 624
Gestalt therapy 625
behavior therapies 626
systematic desensitization 627
token economies 628
cognitive therapy 629
rational-emotive therapy
  (RET) 630
cognitive behavior therapy 630

- Psychotherapies are forms of therapy in which a trained professional establishes a special relationship with a person experiencing psychological distress and makes efforts to bring about beneficial changes in the behavior, feelings, or thoughts of this person.
- Psychodynamic therapies such as psychoanalysis are based on the view that psychological disorders stem largely from hidden conflicts. Classical Freudian psychoanalysis is very famous, but there is little evidence that it is effective. Modern versions of psychodynamic therapy focus more on patients' current problems than on their past histories.
- Humanistic therapies assume that psychological disorders stem from interference by the environment with personal growth. Rogers's client-centered therapy focuses on eliminating unrealistic conditions of worth in a therapeutic environment of unconditional positive regard. Gestalt therapy focuses on helping clients acknowledge disowned parts of their own personalities and feelings.
- Humanistic approaches have been criticized for being vague; but several of their concepts have been validated in ongoing research.
- Behavior therapies assume that psychological disorders stem from faulty learning. Behavior therapies based on principles of classical conditioning attempt to eliminate maladaptive reactions through extinction or desensitization. Therapies based on operant conditioning offer positive reinforcement for adaptive behavior. Therapies based on observational learning employ modeling to change behavior.
- Cognitive therapies assume that psychological disorders stem from irrational thoughts. Rational–emotive therapy focuses on inducing individuals to recognize and reject irrational assumptions and thoughts. Cognitive–behavior therapy for depression seeks to eliminate self-defeating modes of thought. Specialized versions of cognitive theory such as stress inoculation training can be used to manage anxiety and other emotional reactions.

GROUP THERAPIES: WORKING WITH OTHERS TO SOLVE PERSONAL PROBLEMS

group therapies 633
psychodrama 633
encounter groups 634
sensitivity-training groups 634
self-help groups 634

- Psychodynamic group therapies such as psychodrama are designed to help individuals bring inner conflicts to the surface. Behavioral group therapies focus on changing specific aspects of behavior, such as social skills or assertiveness. Humanistic group therapies focus on enhancing personal growth and improving self-knowledge.
- Self-help groups consist of people who share a problem. Such groups provide social support for members and may be helpful.
- There is evidence that subliminal stimuli can affect our moods and attitudes, but careful tests provide no support for the view that subliminal self-help audiotapes can produce beneficial effects.

THERAPIES FOCUSED ON INTERPERSONAL RELATIONS: MARITAL AND FAMILY THERAPY marital therapy 637 family therapy 638	• Marital or couple therapy focuses on improving communication and changing faulty attributions within couples. • Family therapy focuses on improving relations among family members by reducing contradictory communication and by altering family structure.
PSYCHOTHERAPY: SOME CURRENT ISSUES	• Growing evidence indicates that psychotherapy is effective. However, there is little evidence that contrasting types of therapy differ in overall success. This may be because all forms of therapy share certain crucial features. • There is a pressing need for a multicultural perspective in psychotherapy, and psychologists are devoting increasing attention to this issue.
BIOLOGICALLY BASED THERAPIES biologically based therapies 645 electroconvulsive therapy (ECT) 645 psychosurgery 646 drug therapy 647 tardive dyskinesia 648	• Early forms of biological therapy involved electric shock, insulin therapy, and psychosurgery. Electroconvulsive therapy, which is still used to treat depression, involves delivering an electric current to the brain. Psychosurgery is a radical procedure that is now rarely used. • Drug therapy provides an effective means for treating many psychological disorders. • Antipsychotic drugs reduce a wide range of symptoms, including hallucinations and extreme hostility. Antidepressant drugs are effective in countering depression but may produce side effects such as hypertension. Antianxiety drugs are widely prescribed and may be effective, but are habit-forming and often produce side effects. Lithium is effective in countering manic disorders.
THE SETTING FOR MAJOR THERAPY revolving door 651 primary prevention 651 secondary prevention 651 tertiary prevention 651	• Initially, large provincial institutions provided primarily custodial care for seriously disturbed patients. With the advent of drug therapies, large numbers of people no longer required permanent hospitalization. • Treatment shifted to psychiatric units of general hospitals and, in some centers, to community clinics administered by these hospitals. Typically, patients stay for a relatively short period of time, until drug therapies alleviate symptoms, and then are released. • The absence, in many urban centers, of community support systems to help the seriously ill on discharge fosters a revolving door cycle of release and readmission. • More attention has been focused recently on the prevention of psychological disorders and closely related social problems, including child abuse.

CRITICAL THINKING QUESTIONS

APPRAISAL	If various forms of therapy are as effective as suggested in this chapter, then why are psychological disorders so common? Why, in short, don't more people seek out appropriate treatment for their psychological problems?
CONTROVERSY	There is a huge market for self-help books and audiotapes, and many people continue to believe that they can solve their own psychological problems with the aid of these materials. Yet existing evidence indicates that most of these products are useless, and that some may do more harm than good. In view of this fact, do you think that steps should be taken to ban their sale?
MAKING PSYCHOLOGY PART OF YOUR LIFE	Now that you know something about how various forms of therapy work, do you think you are more likely to seek out the help of a trained psychologist or other professional if *you* experience psychological distress? If not, what factors would deter you from doing so?

Social Thought

How We Think About Others ...
and the Social World

SOCIAL THOUGHT: THINKING ABOUT OTHER PEOPLE 661
Attribution: Understanding the Causes of "Their" Behavior
Social Cognition: How We Process Social Information
Basic Aspects of Social Thought: How We Think About Other People
Automatic Vigilance: Noticing the Negative
Attitudes: Evaluating the Social World

GROUP BEHAVIOR: INTERACTING WITH OTHERS 679
Prejudice: Distorted Views of the Social World
Challenging Prejudice: Some Potential Plans of Action
Social Influence: Changing Behavior
Gender Differences and Conformity: The Myth of Female/Male Differences
Compliance: To Ask—Sometimes—Is to Receive
Prosocial Behavior: When We Help ... and When We Don't
Feeling Good and Feeling Bad and Helping: Mood and Prosocial Behavior

ATTRACTION, LOVE, AND CLOSE RELATIONSHIPS 701
Love: The Most Intense Form of Attraction

SUMMARY AND REVIEW OF KEY POINTS 709

THE POINT OF IT ALL—PRACTICAL USES OF DISSONANCE THEORY: HYPOCRISY AND THE ALTERATION OF SOCIETALLY IMPORTANT ATTITUDES 678

PERSPECTIVES ON DIVERSITY—THE EFFECTS OF PREJUDICE: GROUP IDENTIFICATION AMONG AFRICAN AMERICANS 685

THE RESEARCH PROCESS—LINEUPS AND LINES 688

KEY CONCEPT—MAJOR FORMS OF SOCIAL INFLUENCE 696

CANADIAN FOCUS—WHERE CHARITY BEGINS ... AND CONTINUES 697

THE RESEARCH PROCESS—IS PHYSICAL ATTRACTIVENESS ONLY SKIN DEEP? 703

MAKING PSYCHOLOGY PART OF YOUR LIFE—ENHANCING THE ACCURACY OF YOUR SOCIAL JUDGMENTS 708

THIRD WORLD STUDENTS HELPED BY RECYCLING PROGRAM

Ottawa Citizen:
November 14, 1994

A Citizen article tells about one service club—in the Ottawa area—which has established a collection and sorting center for "textbooks and educational magazines of all types, from preschool readers and story books to National Geographic and college texts." Already about 80 tons of textbooks and magazines have been sent away to support educational programs in other countries.

Through the Volunteer Center of Ottawa-Carleton, there are many other opportunities to volunteer: for example, as a literacy tutor, a fundraiser, a youth supervisor.

Psychologists call these kinds of activities "prosocial" behavior—that is when people help other people without any expectation of personal gain.

Sometimes the opposite occurs. Help is obviously required, but people fail to provide assistance. This is known as bystander apathy.

Both prosocial behavior and bystander apathy are reactions we have to other people. In Chapter 16 you will find current knowledge about the very many ways in which other people influence the way we behave—and why.

WE DO NOT MERELY INTERACT WITH OTHER PEOPLE; WE ALSO SPEND LOTS OF TIME THINKING ABOUT THEM.

*T*here is no doubt that other people are important to us. They are the source of many of our most valued forms of reward—praise, approval, sympathy, affection; and of our most devastating forms of punishment—criticism, rejection, disapproval. They are also the focus of our most common and most intense emotions: love, anger, envy, jealousy.

What would it be like to be totally cut off from other people? That has been the theme of many books, movies, and songs. Whether the story takes place in a remote mountain valley, on a desert island, or on the seacoast of Bohemia, our reactions are much the same. We feel for the people so isolated, and we shudder at the thought of being cut off like that. Sometimes we do find ourselves in this very situation, even though we are surrounded by other people. Loneliness is what we feel at such times. You may have felt it when you first arrived at college or university, when you entered a large class, when you stood looking for a place to put your tray in the new-to-you dining hall.

At the University of New Brunswick, DiTommaso and Spinner (1992) have begun to develop a SELSA (Social and Emotional Loneliness Rating Scale) for young adults. (Others had been developed for children—Heinlein & Spinner, 1985; and for older adults—Spinner & Byers, 1986.) These researchers asked students at the University of New Brunswick and at St. Thomas University in Fredericton how strongly they agreed or disagreed with statements such as these: "I feel alone when I'm with my family," "I really belong in my family,"

Leon Festinger

Festinger is well known in psychology for his theory of cognitive dissonance. According to this theory, individuals experience an unpleasant state known as cognitive dissonance when they notice that their attitudes and their behavior, or various attitudes that they hold, are inconsistent. They may then change either their attitudes or their behavior in order to reduce the cognitive dissonance.

Kenneth B. Clark

Clark is a noted researcher of prejudice. His work on the harmful effects of segregation was cited by the U.S. Supreme Court in its 1954 decision *Brown v. Board of Education*. Clark is past president of the American Psychological Association (1970–71), the first African American to hold the position.

Stanley Milgram

Milgram's research focused on the concept of obedience. In a series of chilling (and ethically questionable) experiments, he showed that ordinary people were surprisingly willing to comply with instructions to inflict pain on another person when ordered to do so by someone with authority.

PSYCHOLOGISTS OF NOTE

"I like the people I hang out with," "I'm not part of a group of friends and I wish I were," "I am an important part of someone else's life," "I find myself wishing for someone with whom to share my life." Then they subjected those responses to statistical analyses which showed that loneliness had three components. Two of these—family and romantic loneliness—together reflected emotional isolation. The third, social loneliness—the individual's perception of their friends and friendships—reflected social isolation. They concluded that "different types of loneliness have distinct determinants and are associated with different affective and behavioral reactions." Furthermore, different types of loneliness call for different kinds of changes: in the one case, adequate social relationships, in the other case, close emotional attachments.

Life without other people is, in a very real sense, painful to imagine. Even so, other people remain a mystery to us. They say and do things we do not expect, they have motives we don't understand, and they often see the world very differently. For those reasons, we spend a lot of time thinking about them as well as interacting with them. Two topics—social thought and social interaction—are central to the study of **social psychology**, which is that branch of psychology that investigates how other people affect our behavior.

Social psychology is a very diverse field; indeed, it goes the distance from love to hate and includes all that is in between. On the following pages you will find out how we explain why other people behave the way they do, how we process social information, and why we have the attitudes and opinions that we do. Then we will discuss psychological findings about negative attitudes toward the members of various social groups—that is, prejudice; about the many ways in which people attempt to change one another's behavior—that is, social influence; about the things we do to benefit other people without expectation of reward—that is, prosocial behavior; and about why we like or dislike others, why we fall in (and out) of love, and how we form close relationships with friends and lovers—that is interpersonal attraction. Chapter 17 will continue our discussion of social psychology, with the focus on psychology "at work."

Social Thought: Thinking About Other People

Do you ever try to figure out why people act the way they do? Do you ever try to change people's opinions? Do you make judgments about people—for example, about their suitability as a roommate or as a romantic mate? When you do, you are making *attributions*, attempting influence, and expressing attitudes. Let us survey current knowledge about those topics as revealed by research in social psychology.

Attribution: Understanding the Causes of "Their" Behavior

Imagine the following situation. You are standing at the ticket counter of a movie theater. Another student walks up to the counter and without a "by your leave" puts down money for tickets. How would you react? While your first guess is probably "Not!" the way you would really respond depends on what you take to be the reason for the rude behavior. What was the intent? What was the motive? What was the reason? The process by which we attempt to answer these questions—to make judgments about the causes of behavior—

Social Psychology: The branch of psychology that studies all aspects of social behavior and social thought.

is known as **attribution.** We attribute causes and reasons, intentions and motives, to other people in order to explain their behavior to ourselves.

Many variables influence the attributions we make. Here are two examples. At the beginning of the school year at the Royal Military College in Kingston, Ontario, Guimond and Palmer (1990) studied the ideas that students enrolled in commerce, social science, and engineering had about the causes of poverty and unemployment. The data showed no differences among these three groups with respect to the explanations they gave for these social problems. However, within six months, this had changed, the main reason being that more social science students now blamed "the system" for poverty and unemployment. The researchers suggested that social science students in university are exposed to an ideology that attributes blame to social circumstances. In another study, Guimond and colleagues (1989) made the remarkable finding that poor and unemployed youth "blamed the poor and the unemployed [for poverty and unemployment] significantly more than did the social science students," who blamed the situations in which the poor and the unemployed found themselves.

In a very different study, the "excuses" of child molesters were studied at the Clarke Institute of Psychiatry in Toronto (Pollock & Hashmall, 1991). Researchers found that attributions made in these cases could be classified as follows: "denial of fact, of responsibility, of sexual intent, of wrongfulness, and of self-determination." These attributions are of special interest because they could be useful (along with other information) in predicting whether it is likely that there will be a repeat of the original criminal behavior.

Political attributions have been studied as well. At the University of Manitoba, Sande and colleagues conducted an interesting comparison of the political attributions made by Canadian and American students (1989). Undergraduates from both countries were given information that their countries (Canada and the United States together) had engaged in either positive behavior (sending aid to Tanzania or sending an icebreaker to save whales) or negative behavior (sending arms to Tanzania or building a new fleet of nuclear-powered submarines). The students in both countries gave the same explanations for negative behavior: "Our side is good and the other side is bad." In addition, however, the Canadian students saw the United States (but not Canada) as self-serving, even when the American political actions were positive.

People make judgments about many, many other matters that come up in daily living. The topics addressed in studies of attribution have been as diverse. Recent examples include judgments about creativity of particular people (Katz & Thompson, 1993); about ability, effort, and luck among disabled athletes (Crocker, 1993); about who is to blame—the offender, the victim, alcohol, or drugs—in a case of rape (Loza, 1993); about audience support for political figures (Pancer et al., 1992); about the knowledge of the person who is doing the listening while engaged in conversation (Slugoski et al., 1993); about medical symptoms (Robbins & Kirmayer, 1991); about why mother is angry (Covell & Movitch, 1987); about unexpected life stress (Flett et al., 1991); about sexual harassment (Summers, 1991); about memory in older and younger adults (Devolder & Pressley, 1992); about hyperactive and aggressive children (Johnston et al., 1992); about the losses by video poker players (Coulombe et al., 1992); about making decisions on job candidates (Struthers et al., 1992); about what young people think about whether older people (aged seventy) will succeed or fail in learning to use computers (Ryan et al., 1992); about parental influence on career development (Young et al., 1991); about sports (Leith, 1989); about arousal (Ellis & Zanna, 1990); about the personalities of smokers and nonsmokers (Dion et al., 1990); and about refusals of sexual advances (Byers & Wilson, 1985).

Attribution: The processes through which we seek to determine the causes behind others' behavior.

The subjects in studies of attribution have been many and varied as well. Along with college and university students in every corner of Canada, included in these experiments have been disabled athletes, soccer players (Robinson & How, 1987), married couples (Alain, 1985), identical and fraternal twins (Vernon & Jang, 1993), marketing managers (Chebat et al., 1992), and many other very specific populations—for example, correctional workers, alcohol abusers, rapists, and child molesters.

CAUSAL ATTRIBUTION: HOW DO WE ANSWER THE QUESTION "WHY"? Our efforts to understand behavior are varied. Sometimes, in trying to explain people, we draw conclusions about their personal traits (Gilbert et al., 1992; Jones & Davis, 1965). That is, we ask ourselves, what is that stranger—the one who just winked at me across the crowded room—really like? Other times, "why" really means "What happened that made them do what they did? Was it a bit of dust in the eye or did they wink at me on a dare?" In short, the basic judgment here is this: Is the observed behavior the result of internal dispositions (personality characteristics, motives, intentions) or external situations (some event in the physical or social world), or is it perhaps some combination of both?

In this, how do we go about reaching conclusions? This is what Kelley addressed in his theory of causal attribution (Kelley, 1972; Hilton & Slugoski, 1986). According to Kelley, we choose between internal and external causes (for someone butting into line, for example) by considering three kinds of information. The first of these relates to **consensus**—the extent to which all people react in the same manner. Is jumping the queue at this theater done often, by all kinds of people? The second relates to **consistency**—the extent to which the person reacts in the same way on other occasions. Does our intruder butt into line every week? And finally, there is **distinctiveness**—the extent to which the person reacts in the same manner in different circumstances—in the Superstore, on the exit ramp, at the registrar's office, and so on.

According to Kelley, we are most likely to attribute behavior to internal causes when consensus and distinctiveness are low but consistency is high. In contrast, we are most likely to attribute behavior to external causes when consensus, consistency, and distinctiveness are all high. Finally, we attribute behavior to a combination of those factors when consensus is low but consistency and distinctiveness are high. What that means in a real example is this:

Assume that consistency is high [in the movie lineup, the student who cuts in front of you does so on other occasions] but consensus is low [other people do not queue jump] and distinctiveness is low [our student pushes ahead in different places, such as the cafeteria] Here, Kelley's theory predicts that you will attribute the stranger's behavior to internal factors, concluding perhaps that he is rude and inconsiderate and needs to get a life.

If consistency, consensus, and distinctiveness are all high, that means that our buddy pushes ahead every Saturday night (high consistency), but so do other people (high consensus), but not in other places (high distinctiveness). Here, Kelley's theory predicts that you will attribute the stranger's behavior to external factors—to something about the current situation, perhaps the fact that you have left a large space in front of you that seems to invite other people to go ahead of you. (See Figure 16.1 for a summary of these suggestions.)

Are consistency, consensus, and distinctiveness all equally useful in making inferences about various matters? The answer to that question is not clear; however, a very interesting study by Chebat and Filiatrault (1986) studied the voting patterns of students at the University of Quebec at Montreal.

Consensus: The extent to which behavior by one person is shown by others as well.

Consistency: The extent to which a given person responds in the same way to a given stimulus across time.

Distinctiveness: The extent to which a given person reacts in the same manner to different stimuli or situations.

ATTRIBUTION: DETERMINING THE CAUSES BEHIND OTHERS' BEHAVIOR

Why do other people act as they do? This is a question we often ask during social interaction. This woman has received a clear-cut answer to this question—but we doubt that she likes it!
(Source: Drawing by Bruce Eric Kaplan, © 1993 The New Yorker Magazine, Inc.)

"I'll be straight with you. I was put on this planet to make your life miserable."

The participants were exposed to consensus, consistency, and distinctiveness statements about political issues. Consensus statements such as, "All economists agree that ..." were most effective, and distinctiveness statements such as, "The present provincial government is responsible for ..." were least effective in influencing how the students voted in this mock election.

Do we really think about other people and the causes of their actions in that way? Doing the kind of analysis described by Kelley requires a lot of effort; and the fact of the matter is that, in general, people tend to avoid unnecessary cognitive effort. So it is not surprising that other studies (e.g., Hansen, 1980; Lupfer, Clark, & Hutcherson, 1990) point to these limited conclusions: We do use the Kelley kind of analysis when we feel that a lot of cognitive effort is justified, which is primarily in situations where it is important for us to understand why other people acted as they did, or when we cannot readily explain their actions from what we already know. In many other cases, however, we don't bother because, quite simply, it involves too much mental effort.

ATTRIBUTION: SOME BASIC SOURCES OF BIAS In theory, attribution is a rational process. However, attribution is not always accurate. We make different

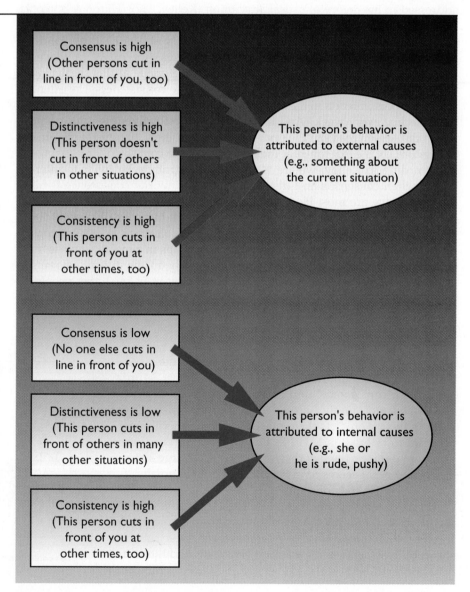

FIGURE 16.1

Kelley's Theory of Causal Attribution: An Overview

Kelley's theory indicates that when consensus, distinctiveness, and consistency are all high, we attribute others' behavior to external causes (upper diagram). When consensus and distinctiveness are low while consistency is high, however, we attribute others' behavior to internal causes (lower diagram).

Consensus is high
(Other persons cut in line in front of you, too)

Distinctiveness is high
(This person doesn't cut in front of others in other situations)

Consistency is high
(This person cuts in front of you at other times, too)

This person's behavior is attributed to external causes (e.g., something about the current situation)

Consensus is low
(No one else cuts in line in front of you)

Distinctiveness is low
(This person cuts in front of others in many other situations)

Consistency is high
(This person cuts in front of you at other times, too)

This person's behavior is attributed to internal causes (e.g., she or he is rude, pushy)

kinds of errors in our judgments about other people and about why they behave the way they do. As you can see from the cartoon below, even Charlie Brown is not free of that very human foible.

We are all subject to various forms of bias in our judgments. This is true even of Olympic-level skating judges, as was revealed by Whissell and colleagues (1993). These researchers pointed out that the judges at Olympic competitions are exceedingly well-trained in making judgments about the quality of skating. They are highly skilled and experienced at ignoring "expectations … order of appearance, or national bias." Nevertheless, at the 1984 (Sarajevo) and 1988 (Calgary) Olympic Games, according to four methods of analysis, some judges were nationally biased in "both men's and women's competitions, in the compulsory figures, short program, free skate, and final placements." They recommended that computerized monitoring of scores be used to eliminate those judges who continued to use criteria other than the competitor's merit.

Several more common errors in social judgment, which we all make regularly, are worth careful consideration.

THE FUNDAMENTAL ATTRIBUTION ERROR: OVERESTIMATING THE ROLE OF DISPOSITIONAL CAUSES   Imagine that you are a witness to the following: A newcomer arrives at a meeting thirty minutes late. On entering the room he drops his notes on the floor. While attempting to pick them up, he falls over and breaks his glasses. How would you explain his behavior? Most likely you would conclude that he is disorganized, clumsy, and generally a klutz. That is, most of us would think of him as "that kind of person," and we would emphasize the internal reasons for his odd conduct.

Would that be correct? Perhaps. But it is also possible that he was late because of unavoidable delays in traffic, that his materials slid out of his hands because they were transparencies, and that he fell down because the floor had just been waxed. These are external reasons that would explain his behavior. Still, our inclination is to explain the actions of other people in terms of internal rather than external causes. This is referred to as the **fundamental attribution error**. When we think about other people, we most often conclude that they act the way they do *because they are that kind of person*, though other reasons may well be more correct. This is a fundamental error in our social thinking.

Why do we have that fundamental bias? One suggested explanation is that when we observe other people, we focus on their actions specifically rather than on the context in which their actions take place. As a result, we play down situational causes. (When we observe ourselves, quite the opposite happens.) Also, we may notice the situational factors that face other people but decide that they are not important (Gilbert & Jones, 1986). Whatever the precise basis for the fundamental attribution error, it has important implications. It means, for example, that even when we are aware of situational factors that harm some people in our society—poor diet, disrupted family life, and exposure to lawless and violent peer models—we still perceive such people as bad and as responsible for their own difficulties. In this respect, the fundamental attribution error has far-reaching social consequences for all of us.

Fundamental Attribution Error: The tendency to attribute behavior to internal causes to a greater extent than is actually justified.

ATTRIBUTION

As Charlie Brown finds out here, we can't always predict why people do what they do.

Remarkably, our tendency to make our attributions to internal causes tends to change over time (Burger, 1986; Frank & Gilovich, 1988). While we blame internal causes soon after an event has taken place, we take more account of situational causes with the passage of time. In other words, we forget personal information more rapidly that situational information. Research conducted by Burger and Pavelich (1993) demonstrated this time-related shift.

These investigators surveyed the explanations given for the results of several presidential elections in the editorials of major American newspapers (the *New York Times*, *Wall Street Journal*, and *Christian Science Monitor*). The survey was done twice: once within five days of the election, and again two or three years later. The purpose was to determine whether the editorials attributed the election results to the personal characteristics of the candidates (internal causes) or to the circumstances surrounding the election (external factors). Here is an example of a personal cause: "Candidate A made the outcome worse by the ineptitude of his campaign." Here is an example of a situational cause: "The shadows of scandal ... cleared the way for Candidate B to climb to the presidency." The results were clear: Explanations printed a few days after an election emphasized internal factors; nearly two-thirds mentioned such causes. Two or three years later, however, the opposite was true: Two-thirds of the explanations referred to situational factors. So over time, the fundamental attribution error does tend to diminish, even in the realm of politics.

THE SELF-SERVING BIAS: I CAN DO NO WRONG, YOU CAN DO NO RIGHT Suppose that you write a paper for one of your classes. Your professor tells you it was great. To what would you explain such success? If you are like most people, you would attribute it to internal causes—your own talent for doing library research or your effort in preparing the report.

Imagine, however, that your instructor dislikes the report and criticizes it harshly. How would you explain that outcome? Here it is likely that you will focus mainly on situational causes—the difficulty of the assignment, the instructor's too-high standards, and so on. That is, you would make another type of attributional error: the **self-serving bias** (Miller & Ross, 1975), which is the tendency to take credit for positive outcomes by attributing them to internal causes, but to blame negative ones on external causes—particularly on factors beyond your control (Baumgardner, Hepner, & Arkin, 1986; Brown & Rogers, 1991). Guimond and colleagues studied the attribution patterns of Anglophones and Francophones in Quebec (1989) and found that there was a self-serving bias to attribute internal causes to the other language group and external causes to one's own.

Why does this "tilt" in attributions occur? The most important factor seems to be the need to protect and enhance self-esteem, and the related desire to look good to others (Brown & Rogers, 1991; Greenberg, Pyszczynski, & Solomon, 1982). Attributing our successes to internal causes, while attributing our failures to external causes, permits us to accomplish these ego-protective goals. However, sometimes that ego protection may be missing. In individuals suffering from depression (e.g., Gotlib et al., 1988), there is an "evenhandedness" of social perceptions; attributions to internal and external causes do not follow the normal pattern. This suggests a possible treatment for those with disordered mood—the retraining of patterns of attribution. Even though those normal patterns are actually "errors" (as we have described them), they serve an essential function in the regulation of mood from day to day.

In one program, this attribution retraining consists of a twenty-five minute videotape of a professor who makes these personal statements about his first year in university. During that year, he failed repeatedly. After a conversation with a friend, he got the idea that he could control the amount of effort

Self-Serving Bias: The tendency to attribute positive outcomes to our own traits or characteristics but negative outcomes to factors beyond our control.

he put into his studies—that people can actually change that part of their behavior. He makes these four points:

1. His poor performance was a matter of lack of effort (internal attribution).

2. His better performance was a matter of ability and good effort (external attribution).

3. Ability can be enhanced by trying hard.

4. Persistence (i.e., good effort) can enhance achievement.

Whatever its precise origins, the self-serving bias causes various interpersonal complications. For example, people who work together on a joint project may overestimate their own contributions, while underestimating those of their co-workers by attributing those contributions to external events. Similarly, the self-serving bias leads individuals to view their own successes as resulting from internal factors and thus well deserved, but the successes of others as resulting from external factors and so less admirable. Also, and again because of the self-serving bias, people may perceive their own negative actions as justified and excusable, but identical actions by others as irrational and inexcusable (Baumeister, Stillwell, & Wotman, 1990). In these ways, the self-serving bias has important consequences for interpersonal relations.

Social Cognition: How We Process Social Information

In thinking about other people, we do not merely make attributions—we also note important particulars about them. Moreover, we save that information in long-term memory so that we will be able to retrieve it when we need it later on. And we combine those memories in various ways in order to make different social judgments. Thus, we notice, interpret, remember, and then use social information (Gilovich, 1990; Ross, 1989). These processes are the focus of research in **social cognition.**

The information we process about people is of crucial importance in many aspects of our lives. Just how accurate are we at social cognition? The research results here are somewhat mixed. On the one hand, we do seem to be quite good at sorting, combining, and remembering a wealth of social information (Fiske & Taylor, 1991). On the other hand, social cognition is subject to a number of different kinds of errors. For example, we make mistakes when we judge political candidates as to their height. In 1980, Keyes asked students at the University of New Brunswick to estimate the height of the two main candidates in that year's federal election—Pierre Trudeau and Joe Clark. The estimates were precisely the opposite of the actual heights of these two men.

Most of our errors in social cognition are the result of mental shortcuts—strategies we use to extract the maximum value from the widest range of information with the least amount of mental effort. We examined some of these shortcuts in Chapter 7, in our discussion of heuristics. As you may recall, heuristics are mental rules of thumb we use for making decisions quickly. In this section, we will focus on other ways we make sense out of other people.

Basic Aspects of Social Thought: How We Think About Other People

Human beings are definitely not computers. We can imagine people who reason in a perfectly logical manner, like Mr. Spock of the starship *Enterprise*, but

Social Cognition: The processes through which we notice, interpret, remember, and later use social information.

it is unlikely that we will ever meet one—at least not on our planet. As a rule, being human, we make mistakes. Let us consider some of the ways in which human thinking about other people departs from total rationality.

THE FALSE CONSENSUS EFFECT: THE TENDENCY TO ASSUME THAT OTHERS THINK AS WE DO   On a scale ranging from 1 (strongly against) to 7 (strongly in favor), what is your view about permitting homosexuals to serve in the Canadian Forces? Now, out of 100 other students, how many do you think share your view, whatever it is? If you are like most people, your estimate of the degree to which your opinion is shared by others is higher than would be revealed by an actual survey. In other words, regardless of how you think about this issue, fewer people agree with you than you think (e.g., Conway et al., 1990).

This error, which we all make in many judgments, is known as the **false consensus effect**. Students tend to overestimate the number of classmates who share their attitudes toward drugs, abortion, seat belt use, university policies, politics, color preferences, ethnic foods, and even Ritz crackers or Oreo cookies (Gilovich, 1990; Marks & Miller, 1987; Suls, Wan, & Sanders, 1988). Although the error we make is not large in absolute terms—people do not grossly overestimate the extent to which others agree with them—it is a common miscalculation.

Why do we assume that others think as we do? The most important reason relates to the availability heuristic, described in Chapter 7. The more important we judge information to be, the easier it is to bring it to mind. Thus, we are more likely to remember instances in which other people have agreed with us than instances in which they have not. As a result, we tend to overestimate the extent to which our views are shared by others (see Figure 16.2).

While the false consensus effect is very common, it does not occur in all situations. Where highly desirable attributes are concerned, people tend to perceive themselves as unique, and as more gifted relative to others than they actually are (Suls & Wan, 1987). As a result, they tend to perceive themselves as happier, more intelligent, more ethical, and less prejudiced than the people

False Consensus Effect: The tendency to believe that other people share our attitudes to a greater extent than is true.

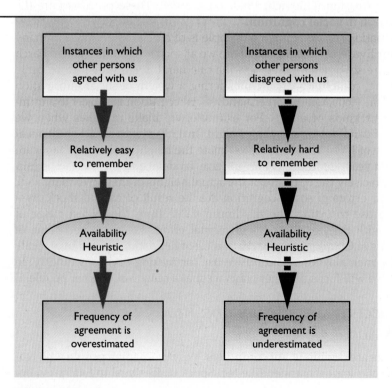

FIGURE 16.2

One Possible Basis for the False Consensus Effect

We often find it easier to remember instances in which others agreed with us than instances in which they disagreed with us. The availability heuristic indicates that the easier it is to remember information, the more weight we attach to it. As a result, we tend to overestimate the extent to which others share our opinions—which is the *false consensus effect.*

Instances in which other persons agreed with us

Relatively easy to remember

Availability Heuristic

Frequency of agreement is overestimated

Instances in which other persons disagreed with us

Relatively hard to remember

Availability Heuristic

Frequency of agreement is underestimated

around them (Miller & McFarland, 1987). Ask ten of your friends to rate themselves on leadership ability; chances are good that almost all will rate themselves as above average.

Automatic Vigilance: Noticing the Negative

Read the following information about someone named Jim:

> Jim, a third-year student at Provincial U, is a biology major with an A average. He hopes to enter medical school after graduation. He is a friendly person with a good sense of humor, so his friends think that he'll make a great doctor. Jim's hobby is music, and he has a large collection of CDs. He works part-time to help pay for his education and to cover the insurance on his car, which is high because of several speeding tickets. Jim grew up in a small town and has one sister, who is a junior in high school. He is neat and easygoing, so he never has any trouble getting roommates. He is currently living with two other men in Howe Hall.

Which piece of information stands out most when you think about Jim? If you said those speeding tickets, you are reacting like most people, because in general, we pay much more attention to negative information about others than to positive information about them. In fact, it is fair to say that we are highly sensitive to negative social information. If one of our friends describes a new acquaintance and makes ten positive statements and one negative statement about her, it is the negative one we will tend to remember. We have a powerful and automatic tendency to pay particular attention to undesirable events (e.g., Shiffrin, 1988). This characteristic of social information processing is so strong that some researchers refer to it as **automatic vigilance**.

In an important sense, this tendency is useful. Negative information may alert us to potential danger, and it is crucial that we recognize it and respond as quickly as possible (Pratto & John, 1991). But our attentional capacity is limited, and when we direct attention to negative social information, we run the risk of overlooking other, positive details that are of value as well. Thus, as is true with all the different ways social cognition operates, automatic vigilance has an upside and a downside. Although it saves us cognitive effort, it causes errors in our judgment of other people.

One final point: Automatic vigilance helps to explain why it is so important to make a good first impression. Since people are highly sensitive to negative information, anything we say or do during a first meeting that triggers a negative reaction is likely to make a lasting impression. In that respect, automatic vigilance can have a very important effect on our social well-being.

MOTIVATED SKEPTICISM   Suppose that you are listening to a political debate between two candidates for federal, provincial, municipal, or student government office. You have not made up your mind as to which one you prefer, but you are leaning toward one candidate because her views seem closer to your own. What would it take for you to make up your mind to vote for her? And how does that compare with what it would require for you to switch? Since you already have a preference for the first candidate, it will not take much additional information to move you firmly into her camp—a relatively small amount will be enough. But what about the other candidate? Clearly, that person has a tough row to hoe: He will have to say a lot of things with which you agree before you reverse your initial preference and vote for him.

In general, we are skeptical about information that is not consistent with our initial preferences, but quite open to information that supports them. Put another way, we examine information that supports our preferred conclusions

Automatic Vigilance: The strong tendency to pay attention to negative social information.

much less carefully—and less skeptically—than information that undercuts them. Evidence for this **motivated skepticism** has been provided by many studies (e.g., Ditto et al., 1988; Ditto & Lopez, 1992; Kruglanski, 1990). Thus, motivated skepticism appears to be yet another important tilt in social cognition. This does not mean that we never acknowledge the accuracy or usefulness of information contrary to our preferences. It does mean that we seem to possess several kinds of cognitive filters that shape our conclusions. Motivated skepticism is one of those filters.

COUNTERFACTUAL THINKING: THE EFFECTS OF CONSIDERING WHAT MIGHT HAVE BEEN
Consider the following incidents:

- Mr. Caution never picks up hitchhikers. Yesterday, however, he gave a stranger a ride. The stranger robbed Mr. Caution and stole the car.

- Mr. Risk frequently picks up hitchhikers. Yesterday, he gave a stranger a ride. The stranger robbed Mr. Risk and stole the car.

Which of these two men will experience greater regret? The outcome was precisely the same for both individuals, but if you are like most people, you probably answered that Mr. Caution will be more upset. Why? Briefly, it is because our reaction to a given event depends not only on the event itself but also on what that event brings to mind (Kahneman & Miller, 1986). When we have an experience, we do not think only about the experience itself. We also engage in **counterfactual thinking,** imagining what might have been (Roese & Olson, 1993; Gleicher et al., 1990). We do this in a number of ways. For example, sometimes we add prior conditions that would have prevented the negative event from happening, and sometimes we subtract prior conditions that would have had the same effect. At the University of Alberta, Wells and colleagues (1987) found that, in most cases, it is the first event in a series that we try to undo, and the events that are exceptional are those that are undone in counterfactual thinking.

Now consider how those research findings apply to Mr. Caution and Mr. Risk. In one case we think, "If only Mr. Caution had not violated his usual rule against picking up hitchhikers, he would have avoided this frightening incident." Alternatively, we may imagine, "If only Mr. Risk had read the papers, he might have realized how dangerous it is to pick up hitchhikers. Then he might have acted differently."

But why does such counterfactual thinking lead us to conclude that Mr. Caution will experience greater regret? In part because we find it easier to imagine alternatives to unusual forms of behavior than to usual or typical ones. In other words, it requires less mental effort to imagine Mr. Caution driving right by the hitchhiker—his usual behavior—than to imagine Mr. Risk *not* stopping for him, which would have been an unusual action for him. We conclude that Mr. Caution experienced more regret because it is easier to imagine him acting in a different way—sticking to his rule—than it is to imagine Mr. Risk acting differently. After all, Mr. Risk always picks up hitchhikers; it was just his bad luck that it finally caught up with him.

This reasoning about counterfactual thinking leads to the following prediction: Negative outcomes that follow unusual behavior should generate more sympathy than negative outcomes that follow usual or typical behavior. This prediction has been confirmed by research in social psychology (e.g., Miller & McFarland, 1987). For example, in one study, Macrae (1992) had two groups of students read different versions of an incident in which a young woman got food poisoning after eating in a restaurant. In one condition the restaurant was described as one she regularly visited. In the other it was her first visit to that restaurant—that is, her going there was unusual. Participants were then

Motivated Skepticism: The tendency to require more information to make a decision contrary to one's initial preferences than for a decision consistent with one's initial preferences.

Counterfactual Thinking: The tendency to evaluate events by thinking about alternatives to them—"what might have been."

asked to indicate how much compensation the victim should receive and how large a fine the restaurant should pay for its negligence. As shown in Figure 16.3, both amounts were larger in the "unusual behavior" condition than in the "usual behavior" condition.

In short, our tendency to imagine events other than those that have actually occurred is another important aspect of social cognition. In terms of our judgments of and conclusions about others, "What might have been" may sometimes be just as important as what actually *did* occur.

SOME POSITIVE THOUGHTS ON SOCIAL COGNITION In our efforts to make sense out of the social world, we use many mental shortcuts; and these can often lead us to draw false conclusions and make inaccurate judgments. Nevertheless, there is growing support for a more positive conclusion—that errors in social cognition are more the exception than the rule. More typically, our mental shortcuts allow us to have our cake and eat it, too—that is, to process complex information quickly and efficiently without making serious errors. So we should view these ways of thinking about people not as errors, but as useful working compromises that allow us to deal with persistent *information overload*—that is, to process more social input than we otherwise might (Funder, 1987).

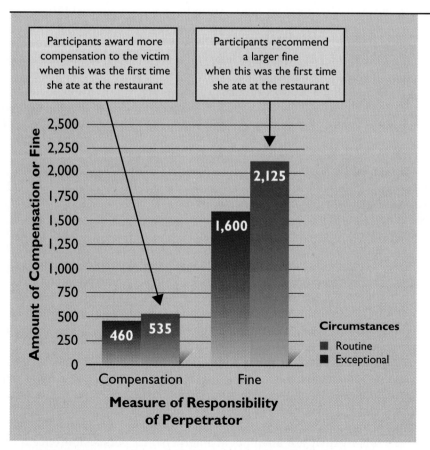

FIGURE 16.3

Counterfactual Thinking in Operation

Research participants indicated that a restaurant that had served tainted food should pay a larger fine to the victim when she had never eaten there before than when she had eaten there often. This is because when the customer's behavior was unusual, it was easier for participants to imagine a different outcome— one in which she did *not* experience food poisoning.
(Source: Based on data from Macrae, 1992.)

PERSUASION IN ACTION

Efforts to change attitudes and behavior through persuasion are all around us.

Attitudes: *Evaluating the Social World*

Consider the following list:

Jean Chrétien

Leonard Cohen

U2

AIDS

Erika Ehm

Do you react to these items? Unless you have been living a life of total isolation, you probably do. At one time or other you have probably thought about the items on the list and have developed opinions about them. You may like or not like Prime Minister Chrétien, be worried or not about the spread of AIDS, and find Erika Ehm knowledgeable or not. Such reactions are generally known as **attitudes**, which are our evaluations of the various features—including the human inhabitants—of the social world in which we live (Judd et al., 1991). As normal humans, we have opinions about many things, and those opinions have important effects. For example, in St. John's, Newfoundland, a newspaper began making public the names of people who were convicted of selected crimes. Shoplifting and impaired driving were two of them. Ross and White (1987) studied the effects of this publicity and found that shoplifting decreased but impaired driving did not. They suggested that social attitudes toward the two crimes are different, and that tolerance of one and not the other caused the different results of the publicity campaign.

Attitudes are acquired through the basic learning processes we considered in Chapter 5. For example, through *operant conditioning* we are rewarded by our parents, teachers, or friends for expressing the "correct views"—that is, the views they themselves hold. Attitudes are also acquired through *observational learning*; at every age, we copy the preferences expressed by people we like or respect, as a result of being exposed to these views. *Classical conditioning* also plays a role; it is especially influential in shaping an attitude's *emotional* or *affective* component (e.g., Betz & Krosnick, 1993; Krosnick et al., 1992)

Whatever their various origins, attitudes are important in social thought and have long been the subject of systematic study by social psychologists (Olson & Zanna, 1993). For example, mood affects attitudes—that is, people make evaluations that are consistent with their mood, be it positive or negative (Finegan & Seligman, 1993). In the next section of this chapter we will consider the social psychology of attitude change under these two headings: *persuasion*—how attitudes can be changed by other people; and *cognitive dissonance*—how we change our attitudes ourselves.

PERSUASION: THE PROCESS OF CHANGING ATTITUDES As the twentieth century draws to a close, the effort to change attitudes—or at least try to change them—seems to grow ever more intense. Television commercials, magazine ads, giant billboards, political campaigns, public service announcements, and even documentary films (Linton, 1992) are all used to urge people to do something—for example, to vote one way or another, to stop smoking, or to start exercising. The messages and the media vary, but the goal remains the same: to change people's beliefs and, ultimately, their behavior.

At the University of British Columbia, Crowhurst has studied how elementary students write persuasive messages. She found a typical weakness in their messages to be lack of support for the arguments. However, she noted that the basics for persuasive argumentation can be seen early in children's language development.

To what extent are attempts at interpersonal **persuasion** effective? And what determines whether persuasion will succeed?

Attitudes: Mental representations and evaluations of features of the social or physical world.

Persuasion: The process through which one or more people attempt to alter the attitudes of one or more others.

Persuasion: The traditional approach In most cases, attempts at persuasion involve a *source* directing a *message* to a target *audience*. Early research on persuasion, therefore, focused on those basic components and addressed various aspects of this question: *"Who* says *what* to *whom* and with *what effect?"* (Hovland, Janis, & Kelley, 1953). The findings of such research were complex, but among the most important were these:

1. Experts are more persuasive than nonexperts (Hovland & Weiss, 1951). We give more weight to arguments delivered by those who seem to know what they are talking about.

2. Messages that appear not to be designed to change our attitudes are often more successful than ones that seem intended to manipulate us (Walster & Festinger, 1962). We do not trust information that we believe was meant to be persuasive.

3. Popular and attractive sources are more effective in changing attitudes than unpopular or unattractive ones (Kiesler & Kiesler, 1969). Personal appeal is important, particularly in politics, as many of our politicians have found out.

4. Individuals who are relatively low in self-esteem are often easier to persuade than those who are high in self-esteem (Janis, 1954). These people are more susceptible to persuasion from high-status or attractive sources.

5. When an audience holds attitudes contrary to those of a would-be persuader, it is often more effective to adopt a *two-sided approach*, in which both sides of an issue are presented, rather than a *one-sided approach*, in which only one side is presented. When members of an audience hold attitudes consistent with those of a would-be persuader, however, a one-sided approach is often more effective.

6. People who speak rapidly are generally more persuasive than ones who speak slowly (Miller et al., 1976), partly because they seem more competent and confident and expert.

These findings have generally withstood the test of research, which makes them useful basic principles and an important part of our knowledge about the process of persuasion. Here is one word of caution, however: Changing attitudes is a complex and tricky business. Many factors, including all of those listed above and others as well, play different roles. Moreover, these variables can and often do interact with one another. For example, researchers at the University of Quebec at Montreal showed that together, low levels of voice intonation and low levels of voice intensity are more effective in persuading students about automated teller machines and student loans. In other words, simplistic generalizations about persuasion are risky at best.

Persuasion: The cognitive approach The traditional approach to research on persuasion has provided a wealth of useful information about the "who" and "how" of persuasion. That approach has been less helpful, however, in answering the question "why"—that is, why people change their attitudes in response to persuasive messages.

A contemporary approach known as the **cognitive perspective on persuasion** is being used to answer that question (Petty & Cacioppo, 1986). Those who take the cognitive perspective ask this: *Which cognitive processes determine when someone is actually persuaded?* In other words, this newer perspective seeks to understand (1) what people think about when they are exposed to persuasive appeals, and (2) how these thoughts and cognitive processes determine the extent to which attitude change occurs.

Cognitive Perspective on Persuasion: An approach that seeks to understand persuasion by identifying the cognitive processes that play a role in it.

One theory that has adopted the cognitive perspective is known as the **elaboration likelihood model (ELM)** (Petty & Cacioppo, 1986). According to the ELM model, it is not the persuasive message itself but the thinking it produces that results in either attitude change or resistance to attitude change. The model also predicts that when persuasive messages deal with issues that are important or have personal relevance, people are likely to give careful attention to the message and to the arguments it makes. In such cases, persuasion occurs through the **central route**. This route involves an evaluation of (a) the strength or rationality of the argument, and (b) how closely that argument agrees or disagrees with our current beliefs. When messages are processed via this central route, attitude change may occur, to the extent that the arguments presented are strong and the facts that are marshalled are convincing.

In contrast, when messages deal with issues that are relatively unimportant and not personally relevant, persuasion occurs through the **peripheral route**. Here, little cognitive work is performed, and attitude change, when it takes place, is a seemingly automatic response to the prestige of the source and the credibility, likability, or style (or form) of the message. Attitude change is more likely to occur through the peripheral route when people are distracted and therefore do not take the time to do a careful analysis of the the message itself (see Figure 16.4).

Elaboration Likelihood Model (of persuasion): A theory suggesting that there are two distinct routes to persuasion involving different amounts of cognitive elaboration in response to a persuasive message.

Central Route (to persuasion): Attitude change resulting from systematic processing of information contained in persuasive messages.

Peripheral Route (to persuasion): Attitude change resulting from peripheral persuasion cues—information concerning the expertise, status, or attractiveness of would-be persuaders.

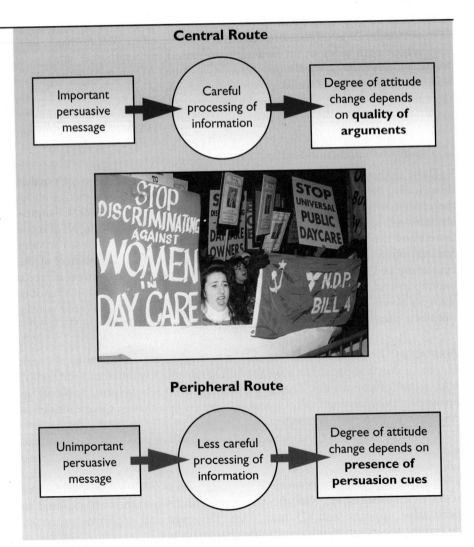

FIGURE 16.4

The Elaboration Likelihood Model: An Overview

According to the ELM, persuasion can occur through two different processes. If persuasive messages are important or personally relevant to us, we pay careful attention to the arguments, and persuasion can occur through the *central route*. If we find messages unimportant or irrelevant, however, persuasion occurs through the *peripheral route*, largely in response to persuasion cues.
(Source: Based on suggestions by Petty & Cacioppo, 1986.)

There is growing evidence that the ELM analysis is accurate (e.g., DeBono, 1992; Roskos-Ewoldsen & Fazio, 1992; Chebat et al., 1990). For example, student subjects at the University of Quebec at Montreal (Gelinas-Chebat & Chebat, 1992) confirmed this model in a study that compared two messages about ATMs and student loans. The cognitive perspective has added to our understanding of persuasion, in that we are now beginning to understand *why* it takes place.

COGNITIVE DISSONANCE: HOW WE SOMETIMES CHANGE OUR OWN ATTITUDES There are many occasions in everyday life when we feel compelled to say or do things that are not consistent with our true attitudes. Here are two examples:

- Your friend buys a new computer and proudly asks how you like it. You have just read an article indicating that this particular model is such a lemon that the manufacturer should put a large bottle of aspirin in each shipping carton. What do you say?

- You are writing a term paper, and your professor has given you one of his own articles to read. You find it muddled beyond belief. Later he asks you, "How did you like my paper?" What is your answer?

Unless you are a very special person, the chances are good that in situations like this, you will say the "correct" thing: You will tell your friend that the computer is awesome, and you will say something good about the professor's article. Social psychologists describe such behaviors as **forced compliance**, in the sense that we feel compelled to say or do things that aren't consistent with our true attitudes. Does forced compliance have any effect on our underlying attitudes? According to a theory known as cognitive dissonance, it may serve to change them (Festinger, 1957).

The term **cognitive dissonance** refers to the discomfort we experience as a result of the obvious gap between our attitudes and our actions, or between two attitudes that are contradictory (see Figure 16.5). Such dissonance, the theory holds, is *motivational*: People experiencing dissonance try to reduce it. They do so in several ways—for example, by minimizing the importance of the inconsistency. By far the most intriguing method is this: *People experiencing dissonance because they have done something inconsistent with their own attitudes may change those attitudes, because that helps to reduce dissonance.* In short, after praising your friend's lemon or your professor's jargon-studded paper, you may actually persuade yourself that these items are better than you thought. In this way, you may develop a more favorable attitude toward the computer, and toward the paper in question (McCann et al., 1991; Wright et al., 1992). Doing so reduces the discomfort of cognitive dissonance (Chebat & Picard, 1991).

Sometimes, after a decision is made, you may experience post-decision dissonance. You may ask yourself, "Why did I agree to go out the night before the test?" You need to reduce this dissonance, and you do so by thinking about the decision in a positive way. For example, once they have made their decision and cast their ballot, voters are more confident that their candidate will prevail (Frenkel & Doob, 1976). And after betting in a game of chance at the Canadian National Exhibition in Toronto, people are more confident of winning than they were before placing their bet (Younger et al., 1977).

DISSONANCE AND THE LESS-LEADS-TO-MORE EFFECT The prediction that people will change their attitudes as a result of their own behavior is surprising enough. However, when people act in ways that are contrary to their own views, there is another variable to be considered: How strong are their reasons for doing that? If their reasons are very good, then little or no dissonance will be generated. After all, there are good reasons for not telling your

Forced Compliance: A sense of obligation to say or do things inconsistent with our true attitudes.

Cognitive Dissonance: The state experienced by individuals when they discover inconsistency between two attitudes they hold or between their attitudes and their behavior.

FIGURE 16.5

Cognitive Dissonance

When people notice that two attitudes they hold are somehow inconsistent, they may experience *cognitive dissonance*—an unpleasant motivational state. In order to reduce cognitive dissonance, individuals may change one or both of the inconsistent methods.

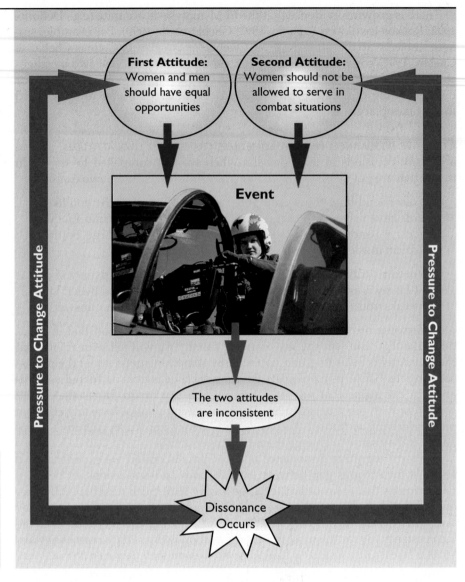

First Attitude: Women and men should have equal opportunities

Second Attitude: Women should not be allowed to serve in combat situations

Pressure to Change Attitude

Pressure to Change Attitude

Event

The two attitudes are inconsistent

Dissonance Occurs

Less-Leads-to-More Effect: *The fact that rewards just barely sufficient to induce individuals to state positions contrary to their own views often generate more attitude change than larger rewards*

friend that her new computer is a dud, and for not telling your professor that his paper was boring. Those comments could prove costly—at the very least, in terms of embarrassment. In sum, the better the original reasons for saying what you do not believe, the less dissonance you will experience, and the weaker the pressure to change your own views.

Social psychologists describe this paradoxical state of affairs as the **less-leads-to-more effect:** The stronger the reasons for engaging in attitude-discrepant (or counterattitudinal) behavior, the weaker the pressures to change the underlying attitudes, and vice versa (see Figure 16.6). Surprising as this outcome may seem, it has been confirmed in many studies (e.g., Riess & Schlenker, 1977). In all of those investigations, stating opinions that were contrary to one's own views changed attitudes in the direction of the contrary views that had originally been expressed at the request of the researcher—perhaps in return for a small reward. Surprisingly to some, the strategies men and women use for persuasion are similar—at least according to the data collected by Bisanz and Rule (1989).

- Attitudes play an important role in many aspects of social thought.
- Early research on persuasion focused primarily on how aspects of the source, the message, and the audience influence persuasion.
- Modern cognitive models of persuasion, such as the elaboration likelihood model, emphasize the role of cognitive processes.

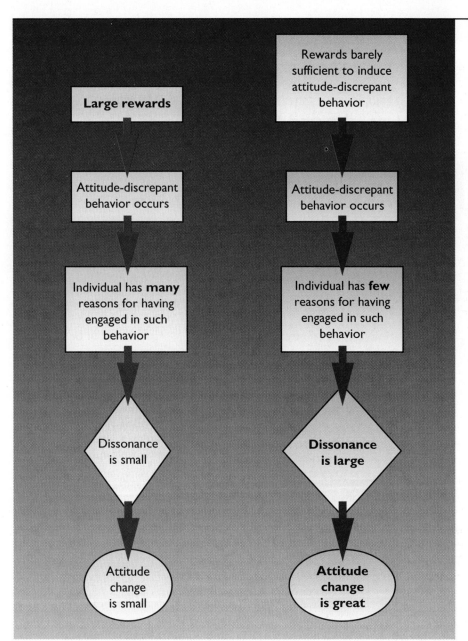

FIGURE 16.6

Rewards and Forced Compliance: Why Less Sometimes Leads to More

When individuals receive *large* rewards for engaging in attitude-discrepant behavior, they experience little or no dissonance. Thus, there is little pressure for them to change their attitudes (shown on the left). In contrast, when individuals receive *small* rewards for engaging in attitude-discrepant behavior (ones just barely sufficient to induce them to perform such actions), they experience much greater dissonance and much greater pressure to change their attitudes (shown on the right). In short, less (smaller rewards) can really be more (produce more attitudinal change) in such situations.

The less-leads-to-more effect does not happen in all cases, however. In order for it to occur, people must feel that they had a choice whether to perform the attitude-discrepant behavior or not, and they must believe that they were personally responsible both for the chosen course of action and for any negative effects it produced (Cooper & Scher, 1990; Goethals, Cooper, & Naficy, 1979). When those conditions exist—and they often do—the less-leads-to-more effect occurs. In short, offering people small rewards for saying or doing what they do not believe will produce greater change in their attitudes than offering them larger rewards directly. For information on the practical uses of dissonance theory, see **The Point of It All**.

KEY POINTS

- When individuals notice that attitudes they hold (or their attitudes and their behavior) are somehow inconsistent, they experience cognitive dissonance, a state that can cause them to change their attitudes.

- Providing individuals with small rewards for expressing views they don't really hold—forced compliance—sometimes leads to greater attitude change than if they were provided with relatively large rewards.

The Point of It All

Practical Uses of Dissonance Theory: Hypocrisy and the Alteration of Societally Important Attitudes

Most efforts to alter our attitudes stem from selfish motives—someone wants to sell us something, to win our vote, and so on. But other persuasive efforts have more socially beneficial goals. For example, public service organizations attempt to change our attitudes toward various unhealthy practices such as smoking, unsafe sex, and too much sun. A very practical question arises in connection with campaigns like this: Since people are so good at resisting persuasion, how can the effectiveness of these efforts to change attitudes be maximized? Research by Aronson and his colleagues (e.g., Aronson, 1992; Stone et al., 1994) suggests that techniques based on dissonance theory may be very helpful in this regard.

Most people already agree with such views as, "Smoking can be harmful to your health," or, "Too much sun can cause permanent harm to your skin." The problem is that their actions do not match their beliefs. What is important, then, is for people to recognize the gap between their stated attitudes and their behavior—a gap often referred to as *hypocrisy*. Presumably, when people become aware of the gap between what they practice and what they preach, they feel strong pressures to eliminate it—to bring their actions into line with their attitudes. As an example, let's consider a study concerned with one important environmental issue—water conservation (Dickerson et al., 1992; Dwyer, Leeming, Cobern, & Porter, 1993).

This experiment was conducted in California in the early 1990s, a time of severe drought. Researchers designed an experiment to make female college

FIGURE 16.7

Dissonance, Hypocrisy, and Attitudinal Change

Participants who both endorsed water-saving actions and answered questions about their own behavior (*hypocrisy* condition) actually took shorter showers than those who merely endorsed the flyer (*commitment-only* condition) or who merely answered questions about their behavior (*mindfulness-only* condition). These findings indicate that dissonance, induced by making people aware of their own hypocrisy, can be a powerful technique for changing socially important attitudes and behaviors.
(Source: Based on data from Dickerson et al., 1992.)

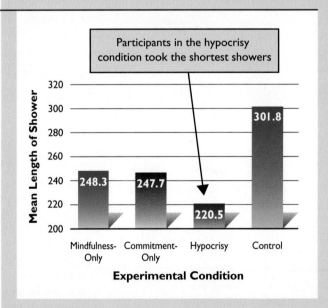

athletes (swimmers) feel hypocritical about how much water they used to shower. The swimmers in the *commitment-only* condition were asked to endorse a flyer reading: "Please conserve water. Take shorter showers. Turn showers off while soaping up." Swimmers in a second group, the *mindfulness-only* condition, answered questions about their own showering practices, such as, "Do you always turn off the water while soaping up or shampooing?" These questions were designed to remind participants about their own past failures to conserve water. A third group (the *hypocrisy* condition) was asked not only to sign the flyer, but also to answer the questions. This group, of course, was expected to feel the most hypocritical, because the members' attitudes as confirmed by their signatures on the flyer were likely to contradict their behaviors as revealed on the personal questionnaire. Finally, athletes in a fourth group (the *control* condition) were not asked to do anything. A female experimenter present in the shower room timed the length of showers taken by participants in these four groups. As shown in Figure 16.7, those in the hypocrisy condition took the shorter showers.

Group Behavior: *Interacting with Others*

*I*n this section you will learn about three aspects of social interaction: prejudice and how it works; social influence and what it does; and interpersonal attraction and when it happens.

Prejudice: *Distorted Views of the Social World*

As Anne Murray tells us in song, most days we could use a little good news. Ethnic cleansing in Bosnia, slaughter in Rwanda, civil war in Angola ... every day brings new evidence of the tragic consequences of racial, ethnic, or religious hatred. Such actions arise out of **prejudice**—negative attitudes toward the members of a specific group that are based solely on their membership in that group. Where do such attitudes come from? And what can be done to reduce their influence on behavior?

Many different explanations of prejudice have been proposed. Here are the four that have received most support.

DIRECT INTERGROUP CONFLICT: COMPETITION AS A SOURCE OF BIAS   It is sad but true that some of the things we value—a good job, a comfortable home, status, and success—are often in short supply. There is never enough for everybody. That is the basis for the first explanation of prejudice—**realistic conflict theory**. According to this theory, prejudice stems from competition between social groups over desired commodities or valued opportunities (Grant, 1992). The theory suggests further that, as such competition persists, the members of competing groups come to view each other in increasingly negative ways (White, 1977). They label their competitors "enemies," they view their own group as morally superior, and they draw the boundaries between

Prejudice: Negative attitudes toward the members of some social group based on their membership in that group.

Realistic Conflict Theory: A theory proposing that prejudice stems, at least in part, from economic competition between social groups.

themselves and their opponents more and more firmly. In short, economic competition gradually increases ethnocentrism until full-scale prejudice results, with the hatred and anger that implies.

A study by researchers at Concordia University (Hilton et al., 1989) found that these factors were at work in the thinking of French-Canadian landlords in Montreal and some ethnic groups (e.g., Asians, Haitians, and Italians).

Please don't misunderstand: The fact that conflict between groups can be a source of prejudice does not mean that it *always* is. Indeed, Abra (1993) at the University of Calgary takes the position that interpersonal competition is both enjoyable and productive, and moreover that competition provides much of the motivation for creative work. However, groups in competition often do perceive each other in increasingly negative ways. The reality conflict theory sees this as where prejudice begins.

THE US-VERSUS-THEM EFFECT: SOCIAL CATEGORIZATION AS A BASIS FOR PREJUDICE

A second opinion about the origins of prejudice proposes this as its starting point: Just as our perception of external form follows orderly rules—for example, from outside to inside lines—(Earhard, 1990; Earhard & Walker, 1985), so too does our perception of other people. For example, we concentrate on the eyes and mouth when we inspect the face of another person because that is where the useful information is located. In the same way, our perception of the social world also uses categories—for example, young and old, male and female (Bourhis et al., 1992). That is, "We all belong to many more categories than we probably even realize, categories based not only on gender, nationality, colour, and occupation, but also on religion, age group, ethnic group, geographical origin, or marital status" (Alcott, Carment, & Sadava, 1994).

Warm and cold are categories we give much meaning. At the University of Waterloo, Widmeyer and Loy (1988) announced to their students that the lecture that day would be given by a visiting professor. The students were told either that he was a warm person or that he was a cold person; and either that he was a professor of physical education or that he was a professor of social psychology. The department name had no effect on the students' perceptions, nor did whether the students were male or female; however, the students perceived the "warm professor" as a better teacher, more sociable, more humorous, more humane, less unpleasant, less irritable, less ruthless, and less formal than the "cold professor," even though all of the students were taking the same lecture. Thus, social classifications like warm and cold are really mini-theories about people and their behavior, and the two special classifications—*us* and *them*—are no exception to this rule (Turner et al., 1987).

People consider others as belonging either to their own social group (the ingroup), or not (the outgroup). Such distinctions may be along one or more dimensions, including ethnicity, religion, sex, age, occupation, and even the town or neighborhood in which people happen to live. If the process of **social categorization**—dividing the world into distinct social categories—stopped there, it would have little connection to prejudice. Unfortunately, it does not. Sharply contrasting feelings and beliefs are usually attached to members of the ingroup and to members of various outgroups. People in the former (us) category are viewed in largely favorable terms, while those in the latter (them) category are perceived negatively. For example, members of a last-place hockey team might perceive their opponents as "dirty players," even while realizing that they themselves are not as skilled at the game (Lalonde, 1992). Such effects also occur in research settings, even if the people in the two categories never meet.

The *basis* of social categorization may be trivial, like a preference for butter or margarine; or it may be serious, as in, "The right to work is more important

Social Categorization: Our tendency to divide the social world into two distinct categories: "us" and "them."

than the right to vote." (Moghaddam & Stringer, 1988). In both of these cases, nevertheless, outgroup members are perceived as "all alike," are assumed to possess undesirable traits, and are often strongly disliked (Judd, Ryan, & Park, 1991; Linville, Fischer, & Salovey, 1989). Because of the sets of beliefs that we attach to groups other than our own (e.g., Tajfel, 1982), categorizing the social world into distinct ingroups and outgroups can become the basis for prejudice. In the study of landlords in Montreal cited earlier, social categorization was another factor that contributed to discrimination in housing.

THE ROLE OF SOCIAL LEARNING   A third perspective on the origins of prejudice begins with the observation that infants are not born prejudiced. This theory suggests that children acquire negative reactions to others through the process of social learning.

For example, instead of learning what is positive about real differences between the sexes, children acquire the sex-role stereotype used in their own social world (Bowen, 1973).

In a study of young children, Aboud (1988) found that awareness of ethnic groups is present by age four or five. Aboud put forward the suggestion that there are three stages in the development of prejudice. Children base their reactions to other people first upon their needs and emotional state, then on perceptions of differences in appearance and behavior, and finally (by age eight) on ideas about characteristics shared by members of a group.

Prejudice emerges when children hear or observe their parents, friends, teachers, and others expressing biased views; or because they are directly rewarded, with praise and approval, for adopting those views. While the people with whom children interact certainly play a key role in this process, the mass media, too, are important. What views would young viewers form from the scene shown in the photograph below? Where acquisition of prejudiced views is concerned, the impact of many hours of television viewing cannot be ignored.

COGNITIVE SOURCES OF PREJUDICE: THE ROLE OF STEREOTYPES   The last suggested source of prejudice is in some ways the most unsettling of all. It is very likely that prejudice stems, at least in part, from the basic ways in which we handle social information (Bodenhausen, 1988). While several processes may play an important role, perhaps the most important of these is the influence of **stereotypes** (e.g., Bodenhausen, 1988; Devine, 1989; Gilbert & Hixon, 1991).

A stereotype is a set of beliefs about a specific social group—one which posits that by and large, all members of the group have certain characteristics in common (Judd, Ryan, & Park, 1991). We have stereotypes, for example, for attractive people—particularly attractive males, whom we expect to have

Stereotypes: Cognitive frameworks suggesting that all members of specific social groups share certain characteristics.

THE MASS MEDIA AND PREJUDICE

What stereotype of visible minorities does this movie show? Has the mass media changed its portrayal of minority groups since this movie?

better personalities than unattractive ones (Dion & Dion, 1987). We think in stereotypes about women who prefer to be addressed formally as Ms. rather than Miss or Mrs. In a 1991 study, Dion and Schuller gave subjects a short résumé of a woman who was given the title Ms., Miss, or Mrs. They found a Ms. stereotype, in that those women who used Ms. were perceived as more masculine and not as likable as those who used the other titles.

As with other cognitive schemas, thinking in stereotypes determines how we process social information. For example, information that is relevant to a stereotype is processed more quickly than information that is unrelated to it (Dovidio, Evans, & Tyler, 1986). Similarly, we pay attention to specific kinds of information—usually to information that does not contradict the ideas we already have. And these ideas may block our ability to pay attention to stereotype-inconsistent information (Sanbonmatsu, Akimoto, & Gibson, 1994). Finally, stereotypes also determine what we remember best. You guessed it—we remember best the information that is consistent with the beliefs we already hold (Seta & Hayes, 1994).

What is the relevance of these results to prejudice? Together, they tell us that stereotypes are self-confirming. Once we engage in stereotypic thinking about a social group, we notice only details that fit, and we remember as "facts" those particulars which are consistent more readily than those which are not. As a result, the stereotype becomes more and more inflexible over time. Indeed, even exceptions tend to make it stronger, for our response then is not to change but rather to seek more supporting information. In short, the basic ways in which we create, organize, and remember social information may contribute to the development and persistence of prejudice. This makes challenging prejudice hard work.

Challenging Prejudice: Some Potential Plans of Action

Whatever the precise roots of prejudice, there can be no doubt about one fact: It is a brutal—and brutalizing—force. A poll conducted by Gallup Canada in the summer of 1993 found that five out of every ten Canadian adults thought intolerance in our country had increased in the past five years, and that six out of every ten thought that it would increase even more in the next five years. Countering and reducing the impact of prejudice, therefore, is an important human goal, not only in other countries but also in our own. There are some effective strategies for combating prejudice. No single one is capable of eliminating it all, but used together, they can help.

BREAKING THE CYCLE OF PREJUDICE: LEARNING NOT TO HATE Bigots are made, not born. This means that children acquire negative attitudes toward specific social groups from other people—from their parents, friends, teachers, and others. Given this, one way to reduce prejudice would be to discourage the transmission of bigotry from one generation to another and to encourage more positive attitudes as well. But how can we encourage parents who are themselves highly prejudiced to change the message they transmit to their children from "People in those groups are bad" to "People should be judged on their own merits—not on the basis of the group to which they belong"?

One suggestion begins with the fact that few people are willing to admit that they themselves are prejudiced. Instead, they believe that their negative attitudes toward others are justified. A first step, therefore, is to raise parents' awareness of their own biased beliefs and their own consequent behaviors (which are what children copy). Once they do that, many parents are willing to modify their words and actions. True, some die-hard bigots actually want to turn their children into hate-filled fanatics. Most people, however, genuinely wish to provide their children with a positive view of the social world. For that reason, campaigns designed to enhance parents' awareness of prejudice and its harmful effects may yield desirable results (Aronson, 1990).

Schools and teachers, too, have a role to play. By calling attention to the ways in which prejudice works, and by using role-playing (McGregor, 1993), they may increase children's awareness of the negative effects of prejudice and also promote tolerance (Aboud, 1993). Where prejudice is concerned, awareness of the problem is a crucial first step toward its elimination.

DIRECT INTERGROUP CONTACT: THE POTENTIAL BENEFITS OF CLOSE ACQUAINTANCE
Prejudice builds social walls between people. Once these exist, members of different ethnic or religious groups restrict their contact with one another. Such limited contact, in turn, makes it easier for stereotypes to persist. How do we break out of this vicious circle? The **contact hypothesis** suggests that intergroup exposure is a key requirement (Stephan, 1987). According to this hypothesis, increased contact between members of various groups works to reduce prejudice and prejudiced behavior—for example, the negative statements of some Westerners about Ontarians, of some New Brunswickers about Quebeckers, of some Cape Bretoners about other Nova Scotians—provided that it occurs under the following conditions:

1. The groups that interact are roughly equal in social, economic, or task-related status.

2. The contact situation involves cooperation and interdependence so that the groups work toward shared goals.

3. Contact between the groups is informal, so they can get to know one another on a one-to-one basis.

4. Contact occurs in a setting where existing norms favor group equality.

5. The people involved view one another as typical members of their respective groups.

When contact between initially hostile groups occurs under these conditions, prejudice between them does seem to decrease (Cook, 1985). For example, increased contact between Jews of Middle Eastern origin and Jews of European or American origin has been found to reduce ingroup bias among Israeli soldiers (Schwarzwald, Amir, & Crain, 1992). Similarly, increased contact between African Americans and European Americans has been found to reduce prejudice between them (Aronson, Bridgeman, & Geffner, 1978). Thus, increased social contact, under appropriate conditions, offers another useful means for reducing prejudice.

RECATEGORIZATION: REDRAWING THE BOUNDARY BETWEEN "THEM" AND "US"
Suppose that a team from your school played against a team from a rival school. Which would be "us" and which would be "them"? The answer is obvious: Your own school's team would constitute your ingroup, while the other school's team would be the outgroup. Lalonde and colleagues (1987) studied that distinction by asking fans of the McGill University Redmen at four home games to rate opponents on a number of items relevant to the game of hockey: speedy, hard-working, aggressive/clean, aggressive/dirty, arrogant, and so on. The results are shown in Figure 16.8, where you can see the loyalty of the McGill fans to their own team (ingroup) and their negative views about opponents (outgroups).

But now imagine that the other team had won a whole series of games and was chosen to represent the province or territory in a national series. How would your definition of them and us change? Under those circumstances,

Contact Hypothesis: The suggestion that increased contact between members of different social groups will reduce prejudice between them.

RECATEGORIZATION: THE BOUNDARY BETWEEN "US" AND "THEM"

The greater the extent to which students at a multicultural school perceive themselves as part of a single group, the more positive their feelings toward other students outside their own cultural group. Recategorization, which involves redrawing the boundary between ingroups and outgroups to include formerly excluded people, can by very effective in reducing prejudice.

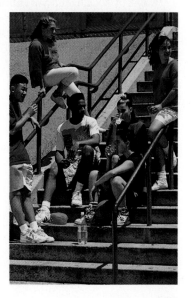

FIGURE 16.8

Ingroup and Outgroup Ratings

Ratings of ingroup and outgroup across periods on the four characteristics that involved significant interactions.
(Source: Lalonde, Moghaddam, Taylor, *Journal of Social Psychology* 1986 127 (3), 273–287)

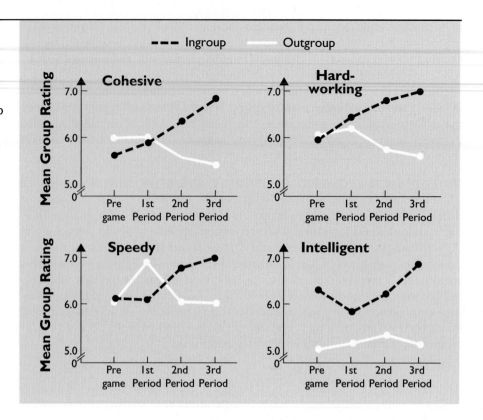

- Prejudice—negative attitudes toward members of specific social groups—may arise out of economic competition between groups, social categorization, social learning, and cognitive factors (stereotypes).
- Prejudice can be reduced, and its harmful effects countered, in several ways: by socialization of children to be tolerant, by increased contact between groups, and by recategorization—changing the boundaries between ingroups and outgroups.

Recategorization: Shifting the boundary between "us" and "them" so that people previously seen as belonging to outgroups are now seen as belonging to the ingroup.

many people would view the other team now as their ingroup. This suggests that the boundary between "us" and "them" is not fixed or inflexible. Apparently, it can be shifted to include or exclude various groups of people. Can such shifts or **recategorization** of the social world be used to reduce prejudice in other contexts? Studies conducted by Gaertner and his colleagues (1989, 1990) suggest that it can.

For example, in one of those projects (Gaertner et al., 1993), researchers investigated the attitudes of students at a multicultural high school in the United States. The students came from many different backgrounds—African American, Caucasian, Chinese, Hispanic, Japanese, Korean, and Vietnamese. More than 1,300 young people completed a survey designed to determine their perceptions of the student body at the school. Was it a single group, several distinct groups, or many separate individuals? The more the participants believed that the student body was a single integrated group, the stronger their perception was that students from all groups worked well together, and the more positive were their feelings toward students from ethnic groups other than their own. Indeed, the stronger the students' beliefs that they all belonged to one group, the smaller the differences between their feelings about members of their own ethnic group (ingroup) and their feelings about other ethnic groups (outgroups). When combined with the results of systematic laboratory studies (Gaertner et al., 1989, 1990), these findings suggest that efforts to induce people belonging to different groups to engage in recategorization may be an important first step in the reduction of prejudice.

What are the effects of prejudice on groups who are its victims? For information on this, see **Perspectives on Diversity**.

PERSPECTIVES ON DIVERSITY

The Effects of Prejudice: Group Identification Among African Americans

Important work in social psychology has centered on one particular group—African Americans. However, the principles below are universal and can be applied to Canadian social realities as they relate to French and English Canadians, Easterners and Westerners, citizens and landed immigrants, younger and older Canadians, environmentalists and logging companies, foreign students from countries in Africa and Asia (Hekinheimo & Shute, 1986), and Jays fans and Expos fans.

Many of the effects of prejudice on the groups toward which it is directed are known: discrimination in employment, housing, and schools; second-class treatment by the courts and other public institutions; stereotyping in the mass media; and, of course, senseless acts of violence. These are illegal, of course. The Canadian Charter of Rights and Freedoms ensures that. However, important as high principles and legal rights are, they have their limitations in practice (Hughes, 1989).

More to the point, however, there are consequences of prejudice that, while subtle in form, have a serious impact. These arise out of the reactions of victims of prejudice to their mistreatment. What does prejudice do to self-concept, self-esteem, and self-identification? How do people cope with being outsiders in their own society?

Classic studies of the effects of prejudice in the United States on the self-concepts of African Americans were conducted in the 1940s (e.g., Clark & Clark, 1947). After that early work, the topic was largely neglected. It has reappeared, in much more sophisticated form, only in the past decade (McMillan, 1988). Since then, research on the reactions to prejudice of other minority groups has also begun.

While prejudice may influence its victims in many ways, **minority identification** is very important. This term refers to the extent to which individuals are conscious of belonging to a specific minority. That such feelings are indeed part of the experience of visible minorities seems obvious (e.g., Asante, 1980; Williams, 1976). But what, precisely, does minority identification involve? Does it consist of distinct components? And what factors affect it? Systematic research has begun to investigate all of these questions (e.g., Hilliard, 1985).

In 1988 at Trent University, Paul Wong and colleagues reported the results of an experiment that had been done in the United States with African- and European-American undergraduates as subjects. These students, who were enrolled in psychology or education, were told that they were participating in a study of "social perception." Each subject read four different "vignettes," which differed in whether the child in the story was black or white, and whether the child in the story had passed or failed a test. After reading each story, the students completed a questionnaire about their reactions to what they had read, their ideas about what had caused the success or failure of the child in the story, and their expectations with respect to the child's future performance. Here is the "major finding" of this research: Black *and* white students expected black children to do worse than white children in a future lesson on health, in academic achievement in school, and in their future careers. This was true whether the child in the story had succeeded or failed. Wong pointed out that these achievement expectancies are a key component of minority bias and stereotypic thinking. These data had been collected several years before; they represented the expectations of black and white students in the late 1970s and early 1980s.

The most influential current model of minority identification is that of Thompson (1991), who suggests that it has three components: physical, psychological, and sociocultural. The physical component refers to a sense of acceptance and comfort with physical attributes (skin color, hair texture, and so on). The psychological component refers to the individual's sense of concern for and commitment

Minority Identification: The extent to which individuals identify with their own minority group.

to the minority group. Group pride and feelings of group membership are central to this aspect of minority identity. Finally, the sociocultural aspect refers to individuals' attitudes toward cultural, social, and economic issues. These include expressions of cultural heritage as well as attitudes concerning economic and political advancement. According to Thompson (1990, 1991), all three are essential components of African-Americans' minority identification (see Figure 16.9).

Which factors determine the extent to which people actually develop the physical, psychological, and sociocultural reactions described above? In order to find out, Thompson studied a large sample of African-Americans and, through interviews and a questionnaire, asked about matters that might potentially influence the degree to which people identify with their subgroup. These included demographics (age, income, level of education, and so on) as well as many social factors, such as when and to what extent respondents had personally experienced prejudice, whether there had been conflict with their families relating to skin color or social class, and the extent that respondents interacted with European Americans—the proportion of whites in their neighborhood and school, their experience with interracial dating, and so on.

The results indicated that by far the most important predictor of all three aspects of minority identification was personal exposure to prejudice. The more prejudice the subject had experienced, the stronger the minority identification. Demographic factors such as age, income, and education were less important, although they did play some role in the psychological aspect of minority identification. Not surprisingly, conflicts within one's own family relating to skin color or social class affected physical identification.

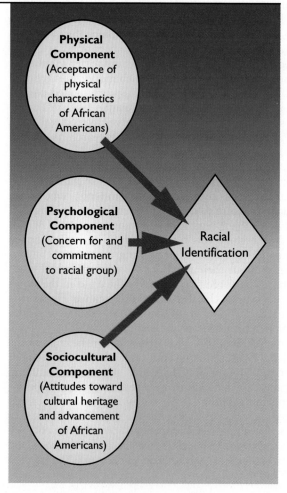

FIGURE 16.9

Minority Identification

According to Sanders Thompson (1991), minority identification involves three basic components: physical, psychological, and sociocultural. This research indicates that the greater the exposure African Americans have had to prejudice, the stronger their minority identification.

Physical Component (Acceptance of physical characteristics of African Americans)

Psychological Component (Concern for and commitment to racial group)

Sociocultural Component (Attitudes toward cultural heritage and advancement of African Americans)

Racial Identification

What do these findings mean? It is clear that exposure to prejudice is a key factor in the development of a strong sense of minority identification. This, in turn, leads many African Americans to identify strongly with their own group. Such identification can then serve as a source of personal strength and support for the individuals involved (White & Parham, 1990). Therefore, in one sense, prejudice may have a surprising—and certainly unintended—effect: It can actually serve to strengthen the sense of group cohesion of the target group and thus enhance its ability to deal effectively with bigotry. Of course, heightened minority identification in a culturally diverse society is not an unmixed blessing. The ultimate goal of Canadians is coexistence—that is, multiculturalism with a high degree of tolerance, cooperation, and appreciation—not a set of separate and distinct groups fortified within the limits of their own cultures.

Social Influence: Changing Behavior

How many times each day do other people try to get you to act in some way? And how often do you do that to them? If you stop and count, you will probably reach a surprisingly large number, for attempts at **social influence** are very common. Moreover, they take many different forms and sometimes have unexpected outcomes. For example, in the mid-1980s the Coca Cola company began an advertising campaign for the "New Coke" label. The results were favorable with subjects who were not cola drinkers; however, there was a "boomerang effect" for subjects who liked cola drinks, whose response to the new label was negative (Pierce, 1987). In this section we'll examine some of the more common techniques of social influence that have been studied by social psychologists.

Social Influence: Efforts by one or more individuals to change the attitudes of behavior of one or more others.

Conformity: A type of social influence in which individuals experience pressure to adhere to existing social norms.

Social Norms: Rules in a given group or society indicating how individuals ought to behave in specific situations.

CONFORMITY: TO GET ALONG, OFTEN, WE MUST GO ALONG   Have you ever been in a social situation where you felt that you stuck out like a sore thumb? If so, you know how uncomfortable that can be. In these kinds of circumstances, there are powerful pressures to act or think like those around us—in other words, to practice **conformity**. In many situations, there are spoken or unspoken rules of behavior. These rules are known as **social norms.** Some norms are both detailed and precise—for example, written constitutions, sports rules, traffic signs. Other norms—"No eye contact with people in an elevator," "Never show up for a party early," and so on—are implicit but still exert powerful effects on our behavior. Whatever form they take, social norms are obeyed by most of us most of the time (Cialdini, 1988).

One set of social norms has to do with which people should be ignored or excluded. As Dion (1985) has stated: "Every culture prescribes avoidance of some persons." What, then, determines the social distance between people? In his study of undergraduate students at the University of Toronto, Dion found that occupational status was most important in determining the more attractive and socially desirable individuals.

"Gotta run, Peter. A new client is on his way up."

ONE UNUSUAL FORM OF SOCIAL INFLUENCE

Social influence—efforts to change others' behavior—takes many different forms.
(Source: Drawing by Shanahan; © 1993 The New Yorker Magazine, Inc.)

In explaining his finding, Dion argued that "merely knowing that someone belongs to a different occupational class … leads one to assume that they possess different beliefs."

Are social norms necessarily bad? Not at all. If most people did not follow such rules on most occasions, we would not know how to behave or what to expect. Waiting to pay for their groceries, shoppers would fail to form lines; motorists would drive on whichever side of the road they liked; people would come to class whenever the spirit moved them. So norms, along with the conformity they produce, are a necessary part of social life. Nevertheless, when they are based on false assumptions, or when they impose unnecessary uniformity—for example, with respect to styles of dress or personal appearance—social norms, and other pressures toward conformity, may be objectionable.

How early do norms govern behavior? An inventory of the social rules that six- to thirteen-year-olds used among themselves was compiled at schools in Sudbury, Ontario, by Bigelow and colleagues (1992), and by Tesson and colleagues (1987). They developed a social-rules checklist that children applied to their relationships with parents, siblings, peers, and teachers. They found that they could place the rules they gathered in a number of "megacategories," which included compliance (do your best), revealing feelings (tell about them), conflict management (don't bug them), prosocial behaviors (share things), loyalty (trust them), and autonomy (try to do things on your own).

THE RESEARCH PROCESS

Lineups and Lines

The fact that we conform to most social norms most of the time is hardly surprising; failure to do so can lead to disapproval or rejection. Other people affect our behavior in many social systems—for instance, in lineups. A lineup is a social system in miniature, in which there are social rules about how to behave when we queue up to wait our turn. A study of the social behaviors that people engage in while waiting in line was conducted by Milgram and colleagues in 1986. A paid employee of the experimenter intruded into 129 actual lines (average length: six people) waiting at railway ticket counters and so on in New York City. The intruder entered between the third and fourth person in line and said, "Excuse me, I'd like to get in here."

The researchers noted a number of characteristics of the defensive reactions of those in line. First, they found that these reactions were "local," in that most often by far the response was from the person right

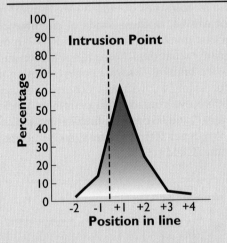

FIGURE 16.10

Social rules and lineups

The percentage of people objecting to intrusion into lineups is highest immediately after the intrusion point.
(Source: Milgram, *Journal of Personality and Social Psychology* 51 (4), 683-689.)

after the point in the line where the intrusion had taken place (see Figure 16.10).

Second, they found that two intruders drew a much stronger defensive response than did one. Finally, if the people immediately after the intruder were quiet about it (because they were paid also by the experimenter), there was much less of a response anywhere else. Milgram and his associates concluded that because it is composed of people who are strangers to one another, a queue is made up of repeated segments. The space people would defend most is the space just in front of themselves, and they defend it by different kinds of defensive reactions. The verbal reactions recorded in this study varied from "Get to the end of the line" to "Are you waiting to buy a ticket?" Nonverbal objections included hostile gestures and stares. Physical responses were tugging and pushing. Finally, the fact that three out of every four defensive reactions came from people behind the intruder led Milgram to conclude that what fueled the defensive reaction was not moral outrage so much as the fact that the people most affected had to wait longer.

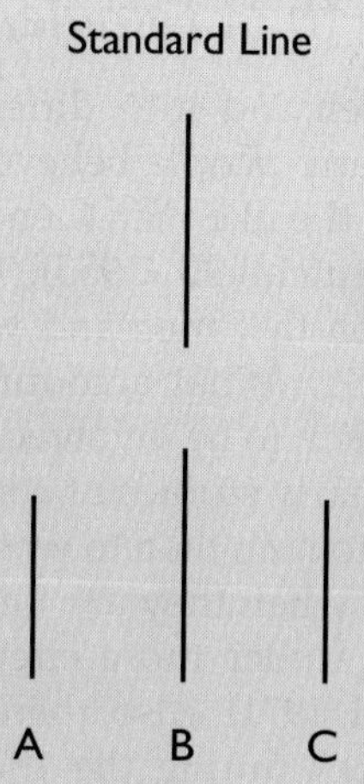

In the Milgram study, the pressures to conform placed on intruders into a line were overt. More unexpected is that pressures to conform are so powerful that we surrender to them even when the costs of failing to conform are minimal. This was first revealed by Solomon Asch (1951) in research that is classic in social psychology.

To investigate conformity, Asch asked male students to respond to a series of simple perceptual problems in which they were to indicate which of three comparison lines matched a standard line in length (see Figure 16.11). Six to eight other people were also present, but all of them were accomplices of the exper-

Standard Line

FIGURE 16.11

Asch's Line-Judging Task: An Example

In one of the problems used by Asch in his famous research on conformity, the participants' task was to indicate which of the three comparison lines (A, B, or C) best matched the standard line in terms of length.

imenter. These "subjects" gave their answers before the participant gave his, and on 12 out of the 18 problems, their answers were clearly wrong. On these trials, fully 76 percent of the participants went along with wrong answers at least once. In contrast, only 5 percent of people in the control group (who responded to the same problems in the absence of any accomplices) made any such errors.

These findings demonstrate that pressures to conform may be so strong that, faced with a group of strangers who unanimously voice one opinion, most people will agree, even when doing so requires them to contradict what their own eyes are telling them.

FACTORS AFFECTING THE DEGREE OF CONFORMITY Several factors are important in determining when, and to what extent, conformity occurs. One of these is the number of people exerting social pressure. Up to a point, the more people around us who agree with each other, the more the pressure to do as they do. However, after the number reaches three or four, the pressure to go along with the group increases very little. The reason is this: Beyond three or four, we begin to suspect collusion—that is, we start to conclude that, rather than giving independent judgments, people are working together to influence us (Wilder, 1977).

Participants in Asch's studies faced a unanimous (albeit erroneous) opinion about the size of the stimulus. But what would have happened if some of the others who gave earlier answers had given the correct one? Several studies have investigated that question, and the results are clear. Under those conditions, conformity is greatly reduced (Allen & Levine, 1971; Morris & Miller, 1975). In short, in order to resist group pressure to conform, at least one more supporter is required; unfortunately, one contrary opinion alone is one too few.

A factor that was once linked to conformity is no longer relevant. Read the next section to find out why the idea that there are differences between women and men in conformity to social pressure is not correct.

KEY POINTS

- Social influence—that is, attempts to change others' attitudes or behavior—takes many different forms.
- Social norms often exert strong pressures toward conformity. Group size and the unanimity of the influencing group are factors in conformity, but gender is not.

Gender Differences and Conformity: The Myth of Female/Male Differences

Do women and men differ in terms of their tendencies to conform? Even today many people believe that women are more susceptible to sales pressure and the like than men. Moreover, early studies offered support for such ideas (Crutchfield, 1955). More recent experiments, however, point to the conclusion that men and women do not differ in this respect (e.g., Eagly & Carli, 1981). What accounts for these sharply contrasting findings? Several factors seem to be involved.

First, early studies of conformity used tasks and materials that were more familiar to men than to women. Since people are more likely to yield to social pressure when they are uncertain about how to behave, it is hardly surprising that, under those circumstances, women conformed more (Sistrunk & McDavid, 1971). Also, there was a major shift in gender roles and gender-role stereotypes during the 1970s and 1980s. As an ever-increasing number of women moved into jobs and fields once dominated by men, stereotypes that women are less ambitious, less competent, and less independent changed (Maupin & Fisher, 1989). Moreover, women generally have had lower economic status than men (Eagly, 1987). Since those of lower status are often easier to influence than those of higher status, this difference may account, at least in part, for the original finding that women were more susceptible to social pressure (e.g., Steffen & Eagly, 1985). In fact, under conditions where women have superior knowledge or expertise, men are more likely to yield to their judgments. That particular result occurred in a study conducted by Maupin and Fisher (1989) at the University of Saskatchewan. These researchers provided pairs of participants (one man, one woman) with information suggesting that the woman had performed better than her partner on a task related to intellectual ability. Then both participants completed a questionnaire about a number of different issues. When the questionnaire was completed, they were told that their partner had disagreed with them on several of the items. Afterwards, they responded to the questions once again.

In this study, yielding to social pressure was measured by the number of items on which participants changed their initial responses to agree with their partner. As shown in Figure 16.12, men confronted with women who had outperformed them on the initial task changed more items. That is, the males yielded to the social pressure to conform to the opinions of their female partners.

This recent and more sophisticated research indicates that men and women do not differ with respect to the tendency to yield to conformity pressure. This does not deny, however, that gender is a category we use for our social judgments, social expectations, and social explanations. Moreover, these preconceived expectations are stereotypes, according to which many people model their own behavior, thus causing gender-based differences to continue nevertheless.

Compliance: To Ask—Sometimes—Is to Receive

How many times a day does somebody ask you to do something? Our friends, co-workers, family members, and co-inhabitants of the earth frequently ask us to comply with their requests, and not infrequently, we do the same of them. Social psychologists call this kind of social interaction **compliance.** There are different ways to gain compliance. Let's consider several special maneuvers.

Compliance: A form of social influence in which one or more people accept direct requests from one or more others.

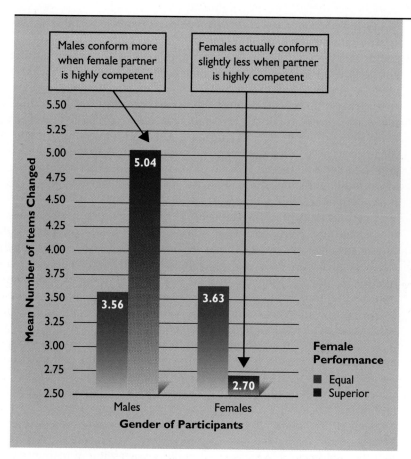

FIGURE 16.12

Evidence Against the Existence of Gender Differences in Conformity

Males faced with a female partner who outperformed them on an initial task were more likely to conform to her views than were males faced with a partner whose performance equalled their own. Females who learned that their performance was superior to that of a male partner showed less conformity to his views than those who learned that their score was equal to their partner's.

Chart labels:
- Males conform more when female partner is highly competent
- Females actually conform slightly less when partner is highly competent
- Mean Number of Items Changed
- Gender of Participants
- Males: 3.56, 5.04
- Females: 3.63, 2.70
- Female Performance: Equal, Superior

INGRATIATION: LIKING AS A CONDITION FOR GAINING COMPLIANCE   People are more likely to do a favor for someone they like. That is the basis for one important technique for gaining compliance: **ingratiation**—a tactic aimed at increasing liking before a request is made (Liden & Mitchell, 1988; Wortman & Linsenmeier, 1977). Which efforts are most successful for ingratiating oneself before asking for a raise in pay, a reconsideration of a grade, a donation at the door? Research on ingratiation—and on the related field of **impression management**—studies the steps people take to enhance the impressions they make.

These have been found to work when used in moderation:

- Agreement—the sharing of common views on various issues.
- Praise or flattery (very carefully).
- Enhancement of personal appearance—for example, dress and grooming.
- Connections with important or respected people—name dropping, for example.
- Positive nonverbal cues—smiles and eye contact.
- Self-deprecating remarks (i.e., mild put-downs of ourselves) indicating modesty as well as recognition that we are not perfect.

Would you like a stranger who engaged in such tactics better? Research findings suggest that you would (e.g., Baron et al., 1990; Godfrey, Jones, & Lord, 1986; Liden & Mitchell, 1988). So when people who have something to gain from influencing you—when you walk into a store, for example—use such methods to increase your liking for them, beware: Attempts to gain compliance cannot be far behind.

Ingratiation: A technique of social influence based on inducing increased liking in the target person before influence is attempted.

Impression Management: Efforts by individuals to enhance the impression they make on others.

MULTIPLE REQUESTS: COMPLIANCE AS A TWO-STEP PROCESS Suppose you wanted a fairly large favor from one of your friends. You might ask directly, or you could do something to tip the balance in your favor before putting forward your request. What would help? Here are three different strategies that seem to work—in some situations.

The first of these is the **foot-in-the-door technique.** Many studies indicate that starting with small request (e.g., to donate a couple of loonies) increases the likelihood that people will agree to a second request for a larger donation (Beaman et al., 1983; Freedman & Fraser, 1966). Apparently, this is because after people have agreed to a small favor, they feel that saying no to another one would threaten the enhanced self-image they have of themselves (Eisenberg et al., 1987).

A second and quite the opposite technique is known as the **door-in-the-face technique.** Here, you make a large request first—for example, keep my cat for me over the winter break. When that request is rejected, make the much smaller one—keep my cat for the weekend. This technique is also effective for gaining compliance, primarily because when you make the reduced request, that puts subtle social pressure on the other person to make a similar concession. They will feel that they should reciprocate in some manner (Cialdini et al., 1975; Pendleton & Batson, 1979).

A third tactic for gaining compliance is known as the **that's-not-all approach.** The basic idea here is to throw in something extra just before you get a yes or no. This extra "deal sweetener" may be trivial. For example, many salespeople will throw in floor mats when a potential buyer of an automobile hesitates before buying the car. In economic terms, that little extra costs about 35 dollars. Even so, the technique is often enough to change the likelihood of closing the sale (Burger, 1986). Again, the reason seems to be that the customer feels pressure to make a concession in response to the very slightly improved offer.

COMPLAINING: GRIPING ONE'S WAY TO COMPLIANCE There is one additional tactic that most people occasionally use to achieve social influence—**complaining,** which as you know involves expressing discontent or dissatisfaction. Research indicates that it is often quite effective (Alicke et al., 1992). These researchers had university students keep a record of the complaints they made over a number of days at two points during a school term. They wrote the complaint, the reason for it, and what the response was. While most complaints were made to gain sympathy, or to vent the emotions, almost 10 percent were directed at changing another person's behavior. The students reported that their complaining succeeded about 25 percent of the time (Alicke et al., 1992; and see Figure 16.13).

Researchers have found that women and men complain about somewhat different topics. Women complain about themselves—their appearance or feelings—more often than men, who complain more often about other people (Klotz & Alicke, 1993). And women react more to complaints than do men. They offer more suggestions for dealing with the substance of a complaint, as well as more emotional support (e.g., "I know how you feel"). In contrast, men are more likely to ignore complaints made by other people or to reject them—for example, "Do I care about that?" So, while both sexes use complaints in their dealings with others, there appear to be some differences in precisely how they use this technique for gaining compliance.

OBEDIENCE: SOCIAL INFLUENCE BY DEMAND What is the most direct technique one person can use to change the behavior of another? One answer is give direct orders—that is, tell the other person what to do. This approach is less

Foot-in-the-Door Technique:
A technique for gaining compliance in which a small request is followed by a larger one.

Door-in-the-Face Technique:
A technique for gaining compliance in which a large request is followed by a smaller one.

That's-Not-All Approach: A technique for gaining compliance in which a small extra incentive is offered before the target person has agreed to or rejected a request.

Complaining: Expressing discontent or dissatisfaction with oneself or with some aspect of the external world.

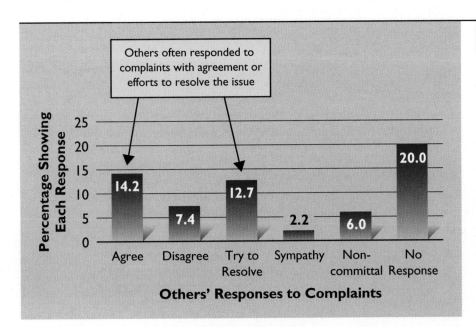

FIGURE 16.13

Complaining as a Technique for Gaining Compliance

Individuals often complain as a means of changing other's behavior. As shown here, students who kept a diary of their complaints reported that other people often complied with the changes requested implicitly or explicitly in the complaints. (Source: Based on data from Alicke et al., 1992.)

common than either conformity pressure or tactics for gaining compliance, but it is far from rare. Executives issue orders to their subordinates; military officers shout out commands, which they expect to be obeyed. Our police officers and our sports coaches tell us to do what we are told. **Obedience** to authority is far from surprising. These folks have power by virtue of their ability to enforce their orders. However, even people lacking in such authority can sometimes command high levels of obedience. Evidence of this was first reported by Milgram in a series of famous and controversial experiments (Milgram, 1963, 1974).

DESTRUCTIVE OBEDIENCE: BASIC FINDINGS   In order to find out when people will obey commands, Milgram used the following procedure. Participants in his studies (male students) were told that they were taking part in an experiment about the effects of punishment on learning. Their role was that of the "teacher," who delivered electric shocks to a male "learner" (in reality an assistant of the experimenter) each time he made an error in a simple learning task. These shocks were to be delivered by means of switches on a special panel shown in the photo on page 694. Each time the learner made a mistake, the teacher was to deliver the next level of shock. The first switch delivered a shock of 15 volts, the second a shock of 30, and so on up to the last switch, which supposedly delivered a shock of fully 450 volts. (The only real shock was a mild demonstration pulse from Button No. 3, used in the instructions to convince participants that the equipment was real.)

During the session, the learner seemed to make many errors, so participants soon faced a dilemma: Should they proceed with increasingly painful shocks, or should they refuse to continue? The choice was not easy for them, because when they hesitated, the experimenter pressured them to continue. Since participants were volunteers (albeit paid in advance), they might have opted out. Even so, 65 percent of them continued through the entire series of switches to the final 450-volt shock (see Figure 16.14). Of course, many protested, and expressed concern over the learner's welfare. When ordered to proceed, however, most yielded and continued to obey. Indeed, they did so even when the victim pounded on the wall as if to protest the pain he was

Obedience: A form of social influence in which one individual follows orders from another to behave in a specific way.

FIGURE 16.14

Milgram's Research on Obedience

The graph illustrates the proportion of participants who obeyed the experimenter's commands at various levels of shock. Fully 65 percent obeyed at the highest shock level—supposedly 450 volts.
(Source: Based on data from Milgram.)

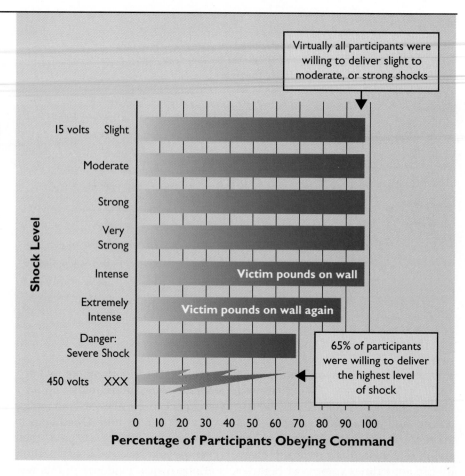

Virtually all participants were willing to deliver slight to moderate, or strong shocks

Victim pounds on wall

Victim pounds on wall again

65% of participants were willing to deliver the highest level of shock

Shock Level

15 volts — Slight
Moderate
Strong
Very Strong
Intense
Extremely Intense
Danger: Severe Shock
450 volts — XXX

0 10 20 30 40 50 60 70 80 90 100
Percentage of Participants Obeying Command

MILGRAM'S EQUIPMENT AND PROCEDURE

The photo on the left shows the apparatus that was used by Milgram in his famous studies of obedience. The photo on the right shows the experimenter (Milgram, in a white coat) and a participant (rear) attaching the electrodes to the learner's (accomplice's) wrists.
(Source: From the film *Obedience*, distributed by the New York University Film Library. Copyright 1965 by Stanley Milgram. Reprinted by permission of the copyright holder.)

enduring. Similar findings have been obtained in studies conducted around the world (Jordan, Germany, Australia), and with children as well as with adults. This tendency to obey even seemingly dangerous commands—and from a relatively powerless source of authority—appears to be quite general (e.g., Kilham & Mann, 1974; Shanab & Yahya, 1977).

How do men and women respond when observing the Milgram experiment in progress? In a study conducted at the University of British Columbia, the emotional responses of male and female undergraduates to videotapes of the Milgram obedience experiment differed (Dutton & Aron, 1989). Typically, as they watched, men became angry and women became anxious.

DESTRUCTIVE OBEDIENCE   The results obtained by Milgram are very disturbing. The parallels between the behavior of participants in his studies and atrocities against civilians during time of war or civil unrest are clear. Why does obedience occur? More importantly, perhaps, how can it be resisted? Several factors seem to have played a role in gaining obedience in these studies. First, the experimenter deliberately and expressedly relieved participants of all personal responsibility. He indicated that he, not they, would take responsibility for the learner's welfare. Thus, the subjects could say, "I was only following orders." An analysis of real-life situations, in which people obey commands that violate widely accepted moral or ethical standards (Kelman & Hamilton, 1989), suggests that the diffusion of personal responsibility, or its absence, plays a major role. Indeed, that may be a central factor in the occurrence of what Kelman and Hamilton (1989) have called "crimes of obedience" (Hans, 1992).

Second, the experimenter presented clear and visible signs of his authority, and we know that people with authority must be obeyed (Bushman, 1984, 1988). In one experiment, Bushman had a forty-seven-year old man ask adult pedestrians to give money for a parking meter to a twenty-three-year-old man dressed in blue jeans. The older man dressed either as a "business executive, a bum or a fire-fighter." Power dressing made a difference to whether people gave the money and why they did. In a further experiment, Bushman studied the effect of female dress on compliance. The pedestrians were most likely to give the money to a woman in a uniform. So dress does make a difference when it signals authority either directly or indirectly.

On the other hand, sometimes dress does not make a difference. McKelvie and colleagues (1993) had undergraduates at Bishop's University read a transcript of a murder trial and choose the length of sentence and other details about the resolution of the case. They found that motive made a difference to the length of the sentence, but that dress of the defendant did not.

Third, in Milgram's studies, the experimenter's commands escalated gradually. He did not request that participants administer the 450-volt shock immediately; rather, he proceeded toward that level of punishment one step at a time. This gradual approach is very effective in achieving obedience.

In short, several factors probably contributed to the high levels of obedience observed in Milgram's research and related studies. These factors merge into a powerful force that most people find difficult to resist. But this does not deny that commands from authority figures can be resisted. In fact, events in 1989 and afterwards in Germany, the former Soviet Union, Poland, and many other countries suggest that civil disobedience is sometimes a viable option. In those countries, repressive regimes that had ruled for decades disappeared seemingly overnight when very large numbers of citizens refused to obey any longer. What made these dramatic changes possible? Systematic research indicates that exposure to disobedient models—to people who refuse to obey—makes disobedience by others more probable; so does increased personal responsibility for the outcome produced (Hamilton, 1978); and so does clear evidence that those in authority are pursuing selfish rather than prosocial goals (Saks, 1992). When such conditions prevail, the power of those in authority may be sharply curtailed, even though they may have the military capability to enforce obedience. See **Key Concept** on page 696 for an overview of major techniques of social influence.

KEY POINTS

- Compliance is often gained through techniques such as ingratiation or through multiple requests, as in the foot-in-the-door or door-in-the-face techniques. Also useful in compliance are the that's-not-all approach and complaining.

- Obedience is a form of social influence in which one person follows direct orders from another.

- Research findings indicate that many people will obey commands to harm another person.

- Destructive obedience is reduced by exposure to disobedient models, acceptance of personal responsibility, and evidence that authority figures are seeking selfish ends.

Major Forms of Social Influence

Conformity

Individuals experience pressure to "stay in line"—to adhere to widely accepted social norms.

Compliance

Ingratiation

An individual tries to get a target person to like him or her and then uses this liking as a basis for exerting influence (e.g., making requests).

Foot-in-the-Door Technique

The requester makes an initial small request, one with which the target person is almost certain to comply. This is followed by a larger request—the one the requester really wants.

Door-in-the-Face Technique

The requester makes a large initial request, one that the target person is almost certain to reject. This is followed by a smaller request—the one the requester really wants.

That's-Not-All Approach

Initial request or offer is made and then, before the target person can respond, a small "extra" is added.

Obedience

One person issues direct orders to another.

Prosocial Behavior: When We Help ... and When We Don't

In Chapter 10 we examined human aggression—the special social behaviors by which people harm each other (Baron & Richardson, 1994). Here, to balance the picture, we will focus on behaviors that are in some respects quite opposite. **Prosocial behaviors** are actions we perform for the benefit other people, without any direct advantage to ourselves (Spacapan & Oskamp, 1992). Fortunately, prosocial behavior, or *altruism*, is a common part of social life. Each day we help each other in various ways. Most often we do so without expectation of direct or immediate repayment for such favors. At the same time, people sometimes do not respond when assistance is needed, and they may ignore direct pleas for help. We all have refused someone at the door seeking a donation or walked by a homeless person asking for small change (Steinfels, 1992). So prosocial behavior is neither automatic nor assured. For this reason, social psychologists have asked this question: What determines whether people do help one another? We will answer this question in two ways. First, we will look at current thinking about how prosocial behavior develops. Then we will consider the factors at work when prosocial behavior fails to occur.

> **Prosocial Behaviors:** Actions that benefit others without necessarily providing any direct benefit to the people who perform them.

PROSOCIAL BEHAVIOR: NOT A CERTAINTY

While prosocial behavior is common, it is far from guaranteed. In fact, in many instances, many people ignore direct requests for help from others.

CANADIAN FOCUS

Where Charity Begins ... and Continues

Canadians donated an estimated $3 to 5 billion to charities in 1991, 85 percent of which came from individual donors. This, even though Canadians that year in every walk of life were suffering through a severe economic recession. Newfoundlanders, who have a strong tradition of giving, were the most generous of all; on average, they gave $230 each. In July 1994 the Employee Charitable Society of a Calgary bank raised over $100,000 for twenty local charities, and the Foothills Hospital Employee Charity Fund donated a similar amount.

In every community, large, medium, or small, there are groups of people dedicated to assisting those in need. These groups vary from the United Way, which is a consortium of many not-for-profit agencies, to several involved in the relief of specific diseases (the Canadian Cancer Society, the Asthma Society of Canada, the Canadian Heart and Stroke Foundation), to agencies such as Oxfam, which are dedicated to international relief.

Of course, money is just one way we help. Almost one million Canadians donate blood every year. Montreal Harvest collects 20 tons of food a day and delivers to over 170 food banks to meet the needs of 18,000 young Montrealers and as many older ones who would otherwise go hungry each day. Millions of people donate their time and effort as well, and students are among the most generous. Whether the community service is at the school itself—for example, the Campus Tiger Patrol—or in a hospital, a geriatric home, a youth shelter, or a school for the deaf, college and university students are generously helping out to such a degree that it can be said, as one magazine did, "Altruism is in."

At some universities, community service is part of the curriculum; for example, at Dalhousie in Halifax there is a special program for "Presidents' Scholars" that includes a special commitment to community work. Other students work at Frontier College—the "university in overalls"—in the summer, laboring during the day and tutoring farm workers in the evening. In its brochure, that college promises "Hard work, low pay, and the experience of a lifetime."

How do people acquire generosity? Learning—through imitation, reinforcement, and instruction—plays a part. At some point, generosity becomes self-rewarding. Through the processes of approval and recognition, it raises our feelings of self-worth and makes us feel good about ourselves (Batson et al., 1991; Batson & Shaw, 1991; Alcock, Carment, & Sadava, 1994).

How we explain our generous acts to ourselves says much about whether we will repeat them or not. For instance, Grusec and Redler (1980) studied the generous acts of children and found that children who attributed their generosity to internal causes were more likely to share again a week or more later.

At Simon Fraser University, Janet Strayer has studied the development of *empathy*—the understanding of other people's needs—and its relationship to the prosocial behavior of children. Strayer's idea is that, in order to help, children first need to understand the emotional states (fear, pain, anger) of other people. "Direct" training of empathy in the home is not common (Grusec,

1991). Empathy comes from understanding how people express themselves, both verbally and nonverbally, and how they behave, as well as from the specific circumstances surrounding a request for help.

Of course, there are other social understandings that children develop as they grow up. For example, at about age four or five, children begin to understand that beliefs and expectations can be false. Therefore, they are able to understand surprise and disappointment, and what would cause other people to be surprised or disappointed (MacLaren & Olson, 1993). In a 1989 study, Strayer and Schroeder showed children aged five, nine, and thirteen a number of short, videotaped stories to determine whether they understood the emotions illustrated—that is, whether they had empathy. Then they asked the children what kind of help they might give. There were two noteworthy findings. First, the children who offered helpful suggestions also had empathy, in the sense that they understood the emotion that was portrayed. Second, the most frequent kind of suggestion was direct assistance (e.g., calling the emergency number). Verbal reassurance, social support (offering to be a friend), and aggressive support (offering to "kick the man and run away") were much less common. Strayer reasoned that direct assistance was what the children's parents provided them when they were distressed. She concluded: "It may be that children do most readily for others what has been done for them."

BYSTANDER EFFECT: THERE IS NOT ALWAYS SAFETY IN NUMBERS While prosocial behavior develops in childhood and is very common, there are times when it fails to occur. Let's now consider when that happens.

The attention of researchers in social psychology (and of the rest of the world) was captured by a dramatic incident in New York City in the mid-1960s. A young woman named Catherine (Kitty) Genovese was stabbed to death as she was returning home from work. Here is how it happened: She was attacked on the street by a man with a knife. She ran, but he chased her and stabbed her again. Genovese screamed for help, and lights came on in many windows in nearby buildings. Seeing those, the attacker fled. However, when no one actually came out, he returned and stabbed her again. Once more Genovese screamed for help. Again not a single person came to her assistance and no one called the police. The attack continued until she died. The case of Kitty Genovese is not unique. For example, in 1973, in the Toronto subway, thirty people watched three youths assault another passenger. In 1978, Ross produced a film with an actor and a hidden camera. When the actor collapsed on Yonge Street, and later snatched a woman's purse in front of Toronto City Hall, many people saw but no one helped (see Alcock et al., 1994).

Why did no one come to the victim's assistance in these cases? Why did not one person alert the police? Clearly, there were invisible barriers that prevented all of the law-abiding citizens who witnessed those crimes from doing something about them. What were those barriers? What first comes to mind is the physical risk involved. For example, in 1994 a University of King's College student in Halifax was beaten badly. There were thirty-eight witnesses but they stayed in the shadows and would not come forward. They were afraid for themselves. In other cases, however, help is withheld *even when there is no risk.*

Two social psychologists sought an answer to the Genovese case. Darley and Latane (1968) suggested that perhaps no one came to her assistance because all of the witnesses assumed that someone else would; after all, there were many other potential helpers. In effect, there may be danger, not safety, in numbers.

Was their hypothesis correct? To find out, they conducted a famous experiment (Darley & Latane, 1968) in which male participants seated alone in separate rooms overheard another person experience what seemed to be an intense epileptic seizure. The incident was staged by means of a special tape recording, but to the subjects it was frighteningly real.

To examine the impact of the presence of other bystanders on willingness to help, participants in three separate conditions were led to believe that (1) only they and the victim were present; (2) they, the victim, and one other person were present; or (3) they, the victim, and four other people were present. As the number of presumed bystanders increased, the percentage of participants who rushed from their room to offer assistance dropped sharply (from 85 to 31 percent), and more time passed before help was offered (from 52 to 166 seconds). These results offered strong support for what has come to be known as the **bystander effect**: Witnesses to an emergency fail to help when they believe there are other people present.

These results were soon confirmed in many other studies. It appeared that **diffusion of responsibility**—a sharing of responsibility among all potential helpers—is a determinant of whether and how quickly people offer aid in emergencies. Diffusion of responsibility occurs in many other circumstances as well. For example, how close pedestrians stand to the curb and how likely they are to look for traffic before crossing depends on whether there are other people crossing (at least, that is the case at traffic lights in Edmonton, Alberta; Harrell, 1991). However, diffusion of responsibility is not the entire story. Several other factors also enter into the equation. Surprisingly, one of the most important of these is the potential helper's mood at the time.

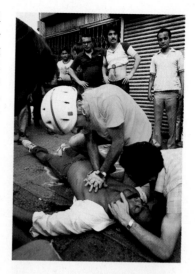

WHO HELPS IN EMERGENCIES? PERSONAL CHARACTERISTICS DO MATTER

People who rush forward to help victims of accidents appear to differ from those who fail to help in several important respects.

Feeling Good and Feeling Bad and Helping: Mood and Prosocial Behavior

Are you more likely to offer help to others when you are in a good mood or in a bad mood? The answer, according to Isen (1987), is this: Virtually anything that elevates mood—finding coins in a phone booth, watching funny movies, even smelling pleasant smells—increases the likelihood that people will help (Baron & Thomley, 1994; Wilson, 1981). This is not always the case, however. When the helping may be unpleasant—for example, when the victim is bleeding or sick—people in a good mood are actually less likely to help. Apparently, this is because they are reluctant to undertake actions that will interfere with their good mood (Shaffer & Graziano, 1983).

What about being in a bad mood—how does that influence whether help will be offered? The answer is that it depends. A bad mood tends to oppose

Bystander Effect: A reduced tendency of witnesses to an emergency to help when they believe that there are other potential helpers present.

Diffusion of Responsibility: A sharing of responsibility among all potential helpers who witness an emergency; the result is that each feels less responsible for helping victims.

helping when potential helpers focus on their own needs or misfortunes or the consequences of helping (Millar et al., 1988; Thompson, Cowan, & Rosenhan, 1980). Under other conditions, a bad mood can have the opposite effect because, simply stated, helping other people makes us feel good. We observe the positive effects of our assistance and receive thanks, and we also pat ourselves on the back for engaging in prosocial behavior. These rewards may counter a negative mood and provide "negative state relief." That is, sometimes we are motivated to help by understanding that in helping other people, we may make ourselves feel better (Cialdini, Kenrick, & Bauman, 1982; Cunningham et al., 1990).

Embarrassment, however, makes us feel worse, not better. When the choice is between helping and embarrassment, sometimes we do not bother. A study by Bishop's University in Quebec by McDonald and McKelvie (1992) illustrated this point. At a shopping mall, a young adult male, casually dressed, dropped either a glove or a box of condoms in front of an approaching shopper. He then walked on, leaving the dropped article behind him. Of the sixty subjects who noticed the article, only eighteen helped—nine men and nine women—and more than twice as many with the glove as with the condoms. (One male helped with the condoms by kicking the box along the floor to the experimenter's feet!) This experiment replicated similar findings by Edwards (1975), whose two dropped objects (in a South African shopping area) were a box of tampons and a purse.

PERSONAL CHARACTERISTICS AND HELPING Some individuals are on the mailing list of every charity; they donate regularly to as many of them as they can. Others proclaim that they do not believe at all in giving money to strangers. In matters of the tendency to help, there are large individual differences among human beings. In other words, some people are much more likely than others to engage in prosocial behavior. Which personality characteristics are related to these individual differences? An intriguing study conducted by Bierhoff, Klein, and Kramp (1991) provided some ideas about this.

These researchers asked members of an ambulance team for the names of people who had administered first aid to accident victims before the ambulance arrived. Then they made contact with those individuals and asked them to complete a questionnaire about a number of personal characteristics they believed might be involved in helping. A second group, who had witnessed accidents but failed to help, also completed the questionnaire. When the responses of the two groups were compared, interesting differences emerged.

For example, those who had offered first aid had stronger beliefs in a just world—that is, they believed more firmly that the world is a fair and predictable place in which good behavior is rewarded and bad behavior is punished. In addition, they scored higher on items that tested their belief that people control their own fate; in other words, their locus of control was internal. Third, they scored higher on items testing their sense of social responsibility—that is, the idea that we are responsible for others and should help them whenever and wherever the need arises. Finally, those who had helped were lower than the control group in egocentrism—they were less concerned with themselves and with their own problems. In short, the people who are most likely to engage in prosocial behavior appear to be characterized by a combination of beliefs and personal qualities. Clearly, these are the people we all hope will be around if and when we find ourselves faced with a natural disaster, an accident, or a crime.

KEY POINTS

- Prosocial behavior involves actions that benefit others without necessarily providing any direct benefit to the people who perform them.
- The more witnesses present at the scene of an emergency, the less likely is the victim to receive aid; this is known as the bystander effect.
- Other influences on helping include the current moods, beliefs, and characteristics of potential helpers.

Attraction, Love, and Close Relationships

*A*ccording to the lyrics of one old song, "Love makes the world go round." And most people agree. **Love**—the intense emotional state that includes attraction, sexual desire, and deep concern for another person—exerts a profound influence on our social lives (Hatfield & Rapson, 1993; Hendrick & Hendrick, 1992). Here, we will consider what psychologists have discovered not only about love but also about interpersonal attraction—the extent to which we like or dislike others—and about close relationships (Baron & Byrne, 1994).

INTERPERSONAL ATTRACTION: LIKING AND DISLIKING OTHERS   Think of someone you like very much, someone you strongly dislike, and someone who is about in the middle. Now, ask yourself this question: Why do I react to them in that way? Research in social psychology about the nature of **interpersonal attraction** has given us some expected and some unexpected answers.

PROPINQUITY: NEARNESS MAKES THE HEART GROW FONDER   In general, the closer to one another people live, work, or even sit in a large university classroom, the more likely they are to form friendships and grow to like one another. Many friendships and romances start when individuals find themselves sitting near each another, often by chance (Festinger, Schachter, & Back, 1950).

Why does **propinquity** often lead to attraction? The more often we are exposed to others, the more familiar they become, the more comfortable we feel in their presence, and the more we tend to like them (e.g., Moreland & Beach, 1992). This finding is known as the **repeated exposure effect,** and it operates with respect to people as well as to other features of our physical and psychological world (Bornstein, 1989; Zajonc, 1968).

The point here is that the past influences our perceptions of the present, and vice versa. In an experiment conducted at McMaster University, Jacoby and colleagues (1989) showed how unknown people became "famous overnight." The names of known and unknown people were read out to subjects one or four times on Day 1. The subjects judged them accurately as famous or not famous. However, when the judgments were postponed for twenty-four hours after the names were read, errors in judgment occurred, for the following reason. Reading the name on the previous day had increased its familiarity, and therefore it was misjudged later as more famous than it really was. The names that had been exposed four times were more likely to be misjudged—as famous—than the ones that had been exposed once. This confirms the repeated exposure effect.

SIMILARITY: LIKING OTHERS WHO ARE LIKE OURSELVES   You've probably heard the following proverbs: "Birds of a feather flock together" and "Opposites attract." Which is true? Psychological research leaves little room for doubt: Similarity wins hands down (Byrne, 1971; Park & Fink, 1989). Moreover, this is true whether similarity pertains to attitudes and beliefs, personality traits, success in school, personal habits such as drinking and smoking, or even circadian rhythms (Jamieson, Lydon, & Zanna, 1987). For example, Lydon and colleagues (1988) studied the first impressions of undergraduates at the University of Waterloo. Their interesting finding was that people liked those who were similar to them in their preferences about activities, and respected those who were similar to them in their attitudes.

Love: A strong emotional state involving attraction, sexual desire, and concern for another person.

Interpersonal Attraction: The extent to which we like or dislike other people.

Propinquity: Physical proximity and the interpersonal contact it produces.

Repeated Exposure Effect: The fact that the more frequently we are exposed to various stimuli (at least up to a point), the more we tend to like them.

Why do we like people who are similar to ourselves better? The most plausible explanation is that they validate our views or our personal characteristics (Goethals, 1986). If they agree with us, it indicates that our views are correct; and if they share our traits, it indicates that our traits are desirable—at least the ones we have in common. Whatever the precise reason, however, it is clear that similarity is an important determinant of interpersonal attraction.

Similarity works for attraction between groups as well. When groups believe their views are similar, they profess more liking for each other, even if they have never actually met (Grant, 1993). This finding has implications for Canadian society, as Grant (p. 42) points out:

> ... emphasizing intergroup similarities can improve intergroup relations provided that the members of both groups do not feel that their social identify is threatened. For example, it is likely that highlighting values and beliefs shared by different ethnic groups in Canada's multicultural society will minimize ethnocentrism and foster positive intergroup relations. This is because the Canadian government's multicultural policy tries to create a social milieu which encourages strong ethnic identities by providing support for cultural and ethnic diversity.

In Canada, we are really talented at celebrating our intergroup differences. However, we seem to take for granted the values and beliefs *that we hold in common as members of the same nation*—to the point that sometimes we wonder if there are any of those. And that may be precisely what we all have in common, aside from the CBC. In addition, according to Lipset (1989) and Rokeach (1973), Canadians are more conservative and cheerful, less concerned with competition and ambition.

RECIPROCITY: LIKING OTHERS WHO LIKE US   It may seem strange, but one important determinant of how attracted you are to another person is the person's opinions about you. The more other people like you, the more, in general, you like them (Condon & Crano, 1988; Curtis & Miller, 1986). This is mainly because all of us find positive evaluations rewarding and negative ones unpleasant. This effect happens even when we believe that other people's assessments of us are not accurate (Swann et al., 1987) or that they are making an obvious attempt to use flattery (Drachman, DeCarufel, & Insko, 1978)!

Reciprocity goes beyond reciprocal liking. Social bonds require that confidences, or "disclosures," between friends be reciprocal rather than one-sided. The development of this social rule was studied by Rotenberg and Chase (1992) at Lakehead University. They showed videotapes of some disclosures by three children to boys and girls in kindergarten and in grades two, four, and six. These children sent a message back to each child in the videotape. The children in kindergarten and grade two did not reciprocate, but those in the higher grades did, indicating that somewhere between ages seven and nine, reciprocity had developed. Also, they found that intimate disclosures were more commonly made by girls than by boys.

People who appear anxious, fidgety, and uncomfortable are more difficult to like than calmer people. One possible reason why is that anxious people are so self-protective that they do not make disclosures about themselves when others do (Meleshko & Alden, 1993).

PHYSICAL ATTRACTIVENESS   Beauty may be only skin deep, but we pay lots of attention to skin. Perhaps the most immediate determinant of interpersonal attraction is physical beauty (e.g., Hatfield & Rapson, 1993). Moreover, this is true for both women and men, although the conclusion seems to be somewhat clearer for men (Feingold, 1990; Pierce, 1992). Interestingly, the impact of physical attractiveness occurs across the entire life span. For example, twelve-month-old infants demonstrate more positive reactions to a stranger wearing an attractive mask than to a stranger wearing an unattractive mask (Langlois & Roggman, 1990), and people in their seventies and eighties still report a preference for those who are high in physical attractiveness (Pittenger, Mark, & Johnson, 1989).

Some young women in late adolescence and early adulthood suffer from appearance anxiety (Keelan et al., 1992). These women have low self-esteem and are shy and self-conscious in public. Their discomfort with their own appearance has been linked to their having experienced critical remarks about their appearance, and to their lack of success in dating and romantic relationships during their high school years (Dion et al., 1990).

> **Just World:** *The belief that "people get what they deserve" and "deserve what they get."*

THE RESEARCH PROCESS

Is Physical Attractiveness Only Skin Deep?

In actual fact, the physical attractiveness stereotype goes well beyond looks. We have a definite bias in favor of individuals whom we judge to be physically attractive. We also judge them to have better personalities and to be more socially desirable, more suitable for marriage and parenthood, and more likely to find happiness and success in life. Those were the findings of Dion and colleagues (1972). Dion summarized the implications of her findings in the title of her published report: "What Is Beautiful Is Good."

At Bishop's University, Stuart McKelvie and his students (McKelvie & Coley, 1993; McLennan & McKelvie, 1993) conducted a series of studies in which undergraduate students provided ratings, rankings, and classifications of facial attractiveness. They confirmed that, in general, what is beautiful is good—that is, pleasant, positive, and young. McKelvie and Coley also studied the facial attractiveness of defendants and the treatments recommended for them by Bishop's undergraduates. His students recommended punishments of similar severity for attractive and unattractive defendants; however, the less attractive the defendant, the more frequently the students recommended him (or her) for psychiatric care. This may indicate that we have a stereotypic view of the appearance of people suffering from behavior disorders, and that facial attractiveness is part of that view.

Why do we hold such strong ideas about physical attractiveness? What purpose does such stereotyping serve? That question was asked by Dion and Dion (1987), and here is how they arrived at their answer. First, visitors to the Ontario Science Centre gave permission for their photographs to be taken for use in research. Next, volunteers rated those photographs on eighteen personality dimensions, for example: interesting–boring, warm–cold, sensitive–insensitive, and so on. Then the volunteers judged how likely it was that the people in the photos would succeed in achieving life objectives such as happiness, self-fulfillment, career success, and parenthood. Finally, they provided ratings for themselves on the items in the Just World Scale (Rubin & Peplau, 1975), which measures the individual's belief that the world is a just and fair place. For example, it measures how strongly they believe that people really deserve the reputation (or the good fortune) they have achieved.

The results of this study indicated that the more the subjects believed in a **just world**—that is, the more strongly they believed that "people get what they deserve" and "deserve what they get" (Lerner, 1980)—the more closely they linked physical attractiveness with the good things in life.

Why do people link these? Dion and Dion suggested that the physical attractiveness stereotype is applied so broadly because it supports the idea some people hold that the world is a just, reliable, and stable place—one in which "winners" are winners, not only where beauty is concerned but also where life is concerned.

Standards of physical attractiveness are not universal across cultures. While most cultures have ideas about who is beautiful, those ideas differ from society to society and from group to group. Dion (1986) suggested that facial attractiveness stereotypes may occur more in societies that identify each person as an individual (e.g., Canada, the United States, and Australia) than in societies "where traditionally an individual's personal identity has been defined by one's family, social position, and group allegiances" (e.g., Taiwan, Hong Kong, People's Republic of China, Japan).

That idea was confirmed in a study, by Dion, Pak, and Dion (1990), of Chinese undergraduate students at the University of Toronto who had been born in the Far East. Those Chinese students who were very involved with Chinese culture (Chinese movies, TV, newspapers, food, friends) were less likely to categorize a person with an attractive face as also having an attractive personality. Those students who were less involved with the Chinese ethnic community were more likely to hold the physical attractiveness stereotype, thus confirming the sociocultural hypothesis which states that stereotypes emerge from individualistic cultures.

In short, then, physical attractiveness is indeed in the eye of the beholder, and depending upon sociocultural conditions, that eye may be trained in a variety of ways—to see the beauty in people as they are—or as they compare with an artificial ideal.

PHYSICAL ATTRACTIVENESS IN DIFFERENT CULTURES

Different cultures may have sharply contrasting views about what makes a person physically attractive.

Love: The Most Intense Form of Attraction

And now at last we come to what many would consider the heart of the matter: true love. Countless poets, novelists, and philosophers, as well as billions of ordinary human beings, have pondered the nature of love since forever ago. Yet surprisingly, it is only within the past few decades that love has become the topic of systematic research by psychologists (e.g., Hatfield & Rapson, 1993; Hendrick & Hendrick, 1992). While most of the research has focused on romantic or passionate love, please note that this is not the only kind of love. There is also the love of parents for their children and the love that remains in stable relationships long after first passions have subsided (Borello & Thompson, 1990; Hatfield, 1988). However, romantic love is what we sing about, so let us turn our attention to the findings of social psychologists on this ever-intriguing topic.

ROMANTIC LOVE: ITS BASIC NATURE Under what conditions do individuals conclude that they are in love? Research has provided three answers to that question (Hatfield, 1988; Hatfield & Walster, 1981). First, there must be strong emotional arousal. Love, after all, is an intense emotional state. Second, such

TYPE OF LOVE	TEST ITEM THAT MEASURES THIS TYPE OF LOVE
Eros (passionate love)	My lover and I were attracted to each other after we first met.
Friendship love	Love is really a deep friendship, not a mysterious, mystical deep emotion.
Ludos (game-playing love)	I have sometimes had to keep two of my lovers from finding out about each other.
Mania (possessive love)	I cannot relax if I suspect that my lover is with someone else.
Pragma (logical love)	It is best to love someone with a similar background.
Agape (selfless love)	I would rather suffer myself than let my lover suffer.

TABLE 16.1

feelings must occur in the presence of an appropriate person—someone defined by the culture as a suitable object of one's affections. Third, the idea of **romantic love** must be present in the culture, which is in fact the case for most human societies—89 percent of them, according to anthropologist William Wankowiak (1992). However, not all cultures contain the concept of romantic love; and when that is lacking, it is difficult for people to say that they have "fallen" in love, since, like Mr. Spock, they have no idea of how it feels.

Although the idea of romantic love is found around the world, different cultures have different notions about whether romantic love is an acceptable and proper basis for marriage—remember the plot line in *Romeo and Juliet* or *West Side Story*. Often seen as more important are the social goals of the families involved and their internal allegiances, although even in remote places, such as among the aborigines of Australia, the institution of "arranged marriage" is becoming less common.

Clearly, then, love obviously means different things to different people. This is equally true for those within the same society; such differences are reflected in modern theories, which describe several types of love rather than only one (e.g., Jacobs, 1992; Sternberg, 1988). For example, some theories distinguish between various forms of **passionate love**—love dominated by strong physical attraction—and **companionate love**—love that reflects "the affection we feel for those with whom our lives are deeply entwined" (Hatfield, 1988, p. 205). Companionate love emphasizes commitment and concern for the loved one's well-being. Other models of love exist; one of these is summarized in Table 16.1, in which six distinct types of love are evident.

LOVE: *A BIOCHEMICAL INTERPRETATION* In the musical *Guys and Dolls*, the hero Sky Masterson sings about love and chemistry. Now there is one additional explanation of love, based largely on *bio*chemistry. According to this view (Gray, 1993), intense attraction to another person triggers the release of amphetamine-like substances within the body, especially phenylethylamine (PEA). Those substances, in turn, play an important role in the emotional high of love—the rush of excitement and wonderful feelings we experience when we first fall in love. Over time, however, the release of those substances in the presence of one's lover diminishes. In some cases this leads to the demise of the romantic relationship. When the excitement is gone, one partner seeks a new love, or both do. That is, people seek again the emotional high that comes with first falling in love.

Types of Love: One Model
A model of love proposed by Hendrick and Hendrick (1986) suggests that there are distinct types of love. Test items designed to measure each of these types are shown in the right-hand column.
(Source: Based on suggestions by Hendrick & Hendrick, 1986, and Lasswell & Lobsenz, 1980.)

Romantic Love: A form of love in which feelings of strong attraction and sexual desire toward another person are dominant.

Passionate Love: Love dominated by strong physical attraction.

Companionate Love: A form of love involving a high degree of commitment and deep concern for the well-being of the beloved.

In other cases, however, the presence of one's lover becomes a stimulus for the production of endorphins, substances that are soothing and that generate feelings of calm and contentment. Those feelings, in turn, serve as a basis for companionate love. The intense pain and misery many long-married people suffer after the death of a spouse may result from a sharp reduction in those endorphins.

Is this biochemical theory of love accurate? At present, there is not sufficient scientific evidence to tell. In her book *Anatomy of Love*, anthropologist Helen Fisher (1992) argues that the bonding which occurs when people pair off is based on a brain chemistry that developed millions of years ago to help the human species survive. In her view, part of that brain chemistry governs romantic love. If that is the case, then the potential for romantic love is universal in human beings. Whatever the psychological research will show specifically, there is no doubt that love, like all other aspects of human experience, is biologically based, and that a full account of love will need to encompass that fact.

TROUBLED RELATIONSHIPS: WHEN LOVE DIES "… and they lived happily ever after." That is the way many fairy tales end—with the characters riding off into a glowing, love-filled future. Some romantic relationships do blossom into lifelong commitment. But all too often, the glow of love fades and left behind are empty relationships from which one or both partners soon withdraw. What causes such outcomes? Research on intimate relationships has revealed several possibilities.

First, there is jealousy, which we considered in Chapter 10. High levels of jealousy often mean that a relationship is in jeopardy (Kasian & Painter, 1992). In 1989, Pfeiffer and Wong isolated cognitive, emotional, and behavioral components of jealousy. They found that all three components predicted that couples would dislike each other.

Second, dissimilarities are also important. As time progresses, some couples discover they are facing important dissimilarities that were not previously apparent. Irreconcilable differences may emerge as the two people get on with the task of living together (Byrne & Murnen, 1988). In addition, some differences may develop as the relationship continues over the years. One or both partners may change significantly—for example, in their religious beliefs, political views, drinking behavior, or sexual preferences. In such cases, initial similarity gradually shifts into dissimilarity (Levinger, 1988), with negative implications for the relationship.

A third problem, faced after a while by many couples, is boredom. Over time, the routine nature of daily life may lead people to feel that they are in a rut. The boredom that results may become a major cause of marital dissatisfaction, the final result being dissolution of the partnership (Fincham & Bradbury, 1992). However, some people are more prone to boredom than others (Ahmed, 1990). Also, boredom can be overcome, although it takes effort and early detection is important. Happily married couples report that they avoid boredom by seeking new projects: new learning experiences, new challenges, and new places, to mention just a few.

Finally, as relationships persist, patterns of behavior that are self-defeating sometimes develop. New couples and newlyweds frequently express positive thoughts and feelings toward each other. As time passes, however, these may

KEY POINTS

- Interpersonal attraction is influenced by many different factors, including propinquity, similarity, reciprocity, and physical attractiveness.

- Several conditions must be met before people can conclude that they are in love: strong emotional arousal, the presence of an appropriate love object, and presence of the cultural concept of love.

- Several kinds of love exist. Among these, passionate love and companionate love appear to be most important. Love may have important biochemical roots.

- Among the many factors that contribute to the dissolution of relationships and the ending of love are boredom, jealousy, increasing dissimilarity, and shifts in patterns of communication.

be replaced by negative statements. The partners whine and lay blame on each other, and "It's all your fault!"—either stated or implied—becomes a frequent message. Couples spend less time praising and more time criticizing each other (Miller, 1991; and see Figure 16.15). These kinds of interactions, and the biting, caustic remarks that characterize them, predict that the relationship is likely to terminate (Kasian & Painter, 1992).

Fortunately, additional research suggests that people committed to maintaining happy long-term relationships can avoid those pitfalls (Hatfield & Rapson, 1993). The effort required is far from trivial, but the rewards of maintaining love, and remaining in loving relationships, make this one of the most important tasks you will ever undertake.

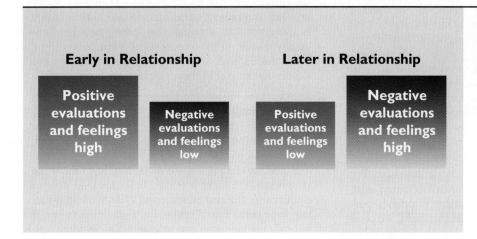

Early in Relationship

Positive evaluations and feelings high

Negative evaluations and feelings low

Later in Relationship

Positive evaluations and feelings low

Negative evaluations and feelings high

FIGURE 16.15

Self-Defeating Behavior: One Reason Why Relationships Dissolve

Initially, dating couples and newlyweds express mostly positive evaluations and feelings to each other. Over time this pattern may change so that a couple expresses mostly negative evaluations and feelings. If this change goes too far, the relationship may dissolve.

MAKING PSYCHOLOGY PART OF YOUR LIFE

Enhancing the Accuracy of Your Social Judgments

During the course of daily life, you make many judgments about others. Some of these are informal and have no lasting impact: *Will a friend loan me 25 dollars? Will two people hit it off if I arrange for them to meet?* Other judgments have more serious implications: *Which of the two roommates will be easier to live with? Should I recommend one of our friends for a job where we work?* In making such judgments it is important to be as accurate as possible. Yet, as we have seen, social cognition is subject to many potential sources of error and bias. Can you take concrete steps to minimize the occurrence of such errors? A considerable body of research indicates that you can (Srull & Wyer, 1991). Keep the following points in mind, and the chances are good that the accuracy of your judgments about others will be markedly improved.

1. *Be aware—and beware—of the impact of heuristics* Try to avoid the path of least resistance associated with the use of heuristics. In evaluating another's performance on a job, on the playing field, or elsewhere, it is tempting to follow the availability heuristic and weight information that comes readily to mind more heavily than information that is harder to recall. *This can be a serious mistake.* In making such judgments, try to remember as much information about people as possible *before* forming conclusions. This requires extra work, but increased accuracy may well justify the effort.

2. *Avoid errors of attribution* It is often tempting to assume that other people act as they do because they are "that kind of person"—that their overt actions stem from internal traits. Frequently this is *not* the case. Yet because of the *fundamental attribution error*, we tend to assume that we know more about others than we do. Try to consider the context of others' behavior and the impact of potential

external causes. Doing so may help you avoid jumping to false conclusions.

3. *Remember that not everyone shares your views* Because of the *false consensus effect*, it is tempting to assume that others are more similar to us than they really are. Try to remind yourself from time to time that it is dangerous to assume that other people share your views, your preferences, and your perspective. The chances are better than fifty–fifty that they are *less* similar to you in these respects than you think.

4. *Recognize the self-serving bias* In almost any situation where we interact with others, it is tempting to view ourselves as the major cause of positive outcomes while blaming others for negative results. In fact, this tendency—the *self-serving bias*—is so powerful and pervasive that we are often totally unaware of its presence. *Do not overlook it!* It can lead you to undervalue the contributions of others while inflating your own. Try to remember that in their eyes, it is probably *you* who are to blame for negative outcomes while *they* are responsible for positive ones.

5. *Remember that no one—not even you—is totally immune to prejudice* Growing evidence indicates that prejudice has deep roots in basic social cognition and cannot be easily avoided by anyone (Anderson, Klatzky, & Murray, 1990). Stereotypes, and the tendency to divide the social world into "us" and "them," are matters of fact in social thought. Recognizing them can help combat them. In thinking about others, ask yourself, "Am I assuming that they have certain traits because they belong to some group?" and, "Am I judging them on the basis of their background?" If you keep asking these questions and answer them honestly, you can lessen the impact of prejudice on your thoughts and judgments.

SOCIAL THOUGHT: THINKING ABOUT OTHER PEOPLE

social psychology 661

attribution 662

consensus 663

consistency 663

distinctiveness 633

fundamental attribution
  error 665

self-serving bias 666

social cognition 667

false consensus effect 668

automatic vigilance 669

motivated skepticism 670

counterfactual thinking 670

attitudes 672

persuasion 672

cognitive perspective on
  persuasion 673

elaboration likelihood model 674

central route 674

peripheral route 674

forced compliance 675

cognitive dissonance 675

less-leads-to-more effect 676

- Attribution is the process through which we seek to identify the causes behind others' behavior. According to a theory proposed by Kelley, we accomplish this by focusing on information relating to consensus, consistency, and distinctiveness.

- Attribution is influenced by several tendencies that can reduce its accuracy. The fundamental attribution error leads us to overestimate the importance of dispositional causes of others' behavior. The self-serving bias leads us to attribute our own positive outcomes to internal causes, but negative outcomes to external factors.

- Social cognition consists of the processes through which we notice, interpret, remember, and then use social information. These processes are subject to several tendencies that can reduce their accuracy.

- The false consensus effect leads us to assume that others share our views to a greater extent than is really the case. We are especially sensitive to negative social information—a tendency known as automatic vigilance. In general, we are much more open to information that is consistent with our initial preferences than to information that is inconsistent with these preferences; this is known as motivated skepticism.

- Engaging in counterfactual thinking—imagining events and outcomes that didn't occur—can affect our interpretation of the events that actually did occur and our subsequent decisions or judgments concerning these outcomes.

- Attitudes—lasting beliefs about and evaluations of aspects of the world—play an important role in many aspects of social thought.

- Early research on persuasion focused primarily on how aspects of the source, the message, and the audience influence this process. Modern cognitive models of persuasion, such as the elaboration likelihood model, emphasize the role of cognitive processes.

- When individuals notice that attitudes they hold, or their attitudes and their behavior, are inconsistent, they experience cognitive dissonance. This state, in turn, can lead to attitude change. Providing individuals with small rewards for expressing views they do not really believe sometimes leads to greater attitude change than providing them with relatively large rewards.

GROUP BEHAVIOR: INTERACTING WITH OTHERS	• Prejudices—negative attitudes toward members of specific social groups—stem from many different sources. These include economic competition between groups, social categorization, social learning, and cognitive factors such as stereotypes.
prejudice 679 realistic conflict theory 679 social categorization 680 stereotypes 681 contact hypothesis 683 recategorization 684 minority identification 685 social influence 687 conformity 687 social norms 687 compliance 690 ingratiation 691 impression management 691 foot-in-the-door technique 692 door-in-the-face technique 692 that's-not-all approach 692 complaining 692 obedience 693 prosocial behaviors 697 bystander effect 699 diffusion of responsibility 699	• Prejudice can be reduced by socialization of children for tolerance, greater intergroup contact, and recategorization—shifting the boundaries between ingroups and outgroups so as to include people previously excluded from one's own group. • Social influence, or attempts to change others' behavior, takes many different forms. Social norms often exert strong pressures toward conformity. Group size and the unanimity of the influencing group are factors in conformity, but gender is not. • Compliance is often gained through techniques such as ingratiation, or through multiple requests, as in the foot-in-the-door and door-in-the-face techniques. Adding a small extra incentive often increases compliance through the that's-not-all effect. Finally, compliance can often be gained through complaining. • Obedience is a form of social influence in which one person follows direct orders from another. Research findings indicate that many people will obey commands to harm another person. • Destructive obedience is reduced by exposure to disobedient models, acceptance of personal responsibility, and evidence that authority figures are seeking selfish ends. • Prosocial behavior involves actions that benefit others without necessarily providing any direct benefit to the people who perform them. • The more witnesses present at the scene of an accident, the less likely is the victim to receive aid; this is known as the bystander effect. • Other influences on helping include current moods, beliefs, and personal characteristics of potential helpers.
ATTRACTION, LOVE, AND CLOSE RELATIONSHIPS	• Interpersonal attraction—our liking for others—is influenced by many different factors. Among the most important of these are propinquity, similarity, reciprocity, and physical attractiveness.
love 701 interpersonal attraction 701 propinquity 701 repeated exposure effect 701 just world 703 romantic love 705 passionate love 705 companionate love 705	• Several types of love exist, including passionate love, which is dominated by strong physical attraction, and companionate love, which emphasizes commitment and concern for the loved one's well-being. • Several conditions must be met before people conclude that they are in love: strong emotional arousal, the presence of an appropriate love object, and the presence of the cultural concept of love. Biological processes may play a role in both passionate and companionate love. • Several factors can lead to the dissolution of romantic relationships. These include jealousy, boredom, growing dissimilarity between the people involved, and a pattern in which negative statements and interactions replace positive ones. All of these factors are lessened or prevented in happy long-term relationships.

CRITICAL THINKING QUESTIONS

APPRAISAL	Social thought and social interaction occur together in a seamless fashion in everyday life. Do you think that studying them separately, as social psychologists have often done, makes any sense? If so, why? If not, how could they be studied simultaneously?
CONTROVERSY	Many people believe that love is beyond the realm of science—that we will never be able to understand it fully through scientific research. Do you agree? Or do you think that love can be investigated in a systematic manner through the methods of modern psychology?
MAKING PSYCHOLOGY PART OF YOUR LIFE	Now that you know more about the many techniques people use to influence each other, do you think that you can use this information to (1) be more effective in exerting influence over others, and (2) resist such influence yourself? What techniques do you think might be most useful to you in your own life? Which do you feel might be hardest to resist when used by other people?

Psychology at Work
Industrial/Organizational Psychology: Human Factors, the Environment, and the Law.

INDUSTRIAL/ORGANIZATIONAL PSYCHOLOGY: THE
SYSTEMATIC STUDY OF BEHAVIOR AT WORK
SETTINGS 715
Work Motivation: Theories and Techniques
Performance Appraisal: Tying Rewards to
    Performance
Performance Appraisals: Techniques for
    Reducing Errors
Work-Related Attitudes: The Prevalence,
    Causes, and Effects of Job Satisfaction
Leadership: Its Nature and Impact

APPLIED PSYCHOLOGY: PUTTING KNOWLEDGE
ABOUT BEHAVIOR TO WORK 741
Environmental Psychology: The Physical
    Environment and Behavior
Crowding: The Effects of Close Encounters
    with Other People
Other Aspects of the Physical Environment:
    Noise, Temperature, and Light

HUMAN FACTORS: DESIGNING FOR
EFFECTIVENESS AND SAFETY 745
Visual Displays: Principles and Applications
Controls: "What Happens When I Turn
    This Dial ...?"
Workplace Environments: Planning for
    Productivity and Well-Being

PSYCHOLOGY AND THE LEGAL SYSTEM: WHERE
LAW AND PSYCHOLOGY MEET 756
Sources of Bias in Legal Proceedings:
    Characteristics of Defendants
Sources of Bias in Legal Proceedings: The
    Procedures Themselves

SUMMARY AND REVIEW OF KEY POINTS 761

KEY CONCEPT—THEORIES OF WORK
MOTIVATION 721

THE POINT OF IT ALL—COMPUTERS AT
WORK 723

PERSPECTIVES ON DIVERSITY—NEGATIVE
EFFECTS OF GENDER STEREOTYPES: WHY MEN
OFTEN GET THE JOB 727

THE RESEARCH PROCESS—JOB
SATISFACTION AND TASK PERFORMANCE 736

CANADIAN FOCUS—ETHNIC DIFFERENCES IN
REACTIONS TO CROWDING 743

THE RESEARCH PROCESS—COMPUTERS
AND STRESS 754

MAKING PSYCHOLOGY PART OF YOUR
LIFE—COMPUTERS AND REPETITIVE STRAIN
INJURY: KEYBOARDS CAN HURT YOU 758

SASKATCHEWAN JOBLESS RATE UP

**The Regina Leader-Post:
November 5, 1994**

Each month Statistics Canada reports the change in unemployment rate in each province and in the country overall. We compare the unemployment rate this month this year to the unemployment rate this month last year—to see how we are doing.

As The Leader-Post reported, in October of 1994, Statistics Canada found that the unemployment rate for Saskatchewan was slightly up— from 6.1 to 6.2—over October of 1993. That was the bad news. The good news was that Saskatchewan "continues to enjoy the lowest unemployment rate in the country." Indeed, in the same month, the national unemployment rate in October was 9.1 percent. Quite a difference, eh?

Work is central to our lives. I work therefore I am is the way many of us think about ourselves.

In Chapter 17 you will study psychology at several different kinds of work: Employment, environment, and jury duty are examples.

**FOR MANY OF US,
WORK IS AT THE CORE
OF OUR SELF-CONCEPT.**

Which single activity occupies more of your time than any other? Did you say sleep? In Chapter 4, we saw that that's one possible answer, and for young people who sleep eight, nine, or even more hours each day, it may well be correct. However, after we leave school, another answer is more likely to be accurate: *Work* is what we spend most of our time doing. Most adults spend more of their time on work-related activities—traveling to work, doing their work, traveling

home, finishing at home the work they didn't finish at the office, and on and on. Although many people complain loud and long about having to work, most simply cannot imagine life otherwise—that is, life without some kind of productive activity around which to center their daily routine. Furthermore—as researchers at the University of Western Ontario have demonstrated most recently—occupation is an integral part of our self-concept (Meyer, Allen, & Smith, 1993). When asked, "Who am I?" they answer in

**WORK: A CENTRAL PART OF
ONE'S SELF-CONCEPT**

When asked, "Who are you?" many people reply in terms of their occupation. Work-related activities play a central role in most people's lives.

terms of their job or their career: "I'm an engineer," "I'm a data entry clerk," "I'm a dentist," "I'm a salesperson" (Greenberg & Baron, 1993). Or "I'm an undergraduate [or graduate, or postgraduate] student," of course.

People do plenty of other work besides the kind that earns money directly. They work when they are at school, when they clean up the environment, and when they are on jury duty. Moreover, although there are general principles involved here, every kind of work—paid or nonpaid—is special in some way, whether it is performed by social workers in the Yukon (Zapf, 1993), by university faculty women (Stark-Adamec et al., 1993), by advertising agencies in Canada, the United Kingdom, and the United States (West, 1993), or by police officers (Stark-Adamec et al, 1994).

Given the importance of work in our lives, it is not surprising that this subject is now a special subdiscipline called **industrial/organizational psychology** ("I/O" for short). Industrial/organizational research focuses on the kinds of *behaviors* that are found at work and on the *conditions* under which people work—that is, the procedures, policies, and practices followed within the workplace.

Why do some employees come to work even when it's difficult, while others are often absent? Why do workers in some companies remain loyal even when their incomes decrease and their responsibilities increase, while in other companies, employees often leave or just stop working? These are some of the real-life questions that I/O psychologists try to answer.

The trends in I/O psychology, particularly in Canada, were reviewed in *Canadian Psychology* (1988). In a special issue devoted to I/O, six topics were identified as central to the study of work in Canada: job analysis and classification, performance appraisals, personnel selection, training and development, job evaluation/equal pay, and affirmative action/employment equity Two future directions for research were identified: increased productivity, and nondiscriminatory personnel practices. In the years since, progress has been made in all of these.

Industrial/Organizational Psychology: The branch of psychology that studies all aspects of behavior in work settings and the nature of work settings themselves.

In the sections of this chapter devoted to I/O psychology, we will examine four topics in detail: work motivation; performance appraisal (i.e., techniques for evaluating work performance and providing feedback); people's attitudes toward their work and their employer; and leadership, which is a particular form of influence over others.

A second subdiscipline of I/O psychology is known as **human factors** psychology (or ergonomics) and has a somewhat different focus. Psychologists who study human factors measure people's abilities (e.g., sensory, or cognitive) and apply that information to the design of tools, systems, tasks, jobs, and working environments. The goal is to ensure safe, productive, comfortable, and useful machines. If you find that some computers are user friendly while others are intimidating and difficult to operate, or that the controls on your VCR are confusing, or if you forget which button on your microwave does what when, you will appreciate how important human factors are in the design of products and environments for human use.

In this chapter, you will study some of the major findings of I/O psychology and ergonomics and how they relate to work. Although both subfields are distinct branches of psychology, they overlap in important ways. Both share a basic interest in factors affecting human performance; both recognize the importance of cognitive abilities and processes in work-related activities; and both share an interest in the physical design of the human environment. You will also study how people work on other occasions: on jury duty and on environmental issues.

Industrial/Organizational Psychology: The Systematic Study of Behavior at Work

Here is the recollection of one psychologist/author (R.A.B.), about his early work experience:

> Although I had various part-time jobs from the time I was fourteen, my first full-time job was the summer after high school graduation. It was, in a word, boring. In those days the work week was a full forty hours, so I would arrive every morning before 8:00 a.m. and would leave precisely at 5:00 p.m. Since I was a summer fill-in, I was given the most tedious work to do. Each day—for hours—I would place letters and documents in file cabinets. I soon discovered that I could finish the work in about two hours, but if I did that, there was nothing else for me to do—sometimes, for the rest of the day. The result? I learned to learn to work in slow motion with my brain turned off. The only high points of the day were the breaks: fifteen-minutes at mid-morning and mid-afternoon and 60 minutes at lunchtime. Because I needed the money for college, I stuck it out for the entire summer, but what a relief—when the fall finally came—and I could go back to school!

What was wrong with that job? The answer: almost everything. It's almost as though it was designed deliberately to reduce motivation, create negative attitudes, and undermine performance in every way possible. Let's see how, from the perspective of I/O psychology, this work situation might have been improved.

Human Factors: *The branch of psychology that applies basic knowledge about human abilities and limitations to the design of tools, equipment, systems, and products.*

Work Motivation: Theories and Techniques

Every organization—profit or not-for-profit, Microsoft or Apple, the Salvation Army or the Scouts—requires a motivated work force. Unless people are willing to put effort into their jobs, little or nothing will get done, and what does get done may be done badly. So a very basic question is this: How can people be motivated to work hard, whatever their work may be?

I/O psychologists believe that to answer this question, we must first understand the basic nature of motivation (Evans, 1986). This requires us to construct and test valid theories. Think about the anxiety you feel when you anticipate earning a negative evaluation—a poor test grade, for example. Does that influence your effort to prepare for that very test? Does it increase or decrease how hard you try? Keep your answer in mind as you read on about the role of needs and expectancies relating to work.

In Chapter 16, you learned that interpersonal competition and cooperation provide energy to create and produce (Abra, 1993). In Chapter 10, you learned about the motivational powers of expectancies and needs (as incorporated into theories like Maslow's). And in Chapter 4, you learned about the links between expectancies and responses during hypnosis (Spanos et al., 1993). Both expectancy and needs theories have been used to explain work motivation (Mitchell, 1983; Vroom, 1964).

Expectancy theory holds that the motivation to work is a function of three factors: *expectancy*, of course, which in this particular case is the assumption that effort will result in better performance; *instrumentality*, which is the belief that better performance will be recognized and rewarded; and *valence*, which is the perceived value of the rewards we expect to acquire for that better performance (see Figure 17.1).

Expectancy theory has been tested in many different studies (e.g., Tubbs, Boehne, & Dahl, 1993; Klein, 1991). In general, the results have supported the idea that people work hardest when they expect that doing so will improve

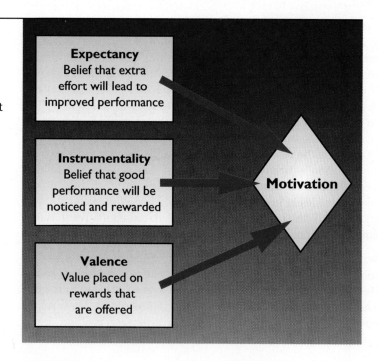

FIGURE 17.1

Expectancy Theory: An Overview

Expectancy theory suggests that work motivation is strongly affected by three factors: *expectancy*, *instrumentality*, and *valence*.

their performance, when they believe that good performance will be rewarded, and when they value the rewards to be gained for quality performance (e.g., Kanungo & Hartwick, 1987). In contrast, they are much less likely to work hard when any one of these is not the case (Greenberg & Baron, 1993).

From the point of view of expectancy theory, the summer job described earlier was a disaster. The student knew that working harder would not improve performance—it would simply lead to greater boredom. Furthermore, if it did improve his performance, no one cared and no reward would be gotten. The result was that motivation sank to a very low level.

Now that we have briefly reviewed expectancy theory, let's turn to two other ideas developed by I/O psychologists to explain work motivation.

GOAL-SETTING THEORY   When you study for an important exam, do you tell yourself that you won't stop until you have read a certain number of chapters, solved a fixed number of problems, or memorized some number of definitions? It is likely that you do, because most people find that they accomplish more when they set specific goals. This basic notion is central to the second major idea about work motivation—**goal-setting theory** (Latham & Locke, 1991; Locke & Latham, 1990).

The original research finding that led to this theory was both straightforward and impressive: On a wide variety of tasks, people performed better when they were given specific goals than when they were simply told to do their best (Wood & Locke, 1990). For example, in one early study done in Oklahoma (Latham & Baldes, 1975), the participants were workers in lumber-camp crews, who hauled logs from forests to a nearby sawmill. Before the study began, these crews loaded the log-hauling trucks to about 60 percent of capacity. That was very wasteful, because the trucks were huge and used large amounts of fuel. To change the situation, Latham (a native Nova Scotian) and Baldes set a specific goal for the loggers: to load the trucks to 94 percent of capacity before driving them to the mill.

What happened? The crews quickly improved their performance to that level and then maintained it (refer to Figure 17.2). In a follow-up study seven years later, they were still loading the trucks almost full.

Notice that in this study (as in many others), challenging goals were set—goals that made people stretch. Surprisingly, such goals are generally more effective. There are, of course, individual differences in the need for personal growth (Das, 1991). Also, goals must be perceived as attainable—otherwise, they are likely to be ignored. Moreover, it is important that goals be as specific as possible. Merely saying "Do better!" is not a good way to state a goal. Far more helpful is a call for a specific, measurable improvement, such as a 10 percent increase in sales (ten more pairs of shoes per week) or a 25 percent reduction in errors (ten fewer typos per page). Finally, regular feedback is important, so that people know whether they are making progress, and how much. When these conditions are present, goal setting is a highly effective technique for increasing motivation and performance.

Why, precisely, is goal setting so effective? According to Locke and Latham (1990), goals work in several ways. First, the existence of a goal clarifies the level of performance required. Once that level is established, individuals develop effective strategies for attaining it. Without a clear goal, it is much more difficult to devise such strategies. Second, goals lead people to compare their present performance with a new target. To the extent that people fall short of the goal, they feel dissatisfied and work harder to attain it—that is, as long as they believe it is possible for them to do so. Third, when people succeed in reaching a goal, they feel competent and successful. These feelings are desirable and can serve as a strong incentive to extra effort.

Research in Canada

Gary P. Latham
University of Toronto

Goal-Setting Theory: A theory that explains why setting specific, challenging goals for a given task often leads to improvements in performance.

FIGURE 17.2

Goal Setting: An Illustration of Its Effects

As shown here, performance improved sharply after a specific challenging goal was set for loading giant logging trucks. Moreover, these gains were still present in a follow-up study conducted seven years later.
(Source: Based on data from Latham & Baldes, 1975.)

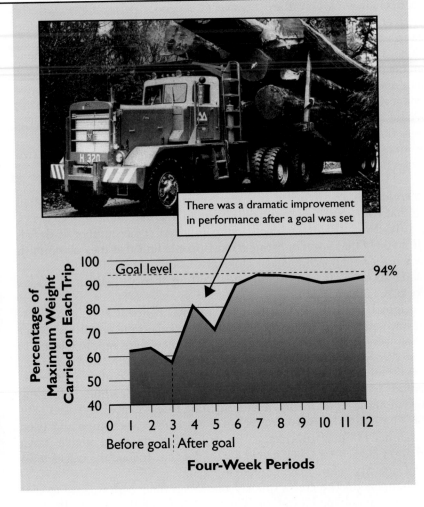

There was a dramatic improvement in performance after a goal was set

Goals aren't necessarily just for individuals. Incentive programs may be designed for an organization as a whole, or for smaller groups within it (Latham & Huber, 1991).

How does goal setting work? According to Gellatly and Meyer (1992), the physiological arousal (e.g., increased heart rate) that occurs when difficult goals are set may be fundamental to successful goal setting.

In goal-setting theory there is an important role for self-efficacy—that is, self-confidence matters a lot. If people conclude that no matter what they do or how hard they try, they will be unable to reach a particular goal, their effort (and performance) will decrease. The reverse is also true: If they conclude that they are capable of reaching that goal, their motivation and performance will increase. This is true in many kinds of work, from caring for one's own children (Grusec & Mammone, 1994), to training for new technology (Taylor et al., 1990), to managing co-op housing (Cooper & Rodman, 1994), to achieving academic and social goals. Jordan and colleagues (1993) studied elementary teachers who worked with exceptional students. The teachers who had low self-efficacy attributed their students' problems to internal causes and preferred that problem pupils be removed from the classroom; the teachers who had high self-efficacy attributed their students' problems to external causes and preferred to deal with them in the classroom. Obviously, this finding has relevance for the treatment of those children and their well-being.

Finally, goal-setting theory maintains that goals will guide behavior only when they are accepted. Similarly, if you set *yourself* a goal that you don't really accept (e.g., "Lose fifteen pounds before Tuesday"), the effect on your behavior will be minimal. To increase motivation and improve performance, goals must be perceived as realistic.

EQUITY THEORY Sometimes people are not treated equitably at work. That is the focus of another important theory of work motivation—**equity theory** (Cropanzano & Randall, 1993; Greenberg, 1990; Stewart, 1989). The central issue here is perceived fairness.

Equity theory holds that people are deeply concerned about fairness. This certainly fits with everyday experience. For example, a recent study examined the hiring practices of twenty-two Western Canadian municipal police departments (Nelson, 1992). These particular departments were selected because statistics showed that they were very slow to hire women and visible minorities. Nelson concluded that "[those police] forces seemed to be ... open to accusations of discrimination and/or favoritism," even though they might not have thought so when they hired new officers.

How do we determine whether we are being treated fairly? Equity theory suggests that we begin by comparing ourselves to other people in the workplace. More specifically, we compare the ratio of our inputs and outcomes— what we contribute and what we receive—with the corresponding ratios for the other people we have chosen to compare ourselves with (Kulik & Ambrose, 1992). However, a beginning salesperson, for example, does not normally compare his or her inputs and outcomes with those of the manager of the store. Rather, the comparison is with someone who is similar in important respects—perhaps another fairly new employee.

Equity theory suggests that if these ratios are about equal, we perceive our treatment as being basically fair. If these ratios are off by much, however, a state known as inequity exists. One of its consequences is a sharp drop in motivation.

It is important to bear in mind that inequity exists first in the eye of the beholder. People make personal judgments about the way in which their inputs and outcomes compare with those of others. It is quite possible (and quite human) for every person in a group to feel that he or she is contributing more than anybody else. Moreover, feelings of inequity may arise in very different situations. In one, we may feel underrewarded relative to others; in the second, we may feel overrewarded.

As you can probably guess, however, we are far less sensitive to this second kind of inequity (Cropanzano, 1993). Indeed, when we enjoy a higher inputs-to-outcomes ratio than others, we tend to reason that we deserve the extra benefits. This is another illustration of the self-serving bias (see Chapter 16).

Why do feelings of inequity interfere with work motivation? The theory provides the following answer: When individuals perceive themselves as receiving less than they deserve, they experience the negative feelings associated with unfairness: discomfort, anger, and resentment, for example. To reduce that discomfort, they take steps to remedy the situation. One such step is to try to increase outcomes: to ask for a raise, or a bonus, or some other increased benefit. Another is to leave: to quit and find another job. Still a third is to reduce inputs: to expend less effort on the job. Many studies indicate that this last tactic is a very common reaction to feelings of being underrewarded. That is, people who conclude that they are being underrewarded reduce their performance relative to others who feel that they are being treated fairly (Pritchard, Dunnette, & Jorgenson, 1972). Such effects have even been noted among professional basketball players (Harder, 1992).

There are other ways besides reduced performance that employees may demonstrate reduced motivation. For example, they may take actions that

Equity Theory: A theory suggesting that individuals compare the ratio of their inputs and outcomes in any relationship with the ratios of other persons. If these ratios are not approximately equal, they may experience feelings of inequity which can reduce work motivation.

provide them with extra benefits. Perhaps the most revealing evidence on this point was gathered by Greenberg (1990).

This study focused on three manufacturing plants. In plants A and B, poor economic conditions made it necessary for management to lower employees' pay by 15 percent. In plant C, business was better, so no pay cut was necessary. In plant A, management gave employees a thorough explanation of why the pay cut was essential, showed concern over the cut, and expressed sympathy for the employees. In plant B, management gave employees a brief explanation and showed little sympathy for the personal hardship the cuts would cause.

Greenberg employed an unusual measure of the effect of inequity: theft of company tools, supplies, equipment, and products by employees. He reasoned that employees in plant B would experience strong feelings of inequity and would more likely engage in efforts to reduce these feelings. He predicted that the incidence of theft would be greater in plant B than in plants A and C. As shown in Figure 17.3, that was exactly the case.

In short, when individuals conclude that they are being treated unfairly, their work motivation decreases sharply. Thus, there are in all workplaces important practical reasons, as well as moral and ethical ones, for ensuring that a high standard of fairness is not only applied but *seen* to be applied. See **Key Concept** on page 721 for an overview of theories of work motivation.

WORK MOTIVATION: HOW CAN IT BE ENHANCED? I/O psychology is a field of applied psychology as well as an important branch of scientific psychology. Thus, when seeking to understand the basic nature of work motivation, I/O psychologists also seek and test ways of improving workplaces. Several methods of doing this are closely linked to theories we have already considered. For example, goal setting is a means of increasing motivation and performance in a wide variety of work settings (e.g., Locke & Latham, 1990; Gosse et al., 1992). Furthermore, principles derived from expectancy theory are effective. Many

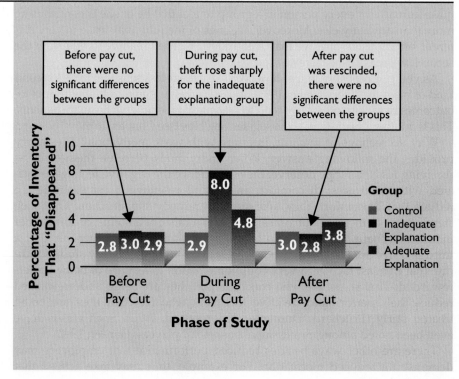

FIGURE 17.3

Employee Theft: One Reaction to Feelings of Inequity

Theft of company property increased among employees who received a pay cut without a clear explanation of why it was necessary. In contrast, theft increased to a much lesser degree among employees who were given an identical pay cut but who received a clear explanation why. (Source: Based on data from Greenberg, 1990.)

KEY CONCEPT

Theories of Work Motivation

Need Theory

Individuals will work hard only if their basic (deficiency) needs are met—for example, physiological needs, needs for money.

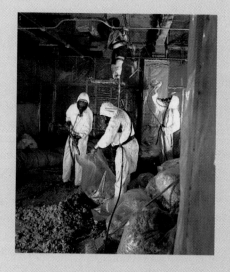

The removal of harmful substances such as asbestos from homes, schools, and factories contributes to satisfaction of our safety needs.

Goal-Setting Theory

Individuals will work hard when they:
• Accept challenging goals
• Compare their present performance with these goals
• Believe that they can perform at the level required to reach these goals.

Expectancy Theory

Individuals will work hard only to the extent that:
• They believe effort will improve performance.
• They believe good performance will be rewarded.
• They value the reward offered.

When individuals work toward concrete goals and are rewarded for them, their performance—and achievement—is often improved.

Equity Theory

Individuals will work hard only to the extent that they believe they are being treated fairly.

When individuals believe that they have been treated unfairly, they may take actions designed to correct this situation—to restore fairness.

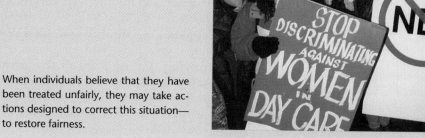

Cafeteria-Style Benefit Plans: *Pay plans that permit employees to choose the specific fringe benefits they prefer.*

Job Design: *Efforts to make jobs more motivating to the persons who hold them by making them more interesting and appealing.*

Job Enlargement: *Adding more varied tasks, at the same level of responsibility or skill, to a given job.*

Job Enrichment: *Expanding a given job to include additional tasks at higher levels of skill or responsibility.*

KEY POINTS

- Industrial/organizational psychology studies all aspects of behavior in work settings and the nature of the work settings themselves.
- Work motivation plays an important role in the performance of many work-related tasks. Expectancy theory suggests that people will expend effort on various tasks only to the extent that they expect such effort to improve performance, believe that good performance will be rewarded, and desire the rewards offered.
- Goal setting—the process of establishing clear goals for various tasks—often greatly increases performance. Goal-setting theory proposes that the beneficial effects of goal setting stem from several factors, including comparisons between present performance and the goal, feelings of self-efficacy, clarification of expected performance, and improved strategies for task performance.
- Equity theory suggests that people compare the ratio of their own inputs and outcomes to the ratio of inputs and outcomes for other people comparable to themselves.
- If these ratios are unequal, feelings of inequity may arise.
- In addition to formulating theories of work motivation, I/O psychologists have focused on devising techniques for enhancing such motivation. Such procedures include job design, including job enlargement and job enrichment.

companies have found that **cafeteria-style benefit plans** are very effective. In these plans, employees choose the rewards they receive for good performance, such as more vacation time. These plans maximize valence—an important component of expectancy theory (e.g., Stern & Stewart, 1993).

Other changes in work motivation have different origins. I/O researchers are now looking at **job design**—how jobs can be changed so that the work is more interesting and appealing (Griffin & McMahan, in press; Johns, et al., 1992).

There are many ways to redesign jobs, but the two that have received the most attention are job enlargement and job enrichment (Swanson, 1987; Ondrack & Evans, 1987, 1986). **Job enlargement** involves expanding a job's scope to include a larger variety of *different tasks requiring the same level of skill*. For instance, consider people working at a greeting card company, repeatedly designing birthday cards day after day. Their jobs might be enlarged to include designing cards for other occasions, and humorous coffee mugs as well. This would increase their motivation at work and therefore their productivity.

Recent studies indicate that job enlargement does increase motivation, at least temporarily (Campion & McClelland, 1991). Once employees get used to their enlarged jobs, though, improvements may decrease, so job enlargement is not a one-step process; it may be necessary to redesign jobs periodically and regularly to maintain motivation levels. Based on these findings, what advice would I/O psychology have for professors required to teach the same courses year after year?

In contrast, **job enrichment** gives employees not only more tasks, but tasks that demand *greater skill and responsibility*. It also offers employees greater control over how they do their work. For example, in many manufacturing plants now, teams of workers decide among themselves how they will do various tasks; they are no longer simply told how by a supervisor.

Job design, then, is a useful means for enhancing work motivation. There is no guarantee of universal success. That being said, we live at a time of rising international competition; there is a strong need to maximize work motivation; and the innovations being suggested by I/O psychologists are of key relevance. For a discussion of one highly controversial technique for increasing productivity, see **The Point of It All**.

One final point: Throughout this discussion we have focused on ways of increasing motivation. The underlying assumption is that increments in motivation will lead to improvements in performance. Most often that is true. But it is important to recognize that there is no hard-and-fast relationship between motivation and performance; rather, motivation is only one of many factors involved. Thus, even when motivation increases, performance may not, because of the impact of other variables. For example, increased motivation will not lead to improved performance if the employees lack necessary skills. If you've ever tried to use a new computer program without the manual—or even with the manual—then you have had firsthand experience with this. Alternatively, if people are already performing at very high levels, increased motivation may fail to better performance any further, because there is no room left for improvement. So remember: Increased motivation is an important contributor to improved performance but by no means a guarantee.

THE POINT OF IT ALL

Computers at Work

Fifteen years ago, the idea that millions of people would be working at desktop computers was farfetched, to say the least. In the 1990s, however, it is reality. There are hundreds of thousands of personal computers and workstations across Canada, and that number is increasing rapidly. A survey in 1991 found that 88 percent of office workers in Canada used a PC or a computer terminal in their work. But that is not all: Computers now operate traffic lights, assembly lines, automated teller machines, and medical equipment. Moreover, they check the T-4s and T-4As you submit with your income tax return, and they decide who gets audited by Revenue Canada.

The psychological impact of this technology in the workplace and at home has been powerful. As in all things, there is an upside and a downside. On the upside: A study of 253 employees at 112 Canadian companies was done by Richard Long of the University of Saskatchewan (Long, 1993). He found important increases in job quality (variety, autonomy, motivation), particularly for female clerical and secretarial employees; for these workers, the new technology offered a dramatic change. Also, more and more people are working at home (Gurstein, 1991). In some cases a corporation will establish an office at home—for an employee who has a new baby, for example. On the downside: The use of computers is producing special kinds of stress, not only on the minds of those who use them but also on their bodies.

Computers are powerful tools (Matheson, 1993), and that is how they have primarily been used. One source of stress, low performance, and greater cost has been lack of training for the new technology. Until recently, it was common for undertrained employees to waste time trying to help each other—often, when no one really knew what to do. More recently, many computer hardware and software companies have established free user support by telephone, fax, or e-mail.

Computer-Based Work Monitoring: Big Brother Is On-Line

Because many jobs involve constant use of computers—for data entry and retrieval, inventory control, customer service, and so on—some companies are now using computers to track employee performance electronically. Proponents of this contend that it enhances motivation and thereby boosts performance. The information about performance levels from moment to moment provides immediate and accurate feedback to employees—something that both expectancy theory and goal-setting theory view as a major benefit. Moreover, it discourages employees from slacking off. Critics of computer-based monitoring contend that it is an invasion of privacy, induces high levels of stress among employees, and results in dissatisfaction, low morale, and poor teamwork (Aiello, 1993). Would you take time to help a fellow employee if you knew that the time you spent away from your own keyboard would be recorded, to the hundredth of a second, for your boss to see? While this argument continues, many companies have adopted **computer-based work monitoring**.

By 1990, more than 10 million workers in the United States were being monitored in this way (Halpern, 1992). Do such procedures work? Psychologists have only just begun to study this question, and the results to date have been mixed. Some studies have reported improvements in performance (Nebeker & Tatum, 1993); others have reported increased stress and anxiety and corresponding reductions in performance (Aiello & Svec, 1993). At Bell Canada in Montreal, DiTecco and colleagues (1992) found work-

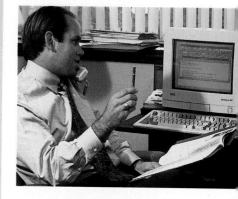

COMPUTER-BASED WORK MONITORING: AN EFFECTIVE WAY TO ADVANCE PERFORMANCE

A growing number of companies have adopted computer-based monitoring of their employees' work. Existing evidence suggests that this technique may improve performance on simple tasks but interferes with performance on more complex tasks.

Computer-Based Work Monitoring: Use of computers to monitor the performance of employees.

related stress in one of every two telephone operators—stress arising from computer monitoring, telephone surveillance, and the pressure to keep call-time to a minimum while serving the customer well.

Here is another thought: Computer monitoring of performance has effects similar to the presence of other people—effects described in psychology by the term **social facilitation** (e.g., Geen, 1989). Research indicates that the presence of others improves performance on simple or well-learned tasks, such as entering simple information through a keyboard (Nebeker & Tatum, 1993) or coding single digits (Griffith, 1993); but impairs performance on tasks still being learned, and on complex tasks such as solving anagrams (unscrambling scrambled words). These are the findings obtained in many studies concerned with the effects of computer monitoring at work (Aiello & Svec, 1993).

However, even if work monitoring improves performance, it is not clear that increased work motivation is the actual reason. It may have more to do with increased anxiety and activation. In short, the jury—both legal and scientific—is still out where these procedures are concerned. In the long run the indirect costs may well outweigh the benefits.

Performance Appraisal: *Tying Rewards to Performance*

Years ago, New York City had a mayor whose favorite question to reporters was, "How am I doing?" He was not alone in wanting feedback on his performance. We all want to know how we're doing. This is perfectly natural, because knowing how we are doing helps us do better. The **performance appraisals** we are provided vary according to our work. For students they mean comments on papers, or grade-point averages; for profs they mean student comments, or course evaluations; for ballplayers they mean RBIs or three-pointers; for musicians like k.d. lang or Roch Voisine, they mean the number of platinum albums. Across Canada, and indeed across the world, in fast food outlets and fancy restaurants, in hotel rooms and auto repair shops, in university and college libraries and in registrars' offices, we find cards that ask, "Tell us how we are doing."

Feedback may take a variety of forms—for example, the appraisals we get from other people as individuals and collectively, and the appraisals we give ourselves. O'Connor and Dyce (1993) of Lakehead University studied appraisals of musical ability of forty bar bands across Canada and the United States. They asked the musicians themselves, other musicians, and other people to rate both ability and performance and found that self-appraisals and actual appraisals were related, although there were differences due to faulty communication and cognitive distortion among the musicians.

In other workplaces, feedback is often provided by means of formal appraisals: annual or semi-annual performance ratings that incorporate reasons for the ratings (Balzer & Sulsky, 1990; DeNisi, Cafferty, & Meglino, 1984). As you might imagine, evaluating employees is a difficult and tricky process, because—as you already know—the way we think about other people is complex. Moreover, because we tend to take cognitive shortcuts (Dumont, 1993, 1987) and to expend the least amount of cognitive effort, we often make errors when we draw conclusions about other people and about the reasons for their actions (e.g., Ditto & Lopez, 1992; Macrae, 1992). Clearly, we want to avoid

Social Facilitation: Effects on behavior stemming from the mere presence of others.

Performance Appraisal: Annual or semi-annual evaluations of employees' performance coupled with feedback about the ratings they have received.

errors in evaluating job performance, since so much—raises in pay, promotions in rank, and ultimately career progress—depends on the process.

PERFORMANCE APPRAISALS: POTENTIAL SOURCES OF ERROR Suppose that you are called upon to evaluate the performance of several people who work under your direction. How would you proceed? What would you consider? And how would you combine that information into an overall evaluation? Further, how would you then compare the work of the different individuals in question? As you can readily see, this is a complex process (although it may not seem so when you are asked to evaluate a teacher or coach). However, from what you learned about how people remember and why they forget (in Chapter 6) and about social judgments (in Chapter 16), you already know that there are many potential sources of error and distortion in evaluating people. Let's consider several of those now.

ERRORS IN ATTRIBUTION Suppose now that you are faced with the task of evaluating two people who work under your supervision. Thinking back over the past year, you conclude that both have shown average performance. However, you also know that employee A is highly talented and has a lot of experience; he has "coasted" at an average level of performance. In contrast, employee B is quite low in natural ability and has little experience; he has had to work very hard to achieve average performance.

Would you assign equal ratings to these two people? More likely, you would assign a higher rating to the person who was lacking in talent but trying very hard. This is because when we evaluate others, we consider also the explanations for the performance. Research suggests that we often award high motivation and extra effort a better rating than natural talent or past experience (Mitchell, Green, & Wood, 1982). Therefore, the way we attribute causes to work performance is a potential source of error. This may cause us to evaluate two people with identical levels of performance quite differently.

HALO EFFECTS: WHEN OVERALL IMPRESSIONS SHAPE SPECIFIC JUDGMENTS Once we have formed a general impression of another person, that impression has important consequences for our future judgments about them. These are **halo effects** and they may be either positive or negative. If an impression is favorable, we tend to see everything else about the person in a positive light—a kind of golden halo. If our impression is unfavorable, we tend to perceive all of their actions negatively—a kind of rusty horns effect (Feldman, 1986; Nathan & Lord, 1983). Statistically, halo effects can be seen in inflated correlations between various scales of a performance appraisal.

Halo Effects: The tendency to evaluate all traits of aspects of performance by another person in a manner consistent with our overall impression of this person.

FRANK and ERNEST   By Bob Thaves

ANY AWARDS OR HONORS FROM ANYBODY OTHER THAN YOUR MOM?

THAVES 9-4

A HALO EFFECT IN OPERATION
(Source: FRANK & ERNEST reprinted by permission of NEA, Inc.)

Many studies have found that halo effects reduce the accuracy of performance appraisals (e.g., Binning et al., 1988; Nathan & Tippins, 1990). However, some experts believe that mechanical halo effects are not as common as has often been assumed. They note that supervisors sometimes intentionally rate a particular employee high (or low) on all measures when they wish to recommend promotion—or dismissal—because doing so will make a strong case for the change they plan to recommend (Murphy, Jako, & Anhalt, 1993, p. 222). In these circumstances, it is not the halo effect that is at work, although it may seem so.

LENIENCY ERRORS: INFLATED RATINGS OF OTHERS   Have you ever heard the expression "grade inflation"? It refers to the finding that at many colleges and universities in recent decades, the overall grade-point average of students has risen considerably. Is this because current students are smarter or study harder? Probably not. Rather, professors have increased the number of As and Bs they give. The reasons why are complex, but in recent years, it has become more and more common for students to "discuss" their grades with faculty members; also, there are now procedures (both formal and informal) to appeal a grade.

Leniency effects are at work when people who evaluate performance inflate the ratings they give. In these circumstances almost everybody gets high ratings, no matter which measure of performance is used, and it is impossible to differentiate between employees with respect to raises, promotions, and other benefits.

Why does the systematic inflation of performance appraisals occur? Partly that is because, in the process of providing people with feedback, supervisors must disclose their evaluations to the people they rate. This is a difficult thing to do when there are faults; as a result, ratings are sometimes inflated in order to avoid the unpleasantness of a confrontation (Banks & Murphy, 1985; Murphy & Cleveland, 1991). Also, because managers must share their evaluation with the employee, they may remember good performance preferentially. In other words, people focus on information that will make their task easier, since this allows them to assign favorable evaluations (Hauenstein, 1992) and avoid discomfort. No matter why they occur, leniency effects reduce the accuracy of performance ratings.

Are people lenient when they evaluate themselves? That was one question asked by Nhundo (1992) in a study of the Edmonton public school system. This researcher compared the self-ratings of teaching interns with the appraisals done by their teaching supervisors. Nhundo found that, when appraising themselves, the teaching interns were *less* lenient than the supervisors!

STEREOTYPES   How do stereotypes, another source of error in social cognition, affect performance appraisals? In Chapter 16 you learned that when we create stereotypes, we organize our knowledge and beliefs around specific social groups, with our conclusion being that, generally, all members of these groups possess certain traits (Judd, Ryan, & Park, 1991). Stereotypes greatly affect how we process social information; for example, we process information that is relevant to a particular stereotype more quickly than information that is irrelevant to it (Dovidio, Evans, & Tyler, 1986). Similarly, stereotypes cause us to pay attention to specific types of information—usually information that is consistent. Stereotypes also determine what we remember—usually, information that is consistent with these stereotypes as well.

Stereotypes exist for many minority and religious groups, and even for occupations or professions. Moreover, stereotypic thinking may be responsible for lower performance appraisals of members of particular groups (e.g., Gilbert & Hixon, 1991). For example, at some engineering and polytechnical schools, there is a negative stereotype for *psychology prof.*: "a faculty member

Leniency Effects: Tendencies to assign higher ratings to persons being evaluated than they actually deserve.

who is unfamiliar with science and mathematics, muddled in thinking, and somewhat flaky." Of course, in other places, quite the opposite may be true; there, a psychologist may be "a faculty member who is familiar with science and mathematics, clear in thinking, and perhaps somewhat not flaky."

Other stereotypes with important implications for performance appraisals center on age and gender. How do we think about younger and older people at work? To check that out, Gibson and his associates at the Center for Studies of Aging at the University of Toronto gave Canadian employers twenty-one work-related attributes and asked them to rate younger and older workers. The results showed that younger workers were expected to have greater potential for future development; however, older workers were rated higher with respect to initiative and stability. Another analysis revealed an interesting qualification that will not surprise you, given what you learned in Chapter 16: Younger employers thought better of younger employees, and older employers thought better of older employees. The effects of gender-based stereotypes are considered in detail in **Perspectives on Diversity**.

In short, many different factors contribute to the errors we make in appraising the performance of employees. Many of those errors are characteristic of the way people think generally about each other—that is, characteristic of social thought in general. In fact, research on performance appraisals has drawn heavily on our fundamental scientific knowledge about social cognition. Moreover, efforts to improve the accuracy and fairness of performance appraisals have called upon important links within psychology between basic research and its application to important practical problems.

PERSPECTIVES ON DIVERSITY

Negative Effects of Gender Stereotypes: Why Men Often Get the Job

Human beings use social stereotypes to think about other people at work. One consequence has been that, past and present, women have been subject to the prejudice and discrimination that arises from gender stereotypes—in hiring, pay, promotion, training, and treatment (Lips & Colwill, 1988). Men, too, are perceived as being "all alike" in certain respects—for example, many people believe that men who sell used cars are all pushy and dishonest. By and large, however, in many cultures, males are assumed to possess such desirable traits as decisiveness, forcefulness, confidence, ambition, and rationality. In contrast, females are assumed to possess less desirable traits such as passivity, submissiveness, indecisiveness, emotionality, and dependence. Of course, stereotypes for females include positive traits as well, such as kindness, sensitivity, nurturance, gentleness, warmth, and kindness (e.g., Cota et al., 1991; Aube & Koestner, 1992). However, women's abilities to foster cooperation are undervalued or unrecognized, according to Ferguson-Pare (1993). As a result, there are inequities—for example, in the federal government in 1991, women constituted 44 percent of all employees but only 8 percent of upper management.

Psychologists have investigated stereotypic thinking about males and females at work. For example, at the University College of Cape Breton, Joanne Gallivan (1991) gave students sample essays to read. The same essays had either a man's or a woman's name as author. She found that "males were rated as less biased and more knowledgeable than females, but not as having better writing skills." Here we have the same student work being judged differently, depending on whether the author was thought to be a man or a woman. In some studies, subjects are asked to imagine that they are guidance teachers. They then rate the suitability of men and women who are said to be job candidates. Certain kinds of occupations continue to be perceived as "men's work"—for example, research careers in science, engineering, and technology (Stark-Adamec & Pullin, 1995). Furthermore, women continue to be reluctant to enter those occupations—perhaps, as Kimball (1985) concludes, because they do not feel they will be able to live up to expectations, given their intent to have families as well. Finding time to do everything is an occupational barrier for women in these predominantly male occupations (Stark-Adamec et al., 1993, 1994).

The female stereotype affects the status assigned to employees (Heilman, Martell, & Simon, 1988). Consider the traits most people consider necessary for career success at a high level—leadership and authority. These traits demand people who are bold, tough, decisive, and even aggressive. Clearly, these are positive traits of the gender stereotype for males. The result: Females are often perceived as less suited for positions of leadership and authority, even though, as we saw in Chapter 11, they do just as well in them (Heilman Martell, & Simon, 1988). The result is less favorable evaluations for women in high-level positions, slower promotion, and lower pay (Stroh, Brett, & Reilly, 1992).

As always, once a stereotype has been established, it matters little whether it has any basis in reality. As a specific example, consider this question. In a social conversation or in a planning session at work, who would you expect to interrupt more, John or Jane? Included in our thinking about males and females, in the workplace and elsewhere, is the notion that males interrupt females more often than vice versa. Several studies have in fact found that women are interrupted more—by men. Indeed, some argue that males use this kind of behavior to achieve dominance, power, and control, both in the workplace and in social situations. Recently, however, Tammy Marche and Carol Peterson, working with elementary, high school, and university students in St. John's, obtained a different result. They studied same-sex and mixed-sex pairs in conversation and observed the interruptions that occurred. They found that males and females "butted in" equally often regardless of the pairing. Moreover, this was true generally as development proceeded from grade four to university age. The conclusion reached was that "wholesale acceptance of sex differences in interruption behavior ... is not warranted ... [Only] when we know why an individual interrupts, will we be able to say [which] interpretation is appropriate."

More research is needed to establish who interrupts whom more often and when. Whatever the answer turns out to be, work-related stereotypes, particularly those about how well-suited women are for senior positions—whether correct or not—are holding women back.

Clear evidence of the negative influence of gender stereotypes was provided in a Dutch study that examined the decisions of employment boards (Van Vianen & Willemsen, 1992). The board members—some of whom were female, some male—interviewed applicants for high-level scientific and technical jobs at a university. The board members completed two questionnaires. On one they rated the attributes of ideal candidates for these jobs; on the other they rated the qualities of each job applicant as they saw them. Traits on both questionnaires were taken from the gender stereotypes. For example, positive traits taken from the masculine gender stereotype included daring, forceful, logical, and confident; negative traits included arrogant, dominating, and reckless. Positive traits of the feminine gender stereotype were understanding, sociable, spontaneous, warm, and gentle; negative traits included dependent, dreamy, changeable, and affected.

The results supported the view that gender stereotypes influence both ideas about ideal job candidates and the evaluation of the actual candidates. First, the ideal candidates as judged by the board members had mainly traits of the male gender stereotype. The traits judged necessary for high-level career success were primarily those usually attributed to males. Second, the actual candidates that were recommended for hiring possessed masculine attributes to a greater extent than the candidates that were rejected. Third, as shown in Figure 17.4, the women who were hired were much closer to the description of the ideal candidate—and hence closer to the masculine stereotype—than the women who were rejected.

The impact of the female gender stereotype may be diminished by clear evidence of a woman's ability or competence (Heilman, Martell, & Simon, 1988).

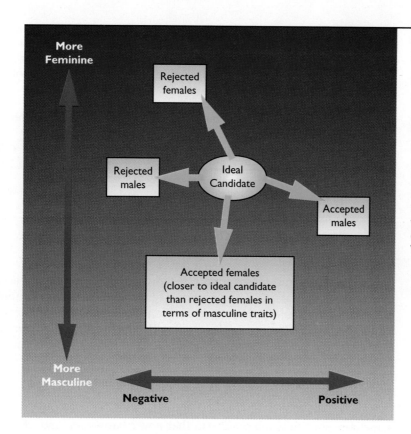

FIGURE 17.4

One Way in Which Gender Stereotypes Affect Employment Opportunities

Female applicants who were selected for a job were perceived as possessing more traits typically associated with males relative to female applicants who were rejected.
(Source: Based on data from Van Vianen & Willemsen, 1992.)

Even so, the Dutch findings, and other studies, indicate that gender stereotypes have the potential to harm the career prospects of working women.

A number of efforts have been made to counteract gender bias during hiring. Tougas and colleagues (1989) worked with female students at the University of Ottawa. They provided information about the negative effects of stereotypes; they also held discussions on the use of personal appearance as a criterion for hiring women, on sexual discrimination, and on various other topics.

A different approach was taken by Kunda and Sherwin-Williams (1993). They were interested in how stereotypic thinking is contradicted by *individuating information*—that is, by information that sets people apart as individuals. They found that a "construction worker" was rated as more aggressive than a "housewife" when subjects relied only on the stereotype—that is, when they were told simply that the person (construction worker or housewife) had gotten annoyed and hit somebody. However, there was no difference between these two "actors" when details about the individual events were given, as in "the housewife [or construction worker] hit someone who was taunting [them] about [their] marriage and … [they] decked the neighbour." The researchers' interpretation was that stereotypes are most powerful when the information available is vague and ambiguous. That suggests that, to counteract a stereotype, as much individuating information as possible should be included—for example, in a résumé.

Yet another approach involves affirmative action programs. These have been implemented in various work settings (Tougas & Beaton, 1993; Tougas & Veilleux, 1988), and they open the competition for jobs widely. If there is a tie between two job candidates, and both are equally qualified, preference is given to a member of a group that is underrepresented among employees. The goal of Ontario's employment equity legislation is to increase employers' recognition of the talents of designated groups—women, native people, visible minorities, people with disabilities—who have been disadvantaged with respect to employment.

Equitable treatment in gaining employment is the goal of affirmative action programs. The principle involved is that, when job candidates are judged, the biases that occur need to be deliberately contradicted. Otherwise, people of equal merit but different genders, backgrounds, ages, and abilities that are unrelated to the job will not have equal access to employment. A problem here is that knowledge that an affirmative action program is in effect makes people discount the qualifications of the people selected—for example, for management positions. At St. Mary's University, students rated the qualifications of a woman in management higher when they thought she worked for a company that was against affirmative action (Summers, 1991).

Performance Appraisals: *Techniques for Reducing Errors*

Given the errors and biases involved, how can we improve the accuracy of performance appraisals? I/O psychologists have paid much attention to this important question. The basic conclusion is optimistic: The accuracy of performance appraisals can be increased, with much preparation and considerable effort. Several steps, taken together, may increase the accuracy of the ratings assigned to workers.

THE IMPORTANCE OF KEEPING ACCURATE RECORDS   As explained in Chapter 6, memory is uncertain. Sometimes we forget information we want to remember; sometimes we "remember" events that never happened; and often information entered into memory is distorted. For example, in their study of memory over a twenty-four hour delay, Jacoby and his colleagues (1989) demonstrated that they could make a person "famous overnight" by increasing the familiarity of a name that was originally unknown. Clearly, it is important for people who evaluate work performance to keep accurate records, or "diary notes." In these notes should be included information about performance that is either better or worse than average (Balzer & Sulsky, 1990). These records should be consulted when annual or semiannual ratings are made.

Complete and accurate diary notes are valuable for three reasons. First, they counteract the selectivity of human memory—for example, the probability that important information will be omitted. Second, they provide a basis for explaining to people why they received the evaluation they did. When there are specific instances of better and worse work, the reasons for the ratings are more apparent, as are the ways in which improvements may be made. Finally, diary notes provide a written record that can be introduced into legal proceedings by the employee or the employer if a complaint is lodged. Remember, however, that the main purpose of notes is to provide a record that can be used to settle any differences in recollection.

RATING FORMATS: HOW RATINGS ARE ACTUALLY DONE   Have you ever received a formal performance appraisal? If so, you know there are forms for recording ratings and making appropriate comments. Some I/O psychologists conclude that the raters are the reason for evaluation errors (Landy & Farr, 1983; DeNisi et al., 1984). However, recent research suggests that some rating scales may be less accurate than others (Hartel, 1993; Steiner, Rain, & Smalley, 1993). Training may reduce the errors made on some rating scales (Sulsky & Day, 1992).

Here are two types of rating scales that have received much attention in I/O psychology. The first of these—the **behaviorally anchored rating scale**, or BARS (Landy & Farr, 1983)—is based on the idea that, unless there is a clear definition of excellent, good, average, poor, or unacceptable performance, each

Behaviorally Anchored Rating Scales: Performance appraisal scales that provide raters with behavioral examples of various levels of performance (excellent, good, average, and so on).

rater will have a different idea of what these mean and for that reason use the various anchor points quite differently. The result is that people who objectively perform to the same standard may receive quite different ratings.

The BARS was designed to prevent such problems. Here is how they are constructed: First, people familiar with a particular job generate ten to twenty measures of performance. For example, the job of university professor might include teaching large classes, teaching small classes, teaching graduate or undergraduate students, research, counseling students, service on university committees, service on rational committees, service to the university, service to the community, and five or ten more. Next, other people give examples of excellent, good, average, poor, and unacceptable performance for each measure. An example of excellent teaching might be this: 90 percent or better class attendance by students. Poor performance might be this: 70 percent of the class falls asleep during most lectures. An example of excellent research performance might be this: Produces two or more research reports in scientific journals each year. An example of unacceptable behavior might be this: Has never produced any scientific reports and plans never to publish any.

Then these examples are reviewed by still another group of people who are familiar with the job, to establish that these examples are appropriate (to teaching, research, and so on) and that they illustrate different levels of performance (excellent, good, and so on). The result is a rating scale consisting of measures of the job in question—with examples. After an assessment is done, the scale's ability to accurately evaluate performance may be tested statistically (Hakstian et al., 1991). A BARS scale is presented in Table 17.1.

Although it is not entirely clear that the BARS format improves accuracy for all raters (Hartel, 1993), it is certainly an improvement over informal ratings, which are generally unreliable.

The second rating scale provides **distributional ratings of performance** (Jako & Murphy, 1990). This approach takes into account that job performance is better at some times than at others. Raters are asked to indicate the percentage of time the employee's performance is excellent, good, average, poor, and

Distributional Ratings of Performance: Performance appraisal scales that ask raters to indicate what proportion of the time the performance of the persons being evaluated falls into various categories—excellent, good, and so on.

DIMENSION OF JOB PERFORMANCE	EXAMPLES OF BEHAVIOR
Teaching	*Excellent*: Students in the professor's classes score higher than average on department-wide final examination.
	Average: Students in the professor's classes score average on department-wide final examination.
	Poor: Students in the professor's classes score lower than average on department-wide final examination.
Couseling students	*Excellent*: All students counseled by this professor request that the professor continue as their counselor.
	Average: Most students counseled by this professor request that the professor continue as their counselor.
	Poor: All students counseled by this professor request a different counselor.
Service to department	*Excellent*: Serves on two or more important committees; comes to all meetings; contributes actively.
	Average: Serves on one committee; comes to most meetings; contributes.
	Poor: Serves on one committee; rarely comes to meetings; never participates.

TABLE 17.1

Behaviorally Anchored Rating Scales

On a behaviorally anchored rating scale (BARS), raters receive examples on various levels of performance for each job dimension on which they evaluate others. These examples help ensure that all raters have a clear idea of precisely what kinds of actions constitute excellent, good, average, and poor performance.

- Performance appraisals are assessments of employees' performance, coupled with feedback about these ratings. They are subject to many potential forms of bias, such as attributional errors, halo effects, leniency and stereotypes.
- Although many errors in performance appraisal stem from the cognitive limitations of raters, others may involve the nature of the rating forms used.
- Two techniques for reducing such errors are behaviorally anchored rating scales and distributional ratings of performance.

so on. The ratings obtained in this way provide an average or overall evaluation of performance along with some estimate of the person's variability in performance. This is an important consideration, because for many jobs low variability (i.e., high reliability) is very important. For example, most people would object strongly to a dentist whose performance varied widely, so that during some visits she filled cavities perfectly and painlessly, while during others she filled the wrong teeth. To date, there has been little research on distributional rating scales, but present evidence suggests that they may be quite effective (Steiner, Rain, & Smalley, 1993).

Performance appraisal is a complex process and subject to many potential errors. However, by finding sources of possible bias, recognizing them, and showing people how to reduce them, we can increase the accuracy and fairness of job evaluations. This represents a major contribution by I/O psychologists to the welfare of employers and employees.

Work-Related Attitudes: The Prevalence, Causes, and Effects of Job Satisfaction

In Chapter 16 you learned that attitudes are evaluations of various aspects of the social or physical world (Judd et al., 1991). Work plays an important role in most lives, so it is only natural that people have many work-related attitudes—for example, toward their job (Fisher & Locke, 1992), their company (Allen & Meyer, 1993; Gutek & Winter, 1992), their co-workers and subordinates, and their boss. Attitudes to work have long been studied by I/O psychologists. Many consider that the most important of these attitudes involves **job satisfaction**.

Job satisfaction has important social and economic implications and for that reason has been studied in a wide variety of populations: male and female physicians (Burke, 1993; Richardsen & Burke, 1993); women in management (Burke & McKeen, 1993); managers and supervisors at many levels of seniority (e.g., Long, 1993); full-time and part-time employees (Levanoni & Sales, 1990); and so on. It has also been studied by personality type (Greenglass & Burke, 1991),

THE PREVALENCE OF JOB SATISFACTION: DO PEOPLE LIKE THEIR WORK? The results of large-scale surveys conducted in several countries over many years point to a fairly encouraging conclusion: Most people are quite satisfied with their employment situation (Page & Wiseman, 1993). In 1991, Statistics Canada reported that more than eight out of ten working Canadians were at least somewhat satisfied with the work they did. The picture is more complex than that, however; people are not equally satisfied with all aspects of their jobs. They may report a high level of satisfaction overall, but closer examination indicates that they are more satisfied with some aspects than others. For example, they may be satisfied with their pay but less happy about their working conditions or their relations with co-workers. Also, some groups of people enjoy higher job satisfaction than others. Who are these people? Here are some key findings:

- White-collar personnel (managers, technical and professional employees) tend to be more satisfied than blue-collar employees.
- Older people with more job seniority tend to be more satisfied than younger, less experienced workers (Eichar, Noland, Brady, & Fortinsky, 1991).

Job Satisfaction: Individuals' positive or negative attitudes toward their jobs.

- Men and members of majority groups tend to be more satisfied than women and members of minority groups (Lambert, 1991).
- Some individuals are relatively satisfied with their job, whatever that may be; others tend to be dissatisfied no matter what job they hold (Staw & Ross, 1985).
- Job satisfaction seems to be a relatively stable tendency or disposition. People carry it with them from one job to another (Staw & Ross, 1985; Gutek & Winter, 1992). These individual differences play a role in job satisfaction for many people.

A recent—and controversial—suggestion is that genetic factors may be at work here. Arvey and his colleagues (1989) assessed the current job satisfaction of thirty-four pairs of identical twins who had been separated at an early age and then raised apart. Such pairs were identical in genetic makeup but had different life experiences; a correlation between the twins' current levels of job satisfaction was taken as support for the conclusion that genetic factors play a role in job satisfaction. The twins were in fact quite similar on job satisfaction. The conclusions, however, have been questioned by other researchers, who note that although the twins in the study were raised apart, they actually grew up in similar homes; thus, any overlap in job satisfaction could stem from environmental rather than genetic factors (Cropanzano & James, 1990). Furthermore, other studies designed to examine the possible effects of genetic factors on job satisfaction have yielded negative results (e.g., Hershberger, Lichtenstein, & Knox, 1994).

In short, then, attitudes about work are stable differences among individuals. Those differences may or may not have a genetic link.

CAUSES OF JOB SATISFACTION Are there specific aspects of work that influence job satisfaction? Informal experience suggests that there certainly are: Why else would some people express very positive views about their work and choose to remain in one job for decades, while others express dissatisfaction and find other work as soon as possible? Various reasons for job satisfaction have been identified. Generally, they fall into two major groups: those relating to jobs and where they are done, and those relating to employees' personal characteristics.

WORK-RELATED DETERMINANTS OF JOB SATISFACTION Job satisfaction depends on the reward system in place within an organization. It is high when individuals believe that the system is fair and operates equitably; it is low when they believe it is unfair and that there is favoritism (Miceli & Lane, 1991). Another important factor is the extent to which employees believe their supervisors are competent, have their best interests at heart, and treat them with respect and consideration. Related to that point, the more opportunity individuals have to communicate with their supervisors, the higher their job satisfaction tends to be (Callan, 1993). A third important factor is the extent to which individuals feel that they participate in the decisions that affect them (Locke & Schweiger, 1979). Fourth, the level of stimulation provided by the job is important. People report the highest satisfaction in jobs that provide them with a good level of variety—that is, neither so low as to be boring nor so high as to be overwhelming (Wright, 1990). Fifth, job satisfaction varies with the industrial relations that are present at work. Conflict—between employees who are peers, between managers and workers, between company and union—is quite common. When employees are at odds with one another, job satisfaction suffers (Kelloway et al., 1993). As Roger Fisher (1994) of the University of Saskatchewan has written: "Poorly managed intergroup conflict is the world's most costly ... social issue. At low intensity, it is expressed through prejudice, discrimination and oppression, which perpetuate inequality and injustice, sap the resources and underutilize the diversity of human systems."

What can people do to resolve the differences between them? In his book about the social psychology of conflict resolution (1990), Fisher proposes five steps for settling disputes through negotiation: These include a first stage in which the conflict is analyzed as to its origins and its recent history, a second stage in which the conflict is confronted by the opposing parties together, and a third stage in which the issues are resolved through cooperative problem solving. Fisher applies these principles to race relations, but they are equally applicable to conflict in the workplace.

Finally, higher levels of job satisfaction are reported when the work setting is pleasant. Many aspects of the physical environment are included in this: comfortable temperature, adequate lighting, absence of noise, fresh rather than stale air, and adequate space and privacy (Sundstrom & Sundstrom, 1986). We'll return to this issue in our later discussion of ergonomics at work.

PEOPLE-RELATED DETERMINANTS OF JOB SATISFACTION Several aspects of personality have been linked to job satisfaction. For example, individuals who are high in self-esteem and those who are Type A (see Chapter 13) report higher job satisfaction than those who are low in self-esteem and those who are Type B. Also important is the extent to which people see their jobs as consistent with their own interests. The closer this person–job fit, the higher the job satisfaction (Fricko & Beehr, 1992; Burke & Deszka, 1992).

One way of measuring "job fit"—and of helping people choose jobs that are consistent with their interests—was developed by Holland (1973). His tool, sometimes known as the Holland Scales, categorizes people according to the activities they most enjoy—for example, interacting with others (social), or solving problems (investigative)—and categorizes occupational environments on these same kinds of dimensions. Holland contends that people are happiest and most productive when there is a good fit between their interests and the requirements of their work. This idea has been confirmed by research (e.g., Feldman & Arnold, 1985). The six personality types in Holland's theory are shown in Table 17.2.

JOB SATISFACTION AND EMPLOYEE WITHDRAWAL Attitudes often guide our actions; thus, job satisfaction influences work-related behavior. The relationship here is complex, and perhaps more subtle than you might expect. Here we will consider the impact of job satisfaction on two important kinds of work-related behavior: employee withdrawal and task performance.

When people are dissatisfied with their jobs, they find ways to withdraw. Two types of employee withdrawal are absenteeism (i.e., missing work), and voluntary withdrawal (i.e., quitting).

Absenteeism is a major cost to the economy of North America. According to Johns (1987) the direct cost to business may be as high as $30 billion a year—and that was in the mid-1980s. The less job satisfaction, the more absenteeism

PERSON–JOB FIT: AN IMPORTANT DETERMINANT OF JOB SATISFACTION

Research findings indicate that the closer the match between people's jobs and their interests—one aspect of *person–job fit*—the greater their job satisfaction. (Source: © 1990 by King Features Syndicate, Inc. World rights reserved. Reprinted with special permission of King Features Syndicate.)

PERSONALITY TYPE	MATCHING OCCUPATIONAL ENVIRONMENT	TABLE 17.2
Realistic: Use of tools and machines; physical activity requiring skill, strength, coordination.	Forestry, farming, architecture, police work, carpentry.	
Investigative: Observing, organizing, engineering, understanding data.	Biology, mathematics, geology, dentistry.	
Social: Interpersonal activities; enjoys informing, training, and instructing others.	Clinical psychology, education, foreign service, social work.	
Conventional: Structured, rule regulated; enjoys ordered, systematic activities.	Accounting, finance, bookkeeping, clerical work, military.	
Enterprising: Verbal activities to influence others, to attain power and status. Activity rather than observation.	Management, law, labor relations, sales.	
Artistic: Self-expression, artistic creation, expression of emotions, individual activities. Dislikes repetitive, ordered activities.	Art, music, advertising, interior design.	

Person–Job Fit: The Holland Model

According to a model proposed by Holland (1973), people are most productive and happiest when their interests match the requirements of their work. This table shows careers that offer a good person–job fit for individuals with six contrasting patterns of interests.
(Source: Based on Holland, 1973.)

(Porter & Steers, 1973). That is not necessarily the more days away at a time; it also involves people staying home for a day or two (Johns, 1987).

Why do people miss work? When we consider the absence of a co-worker, we follow the rules of social thinking. We believe that other people stay home from work because they are malingering, or that they are lazy—that is, we give dispositional reasons; we give situational reasons for our own absences. Social comparison also takes place: We estimate how many days other workers miss and adjust our own attendance accordingly. Also, absenteeism may vary from plant to plant in similar departments (e.g., shipping). Johns also suggests that there may be an "absence culture"—that is, social rules that set the standard for a department with respect to absence from work.

However, low job satisfaction alone does not always determine which employees will be absent. For example, people with relatively high job satisfaction may miss work when their car breaks down, or their child is ill, as Haccoun and Desgent (1993) found in their study of hundreds of French-speaking workers in the Greater Montreal area. Furthermore, people who dislike their jobs intensely will still come to work every day, sometimes because they are not paid when they are away. Within small units at production plants, there may be dramatic differences in absenteeism. This may be the result of social pressures to stay away an average amount or to come to work regularly.

Many places of business have on-site fitness programs (Shephard, 1992). These have been found useful in increasing employee job satisfaction. Many firms enter a corporate team in the Vancouver Sun Run, for example, because fitness has been linked to job satisfaction, reduced absenteeism, and higher productivity, and therefore to greater consumer satisfaction. Also, employee assistance programs (EAPs) can help workers cope with stress and other circumstances that lead to absenteeism. Loo and Watts (1993) found that about seven out of ten medium and large Canadian corporations (including Molson and Canada's Wonderland) had such programs and that employees did make use of the information and services they provided. EAPs are often used by employees whose personal difficulties include substance abuse, but legal and marital problems, and specific issues relating to work stress management, may also be included (Wong, 1992). For example, the EAP at the National

Bank of Canada helped employees deal with the psychological aftermath of a bank robbery. At the University of New Brunswick, the introduction of an EAP is credited with increasing employee morale and productivity.

EAPs also provide a number of other services, such as cross-cultural counseling. It is critical that people who work together value and respect the diversity they encounter among their co-workers. According to Pare (1990), in the homes of students at Dawson College in Montreal, thirty-nine different languages are found. Linguistic and cultural differences influence the way we think and the way we behave and are the source of conflicting practices. Given that diversity, it is imperative that cross-cultural counseling be available.

EAP programs also help the bottom line. Warner-Lambert Canada calculated that it had saved $220,000 by investing an initial $36,000 (MacLeod, 1988).

Voluntary turnover is also related to job satisfaction (Tett & Meyer, 1993). This is the case when there are many good jobs available, not when the job market is tight (Carsten & Spector, 1987). Given that qualification, however, there is another factor at work here. Which workers do you think would be more likely to quit their jobs when dissatisfied—those who are satisfied or dissatisfied with their lives generally? Surprisingly, it appears that people who are negatively disposed toward life in general realize that changing jobs won't help—they will still be unhappy. This means that those with negative dispositions; and who are dissatisfied at work, change jobs less often. In contrast, those who are generally happy (perhaps with good reason), yet who are dissatisfied at work, believe that changing jobs will help; after all, they're quite satisfied with other aspects of their lives. Among a group of nurses and medical technicians who reported low job satisfaction, those with a positive disposition were actually more likely to quit than those with a negative disposition (Judge, 1993).

In short, voluntary withdrawal most often occurs when employees are not satisfied, but other factors also enter into the decision. As will be explained in **The Research Process**, one of these is commitment (or loyalty) to the organization.

> **KEY POINT**
>
> • Job satisfaction, the extent to which people like or dislike their work, is an important work-related attitude. It is influenced by many different variables; even inheritance may play a role.

THE RESEARCH PROCESS

Job Satisfaction and Task Performance

A re "happy employees productive employees"? Surprisingly, studies designed to examine this relationship have often reported mixed results.

As was true for voluntary turnover, many factors other than job satisfaction influence productivity. For example, employees may be unable to perform at high levels if needed supplies are missing, or equipment breaks down frequently, no matter how satisfied they are. Moreover, both job satisfaction and high levels of performance may depend on being rewarded for work done. When the rewards are high and are perceived as fair, both performance and job satisfaction increase (Porter & Lawler, 1968).

Job Satisfaction and Performance: Individuals or Organizations?

Ostroff studied job satisfaction among principals, teachers, and students in hundreds of schools throughout Canada and the United States. Then she took measures of the schools' performance: academic achievement (scores on standard achievement tests), student behavior (dropout rates, average daily attendance), teacher turnover, performance of school administrators, and so on. As you can see from Figure 17.5, job satisfaction depended more on school performance and less on individual performance.

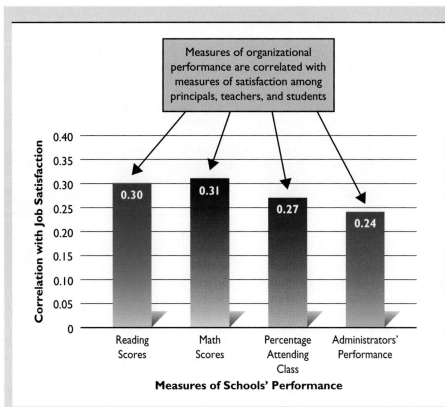

FIGURE 17.5

Measures of organizational performance are correlated with measures of satisfaction among principals, teachers, and students

Job Satisfaction and Organizational Performance

Job satisfaction among principals, teachers, and students was correlated with various measures of school performance. These findings indicate that the link between job satisfaction and *organizational* performance may be somewhat stronger than the link between job satisfaction and *individual* performance.
(Source: Based on data from Ostroff, 1992.)

Why so? Ostroff (1992, p. 969) suggested that people who are satisfied with their jobs help their co-workers, cooperate with them, make constructive suggestions, and contribute their energies to public relations. Those behaviors do not necessarily improve individual performance, but they do contribute to the success of the entire organization. Such actions, which are sometimes described as **organizational citizenship behavior**, have a positive effect on the performance of the organization as a whole (George & Brief, 1992; Organ, 1988). In short, job satisfaction is linked to performance in some ways, but the relationship is much more complex than common sense might suggest. Job satisfaction is modestly related to absenteeism and voluntary withdrawal.

Commitment in the Workplace

Other kinds of goals besides individual ones contribute to people's work performance. These include organizational and professional goals—of the place of employment, the business, the educational institution, the union, the profession, the political party, the team, or the supervisor. This kind of loyalty is often called *commitment*. At the University of Western Ontario, John Meyer and Natalie Allen (e.g., Meyer, Allen, & Smith, 1993) have developed a theory of how commitment affects workplace behavior. In general, the higher the level of commitment to the goals of the workplace, the greater the job satisfaction. Employees with greater commitment perform better. They need less close supervision, are less likely to be absent from

work, and are less likely to leave for another job.

Commitment to an organization may take a variety of forms: an emotional attachment (i.e., affection, loyalty, pride) to the company; a need to remain with the company; or an obligation to the company. In the words of Meyer and Allen, "Employees ... remain because they want to ... because they need to ... or because they feel they ought to do so." These motives are not mutually exclusive; rather, people may feel various levels of all three.

In their 1993 paper, these researchers reported their findings regarding occupational and organizational commitment among registered nurses who were members of the College of Nurses of Ontario, and among student nurses. They asked participants to rate their agreement with statements such as these:

- I am enthusiastic about nursing.

- Changing professions now would be difficult for me.

- I would feel guilty if I left nursing.

- This organization [e.g., hospital] has a great deal of personal meaning for me.

- Staying with this organization is a matter of necessity.

- I would feel guilty if I left this organization now.

The results showed that nurses are committed both to their organization and to their occupation, and that both commitments contributed to their job satisfaction and to their intention to remain in their current jobs.

1. Can you think of additional reasons, besides those mentioned above, why job satisfaction might not be closely linked to performance in some situations?

2. Are there any factors other than high rewards that might produce both high levels of job satisfaction and high levels of performance, thus creating the appearance that these two variables are directly linked?

3. Ultimately, the performance of an organization depends on the performance of the people in it. So in a sense, Ostroff's 1992 findings indicate that job satisfaction does affect the performance of individuals as well as the performance of the organization as a whole. If you agree, why? If not, why not?

4. In many organizations, if people help others, their own work may suffer. Also, they may be competing with others for the same promotions, bonuses, and so on. How could high levels of job satisfaction encourage reciprocal helping even under these conditions?

Research in Canada

John Meyer
University of Western Ontario

Natalie Allen
University of Western Ontario

Leadership: *Its Nature and Impact*

Suppose you asked many different people the following question: "What is the difference between a highly successful company and a mediocre one?" The chances are good that people would reply: "Good leadership!" There is a widespread agreement that **leadership** is the key to success in many areas of life, not only in business but also in sports, politics, and many other fields.

But what precisely is leadership? Like love, it is something we can recognize but cannot easily define. Psychologists who have studied leadership define it as follows: A leader is an important member of a group who influences most other group members toward shared group goals (Yukl, 1989). Who becomes a leader, and why? And what makes a leader effective? Let's turn to the results of psychological research and see what is known about this topic. Although what you will learn has to do with leadership in general, the principles are equally applicable to leadership in the workplace.

ARE LEADERS BORN OR MADE? A NEW LOOK AT THE GREAT PERSON THEORY Are some people born to lead? Common sense suggests that is the case. Acknowledged leaders—for example, Moses, Alexander the Great, Napoleon, Winston Churchill, Nelson Mandela, and Louis Riel—do seem to differ from other people in many respects. For this reason, early researchers formulated the **great person theory of leadership**. According to this idea, great leaders possess traits that set them apart from other human beings. And those traits remain stable over time and are shared across cultures.

Is this view correct? On the one hand, decades of research (mostly conducted before 1950) failed to yield a short, agreed-upon list of traits that are shared by all leaders (Yukl, 1981). On the other hand, there is mounting evidence that leaders actually do differ from other people in several respects that are both important and measurable. For example, Kirkpatrick and Locke (1991) have concluded that in business settings, certain leadership traits do matter and contribute to a leader's success. They are summarized in Table 17.3.

Most of the leadership traits listed in Table 17.3 are personal characteristics that you will readily recognize: honesty, drive, self-confidence, creativity, and sense of purpose (Morris, 1993). One trait, however, seems to be especially important: flexibility, which in this context means the ability to recognize the needs of a given situation and to adopt the style of leadership that is required (Zaccaro, Foti, & Kenny, 1991; Mumford et al., 1993). People who are flexible rise quickly to positions of leadership and are readily recognized as leaders by others. Moreover, they are recognized because they offer their followers just

Trait	Description
Drive	Desire for achievement; ambition; high energy; tenacity; initiative.
Honesty and integrity	Trustworthiness; reliability; openness.
Leadership motivation	Desire to exercise influence over others to reach goals.
Self-confidence	Trust in own abilities.
Cognitive ability	Intelligence; ability to integrate and interpret large amounts of information.
Expertise	Knowledge of the group's activities; knowledge of relevant technical matters.
Creativity	Originality.
Flexibility	Ability to adapt to needs of followers and to changing demands of the situation.

TABLE 17.3

Traits Associated with Leadership

Research findings indicate that successful leaders show the traits listed here.
(Source: Based on suggestions by Kirkpatrick & Locke, 1991.)

the kind of direction they need—firm guidance if that will work, a more democratic approach if that is most appropriate, and so on.

Leadership style varies along several dimensions. These include the extent to which a leader adopts a democratic rather than an autocratic approach, and the extent to which he or she focuses on personal relationships rather than on performance and success (Howell & Frost, 1989). As you can probably guess, neither one is always best. Rather, effective leadership depends on the specific challenges that the leaders and their groups face (Blake & Mouton, 1985; Yukl, 1989).

THEORIES OF LEADER EFFECTIVENESS The importance of flexibility is echoed in several major theories about leader effectiveness. For example, flexibility is central to **normative theory**, which explains how leaders make good decisions (Vroom & Yetton, 1973). According to this theory, leaders take different approaches to decision-making; these range from the autocratic (decisions are made without consulting others) to the group approach (the leader and followers reach decisions through consensus). An intermediate approach is consultative (the leader seeks input from followers but makes the decision alone).

Which kind of approach is best? According to normative theory, that depends on the situation. If a decision must be accepted for it to be implemented, or if a leader lacks sufficient information to make a solo decision, then a purely autocratic approach is inappropriate. So once again it is important that leaders be flexible—that they match their decision-making style to the requirements of the situation (Crouch & Yetton, 1987; Field & House, 1990).

The importance of flexibility is also emphasized in **situational leadership theory** (Hersey & Blanchard, 1982). Here, it is recognized that relationships between leaders and their followers or subordinates change over time, just as all relationships do. As subordinates gain in skill and experience, they require less and less direction. In fact, they may ultimately come to resent firm direction as unnecessary meddling, just as teens in their late adolescence do. Thus, to maximize their effectiveness, leaders must adjust their style over time, from task-oriented and directive to relations-oriented and less directive.

As you can see, the importance of flexibility on the part of leaders is emphasized in several theories of leader effectiveness. This may ultimately be shown to be the key to successful leadership in general.

TRANSFORMATIONAL LEADERSHIP: VISION AND CHARISMA Down through the ages, some leaders have been able to influence their followers profoundly.

Organizational Citizenship Behavior: Actions performed by individuals that are not part of their regular jobs, but which contribute to the success of the organization.

Leadership: The process through which one member of a group (its leader) exerts influence over other group members with respect to the attainment of shared group goals.

Great Person Theory of Leadership: A theory suggesting that all great leaders share certain traits.

Normative Theory: A theory suggesting that to maximize their effectiveness, leaders must adopt a decision-making approach or style consistent with the needs of their group.

Situational Leadership Theory: A theory of leadership indicating that as their followers gain increasing experience, leaders should shift from a directive to a nondirective style of leadership.

For example, through his radio speeches during the Second World War, Sir Winston Churchill brought the world back to life. Similarly, through his personal example and his persistence in the face of adversity, Nelson Mandela stirred people all over the world to cooperate in taking action against racial oppression in South Africa. History is filled with leaders who inspired others to acts of extraordinary courage—or, in some cases, to acts of extraordinary evil, such as the atrocities the Nazis committed under the leadership of Adolf Hitler. Individuals who exert such profound effects are described as **transformational** (or **charismatic**) **leaders**. That term seems fitting, for they do indeed transform social, political, and economic realities.

THE BASIC NATURE OF CHARISMA   Do transformational or charismatic leaders possess special traits that contribute to their profound impact on followers? How do they exert their profound effects on others? Can such leadership be understood as an extension of the great person theory? Systematic psychological research has begun to yield some insights into these questions.

On the one hand, charismatic leaders are naturally gifted with unusual skills. Indeed, *charisma* is the ancient Greek word for "gift." Charismatic leaders do seem to possess unusually effective social skills. They are particularly good at "reading" other people (especially their nonverbal cues); they also have high levels of achievement and power motivation and exceptional levels of energy and vigor (House, Spangler, & Woycke, 1991). Moreover, they actively support innovation (Howell & Avolio, 1993).

Charismatic leaders inspire specific types of responses. Followers show heightened performance (Howell & Avolio, 1993); loyalty and devotion toward both the leader and his or her ideas; and a willingness to sacrifice personal interests for the sake of a common goal. In short, charismatic leaders create a special kind of leader–follower relationship. Many authorities believe that it is this relationship, rather than any specific traits, that accounts for the immense impact a charismatic leader exerts on other people (House, 1977).

What do charismatic individuals actually do when they lead? That was discussed in a book called *Charismatic Leadership* by Rabi Kanugo and Jay Conger of McGill University (1992). These two suggest that there are three steps in the work of a charismatic leader. The first is to evaluate carefully the present situation; the second is to formulate goals with and for the group; the third is to generate the means to accomplish those goals.

THE BEHAVIOR OF CHARISMATIC LEADERS: THE IMPORTANCE OF A VISION   What do charismatic leaders do to generate that special relationship with their

Transformational Leaders: Leaders who exert profound effects on their followers and establish special types of relationships with them.

TRANSFORMATIONAL LEADERS: MARTIN LUTHER KING, JR., AND MARGARET THATCHER

Both of the people shown here were transformational or charismatic leaders—they exerted profound effects on their societies. Can you think of additional examples of transformational leaders in history?

subordinates? First and foremost, they possess a vision—an idea of what their company, or political group, or country, could and should become (Howell & Frost, 1989).

In 1985, Bob Geldoff used the Live Aid Concert to mobilize people to give generously to victims of famine in Ethiopia. Westhey (1991) studied that case of leadership and how Geldoff used the emotional impact of music to create a "global social innovation."

Transformational leaders do more than simply describe a dream or vision; they also offer a plan for making it a reality. And they engage in framing (Conger, 1991)—that is, they define their purpose in a way that gives meaning to the actions they propose. That is crucial, for a vision that seems impossible to attain is unlikely to spur people toward achieving it. Perhaps the nature of framing is best illustrated by the story of two stonecutters who were working on a cathedral during the Middle Ages. When asked what they were doing, one replied, "Cutting stone, of course." The other replied, "Building the world's most beautiful temple to the glory of God." Which person do you think would be more likely to elicit extraordinary effort?

In short, the profound influence of charismatic leaders is not a mystery. They have a combination of traits and behaviors, as well as the means of building a special relationship with their followers. All of this permits them to change their group, their society, and their world. That is why we read about them in history books years, decades, and even centuries afterwards.

KEY POINTS

- Leadership is a process in which one member of a group (its leader) exerts influence over other members for the attainment of common goals.

- Growing evidence suggests that leaders do differ from other people in certain respects.

- One characteristic that plays a key role in leader effectiveness is flexibility.

- Transformational or charismatic leaders exert profound effects on their followers, and often upon entire societies.

Applied Psychology: *Putting Knowledge About Behavior to Work*

If psychology is anything, it is *diverse*, with respect to how basic knowledge is applied directly to real-world problems. A major trend in social psychology, especially since the 1970s, has been the emphasis on applying research results to a host of practical problems (Lambert, 1992; Baron & Byrne, 1991). In this section we will look at environmental psychology, which involves efforts to understand how the physical environment affects human behavior (Bell, Fisher, & Baum, 1990); at ergonomics, which studies the interface between people and their environment; and at psychological principles as they apply to how the legal system works (Kassin & Wrightsman, 1988).

Environmental Psychology: *The Physical Environment and Behavior*

Think of it: There are two billion (2,000,000,000) more people on this planet now than there were three decades ago. At present, the world population is growing at slightly less than 2 percent per year. That may not sound like much, but it means that our numbers will double again in only forty more years. And then they will double again, and again ... Needless to say, the earth's capacity to support 10, 20, or 40 billion human beings is doubtful. Something will probably happen naturally to slow that rate of growth (McKibben, 1989).

HUMAN ACTIVITY: AFFECTING THE PHYSICAL ENVIRONMENT
Human activity—especially heavy industrialization and the pollution it produces—is changing the physical environment in which we all must live.

The human race, through cultural evolution, industrial development, and population growth, has reconfigured the physical environment in crucial ways. For example, in March 1993, Environment Canada reported that in January and February, the ozone layer had become thinner over a large area of our country. Your have probably heard of the consequence of that—the *greenhouse effect*, which may already be increasing the earth's average temperature. This is only one of the many ways in which human activity is affecting the only home planet of our species. As we examine how the physical environment influences human behavior, you will see again that human activity also affects the environment in which we live.

Crowding: The Effects of Close Encounters with Other People

Imagine two scenes. In the first, you are part of a huge, densely packed crowd at a football game. In the second you are part of a crowd pushing onto an already filled bus or train. Will you feel equally crowded in both circumstances? Probably not. In all likelihood you will feel crowded only in the second example. **Crowding** refers to the subjective judgment that we are surrounded by too many people (Paulus, 1980); it is quite different from *density*, which refers only to the number of people in a given space.

Often, of course, density and crowding go together. But there are also exceptions—times when we are packed close together with others but do not experience any unpleasant feelings, such as at a sports event or a rock concert.

As you know yourself, the subjective feeling of crowding, whatever its source, has negative effects on us. Feeling crowded threatens our confidence that we have control over what happens to us (Bell, Fisher, & Baum, 1990). And it may lead us to experience *information overload*—the feeling that the environment is providing more information than we can comfortably handle in a given period of time (Baum & Valins, 1979).

EFFECTS OF EXTENDED EXPOSURE TO CROWDING Most people can tolerate short periods of crowding. The most dramatic effects develop over time. College and university dormitories are living laboratories for the study of such effects. Most of these studies report the following results: When three students are assigned to a room designed for two, and report feeling more crowded, they dislike their roommates to a greater degree, feel more dissatisfied with educational life, and even obtain lower grades (Gormley & Aiello, 1982). Similar findings have come from studies in junior high schools. For example, McCain and his colleagues (1985) compared two originally identical schools, one of which had experienced a 43 percent drop in enrollment. At the school where enrollment had dropped and crowding had decreased, there were several benefits. The students expressed more favorable attitudes about the environment. Also, absenteeism decreased among the teachers.

Additional research has found that crowding has negative effects in prisons. This is a serious problem, particularly in the United States, where prison populations have increased rapidly in recent years. The construction of new facilities has lagged behind the growing number of prisoners, and more inmates have been placed into existing cells. This has increased the levels of stress and frequency of aggressive behavior among prisoners (Ruback, Carr, & Hopper, 1986; Schaeffer et al., 1988). Clearly, crowding will be a serious issue for society in the years ahead.

Crowding: The subjective judgment that we are surrounded by too many people.

Ethnic Differences in Reactions to Crowding

People who have been used to wide-open spaces and an extremely low population density typically perceive suburban settings as crowded. In contrast, people who live in the downtown core of a large city typically perceive suburbia as wide-open countryside. In sum, individuals vary widely in their reactions to the same social density. For this reason, we might expect people from very crowded nations such as Japan to be less sensitive to overcrowding than those from Canada.

To test that possibility, Gillis, Richard, and Hagan (1986) studied Toronto high school students whose parents were of British background; Southern European background (Italian, Greek, Spanish); or Asian background (Japanese, Chinese, Vietnamese). The students reported on the number of people who shared their bedroom and on whether they lived in a single detached house, a duplex, a row house, or a highrise apartment. They also completed questionnaires designed to measure physical symptoms that often indicate psychological strain—loss of appetite, sleep problems, headache, and so on.

Results suggested that among the students of British descent, high density was indeed related to strain; for those of Southern European descent, this was true but to a lesser degree. No relationship was noted between density and strain for the students of Asian descent. These differences remained even when differences in socioeconomic level were statistically removed. So it appears that there are different cultural views with respect to crowding (i.e., different standards for whether an environment is crowded) and that people from different cultures can and do have sharply contrasting reactions to the same physical conditions.

CROWDING, UNLIKE DENSITY, IS A SUBJECTIVE JUDGMENT
The Norwegian fisherman probably has a very different perception of crowding than do these Indonesian commuters.

Other Aspects of the Physical Environment: *Noise, Temperature, and Light*

Many aspects of the physical environment have the potential to influence our behavior. Research findings suggest that of these, several are especially important.

Annabel Cohen
University of Prince Edward Island

NOISE: SOUND THAT HARMS In the 1990s we are every day exposed to higher levels of noise than our ancestors probably experienced at any time in their lives. That noise is produced by car engines, hair dryers, vacuum cleaners, fans, coffee grinders, electric razors, lawn mowers, jet planes, sound amplifiers, and countless other objects in the environment. How does all of this noise pollution affect behavior?

Hearing loss, which is gradual and insidious, is the obvious answer; but there are other effects as well. First, there is growing evidence that exposure to noise—especially the high and unpredictable levels encountered in larger cities—may be harmful to health. People who live near large factories or airports have higher blood pressure and a higher incidence of strokes (Topf, 1989). Apparently, the high levels of arousal produced by such noise take a heavy physical toll on us. Such effects do not seem related to the fact that people living in such areas are often poorer than those living elsewhere; they occur even when level of income and several other factors are taken into account statistically (Cohen et al., 1986).

Second, prolonged exposure to loud noise interferes with the performance of at least some cognitive tasks. Cohen and colleagues (1986) spent several years studying children attending school near a busy airport. One of their findings: Such children have lower scores on several standard achievement tests and solve puzzles with more difficulty than children from schools in quieter areas. Adults, too, may experience these effects. Male participants were exposed to three different levels of noise while performing two cognitive tasks: reading a story and answering questions about it; and unscrambling anagrams. The higher the level of noise, the poorer was the cognitive performance (Nagar & Pandey, 1987).

Noise also seems to influence social behavior. Individuals exposed to loud, irritating noise lose their temper more easily and are less willing to help others (Donnerstein & Wilson, 1976).

TEMPERATURE: ARE HEAT AND VIOLENCE LINKED? Hot under the collar ... The heat of anger ... Phrases like these suggest that there is a link between high temperature and irritability—and perhaps overt aggression. Do research findings support this idea? In one study, researchers at the University of Alberta assigned participants to work either in 21°C or 33°C (Rule et al., 1987). They were given story "stems" (incomplete stories) and asked to write endings for them. Some of the stems hinted that aggression might occur; some did not. The participants who were working in the hot environment used more "negative emotions, frustrators, and aggression" in the story endings they wrote.

In a different type of study, Anderson and Anderson (1984) obtained records of violent crimes (murder and rape) and nonviolent crimes (robbery and arson) over a two-year period in Houston, Texas. They also obtained daily maximum temperatures during that period. They found that the higher the daily temperature, the higher the incidence of violent crimes; also, violence peaked during the group of days with the highest temperature. Nonviolent crimes did not increase in this way. Similar results have been obtained in several other studies (Anderson, 1987; Cohn, 1990; Perry & Simpson, 1987). Moreover, data collected over several decades indicate that more aggression occurs during hotter years, quarters of years, seasons, months, and days than during cooler ones (Anderson, 1989).

In other studies (Baron, 1978; Bell & Fusco, 1986), the incidence of aggression increased with temperature (to about 25°C), but fell off when people become so uncomfortable (30°C) that escape from the heat became a goal. Of course, exposure to extreme heat has harmful consequences, and these render people unable to engage in any effortful physical activity (Bell, Fisher, &

Baum, 1990). At present, then, it appears that increased aggression may be linked to rising temperature, up to temperature levels that most people find very uncomfortable. It is likely that those levels vary with the task and the individual's tolerance for heat.

LIGHT: CHANGING ONE ASPECT OF THE INDOOR ENVIRONMENT   Have you ever felt depressed during the winter as one gray, dreary day follows another? If so, you may have experienced **seasonal affective disorder**, which, as you learned in Chapter 4, is depression brought on by lack of sunlight (Rosenthal, 1985). Such effects of light called psychologists' attention to another light source. Indoor lighting provides more than just the illumination necessary to perform certain tasks; it may also influence moods (Boyce et al., 1989). If it does, indoor lighting conditions may have much more general effects, because our current mood influences both our thinking and our social behavior (Isen & Baron, 1991; and see Chapter 16).

But do lighting conditions actually influence mood? Only in recent years has systematic research considered this question (Davis & Ginthner, 1990). Studies point to two conclusions: indoor lighting may indeed shift people's moods; and those mood changes have strong effects on behavior (Baron, 1990). In particular, relatively dim light and "warm" light elicit more positive moods than bright light and "cool" light. Moreover, light-induced mood shifts influence performance on a wide range of cognitive tasks (Baron, Ray, & Daniels, 1991).

Does the color of the environment influence people's moods and therefore their behavior? In their work, interior designers use this kind of information, much of which is based on psychological research. For example, fast food restaurants use colors like red, yellow, and orange because research suggests that these colors tend to activate people and increase their appetites. Blues and greens are not often found in fast food restaurants because these colors tend to be calming. If you run a fast food restaurant, you may not want to encourage people to linger over their meals.

Human Factors: Designing for Effectiveness and Safety

Notwithstanding the effects of crowding, noise, and light on our behavior, generally speaking, human beings are remarkably adaptive with respect to the environment. For example, high-altitude mountaineers expose themselves to drastically reduced oxygen levels. The temporary effects of lack of oxygen may result in poor decisions and bad judgment. In 1989, Gregor Jason and his colleagues at the University of Calgary tested twelve Canadian climbers on a variety of psychological measures, both before and after they attempted to climb 8848 meters up Mount Everest. The climbers also completed some paper-and-pencil tests of tracking and concentration at various altitudes on the mountain. Despite the thin air, there were no deficits in the climbers' mental performance on any of the tests. Jason concluded that "well-acclimatized climbers can tolerate short periods of time ... but prolonged stays at high altitude may be harmful."

Seasonal Affective Disorder: Depression brought on by lack of sunlight.

Our adaptive cognitive abilities—to perceive the external world, and to acquire, remember, and reason about new information—are also excellent. Yet, like all other animals, we also have limitations. Those limitations are a central focus of psychological research in the field of human factors and ergonomics. The guiding principle of this field is as follows: All tools, equipment, and systems for human beings should maximize ease, safety, and effectiveness of use. This means that careful attention must be paid to the limitations of human abilities (Sanders & McCormick, 1993). In their research and consulting activities, psychologists and ergonomists apply their knowledge about basic aspects of human behavior to the design of the environment.

For example, at the Center for Research in Human Factors at Carleton University, Momtahan, Hetu, and Tansley (1993) applied their knowledge about the detection and identification of auditory signals to more than twenty alarms in a hospital's intensive care units and operating rooms. They found that operating room staff identified only some of the sounds made by the alarms and concluded that warning systems in hospitals and alarms on medical equipment are poorly designed and need to be standardized.

A different setting altogether: Two kinds of control systems for a log loader were compared in British Columbia by researchers at Ergo Systems Canada. The question at hand was whether experienced operators could change to a control system that suited novice operators better. The researchers found that the skills could be transferred in a short time (Wallersteiner et al., 1993). At the Aging and Vision Laboratory at the University of Calgary, Kline and Fuchs compared the visibility and comprehension of highway signs for people at difference ages. In Toronto, at the Defence and Civil Institute of Environmental Medicine, ergonomists studied which value, for different colors, is perceived as best for electronic displays (Kaufmann & O'Neill, 1993). In Calgary, new designs for park benches, lighting, and telephones are being used to increase safety and reduce crime. Below, you will read more about recommendations for displaying information and designing controls and for planning work and living environments. You will also learn what may happen when these recommendations are ignored.

Visual Displays: *Principles and Applications*

In 1985, many new automobiles began featuring a new kind of speedometer. Instead of the standard round gauge with a pointer, they now had a digital display in which bars of light moved across the screen. The bars changed color, from green to amber to red, as speed increased. It seemed like a nice design, but drivers found it both distracting and irritating. As a result, many people who bought a new car that year specified the standard speedometer. By the mid-1990s, millions of drivers had done so. The "improved" speedometer has now largely vanished.

This example calls attention to an important fact: Some kinds of **visual displays** are better than others. This is true both when the information is static (e.g., when a red light indicates that the battery of your portable phone is low) and when it is dynamic (i.e., when the information is changing and the display shows you the change). Dynamic information is often very important; there are gauges that indicate the temperature of various fluids, the pounds of pressure inside a system, and the altitude (as in a plane). The indicator on a moving elevator is a common dynamic display. How should such displays be designed so that they can be read easily and accurately by the people who use them?

Visual Displays: *Displays that present information visually.*

Hundreds of studies have been conducted to answer the question, and several basic principles have emerged from that work (Sanders & McCormick, 1993). First, pointers moving against a fixed scale are usually easier to read. Thus, the moving needle of a speedometer is a more useful arrangement than a moving scale and static needle. Second, increases are perceived more easily if they are displayed going up, and decreases are perceived more easily if they are going down. Since we tend to interpret the clockwise directions as moving from low to high, standard speedometers are effective because they follow that rule as well. (Imagine trying to read a speedometer on which 0 was to the right and 100 km to the left.) Third, the scale must be clear and easy to read. If you've ever had to hold a thermometer closer to your eyes (or farther away) because you could not tell where the mercury level was, you are familiar with the importance of clear scale indicators.

Many other variables influence the ease with which people read dynamic displays of visual information. For example, it is helpful to have different colors for different zones—for example, one color for "Normal," another for "Caution," and a third for "Danger" (Sanders & McCormick, 1993). Similarly, when individuals must respond quickly to a large amount of incoming information, that information should be presented in the same location rather than at different locations (Uhlarik & Joseph, 1992).

Of course, the visual modality is not our only source of information from the environment. We also receive auditory instructions. In some automated trains around large airports, for example, a simulated voice says, "Step to the rear of the train, please. Next stop is Air Canada and Canadian Airlines …" Over the telephone, voices are constantly telling us to press 1 for English, 2 for French, and 3 for none of the above. Warnings may also be visual or auditory. For example, some automobiles show a red key and make a rude noise when you open the car door with the key still in the ignition. Is it more effective to use both warnings at the same time? In a cockpit environment, Byblow (1990) found that for some kinds of information, presenting both warnings increased rather than decreased reaction times. However, another study—this one of subjects who were at various levels of consciousness (under general anesthesia)—found that the reaction time was faster to an auditory warning signal (Letourneau et al., 1986). Which type of warning signal is best is a complex question that depends on a number of human factors that are now being revealed in this very important field of research.

What is certain, however, is there do appear to be right and wrong ways to design visual displays, and careful attention to basic principles is essential so that we humans can use machines as easily and as safely as possible.

DESIGNING EFFECTIVE WARNINGS: DANGER!—UNLESS HUMAN FACTORS PRINCIPLES ARE CONSIDERED   One especially important use of visual displays is in **warnings**—messages designed to alert us to hazards in the environment. Warnings often present information about how to avoid these hazards, as well as some indication of when and where the danger is most likely to be encountered. Unfortunately, many people tend to ignore warnings, thus placing themselves and others needlessly at risk.

That raises an important practical question: How can compliance with warnings be increased? We considered this topic briefly in Chapter 3, but it is so important that it is worth returning to here, especially since it is a major topic of current research in human factors psychology.

First, as was pointed out in Chapter 3, in order for a warning to influence behavior, it must be noticed by its intended audience. This means that warning signs and messages must be both perceptible (i.e., legible and/or audible) and attention-getting. Some factors that increase attention to warnings are

Warnings: Messages designed to alert users of various products and services, or the general public, to potential hazards.

WARNINGS: OFTEN IGNORED
People often ignore signs warning them of danger. How can compliance with such warnings be increased? This is one important research topic in the field of human factors.

size, design, color, and "active" elements such as blinking lights or flags. An amusing and attention-getting type of road sign in the south of France is a larger-than-life model of a police officer waving a large red flag.

After noticing a warning, people must understand it, so it is essential that warnings be clear, brief, and to the point. Finally, noticing and understanding a warning is not enough—people must be induced to comply with it. What are the factors that increase such compliance? Fortunately, there are many. For example, interactive warnings—those which require users to do something either before or while using a product—are effective (Hunn & Dingus, 1992). The benefits of such warnings were illustrated very clearly in a recent study by Duffy, Kalsher, and Wogalter (1993).

These researchers placed three different warnings on an extension cord. One of these was simply a tag indicating that no more than two plugs should be connected to the extension cord at one time. Two others were interactive labels: They contained the same message as the tag, but users had to remove the plastic pieces on which these words were written before an appliance could be plugged into the extension cord. One of the interactive warnings was brightly colored in orange, while the other was gray. (There was also a control condition in which no warning was present.) When the experimenter left the room, participants were asked to help out by plugging in a television, a VCR, and a videotape rewinder. By observing how participants had accomplished these tasks, the experimenter could see whether they had complied with the warning on the extension cord. As shown in Figure 17.6, results were clear: Participants were much more likely to comply with the warning in the two interactive conditions than in the tag condition or in the control condition. These results indicate that interactive labels, because they require users actually to do something, may be especially effective warnings.

Additional findings are that we increase the effectiveness of warnings by personalizing them—that is, by placing names on them (Wogalter et al., 1993)—and by placing them where they don't compete with a lot of visual clutter (Wogalter, Kalsher, & Racicot, 1993). Finally, there appear to be some interesting gender differences with respect to compliance with warnings. Specifically, although

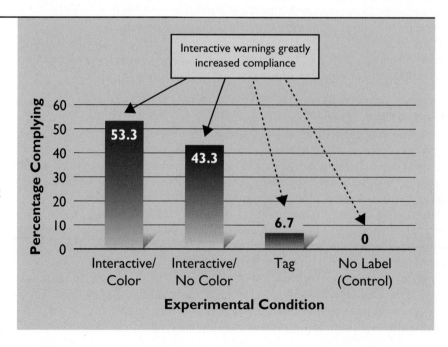

FIGURE 17.6

The Benefits of Interactive Warnings

Interactive warnings—ones that required participants to remove a warning tag before using an extension cord—increased participants' compliance with the message on the tag.
(Source: Based on data from Duffy et al., 1993.)

women and men report noticing warning signs about equally, women are more likely to comply with them. Since women also view various high-risk activities (e.g., skiing and scuba diving) as more dangerous than men do, these findings may not be surprising (Vredenburgh & Cohen, 1993).

In short, there are many steps that can be taken to increase the likelihood that people will notice, understand, and comply with warnings. Sometimes the difficult task is not in determining what these are; rather, it is getting government and industry to use the findings available.

Controls: "What Happens When I Turn This Dial ... "?

Look at the controls in Figure 17.7. All are from recent automobiles, and all serve the same function: to control power seats in these vehicles. It's obvious, however, that they are not equally easy to use. Which would you find simplest? If you are like most people, you would choose the one in photo 2. Looking at it, you can tell at a glance what will happen to the seat when you push each button. In contrast, there will be trial and error in determining just what the controls in photos 1 and 3 do. Most confusing of all are the controls in photo 4. As two ergonomists put it: "Faced with the ... seat control pictured in this photo, we wondered: Is this a seat control or a chiropractor's textbook?" (Andre & Segal, 1993, p. 6).

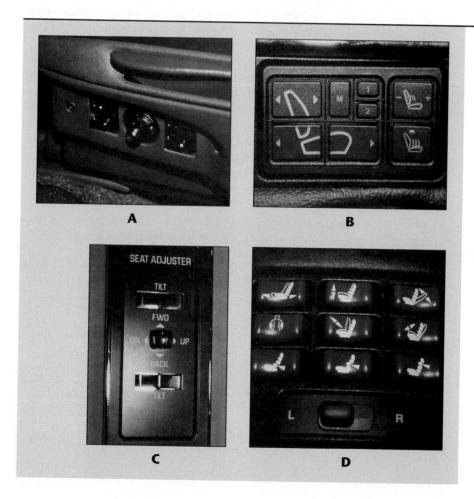

FIGURE 17.7

Controls: Careful Design is Essential

All these controls were designed to operate power seats in automobiles. However, they differ greatly in clarity and ease of use. The one in photo B is best; the one in photo D is worst.
(Source: Andre & Segal, 1993, p. 5. Reprinted with permission from *Ergonomics in Design*, April 1993. Copyright 1993 by the Human Factors and Ergonomics Society. All rights reserved.)

Unfortunately, confusing or misleading **controls** are far from rare. Careful studies of the Three Mile Island accident, in which a major nuclear-powered electric plant in the United States came very close to melting down, found that some of the human errors in that plant could be traced to poor design (Seminara, 1993). For instance, some controls had three positions labeled OFF, AUTO, and ON. Yet when the dial was pointing to auto, the control was actually off, because it automatically returned to the middle position after being set to the left—that is, to OFF. Obviously, controls that say what they mean are important in the design of tools, equipment, and systems.

Are there general psychological principles that should guide the design of controls? Yes, there are. Paramount is **compatibility**—the degree to which controls are consistent with human expectations. For example, people expect that when they turn a knob in a clockwise direction, it will increase whatever function is being controlled—a light will get brighter, the temperature in an oven will increase, and so on. Similarly, people seem naturally to expect that pushing a lever, like an accelerator or a brake, forward will increase its action, while releasing the lever back will reduce it. So a basic rule of design where controls are concerned is this: Make sure that they follow the compatibility principle (i.e., that they work the way most people expect them to).

That sounds so simple and natural that you may be wondering why complications ever arise. However, in some situations, we do not have clear-cut human expectations about the operation of controls. Look at the controls in the left-hand drawing of Figure 17.8. Which knob controls which burner? Several answers are possible, so there is considerable uncertainty and therefore lots of room for error, and that is compounded by the fact that different stove manufacturers use different arrangements. In cases such as this one, extra information is needed and should be provided. Drawing lines from the controls to the burners virtually eliminates errors (Osborne & Ellingstad, 1987).

In other situations, we *do* have expectations about how controls operate; unfortunately, however, our expectations are out of sync with the way the controls actually operate. A dramatic illustration is the case of antilock brakes, which are designed to prevent accident-causing skids on wet or icy pavements. When those brakes were introduced, it was expected that they would prevent many accidents. As a result, some insurance companies offered reduced premiums for cars equipped with them. Studies of the accident rates of cars with and without such brakes have now found that there is no difference.

How can this be so? Human factors research has provided a ready answer— one that was largely overlooked by safety experts without training in ergonomics (Miller, 1994). Apparently, when they feel their vehicle beginning to skid, most drivers instinctively pump the brakes—the correct response with regular

Controls: Devices that permit human beings to operate and direct tools, equipment, or systems.

Compatibility: The degree to which controls operate in a manner consistent with human expectations or tendencies.

FIGURE 17.8

When Compatibility Needs a Boost

Look at the left-hand drawing. Can you guess which knob controls each burner? Some people differ in their expectations concerning this relationship. Adding lines such as those in the right-hand drawing can be very helpful.

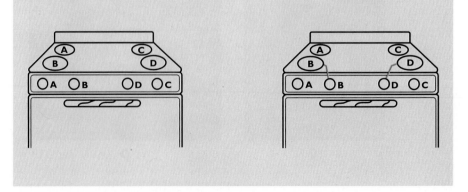

brakes. But that is the wrong thing to do with antilock brakes, for which the correct response is to apply steady pressure to the brake pedal. Before the benefits of antilock brakes can be fully realized, therefore, it will be necessary either to change the way such brakes operate, so that pumping the brake is correct, or to retrain millions of drivers to use the brake pedal in a new way.

People are often called upon to perform another task where controls are used—**tracking**. This involves continuous effort to stay as close to a target as possible. Whenever you drive a car you are tracking—constantly making small adjustments in the steering wheel to remain in your own lane. Human beings are quite good at tracking, but there is a time delay. That delay often plays a role in automobile accidents. Tracking is also an important consideration in flying an airplane, which, during landing, involves simultaneous tracking of speed, altitude, and position. Predictor displays provide us with indications of where our vehicle, or the system, will be in five, ten, or twenty seconds, and this helps us counteract the delay in responding to those changes and make the rapid adjustments necessary to stay on track (Sanders & McCormick, 1993).

As the role of computers increases in our lives, a new set of questions about controls arises. In their interactions with computers, humans exert supervisory control: They tell the machine what they wish to accomplish—for example, when you strike "wp" for WordPerfect, the program takes over. This is the process not only with computers but also with automatic washing machines—a very simple case of supervisory control. When you choose a specific cycle, the washer takes over and controls water temperature, length of washing and spinning cycles, and so on.

Supervisory control is increasingly common in manufacturing processes, where machines, under the guidance of computers, perform more and more of the functions previously carried out by people. Even when computers control production, however, human beings must still be present to program and oversee the computers. Therefore, although the particular questions about controls may change, their effective design remains an important concern even in the most modern automated factories.

Workplace Environments: *Planning for Productivity and Well-Being*

People do not do their best under adverse environmental conditions. Thus, workplace design is deserving of careful attention. Actually, there are many aspects of the workplace to be considered, including environmental factors such as temperature, lighting, air quality, and noise; interpersonal factors, including crowding, privacy, and general office layout; and the arrangement of work spaces relative to the dimensions and characteristics of the human body. As you will find out, all three of these are important aspects of work. It is also essential to take into account the special needs of employees who are disabled or disadvantaged relative to others.

THE PHYSICAL ENVIRONMENT OF WORK SPACES: EFFECTS ON PERFORMANCE
Temperature, air quality, illumination, and noise affect performance on many different tasks (Baron, 1994; Sundstrom & Sundstrom, 1986).

Tracking: Tasks, such as driving, in which individuals make adjustments to approach as closely as possible to some target value.

Polluted air has negative effects on both personal health and performance at work. Some workers, such as smelter workers who are exposed to lead, are at special risk. Braun and Daigneault (1991) found that these workers had blood-lead levels six times the Canadian urban average; the effects were most obvious in tests of motor function and in their own reports of negative mood states.

In early 1989, Toronto had the worst air quality of six cities in North America of equivalent size. All major cities on this continent have air quality problems. Farther south, Mexico City is extremely polluted. Carbon monoxide, airborne particles such as dust and pollen, and oxides of nitrogen and sulfur are common in major cities and in many industrial settings. Exposure to such substances can produce an air pollution syndrome that includes headache, fatigue, insomnia, irritability, and depression and that can adversely affect performance on many tasks, especially those involving quick reaction time and manual dexterity (Baron, 1994; Briesacher, 1971). In addition, smoke serves as both a distractor and a source of annoyance (Zillmann, Baron, & Tamborini, 1981).

Temperatures that people find uncomfortably warm or uncomfortably cool may reduce performance on a wide range of tasks, especially ones requiring considerable cognitive effort. Tasks that temperature commonly affects include those requiring the recording and decoding of signals, fine eye–hand coordination, and "vigilance" (i.e., heightened alertness to changes in events or displays) (e.g., Bell et al., 1990).

But what, precisely, are comfortable temperatures? Large individual differences exist, but many people dressed in normal clothing report feeling most comfortable at a temperature between 18 and 22°C. Men tend to prefer slightly lower temperatures than women, perhaps because they have higher blood pressure and greater blood circulation to the extremities (Grivel & Candas, 1991). Preferred temperature ranges also vary with the kinds of activities being performed: The more strenuous work activities are, the lower the preferred temperature (Ramsey & Kwon, 1988). Nevertheless, people do become acclimatized to both high and low temperatures after several days' exposure. As a result, they can work more productively than they could when first exposed to the extreme temperatures (Strydom et al., 1986).

Prolonged exposure to high levels of *noise* (approximately 85 decibels or higher, depending on length of exposure) can produce permanent damage to our hearing, and that is a serious matter in the design of any work setting. In addition, noise well below the levels that produce hearing loss may interfere with performance on many kinds of tasks, especially those requiring much cognitive effort (Sanders & McCormick, 1993). This is especially pronounced when the noise is unpredictable—that is, when it occurs irregularly and without warning—as Linden (1991) found in his studies of arithmetic stress.

A very clear illustration of the detrimental impact of noise was provided by Nagar and Pandey (1987). These researchers exposed male participants to different noise levels while they performed two cognitive tasks: answering questions about a story they read, and unscrambling word puzzles. Results indicated that the higher the level of noise, the worse participants' performance in both tasks.

COUNTERING THE EFFECTS OF NEGATIVE WORK ENVIRONMENTS Fortunately, means exist for countering the adverse effects of all of the factors described above, and thus for enhancing the performance and well-being of workers. Heating and air-conditioning equipment offers excellent (and energy-efficient) control over indoor temperatures. New insulating materials can also be highly effective.

Similarly, devices and systems have been developed for removing many pollutants from the air in work settings. Some of these make use of true-HEPA (high efficient particular arresting) filters to remove from the air more than 99.75 percent of all dust and other particles down to a size of 0.3 microns. (Many bacteria are larger in diameter than 0.3 microns.)

People can be protected from exposure to dangerously high levels of noise through the use of effective ear-covering devices. And distracting and unpleasant noise at lower levels can be reduced in several ways. For example, equipment can be designed so that it emits less noise. Also, sound-absorbing materials can be used in barriers and on large surfaces; and equipment can be provided that emits white noise—a mixture of many different frequencies— to mask distracting sounds produced by equipment, ringing telephones, the human voice, and so on.

In a study at the University of British Columbia, Loewen and Suedfeld (1992) investigated the effects of office noise on arousal, stress, and work. Students in the group that worked with office noise that was masked not only performed better but also reported being less stressed and less distracted by the noise in the environment.

A device that combines air filtration, noise control, and other environment-enhancing features is shown on this page. While this product is designed primarily for use in relatively small rooms (e.g., private offices, dorm rooms, bedrooms), the principles it incorporates can readily be applied to larger areas as well.

INTERPERSONAL ASPECTS OF WORK SPACE DESIGN   Look at the photos at the bottom of this page. In which office would you most prefer to work? Most people express a preference either for an individual room or cubicle (photo 2), or for the large open or landscaped office design shown in photo 3—a design in which people who work together are grouped near each other. Few people prefer the "bullpen" layout shown in photo 1, although this design is still quite common in many work settings.

Why do most people dislike the design in photo 1? Partly because there is a total uniformity of work space, except for higher-status employees, who generally occupy offices arranged around the outside of the bullpen. Partly because there is no privacy and no way to personalize the individual work areas (Sundstrom & Sundstrom, 1986). In addition, people feel more crowded in the bullpen arrangement—a reaction that has been linked to reduced productivity (Bell et al., 1990; Nagar, Pandey, & Paulus, 1988).

Because open designs offer certain advantages (e.g., they enhance communication), they have been adopted by many organizations. Yet they are not without disadvantages, too; for example, relative to private offices or cubicles,

ONE PRODUCT FOR IMPROVING THE PHYSICAL ENVIRONMENT OF WORK SETTINGS

The device shown here (patented by R.A. Baron and F. Haber) combines high-efficiency air filtration with noise control and other features to improve the physical environment of an office—or any other small room, such as a bedroom or dorm room.

OFFICE DESIGN: AN IMPORTANT FACTOR IN PRODUCTIVITY

In which of these three offices would you prefer to work? All three designs offer some advantages and disadvantages, but the one on the right—a landscaped office—has been adopted by a growing number of companies in recent years.

A

B

C

there are greater distractions and higher levels of noise. How can an organization maximize the benefits of an office layout while reducing the potential disadvantages? Research findings suggest that these goals may be reached by applying the following procedures:

- Take active steps to reduce noise—for example, use sound-absorbing materials on all major surfaces, and introduce noise-reducing equipment.
- Provide surfaces (horizontal or vertical) on which individuals can display their belongings and otherwise personalize their space.
- Provide several easily accessible islands of privacy—rooms where people can go to be alone, to hold confidential conversations, or to work undisturbed.
- Design workstations so that visitors can sit while consulting.
- Provide adequate storage space—something that is often overlooked in the design of landscaped or open offices.
- Install telephones that ring silently.

Through careful attention to these factors and to the environmental conditions discussed earlier, work spaces can be made comfortable and pleasant so that they offer workers the kind of satisfaction that leads to maximum productivity. Psychologists already know much about how to create good work places. Often, the most difficult part of the psychologist's job is convincing business that the cost of providing them is an excellent investment (Johns, 1993).

KEY POINTS

- Many environmental variables, including temperature, noise, and air quality, influence performance in work settings.
- The design of workplaces also affects performance. Landscaped or open offices have become increasingly popular. This type of layout involves decreased privacy and increased noise and distraction; however, it also offers benefits.

THE RESEARCH PROCESS

Computers and Stress

Stress is a problem in almost any workplace where computers are used heavily. The following study provides a good example of human factors research in this area. At the University of Toronto in 1993, Muter, Furedy, Vincent, and Pelcowitz gathered twenty-five volunteers from an introductory psychology class. They all had used a personal computer: a PC or a Macintosh.

These students were given four tasks to perform for six minutes each. Two of the tasks involved recalling series of numbers. There were two kinds of series: those which they had to recite in the same order as they had been presented (the easy memory task) and those which they had to recite in reverse order (the hard memory task).

The other two assignments involved using a computer as if it were a bank machine, to type in a set of transactions. In this case, the "user-friendly" computer program worked like one at a bank but even more simply. The "user-hostile" program presented a screen that looked the one in Figure 17.9. The instructions were difficult to read, there was no menu to follow, and time limits were imposed. There was no positive feedback when the student performed correctly, but when an error was made, the computer buzzed loudly and flashed FATAL ERROR or TOO SLOW.

Muter and his colleagues took readings of the heart rate and the spontaneous conductance of the skim in order to measure the psychophysiological responses of the subjects to the tasks they had to perform. They

FIGURE 17.9

YOUR CHEQUING ACCOUNT IS NUMBER 1. YOUR SAVINGS ACCOUNT IS NUMBER 2, AND YOUR CREDIT CARD ACCOUNT IS NUMBER 3. THE KEYWORD FOR WITHDRAW IS 'With'. (CASE IS IMPORTANT.) THE KEYWORD FOR DEPOSIT IS 'Dpos'. THE KEYWORD FOR TRANSFER IS 'Trfr'. THE KEYWORD FOR ACCOUNT BALANCE IS 'Bala'. TO ERASE, SIMULTANEOUSLY PRESS THE CLOVER-LEAF KEY AND 'H'. TO MAKE A TRANSACTION, ENTER TRANSACTION TYPE, FOLLOWED BY ACCOUNT TYPE, FOLLOWED BY AMOUNT OF MONEY (IF RELEVANT), INCLUDING DECIMAL POINT AND CENTS. TO TRANSFER, SPECIFY TWO ACCOUNTS, FIRST THE FROM ACCOUNT AND THEN THE TO ACCOUNT. THUS THERE ARE 2,3, OR 4 FIELDS. TO DENOTE THE END OF A FIELD, TYPE A COLON. IMPORTANT: IT MAY BE NECESSARY TO UNPACK BYTES.

FIGURE 17.9

On-Screen Instructions for User-Hostile Condition

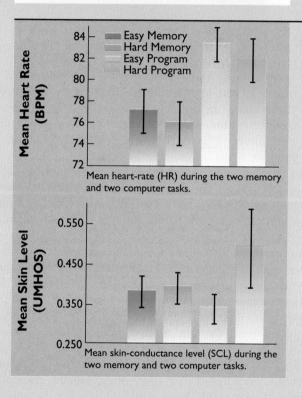

Mean heart-rate (HR) during the two memory and two computer tasks.

Mean skin-conductance level (SCL) during the two memory and two computer tasks.

FIGURE 17.10

Stress and Computers

Clearly, in the study, the user-hostile computer program had the greatest effect on skin conductance. Memory tasks had less effect on heart rate than either computer task.

found that, in general, heart rate was higher for the two computer tasks than for the two memory tasks. Also, skin conductance increased greatly for the hard computer program alone (see Figure 17.10). These results were taken as meaning that, perhaps, user-hostile systems "may produce the increased sympathetic excitation that typically accompanies human fight-or-flight responses."

Whether that interpretation is correct or not remains to be seen. What is clear is that the interactions between humans and computers may affect the most fundamental biopsychology of the computer user and that information provided by psychological research can contribute much to our general well-being.

For still more information about computers and stress, see **Making Psychology Part of Your Life**.

Psychology and the Legal System:
Where Law and Psychology Meet

People do not only work at work. For example, they work when they serve on a jury. Here are some findings of psychological research to do with that kind of work.

Canada's legal system is the result of centuries of thought and tradition and is fundamental to democracy. Is justice blind, fair, and impartial in all cases and for everyone (Ungerleider, 1992)? Although we would like to believe it is just and that it works properly (i.e., that it yields the kind of objective, unbiased decisions we expect), the fact is that it is not perfect. Because trials and other legal proceedings involve people, there is ample room for a wide range of social factors to influence—and bias—outcomes. For example, the royal commission into the case of Donald Marshall found that no native person had ever sat on a jury in Nova Scotia.

Sources of Bias in Legal Proceedings:
Characteristics of Defendants

One basic principle of our legal system is that defendants must be judged according to the evidence rather than their background or personal characteristics. At the same time, jurors, lawyers, and judges cannot help but notice—and perhaps be affected by—a defendant's physical appearance, gender, age, and race.

As Daniel Yarmey at the University of Guelph has shown, people agree on which faces and voices are the "good guys" and which are the "bad guys." Yarmey had undergraduates select faces and voices that fit criminal and non-criminal occupations. Not only could subjects differentiate, but they were quite confident in their judgments.

Clearly, many factors other than the evidence may enter into jurors' deliberations as to the guilt or innocence of a defendant. For example, juries are usually more sympathetic to attractive defendants (McKelvie & Coley, 1993a, 1993b), viewing them as less dangerous and less likely to engage in future criminal acts (Esses & Webster, 1988). Some studies show that attractive defendants are acquitted more often and receive lighter sentences (Stewart, 1980).

The gender of the defendant often plays a role as well. While you might predict that juries would show more leniency toward female defendants, the situation is more complicated than that. Often, females do seem to have an edge in terms of sympathy from juries (Michelini & Snodgrass, 1980). However, that is not the case when females are charged with crimes that are not consistent with traditional sex-role stereotypes (Cruse & Leigh, 1987).

Finally, as you might guess, the defendant's ethnic background may influence the process. For example, defendants of northern European background are less likely to be convicted and less likely to receive a prison sentence (Stewart, 1980). This may stem from prejudice (Stephan & Stephan, 1986), or it may reflect also that for economic reasons, defendants from some minority groups are less able to obtain high-quality legal assistance (Welch, Gruhl, & Spohn, 1984). It is clear, however, that minority stereotypes do influence social judgments on the part of jurors, and this plays at least some role in the greater conviction rates for members of visible minorities (Bodenhausen, 1990).

Stereotypes are also a factor in the jury-selection process. In the recent

DEFENDANTS' PERSONAL CHARACTERISTICS

Shown here is one potential source of bias in the legal system. Jurors, lawyers, and even judges can be influenced by personal characteristics of defendants. (Source: Drawing by Chas. Addams; © The New Yorker Magazine, Inc.)

Menendez case in California, the jury split six to six, with all the women voting for a more lenient outcome than the men. Witnesses may also be subject to stereotypic thinking. In 1988, Yarmey and Popiel surveyed about a hundred Canadian psychologists, psychiatrists, prosecutors, and defence lawyers about the value of various expert witnesses. Psychiatrists and clinical psychologists were judged best. In another study, Yarmey (1986) investigated the credibility of police officers as eyewitnesses.

Sources of Bias in Legal Proceedings: The Procedures Themselves

Perhaps even more disturbing than sources of bias relating to the personal characteristics of defendants are problems that seem built into the legal system itself. First, the order in which juries are instructed to consider potential verdicts is important. Several studies indicate that considering the most serious verdict first yields harsher decisions than considering the mildest verdict first (Greenberg, Williams, & O'Brien, 1986).

Second, the range of possible verdicts available to jurors may also influence their decisions. For example, jurors given the option of such verdicts as "not guilty by reason of insanity" or "guilty but mentally incompetent" are more likely to convict a defendant than ones given only the traditional verdicts of guilty or innocent (Savistky & Lindblom, 1986). Apparently, that is because these additional options allow jurors to break potential deadlocks and agree on a guilty verdict.

While Canada does not have the death penalty, research relating to this form of punishment is worth noting here. When the death penalty is included in a range of possible verdicts, many American jurors become even more reluctant to offer a "guilty" verdict than they would otherwise be. In 1990, Jonathan Freedman at the University of Toronto asked people who had already served on juries that had convicted defendants of first-degree murder whether they would have changed their decisions if the death penalty had existed at that time and in that place. Fully 30 percent indicated that they would have been less likely to vote guilty if the death penalty had been in force at the time of the trial. These findings suggest that when jurors know that a guilty verdict may result in the execution of a defendant, they make every effort to avoid a conviction.

A third potential source of difficulty in the legal system itself is the *presumption of innocence* (Dane, 1985). Most legal systems operate under the assumption that defendants are presumed innocent until there is compelling evidence that they are guilty. Jurors are often reminded of that when the trial begins, but do they really adhere to it? There is evidence to indicate that they may not (Ostrom, Werner, & Saks, 1978). For example, consider the results of a study conducted by Helgeson and Shaver (1990), who provided participants with written information about four defendants. For two of the defendants, the crime fit with their occupation; for example, a physician was charged with a drug offense, and a politician was charged with bribery. For two others, the crime did not fit with their occupation; for example, a salesman was charged with arson, and a lawyer was charged with auto theft. After reading the information, participants answered several question designed to determine the extent to which they presumed that the defendant was innocent. For all four occupations, the defendant was more likely to be viewed as guilty when the crime and the occupation were congruent (see Figure 17.11).

Subsequently, Helgeson and Shaver found that, under more realistic conditions, where subjects watched tapes of simulated trials in a courtroom setting,

FIGURE 17.11

The Presumption of Innocence

Innocence is not always presumed by jurors. When individuals were charged with crimes that were congruent with their occupation, mock jurors were less likely to adhere to the principle of *presumed innocence* than when defendants were charged with crimes that were not congruent with their occupation.
(Source: Based on data from Helgeson & Shaver, 1990).

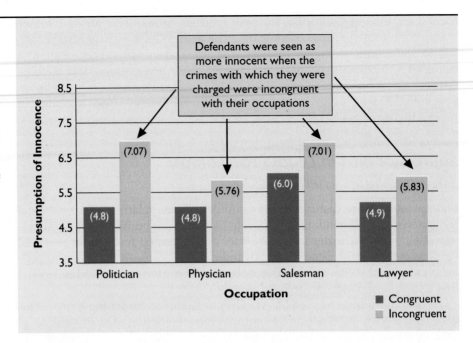

- The outcomes of legal proceedings are often influenced by personal characteristics of defendants as well as by the evidence.

- Several aspects of legal proceedings themselves may bias the outcomes. These include the range of verdicts available to jurors, presence of the death penalty, and factors that influence the presumption of innocence.

the congruency mattered less. This suggests that there are other factors present during actual trials, and these may tend to strengthen the jurors' commitment to keeping as open a mind as possible. However, given the powerful impact of stereotypes, expectations, priming, and other aspects of social cognition, it seems risky to assume that jurors always, or even usually, adhere to the principle that defendants must be presumed innocent. Clearly, this issue deserves further careful attention as psychologists attempt to apply their knowledge to improving the fairness of legal proceedings.

MAKING PSYCHOLOGY PART OF YOUR LIFE

Computers and Repetitive Strain Injury: Keyboards Can Hurt You

When human muscles are used over and over again, in precisely the same way, for long periods of time, they become overreactive, and instead of relaxing, they remain tense. The result is a variety of symptoms, such as tingling in the fingers, hands, and arms and pain in the back and the neck. The general term for these kinds of disorders is repetitive

strain injury. The incidence of RSI in its various forms is increasing rapidly among those who use computers at work—for example, in the newsroom, at the office, and even in the labs of authors of psychology textbooks.

This disorder is of interest to psychologists because it is stress-related and because changes in behavior are required to prevent or remedy this situation.

Choosing the Right Angles to Prevent Keyboard Injury

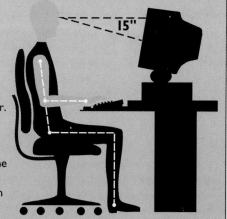

Posture

Arms relaxed and loose at sides; forearms and hands parallel to floor.

Thighs at right angle to torso.

Knees at right angle to thighs.

Arm and hand supports can take the load off back muscles, but ergonomists cannot agree on which ones are best.

Limbering Up:
Exercises for the Hands, Wrists, and Fingers

Massage inside and outside of hand with thumb and fingers.

Grasp fingers and gently bend back wrist. Hold for five seconds.

Gently pull thumb down and back until you feel the stretch. Hold for five seconds.

Clench fist tightly, then release, fanning out fingers. Repeat five times.

By sitting with the correct posture at a well-designed workstation, you can avoid RSI.
(Sources: John Kella, Ph.D., Miller Health Care Institute for the Performing Arts; Joyce Institute; *New York Times*)

---

cles, which are responsible for holding the arms in a steady position at the keyboard (Pascarelli & Quilter, 1994). Little by little, the trauma those muscles experience from their inability to relax accumulates, and the electrical messages between muscle and brain begin to falter. "With a repetitive strain injury," wrote Taylor in 1993, "... these [electrical] messages get mixed up. The muscles will contract, or they contract out of sequence. Or they may contract and then be unable to relax." If this continues, scar tissue and permanent damage may occur.

A number of symptoms may appear at any stage, including annoying to severe pains in the neck and back and tingling and weakness of the hands and arms. Eventually the employee can no longer use the arms or the hands, even to hold a book or use cutlery or a hair dryer. In part, the stress of this disorder occurs because it is not commonly understood and does not show up on X-rays (see the sections on stress in Chapter 13).

The diagnosis of RSI has been made simpler by electromyography (EMG), a procedure in which a surface electrode is used to identify which muscles are not working properly. There are now treatment centers in at least four centers in Canada—Toronto, Hamilton, Calgary, and Vancouver. The general idea is to start the muscles working again, to reestablish the flow of electrical information between the muscles and the brain.

One way of doing that is to pass a mild electrical current into the muscle itself. This therapy was developed by Chan Gunn, a Vancouver researcher and physician. Various professionals, including medical doctors, human factors specialists, and occupational and physical therapists, are now doing research on RSI.

The clinic in Calgary is of special interest here because it is directed by Stuart Donaldson, a clinical psychologist who has applied his knowledge about how the brain and the body work to design treatment and rehabilitation programs for people with RSI. Donaldson's theory is being tested by industries where RSI occurs—for example, at a Ford plant in the United States where 10 percent of the production-line workers have RSI symptoms.

In 1993, Paul Taylor, the medical reporter for *The Globe and Mail*, developed RSI. The results of his efforts to understand the disorder were published in his newspaper in a five-part series titled "Keyboard Grief: Coping with Computer-Caused Injuries." Taylor found that RSI is not unique to computer operators. Any occupation that requires the same movements to be made repetitively for long periods of time involves risk. RSI is also found among musicians (drummers), factory workers (on assembly lines), and athletes (tennis players).

In their study of 800 sewing-machine operators in Quebec, Brisson, Vezina, and Vinet (1992) found a population of women under psychological and ergonomic stress. The psychological stress related to their having to perform a complex task under serious time pressure. The ergonomic stress they described this way: They had to sit with their head forward for a long time while continuously repeating the same upper-limb movements. The researchers found that "the psychological tension associated with the time pressure may play a direct role in the development of musculoskeletal disorders ... in that muscle tension ... increases with psychological tension." They pointed out also the significant cost to the health care system of work-related health problems.

In the 1990s, the health hazards of sewing machines have been linked to computers. Researchers and therapists believe that the difficulty begins with the muscles of the back and neck, particularly the trapezius mus-

What can you do to prevent RSI? What can you do if you have noticed what you think may be mild symptoms of RSI? Here are five ways of applying current knowledge to your situation:

1. Check out the ergonomics of your computer station. The drawing on the previous page shows you the general idea: monitor at eye level, keyboard at the proper height.

2. Check out the way you use your body: how you hold the telephone receiver, how you pound the keys. Hold your head up naturally, your wrists at neutral rather than bent or twisted to the right or the left, your arms and legs at right angles. Notice that over time your shoulders will rise up; lower them often.

3. Check out the chair you use. Do you need a wrist rest, a copy holder, a specially designed back support, or a specially designed pillow that may provide relief to the muscles of your head, neck, and back while you sleep?

4. Take regular breaks, during which you can relax and move your body in different ways and with different muscles.

5. Check out the exercises that are recommended for RSI. Some of these are presented on the previous page. These are designed to stretch the taut muscles and to encourage them to continue functioning normally. They will make you feel better whether you have RSI or not, and they will contribute to prevention if you are at risk.

The prevention and treatment of RSI requires people to change their behavior at work and at play. Undoubtedly, making that happen will require future research and the application of the principles to which you have been introduced in this introduction to psychology.

INDUSTRIAL/ ORGANIZATIONAL PSYCHOLOGY: THE SYSTEMATIC STUDY OF BEHAVIOR AT WORK industrial/organizational psychology 714 human factors 715 goal-setting theory 717 equity theory 719 cafeteria-style benefit plans 722 job design 722 job enlargement 722 job enrichment 722 computer-based work monitoring 723 social facilitation 724 performance appraisals 724 halo effects 725 leniency effects 726 behaviorally anchored rating scales 730 distributional ratings of performance 731 job satisfaction 732 organizational citizenship behavior 739 leadership 739 great person theory of leadership 739 normative theory 739 situational leadership theory 739 transformational (charismatic) leaders 740	• Industrial/organizational psychology studies all aspects of behavior in work settings and the nature of work settings themselves. • Work motivation plays an important role in the performance of many work-related tasks. Expectancy theory suggests that people will expend effort on various tasks only to the extent that they expect such effort to improve performance, believe that good performance will be rewarded, and desire the rewards offered. • Goal setting—the process of establishing clear goals for various tasks—often greatly increases performance. Goal-setting theory proposes that the beneficial effects of goal setting stem from several factors, including comparison between present performance and the goal, feelings of self-efficacy, clarification of expected performance, and improved strategies for task performance. • Equity theory suggests that people compare the ratio of their own inputs and outcomes to the ratio of inputs and outcomes for other comparable individuals. If these ratios are roughly equal, then equity exists. If the ratios are not equal, feelings of inequity may arise. • I/O psychologists have not only developed theories of work motivation but also devised several techniques for enhancing motivation. In addition to goal setting, such procedures include job design, which involves enhancing jobs to maximize motivation. This can involve job enlargement or job enrichment. Another technique is computer-based work monitoring, which is somewhat controversial at present. • Performance appraisals involve assessments of employees' performance coupled with feedback about these ratings. Performance appraisals are subject to many potential forms of bias, including attributional errors, halo effects, the leniency effect, and stereotypes. • Many errors in performance appraisal stem from the cognitive limitations of raters. Others may involve the nature of the rating forms used. Two techniques for reducing such errors are behaviorally anchored rating scales (BARSs) and distributional ratings of performance. • Job satisfaction—the extent to which people like or dislike their work—is an important work-related attitude. Job satisfaction is influenced by both person-related and organization-related factors; even genetic factors seem to play a role. • Job satisfaction is modestly related to absenteeism and voluntary withdrawal by employees. It is also modestly related to individual performance. Recent findings indicate that it may be more strongly linked to organizational performance. • Leadership is a process in which one member of a group exerts influence over other members toward the attainment of common goals. Growing evidence offers support for the view that certain traits play a role in leadership. Among these, flexibility is one of the most important. • Transformational or charismatic leaders exert profound effects on their followers and often on entire societies. This impact stems both from traits they possess and from the special relationships they establish with their followers.
ENVIRONMENTAL PSYCHOLOGY: THE PHYSICAL ENVIRONMENT AND BEHAVIOR crowding 742 seasonal affective disorder 745	• Many environmental variables, including temperature, noise, and air quality, influence performance in work settings. The design of workplaces also affects performance. Landscaped or open offices have become increasingly popular. This type of layout involves reduced privacy as well as increased noise and distraction, but it also offers obvious benefits.

| HUMAN FACTORS: DESIGNING FOR EFFECTIVENESS

visual displays 746
warnings 747
controls 750
compatibility 750
tracking 751 | • Visual displays present information visually. Many factors influence the clarity of such displays. Dynamic displays present information about changing values such as speed or altitude. Such displays are usually easier to read when they use a moving pointer against a fixed scale and when higher values are consistent with what we normally expect to be higher.
• Warnings alert users of products, or the general public, to the presence of hazards. Several factors influence the extent to which warnings are noticed, understood, and obeyed. Interactive warnings seem to be especially effective.
• Controls permit human beings to operate tools, equipment, and systems. If controls do not follow the compatibility principle (i.e., if they don't operate in the ways we expect) they can be very confusing.
• We often use controls for tracking, in which we attempt to stay as close as possible to some target value, as when we drive. Controls may also involve supervisory control, in which users set basic values and then some intermediary mechanism, such as a computer, actually operates the equipment. |
| PSYCHOLOGY AND THE LEGAL SYSTEM: WHERE LAW AND PSYCHOLOGY MEET | • The outcomes of legal proceedings are often influenced by personal characteristics of defendants as well as by the evidence.
• Several aspects of legal proceedings themselves may bias the outcomes. These include the range of verdicts available to jurors, presence of the death penalty, and factors that influence the presumption of innocence. |

CRITICAL THINKING QUESTIONS

APPRAISAL	Work and work-related activities play an extremely important role in most people's lives. Yet the field of industrial/organizational psychology has often been neglected in textbooks like this one. Why do you think this was true in the past? And why is the situation changing now, so that more texts include coverage of this field?
CONTROVERSY	Industrial/organizational psychologists have sometimes been accused of being "tools of management," because they devote so much attention to finding ways of increasing work motivation and productivity. In their own defense, I/O psychologists point out that they also study ways of making work and work settings more pleasant for employees. What are your views on this controversy?
MAKING PSYCHOLOGY PART OF YOUR LIFE	The chances are quite good that at some point in your career, you will be asked to evaluate others—to assess their performance. Now that you know how complex this process can be, and how easily it can be affected by various forms of error, do you think you will approach it differently than might otherwise have been the case? For example, what safeguards might you adopt to help yourself do better at this important task?

Appendix

Statistics: Uses and Potential Abuses

At many points in this text, it has been noted that one benefit you should gain from your first course in psychology is the ability to think about human behavior in a new way. This appendix will expand on that theme by offering a basic introduction to one essential aspect of psychological thinking: **statistics**.

What does this special form of mathematics have to do with psychology or with thinking like a psychologist? The answer involves the fact that all fields of science require two major types of tools. First, scientists need various kinds of equipment to gather the data they seek. Obviously, this equipment differs from field to field; for example, biologists use microscopes, astronomers employ telescopes, and geologists wield hammers (or even dynamite!) in their work.

Second, all scientists need some means for interpreting the findings of their research—for determining the *meaning* of the information they have acquired and its relationship to important theories in their field. Again, this varies from one science to another. In most cases, though, some type of mathematics is involved. Psychology is no exception to this general rule: To understand the findings of their research (and, hence, important aspects of human behavior), psychologists perform *statistical analysis* of the data they collect.

As you'll soon see, statistics are a flexible tool and can be used for many different purposes. In psychology, however, they are usually employed to accomplish one or more of the following tasks: (1) *summarizing* or *describing* large amounts of data; (2) *comparing* individuals or groups of individuals in various ways; (3) determining whether certain aspects of behavior are *related* (whether they vary together in a systematic manner); and (4) *predicting* future behavior from current information. In the pages that follow we'll consider each of these major uses of statistics by psychologists. After doing so, we'll explore several ways in which statistics can be abused—how they can be employed to disguise or conceal important facts rather than to clarify them.

Descriptive Statistics:
Summarizing Data

Suppose that a psychologist conducts an experiment concerned with the effects of staring at others in public places. The procedures of the study are simple. He stares at people in stores, airports, and a variety of other locations, and he records the number of seconds until they look away—or until they approach to make him stop! After carrying out these procedures twenty times, he obtains the data shown in Table A.1. Presented in this form, the scores seem meaningless. If

Statistics: Mathematical procedures used to describe data and draw references from them.

Raw Data from a Simple Experiment

When a psychologist stares at strangers in a public place, these people either look away or approach him in the number of seconds shown. Note that more people look away or approach after 4 seconds than at any other value.

	NUMBER OF SECONDS UNTIL PERSON EITHER LOOKS AWAY OR APPROACHES
Person 1	4
Person 2	4
Person 3	1
Person 4	4
Person 5	3
Person 6	2
Person 7	5
Person 8	3
Person 9	6
Person 10	5
Person 11	4
Person 12	4
Person 13	3
Person 14	3
Person 15	5
Person 16	4
Person 17	4
Person 18	2
Person 19	6
Person 20	5

they are grouped together in the manner shown in Figure A.1 (on page 765), however, a much clearer picture emerges. Now we can see at a glance that the most frequent score is about 4 seconds; that fewer people look away after 3 or 5 seconds; and that even fewer look away very quickly (after 2 seconds) or after a longer delay (6 seconds). This graph presents a **frequency distribution**: It indicates the number of times each score occurs within an entire set of scores. Here, the frequency distribution indicates how many times scores of 1, 2, 3, 4, 5, or 6 seconds were recorded in the study of staring.

A graph such as the one in Figure A.1 provides a rough idea of the way a set of scores is distributed. In science, however, a rough idea is not sufficient; more precision is required. In particular, it would be useful to have an index of (1) the middle score of the distribution of scores (their **central tendency**) and (2) the extent to which the scores spread out around this point (their **dispersion**). Such measures are provided by **descriptive statistics.**

Measures of Central Tendency: Finding the Center

You are already familiar with one important measure of central tendency: the **mean,** or average. We calculate a mean by adding all scores and then dividing by the total number of scores. The mean represents the typical score in a distribution and in this respect is often quite useful. Sometimes, though, it can be misleading. This is because the mean can be strongly affected by one or a few extreme scores. To see why this is so, consider the following example. Ten families live on a block. The number of children in each family is shown in Table A.2 (on page 765). Adding these numbers together and dividing by ten yields a mean of four. Yet, as you can see, *not one family actually has four children.* Most have none or two, but one has eight and another has nineteen.

In cases such as this, it is better to refer to other measures of central tendency. One of these is the **mode**—the most frequently occurring score. As you can see, the mode of the data in Table A.2 is 2: More families have two children than have any other number. Another useful measure of central tendency is the **median**—the midpoint of the distribution. Fifty percent of the scores fall at or above the median, while 50 percent fall at or below this value. Returning to the data in Table A.2, the median also happens to be 2: Half the scores fall at or below this value, while half fall at or above it.

As you can readily see, both the mode and the median provide more accurate descriptions of the data than does the mean in this particular example. But please note that this is *not* always or even usually the case. It is true only in instances where extreme scores distort the mean. In fact, there is no single

Frequency Distribution: The frequency with which each score occurs within an entire distribution of scores.

Central Tendency: The middle (center) of a distribution of scores.

Dispersion: The extent to which scores in a distribution spread out or vary around the center.

Descriptive Statistics: Statistics that summarize the major characteristics of an array of scores.

Mean: A measure of central tendency derived by adding all scores and dividing by the number of scores.

Mode: A measure of central tendency indicating the most frequent score in an array of scores.

Median: A measure of central tendency indicating the midpoint of an array of scores.

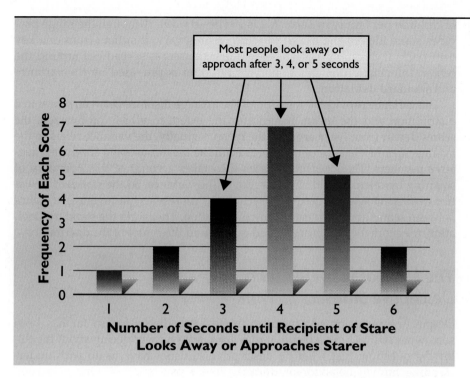

A Frequency Distribution

In a *frequency distribution*, scores are grouped together according to the number of times each occurs. This one suggests that most people react to being stared at within about four seconds.

Most people look away or approach after 3, 4, or 5 seconds

Frequency of Each Score

Number of Seconds until Recipient of Stare Looks Away or Approaches Starer

	NUMBER OF CHILDREN
Family 1	0
Family 2	0
Family 3	2
Family 4	2
Family 5	2
Family 6	2
Family 7	2
Family 8	3
Family 9	19
Family 10	8
	Total = 40 children
	Mean = 40/10 = 4.0

TABLE A.2

How the Mean Can Sometimes Be Misleading

Ten families have a total of forty children among them. The mean is 4.0, but, as you can see, not one family has this number of children. This illustrates the fact that the *mean*, while a useful measure of central tendency, can be distorted by a few extreme scores.

rule for choosing among these measures. The decision to employ one over the others should be made only after careful study of frequency distributions such as the one shown in Figure A.1.

Measures of Dispersion: Assessing the Spread

The mean, median, and mode each tell us something about the center of a distribution, but they provide no indication of its shape. Are the scores bunched together? Do they spread out over a wide range? This issue is addressed by measures of *dispersion*.

The simplest measure of dispersion is the **range**—the difference between the highest and lowest scores. For example, the range for the data on number

Range: The difference between the highest and lowest scores in a distribution of scores.

of children per family in Table A.2 is 19 (19 − 0 = 19). Although the range provides some idea of the extent to which scores vary, it suffers from one key drawback: It does not indicate how much the scores spread out around the center. Information on this important question is provided by the **variance** and **standard deviation**.

The variance provides a measure of the average distance between scores in a distribution and the mean. It indicates the extent to which, on average, the scores depart from (vary around) the mean. Actually, the variance refers to the average *squared* distance of the scores from the mean; squaring eliminates negative numbers. The *standard deviation* then takes account of this operation of squaring by calculating the square root of the variance. So the standard deviation, which is widely used in psychology, represents the average distance between scores and the mean in any distribution. The larger the standard deviation, the more the scores are spread out around the center of the distribution.

The Normal Curve: Putting Descriptive Statistics to Work

Despite the inclusion of several examples, this discussion so far has been somewhat abstract. As a result, it may have left you wondering about the following question: Just what do descriptive statistics have to do with understanding human behavior or thinking like a psychologist? One important answer involves their relationship to a special type of frequency distribution known as the **normal curve**.

While you may never have seen this term before, you are probably quite familiar with the concept it describes. Consider the following characteristics: height, size of vocabulary, strength of motivation to attain success. Suppose you obtained measurements of each from thousands of individuals. What would be the shape of each of these distributions? If you guessed that they would all take the form shown in Figure A.2, you are correct. In fact, on each dimension most scores would pile up in the middle, and fewer and fewer scores would occur farther away from this value. In short, most people

Variance: A measure of dispersion reflecting the average squared distance between each score and the mean.

Standard Deviation: A measure of dispersion reflecting the average distance between each score and the mean.

Normal Curve: A symmetrical, bell-shaped frequency distribution. Most scores are found near the middle, and fewer and fewer occur toward the extremes. Many psychological characteristics are distributed in this manner.

FIGURE A.2

The Normal Curve

On many dimensions relating to behavior, scores show the kind of frequency distribution illustrated here: the *normal curve*. Most scores pile up in the middle, and fewer and fewer occur toward the extremes.

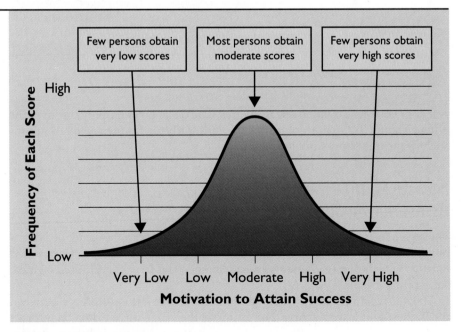

would be found to be average height, would have average vocabularies, and would show average desire for success; very few would be extremely high or low on these characteristics. We should add, by the way, that the normal curve applies to an amazingly wide range of human characteristics—everything from personality traits to cognitive abilities and physical attributes.

What does the normal curve have to do with the use of descriptive statistics? A great deal. One key property of the normal curve is as follows: Specific proportions of the scores within it are contained in certain areas of the curve; moreover, these portions can be defined in terms of the standard deviation of all of the scores. Therefore, once we know the mean of a normal distribution and its standard deviation, we can determine the relative standing of any specific score within it. Perhaps a concrete example will help clarify both the nature and the value of this relationship.

Figure A.3 presents a normal distribution with a mean of 5.0 and a standard deviation of 1.0. Let's assume that the scores shown are those on a test of desire for power. Suppose that we now encounter an individual with a score of 7.0. We know that she is high on this characteristic, but *how* high? On the basis of descriptive statistics—the mean and standard deviation—and of the properties of the normal curve, we can tell. Statisticians have found that 68 percent of the scores in a normal distribution fall within one standard deviation of the mean, either above or below it. Similarly, fully 96 percent of the scores fall within two standard deviations of the mean. Given this information, we can conclude that a score of 7 on this test is very high indeed: Only 2 percent of individuals taking the test attain a score equal to or higher than this one (refer to Figure A.3).

In a similar manner, descriptive statistics can be used to interpret scores in any other distribution, providing it approaches the normal curve in form. As

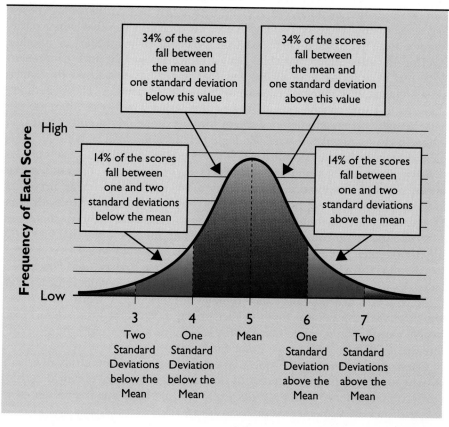

FIGURE A.3

Interpreting Scores by Means of the Normal Distribution

Sixty-eight percent of the scores in a normal distribution fall within one standard deviation of the mean (above or below it). Similarly, fully 96 percent of the scores fall within two standard deviations of the mean. Thus, on a test with a mean of 5.0 and a standard deviation of 1.0, only 2 percent of individuals attain a score of 7.0 or higher.

34% of the scores fall between the mean and one standard deviation below this value

34% of the scores fall between the mean and one standard deviation above this value

14% of the scores fall between one and two standard deviations below the mean

14% of the scores fall between one and two standard deviations above the mean

Frequency of Each Score

High

Low

3 — Two Standard Deviations below the Mean

4 — One Standard Deviation below the Mean

5 — Mean

6 — One Standard Deviation above the Mean

7 — Two Standard Deviations above the Mean

noted above, a vast array of psychological characteristics and behaviors do seem to be distributed in this manner. The result: We can readily determine an individual's relative standing on any of these dimensions from just two pieces of information: the mean of all scores in the distribution and the standard deviation. Little wonder, then, that the normal curve has sometimes been described as a statistician's or psychologist's delight.

Now imagine that your first psychology test contains fifty multiple-choice items. You obtain a score of 40. Did you do well or poorly? If your instructor provides two additional pieces of information—the mean of all the scores in the class and the standard deviation—you can tell. Suppose that the mean is 35 and the standard deviation is 2.50. The mean indicates that most people got a lower score than you did. The relatively small standard deviation indicates that most scores were quite close to the mean—only about twice this distance *above* the mean. Further—and here is a key point—this conclusion would be accurate whether there were 30, 100, or 500 students in the class, assuming the mean and standard deviation remained unchanged. It is precisely this type of efficiency that makes descriptive statistics so useful for summarizing even large amounts of information.

Inferential Statistics: *Determining Whether Differences Are or Are Not Real*

*T*hroughout this book, the results of many experiments have been described. When these studies were discussed, differences between various conditions or groups were often mentioned. For example, we saw that participants exposed to one set of conditions or one level of an independent variable behaved differently from participants exposed to another set of conditions or another level of an independent variable. How did we know that such differences were real ones rather than differences that might have occurred by chance alone? The answer involves the use of **inferential statistics**. These methods allow us to reach conclusions about just this issue: whether a difference we have actually observed is large enough for us to conclude (to *infer*) that it is indeed a real or *significant* one. The logic behind inferential statistics is complex, but some of its key points can be illustrated by the following example.

Suppose that a psychologist conducts an experiment to examine the impact of mood on memory. (As you may recall, such research was discussed in Chapter 6.) To do so, he exposes one group of participants to conditions designed to place them in a good mood: They watch a very funny videotape. A second group, in contrast, is exposed to a neutral tape—one that has little impact on their mood. Both groups are then asked to memorize lists of words, some of which refer to happy events, such as "party" and "success." Later, both groups are tested for recall of these words. Results indicate that those who watched the funny tape remember more happy words than those who watched the neutral tape; in fact, those in the first group remember twelve happy words, while those in the second remember only eight—a difference of 4.0. Is this difference a real one?

One way of answering this question would be to repeat the study over and over again. If a difference in favor of the happy group were obtained consistently, our confidence that it is indeed real (and perhaps due to differences in subjects' mood) would increase. As you can see, however, this would be a

Inferential Statistics: *Statistical procedures that permit us to determine whether differences between individuals or groups are ones that are likely or unlikely to have occurred by chance.*

costly procedure. Is there any way of avoiding it? One answer is provided by inferential statistics. These methods assume that if we repeated the study over and over again, the size of the difference between the two groups obtained each time would vary; moreover, these differences would be normally distributed. Most would fall near the mean, and only a few would be quite large. When applying inferential statistics to the interpretation of psychological research, we make a very conservative assumption: We begin by assuming that there is no difference between the groups—that the mean of this distribution is zero. Through methods that are beyond the scope of this discussion, we then estimate the size of the standard deviation. Once we do, we can readily evaluate the difference obtained in an actual study. If an observed difference is large enough that it would occur by chance only 5 percent (or less) of the time, we can view it as significant. For example, assume that in the study we have been discussing, this standard deviation (a standard deviation of mean differences) is 2.0. This indicates that the difference we observed (4.0) is two standard deviations above the expected mean of zero (please refer to Figure A.4). As you'll recall from our discussion of the normal curve, this means that the difference is quite large and would occur by chance less than 2 percent of the time. Our conclusion: The difference between the two groups in our study is *probably* real. Thus, mood does indeed seem to affect memory.

Please note that the word *probably* is being used here. Since the tails of the normal curve never entirely level off, there is always some chance—no matter how slight—that even a huge observed difference is due to chance. If we accept a difference that really occurred by chance as being real, we make what statisticians describe as a Type I error. If, in contrast, we interpret a real difference as being one that occurred by chance, we make a Type II error. Clearly, both kinds can lead us to false conclusions about the findings of a research project.

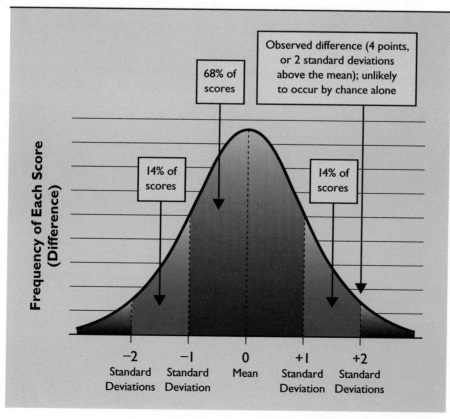

FIGURE A.4

Using Inferential Statistics to Determine Whether an Observed Difference Is a Real One

Two groups in a study concerned with the effects of mood on memory attain mean scores of 12.0 and 8.0, respectively. Is this difference *significant* (real)? Through inferential statistics, we can tell. If the study were repeated over and over, and the two groups did not really differ, the mean difference in their scores would be zero. Assuming that the standard deviation is 2.0, we know that the probability of a difference this large is very small—less than 2 percent. In view of this fact, we conclude that this finding is indeed significant.

Correlation and Prediction

Does crime increase as temperatures rise? Does the chance of winning elections increase with a candidate's height? Does our ability to solve certain kinds of problems change with age? Psychologists are often interested in such questions. In short, they are concerned with whether two or more variables are *related*, so that changes in one are associated with changes in the other. Remember: This is quite different from the issue of whether changes in one variable *cause* changes in another. (If you're unclear about this distinction, refresh your memory by referring to Chapter 1.)

In order to answer such questions, we must gather information on each variable. For example, assume that we wanted to find out if political fortunes are indeed related to height. To do so, we might obtain information on (1) the height of hundreds of candidates and (2) the percentage of votes they obtained in recent elections. Then we'd plot these two variables, height against votes, by entering a single point for each candidate on a graph such as the one in Figure A.5. As you can see, the first graph in this figure indicates that tallness is positively associated with political success. The second points to the opposite conclusion, and the third suggests that there is no relationship at all between height and political popularity.

FIGURE A.5

Illustrating Relationships Through Scatterplots

Is height related to success in politics? To find out, we measure the height of many candidates and obtain records of the percentage of votes they obtained. We then plot height against votes in a scatterplot. Plot A indicates a positive relationship between height and political success: The taller candidates are, the more votes they get. Plot B indicates a negative relationship between these variables. Plot C suggests that there is no relationship between these variables.

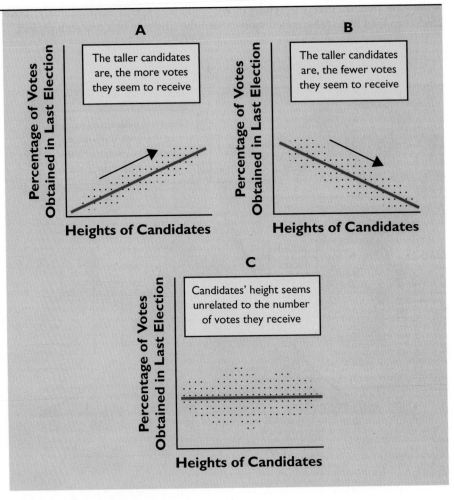

APPENDIX

While such graphs, known as *scatterplots,* are useful, they don't by themselves provide a precise index of the strength of the relationship between two or more variables. To obtain such an index, we often calculate a statistic known as a **correlation coefficient**. Such coefficients can range from –1.00 to +1.00. Positive numbers indicate that as one variable increases, so does the other. Negative numbers indicate that as one factor increases, the other decreases. The greater the departure from 0.00 in either direction, the stronger the relationship between the two variables. Thus, a correlation of +0.80 is stronger than one of +0.39. Similarly, a correlation of –0.76 is stronger than one of –0.51.

Once we've computed a correlation coefficient, we can test its significance: We can determine whether it is large enough to be viewed as unlikely to occur by chance alone. Further, we can also compare correlations to determine if, in fact, one is significantly larger or smaller than another. The methods used for completing these tasks are somewhat different from those used for comparing means, but the logic is much the same.

In addition to determining the extent to which two or more variables are related, statistical procedures also exist for determining the degree to which a specific variable can be *predicted* from one or more others. These methods of *regression analysis* are complex, but they are of great practical value. Knowing the extent to which performance can be predicted from currently available information—such as grades, past performance, or scores on psychological tests—can aid companies, schools, and many other organizations in selecting the best people for employment or educational opportunities.

The Misuse of Statistics: *Numbers Don't Lie ... or Do They?*

A public figure once remarked, "There are lies, damned lies, and statistics!" By this, he meant that statistics are often used for purposes quite different from the ones we've discussed here. Instead of serving as a valuable basis for understanding scientific data, interpreting test scores, or making predictions about behavior, statistics are sometimes employed to confuse, deceive, or mislead their intended victims. To make matters worse, in the wrong hands statistics can be quite effective in this role. The reason for such success lies in the fact that most of us firmly accept another popular saying: "Numbers don't lie." Thus, when confronted with what appear to be mathematical data and facts, we surrender our usual skepticism and readily accept what we are told. Since the costs of doing so can be quite high, let's conclude this brief discussion of statistics by examining some of the more common—and blatant—*mis*uses of statistics. Here, too, thinking like a psychologist can be of considerable practical value. If you keep the principles outlined here firmly in mind, you'll often be able to spot such statistical abuses and can avoid being deceived by them.

Random Events Don't Always Seem Random

You pick up the paper and read an account of a young woman who won more than one million dollars at a gambling casino. She placed sixteen bets in a row at a roulette table and won on every spin of the wheel. Why? Was she incredibly lucky? Did she have a system? If you are like many people, you may jump to the conclusion that there is indeed something special about her. After all, how else can this incredible series of events be explained?

Correlation Coefficient: A statistic indicating the degree of relationship between two or more variables.

If you do jump to such conclusions, you are probably making a serious mistake. Here's why. For any single player, the odds of winning so many times in succession are indeed slight. But consider the vast number of players and the number of occasions on which they play; some casinos remain open around the clock. Also, remember the shape of the normal curve. The mean number of wins in a series of sixteen bets is indeed low—perhaps one or two. But the tails of the curve never level off, so there is some probability, however slight, of even sixteen wins occurring in a row. In short, even events that would be expected to occur by chance *do* occur albeit very rarely. The moral is clear: Don't overinterpret events that seem, at first glance, to border on impossible. They may actually be rare chance occurrences with no special significance of their own.

Large Samples Provide a Better Basis for Reaching Conclusions Than Small Ones

Many television commercials take the following form. A single consumer is asked to compare three unlabeled brands of facial tissue or to compare the whiteness of three loads of wash. She then makes the "right" choice, selecting the sponsor's product as softest, brightest, or whitest. The commercial ends with a statement of the following type: "Here's proof. Our brand is the one most shoppers prefer." Should you take such evidence seriously? Caution is advised. In most cases, it is not possible to reach firm statistical conclusions on the basis of the reactions of a single individual, or even of several individuals. Rather, a much larger number of cooperative participants is necessary. After watching such a commercial, then, you should ask what would happen if the same procedures were repeated with 20, 50, or 500 shoppers. Would the sponsor's brand actually be chosen significantly more often than the others? The commercials leave the impression that it would; but, as you should realize by now, jumping to such conclusions is risky. So be skeptical of claims based on very small samples. They are on shaky grounds at best, and they may be designed to be purposely misleading.

Unbiased Samples Provide a Better Basis for Reaching Conclusions Than Biased Ones

Here's another popular type of commercial, and another common misuse of statistics. An announcer, usually dressed in a white coat, states: "Three out of four dentists surveyed recommend Jawbreak sugarless gum." At first glance, the meaning of this message seems clear: Most dentists prefer that their patients chew a specific brand of gum. But look more closely: There's an important catch. Notice that the announcer says, "Three out of four dentists *surveyed* ..." Who were these people? A fair and representative sample of all dentists? Major stockholders in the Jawbreak company? Close relatives of the person holding the patent on this product? From the information given, it's impossible to tell. To the extent these or many other possibilities are true, the dentists surveyed represent a *biased* sample; they are *not* representative of the population to which the sponsor wishes us to generalize: all dentists.

So whenever you encounter claims about the results of a survey, ask two questions: (1) Who were the people surveyed? (2) How were they chosen? If these questions can't be answered to your satisfaction, be on guard: Someone may be trying to mislead you.

Unexpressed Comparisons Are Often Meaningless

Another all-too-common misuse of statistics involves what might be described as "errors of omission." People using this tactic mention a comparison but then fail to specify all of the groups or items involved. For example, consider the following statement: "In recent laboratory tests, Plasti-spred was found to contain fully 82 percent less cholesterol! So, if you care about your family's health, buy Plasti-spred, the margarine for modern life." Impressive, right? After all, Plasti-spred seems to contain much less of a dangerous substance than—what? There, in fact, is the rub: We have no idea as to the identity of the other substances in the comparison. Were they other brands of margarine? Butter? A jar of bacon drippings? A beaker full of cholesterol?

The lesson offered by such claims is clear. Whenever you are told that a product, candidate, or anything else is better or superior in some way, always ask the following question: Better than *what*?

Some Differences Aren't Really There

Here's yet another type of commercial you've probably seen before. An announcer points to lines on a graph that diverge before your eyes and states, "Here's proof! Gasaway neutralizes stomach acid twice as fast as the other leading brand." And in fact, the line labeled Gasaway does seem to rise more quickly, leaving its poor competitor in the dust. Should you take such claims seriously? Again, the answer is no. First, such graphs are usually unlabeled. As a result, we have no idea as to what measure of neutralizing acids is being applied or how much time is involved. It is quite possible that the curves illustrate only the first few seconds after the medicine is taken and that beyond that period the advantage for the sponsor's product disappears.

Second, and even more important, there are no grounds for assuming that the differences shown are *significant*—that they could not have occurred by chance. Perhaps there is no difference whatsoever in the speed with which the two products neutralize acid, but the comparison was run over and over again until—by chance—a seemingly large difference in favor of the sponsor's brand occurred. This is not to say that all advertisers, or even most, engage in such practices. Perhaps the differences shown in some commercials are indeed real. Still, given the strong temptation companies face to stress the benefits of their own products, the following policy is probably best: Assume that all differences reported in ads and similar sources are *not* significant—that is, not real—unless specific information to the contrary is provided.

Graphs May Distort (or At Least Bend) Reality

The results of psychological research are often represented in graphs; graphs can communicate major findings efficiently and can readily present complex relationships that are difficult to describe verbally. Unfortunately, however, graphs are often used for another purpose: to alter the conclusions drawn from a given set of data. There are many ways to do this, but the most common involves altering the meaning of the axes—the horizontal or vertical boundaries of the graph. A specific example may help clarify this process.

During the last Canadian federal election, there was much dispute over the growth of the national debt under Mulroney's Conservative government. In Figure A.6, two different ways of graphically representing the debt figures for most of the Conservatives' years in power are shown.

If you were a supporter of the Liberals in the last election and had been presented with the graph on the left, it would have likely served to confirm your worst expectations about uncontrolled debt growth under the Conservative government. On the other hand, if you were a Conservative supporter, and had been presented with the graph on the right, you would have found it relatively reassuring: An increase in the debt is apparent, but it seems relatively modest and controlled. If you had no strong party affiliation, but were concerned about the debt, selective exposure to one or the other of these graphs, with a little political rhetoric, might well have been decisive in moving you to support one party or the other. How can these graphs seemingly support two different positions? The same numbers are presented in both. It is evident that the national debt rose from approximately $161 billion in 1984 to about $423 billion in 1992. This rise seems much larger and more dramatic in the left-hand graph. The reason for this has to do with the size of the units along the vertical axis. These are small in the left-hand graph but very large in the right-hand one. Small units magnify differences, large units diminish them.

Sadly, such fine-tuning of graphs is common in magazines, political mailings, and many other sources. Thus, it is important to pay careful attention to the scale employed in any graph, the precise quantities being measured, and all labels employed. If you overlook such factors, you may be a sitting duck for those who wish to lead you to false conclusions.

FIGURE A.6

Misleading Graphs: One Common Technique

A change in the scale of the vertical axis can make graphs representing the same data seem to convey very different information. The growth of the national debt appears to be huge in the left-hand graph but quite modest in the right-hand graph.

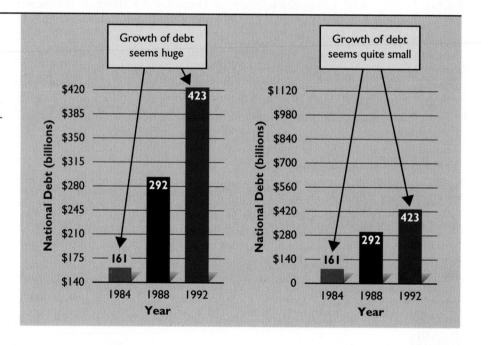

SUMMARY AND REVIEW OF KEY POINTS

DESCRIPTIVE STATISTICS: SUMMARIZING DATA statistics 763 frequency distribution 764 central tendency 764 dispersion 764 descriptive statistics 764 mean 764 mode 764 median 764 range 765 variance 766 standard deviation 766 normal curve 766	• All scientists require two types of tools in their research: equipment for collecting data and some means of interpreting their findings. In psychology, statistics are often used for the latter purpose. • Large quantities of data can be grouped into frequency distributions indicating the number of times each score occurs. Two important facts about any frequency distribution are its central tendency—its center—and its dispersion, or the extent to which scores spread out around this value. • Common measures of central tendency include the mean, mode, and median. Dispersion is often measured in terms of variance and the standard deviation. This latter term refers to the average distance of each score from the mean. • The frequency distributions for many behavioral characteristics show a bell-shaped form known as the normal distribution or normal curve. Most scores fall near the middle, and fewer occur at increasing distances from this value. Specific proportions of the scores are found under certain parts of the curve.
INFERENTIAL STATISTICS: DETERMINING WHETHER DIFFERENCES ARE OR ARE NOT REAL inferential statistics 768	• Psychologists use inferential statistics to determine whether differences between individuals or groups are significant, or real. Inferential statistics assume that the mean difference in question is zero and that observed differences are distributed normally around this value. • If an observed difference is large enough that it would occur by chance only 5 percent of the time, it is viewed as significant.
CORRELATION AND PREDICTION correlation coefficient 771	• To determine whether two or more variables are related, psychologists compute correlation coefficients. These range from –1.00 to +1.00. The larger the departure from 0.00, the stronger the correlation between the variables in question. • Correlations, and statistics derived from them, can be used to predict future behavior from current information. Such predictions are of great practical benefit to schools, companies, and others wishing to predict future performance from current behavior.
THE MISUSE OF STATISTICS: NUMBERS DON'T LIE ... OR DO THEY?	• Although statistics have many beneficial uses, they are often employed to deceive or mislead. • Misuse of statistics can involve the use of extremely small or biased samples, unexpressed comparisons, and misleading graphs and presentations.

References

Aaronson, L. S., & MacNee, C. L. (1989). Tobacco, alcohol, and caffeine use during pregnancy. *Journal of Obstetrics, Gynecology, and Neonatal Nursing, 18,* 279–287.

Abbey, S. E., Hood, E., Young, L. T., & Malcolmson, S. A. (1993). Psychiatric Consultation in the Eastern Canadian Arctic III. Mental health issues in Inuit women in the Eastern Arctic. III. *Canadian Journal of Psychiatry, 38,* 32–35.

Abelson, R. P., Loftus, E. F., & Greenwald, A. G. (1992). Attempts to improve the accuracy of self-reports of voting. In J. M. Tanur (Ed.), *Questions about survey questions: Meaning, memory, expression, and social interactions in surveys* (pp. 138–153). New York: Russell Sage Foundation.

Aboud, F.E. (1989). Disagreement between friends. *International Journal of Behavioral Development, 12(4),* 495–508.

Aboud, F.E. (1993). The developmental psychology of racial prejudice. *Transcultural Psychiatric Research Review, 30(3),* 229–242.

Aboud, F.E., Kubaysi, J.I., Tabbarah, D.H., Rubays, J.A. (1986). Beliefs about laws and legal justice among Lebanese college students. *Journal of Social Psychology, 126(3),* 317–320.

Aboud, F.E., Samuel, M., Hadera, A., Addus, A. (1991). Intellectual, social and nutritional status of children in an Ethiopian orphanage. *Social Science and Medicine, 33(11),* 1275–1280.

Abra, J.C. (1993). Competition: Creativity's vilified motive. *Genetic, Social, and General Psychology Monographs, 119(3),* 289–342.

Abra, J.C. (1989). Changes in creativity with age: data, explanations, and further predictions. *International Journal of Aging and Human Development, 28(2),* 105–126.

Abramovitch, R., Freedman, J.L., Pliner, P. (1991). Children and money: Getting an allowance, credit versus cash, and knowledge of pricing. *Journal of Economic Psychology, 12(1),* 27–45.

Abramovitch, R., Freedman, J.L., Thoden, K., Nikolich, C. (1991). Children's capacity to consent to participation in psychological research: Empirical findings. *Child Development, 62(5),* 1100–1109.

Abramowitz, S. I. (1986). Psychosocial outcomes of sexual reassignment surgery. *Journal of Consulting and Clinical Psychology, 54,* 183–189.

Abramowitz, S. I., & Murray, J. (1983). Race effects in psychotherapy. In J. Murray & P. R. Abramson (Eds.), *Bias in psychotherapy* (pp. 215–255). New York: Academic Press.

Abramson, L. Y., Seligman M. E. P., & Teasdale, J. D. (1978). Learned helplessness in humans: Critique and reformation. *Journal of Abnormal Psychology, 87,* 49–74.

Absi-Semaan, N., Crombie, G., Freeman, C. (1993). Masculinity and femininity in middle childhood: Developmental and factor analyses. *Sex Roles, 28(3–4),* 187–206.

Adamec, R.E. (1990). Role of the amygdala and medial hypothalamus in spontaneous feline aggression and defense. *Aggressive Behavior, 16(3–4),* 207–222.

Adamec, R.E. (1991). Corticotropin releasing factor: a peptide link between stress and psychopathology associated with epilepsy? *Journal of Psychopharmacology, 5(2),* 96–104.

Adams, R.J., (1987). An evaluation of color preference in early infancy. *Infant Behavior and Development, 10(2),* 143–150.

Addington, J. (1992). Separation group. *Journal for Specialists in Group Work, 17(1),* 20–28.

Addington, J.M. (1986). The development of children and adolescents from divorced homes. *Journal of Child Care, 2(5),* 83–97.

Adelstein, A. & Crowne, D.P. 1991. Visuospatial asymmetries and interocular transfer in the split-brain rat. *Behavioral Neuroscience, 105(3),* 459–469.

Ader, R., & Cohen, N. (1984). Behavior and the immune system. In W. D. Gentry (Ed.), *Handbook of behavioral medicine.* New York: Guilford.

Adlaf, E.M., Smart, R.G., Walsh, G.W. (1993). Ontario Student Drug Use Survey, 1977–1993. The Addiction Research Foundation of Ontario.

Adler, N. J., & Bartholomew, S. (1992). Managing globally competent people. *Academy of Management Executive, 6,* 52–65.

Ahmed, S.M. (1990). Psychometric properties of the boredom proneness scale. *Perceptual and Motor Skills, 71(3 pt. 1),* 963–966.

Ahmed, S.M. & Mapletoft, S.J. (1989). A new approach to explain aggression. *Perceptual and Motor Skills, 69(2),* 403–408.

Ahmed, S.M. (1992). Fraisse's theory of emotion and aggression. *Journal of Social Psychology, 132(2),* 257–260.

Aiello, J. R. (1993). Computer-based work monitoring: Electronic surveillance and its effects. *Journal of Applied Social Psychology, 23,* 499–507.

Aiello, J. R., & Svec, C. M. (1993). Computer monitoring of work performance: Extending the social facilitation framework to electronic presence. *Journal of Applied Social Psychology, 23,* 537–548.

Aiken, L. R. (1991). *Psychological testing and assessment* (7th ed.) Boston: Allyn & Bacon.

Ainsworth, M. D. S. (1969). Object relations, dependency, and attachment: A theoretical review of the infant-mother relationship. *Child Development, 40,* 969–1025.

Ainsworth, M. D. S. (1973). The development of infant-mother attachment. In B. Caldwell & H. Riciutti (Eds.), *Review of child development research* (Vol. 3, pp. 1–94). Chicago: University of Chicago Press.

Ainsworth, M. D. S., Blehar, M. C., Waters, E., & Wall, S. (1978). *Patterns of attachment.* Hillsdale, NJ: Erlbaum.

Akerstedt, T., & Froberg, J. E. (1976). Interindividual differences in circadian pattern of catecholamine excretion, body temperature, performance, and subjective arousal. *Biological Psychology, 4,* 277–292.

Akil, J., Watson, S. J., Young, E., Lewis, M. E., Kachaturian, H., & Walker, M. W. (1984). Endogenous opiates: Biology and function. *Annual Review of Neuroscience, 7,* 223–256.

Al-Issa, I. (1982). Does culture make a difference in psychopathology? In I. Al-Issa (Ed.), *Culture and psychopathology.* Baltimore: University Park Press.

Alagna, F. J., Whitcher, S. J., & Fisher, J. D. (1979). Evaluative reactions to interpersonal touch in a counseling interview. *Journal of Counseling Psychology, 26,* 465–472.

Alain, M. (1985). Une application des theories d'attributions: les conflits conjugaux. (An application of the attribution theories: Marital conflicts.) *Revue Quebecoise de Psychologie, 6(2),* 102–113.

Alberts-Corush, J., Firestone, P., Goodman, J.T., (1986). Attention and impulsivity characteristics of the biological and adoptive parents of hyperactive and normal control children. *American Journal of Orthopsychiatry, 56(3),* 413–423.

Aldridge, D., & Kimberly, St.J. (1991). Adolescent and pre-adolescent suicide in Newfoundland and Labrador. *Canadian Journal of Psychiatry, 36,* 432–436.

Alicke, M.D., Braun, J.C., Glor, J.E., Klotz, M.L., et al. (1992). Complaining behavior in social interaction. *Personality and Social Psychology Bulletin, 18(3),* 286–295.

Allan, L.G. & Siegel, S. (1993). McCollough effects as conditioned responses: Reply to Dodwell and Humphrey, *Psychological Review, 100.* 342–346.

Allen, N.J., Meyer, J.P. (1993). Organizational commitment: Evidence of career stage effects? Special Issue: Loyalty in a multi-commitment world. *Journal of Business Research, 26(1),* 49–61.

Allen, V. L., & Levine, J. M. (1971). Social support and conformity: The role of independent assessment of reality. *Journal of Experimental Social Psychology, 4,* 48–58.

Allgood-Merton, B., Lewinsohn, P.M. & Hops, H. (1990). Sex differences and adolescent depression. *Journal of Abnormal Psychology, 99(1),* 55–63.

Alloy, L.B., Abramson, L., Metalsky, G., & Bartlage, S. (1988). The hopelessness theory of depression: Attributional aspects. *British Journal of Clinical Psychology, 27,* 5–21.

Allport, G. W. (1965). *Letters from Jenny.* New York: Harcourt, Brace & World.

Allport, G. W., & Odbert, H. S. (1936). Trait names: A psycholexical study. *Psychological Monographs, 47,* 211.

Altman, I., & Taylor, D. A. (1973). *Social penetration: The development of interpersonal relationships.* New York: Holt, Rinehart & Winston.

Altshuler, J.L., Ruble, D.N., (1989). Developmental changes in children's awareness of strategies for coping with uncontrollable stress. *Child Development, 60(6),* 1337–1349.

American Psychiatric Association (1993). DSM-IV Draft Criteria. Washington, DC: Author.

Amoore, J. (1970). *Molecular basis of odor.* Springfield, IL: Thomas.

Amoore, J. (1982). Odor theory and odor classification. In E. Theimer (Ed.), *Fragrance chemistry—The science of the sense of smell.* New York: Academic Press.

Amundson, N.E. (1993). Mattering: a foundation for employment counselling and training. Special issue: Employment counselling training. *Journal of Employment Counselling, 30(4),* 146–152.

Anderson, C.A., Anderson, D.C. (1984). Ambient temperature and violent crime: Tests of the linear and curvilinear hypotheses. *Journal of Personality and Social Psychology, 46(1),* 91–97.

Anderson, C. A., & DeNeve, K. M. (1992). Temperature, aggression, and the negative affect escape model. *Psychological Bulletin, 111,* 347–351.

Anderson, J.L. & Crawford, C.B. (1992). Modeling costs and benefits of adolescent weight control as a mechanism for reproductive suppression. *Human Nature, 3(4),* 299–334.

Andreasen, N. C., Flaum, M., Swayze, V., II, O'Leary, D. S., Alliger, R., Cohen, J., Ehrhardt, J., & Yuhn, W. T. C. (1993). Intelligence and brain structure in normal individuals. *American Journal of Psychiatry, 150,* 130–134.

✤ indicates Canadian reference

Andrews, J. D. W. (1967). The achievement motive and advancement in two types of organization. *Journal of Personality and Social Psychology, 6*, 163–168.

Angerspach, D., Knauth, P., Karvonen, M. J., & Undeutsch, K. (1980). A retrospective cohort study comparing complaints and diseases in day and shift workers. *International Archives of Occupational and Environmental Health, 45*, 127–140.

Ankney, C.D. (1992). Sex differences in relative brain size: a mismeasure of woman, too? Special issue: biology and intelligence. *Intelligence, 16(3–4)*, 329–336.

Anson, A. R., Cook, T. D., Habib, F., Grady, M. K., Haynes, N., & Comer, P. (1991). The Comer school development program: A theoretical analysis. *Urban Education, 26*, 56–82.

Anstis, S. (1992). Adaptation to a negative, brightness-reversed world: Some preliminary observations. In G. A. Carpenter & S. Grossberg (Eds.), *Neural networks for vision and image processing*. Cambridge: MIT Press.

❀ Anstis, S., & Hutahajan, P. (1991). Visual adaption to a negative, brightness-reversed world. Paper presented at the Association for Researach in Vision and Opthalmology Conference, Sarasota, Florida.

Antrobus, J. (1991). Dreaming: Cognitive processes during cortical activation and high afferent thresholds. *Psychological Review, 98*, 96–212.

Appley, M. H., & Rickwood, J. (1967). *Psychology in Canada. Special Study No. 3*, Science Secretariat, Privy Council Office, Ottawa, p. 61.

Arato, M., Frecska, E., Tekes, K. & MacCrimmon, D.J. (1991). Serotonergic interhemispheric asymmetry: gender difference in the orbital cortex. *Acta Psychiatrica Scandinavica, 84(1)*, 110–111.

Arbuckle, T.Y. & Gold, D.P. (1993). Aging, inhibition, and verbosity. *Journals of Gerontology, 48(5)*, 225–232.

❀ Arbuckle, T.Y., Gold, D.P., Andres, D., Schwartzman, A., Chaikelson, J. (1992). The role of psychosocial context, age, and intelligence in memory performance of older men. *Psychology and Aging, 7(1)*, 25–36.

❀ Archer, L.A., Cunningham, C.E. & Whelan, D.T. (1988). Coping with dietary therapy in phenylketonuria: A case report. Special issue: Child and adolescent health. *Canadian Journal of Behavioral Science, 20(4)*, 461–466.

Arieti, S. (1974). *Interpretation of schizophrenia*. New York: Basic Books.

Arkes, H. R., Herren, L. T., & Isen, A. M. (1988). The role of potential loss in the influence of affect on risk-taking behavior. *Organizational Behavior and Human Decision Processes, 42*, 181–193.

Arkin, R. M., Lake, E. A., & Baumgardner, A. H. (1986). Shyness and self-presentation. In W. Jones, J. Cheek, & S. Briggs (Eds.), *Shyness: Perspectives on research and treatment* (pp. 189–203). New York: Plenum Press.

Armstrong, C. (1991). Emotional changes following brain injury: Psychological and neurological components of depression, denial and anxiety. *Journal of Rehabilitation, 2*, 15–22.

Aronoff, J., Woike, B. A., & Hyman, L. M. (1992). Which are the stimuli in facial displays of anger and happiness? Configurational bases of emotional recognition. *Journal of Personality and Social Psychology, 62*, 1050–1066.

Aronoff, S. R., & Spilka, B. (1984–1985). Patterning of facial expressions among terminal cancer patients. *Omega, 15*, 101–108.

Aronson, E. (1990). Applying social psychology to desegregation and energy conservation. Special Issue: Illustrating the value of basic research. *Personality and Social Psychology Bulletin, 16(1)*, 118–132.

Aronson, E. (1992). The return of the repressed: Dissonance theory makes a comeback. *Psychological Inquiry, 3(4)*, 303–311.

Aronson, E., Bridgeman, D.L., Geffner, R. (1978). Interdependent interactions and prosocial behavior. *Journal of Research and Development in Education, 12(1)*, 16–27.

Arvey, R.D., Bouchard, T.J., Segal, N.L., Abraham, L.M. (1989). Job satisfaction: Environmental and genetic components. *Journal of Applied Psychology, 74(2)*, 187–192.

❀ Asante, M. K. (1980). Afrocentricity: The theory of social change. Buffalo, NY: Amulefi Publishing Company.

Asarnow, R. F., Granholm, E., & Sherman, T. (1991). Span of apprehension in schizophrenia. In J. Zubin, S. Steinhauer, & J. Gruzelier (Eds.), *Handbook of schizophrenia: Vol. 5. Neuropsychology, psychophysiology, and information-processing* (pp. 335–370). Amsterdam: Elsevier Science.

Asch, S. E. (1951). Effects of group pressure upon the modification and distortion of judgment. In H. Guetzkow (Ed.), *Groups, leadership, and men*. Pittsburgh, PA: Carnegie.

Assogba, Y. (1992). Raccrocher l'autre jeunesse: une experience comunautaire de raccrochage scolaire dans l'Outaouais. (Rehabilitating the "other" youth: a community experiment in educational rehabilitation in the Outaouais region.) *Apprentissage et Socialisation, 15(1)*, 39–48.

❀ Astley, S. J., Claaren, S. K., Little, R. E., Sampson, P. D., & Daling, J. R. (1992). Analysis of racial shape in children gestationally exposed to marijuana, alcohol, and/or cocaine. *Pediatrics, 89*, 67–77.

Astley, S. L., & Wasserman, E. A. (1992). Categorical discrimination and generalization in pigeons: All negative stimuli are not created equal. *Journal of Experimental Psychology: Animal Behavior Processes, 18* 193–207.

Atkinson, J. W., & Litwin, G. H. (1960). Achievement motive and test anxiety conceived as motive to approach success and motive to avoid failure. *Journal of Abnormal and Social Psychology, 60*, 52–63.

Atkinson, R. C., & Shiffrin, R. M. (1968). Human memory: A proposed system and its control processes. In K. W. Spence (Ed.), *The psychology of learning and motivation: Advances in research and theory* (Vol. 2, pp. 89–195). New York: Academic Press.

Aubé, J., & Koestner, R. (1992). Gender characteristics and adjustment: A longitudinal study. *Journal of Personality and Social Psychology, 63*, 485–493.

Austin, J., Hatfield, D. B., Grindle, A. C., & Bailey, J. S. (1993). Increasing recycling in office environments: The effects of specific, informative cues. *Journal of Applied Behavior Analysis, 26*, 247–253.

Avis, J. M. (1992). Where are all the family therapists? Abuse and violence within families and family therapy's response. *Journal of Marital and Family Therapy, 18*, 225–232.

Babcock, R. L., & Salthouse, T. A. (1990). Effects of increased processing demands on age differences in working memory. *Psychology and Aging, 5*, 421–428.

Bachetti, P. (1990). Estimating the incubation period of AIDS by comparing population infection and diagnosis patterns. *Journal of the American Statistical Association, 85*, 1002–1008.

Bachman, J. G. (1987, February). An eye on the future. *Psychology Today*, pp. 6–7.

Baddeley, A. (1990). *Human memory: Theory and practice*. Boston: Allyn & Bacon.

Bahrick, H. P. (1984). Memory for people. In J. E. Harris & P. E. Morris (Eds.), *Everyday memory actions and absent-mindedness* (pp. 19–34). London: Academic Press.

Bahrick, H. P., Bahrick, P. O., & Wittlinger, R. P. (1975). Fifty years of memory for names and faces: A cross-sectional approach. *Journal of Experimental Psychology: General, 104*, 54–75.

Bailey, M. J., & Pillard, R. C. (1991). A genetic study of male sexual orientation. *Archives of General Psychiatry, 48*, 1089–1096.

Baillargeon, R., (1987). Object permanence in 3 1/2–4 1/2 month old infants. *Developmental Psychology, 23(5)*, 655–664.

Baker, A. G., & Mackintosh, N. J. (1977). Excitatory and inhibitory conditioning following uncorrelated presentations of CS and US. *Animal Learning and Behavior, 5(3)*, 315–319.

Baker, A., Mercier, P., Vallee-Tourangeau, F., Frank, R. Pan, M. (1993). Selective associations and causality judgments: Presence of a strong causal factor may reduce judgments of a weaker one. *Journal of Experimental Psychology Learning, Memory and Cognition, 19*, 414–432.

❀ Baker, B., Dorian, P., Woloshyn, N., Kazarian, S.,Lanphier, C. (1991). Psychiatric treatment strategies for patients at risk of dying suddenly. *Psychotherapy and Pyschsomatics, 56(4)*, 242–246.

❀ Baker-Ward, L., Ornstein, P.A., Holden, D.J., (1984). The expression of memorization in early childhood. *Journal of Experimental Child Psychology, 37(3)*, 555–575.

Ball, S. A., & Zuckerman, M. (1992). Sensation seeking and selective attention: Focused and divided attention on a dichotic listening task. *Journal of Personality and Social Psychology, 63*, 825–831.

Balogh, R. D., & Porter, R. H. (1986). Olfactory preferences resulting from mere exposure in human neonates. *Infant Behavior and Development, 9*, 395–401.

Balzer, W. K., & Sulsky, L. M. (1990). Performance appraisal effectiveness. In K. Murphy & F. Saal (Eds.), *Psychology in organizations: Integrating science and practice* (pp. 133–156). Hillsdale, NJ: Erlbaum.

Bandura, A. (1977). *Social learning theory*. Englewood Cliffs, NJ: Prentice Hall.

Bandura, A. (1986). *Social foundations of thought and action: A social cognitive theory*. Englewood Cliffs, NJ: Prentice Hall.

Bandura, A., Adams, N. E., & Beyer, J. (1977). Cognitive processes mediating behavioral change. *Journal of Personality and Social Psychology, 35*, 125–139.

Bandura, A., Blanchard, E. B., & Ritter, B. (1969). Relative efficacy of desensitization and modeling approaches for inducing behavioral, affective, and attitudinal change. *Journal of Personality and Social Psychology, 13*, 173–199.

Bandura, A., Ross, D., & Ross, S. (1963). Imitation of film-mediated aggressive models. *Journal of Abnormal and Social Psychology, 66*, 3–11.

Banich, M. T., & Belger, A. (1990). Inter-hemispheric interaction: How do the hemispheres divide and conquer a task? *Cortex, 26*, 77–94.

Banks, C.G., Murphy, K.R. (1985). Toward narrowing the research-practice gap in performance appraisal. *Personnel Psychology, 38(2)*, 335–345.

❀ Bardwell, J. R., Cochran, S. W., & Walker, S. (1986). Relationship of parental education, race, and gender to sex role stereotyping in five-year-old kindergarteners. *Sex Roles, 15*, 275–281.

Barkley, R. A. (1990). *Attention deficit hyperactivity disorder: A handbook for diagnosis and treatment*. New York: Guilford.

Barling, J. (1988). Industrial relations: A "blind spot" in the teaching, research and practice of industrial/organizational psychology, Special Issue: Industrial/organizational psychology in *Canada*. *Canadian Psychology, 29(1)*, 103–108.

Barling, J., Kryl, I.P. (1990). Moderator's of the relationship between daily work stressors and mood. *Work and Stress, 4(4)*, 319–329.

Barlow, D. H. (1988) *Anxiety and its disorders: The nature and treatment of anxiety and panic* New York: Guilford Press.

Barlow, D. H. (1991). Introduction to the special issue on diagnoses, dimensions, and DSM-IV: The science of classification. *Journal of Abnormal Psychology, 100*, 243–244.

Barlow, D. H. (1992). An integrated model of panic. Described in Antony, M. M., Brown, T. A., & Barlow, D. H. Current perspectives on panic and panic disorder. *Journal of Abnormal Psychology, 100*, 79–82.

Barnes, R., Barrett, C., Weintraub, S., Holowacz, G., et al. (1993). Hospital response to psychosocial needs of AIDS inpatients. *Journal of Palliative Care, 9(2)*, 22–28.

Baron, J. (1988). *Thinking and deciding*. Cambridge, England: Cambridge University Press.

Baron, R. A. (1970). Attraction toward the model and model's competence as determinants of adult imitative behavior. *Journal of Personality and Social Psychology, 14*, 335–344.

Baron, R. A. (1972). Aggression as a function of ambient temperature and prior anger arousal. *Journal of Personality and Social Psychology, 21*, 183–189.

Baron, R. A. (1978). Aggression and heat: The "long hot summer" revisited. In A. Baum, S. Valins, and J. E. Singer (Eds.), *Advances in environmental research* (Vol. 1). Hillsdale, NJ: Erlbaum.

Baron, R. A. (1983). The "sweet smell of success"? The impact of pleasant artificial scents (perfume or cologne) on evaluations of job applicants. *Journal of Applied Psychology, 68*, 709–713.

Baron, R. A. (1986). Self-presentation in job interviews: When there can be "too much of a good thing." *Journal of Applied Social Psychology, 16*, 16–28

Baron, R. A. (1987). Mood of interviewer and the evaluation of job candidates. *Journal of Applied Social Psychology, 17*, 911–926.

Baron, R. A. (1990). Environmentally induced positive affect: The impact on self-efficacy, task performance, negotiation, and conflict. *Journal of Applied Social Psychology, 20*, 368–384.

Baron, R. A. (1993). Interviewers' moods and evaluations of job applicants: The role of applicant qualifications. *Journal of Applied Psychology, 23(4)*, 253–271.

Baron, R. A., & Bell, P. A. (1975). Aggression and heat: Mediating effects of prior provocation and exposure to an aggressive model. *Journal of Personality and Social Psychology, 31*, 825–832.

Baron, R. A., & Bronfen, M. I. (1994). A whiff of reality: Empirical evidence concerning the effects of pleasant fragrances on work-related behavior. Manuscript submitted for publication.

Baron, R. A., & Byrne, D. (1994). *Social psychology: Understanding human interaction* (7th ed.). Boston: Allyn & Bacon.

Baron, R. A., Fortin, S. P., Frei, R. L., Haver, L. A., & Shack, M. L. (1990). Reducing organizational conflict: The potential role of socially induced positive affect. *International Journal of Conflict Management, 1*, 133–152.

Baron, R. A., Rea, M. S., & Daniels, S. G. (1992). Effects of indoor lighting (illuminance and spectral distribution) on the performance of cognitive tasks and interpersonal behavior: The potential mediating role of positive affect. *Motivation and Emotion, 16*, 1–33.

Baron, R. A., & Richardson, D. R. (1994). *Human aggression*, (2nd ed.). New York: Plenum.

Baron, R. A., & Thomley, J. (1994). A whiff of reality: Positive affect as a potential mediator of the effects of pleasant fragrances on task performance and helping. Manuscript submitted for publication.

Barrera, M.E., Maurer, D., (1981a). Discrimination of strangers by the three-month-old. *Child Development. 52(2)*, 558–563.

Barsky, A. J., & Wyshak, G. (1989). Hypochondriasis and related health attitudes. *Psychosomatics, 330*, 412–420.

Barta, P. E., Pearlson, G. D., Powers, R. E., Richards, S. S., & Tune, L. E. (1990). Auditory hallucinations and smaller superior temporal gyral volume in schizophrenia. *American Journal of Psychiatry, 147*, 1457–1462.

Barth, R. J., & Kinder, B. N. (1988). A theoretical analysis of sex differences in same-sex friendships. *Sex Roles, 19*, 343–363.

Baruch, G. (1984). The psychological well-being of women in the middle years. In G. Baruch & J. Brooks-Gunn (Eds.), *Women in midlife* (pp. 161–180). New York: Plenum Press.

Bates, S., & Bates, D. F. (1971). ... And a child shall lead them. Stephanie's chart story. *Teaching Exceptional Children, 3*, 24–27.

Batson, C.D., Batson, J.G., Stingsby, J.K., Harrell, K.L., Peekna, H., Todd, R. (1991). Empathic joy and the empathy-altruism hypothesis. *Journal of Personality and Social Psychology, 61(3)*, 413–426.

Batson, C.D., Shaw, L.L. (1991). Evidence for altruism: Toward a pluralism of prosocial motives. *Psychological Inquiry, 2(2)*, 107–122.

Bauer, P.J., Mandler, J.M., (1992). Putting the horse before the cart: The use of temporal order in recall of events by one- year-old children. *Developmental Psychology, 28(3)*, 441–452.

Baum, A., & Fleming, I. (1993). Implications of psychological research on stress and technological accidents. *American Psychologist, 48*, 665–672.

Baum, S.R. & Ryan, L. (1993). Rate of speech effects in aphasia: voice onset time. *Brain and Language, 44(4)*, 431–445.

Baumeister, R. F. (1990). Suicide as escape from self. *Psychological Review, 97*, 90–113.

Baumeister, R. F., & Scher, S. J. (1988). Self-defeating behavior patterns among normal individuals: Review and analysis of common self-destructive tendencies. *Psychological Bulletin, 104*, 3–22.

Baumeister, R. F., & Steinhilber, A. (1984). Paradoxical effects of supportive audiences on performance under pressure: The home field disadvantage in sports championships. *Journal of Personality and Social Psychology, 47*, 85–93.

Baumeister, R. F., & Tice, D. M. (1988). Metatraits. *Journal of Personality, 64*, 141–156.

Baumeister, R.F., Stillwell, A., Wotman, S.R. (1990). Victim and perpetrator accounts of interpersonal conflict: Autobiographical narratives about anger. *Journal of Personality and Social Psychology, 59(5)*, 994–1005.

Baumgardner, A.H., Heppner, P.P., Arkin, R.M. (1986). Role of causal attribution in personal problem solving. *Journal of Personality and Social Psychology, 50(3)*, 636–643.

Baumrind, D. (1984). A developmental perspective on adolescent drug use. Unpublished manuscript, University of California, Berkeley.

Baumrind, D. (1985). Research using intentional deception: Ethical issues revisited. *American Psychologist, 40*, 165–174.

Beaman, A.L., Cole, C.M., Preston, M., Klentz, B., Stebloy, N.M. (1983). Fifteen years of foot-in-the-door research: A meta-analysis. *Personality and Social Psychology Bulletin, 9(2)*, 181–196.

Bebko, J.M., McKinnon, E.E., (1990). The language experience of deaf children: Its relation to spontaneous rehearsal in a memory task. *Child Development, 61(6)*, 1744–1752.

Beck, A. T. (1976). *Cognitive therapy and the emotional disorders*. New York: International Universities Press.

Beck, A. T. (1985). *Anxiety disorders and phobias: A cognitive perspective*. New York: Basic Books.

Beck, A. T., Rush, A. J., Shaw, B. F., & Emery, G. (1979). *Cognitive theory of depression*. New York: Guilford Press.

Becklen, R., & Cerone, D. (1983). Selective looking and the noticing of unexpected events. *Memory & Cognition, 11*, 601–608.

Beckstead, J.W. (1991). Psychological factors influencing judgments and attitudes regarding animal research: An application of functional measurement and structural equation modeling. Unpublished doctoral dissertation, State University of New York, Albany.

Bedard, M.A., Montplaisir, J., Malo, J., & Richer, F. (1993). Persistent neuropsychological deficits and vigilance impairment in sleep apnea syndrome after treatment with continuous positive airways pressure (CPAP). *Journal of Clinical and Experimental Neuropsychology, 15*, 330–341.

Begg, I. M., Needham, D. R. & Bookbinder, M. (1993). Do backward messages unconsciously affect listeners? No. *Canadian Journal of Experimental Psychology, 47*, 1–14.

Beggan, J.K. (1992). On the social nature of nonsocial perception: The mere ownership effect. *Journal of Personality and Social Psychology, 62(2)*, 229–237.

Behrend, D.A., Rosengren, K. S., & Perlmutter, M. (1992). The relation between private speech and parental interactive style. In R. M. Diaz & L. E. Berk (Eds.), *Private speech: From social interaction to self-regulation* (pp. 85–100). Hillsdale, NJ: Erlbaum.

Bekesy, G. von. (1960). *Experiments in hearing*. New York: McGraw-Hill.

Bell, P. A. (1992). In defense of the negative affect escape model of heat and aggression. *Psychological Bulletin, 111*, 342–346.

Bell, P. A., Fisher, J. D., Baum, A., & Green, T. E., (1990). *Environmental psychology* (3rd ed.). New York: Holt, Rinehart, & Winston.

Bellak, L. (1994). The schizophrenic syndrome and attention deficit disorder. *American Psychologist, 49*, 25–29.

Bellisimo, A., & Tunks, E. (1984). *Chronic pain*. New York: Praeger.

Belsky, J., Braungart, J.M., (1991). Are insecure-avoidant infants with extensive day-care experience less stressed by and more independent in the Strange Situation? *Child Development, 62(3)*, 567–571.

Bem, D. J., & Honorton, C. (1994). Does psi exist? Replicable evidence for an anomalous process of information transfer. *Psychological Bulletin, 115*, 4–18.

Bem, S. L. (1974). The measurement of psychological androgyny. *Journal of Consulting and Clinical Psychology, 42*, 155–162.

Bem, S.L., (1981). Gender schema theory: A cognitive account of sex typing. *Psychological Review, 88(4)*, 354–364.

Bem, S. L. (1984). Adrogyny and gender schema theory: A conceptual and empirical integration. In R. A. Dientsbier & T. B. Sondregger

(Eds.), *Nebraska Symposium on Motivation* (Vol. 34, pp. 179–226). Lincoln: University of Nebraska Press.

Bem, S.L., (1989). Genital knowledge and gender constancy in preschool children. *Child Development, 60(3)*, 649–662.

Bemis, K. M. (1987). The present status of operant conditioning for the treatment of anorexia nervosa. *Behavior Modification, 11*, 432–463.

Benesch, K. F., & Page, M. M. (1989). Self-construct systems and interpersonal congruence. *Journal of Personality, 57*, 139–173.

Beninger, R.J. (1992). D-1 receptor involvement in reward-related learning. *Journal of Psychopharmacology, 6*, 34–42.

Beninger, R.J., Wirsching, B.A., Jhamandas, K. & Boegman, R.J. 1989. Animal studies of brain acetylcholine and memory. Symposium: Memory and aging (1988, Lausanne, Switzerland). *Archives of Gerontology and Geriatrics, supp 1*, 71–89.

Benoit, D., Zeanah, C.H., Barton, M.L., (1989). Maternal attachment disturbances in failure to thrive. Special Issue: Internal representations and parent-infant relationships. *Infant Mental Health Journal, 10(3)*, 185–202.

Benson, H., & Friedman, R. (1985). A rebuttal to the conclusions of David S. Holmes's article: "Meditation and somatic arousal reductions." *American Psychologist, 40*, 725–728.

Bentall, R. P. (1990). The illusion of reality: A review and integration of psychological research on hallucinations. *Psychological Bulletin, 107*, 82–95.

Berenbaum, S. A., & Hines, M. (1992). Early androgens are related to childhood sex-typed toy preferences. *Psychological Science, 3*, 203–206.

Berg, K.S., Vidmar, N. (1975). Authoritarianism and recall of evidence about criminal behavior. *Journal of Research in Personality, 9(2)*, 147–157.

Bergin, A. E., & Lambert, M. J. (1978). The evaluation of therapeutic outcomes. In S. L. Garfield & A. E. Bergin (Eds.), *Handbook of psychotherapy and behavior change: An empirical analysis*, (2nd ed., pp. 139–190). New York: Wiley.

Berk, L. E. (1993). *Infants, children and adolescents*. Boston: Allyn and Bacon.

Berkowitz, L. (1984). Some effects of thoughts on anti- and pro-social influences of media events: A cognitive-neoassociation analysis, *Psychological Bulletin, 95*, 410–427.

Berkowitz, L. (1989). Frustration-aggression hypothesis: Examination and reformulation. *Psychological Bulletin, 106*, 59–73.

Berkowitz, L. (1990). On the formation and regulation of anger and aggression. *American Psychologist, 45*, 494–503.

Berlyne, D. E. (1967). Arousal and reinforcement. In D. Levine (Ed.), *Nebraska Symposium on Motivation* (Vol. 15, pp. 279–286). Lincoln: University of Nebraska Press.

Berman, A. L., & Jobes, D. A. (1991). *Adolescent suicide: Assessment and intervention*. Washington, DC: American Psychological Association.

Berndt, T. J. (1992). Friendship and friends' influence in adolescence. *Current Directions in Psychological Science, 1*, 156–159.

Bernstein, A. S. (1987). Orienting response research in schizophrenia: Where we have come and where we might go. *Schizophrenia Bulletin, 13*, 623–641.

Bernstein, I. L. (1978). Learned taste aversion in children receiving chemotherapy. *Science, 200*, 1302–1303.

Berry, D. S. (1991). Attractive faces are not all created equal: Joint effects of facial babyishness and attractiveness on social perception. *Personality and Social Psychology Bulletin, 17*, 523–531.

Berry, D. S., & McArthur, L. Z. (1986). Perceiving character in faces: The impact of age-related craniofacial changes on social perception. *Psychological Bulletin, 100*, 3–18.

Berry, D. S., & Zebrowitz-McArthur, L. (1988). What's in a face? Facial maturity and the attribution of legal responsibility. *Personality and Social Psychology Bulletin, 14*, 23–33.

Berry, D. T. R., & Webb, W. B. (1985). Mood and sleep in aging women. *Journal of Personality and Social Psychology, 49*, 1724–1727.

Berscheid, E., Dion, K., Walster, E., & Walster, G. W. (1971). Physical attractiveness and dating choice: A test of the matching hypothesis. *Journal of Experimental Social Psychology, 7*, 173–189.

Besson, J., & Chaouch, A. (1987). Peripheral spinal mechanisms of nociception. *Psychological Review, 67*, 67–186.

Best, D. L., Williams, J. E., Cloud, J. M., Davis, S. W., Robertson, L. S., Edwards, J. R., Giles, H., & Fowles, J. (1977). Development of sex-trait stereotypes among young children in the United States, England, and Ireland. *Child Development, 48*, 1375–1384.

Betz, A. L., & Krosnick, J. A. (1993). *A test of the primacy of affect: does detection of the affective tone of a stimulus precede detection of stimulus presence or content?* Unpublished manuscript, Ohio State University.

Betz, E. L. (1982). Need fulfillment in the career development of women. *Journal of Vocational Behavior, 20*, 53–66.

Beutler, L. E., Crago, M., & Arizmendi, T. G. (1986). Research on therapist variables in psychotherapy. In S. L. Garfield & A. E. Bergin (Eds.), *Handbook of psychotherapy and behavior change: An evaluative analysis* (3rd ed.). New York: Wiley.

Beyth-Marom, R., Austin, L., Fischoff, B., Palmgren, C., & Quadrel, M. (in press). Perceived consequences of risky behaviors: Adolescents and adults. *Developmental Psychology*.

Bhatia, S., Hendricks, S. & Bhatia, S. (1993). Attitudes toward and beliefs about smoking in grade school children. *International Journal of the Addictions, 28(3)*, 271–280.

Bhatt, R. S., Wasserman, E. A., Reynolds, W. F., Jr., & Knauss, K. S. (1988). Conceptual behavior in pigeons: Categorization of both familiar and novel examples from four classes of natural and artificial stimuli. *Journal of Experimental Psychology: Animal Behavior Proccesses, 14*, 219–234.

Bialystok, E., (1992). The emergence of symbolic thought: Introduction. Meeting of the Society for Research in Child Development: Symposium on the emergence of symbolic thought (1991, Seattle, Washington). *Cognitive Development, 7(3)*, 269–272.

Bichard, S.L., Alden, L., Walker, L.J. & Mcmahon, R.J. (1988). Friendship understanding in socially accepted, rejected, and neglected children. *Merrill Palmer Quarterly, 34(1)*, 33–46.

Bickman, J. (1992) Female lives, feminist deaths: The relationship of the Montreal Massacre to dissociation, incest, and violence against women. *Canadian Psychology 33*, 128–143.

Bienert, H., & Schneider, B. H. (in press). Diagnosis-specific social skill: Training with peer-nominated aggressive-disruptive and sensitive-isolated preadolescents. *Journal of Applied Developmental Psychology*.

Bierhoff, H.W., Klein, R., Kramp, P. (1991). Evidence for the altruistic personality from data on accident research. *Journal of Personality, 59(2)*, 263–280.

Bigelow, A., (1986). The development of reaching in blind children. *British Journal of Developmental Psychology, 4(4)*, 355–366.

Bigelow, A., (1990). Relationship between the development of language and thought in young blind children. *Journal of Visual Impairment and Blindness, 84(8)*, 414–419.

Bigelow, B.J., Tesson, G., Lewko, J.H. (1992). The social rules that children use: Close friends, other friends, and "other kids" compared to parents, teachers and siblings. *International Journal of Behavioral Development, 15(3)*, 315–335.

Binet, A., & Simon, T. (1905). Methodes nouvelles pour le diagnostic du niveau intellectual des anormaux. *L'année Psychologique, 11*, 191–244.

Bini, L. (1938). Experimental researches on epileptic attacks induced by the electric current. *American Journal of Psychiatry* (Suppl. 94), 172–183.

Binning, J.F., Goldstein, M.A., Garcia, M.F., Scattaregia, J.H. (1988). Effects of preinterview impressions on questioning strategies in same- and opposite-sex employment interviews. *Journal of Applied Psychology, 73(1)*, 30–37.

Birnbaum, I. M., & Parker, E. D. (Eds.). (1977). *Alcohol and human memory*. Hillsdale, NJ: Erlbaum.

Bisanz, G.L., Rule, B.G. (1989). Gender and the persuasion schema: A search for cognitive invariants. *Personality and Social Psychology, 15(1)*, 4–18.

Bisnaire, L.M., Firestone, P. & Rynard, D. (1990). Factors associated with academic achievement in children following parental separation. *American Journal of Orthopsychiatry, 60(1)*, 67–76.

Bisson, C. & Whissell, C. (1989). Will premenstrual syndrome produce a Ms Hyde? Evidence from the daily administrations of the Emotions Profile Index. *Psychological Reports, 65(1)*, 179–184.

Bivens, J.A., Berk, L.E., (1990). A longitudinal study of the development of elementary school children's private speech. *Merrill-Palmer Quarterly, 36(4)*, 443–463.

Bixler, E. O., Kales, A., Soldatos, C. R., Kales, J. D., & Healey, S. (1979). Prevalence of sleep disorders in the Los Angeles metropolitan area. *American Journal of Psychiatry, 136*, 1257–1262.

Bjorklund, D.F., (1987). How age changes in knowledge base contribute to the development of children's memory: An interpretive review. *Developmental Review, 7(2)*, 93–130.

Bjorklund, D. F., & Muir, J. E. (1988). Children's development of free recall memory: Remembering on their own. In R. Vasta (Ed.), *Annals of child development* (Vol. 5, pp. 79–123). Greenwich, CT: JAI Press.

Bjorkqvist, K., Lagerspetz, K. M. J., & Kaukiainen, A. (1992). Do girls manipulate and boys fight? Developmental trends in regard to direct and indirect aggression. *Aggressive Behavior, 18*, 37–45.

Black, J. S., & Mendenhall, M. (1990). Cross-cultural training effectivness: A review and a theoretical framework for future research. *Academy of Management Review, 15*, 113–136.

Blackmore, S. (1986). A critical guide to parapsychology. *Skeptical Inquirer, 11(1)*, 97–102.

Blade, L. (1993). as in: Research pursues timing of puberty, menstruation by Pamela Fayerman in *Vancouver Sun*, July 31, page B10.

Blain, M.D., Thompson, J.M., Whiffen, V.E., (1993). Attachment and perceived social support in late adolescence: The interaction between working models of self and others. *Journal of Adolescent Research, 8(2)*, 226–241.

Blakemore, B., Shindler, S., Conte, R., (1993). A problem solving training program for parents of children with attention deficit hyperactivity disorder. *Canadian Journal of School Psychology, 9(1)*, special issue 66–85.

Blakeslee, S. (1993, September 7). Human nose may hold an additional organ for a real sixth sense: Odorless skin chemicals may draw or repel other people. *New York Times*, pp. C1, C3.

Blanchard, R. (1993). Varieties of autogynephilia and their relationship to gender dysphoria. *Archives of Sexual Behavior, 22(3)*, 241–251.

Bland, R. C., Newman, S. C., & Orn, H. (1988). Period prevalence of psychiatric disorders in Edmonton. *Acta Psychiatrica Scandinavica. 77(suppl.388)*, 33–42. © Munksgaard International Publishers Ltd., Copenhagen, Denmark.

Bland, R.C., Orn, H., & Newman, S.C. (1988). Lifetime prevalence of psychiatric disorders in Edmonton. *Acta Psychiatrica Scandinavica. 77(suppl.388)*, 24–32.

Blashko, C.A. & Peterson, J.G. (1990). You and your heart: promoting preventive health education through the mass media. *International Journal fot the Advancement of Counselling, 13(1)*, 49–59.

Bless, H., Bohner, G., Schwarz, N., & Stracik, F. (1990). Mood and persuasion: A cognitive response analysis. *Personality and Social Psychology Bulletin, 16*, 331–345.

Bliss, E.L. (1991). A reexamination of Freud's basic concepts from studies of multiple personality disorder. *Dissociation Progress in the Dissociative Disorders, 1(3)*, 36–40.

Bliss, R. E., Garvey, A. J., Heinhold, J. W., & Hitchcock, J. L. (1989). The influence of situation and coping on relapse crisis outcomes after smoking cessation. *Journal of Consulting and Clinical Psychology, 57*, 443–449.

Blyth, D. A., Bulcroft, R., & Simmons, R. G. (1981, August). *The impact of puberty on adolescents: A longitudinal study*. Paper presented at the annual meetings of the American Psychological Association, Los Angeles.

Bodenhausen, G.V. (1988). Stereotypic biases in social decision making and memory: Testing process models of stereotype use. *Journal of Personality and Social Psychology, 55(5)*, 726–737.

Bogard, N. (1990). Why we need gender to understand human violence. *Journal of Interpersonal Violence, 5*, 132–135.

Boles, D. B. (1992). Factor analysis and the cerebral hemispheres: Temporal, occipital and frontal functions. *Neuropsychologia, 30*, 963–988.

Bootzin, R. R., Acocella, J. R., & Alloy, L. B. (1993). *Abnormal psychology* (6th ed.). New York: McGraw-Hill.

Borbely, A. A., Achermann, P., Trqachsel, L., & Tobler, I. (1989). Sleep initiation and initial sleep intensity: Interactions of homeostatic and circadian mechanisms. *Journal of Biological Rhythms, 4*, 149–160.

Bordeleau, Y., Morin, E.M. (1988). La psychologie industrielle et organisationnelle au Canada francais: Enseignement, recherche et pratique. (Industrial and organizational psychology in French Canada: Teaching, research, and practice.) Special Issue: Industrial/organizational psychology in Canada. *Canadian Psychology, 29(1)*, 44–56.

Borello, G. M., & Thompson, B. (1990). An hierarchical analysis of the Hendrick-Hendrick measure of Lee's typology of love. *Journal of Social Behavior and Personality, 5*, 327–342.

Borkovec, T. D. (1982). Insomnia. *Journal of Consulting and Clinical Psychology, 50*, 880–895.

Bornstein, R. F. (1989). Subliminal techniques as propaganda tools: Review and critique. *Journal of Mind and Behavior, 10*, 231–262.

Bortolotti, S., D'Elia, P., Whissell, C.M. (1993). When children talk about the causes of their emotions, how well do adults and other children understand which emotion they are talking about? *Perceptual and Motor Skills, 77(1)*, 67–78.

Boshier, R. (1992). Popular discourse concerning AIDS: Its implications for adult education. *Adult Education Quarterly, 42(3)*, 125–135.

Bosman, E.A. (1993). Age-related differences in the motoric aspects of transcription typing skill. *Psychology and Aging, 8(1)*, 87–102.

Bouchard, T. J. (1987). *Information about the Minnesota Center for Twin and Adoption Research*. Minneapolis: University of Minnesota.

Bouchard, T. J., & McGue, M. (1981). Familial studies of intelligence: A review. *Science, 212*, 1055–1059.

Bouchard, T. J., & Segal, N. L. (1985). Environment and IQ. In B. B. Wolman (Ed.), *Handbook of intelligence: Theories, measurements, and applications*. New York: Wiley.

Bouchard, T. J., Lykken, D. T., McGue, M., Segal, N. L., & Tellegen, A. (1990). Sources of human psychological differences: The Minnesota Study of Twins Reared Apart. *Science, 250*, 223–228.

Bourhis, R.Y., Cole, R., Gagnon, A. (1992). Sexe, pouvoir et discrimination: analyse intergroupe des rapports femmes-hommes. (Sex, power, and discrimination: Intergroup analysis of rapport between men and women.) *Revue Quebecoise de Psychologie, 13(1)*, 103–127.

Bowd, A. D. (1990). A decade of debate on animal research in psychology: Room for consensus? *Canadian Psychology, 31*, 74–82.

Bowen, B. (1986, September 18). Hong Kong students in Canada suffer high stress, study shows. *The Globe and Mail*, A23.

Bower, G. H., Clark, M. C., Lesgold, A. M., & Winzenz, D. (1969). Hierarchical retrieval schemes in recall of categorized word lists. *Journal of Verbal Learning and Verbal Behavior, 8*, 323–343.

Bowers, K. S. (1990). Unconscious influences and hypnosis. In J. L. Singer (Ed.)., *Repression and dissociation: Implications for personality theory, psychopathology, and health* (pp. 143–178). Chicago: University of Chicago Press.

Bowlby, J. (1969). *Attachment and loss: Vol. 1. Attachment*. New York: Basic Books.

Bowles, N., & Hynds, F. (1978). *Psy search: The comprehensive guide to psychic phenomena*. New York: Harper & Row.

Boyanowski, E. O. (1991). Grains of truth in a wasteland of fear. *Canadian Psychology, 32*, 188–189.

Boyes, M.C., Allen, S.G. (1993). Styles of parent-child interaction and moral reasoning in adolescence. *Merrill Palmer Quarterly, 39(4)*, 551–570.

Boyes, M.C., Walker, L.J., (1988). Implications of culture diversity for the universality claims of Kohlberg's theory of moral reasoning. *Human Development, 31(1)*, 44–59.

Boyle, P. (1993). The hazards of passive—and active—smoking. *New England Journal of Medicine, 328*, 1708–1709.

Bradbury, T. N., & Fincham, F. D. (1992). Attributions and behavior in marital interaction. *Journal of Personality and Social Psychology, 63*, 613–628.

Bradley, B., & Mathews, A. (1983). Negative self-schemata in clinical depression. *British Journal of Clinical Psychology 22*, 173–181.

Bradley, M.T. & Rettinger, J. (1992). Awareness of crime-relevant information and the Guilty Knowledge Test. *Journal of Applied Psychology, 77(1)*, 55–59.

Bradshaw, R.H., Bubier, N.E., Sullivan, M. (1994). The effects of age and gender on perceived facial attractiveness: A reply to McLellan and McKelvie. *Canadian Journal of Behavioural Science, 26(2)*, 199–204.

Braff, D. L. (1989). Sensory input deficits and negative symptoms in schizophrenic patients. *American Journal of Psychiatry, 146*, 1006–1011.

Braff, D. L., & Geyer, M. A. (1990). Sensorimotor gating and schizophrenia: Human and animal model studies. *Archives of General Psychiatry, 47*, 181–188.

Braun, C.M. & Giroux, J. (1989) Arcade video games: Proxemic, cognitive and content analyses. *Journal of Leisure Research, 21*, 92–105.

Braun, C.M., Daigneault, S. (1991). Sparing of cognitive executive functions and impairment of motor functions after industrial exposure to lead: A field study with control group. *Neuropsychology, 5(3)*, 179–193.

Braverman, N. S., & Bronstein, P. (Eds.). (1985). Experimental assessments and clinical applications of conditioned food aversions. *Annals of the New York Academy of Sciences, 443*, 1–41.

Bravo, M., Rubio-Stipec, M., Canino, G. J., Woodbury, M. A., & Ribera, J. C. (1990). The psychological sequelae of disaster prospectively and retrospectively evaluated. *American Journal of Community Psychology, 18*, 661–680.

Brean, H. (1958, March 31). What hidden sell is all about. *Life*, 104–114.

Breggin, P. R. (1979). *Electroshock: Its brain-disabling effects*. New York: Springer.

Brehm, J. W., & Self, E. A. (1989). The intensity of motivation. *Annual Review of Psychology, 40*, 109–131.

Brehm, S. (1992). *Intimate relationships*. New York: McGraw-Hill.

Brennan, W. M., Ames, E. W., & Moore, R. W. (1966). Age differences in infants' attention to patterns of different complexities. *Science, 151*, 354–356.

Brickman, J. & Briere, J. (1984). Incidence of rape and sexual assault in an urban Canadian population. *International Journal of Women's Studies, 7*, 195–206.

Briggs, R. (1990). Biological aging. In J. Bond & P. Coleman (Eds.), *Aging in society*. Newbury Park, CA: Sage.

Briggs, S. R., & Cheek, J. M. (1988). On the nature of self-monitoring: Problems with assessment, problems with validity. *Journal of Personality and Social Psychology, 54*, 663–678.

Brisson, C., Vezina, M., Vinet, A. (1992). Health problems of women employed in jobs involving psychological and ergonomic stressors: The case of garment workers in Quebec. *Women & Health, 18(3)*, 49–65.

Britt, T. W. (1992). The self-consciousness scale: On the stability of the three-factor structure. *Personality and Social Psychology Bulletin, 18*, 748–755.

Brockner, J., & Rubin, J. Z. (1985). *Entrapment in escalating conflicts*. New York: Springer-Verlag.

Brodbeck, D.R., Burack, O.R. and Shettleworth, S.J. (1992). One trial associative memory in black-capped chickadees. *Journal of Experimental Psychology: Animal Behaviour Processes, 18*, 12–21.

Brody, G. H., Neubaum, E., & Forehand, R. (1988). Serial marriage: A heuristic analysis of an emerging family form. *Psychological Bulletin, 103*, 211–222.

Broughton, R.J. (1992). Psychosocial impact of narcolepsy-cataplexy. *Loss, Grief and Care, 5*, 33–35.

Brown, J. D., & McGill, K. L. (1989). The cost of good fortune: When positive life events produce negative health consequences. *Journal of Personality and Social Psychology, 57*, 1103–1110.

Brown, J. D., & Smart, S. A. (1989). *Role of self-concept certainty in buffering the adverse impact of stressful life events*. Unpublished manuscript, University of Washington, Seattle.

Brown, J.D., Rogers, R.J. (1991). "Self-serving attributions: The role of physiological arousal": Erratum. *Personality and Social Psychology Bulletin, 17(6)*, 717.

Brown, N. R., Shevell, S. K., & Rips, L. J. (1986). Public memories and their personal context. In D. C. Rubin (Ed.), *Autobiographical memory* (pp. 137–158). Cambridge, England: Cambridge University Press.

Brown, R. (1973). *A first language: The early stages.* Cambridge, MA: Harvard University Press.

Brown, R. W., & Kulik, J. (1977). Flashbulb memories. *Cognition, 5*, 73–99.

Brown, R. W., & McNeill, D. (1966). The "tip of the tongue" phenemonon. *Journal of Verbal Learning and Verbal Behavior, 5*, 325–337.

Bruhn, J. G., & Phillips, B. U. (1987). A developmental basis for social support. *Journal of Behavioral Medicine, 10*, 213–229.

Bryden, J. P., Ley, R. G., & Sugarman, J. H. (1982). A left ear advantage for identifying the emotional quality of tonal sequences. *Neuropsychologia, 20*, 83–87.

Bryden, M.P. & MacRae, L. (1988). Dichotic laterality effects obtained with emotional words. *Neuropsychiatry, Neuropsychology, and Behavioral Neurology, 1(3)*, 171–176.

Bryden, M.P., Free, T., Gagne, S. & Groff, P. 1991. Handedness effects in the detection of dichotically-presented words and emotions. *Cortex, 27(2)*, 229–235.

Bucher, B., & Lovaas, O. N. I. (1968) Use of aversive stimulation in behavior modification. In M. R. Jones (Ed.), *Miami symposium on the prediction of behavior, 1967: Aversive stimulation.* Coral Gables, FL: University of Miami Press.

Burger, J. M. (1986). Temporal effects on attributions: Actor and observer differences. *Social Cognition, 4*, 377–387.

Burger, J. M. (1990). *Personality,* (2nd ed.). Belmont, CA: Wadsworth.

Burger, J. M., & Pavelich, J. L. (1993). *Attributions for presidential elections: The situational shift over time.* Unpublished manuscript, Santa Clara University.

Burish, T. G., & Carey, M. P. (1986). Conditioned aversive response in cancer chemotherapy patients: Theoretical and developmental analysis. *Journal of Consulting and Clinical Psychology, 54*, 593–600.

Burke, R.J. (1993). Stress, work and professional satisfaction and militancy among Canadian physicians. Special Issue: Integrating domains of work stress and industrial relations: Evidence from five countries. *Journal of Organizational Behavior, 14(5)*, 459–472.

Burke, R.J., Deszka, G. (1992). Career orientations, satisfaction and health among police officers: Some consequences of person-job misfit. *Psychological Reports, 62(2)*, 639–649.

Burke, R.J., McKeen, C.A. (1993). Career priority patterns among managerial and professional women. Special Issue: Women in management. *Applied Psychology: An International Review, 42(4)*, 341–352.

Burton, I. (1990). Factors in urban stress. *Journal of Sociology and Social Welfare, 17(1)*, 79–92.

Bushman, B.J. (1984). Perceived symbols of authority and their influence on compliance. *Journal of Applied Social Psychology, 14(6)*, 501–508.

Bushman, B.J. (1988). The effects of apparel on compliance: A field experiment with a female authority figure. *Personality and Social Psychology Bulletin, 14(3)*, 459–467.

Buss, D. M. (1989). Sex differences in human mate preferences: Evolutionary hypotheses tested in 37 cultures. *Behavioral and Brain Sciences, 12*, 1–49.

Buss, D. M. (1990). Evolutionary social psychology: Prospects and pitfalls. *Motivation and Emotion, 14*, 265–286.

Buss, D. M., et al. (1990). International preferences in selecting mates: A study of 37 cultures. *Journal of Cross-cultural Psychology, 21*, 5–47.

Buss, D. M., Larsen, R. J., Westen, D., & Semmelroth, J. (1992). Sex differences in jealousy: Evolution, physiology, and psychology. *Psychological Science, 3*, 251–258.

Butt, D.S. & Beiser, M. (1987). Successful aging: a theme for international psychology. *Psychology and Aging, 2(1)*, 87–94.

Byblow, W.D. (1990). Effects of redundancy in the comparison of speech and pictorial displays in the cockpit environment. *Applied Ergonomics, 21(2)*, 121–128.

Byers, E. S. and Wilson, P. (1985). Accuracy of women's expectations regarding men's responses to refusals of sexual advances in dating situations. Special Issue: Women in groups and aggression against women. *International Journal of Women's Studies, 8*, 376-387.

Byrne, D. (1971). *The attraction paradigm.* New York: Academic Press.

Byrne, D. (1982). Predicting human sexual behavior. In A. G. Kraut (Ed.), *The G. Stanley Hall Lecture Series* (Vol. 2, pp. 363–364, 368). Washington, DC: American Psychological Association.

Byrne, D., & Murnen, S. K. (1988). Maintaining loving relationships. In R. J. Sternberg & M. I. Barnes (Eds.), *The psychology of love* (pp. 293–310). New Haven, CT: Yale University Press.

Byrne, B.M. (1993). The Maslach Burnout Inventory: testing for factual validity and invariance across elementary, intermediate and secondary teachers. *Journal of Occupational and Organizational Psychology, 66(3)*, 197–212.

Cacioppo, J. T., Petty, R. E., & Quintanar, L. R. (1982). Individual differences in relative hemisphere alpha abundance and cognitive

responses persuasive communications. *Journal of Personality and Social Psychology, 43*, 623–626.

Cain, W. S. (1988). Olfaction. In R. C. Atkinson, R. J. Herrnstein, G. Lindzey, & R. D. Luce (Eds.), *Stevens' handbook of experimental psychology: Vol. 1. Perception and motivation* (rev. ed., pp. 409–459). New York: Wiley.

Cairns, K.V., Woodward, J.B. & Hashizume, L.G. (1992). Employment councellors' and youths' views of the transition to work: preparing to develop a work skills simulation. *Canadian Journal of Counselling, 26(4)*, 222–239.

Callan, V.J. (1993). Subordinate-manager communication in different sex dyads: Consequences for job satisfaction. *Journal of Occupational and Organizational Psychology, 66(1)*, 13–27.

Came, B., Burke, D., Ferzoco, G., O'Farrell, B., & Wallace, B. (1989). Montreal Massacre. *Maclean's 102*, 14–17.

Campbell, J. D. (1990). Self-esteem and clarity of the self-concept. *Journal of Personality and Social Psychology, 59*, 538–549.

Campbell, J. N., & LaMotte, R. H. (1983). Latency to detection of first pain. *Brain Research, 266*, 203–208.

Campbell, M., Perry, R., & Green, W. H. (1984). Use of lithium in children and adolescents. *Psychosomatics, 25*, 95–106.

Campbell, P. E., Batsche, C. J., & Batsche, G. M. (1972). Spaced-trials reward magnitude effects in the rat: Single versus multiple food pellets. *Journal of Comparative and Physiological Psychology, 81*, 360–364.

Campbell, R.L., & Svenson, L.W. (1992). Drug use among university undergraduate students. *Psychological Reports, 70*, 1039–1042.

Campion, M. A., & McClelland, C. L. (1991). Interdisciplinary examination of the costs and benefits of enlarged jobs: A job design quasi-experiment. *Journal of Applied Psychology, 76*, 186–198.

Canadian Psychological Association (1991). Canadian Code of Ethics for Psychologists. Old Chelsea, Quebec: Author.

Cannon, W. B., Lewis, J. T., & Britton, S. W. (1927). The dispensability of the sympathetic division of the autonomic nervous system. *Boston Medical Surgery Journal, 197*, 514.

Capaldi, E. J. (1978). Effects of schedule and delay of reinforcement on acquisition speed. *Animal Learning and Behavior, 6*, 330–334.

Capaldi, E. J., & Miller, D. J. (1988). Counting in rats: Its functional significance and the independent cognitive processes that constitute it. *Journal of Experimental Psychology: Animal Behavior Processes, 14*, 3–17.

Carbonneau, L. (1994) When bullets have ceased, critical incident stress is the biggest source of morbitity in Canada's peacekeepers. *Medical post, 30*, p. 9

Carlson, N. R. (1994). *Physiology of behavior* (5th ed.). Boston: Allyn & Bacon.

Carlson, N.E. (1993). *Foundations of physiological psychology* (4th ed.). Boston: Allyn & Bacon.

Carney, J.M., Starke-Reed, P.E., Oliver, C.N., Landum, R.W., Cheng, M.S., Wu, J.F. & Floyd, R.A. 1991. Reversal of age- related increases in brain protein oxidation, decrease in enzyme activity, and loss in temporal and spatial memory by chronic administration of the spin-trapping compound N-tert- butyl-alpha-phenylnitrone. *Proceedings of the National Academy of Sciences, U.S.A., 88(9)*, 3633–3636.

Carr, E. G. (1977). The motivation of self-injurious behavior: A review of some hypotheses. *Psychological Bulletin, 84*, 800–816.

Carson, R. C., Butcher, J. N., & Coleman, J. C. (1988). *Abnormal psychology and modern life* (8th ed.). Glenview, IL: Scott, Foresman.

Carsten, J. M., & Spector, P. E. (1987). Unemployment, job satisfaction, and employee turnover: A meta-analytic test of the Muchinsky model. *Journal of Applied Psychology, 72*, 75–80.

Carver, C. S., & Scheier, M. F. (1992). *Perspectives on personality* (2nd ed.). Boston: Allyn & Bacon.

Carver, C. S., Pozo, C., Harris, S. D., Noriega, V., Scheier, M. F., Robinson, D. S., Ketcham, A. S., Moffat, F. L., & Clark, K. C. (1993). How coping mediates the effect of optimism on distress: A study of women with early stage breast cancer. *Journal of Personality and Social Psychology, 65*, 375–390.

Carver, C. S., & Scheier, M. F. (1981). *Attention and self-regulation: A control-theory approach to human behavior.* New York: Springer-Verlag.

Carver, C. S., & Scheier, M. F. (1990). Origins and functions of positive and negative affect: A control-process view. *Journal of Personality and Social Psychology, 97*, 19–35.

Carver, C. S., Scheier, M. F., & Weintraub, J. K. (1989). Assessing coping strategies: A theoretically based approach. *Journal of Personality and Social Psychology, 56*, 267–283.

Case, R. (1991). *The mind's staircase: Exploring the conceptual underpinnings of children's thought and knowledge.* Hillsdale, NJ: Erlbaum.

Casper, R.C. (1990). Personality features in women with good outcome from restricting anorexia nervosa. *Psychosomatic Medicine, 52(2)*, 156–170.

Cattell, R. B. (1963). Theory of fluid and crystallized intelligence: A critical experiment. *Journal of Educational Psychology, 54*, 1–22.

Cattell, R. B. (1987). *Intelligence: Its structure, growth and action.* Amsterdam: North-Holland.

Cattell, R. B., & Dreger, R. M. (Eds.). (1977). *Handbook of modern personality theory.* Washington, DC: Hemisphere.

Cautela, J. R. (1985). Covert modeling. In A. S. Bellack & M. Hersen (Eds.), *Dictionary of behavior therapy techniques*. New York: Pergamon.

Ceci, S. J. (1991) How much does schooling influence general intelligence and its cognitive components? A resassessment of the evidence. *Developmental Psychology, 27*, 703–722.

Ceci, S. J., Baker, J. E., & Bronfenbrenner, U. (1988). Prospective remembering, temporal calibration, and context. In M. M. Gruneberg, P. E. Morris, & R. N. Sykes (Eds.), *Practical aspects of memory: Current research and issues* (pp. 360–365). Chichester, England: John Wiley & Sons.

Centerwall, B. S. (1989). Exposure to television as a cause of violence. In G. Comstock (Ed.), *Public communication and behavior* (Vol. 2). San Diego: Academic Press.

Cerelli, E. (1989). *Older drivers, the age factor in traffic safety* (DOT HS-807-402). Washington, DC: National Highway Traffic and Safety Administration.

Challis, G.B. & Stam, H.J. (1992). A longitudinal study of the development of anticipatory nausea and vomiting in cancer chemotherapy patients: The role of absorption and autonomic perception. *Health Psychology, 11*, 181–189.

Chapman, S., Wong, W.L. & Smith, W. (1993). Self-exempting beliefs about smoking and health: differences between smokers and ex-smokers. *American Journal of Public Health, 83(2)*, 215–219.

Charness, N. (1987). Component processes in bridge bidding and novel problem-solving tasks. Special Issue: Aging and cognition. *Canadian Journal of Psychology, 41(2)*, 223–243.

Charness, N. (1989). Age and expertise: Responding to Talland's challenge. In L. W. Poon, D. C. Rubin, & B. A. Wilson (Eds.), *Everyday cognition in adulthood and old age*. New York: Cambridge University Press.

Charness, N., Clifton, J., & MacDonald, L. (1988). Case study of a musical "Mono-savant": A cognitive-psychological focus. In L. K. Obler & D. Fein (Eds.), *The Exceptional Brain*. New York: Guilford.

Chasnoff, I. J., Griffith, D. R., MacGregor, S., Dirkes, K., & Burns, K. S. (1989). Temporal patterns of cocaine use in pregnancy: Perinatal outcome. *Journal of the American Medical Association, 261*, 1741–1744.

Chataway, C. J., & Berry, J. W. (1989). Acculturation experiences, appraisal, coping and adaptation: A comparison of Hong Kong Chinese, French, and English students in Canada. *Canadian Journal of Behavioral Science, 21*, 295–309.

Chaves, J. F., & Brown, J. M. (1987). Spontaneous cognitive strategies for the control of clinical pain and stress. *Journal of Behavioral Medicine, 10*, 263–276.

Chebat, J.C., Filiatrault, P. (1986). Preference for forms of political causal attributions. *Journal of Social Psychology, 126(5)*, 633–638.

Chebat, J.C., Filiatrault, P., Perrien J. (1990). Limits of credibility: The case of political persuasion. *Journal of Social Psychology, 130(2)*, 157–167.

Chebat, J.C., Picard, J. (1991). Does prenotification increase response rates in mail surveys? A self-perception approach. *Journal of Social Psychology, 131(4)*, 477–481.

Chebat, J.C., Zuccaro, C., Filiatrault, P. (1992). Locus of control as a moderator variable for the attribution and learning processes of marketing managers. *Journal of Social Psychology, 132(5)*, 597–608.

Chenard, J.R., Marchand, S., Charest, J., Li, J., et al. 1991. Evaluation d'un traitement comportemental de la lombalgie chronique: l' "ecole inter-actionelle du dos". (Evaluation of a behavioral intervention for chronic low-back pain: the "interactional back school".) Special issue: behavioral medicine. *Science et Comportement, 21(4)*, 225–238.

Cherry, E. C. (1953). Some experiments on the recognition of speech with one and with two ears. *Journal of Acoustical Society of America, 25*, 975–979.

Chess, S., & Thomas, A. (1984). *Origins and evolution of behavior disorders*. New York: Brunner/Mazel.

Chilmonczyk, B. A., Salmun, L. M., Megathlin, K. N., Neveux, L. M., Palomaki, G. E., Knight, G. J., Pulkkinen, M. S., & Haddow, J. E. (1993). Association between exposure to environmental tobacco smoke and exacerbations of asthma in children. *New England Journal of Medicine, 328*, 1665–1669.

Chipman, S. F., Brush, L. R., & Wilson, D. M. (Eds.). (1985). *Women and mathematics: Balancing the equation*. Hillsdale, NJ: Erlbaum.

Chipperfield, J.G. (1993). Percieved barriers in coping with health problems: a twelve-year longitudinal study of survival among elderly individuals. *Journal of Aging and Health, 5(1)*, 123–139.

Chisholm, G., Jung, S.O., Cumming, C.E., Fox, E.E., Cumming, D.C. (1990). Premenstrual anxiety and depression: comparison of objective psychological tests with a retrospective questionnaire. *Acta Psychiatrica Scandinavica, 81(1)*, 52–57.

Chomsky, N. (1968). *Language and mind*. New York: Harcourt Brace.

Christensen, A., & Jacobson, N. S. (1994). Who (or what) can do psychotherapy: The status and challenge of nonprofessional therapies. *Psychological Science, 5*, 8–14.

Christianson, S.-A., Goodman, J. & Loftus, E. F. (1992). Eyewitness memory for stressful events: Methodological quandaries and ethical dilemmas. In S.-A. Christianson (Ed.), *The handbook of emotion and learning: Research and theory*. Hillsdale, NJ: Erlbaum.

Chuang, H.T., Devins, G.M., Hunsley, J., Gill, M.J. (1989). Psychosocial distress and well-being among gay and bisexual men with human immunodeficiency virus infection. *American Journal of Psychiatry, 146(7)*, 876–880.

Chuang, H.T., Jason, G.W., Pajurkova, E.M., Gill, M.J. (1992). Psychiatric morbidity in patients with HIV infection. *Canadian Journal of Psychiatry, 37(2)*, 109–115.

Church, A. T., & Burke, P. J. (1994). Exploratory and confirmatory tests of the big five and Tellegen's three- and four-dimensional models. *Journal of Personality and Social Psychology, 66* 93–114

Church, R. M. (1993). Human models of animal behavior. *Psychological Science, 4*, 170–173.

Cialdini, R. B. (1988). *Influence: Science and practice* (2nd ed.). Glenview, IL: Scott, Foresman.

Cialdini, R. B., Kenrick, D. T., & Bauman, D. J. (1982). Effects of mood on prosocial behavior in children and adults. In N. Eisenberg-Berg (Ed.), *Development of prosocial behavior*. New York: Academic Press.

Cialdini, R. B., Vincent, J. E., Lewis, S. K., Catalan, J., Wheeler, D., & Darby, B. L. (1975). Reciprocal concession procedure for inducing compliance: The door-in-the-face technique. *Journal of Personality and Social Psychology, 31*, 206–215.

Claes, M.E. 1992. Friendship and personal adjustment during adolescence. Journal of Adolescence, 15(1), 39–55.

Clark, D. A., Beck, A. T, & Brown, G. (1989). Cognitive mediation in general psychiatric outpatients: A test of the content-specificity hypothesis. *Journal of Personality and Social Psychology, 56*, 958–964.

Clark, D. M. (1988). A cognitive model of panic attacks. In S. Rachman & J. D. Maser (Eds.), *Panic: Psychological perspectives*. Hillsdale, NJ: Erlbaum.

Clark, E. V. (1973). Nonlinguistic strategies and the acquisition of word meanings. *Cognition, 2*, 161–182.

Clark, H. H., & Chase, W. G. (1972). On the process of comparing sentences against pictures. *Cognitive Psychology, 3*, 472–517.

Clark, K., & Clark, M. (1947). Racial identification and racial preferences in Negro children. In T. M. Newcomb & E. L. Hartley, *Readings in social psychology* (pp. 169–178). New York: Holt.

Clark, W., & Clark, S. (1980). Pain response in Nepalese porters. *Science, 209*, 410–412.

Clarke, J.N. (1992). Cancer, heart disease, and AIDS: What do the media tell us about these diseases? *Health Communication, 4(2)*, 105–120.

Clarke, J.T., Gates, R.D., Hogan, S.E., Barrett, M., et al. 1987. Neuropsychological studies on adolescents with phenylketonuria returned to phenylalanine-resticted diets. *American Journal on Mental Retardation, 92(3)*, 255–262.

Clum, G. A., & Bowers, T. G. (1990). Behavior therapy better than placebo treatments: Fact or artifact? *Psychological Bulletin, 107*, 110–113.

Coderre, T.J., Katz, J., Vaccarino, A.L. & Melzack, R. 1993. Contribution of central neuroplasticity to pathological pain: review of clinical and experimental evidence. *Pain, 52(3)*, 259–285.

Cohen, A.J., Thorpe, L.A., Trehub, S.E. (1987). Infants' perception of musical relations in short transposed tome sequences. *Canadian Journal of Psychology, 41(1)*, 33–47.

Cohen, J. (1993). AIDS research: The mood is uncertain. *Science, 260*, 1254–1265.

Cohen, R. J., Montague, P., Nathanson, L. S., & Swerdlik, M. E. (1988). *Psychological testing: An introduction to test & measurement*. Mountain View, CA: Mayfield Publishing Company.

Cohen, R.L., Griffiths, K. (1987). Release from PI in running memory: What does this tell us about developmental STM: *Intelligence, 11(4)*, 317–331.

Cohen, S., Kaplan, J. R., Cunnick, J. E., Manuck, S. B., & Rabin, B. S. (1992). Chronic social stress, affiliation, and cellular immune response in nonhuman primates. *Psychological Science, 3*, 301–304.

Cohen, S., Tyrrell, D. A., & Smith, A. P. (1993). Negative life events, perceived stress, negative affect, and susceptibility to the common cold. *Journal of Personality and Social Psychology, 64*, 131–140.

Cohen, S., & Wills, T. A. (1985). Stress, social support, and the buffering hypothesis. *Psychological Bulletin, 98*, 310–357.

Colby, A., Kohlberg, L., Feonton, E., Speicher-Dubin, B., & Lieberman, M. (1983). A longitudinal study of moral judgment. *Monographs of the Society for Research in Child Development, 48*, (1–2, Serial No. 200).

Colby, A., Kohlberg, L., Gibbs, J., Liegerman, M., (1983). A longitudinal study of maorl judgement. *Monographs of the Society for Research in Child Development, 48(1–2)*, 124p.

Cole, M., & Scribner, S. (1974). *Culture and thought: A psychological introduction*. New York: John Wiley.

Cole, W.A. & Bradford, J.M. (1992). Abduction during custody and access disputes. *Canadian Journal of Psychiatry, 37(4)*, 264–266.

Colwill, R. M. (1993). An associative analysis of instrumental learning. *Current Directions in Psychological Science, 2*, 111–116.

Colwill, R. M., & Rescorla, R. A. (1985). Postconditioning devaluation of a reinforcer affects instrumental responding. *Journal of Experimental Psychology, 11*, 120–132.

Colwill, R. M., & Rescorla, R. A. (1988). Associations between the discriminative stimulus and the reinforcer in instrumental learning. *Journal of Experimental Psychology, 14,* 155–164.

Condon, J.W., Crano, W.D. (1988). Inferred evaluation and the relation between attitude similarity and interpersonal attraction. *Journal of Personality and Social Psychology, 54(5),* 789–797.

Conger, J.A., Kanungo, R.N. (1987). Toward a behavioral theory of charismatic leadership in organizational settings. *Academy of Management Review, 12(4),* 637–647.

Conger, J.A., Kanungo, R.N. (1992). Perceived behavioural attributes of charismatic leadership. *Canadian Journal of Behavioural Science, 24(1),* 86–102.

Contrada, R. J. (1989). Type A behavior, personality hardiness, and cardiovascular responses to stress. *Journal of Personality and Social Psychology, 57,* 895–903.

Conway, M., & Giannopoulos, C. (1993). Self-esteem and specificity in self-focused attention. *Journal of Social Psychology, 133,* 121–123.

Conway, M., DiFazio, R., Bonneville, F. (1990). Consensus and causal attributions for negative affect. *Journal of Social Psychology, 130(3),* 375–384.

Conway, M., Giannopoulos, C., Csank, P., & Mendelson, M. (1993). Dysphoria and specificity in self-focused attention. *Personality and Social Psychology Bulletin, 19,* 265–268.

Cook, R. G. (1993). The experimental analysis of cognition in animals. *Psychological Science, 4,* 174–178.

Cook, S. W. (1985). Experimenting on social issues: The case of school desegregation. *American Psychologist, 40,* 452–460.

Cooper, J., & Scher, S. J. (1990). Actions and attitude: The role of responsibility and aversive consequences in persuasion. In T. Brock & S. Shavitt (Eds.), *The psychology of persuasion.* San Francisco: Freeman.

Cooper, B.A., Ward, M., Gowland, C.A. & McIntosh, J.M. (1991). The use of the Lanthony New Color Test in determining the effects of aging on color vision. *Journals of Gerontology, 46(6),* 320–324.

Cooper, M., Rodman, M.C. (1994). Accessibility and quality of life in housing cooperatives. *Environment and Behavior, 26(1),* 49–70.

Cooper, M., Corrado, R., Karlberg,A. M., & Adams,L. P.(1992). Aboriginal suicide in British Columbia: An overview. *Canada's Mental Health, 40,* 19–23.

Corballis, M.C. & Sergent, J. (1992). Judgements about numerosity by a commissurotomized subject. *Neuropsychologia, 30(10),* 865–876.

Corbett, D. (1991). Cocaine enhances the reward value of medial prefrontal cortex self-stimulation. Neuroreport An *International Journal for the Rapid Communication of Research in Neuroscience, 2(12),* 215–218.

Coren, S. & Mah, K.B. (1993). Prediction of physiological arousability: a validation of the Arousal Predisposition Scale. *Behavior Research and Therapy, 31(2),* 215–219.

Coren, S. & Russel, J.A. (1992). The relative dominance of different facial expressions of emotion under conditions of perceptual ambiguity. *Cognition and Emotion, 6(5),* 339–356.

Coren, S. (1993). The lateral preference inventory for measurement of handedness, footedness, eyedness, and earedness: norms for young adults. *Bulletin of the Psychnomic Society, 31(1),* 1–3.

Coren, S., & Girgus, J. S. (1978). *Seeing is deceiving: The psychology of visual illusion.* Hillsdale, N.J.: Lawrence Erlbaum.

Coren, S., & Ward, L. M. (1989). *Sensation and Perception* (3rd ed.). San Diego: Harcourt Brace Jovanovich.

Coren, S., Girgus, J. S., Erlichman, H., & Hakstean, A. R. (1976). An empirical taxonomy of visual illusions. *Perception & Psychophysics, 20,* 129–137.

Cornelius, S. W., & Caspi, A. (1987). Everyday problem solving in adulthood and old age. *Psychology and Aging, 2,* 144–153.

Corrigall, W.A., Coen, K.M. (1991). Cocain self-administration is incresed by both D1 and D2 dopamine antagonists. *Pharmacology, Biochemistry and Behavior. 39(3),* 799–802.

Corso, J. F. (1977). Auditory perception and communication. In J. E. Birren & K. W. Schaie (Eds.), *Handbook of the psychology of aging* (pp. 535–553). New York: Van Nostrand Reinhold.

Costa, P. T., Jr., & McCrae, R. R. (1988). Personality in adulthood: A six-year longitudinal study of self-reports and spouse ratings on the NEO Personality Inventory. *Journal of Personality and Social Psychology, 54,* 853–863.

Costa, P. T., Jr., & McCrae, R. R. (1994). The Revised NEO Personality Inventory (NEO-PI-R). In R. Briggs & J. M. Cheek (Eds.), *Personality measures: Development and evaluation* (Vol. 1.). Greenwich, CT: JAI Press.

Cota, A.A., Dion, K.L. (1986). Salience of gender and sex composition of ad hoc groups: An experimental test of distinctiveness theory. *Journal of Personality and Social Psychology, 50(4),* 770–776.

Cota, A.A., Reid, A., Dion, K.L. (1991). Construct validity of a diagnostic ratio measure of gender stereotypes. *Sex Roles, 25(3–4),* 225–235.

Cottrell, N., Eisenberg, R., & Speicher, H. (1992). Inhibiting effects of reciprocation wariness on interpersonal relationships. *Journal of Personality and Social Psychology, 62,* 658–668.

Coulombe, A., Ladouceur, R., Desharnais, R. Jobin, J. (1992). Erroneous perceptions and arousal among regular and occasional video poker players. *Journal of Gambling Studies, 8(3),* 235–244.

Counts, D.A., Counts, D.R. (1992). "They're my family now": The creation of communtiy among RVers. *Anthropologica, 34(2),* 153–182.

Cousins, L.S., Weiss, G., (1993). Parent training and social skills training for children with attention deficit hyperactivity disorder: How can they be combined for greater effectiveness? *Canadian Journal of Psychiatry, 38(6),* 449–457.

Cousins, S.O. & Burgess, A. (1992). Perspectives on older adults in physical activity and sports. Special Issue: Educational gerontology in Canada. *Educational Gerontology, 18(5),* 461–481.

Covell, K., Abramovitch, R. (1987). Understanding emotion in the family: Children's and parents' attributions of happiness, sadness, and anger. *Child Development, 58(4),* 985–991.

Covell, K., Miles, B., (1992). Children's beliefs about strategies to reduce parental anger. *Child Development, 63(2),* 381–390.

Cowan, N. (1984). On short and long auditory stores. *Psychological Bulletin, 96,* 341–370.

Coyle, J. T., Price, D. L., & DeLong, M. R. (1983). Alzheimer's disease: A disorder of cortical cholinergic innervation. *Science, 219,* 1184–1190.

Coyle, J. T. (1987). Alzheimer's disease. In G. Adelman (Ed.), *Encyclopedia of neuroscience* (pp. 29–31). Boston: Birkhauser.

Craig, K. D., & Prkachin, K. M. (1978). Social modeling influences on pain thresholds influenced by social modeling. *Journal of Personality and Social Psychology, 36,* 805–815.

Craig, K.D., Grunau, R.V., Aquan-Assee, J., (1988). Judgement of facial pain in newborns: Facial activity and cry as determinants. Special Issue: Child and adolescent health. *Canadian Journal of Behavioral Science, 20(4),* 442–451.

Craik, F. I. M., & Lockhardt, R. S. (1972). Levels of processing: A framework for memory research. *Journal of Verbal Learning and Verbal Behavior, 11,* 671–684.

Craik, F. I. M., & Tulving, E. (1975). Depth of processing and the retention of words in episodic memory. *Journal of Experimental Psychology: General, 104,* 268–294.

Craik, F.I.M. & Dirkx, E. (1992). Age-related differences in three tests of visual imagery. *Psychology and Aging, 7(4),* 661–665.

Craik, F.I.M. & McDowd, J.M. (1987). Age difference in recall and recognition. *Journal of Experimental Psychology Learning, Memory, and Cognition, 13(3),* 474–479.

Cram, S. J., & Dobson, K. S. (1993). Confidentiality: Ethical and legal aspects for Canadian law. *Canadian Psychologist, 34,* 347–363.

Crespi, L. P. (1942). Quantitative variation of incentive and performance in the white rat. *American Journal of Psychology, 55,* 467–517.

Cristofalo, V. J. (1988). An overview of the theories of biological aging. In J. E. Birren & V. L. Bengtson (Eds.), *Emergent theories of aging* (pp. 118–127). New York: Springer.

Crocker, P.R. (1993). Sport and exercise psychology and research with individuals with disabilities: using theory to advance knowledge. Special issue: research with special populations: part of an ongoing research program. *Adapted Physical Activity Quarterly, 10(4),* 324–335.

Cromwell, R. L. (1992). Searching for the original of schizophrenia. *Psychological Science, 4,* 276–279.

Cronshaw, S.F. (1988). Future directions for industrial psychology in Canada. Special Issue: Industrial/organizational psychology in Canada. *Canadian Psychology, 29(1),* 30–43.

Cropanzano, R. (Ed.). (1993). *Justice in the workplace: Approaching fairness in human resource management.* Hillsdale, NJ: Erlbaum.

Cropanzano, R., & James, K. (1990). Some methodological considerations for the behavioral-genetic analysis of work attitudes. *Journal of Applied Psychology, 21,* 433–439.

Cropanzano, R., & Randall, M. L. (1993). Injustice and work behavior: A historical review. In R. Cropanzano (Ed.), *Justice in the workplace* (pp. 3–20). Hillsdale, NJ: Erlbaum.

Crossman, J. & Eyjolfsson, K. (1991). Perceptions of participants regarding the long-term impact of an education and support program for heart attack and heart surgery patients and their partners. *Journal of Community Psychology, 19(4),* 333–336.

Crouch, A.G., Yetton, P. (1987). Manager behavior, leadership style, and subordinate performance: An empirical extension of the Vroom-Yetton conflict rule. *Organizational Behavior and Human Decision Processes, 39(3),* 384–396.

Crowhurst, M. (1990). Teaching and learning the writing of persuasive/ argumentative discourse. *Canadian Journal of Education, 15(4),* 384–359.

Crownshaw, S. F., & Ellis, R. J. (1991). A process investigation of self-monitoring and leaders emergence. *Small Group Research, 22,* 403–420.

Croyle, R. T. (1992). Appraisal of health threats: Cognition, motivation, and social comparison. *Cognitive Therapy and Research, 16,* 165–182.

Crusco, A. H., & Wetzel, C. G. (1984). The Midas touch: The effects of interpersonal touch on restaurant tipping. *Personality and Social Psychology Bulletin, 10,* 512–517.

Crutchfield, R. A. (1955). Conformity and character. *American Psychologist, 10,* 191–198.

Csikszentmihalyi, M., & Larson, R. (1984). *Being adolescent: Conflict and growth in the teenage years.* New York: Basic Books.

Cuneo, D., (1980). A general strategy for quantity judgements: The height and width rule. *Child Development, 51(1),* 299–301.

Cunningham, J.B. (1989) A compressed shift schedule: Dealing with some of the problems of shift-work. *Journal of Organizational Behavior, 10.* 231–245.

Cunningham, M.R. (1986). Measuring the physical in physical attractiveness: Quasi-experiments on the sociobiology of female facial beauty. *Journal of Personality and Social Psychology, 50(5),* 925–935.

Cunningham, M. R., Shaffer, D. R., Barbee, A., Wolff, P. L., & Kelley, D. J. (1990). Separate processes in the relation of elation and depression to helping: Social versus personal concerns. *Journal of Experimental Social Psychology, 26,* 13–33.

Curtis, R.C., Miller, K. (1986). Believing another likes or dislikes you: Behaviors making the beliefs come true. *Journal of Personality and Social Psychology, 51(2),* 284–290.

Cynader, M., & Chen, Z., as in cited in *Science News,* Nov. 27, 1993, 144(22), 367.

Czeisler, C. A., Moore-Ede, M. C., & Coleman, R. M. (1982). Rotating shift work schedules that disrupt sleep are improved by applying Circadian principles. *Science, 217,* 460–462.

Dahl, O. (1985). Testicular carcinoma: A curable malignancy. *Acta Radiology and Oncology, 24,* 3–15.

Daniel, J., & Potasova, A. (1989). Oral temperature and performance in 8 hour and 12 hour shifts. *Ergonomics, 32,* 689–696.

Darke, P.R., Freedman, J.L. (1993). Deciding whether to seek a bargain: Effects of both amount and percentage off. *Journal of Applied Psychology, 78(6),* 960–965.

Darley, J. M., & Latané, B. (1968). Bystander intervention in emergencies: Diffusion of responsibility. *Journal of Personality and Social Psychology, 8,* 377–383.

Darou, W. G. Native Canadians and intelligence testing. *Canadian Journal of Counselling, 26,* 96–99.

Das, B. (1991). Individual growth need strength as a moderator of the relationship of worker satisfaction and attitudes to worker productivity. *Journal of Human Ergology, 20(1),* 89–94.

Das, J. P. (1992). Beyond a unidimensional scale of merit *Intelligence, 16,* 137–149.

DasGupta, B. (1992). Percieved control and examination stress. *Psychology- A Journal of Human Behavior, 29(1),* 31–34.

Datan, N., Antonovsky, A., & Moaz, B. (1984). Love, war, and the life cycle of the family. In K. A. McCluskey & H. W. Reese (Eds.), *Life-span developmental psychology: Historical and generational effects* (pp. 143–159). New York: Academic Press.

Daum, I., Ackermann, H., Schugens, M. M., Reimold, C., Dichgans, J., & Birbaumer, N. (1993). The cerebellum and cognitive functions in humans. *Behavioral Neuroscience, 104,* 411–419.

Davey, G. C. L. (1992). Classical conditioning and the acquisition of human fears and phobias: A review and synthesis of the literature. *Advances in Behavior Research Therapy, 14,* 29–66.

Davey, V.A. & Biederman, G.B. (1991). Methodological issues in drug conditioning in rats: Nonassociative factors in heart rate and avfail. *Behavioral Neuroscience, 105,* 850–859.

Davidson, J. K., Sr., & Hoffman, L. E. (1986). Sexual fantasies and sexual satisfaction: An empirical analysis of erotic thought. *Journal of Sex Research, 22,* 184–205.

Davidson, K., & Hopson, J. L. (1988). Gorilla business. *Image* (San Francisco Chronicle), 14–18.

Davidson, R. J. (1992). Emotion and affective style: Hemispheric substrates. *Psychological Science, 3,* 39–43.

Davidson, R. J., Finman, R., Straus, A., & Kagan, J. (1991). *Childhood temperament and frontal lobe activity: Patterns of asymmetry differentiate between wary and outgoing children.* Manuscript submitted for publication.

Davidson, R. J., & Fox, N. A. (1988). Cerebral asymmetry and emotion: Developmental and individual differences. In D. L. Molfese & S. J. Segalowitz (Eds.), *Brain lateralization in children: Developmental implications* (pp. 191–206). New York: Guilford Press.

Davies, M. F. (1987). Reduction of hindsight bias by restoration of foresight perspective. *Organizational Behavior & Human Decision Processes, 40,* 50–68.

Davis, C. (1994). Seventh International Congres on Obesity, as quoted in the *Globe and Mail,* August 24, 1994.

Davis, C., Brewer, H. & Weinstein, M. (1993). A study of appearance anxiety in young men. *Social Behavior and Personality, 21(1),* 63–74.

Davis, H. (1990). Cognitive style and nonsport imagery in elite ice hockey performance. *Perceptual and Motor Skills, 71(3, Pt 1),* 795–801.

Davis, H. (1991). Criterion validity of the Athletic Motivation Inventory: issues in professional sport. *Journal of Applied Sport Psychology, 3(2),* 176–182.

Davis, J.R., & Tunks, E. (1990–91). Environments and addiction: A proposed taxonomy. *International Journal of the Addictions, 25,* 805–826.

Davis, M. H., & Franzoi, S. L. (1986). Adolescent loneliness, self-disclosure and private self-consciousenss: A longitudinal investigation. *Journal of Personality and Social Psychology, 51,* 595–608.

De Villiers, J. G., & De Villiers, P. A. (1978). *Language acquisition.* Cambridge, MA: Harvard University Press.

de Montigny, J. (1993). Distress, stress and solidarity in palliative care. *Omega Journal of Death and Dying, 27(1),* 5–15.

de Vries, B., Bluck, S. & Birren, J.E. (1993). The understanding of death and dying in a life-span perspective. *Gerontologist, 33(3),* 366–372.

de-Koninck, J. (1991). Les rythmes biologiques lies au sommeil et l'adaptation physchologique, (Biological rhythms linked to sleep and psychological adaptation.) *Journal of Psychiatry and Neuroscience, 16,* 115–122.

Deaux, K. (1993). Commentary: Sorry, wrong number—a reply to Gentile's call. *Psychological Science, 4,* 125–126.

Deaux, K., & Lewis, L. L. (1986). The structure of gender stereotypes: Interrelationships among components and gender label. *Journal of Personality and Social Psychology, 46,* 991–1005.

DeBono, K.G. (1992). Pleasant scents and persuasion: An information processing approach. *Journal of Applied Social Psychology, 22(11),* 910–919.

deCantanzaro, D., MacNiven, E., (1992). Psychogenic pregnancy disruptions in mammals. *Neuroscience and Behavioral Reviews, 16(1),* 43–53.

DeCasper, A. J., & Fifer, W. P. (1980). Of human bonding: Newborns prefer their mothers' voices. *Science, 208,* 991–1004.

DeCasper, A. J., & Spence, M. J. (1986). Prenatal maternal speech influences newborns' perception of speech sounds. *Infant Behavior and Development, 9,* 133–150.

Deci, E. L. (1975). *Intrinsic motivation.* New York: Plenum.

Deci, E. L., & Ryan, R. M. (1985). *Intrinsic motivation and self–determination in human behavior.* New York: Plenum Press.

Deckers, L., & Carr, D. E. (1986). Cartoons varying in low-level pain ratings, not aggression ratings, correlate positively with funniness ratings. *Motivation and Emotion, 10,* 207–216.

DeGroot, J.M., Kennedy, S., Rodin, G. & McVey, G. (1992). Correlates of sexual abuse in women with anorexia nervosa and bulimia nervosa. *Canadian Journal of Psychiatry, 37(7),* 516–518.

Delgado, P. L., Charney, D. S., Price, L. H., Aghajanian, G. K., Landis, H., & Heninger, G. R. (1990). Serotonin function and mechanism of antidepressant action: Reversal of antidepressant-induced remission by rapid depletion of plasma atryptophan. *Archives of General Psychiatry 47,* 411–418.

DeLongis, A., Folkman, S. & Lazarus, R.S. (1988). The impact of daily stress on health and mood: psychological and social sources as mediators. *Journal of Personality and Social Psychology, 54(3),* 486–495.

Dembrowski, T. M., & Williams, R. B. (1989). Definition and assessment of coronary-prone behavior. In N. Schneiderman, P. Kaufmann, & S. M. Wiess (Eds.), *Handbook of research methods in cardiovascular behavioral medicine.* New York: Plenum.

Dement, W. C. (1975). *Some must watch while some must sleep.* San Francisco: W. H. Freeman.

Dement, W. C., & Wolpert, E. A. (1958). The relation of eye movements, body mobility and external stimuli to dream content. *Journal of Experimental Psychology, 55,* 543–553.

DeNisi, A.S., Cafferty, T.P., Meglino, B.M. (1984). A cognitive view of the performance appraisal process: A model and research propositions. *Organizational Behavior and Human Performance, 33(3),* 360–396.

Denney, N. W., & Palmer A. M. (1981). Adult age differences on traditional and practical problem-solving measures. *Journal of Gerontology, 36,* 323–328.

Denning, P. J. (1992). Neural networks. *American Scientist, 80,* 426–429.

DePaulo, B.M. 1992. Nonverbal behavior and self-presentation. *Psychological Bulletin, 111(2),* 203–243.

Derksen, L. & Gartrell, J. (1993). The social context of recycling. *American Sociological Review, 58,* 434–442.

Dermer, M.L. & Jacobsen, E. (1986). Some potential negative social consequences of cigarette smoking: marketing research in reverse. *Journal of Applied Social Psychology, 16(8),* 702–725.

Deutsch, A. (1949). *The mentally ill in America* (2nd ed.). New York and London: Columbia University Press.

DeValois, R. L., & DeValois, K. K. (1975). Neural coding of color. In E. C. Carterette & M. P. Friedman (Eds.), *Handbook of perception* (pp. 117–166). New York: Academic Press.

Devine, P.G. (1989). Stereotypes and prejudice: Their automatic and controlled components. *Journal of Personality and Social Psychology, 56(1),* 5–18.

Devins, G.M. 1992. Social cognitive analysis of recovery from a lapse after smoking cessation: comment on Haaga & Stewart (1992). *Journal of Consulting and Clinical Psychology, 60(1),* 29–31.

Devitt, M., McKelvie, S.J. (1991). Effects of physical attractiveness on perceived support for women's rights. *Social Behavior and Personality, 19(3),* 151–156.

Devolder, P.A., Pressley, M. (1992). Causal attributions and strategy use in relation to memory performance differences in younger and older adults. *Applied Cognitive Psychology, 6(7),* 629–642.

Diamond, J. (1990). The Cost of Living. *Discover,* June 1990, 11, 62–67.

Dickerson, C.A., Thibodeau, R., Aronson, E., Miller, D. (1992). Using cognitive dissonance to encourage water conservation. *Journal of Applied Social Psychology, 22(11),* 841–854.

Digman, J. M. (1990). Personality structure: Emergence of the five-factor model. *Annual Review of Psychology, 41,* 417–440.

Dillard, J.P. (1991). The current status of research on sequential-request compliance techniques. *Personality and Social Psychology Bulletin, 17,* 283–288.

Dindia, K., & Allen, M. (1992). Sex differences in self-disclosure: A meta-analysis. *Psychological Bulletin, 112,* 106–124.

Dion, K. K., & Dion, K. L. (1991). Psychological individualism and romantic love. *Journal of Social Behavior and Personality, 6,* 17–33.

Dion, K. K., & Dion, K. L. (1993). Individualistic and collectivitist perspectives on gender and the cultural context of love and intimacy. *Journal of Social Issues, 49,* 53–69.

Dion, K. L., & Giordano, C. (1990). Ethnicity and sex as correlates of depression symptoms in a Canadian university sample. *International Journal of Social Psychiatry, 36,* 30–41.

Dion, K. L., Dion, K. K., & Pak, A. W.-P. (1992). Personality-based hardiness as a buffer for discrimination-related stress in members of Toronto's Chinese community. *Canadian Journal of Behavioral Science, 24,* 517–536.

Dion, K.K., and Dion, K.L. (1993). Individualistic and collectivistic perspectives on gender and the cultural context of love and intimacy. *Journal of Social Issues, 49(3),* 53–69.

Dion, K.K., Pak, A.W., Dion, K.L. (1990). Stereotyping physical sttractiveness: A sociocultural perspective. *Journal of Cross Cultural Psychology, 21(2),* 158–179.

Dion, K.K., Wan-Ping Pak, A., Dion, K.L. (1990). Stereotyping Physical Attractiveness: A Sociocultural Perspective. *Journal of Cross-Cultural Psychology, 21(2),* 158–179.

Dion, K.L. (1985). Social distance norms in Canada: Effects of stimulus characteristics and dogmatism. *International Journal of Psychology, 20(6),* 743–749.

Dion, K.L., Dion, K.K. (1987). Belief in a just world and physical attractiveness stereotyping. *Journal of Personality and Social Psychology, 52(4),* 775–780.

Dion, K.L., Dion, K.K., Keelan, J.P. (1990). Appearance anxiety as a dimension of social-evaluative anxiety: Exploring the ugly duckling syndrome. *Contemporary Social Psychology, 14(4),* 220–224.

Dion, K.L., Dion, K.K., Pak, A.W. (1992). Personality-based hardiness as a buffer for discrimination-related stress in members of Toronto's Chinese community. *Canadian Journal of Behavioural Science, 24(4),* 517–536.

Dion, K.L., Schuller, R.A. (1991). The Ms. stereotype: Its generality and is relation to managerial and marital status stereotypes. *Canadian Journal of Behavioural Science, 23(1),* 25–40.

DiTecco, D., Cwitco, G., Arsenault, A., Andre, M. (1992). Operator stress and monitoring practices. special Issue: Electronic performance monitoring. *Applied Ergonomics, 23(1),* 29–34.

DiTommaso, E., Spinner, B. (1992). The development and initial validation of the social and emotional loneliness scale for adults (SELSA). *Personality and Individual Difference, 14(1),* 127–134.

Ditto, P.H., Jemmott, J.B., Darley, J.M. (1988). Appraising the threat of illness: A mental representational approach. *Health Psychology, 7(2),* 183–201.

Ditto, P.H., Lopez, D.F. (1992). Motivated skepticism: Use of differential decision criteria for preferred and nonpreferred conclusions. *Journal of Personality and Social Psychology, 63(4),* 568–584.

Dobbs, A.R. & Rule, B.G. (1987). Prospective memory and self- reports of memory abilities in older adults. Special issue: Aging and cognition. *Canadian Journal of Psychology, 41(2),* 209–222.

Donovan, J.M., Hill, E., Jankowiak, W.R. (1989). Gender, sexual orientation, and truth-of-donsensus in studies of physical attractiveness. *Journal of Sex Research, 26(2),* 264–271.

Dore, F.Y. & Goulet, S. (1992). Cognition chez les mammiferes carnivores (chats et chiens). (Cognition in carnivorous mammals: Cats and dogs. *Psychologie Francaise, 37,* 65–72.

Doty, R. L., Shaman, P., Applebaum, S. L., Giberson, R., Sikorski, L., & Rosenberg, L. (1984). Smell identification ability: Changes with age. *Science, 226,* 141–143.

Douek, E. (1988). Olfaction and medicine. In S. Van Toller & G. Doll (Eds.), *Perfumery: The psychology and biology of fragrance.* London: Chapman Hall.

Dovidio, J. F., Evans, N., & Tyler, R. B. (1986). Racial stereotypes: The contents of their cognitive representations. *Journal of Experimental Social Psychology, 22,* 22–37.

Dovidio, J. F., & Gaertner, S. L. (Eds.). (1986). *Prejudice, discrimination, and racism.* Orlando, FL: Academic Press.

Doyle, A.B., Aboud, F.E., Sufrategui, M. (1992). Le developpement des prejuges ethniques durant l'enfance. (The development of ethnic prejudices in childhood.) *Revue Quebecoise de Psychologie, 13(1),* 63–73.

Doyle, A.B., Beaudet, J., Aboud, F.E. (1988). Developmental patterns in the flexibility of children's ethnic attitudes. *Journal of Cross Cultural Psychology, 19(1),* 3–18.

Doyle, A.B., Connolly, J., (1989). Negotiation and enactment in social pretend play: Relations to social acceptance and social cognition. *Early Childhood Research Quarterly, 4(3),* 289–302.

Drachman, D., DeCarufel, A., Insko, C.A. (1978). The extra credit effect in interpersonal attraction. *Journal of Experimental Social Psychology, 14(5),* 458–465.

Dreidger, L. (1989).*The ethnic factor: Identity in diversity.* Toronto: McGraw-Hill Ryerson, p. 82.

Droungas, A. & LoLordo, V.M. (1991). Taste-mediated potentiation of odor aversion induced by lithium chloride: Aspects of preconditioning exposure to the conditioned stimulus and postconditioning extinction of the taste aversion. *Learning and Motivation, 22,* 291–310.

Dubbert, P. M. (1992). Exercise in behavioral medicine. *Journal of Consulting and Clinical Psychology, 60,* 613–618.

Duck, S., & Barnes, M. H. (1992). Disagreeing about agreement: Reconciling differences about similarity. *Communication Monographs, 59,* 199 208.

Dudek, S.Z. & Hall, W.B. (1991). Personality consistency: eminent architects 25 years later. *Creativity Research Journal, 4(3),* 213–231.

Duffy, D. L., Hamerman, D., & Cohen, M. A. (1980). Communication skills of house officers: A study in a medical clinic. *Annals of Internal Medicine, 93,* 354–357.

Duffy, R. D., Kalsher, M. J., & Wogalter, M. S. (1993). The effectiveness of an interactive warning in a realistic product-use situation. *Proceedings of the Human Factors and Ergonomics Society, 37th Annual Meeting,* 935–939.

Dumas, C., Dore, F.Y., (1989). Cognitive development in kittens (Felis catus): A cross-sectional study of object permanence. *Journal of Comparative Psychology, 103(2),* 191–200.

Dumont, F. (1993). Inferential heuristics in clinical problem formulation: Selective review of their strengths and weaknesses. *Professional Psychology Research and Practice, 24(2),* 196–205.

Dumont, M. (1987). Acquisition des connaisances sociales et developpement des habiletes interactives chez l'enfant de l'age prescolaire. (Acquisition of social knowledge and development of interactive skills in preschoolers). *Apprentissage et Socialization, 10(4),* 219–223.

Dumont, M. & Ladouceur, R. (1990). Evaluation of motivation among video-poker players. *Psychological Reports, 66,* 95–98.

Duncker, K. (1945). On problem solving. *Psychological Monographs* (whole No. 270).

Dunn, K. (1991, October 17). City's homeless now top 15,000: Study. *The Gazette* (Montreal), A3.

Dussault, C. (1990). Effectiveness of a Selective Traffic Enforcement Program combined with incentives for seat belt use in Quebec. *Health Education Research, 5,* 217–223.

Dutton, D.G. & Aron, A.P. (1974). Some evidence for heightened sexual attraction under conditions of high anxiety. *Journal of Personality and Social Psychology, 30(4),* 510–517.

Dutton, D.G. & Strachan, C.E. (1987). Motivational needs for power and spouse-specific assertiveness in assaultive and nonassaultive men. *Violence and Victims, 2(3),* 145–156.

Dutton, D.G. & Hart, S.D. (1992). Risk markers for family violence in a federally incarcerated population. *International Journal of Law and Psychiatry, 15,* 102–112.

Dutton, D.G., Aron, A. (1989). Romantic attraction and generalized liking for others who are sources of conflict-based arousal.

Dweck, C. S., & Licht, B. G. (1980). Learned helplessness and intellectual achievement. In M. E. P. Seligman & J. Garber (Eds.), *Human helplessness: Theory and application.* New York: Academic Press.

Dwyer, W. L., Leeming F. C., Cobern, M. K., & Porter, B. E. (1993). Critical review of behavioral interventions to preserve the environment. *Environment and Behavior, 225,* 275–321.

Dworkin, E. S., & Efran, J. S. (1967). The angered: Their susceptibility to varieties of humor. *Journal of Personality and Social Psychology, 34,* 510–518.

Dyck, R. J., Bland, R. C., Newman, S. C., & Orn, H. Suicide attempts and psychiatric disorders in Edmonton. *Acta Psychiatrica Scandinavica. 77(suppl.388),* 64–71.

Dyer, F. C. (1991). Bees acquire route-based memories but not cognitive maps in a familiar landscape. *Animal Behaviour, 41,* 239–246.

Eagly, A. E., & Carli, L. (1981). Sex of researchers and sex-typed communications as determinants of sex differences in influence ability: A meta-analysis of social influence studies. *Psychological Bulletin, 90,* 1–20.

Eagly, A. H. (1987). *Sex differences in social behavior: A social-role interpretation.* Hillsdale, NJ: Erlbaum.

Eagly, A. H., & Johnson, B. T. (1990). Gender and leadership style: A meta-analysis. *Psychological Bulletin, 108*, 233–256.

Eagly, A. H., Makhijani, M. G., & Klonsky, B. G. (1992). Gender and the evaluation of leaders: A meta-analysis. *Psychological Bulletin, 111*, 3–22.

Eagly, A.H., Carli, L.L. (1981). Sex of researchers and sex-typed communications as determinants of sex differences in influenceability: A meta-analysis of social influence studies. *Psychological Bulletin, 90(1)*, 1–20.

Earhard, B. (1990a). The object-line effect: Is it attributable to intercontext differences or the structural properties of contexts and task demands? *Canadian Journal of Psychology, 44(3)*, 384–399.

Earhard, B. (1990b). The generality of outside-in processing routines in the analysis of form. *Canadian Journal of Psychology, 44(1)*, 14–29.

Earhard, B., Walker, H. (1985). An "outside-in" processing strategy in the perception of form. *Perception and Psychophysics, 38(3)*, 249–260.

Earle, S.S. (1993). Assessing the needs of persons of advanced age: The Weston, Masseachusetts Council on Aging "over 80" outreach survey. *Pride Institute Journal of Long Term Home Health Care, 12(3)*, 33–36.

Eastwood, R., Nobbs, H., Lindsay, J. & McDowell, I. (1992). Canadian Study of Health and Aging. *Dementia, 3(4)*, 209–212.

Ebbesen, B.L., Prkachin, K.M. & Mills, D.E. (1992). Effects of acute exercise on cardiovascular reactivity. *Journal of Behavioral Medicine, 15(5)*, 489–507.

Ebbinghaus, H. (1885). *Über das Gedachtnis.* Leipzig: Dunker. (Translation by H. Ruyer & C. E. Bussenius (1913), *Memory.* New York: Teachers College, Columbia University.)

Eberhardt, C. A., & Schill, T. (1984). Differences in sexual attitudes and likeliness of sexual behavior of black lower-socioeconomic father-present vs. father-absent female adolescents. *Adolescence, 19*, 99–105.

Edwards, J. R., & Harrison, R. V. (1993). Job demands and worker health: Three-dimensional reexamination of the relationship between person-environment fit and strain. *Journal of Applied Psychology, 78*, 628–648.

Egeland, J. A., Gerhard, D. S., Pauls, D. L., Sussex, J. N., Kidd, K. K., Allen, C. R., Hostetter, A. M., & Housman, D. E. (1987). Bipolar affective disorders linked to DNA markers on chromosome 11. *Nature, 325*, 783–787.

Ehrlichman, H., & Bastone, L. (1990). Olfaction and emotion. In M. Serby & K. Chobor (Eds), *Olfaction and the central nervous system.* Hillsdale, NJ: Erlbaum.

Ehrman, R. N., Robbins, S. J., Childress, A. R., & O'Brien, C. P. (1992). Conditioned responses to cocaine-related stimuli in cocaine abuse patients. *Psychopharmacology, 107*, 523–529.

Eich, J. E. (1980). The cue-dependent nature of state-dependent retrieval. *Memory & Cognition, 8*, 157–173.

Eichar, D.M., Norland, S., Brady, E.M., Fortinsky, R.H. (1991). The job satisfaction of older workers. *Journal of Organizational Behaviour, 12(7)*, 609–620.

Eimas, P. D., & Tarter, V. C. (1979). The development of speech perception. In H. W. Reese & L. P. Lipsitt (Eds.), *Advances in child development and behavior* (Vol. 13, pp. 155–193). New York: Academic Press.

Eisenberg, N., Cialdini, R.B., McCreath, H., Shell, R. (1987). Consistency-based compliance in children: When and why do consistency procedures have immediate effects? *International Journal of Behavioral Development, 12(3)*, 351–367.

Ekman, P. as in: The fine art of catching liars, *Time*, April 22, (1985), page 63.

Ekman, P. (1992). Facial expressions of emotion: New findings, new questions. *Psychological Science, 3*, 34–38.

Ekman, P., Davidson, R. J., & Friesen, W. V. (1990). The Duchenne smile: Emotional expression and brain physiology II. *Journal of Personality and Social Psychology, 58*, 231–242.

Eldridge, G.D. & Pear, J.J. (1987). Topographical variations in behavior during autoshaping, automaintenance, and omission training. *Journal of the Experimental Analysis of Behavior, 47*, 319–333.

Elkin, J., Shea, T., Watkins, J. T., Imber, S. D., Stotsky, S. M., Collins, J. F., Glass, D. R., Pilkonis, P. A., Leber, W. R., Docherty, J. P., Fiester, S. J., & Parloff, M. B. (1989). National Institutes of Mental Health treatment of depression and collaborative research program. *Archives of General Psychiatry, 46*, 971–982.

Elkind, D. (1967). Egocentrism in adolescence. *Child Development, 38*, 1025–1034.

Elkins, I. J., Cromwell, R. L., & Asarnow, R. F. (1992). Span of apprehension in schizophrenic patients as a function of distracter masking and laterality. *Journal of Abnormal Psychology, 101*, 53–60.

Elkins, L. E., & Peterson, C. (1993). Gender differences in best friendships. *Sex Roles, 29*, 497–508.

Ellington, R. J. (1954). Incidence of EEG abnormality among patients with mental disorders of apparently nonorganic origin: A criminal review. *American Journal of Psychiatry, 3*, 263–275.

Ellins, von Kluge, & Cramer (1990), *Behavioral Neuroscience, 104*, 233–234.

Elliot, A. J. (1981) *Child language.* Cambridge, England: Cambridge University Press.

Ellis, A. (1987). The impossibility of achieving consistently good mental health. *American Psychologist, 42*, 364–375.

Ellis, R. J. (1988). Self-monitoring and leadership emergence in groups. *Personality and Social Psychology, 14*, 681–693.

Ellis, R.J., Zanna, M.P. (1990). Arousal and causal attribution. *Canadian Journal of Behavioural Science, 22(1)*, 1–12.

Ellsworth, C.P., Muir, D.W., Hains, S.M., (1993). Social competence and person-object differentiation: An analysis of the still-face effect. *Developmental Psychology, 29(1)*, 63–73.

Ellsworth, P. C., & Carlsmith, J. M. (1973). Eye contact and gaze aversion in aggressive encounter. *Journal of Personality and Social Psychology, 33*, 117–122.

Elmer-Dewitt, P. (1985, October 28). Kings, queens, and silicon chips. *Time.*

Empson, J. A. C. (1984). Sleep and its disorders. In R. Stevens (Ed.), *Aspects of consciousness.* New York: Academic Press.

Empsom-Warner, S. & Krahn, H. 1992. Unemployment and occupational aspirations: a panel study of high school graduates. *Canadian Review of Sociology and Anthropology, 29(1)*, 38–54.

Endler , N. S. (1982). *Holiday of darkness: A psychologist's personal journey out of his depression.* Toronto: Wiley.

Endler, N. S., & Persad, E. (1999). *Electroconvulsive therapy: The myths and the realities.* Toronto: Hans Huber.

Endler, N.S., Crooks, D.S. & Parker, J.D. (1992). The interaction model of anxiety: an empirical test in a parachute training situation. *Anxiety, Stress and Coping; An International Journal, 5(4)*, 301–311.

Engel, G. L. (1980). The clinical application of a biopsychosocial model. *American Journal of Psychiatry, 137*, 535–544.

Engen, T. (1982). *The perception of odors.* New York: Academic Press.

Engen, T. (1986). *Remembering odors and their names.* Paper presented at the First International Conference on the Psychology of Perfumery, University of Warwick, England.

Engen, T. (1987). Remembering odors and their names. *American Scientist, 75*, 497–503.

Engen, T., & Ross, B. M. (1973). Long-term memory of odors with and without verbal descriptions. *Journal of Experimental Psychology, 100*, 221–227.

Enns, M. W., & Reiss, J. P. R. (1992). Electroconvulsive therapy. *Canadian Journal of Psychiatry, 37*, 671–678.

Enzle, M.E., Hawkins, W.L. (1992). A priori actor negligence mediates a posteriori outcome effects on moral judgement. *Journal of Experimental Social Psychology, 28(2)*, 169–185.

Epstein, L. H. (1992). Role of behavior theory in behavioral medicine. Special Issue: Behavioral medicine: An update for the 1990s. *Journal of Consulting and Clinical Psychology, 60*, 493–498.

Epstein, S. (1983). Aggregation and beyond: Some basic issues on the prediction of behavior. *Journal of Personality, 51*, 360–392.

Erikson, E. H. (1950). *Childhood and society.* New York: Norton.

Erikson, E. H. (1987). *A way of looking at things: Selected papers from 1930 to 1980* (S. Schlein, Ed.). New York: Norton.

Erlenmeyer-Kimling, L., & Jarvik, L. F. (1963). Genetics and intelligence. *Science, 142*, 1477–1479.

Eron, L. D. (1987). The development of aggressive behavior from the perspective of a developing behaviorist. *American Psychologist, 42*, 435–442.

Etaugh, C., & Liss, M. B. (1992). Home, school, and playroom: Training grounds for adult gender roles. *Sex Roles, 26*, 129–147.

Evans, B.K. & Fischer, D.G. (1993). The nature of burnout: a study of the three factor model of burnout in human service and non-human service samples. *Journal of Occupational and Organizational Psychology, 66(1)*, 29–38.

Evans, M.G. (1986). Organizational behavior: The central role of motivation. *Journal of Management, 12(2)*, 203–222.

Eysenck, H. J. (1952). The effects of psychotherapy: An evaluation. *Journal of Consulting Psychology, 16*, 319–324.

Eysenck, H. J., & Eysenck, M. W. (1985). *Personality and individual differences.* New York: Plenum.

Fagot, B.I., Kabanaugh, K., (1990). The prediction of antisocial behavior from avoidant attachment classification. *Child Development, 61(3)*, 864–873.

Fallon, A.E. & Rozin, P. (1985). Sex differences in perceptions of desirable body shape. *Journal of Abnormal Psychology, 94(1)*, 102–105.

Family, G. (1992). Projected image and observed behavior of physicians in terminal cancer care. *Omega Journal of Death and Dying, 26(2)*, 129–136.

Fantz, R. L. (1961). The origin of form perception. *Scientific American, 204*, 66–72.

Faraone, S. V., Kremen, W. S., & Tsuang, M. T. (1990). Genetic transmission of major affective disorders: Quantitative models and linkage analyses. *Psychological Bulletin, 108*, 109–127.

Farde, L., Wiesel, F., Halldin, C., & Sevdall, G. (1988). Central D2-dopamine receptor occupancy in schizophrenic patients treated with antipsychotic drugs. *Archives of General Psychiatry 45*, 71–76.

Farquhar, J. W., Maccoby, N., & Solomon, D. S. (1984). Community applications of behavioral medicine. In W. D. Gentry (Ed.), *Handbook of behavioral medicine.* New York: Guilford Press.

Feather, N. T., & Volkmer, R. E. (1988). Preference for situations involving effort, time pressure, and feedback in relation to Type A behavior, locus of control, and test anxiety. *Journal of Personality and Social Psychology, 55*, 266–271.

Fechner, G. T. (1860). *Elementse der psychophysik.* Leipzig: Breitkops & Harterl.

Feehan, G.G. & Enzle, M.E. (1991). Subjective control over rewards: effects of percieved choice of reward schedule on intrinsic motivation and maintenance. *Perceptual and Motor Skills, 72(3, Pt 1)*, 995–1006.

Feingold, A. (1990). Gender differences in effects of physical attractiveness on romantic attraction: A comparison across five research paradigms. *Journal of Personality and Social Psychology, 59(5)*, 981–993.

Feingold, A. (1992a). Gender differences in mate selection preferences: A test of the parental investment model. *Psychological Bulletin, 112*, 125–139.

Feingold, A. (1992b). Cognitive gender differences: A developmental perspective. *Sex roles, 29*, 91–112.

Feldman, D. C., & Arnold, H. J. (1985). Personality types and career patterns: Some empirical evidence on Holland's model. *Canadian Journal of Administraive Sciences, 2*, 192–210.

Feldman, D. C., & Tompson, H. B. (1993). Entry shock, culture shock: Socializing the new breed of global managers. *Human Resource Management, 31*, 345–362.

Fenton, W. S., & McGlashan, T. H. (1991). Natural history of schizophrenia subtypes: II. Positive and negative symptoms and long-term course. *Archives of General Psychiatry, 48*, 978–986.

Ferguson-Pare, M. (1993). Women ready to bring excellence to CEO role. *Leadership in Health Services, 2(3)*, 12–13.

Fernandez, E., & Turk, D. C. (1992). Sensory and affective components of pain: Separation and synthesis. *Psychological Bulletin, 113*, 205–217.

Ferster, C. B., & Skinner, B. F. (1957). *Schedules of reinforcement.* New York: Appleton-Century-Crofts.

Festinger, L. (1957). *A theory of cognitive dissonance.* Evanston, IL: Row, Peterson.

Festinger, L., Schachter, S., & Back, K. (1950). *Social pressures in informal groups: A study of a housing community.* New York: Harper.

Feuerstein, M., Labbé, E. E., & Kuczmierczyk, A. R. (1986). *Health psychology: A psychobiological perspective.* New York: Plenum.

Fibiger, H. C., Murray, C. L., & Phillips, A. G. (1983). Lesions of the nucleus basalis magoncellularis impair long-term memory in rats. *Society for Neuroscience Abstracts, 9*, 332.

Fichten, C.S., Tagalakis, V., Judd, D., Wright, J., Amsel, R. 1992. Verbal and nonverbal communication cues in daily conversations and dating. *Journal of Social Psychology, 132(6)*, 751–769.

Field, R.H., House, R.J. (1990). A test of the Vroom-Tetton model using manager and subordinate reports. *Journal of Applied Psychology,. 75(3)*, 362–366.

Fielder, F. E., Mitchell, T., & Triandis, H. C. (1971). The culture assimilator: An approach to cross-cultural training. *Journal of Applied Psychology, 55*, 95–102.

Fields, H. L., & Basbaum, A. (1984). Endogenous pain control mechanisms. In P. D. Wall & R. Melzack (Eds.), *Textbook of pain* (pp. 142–152). Edinburgh: Churchill Livingstone.

Fiez, J. A., & Petersen, S. E. (1993). PET as part of an interdisciplinary approach to understanding processes involved in reading. *Psychological Science, 4*, 287–293.

Fincham, F.D., Bradbury, T.N. (1992). Assessing attributions in marriage: The Relationship Attribution Measure. *Journal of Personality and Social Psychology, 62(3)*, 457–468.

Finegan, J.E., Seligman, C. (1993). Mood and the formation of attitudes. *Canadian Journal of Behaviour Science, 25(3)*, 421–445.

Fischoff, B. (1975). Hindsight-foresight: The effect of outcome knowledge on judgment under uncertainty. *Journal of Experimental Psychology: Human Perception and Performance, 1*, 288–299.

Fischoff, B. (1992). Risk taking: A developmental perspective. In J. F. Yates (Ed.), *Risk taking.* New York: Wiley.

Fisher, J. D., & Fisher, W. A. (1992). Changing AIDS-risk behavior. *Psychological Bulletin, 3*, 455–474.

Fisher, J. D., & Misovich, S. J. (1989). Social influence and AIDS-preventive behavior. In J. Edwards (Ed.), *Applied social psychology annual* (Vol. 9). New York: Plenum.

Fisher, R. P., & Geiselman, R. E. (1988). Enhancing eyewitness memory with the cognitive interview. In M. M. Gruneberg, P. E. Morris, & R. N. Sykes (Eds.), *Practical aspects of memory: Current research and issues: Vol. 1. Memory in everyday life* (pp. 34–39). Chichester, England: John Wiley & Sons.

Fisher, R. P., Geiselman, R. E., & Amador, M. (1989). Field test of the cognitive interview: Enhancing the recollection of actual victims and witnesses of crime. *Journal of Applied Psychology, 75*, 722–727.

Fisher, R.J. (1990). The Social Psychology of Intergroup and International Conflict Resolution. New York, NY: Springer-Verlag.

Fiske, S. T., & Neuberg, S. L. (1990). A continuum model of impression formation, from category based to individuating processes: Influences of information and motivation in attention and interpretation. In M. P. Zanna (Ed.), *Advances in experimental social psychology* (Vol. 23). New York: Academic Press.

Fiske, S. T., & Taylor, S. (1991). *Social cognition* (2nd ed.). New York: Random House.

Fivusch, R., Gray, J. T., & Fromhoff, F. A. (1987). Two-year-olds talk about the past. *Cognitive Development, 2*, 393–409.

Flaherty, C. F., & Largen, J. (1975). Within-subjects positive and negative contrast effects in rats. *Journal of Comparative and Physiological Psychology, 88*, 653–664.

Flavell, J. H. (1973). The development of inferences about others. In T. Misebel (Ed.), *Understanding other persons.* Oxford: Blackwell, Basic, & Mott.

Flavell, J. H. (1982). Structures, stage and sequences in cognitive development. In W. A. Collins (Ed.), *Minnesota Symposia on Child Psychology* (Vol. 15, pp. 1–28). Hillsdale, NJ: Erlbaum.

Fleming, A.S., Corter, C., Franks, P., Surbey, M., et al., (1993). Postpartum factors related to mothers' attraction to newborn infant odors. Developmental Psychology, 26(2), 115–132.

Flemming, J.A. (1993). The difficult to treat insomniac patient. *Journal of Psychosomatic Research, 37*, 45–54.

Flessati, S. L., & Jamieson, J. (1991). Gender differences in mathematics anxiety: An artifact of response bias? *Anxiety Research, 3*, 303–312.

Flett, G.L., Blankstein, K.R., Kleinfeldt, S. (1991). Depression and causal attributions for unexpected stressful events. *Social Behavior and Personality, 19(1)*, 53–64.

Flett, G.L., Hewitt, P.L., Blankstein, K.R. & Mosher, S.W. (1991). Perfectionism, self-actualization, and personal adjustment. Special issue: handbook of self-actualization. *Journal of Social Behavior and Personality, 6(5)*, 147–160.

Flor-Henry, P. (1990). Influence of gender in schizophrenia as related to other psychopathological syndromes. *Schizophrenia Bulletin, 16(2)*, 211–227.

Flynn, J. R. (1987). Massive IQ gains in 14 nations: What IQ tests really measure. *Psychological Bulletin, 101*, 171–191.

Foderaro, L. W. (1988, February 4). The fragrant house: An expanding market for every mood. *The New York Times*, pp. C1, C10.

Folkman, S., Lazarus, R. S., Dunkel-Schetter, C., DeLongis, A., & Gruen, R. J. (1986). Dynamics of a stressful encounter: Cognitive appraisal, coping, and encounter outcomes. *Journal of Personality and Social Psychology, 50*, 992–1003.

Forest, M. (1992). La differenciation des affects: une nouvelle approche de la crise de rupture. (Differentiation of emotions: a new approach to the crisis of marital separation.) *Revue Quebecoise de Psychologie, 13(3)*, 119–145.

Forgas, J. P. (1991). Affect and social perception: Research evidence and an integrative theory. In W. Stroebe & M. Newstone (Eds.), *European review of social psychology.* New York: Wiley.

Forgas, J. P. (1991). Affective influences on partner choice: Role of mood in social interviewer's selection decisions. *Journal of Applied Psychology, 70*, 374–378.

Forgas, J. P. (1993). On making sense of odd couples: Mood effects on the perception of mismatched relationships. *Personality and Social Psychology Bulletin, 19*, 59–70.

Forgas, J. P., & Bower, G. H. (1988). Affect in social and personal judgments. In K. Fiedler & J. P. Forgas (Eds.), *Affect, cognition, and social behavior.* Toronto: Horgrefe.

Forgas, J.P. (1991). Effective influences on partner choice: role of mood in social decisions. *Journal of Personality and Social Psychology, 61(5)*, 708–720.

Foulkes, D. (1985). *Dreaming: A cognitive-psychological analysis.* Hillsdale, NJ: Erlbaum.

Fowler, B. & Lindeis, A.E. (1992). The effects of hypoxia on auditory reaction time and P300 latency. *Aviation, Space and Environmental Medicine, 63(11)*,976–981.

Fowler, R. D. (1993). 1992 report of the chief executive officers. *American Psychologist, 48*, 726–735.

Fox, R., Aslin, R.N., Shea, S.L., Dumais, S.T., (1980). Stereopsis in human infants. *Science 207 (4428)*, 323–324.

Fraczek, A., & Kirwil, L. (1992). Living in the family and child aggression: Studies on some socialization conditions of development of aggression. In A. Fraczek & H. Zumky (Eds.), *Socialization and aggression.* Berlin: Springer-Verlag.

Frank, M. G., & Gilovich, T. (1988). The dark side of self and social perception: Black uniforms and aggression in professional sports. *Journal of Personality and Social Psychology, 54*, 74–85.

Franks, J. J., & Bransford, J. D. (1971). Abstraction of visual patterns. *Journal of Experimental Psychology, 90*, 65–74.

Franzoi, S.L., Herzog, M.E. (1987). Judging physical attractiveness: What body aspects do we use? *Personality and Social Psychology Bulletin, 13(1)*, 19–33.

Frederick, D., & Libby, R. (1986). Expertise and auditors' judgments of conjunctive events. *Journal of Accounting Research, 24*, 270–290.

Freedman, J.A. (1986). Television violence and aggression: A rejoinder. *Psychological Bulletin, 100(3)*, 372–378.

Freedman, J.A. (1988). Cross cultural intervention: The case of the hexed hair. *Clinical Sociology Review, 6*, 159–166.

Freedman, J. L. (1986). Television violence and aggression: A rejoinder. *Psychological Bulletin, 100*, 372–378.

Freedman, J. L., & Fraser, S. C. (1966). Compliance without pressure: The foot-in-the-door technique. *Journal of Personality and Social Psychology, 4*, 195–202.

Freedman, J.L. (1990). The effect of captial punishment on juror's willingness to convict. *Journal of Applied Social Psychology, 20(6 pt 1)*, 465–477.

Freedman, J.L., Cunningham, J.A., Krismer, K. (1992). Inferred values and the revers-incentive effect in induced compliance. *Journal of Personality and Social Psychology, 62(3)*, 357–368.

Frenkel, O.J., Doob, A.N. (1976). Post-decision dissonance at the polling booth. *Canadian Journal of Behavioural Science, 8(4)*, 347–350

Frese, M. (1985). Stress at work and psychosomatic complaints: A causal interpretation. *Journal of Applied Psychology, 70*, 314–328.

Freud, S. (1901). *The interpretation of dreams*. In J. Strachey (Ed.), *The standard edition of the complete psychological works of Sigmund Freud*. (Vols. 4, 5). London: Hogarth.

Freud, S. (1915). Instincts and their vicissitudes. In E. Jones (Ed.), *The collected papers of Sigmund Freud* (Vol. 4). New York: Basic Books.

Freund, K. & Blanchard, R. (1993). Erotic target location errors in male gender dysphorics, paedophiles, and fetishists. *British Journal of Psychiatry, 162*, 558–563.

Fricko, M.A., Beehr, T.A. (1992). A longitudinal investigation of interest congruence and gender concentration as predictors of job satisfaction. *Personnel Psychology, 45(1)*, 99–117.

Fried, P.A., Watkinson, B., & Gray, R. (1992). A follow-up study of attentional behavior in 6-year-old children exposed prenatally to marijuana, cigarettes, and alcohol. *Neurotoxicology and Teratology, 14*, 299–311.

Fried, P.A., Watkinson, B., (1988). 12 and 24 month neurobehavioral follow-up of children prenatally exposed to marijuana, cigarettes and alcohol. *Neurotoxicology and Teratology, 10(4)*, 305–313.

Fried, P.A., Watkinson, B., (1990). 36 and 48 month neurobehavioral follow-up of children prenatally exposed to marijuana, cigarettes and alcohol. *Journal of Developmental and Behavioral Pediatrics, 11(2)*, 49–58.

Friedman, H. S., & Miller-Herringer, T. (1991). Nonverbal display of emotion in public and private: Self-monitoring, personality, and expressive cues. *Journal of Personality and Social Psychology, 62*, 766–775.

Friedman, H. W., Tucker, J. S., Tomlinson-Keasey, C., Schwartz, J.E., Wingard, D. L., & Criqui, M. H. (1993). Does childhood personality predict longevity? *Journal of Personaltiy and Social Psychology, 65*, 176–185.

Friedman, H., & Zebrowitz, L. A. (1992). *Personality and Social Psychology Bulletin, 18*, 430–438.

Friedman, W. J. (1993). Memory for the time of past events. *Psychological Bulletin, 113*, 44–66.

Fuchs, I., Eisenberg, N., Hertz-Lazarowitz, R., Sharabany, R., (1986). Kibbutz, Israeli city, and American children's moral reasoning about prosocial moral conflicts. *Merrill-Palmer Quarterly, 32(1)*, 37–50.

Funder, D. C., & Colvin, C. R. (1991). Explorations in behavioral consistency: Properties of persons, situations, and behavior. *Journal of Personaltiy and Social Psychology, 60*, 773–794.

Funder, D. C., & Sneed, C. D. (1993). Behavioral manifestations of personality: An ecological approach to judgmental accuracy. *Journal of Personality and Social Psychology, 64* 479–490.

Funder, D.C. (1987). Errors and mistakes: Evaluating the accuracy of social judgment. *Psychological Bulletin, 101(1)*, 75–90.

Furomoto, L., & Scarborough, E. (1986). Placing women in the history of psychology. *American Psychologist, 41*, 35–42.

Furstenberg, F. F., Jr. (in press). How families manage risk and opportunity in dangerous neighborhoods. In W. J. Wilson (Ed.), *Sociology and the public agenda*. Newbury Park, CA: Sage.

Gaboury, A. & Ladouceur, R. (1993). Evaluation of a prevention program for pathological gambling among adolescents. *Journal of Primary Prevention, 14*, 21–28.

Gaertner, S. L., Dovidio, J. F., Anastasio, P. A., Bachman, B. A., & Rust, M. C. (in press). The common ingroup identity model: Recategorization and the reduction of intergroup bias. In W. Stroebe & H. Hewstone (Eds.), *European Review of Social Psychology*.

Gaertner, S.L., Mann, J., Murrell, A., Dovidio, J.F. (1989). Reducing intergroup bias: The benefits of recategorization. *Journal of Personality and Social Psychology, 57(2)*, 239–249.

Gaertner, S.L., Mann, J.A., Dovidio, J.F., Murrell, A.J., Pomare, M. (1990). How does cooperation reduce intergroup bias? *Journal of Personality and Social Psychology, 59(4)*, 692–704.

Gaines, J., & Jermier, J. M. (1983). Emotional exhaustion in a high stress organization. *Academy of Management Journal, 26*, 567–586.

Galambos, N. I. (1992). Parent-adolescent relations. *Current Directions in Psychological Science, 1*, 146–149.

Galambos, N.L. & Walters, B.J. (1992). Work hours, schedule inflexibility and stress in dual-earner spouses. *Canadian Journal of Behavioral Science, 24(3)*, 290–302.

Galambos, N.L., Almeida, D.M. & Petersen, A.C. 1991. Masculinity, feminity, and sex role attitudes in early adolescence: Exploring gender intensification. *Annual Progress in Child Psychiatry and Child Development, 1991*, 77–91.

Galanter, E. (1962). Contemporary psychophysics. In R. Brown, E. Galnater, E. G. Hess, & G. Mandler (Eds.), *New Directions in Psychology*. New York: Holt, Rinehart, & Winston.

Galef, B.G. (1990). Necessary and sufficient conditions for communication of diet preferences by Norway rats. *Animal Learning and Behavior, 18*, 347–351.

Galef, B.G. (1993). Functions of social learning about food: A causal analysis of effects of diet novelty on preference transmission. *Animal Behaviour, 46(2)*, 257–265.

Galef, B.G., McQuoid, L.M. & Whiskin, E.E. (1990). Further evidence that Norway rats do not socially transmit learned aversions to toxic baits. *Animal Learning and Behavior, 18*, 199–205.

Gallivan, J. (1991). Gender bias in students' ratings of essays. *Journal of Social Behavior and Personality, 6(1)*, 119–124.

Gallo, L.C., & Eastman, C.I. (1993) Circadian rhythms during gradually delaying and advancing sleep and light schedules. *Physiology and Behavior, 53*, 119–126.

Gallop, R.M., Lancee, W.J., Taerk, G., Coates, R.A., et al. (1992). Fear of contagion and AIDS: Nurses' perception of risk. *AIDS Care, 4(1)*, 103–109.

Gallop, R.M., Taerk, G., Lancee, W.J., Coates, R.A., et al. (1992). A randomized trial of group interventions for hospital staff caring for persons with AIDS. *AIDS Care, 4(2)*, 117–185.

Galotti, K. (1989). Approaches to studying formal and everyday reasoning. *Psychological Bulletin, 105*, 331–351.

Galotti, K.M., Kozberg, S.F., Farmer, M.C., (1991). Gender and developmental differences in adolescents' conception of moral reasoning. *Journal of Youth and Adolescence, 20(1)*, 13–30.

Gannon, L., Luchetta, T., Rhodes, K., Pardie, L., & Segrist, D. (1992). Sex bias in psychological research: Progress or complacency? *American Psychologist, 47*, 389–396.

Gara, M. A., Woolfolk, R. L., Cohen, B. D.,Goldston, R. B., Allen, L. A., & Novalany, J. (1993). Perception of self and other in major depression. *Journal of Abnormal Psychology, 102*, 93–100.

Garb, J. L., & Stunkard, A. J. (1974). Taste aversion in man. *American Journal of Psychiatry, 131*, 1204–1207.

Garcia, J., Hankins, W. G., & Rusiniak, K. W. (1974). Behavioral regulation of the milieu interne in man and rat. *Science, 185*, 824–831.

Garcia, J., & Koelling, R. A. (1966). Relation of cue to consequence in avoidance learning. *Psychonomic Science, 4*, 123.

Garcia, J., Rusiniak, K. W., & Brett, L. P. (1977). Conditioning food-illness aversions in wild animals: Caveat Canonici. In H. Davis & H. M. B. Hurwitz (Eds.), *Operant-Pavlovian interactions*. Hillsdale, NJ: Erlbaum.

Gardner, B. T., & Gardner, R. A. (1975). Evidence for sentence constituents in the early utterances of child and chimpanzee. *Journal of Experimental Psychology: General, 4*, 244–267.

Gardner, H. (1983). *Frames of mind: The theory of multiple intelligences*. New York: Basic Books.

Garfinkel, P.E. & Goldbloom, D.S. 1993. Bulimia nervosa: a review of therapy research. *Journal of Psychotherapy Practice and Research, 2(1)*, 38–50.

Garland, H., & Newport, S. (1991). Effects of absolute and relative sunk costs on the decision to persist with a course of action. *Organizational Behavior and Human Decision Processes, 48*, 55–69.

Garner, D.M., Garfinkel, P.E., Irvine, M.J. (1986). Integration and sequencing of treatment approaches for eating disorders. *Psychotherapy and Psychosomatics, 46*, 67–75.

Garside, B. (1993). Physicians Mutual Aid Group: A response to AIDS-related burnout. *Health and Social Work, 18(4)*, 259–267.

Gatchel, R. J., Baum, A., & Krantz, D. S. (1989). *An introduction to health psychology* (2nd ed.). New York: Random House.

Gatchel, R. J., Schaeffer, M. A., & Baum, A. (1985). A psychophysiological field study of stress at Three Mile Island. *Psychophysiology, 22*, 175–181.

Gauvain, M., & Rogoff, B. (1989). Collaborative problem solving and children's planning skills. *Developmental Psychology, 25*, 139–151.

Gauvin, L. (1990). An experiential perspective on the motivational features of exercise and lifestyle. *Canadian Journal of Sport Sciences, 15(1)*, 51–58.

Gazzaniga, M. S. (1984). Right hemisphere language: Remaining problems. *American Psychologist, 39*, 1494–1495.

Geary, D. C., & Widaman, K. F. (1992). Numerical cognition: on the convergence of componential and psychometric models. *Intelligence, 16*, 47–80.

Geary, D. C., Fan, L., & Bow-Thomas, C. C. (1992). Numerical cognition: Loci of ability differences comparing children from China and the United States. *Psychological Science, 3*, 180–185.

Geen, R. G. (1989). Alternative conceptions of social facilitation. In P. B. Paulus (Ed.), *Psychology of group influence* (2nd ed., pp. 1–37). New York: Academic Press.

Geen, R. G., Beatty, W. W., & Arkin, R. M. (1984). *Human motivation.* Boston: Allyn and Bacon.

Geiselman, R. E., Fisher, R. P., Mackinnon, D. P., & Holland, H. L. (1985). Eyewitness memory enhancement in the police interview: Cognitive retrieval mnemonics versus hypnosis. *Journal of Applied Psychology, 70,* 401–412.

Gelinas-Chebat, C., Chebat, J.C. (1992). Effects of two voice characteristics on the attitudes toward advertising messages. *Journal of Social Psychology, 132(4),* 447–459.

Gellatly, I.R., Meyer, J.P. (1992). The effects of goal difficulty on physiological arousal, cognition, and task performance. *Journal of Applied Psychology, 77(5),* 694–704.

Geller, E. S. (1988). A behavioral science approach to transportation safety. *Bulletin of the New York Academy of Medicine, 64(7),* 632–661.

Geller, E. S., Winett, R. A., & Everett, P. B. (1982). *Preserving the environment: New strategies for behavior change.* New York: Pergamon Press.

George, J.M., Brief, A.P. (1992). Feeling good-doing good: A conceptual analysis of the mood at work-organizational spontaneity relationship. *Psychological Bulletin, 112(2),* 310–329.

George, J. T., & Hopkins, B. L. (1989). Multiple effects of performance-contingent pay for waitpersons. *Journal of Applied Behavior Analysis, 22,* 131–142.

Gerrard, M. (1986). Are men and women really different? In K. Kelley (Ed.), *Females, males, and sexuality.* Albany, NY: SUNY Press.

Geschwind, N. (1972). Language and the brain. *Scientific American, 226,* 76–83.

Giancola, P.R., Peterson, J.B. & Pihl, R.O. (1993). Risk for alcoholism, antisocial behavior, and response perseveration. *Journal of Clinical Psychology, 49(3),* 423–428.

Gibbons, B. (1986). The intimate sense of smell. *National Geographic, 170,* 324–361.

Gibbs, S. (1993, June 28). Bringing up father. *Time,* pp. 53–61.

Gibson, E. J., & Walk, R. D. (1960). The "visual cliff." *Scientific American, 202,* 64–71.

Gibson, K.J., Zerbe, W.J. & Franken, R.E. (1992). Job search strategies for older job hunters: addressing employers' perceptions. *Canadian Journal of Counselling, 26(3),* 166–176.

Gibson, K.J., Zerbe, W.J., Franken, R.E. (1993). The influence of rater and ratee age on judgments of work-related attributes. *Journal of Psychology, 127(3),* 271–280.

Gilbert, A. N., & Wysocki, C. J. (1987). The smell survey results. *National Geographic, 172,* 514–525.

Gilbert, D.T., Hixon, J.G. (1991). The trouble of thinking: Activation and application of stereotypic beliefs. *Journal of Personality and Social Psychology, 60(4),* 509–517.

Gilbert, D.T., Jones, E.E. (1986). Perceiver-induced constraint: Interpretations of self-generated reality. *Journal of Personality and Social Psychology, 50(2),* 269–280.

Gilbert, D.T., McNulty, S.E., Giuliano, T.A., Benson, J.E. (1992). Blurry words and fuzzy deeds: The attribution of obscure behavior. *Journal of Personality and Social Psychology, 62(1),* 18–25.

Gill, J. (1985, August, 22). Czechpoints. *Time Out,* p. 15.

Gillett, J. & White, P.G. (1992). Male bodybuilding and the reassertion of hegemonic masculinity: a critical feminist perspective. *Play and Culture, 5(4),* 358–369.

Gilligan, C. F. (1982). *In a different voice.* Cambridge, MA: Harvard University Press.

Gilovich, T. (1990). Differential construal and the false consensus effect. *Journal of Personality and Social Psychology, 59(4),* 623–634.

Gisiner, R., & Schusterman, R. J. (1992). Sequence, syntax, and semantics: Responses of a language-trained sea lion (*Zalophus californianus*) to novel sign combinations. *Journal of Comparative Psychology, 106,* 78–91.

Gladue, B. A. (1991). Aggressive behavioral characteristics, hormones, and sexual orientation in men and women. *Aggressive Behavior, 17,* 313–326.

Glazer, S. (1993). Intelligence testing. *CQ Researcher, 3,* 651–659.

Gleicher, F., Kost, K.A., Baker, S.M., Strathman, A.J., Richman, S.A., Sherman, S.J. (1990). The role of counterfactual thinking in judgments of affect. *Personality and Social Psychology Bulletin, 16(2),* 284–295.

Glenn, N. D., & Kramer, K. B. (1987). The marriages and divorces of the children of divorce. *Journal of Marriage and the Family, 48,* 737–747.

Globe and Mail , June 19, 1992, p. A1.

Gloor, P., Salanova, V., Oliver, A., Quesney, L.F. (1993). The human dorsal hippocampal commissure. An anatomically identifable an functional pathway. *Brain, 116,* (pt5), 1249–1273.

Goddard, E. (1992). Why children start smoking. *British Journal of Addiction, 87(1),* 17–18.

Godden, D., & Baddeley, A. D. (1975). Context-dependent memory in two natural environments: On land and under water. *British Journal of Psychology, 66,* 325–331.

Godden, D., & Baddeley, A. D. (1980). When does context influence recognition memory? *British Journal of Psychology, 71,* 99–104.

Godfrey, D.K., Jones, E.E., Lord, C.G. (1986). Self-promotion is not ingratiating. *Journal of Personality and Social Psychology, 50(1),* 106–115

Godin, G., Boyer, R., Duval, B., Fortin, C., et al. (1992). Understanding physicians' decision to perform a clinical examination on an HIV seropositive patient. First International Congress of Behavioral Medicine (1990, Uppsala, Sweden). *Medical Care, 30(3),* 199–207.

Goethals, G.R. (1986). Social comparison theory: Psychology from the lost and found. American Psychological Association Convention (1984, Toronto, Canada). *Personality and Social Psychology Bulletin, 12(3),* 261–278.

Goethals, G.R., Cooper, J., Naficy, A. (1979). Role of foreseen, foreseeable, and unforeseeable behavioral consequences in the arousal of cognitive dissonance. *Journal of Personality and Social Psychology, 37(7),* 1179–1185.

Gold, E. B., Leviton, A., Lopez, R., Gilles, F. H., Hedley-White, E. T., Kolonel, L. N., Lyon, J. L., Swanson, G. M., Weiss, N. S., West, D., Aschenbrener, C., & Austin, D. F. (1993). Parental smoking and risk of childhood brain tumors. *American Journal of Epidemiology, 137,* 620–628.

Goldberg, J. (1992, May). The empty mirror. *Omni,* p. 16.

Goldbloom, D.S. & Garfinkel, P.E. 1990. The serotonin hypothesis of bulimia nervosa: theory and evidence. *Canadian Journal of Psychiatry, 35(9),* 741–744.

Goldenberg, I., & Goldenberg, H. (1985). *Family therapy: An overview,* (2nd ed.). Monterey, CA: Brooks/Cole.

Goldenring, J. M., & Purtell, E. (1984). Knowledge of testicular cancer risk and need for self-examination in college students: A call for equal time for men in teaching early cancer detection techniques. *Pediatrics, 74,* 1093–1096.

Goldman, S.J., Herman, C.P. & Polivy, J. 1991. Is the effect of a social model on eating attenuated by hunger? *Appetite, 17(2),* 129–140.

Goleman, D. (1993, June 11). Studies reveal suggestibility of very young as witnesses. *New York Times,* pp. A1, A23, A24.

Goleman, D. (1993, November 9). The secret of long life? Be dour and dependable. *New York Times,* p. C3.

Goleman, O. (1980, February). 1,528 little geniuses and how they grew. *Psychology Today* pp. 28–53.

Goodale, M.A. & Milner, A.D. (1992). Separate visual pathways for perception and action. *Trends in Neuroscience, 15(1)(163),* 20–25.

Goodale, M.A. (Ed.). (1990). *Vision and Action: The Control of Grasping.* Norwood, NJ: Ablex Publishing Corps.

Goodale, M.A., Milner, A.D., Jacobson,L.S. & Carey, D.P. (1991). A neurological dissociation between percieving objects and grasping them. *Nature, 349(6305),* 154–156.

Goode, E. (1990, May 14). Getting slim. *U.S. News & World Report,* pp. 56–59.

Goodstein, L. D., & Calhoun, J. F. (1982). *Understanding abnormal behavior.* Reading, MA: Addison-Wesley.

Gopnick, M. & Crago, M. B. (1991). Familial aggregation of a developmental language disorder. *Cognition, 39,* 1–50.

Gopnick, M. (1990). Feature-blind grammar and dysphasia. *Nature, 344,* 715.

Gordon, A. & Baum, M. (1987). Shuttlebox avoidance in rats and response prevention (flooding): Persistence of fear following reduced instrucmental responding. *Journal of General Psychology, 114,* 263–272.

Gordon, W. C. (1989). *Learning and memory.* Belmont, CA: Brooks/Cole Publishing Company.

Gosse, V.F., Sullivan, A.M., Ross, A.S., Simmonds, A.J., et al. (1992). Evaluation of the Goal Oriented Adult Learning (GOAL) program. *Psychosocial Rehabilitation Journal, 15(4),* 97–100.

Gotlib, I.H., McLachlan, A.L., Katz, A.N. (1988). Biases in visual attention in depressed and nondepressed individuals. Special Issue: Information processing and the emotional disorders. *Cognition and Emotion, 2(3),* 185–200.

Gottesman, I. I., & Bertelsen, A. (1989). confirming unexpressed genotypes for schizophrenia. *Archives of General Psychiatry, 46,* 867–872.

Gottfried (Ed.). (1984). *Home environment and early cognitive development.* San Francisco: Academic.

Gould, R. L. (1978). *Transformations, growth, and change in adult life.* New York: Simon & Schuster.

Graf, P., & Schacter, D. L. (1985). Implicit and explicit memory for new associations in normal and amnesic subjects. *Journal of Experimental Psychology: Learning, Memory, and Cognition, 11,* 501–518.

Graffi, S. & Minnes, P. (1989). Stress and coping in caregivers of persons with traumatic head injuries. *Journal of Applied Social Sciences, 13(2),* 293–316.

Graham, C. H., & Hsia, Y. (1958). Color defect and color theory. *Science, 127,* 675–682.

Granchrow, J.R., Steiner, J.E., Daher, M., (1983). Neonatal facial expressions in response to different qualities and intensities of gustatory stimuli. *Infant Behavior and Development, 6(4),* 473–484.

Granger, L. (1993). The Department de Psychologie at the University of Montreal: 50 years of quality and diversity. *Canadian Psychology, 34,* 1–2.

Grant, P.R. (1992). Ethnocentrism between groups of unequal power in response to perceived threat to social identity and valued resources. *Canadian Journal of Behavioural Science, 24(3)*, 348–370.

Grant, P.R. (1993). Reactions to intergroup similarity: Examination of the similarity-differentiation and the similarity-attraction hypotheses. *Canadian Journal of Behavioural Science, 25(1)*, 28–44.

Gray, P. (1993, February 15). What is love? *Time*, pp. 47–51.

Gray, T. A., & Morley, J. E. (1986). Minireview: Neuropeptide Y: Anatomical distribution and possible function in mammalian nervous system. *Life Sciences, 38*, 389–401.

Graziano, W. G., Jensen-Campbell, L. A., Shebilske, L. J., & Lundgren, S. R. (1993). Social influence, sex differences, and judgments of beauty: Putting the interpersonal back in interpersonal attraction. *Journal of Personality and Social Psychology, 65*, 522–531.

Green, R., & Fleming, D. T. (1990). Transsexual surgery follow-up: Status in the 1990s. *Annual review of sex research, 1*, 163–174.

Greenberg, J. (1990). "Employee theft as a reaction to underpayment inequity: The hidden cost of pay cuts": Correction. *Journal of Applied Psychology, 75(6)*, 667.

Greenberg, J., & Baron, R. A. (1993). *Behavior in organizations* (5th ed.). Boston: Allyn and Bacon.

Greenberg, J., Pyszczynski, T.A., Solomon, S. (1982). The self-serving attributional bias: Beyond self-presentation. *Journal of Experimental Social Psychology, 18(1)*, 56–67.

Greenberg, J. S. (1991). *Comprehensive stress management* (3rd ed.). Madison, WI: William C. Brown.

Greenglass, E. R., Burke, R. J., (1991). The relationship between stress and coping among Type As. Special Issue: Handbook on job stress. *Journal of Social Behavior and Personality, 6(7)*, 361–373.

Greenwald, A. G. (1992). New look 3: Unconscious cognition reclaimed. *American Psychologist, 47*, 766–779.

Greenwald, A. G., Spangenberg, E. R., Pratkanis, A. R., & Eskenazi, J. (1991). Double-blind tests of subliminal self-help audiotapes. *Psychological Science, 2*, 119–122.

Gregg, W., Foote, A., Erfurt, J. C., & Heirich, M. A. (1990). Worksite follow-up and engagement strategies for initiating health risk behavior changes. *Health Education Quarterly, 17*, 455–478.

Greist-Bousquet, S., Watson, M., & Schiffman, H. R. (1990). *An examination of illusion decrement with inspection of wings-in and wings-out Müller-Lyer figures: The role of corrective and contextual information perception.* New York: Wiley.

Griffin, R. W., & McMahan, G. C. (in press). Motivation through job design. In J. Greenberg (Ed.), *Organizational behavior: The state of the science.* Hillsdale, NJ: Erlbaum.

Griffith, T. L. (1993). Monitoring and performance: A comparison of computer and supervisor monitoring. *Journal of Applied Social Psychology, 23*, 549–572.

Grillon, C., Courchesne, E., Ameli, R., Geyer, M. A., & Braff, D. L. (1990). Increased distractibility in schizophrenic patients: Electrophysiologic and behavioral evidence. *Archives of General Psychiatry, 47*, 171–179.

Grobe, C. & Campbell, E. 1990. Who is using what in the public schools: the interrelationships among alcohol, drug and tobacco use by adolescents in New Brunswick classrooms. *Journal of Alcohol and Drug Education, 35(3)*, 1–11.

Gross, P. (1986). Defining post-divorce remarriage families: A typology based on the subjective perceptions of children. Special Issue: The divorce process: A handbook for clinicians. *Journal of Divorce, 10(1–2)*, 205–217.

Grosskurth, P. (1991). *The secret ring: Freud's inner circle and the politics of psychoanalysis.* Reading, Ma.: Addison-Wesley.

Gruneberg, M. M. (1978). The feeling of knowing, memory blocks, and memory aids. In M. M. Greenberg & P. Morris (Eds.), *Aspects of memory.* London: Methuen.

Gruneberg, M. M., Morris, P., & Sykes, R. N. (1988). *Practical aspects of memory: Current research and issues* (Vols. 1, 2). Chichester, England: Wiley Interscience.

Grusec, J.E. (1991). Socializing concern for others in the home. *Developmental Psychology, 27(2)*, 338–342.

Grusec, J.E., Goodnow, J.J., (1994). Impact of parental discipline methods on the child's internalization of values: A reconceptualization on current points of view. *Developmental Psychology, 30(1)*, 4–19. © by the American Psychological Association. Reprinted by permission.

Grusec, J.E., Mammone, N. (1993). Features and sources of parents' attributions themselves and their children. Review of Personality and Social Psychology, 15, Thousand Oaks, CA: Sage, 49–73.

Guilford, J. (1967). *The nature of human intelligence.* New York: McGraw-Hill.

Guilford, J. (1985). Cognitive psychology's ambiguities: Some suggested remedies. *Psychological Review, 89*, 48–59.

Guimond, S., Begin, G., Palmer, D.L. (1989). Education and causal attributions: The development of "person-blame" and "system-blame" ideology. *Social Psychology Quarterly, 52(2)*, 126–140.

Guimond, S., Dube, L. (1989). La representation des causes de l'inferiorite economique des quebecois Francophones. (Representation of the causes of economic inferiority of french speaking Canadians from Quebec.) *Canadian Journal of Behavioural Science, 21(1)*, 28–39.

Guimond, S., Palmer, D.L. (1990). Type of academic training and causal attributions for social problems. *European Journal of Social Psychology, 20(1)*, 61–75.

Gunn, K. P. (1993). A correlation between attendance and grades in a first-year psychology class. *Canadian Psychology, 34*, 201–202.

Gurman, A. S., Kniskern, D. P., & Pinsof, W. M. (1986). Research on marital and family therapies. In S. L. Garfield & A. E. Bergin (Eds.), *Handbook of psychotherapy and behavior change.* (pp. 565–626). New York: Wiley.

Gurstein, P. (1991). Working at home and living at home: Emerging scenarios. Special Issue: the meaning and use of home. *Journal of Architectural and Planning Research, 8(2)*, 164–180.

Gustavson, C. R., Garcia, J., Hawkins, W. G., & Rusiniak, K. W. (1974). Coyote predation control by aversive conditioning. *Science, 184*, 581–583.

Gutek, B.A., Winter, S.J. (1992). Consistency of job satisfaction across situations: Fact or framing artifact? *Journal of Vocational Behavior, 41(1)*, 61–78.

Guttman, H.A. (1991). Parental death as a precipitant of marital conflict in middle age. *Journal of Marital and Family Therapy, 17(1)*, 81–87.

Haas, K., & Haas, A. (1993). *Understanding sexuality.* St. Louis, MO: Mosby.

Haccoun, R.R., Desgent, C. (1993). Perceived reasons and consequences of work absence: A survey of French-speaking employees in Quebec. *International Journal of Psychology, 28(1)*, 97–117.

Haddock, G., Zanna, M.P., Esses, V.M. (1993). Assessing the structure of prejudicial attitudes: The case of attitudes toward homosexuals. *Journal of Personality and Social Psychology, 65(6)*, 1105–1118.

Hagan, J. & Wheaton, B. (1993). The search for adolescent role exits and the traqnsition to adulthood. *Social Forces, 71(4)*, 955–979.

Hagen, R. (1993). Clinical files, Florida State University. Quoted in R. R. Bootzin, J. R. Acocella, & L. B. Alloy, *Abnormal psychology* (6th ed.). New York: McGraw-Hill.

Haier, R. J., Siegel, B. V., Tang, C., Abel, L., & Buchsabum, M. S. (1992). Intelligence and changes in regional cerebral glucose metabolic rate following learning. *Intelligence, 16*, 415–526.

Hajek, P., & Belcher, M. (1991). Dream of absent-minded transgression: An empirical study of a cognitive withdrawal symptom. *Journal of Abnormal Psychology, 100*, 487–491.

Hakstain, A.R., Woolley, R.M., Woolsey, L.K., Kryger, B.R. (1991). Management selection by multiple-domain assessment: I. Concurrent validity. *Educational and Psychological Measurement, 51(4)*, 883–898.

Hall, C. S. (1984). "A ubiquitous sex difference in dreams" revisited. *Journal of Personality and Social Psychology, 46*, 1109–1117.

Hall, J. A., Roter, D. L., & Katz, N. R. (1987). Task versus socioemotional behaviors in physicians. *Medical Care, 25*, 399–412.

Hall, J. A., & Veccia, E. M. (1990). More "touching" observations: New insights on men, women, and interpersonal touch. *Journal of Personality and Social Psychology, 59*, 1155–1162.

Halpern, S. (1992, May 6). Big boss is watching you. *Details*, pp. 18–23.

Hamer, D. H., Hu, S., Magnuson, V. L., Hu, N., & Pattatucci, A. J. (1993). A linkage between DNA markers on the X chromosome and male sexual orientation. *Science, 261*, 321–327.

Hamilton, J. A. (1983). Development of interest and enjoyment in adolescence: II. Boredom and psychopathology. *Journal of Youth and Adolescence, 12*, 363–372.

Hamilton, V.L. (1978). Obedience and responsibility: A jury simulation. *Journal of Personality and Social Psychology, 36(2)*, 126–146.

Hammersmith, S. K. (1982). *Sexual preference: An empirical study from the Alfred C. Kinsey Institute for Sex Research.* Paper presented at the meetings of the American Psychological Association, Washington, D.C.

Hanly, C. 1978. Instincts and hostile affects. 30th International Psycho-Analytical Congress (1977, Jerusalem, Israel). *International Journal of Psycho-Analysis, 59(2–3)*, 149–156.

Hans, V. P. (1992). Obedience, justice, and the law: PS reviews recent contributions to a field ripe for new research efforts by psychological scientists. *Psychological Science, 3*, 218–221.

Hansen, R. D. (1980). Common sense attribution. *Journal of Personality and Social Psychology, 17*, 398–411.

Harder, J. W. (1992). Play for pay: Effects of inequity in a pay-for-performance context. *Administrative Science Quarterly, 37*, 321–335.

Harder, L.D. (1988). Choice of individual flowers by bumble bees: Interaction of morphology time and energy. *Behaviour, 104*, 60–77.

Harlow, H. F., & Harlow, M. H. (1966). Learning to love. *American Scientist, 54*, 244–272.

Harpur, T. J., & Hare, R. D. (1990). Psychopathy and attention. In J. Enns (Ed.) *The development of attention: Research and theory* (pp. 429–444). New York: North Holland.

Harrell, W.A. (1992). Older motorist yielding to pedestrians: Are older inattentive and unwilling to stop? *International Journal of Aging and Human Development, 36(2),* 115–127.

Harrell, W.A. (1991). Factors influencing pedestrian cautiousness in crossing streets. *Journal of Social Psychology, 131(3),* 367–372.

Harrigan, J. A. (1987). Self-touching as a indicator of underlying affect and language processing. *Social Science and Medicine, 20,* 1161–1168.

Harris, J., & Wilkins, A. J. (1982). Remembering to do things: A theoretical framework and illustrative experiment. *Human Learning, 1,* 1–14.

Harris, M. B. (1992). Sex, race, and experiences of aggression. *Aggressive Behavior, 18,* 201–217.

Harris, P. L. (1991). The work of the imagination. In A. Whiten (Ed.), *Natural theories of mind* (pp. 283–304). Oxford: Blackwell.

Harris, P. R. (1979, March). Cultural awareness training for human resource development. *Training and Development Journal,* 64–74.

Harrison, R. V. (1985). The person-environment fit model and the study of job stress. In T. A. Beehr & R. S. Bhagat (Eds.), *Human stress and cognition in organizations* (pp. 23–55). New York: Wiley.

Hartel, C.E. (1993). Rating format research revisited: Format effectiveness and acceptability depend on rater characteristics. *Journal of Applied Psychology, 78(2),* 212–217.

Hartley, J. T. (1986). Reader and text variables as determinants of discourse memory in adulthood. *Psychology and Aging, 1,* 150–158.

Hartmann, E. L. (1973). *The functions of sleep.* New Haven: Yale University Press.

Harvey, S. M. (1987). Female sexual behavior: Fluctuations during the menstrual cycle. *Journal of Psychosomatic Research, 31,* 101–111.

Haskins, R. (1989). Beyond metaphor: The efficacy of early childhood education. *American Psychologist, 44,* 274–282.

Hassett, J. (1978). Sex and smell. *Psychology Today, 11,* 40, 42, 45.

Hatfield, E. (1988). Passionate and companionate love. In R. J. Sternberg & M. I. Barnes (Eds.), *The psychology of love* (pp. 191–217). New Haven, CT: Yale University Press.

Hatfield, E., & Rapson, R. L. (1993). *Love, sex, and intimacy: Their psychology, biology, and history.* New York: Harper Collins.

Hatfield, E., & Walster, G. W. (1981). *A new look at love.* Reading, MA: Addison-Wesley.

Hauenstein, N.M. (1992). An information-processing approach to leniency in performance judgments. *Journal of Applied Psychology, 77(4),* 485–493.

Haugaard, J. J., Repucci, N. D., Laurd, J., & Nauful, T. (1991). Children's definitions of the truth and their competency as witnesses in legal proceedings. *Law and Human Behavior, 15,* 253–273.

Havel, V. (1992, June 3). Rio and the new millennium. *New York Times,* p. A21.

Hawkins, S. A., & Hastie, R. (1990). Hindsight: Biased judgments of past events after the outcomes are known. *Psychological Bulletin, 107,* 311–327.

Hawranik, P. (1991). A clinical possibility: preventing health problems after the age of 65. *Journal of Gerontological Nursing, 17(11),* 20–25.

Hazelrigg, M. D., Cooper, H. M., & Borduin, C. M. (1987). Evaluating the effectiveness of family therapies: An integrative review and analysis. *Psychological Bulletin, 101,* 428–442.

Hearty, R. (1989). A further development of the relation between mourning and manic-depression. *Melanie Klien and Object Relations, 7(2),* 83–94.

Hecaen, H., & Angelergues, R. (1964). Localization of symptoms in aphasia. In A. V. S. de Reuck & M. O'Connor (Eds.), *CIBA foundation symposium on the disorders of language* (pp.222–256). London: Churchill Press.

Heilman, M.E., Martell, R.F., Simon, M.C. (1988). the vagaries of sex bias: Conditions regulating the undervaluation, equivaluation, and overvaluation of female job applicants. *Organizational Behavior and Human Decision Processes, 41(1),* 98–110.

Heinrichs, R. W. (1993). Schizophrenia and the brain: Conditions for a neuropsychology of madness. *American Psychologist, 48,* 221–233.

Heller, R.B., Dobbs, A.R. & Rule, B.G. 1992. Communicative function in patients with questionable Alzheimer's diseases. *Psychology and Aging, 7(3),* 395–400.

Hellige, J.B. (1993). Unity of thought and action: varieties of interaction between the left and right cerebral hemispheres. *Current Directions in Psychological Science, 2(1),* 21–25.

Helms, J. E. (1989). Oral and literate traditions among black Americans living in poverty. *American Psychologist, 44,* 367–373.

Helms, J. E. (1992). Why is there no study of cultural equivalence in standardized cognitive ability testing? *American Psychologist, 47,* 1083–1101.

Hendrick, C. (Ed.) (1989). *Close relationships.* Newbury Park, CA: Sage.

Hendrick, C., Hendrick, S. (1992). A theory and method of love. *Journal of Personality and Social Psychology, 50(2),* 392–402.

Heneman, R.L., Greenberger, D.B., Anonyuo, C. (1989). Attributions and exchanges: The effects of interpersonal factors on the diagnosis of employee performance. *Academy of Management Journal, 32(2),* 466–476.

Henker, B., Whalen, C.K., (1989). Hyperactivity and attention deficits. Special Issue: Children and their development: Knowledge base, research agenda, and social policy application. *American Psychologist, 44(2),* 216–223.

Henriques, J. B., & Davidson, R. J. (1990). Regional brain electrical asymmetries discriminate between previously depressed and healthy control subjects. *Journal of Abnormal Psychology, 99,* 22–31.

Henriques, J. B., & Davidson, R. J. (1991). Left frontal hypoactivation in depression. *Journal of Abnormal Psychology, 100,* 535–545.

Henry, J. (1982). Circulating opiods: Possible physiological roles in central nervous function. *Neuroscience and Behavioral Reviews, 6(3),* 229–245.

Henry, W. A., (1993, July 26). Born gay? *Time,* pp. 36–39.

Herman, L. M., Kuczaj, S. A., & Holder, M. D. (1993). Responses to anomalous gestural sequences by a language-trained dolphin: Evidence for processing of semantic relations and syntactic information. *Journal Experimental Psychology: General, 122,* 184–194.

Herman, L. M., Richards, D. G., & Wolz, J. P. (1984). Comprehension of sentences by bottlenosed dolphins. *Cognition, 16,* 129–219.

Herold, E.S., Mewhinney, D.M.K. (1993). Gender differences in casual sex and AIDS prevention: A survey of dating bars. *Journal of Sex Research, 30(1),* 36–42.

Herrnstein, R. J. (1973). *IQ in the meritocracy.* Boston: Little, Brown.

Hershberger, S. L., Lichtenstein, P., & Knox, S. S. (1994). Genetic and environmental influences on perceptions of organizational climate. *Journal of Applied Psychology, 79,* 24–33.

Hetzel, B., & McMichael, T. (1987). *The LS factor: Lifestyle and health.* Ringwood, Victoria: Penguin.

Hewitt, P.L. & Flett, G.L. (1993). Dimensions of perfectionism, daily stress and depression: a test of the specific vulnerability hypothesis. *Journal of Abnormal Psychology, 102(1),* 58–65.

Hicks, R.A., & Pellegrini, R.J. (1991). The changing sleep habits of college students. *Perceptual and Motor Skills, 72,* 1106.

Hiew, C.C. & McDonald, G. (1986). Delinquency prevention through promoting social competence in adolescents. *Canadian Journal of Criminology, 28(3),* 291–302.

Higgins, A. T., & Turnure, J. E. (1984). Distractibility and concentration of attention in children's development. *Child Development, 55,* 1799–1810.

Higham, P.A., Carment, W. (1992). The rise and fall of politicians: the judged heights of Broadbent, Mulroney and Turner before and after the 1988 Canadian Federal Election. *Canadian Journal of Behavioural Science, 24(3),* 404–409.

Hilgard, E. R. (1977). *Divided consciousness: Multiple controls in human thought and action.* New York: Wiley.

Hilgard, E. R. (1979). Divided consciousness in hypnosis: Implications of the hidden observer. In E. Fromm & R. E. Shor (Eds.), *Hypnosis: Developments in research and new perspectives* (2nd ed). Chicago: Aldine.

Hill, R. (1945). Campus values in mate selection. *Journal of Home Economics, 37,* 554–558.

Hilliard, A. (1985). *Parameters affecting the African-American child.* Paper presented at the Black Psychology seminar, Duke University, Durham, NC.

Hillier, L.M., Hewitt, K.L., Morrongiello, B.A., (1992). Infants' perception of illusions in sound localization: Reaching to sounds in the dark. *Journal of Experimental Child Psychology, 53(2),* 159–179.

Hilton, A., Potvin, L., Sachdev, I. (1989). Ethnic relations in rental housing: A social psychological approach. *Canadian Journal of Behavioural Science, 21(2),* 121–131.

Hilton, D.J., Slugoski, B.R. (1986). Knowledge-based causal attribution: The abnormal conditions focus model. *Psychological Review, 93(1),* 75–88.

Hilton, M. E. (1993). An overview of recent findings on alcoholic beverage warning labels. *Journal of Public Policy and Marketing, 12,* 1–9.

Hilton, N.Z. (1993). Childhood sexual victimization and lack of empathy in child molesters: Explanation or excuse? *International Journal of Offender Therapy and Comparative Criminology, 37(4),* 287–296.

Hines, M., Chiu, L., McAdams, L. A., Bentler, P. M., & Lipcamon, J. (1992). Cognition and the corpus callosum: Verbal fluency, visuospatial ability, and language lateralization related to midsagittal surface areas of callosal subregions. *Behavioral Neuroscience, 106,* 3–14.

Hines, M., McAdams, L.A., Chiu, L., Bentler, P.M. & Lipcamon, J. (1992). Cognition and the corpus callosum: Verbal fluency, visuospatial ability, and language lateralization related to midsagittal surface areas of the callosal subregions. *Behavioral Neuroscience, 106(1),* 3–14.

Hingson, R., Strunin, L., Berlin, B., & Heeren, T. (1990). Beliefs about AIDS, use of alcohol and drugs, and unprotected sex among Massachusetts adolescents. *American Journal of Public Health, 80,* 295–299.

Hinsz, L. D., & Williamson, D. A. (1987). Bulimia and depression: A review of the affective variant hypothesis. *Psychological Bulletin, 102,* 150–158.

Hinton, G. E., & Parsons, L. M. (1988). Scene based and viewer centered representations for comparing shapes. *Cognition, 30,* 1–35.

Hinton, G. E., & Shallice, T. (1991). Lesioning an attractor network: Investigations of acquired dyslexia. *Psychological Review, 98,* 74–95.

Hinz, L.D. & Williamson, D.A. (1987). Bulimia and depression: A review of the affective variant hypothesis. *Psychological Bulletin, 102(1),* 150–158.

Hirsch-Pasek, K., Treiman, R., & Schneiderman, M. (1984). Brown and Hanlon revisited: Mothers' sensitivity to ungrammatical forms. *Journal of Child Language, 11*, 81–88.

Hixon, J. G., & Swann, W. B., Jr. (1993). When does introspection bear fruit? Self-reflection, self-insight, and interpersonal choices. *Journal of Personality and Social Psychology, 64*, 35–43.

Hobart, C. (1992). How they handle it: Young Canadians, sex, and AIDS. *Youth and Society, 23(4)*, 411–433.

Hobson, J. A. (1988). *The dreaming brain.* New York: Basic Books.

Hodges, J., Tizard, B., (1989). Social and family relationships of ex-institutional adolescents. *Journal of Child Psychology and Psychiatry and Allied Disciplines, 30(1)*, 77–97.

Hoffman, D.C. & Beninger, R.J. (1988). Selective D1 and D2 dopamine agonists produce opposing effects in place conditioning but not in conditioned taste aversion learning. *Pharmacology, Biochemistry and Behavior, 31*, 1–8.

Hofstede, G. (1980). *Culture's consequences: International differences in work-related values.* Beverly Hills, CA: Sage.

Hofstede, G., Bond, M.H., Luk, C. (1993). Individual perceptions of organizational cultures: A methodological treatise on levels of analysis. *Organization Studies, 14(4)*, 483–503.

Holland, J. L. (1973). *Making vocational choices: A theory of careers.* Englewood Cliffs, NJ: Prentice Hall.

Hollon, S. D., DeRubeis, R. J., & Evans, M. D. (1987). Causal mediation of change in treatment for depression: Discriminating between non-specificity and noncausality. *Psychological Bulletin, 102*, 139–149.

Hollon, S. D., Shelton, R. C., & Loosen, P. T. (1991). Cognitive therapy and pharmacotherapy for depression. *Journal of Consulting and Clinical Psychology, 59*, 88–99.

Holmes, D. (1990). The evidence for repression: An examination of sixty years of research. In J. Singer (Ed.), *Repression and dissociation: Implications for personality theory, psychopathology, and health* (pp. 85–102). Chicago: University of Chicago Press.

Holmes, D. S. (1984). Meditation and somatic arousal reduction: A review of the experimental evidence. *American Psychologist, 39*, 1–10.

Holmes, T. H., & Masuda, M. (1974). Life change and illness susceptibility. In B. S. Dohrenwend and B. P. Dohrenwend (Eds.), *Stressful life events: Their nature and effects.* New York: Wiley.

Holmes, T. H., & Rahe, R. H. (1967). The social readjustment rating scale. *Journal of Psychosomatic Research, 11*, 213–218.

Holtzworth-Munroe, A., & Jacobson, N. S. (1985). Causal attributions of married couples: When do they search for causes? What do they conclude when they do? *Journal of Personality and Social Psychology, 50*, 537–542.

Honig, W. K., & Staddon, J. E. R. (Eds.). (1977). *Handbook of operant behavior.* Englewood Cliffs, NJ: Prentice-Hall.

Honig, W. K., & Urcuioli, P. J. (1981). The legacy of Guttman and Kalish: Twenty-five years of research on stimulus generalization. *Journal of the Experimental Analysis of Behavior, 36*, 405–445.

Hoppe, R. B. (1988). In search of a phenomenon: Research in parapsychology. *Contemporary Psychology, 33*, 129–130.

Hopson, J., & Rosenfeld, A. (1984, August). PMS: Puzzling monthly symptoms. *Psychology Today*, 30–35.

Horner, M. (1970). Femininity and successful achievement: A basic inconsistency. In J. M. Bardwicks, E. Douvan, M. Horner, & D. Gutmann (Eds.), *Feminine personality and conflict.* Belmont, CA: Wadsworth.

Horner, M. (1972). Toward an understanding of achievement-related conflicts in women. *Journal of Social Issues, 28*, 157–176.

Horney, K. E. (1967). *Feminine psychology.* New York: Norton.

Hornick, J.P., Devlin, M.C., Downey, M.K., Baynham, T. (1985–1986). as in: Successful and unsuccessful contraceptors: A multivariate typology. Special Issue: Social work practice in sexual problems. *Journal of Social Work and Human Sexuality 4(1–2)*, 17–31.

Hornstein, G. A. (1992). The return of the repressed: Psychology's problematic relations with psychoanalysis, 1909–1960. *American Psychologist, 47*, 254–263.

Hosman, L. A. (1986). *A meta-analysis of sex differences in self-disclosure.* Paper presented at the meetings of the Southern Speech Communication Association, Houston.

Houfman, L. G., House, J. & Ryan, J. B. (1981). Dynamic visual acuity: A review. *Journal of the American Optometric Association, 52*, 883–887.

House, R.J., Spangler, W.D., Woycke, J. (1991). Personality and charisma in the U.S. presidency: A psychological theory of leader effectiveness. *Administrative Science Quarterly, 36(3)*, 364–396.

Hovland, C., Janis, I. L., & Kelley, H. H. (1953). *Communication and Persuasion: Psychological studies of one on one.* New Haven, CT: Yale University Press.

Hovland, C. I., & Weiss, W. (1951). The influence of source credibility on communication effectiveness. *Public Opinion Quarterly, 1*, 635–650.

Howard, G. S. (1985). The role of values in the science of psychology. *American Psychologist, 40*, 255–265.

Howard, K. I., Kopta, S. M., Krause, M. S., & Orlinsky, D. E. (1986). The dose-effect relationship in psychotherapy. *American Psychologist, 41*, 159–164.

Howe, B. & Poole, R. (1992). Goal proximity and achievement motivation of high school boys in a basketball shooting task. *Journal of Teaching in Physical Education, 11(3)*, 248–255.

Howe, M. L., & Courage, M. L. (1993). On resolving the enigma of infantile amnesia. *Psychological Bulletin. 113*, 305–326.

Howell, J.M., Avolio, B.J. (1993). Transformational leadership, transactional leadership, locus of control, and support for innovation: Key predictors of consolidated-business-unit performance. *Journal of Applied Psychology, 78(6)*, 891–902.

Howell, J.M., Frost, P.J. (1989). A laboratory study of charismatic leadership. *Organizational Behavior and Human Decision Processes, 43(2)*, 243–269.

Howes, J.L. & Katz, A.N. (1992). Remote memory: Recalling autobiographical and public events from across the lifespan. *Canadian Journal of Psychology, 46(1)*, 92–116.

Hoyseth, K.S., Jones, P.J., (1989). Ethanol induced teratogenesis: characterization, mechanisms and diagnostic approaches. *Life Sciences, 44(10)*, 643–649.

Hsu, L.G. 1986. The treatment of anorexia nervosa. *American Journal of Psychiatry, 143(5)*, 573–581.

Hubble, L. M., & Groff, M. G. (1982). WISC-R verbal performance IQ discrepancies among Quay-classified adolescent male delinquents. *Journal of Youth and Adolescence, 11*, 503–508.

Hubel, D. H., & Wiesel, T. N. (1979). Brain mechanisms of vision. *Scientific American, 241*, 150–162.

Huddleston, R.J. & Hawkings, L. (1993). The reaction of friends and family to divorce. *Journal of Divorce and Remarriage, 19(1–2)*, 195–207.

Hughes, J. R., Smith, T. W., Kosterlitz, H. W., Fothergill, L. A., Morgan, B. A., & Morris, H. R. (1975). Identification of two related pentapeptides from the brain with potent opiate agonist activity. *Nature, 258*, 577–581.

Hughes, P. (1989). The development of social policy: The impact of the charter of rights. Special Issue: Public policy, social and economic development, and the power of ideas. *Canadian Journal of Community Mental Health, 8(2)*, 13–23.

Hull, C. L. (1943). *Principles of behavior theory.* New York: Appleton-Century-Crofts.

Hultsch, D. F., & Dixon, R. A. (1990). Learning and memory in aging. In J. E. Birren & K. W. Schaie (Eds.), *Handbook of the psychology of aging* (3rd ed., pp. 359–374). San Diego: Academic Press.

Hultsch, D.F., Hammer, M. & Small, B.J. (1993). Age differences in cognitive performance in later life: Relationships to self- reported health and activity life style. *Journals of Gerontology, 48(1)*, 1–11.

Hultsch, D.F., Hertzog, C. & Dixon, R.A. (1987). Age differences in metamemory: resolving the inconsistencies. Special issue: Aging and cognition. *Canadian Journal of Psychology, 41(2)*, 193–208.

Hume, K.M. & Crossman, J. (1992). Musical reinforcement of practice behaviors among competitive swimmers. *Journal of Applied Behavior Analysis, 25*, 665–670.

Hundleby, J.D. & Mercer, G.W. (1987). Family and friends as social environments and their relationship to young adolescents' use of alcohol, tobacco, and marijuana. *Journal of Marriage and the Family, 49(1)*, 151–164.

Hundleby, J.D., Misumi, L., Van Kampen, J. & Keating, L.J. (1993). The generality of individual differences in the estimation of size. *Journal of Psychology, 127(2)*, 233–242.

Hunn, B.P., Dingus, T.A. (1992). Interactivity, information, and compliance cost in a consumer product warning scenario. *Accident Analysis and Prevention, 24(5)*, 497–505.

Huntingford, F. A. (1976). The relationship between anti-predator behavior and aggression among conspecifics in the three-spined stickleback (Gasterosteus aculeatus). *Animal behavior, 24*, 245–260.

Hurvich, L. M. (1981). *Color vision.* Sunderland, MA: Sinauer Associates.

Hwang, K. (1986). Behavior of Swedish primary and secondary caretaking fathers in relation to mother's presence. *Developmental Psychology, 22*, 739–751.

Hyde, J. S., & Linn, M. (1988). Gender differences in verbal stability: A meta-analysis. *Psychological Bulletin, 104*, 53–69.

Hyde, J. S., Fennema, E., & Lamon, S. J. (1990). Gender differences in mathematics performance: A meta-analysis. *Psychological Bulletin, 107*, 130–155.

Hyman, R. (1994). Anomaly or artifact? Comments on Bem and Honorton. *Psychological Bulletin, 115*, 19–24.

Indicators of "victims" or "copers" on-the-job stressors? Special Issue: Career decision making and career indecision. *Journal of Vocational Behavior, 41(3)*, 270–281.

Intons-Peterson, M. J., & Roskos-Ewoldsen, B. (1988). *Sensory/perceptual qualities of images.* Paper presented at the 29th annual meeting of the Psychonomics Society, Chicago.

Irving, H.H. & Benjamin, M. (1988). Divorce mediation in a court- based fee for service agency: an empirical study. *Conciliation Courts Review, 26(1)*, 43–47.

Irving-Neto, R.L. & Verny, T.R. (1992). Pre- and perinatal experiences and personality: a retrospective analysis. *Pre- and Perinatal Psychology Journal, 7(2)*, 139–172.

Isabella, R.A., Belsky, J., (1991). Interactional sychrony and the origins of infant-mothe attachment: A replication study. *Child Development, 62(2)*, 373–384.

Isen, A. M. (1987). Positive affect, cognitive processes, and social behavior. In L. Berkowitz (Ed.), *Advances in experimental social psychology* (Vol. 20, pp. 203–253). New York: Academic Press.

Isen, A. M., & Baron, R. A. (1991). Positive affect and organizational behavior. In B. M. Staw & L. L. Cummings (Eds.), *Research in organizational behavior* (Vol. 14, pp. 1–48). Greenwich, CT: JAI Press.

Isen, A. M., & Daubman, K. A. (1984). The influence of affect on categorization. *Journal of Personality and Social Psychology, 47*, 1206–1217.

Isen, A. M., Daubman, K. A., & Nowicki, G. P. (1987). Positive affect facilitates creative problem solving: When we are glad, we feel as if the light has increased. Journal of *Personality and Social Psychology, 52*, 1122–1131.

Isen, A. M., & Johnson, N. M. S., Merz, E., & Robinson, G. (1985). The influence of positive affect on the usualness of word associations. *Journal of Personality and Social Psychology, 48*, 1413–1426.

Isen, A. M., & Shalker, T. E. (1982). Do you "accentuate the positive, eliminate the negative" when you are in a good mood? *Social Psychology Quarterly, 41*, 345–349.

Isher, R.J. (1994). Generic principles for resolving intergroup conflict. *Journal of Social Issues, 50(1)*, 47–66.

Iwahashi, M. (1992). Scents and science. *Vogue*, pp. 212–214.

Izard, C. E. (1992). *Human emotions* (2nd ed.). New York: Plenum.

Izard, C.E., Hembree, E.A., Huebner, R.R., (1987). Infants' emotion expressions acute to pain: Developmental change and stability of indivual differences. *Developmental Psychology, 23(1)*, 105–113.

Izard, C. I. (1992). *The psychology of emotion.* New York: Plenum.

Jaccard, J. (1992, November). *Women and AIDS.* Paper presented at the meetings of the Society for the Scientific Study of Sex, San Diego.

Jackson, S. E., Schwab, R. L., & Schuler, R. S. (1986). Toward an understanding of the burnout phenomenon. *Journal of Applied Psychology, 71*, 630–640.

Jacobs, J.R. (1992). Facilitators of romantic attraction and their relation to lovestyle. *Social Behavior and Personality, 20(3)*, 227–233.

Jacobson, E. (1938). *Progressive relaxation.* Chicago: University of Chicago Press.

Jacobson, S., Fein, G., Jacobson, J., Schwartz, P., & Dowler, J. (1984). Neonatal correlates of prenatal exposure to smoking, caffeine, and alcohol. *Infant Behavior and Development, 7*, 253–265.

Jacoby, L.L., Kelley, C., Brown, J., Jasechko, J. (1989). Becoming famous overnight: Limits on the ability to avoid unconscious influences of the past. *Journal of Personality and Social Psychology, 56(3)*, 326–338.

Jacoby, L.L., Levy, B.A., & Steinbach, K. (1992). Episodic transfer: Automaticity: Integration of data-driven and conceptually-driven processing in rereading. *Journal of Experimental Psychology: Learning, Memory and Cognition, 18*, 15–24.

Jako, R.A., Murphy, K.R. (1990). Distributional ratings, judgment decomposition, and their impact of interrater agreement and rating accuracy. *Journal of Applied Psychology, 75(5)*, 500–505.

James, W. J. (1890). *Principles of psychology.* New York: Holt.

Jameson, D., & Hurvich, L. M. (1989). Essay concerning color constancy. *Annual Review of Psychology, 40*, 1–22.

Jamieson, D. W., Lydon, J. E., & Zanna, M. P. (1987). Attitude and activity preference similarity: Differential bases of interpersonal attraction for low and high self-monitors. *Journal of Personality and Social Psychology, 53*, 1052–1060.

Jamieson, D.G. & Morosan, D.E. (1986). Training non-native speech contrasts in adults: acquisition of the English /o/-/O/ contrast by francophones. *Perception and Psychophysics, 40(4)*, 205–215.

Jamieson, D.W., Lydon, J.E., Zanna, M.P. (1987). Attitude and activity preference similarity: Differential bases of interpersonal attraction for low and high self-monitors. Special Issue: Integrating personality and social psychology. *Journal of Personality and Social Psychology, 53(6)*, 1052–1060.

Janis, I. L. (1954). Personality correlates of susceptibility to persuasion. *Journal of Personality, 22*, 504–518.

Jankowiak, W.R., Hill, E.M., Donovan, J.M. (1992). The effects of sex and sexual orientation on attractiveness judgments: An evolutionary interpretation. *Ethology and Sociobiology, 13(2)*, 73–85.

Jason, G.W., Pajurkova, E.M. (1992). Failure of metacontrol: Breakdown in behavioural unity after lesion of the corpus callosum and inferomedial fronal lobes. *Cortex, 28(2)*, 241–260.

Jason, G.W., Pajurkova, E.M., Lee, R.G. (1989). High-altitude mountaineering and brain function: Neuropsychological testing of members of a Mount Everest expedition. *Aviation, Space, and Environmental Medicine, 60(2)*, 170–173

Jefferson, D. J. (1993, August 12). Dr. Brown treats what ails the rides at amusement parks. *The Wall Street Journal.* p. 1.

Jencks, D. (1972). *Inequality: A reassessment of the effect of family and school in America.* New York: Basic Books.

Jenkins, C. D., Zyzanski, S. J., & Rosenman, R. H. (1979). *Jenkins Activity Survey.* Cleveland, OH: Psychological Corp.

Jenkins, J. G., & Dallenbach, K. M. (1924). Obliviscence during sleep and waking. *American Journal of Psychology, 35*, 605–612.

Jenkins, J.M. & Smith, M.A. (1993). A prospective study of behavioral disturbance in children who subsequently experience parental divorce: a research note. *Journal of Divorce and Remarriage, 19(1–2)*, 143–160.

Jennings, J.M. & Jacoby, L.L. (1993). Automatic versus intentional uses of memory: Aging, attention, and control. *Psychology and Aging, 8(2)*, 283–293.

Jernigan, T. L., Zisook, S., Heaton, R. K., Moranville, J. T., Hesselkink, J. R., & Braff, D. L. (1991). Magnetic resonance imaging abnormalities in lenticular nuclei and cerebral cortex in schizophrenia. *Archives of General Psychiatry, 48*, 881–890.

Jemmott, J. B., III, & Magloire, K. (1988). Academic stress, social support, and secretory immunoglobulin A. *Journal of Personality and Social Psychology, 55*, 803–810.

Jessor, R. (1993). Successful adolescent development among youth in high-risk settings. *American Psychologist, 48*, 117–126.

Jiujias, A., & Horvath, P. (1991). The evaluation of self-monitoring attributes. *Social Behavior and Personality, 19*, 204–215.

Joffe, R.T., Moul, D.E., Lam, R.W., & Levitt, A.J. (1993). Light visor treatment for seasonal affective disorder: A multicenter study. *Psychiatry Research, 46*, 29–39.

Joffe, R. T., Offord, D. R., & Boyle, M. H. (1988). Ontario child health study: Suicidal behavior in youth age 12–16 years. *American Journal of Psychiatry, 145*, 1420–1423

Johansson, F., Almay, B. G. L., von Knorring, L., Terenius, L., & Astrom, M. (1979). Personality traits in chronic pain patients related to endorphin levels in cerebrospinal fluid. *Psychiatry Research, 1*, 231–239.

Johns, G. (1991). Substantive and methodological constraints of behavior and attitudes in organizational research. *Organizational Behavior and Human Decision Processes, 49*, 80–104.

Johns, G. (1993). Constraints on the adoption of psychology-based personnel practices: Lessons from organizational innovation. Special Issue: Innovations in research methods for field settings. *Personnel Psychology, 46(3)*, 569–592.

Johns, G., (1987). The great Escape. *Psychology Today*, October 1987 issue, 30–33.

Johns, G., Xie, J.L., Fang, Y. (1992). Mediating and moderating effects in job design. *Journal of Management, 18(4)*, 657–676.

Johnson, E. J. (1985). Expertise and decision under uncertainty: Performance and process. In M. Chi, R. Glasse & M. Farr (Eds.), *The nature of expertise.* Columbus, OH: National Center for Research in Vocational Education.

Johnson-Laird, P. N., Byrne, R. M. J., & Tabossi, P. (1989). Reasoning by model: The case of multiple quantification. *Psychological Review, 96*, 658–673.

Johnston, C., Patenaude, R.L., Inman, G.A. (1992). Attributions for hyperactive and aggressive child behaviors. *Social Cognition, 10(3)*, 255–270.

Johnston, C.C., Stevens, B., Craig, K.D., Grunau, R.V., (1993). Developmental changes in pain expression in premature, full- term, two-and four-month-old infants. *Pain, 52(2)*, 201–208.

Johnston, W., & Dark, V. (1986). Selective attention. *Annual Review of Psychology, 37*, 43–75.

Joiner, T. E., Jr., Alfano, M. S., & Metalsky, G. I. (1993). When depression breeds contempt: Reassurance seeking, self-esteem, and rejection of depressed college students by their roommates. *Journal of Abnormal Psychology, 101* 165–173.

Jones, D. M., & Broadbent, D. E. (1987). Noise. In G. Salvendy (Ed.), *Handbook of human factors.* New York: John Wiley & Sons.

Jones, E. E., & Davis, K. E. (1965). From acts to dispositions: The attribution process in person perception. In L. Berkowitz (Ed.), *Advances in experimental social psychology* (Vol. 2, pp. 219–266). New York: Academic Press.

Jones, I.L. & Hunter, F.M. (1993). Mutual sexual selection in a monogamous seabird. *Nature, 362(6417)*, 238–239.

Jones, M. M. (1980). Conversion reaction: Anachronism or evolutionary form? Review of the neurological, behavioral, and psychoanalytic literature. *Psychological Bulletin, 87*, 427–441.

Jones-Gotman, M. & Zatorre, R.J. (1993). Odor recognition memory in humans: Role of right temporal and orbitofrontal regions. *Brain and Cognition, 22(2)*, 182–198.

Jordan, A., Kircaali, I.G., Diamond, C.P. (1993). Who has a problem, the student or the teacher? Differences in teachers' beliefs about their work with at-risk and integrated exceptional students. Special Issue: Festschrift for Professor John McLeod. *International Journal of Disability, Development and Education, 40(1)*, 45–62.

Joseph, J.A. (1992). The putative role of free radicals in the loss of neuronal functioning in senescence. *Intergrative Physiological and Behavioral Science, 27(3),* 216–227.

❋ Jourard, S. M. (1971). *Self-disclosure.* New York: Wiley.

Judd, C.M., Drake, R.A., Downing, J.W., Krosnick, J.A. (1991). Some dynamic properties of attitude structures: Context-induced response facilitation and polarization. *Journal of Personality and Social Psychology, 60(2),* 193–202.

Judd, C.M., Ryan, C.S., Park, B. (1991). Accuracy in the judgment of ingroup and out-group variability. *Journal of Personality and Social Psychology, 61(3),* 366–379.

Judge, T. A. (1993). Does affective disposition moderate the relationship between job satisfaction and voluntary turnover? *Journal of Applied Psychology, 78,* 395–401.

❋ Jusczyk, P.W., (1993). From general to language-specific capacities: The WRAPSA model of how speech perception develops. Special Issue: Phonetic development. *Journal of Phonetics, 21(1–2),* 3–28.

Just, M. A., & Carpenter, P. A. (1987). *The psychology of reading and language comprehension.* Newton, MA: Allyn & Bacon.

Kafer, R., Hodkin, B., Furrow, D. & Landry, T. (1993). What do the Montreal murders mean? Attitudinal and demographic predictors of attribution. *Canadian Journal of Behavioral Science, 25,* 541–558

Kagan, J., Reznick, J.S., Gibbons, J., (1989). Inhibited and uninhibited types of children. Child Development, 60(4), 838–845.

Kagan, J., Reznick, J.S., Snidman, N., (1988). Biological bases of childhood shyness. *Science, 240(4849),* 167–171.

Kagan, J., Snidman, N., (1991). Temperamental factors in human development. *American Psychologist, 46(8),* 856–862.

Kagan, J., Snidman, N., Arcus, D.M., (1992). Initial reactions to unfamiliarity. *Current Directions in Psychological Science, 1(6),* 171–174.

Kahnemann, D., & Miller, D. T. (1986). Norm theory: Comparing reality to its alternatives. *Psychological Review, 93,* 136–153.

❋ Kahneman, D., & Tversky, A. (1982). Judgment under uncertainty: Heuristics and biases. In D. Kahneman, P. Slovic, & A. Tversky (Eds.), *Judgment under uncertainty: Heuristics and biases* (pp. 3–22). Cambridge, England: Cambridge University Press.

Kalick, S. M., & Hamilton, T. E. (1986). The matching hypothesis reexamined. *Journal of Experimental Social Psychology, 24,* 469–489.

Kalivas, P. W., & Samson, H. H. (Eds.). (1992). *The neurobiology of drug and alcohol addiction.* Annals of the New York Academy of Sciences, Vol. 654. New York: Academy of Sciences.

❋ Kalsher, M. J., Clarke, S. W., & Wogalter, M. S. (1993). Communication of alcohol facts and hazards by a warning poster. *Journal of Public Policy and Marketing, 12,* 78–90.

Kalsher, M. J., Rodocker, A. J., Racicot, B. M., & Wogalter, M. S. (1993). Promoting recycling behavior in office environments. *Proceedings of the Human Factors and Ergonomics Society, 37,* 484–488.

Kamin, L. J. (1978). Comment on Munsinger's review of adoption studies. *Psychological Bulletin, 85,* 194–201.

Kaniasty, K., & Norris, F. H. (1993). A test of the social support deterioration model in the context of natural disaster. *Journal of Personality and Social Psychology, 64,* 395–408.

Kanner, A. D., Coyne, J. C., Schaefer, C., & Lazarus, R. S. (1981). Comparison of two modes of stress measurement: Daily hassles and uplifts versus major life events. *Journal of Behavioral Medicine, 4,* 1–39.

Kanungo, R.N., Conger, J.A. (1989). Dimensions of executive charisma. *Vikalpa, 14(4),* 3–8.

❋ Kanungo, R.N., Conger, J.A. (1992). Charisma: Exploring new dimensions of leadership behaviour. Special Issue: In honour of Professor Durganand Sinha. *Psychology and Developing Societies, 4(1),* 21–38.

❋ Kanungo, R.N., Hartwick, J. (1987). An alternative to the intrinsic-extrinsic dichotomy of work rewards. *Journal of Management, 13(4),* 751–766.

❋ Kaplan, H. I., & Sadock, B. J. (1991). *Synopsis of psychiatry: Behavioral sciences, clinical psychiatry* (6th ed.). Baltimore: Williams & Wilkins.

Kaplan, R. E. (1982). The dynamics of injury in encounter groups: Power, splitting, and the mismanagement of resistance. *International Journal of Group Psychotherapy, 32,* 163–187.

Karacan, I., Goodenough, D. R., Shapiro, A., & Starker, S. (1966). Erection cycle during sleep in relation to dream anxiety. *Archives of General Psychiatry, 15,* 183–189.

Karasek, R., & Theorell, T. (1990). *Healthy work: Job stress, productivity, and the reconstruction of working life.* New York: Basic Books.

Kasian, M., Painter, S.L. (1992). Frequency and severity of psychological abuse in a dating population. *Journal of Interpersonal Violence, 7(3),* 350–364.

❋ Katz, A.N., Thompson, M. (1993). On judging creativity: By one's acts shall ye be known (and vice versa). *Creativity Research Journal, 6(4),* 345–364.

Katz, J. (1992). Psychophysiological contributions to phantom limbs. *Canadian Journal of Psychiatry, 37(5),* 282–298.

Kaufman, A. S. (1983). Some questions and answers about the Kaufman Assessment Battery for Children (K-ABC). *Journal of Psychoeducational Assessment, 1,* 205–218.

Kaufman, A. S. (1990). V-PIQ discrepancies in brain-damaged adults: Interactions with gender, race, and other patient variables. In *Assessing adolescent and adult intelligence* (pp. 301–343). Boston: Allyn & Bacon.

Kaufman, K., Gregory, W. L., & Stephan, W. G. (1990). Maladjustment in statistical minorities within ethnically unbalanced classrooms. *American Journal of Community Psychology, 18,* 757–765.

Kaufman, M. T. (1980, November 16). Love upsetting Bombay's view of path to altar. *New York Times,* p. 12.

Kaufmann, R., O'Neill, M.C. (1993). Colour names and focal colours on electronic displays. Special Issue: Ergonomics in Canada: Managing your environment. *Ergonomics, 36(8),* 881–890.

❋ Kazdin, A. E. (1982). The token economy: A decade later. *Journal of Applied Behavior Analysis, 15,* 431–446.

Kazdin, A. E. (1993). Psychotherapy for children and adolescents: Current progress and future research directions. *American Psychologist, 48,* 644–657.

Keegstra, H.J. (1986). Depressive desorders in Ethiopia: A standardized assessment using the SADD schedule. *Acta Psychiatrica Scandinavica, 73(6),* 658–664.

❋ Keelan, J.P., Dion, K.K., Dion, K.L. (1992). Correlates of appearance anxiety in late adolescence and early adulthood among young women. *Journal of Adolescence, 15(2),* 193–205.

Keesling, B. & Friedman, H.S. (1987). Psychosocial factors in sunbathing and sunscreen use. *Health Psychology, 6(5),* 477–493.

❋ Keller, L. M., Bouchard, T. J., Jr., Arvey, R. D., Segal, N. L., & Dawis, R. V. (1992). Work values: Genetic and environmental influences. *Journal of Applied Psychology, 77,* 79–88.

Kelley, H. H. (1972). Attribution in social interaction. In E. E. Jones et al. (Eds.), *Attribution: Perceiving the causes of behavior.* Morristown, NJ: General Learning Press.

Kelley, K., & Byrne, D. (1992). *Exploring human sexuality.* Englewood Cliffs, NJ: Prentice-Hall.

❋ Kelloway, E.K., Barling, J. & Shah, A. (1993). Industrial relations, stress and job satisfaction: concurrent effects and mediation. Special Issue: integrating domains of work stress and industrial relations: evidence from five countries. *Journal of Organizational Behavior, 14(5),* 447–457.

Kelman, H. C. (1967). Human use of human subjects: The problem of deception in social psychological experiments. *Psychological Bulletin, 67,* 1–11.

Kelman, H. C., & Hamilton, V. L. (1989). *Crimes of obedience.* New Haven, CT: Yale University Press.

❋ Kelner, M.J. & Bourgeault, I.L. (1993). Patient control over dying: responses of health care professionals. *Social Science and Medicine, 36(6),* 757–765.

❋ Kelsey, F. O. (1969). Drugs and pregnancy. *Mental Retardation, 7,* 7–10.

Kendall-Tackett, K. A. (1991). Characteristics of abuse that influence when adults molested as children seek treatment. *Journal of Interpersonal Violence, 6,* 486–493.

Kendall-Tackett, K. A., Williams, L. M., & Finkelhor, D. (1993). Impact of sexual abuse on children: A review and synthesis of recent empirical studies. *Psychological Bulletin, 113,* 164–180.

Kendler, K. S., & Robinette, C. D. (1983). Schizophrenia in the National Academy of Sciences' National Research Council twin registry: A 16-year update. *American Journal of Psychiatry, 1140,* 1551–1563.

Kennedy, S.H. & Garfinkel, P.E. (1992). Advances in diagnosis and treatment of anorexia nervosa and bulimia nervosa. *Canadian Journal of Psychiatry, 37(5),* 309–315.

Kenrick, D. T., & Keefe, R. C. (1992). Age preferences in mates reflect sex differences in human reproductive strategies. *Behavioral and Brain Science, 15,* 75–133.

❋ Kenrick, D. T., Groth, G. E., Trost, M. R., & Sadalla, E. K. (1993). Integrating evolutionary and social exchange perspectives on relationships: Effects of gender, self-appraisal, and involvement level on mate selection criteria. *Journal of Personality and Social Psychology, 64,* 951–969.

Kerig, P.K., Cowan, P.A., Cowan, C.P., (1993). Marital quality and gender differences in parent-child interaction. *Developmental Psychology, 29(6),* 931–939.

Kerr, D., & Ram, B. (1994). *Focus on Canada: Population Dynamics in Canada.* Toronto: Prentice Hall.

❋ Kerr, G. & Leith, L. (1993). Stress management and athletic performance. *Sport Psychologist, 7(3),* 221–231.

Kerr, G. & Minden, H. (1988). Psychological factors related to the occurrence of athletic injuries. *Journal of Sport and Exercise Psychology, 10(2),* 167–173.

❋ Kerr, S. L., & Neale, J. M. (1993). Emotion perception in schizophrenia: specific deficit or further evidence of generalized poor performance? *Journal of Abnormal Psychology, 102,* 312–318.

Kerr, J.H. & Cox, T. (1991). Arousal and individual differences in sport. *Personality and Individual Differences, 12(10),* 1075–1085.

Kertesz, A. & Benke, T. (1989). Sex equality in intrahemispheric language organization. *Brain and Language, 37(3)*, 401–408.

Kertesz, A., Lau, W.K. & Polk, M. (1993). The structural determinants of recovery in Wernicke's aphasia. *Brain and Language, 44(2)*, 153–164.

Kessler, C. R. (1994). Incidence of mental disorders in a non-institutionalized population. *Archives of General Psychiatry, 50*, in press.

Kessler, R. C., McGonagle, K. A., Zhao, S., Nelson, C. B., Hughes, M., Eshleman, S., Witchen, H. U., & Kendler, K. S. (1994). Lifetime and 12–month prevalence of DSM-III-R psychiatric disorders in the United States. *Archives of General Psychiatry, 5*, 8–19.

Kety, S. S. (1988). Schizophrenic illness in the families of schizophrenic adoptees: Findings from the Danish national sample. *Schizophrenic Bulletin, 14*, 217–222.

Kiecolt-Glaser, J. K., Fisher, L., Ogrocki, P., Stout, J. C., Speicher, C. E., & Glaser, R. (1987). Marital quality, marital disruption, and immune function. *Psychosomatic Medicine, 49*, 13–34.

Kiecolt-Glaser, J.K. & Glaser, R. (1992). Psychoneuroimmunology: can psychological interventions modulate? Special issue: behavioral medicine: an update for the 1990s. *Journal of Consulting and Clinical Psychology, 60(4)*, 569–575.

Kiecolt-Glaser, J. K., Kennedy, S., Malkoff, S., Fisher, L., Speicher, C. E., & Glaser, R. (1988). Marital discord and immunity in males. *Psychosomatic Medicine, 50*, 213–229.

Kienker, P. K, Sejinowski, T. J. Hinton, G. E., & Scumacher, L. E. (1986). Separating figure from ground with a parallel network. *Perception, 15*, 197–216.

Kieren, D.K. & Morse, J.M. (1992). Preparation factors and menstrual attitudes of pre- and postmenarcheal girls. *Journal of Sex Education and Therapy, 18(3)*, 155–174.

Kiesler, C. A., & Kiesler, S. B. (1969). *Conformity*. Reading, MA: Addison-Wesley.

Kiesler, D. J. (1966). Some myths of psychotherapy research and the search for a paradigm. *Psychological Bulletin, 65*, 110–136.

Kiesler, D. J. (1985). Meta-analysis, clinical psychology, and social policy. *Clinical Psychology Review, 5*, 3–12.

Kihlstrom, J. F., Tataryn, D. J., & Hoyt, I. P. (1993). Dissociative disorders. In P. B. Sutker & H. E. Adams. (Eds.), *Comprehensive handbook of psychopathology* (2nd ed.). New York: Plenum Press.

Kilham, W., Mann, L. (1974). Level of destructive obedience as a function of transmitter and executant roles in the Milgram obedience paradigm. *Journal of Personality and Social Psychology, 29(5)*, 696–702.

Kim, C.K., Pinel, J.P., & Roese, N.R. (1992). *Pharmacology, Biochemistry and Behavior, 4*, 127–132.

Kimball, M. M. (1986). Developing a feminist psychology of women: Past and future accomplishments. *Canadian Psychology. 27*, 248–259.

Kimura, D. (1987). Are men's and women's brains really different? Annual meeting of the Canadian Psychological Association (1986, Toronto, Canada). *Canadian Psychology, 28(2)*, 133–147.

Kinsey, A. C., Pomeroy, W., & Martin, C. (1984). *Sexual behavior in the human male*. Philadelphia: W. B. Saunders.

Kinsey, A. C., Pomeroy, W., Martin, C., & Gebhard, P. (1953). *Sexual behavior in the human female*. Philadelphia: W. B. Saunders.

Kirby, J. R. & Das, J. P. (1990). A cognitive approach to intelligence: Attention, coding and planning. *Canadian Psychology, 31*, 320–333.

Kirchmeyer, C. (1990). A profile of managers active in office politics. *Basic and Applied Social Psychology,11*, 339–356.

Kisilevsky, B.S., Muir, D.W., Low, J.A., (1992). Maturation of human fetal responses to vibroacoustic stimulation. *Child Development, 63(6)*, 1497–1508.

Klayman, J., & Ha, Y. W. (1987). Confirmation, disconfirmation, and information in hypothesis testing. *Psychological Review, 94*, 211–228.

Klein, H.J. (1991). Further evidence on the relationship between goal setting and expectancy theories. *Organizational Behavior and Human Decision Processes, 49(2)*, 230–257.

Klein, R., Armitage, R. (1979). Rhythms in human performance: 1 1/2–hour oscillations in cognitive style. *Science, 204(4399)*, 1326–1328.

Kleinke, C. L. (1986). Gaze and eye contact: A research review. *Psychological Bulletin, 100*, 78–100.

Kleinman, A. (1986). *Social origins of distress and disease*. New Haven, CT: Yale University Press.

Kleinplatz, P., McCarvey, M., Kateb, C., (1992). The impact of gender-role identity on women's self-esteem, lifestyle staisfaction and conflict. *Canadian Journal of Behavioral Science, 24(3)*.

Kline, D.W., Fuchs, P. (1993). The visibility of symbolic highway signs can be increased among drivers of all ages. *Human Factors, 35(1)*, 25–34.

Kline, D.W., Kline, T.J., Fozard, J.L., Kosnik, W., Shieber, F., Sekuler, R. (1992). Vision, aging, and driving: The problems of older drivers. *Journals of Gerontology, 47(1)*, 27–34.

Klotz, M. L., & Alicke, M. D. (1993). Complaining in close relationships. Unpublished manuscript.

Knowlton, B. J., Ramus, S. J., & Squire, L. R. (1992). Intact artificial grammar learning in amnesia: Dissociation of classification learning and explicit memory for specific instances. *Psychological Science, 3*, 172–179.

Kobasa, S. C. (1979). Stressful life events, personality, and health: An inquiry into hardiness. *Journal of Personality and Social Psychology, 37*, 1–11.

Koestner, R., Bernieri, F., & Zuckerman, M. (1992). Self-regulation and consistency between attitudes, traits, and behaviors. *Personality and Social Psychology Bulletin, 18*, 52–59.

Kohler, I. (1962, May). Experiments with goggles. *Scientific American*, pp. 62–72.

Kohlberg, L. (1984). *Essays on moral development: Vol. 2. The Psychology of moral development*. San Francisco: Harper & Row.

Kohn, A. (1989). Do religious people help more? Not so you'd notice. *Psychology Today, 66–68*.

Kohn, P.M., Lafreniere, K. & Gurevich, M. (1990). The inventory of college student's recent life experiences: a decontaminated hassles scale for a special population. *Journal of Behavioral Medicine, 13(6)*, 619–630.

Kolata, G. (1985). Obesity declared a disease. *Science, 227*, 1019–1020.

Kolata, G. B. (1986). Manic depression: Is it inherited? *Science 232*, 448–450.

Kolb, B. (1989). Brain development, plasticity, and behavior. *American Psychologist, 44(9)*, 1203–1212.

Kolb, B. (1990). Recovery from occipital stroke: a self-report and an inquiry into visual processes. *Canadian Journal of Psychology, 44(2)*, 130–147.

Kolb, B., Wilson, B. & Taylor, L. (1992). Developmental changes in the recognition and comprehension of facial expression: implications for frontal lobe function. Special issue: the role of frontal lobe maturation in cognitive and social development. *Brain and Cognition, 20(1)*, 74–84.

Komaki, J. L. (1986). Toward effective supervision: An operant analysis and comparison of managers at work. *Journal of Applied Psychology, 36*, 271–279.

Konovsky, M. A., & Brockner, J. (1993). Managing victim and survivor layoff reactions: A procedural justice perspective. In R. Cropanzano (Ed.), *Justice in the workplace* (pp. 133–155). Hillsdale, NJ: Erlbaum.

Kopala, L., Clark, C. & Hurwitz, T.A. (1989). Sex differences in olfactory function in schizophrenia. *American Journal of Psychiatry, 146(10)*, 1320–1322.

Korabik, K.; Baril, G. L. & Watson, C. (1993) Managers' conflict management style and leadership effectiveness: The moderating effects of gender. *Sex Roles, 29*, 405–420.

Kosaka, B., Hiscock, M., Strauss, E., Wada, J.A., Purves, S. (1993). Dual task performance by patients with left or right speech dominance as determined by amytal tests. *Neuropsychologia, 31(2)*, 127–136.

Kosslyn, S. M. (1980). *Image and mind*. Cambridge, MA: Harvard University Press.

Kosslyn, S. M. (1987). Seeing and imagining in the cerebral hemispheres: A computational approach. *Psychological Review, 14*, 148–175.

Koulack, D. (1991). *To Catch a Dream: Explorations of Dreaming*. Albany: SUNY Press.

Krakoff, L. R., Dziedzic, S., Mann, S. J., Felton, K., & Yeager, K. (1985). Plasma epinephrine concentrations in healthy men: Correlation with systolic blood pressure and rate-pressure product. *Journal of American College of Cardiology, 5*, 352.

Krank, M.D. & Perkins, W.L. (1993). Conditioned withdrawal signs elicited by contextual cues for morphine administration. *Psychobiology, 21*, 113–119.

Krause, A.M. & Long, B.C. (1993). Predictors of coping for mothers of separated/ divorced offspring. *Canadian Journal on Aging, 12(1)*, 50–66.

Krech, K.H. & Johnston, C. (1992). The relationship of depressed mood and life stress to materal perceptions of child behavior. *Journal of Clinical Child Psychology, 21(2)*, 115–122.

Kroger, W. S., & Douce, R. G. (1979). Hypnosis in criminal investigation. *International Journal of Clinical and Experimental Hypnosis, 27*, 358–384.

Krosnick, J. A., Betz, A. L., Jussim, L. J., & Lynn, A. R. (1992). Subliminal conditioning of attitudes. *Personality and Social Psychology Bulletin, 18*, 152–162.

Krosnick, J.A., Betz, A.L., Jussim, L.J., Lynn, A.R. (1992). Subliminal conditioning of attitudes. *Personality and Social Psychology Bulletin, 18(2)*, 152–162.

Krugman, R., & Davidson, H. (1990). *Child abuse and neglect: Critical first steps in response to a national emergency*. Washington, DC: U.S. Advisory Board on Child Abuse and Neglect.

Kruglanski, A. W. (1990). Motivations for judging and knowing: Implications for causal attribution. In E. T. Higgins & R. M. Sorrentino (Eds.), *The handbook of motivation and cognition: Foundations of social behavior* (Vol. 2, pp. 333–368). New York: Guilford Press.

Kruk, E. (1993). Promoting co-operative parenting after separation: a therapeutic/ interventionist model of family mediation. *Journal of Family Therapy, 15(3)*, 235–261.

Kruk, E. (1994). The disengaged noncustodial father: implications for social work practice with the divorced family. *Social Work, 39(1)*, 15–25.

Kuhn, D., (1989). Children and adults as intuitive scientists. *Psychologial Review, 96(4)*, 674–689.

Kuiper, N. A., Olinger, L. J., & MacDonald, M. R. (1987). Depressive schemata and the processing of personal and social information. In L. B. Alloy (Ed.), *Cognitive processes in depression* New York: Guilford Press.

Kuiper, N.A., Martin, R.A. & Olinger, L.J. (1993). Coping humour, stress and cognitive appraisals. *Canadian Journal of Behavioral Science, 25(1),* 81–96.

Kulik, C.T., Ambrose, M.L. (1992). Personal and situational determinants of referent choice. *Academy of Management Review, 17(2),* 212–237.

Kunce, J. T., Ryan, J., & Eckelman, C. C. (1976). Violent behavior and differential WAIS characteristics. *Journal of Consulting and Clinical Psychology, 44,* 42–45.

Kunda, Z., & Nisbett, R. E. (1986). The psychometrics of everyday life. *Cognitive Psychology, 18,* 195–224.

Kunda, Z., Sherman-Williams, B. (1993). Stereotypes and the construal of individuating information. *Personality and Social Psychology Bulletin, 19(1),* 90–99.

Kunzinger, E.L., (1985). A short-term longitudinal study of memorial development during early grade school. *Developmental Psychology, 21(4),* 642–646.

Kupych, W.N., MacFalane, J.G., & Shapiro, C.M. (1993). A group approach for the management of insomnia. *Journal of Psychosomatic Research, 37,* 39–44.

Kurtz, L. & Derevensky, J.L. (1993). Stress and coping in adolescents: The effects of family configuration and environment on suicidality. Second International Conference for the Child of the Organization for the Protection of Children's Rights (1992, Montreal, Canada). *Canadian Journal of School Psychology, 9(2),* 204–216.

Kutcher, S., Williamson, P., Marton, P., Szalai, J. (1992). REM latency in endogenously depressed adolescents. *British Journal of Psychiatry, 161,* 399–402.

Kutchinsky, B. (1992). The child sexual abuse panic. *Nordisk Sexologist, 10,* 30–42.

Laboratory Centre for Disease Control, Health and Welfare Canada, 1994.

Labouvie-Vief, G. M., & Hakim-Larson, J. (1989). Developmental shifts in adult thought. In S. Hunter & M. Sundel (Eds.), *Midlife myths: Issues, findings, and practical implications* (pp. 690–696). Newbury Park, CA: Sage.

Lafonde, J.S., Mensah, M.N., Badeau, D. (1992). Women and AIDS: Reality or myth. *Canada's Mental Health, 40(4),* 23–25.

Lagerspetz, K. M., Bjorkqvist, K., & Peitonen, T. (1988). Is indirect aggression typical of females? Gender differences in aggressiveness in 11–12 year old children. *Aggressive Behavior, 14,* 403–414.

Laird, J. D. (1984). The real role of facial response in the experience of emotion: A reply to Tourangeua and Ellsworth, and others. *Journal of Personality and Social Psychology, 47,* 909–917.

Lalande, S., Braun, C.M., Charlebois, N. & Whitaker, H.A. (1992). Effects of right and left hemisphere cerebrovascular lesions on the prosodic and semantic aspects of affect in sentences. *Brain and Language, 42(2),* 165–186.

Lalonde, M. (1974). *A new perspective on the health of Canadians.* Ottawa: Canadian Government Printing Office.

Lalonde, R.N. (1992). The dynamics of group differentiation in the face of defeat. *Personality and Social Psychology Bulletin, 18(3),* 336–342.

Lalonde, R.N., Moghaddam, F.M., Taylor, D.M. (1987). The process of group differentiation in a dynamic intergroup setting. *Journal of Social Psychology, 127(3),* 273–287. Reprinted with permission of Helen Dwight Reid Educational Foundation. Published by HeldreF Publications, 1319 Eighteenth St., N.W. Washington, D.C. 20036–1802. Copyright © 1987.

Lamb, M. E. (1977). Father-infant and mother-infant interactions in the first year of life. *Child Development, 48,* 167–181.

Lambert, M. J., Shapiro, D. A., & Bergin, A. E. (1986). The effectiveness of psychotherapy. In S. L. Garfield & A. E. Bergin (Eds.), *Handbook of psychotherapy and behavior change: An evaluative analysis,* (3rd ed.). New York: Wiley.

Lambert, S.J. (1991). The combined effects of job and family characteristics on the job satisfaction, job involvement, and intrinsic motivation of men and women workers. *Journal of Organizational Behavior, 12(4),* 341–363.

Landau, S., Lorch, E.P., Milich, R., (1992). Visual attention to and comprhension of television in attention deficit hyperactivity disordered and mormal boys. *Child Development, 63(40),* 928–937.

Landreville, P. & Vezina, J. (1992). A comparison between daily hassles and major life events as correlates of well-being in older adults. *Canadian Journal on Aging, 1(2),* 137–149.

Landsbergis, P. A., Schnall, P. L., Deitz, D., Friedman, R., & Pickering, T. (1992). The patterning of psychological attributes and distress by job strain and social support in a sample of working men. *Journal of Behavioral Medicine, 15,* 379–405.

Landy, F. J., & Farr, J. L. (1983). *The measurement of work performance: Methods, theory, and applications.* New York: Academic Press.

Lange, J. D., Brown, W. A., Wincze, J. P., & Zwick W. (1980). Serum testosterone concentration and penile tumescence changes in men. *Hormones and Behavior, 14,* 267–270.

Langlois, J.H., Roggman, L.A. (1990). Attractive faces are only average. *Psychological Science, 1(2),* 115–121.

Langlois, J. H., Roggmann, L. A., & Reisser-Danner, L. A. (1990). Infants' differential social responses to attractive and unattractive faces. *Developmental Psychology, 26,* 153–159.

Lapsley, D.K. (1993). Toward an integrated theory of adolescent ego development: The "new look". *American Journal of Orthopsychiatry, 63(4),* 562–571.

Larose, H., Tracy, J., McKelvie, S.J. (1993). Effects of gender on the physical attractiveness stereotype. *The Journal of Psychology, 127(6),* 677–680.

Larrick, R. P. (1993). Motivational factors in decision theories: The role of self-protection. *Psychological Bulletin, 113,* 440–450.

Lashley, K. S., Chow, K. L., & Semmes, J. (1951). An examination of the electrical field theory of cerebral integration. *Psychological Review, 58,* 123–136.

Lassonde, M., Bryden, M.P. & Demers, P. (1990). The corpus collsum and cerebral speech lateralization. *Brain and Language, 38(2),* 195–206.

Latham, G.P. & Huber, V.L. (1992). Schedules of reinforcement: Lessons from the past and issues for the future. *Journal of Organizational Behavior Management, 12,* 125–149.

Latham, G.P., Baldes, J.J. (1975). The "practical significance" of Locke's theory of goal setting. *Journal of Applied Psychology, 60(1),* 122–124.

Latham, G.P., Huber, V.L. (1992). Schedules of reinforcement: Lessons from the past and issues for the future. Special Issue: Pay for performance: History, controversy, and evidence. *Journal of Organizational Behavior Management, 12(1),* 125–149.

Latham, G.P., Locke, E.A. (1991). Self-regulation through goal setting. Special Issue: Theories of cognitive self-regulation. *Organizational Behavior and Human Decision Processes, 50(2),* 212–247.

Lauer, J., & Lauer, R. (1985, June). Marriages made to last. *Psychology Today,* pp. 22–26.

LaVecchia, C., Lucchini, F., Negri, E., Boyle, P., & Levi, F. (1993). Trends in cancer mortality in the Americas, 1955–1989. *European Journal of Cancer, 29,* 431–470.

LaVecchia, C., Lucchini, F., Negri, E., Boyle, P., Maisonneuve, P., & Levi, F. (1992). Trends of cancer mortality in Europe, 1955-1989: II, Respiratory tract, bone, connective and soft tissue sarcomas, and skin. *European Journal of Cancer, 23,* 514–599.

Lavrakas, P.J. (1975). Female preferences for male physiques. *Journal of Research in Personality, 9(4),* 324–334.

Law, D. J., Pellegrino, J. W., & Hunt, E. B. (1993). Comparing the tortoise and the hare: Gender differences and experience in dynamic spatial reasoning tasks. *Psychological Sciences, 4,* 35–40.

Lawless, H., & Engen, T. (1977). Associations to odors: Interference, mnemonics, and verbal labeling. *Journal of Experimental Psychology: Human Learning and Memory, 3,* 52–59.

Lay, C. (1974). The responsive bystander in emergencies: Some preliminary data. *Canadian Psychologist, 15(3),* 220–227.

Lazarus, R. S., & Folkman, S. (1984). *Stress, appraisal, and coping.* New York: Springer.

Lazarus, R. S., Opton, E. M., Nomikos, M. S., & Rankin, N. O. (1985). The principle of short-circuiting of threat: Further evidence. *Journal of Personality, 33,* 622–635.

Ledingham, J. & Crombie, G. 1988. Promoting the mental health of children and youth: A critical review of recent literature. *Canada's Mental Health, 36(1),* 9–17.

Lee, J.M. & Hett, G.G. (1990). Post-divorce adjustment: an assessment of a group intervention. *Canadian Journal of Counselling, 24(3),* 199–209.

Lee, P. C., Senders, C. W., Gantz, B. J., & Otto, S. R. (1985). Transient sensorineural hearing loss after overuse of portable headphone cassette radios. *Otolaryngology, 93,* 622–625.

Lee, R. T., & Ashforth, B. E. (1990). On the meaning of Maslach's three dimensions of burnout. *Journal of Applied Psychology, 75,* 743–747.

Lee, R.T. & Ashforth, B.E. (1993). A longitudinal study of burnout among supervisors and managers: comparisons between the Lieter & Maslach (1988) and Golembiewski et al (1986) models. *Organizational Behavior and Human Decision Processes, 54(3),* 369–398.

Leenaars, A.A. & Lester, D. (1990). Suicide in adolescents: A comparison of Canada and the United States. *Psychological Reports, 67(3, pt 1),* 867–873.

LeFevre, J. A., Kulak, A.G., & Heymans, S. L. Factors influencing the selection of university majors varying in mathematical content. *Canadian Journal of Behavioral Science. 24,* 276–289.

Legerstee, M., (1990). Infants use multimodial information to imitate speech sounds. *Infant Behavior and Development, 13(3),* 343–354.

Legerstee, M., (1991). The role of the person and object in eliciting early imitation. *Journal of Experimental Child Psychology, 51(3),* 423–433.

Lehman, D.R. & Taylor, S.E. (1987). Date with an earthquake: coping with a probable, unpredictable disaster. *Personality and Social Psychology Bulletin, 13(4),* 546–555.

Lehman, D.R., Davis, C.G., DeLongis, A., Wortman, C.B. Bluck, S., Mandel, D.R., Ellard, J.H. (1993). Positive and negative life changes following bereavement and their relations to adjustment. *Journal of Social and Clinical Psychology, 12(1)*, 90–112.

Lehman, H. C. (1953). *Age and achievement*. Philadelphia: W. B. Saunders.

Leighton, A. H. (1959). *My name is legion: The Stirling County study of psychiatric disorder and social environment*. New York: Basic Books, Vol. 1.

Leith, L.M. (1989). Causal attribution and sport behavior: Implications for practitioners. *Journal of Sport Behavior, 12(4)*, 213–225.

Lempers, J. D., Flavell, E. R., & Flavell, J. H. (1977). The development in very young of tacit knowledge concerning visual perception. *Genetic Psychology Monographs 95*, 3–53.

Lennox, R. D., & Wolfe, R. N. (1984). Revision of the self-monitoring scale. *Journal of Personality and Social Psychology, 46*, 1349–1364.

Lepper, M. R., & Cordova, D. I. (1992). A desire to be taught: Instructional consequences of intrinsic motivation. *Motivation and Emotion, 16*, 187–208.

Lepper, M. R., & Hoddell, M. (1992). *Instructional games: Effects of sex-typed fantasy contexts on boys' and girls' learning and instruction.* Unpublished manuscript, Stanford University.

Lerner, R. M. (1990). Plasticity, person-context relations, and cognitive training in the aged years: A developmental contextual perspective. *Developmental Psychology, 26*, 911–915.

Lerner, R. M. (1993). The demise of the nature-nurture dichotomy. *Human Development, 36*, 119–124.

Leroux, J.A., (1986). Making theory real: Developmental theory and implications for education of gifted adolescents. *Roeper-Review, 9(2)*, 72–77.

Letourneau, J.E., Denis, R., Londorf, D. (1986). Influence of auditory or visual warning on visual reaction time with variations of subjects' alertness. *Perceptual and Motor Skills, 62(2)*, 667–674.

Lett, B. (1992). Pairings of a drug or place conditioned stimulus with lithium chloride produce conditioned sickness, not antisickness. *Behavioral Neuroscience, 106*, 106–111.

Leung, A.K., & Robson, W.L. (1993). Nightmares. *Journal of the National Medical Association, 85*, 233–235.

Levanoni, E., Sales, C.A. (1990). Differences in job attitudes between full-time and part-time Canadian employees. *Journal of Social Psychology, 130(2)*, 231–237.

LeVay, S. (1991). A difference in hypothalamic structure between heterosexual and homosexual men. *Science, 253*, 1034–1037.

Levenson, R. W. (1992). Autonomic nervous system differences among emotions. *Psychological Science, 3*, 23–27.

Levenson, R. W., Carstensen, L. L., Friesen, W. V., & Ekman, P. (1991). Emotion, physiology, and expression in old age. *Psychology and Aging, 6*, 28–35.

Levine, D. S. (1991). *Introduction to neural and cognitive modeling*. Hillsdale, NJ: Erlbaum.

Levine, J. M., & McBurney, D. H. (1982). *The role of olfaction in social perception and behavior*. Paper presented at the Third Ontario Symposium in Personality and Social Psychology, Toronto.

Levine, S.V. (1987). The myths and needs of contemporary youth. *Adolescent Psychiatry, 14*, 48–62.

Levinger, G. (1988). Can we picture "love"? In R. J. Sternberg & M. I. Barnes (Eds.), *The psychology of love* (pp. 139–158). New Haven, CT: Yale University Press.

Levinson, D. J. (1986). A conception of adult development. *American Psychologist, 41*, 3–13.

Levis, D. J. (1985). Implosive theory: A comprehensive extension of conditioning theory of fear/anxiety to psychology. In S. Reiss & R. R. Bootzin (Eds.), *Theoretical issues in behavior therapy*. New York: Academic Press.

Levitt, A.J., Joffe, R.T., Moul, D.E., Lam, R.W. Teicher, M.H., Lebegue, B., Murray, M.G., Oren, D.A., Schwartz, P., Buchanan, A., Glod, C.A., Brown, J. (1993). Side effects of light therapy in seasonal affective disorder. *American Journal of Psychiatry, 150*, 650–652.

Levitt, A.J. Joffe. R.T., Brecher, D., & MacDonald, C. (1993). Anxiety disorders and anxiety symptoms in a clinic sample of seasonal and nonseasonal depressives. *Journal of Affective Disorders, 28*, 51–56

Levy, S. M. (1990). Psychosocial risk factors and cancer progression: Mediating pathways linking behavior and disease. In K. D. Craig & S. M. Weiss (Eds.), *Health enhancement, disease prevention, and early intervention: Biobehavioral perspectives*. New York: Springer.

Levy, S.M., Herberman, R.B., Maluish, A.M., Schlien, B., Lippman, M. (1985). Prognostic risk assessment in primary breast cancer by behavioral and immunological parameters. *Health Psychology, 4(2)*, 99–113.

Lewin, K. (1947). Group decision and social change. In T. N. Newcomb & E. L. Hartley (Eds.), *Readings in social psychology*. New York: Holt, Rinehart, & Winston.

Lewis, M., Sullivan, M. W., Stanger, C., & Weiss, M. (1989). Self-development and self-consciousness emotions. *Child Development, 60*, 146–156.

Lewis, T.L., Maurer, D., (1992). The Development of the temporal and nasal visual fields during infancy. *Vision Research, 32(5)*, 903–911.

Ley, P. (1988). *Communicating with patients*. London: Croom Helm.

Liddell, A. & Locker, D. (1993). Dental anxiety in the elderly. Special issue: dental health psychology. *Psychology and Health, 8(2–3)*, 175–183.

Liddell, F. D. K. (1982). Motor vehicle accidents (1973–6) in a cohort of Montreal drivers. *Journal of Epidemiological Community Health, 36*, 140–145.

Liden, R. C., & Mitchell, T. R. (1988). Ingratiatory behaviors in organizational settings. *Academy of Management Review, 13*, 572–587.

Lieberman, D. A. (1990). *Learning: Behavior and cognition*. Belmont, CA: Wadsworth Publishing Company.

Lieter, M.P. & Maslach, C. (1988). The impact of interpersonal environment on burnout and organizational commitment. *Journal of Organizational Behavior, 9(4)*, 297–308.

Lightdale, J. R., & Prentice, D. A. (1994). Rethinking sex differences aggression: Aggressive behavior in the absence of social roles. *Personality and Social Psychology Bulletin, 20*, 34–44.

Linden, E. (1993, March 22). Can animals think? *Time*.

Linden, W. (1991). What do arithmetic stress tests measure? Protocol variations and cardiovascular responses. *Psychophysiology, 28(1)*, 91–102.

Lindsley, O. (1992). Precision teaching: Discoveries and effects. *Journal of Applied Behavior Analysis, 25*, 51–57.

Lindy, J. D., Green, B. L., & Grace, M. C. (1987). Commentary: The stressor criterion and post–traumatic stress disorder. *Journal of Nervous and Mental Disease, 175(5)*, 269–272.

Links, P.S. & Van Reekum, R. (1993). Childhood sexual abuse, parental impairment and the development of borderline personality disorder. *Canadian Journal of Psychiatry, 38(7)*, 472–474.

Linseman, M.A. (1989). Central versus peripheral mediation of opioid effects on alcohol consumption in free-feeding rats. *Pharmacology, Biochemistry and Behavior, 33(2)*, 407–413.

Linton, J.M. (1992). Documentary film research's unrealized potential in the communication field. *Communication, 13(2)*, 85–93.

Linton, M. (1975). Memory for real-world events. In D. A. Norman & D. E. Rumelhart (Eds.), *Explorations in cognition,* Chapter 14. San Francisco: Freeman.

Linville, P.W., Fischer, G.W., Salovey, P. (1989). Perceived distributions of the characteristics of in-group and out-group members: Empirical evidence and a computer simulation. *Journal of Personality and Social Psychology, 57(2)*, 165–188.

Lips, H.M., Colwill, N.L. (1988). Psychology addresses women and work: Canadian research in 1980s. Special Issue: Industrial/organizational psychology in *Canada. Canadian Psychology, 29(1)*, 57–68.

List, W. (1993). Work-related stress remains a costly problem. *Canadian Occupational Safety, 31(3)*, 6–7.

Livesley, W. J., Schroeder, M. L., Jackson, D. N., & Jang, K. L. (1994). Categorial distinctions in the study of personality disorder: Implications for classification. *Journal of Abnormal Psychology, 103*, 6–17.

Locke, B. Z., & Slaby, A. E. (1982). Preface. In D. Mechanic (Ed.), *Symptoms, illness behavior, and help-seeking* (pp. xi–xv). New York: Prodist.

Locke, E. A., & Latham, G. P. (1990). *A theory of goal setting and task performance*. Englewood Cliffs, NJ: Prentice Hall.

Locke, E. A., & Schweiger, D. M. (1979) Participation in decision-making: One more look. In B. M. Staw & L. L. Cummings (Eds.), *Research on organizational behavior* (Vol. 1, pp. 265–339). Greenwich, CT: JAI Press.

Loewen, L.J., Suedfeld, P. (1992). Cognitive and arousal effects of masking office noise. *Environment and Behavior, 24(3)*, 381–395.

Loftus, E. F. & Loftus, G. R. (1980). On the permanence of stored information in the human brain. *American Psychologist, 35*, 409–420.

Loftus, E. F. (1991). The glitter of everyday memory … and the gold. *American Psychologist, 46*, 16–18.

Loftus, E. F. (1992). When a lie becomes memory's truth: Memory distortion after exposure to misinformation. *Current Directions in Psychological Science, 1*, 121–123.

Loftus, E. F. (1993). The reality of repressed memories. *American Psychologist, 48*, 518–537.

Loftus, E. F., & Coan, D. (in press). The construction of childhood memories. In D. Peters (Ed.), *The child in context: Cognitive, social and legal perspectives*. New York: Kluwer.

Loftus, E. F., & Herzog, C. (1991). Unpublished data, University of Washington. Cited in Loftus, E. F. (1993). The reality of repressed memories. *American Psychologist, 48*, 518–537.

Logan, G. D. (1985). Skill and automaticity: Relations, implications, and future directions. *Canadian Journal of Psychology, 39*, 367–386.

Logan, G. D. (1988). Toward an instance theory of automotization. *Psychological Review, 95*, 492–527.

Logue, A. W. (1979). Taste aversion and the generality of the laws of learning. *Psychological Bulletin, 86*, 27–296.

Logue, A. W., Logue, K. R., & Strauss, K. E. (1983). The acquisition of taste aversion in humans with eating and drinking disorders. *Behavioral Research and Therapy, 21*, 275–289.

Logue, A. W., Ophir, I., & Strauss, K. E. (1981). The acquisition of taste aversion in humans. *Behavior Research and Therapy, 19*, 319–333.

Long, B.C. (1993). Coping strategies of male managers: A prospective analysis of predictors of psychosomatic symptoms and job satisfaction. *Journal of Vocational Behavior, 42(2),* 184–199.

Long, B.C., Kahn, S.E. & Schutz, R.W. (1992). Causal model of stress and coping: women and management. *Journal of Counselling Psychology, 39(2),* 227–239.

Long, G. M., & Crambert, R. F. (1990). The nature and basis of age-related change in dynamic visual acuity. *Psychology and Aging, 5,* 138–143.

Long, R.J. (1993). The impact of new office information technology on job quality of female and male employees. *Human Relations, 46(8),* 939–961.

Lonner, W. J., & Malpass, R. (Eds.) (1994). *Psychology and Culture.* Boston: Allyn and Bacon.

Loo, R., Watts, T. (1993). A survey of employee assistance programs in medium and large Canadian organizations. *Employee Assistance Quarterly, 8(3),* 65–71.

Looy, H., Callaghan, S., & Weingarten, H.P. (1992). Hedonic response of sucrose likers and dislikers to ther gustatory stimuli. *Physiology and Behavior, 52,* 219–225.

Lopez, S. R. (1989). Patient variable biases in clinical judgment; conceptual overview and methodological considerations. *Psychological Bulletin, 106,* 184–203.

Loranger, M., Arsenault, R., Plante, C., (1989). A srudy of classroom scripts. Canadian Journal of Education, 14(3), 277–294.

Lovaas, O. I. (1977). *The autistic child: Language development through behavior modification.* New York: Halsted Press.

Lovaas, O. I. (1982). Comments on self-destructive behaviors. *Analysis and Intervention in Developmental Disabilities, 2,* 115–124.

Loza, W. (1993). Attributions of blame toward incarcerated rapists among correctional workers: Implications for staffing. *Canadian Journal of Criminology, 35(1),* 59–60.

Luborsky, L., Singer, B., & Luborsky, L. (1975). Comparative studies of psychotherapies: Is it true that "everyone has won and all must have prizes"? *Archives of General Psychiatry, 32,* 49–62.

Luchins, A. S. (1942). Mechanization in problem solving. *Psychological Monographs, 54* (whole No. 248).

Lupfer, M.B., Clark, L.F., Hutcherson, H.W. (1990). Impact of context on spontaneous trait and situational attributions. *Journal of Personality and Social Psychology, 58(2),* 239–249.

Lupker, S.J., Fleet, G.J. & Shelton, B.R. (1988). Callers' perceptions of post-dialling delays: The effectys of new signaling technology. *Behaviour and Information Technology, 7,* 263–274.

Luthans, F., Paul, R., & Baker, D. (1981). An experimental analysis of the impact of a contingent reinforcement intervention on salespersons' performance behaviors. *Journal of Applied Psychology, 66,* 314–323.

Lyden, J.E., Jamieson, D.W., Zanna, M.P. (1998). Interpersonal similarity and the social and intellectual dimensions of first impressions. *Social Cognition, 6(4),* 269–286.

Lykken, D. T. (1957). A study of anxiety in the sociopathic personality. *Journal of Abnormal and Social Psychology, 55,* 6–10.

Lykken, D. T. (1985). The probity of the polygraph. In S. M. Kassin & L. S. Wrightsman (Eds.), *The psychology of evidence and trial procedure.* Beverly Hills, CA: Sage.

Lykken, D. T., McGue, M., Tellegen, A., & Bouchard, T. J. (1992). Emergenesis: Genetic traits that may not run in families. *American Psychologist, 47,* 1565–1577.

Lyman, B. J., & McDaniel, M. A. (1986). Effects of encoding strategy on long-term memory for odours. *Quarterly Journal of Experimental Psychology, 38A,* 753–765.

Lyman, B. J., & McDaniel, M. A. (1987, April). Effects of experimenter and subject provided verbal and visual elaborations on long-term memory for odors. Paper presented at the annual meeting of the Eastern Psychological Association, Arlington, VA.

Lyness, S. A. (1993). Predictors of differences between Type A and B individuals in heart rate and blood pressure reactivity. *Psychological Bulletin, 114,* 266–295.

Lynn, S. J., & Rhue, J. W. (1986). The fantasy-prone person: Hypnosis, imagination, and creativity. *Journal of Personality and Social Psychology, 51,* 404–408.

Lynn, S. J., Rhue, J. W., & Weekes, J. R. (1990). Hypnotic involuntariness: A social cognitive analysis. *Psychological Review, 974,* 169–184.

Lytton, H., Romney, D.M., (1991). Parents' differential socialization of boys and girls: A meta-analysis. *Psychological Bulletin, 109(2),* 267–296.

Maccoby, E. E., (1990). Gender and relationships: A development account. American Psychological Association: Distinguished Scientific Contributions Award Address (1989, New Orleans, Louisiana). *American Psychologist, 45(4),* 513–520.

Maccoby, E. E., & Jacklin, C. N. (1987). Gender segregation in childhood. In H. W. Reese (Ed.), *Advances in child development and behavior* (Vol. 20, pp. 239–288). New York: Academic Press.

Macguire, P., Fairburn, S., & Fletcher, C. (1986). Consultation skills of young doctors: I. Benefits of feedback training in interviewing as

students persists. *British Medical Journal, 292,* 1573–1576.

Mackay, A. V. P., Iversen, L. L., Rossor, M., Spokes, E., Bird, E., Arregui, A., Creese, I., & Snyder, S. (1982). Increased brain dopamine and dopamine receptors in schizophrenia. *Archives of General Psychiatry, 39,* 991–997.

Mackie, D. M., & Worth, L. T. (1989). Processing deficits and the mediation of positive affect in persuasion. *Journal of Personality and Social Psychology, 57,* 27–40.

MacLaren, R., Olson, D. (1993). Trick or Treat: Children's understanding of surprise. *Cognitive Development, 8,* 27–46.

Macnamara, J., Austin, G., (1993). Physics and plasticine. *Canadian Psychology, 34(3),* 225–232.

Macrae, C.N. (1992). A tale of two curries: Counterfactual thinking and accident-related judgments. *Personality and Social Psychology Bulletin, 18(1),* 84–87.

Maher, B. A., & Maher, W. B. (1985). Psychopathology: II. From the eighteenth century to modern times. In G. A. Kimble & K. Schlesinger (Eds.), *Topics in the history of psychology* (Vol. 2). Hillsdale, NJ: Erlbaum.

Mahoney, M. J. (1991). *Human change process: The scientific foundations of psychotherapy.* New York: Basic Books.

Maier, S. F., & Jackson, R. L. (1979). Learned helplessness: All of us were right (and wrong): Inescapable shock has multiple effects. In G. H. Bower (Ed.), *The psychology of learning and motivation* (Vol. 13). New York: Academic Press.

Major, B., Carnevale, P. J. D., & Deaux, K. (1981). A different perspective on androgyny: Evaluation of masculine and feminine personality characteristics. *Journal of Personality and Social Psychology, 41,* 988–1001.

Malan, J. R., Norton, G. R., & Cox, B. J. (1993). Panic attacks and alcoholism: Primacy and frequency of attacks. *Alcoholism Treatment Quarterly, 10,* 95–105.

Malenfant, L. & Van Houten, R. (1990). Increasing the percentage of drivers yielding tp pedestrians in three Canadian cities with a multifaceted safety program. *Health Education Research, 5,* 275–279.

Malinowski, B. (1927). *Sex and repression in savage society.* London: Humanities Press.

Malla, A.K. & Norman, R.M. (1992). Relationship of major life events and daily stressors to symptomology in schizophrenia. *Journal of Nervous and Mental Disease, 180(10),* 664–667.

Mallory, B.L., Schein, J.D. & Zingle, H.W. (1992). Hearing offspring as visual language mediators in deaf-parented families. *Sign Language Studies, 76,* 193–213.

Malpass, R. S., & Devine, P. G. (1981). Guided memory in eyewitness identification research. *Journal of Applied Psychology 66,* 343–350.

Mamelak, M. (1992). A perspective on narcolepsy. *Encephale, 18,* 347–351.

Mann, J. (1992). *AIDS in the world 1992: A global epidemic out of control?* Report of the Global AIDS Policy Coalition. Cambridge, MA: Harvard University School of Public Health.

Mann, L. M., Chassin, L., & Sher, K. J. (1987). Alcohol, expectancies and risk for alcoholism. *Journal of Consulting and Clinical Psychology, 55,* 411–417.

Marche, T.A., Peterson, C. (1993). The development and sex-related use of interruption behavior. *Human Communication Research, 19(3),* 388–408.

Marek, G. R. (1975). *Toscanini.* London: Vision Press.

Margolin, G., & Wampold, B. E. (1981). Sequential analysis of conflict and accord in distressed and non-distressed marital partners. *Journal of Consulting and Clinical Psychology, 49,* 554–567.

Markovits, H., (1993). Piaget and plasticine: Who's right about conservation? *Canadian Psychology, 34(3),* 233–238.

Marks, G., Miller, N. (1987). Ten years of research on the false-consensus effect: An empirical and theoretical review. *Psychological Bulletin, 102(1),* 72–90.

Marks, I. (1994). Behavior therapy as an aid to self-care. *Current Directions in Psychological Science, 3,* 19–22.

Markus, H. M. & Nurius, P. (1986). Possible selves. *American Psychologist, 41,* 954–969.

Marlatt, G. A., Baer, J. S., Donovan, D. M., & Kivlahan, D. R. (1988). Addictive behaviors: Etiology and treatment. *Annual Review of Psychology, 58,* 265–272.

Marr, D. (1982). *Vision: A computational investigation into the human representation and processing of visual information.* San Francisco: W. H. Freeman.

Martin, C.L., Little, J.K., (1990). The relation of gender understanding to children's sex-typed preferences and gender stereotypes. *Child Development, 61(5),* 1427–1439.

Martin, M. (1986). Individual differences in sensation seeking attentional ability. *Personality and Individual Differences, 6,* 637–649.

Martin, M., Williams, R., & Clark, D. (1991). Does anxiety lead to selective processing of threat-related information? *Behaviour Research and Therapy, 29,* 147–160.

Martin, R. L., Cloninger, R., Guze, S. B., & Clayton, P. J. (1985). Mortality in a follow-up of 500 psychiatric outpatients: I. Total mortality. *Archives of General Psychiatry, 42,* 47–54.

Marton, P., Golombek, H., Stein, B., & Korenblum, M. (1988). The relation of personality functions and adaptive skills to self-esteem in early adolescence. *Journal of Youth and Adolescence, 17*, 393–401.

Marzetta, B. R., Benson, H., & Wallace, R. K. (1972). Combatting drug dependency in young people: A new approach. *Medical Counterpoint, 4*, 13–37.

Maser, J. D., Kaelber, C., & Weise, R. E. (1991). International use and attitudes toward DSM-III and DSM-III-R: Growing consensus in psychiatric classification. *Journal of Abnormal Psychology, 100*, 271–279.

Maslach, C. (1982). *Burnout: The cost of caring.* Englewood Cliffs, NJ: Prentice-Hall.

Maslach, C., & Jackson, S. E. (1984). Burnout in organizational settings. In S. Oskamp (Ed.), *Applied social psychology annual* (Vol. 5, pp. 135–154). Beverly Hills: Sage.

Maslow, A. H. (1970). *Motivation and personality,* (2nd ed.). New York: Harper & Row.

Masters, W. H., & Johnson, V. E. (1966). *Human sexual response.* Boston: Little, Brown.

Matarazzo, J. D. (1980). Behavioral health and behavioral medicine: Frontiers for a new health psychology. *American Psychologist, 35*, 807–817.

Mather, J. A., & Anderson, R. C. (1993). Personalities of octopuses (Octopus rubescens). *Journal of Comparative Psychology, 107*, 336–340.

Matheson, A.D. (1993). Innovative use of computers for planning in human service organizations. *Computers in Human Services, 9(3–4)*, 383–395.

Mathews, A. (1990). Why worry? The cognitive function of anxiety. *Behavior Research and Therapy, 28*, 455–468.

Maticka-Tyndale, E. (1992). Social construction of HIV transmission and prevention among heterosexual young adults. *Social Problems, 39(3)*, 238–252.

Maticka-Tyndale, E. (1991). Sexual scripts and AIDS prevention: variations in adherence to safer sex guidelines by heterosexual adolescents. *Journal of Sex Research, 28*, 45–66.

Matlin, M. E. (1990). *Cognition* (3rd ed.). New York: Holt, Rinehart & Winston.

Matlin, M. W., & Foley, H. J. (1992). *Sensation and perception* (3rd ed.). Needham Heights, MA: Allyn & Bacon.

Maturi, R. (1992, July 20). Stress can be beaten. *Industry Week*, pp. 23–26.

Maupin, H.E., Fisher, R.J. (1989). The effects of superior female performance and sex-role orientation on gender conformity. *Canadian Journal of Behavioural Science, 21(1)*, 55–69.

Maurer, D., Barrera, M.E., (1981). Infant's perception of natural and distorted arrangements of a schematic face. *Child Development, 52(1)*, 196–202.

Mauri, M., Reid, R.L. & MacLean, A.W. (1988). Sleep in the premenstrual phase: a self-report study of PMS patients and normal controls. *Acta Psychiatrica Scandinavica, 78(1)*, 82–86.

Maurice, P., & Trudel, G. (1982). Self-injurious behavior prevalence and relationships to environmental events. In J. H. Hollis & C. E. Meyers (Eds.), *Life-threatening behavior: Analysis and intervention.* Washington, DC: American Association on Mental Deficiency, Monograph No. 5, 81–103.

May, C. P., Hasher, L., & Stoltzfus, E. R. (1993). Optimal time of day and the magnitude of age differences in memory. *Psychological Science, 4*, 326–330.

Mayer, R. E., Tajika, H., & Stanley, C. (1991). Mathematical problem solving in Japan and the United States: A controlled comparison. *Journal of Educational Psychology, 1*, 69–72.

Mazursky, D., & Ofir, C. (1989). "I could never have expected it to happen": The reversal of the hindsight bias. *Organizational Behavior and Human Decision Processes, 46*, 20–33.

McCall, R. B. (1994). Academic underachievers. *Current Directions in Psychological Science, 3*, 15–19.

McCann, C.D., Higgins, E.T., Fondacaro, R.A. (1991). Primacy and recency in communication and self-persuasion: How successive audiences and multiple encodings influence subsequent evaluative judgments. Special Issue: Social cognition and communication: Human judgment in its social context. *Social Cognition, 9(1)*, 47–66.

McCanne, T. R., & Anderson, J. A. (1987). Emotional responding following experimental manipulation of facial electromyographic activity. *Journal of Personality and Social Psychology, 52*, 759–768.

McCarley, R. W., & Hobson, R. W. (1981). REM sleep dreams and the activation hypothesis. *American Journal of Psychiatry, 138*, 904–912.

McCarthy, B. & Hagan, J. (1991). Homelessness: A criminogenic situation? *British Journal of Criminology, 31(4)*, 393–410.

McCarthy, B. & Hagan, J. (1992). Surviving on the street: The experiences of homeless youth. *Journal of Adolescent Research, 7(4)*, 412–430.

McCarthy, R. L., Finnegan, J. P., Krumm-Scott, S., & McCarthy, G. E. (1984). Product information presentation, user behavior, and safety. In *Proceedings of the Human Factors Society 28th Annual Meeting* (pp. 81–85). Santa Monica, CA: Human Factors Society.

McClearn, G. E., Plomin, R., Gora-Maslak, G., & Crabbe, J. C. (1991). The gene chase in behavioral science. *Psychological Science, 2*, 222–229.

McClelland, D. C. (1961). *The achieving society.* Princeton, NJ: Van Nostrand.

McClelland, D. C. (1975). *Power: The inner experience.* New York: Irvington.

McClelland, D. C., Atkinson, J. W., Clark, R. W., & Lowell, E. L. (1953). *The achievement motive.* New York: Appleton-Century-Crofts.

McConkie, G. W., & Zola, D. (1984). Eye movement control during reading. The effect of word units. In W. Prinz & A. F. Sanders (Eds.), *Cognition and motor processes* (pp. 63–74). Berlin: Springer-Verlag.

McConkie, G. W., Kerr, P. W., Reddix, M. D., Zola, D., & Jacobs, A. M. (1989). Eye movement control during reading: II. Frequency of refixating a word. *Perception & Psychophysics, 46*, 245–253.

McCrae, R. R. (1989). Why I advocate the five-factor model. Joint factor analyses of the NEO-PI with other instruments. In D. M. Buss & N. Cantor (Eds.), *Personality psychology: Recent trends and emerging directions* (pp. 237–245). New York: Springer-Verlag.

McDonald, J., McKelvie, S.J. (1992). Playing safe: Helping rates for a dropped mitten and a box of condoms. *Psychological Reports, 71*, 113–114.

McDonald, R.J. & White, N.M. (1993). A triple dissociation of memory systems: hippocampus, amygdala, and dorsal striatum. *Behavioral Neuroscience, 107(1)*, 3–22.

McDonnell, P.M., (1988). Developmental response to limb deficiency and limb replacement. Special Issue: Child development: When things go wrong. *Canadian Journal of Psychology, 42(2)*, 120–143.

McEwan, N. H., & Yuille, J. C. (1982). *The effect of hypnosis as an interview technique on eyewitness memory.* Paper presented at the annual meeting of the Canadian Psychological Association, Montreal.

McFarland, C., Ross, M., & DeCourville, N. (1989). Women's theories of menstruation and biases in recall of menstrual symptoms. *Journal of Personality and Social Psychology, 576*, 522–531.

McGinnis, R. (1958). Campus values in mate selection: A repeat study. *Social Forces, 36*, 368–373.

McGlone, J. & MacDonald, B.H. (1989). Reliability of the sodium amobarbital test for memory. *Journal of Epilepsy, 2(1)*, 31–39.

McGrath, J. E., & Cohen, D. B. (1978). REM sleep facilitation of adaptive waking behavior: A review of the literature. *Psychological Bulletin, 85*, 24–57.

McGrath, P.J., McAlpine, L, (1993). Psychologic perspectives on pediatric pain. *The Journal of Pediatrics, 122*, S2–S8.

McGregor, J. (1993). Effectiveness of role playing and antiracist teaching in reducing student prejudice. *Journal of Educational Research, 86(4)*, 215–226.

McGue, M., & Lykken, D. T. (1992). Genetic influence on risk of divorce. *Psychological Science, 3*, 368–373.

McGuire, J., (1988). Gender stereotypes of parents with two-year- olds and beliefs about gender differences in behavior. *Sex Roles, 19(34)*, 233–240.

McIntyre, J.S. & Craik, F.I. (1987). Age differences in memory for item and source information. Special issue: Aging and cognition. *Canadian Journal of Psychology, 41(2)*, 175–192

McKelvie, S. J., & Aikins, S. Why does coin head orientation tend to be misremembered? Tests of schema interference and handedness hypothesis. *British Journal of Psychology, 84*, 355–363.

McKelvie, S.J. (1993). Effects of feature variations on attributions for schematic faces. *Psychological Reports, 73(1)*, 275–288.

McKelvie, S.J. (1993). Perceived cuteness, activity level, and gender in schematic babyfaces. *Journal of Social Behavior and Personality, 8(2)*, 297–310.

McKelvie, S.J. (1993). Stereotyping in perception of attractiveness, age, and gender in schematic faces. *Social Behavior and Personality, 21(2)*, 121–128.

McKelvie, S.J., Coley, J. (1993). Effects of crime seriousness and offender facial attractiveness on recommended treatment. *Social Behavior and Personality, 21(4)*, 265–277.

McKenna, S. P., & Glendon, A.I. (1985). Occupational first aid training: Decay in cardiopulmonary resuscitation (CPR) skills. *Journal of Occupational Psychology, 58*, 109–117.

McKenry, P. C., Kotch, J. B., & Browne, D. H. (1991). Correlates of dysfunctional parenting attitudes among low-income adolescent mothers. *Journal of Adolescent Research, 6*, 212–234.

McKey, R., Condelli, L., Ganson, H., Barrett, B., McConkey, C., & Plantz, M. (1985). The impact of Head Start on children, families, and communities: Final report of the Head Start Evaluation, Synthesis and Utilization Project (No. OHDS 85–31193). Washington, DC: U.S. Government Printing Office.

McLaren, J. & Bryson, S.E. (1987). Hemispheric asymmetries in the perception of emotional and neutral faces. *Cortex, 23(4)*, 645–654.

McLellan, B., McKelvie, S.J. (1993). Effects of age and gender on perceived facial attractiveness. *Canadian Journal of Behavioural Science, 25(1)*, 135–142.

McLeod, K. (1988). Somewhere to turn: When an employee's personal problems affect how he works in the office, it may be time for a helping hand. OA: *Office Management and Automation, 4(9)*, 46–48.

McLeod, L. (1989). The city for women: No safe place. Secretary of State, Canada.

McLeod, P.J., (1993). What studies of communication with infants ask us about psychology: Baby-talk and other speech registers. *Canadian Psychology, 34(3),* 282–292.

McMillan, M. (1988). The doll test studies—from cabbage patch to self-concept. *Journal of Black Psychology, 25,* 69–72.

McNeal, E. T., & Cimbolic, P. (1986). Antidepressants and biochemical theories of depression. *Psychological Bulletin, 99,* 361–374.

McReynolds, W. T. (1980). Learned helplessness as a schedule-shift effect. *Journal of Research in Personality, 14,* 139–157.

Medcof, J.W. & Wegener, J.G. (1992). Work technology and the needs for achievement and nurturance among nurses. *Journal of Organizational Behavior, 13(4),* 413–423.

Medin, D. L., Ross, B. H. (1992). *Cognitive psychology.* Fort Worth, TX: Harcourt Brace Jovanovich.

Meehan, P. J., Lamb, J. A., Saltzman, L. E., & O'Carroll, P. W. (1992). Attempted suicide among young adults: Progress towards a meaningful estimate of prevalence. *American Journal of psychiatry, 149,* 41–44.

Meichenbaum, D. H. (1977). *Cognitive-behavior modification.* New York: Plenum.

Meichenbaum, D. K., & Deffenbacher, J. L. (1988). Stress inoculation training. *Counseling Psychologist, 16,* 69–90.

Meier, S. T. (1991). Vocational behavior, 1988–1990: Vocational choice, decision-making, career development interventions, and assessment. *Journal of Vocational Behavior, 39,* 459–484.

Melamed, S., Kushnir, T., & Shirom, A. (1992). Burnout and risk factors for cardiovascular diseases. *Behavioral Medicine, 18,* 53–60.

Meleshko, K. G. A., & Alden, L. E. (1993). Anxiety and self-disclosure: Toward a motivational model. *Journal of Personality and Social Psychology, 64,* 1000–1009.

Meltzoff, A. N. (1990). Towards a developmental cognitive science: The implications of cross-modal matching and imitation for the development of representation and memory in infancy. In A. Diamond (Ed.), *Annals of the New York Academy of Sciences: Vol 608. The development and neural bases of higher cognitive functions* (pp. 1–37). New York: New York Academy of Sciences

Meltzoff, A. N., & Moore, M. K. (1977). Imitation of facial and manual gestures by human neonates. *Science, 198,* 75–78.

Meltzoff, A. N., & Moore, M. K. (1989). Imitation in newborn infants: Exploring the range of gestures imitated and the underlying mechanisms. *Developmental Psychology, 25,* 954–962.

Melzack, R. (1976). Pain: Past, present, and future. In M. Weisenberg & B. Tursky (Eds.), *Pain: New perspectives in therapy and research.* New York: Plenum.

Melzack, R. (1990, Special Issue). The tragedy of needless pain. *Medicine,* pp. 45–51.

Melzack, R. (1989). Phantom limbs, the self and the brain (the D. O. Hebb Memorial Lecture). *Canadian Psychology, 30(1),* 1–16.

Melzack, R., & Wall, P. D. (1982). *The challenge of pain.* New York: Basic.

Mendolia, M., & Kleck, R. E. (1993). Effects of talking about a stressful event on arousal: Does what we talk about make a difference? *Journal of Personality and Social Psychology, 64,* 283–292.

Merikle, P. M. (1992). Perception without awareness. *American Psychologist, 47,* 792–795.

Mestre, D. R., Brouchon, M., Ceccaldi, M., & Poncet, M. (1992). Perception of optical flow in cortical blindness: A case report. *Neuropsychologia, 30,* 783–795.

Metzger, A. M. (1980). A methodological study of the Kübler-Ross stage theory. *Omega, 10,* 291–301.

Meyer, A. J., Maccoby, N., & Farquhar, J. W. (1980). Skills training in a cardiovascular health education campaign. *Journal of Consulting and Clinical Psychology, 48,* 129–142.

Meyer, J.P. (1988). Organizational psychology in the 1980s: A Canadian perspective. Special Issue: Industrial/organizational psychology in Canada. *Canadian Psychology, 29(1),* 18–29.

Meyer, J.P., Allen, N.J., Gellatly, I.R. (1990). Affective and continuance commitment to the organizatio: Evaluation of measures and analysis of concurrent and time-lagged relations. *Journal of Applied Psychology, 75(6),* 710–720.

Meyer, J.P., Allen, N.J., Smith, C.A. (1993). Commitment to organizations and occupations: Extension and test of a three-component conceptualization. *Journal of Applied Psychology, 78(4),* 538–551.

Miceli, M. P., & Lane, M. C. (1991). Antecedents of pay satisfaction: A review and extensions. In K. Rowland & O. R. Ferris (Eds.), *Research in personnel and human resources management* (Vol. 9, pp. 235–309). Greenwich, CT: JAI Press.

Miklowitz, D. J., Goldstein, M. J., Doane, J. A., Neuchterlein, K. H., Strachan, A. M., Snyder, K. S., & Magana-Amato, A. (1989). Is expressed emotion an index of a transactional process? I. Parents, affective style. *Family Process, 22,* 153–167.

Milgram, S. (1963). Behavioral study of obedience. *Journal of Abnormal and Social Psychology, 67,* 371–378.

Milgram, S. (1974). *Obedience to authority.* New York: Harper.

Milgram, S., Liberty, H.J., Toledo, R., Wackenhut, J. (1986). Response to intrusion into waiting lines. Journal of *Personality and Social Psychology, 51(4),* 683–689. © by the American Psychological Association. Reprinted by permission.

Millan, M. J. (1986). Multiple opioid systems and pain. *Pain, 27,* 303–347.

Millar, K. U., & Millar, M. G. (1988). Sex differences in perceived self- and other-disclosure: A case where inequity increases satisfaction. *Social Behavior and Personality, 16,* 59–64.

Millar, M.G., Millar, K.U., Tesser, A. (1988). The effects of helping and focus of attention on mood states. *Personality and Social Psychology Bulletin, 14(3),* 536–543.

Millar, W.J. & Hunter, L. 1990. Relationship between socioeconomic status and household smoking patterns in Canada. *American Journal of Health Promotion, 5(1),* 36–43.

Miller, D. T., & McFarland, C. (1987). Counterfactual thinking and victim compensation: A test of norm theory. *Personality and Social Psychology Bulletin, 12,* 513–519.

Miller, D.T., Ross, M. (1975). Self-serving biases in the attribution of causality: Fact or fiction? *Psychological Bulletin, 82(2),* 213–225.

Miller, L. (1987). The emotional brain. *Psychology Today, 22,* 35–42.

Miller, L. L., Cornelius, T., & McFarland, D. (1978). Marijuana: An analysis of storage and retrieval deficits in memory with the technique of restricted reminding. *Pharmacology, Biochemistry, and Behavior, 8,* 441–457.

Miller, M. E., & Bowers, K. S. (1993). Hypnotic analgesia: Dissociated experience or dissociated control? *Journal of Abnormal Psychology, 102,* 29–38.

Miller, N. E. (1985). The value of behavioral research on animals. *American Psychologist, 40,* 423–440.

Miller, N., Maruyama, G., Beaber, R.J., Valone, K. (1976). Speed of speech and persuasion. *Journal of Personality and Social Psychology, 34(4),* 615–624.

Miller, P.H., Zalenski, R., (1982). Preschooler's knowledge about attention. *Developmental Psychology, 18(6),* 871–875.

Miller, R. S. (1991). On decorum in close relationships: Why aren't we polite to those we love? *Contemporary Social Psychology, 15,* 63–65.

Miller, S.B. (1992). Affective moderators of the cardiovascular response to stress in offspring of hypertensives. *Journal of Psychosomatic Research, 36(2),* 149–157.

Millon, T. (1991). Classification psychopathology: Rationale, alternatives, and standards. *Journal of Abnormal Psychology, 100,* 245–261.

Milner, B. (1974). Hemispheric specialization: Scope and limits. In F. O. Schmitt & F. G. Worden (Eds.), *The neurosciences: Third study program* (pp. 75–89). Cambridge, MA: MIT Press.

Milner, B., Corkin, S., & Teuber, H.-L. (1968). Further analysis of the hippocampal amnesic syndrome: 14-year follow-up study of H.M. *Neuropsychologia, 1968, 6,* 215–234.

Minami, H., & Dallenbach, K. M. (1946). The effect of activity upon learning and retention in the cockroach. *American Journal of Psychology, 59,* 1–58.

Minkoff, H., Deepak, N., Menez, R., & Fikrig, S. (1987). Pregnancies resulting in infants with acquired immunodeficiency syndrome or AIDS-related complex: Follow-up of mothers, children, and subsequently born siblings. *Obstetrics and Gynecology, 69,* 288–291.

Minuchin, P., & Shapiro, E. K. (1983). The school as a context for social development. In P. Mussen & E. M. Heatherington (Eds.), *Handbook of child psychology* (Vol. 4, 4th ed., pp. 197–172). New York: Wiley.

Minuchin, S., & Fishman, H. C. (1981). *Family therapy techniques.* Cambrdige, MA: Harvard University Press.

Mischel, W. (1977). On the future of personality measurement. *American Psychologist, 32,* 246–254.

Mischel, W. (1985). *Personality: Lost or found? Identifying when individual differences make a difference.* Paper presented at the meetings of the American Psychological Association, Los Angeles.

Mistlberger, R.E. (1991). Sceduled daily exercise or feeding alters the phase of photic entrainment in syrian hamsters. *Physiology and Behavior, 50,* 1257–1260.

Mistlberger, R.E. (1992). Nonphotic entrainment of circadian activity rhythms in suprachiasmatic nuclei-ablated hamsters. *Behavioral Neuroscience, 106,* 192–202.

Mistler-Lachman, J. L. (1975). Queer sentences, ambiguity, and levels of processing. *Memory and Cognition, 3,* 395–400.

Mitchell, D. J., Russo, J. E., & Pennington, N. (1989). Back to the future: Temporal perspective in the explanation of events. *Journal of Behavioral Decision Making. 2,* 25–38.

Mitchell, H. (1988, February). Why are women still dying of cervical cancer? *Australian Society,* pp. 34–35.

Mitchell, T. R. (1983). Expectancy-value models in organizational psychology. In N. Feather (Ed.), *Expectancy, incentive, and action* (pp. 293–314). Hillsdale, NJ: Erlbaum.

Mitchell, T. R., Green, S. G., & Wood, R. S. (1982). An attributional model of leadership and the poor performing subordinate: Development and validation. In B. M. Staw and L. L. Cummings (Eds.), *Research in organizational behavior* (Vol. 3). Greenwich, CT: JAI Press.

Mitchell, T. R., & Larson, J. R., Jr. (1987). *People in organizations: An introduction to organizational behavior* (3rd ed.). New York: McGraw-Hill.

Mittelstaetd, M. (1993, June 17). Ontario revamps psychiatric care. *The Globe and Mail*, p. A10.

Miura, I., & Okamoto, Y. (1989). Comparisons of U.S. and Japanese first graders' cognitive representation of number and understanding of place value. *Journal of Educational Psychology, 81,* 109–113.

Moffitt, A., Kramer, M., & Hoffmann, R. (Eds.). (1993). The *Functions of Dreaming.* Albany: SUNY Press.

Mogg, K., Bradley, B. P., Williams, R., & Mathews, A. (1993). Subliminal processing of emotional information in anxiety and depression. *Journal of Abnormal Psychology, 102,* 304–311.

Moghaddam, F.M., Stringer, P. (1987). Out-group similarity and inter-group bias. *Journal of Social Psychology, 128(1),* 105–115.

Momtahan, K., Hetu, R., Tansley, B. (1993). Audibility and identification of auditory alarms in the operating room and intensive care unit. *Ergonomics, 36(10),* 1159–1176.

Money, J. (1980). *Love and love sickness.* Baltimore: Johns Hopkins University Press.

Money, J. (1985). *Pornography as related to criminal sex offenses and the history of medical degeneracy theory.* Paper presented at the U.S. Justice Department Hearings, Houston.

Money, J., & Ehrhardt, A. A. (1972). *Man and woman, boy and girl.* Baltimore: Johns Hopkins University Press.

Monk, T. H., & Folkard, S. (1983). Circadian rhythms and shiftwork. In G. R. J. Hockey (Ed.), *Stress and fatigue in human performance* (pp. 97–121). New York: Wiley.

Monroe, L. R. (1990, January 3). Listen to the music: Headsets for children strike a harmful note. *Los Angeles Times,* p.3.

Moore, B. C. J. (1982). *An introduction to the psychology of hearing* (2nd ed.). New York: Academic.

Moore, C., Corkum, V. (1994). Social Understanding at the end of the first year of life. *Developmental Review, 14.*

Moore-Ede, M. C., Sulzman, F. M., & Fuller, C. A. (1982). *The clocks that time us.* Cambridge, MA: Harvard University Press.

Moran, G., Pederson, D.R., Pettit, P., Krupka, A., (1992). Maternal sensitivity and infant-mother attachment in a developmentally delayed sample. *Infant Behavior and Development, 15(4),* 427–442.

Moran, J. S., Janes, H. R., Peterman, T. A., & Stone, K. M. (1990). Increase in condom sales following AIDS education and publicity, United States. *American Journal of Public Health, 80,* 607–608.

Moran, S.M., Cockram, L.L., Walker, B., McPherson, F.M. (1990). Prediction of survival by the Clifton Assessment Procedures for the elderly (CAPE). *British Journal of Clinical Psychology, 29(2),* 225–226.

Moray, N. (1959). Attention in dichotic listening: Affective cues and the influence of instruction. *Quarterly Journal of Experimental Psychology, 11,* 59–60.

Moreland, R. L., & Beach, S. R. (1992). Exposure effects in the classroom: the development of affinity among students. *Journal of Experimental Social Psychology, 28,* 255–276.

Morganstern, K. P. (1973). Implosive therapy and flooding procedures: A critical review. *Psychological Bulletin, 79,* 318–334.

Morris, B., et al. (1993). as in: Genetic Link to obesity could lead to therapy, by Chris Pritchard, Medical Post, February, 1993, page 24.

Morris, G.B., (1993). A rational-emotive treatment program with conduct disorder and attention deficit hyperactivity disorder adolescents. *Journal of Rational-Emotive and Cognitive Behavioral Therapy, 11(3),* 123–134.

Morris, W.N., Miller, R.S. (1975). The effects of consensus-breaking and consensus-preempting partners on reduction of conformity. *Journal of Experimental Social Psychology, 11(3),* 215–223.

Morrison, R. L., Bellack, A. S., & Mueser, K. T. (1988). Deficits in facial-affect recognition in schizophrenia. *Schizophrenia Bulletin, 14,* 67–83.

Morrongiello, B.A., Clifton, R.K., (1984). Effects of sound frequency on behavioral and cardiac orienting in newborn- and five-month-old infants. *Journal of Experimental Child Psychology, 38(3),* 429–446.

Morrow, K. B., & Sorell G. T. (1989). Factors affecting self-esteem, depression, and negative behaviors in sexually abused female adolescents. *Journal of Marriage and the Family, 51,* 677–686.

Morse, J. M., & Morse, R. M. (1988). Cultural variation in the inference of pain. *Journal of Cross Cultural Psychology, 19,* 232–242.

Moscarello, R. (1991). Posttraumatic stress disorder after sexual assault: its psychodynamics and treatment. *Journal of the American Academy of Psychoanalysis, 19(2),* 235–253.

Moscovitch, M. (1985). Memory from infancy to old age: Implications for theories of normal and pathological memory. *Annals of the New York Academy of Sciences, 444,* 79–96.

Motley, M. T., & Camden, C. T. (1985). Nonlinguistic influences on lexical selection: Evidence from double entendres. *Communication Monographs, 52,* 124–135.

Motowidlo, S. J., Packard, J. S., & Manning, M. R. (1986). Occupational stress: Its causes and consequences for job performance. *Journal of Applied Psychology, 71,* 618–629.

Mottron, L., & Belleville, S. (1993). A study of perceptual analysis in a high-level autistic subjects with exceptional graphic ability. *Brain and Cognition, 23,* 279–309.

Mrosovsky, N. (1986). Sleep researchers caught napping. *Nature, 319,* 536–537.

Mrosovsky, N. (1988). Seasonal affective disorder, hibernation, and annual cycles in animals: Chipmunks in the sky. *Journal of Biological Rhythms, 3,* 189–207.

Muir, D. W. & Mitchell, D. E. (1974) Behavioral deficits in cats following early selected visual exposure to contours of a single orientation. *Brain Research, 85,* 459–477.

Mullaney, D. J., Johnson, L. C., Naitoh, P., Friedman, J. K., & Globus, G. G. (1977). Sleep during and after gradual sleep reduction. *Psychophysiology, 14,* 237–244.

Mumby, D.G., Pinel, J.P. & Wood, E.R. (1990). Nonrecurring-items delayed nonmatching-to-sample in rats: A new paradigm for testing nonspatial working memory. *Psychobiology, 18,* 321–326.

Munsinger, H. A. (1978). The adopted child's IQ: A crucial review. *Psychological Bulletin, 82,* 623–659.

Murdoch, D. D., & Pihl, R. O. (1988). The influence of beverage type on aggression in males in the natural setting. *Aggressive Behavior, 14,* 325–335.

Murdoch, D., Pihl, R.O. & Ross, D. (1990). Alcohol and crimes of violence: present issues. *International Journal of the Addictions, 25(9),* 1065–1081.

Murphy, J. M. (1980). Continuities in community-based psychiatric epidemiology. *Archives of General Psychiatry, 37,* 1215–1223.

Murphy K. R., & Cleveland, N. J. (1991). *Performance appraisal: An organizational perspective.* Boston: Allyn and Bacon.

Murphy, K.R., Jako, R.A., Anhalt, R.L. (1993). Nature and consequences of halo error: a critical analysis. *Journal of Applied Psychology, 78(2),* 218–225.

Murrey, G. J., Cross, H. J., & Whipple, J. (1992). Hypnotically created pseudomemories: Further investigation into the "memory distortion or response bias" question. *Journal of Abnormal Psychology, 101,* 75–77.

Muter, Furedy, Vincent, & Pelcowitz (1993). User-Hostile Systems and Patterns of Psychophysiological Activity. *Computers in Human Activity, 9,* 105–111. Reprinted with kind permission from Elsevier Science Ltd, The Boulevard, Langford Lane, Kidlington OXS 1GB, UK

Myers, M.F. (1991). Marital therapy with HIV-infected men and their wives. *Psychiatric Annals, 21(8),* 466–470.

Myers, T., Orr, K.W., Locker, D., Jackson, E.A. (1993), Factors affecting gay and bisexual men's decisions and intentions to seek HIV testing. *American Journal of Public Health, 83(5),* 701–704.

Nadis, S. (1992, February). The energy-efficient brain: PET scans reveal how the brain delegates mental tasks. *Omni,* p. 16.

Nagar, D., Pandey, J. (1987). Affect and performance on cognitive task as a function of crowding and noise. *Journal of Applied Social Psychology, 17(2),* 147–157.

Nagar, D., Pandey, J., Paulus, P.B. (1988). The effects of residential crowding experience on reactivity to laboratory crowding and noise. *Journal of Applied Social Psychology, 18(16, pt 2),* 1423–1442.

Naglieri, J. A., & Das, J. P. (1990). Planning, attention, simultaneous and successive (PASS) cognitive processes. *Journal of Psychoeducational Assessment, 8,* 303–337.

Nakajima, S. & O'Regan, N.B. (1991). The effects of dopaminergic agonists and antagonists on the frequency-response function for hypothalamic self-stimulation in the rat. *Pharmacology, Biochemistry and Behavior, 39,* 465–468.

Nakajima, S. (1986). Suppression of operant responding in the rat by dopamine D1 receptor blockade with SCH 23390. *Physiological Psychology, 14,* 111–114.

Nakajima, S., Liu, S., & Lau, C.L. (1993). Synergistic interaction of D1 and D2 dopamine receptors in the modulation of the reinforcing effect of brain stimulation. *Behavioral Neuroscience, 107(1),* 161–165.

Nanson, J.L., Hiscock, M., (1990). Attention deficits in children exposed to alcohol prenatally. *Alcoholism-Clinical and Experimental Research, 14(5),* 656–661.

Naranjo, C.A. & Bremner, K.E. (1993). Behavioral correlates of alcohol intoxication. *Addiction, 88(1),* 25–35.

Nash, J. E., & Persaud, T. V. N. (1988). Embryopathic risks of cigarette smoking. *Experimental Pathology, 33,* 65–73.

Nathan, B.R., Tippins, N. (1990). The consequences of halo "error" in performance ratings: A field study of the moderating effect of halo on test validation results. *Journal of Applied Psychology, 75(3),* 290–296.

Nathans, J. (1989). The genes for color vision. *Scientific American, 260,* 42–49.

Nathans, J., Thomas, D., & Hogness, D. S. (1986). Molecular genetics of human color vision: The genes encoding blue, green, and red pigments. *Science, 232,* 193–202.

National Institutes of Mental Health. (1985). *Electroconvulsive therapy: Consensus development conference statement.* Bethesda, MD: Office of Medical Applications of Research.

Navarro, R. (1990). *Sound pressure levels of portable stereo headphones.* Indianapolis: Ear Institute of Indiana.

Neale, J. H., Barker, J. L., Uhl, G. R., & Snyder, S. H. (1978). Enkephalin-containing neurons visualized in spinal cord cultures. *Science, 201,* 467–469.

Neale, M. A., & Bazerman, M. H. (1985). The effects of framing and negotiator overconfidence on bargaining behaviors and outcomes. *Academy of Management Journal, 28,* 34–49.

Nebeker, D. M., & Tatum, B. C. (1993). The effects of computer monitoring, standards, and rewards on work performance, job satisfaction, and stress. *Journal of Applied Social Psychology, 23,* 508–536.

Neimeyer, G. J., & Banikiotes, P. G. (1981). Self-disclosure flexibility, empathy, and perceptions of adjustment and attraction. *Journal of Counseling Psychology, 28,* 272–275.

Neisser, U. (1991). A case of misplaced nostalgia. *American Psychologist, 46,* 34–36.

Nelson, E.D. (1992). "Employment equity" and the red queen's hypothesis: Recruitment and hiring in Western Canadian municipal police departments. *Canadian Police College Journal, 16(3),* 184–203.

Nelson, M. J., Lamke, T. A., & French, J. L. (1973). *The Henmon-Nelson Tests of Mental Ability.* Riverside, CA: Riverside Publishing.

Nelson, T.M., Evelyn, B. & Taylor, R. (1992). Experimental intercomparisons of younger and older driver perception. *International Journal of Aging and Human Development, 36(3),* 239–253.

Netting, N.S. (1992). Sexuality in youth culture: Identity and change. *Adolescence, 27(108),* 961–976.

Neugarten, B. L. (1979). Time, age, and the life cycle. *American Journal of Psychiatry, 136,* 887–894.

Neugarten, B. L. (1987). The changing meaning of age. *Psychology Today, 21,* 29–33.

Newell, A., & Rosenbloom, P. S. (1981). Mechanisms of skill acquisition and the law of practice. In J. R. Anderson (Ed.), *Cognitive skills and their acquisition* (pp. 1–55). Hillsdale, NJ: Erlbaum.

Newman, J. P., Widom, C. S., & Nathan, S. (1985). Passive avoidance in syndromes of disinhibition: Psychopathy and extraversion. *Journal of Personality and Social Psychology, 48,* 1316–1327.

Ney, P.G., Fung, T. & Wickett, A.R. (1993). Child neglect: The precursor to child abuse. *Pre- and Peri-Natal Psychology Journal, 8(2),* 95–112.

Nhundu, T.J. (1992). Job performance, role clarity, and satisfaction among teacher interns in the Edmonton Public School System. *Alberta Journal of Educational Research, 38(4),* 335–354.

Nicher & Parker. (1994). *Psychology Today,* September/October 1994, page 9.

Nicholls, A.L., Kennedy, J.M., (1992). Drawing development: From similarity of features to direction. *Child Development, 63(1),* 227–241. © Society for Research in Child Development Inc.

Nichols, M. (1994). Questioning Prozac. *Maclean's 107,* 36–41.

Nicoli, S. E., & Gottesman, I. I. (1983). Clues to the genetics and neurobiology of schizophrenia. *American Scientist, 71,* 398–404.

Niedenthal, P. M. (1990). Implicit perception of affective information. *Journal of Experimental Social Psychology, 26,* 505–527.

Nielsen, T.A. (1993). Changes in the kinesthetic content of dreams following somatosensory stimulation of leg muscles during REM sleep. *Dreaming Journal of the Association for the Study of Dreams. 3,* 99–113.

Nietzel, M. T., & Himelein, M. J. (1986). Prevention of crime and delinquency. In B. A. Edelstein and L. Mitchelson (Eds.), *Handbook of prevention.* New York: Plenum.

Nilsson, L. G., & Cohen, R. L. (1988). Enrichment and generation in the recall of enacted and non-enacted instructions. In M. M. Gruneberg, P. E. Morris, & R. N. Sykes (Eds.), *Practical aspects of memory: Current research and issues: Vol. 1. Memory in everyday life* (pp. 427–432). Chichester, England: John Wiley & Sons.

Nisbett, R. E. (1990). Evolutionary psychology, biology, and cultural evolution. *Motivation and Emotion, 14,* 255–264.

Noble, B. P. (1993, June 13). Staying bright-eyed in the wee hours. *New York Times,* pp. F1, F11.

Noble, E.K., et al. (1994). as in: Big Brothers find gene blamed for obesity, by Susan Peterson, *Toronto Star,* March 15, 1994, page C2

Nolen-Hoeksema, S. (1987). Sex differences in unipolar depression: Evidence and theory. *Psychological Bulletin, 101,* 259–282.

Nolen-Hoeksema, S. (1990). *Sex differences in depression.* Stanford, CA: Stanford University Press.

Noller, P., Law, H., & Comrey A. L. (1987). Cattell, Comrey, and Eysenck personality factors compared: More evidence for the five robust factors? *Journal of Personality and Social Psychology, 53,* 775–782.

Norman, D. A., & Shallice, T. (1985). Attention to action: Willed and automatic control of behavior. In R. J. Davidson, G. E. Schwartz, & D. Shapiro (Eds.), *Consciousness and self-regulation: Vol. 4. Advances in research and theory* (pp. 2–18). New York: Plenum Press.

Norris, F. H., & Murrell, S. A. (1990). Social support, life events, and stress as modifiers of adjustment to bereavement by older adults. *Psychology and Aging, 5,* 429–436.

Norris, F. H., & Uhl, G. A. (1993). Chronic stress as a mediator of acute stress: The case of hurricane Hugo. *Journal of Applied Social Psychology, 23,* 1263–1284.

Northcraft, G. B., & Neale, M. A. (1987). Experts, amateurs, and real estate: An anchoring-and-adjustment perspective on property pricing in decision. *Organizational Behavior and Human Decision Processes, 39,* 94–97.

Norton, A., & Moorman, J. E. (1987). Current trends in marriage and divorce among American women. *Journal of Marriage and the Family, 49,* 3–14.

Novick, B. E. (1989). Pediatric AIDS: A medical overview. In J. M. Seibert & R. A. Olson (Eds.), *Children, adolescents, and AIDS* (pp. 1–23). Lincoln: University of Nebraska Press.

Nyhan, W. L. (1987). Phenylalanine and mental retardation (PKU). In G. Adelman (Ed.), *Encyclopedia of neuroscience* (Vol. 2, pp. 940–942). Boston: Birkhauser.

O'Brien, S.J. & Vertinsky, P.A. (1991). Unfit survivors: exercise as a resource for aging women. *Gerontologist, 31(3),* 347–357.

O'Brien-Cousins, S., as in Tomboys can beat the aging odds, by Liane Faulder, *Vancouver Sun,* February 27,1993, D16.

O'Connor, B.P, Dyce, J. (1993). Appraisals of musical ability in bar bands: Identifying the weak link in the looking-glass self chain. *Basic and Applied Social Psychology, 14(1),* 69–86.

Offer, D., & Sabshin, M. (1984). Adolescence: empirical perspectives. In D. Offer & M. Sabshin (Eds.), *Normality and the life cycle.* New York: Basic Books.

Ofshe, R. J. (1992). Inadvertent hypnosis during interrogation: False confession due to dissociative state, misidentified multiple personality, and the satanic cult hypothesis. *International Journal of Clinical and Experimental Hypnosis, 40,* 125–156.

Ogloff, J. R., & Wong, S. (1990). Electrodermal and cardiovascular evidence of a coping response in psychopaths. *Criminal Justice and Behavior, 17,* 231–245.

Ogloff, J.R.P. (1990). Law and psychology in Canada: The need for training and research. *Canadian Psychology, 31(1),* 61–73.

Ogus, E.D. (1992). Burnout and coping strategies: a comparative study of ward nurses. *Journal of Social Behavior and Personality, 7(1),* 111–124.

Olders, H. (1989). Mourning and grief as healing processes in psychotherapy. *Canadian Journal of Psychiatry, 34(4),* 271–278.

Olioff, M., Aboud, F.E., (1991). Predicting postpartum dysphoria in primiparous mothers: Roles of perceived parenting self- efficacy and self-esteem. *Journal of Cognitive Psychotherapy, 5(1),* 3–14.

Oliver, M. B., & Hyde, J. S. (1993). Gender differences in sexuality: A meta-analysis. *Psychological Bulletin, 114,* 29–51.

Olson, J.M., Zanna, M.P. (1993). Attitudes and attitude change. Annual Review of Psychology, 44, 117–154.

Olsson, P. A. (1989). Psychodrama and group therapy approaches to alexithymia. In D. A. Halperin (Ed.), *Group Psychodynamics: New paradigms and new perspectives.* Chicago: Year Book Medical.

Ondrack, D.A., Evans, M.G. (1986). Job enrichment and job satisfaction in quality of working life and nonquality of working life work sites. *Human Relations, 39(9),* 871–889.

Ondrack, D.A., Evans, M.G. (1987). Job enrichment and job satisfaction in greenfield and redesign QWL sites. *Group and Organization Studies, 12(1),* 5–22.

O'Neill, P., Duffy, C., Enman, M., Blackmer, E., & Goodwin, J. (1988). Cognition and citizen participation in social action. *Journal of Applied Social psychology, 18,* 1067–1083.

Orbach, I., Kedem, P., Gorchover, O., Apter, A., & Tyano, S. (1993). Fears of death in suicidal and nonsuicidal adolescents. *Journal of Abnormal Psychology, 102,* 553–558.

Organ, D. W. (1988). *Organizational citizenship behavior: The good soldier syndrome.* Lexington, MA: Lexington Books.

Orlinsky, D. E., & Howard, K. E. (1987). The relation of process to outcome in psychotherapy. In S. L. Garfield & A. E. Bergin (Eds.), *Handbook of psychotherapy and behavior change* (3rd ed.). New York: Wiley.

Orlofsky, J. L., & O'Heron, C. A. (1987). Stereotypic and nonstereotypic sex role trait and behavior orientations: Implications for personal adjustment. *Journal of Personality and Social Psychology, 52,* 1034–1042.

Ornsetin, M. (1989). *AIDS in Canada: Knowledge, behavior, and attitudes of adults.* Toronto: University of Toronto Press.

Ostroff, C. (1992). The relationship between satisfaction, attitudes, and performance: An organizational level analysis. *Journal of Applied Psychology, 77(6),* 963–974.

Osterwell, Z., & Nagano-Nakamura, I. K. (1992). Maternal views on aggression: Japan and Israel. *Aggressive Behavior, 18,* 263–270.

O'Sullivan, J.T., (1993). Preschooler's beliefs about effort, incentives, and recall. *Journal of Experimental Child Psychology, 53(3),* 396–414.

O'Sullivan, L. F. and Byers, E. S. (1993). Eroding stereotypes: College women's attempts to influence reluctant male sexual partners. *Journal of Sex Research, 30,* 270-282.

Otaki, M., Durrett, M., Richards, P., Nyquist, L., & Pennebaker, J. (1986). Maternal and infant behavior in Japan and America: A partial replication. *Journal of Cross-Cultural Psychology, 17,* 251–268.

Otis, A. S., & Lennon, R. T. (1967). *The Otis-Lennon Mental Ability Tests.* Los Angeles: Psychological Corp.

Oulette-Kobasa, S. C., & Puccetti, M. C. (1983). Personality and social resources in stress resistance. *Journal of Personality and Social Psychology, 45,* 836–850.

Page, J. B., Fletcher, J., & True, W. R. (1988). Psychosociocultural perspectives on chronic cannabis use: The Costa Rica follow-up. *Journal of Psychoactive Drugs, 20,* 57–65.

Page, N. R., & Wiseman, R. L. (1993). Supervisory behavior and worker satisfaction in the United States, Mexico, and Spain. *Journal of Business Communication, 30,* 161–180.

Paivio, A. (1983).The mind's eye in arts and science. *Poetics ,12,* 1–18

Paivio, A. (1990). *Mental representations: A dual coding approach.* New York: Oxford.

Palmer, C.T. (1993). Anger, aggression, and humor in Newfoundland floor hockey: an evolutionary analysis. *Aggressive Behavior, 19(3),* 167–173.

Palmer, S. E. (1992). Common region: A new principle of perceptual grouping. *Cognitive Psychology, 24,* 436–447.

Pancer, S.M., Brown, S.D., Gregor, P., Claxton-Oldfield, S.P. (1992). Causal attributions and the perception of political figures. *Canadian Journal of Behavioural Science, 24(3),* 371–381.

Pare, D. (1990). The EAP cross-cultural counselling. *Human Resource, 7(1),* 11.

Park, B., & Fink, C. (1989). A social relations analysis of agreement in liking judgments. *Journal of Personality and Social Psychology, 56,* 506–518.

Parker, L. E., & Lepper, M. R. (1992). The effects of fantasy contexts on children's learning and motivation: Making learning more fun. *Journal of Personality and Social Psychology, 62,* 625–633.

Passman, R.H., Weisberg, P., (1975). Mothers and blankets as agents for promoting play and exploration by young children in a novel environment: The effects of social and nonsocial attachment objects. *Developmental Psychology, 11(2),* 170–177.

Pastor, D. L. (1981). The quality of mother-infant attachment and its relationship to toddlers' initial sociability with peers. *Developmental Psychology, 17,* 326–335.

Patrick, C. J., Bradley, M. M., & Lang, P. J. (1993). Emotion in the criminal psychopath: Startle reflex modulation. *Journal of Abnormal Psychology, 102,* 83–92.

Patrick, C.J. & Iacono, W.G. (1989). Psychopathy, threat, and polygraph test accuracy. *Journal of Applied Psychology, 74(2),* 347–355.

Patterson, F. (1978). Conversations with a gorilla. *National Geographic, 154,* 438–465.

Paul, G. L. (1982). *The development of a "transportable" system of behavioral assessment for chronic patients.* Invited address, University of Minnesota, Minneapolis.

Paul, G. L., & Lentz, R. J. (1977). *Psychosocial treatment of chronic mental patients: Milieu versus social-learning programs.* Cambridge, MA: Harvard University Press.

Paul, J. (1990). *Critical thinking: What every person needs to survive in a rapidly changing world.* Rohnert Park, CA: Sonoma State University.

Paul, S. M. (1985). The Advanced Raven's Progressive Matrices: Normative data for an American university population and an examination of the relationship with Spearman's "g." *Journal of Experimental Education, 54,* 95–100.

Pavlov, I. P. (1927). Conditioned reflexes. (G. V. Anrep, Trans.). London: Oxford University Press.

Payne, D.G. (1987). Hyperamnesia and reminiscence in recall: A historical and empirical review. *Psychological Bulletin, 101,* 5–27.

Pearce, J. M. (1986). A model for stimulus generalization in Pavlovian conditioning. *Psychological Review, 94,* 61–73.

Pederson, D.R., Moran, G., Sitka, C., Compbell, K., Ghesquire, K., Acton, H. (1990). Maternal sensitivity and the security of infant-mother attachment: A Q-sort study. *Child Development, 61(6),* 1974–1983.

Pegg, J.E., Werker, J.F., McLeod, P.J., (1992). Preference for infant-directed over adult-directed speech: Evidence from 7 week-old infants. *Infant Behavior and Development, 15(3),* 325–345.

Pelletier, K. R. (1986). Longevity: What can centenarians teach us? In K. Dychtwald (Ed.), *Wellness and health promotion for the elderly.* Rockville, MD: Aspen Publishers.

Pelletier, L.G., & Vallerand, R.J. (1990). L'Echelle Revisee de Conscience de Soi: Une traduction et une validitation Canadienne-Francaise due Revised Self-Consiousness Scale. (The Revised Self-Consciousness Scale: A translation and a French Canadian validation of the Revised Self-Consciousness scale.) *Canadian Journal of Behavioural Science, 22,* 191–206.

Pelsser, R. 1991. La method des cas dans l'apprentissage de la relation patient-medecin. Discussion of clinical cases in doctor-patient relationship training. 33rd Colloquium of the French Language Medical Psychology Society: pedagogy and medical psychology for the doctor... for the patient (1990, Montreal). *Psychologie Medicale, 23(6),* 615–617.

Pendleton, M.G., Batson, C.D. (1979). Self-presentation and the door-in-the-face technique for inducing compliance. *Personality and Social Psychology Bulletin, 5(1),* 77–81.

Penfield, W. & Milner, B. (1958). Memory deficit produced by bilateral lesions in the hippocampal zone. *Archives of Neurology & Psychiatry. 79,* 475–497.

Pennebaker, J. W. (1983). Accuracy of symptom perception. In A. Baum, S. E. Taylor, & J. Singer (Eds.), *Handbook of psychology and health* (Vol. 4, pp. 189–218). Hillsdale, NJ: Erlbaum.

Pennebaker, J. W. (1990). *Opening up: The healing power of confiding in others.* New York: William Morrow.

Pennebaker, J. W., Hughes, C. F., & O'Heeron, R. C. (1987). The psychophysiology of confession: Linking inhibitory and psychosomatic processes. *Journal of Personality and Social Psychology, 52,* 718–793.

Pennebaker, J. W., Kiecolt-Glaser, J. H. K., & Glaser, R. (1988). Disclosure of traumas and immune function: Health implications for psychotherapy. *Journal of Consulting and Clinical Psychology, 56,* 239–245.

Perceived benefits of marathon running in males and females. *Sex Roles, 25(3–4),* 119–127.

Perls, F. S. (1969). *Gestalt therapy verbatim.* Lafayette, CA: Real People Press.

Perry, R.P., Penner, K.S. (1990). Enhancing academic achievement in college students through attributional retraining and instruction. *Journal of Educational Psychology, 82(2),* 262–271.

Persad, S.M. & Polivy, J. (1993). Differences between depressed and non-depressed individuals in the recognition of and response to facial emotional cues. *Journal of Abnormal Psychology, 102(3),* 358–368.

Persinger, M.A. (1993) Transcendental Meditation-super (TM) and general meditation are associated with enhanced complex partial epileptic-like signs: Evidence for "cognitive" kindling? *Perceptual and Motor Skills, 76,* 80–82.

Peters, D.A. (1990). Maternal stress increases fetal brain and neonatal cerebral cortex 5-hydroxytryptamine synthesis in rats: a possible mechanism by which stress influences brain development. *Pharmacology, Biochemistry and Behavior, 35(4),* 943–947.

Peters, J.F. (1987). Youth, family and employment. *Adolescence, 22(86),* 465–473.

Peters, M. (1991). Sex differences in human brain size and the general meaning of differences in brain size. *Canadian Journal of Psychology, 45(4),* 507–522.

Peterson, A. C. (1987, September). Those gangly years. *Psychology Today,* pp. 28–34.

Peterson, L. R., & Peterson, M. J. (1959). Short-term retention of individual verbal items. *Journal of Experimental Psychology, 58,* 193–198.

Peterson, S. E., Fox, P. T., Mintun, M. A., Posner, J. I., & Raichle, M. E. (1989). Studies of the processing of single words using averaged positron emission tomographic measurements of cerebral blood flow change. *Journal of Cognitive Neuroscience, 1,* 153–170.

Petit, D., Montplaisir, J., Lorrain, D., Gauthier, S. (1992). Spectral analysis of the rapid eye movement sleep electroencephalogram in right and left temporal regions: A biological marker of Alzheimer's disease. *Annals of Neurology, 32,* 172–176.

Peto, R., Lopez, A. D., Boreham, J., Thun, M., & Heath, C. (1992). Mortality from tobacco in developed countries: Indirect estimation from national vital statistics. *Lancet, 339,* 1268–1278.

Petty, M. M., Singleton, B., & Connell, D. W. (1992). An experimental evaluation of an organizational incentive plan in the electric utility industry. *Journal of Applied Psychology, 77,* 427–436.

Petty, R. E., & Cacioppo, J. T. (1986). The elaboration likelihood model of persuasion. In L. Berkowitz (Ed.), *Advances in experimental social psychology* (Vol. 19, pp. 123–205). New York: Academic Press.

Pfaffman, C. (1978). The vertebrate phylogyny, neural code, and integrative processess of taste. In E. C. Carterrette & M. P. Friedman (Eds.), *Handbook of perception* (Vol. 6A). New York: Academic.

Pfeiffer, S.M., Wong, P.T. (1989). Multidimensional jealousy. *Journal of Social and Personal Relationships, 6(2),* 181–196.

Phares, V., Compas, B.E., (1992). The role of fathers in child and adolescent psycholathology: Make room for daddy. *Psychological Bulletin, 111(3),* 387–412.

Phillips, D. P., & Brugge, J. F. (1985). Progress in neurophysiology of sound localization. *Annual Review of Psychology, 36,* 245–274.

Phillips, D. P., & Fibiger, H. C. (1989). Neuroanatomical bases of intracranial self-stimulation: Untangling the Gordian knot. In J. M. Leibman & S. J. Cooper (Eds.), *The neuropharmacological bases of reward* (pp. 66–105). Oxford, England: Clarendon Press.

Phillips, D.P. & Fibiger, H.C. (1990). Role of reward and enhancement of conditioned reward in persistance of responding for cocaine. *Behavioral Pharmacology, 1 (4),* 269–282.

Piaget, J. (1965). *The moral judgment of the child.* New York: Free Press. (Original work published 1932.)

Piaget, J. (1975). *The child's conception of the world.* Totowa, NJ: Littlefield, Adams. (Originally published in 1929.)

Pickar, D. (1988). Perspectives on a time-dependent model of neuroleptic action. *Schizophrenia Bulletin 14,* 255–265.

Pierce, C. A. (1992). *The effects of physical attractiveness and height on dating choice: Meta-analysis.* Unpublished masters thesis, University at Albany, State University of New York, Albany.

Pierce, J. P., Macaskill, P., & Hill, D. (1990). Long-term effectiveness of mass media led antismoking campaigns in Australia. *American Journal of Public Health, 80,* 565–569.

Pierce, W.D. (1987). Which Coke is it? Social influence in the marketplace. *Psychological Reports, 60(1),* 279–286.

Pihl, R.O., Peterson, J.B. & Lau, M.A. 1993. A biosocial model of the alcohol-aggression relationship. *Journal of Studies of Alcohol, sep suppl 11,* 128–139.

Pinel, J. P. (1993). *Biopsychology* (2nd ed.). Boston: Allyn and Bacon.

Pinker, S. (1984). Visual cognition: An introduction. *Cognition: International Journal of Cognitive Science, 18,* 1–63.

Piper, W.E. & McCallum, M. 1991. Group interventions for persons who have experienced loss: description and evaluative research. *Group Analysis, 24(4),* 363–373.

Pitman, R. K., Orr, S. P., Forgue, D. F., Altman, B., deJong, J. B., & Hgerz, L. R. (1990). Psychophysiologic responses to combat imagery of Vietnam veterans with posttraumatic stress disorder versus other anxiety disorders. *Journal of Abnormal Psychology, 99,* 49–54.

Pittenger, J.B., Mark, L.S., Johnson, D.F. (1989). Longitudinal stability of facial attractiveness. *Bulletin of the Psychonomic Society, 27(2),* 171–174.

Plante, T. G., & Rodin, J. (1990). Physical fitness and enhanced psychological health. *Current Psychology: Research & Reviews, 9,* 3–24.

Plechaty, M. 1988. A conjugal curriculum vitae method: behavioral assessment and treatment of marital problems. *Psychological Reports, 63(1),* 151–159.

Pliner, P. & Chaiken, S. 1990. Eating, social motives, and self-presentation in women and men. *Journal of Experimental Social Psychology, 26(3),* 240–254.

Plomin, R. (1989). Environment and genes: Determinants of behavior. *American Psychologist, 44,* 105–111.

Plouffe, L. & Gravelle, F. 1989. Age, sex, and personality correlates of self-actualization in elderly adults. *Psychological Reports, 65(2),* 643–647.

Pollack, E. S., Nomura, A. M., Heilbrun, L. K., Stemmermann, G. N., & Green, S. B. (1984). Prospective study of alcohol consumption and cancer. *New England Journal of Medicine, 310,* 617–621.

Pollock, N.L., Hashmall, J.M. (1991). The excuses of child molesters. *Behavioral Sciences and the law, 9(1),* 53–59.

Pomerleau, A., Bolduc, D., Malcuit, G., Cossette, L., (1990). Pink or blue: Environmental gender stereotypes in the first two years of life. *Sex Roles, 22(5–6),* 359–367.

Pomerleau, A., Malcuit, G. Chamberland, C., Laurendeau, M.C., Lamarre, G. (1992). Methodological problems in operant learning research with human infants. *International Journal of Psychology, 27(6),* 417–432.

Pomerleau, O. F., & Pomerleau, C. S. (1984). Neuro-regulators and the reinforcement of smoking: Towards a biobehavioral explanation. *Neuroscience and Biobehavioral Reviews, 8,* 503–513.

Poole, G.D. & Craig, K.D. 1992. Judgements of genuine, suppressed, and faked facial expressions of pain. *Journal of Personality and Social Psychology, 63(5),* 797–805.

Poon, L. W., & Fozard, J. L. (1980). Age and word frequency effects in continuous recognition memory. *Journal of Gerontology, 35,* 77–86.

Pope, K. S., & Vetter, V. A. (1992). Ethical dilemmas encountered by members of the American Psychological Association. *American Psychologist, 47,* 397–411.

Popper, K. (1959). *The logic of scientific discovery.* London: Hutchinson.

Porac, C. & Buller, T. 1990. Overt attempts to change hand preference: a study of group and individual characteristics. *Canadian Journal of Psychology, 44(4),* 512–521.

Porac, C. 1993. Hand preference and the incidence of accidental unilateral hand injury. *Neuropsychologia, 31(4),* 355–362.

Porter, J. & Weisberg, J. 1992. Overcoming destructive societal values in the treatment of anorexia nervosa: an intensive day treatment model. *Journal of Contemporary Psychotherapy, 22(2),* 77–88.

Porter, L. W., & Lawler, E. E., III. (1968). *Managerial attitudes and performance.* Homewood, IL: Dorsey Press.

Porter, L. W., & Steers, R. M. (1973). Organizational work and personal factors in employee turnover and absenteeism. *Psychological Bulletin, 80,* 151–176.

Posner, M. I., & McCandliss, B. D. (1993). Converging methods for investigating lexical access. *Psychological Science, 4,* 305–309.

Postman, L., & Phillips, L. W. (1965). Short-term temporal changes in free recall. *Quarterly Journal of Experimental Psychology, 17,* 132–138.

Poucet, B. (1993). Spatial cognitive maps in animals: New hypotheses on their structure and neural mechanisms. *Psychological Review, 100,* 163–182.

Powell, G. N. (1990). One more time: Do female and male managers differ? *Academy of Management Executive, 4(3),* 68–75.

Powley, T. L., Opsahl, C. A., Cox, J. E., & Weingarten, H. P. (1980). The role of the hypothalamus in energy homeostasis. In P. J. Morgane & J.

Panskepp (Eds.), *Handbook of the hypothalamus. 3A: Behavioral studies of the hypothalamus* (pp. 211–298). New York: Marcel Dekker.

Pranger, T. & Brown, G.T. 1992. Burnout: an issue for psychiatric occupational therapy personnel? *Occupational Therapy in Mental Health, 12(1),* 77–92.

Pratt, M.W., Golding, G., Hunter, W., Norris, J., (1988). From inquiry to judgement: Age and sex differences in patterns of adult moral thinking and information seeking. International *Journal of Aging and Human Development, 27(2),* 109–124.

Pratto, F., John, O.P. (1991). Automatic vigilance: The attention-grabbing power of negative social information. Journal of *Personality and Social Psychology, 61(3),* 380–391.

Preston, R. (1992, October 26). Crisis in the hot zone. *New Yorker,* pp. 58–62, 64–76, 78–81.

Pretty, G.M., McCarthy, M.E., Catano, V.M. (1992). Psychological environments and burnout: Gender considerations within the corporation. *Journal of Organizational Behavior, 13(7),* 701–711.

Priest, K. 1985. Adolescents' response to parents' alcoholism. *Social Casework, 66(9),* 533–539.

Prigatano, G. P. (1992). Personality disturbances associated with traumatic brain injury. *Journal of Consulting and Clinical Psychology, 3,* 360–368.

Pritchard, C. Gene linked to heart attack deaths in fit young patients. *Medical Post, 30(11),* 33.

Pritchard, R. D., Dunnette, M. D., & Jorgenson, D. O. (1972). Effects of perceptions of equity and inequity on work performance and satisfaction. *Journal of Applied Psychology, 57,* 75–94.

Prkachin, K.M. 1992a. The consistency of facial expressions of pain: a comparison across modalities. *Pain, 51(3),* 297–306.

Prkachin, K.M. 1992b. Dissociating spontaneous and deliberate expressions of pain: signal detection analysis. *Pain, 51(1),* 57–65.

Pruitt, D. G., & Rubin, J. Z. (1986). *Social conflict: Escalation, stalemate, settlement.* New York: Random House.

Purvis, A. (1993, December 6). Cursed, yet blessed. *Time,* p. 67.

Putnam, F. W. (1991). Dissociative phenomena. In A. Tasman & S. M. Goldfinger (Eds.), *Review of psychiatry* (Vol. 10, pp. 144–164). Washington, D.C.: American Psychiatric Press.

Putnam, F. W., Guroff, J. J., Silberman, E. K., Barban, L., & Post, R. M. (1986). The clinical phenomenology of multiple personality disorder: Review of 100 recent cases. *Journal of Clinical Psychiatry, 47,* 285–293.

Pyke, S. W. (1992). The more things change … *Canadian Psychology, 33,* 713–720.

Pyke, S. W., & Stark-Ademac, C. (1981). Canadian feminism and psychology: The first decade. *Canadian Psychology, 22,* 35–54.

Pylyshyn, Z. W. (1973). What the mind's eye tells the mind's brain: A critique of mental imagery. *Psychological Bulletin, 80,* 1–24.

Pylyshyn, Z. W. (1981). The imagery debate: Analogue media versus tacit knowledge. *Psychological Review, 88,* 16–45.

Pyryt, M. C. (1993). The fulfillment of promise revisited: A discriminant analysis of factors predicting success in the Terman study. *Roeper Review, 15,* 178–179

Quadrel, M. J. (1990). *Elicitations of adolescents' risk perceptions: Qualitative and quantitative dimensions.* Unpublished doctoral dissertation, Carnegie Mellon University.

Quadrel, M. J., Fischoff, B., & Davis, W. (1993). Adolescent (in)vulnerability. *American Psychologist, 48,* 102–116.

Rabin, M. D., & Cain, W. S. (1984). Determinants of measured olfactory sensitivity. *Perception & Psychophysics, 39,* 281–286.

Rachman, S. J. (1990). The determinants of treatment of simple phobias. *Advances in Behaviour Research and Therapy, 12,* 1–30.

Rachman, S. J. (1991) Neo-conditioning and the classical theory of fear acquisition. *Clinical Psychology Review, 11,* 155–173.

Rachman, S. J., & Hodgson, R. J. (1980). *Obsessions and compulsions.* Englewood Cliffs, NJ: Prentice Hall.

Rae G.Q., & Robson, B.E. 1988. Moderating the morbidity of divorce. *Canadian Journal of Psychiatry, 33(6),* 443–452.

Ragland, D. R., & Brand, R. J. (1988). Type A behavior and mortality from coronary heart disease. *New England Journal of Medicine, 318,* 65–69.

Ramirez, V., & Bartoshuk, L. M. (1987). *Effects of HCl on taste: Possible role in bulimia.* Poster presented at the 95th annual meeting of the American Psychological Association, New York.

Raphael, B., Cubis, J., Dunne, M., Lewin, T., & Kelly, B. (1990). The impact of parental loss on adolescents' psychosocial characteristics. *Adolescence, 25,* 689–700.

Rasmussen, T., & Milner, B. (1975). Excision of Broca's area without persistent aphasia. In K. J. Zulch, O. Creutzfeldt, & G. C. Gailbraith (Eds.), *Central localization* (pp. 258–263). New York: Springer-Verlag.

Raven, J. C. (1977). *Raven Progressive Matrices.* Los Angeles: Psychological Corp.

Raynor, J. O. (1970). Relationships between achievement-related motives, future orientation, and academic performance. *Journal of Personality and Social Psychology, 15,* 28–33.

Raz, S. (1993). Structural cerebral pathology in schizophrenia: Regional or diffuse? *Journal of Abnormal Psychology, 102*, 445–452.

Raz, S., & Raz, N. (1990). Structural brain abnormalities in the major psychoses: A quantitative review of the evidence from computerized imaging. *Psychological Bulletin, 108*, 93–108.

Read, D.E. 1987. Neuropsychological assessment of memory in the elderly. Special issue: Aging and cognition. *Canadian Journal of Psychology, 41(2)*, 158–174.

Reason, J. T., & Lucas, D. (1984). Using cognitive diaries to investigate naturally occurring memory blocks. In J. E. Harris & P. E. Morris (Eds.), *Everyday memory actions and absent-mindedness* (pp. 53–70). London: Academic Press.

Rechtschaffen, A., Gilliland, M. A., Bergmann, B. M., & Winter, J. B. (1983). Physiological correlates of prolonged sleep deprivation in rats. *Science, 221*, 182–184.

Reed, T. E., & Jensen, A. R. (in press). Conduction velocity in a brain nerve pathway of normal adults correlates with intelligence level. *Intelligence*.

Reed, T.E. & Jensen, A.R., 1991. Arm nerve conduction velocity (NCV), brain NCV, reaction time, and intelligence. *Intelligence, 15 (1)*, 33–47.

Reeder, G. D., Fletcher, G. J. O., & Furman, K. (1989). The role of observers: Expectations in attitude attribution. *Journal of Experimental Social Psychology, 25*, 168–188.

Reese, H. W., & Rodeheaver, D. (1985). Problem solving and complex decision making. In J. E. Birren & K. W. Schaie (Eds.), *Handbook of the psychology of aging* (2nd ed., pp. 474–499). New York: Van Nostrand Reinhold.

Reeves, A., & Sperling, G. (1986). Attention gating in short-term retention of individual verbal items. *Psychological Review, 93*, 180–206.

Reich, C., Purbhoo, M. (1975). The effect of cross-cultural contact. *Canadian Journal of Behavioural Science, 7(4)*, 313–327.

Reid, I.S., Crompton, J.L. (1993). A taxonomy of leisure purchase decision paradigms based on level of involvement. *Journal of Leisure Research, 25(2)*, 182–202.

Reid, L. D. (1990). Rates of cocaine addiction among newborns. Personal communication, Rensselaer Polytechnic Institute.

Reid, L. D. (Ed.) (1990). *Opioids, bulimia, and alcohol abuse.* New York: Springer-Verlag.

Reid, L. D., & Carpenter, D. J. (1990). Alcohol-abuse and alcoholism. In L. D. Reid (Ed.), *Opioids, bulimia, and alcohol abuse & alcoholism* (pp. 23–48). New York: Springer-Verlag.

Reifman, A. S., Larrick, R. P., & Fein, S. (1991). Temper and temperature on the diamond: The heat-aggression relationship in major league baseball. *Personality and Social Psychology Bulletin, 17*, 580–585.

Reis, H. T., Senchak, M., & Solomon, B. (1985). Sex differences in the intimacy of social interaction: Further examination of potential explanations. *J, 48*, 1204–1217.

Reissland, N. (1988). Neonatal imitation in the first hour of life: Observations in rural Nepal. *Developmental Psychology, 24*, 464–469.

Reitman, J. S. (1974). Without surreptitious rehearsal, information in short-term memory decays. *Journal of Verbal Learning and Verbal Behavior, 13*, 365–377.

Rensberger, B. (1993, May 3). The quest for machines that not only listen, but also understand. *Washington Post*, p.3.

Rescorla, R. A. (1988). Pavlovian conditioning: It's not what you think it is. *American Psychologist, 43*, 151–160.

Rescorla, R. A., & Wagner, A. R. (1972). A theory of Pavlovian conditioning: Variations in the effectiveness of reinforcement and non-reinforcement. In A. Black & W. F. Prokasy (Eds.), *Classical conditioning: II. Current research and theory.* New York: Appleton.

Resnick, S. M. (1992). Positron emission tomography in psychiatric illness. *Current Directions in Psychological Science, 1*, 92–98.

Rest, J. R., & Thomas, S. J. (1985). Relation of moral judgment to formal education. *Developmental Psychology, 21*, 709–714.

Revusky, S. & Reilly, S. (1990). Dose effects on heart rate conditioning when phenobarbital is the CS and amphetamine is the US. *Pharmacology, Biochemistry and Behavior, 36*, 933–936.

Rice, C. G., Breslin, M., & Roper, R. G. (1987). Sound levels from personal cassette players. *British Journal of Audiology, 21*, 273–278.

Rice, F. P. (1992). *Intimate relationships, marriages, and families.* Mountain View, CA: Mayfield.

Richardsen, A.M., Burke, R.J. (1993). Occupational stress and work satisfaction among Canadian women pysicians. *Psychological Reports, 72(3, pt1)*, 811–821.

Richardson, J. T. E., & Zucco, G. M. (1989). Cognition and olfaction: A review. *Psychological Bulletin, 105(3)*, 352–360.

Richer, S., (1988). Schooling and the gendered subject: An exercise in planned social change. *Canadian Review of Sociology and Anthropology, 25(1)*, 98–107.

Riess, M., Schlenker, B.R. (1977). Attitude change and responsibility avoidance as modes of dilemma resolution in forced-compliance situations. *Journal of Personality and Social Psychology, 35(1)*, 21–30.

Rigby, C. S., Deci, E. L., Patrick, B. C., & Ryan, R. M. (1992). Beyond the intrinsic-extrinsic dichotomy: Self-determination in motivation and learning. *Motivation and Emotion, 16*, 165–185.

Riley, D. A., & Langley, C. M. (1993). The logic of species comparisons. *Psychological Science, 4*, 185–189.

Riley, R. (1992). Mental disorders. *Health Reports, 4*, 201–203.

Robbins, J.M., Kirmayer, L.J. (1991). Attributions of common somatic symptoms. *Psychological Medicine, 21(4)*, 1029–1045.

Robert, M. (1990). Observational learning in fish, birds, and mammals: A classified bibliography spanning over 100 years of research. *Psychological Record, 40*, 289–311.

Roberts, D.C., & Bennett, S.A. 1993. Heroin self-administration in rats under a progerssive ratio schedule of reinforcement. *Psychopharmacology, 111(2)*, 215–218.

Roberts, J.V., Doob, A.N. (1990). News media influences on public views of sentencing. Special Issue: Law and the media. *Law and Human Behavior, 14(5)*, 451–468.

Roberts, P., & Newton, P. M. (1987). Levinsonian studies of women's adult development. *Psychology and Aging, 2*, 154–163.

Roberts, T. A. (1991). Gender and the influence of evaluations on self-assessments in achievement settings. *Psychological Bulletin, 109*, 297–308.

Roberts, T. A., & Nolen-Hoeksema, S. (1990). Gender differences in construals of and responsiveness to evaluations in an achievement situation. Unpublished manuscript, Stanford University.

Robins, L. N., & Regier, D. A. (1991). *Psychiatric disorders in America: The epidemiological catchment area.* New York: The Free Press.

Robinson, D.W., Howe, B.L. (1987). Causal attribution and mood state relationships of soccer players in a sport achievement setting. *Journal of Sport Behavior, 10(3)*, 137–146.

Robinson, L. A., Berman, J. S., & Neimeyer, R. A. (1990). Psychotherapy for the treatment of depression: A comprehensive review of controlled outcome research. *Psychological Bulletin, 108*, 30–49.

Robinson, P.J. & Fleming, S. 1992. Depressotypic cognitive patterns in major depression and conjugal bereavement. *Omega Journal of Death and Dying, 25(4)*, 291–305.

Robinson, R. G., Kubos, K. L., Starr, L. B., Rao, K., & Price, T. R. (1984). Mood disorders in stroke patients: Importance of location of lesion. *Brain, 107*, 81–93.

Robotics Institute. (1984). *Some common types of defects in printed wiring.* Pittsburgh, PA: Carnegie Mellon University.

Rochefort, D. A., & Portz, J. H. (1993). Different systems, shared challenges: assessing Canadian mental health care from a U.S. perspective. *American Review of Canadian Studies, 23*, 65–82.

Rochefort, D.A. (1992). More lessons, of a different kind: Canadian mental health policy in comparative perspective. *Hospital and Community Psychiatry, 43*, 1083–1090.

Rodgers, W.M. & Brawley, L.R. 1991. The role of outcome expectancies in participation motivation. *Journal of Exercise and Sport Psychology, 13(4)*, 411–427.

Rodin, J. (1984, April). A sense of control. *Psychology Today*, 38–45.

Rodin, J., Bartoshuk, L., Peterson, C., & Schank, D. (1990). Bulimia and taste: Possible interactions. *Journal of Abnormal Psychology, 99*, 32–39.

Rodin, J., & Plante, T. (1989). The psychological effects of exercise. In R. S. Williams & A. Wellece (Eds.), *Biological effects of physical activity.* Champaign, IL: Human Kinetics.

Rodin, J., & Salovey, P. (1989). Health psychology. *Annual Review of Psychology, 40*, 533–580.

Rodin, J., & Slochower, J. (1976). Externality in the nonobese: Effects of environmental responsiveness on weight. *Journal of Personality and Social Psychology, 33*, 338–344.

Roediger, H. L., III, & Wheeler, M. A. (1993). Hypermnesia in episodic and semantic memory: Response to Bahrick and Hall. *Psychological Science, 4*, 207–208.

Roese, N.J., Olsen, J.M., Borenstein, M.N., Martin, A., Shores, A.L. 1992. Same sex touching behavior: the moderating role of homophobic attitudes. *Journal of Nonverbal Behavior, 16(4)*, 249–259.

Roese, N.J., Olson, J.M. (1993). Self-esteem and counterfactual thinking. *Journal of Personality and Social Psychology, 65(1)*, 199–206.

Rogers, C. R. (1959). A theory of therapy, personality, and interpersonal relationships as developed in the client-centered framework. In S. Koch (Ed.), *Psychology: A study of a science* (Vol. 3, pp. 184–256). New York: McGraw-Hill.

Rogers, C. R. (1970). *Carl Rogers on encounter groups.* New York: Harper & Row.

Rogers, C. R. (1980). *A way of being.* Boston: Houghton Mifflin.

Rogers, C. R. (1982, August). Nuclear war: A personal response. *American Psychological Association*, pp. 6–7.

Rogers, C.R. (1977). *Carl Rogers on personal power: Inner strength and its revolutionary impact.* New York: Delacorte.

Rogers, R. W. (1980). Subjects' reactions to experimental deception. Unpublished manuscript, University of Alabama.

Roopnarine, J.L, Talukder, E., Jain, D., Joshi, P., Srivastav, P. (1990). Characteristics of holding, patterns of play, and social behaviors between parents and infants in New Dehli, India. *Developmental Psychology, 26(4)*, 667–673.

Rosch, E. H. (1973). Natural categories. *Cognitive Psychology, 4*, 328–349.

Rosch, E. H. (1975). The nature of mental codes for color categories. Journal of *Experimental Psychology: Human Perception and Performance, 1*, 303–322.

Rosen, L.N., Targum, S.D., Terman, M., Bryant, M.J., Hoffman, H., Kasper, S.F., Hamovit, J.R., Docherty, J.P., Welch, B., & Rosenthal, N.E. (1990). Prevalence of seasonal affective disorder at four latitudes. *Psychiatry Research, 31*, 131–144.

Rosenfield, D., Folger, R., & Adelman, H. F. (1980). When rewards reflect competence: A qualification of the overjustification effect. *Journal of Personality and Social Psychology, 39*, 368–376.

Rosenman, R. H. (1988). The impact of certain emotions in cardiovascular disorders. In M. P. Janisse (Ed.), *Individual differences, stress, and health psychology* (pp. 1–23). New York: Springer-Verlag.

Rosenstock, I. M. (1974). The health belief model and preventive health behavior. *Health Education Monographs, 2*, 354–386.

Rosenthal, C.J., Sulman, J. & Marshall, V.W. 1993. Depressive symptoms in family caregivers of long-stay patients. *Gerontologist, 33(2)*, 249–257.

Rosenthal, R. R., & DePaulo, B. M. (1979). Sex differences in eavesdropping on nonverbal cues. *Journal of Personality and Social Psychology, 37*, 273–285.

Rosenzweig, J. M., & Daley, D. M. (1989) Dyadic adjustment/sexual satisfaction in women and men as a function of psychological sex role self-perception. *Journal of Sex and Marital Therapy, 15*, 42–56.

Roskies, E. (1987). *Stress management for the healthy Type A*. New York: Guilford Press.

Roskos-Ewoldsen, D.R., Fazio, R.H. (1992). The accessibility of source likability as a determinant of persuasion. *Personality and Social Psychology Bulletin, 18(1)*, 19–25.

Ross, A.S., White, S. (1987). Shoplifting, impaired driving, and refusing the breathalyser: On seeing one's name in a public place. *Evaluation Review, 11(2)*, 254–260.

Ross, C. A. (1994). The osiris complex: Case studies in multiple personality. Toronto: University of Toronto Press.

Ross, C. A., Miller, S. D., Bjornson, M. A., Reagor, P., Fraser, G. A., & Anderson G. (1991). Abuse histories in 102 cases of multiple personality. *Canadian Journal of Psychiatry, 36*, 97–101.

Ross, C. A., Norton, G. R., & Wozney, K. (1989). Multiple personality disorder: An analysis of 236 cases. *Canadian Journal of Psychiatry, 34*, 413–418.

Ross, C.A. & Anderson, G. 1988. Phenomenological overlap of multiple personality disorder and obsessive-compulsive disorder. *Journal of Nervous and Mental Disease, 176(5)*, 295–299.

Ross, N. (1989). Relation of implicit theories to construction of personal histories. *Psychological Review, 96*, 341–357.

Rossberg-Gempton, I. & Poole, G.D. 1993. The effect of open and closed postures on pleasant and unpleasant emotions. Special issue: research in the creative arts therapies. *Arts in Psychotherapy, 20(1)*, 75–82.

Rotenberg, K.G., Schaut, G.B. & O'Connor, B.P. 1993. The roles of identity development and psychosocial intimacy in marital success. *Journal of Social and Clinical Psychology, 12(2)*, 198–217.

Roter, D. L., & Ewart, C. K. (1992). Emotional inhibition in essential hypertension: Obstacle to communication during medical visits? *Health Psychology, 11*, 163–169.

Roter, D. L., & Hall, J. A. (1989). Studies of doctor-patient interaction. *Annual Review of Public Health, 10*, 163–180.

Rothenberg, R., Nasca, P., Mikl, J., Burnett, W., & Reynolds, B. (1987). In R. W. Amler & H. B. Dull (Eds.), *Closing the gap: The burden of unnecessary Illness*. New York: Oxford University Press.

Rothman, K. R., Cristina, I. C., Flanders, D., & Fried, M. P. (1980). Epidemiology of laryngeal cancer. In P. E. Sartwell (Ed.), *Epidemiologic reviews* (Vol. 2, pp. 195–209). Baltimore: Johns Hopkins University Press.

Rotter, J. B. (1954). *Social learning and clinical psychology*. Englewood Cliffs, NJ: Prentice-Hall.

Rotter, J. B. (1982). *The development and applications of social learning theory: Selected papers*. New York: Praeger.

Rouleau, I., Labrecque, R., Saint-Hilaire, J.M., Cardu, B., Giard, N. 1989. Short-term and long-term memory deficit following intracarotid amytal injection: further support for the memory consolodation hypothesis. *Brain and Cognition, 11(2)*, 167–185.

Rowlison, R. T., & Felner, R. D. (1988). Major life events, hassles, and adaptation in adolescence: Confounding in the conceptualization and measurement of life stress and adjustment revisited. *Journal of Personality and Social Psychology, 55*, 432–444.

Royce, J. M., Darlington, R. B., & Murray, H. W. (1983). Pooled analyses: Findings across studies. In Consortium for Longitudinal Studies, *As the twig is bent. . . Lasting effects of preschool programs*. Hillsdale, NJ: Erlbaum.

Rubin, J. Z. (1985). Deceiving ourselves about deception: Comment on Smith and Richardson's "Amelioration of deception and harm in psychologi-

cal research." *Journal of Personality and Social Psychology, 48*, 252–253.

Ruff, H.A., Lawson, K.R., Parinello, R., Weissberg, R., (1990). Long-term stability of individual differences in sustained attention in the early years. *Child Development, 61(1)*, 60–75.

Rumbaugh, K., & Garrett, J. (1974). Sensation seeking among skydivers. *Perceptual and Motor Skills, 38*, 103–111.

Rumelhart, D. E. (1975). Notes on a schema for stories. In D. G. Bobrow & A. Collins (Eds.), *Representation and understanding* (pp. 211–236). New York: Academic Press.

Rumelhart, D. E., Hinton, G. E., & Williams, R. J. (1986). Learning representations by back propogating errors. *Nature, 323*, 533–536.

Rusak, B. (1990). Biological rhythms: From physiology to behavior. In J. Montplaisir & R. Godbout, Eds.), *Sleep and biological rhythms: Basic mechanisms and applications to psychiatry*. New York: Oxford University Press.

Rushton, W. A. H. (1975). Visual pigments and color blindness. *Scientific American, 232*, 64–74.

Russell, G.W., Mentzel, R.K. (1990). Sympathy and altruism in response to disasters. *Journal of Social Psychology, 130(3)*, 309–316.

Russell, J.A. 1994. Is there universal recognition of emotion from facial expressions? A review of the cross-cultural studies. *Psychological Bulletin, 115(1)*, 102–141.

Russell, L. (1990). Sex and couples therapy: A method of treatment to enhance physical and emotional intimacy. *Journal of Sex and Marital Therapy, 16*, 111–120.

Rutman, D.L., Freedman, J.L. (1988). Anticipating relocation: Coping strategies and the meaning of home for older people. *Canadian Journal on Aging, 7(1)*, 17–31.

Ryan, E.B. & See, S.K. 1993. Age-based beliefs about memory changes for self and others across adulthood. *Journals of Gerontology, 48(4)*, 199–201.

Ryan, E.B. 1992. Beliefs about memory changes across the adult life span. *Journals of Gerontology, 47(1)*, 41–46.

Ryan, E.B., Szechtman, B., Bodkin, J. (1992). Attitudes toward younger and older adults learning to use computers. *Journals of Gerontology, 47(2)*, 96–101.

Ryan, R. M. (1982). Control and information in the intrapersonal sphere: An extension of cognitive evaluation theory. *Journal of Personality and Social Psychology, 43*, 450–561.

Sacks, O. (1993, May 10). To see and not see: A neurologist's notebook. *The New Yorker* pp. 59–73.

Sadava, S.W. & Weithe, H. 1985. Maintainance and attributions about smoking among smokers, non-smokers and ex-smokers. *International Journal of the Addictions, 20(10)*, 1533–1544.

Saks, M. J. (1992). Obedience versus disobedience to legitimate versus illegitimate authorities issuing good versus evil directions. *Psychological Science, 3*, 221–223.

Salame, P., & Baddeley, A. D. (1982). Disruption of short-term memory by unattended speech: Implications for the structure of working memory. *Journal of Verbal Learning and Verbal Behavior, 21*, 150–164.

Salovey, P. (Ed.). (1991). *The psychology of jealousy and envy*. New York: Guilford Press.

Salovey, P. (1992). Mood-induced self-focused attention. *Journal of Personality and Social Psychology, 62*, 699–707.

Salovey, P., & Birnbaum, D. (1989). Influence of mood on health-relevant cognitions. *Journal of Personality and Social Psychology, 57*, 539–551.

Samson, D. & Rachman, S.J. (1992). A search for contrast effects with fear evoking stimuli. *British Journal of Clinical Psychology, 31*, 33–44.

Samson, L. F. (1988). Perinatal viral infections and neonates. *Journal of Perinatal and Neonatal Nursing, 1*, 56–65.

Samson, S., Zatorre, R.J. 1991. Recognition memory for text and melody of songs after unilateral temporal lobe lesion: Evidence for dual encoding. *Journal of Experimental Psychology—Learning, Memory, and Cognition, 17(4)*, 793–804.

Samuels, M., & Samuels, N. (1986). *The well pregnancy book*. New York: Summit.

Sanbonmatsu, D. M., Akimoto, S. A., & Gibson, B. D. (1994). Stereotype-based blocking in social explanation. *Personality and Social Psychology Bulletin, 20*, 71–81.

Sande, G. N., Goethals, G. R., & Radloff, C. E. (1988). Perceiving one's own traits and others': The mulitfaceted self. *Journal of Personality and Social Psychology, 54*, 13–20.

Sande, G.N., Goethals, G.R., Ferrari, L. Worth, L.T. (1989). Value-guided attributions: Maintaining the moral self-image and the diabolical enemy-image. *Journal of Social Issues, 45(2)*, 91–118.

Sandell, M. & Sullivan, K. 1992. Teacher disillusionment and supervision as a part of professional development. *Alberta Journal of Educational Research, 38(2)*, 133–140.

Sanders, M. S., & McCormick, E. J. (1993). *Human factors in engineering and design*. New York: McGraw-Hill.

Santi, S., Best, J.A., Brown, K.S. & Cargo, M. 1990–91. Smoking environment and smoking initiation. Special issue: environmental factors in substance misuse and its treatment. *International Journal of the Addictions, 25(7A–8A)*, 881–903.

Sargent, C. (1984). Between death and shame: Dimensions in pain in Bariba culture. *Social Science Medicine,, 19,* 1299–1304.

Saulnier, K., Perlman, D. (1981). The actor-observer bias is alive and well in prison: A sequel to Wells. *Personality and Social Psychology Bulletin, 7(4),* 559–564.

Savage-Rumbaugh, E. S., Sevcik, R. A., Brakke, K. E., & Rumbaugh, D. M. (1992). Symbols: Their communicative use, communication, and combination by bonobos (*Pan paniscus*). In L. P. Lipsitt & C. Rovee-Collier (Eds.), *Advances in infancy research* (Vol. 7, pp. 221–278). Norwood, NJ: Ablex.

Scarr, S., & Weinberg, R. A. (1976). IQ test performance of black children adopted by white families. *American Psychologist, 31,* 726–739.

Schab, F. R. (1991). Odor memory: Taking stock. *Psychological Bulletin, 109,* 242–251.

Schachter, S., & Singer, J. E. (1962). Cognitive, social, and physiological determinants of emotional states. *Psychological Review, 69,* 379–399.

Schaie, K. W. (1986). *Adult development and aging* (2nd ed.). Boston: Little, Brown.

Schaie, K. W. (1990). Intellectual development in adulthood. In J. E. Birren & K. W. Schaie (Eds.), *Handbook of the psychology of aging* (3rd ed., pp. 291–309). San Diego: Academic Press.

Schaie, K. W. (1993). The Seattle longitudinal studies of adult intelligence. *Current Directions in Psychological Science, 2,* 171–175.

Schaller, G. G. (1986). Secrets of the wild panda. *National Geographic, 169,* 284–309.

Schank, R. (1988). *The creative attitude.* New York: Macmillan.

Scheier, M. F, & Carver, C. S. (1986). A model of self-regulation: Translating intention into action. In L. Berkowitz (Ed.), *Advances in experimental social psychology* (Vol. 20). New York: Academic Press.

Scheier, M. F., & Carver, C. S. (1987). Dispositional optimism and physical well-being: The influence of generalized outcome expectancies in health. *Journal of Personality, 55,* 169–210.

Scheier, M. F., & Carver, C. S. (1988). *Perspectives on personality.* Boston: Allyn and Bacon.

Scheier, M. F., & Carver, C. S. (1992). Effects of optimism on psychological and physical well-being: Theoretical overview and empirical update. *Cognitive Therapy and Research, 16,* 201–228.

Scheier, M. F., Weintraub, J. K., & Carver, C.-S. (1986). Coping with stress: Divergent strategies of optimists and pessimists. *Journal of Personality and Social Psychology, 51,* 1257–1264.

Schell, B.H. & Bonin, L. 1989. Factors affecting censorship by Canadian librarians. *Journal of Psychology, 60(3, Pt 2),* 357–368.

Schell, B.H. & Zinger, J.T. 1985. An investigation of self- actualization: job satisfaction, and job commitment for Ontario funeral directors. *Psychological Reports, 57(2),* 455–464.

Schiff, B.B. & Lamon, M. 1989. Inducing emotion by unilateral contraction of facial muscles: a new look at hemispheric specialization and the experience of emotion. *Neuropsychologia, 27(7),* 923–935.

Schiff, B.B., Esses, V.M. & Lamon, M. 1992. Unilateral facial contractions produce mood effects on social cognitive judgements. *Cognition and Emotion, 6(5),* 357–368.

Schiffman, H. R. (1990). *Sensation and perception: An integrated approach* (3rd ed). New York: John Wiley & Sons.

Schmidt, F.N. & Gifford, R. 1989. A dispositional approach to hazard perception: preliminary development of the Environmental Appraisal Inventory. *Journal of Environmental Psychology, 9(1),* 57–67.

Schmidt, U. (1989). Behavioural psychotherapy of eating disorders. *International Review of Psychiatry, 1,* 245–256.

Schneider, B. H. (1991). A comparison of skill-building and desensitization strategies for intervention with aggressive children. *Aggressive Behavior, 17,* 301–311.

Schneider, B. H., & Byrne, B. M. (1987). Individualizing social skills training for behaviour-disordered children. *Journal of Consulting and Clinical Psychology, 55,* 444–445.

Schneider, S. L. (1992). Framing and conflict: Aspiration level contingency, the status quo, and current theories of risky choice. *Journal of Experimental Psychology: Learning, Memory. and Cognition, 18,* 1040–1057.

Schneider, W., & Shiffrin, R. M. (1977). Controlled and automatic human information processing. I: Detection, search, and attention. *Psychological Review, 84,* 1–66.

Schofield, W. (1964). *Psychotherapy: The purchase of friendship.* Englewood Cliffs, NJ: Prentice Hall.

Schulz, G. & Melzack, R. (1991). The Charles Bonnet syndrome: "Phantom visual images" *Perception, 20,* 809–825.

Schwartzman, A.E., Gold, D., Andres, D., Arbuckle, T.Y., Chailelson, J. 1987. Stability of intelligence: a 40-year follow-up.Special issue: Aging and cognition. *Canadian Journal of Psychology, 41(2),* 244–256.

Schwarzwald, J., Amir, Y., Crain, R.L. (1992). Long-term effects of school desegregation experiences on interpersonal relations in the Israeli Defense Forces. *Personality and Social Psychology Bulletin, 18(3),* 357–368.

Scott, J. P. (1992). Aggression: Functions and control in social systems. *Aggressive Behavior, 18,* 1–20.

Scribner, S. (1977). Recall of classical syllogisms: A cross-cultural investigation of error on logical problems. In R. J. Falmagne (Ed.), *Reasoning: Representation and process.* Hillsdale, NJ: Erlbaum.

Searle, J. (1980). Minds, brains, and programs. *Behavioral and Brain Science, 3,* 417–457.

Seeman, M.V. & Seeman, P. 1988. Psychosis and positron tomography. *Canadian Journal of Psychiatry, 33(4),* 299–306.

Segal, N. L., & Bouchard, T. J. (1993). Grief intensity following the loss of a twin and other relatives: Test of kinship-genetic hypotheses. *Human Biology, 65,* 87–105.

Segal, Z. (1988). Appraisal of the self-schema construct in cognitive models of depression. *Psychological Bulletin, 103,* 147–162.

Segall, M. H., Dasen, P. R,. Berry, J. W., & Poortinga, Y. H. (1990). *Human behavior in global perspective.* Boston: Allyn & Bacon.

Segalowitz, S.J., Unsal, A., Dywan, J. (1992). Cleverness and wisdom in 12-year-olds: Electrophysiological evidence for late maturation of the frontal lobe. Developmental *Neuropsychology, 8(2–3),* 279–298.

Sekuler, R., & Blake, R. (1990). *Perception.* New York: Alfred A. Knopf.

Seligman, M. E. P. (1975). *Helplessness: On depression, development, and death.* San Francisco: Freeman.

Seligman, M. E. P., Castellon, C., Cacciola, J., Schulman, P., Luborsky, L., Ollove, M., & Downing, R. (1988). Explanatory style change during cognitive therapy for unipolar depression. *Journal of Abnormal Psychology, 97,* 13–18.

Seligman, M. E. P., & Hager, J. L. (1972). *Biological boundaries of learning.* New York: Appleton-Century-Crofts.

Selvini-Palazzoli, M., Boscolo, L., Cecchin, G., & Prata, G. (1978). *Paradox.* New York: Aronson.

Selye, H. (1973). The evolution of the stress concept. *American Scientist, 61(6),* 692–699.

Selye, H. (1976). *The stress of life* (2nd ed.). New York: McGraw-Hill.

Sergent, J. & Corballis, M.C. 1990. Generation of multipart images in the disconnected cerebral hemispheres. *Bulletin of the Psychonomic Society, 28(4),* 309–311.

Sergent, J. 1989. Image generation and processing of generated images in the cerebral hemispheres. *Journal of Experimental Psychology: Human Perception and Performance, 15(1),* 170–178.

Sergent, J. 1990. The neuropsychology of visual image generation: data, method, and theory. *Brain and Cognition, 13(1),* 98–129.

Seta, C. E., & Hayes, N. (1994). The influence of impression formation goals on the accuracy of social memory. *Personality and Social Psychology Bulletin, 20,* 93–101.

Sewitch, D. E. (1987). Slow wave sleep deficiency insomnia: A problem in thermo-downregulation at sleep onset. *Psychophysiology, 24,* 200–215.

Shaffer, D., Garland, A., Vieland, V., Underwood, M., & Busner, C. (1991). The impact of curriculum-based suicide prevention programs for teenagers. *Journal of the American Academy of Child and Adolescent Psychiatry, 30,* 588–596.

Shaffer, D.R., Graziano, W.G. (1983). Effects of positive an negative moods on helping tasks having pleasant or unpleasant consequences. Motivation and Emotion, 7(3), 269–278.

Shafir, E. (1993). Choosing versus rejecting: Why some options are both better and worse than others. *Memory and Cognition, 21,* 546–556.

Shanab, M. E., & Spencer, R. E. (1978). Positive and negative contrast effects obtained following shifts in delayed water reward. *Bulletin of the Psychonomic Society, 12,* 199–202.

Shanab, M.E., Yahya, K.A. (1977). A behavioral study of obedience in children. *Journal of Personality and Social Psychology, 35(7),* 530–536.

Shantz, C. U., & Hartup, W. W. (Eds.) 1993. *Conflict in child and adolescent development.* Cambridge: Cambridge University Press.

Shapiro, C.M., MacFarland, J.G., & MacLean, A.W. (1993). Alleviating sleep-related disconinuance symptoms associated with benzodiazepine withdrawal: A new approach. *Journal of Psychosomatic Research. 37,* 55–57.

Shapiro, D. A., & Shapiro, D. (1982). Meta-analysis of comparative therapy outcome studies: A replication and refinement. *Psychological Bulletin, 92,* 581–604.

Shapiro, D. H. (1980). *Meditation: Self-regulation strategy and altered states of consciousness.* New York: Aldine.

Shapiro, I. (1993). Quoted in Gibbs, N. R. (1993, June 28). Bringing up father. *Time,* pp. 53–61.

Sharpe, D., Adair, J.G., & Roese, N.J. (1992). Twenty years of deception research: A decline in subjects' trust? *Personality and Social Psychology Bulletin, 18,* 585–590.

Shepard, R. N. (1964). Circularity in judgments of relative pitch. *Journal of the Acoustical Society of America, 36,* 2346–2353.

Shepard, R. N., & Metzler, J. (1971). Mental rotation of three-dimensional objects. *Science, 171,* 701–703.

Shephard, R.J. (1992). A critical analysis of work-site fitness programs and their postulated economic benefits. *Medicine and Science in Sports and Exercise, 24(3),* 354–370.

Sherif, M. (1935). A study of some social factors in perception. *Archives of Psychology, 27,* 187.

Sherman, W. M. (1990). *Behavior modification*. New York: Harper Collins.

Sherwin, B.B. 1988. A comparative analysis of the role of androgen in human male and female sexual behavior: behavioral specificity, critical thresholds, and sensitivity. Special issue: sexual differentiation and gender-related behaviors. *Psychobiology, 16(4)*, 416–425.

Shettleworth, S. J. (1983). Memory in food-hoarding birds. *Scientific American, 248*, 102–110.

✴ Shettleworth, S. J. (1993). Where is the comparison in comparative cognition? Alternative research programs. *Psychological Science, 4*, 179–183.

Shiffrin, R. M., & Dumais, S. T. (1981). The development of automatism. In J. R. Anderson (Ed.), *Cognitive skills and their acquisition*. Hillsdale, NJ: Erlbaum.

Shiffrin, R. M., & Schneider, W. (1977). Controlled and automatic human information processing. II: Perceptual learning, automatic attending, and a general theory. *Psychological Review, 84*, 127–190.

✴ Shin, W.S. 1993. Self-actualization and wilderness attitudes: a replication. *Journal of Social Behavior and Personality, 8(2)*, 241–256.

Siegel, S. (1975). Evidence from rats that morphine tolerance is a learned response. *Journal of Comparative and Physiological Psychology, 89*, 598–606.

Siegel, S. (1984). Pavlovian conditioning and heroin overdose: Reports by overdose victims. *Bulletin of the Psychonomic Society, 22*, 428–430.

Siegel, S., Hinson, R.E., Krank, M.D., & McCully, J. (1982). Heroin "overdose" death: Contribution of drug-associated environmental cues. *Science, 216*, 436–437.

✴ Siegle, L.S., (1993). Amazing new discovery: Piaget was wrong~. *Canadian Psychology, 34(3)*, 239–245.

Siegler, R. S. (1994). Cognitive variability: A key to understanding cognitive development. *Current Directions in Psychological Science, 3*, 1–5.

Siegler, R. S., & Crowley, K. (in press). Goal sketches constrain children's strategy discoveries. *Cognitive Psychology*.

✴ Siegler, R.S., Jenkins, E., (1989). How children discover new strategies, Lawrence Erlbaum Associated Inc., Hillsdale, NJ, US.

Silva, C. E., & Kirsch, I. (1992). Interpretive sets, expectancy, fantasy proneness, and dissociation as predictors of hypnotic response. *Journal of Personality and Social Psychology, 63*, 847–856.

Silver, R.L., Boon, C., Stones, M.H. (1983). Searching for meaning in misfortune: Making sense of incest. *Journal of Social Issues, 39(2)*, 81–101.

Silver, S., Mitchell, R. M., & Gist, B. (in press). Responses to successful and unsuccessful performance: The relationship between self-efficacy and causal attributions. *Organizational Behavior and Human Decision Processes*.

Simeon, J.G., Wiggins, D.M., (1993). Pharmacotherapy of attention deficit hyperactivity disorder. *Canadian Journal of Psychiatry, 38(6)*, 443–448.

Simonton, D. K. (1990). Creativity and wisdom in aging. In J. E. Birren & K. W. Schaie (Eds.), *Handbook of the psychology of aging* (3rd ed., pp. 320–329). San Diego: Academic Press.

Simpson, J.A., (1990). Influence of attachment styles on romantic relationships. *Journal of Personality and Social Psychology, 59(5)*, 971–980.

Singer, J. L. (1975). Navigating the stream of consciousness: Research in daydreaming and related inner experience. *American Psychologist, 30*, 727–738.

✴ Singer, P.A., Choudhry, S. & Armstrong, J. 1993. Public opinion regarding consent to treatment. *Journal of the American Geriatrics Society, 41(2)*, 112–116.

Sinott, J. D. (1986). Prospective/intentional and incidental everyday memory: Effects of age and passage of time. *Psychology and Aging, 1*, 110–116.

✴ Sistrunk, F., & McDavid, J. W. (1971). Sex variable in conforming behavior. *Journal of Personality and Social Psychology, 29*, 200–207.

✴ Skeels, H. M. (1938). Mental development of children in foster homes. *Journal of Consulting Psychology, 2*, 33–43.

Skeels, H. M. (1966). Ability status of children with contrasting early life experience. *Society for Research in Child Development Monographs, 31(3)*, 1–65.

Skinner, B. F. (1938). *The behavior of organisms*. New York: Appleton-Century-Crofts.

✴ Skinner, B. F. (1953). *The behavior of organisms*. New York: Appleton-Century-Crofts.

Skinner, B. F. (1969). *Contingencies of reinforcement*. New York: Appleton-Century-Crofts.

Skinner, B. F. (1974). *About behaviorism*. New York: Vintage Books.

Sladen-Dew, N., Bigelow, D. A., Buckley, R., & Bornemann, S. (1993). The Greater Vancouver Mental Health Service Society: 20 years' experience in urban community mental health. *Canadian Journal of Psychiatry, 38*, 308–314.

Sloan, E.P., Hauri, P., Bootzin, R. & Morin, C. (1993). The nuts and bolts of behavioral therapy for insomnia. *Journal of Psychosomatic Research, 37*, 19–37.

Sloan, E.P., Hauri, P., Bootzin, r., & Morin, C. and et al. (1993). The nuts and bolts of behavioral therapy for insomnia. *Journal of Psychosomatic Research, 37*, 19–37.

✴ Slobin, D. I. (1979). *Psycholinguistics* (2nd ed.). Glenview, IL: Scott, Foresman.

Slovic, P., Fischoff, B., & Lichtenstein, S. (1977). Behavioral decision theory. *Annual Review of Psychology, 28*, 1–39.

Slugoski, B.R., Lalljee, M., Lamb, R., Ginsburg, G.P. (1993). Attribution in conversational context: Effect of mutual knowledge on explanation-giving. *European Journal of Social Psychology, 23(3)*, 219–238.

✴ Smart, R.G. & Walsh, G.W. 1993. Predictors of depression in street youth. *Adolescence, 28(109)*, 41–53.

✴ Smart, R.G. (1991). Crack cocaine use: A review of prevalence and adverse effects. *American Journal of Drug and Alcohol Abuse, 17*, 13–26.

✴ Smart, R.G., & Adlaf, E.M. (1992). Recent studies of cocaine use and abuse in Canada. *Canadian Journal of Criminology, 34*, 1–13.

✴ Smeaton, D., Byrne, D., & Murnen, S. K. (1989). The revulsion hypothesis revisited: Similarity irrelevance or dissimilarity bias? *Journal of Personality and Social Psychology, 56*, 54–59.

Smith, D. E., Gier, J. A., & Willis, F. N. (1982). Interpersonal touch and compliance with a marketing request. *Basic and Applied Social Psychology, 3*, 35–38.

Smith, J., & Baltes, P. B. (1990). Wisdom-related knowledge: Age/cohort differences in response to life-planning problems. *Developmental Psychology, 26*, 494–505.

Smith, G.N., Macewan, G.W. & Ancill, R.J. 1991. " The role of gender in studies of ventricle enlargement in schizophrenia: a predominantly male effect": comment. *American Journal of Psychiatry, 148(12)*, 1755–1756.

Smith, I.M., McGlone, J. & Fox, A.J. 1993. Intracarotid amobarbital memory protocol: Muteness, dysphasia, and variations in arterial distribution of the drug do not affect recognition results. *Journal of Epilepsy, 6(2)*, 75–84.

Smith, J. F., & Kida, T. (1991). Heuristics and biases: Expertise and task realism in auditing. *Psychological Bulletin, 109*, 472–489.

Smith, M. C. (1983). Hypnotic memory enhancement of witnesses: Does it work? *Psychological Bulletin, 94*, 387–407.

Smith, M. L., Glass, G. V., & Miller, T. J. (1980). *The benefits of psychotherapy*. Baltimore: Johns Hopkins.

Smith, M.L., Minden, D., Lefevbre, A. (1993). Knowledge and attitudes about AIDS and AIDS education in elementary school students and their parents. *Journal of School Psychology, 31(2)*, 281–292.

Smith, P. B., & Bond, N. H. (1993). *Social psychology across cultures*. Boston: Allyn & Bacon.

Smith, R. E., Ptacek, J. T., & Smoll, F. L. (1992). Sensation seeking, stress, and adolescent injuries: A test of stress-buffering, risk-taking, and coping skills hypotheses. *Journal of Personality and Social Psychology, 62*, 1016–1024.

Smith, S. M. (1979). Remembering in and out of context. *Journal of Experimental Psychology: Human Learning and Memory, 5*, 460–471.

Smith, S. M., & Shaffer, D. R. (1991). Celerity and cajolery: Rapid speech may enhance or inhibit persuasion through its impact on message elaboration. *Personality and Social Psychology Bulletin, 17*, 663–669.

Smith, S. M., & Shaffer, D. R. (1991). The effects of good moods on systematic processing: "Willing but not able, or able but not willing?" *Motivation and Emotion, 15*, 243–279.

Smith, S. S., & Richardson, D. (1983). Amelioration of deception and harm in psychological research: The important role of debriefing. *Journal of Personality and Social Psychology, 44*, 1075–1082.

Smith, S. S., & Richardson, D. (1985). On deceiving ourselves about deception: Reply to Rubin. *Journal of Personality and Social Psychology, 48*, 254–255.

Smith, S.M. & Shaffer, D.R. 1991. The effects of good moods on systematic processing: "willing but not able, able but not willing?". *Motivation and Emotion, 15(4)*, 243–279.

Smith, T. W. (1992). Discrepancies between men and women in reporting number of sexual partners: A summary from four countries. *Social Biology, 39*, 203–11.

Snow, W.G., Freedman, L. & Ford, L. 1986. Lateralized brain damage, sex differences, and the Wechsler Intelligence Scales: a reexamination of the literature. *Journal of Clinical and Experimental Neuropsychology, 8(3)*, 179–189.

Snowden, L. R., & Cheung, F. K. (1990). Use of inpatient mental health services by members of ethnic minority groups. *American Psychologist, 45*, 347–355.

Snyder, M. (1987). *Public appearances/private realities: The psychology of self-monitoring*. New York: W. H. Freeman.

Snyder, M., & Gangestad, S. (1986). On the nature of self-monitoring: Matters of assessment, matters of validity. *Journal of Personality and Social Psychology, 51*, 125–139.

Snyder, S.H. (1991). Movies and juvenile delinquency: An overview. *Adolescence, 26*, 121–132.

Snyder, S. H. (1977). The brain's own opiates. *Chemical & Engineering News, 55*, 26–35.

Sobell, L.C., Sobell, M.B., Kozlowski, L.T. & Toneatto, T. 1990. Alcohol or tobacco research versus alcohol and tobacco research. *British Journal of Addiction, 85(2)*, 263–269.

Solomon, R. L. (1982). The opponent-process in acquired motivation. In

D. W. Pfaff (Ed.), *The physiological mechanisms of motivation.* New York: Springer-Verlag.

Solso, R. L. (1991). *Cognitive psychology* (3rd ed.). Boston: Allyn & Bacon.

Sorrentino, R.M., Hewitt, E.C. & Raso-Knott, P.A. 1992. Risk- taking in games of games of chance and skill: informational and affective influences on choice behavior. *Journal of Personality and Social Psychology, 62(3)*, 522–533.

Sorrentino, R.M., Vidmar, N. (1974). Impact of events: Short vs. long term effects of a crisis. *Public Opinion Quarterly, 38(2)*, 271–279.

Sorrentino, R.M., Vidmar, N., Goodstadt, M.S. (1974). Opinion change in a crisis: Effects of the 1970 Canadian kidnapping crisis on political and ethnic attitudes. *Canadian Journal of Behavioural Science, 6(3)*, 199–218.

Spacapan, S., & Oskamp, S. (Eds.). (1992). *Helping and being helped.* Newbury Park, CA: Sage.

Spanos, N. P. (1991). A sociocognitive approach to hypnosis. In S. J. Lynn & J. R. Rhue (Eds.), *Hypnosis theories: Current models and perspectives* (pp. 324–361). New York: Guilford Press.

Spanos, N.P., Burgess, C.A., & Perlini, A.H. (1992). Compliance and suggested deafness in hypnotic and nonhypnotic subjects. *Imagination, Cognition and Personality, 11*, 211–223.

Spanos, N.P., Burgess, C.A., Cross, P., & McCleod, G. (1992). Hypnosis, reporting bias and negative hallucinations. *Journal of Abnormal Psychology 101*, 192–199.

Spanos, N.P., DuBreuil, S.C., & Gabora, N.J. (1991). Fourn-month follow-up of skill-training-induced enhancements in hypnotizablility. *Contemporary Hypnosis, 8*, 25–32.

Spanos, N.P., Flynn, D.M., & Gabora, N.J. (1989). Suggestive negative visual hallucinations in hypnotic subjects: When no means yes. *British Journal of Experimental and Clinical Hypnosis, 6*, 63–67.

Spanos, N.P., Menary, E., Gabora, N.J., DuBreuil, S.C., & Dewhirst, B. (1991). Secondary identity enactments during hypnotic past-life regression: A sociocognitive perspective. *Journal of Personality and Social Psychology, 61*, 308–320.

Spanos, N.P., Perlini, A.H., Patrick, L., Bell, S., & Gwynn, M.I. (1990). The role of compliance and hypnotic and nonhypnotic analgesia. *Journal of Research in Personality.* 24, 433–453.

Spearman, C. E. (1927). *The abilities of man.* London: Macmillan.

Spence, A. P. (1989). *Biology of human aging.* Englewood Cliffs, NJ: Prentice Hall.

Spence, J. T., & Helmreich, R. L. (1972). The Attitudes toward Women Scale: An objective instrument to measure lattitudes toward the rights and roles of women in contemporary society. *JSAS Catalog of Selected Documents in Psychology, 2*, 66 (Ms. No. 153).

Spence, J. T., Helmreich, R., & Stapp, J. A. (1975). A short version of the Attitudes toward Women Scale (AWS). *Bulletin of the Psychonomic Society, 2*, 219–220.

Spencer, J. (1990). Collective violence and everyday practice in Sri Lanka. *Journal of Asian Studies, 24*, 603–623.

Sperling, G. (1960). The information available in brief visual presentations. *Psychological monographs: General and applied, 74*, 1–29.

Sperry, R. W. (1968). Hemisphere deconnection and unity of conscious experience. *American Psychologist, 29*, 723–733.

Spetch, M.L. and Grant, D.S. (1993). Pigeons' memory for event duration in choice and successive matching-to=sample tasks. *Learning and Motivation, 24*, 156–174.

Spetch, M.L. and Wilkie, D.M. (1994). Pigeons' use of landmarks presented in digitized images. *Learning and Motivation, 25*, in press.

Spetch, M.L., Belke, T.W., Barnet, R.C., Dunn, R. Pierce, D. (1990). Suboptimal choice in a percentage-reinforcement procedure: Effects of signal condition and terminal-link length. *Journal of the Experimental Analysis of Behavior, 53*, 219–234.

Spinner, B. and Byers, E. S. (1986). Loneliness and social support in married and unmarried individuals. Presented at the *Annual convention of the Canadian Psychological Association,* Toronto, Canada.

Spirduso, W. W., & MacRae, P.G. (1990). Motor performance and aging. In J. E. Birren & K. W. Schaie (Eds.), *Handbook of the psychology of aging* (3rd ed., pp. 184–200). San Diego: Academic Press.

Springer, S. P., & Deutsch, G. (1985). *Left brain, right brain.* San Francisco: Freeman.

Squire, L. R. (1991). Closing remarks. In L. R. Squire & E. Lindenlaub (Eds.), *The biology of memory* (pp. 643–64). Stuttgart, Germany: F.K. Schattauer Verlag.

Squire, L. R., & McKee, R. (1992). The influence of prior events on cognitive judgments in amnesia. *Journal of Experimental Psychology: Learning, Memory, and Cognition, 18*, 106–115.

Squire, L. R., & Spanis, C. W. (1984). Long gradient of retrograde amnesia in mice: Continuity with the findings in humans. *Behavioral Neuroscience, 98*, 345–348.

Sroufe, L. A., & Waters, E. (1976). The ontogenesis of smiling and laughter on the organization of development in infancy. *Psychological Review, 83*, 173–189.

Stager, J. M. (1988). Menarche and exercise. *Medical Aspects of Human Sexuality, 22*, 118, 133.

Stack, D.M., Muir, D.W., (1990). Tactile stimulation as a component of social interchange: New interpretations for the still-face effect. *British Journal of Developmental Psychology 8(2)*, 131–145.

Stack, D.M., Muir, D.W., (1992). Adult tactile stimulation during face-to-face interactions modulates five-month-olds' affect and attention. *Child Development, 63(6)*, 1509–1525.

Standing, L. G. (1973). Learning 10,000 pictures. *Quarterly Journal of Experimental Psychology, 25*, 207–222.

Stangor, C., & Ruble, D. N. (1989). Strength of expectancies and memory for social information: What we remember depends on how much we know. *Journal of Experimental Social Psychology, 39*, 1408–1423.

Stanton, A. L., & Dunckel-Schetter, C. A. (1991). Psychological adjustment to infertility: An overview of conceptual approaches. In A. L. Standon & C. A. Dunkel-Schetter (Eds.), *Infertility: Perspectives from stress and coping research.* New York: Plenum.

Stanton, W.R., Mahalski, P.A., McGee, R. & Silva, P.A. 1993. Reasons for smoking and not smoking in early adolescents. *Addictive Behaviors, 18(3)*, 321–329.

Stark-Adamec, C. (1994). Women and social science research. Presented at the Canadian Psychological Association Convention, June 30, 1994, Penticton, British Columbia.

Stark-Adamec, C., MacLennan, R., Chadwick, W. (presented at the annual meeting of the Canadian Psychological Association, at Penticton, British Columbia, June 1994).

Stark-Adamec, C., Pullin, W.M. (in press 1994, in The Illusion of Inclusion: Women in Post Secondary Education). Women reflected in the smoke and mirrors of Academia: Grace under fire.

Stark-Adamec, C., Robinson, T.P., Loutzenhiser, L. (1993). Faculty women's allocations of time. *Perceptual and Motor Skills, 77*, 689–690.

Staw, B. M., & Ross, J. (1987). Behavior in escalation situations: Antecedents, prototypes, and solutions. In L. L. Cummings & B. M. Staw (Eds.), *Research in organizational behavior* (Vol. 9, pp. 29–78). Greenwich, CT: JAI Press.

Staw, B. M., & Ross, J. (1989). Understanding behavior in escalation situations. *Science, 246*, 216–220.

Staw, B.M., Ross, J. (1985). Stability in the midst of change: a dispositional approach to job attitudes. *Journal of Applied Psychology, 70(3)*, 469–480.

Stearns, G.M. & Moore, R.J. 1993. The physical and psychological correlates of job burnout in the Royal Canadian Mounted Police. *Canadian Journal of Criminology, 35(2)*, 127–147.

Steers, R. M. (1984). *Organizational behavior* (2nd ed.). Glenview, IL: Scott Foresman.

Steffen, V. J. (1990). Men's motivation to perform the testicular self-exam: Effect of prior knowledge and an educational brochure. *Journal of Applied Social Psychology, 20*, 681–702.

Steffen, V.J., Eagly, A.H. (1985). Implicit theories about influence style: The effects of status and sex. *Personality and Social Psychology Bulletin, 11(2)*, 191–205.

Steiger, H. (1989). An integrated psychotherapy for eating-disorder patients. *American Journal of Psychotherapy, 43*, 229–237.

Stein, B.A., Golombek, H., Marton, P. & Korenblum, M. 1991. Consistency and change in personality characteristics and affect from middle to late adolescence. *Canadian Journal of Psychiatry, 36(1)*, 16–20.

Steiner, D.D., Rain, J.S., Smalley, M.M. (1993). Distributional ratings of performance: Further examination of a new rating format. *Journal of Applied Psychology, 78(3)*, 438–442.

Steinfels, P. (1992, January 20). Apathy is seen toward agony of the homeless. *New York Times*, pp. A1, B7.

Stellar, E. (1985, April). *Hunger in animals and humans.* Lecture to the Eastern Psychological Association, Boston.

Stenson, P. & Anderson, C. 1987. Treating juvenile sex offenders and preventing the cycle of abuse. *Journal of Child Care, 3(2)*, 91–102.

Stephan, W. G. (1987). The contact hypothesis in intergroup relations. In C. Hendrick (Ed.), Group processes and intergroup relations. *Review of Personality and Social Psychology, 9*, 41–67.

Stern, J. M., & Stewart, G. G., III. (1993, June). Pay for performance: Only the theory is easy. *HR Magazine*, pp. 48–49.

Stern, P. C. (1992). Psychological dimensions of global environmental change. In M. R. Rosenzweig & L. W. Porter (Eds.), *Annual review of psychology* (Vol. 43, pp. 269–302). Palo Alto, CA: Annual Reviews.

Sternberg, R. J. (1985). *Beyond IQ.* Cambridge: Cambridge University Press.

Sternberg, R. J. (1986). *Intelligence applied.* New York: Harcourt Brace Jovanovich.

Sternberg, R. J. (1988). Mental self-government: A theory of intellectual styles and their development. *Human Development, 31*, 197–224.

Sternberg, R. J. (1988). Triangulating love. In R. J. Sternberg & H. J. Barnes (Eds.), *The psychology of love* (pp. 119–138). New Haven, CT: Yale University Press.

Sternberg, R. J. (1989). Domain-generality versus domain-specificity: The life and impending death of a false dichotomy. *Merrill-Palmer Quarterly, 35*, 115–130.

Stevens, W. K. (1992, February 25). Global warming threatens to undo decades of conservation efforts. *New York Times*, p. C4.

Stevenson, H. W., Lee, S-Y., & Stigler, J. W. (1986). Mathematics achievement of Chinese, Japanese, and American children. *Science, 321*, 593–699.

Stevenson-Hinde, J., Stillwell-Barnes, R., & Sunz, M. (1980). Subjective assessments of rhesus monkeys over four successive years.*Primates, 21*, 66–82.

Stewart, D.E., Boydell, K.M., Derzko, C. & Marshall, V. 1992. Psychological distress during the menopausal years in women attending a menopause clinic. *International Journal of Psychiatry in Medicine, 22(3)*, 213–220.

Stewart, M.J. (1989). Social support: Diverse theoretical perspectives. *Social Science and Medicine, 28(12)*, 1275–1282.

Stiles, W. B., Shapiro, D. A., & Elliott, R. (1986). "Are all psychotherapies equivalent?" *American Psychologist, 41*, 165–180.

Stipp, D. (1990, May 17). Einstein bird has scientists atwitter over mental feats. *Wall Street Journal*, pp. 1, 7.

Stone, J., Aronson, E., Crain, A. L., Winslow, M. P., & Fried, C. B. (1994). Inducing hypocrisy as a means of encouraging young adults to use condoms. *Personality and Social Psychology Bulletin, 20*, 116–128.

Stoppard, J. M., & Gruchy, C. D. G. (1993). Gender, context, and expression of positive emotion. *Personality and Social Psychology Bulletin, 19*, 143–150.

Storms, M. D. (1981). Theories of sexual orientation. *Journal of Personality and Social Psychology, 38*, 783–792.

Stoutjesdyk, D. & Jevne, R. 1993. Eating disorders among high performance atheletes. *Journal of Youth and Adolescence, 22(3)*, 271–282.

Strachan, H. J., Hohansen, H., Nair, C., & Nargundkar, M. (1990). Canadian suicide mortality rates: First-generation immigrants versus Canadian-born. *Health Reports, 2*, 327–341.

Strauman, T. J., Lemieux, A. M., & Coe, C. L. (1993). Self-discrepancy and natural killer cell activity: Immunological consequences of negative self-evaluation. *Journal of Personality and Social Psychology, 64*, 1042–1052.

Straumann, T. J., & Higgins, E. G. (1988). Self-discrepancies as predictors of vulnerability to distinct syndromes of chronic emotional distress. *Journal of Personality, 56*, 685–707.

Strauss, E., Wada, J.A. & Goldwater, B. 1992. Sex differences in interhemispheric reorganization of speech. *Neuropsychologia, 30(4)*, 353–359.

Strayer, J. (1993). Children's concordant emotions and cognitions in response to observed emotions. *Child Development, 64(1)*, 188–201.

Strayer, J., (1985). Current Research in diffective development. Special Issue: The feeling child: Affective development reconsidered. *Journal of Children in Contemporary Society, 17(4)*, 37–55.

Strayer, J., Schroeder, M. (1989). Children's helping strategies: Influences of emotion, empathy, and age. *New Directions for Child Development, 44*, 85–105.

Strean, H. S. (1985). *Resolving resistances in psychotherapy*. New York: Wiley Interscience.

Striegel-Moore, R.H., Silberstein, L.R. & Rodin, J. 1993. The social self in bulimia nervosa: Public self-consciousness, social anxiety, and percieved fraudulence. *Journal of Abnormal Psychology, 102(2)*, 297–303.

Strickland, B. R. (1992). Women and depression. *Current Directions in Psychological Science, 1*, 132–135.

Stroh, L.K., Brett, J.M., Reilly, A.H. (1992). All the right stuff: A comparison of female and male managers' career progression. *Journal of Applied Psychology, 77(3)*, 251–260.

Struckman-Johnson, C. J., Gilliland, R. C., Struckman-Johnson, D. L., & North, T. C. (1990). The effects of fear of AIDS and gender on responses to fear-arousing condom advertisements. *Journal of Applied Social Psychology, 20*, 1396–1410.

Strupp, H. H., & Binder, J. L. (1984). *Psychotherapy in a new key: A guide to time-limited dynamic psychotherapy*. New York: Basic Books.

Struthers, C.W., Colwill, N.L., Perry, R.P. (1992). An attributional analysis of decision making in a personnel selection interview. *Journal of Applied Social Psychology, 22(10)*, 801–818.

Stuart, R. B. (1977). Self-help group approach to self-management. In R. B. Stuart (Ed.), *Behavioral self-management: Strategies, techniques, and outcome*. New York: Brunner/Mazel.

Stuss, D.T., Benson, D.F. 1984. Neuropsychological studies of the frontal lobes. *Psychological Bulletin, 95(1)*, 3–28.

Stuss, D.T., Gow, C.A. & Hetherington, C.R. 1992. "No longer gage": frontal lobe dysfunction and emotional changes. Special section: the emotional concomitants of brain damage. *Journal of Consulting and Clinical Psychology, 60(3)*, 349–359.

Suboski, M.D. (1992). Releaser-induced recognition learning by amphibians and reptiles. *Animal Learning and Behavior, 20*, 63–82.

Suedfeld, P., Bluck, S., Bullard, E.J. & Baker-Brown, G. 1990. Canadian federal elections: motive profiles and integrative complexity in political speeches and popular media. *Canadian Journal of Behavioral Science, 22(1)*, 26–36.

Sullivan, M.J., Reesor, K., Mikail, S., Fisher, R. 1992. The treatment of depression in chronic low back pain: Review and recommendations. *Pain, 50(1)*, 5–13.

Suls, J., Wan, C.K. (1987) In search of the false-uniqueness phenomenon: Fear and estimates of social consensus. *Journal of Personality and Social Psychology, 52(1)*, 211–217.

Suls, J., Wan, C.K., Sanders, G.S. (1988). False consensus and false uniqueness in estimating the prevalence of health-protective behaviors. *Journal of Applied Social Psychology, 18(1)*, 66–79.

Sulsky, L.M., Day, D.V. (1992). Frame-of-reference training and cognitive categorization: An empirical investigation of rate memory issues. *Journal of Applied Psychology, 77(4)*, 501–510.

Summers, R.J. (1991). The influence of affirmative action on perceptions of a beneficiary's qualifications. *Journal of Applied Psychology, 21(15)*, 1265–1276.

Sundstrom, E., & Sundstrom, M. G. (1986). *Work places: The psychology of the physical environment in offices and factories*. Cambridge, England: Cambridge University Press.

Surbey, M.K. 1990. Family composition, stress, and the timing of human menarche. In Ziegler, T.E. & Bercovitch, F.B. (Eds.), *Socioendocrinology of Primate Reproduction*. New York: Wiley- Liss.

Surridge, D.M., MacLean, A., Coulter, M.E. and Knowles, J.B. (1987). Mood change following an acute delay of sleep. *Psychiatry Research, 22*, 149–158.

Swann, W. B., Jr., Stein-Seroussi, A., & Giesler, R. B. (1992). Why people self-verify. *Journal of Personality and Social Psychology, 62*, 392–401.

Swanson, D. (1987). Stress and burnout: II. Stress in residential rehabilitative services. *Residential Treatment for Children and Youth, 4(3)*, 31–44.

Swartzentruber, D. (1991). Blocking between occasion setters and contextual stimuli. *Journal of Experimental Psychology: Animal Behavior Processes, 12*, 163–173.

Swets, J. A. (1992). The science of choosing the right decision threshold in high-stakes diagnostics. *American Psychologist, 47*, 522–532.

Sylvain, C & Ladouceur, R. Correction cognitive et habitudes de jue chez les joueurs de poker video. (Corrective cognition and gambling habits of players of video poker.) (1992). *Canadian Journal of Behavioural Science, 24*, 479–489.

Szabo, A., Peronnet, F., Boudreau, G., Cote, L., Gauvin, L., Seraganian, P. 1993. Psychophysiological profiles in response to various challenges during recovery from acute aerobic exercise. *International Journal of Psychophysiology, 14(3)*, 285–292.

Sztaba, T.I., Colwill, N.L., (1988). Secretarial and management students: Attitudes, attributes, and career choice considerations. *Sex Roles, 19(9–10)*, 651–665.

Taerk, G., Gallop, R.M., Lancee, W.J., Coates, R.A., et al. (1993). Recurrent themes of concern in groups for health care professionals. *AIDS Care, 5(2)*, 215–222.

Tafari, S., Aboud, F.E., Larson, C.P. (1991). Determinants of mental illness in a rural Ethiopian adult population. *Social Science and Medicine, 32(2)*, 197–201.

Tainturier, M.J., Tremblay, M. & Lecours, A.R. 1989. Aging and the word frequency effect: A lexical decision investigation. *Neuropsychologia, 27(9)*, 1197–1203.

Tajfel, H. (1982). *Social identity and intergroup relations*. Cambridge, England: Cambridge University Press.

Takanishi, R. (1993). The opportunities of adolescence—research, interventions, and policy. *American Psychologist, 48*, 85–87.

Tannock, R., Purvis, K.L., Schachar, R.J., (1993). Narrative abilities in children with attention deficit hyperactivity disorder and normal peers. *Journal of Abnormal Psychology, 21(1)*, 103–117.

Tarquinio, N., Zelazo, P.R., Weiss, M.J. (1989). Recovery of neonatal head turning to decreased sound pressure level. *Developmental Psychology, 26(5)*, 752–758.

Taylor, M.C., Boss, M.W., Bedard, R., Thibault, C.J., Evans, K. (1990). Variables related to the transition of youth from school to work. *Canadian Journal of Counselling, 24(3)*, 153–164.

Taylor, R. L. (1991). Poverty and adolescent Black males: The subculture of disengagement. In P. B. Edelman & J. Ladner (Eds.), *Adolescence and poverty: Challenge for the 1990s* (pp. 139–162). Washington, DC: Center for National Policy Press.

Taylor, S. E. (1991). *Health psychology* (2nd ed.). New York: McGraw-Hill.

Teichman, M., Barnea, Z., & Rahav, G. (1989). Sensation seeking, state and trait anxiety, and depressive mood in adolescent substance abusers. *International Journal of the Addictions, 24*, 87–99.

Tellegen, A., Lykken, D. T., Bouchard, T. J., Wilcox, K. J., Segal, N. L., & Rich, S. (1988). Personality similarity in twins raised apart and together. *Journal of Personality and Social Psychology, 54*, 1031–1039.

Tennen, H., & Eller, S. J. (1977). Attributional components of learned helplessness. *Journal of Personality and Social Psychology, 35*, 265–271.

Terman, L. M. (1954). The discovery and encouragement of exceptional talent. *American Psychologist, 9*, 221–230.

Terrace, H. S. (1985). In the beginning was the "name." *American Psychologist, 40*, 1011–1028.

Terrace, H. S. (1993). The phylogeny and ontogeny of serial memory: List learning by pigeons and monkeys. *Psychological Science, 4*, 162–169.

Tesson, G., Lewko, J.H., Bigelow, B.J. (1987). The social rules that children use in their interpersonal relations. *Contributions to Human Development, 18*, 36–57.

Tett, R.P., Meyer, J.P. (1993). Job satisfaction, organizational commitment, turnover intention, and turnover: Path analyses based on meta-analytic findings. *Personnel Psychology, 46(2)*, 259–293.

Teyler, T. J., & DiScenna, P. (1984). Long-term potentiation as a candidate mnemonic device. *Brain Research Reviews, 7*, 15–28.

Thibault, C. (1992). Preventing suicide in young people … its a matter of life. *Canada's Mental Health, 40*, 2–7

Thiessen, I. 1993. The impact of divorce on children. Special issue: Enhancing young children's lives. *Early Child Development and Care, 96*, 19–26.

Thomas, A., & Chess, S. (1977). *Temperament and development*. New York: Brunner/Mazel.

Thomas, J. L. (1992). *Adulthood and aging*. Boston: Allyn and Bacon.

Thomas, M. H. (1982). Physiological arousal, exposure to a relatively lengthy aggressive film, and aggressive behavior. *Journal of Research in Personality, 16*, 72–181.

Thompson, J. K. (1992). Body image: Extent of disturbance, associated features, theoretical models, assessment methodologies, intervention strategies, and a proposal for a new DSM-IV diagnostic category—Body Image Disorder. In M. Hesen, R. M. Eisler, & P. M. Miller (Eds.), *Progress in behavior modification* (pp. 3–54). Sycamore, IL: Sycamore Publishing.

Thompson, R. A. (1988). The effects of infant day care through the prism of attachment theory: A critical appraisal. *Early Childhood Research Quarterly, 3*, 273–283.

Thompson, R. F. (1989). A model system approach to memory. In P. R. Solomon, G. R. Goethals, C. M., Kelley, & B. R. Stephens (Eds.), *Memory: Interdisciplinary approaches*. New York: Springer–Verlag.

Thompson, V.S. (1990). Factors affecting the level of African American identification. Special Issue: Incorporating and African world view into psychology: I. *Journal of Black Psychology, 17(1)*, 19–35.

Thompson, V.S. (1991). A multidimensional approach to the assessment of African American racial identification. *Western Journal of Black Studies, 15(3)*, 154–158.

Thompson, W.C., Cowan, C.L., Rosenhan, D.L. (1980). Focus of attention mediates the impact of negative affect on altruism. *Journal of Personality and Social Psychology, 38(2)*, 291–300.

Thorndike, R. L., & Hagen, E. (1982). *Ten thousand careers*. New York: Wiley.

Thurstone, E. L. (1938). *Primary mental abilities*. Chicago: University of Chicago Press.

Tice, D. M. (1989). Metatraits: Inherited variance as personality assessment. In D. M. Buss & N. Cantor (Eds.), *Personality psychology: Recent trends and emerging directions* (pp. 194–200). New York: Springer-Verlag.

Tiffany, S. T. (1990). A cognitive model of drug urges and drug-use behavior: Role of automatic and nonautomatic processes. *Psychological Review, 97*, 147–168.

Timney, B., (1990). Effects of brief monocular deprivation on binocular depth perception in the cat: A sensitive period for the loss of stereopsis. *Visual Neuroscience, 5(3)*, 273–280.

Ting-Toomey, S. (1991). Intimacy expressions in three cultures: France, Japan, and the United States. *International Journal of Intercultural Relations, 15*, 29–46.

Tisserand, R. B. (1977). *The art of aromatherapy*. Rochester, VT: Healing Arts Press.

Tobin, D.L., Johnson, C. Steinberg, S., Staats, M., Dennis, A.M. 1991. Multifactorial assessment of bulimia nervosa. *Journal of Abnormal Psychology, 100(1)*, 14–21.

Tolman, E. C., & Honzik, C. H. (1930). Introduction and removal of reward, and maze performance in rats. *University of California Publications in Psychology, 4*, 257–275.

Tomaka, J., Blascovich, J., Kelsey, R. M., & Leitten, C. L. (1993). Subjective, physiological, and behavioral effects of threat and challenge appraisal. *Journal of Personality and Social Psychology, 65*, 248–260.

Tomarken, A. J., Davidson, R. J., & Henriques, J. B. (1990). Resting frontal brain asymmetry predicts affective responses to films. *Journal of Personality and Social Psychology, 59*, 791–801.

Toufexis, A. (1992, April 27). Endangered species. *Time*, pp. 49–51.

Toufexis, A. (1993, February 15). The right chemistry. *Time*, pp. 49–51.

Tougas, F., Veilleux, F. (1988). The influence of identification, collective relative deprivation, and procedure of implementation of women's response to affirmative action: A causal modeling approach. *Canadian Journal of Behavioral Science, 20(1)*, 15–28.

Tougas, R., Dere, M., Veilleux, F., Boudreault, L. (1989). L'effet de l'information sur la privation relative collective dans une situation d'evaluation de candidats. (The effect of information of relative collective deprivation in a situation involving the evaluation of candidates). *Revue Quebecoise de Psychologie, 10(3)*, 54–65.

Tousignant, M., Bastien, M.F. & Hamel, S. 1993. Suicidal attempts and the ideations among adolescents and young adults: The contribution of the father's and mother's care and of parental separation. *Social Psychiatry and Psychiatric Epidemiology, 28(5)*, 256–261.

Towson, S. M. J., & Zanna, M. P. (1982). Toward a situational analysis of gender differences in aggression. *Sex Roles, 8*, 903–914.

Trainor, L.J., & Trehub, S.E., (1992). A comparison of infants' and adults' sensitivity to Western musical structure. *Journal of Experimental Psychology-Human Perception and Performance, 18(2)*, 394–402.

Trainor, L.J., Trehub, S.E., (1993). Musical context effects in infants and adults: Key distance. *Journal of Experimental Psychology-Human Perception and Performance, 19(3)*, 615–626.

Treffert, D. A. (1989). *Extraordinary people*. New York: Harper & Row.

Trehub, S.E., Unyk, A.M., Trainor, L.J., (1993). Adults identify infant directed music across cultures. *Infant Behavior and Development, 16(2)*, 193–211.

Trehub, S.E., Unyk, A.M., Trainor, L.J., (1993). Maternal singing in cross-cultural perspective. *Infant Behavior and Development, 16(3)*, 285–295.

Treit, D. Menard, J. and Royan, C. (1993). Axiogenic stimuli in the elevated-plus maze. *Pharmacology, Biochemistry and Behavior. 44*, 463–469.

Tremblay, S. 1992. Le counseling prenuptial: une invitation a intervenir. (Prenuptial counseling: an invitation for intervention.) *Revue Quebecoise de Psychologie, 13(1)*, 43–57.

Trinder, J. (1988). Subjective insomnia without objective findings: A pseudo diagnostic classification? *Psychological Bulletin, 103*, 87–94.

Trivers, R. (1985). *Social evolution*. Menlo Park, CA: Benjamin/Cummings.

Tronick, E.Z., (1989). Emotions and emotional communication in infants. Special Issue: Children and their development: Knowledge base, research agenda, and social policy application. *American Psychologist, 44(2)*, 112–119.

Trudeau, M., Overbury, O. & Conrod, B. 1990. Perceptual training and figure-ground performance in low vision. *Journal of Visual Impairment and Blindness, 84(5)*, 204–206.

Trudel, M. (1973). *The beginnings of New France 1524–1663*. Toronto: McClelland & Stewart.

Truscott, D. 1992. Intergenerational transmission of violent behavior in adolescent males. *Aggressive Behavior, 18(5)*, 327–335.

Tschann, J. M., Johnston, J. R., & Wallerstein, J. S. (1989). Resources, stressors, and attachment as predictors of adult adjustment after divorce: A longitudinal study. *Journal of Marriage and the Family, 51*, 1033–1046.

Tubbs, M.E., Boehne, D.M, Dahl, J.G. (1993). Expectancy, valence, and motivational force functions in goal-setting research: An empirical test. *Journal of Applied Psychology, 78(3)*, 361–373.

Tudiver, F., Hilditch, J., Permaul, J.A. & McKendree, D.J. 1992. Does mutual help facilitate newly bereaved widowers? Report of a randomized controlled trial. *Evaluation and the Health Professions, 15(2)*, 147–162.

Tudiver, F., Myers, T., Kurtz, R.G., Orr, K., et al. (1992). The talking sex project. *Evaluation and the Health Professions, 15(1)*, 26–42.

Tulving , E. (1989). Remembering and knowing the past. *American Scientist, 77*, 361–367

Tulving , E, Schacter, D. L. McLachlan, D. R. & Moscovitch, M. (1988). Priming of semantic autobiographical memory: A case study of retrograde amnesia. *Brain and Cognition, 8*, 3–20.

Tulving, E. (1993). What is episodic memory? *Current Directions in Psychological Science, 2*, 67–70.

Tulving , E., & Psotka, L. (1971). Retroactive inhibition in free recall: Inaccessibility of information available in the memory store. *Journal of Experimental Psychology, 87*, 1–8.

Tulving, E., & Schacter, D. L. (1990). Priming and human memory systems. *Science, 247*, 301–396

Tulving , E., & Thomson, D. M. (1973). Encoding specificity and retrieval processes in episodic memory. *Psychological Review, 80*, 352–373.

Turk, D. C., & Rudy, T. E. (1992). Cognitive factors and persistent pain: A glimpse into Pandora's box. *Cognitive Therapy and Research, 16*, 99–122.

Turkheimer, E., & Farace, A. (1992). A reanalysis of gender differences in IQ scores following unilateral brain lesions. *Psychological Assessment, 4*, 498–501.

Turner, J. A., & Clancy, S. (1986). Strategies for coping with chronic low back pain: Relationship to pain and disability. *Pain, 24*, 355–362.

Turner, J. C., Hogg, M. A., Oakes, P. J., Richer, S. D., & Wetherell, M. S. (1987). *Rediscovering the social group: A self-categorization theory*. Oxford, England: Blackwell.

Tversky, A., & Kahneman, D. (1974). Judgment under uncertainty: Heuristics and biases. *Science, 185*, 1124–1131.

Tversky, A., & Kahneman, D. (1981). The framing of decisions and the psychology of choice. *Science, 211*, 453–458.

Tyler, T. R., & Cook, F. L. (1984). The mass media and judgment of risk: Distinguishing impact on personal and societal level judgments. *Journal of Personality and Social Psychology, 47*, 693–708.

Unger, R. K. (in press). Alternative conceptions of sex (and sex differences). In M. Haug, R. Whalen, C. Aron, & K. L. Olsen (Eds.), *The development of sex differences and similarities in behavior*. Dordrecht, The Netherlands: Kluwer Academic.

Unger, R. K., & Crawford, M. (1992). *Women and gender: A feminist psychology*. Philadelphia: Temple University Press.

Ungerleider, C.S. (1992). Immigration, multiculturalism, and citizenship: The development of the Canadian social justice infrastructure. *Canadian Ethnic Studies, 24(3)*, 7–22.

Unyk, A. M. (1990) An information-processing analysis of expectancy in music cognition. *Psychomusicology, 9*, 229–240.

Urban, M. J. (1992) Auditory subliminal stimulation: A reexamination. *Perceptual and Motor Skills, 74*, 515–541.

Usher, J. A., & Neisser, U. (1993). Childhood amnesia and the beginnings of memory for four early life events. *Journal of Experimental Psychology: General. 122*, 155–165.

Uttl, B. & Graf, P. 1993. Episodic spatial memory in adulthood. *Psychology and Aging, 8(2)*, 257–273.

Vaccarino et al. 1993. as quoted by Leo Charbonneau in the *Medical Post*, June 22, 1993, page 34.

Vallerand, R.J. & Bissonnette, R. 1992. Intrinsic, extrinsic, and amotivational styles as predictors of behavior: a prospective study. *Journal of Personality, 60(3)*, 599–620.

Vallerand, R.J. & O'Connor, B.P. 1989. Motivation in the elderly: A theoretical framework and some promising findings. Special Issue: Psychology of aging and gerontology. *Canadian Psychology, 30(3)*, 538–550.

Vallerand, R.J., Pelletier, L.G., Blais, M.R., Briere, N.M., Senecal, C., Vallieres, E.F. 1992. The Academic Motivation Scale: a measure of intrinsic, extrinsic, and amotivation in education. *Educational and Psychological Measurement, 52(4)*, 1003–1017.

Vallone, R. P., Griffin, D. W., Lin, S., & Ross, L. (1990). Overconfident prediction of future actions and outcomes by self and others. *Journal of Personality and Social Psychology, 58*, 582–592.

Van Houten, R. (1993). The use of wrist weights to reduce self-injury maintained by sensory reinforcement. *Journal of Applied Behavior Analysis, 26*, 197–203.

Van Roosmalen, E.H. & McDaniel, S.A. 1992. Adolescent smoking intentions: gender differences in peer context. *Adolescence, 27(105)*, 87–105.

Van Vianen, A.E., Willemsen, T.M. (1992). The employment interview: The role of sex stereotypes in the evaluation of male and female job applicants in the Netherlands. *Journal of Applied Social Psychology, 22(6)*, 471–491.

Vance, J., et al. v. Judas Priest et al., No. 86–5844 (2nd Dist. Ct. Nev. 1990).

Vandenburgh, J.G. 1989. Coordination of social signals ovarian function during sexual development. *Journal of Animal Science, 67(7)*, 1841–1847.

Vasudev, J., & Hummel, R. C. (1987). Moral stage sequence and principled reasoning in an Indian sample. *Human Development, 30*, 105–118

Vauclair, J., Fagot, J., & Hopkins, W. D. (1993). Rotation of mental images in baboons when the visual input is directed to the cerebral hemisphere. *Psychological Science, 4*, 99–103.

Vaughan, E. 1993. Individual and cultural differences in adaptation to environmetal risks. *American Psychologist, 48(6)*, 673–680.

Verby, C., Herold, E.S. (1992). Parents and AIDS education. *AIDS Education and Prevention, 4(3)*, 187–196.

Vernon, P. A. (1991). Studying intelligence the hard way. *Intelligence, 15*, 389–395.

Vernon, P. A., & Mori, M. (1992). Intelligence, reaction times, and peripheral nerve conduction velocity. *Intelligence, 16*, 273–288.

Vernon, P.A., Jang, K.L. (1993). Self-rated vs "actual" personality similarity in monozygotic and dizygotic twins and non-twin siblings. *Personality and Individual Differences, 15(2)*, 219–220.

Vidmar, N. (1974). Retributive and utlitarian motives and other correltates of Canadian attitudes toward the death penalty. *Canadian Psychologist, 15(4)*, 337–356.

Vidmar, N., Crinklaw, L.D. (1974). Attributing responsibility for an accident: A methodological and conceptual critique. *Canadian Journal of Behavioural Science, 6(2)*, 112–130.

Vidmar, N., Rokeach, M. (1974). Archie Bunker's bigotry: A study in selective perception and exposure. *Journal of Communication, 24(1)*, 36–47.

Vincente, K. J. & Brewer, W. F. (1993). Reconstructive remembering of the scientific literature. *Cognition, 46*, 101–128.

Vitz, P.C., (1990). The use of stories in moral development: New psychological reasons for an old education method. John Finch Lectures (1990, Pasadena, California). *American Psychologist, 45(6)*, 709–720.

Vogel, L. Z. & Savva, S. (1993). Atlas personality. *British Journal of Medical Psychology, 66*, 323–330.

Volpicelli, J. R., Alterman, A. I., Hayashida, M., & O'Brien, C. P. (1992). Naltrexone in the treatment of alcohol dependence. *Archives of General Psychiatry, 49*, 876–880.

Von Senden, M. (1960). *Space and sign*. Trans. by P. Heath. New York: Free Press.

Vormbrock, J. K. (1993). Attachment theory as applied to wartime and job-related marital separation. *Psychological Bulletin, 114*, 122–144.

Vroom, V. H. (1964). *Work and motivation*. New York: Wiley.

Vygotsky, L. S. (1987). Thinking and speech. In R. W. Rieber, A. S. Carton (Eds.), & N. Minick (Trans.), *The collected works of L. S. Vygotsky: Vol 1. Problems of general psychology* (pp. 37–285). New York: Plenum. (Original work published in 1934.)

Wagenaar, W. A., (1986). My memory: A study of autobiographical memory over six years. *Cognitive Psychology, 18*, 225–522.

Waitzkin, H. (1984). Doctor-patient communication: Clinical implications of social scientific research. *Journal of the American Medical Association, 252*, 2441–2446.

Walden, T.A., Ogan, T.A., (1988). The development of social referencing. *Child Development, 59(5)*, 1230–1240.

Walker, L.J., Taylor, J.H., (1991). Family interactions and the development of moral reasoning. *Child Development, 62(2)*, 264–283.

Walker, L.J., Taylor, J.H., (1991). Stage transitions in moral reasoning: A longitudinal srudy of developmental processes. *Developmental Psychology, 27(2)*, 330–337.

Walker, L. J. (1988). The development of moral reasoning. In R. Vasta (Ed.), *Annals of child development* (Vol. 5, pp. 33–78). Greenwich, CT: JAI Press.

Walker, L. J. & DeVries, B. (1985). *Moral stages/moral orientations: Do the sexes really differ?* Paper presented at the meetings of the American Psychological Association, Los Angeles.

Wall, A.M., Hinson, R.E., Schmidt, E., Johnson, C. et al. (1990). Place conditioning with d-amphetamine: The effect of the CS-UCS interval and evidence of a place avoidance. *Animal Learning and Memory, 18*, 393–400.

Wallace, B. (1993). Day persons, night persons, and variability in hypnotic susceptability. *Journal of Personality and Social Psychology, 64*, 827–833

Wallace, R. K., & Benson, H. (1972). The physiology of meditation. *Scientific American, 236*, 84–90.

Wallace, R. K., & Fisher, L. E. (1987). *Consciousness and behavior* (2nd ed.). Boston: Allyn and Bacon.

Waller, N. G., & Ben-Porath, Y. S. (1987). Is it time for clinical psychology to embrace the five-factor model of personality? *American Psychologist, 42*, 887–889.

Wallersteiner, U., Lawrence, P., Sauder, B. (1993). A human factors evaluation of two different machine control systems for log loaders. Special Issue: Ergonomics in Canada: Managing your environment. *Ergonomics, 36(8)*, 927–934.

Wallman, J. (1992). *Aping Language*. New York : Cambridge.

Walsh, S. (1993). Cited in Toufexis, A. (1993, February 15), *Time*, pp. 49–51.

Walster, E., & Festinger, L. (1962). The effectiveness of "overheard" persuasive communication. *Journal of Abnormal and Social Psychology, 65*, 395–402.

Walton, G. E., & Bower, T. G. R. (1993). Newborns form "prototypes" in less than 1 minute. *Psychological Science, 4*, 203–205.

Walton, G. E., Bower, N. J. A., & Bower, T. G. R. (1992). Recognition of familiar faces by newborns. *Infant Behavior and Development, 15*, 265–269.

Wankel, L.M. 1993. The importance of enjoyment to adherence and psychological benefits from physical activity. Special issue: exercise and psychological well being. *International Journal of Sport Psychology, 24(2)*, 151–169.

Waring, E. M., Stalker, C. A., Carver, C. M., & Gitta, M. Z. (1991). Waiting list controlled trial of cognitive marital therapy in severe marital discord. *Journal of Marital and Family Therapy, 17*, 243–256.

Warm, J. S., Dember, W. N., & Parasuraman, R. (1991). Effects of olfactory stimulation on performance and stress in a visual sustained attention task. *Journal of the Society of Cosmetic Chemists, 12*, 1–12.

Warwick, Z.S., Hall, W.G., Pappas, T.N. & Schiffman, S.S. 1993. Taste and smell sensations enhance the satiating effect of both a high-carbohydrate and a high-fat meal in humans. *Physiology and Behavior, 53(3)*, 553–563.

Wasserman, D., Lempert, R. O., & Hastie, R. (1991). Hindsight and causality. *Personality and Social Psychology Bulletin, 17*, 30–35

Wasserman, E. A. (1993). Comparative cognition: Toward a general understanding of cognition in behavior. *Psychological Science, 4*, 156–161.

Wasserman, E. A., Kiedinger, R. E., & Bhatt, R. S. (1988). Conceptual behavior in pigeons: Categories, subcategories, and pseudocategories. *Journal of Experimental Psychology: Animal Behavior Processes, 14*, 235–246.

Wasylenki, D. A., Goering, P. N., Lemire, D., Lindsey, S., & Lancee, W. (1993). The hostel outreach program: Assertive case management for homeless mentally ill persons. *Hospital and Community Psychiatry, 44*, 848–853.

Watson, C., Anderson, F., Gloor, P., Jones-Gotman, M., Peters, T., Evans, A., Oliver, A., Melanson, D., Leroux, G. 1992. Anatomic basis of amygdaloid and hippocampal volume measurement by magnetic resonance imaging. *Neurology, 42(9)*, 1743–1750.

Watson, D. (1989). Strangers' ratings of the five robust personality factors: Evidence of a surprising convergence with self-report. *Journal of Personality and Social Psychology, 57*, 120–128.

Watson, J. B. (1924). The unverbalized in human behavior. *Psychological Review, 31*, 273–280.

Watson, J. B., & Raynor, R. (1920). Conditioned emotional reactions. *Journal of Experimental Psychology, 3*, 1–14.

Webb, W. (1975). *Sleep: The gentle tyrant*. Englewood Cliffs, NJ: Prentice-Hall.

Webb, W., & Agnew, H. W. (1967). Sleep cycling within the twenty-four hour period. *Journal of Experimental Psychology, 74*, 167–169.

Webster, E.C. (1988). I/O psychology in Canada: From birth to Couchiching. Special Issue: Industrial/organizational psychology in Canada. *Canadian Psychology, 29(1)*, 4–10.

Webster, J.D. & Cappeliez, P. 1993. Reminiscence and autobiographical memory: complementary context for cognitive aging research. *Developmental Review, 13(1)*, 54–91.

Weekes, J. R., Lynn, S. J., Green, J. P., & Brentar, J. T. (1992). Pseudomemory in hypnotized and task-motivated subjects. *Journal of Abnormal Psychology, 101*, 356–360.

Wehner, R., & Menzel, R. (1990). Do insects have cognitive maps? *Annual Review of Neuroscience, 13*, 403–414.

Wehr, T.A., Giesen, H.A., Schulz, P.M., Anderson, J.L., Joseph-Vanderpool, J.R., Kelly, K., Kasper, S., & Rosenthal, N.E. (1991). Contrasts between symptoms of summer depression and winter depression. *Journal of Affective Disorders, 23*, 173–183.

Weinberg, J., (1988). Hyperresponsiveness to stress: Differential effects of prenatal ethanol on males and females. *Alcoholism—Clinical and Experimental Research, 12(5)*, 647–652.

Weinberg, R. A. (1989). Landmark issues and great debates. *American Psychologist, 44(2)*, 98–104.

Weinberger, A. (1989) Ethics: code value and application. *Canadian Psychologist, 30*, 77–85.

Weiner, B. (1989). *Human motivation*. Hillsdale, NJ: Erlbaum.

Weisberg, R., & Suls, J. M. (1973). An information-processing model of Duncker's candle problem. *Cognitive Psychology, 4*, 255–276.

Weisenberg, M. (1982). Cultural and ethnic factors in reaction to pain. In I. Al-Issa (Ed.), *Culture and psychopathology*. Baltimore: University Park Press.

Weisner, T. S., & Wilson-Mitchell, J. E. (1990). Nonconventional family lifestyles and sex typing in six-year-olds. *Child Development, 61*, 1915–1933.

Weiss, R. A. (1993). How does HIV cause AIDS? *Science, 260*, 1273–1278.

Weisz, J. R., Weiss, B., & Donenberg, G. R. (1992). The lab versus the clinic: Effects of child and adolescent psychotherapy. *American Psychologist, 47*, 1578–1585.

Weisz, J. R., Weiss, B., Morton, T., Granger, D., & Han, S. (1992). Metaanalysis of psychotherapy outcome research with children and adolescents. Unpublished manuscript, University of California, Los Angeles.

Wellisch, D. K., & Trock, G. K. (1980). A three-year follow-up of family therapy. *International Journal of Family Therapy, 2*, 169–175.

Wellman, H. M., Somerville, S. C., & Haake, R. J. (1979). Development of search procedures in real-life spatial environments. *Developmental Psychology, 15*, 530–542.

Wells, G. L. (1993). What do we know about eyewitness identification? *American Psychologist, 48*, 553–571.

Wells, G.L., Taylor, B.R., Turtle, J.W. (1987). The undoing of scenarios. *Journal of Personality and Social Psychology, 53(3)*, 421–430

Wells, L. E., & Marwell, G. (1976). *Self-esteem*. Beverly Hills, CA: Sage.

Werker, J. F. (1989). Becoming a native listener. *American Scientist, 77*, 54–59.

Werker, J.F., Tees, R.C., (1992). The organization and reorganization of human speech perception. *Annual Review of Neuroscience, 15*, 377–402.

West, D. C. (1993). Restricted Creativity: Advertising agency work practices in the US, Canada and the UK. *Journal of Creative Behavior, 27(3)*, 200–213.

West, R. 1993. Beneficial effects of nicotine: fact or fiction. *Addiction, 88(5)*, 589–590.

Wheaton, B. 1990. Life transitions, role histories and mental health. *American Sociological Review, 55(2)*, 209–223.

Whiffen, V.E., Gotlib, I.H. (1993). Comparison of postpartum and non-postpartum depression: Clinical presentation, psychiatric history, and psychosocial functioning. *Journal of Consulting and Clinical Psychology, 61(3)*, 485–494.

Whishaw, I.Q., Pellis, S.M. & Gorny, B.P. 1992. Medial frontal cortex lesions impair the aiming component of rat reaching. *Behavioral Brain Research, 50(1–2)*, 93–104.

Whissell, R., Lyons, S., Wilkinson, D., Whissell, C. (1993). National bias in judgments of olympic-level skating. *Perceptual and Motor Skills, 77*, 355–358.

White, G. L., & Mullen, P. E. (1990). *Jealousy: Theory, research, and clinical strategies*. New York: Guilford Press.

White, J. L., & Parham, T. (1990). *The psychology of Blacks: An African-American perspective*. Englewood Cliffs, NJ: Prentice Hall.

White, R.K. (1977). Misperception in the Arab-Israeli conflict. *Journal of Social Issues, 33(1)*, 190–221.

Whorf, B. L. (1956). Science and linguistics. In J. B. Carroll (Ed.), *Language, thought, and reality: Selected writings of Benjamin Whorf*. Cambridge, MA: MIT Press.

Whybrow, P. C., Akiskal, H. S., & McKinney, W. T., Jr. (1984). *Mood disorders: Toward a new psychophysiology*. New York: Plenum.

Whyte, G. (1991). Diffusion of responsibility: Effects on the escalation tendency. *Journal of Applied Psychology, 76*, 408–415.

Whyte, K. (1992). A community in crisis: Will mental health services respond to AIDS? *Canada's Mental Health, 40(4)*, 2–5.

Wickelgren, W. A. (1965). Acoustic similarity and intrusion errors in short-term memory. *Journal of Experimental Psychology, 70*, 102–108.

Widmeyer, W.N., Loy, J.W. (1988). When you're hot, you're hot~ Warm-cold effects in first impressions of persons and teaching effectiveness. *Journal of Educational Psychology, 80(1)*, 118–121.

Widom, C. S. (1989). Does violence beget violence? A critical examination of the literature. *Psychological Bulletin, 106*, 3–28.

Wielkiewicz, R. M., & Calvert, C. R. X. (1989). *Training and habilitating developmentally disabled people: An introduction*. Newbury Park, CA: Sage.

Wiesel, T. N. (1982). Postnatal development of the visual cortex and the influence of environment. *Nature, 299*, 583–591.

Wiggins, J. S. & Pincus, A. L. (1992). Personality; Structure and assessment. *Annual Review of Psychology, 43*, 473–504.

Wiggins, S., Whyte, P., Higgins, M., Adam, S., Theilmann, J., Bloch, M., Sheps, S.B., Schechter, M.T., Hayden, M.R. 1992. The psychological consequences of predictive testing for Huntington's disease. *New England Journal of Medicine, 327(20)*, 1401–1405.

Wilcoxon, H. C., Dragoin, W. B., & Kral, P. A. (1971). Illness-induced aversions in rats and quail: Relative salience of visual and gustatory cues. *Science, 171*, 826–828.

Wilder, D.A. (1977). Perception of groups, size of opposition and social influence. *Journal of Experimental Social Psychology, 13(3)*, 253–268.

Wiley, J. A., & Camacho, T. C. (1980). Life-style and future health: Evidence from the Alameda County study. *Preventive Medicine, 9*, 1–21.

Wilgosh, L. & Mueller, H.H. 1993. Work skills for disadvantaged and unprepared youth and adults. *International Journal for the Advancement of Counselling, 16(2)*, 99–105.

Willett, W. C., & MacMahon, B. (1984). Diet and cancer—an overview. *New England Journal of Medicine, 310*, 633–638.

Williams, D. E., & Page, M. M. (1989). A multi-dimensional measure of Maslow's hierarchy of needs. *Journal of Research in Personality, 23*, 192–213.

Williams, R., Zyzanski, S. J., & Wright, A. L. (1992). Life events and daily hassles and uplifts as predictors of hospitalization and outpatient visitation. *Social Science Medicine, 34*, 763–768.

Williams, R. L. (1976). *Manual of direction for Williams awareness sentence completion*. St. Louis, MO: Robert L. Williams & Associates.

Williamson, D. A. (1990). *Assessment of eating disorders: Obesity, anorexia, and bulimia nervosa*. New York: Pergamon Press.

Williamson, D. A., Cubic, B. A., & Gleaves, D. H. (1993). Equivalence of body image disturbances in anorexia and bulimia nervosa. *Journal of Abnormal Psychology, 102(1)*, 177–180.

Willis, S. L., & Nesselroade, C. S. (1990). Long-term effects of fluid ability training in old-old age. *Developmental Psychology, 26*, 905–910.

Willis, W. D. (1985). *The pain system. The neural basis of nociceptive transmission in the mammalian nervous system*. Basel: Karger.

Wilson, C., Stewin, L.L. (1992). Semantic differential responses to educational posters on Acquired Immune Deficiency Syndrome (AIDS). *Alberta Journal of Educational Research, 38(2)*, 79–89.

Wilson, D. W. (1981). Is helping a laughing matter? *Psychology, 18*, 6–9.

Wilson, R.J. (1990). The relationship of seat belt non-use to personality, lifestyle and driving record. *Health Education Research, 5*, 175–185.

Wilson, T. D., DePaulo, B. M., Mook, D. G., & Klaaren, K. J. (1993). Scientists' evaluations of research: The biasing effects of the importance of the topic. *Psychological Science, 4*, 322–325.

Wilson, T. D., & Klaaren, K. J. (1992). *Effects of affective expectations on willingness to relive pleasant and unpleasant events*. Unpublished data. Cited in Wilson, T. D., & Klaaren, K. J., "Expectation whirls me round": The role of affective expectations in affective experience. In M. S. Clark (Ed.), *Emotion and social behavior* (pp. 1–31). Newbury Park, CA: Sage.

Wilson, T. D., Lisle, D. J., Kraft, D., & Wetzel, C. G. (1989). Preferences as expectation-driven inferences: Effects of affective expectations on affective experience. *Journal of Personality and Social Psychology, 56*, 519–530.

Wilson, T. D., & Schooner, J. (1991). Thinking too much: Introspection can reduce the quality of preferences and decisions. *Journal of Personality and Social Psychology, 60*, 181–192.

Winefield, A. H., & Tiggemann, M. (1991). Employment status and psychological well-being: A longitudinal study. *Journal of Applied Psychology, 75*, 455–459.

Winett, R. A., & Neale, M. S. (1981). Flexible work schedules and family time allocation: Assessment of a system change on individual behavior using self-report logs. *Journal of Applied Behavior Analysis, 14*, 39–46.

Winocur, G. 1992. A comparison of normal old rats and young adult rats with lesions to the hippocampus or prefrontal cortex on a test of matching-to-sample. *Neuropsychologia, 30(9)*, 769–781.

Winocur, G., Moscovitch, M., & Freedman, J. (1987). An investigation of cognitive function in relation to psychosocial variables in institutionalized old people. Special Issue: Aging and cognition. *Canadian Journal of Psychology, 41(2)*, 257–269.

Winograd, E. (1988). Some observations on prospective remembering. In M. M. Gruneberg, P. E. Morris, & R. N. Sykes (Eds.), *Practical aspects of memory: Current research and issues: Vol. 1* (pp. 348–353). Chichester, England: John Wiley & Sons.

Winter, D. G. (1973). *The power motives.* New York: Free Press.

Winter, D. G. (1983). *Development of an integrated system for scoring motives in verbal running text.* Unpublished manuscript, Wesleyan University.

Wise, R. A., & Bozarth, M. A. (1987). A psychomotor stimulant theory of addiction. *Psychological Review, 94*, 469–492.

Witelson, S.E., Kigar, D.L. & McKanna, J.A. 1992. A computer- assisted direct imaging system to obtain numerical densities of neurons in human cortex. *Brain Research Bulletin, 29(3–4)*, 441–447.

Witelson, S.F. & McCulloch, P.B. 1991. Premortem and postmortem measurement to study structure with function: a human brain collection. *Schizophrenia Bulletin, 17(4)*, 583–591.

Witelson, S.F. 1991. Neural sexual mosaicism: sexual differentiation of the human temporo-parietal region for functional assymetry. Special issue: neuroendocrine effects on brain development and cognition. *Psychoneuroendocrinology, 16(1–3)*, 131–153.

Witelson, S.F., McCulloch, P.B. 1991. Premortem and postmortem measurement to study structure with function: A human brain collection. *Schizophrenia Bulletin, 17(4)*, 583–591.

Wogalter, M. S., & Young, S. L. (1991). Behavioural compliance to voice and print warnings. *Ergonomics, 34*, 79–89.

Wogalter, M. S., & Young, S. L. (1993). Using warnings to increase safe behavior: A process approach. *Best's safety directory.* Oldwick, NJ: A. M. Best Company.

Wolberg, L. R. (1977). *The technique of psychotherapy.* New York: Grune & Stratton.

Wolf, M., Risley, T., & Mees, H. (1964). Application of operant conditioning procedures to the behavior problems of an autistic child. *Behavior Research and Therapy, 1*, 305–312.

Wolfe, D. A., Sandler, J., & Kaufman, K. (1981). Competency-based parent training program for child abusers. *Journal of Consulting and Clinical Psychology, 49*, 633–640.

Wolfson, C., Handfield-Jones, R., Glass, K.C., McClaren, J., Keyserlingk, E. 1993. Adult children's perceptions of their responsability to provide care for dependent elderly parents. *Gerontologist, 33(3)*, 315–323.

Wolpe, J. (1958). *Psychotherapy by reciprocal inhibition.* Stanford, CA: Stanford University Press.

Wolpe, J. (1969). *The practice of behavior therapy.* Oxford: Pergamon Press.

Wong, D. F., Gjedde, A., Wagner, H. N., Jr., Tune, L. E., Dannals, R. F., Pearlsson, G. D., Links, J. M., Tamminga, C. A., Broussolle, E. P., Ravert, H. T., Wilson, A. A., Toung, J. K. T., Malat, J., Williams, F. A., O,Touma, L. A., Snyder, S. H., Kuhar, M. J., & Gjedde, A. (1986). Positron emission tomography reveals elevated D2 dopamine receptors in drug-naive schizophrenics. *Science, 234*, 1558–1563.

Wong, P.T. (1993). Effective management of life stress: The resource-congruence model. *Stress Medicine, 9*, 51–60.

Wong, R. & McBride, C.B. (1993). Flavour neophobia in gerbils (Meriones unguiculatus) and hamsters (Mesocricetus auratus). *Quarterly Journal of Experimental Psychology: Comparative and Physiological Psychology, 46B*, 129–143.

Wong, T.P., Derlega, V.J., Colson, W. (1988). The effects of race on expectancies and performance attributions. *Canadian Journal of Behavioural Science, 20(1)*, 29–39.

Wood, C., & Kakuchi, S. (1994). The global gap. *Maclean's 107*, 44–53.

Wood, R. A., & Locke, E. A. (1990). Goal setting and strategy effects on complex tasks. In B. M. Staw & L. L. Cummings (Eds.), *Research in organizational behavior* (Vol. 12, pp. 73–110). Greenwich, CT: JAI Press.

Wood, W., Wong, F. Y., & Chachere, J. G. (1991). Effects of media violence on viewers' aggression in unconstrained social interaction. *Psychological Bulletin, 109*, 373–383.

Woodall, K. L., & Matthews, K. A. (1993). Changes in and stability of hostile characteristics: Results from a 4-year longitudinal study of children. *Journal of Personality and Social Psychology, 64*, 491–499.

Worden, J.W. 1989. As in the *Toronto Star,* January 14, 1989, H4.

Wortman, C. B., & Linsenmeier, H. A. W. (1977). Interpersonal attraction and techniques of ingratiation in organizational settings. In B. N. Staw & G. R. Salancik (Eds.), *New directions in organizational behavior* (pp. 133–178). Chicago: St. Clair Press.

Wright, E.F., Rule, B.G., Ferguson, T.J., McGuire, G.R., Wells, G.L. (1992). Misattribution of dissonance and behaviour-consistent attitude change. *Canadian Journal of Behavioural Science, 24(4)*, 456–464.

Wright, M. J. & Myers, R. C. (1982). *History of academic psychology in Canada.* C. J. Hogrefe, Inc., Toronto, 1982.

Wright, P.L. (1990). Teller job satisfaction and organization commitment as they relate to career orientations. *Human Relations, 43(4)*, 369–381.

Wright, R. W. (1982). *The sense of smell.* Boca Raton, FL: CRC Press.

Wylie, R. (1974). *The self-concept* (Vol. 1). Lincoln: University of Nebraska Press.

Yankner, J., Johnson, S. T., Menerdo, T., Cordell, B., & Firth, C. L. (1990). Relations of neural APP-751/APP-695 in RNA ratio and neuritic plaque density in Alzheimer's disease. *Science, 248*, 854–856.

Yarmey, A.D. (1986). Competence et credibilite des agents de police comme temoins oculaires. / Perceived expertness and credibility of police officers as eyewitnesses. *Canadian Police College Journal, 10(1)*, 36–58.

Yarmey, A.D. (1993). Stereotypes and recognition memory for faces and voices of good guys and bad guys. *Applied Cognitive Psychology, 7(5)*, 419–431.

Yogman, M. W. (1981). Development of the father-infant relationship. In H. Fitzgerald, B. Lester, & M. W. Yogman (Eds.), *Theory and research in behavioral pediatrics* (Vol. 1, pp. 221–279). New York: Plenum.

Yonas, A., Arterberry, M.E., Granrud, C.E., (1987). Four-month- old infants' sensitivity to binocular and kinetic information for three-dimensional-object shape. *Child Development, 58(4)*, 910–917.

Young, A. M., & Herling, S. (1986). Drugs as reinforcers: Studies in laboratory animals. In S. R. Goldberg & I. P. Stolerman (Eds.), *Behavioral analysis of drug dependence* (pp. 9–67). New York: Academic Press.

Young, L. T., Hood, E., Abbey, S. E., & Malcolmson, S. A. (1993). Psychiatric Consultation in the Eastern Canadian Arctic. II. Referral patterns, diagnosis and treatment. *Canadian Journal of Psychiatry, 38*, 28–31.

Young, R.A., Friesen, J.D., Dillabough, J.M. (1991). Personal constructions of parental influence related to career development. XIVth World Congress of the International Association for Educational and Vocational Guidance (1990, Montreal, Canada). *Canadian Journal of Counselling, 25(2)*, 183–190.

Younger, J.C., Walker, L., Arrowood, A.J. (1977). Postdecision dissonance at the fair. *Personality and Social Psychology Bulletin, 3(2)*, 284–287.

Yuille, J. C. & Kim, C. K. (1987). A field study of the forensic use of hypnosis. *Canadian Journal of Behavioral Science, 19*, 418–429.

Yuille, J. C. & Tollestrup, P. A. (1992). A model of the diverse effects of emotion on eyewitness memory. In S.-A. Christianson (Ed.), *The handbook of emotion and learning: Research and theory.* Hillsdale, NJ: Erlbaum.

Yuille, J. C., & Tollestrup, P. A. (1990). Some effects of alcohol on eyewitness memory. *Journal of Applied Psychology, 75*, 268–273.

Zaccaro, S.J., Foti, R.J., Kenny, D.A. (1991). Self-monitoring and trait-based variance in leadership: An investigation of leader flexibility across multiple group situations. *Journal of Applied Psychology, 76(2)*, 308–315.

Zacks, R. T., & Hasher, L. (1988). Capacity theory and the processing of inferences. In L. Light & D. Burke (Eds.), *Language, memory, and aging.* New York: Cambridge University Press.

Zajonc, R. B. (1976). Family configuration and intelligence. *Science, 192*, 226–236.

Zajonc, R. B., & Markus, G. B. (1975). Birth order and intellectual development. *Psychological Review, 82*, 74–88.

Zajonc, R. B. (1968). Attitudinal effects of mere exposure. *Journal of Personality and Social Psychology Monograph Supplement, 9*, 1–27.

Zajonc, R.B. (1986, February). Mining new gold from old research. *Psychology Today.*

Zajonc, R. B., & McIntosh, D. N. (1992). Emotions research: Some promising questions and some questionable promises. *Psychological Science, 3*, 70–74.

Zapf, M.K. (1993). Remote practice and culture shock: Social workers moving to isolated northern regions. *Social Work, 38(6)*, 694–704.

Zarbatany, L., Ghesquiere, K. & Mohr, K. 1992. A context perspective on early adolescents' friendship expectations. *Journal of Early Adolescence, 12(1)*, 111–126.

Zatzick, D. F., & Dimsdale, J. E. (1990). *Psychosomatic Medicine, 52*, 544–557.

Zeki, S. (1992, September). The visual image in mind and brain. *Scientific American,* pp. 69–76.

Zelazo, N.A., Zelazo, P.R., Cohen, K.M., Zelazo, P.D., (1993). Specificity of practice effects on elementary neuromotor patterns. *Developmental Psychology, 29(4)*, 686–691.

Zelazo, P.R., Weiss, M.J., Papageorgiou, A.N., Laplante, D.P., (1989). Recovery and dishabituation of sound localization among normal-, moderate-, and high-risk newborns. Discriminant validity. *Infant Behavior and Development, 12(3)*, 321–340.

Ziegler, S.G. (1987). Comparison of imagery styles and past experience in skills performance. *Perceptual and Motor Skills, 64(2)*, 579–586.

Ziegler, S.G. (1987). Effects of stimulus cueing on the acquisition of groundstrokes by beginning tennis players. *Journal of Applied Behavioral Analysis, 20(4)*, 405–411.

Ziegler, S.G. (1991). Perceived benefits of marathon running in males and females. *Sex Roles, 25(3–4)*, 119–127.

Zigler, E., Berman, W. (1983). Discerning the future of early childhood intervention. *American Psychologist, 38*, 894–906.

Zillmann, D. (1984). *Connections between sex and aggression.* Hillsdale, NJ: Erlbaum.

Zillmann, D. (1988). Cognition-excitation interdependencies in aggressive behavior. *Aggressive Behavior, 14,* 51–64.

Zillmann, D., Baron, R.A., Tamborini, R. (1981). Social costs of smoking: Effects of tobacco smoke on hostile behavior. *Journal of Applied Social Psychology, 11(6),* 548–561.

Zillmann, D., & Bryant, J. (1984). Effects of massive exposure to pornography. In N. M. Malamuth & E. Donnerstein (Eds.), *Pornography and sexual aggression.* New York: Academic Press.

Zillmann, D., & Bryant, J. (1988). Pornography's impact on sexual satisfaction. *Journal of Applied Social Psychology, 18,* 438–453.

Zimbardo, P. G. (1977). *Shyness: What it is and what you can do about it.* Reading, MA: Addison-Wesley.

Zuckerman, M. (1984). Sensation seeking: A comparative approach to a human trait. *Behavioral and Brain Sciences, 7,* 413–471.

Zuckerman, M. (1990). The psychophysiology of sensation seeking. *Journal of Personality, 58,* 313–345.

Zuckerman, M., & Neeb, M. (1980). Demographic influences in sensation seeking and expression of sensation seeking in religion, smoking, and driving habits. *Personality and Individual Differences, 1,* 197–206.

Zuckerman, M., Simons, R. F., & Como, P. (1988). Sensation seeking and stimulus intensity as modulators of cortical, cardiovascular, and electrodermal responses: A cross-modality study. *Personality and Individual Differences, 9,* 361–372.

Glossary

Absolute Threshold: The smallest amount of a stimulus that we can detect 50 percent of the time.

Accommodation: In Piaget's theory, the modification of existing mental frameworks to take account of new information.

Achievement Motivation: The desire to accomplish difficult tasks and meet standards of excellence.

Acquired Immune Deficiency Syndrome (AIDS): A fatal viral infection that reduces the immune system's ability to defend itself against the introduction of foreign matter.

Acquisition: The process by which a conditioned stimulus acquires the ability to elicit a conditioned response through repeated pairings of an unconditioned stimulus with the conditioned stimulus.

Action Potential: A rapid shift in the electrical charge across the cell membrane of neurons. This disturbance along the membrane communicates information within neurons.

Acuity: The visual ability to see fine details.

Adaptation: In Piaget's theory of cognitive development, building mental representations of the world through interaction with it.

Adolescence: A period beginning with the onset of puberty and ending when individuals assume adult roles and responsibilities.

Adolescent Invulnerability: Adolescents' belief that they are immune from the potential harm of high-risk behaviors.

Affect: A person's current mood.

Aggression: Behavior directed toward the goal of harming another living being who wishes to avoid such treatment.

Aggressive Motivation: The desire to inflict harm on others.

Agonist: A drug that mimics the action of a neurotransmitter.

Agoraphobia: Fear of losing control and experiencing a panic attack in specific situations, such as in open places, in a crowd, or on an airplane.

Agreeableness: One of the "big five" dimensions of personality; ranges from good-natured, cooperative, trusting at one end to irritable, suspicious, uncooperative at the other.

Algorithm: A rule that guarantees a solution to a specific type of problem.

Alpha Waves: Brain waves that occur when individuals are awake but relaxed.

Alzheimer's Disease: An illness primarily afflicting individuals over the age of sixty-five and involving severe mental deterioration, including retrograde amnesia.

Amnesia: Loss of memory stemming from illness, accident, drug abuse, or other causes.

Amphetamines: Drugs that act as stimulants, increasing feelings of energy and activation.

Anal Stage: In Freud's theory, a psychosexual stage of development in which pleasure is focused primarily on the anal zone.

Analogy: A strategy for solving problems based on applying solutions that were previously successful with other problems similar in underlying structure.

Anchoring-and-Adjustment Heuristic: A cognitive rule of thumb for decision making in which existing information is accepted as a reference point but then adjusted in light of various factors.

Androgynous: High in both femininity and masculinity.

Anima: According to Jung, the archetype representing the feminine side of males.

Animus: According to Jung, the archetype representing the masculine side of females.

Anorexia Nervosa: An eating disorder in which individuals starve themselves and often lose a dangerous amount of weight.

Antagonist: A drug that inhibits the impact of a neurotransmitter.

Anterograde Amnesia: The inability to store in long-term memory information that occurs after an amnesia-inducing event.

Antisocial Personality Disorder: A personality disorder involving a lack of conscience and sense of responsibility, impulsive behavior, irritability, and aggressiveness.

Anxiety: In Freudian theory, unpleasant feelings of tension or worry experienced by individuals in reaction to unacceptable wishes or impulses; increased arousal accompanied by generalized feelings of fear or apprehension.

Anxiety Disorders: Psychological disorders that center on the occurrence of anxiety and include generalized anxiety, phobias, and obsessive-compulsive disorders.

Apnea: Cessation of breathing during sleep.

Archetypes: According to Jung, inherited images in the collective unconscious that shape our perceptions of the external world.

Arousal Theory: A theory of motivation suggesting that human beings seek an optimal level of arousal, not minimal levels of arousal.

Artificial Intelligence: A branch of science that studies the capacity of computers to demonstrate performance that, if it were produced by human beings, would be described as showing intelligence.

Assimilation: In Piaget's theory, the tendency to understand new information in terms of existing mental frameworks.

Attachment: A strong affectional bond between infants and their caregivers.

Attention-Deficit Hyperactivity Disorder: A psychological disorder in which children are unable to concentrate their attention on any task for more than a few minutes.

Attitudes: Mental representations and evaluations of features of the social or physical world.

Attribution: The processes through which we seek to determine the causes behind others' behavior.

Automatic Processing: Processing of information with minimal conscious awareness.

Automatic Vigilance: The strong tendency to pay attention to negative social information.

Autonomic Nervous System: The part of the peripheral nervous system that connects internal organs, glands, and involuntary muscles to the central nervous system.

Availability Heuristic: A cognitive rule of thumb in which the importance or probability of various events is judged on the basis of how readily they come to mind.

Avoidant Attachment: A pattern of attachment in which infants don't cry when their mother leaves them alone during the Strange Situation Test.

Axon Terminals: Structures at the end of axons that contain transmitter substances.

Axons: The parts of the neurons that conduct the action potential away from the cell body.

Babbling: An early stage of speech development in which infants emit virtually all known sounds of human speech.

Backward Conditioning: A type of conditioning in which the presentation of the unconditioned stimulus precedes and does not overlap with the presentation of the conditioned stimulus.

Barbiturates: Drugs that act as depressants, reducing activity in the nervous system and behavior output.

Behavior Therapies: Forms of psychotherapy that focus on changing maladaptive patterns of behavior through the use of basic principles of learning.

Behaviorally Anchored Rating Scales: Performance appraisal scales that provide raters with behavioral examples of various levels of performance (excellent, good, average, and so on).

Behaviorism: The view that psychology should study only observable behavior.

Binocular Cues: Cues to depth or distance provided by the use of both eyes.

Biological Constraints on Learning: Tendencies of some species to acquire some forms of conditioning less readily than other species do.

Biological Rhythms: Cyclic changes in bodily processes.

Biologically Based Therapies: Forms of therapy that attempt to reduce psychological disorders through biological means such as drug therapy or surgery.

Biopsychology: The branch of psychology concerned with discovering the biological bases of our thoughts, feelings, and behaviors.

Bipolar Disorder: A mood disorder involving swings between depression and mania.

Bisexual (sexual orientation): A sexual orientation in which individuals seek sexual relations with members of both their own and the other sex.

Blended Families: Families resulting from remarriage, consisting of biological parents, step-parents, and biological children of one or both spouses.

Blind Spot: The point in the back of the retina through which the optic nerve exits the eye. This exit point contains no rods or cones and is therefore insensitive to light.

Body Language: Nonverbal cues involving body posture or movement of body parts.

Body-Mass Index: A measure of degree of obesity, based on the ratio between height and weight.

Braille Alphabet: Representation of letters by a system of raised dots, used in reading materials for blind people.

Brightness: The physical intensity of light.

Brightness Constancy: The tendency to perceive objects as having a constant brightness even when they are viewed under different conditions of illumination.

Bulimia: An eating disorder in which periods of binge eating alternate with periods of self-induced purging.

Bystander Effect: A reduced tendency of witnesses to an emergency to help when they believe that there are other potential helpers present.

Cafeteria-Style Benefit Plans: Pay plans that permit employees to choose the specific fringe benefits they prefer.

Cancer: A group of illnesses in which abnormal cells are formed that are able to proliferate, invade, and overwhelm normal tissues and to spread to distant sites in the body.

Cannon-Bard Theory: A theory of emotion suggesting that various emotion-provoking events simultaneously produce subjective reactions labeled as emotions and physiological arousal.

Carcinogens: Cancer-producing agents.

Cardinal Trait: According to Allport, a single trait that dominates an individual's entire personality.

Cardiovascular Disease: All diseases of the heart and blood vessels.

Case Method: A method of research in which detailed information about individuals is used to develop general principles about behavior.

Central Nervous System: The brain and the spinal cord.

Central Route (to persuasion): Attitude change resulting from systematic processing of information contained in persuasive messages.

Central Tendency: The middle (center) of a distribution of scores.

Central Traits: According to Allport, the five or ten traits that best describe an individual's personality.

Cerebellum: A part of the brain concerned with the regulation and coordination of basic motor activities.

Cerebral Cortex: The outer covering of the cerebral hemispheres.

Chaining: A procedure that establishes a sequence of responses, which lead to a reward following the final response in the chain.

Charismatic Leaders: Leaders who exert profound effects on their followers and establish special types of relationships with them.

Childhood: The period between birth and adolescence.

Choking under Pressure: The tendency to perform less well at times when pressures for excellent performance are especially high.

Chromosomes: Threadlike structures containing genetic material, found in nearly every cell of the body.

Chunk: Stimuli perceived as a single unit or a meaningful grouping. Most people can retain seven to nine chunks of information in short-term memory at a given time.

Circadian Rhythms: Cyclic changes in bodily processes occurring within a single day.

Classical Conditioning: A basic form of learning in which one stimulus comes to serve as a signal for the occurrence of a second stimulus. During classical conditioning, organisms acquire information about the relations between various stimuli, not simple associations between them.

Client-Centered Therapy: A form of psychotherapy that concentrates on eliminating irrational conditions of worth—conditions people believe they must meet in order to be loved or accepted.

Climacteric: A period during which the functioning of the reproductive system, and various aspects of sexual activity, change greatly.

Cocaine: A powerful stimulant that produces pleasurable sensations of increased energy and self-confidence.

Cochlea: A portion of the inner ear containing the sensory receptors for sound.

Cognition: The activities involved in thinking, reasoning, decision making, memory, problem solving, and all other forms of higher mental processes.

Cognitive Behavior Therapy: A form of psychotherapy designed to overcome depression by changing self-defeating patterns of thought.

Cognitive Development: Changes in cognitive abilities and functioning occurring as individuals grow older.

Cognitive Disability: Intellectual functioning that is considerably below average.

Cognitive Dissonance: The state experienced by individuals when they discover inconsistency between two attitudes they hold or between their attitudes and their behavior.

Cognitive Perspective on Persuasion: An approach that seeks to understand persuasion by identifying the cognitive processes that play a role in it.

Cognitive Therapy: Psychotherapy that concentrates on altering faulty or distorted modes of thought so as to alleviate psychological disorders.

Cohort Effects: Differences between individuals of different ages stemming from the contrasting social or cultural conditions of the periods in which they grew up.

Collective Unconscious: In Jung's theory, a portion of the unconscious shared by all human beings.

Community Mental Health Centers: Facilities for the delivery of mental health services located in communities where clients live.

Companionate Love: A form of love involving a high degree of commitment and deep concern for the well-being of the beloved.

Compatibility: The degree to which controls operate in a manner consistent with human expectations or tendencies.

Complaining: Expressing discontent or dissatisfaction with oneself or with some aspect of the external world.

Complex Cells: Neurons in the visual cortex that respond to stimuli moving in a particular direction and having a particular orientation.

Compliance: A form of social influence in which one or more individuals accept direct requests from one or more others.

Componential Intelligence: The ability to think analytically.

Computer-Based Work Monitoring: Use of computers to monitor the performance of employees.

Concrete Operations: In Piaget's theory, a stage of cognitive development occurring roughly between the ages of seven and eleven. It is at this stage that children grasp such principles as conservation and that the capacity for logical thought emerges.

Concurrent Validity: The relationship between test scores and current performance relative to some criterion.

Conditioned Response (CR): In classical conditioning, the response to the conditioned stimulus.

Conditioned Stimulus (CS): In classical conditioning, the stimulus that is repeatedly paired with an unconditioned stimulus.

Conditioned Taste Aversion: A type of conditioning in which the UCS (usually internal cues associated with nausea or vomiting) occurs several hours after the CS (often a novel food), leading to a strong CS–UCS association in a single trial.

Conditions of Worth: In Rogers's theory, individuals' beliefs that they must meet certain unrealistic conditions in order to be loved or accepted.

Cones: Sensory receptors in the eye that play a crucial role in sensations of color.

Confirmation Bias: The tendency to pay attention primarily to information that confirms existing views or beliefs.

Confluence Theory: A theory suggesting that IQ tends to decrease across the birth order within a family; first-borns tend to have a higher IQ than second-borns, and so on.

Conformity: A type of social influence in which individuals experience pressure to adhere to existing social norms.

Conscientiousness: One of the "big five" dimensions of personality; this dimension ranges from well-organized, careful, responsible at one end to disorganized, careless, unscrupulous at the other.

Consensus: The extent to which behavior by one person is shown by others as well.

Conservation: Principle that states that certain physical attributes of an object remain unchanged even though its outward appearance changes.

Consistency: The extent to which a given person responds in the same way to a given stimulus across time.

Consolidation of Memory: The process of shifting new information from short-term to long-term storage.

Constancies: Our tendency to perceive physical objects as unchanging despite shifts in the pattern of sensations these objects induce.

Construct Validity: The extent to which a test measures a variable or concept described by a psychological theory.

Constructivist Cognitive Therapy: An approach to psychotherapy that seeks to help individuals understand their own unique views of the world, and to change irrational aspects of these views.

Contact Hypothesis: The suggestion that increased contact between members of different social groups will reduce prejudice between them.

Content Validity: The extent to which the items on a test sample the skills or knowledge needed for achievement in a given field or task.

Context-Dependent Memory: The greater ease of recall of information entered into memory in one context or setting in that same context than in others.

Contextual Intelligence: The ability to adapt to a changing environment.

Continuous Reinforcement Schedule: A schedule of reinforcement in which every occurrence of a particular behavior is reinforced.

Control Theory of Self-Consciousness: A theory suggesting that people compare their current behavior and states with important goals and values. They then alter their behavior to close any gaps they observe.

Controlled Processing: Processing of information with relatively high levels of conscious awareness.

Controls: Devices that permit human beings to operate and direct tools, equipment, or systems.

Conventional Level (of morality): According to Kohlberg, a stage of moral development during which individuals judge morality largely in terms of existing social norms or rules.

Convergent Thinking: Thinking that applies existing knowledge and rules of logic so as to zero in on a single correct solution to a problem.

Conversion Disorder: Psychological disorder in which individuals experience real motor or sensory symptoms for which there is no known organic cause.

Cornea: The curved, transparent layer through which light rays enter the eye.

Corpus Callosum: A band of nerve fibers connecting the two hemispheres of the brain.

Correlation Coefficient: A statistic indicating the degree of relationship between two or more variables.

Correlational Method: A research method in which investigators observe two or more variables to determine whether changes in one are accompanied by changes in the other.

Counterfactual Thinking: The tendency to evaluate events by thinking about alternatives to them—"what might have been."

Crack: A cocaine derivative that can be smoked. It acts as a powerful stimulant.

Creativity: Cognitive activity resulting in new or novel ways of viewing or solving problems.

Criterion-Related Validity: A measure of the validity of any psychological test, determined by correlations between scores on the test and some standard of the characteristic the test supposedly assesses.

Critical Thinking: Careful assessment of available evidence in order to evaluate claims and statements in an objective and reasoned manner.

Cross-Sectional Research: Research comparing groups of individuals of different ages in order to determine how some aspect of behavior or cognition changes with age.

Cross-Tolerance: Increased tolerance for one drug that develops as a result of taking another drug.

Crystallized Intelligence: Aspects of intelligence that draw on previously learned information to make decisions or solve problems.

Cultural Bias: The tendency of items on a test of intelligence to require specific cultural experience or knowledge.

Dark Adaptation: The process by which the visual system increases its sensitivity to light under low illumination.

Daydreams: Imaginary scenes or events that occur while a person is awake.

Debriefing: In psychological research, the provision of complete and accurate information about a study to participants after they have taken part in it.

Deception: Withholding information about a study from participants. Deception is used in situations where the information that is withheld is likely to alter participants' behavior.

Decision Making: The process of choosing among various courses of action or alternatives.

Deep Structure: Information that underlies the form of a sentence and is crucial to its meaning.

Defense Mechanisms: Techniques used by the ego to keep threatening and unacceptable material out of consciousness and so to reduce anxiety.

Delayed Conditioning: A form of forward conditioning in which the presentation of the conditioned stimulus precedes, but overlaps with, the presentation of the unconditioned stimulus.

Delta Waves: High-amplitude, slow brain waves that occur during several stages of sleep, but especially during stage 4.

Delusions: Irrational but firmly held beliefs about the world that have no basis in reality.

Demand Characteristics: Implicit pressure on research participants to act in ways consistent with a researcher's expectations.

Dendrites: The parts of neurons that conduct action potentials toward the cell body.

Dependence: Strong physiological or psychological need for particular drugs.

Dependent Variable: The aspect of behavior that is measured in an experiment.

Depressants: Drugs that reduce activity in the nervous system and therefore slow many bodily and cognitive processes. Depressants include alcohol and barbiturates.

Depression: A psychological disorder involving intense feelings of sadness, lack of energy, and feelings of hopelessness and despair.

Descriptive Statistics: Statistics that summarize the major characteristics of an array of scores.

Developmental Psychology: The branch of psychology that studies all types of changes occurring throughout the life span.

Diagnostic and Statistical Manual of Mental Disorders-IV (DSM-IV): The latest version of a manual widely used for diagnosing various psychological disorders.

Diathesis-Stress Model: A model of schizophrenia suggesting that individuals with inherited dispositions to develop this disorder do so only when subjected to stressful environmental conditions.

Difference Threshold: The amount of change in a stimulus required before a person can detect the shift.

Diffusion of Responsibility: A sharing of responsibility among all potential helpers who witness an emergency; the result is that each feels less responsible for helping victims.

Discriminative Stimulus: Stimulus that signals the availability of reinforcement if a specific response is made.

Disorganized (or Disoriented) Attachment: A pattern of attachment in which infants show contradictory reactions to their mother after being reunited with her during the Strange Situation Test.

Dispersion: The extent to which scores in a distribution spread out or vary around the center.

Dissociative Amnesia: Amnesia for which there is no organic cause.

Dissociative Disorder: Psychological disorder in which individuals experience profound and lengthy losses of identity or memory.

Dissociative Fugue: Form of dissociative amnesia in which individuals forget their identity and virtually all of their past life.

Dissociative Identity Disorder: Multiple personality disorder, in which a single individual seems to possess more than one personality.

Distinctiveness: The extent to which a given person reacts in the same manner to different stimuli or situations.

Distributional Ratings of Performance: Performance appraisal scales that ask raters to indicate what proportion of the time the performance of the people being evaluated falls into various categories—excellent, good, and so on.

Divergent Thinking: Thinking that moves outside conventional solutions or knowledge in an effort to develop novel solutions to a problem.

Door-in-the-Face Technique: A technique for gaining compliance in which a large request is followed by a smaller one.

Dopamine Hypothesis: The hypothesis that schizophrenia is associated with excess activity in those parts of the brain in which dopamine is the primary neurotransmitter.

Double-Blind Procedure: Procedure in which neither the people collecting data nor research participants have knowledge of the experimental conditions to which they have been assigned.

Down Syndrome: A disorder caused by an extra chromosome and characterized by varying degrees of cognitive impairment and physical disorders.

Dream: In Levinson's theory of adult development, a vision of future accomplishments.

Dreams: Cognitive events, often vivid but disconnected, that occur during sleep. Most dreams take place during REM sleep.

Dreams of Absent-Minded Transgression: Dreams in which people attempting to change their own behavior, as in quitting smoking, see themselves unintentionally slipping into the unwanted behavior.

Drive Theory: A theory of motivation suggesting that behavior is "pushed" from within by drives stemming from basic biological needs.

Drug Abuse: Instances in which individuals take drugs purely to change their moods, and in which they experience impaired behavior or social functioning as a result of doing so.

Drug Therapy: Efforts to treat psychological disorders through administration of appropriate drugs.

Drugs: Chemical substances that change the structure or function of biological systems.

Dysfunctional Families: Families that do not meet the needs of children and in fact do them serious harm.

Eating Disorders: Serious disturbances in eating habits or patterns that pose a threat to individuals' physical health and well-being.

Ego: In Freud's theory, the part of personality that takes rational account of external reality in the expression of instinctive sexual and aggressive urges.

Egocentrism: The inability of young children to distinguish their own perspective from that of others.

Elaboration Likelihood Model (of persuasion): A theory suggesting that there are two distinct routes to persuasion involving different amounts of cognitive elaboration in response to a persuasive message.

Elaborative Rehearsal: Rehearsal in which the meaning of information is considered and the information is related to other knowledge already present in memory.

Electroconvulsive Therapy (ECT): A treatment for depression in which patients receive powerful electric shocks to the head.

Electroencephalogram (EEG): A record of electrical activity within the brain. EEGs play an important role in the scientific study of sleep.

Electroencephalography (EEG): A technique for measuring the electrical activity of the brain via electrodes placed at specified locations on the skull.

Embryo: The developing child during the second through the eighth weeks of prenatal development.

Emotional Stability: One of the "big five" dimensions of personality; ranges from poised, calm, composed at one end to nervous, anxious, excitable at the other.

Emotions: Reactions consisting of physiological reactions, subjective cognitive states, and expressive behaviors.

Encoding: The process through which information is converted into a form that can be entered into memory.

Encoding Specificity Principle: The fact that only cues encoded at the time information is entered into memory can later contribute to the retrieval of such information.

Encounter Groups: A form of group therapy in which people are urged to tell other group members exactly how they feel; designed to foster personal growth through increased understanding of one's own behavior and increased honesty and openness in personal relations.

Endocrine Glands: Glands that secrete hormones directly into the bloodstream.

Endorphins: Morphine-like substances produced by the body.

Environmental Psychology: The branch of psychology that investigates the effects of the physical environment on human behavior and the effects of that behavior on the environment.

Episodic Memory: Memories of events that we have experienced personally (sometimes termed autobiographical memory).

Equity Theory: A theory suggesting that individuals compare the ratio of their inputs and outcomes in any relationship with the ratios of other people. If these ratios are not approximately equal, they may experience feelings of inequity, which can reduce work motivation.

Escalation of Commitment: The tendency to become increasingly committed to bad decisions even as losses associated with them increase.

Ethological Theory (of attachment): A theory suggesting that infants are born with a set of behaviors that elicit parental care and so increase their chances of survival.

Evolutionary Psychology: A branch of psychology that studies the adaptive problems humans have faced over the course of evolution and the behavioral mechanisms that have evolved in response to these environmental pressures.

Expectancy Theory: A theory of motivation suggesting that behavior is elicited by expectations of desirable outcomes.

Expected Utility: The product of the subjective value of an event and its predicted probability of occurrence.

Experiential Intelligence: The ability to formulate new ideas or to combine seemingly unrelated information.

Experimentation: A research method where investigators systematically alter one or more variables in order to determine whether such changes will influence some aspect of behavior.

Experimenter Effects: Unintentional influence exerted by researchers on research participants.

Explicit (Declarative) Memory: A memory system that permits us to express the information it contains verbally. It includes both semantic and episodic memory.

Externals: In Rotter's terms, individuals who believe that they have little control over the outcomes they experience.

Extinction: The process through which a conditioned stimulus gradually loses the ability to elicit conditioned responses when it is no longer followed by the unconditioned stimulus.

Extrasensory Perception (ESP): Perception without a basis in sensory input.

Extroversion: One of the "big five" dimensions of personality; ranges from sociable, talkative, fun-loving at one end to sober, reserved, cautious at the other.

Extroverts: Individuals who are talkative and sociable, and who often give free rein to their impulses and feelings.

Eyewitness Testimony: Information provided by witnesses to crimes or accidents.

Facial Feedback Hypothesis: A hypothesis indicating that facial expressions can influence as well as reflect emotional states.

False Consensus Effect: The tendency to believe that other people share our attitudes to a greater extent than is true.

Family Therapy: A form of psychotherapy that focuses on changing interactions or relations among family members.

Fantasies: Imaginary events or scenes that a person experiences while awake.

Farsightedness: A condition in which the visual image of a nearby object is focused behind rather than directly on the retina. Therefore close objects appear out of focus, while distant objects are seen clearly.

Fast Mapping: A process through which children attach a new word to an underlying concept on the basis of a single encounter with it.

Feature Detectors: Neurons at various levels within the visual cortex that respond primarily to stimuli possessing certain features.

Fetus: The developing child during the last seven months of prenatal development.

Figure-Ground Relationship: Our tendency to divide the perceptual world into two distinct parts: discrete figures and the background against which they stand out.

Fixation: Excessive investment of psychic energy in a particular stage of psychosexual development, which results in various types of psychological disorders.

Fixed-Interval Schedule: A schedule of reinforcement in which a specific interval of time must elapse before a response will yield reinforcement.

Fixed-Ratio Schedule: A schedule of reinforcement in which reinforcement occurs only after a fixed number of responses have been emitted.

Flashbulb Memories: Vivid memories of what we were doing at the time of an emotion-provoking event.

Flooding: Procedure for eliminating conditioned fears based on principles of classical conditioning. During flooding an individual is exposed to fear-inducing objects or events. Since no unconditioned stimulus then follows, extinction of fears eventually takes place.

Fluid Intelligence: Aspects of intelligence that involve forming concepts, reasoning, and identifying similarities.

Foot-in-the-Door Technique: A technique for gaining compliance in which a small request is followed by a larger one.

Forced Compliance: A situation in which we feel compelled to say or do things inconsistent with our true attitudes.

Formal Operations: In Piaget's theory, the final stage of cognitive development, during which individuals may acquire the capacity for deductive or propositional reasoning.

Fovea: The area in the center of the retina in which cones are highly concentrated.

Framing: Presentation of information concerning potential outcomes in terms of gains or losses.

Free Association: A key procedure in psychoanalysis in which individuals spontaneously report all thoughts to the therapist.

Frequency Distribution: The frequency with which each score occurs within an entire distribution of scores.

Frequency Theory: A theory of pitch perception suggesting that sounds of different frequencies, heard as differences in pitch, induce different rates of neural activity in the hair cells of the inner ear.

Freudian Slips: Statements that seem to be simple errors in speech, but which in fact reveal unconscious thoughts or impulses.

Frontal Lobe: The portion of the cerebral cortex that lies in front of the central fissure.

Frustration: The blocking of ongoing goal-directed behavior.

Fully Functioning Persons: In Rogers's theory, psychologically healthy people who enjoy life to the fullest.

Functional Autonomy: In Allport's theory, maintenance of patterns of behavior by motives other than the ones originally responsible for the behavior's occurrence.

Functional Fixedness: The tendency to think of using objects only as they have been used in the past.

Functionalism: An early view of psychology suggesting that psychology should study the ways in which the ever-changing stream of conscious experience helps us adapt to a complex and challenging world.

Fundamental Attribution Error: The tendency to attribute behavior to internal causes to a greater extent than is actually justified.

Gate-Control Theory: A theory suggesting that the spinal cord contains a mechanism that can block transmission of pain signals to the brain.

Gender: An individual's membership in one of the two sexes; all the attributes, behaviors, and expectancies associated with each sex in a given society.

Gender Constancy: Children's understanding that gender is stable over time.

Gender Identity: Children's understanding of the fact that they are male or female.

Gender Roles: Beliefs about how males and females are expected to behave in many situations.

Gender Schema Theory: A theory that children develop a cognitive framework, or schema, reflecting the beliefs of their society concerning the characteristics and roles of males and females; this gender schema then strongly affects the processing of new social information.

General Adaptation Syndrome (GAS): A three-phase model of how organisms respond to stress: (1) alarm or mobilization, (2) resistance, and (3) exhaustion.

Genes: Biological "blueprints" that shape development and all basic bodily processes.

Genetic Linkage Analysis: A procedure used to determine the location of specific genes based on their proximity to known reference points on chromosomes.

Genetic Theories of Aging: Theories suggesting that aging results from genetic programming that regulates the aging process.

Genital Stage: In Freud's theory, the final psychosexual stage of development—one in which individuals acquire the adult capacity to combine lust with affection.

Gestalt Psychologists: German psychologists intrigued by our tendency to perceive sensory patterns as well-organized wholes rather than as separate, isolated parts.

Gestalt Therapy: A form of humanistic psychotherapy designed to increase individuals' awareness and understanding of their own feelings.

Gestures: Movements of various body parts that convey a specific meaning to others.

Glial Cells: Cells in the nervous system that surround, support, and protect neurons.

Goal-Setting Theory: A theory that explains why setting specific, challenging goals for a given task often leads to improvements in performance.

Gonads: The primary sex glands.

Graded Potential: A basic type of signal within neurons that results from external physical stimulation of the dendrite or cell body. Unlike the all-or-nothing nature of action potentials, graded potentials vary in proportion to the size of the stimulus that produced them.

Grammar: Rules within a given language indicating how words can be combined into meaningful sentences.

Great Person Theory of Leadership: A theory suggesting that all great leaders share certain traits.

Group Therapies: Therapies conducted with groups of clients.

Hallucinations: Vivid sensory experiences that occur in the absence of external stimuli yet have the full force of impact of real events or stimuli.

Hallucinogens: Drugs that profoundly alter consciousness, such as marijuana and LSD.

Halo Effects: The tendency to evaluate all traits or aspects of performance by another person in a manner consistent with our overall impression of this person.

Hardiness: A personality style characterized by high levels of commitment, a view of change as an opportunity for growth, and a strong sense of being in control.

Health Belief Model: A model predicting that whether a person practices a particular health behavior depends on the degree to which the person believes in a personal health threat and believes that practicing the behavior will reduce that threat.

Health Psychology: The study of the relation between psychological variables and health; reflects the view that both mind and body are important determinants of health and illness.

Heredity: Biologically inherited characteristics.

Heterosexual (sexual orientation): A sexual orientation in which individuals engage in sexual relations only with members of the other sex.

Heuristics: Mental rules of thumb that permit us to make decisions and judgments in a rapid and efficient manner.

Hierarchy of Needs: In Maslow's theory of motivation, an arrangement of needs from the most basic to those at the highest levels.

Hindsight Effect: The tendency to assume that we would have been better at predicting actual events than is really true.

Homeostasis: A state of physiological balance within the body.

Homosexual (sexual orientation): A sexual orientation in which individuals prefer sexual relations with members of their own sex.

Hormones: Substances secreted by endocrine glands that regulate a wide range of bodily processes.

Hue: The color that we experience due to the dominant wavelength of a light.

Human Factors: The branch of psychology that applies basic knowledge about human abilities and limitations to the design of tools, equipment, systems, and products.

Humanistic Perspective: A perspective in modern psychology suggesting that human beings have free will and are not simply under the control of various internal and external factors.

Humanistic Theories: Theories of personality emphasizing personal responsibility and innate tendencies towards personal growth.

Humanistic Therapies: Forms of psychotherapy based on the assumption that psychological disorders stem from environmental conditions that block normal growth and development.

Hunger Motivation: The motivation to obtain and consume food.

Huntington's Disease: A genetically based fatal neuromuscular disorder characterized by the gradual onset of jerky, uncontrollable movements.

Hypercomplex Cells: Neurons in the visual cortex that respond to complex aspects of visual stimuli, such as width, length, and shape.

Hypersomnias: Disorders involving excessive amounts of sleep or an overwhelming urge to fall asleep.

Hypertension: High blood pressure, a condition in which the pressure within the blood vessels is abnormally high.

Hypnosis: An interaction between two persons in which one (the hypnotist) induces changes in the behavior, feelings, or cognitions of the other (the subject) through suggestions. Hypnosis involves subjects' expectations and their attempts to conform to the role of the hypnotized person.

Hypochondriasis: A psychological disorder in which individuals convert anxiety into chronic preoccupations with their health and bodily functions.

Hypothalamus: A small structure deep within the brain that plays a key role in the regulation of the autonomic nervous system and of several forms of motivated behavior such as eating and aggression.

Hypothesis: In psychology, a prediction about behavior that is to be investigated in a research project.

Hypothetico-Deductive Reasoning: In Piaget's theory, a type of reasoning first shown during the stage of formal operations. It involves formulating a general theory and deducing specific hypotheses from it.

Id: In Freud's theory, the portion of personality concerned with immediate gratification of primitive needs.

Illusions: Instances in which perception yields false interpretations of physical reality.

Implicit Memory: A memory system that stores information that we cannot express verbally; sometimes termed procedural memory.

Impression Management: Efforts by individuals to enhance the impression they make on others.

Incentives: Rewards individuals seek to attain.

Independent Variable: The variable that is systematically altered in an experiment.

Individual Differences: Differences between individuals that distinguish them from one another.

Industrial/Organizational Psychology: The branch of psychology that studies all aspects of behavior in work settings and the nature of work settings themselves.

Infantile Amnesia: Inability to remember the first two or three years of life, probably because we did not possess a well-developed self-concept during that period.

Inferential Statistics: Statistical procedures that provide information on the probability that an observed event is due to chance and that permit us to determine whether differences between individuals or groups are ones that are likely or unlikely to have occurred by chance.

Information-Processing Approach: An approach to understanding human memory that emphasizes the encoding, storage, and later retrieval of information.

Informed Consent: Participants' agreement to take part in a research project after they are provided with information about the nature of such participation.

Ingratiation: A technique of social influence based on inducing increased liking in the target person before influence is attempted.

Insomnia: Disorder involving the inability to fall asleep or remain asleep.

Instinct Theory: A theory of motivation suggesting that many forms of behavior stem from innate urges or tendencies.

Instincts: Patterns of behavior assumed to be universal in a species.

Intelligence: The ability to think abstractly and to learn readily from experience.

Internals: In Rotter's terms, individuals who believe that they exert considerable control over the outcomes they experience.

Interpersonal Attraction: The extent to which we like or dislike other persons.

Intrinsic Motivation: The desire to perform activities because they are rewarding in and of themselves.

Introverts: Individuals who are quiet, cautious, and reclusive, and who generally inhibit expression of their impulses and feelings.

IQ: A numerical value that reflects the extent to which an individual's score on an intelligence test departs from the average for other people of the same age.

Iris: The colored part of the eye that adjusts the amount of light that enters by constricting or dilating the pupil.

James-Lange Theory: A theory of emotion suggesting that emotion-provoking events produce various physiological reactions and that recognition of these is responsible for subjective emotional experiences.

Job Design: Efforts to make jobs more motivating to the persons who hold them by making them more interesting and appealing.

Job Enlargement: Adding more varied tasks, at the same level of responsibility or skill, to a given job.

Job Enrichment: Expanding a given job to include additional tasks at higher levels of skill or responsibility.

Job Satisfaction: Individuals' positive or negative attitudes toward their jobs.

Just Noticeable Difference (jnd): The smallest amount of change in a physical stimulus necessary for an individual to notice a difference in the intensity of the stimulus.

Kinesthesia: The sense that gives us information about the location of our body parts with respect to each other and allows us to perform movements.

Korsakoff's Syndrome: An illness caused by long-term abuse of alcohol that often involves profound retrograde amnesia.

Language: A system of symbols, plus rules for combining them, used to communicate information.

Late-Adult Transition: In Levinson's theory of adult development, a transition in which individuals must come to terms with their impending retirement.

Latency Stage: In Freud's theory, the psychosexual stage of development that follows resolution of the Oedipus complex. During this stage, sexual desires are relatively weak.

Latent Content: In Freud's theory, the hidden content of dreams.

Lateralization of Function: Specialization of the two hemispheres of the brain for the performance of different functions.

Laws of Grouping: Simple principles describing how we tend to group discrete stimuli together in the perceptual world.

Leadership: The process through which one member of a group (its leader) exerts influence over other group members with respect to the attainment of shared group goals.

Learned Helplessness: Feelings of helplessness that develop after exposure to situations in which nothing individuals do affects their outcomes. Learned helplessness appears to play a role in the occurrence of depression.

Learning: Any relatively permanent change in behavior (or behavior potential) resulting from experience.

Leniency Effects: Tendencies to assign higher ratings to persons being evaluated than they actually deserve.

Lens: A curved structure behind the pupil that bends light rays, focusing them on the retina.

Less-Leads-to-More Effect: The fact that rewards just barely sufficient to induce individuals to state positions contrary to their own views often generate more attitude change than larger rewards.

Levels of Processing View: A view of memory suggesting that the greater the effort expended in processing information, the more readily it will be recalled at later times.

Libido: According to Freud, the psychic energy that powers all mental activity.

Life Structure: In Levinson's theory of adult development, the underlying pattern or design of a person's life.

Lifestyle: In the context of health psychology, the overall pattern of decisions and behaviors that determine health and quality of life.

Limbic System: Several structures deep within the brain that play a role in emotional reactions and behavior.

Linguistic Relativity Hypothesis: The view that language shapes thought.

Localization: The ability of our auditory system to determine the direction of a sound source.

Longitudinal Research: Research in which the same individuals are studied across relatively substantial periods of time, such as years.

Longitudinal-Sequential Design: A research approach in which several groups of individuals of different ages are studied across time.

Long-Term Memory: A memory system for the retention of large amounts of information over long periods of time.

Love: A strong emotional state involving attraction, sexual desire, and concern for another person.

LSD: A powerful hallucinogen that produces profound shifts in perception; many of these are frightening in nature.

Magnetic Resonance Imaging (MRI): A method for studying the intact brain in which images are obtained by exposure of the brain to a strong magnetic field.

Make-Believe Play: Play in which children pretend to be engaging in various familiar activities, such as eating or going to sleep.

Manifest Content: In Freud's theory, the overt or reported content of dreams.

Marital Therapy: Psychotherapy that attempts to improve relations and understanding in couples.

Matching Hypothesis: The hypothesis that individuals seek romantic partners whose assets are at least equal to their own level of desirability.

Mathematics Anxiety: Fear on the part of individuals that they cannot master the concepts or operations of mathematics.

Mean: A measure of central tendency derived by adding all scores and dividing by the number of scores.

Means-Ends Analysis: A technique for solving problems in which the overall problem is divided into parts and efforts are made to solve each part in turn.

Median: A measure of central tendency indicating the midpoint of an array of scores.

Medical Perspective: The view that psychological disorders have a biological basis and should be viewed as treatable diseases.

Medulla: A brain structure concerned with the regulation of vital bodily functions such as breathing and heartbeat.

Memory: The capacity to retain and later retrieve information.

Menopause: Cessation of the menstrual cycle.

Mental Set: The impact of past experience on present problem solving; specifically, the tendency to retain methods that were successful in the past even if better alternatives now exist.

Mentor: In Levinson's theory of adult development, an older and more experienced individual who helps to guide younger adults.

Meta-Analysis: Statistical procedures for combining the results of many studies in order to determine whether their findings provide support for specific hypotheses.

Metacognition: Awareness and understanding of our own cognitive processes.

Midbrain: A part of the brain containing primitive centers for vision and hearing. It also plays a role in the regulation of visual reflexes.

Midlife Transition: In Levinson's theory of adult development, a turbulent transitional period occurring between the ages of forty and forty-five.

Mitosis: Cell division in which chromosome pairs split and then replicate themselves so that the full number is restored in each of the cells produced by division.

Mode: A measure of central tendency indicating the most frequent score in an array of scores.

Modeling: A basic learning process in which individuals acquire new behaviors by observing others and then put these into action.

Monocular Cues: Cues to depth or distance provided by one eye.

Mood Disorders: Psychological disorders involving intense and prolonged mood shifts.

Moral Development: Changes in the capacity to reason about actions' rightness or wrongness that occur with age.

Morphemes: The smallest units of speech that convey meaning.

Motivated Skepticism: The tendency to require more information to make a decision contrary to one's initial preferences than a decision consistent with one's initial preferences.

Motivation: An inferred internal process that activates, guides, and maintains behavior over time.

Multicultural Perspective: In modern psychology, a perspective that takes note of the fact that many aspects of behavior are strongly influenced by factors related to culture and ethnic identity.

Narcolepsy: A sleep disorder in which individuals are overcome by uncontrollable periods of sleep during waking hours.

Naturalistic Observation: A research method in which various aspects of behavior are carefully observed in the settings where such behavior naturally occurs.

Nearsightedness: A condition in which the visual image of a distant object is focused slightly in front of the retina rather than directly on it. Therefore distant objects appear fuzzy or blurred, whereas near objects can be seen clearly.

Negative Afterimage: A sensation of complementary color that we experience after staring at a stimulus of a given hue.

Negative Reinforcers: Stimuli that strengthen responses that permit an organism to avoid or escape from their presence.

Neodissociation Theory: A theory of hypnosis suggesting that hypnotized individuals enter an altered state of consciousness in which consciousness is divided.

Neo-Freudians: Personality theorists who accepted basic portions of Freud's theory but rejected or modified other portions.

Nervous System: The complex structure that regulates bodily processes and is responsible, ultimately, for all aspects of conscious experience.

Neural Networks: Computer systems modeled after the brain and made up of highly interconnected elementary computational units that work together in parallel.

Neurons: Cells specialized for communicating information, the basic building blocks of the nervous system.

Neurotransmitters: Chemicals, released by neurons, that carry information across the synapse.

Nicotine: The addictive substance in tobacco.

Night Terrors: Extremely frightening dreamlike experiences that occur during non-REM sleep.

Nodes of Ranvier: Small gaps in the myelin sheath surrounding the axons of many neurons.

Nonverbal Cues: Outward signs of others' emotional states. Such cues involve facial expressions, eye contact, and body language.

Normal Curve: A symmetrical, bell-shaped frequency distribution. Most scores are found near the middle, and fewer and fewer occur toward the extremes. Many psychological characteristics are distributed in this manner.

Normative Theory: A theory suggesting that to maximize their effectiveness, leaders must adopt a decision-making approach or style consistent with the situation they face.

Obedience: A form of social influence in which one individual issues orders to another to behave in a specific way.

Obesity: The state of being significantly overweight.

Object Permanence: An understanding of the fact that objects continue to exist when they pass from view.

Observational Learning: The acquisition of new information, concepts, or forms of behavior through exposure to others and the consequences they experience.

Obsessive-Compulsive Disorder: Anxiety disorder in which an individual is unable to stop thinking the same thoughts or performing the same ritualistic behaviors.

Occipital Lobe: A portion of the cerebral cortex involved in vision.

Oedipus Complex: In Freud's theory, a crisis of psychosexual development in which children must give up their sexual attraction to their opposite-sex parent.

Omission Training: A procedure in which a response is weakened through the removal of a desired object or activity.

Openness to Experience: One of the "big five" dimensions of personality; ranges from imaginative, sensitive, intellectual at one end to down-to-earth, insensitive, crude at the other.

Operant Conditioning: A process through which organisms learn to repeat behaviors that yield positive outcomes or permit them to avoid or escape from negative outcomes.

Opiates: Drugs that induce a dreamy, relaxed state and, in some persons, intense feelings of pleasure. Opiates exert their effects by stimulating special receptor sites within the brain.

Opponent-Process Theory: A theory that describes the processing of sensory information related to color at levels above the retina. The theory suggests that we possess six types of neurons, each of which is either stimulated or inhibited by red, green, blue, yellow, black, or white.

Opponent-Process Theory of Emotion: A theory suggesting that an emotional reaction to a stimulus is followed automatically by an opposite reaction.

Optic Nerve: A bundle of nerve fibers that exit the back of the eye and carry visual information to the brain.

Oral Stage: In Freud's theory, a stage of psychosexual development during which pleasure is centered in the region of the mouth.

Organizational Citizenship Behavior: Actions performed by individuals that are not part of their regular job but contribute to the success of the organization.

Oversight Bias: The tendency to overlook flaws if the overall topic or issue is perceived as important.

Panic Attack Disorder: Anxiety disorder characterized by relatively brief periods during which individuals experience unbearably intense anxiety.

Parallel Distributed Processing Model: A model suggesting that our memory systems process information in several different ways simultaneously.

Paranoid Personality Disorder: A personality disorder in which individuals feel that others are out to get them and cannot be trusted.

Paraphilias: Sexual disorders involving choices of inappropriate sexual objects, such as young children, or the inability to experience arousal except in the presence of specific objects or fantasies.

Parapsychologists: Individuals who study psi and other paranormal events.

Parasympathetic Nervous System: The portion of the autonomic nervous system that readies the body for restoration of energy.

Parental Investment Model: The view that males and females adopt contrasting strategies of mate selection because they invest different amounts of resources in their offspring.

Parietal Lobe: A portion of the cerebral cortex, lying behind the central fissure, that plays a major role in the skin senses: touch, temperature, pressure.

PASS Theory: Theory that intelligence involves the three interdependent components of attention, processing, and planning.

Passive Smoking: Inhaling other people's cigarette smoke.

Peak Experiences: In Maslow's theory, intense emotional experiences during which individuals feel at one with the universe.

Perception: The process through which we select, organize, and interpret input from our sensory receptors.

Performance Appraisals: Annual or semiannual evaluations of employees' performance coupled with feedback about the ratings they have received.

Peripheral Nervous System: The portion of the nervous system that connects internal organs and glands, as well as voluntary and involuntary muscles, to the central nervous system.

Peripheral Route (to persuasion): Attitude change resulting from peripheral persuasion cues—information concerning the expertise, status, or attractiveness of would-be persuaders.

Person-Environment (P-E) Fit: The approach that suggests that a misfit between a person and his or her work environment may produce stress.

Personality: Individuals' unique and relatively stable patterns of behavior, thoughts, and feelings.

Personality Disorders: Extreme personality variation associated with the failure to achieve the universal tasks of establishing a personal identity, forming attachments to others, experiencing intimacy with them, and seeking affiliation.

Personality Traits: Specific dimensions along which individuals' personalities differ in consistent, stable ways.

Persuasion: The process through which one or more persons attempt to alter the attitudes of one or more others.

Phallic Stage: In Freud's theory, a psychosexual stage of development during which pleasure is centered in the genital region. It is during this stage that the Oedipus complex develops.

Phenylketonuria (PKU): A genetically based disorder in which a person lacks the enzyme to break down phenylalanine, a substance present in many foods. The gradual buildup of phenylalanine contributes to subsequent outcomes that include retardation.

Phobias: Intense, irrational fears of objects or events.

Phonemes: A set of sounds basic to a given language.

Phonological Development: Development of the ability to produce recognizable speech.

Phonological Strategies: Simplifications used by young children to facilitate the task of producing recognizable speech.

Physical Growth and Development: Physical changes in the size and structure of our bodies between conception and adulthood.

Physiological Dependence: Strong urges to continue using a drug based on organic factors such as changes in metabolism.

Pinna: The external portion of the ear.

Pitch: The characteristic of a sound that is described as high or low. Pitch is mediated by the frequency of a sound.

Pituitary Gland: An endocrine gland that releases hormones to regulate other glands and several basic biological processes.

Place Theory: A theory suggesting that sounds of different frequency stimulate different areas of the basilar membrane.

Placenta: A structure that surrounds, protects, and nourishes the developing fetus.

Pleasure Principle: The principle on which the id operates—immediate pleasure with no attention to possible consequences.

Pons: A portion of the brain through which sensory and motor information passes and which contains structures relating to sleep, arousal, and the regulation of muscle tone and cardiac reflexes.

Positive Reinforcers: Stimuli that strengthen responses that precede them.

Positron Emission Tomography (PET): An imaging technique that detects the activity of the brain by measuring glucose utilization or blood flow.

Postconventional Level (of morality): According to Kohlberg, the final stage of moral development, in which individuals judge morality in terms of abstract principles.

Posttraumatic Stress Disorder: Psychological disorder resulting from a very stressful experience; includes nightmares and flashbacks, distress at exposure to reminders of the event, irritability, difficulty concentrating, and a general unresponsiveness.

Power Motivation: Motivation to be in charge, have high status, and exert influence over others.

Preconventional Level (of morality): According to Kohlberg, the earliest stage of moral development, in which individuals judge morality in terms of the effects produced by various actions.

Predictive Validity: The relationship between scores on a test and later performance relative to a criterion.

Prejudice: Negative attitudes toward the members of some social group based on their membership in this group.

Premack Principle: The principle that a more preferred activity can be used to reinforce a less preferred activity.

Preoperational Stage: In Piaget's theory, a stage of cognitive development during which children become capable of mental representations of the external world.

Prevention Strategies: Techniques designed to reduce the occurrence of physical and psychological problems.

Primary Aging: Aging due to the passage of time and, to some extent, inherited biological factors.

Primary Prevention: Techniques aimed at preventing the occurrence of psychological disorders.

Private Speech: The instructions about what to do next that young children often give themselves as they perform various activities.

Proactive Interference: Interference with the learning or storage of current information by information previously entered into memory.

Problem Solving: Efforts to develop or choose among various responses in order to attain desired goals.

Procedural Memory: A memory system that retains information we cannot readily express verbally—for example, information necessary to perform skilled motor activities such as riding a bicycle.

Propinquity: Physical proximity and the interpersonal contact it produces.

Propositional Reasoning: In Piaget's theory, reasoning during the stage of formal operations, in which individuals can assess the validity of verbal assertions even when these refer to possibilities rather than to actual events.

Propositions: Sentences that relate one concept to another and can stand as separate assertions.

Prosocial Behavior: Actions that benefit others without necessarily providing any direct benefit to the persons who perform them.

Prosopagnosia: A rare condition in which brain damage impairs a person's ability to recognize faces.

Prospective Memory: Remembering to perform certain activities at specific times.

Prototypes: Representations in memory of various objects or stimuli in the physical world; the best or clearest examples of various objects or stimuli in the physical world.

Psi: Unusual processes of information or energy transfer that are currently unexplained in terms of known physical or biological mechanisms. Included under the heading of psi are such supposed abilities as telepathy (reading others' thoughts) and clairvoyance (perceiving unseen objects or unknowable events).

Psychedelics: Drugs that alter sensory perception and so may be considered mind-expanding.

Psychiatry: A branch of medicine that focuses on the diagnosis and treatment of psychological disorders.

Psychoanalysis: A method of therapy based on Freud's theory of personality, in which the therapist attempts to bring repressed unconscious material into consciousness.

Psychodrama: A form of psychodynamic group therapy in which people act out their problems in front of fellow group members.

Psychodynamic Perspective: An approach suggesting that many aspects of behavior stem from hidden forces within our personalities.

Psychodynamic Therapies: Therapies based on the assumption that psychological disorders stem primarily from hidden inner conflicts with repressed urges and impulses.

Psychological Dependence: Strong desires to continue using a drug even though it is not physiologically addicting.

Psychological Disorders: Behaviors or thoughts that are unusual in a given society, that are maladaptive, and that cause the persons who experience them considerable distress.

Psychology: The science of behavior and cognitive processes.

Psychosexual Stages of Development: According to Freud, an innate sequence of stages through which all human beings pass. At each stage, pleasure is focused on a different region of the body.

Psychosurgery: Efforts to alleviate psychological disorders by surgical means.

Psychotherapies: Procedures designed to eliminate or modify psychological disorders through the establishment of a special relationship between a client and a trained therapist.

Puberty: The period of rapid change during which individuals reach sexual maturity and become capable of reproduction.

Punishment: The application or removal of a stimulus so as to decrease the strength of a behavior.

Pupil: An opening in the eye, just behind the cornea, through which light rays enter the eye.

Racial Identification: The extent to which individuals identify with their own racial group.

Random Assignment of Participants to Experimental Conditions: Assuring that all research participants have an equal chance of being assigned to each of the experimental conditions.

Range: The difference between the highest and lowest scores in a distribution of scores.

Rational-Emotive Therapy: A cognitive therapy that focuses on changing irrational beliefs.

Raven Progressive Matrices: One popular "culture-fair" test of intelligence.

Reaction Formation: A defense mechanism in which people act in a manner directly opposite to their unconscious wishes.

Realistic Conflict Theory: A theory proposing that prejudice stems, at least in part, from economic competition between social groups.

Reality Principle: The principle on which the ego operates, according to which the external consequences of behavior are considered in the regulation of expression of impulses from the id.

Reasoning: Cognitive activity that transforms information in order to reach specific conclusions.

Recategorization: Shifting the boundary between "us" and "them" so that persons previously seen as belonging to out-groups are now seen as belonging to the ingroup.

Reconditioning: The rapid recovery of a conditioned response to a CS–UCS pairing following extinction.

Reinforcement: The application or removal of a stimulus so as to increase the strength of a behavior.

Relative Size: A visual cue based on comparison of the size of an unknown object to one of known size.

REM Sleep: A state of sleep in which brain activity resembling waking restfulness is accompanied by deep muscle relaxation and movements of the eyes. Most dreams occur during periods of REM sleep.

Repeated Exposure Effect: The fact that the more frequently we are exposed to various stimuli (at least up to a point), the more we tend to like them.

Representativeness Heuristic: A mental rule of thumb suggesting that the more closely an event or object resembles typical examples of some concept or category, the more likely it is to belong to that concept or category.

Repression: A theory of forgetting that suggests that memories of experiences or events we find threatening are sometimes pushed out of consciousness so that they can no longer be recalled.

Resistance: Efforts by individuals undergoing psychoanalysis to prevent repressed impulses or conflicts from entering consciousness.

Resistant Attachment: A pattern of attachment in which infants reject their mother and refuse to be comforted by her after she leaves them alone during the strange situation test.

Reticular Activating System: A structure within the brain concerned with sleep, arousal, and the regulation of muscle tone and cardiac reflexes.

Retina: The surface at the back of the eye containing the rods and cones.

Retrieval: The process through which information stored in memory is located.

Retrieval Cues: Stimuli associated with information stored in memory that can aid in its retrieval.

Retroactive Interference: Interference with retention of information already present in memory by new information being entered into memory.

Retrograde Amnesia: The inability to store in long-term memory information that occurred before an amnesia-inducing event.

Risk Factors: Aspects of our environment or behavior that influence our chances of developing or contracting a disease, within the limits set by our genetic structure.

Rods: One of the two types of sensory receptors for vision found in the eye.

Romantic Love: A form of love in which feelings of strong attraction and sexual desire toward another person are dominant.

Saccadic Movements: Quick movements of the eyes from one point of fixation to another.

Saturation: The degree of concentration of the hue of light. We experience saturation as the purity of a color.

Savant Syndrome: Condition in which an individual is cognitively impaired but nevertheless demonstrates some normal or above-normal intellectual skills.

Schachter-Singer Theory (two-factor theory): A theory of emotion suggesting that our subjective emotional states are determined, at least in part, by the cognitive labels we attach to feelings of arousal.

Schedules of Reinforcement: Rules determining when and how reinforcements will be delivered.

Schemas: Cognitive frameworks representing our knowledge about aspects of the world.

Schizoid Personality Disorder: A personality disorder in which individuals become almost totally detached from the social world.

Schizophrenia: A group of serious psychological disorders characterized by severe distortions in thought and language, perceptions, and emotion.

Script: Mental representation of the sequence of events in a given situation.

Seasonal Affective Disorder (SAD): Depression experienced during the winter months, supposedly stemming from a lack of exposure to sunlight.

Secondary Aging: Aging due to the effects of disease, disuse, or abuse of the body.

Secondary Prevention: Techniques that focus on early detection of psychological disorders so that minor disturbances will not develop into major ones.

Secondary Traits: According to Allport, traits that exert relatively specific and weak effects upon behavior.

Secure Attachment: A pattern of attachment in which infants actively seek contact with their mother and take comfort from her presence when they are reunited with her during the strange situation test.

Selective Attention: Our ability to pay attention to only some aspects of the world around us while largely ignoring others.

Self-Actualization: A stage of personal development in which individuals reach their maximum potential.

Self-Concept: All the information and beliefs individuals have about their own characteristics and themselves.

Self-Consciousness: Increased awareness of oneself as a social object or of one's own values and attitudes.

Self-Disclosure: The act of revealing information about oneself to another person.

Self-Efficacy: Individuals' expectations concerning their ability to perform various tasks.

Self-Esteem: The extent to which individuals have positive or negative feelings about themselves and their own worth.

Self-Help Groups: Groups of individuals experiencing the same kinds of difficulties that meet to discuss their shared problem and find solutions to it.

Self-Monitoring: A personality trait involving sensitivity to social situations and an ability to adapt one's behavior to the demands of those situations in order to make favorable impressions on others.

Self-Reinforcement: The delivery of rewards to oneself for reaching one's self-set goals.

Self-Schemas: Cognitive frameworks that serve to organize information about the self.

Self-Serving Bias: The tendency to attribute positive outcomes to our own traits or characteristics but negative outcomes to factors beyond our control.

Semantic Development: Development of understanding of the meaning of spoken or written language.

Semantic Memory: The content of our general, abstract knowledge about the world.

Semicircular Canals: Fluid-filled structures that provide information about rotational acceleration of the head or body around three principal axes of rotation.

Sensation: Input about the physical world provided by our sensory receptors.

Sensation Seeking: A trait relating to the extent to which individuals seek and enjoy high levels of stimulation.

Sensitivity-Training Groups: A form of group therapy designed to foster personal growth through increased understanding of one's own behavior and increased honesty and openness in personal relations.

Sensorimotor Stage: In Piaget's theory, the earliest stage of cognitive development.

Sensory Adaptation: Reduced sensitivity to unchanging stimuli over time.

Sensory Memory: A memory system that retains representations of sensory input for brief periods of time.

Sensory Receptors: Cells specialized for the task of transduction—converting physical energy (light, sound) into neural impulses.

Serial Position Curve: The greater accuracy of recall of words or other information early and late in a list than words or information in the middle of the list.

Serum Cholesterol: The amount of cholesterol in one's blood.

Sex-Stereotyped Behavior: Patterns of behavior associated by society with each sex.

Sexual Abuse: Sexual contact or activities forced on children or adolescents by other persons, usually adults.

Sexual Arousal Disorders: Psychological disorders involving inability to attain an erection (males) or absence of vaginal swelling and lubrication (females).

Sexual Desire Disorders: Psychological disorders involving a lack of interest in sex or active aversion to sexual activities.

Sexual Jealousy: A negative state aroused by a perceived threat to one's sexual relationship with another person.

Sexual Motivation: Motivation to engage in various forms of sexual activity.

Shape Constancy: The tendency to perceive a physical object as having a constant shape even when the image it casts on the retina changes.

Shaping: A technique in which closer and closer approximations of desired behavior are required for the delivery of positive reinforcement.

Short-Term Memory: A memory system that holds limited amounts of information for relatively short periods of time.

Signal Detection Theory: A theory suggesting that there are no absolute thresholds for sensations. Rather, detection of stimuli depends on their physical energy and on internal factors such as the relative costs and benefits associated with detecting their presence.

Simple Cells: Cells within the visual system that respond to specific shapes presented in certain orientations (horizontal, vertical, etc.).

Simultaneous Conditioning: A form of conditioning in which the conditioned stimulus and the unconditioned stimulus begin and end at the same time.

Situational Leadership Theory: A theory of leadership indicating that as their followers gain increasing experience, leaders should shift from a directive to a nondirective style of leadership.

Size Constancy: The tendency to perceive a physical object as having a constant size even when the size of the image it casts on the retina changes.

Sleep: A process in which important physiological changes (including shifts in brain activity and slowing of basic bodily functions) are accompanied by major shifts in consciousness.

Social and Emotional Development: Changes in emotional experiences and expressions, and in behaviors and attitudes toward others, occurring with age.

Social Categorization: Our tendency to divide the social world into two distinct categories: "us" and "them."

Social Cognition: The processes through which we notice, interpret, remember, and later use social information.

Social Cognitive Theory: A theory of behavior suggesting that human behavior is influenced by many cognitive factors as well as by reinforcement contingencies, and that human beings have an impressive capacity to regulate their own actions.

Social Facilitation: Effects on behavior stemming from the mere presence of others.

Social Influence: Efforts by one or more individuals to change the attitudes or behavior of one or more others.

Social Norms: Rules in a given group or society indicating how individuals ought to behave in specific situations.

Social Psychology: The branch of psychology that studies all aspects of social behavior and social thought.

Social Referencing: Using others' reactions to appraise an uncertain situation or experience.

Somatic Nervous System: The portion of the peripheral nervous system that connects the brain and spinal cord to voluntary muscles.

Somatization Disorder: A psychological condition in which individuals report physical complaints and symptoms, including aches and pains, problems with their digestive systems, and sexual problems such as sexual indifference or irregular menstruation.

Somatoform Disorders: Category of disorders in which psychological conflicts or other problems take on a physical form.

Somnambulism: A sleep disorder in which individuals actually get up and move about while still asleep.

Source Traits: According to Cattell, key dimensions of personality that underlie many other traits.

Split-Half Reliability: The extent to which an individual attains equivalent scores on two halves of a psychological test.

Spontaneous Recovery: Following extinction, return of a conditioned response upon reinstatement of CS-UCS pairings.

SQUID (Superconducting Quantum Interference Device): An imaging device that captures images of the brain through its ability to detect tiny changes in magnetic fields in the brain.

Stage Theory: Any theory proposing that all human beings move through an orderly and predictable series of changes.

Standard Deviation: A measure of dispersion reflecting the average distance between each score and the mean.

Stanford-Binet Test: A popular test for measuring individual intelligence.

State-Dependent Retrieval: Retrieval of information stored in long-term memory cued by aspects of one's physical state.

States of Consciousness: Varying degrees of awareness of ourselves and the external world.

Statistics: Mathematical procedures used to describe data and draw inferences from them.

Stereotypes: Cognitive frameworks suggesting that all members of specific social groups share certain characteristics.

Stimulants: Drugs that increase activity in the nervous system, including amphetamines, caffeine, and nicotine.

Stimulus: A physical event capable of affecting behavior.

Stimulus Control: Consistent occurrence of a behavior in the presence of a discriminative stimulus.

Stimulus Discrimination: The process by which organisms learn to respond to certain stimuli but not to others.

Stimulus Generalization: The tendency of stimuli similar to a conditioned stimulus to elicit a conditioned response.

Storage: The process through which information is retained in memory.

Strange Situation Test: A procedure for studying attachment in which mothers leave their children alone with a stranger for several minutes and then return.

Stress: The process that occurs in response to events that disrupt, or threaten to disrupt, our physical or psychological functioning.

Stressors: Events or situations in our environment that cause stress.

Striving for Superiority: Attempting to overcome feelings of inferiority. According to Adler, this is the primary motive for human behavior.

Structuralism: An early view suggesting that psychology should focus on conscious experience and on the task of analyzing such experience into its basic parts.

Sublimation: A defense mechanism in which threatening unconscious impulses are channeled into socially acceptable forms of behavior.

Subliminal Perception: The presumed ability to perceive a stimulus that is below the threshold for conscious experience.

Suicide: The act of taking one's own life.

Superego: According to Freud, the portion of human personality representing the conscience.

Suprachiasmatic Nucleus: A portion of the hypothalamus that seems to play an important role in the regulation of circadian rhythms.

Surface Structure: The actual words of which sentences consist.

Survey Method: A research method in which large numbers of people answer questions about aspects of their views or their behavior.

Syllogistic Reasoning: A type of formal reasoning in which two premises are used as the basis for deriving logical conclusions.

Sympathetic Nervous System: The portion of the autonomic nervous system that readies the body for expenditure of energy.

Synapse: A region where the axon of one neuron closely approaches other neurons or the cell membrane of other types of cells such as muscle cells.

Synaptic Vesicles: Structures in the axon terminals that contain various neurotransmitters.

Syntax: Rules about how units of speech can be combined into sentences in a given language.

Systematic Desensitization: A form of behavior therapy in which individuals imagine scenes or events that are increasingly anxiety-provoking and at the same time engage in procedures that induce feelings of relaxation.

Tardive Dyskinesia: A side effect of prolonged exposure to antipsychotic drugs in which individuals experience involuntary muscular movements, especially of the face.

Temperament: Stable individual differences in the quality and intensity of emotional reactions.

Templates: Specific patterns stored in our memories for various visual stimuli that we encounter.

Temporal Lobe: The lobe of the cerebral cortex that is involved in hearing.

Teratogens: Factors in the environment that can harm the developing fetus.

Tertiary Prevention: Techniques designed to minimize the harm done by psychological disorders.

Test-Retest Reliability: The extent to which a psychological test yields similar scores when taken by the same person on different occasions.

Thalamus: A structure deep within the brain that receives sensory input from other portions of the nervous system and then transmits this information to the cerebral hemispheres and other parts of the brain.

That's-Not-All Approach: A technique for gaining compliance in which a small extra incentive is offered before the target person has agreed to or rejected a request.

Thematic Apperception Test (TAT): A psychological test used to assess individual differences in several motives, such as achievement motivation and power motivation.

Theories: In science, frameworks for explaining various phenomena. Theories consists of two major parts: basic concepts and assertions concerning relationships between these concepts.

Therapeutic Alliance: The special relationship between therapist and client that contributes to the effectiveness of many forms of psychotherapy.

Timbre: The quality of a sound, resulting from the complex makeup of a sound wave; timbre helps us to distinguish the sound of a trumpet from that of a saxophone.

Tip-of-the-Tongue Phenomenon: The feeling that we can almost remember some information we wish to retrieve from memory.

Token Economies: Forms of behavior therapy based on operant conditioning, in which hospitalized patients earn tokens they can exchange for valued rewards when they behave in ways the hospital staff consider to be desirable.

Tolerance: Habituation to a drug, causing larger and larger doses to be required to produce effects of the same magnitude.

Trace Conditioning: A form of forward conditioning in which the presentation of the conditioned stimulus precedes and does not overlap with the presentation of the unconditioned stimulus.

Tracking: Tasks, such as driving, in which individuals make adjustments to approach as closely as possible to some target value.

Trait Theories: Theories of personality that focus on identifying the key dimensions along which people differ.

Transduction: The translation of physical energy into electrical signals by specialized receptor cells.

Transference: Strong positive or negative feelings toward the therapist on the part of individuals undergoing psychoanalysis.

Transformational Leaders: Leaders who exert profound effects on their followers and establish special types of relationships with them.

Trephining: An ancient surgical procedure in which holes are cut into the skull.

Trial and Error: A method of solving problems in which possible solutions are tried until one succeeds.

Triarchic Theory: A theory suggesting that there are actually three distinct kinds of intelligence.

Trichromatic Theory: A theory of color perception suggesting that we have three types of cones, each primarily receptive to particular wavelengths of light.

Type A Behavior Pattern: A cluster of traits such as competitiveness, aggressiveness, urgency, and hostility; related to important aspects of health, social behavior, and task performance.

Unconditional Positive Regard: In Rogers's theory, communicating to others that they will be respected or loved regardless of what they say or do.

Unconditioned Response (UCR): In classical conditioning, the response elicited by an unconditioned stimulus.

Unconditioned Stimulus (UCS): In classical conditioning, a stimulus that can elicit an unconditioned response the first time it is presented.

Validity: The extent to which tests actually measure what they claim to measure.

Variable-Interval Schedule: A schedule of reinforcement in which a variable amount of time must elapse before a response will yield reinforcement.

Variable-Ratio Schedule: A schedule of reinforcement in which reinforcement is delivered after a variable number of responses have been performed.

Variance: A measure of dispersion reflecting the average squared distance between each score and the mean.

Vestibular Sacs: Fluid-filled sacs in our inner ear that provide information about the positions and changes in linear movement of our head and body.

Vestibular Sense: Our sense of balance.

Visual Displays: Displays that present information visually.

Visual Images: Mental pictures or representations of objects or events.

Warnings: Messages designed to alert users of various products and services, or the general public, to potential hazards.

Wavelength: The peak-to-peak distance in a sound or light wave.

Wear-and-Tear Theories of Aging: Theories suggesting that aging results from continuous use of cells and organs within our bodies.

Wernicke-Geschwind Theory: A theory of how the brain processes information relating to speech and other verbal abilities. Although the theory has generated a considerable amount of research, recent evidence suggests that it does not provide an adequate picture of this process.

Work Motivation: Motivation to perform and complete various tasks.

Name Index

Aaronson, L.S., 318
Abbey, S.E., 643, 644
Abel, L., 449
Abelson, R.P., 255
Aboud, F.E., 319, 683
Abra, J.C., 382, 680, 716
Abraham, L.M., 84, 733
Abramovitch, R., 662
Abramowitz, S.I., 584, 602
Abramson, L.Y., 589
Absi-Semaan, N., 351
Achermann, P., 160
Ackermann, H., 66
Acocella, J.R., 626
Acton, H., 347
Adair, J.G., 35
Adamec, R.E., 67, 539
Adams, L.P., 591, 592
Adams, N.E., 629
Adams, R.J., 132, 321
Addington, J., 387
Addington, J.M., 368
Adelmen, H.F., 424
Adelstein, A., 75
Ader, R., 546
Adlaf, E.M., 57, 176, 555
Adler, A., 503, 504
Adler, N.J., 221
Aghajanian, G.K., 588
Agnew, H.W., 160
Agyei, Y., 86
Ahmed, S.M., 419, 706
Aiello, J.R., 723, 724, 742
Aiken, L.R., 453, 459, 461
Aikins, S., 264
Ainsworth, M.D.S., 345
Akerstedt, T., 148
Aki, J., 113
Akimoto, S.A., 682
Akiskal, H.S., 588
Al-Issa, I., 580
Alagna, F.J., 434
Alain, M., 663
Alberts-Corush, J., 332
Alcock, J.E., 680, 698
Alden, L.E., 364, 509, 702
Aldridge, D., 591
Alfano, M.S., 589
Alicke, M.D., 20, 692, 693
Allen, C.R., 588
Allen, L.A., 580, 589, 590
Allen, L.E., 188
Allen, M., 509
Allen, N.J., 714, 732, 737
Allen, S.C., 339
Allen, V.L., 689
Allgood-Merton, B., 409
Alliger, R., 450
Alloy, L.B., 589, 626
Allport, G.W., 510, 511
Almay, B.G.L., 523
Almeida, D.M., 360, 361, 364
Altman, I., 508
Altshuler, J.L., 343
Amador, M., 257
Amato, P.R., 369
Ambrose, M.L., 719
Ameli, R., 611
Ames, E.W., 323
Amhalt, R.L., 726
Amir, Y., 683
Amoore, J., 116
Amsel, R., 432
Amundson, N.E., 388
Anderson, 708
Anderson, C., 369, 371
Anderson, C.A., 744
Anderson, D.C., 744
Anderson, G., 74
Anderson, J.A., 427
Anderson, J.L., 147, 410
Anderson, R.C., 514
Andre, A.D., 749
Andre, M., 723
Andreasen, N.C., 450
Andres, D., 381
Andrews, J.D.W., 422
Angelergues, R., 72
Angerspach, D., 149
Angier, 649
Ankney, C.D., 80

Anson, A.R., 371
Anstis, S., 134
Antonovsky, A., 375
Antrobus, J., 165
Applebaum, S.L., 132
Appley, M.H., 11
Apter, A., 592
Aquan-Assee, J., 321
Arato, M., 81
Arbuckle, T.Y., 379
Archer, L.A., 83
Arcus, D.M., 344
Arizmendi, T.G., 626
Arkes, H.R., 436
Arkin, R.M., 403, 509, 666
Armitage, R., 145
Armstrong, C., 87
Armstrong, J., 390
Arnold, H.J., 734
Aron, A.P., 428, 694
Aronoff, J., 433
Aronson, E., 80, 547, 678, 683
Arregui, A., 612
Arrowwood, A.J., 675
Arsenault, A., 723
Arsenault, R., 333
Arterberry, M.E., 323
Arvey, R.D., 13, 84, 733
Asante, M.K., 685
Asarnow, R.F., 611, 612
Aschenbrener, C., 557
Ashforth, B.E., 547
Aslin, R.N., 323
Astley, S.J., 318
Astley, S.L., 280
Astrom, M., 523
Atkinson, J.W., 9, 422
Atkinson, R.C., 229, 231
Aubé, J., 467, 479, 480, 727
Austin, N., 329
Austin, D.F., 557
Austin, J., 212, 213
Austin, L., 362
Avis, J.M., 639
Avolio, B.J., 740

Babcock, R.L., 378
Bachetti, P., 562
Bachman, J.G., 364
Back, K., 701
Baddeley, A.D., 42, 236, 241, 247, 250
Baer, J.S., 428
Bahrick, H.P., 228, 242
Bahrick, P.O., 228
Bailey, J.S., 212, 213
Bailey, M.J., 85, 86
Baillargeon, R., 329
Baker, B., 534
Baker, D., 217
Baker, J.E., 246
Baker, S.M., 670
Baker-Ward, L., 333
Baldes, J.J., 717, 718
Baldwin, J.M., 10
Ball, S.A., 513, 523
Balogh, R.D., 132, 321
Balzer, W.K., 724, 730
Baltes, P.B., 382
Banich, M.T., 77
Banks, C.G., 726
Barban, L., 599
Barbee, A., 700
Bardwell, J.R., 351
Baril, G.L., 470, 471
Barker, J.L., 113
Barker-Brown, G., 422
Barkley, R.A., 332
Barling, J., 544, 733
Barlow, D.H., 581, 593
Barnea, Z., 523
Barnes, M.H., 638
Barnet, R.C., 208
Baron, A., 213
Baron, J., 278, 362
Baron, R.A., 35, 118, 188, 218, 220, 295, 387, 406, 418, 419, 435, 471, 520, 691, 697, 699,

701, 714, 717, 741, 744, 745, 751, 752, 753
Barrera, M., 323
Barrett, B., 465
Barrett, M., 83
Barsky, A.J., 597
Barta, P.E., 613
Barth, R.J., 473
Bartholomew, S., 221
Bartlage, S., 589
Bartohuk, L., 603
Barton, M.L., 347
Baruch, G., 388
Basbaum, A., 56
Bastien, M.F., 368
Bastone, L., 414
Bates, D.F., 215
Bates, S., 215
Batsche, C.J., 207
Batsche, G.M., 207
Batson, C.D., 688
Batson, J.G., 698
Bauer, P.J., 333
Baum, A., 532, 542, 741, 742, 745, 752, 753
Baum, S.R., 73
Bauman, D.T., 700
Bauman, K.E., 217
Baumeister, R.F., 155, 490, 507, 520, 521, 592, 667
Baumgardner, A.H., 509, 666
Baumrind, D., 35, 177
Bayers, 328
Baynham, T., 370
Bazerman, M.H., 286
Beaber, R.J., 673
Beach, S.R., 701
Beaman, A.L., 692
Beaton, 729
Beatty, W.W., 403
Bebko, J.M., et al 326
Beck, A.T., 589, 630, 631, 632
Beckham, A.S., 16, 453
Beckstead, J.W., 36
Bedard, M.A., 161
Bedard, R., 718
Beehr, T.A., 734
Begg, I.M., 99
Behrend, D.A., 329
Beiser, M., 389
Bekesy, G., 110
Belcher, M., 165
Belger, A., 77
Belke, T.W., 208
Bell, A.P., 85
Bell, P.A., 741, 742, 744, 752, 753
Bell, S., 170
Bellack, A.S., 608
Bellak, L., 608
Belleville, S., 446, 447
Bellisimo, A., 114
Belsky, J., 347
Bem, D.J., 134, 136
Bem, S.L., 350, 351, 479
Bemis, K.M., 216
Benesch, K.F., 519
Benezra, E., 332
Beninger, R.J., 55, 194, 202
Benke, T., 81
Bennett, S.A., 58
Benoit, D., 347
Benson, D.F., 69
Benson, H., 180
Benson, J.E., 663
Bentall, R.P., 153
Bentler, P.M., 159
Berk, L.E., 320, 329
Berkowitz, L., 220, 418, 419
Berlin, B., 537, 563
Berlyne, Q.E., 546
Berman, A.L., 652
Berman, J.S., 631, 641, 649
Berman, W., 465
Berndt, T.J., 364
Bernieri, F., 490
Bernstein, A.S., 612
Bernstein, I.L., 196
Berry, D.S., 360
Berry, D.T.R., 160

Berry, J.W., 164, 255, 524
Berscheid, E., 475
Bertelsen, A., 611
Besson, J., 113
Best, D.L., 351
Best, J.A., 555
Betz, A.L., 635, 636, 672
Betz, E.L., 406
Beutler, L.E., 626
Beyer, J., 629
Beyth-Marom, R., 362
Bhatia, S., 555
Bhatt, R.S., 280
Bialystok, E., 329
Bichard, S.L., 364
Biddy, R., 219
Biederman, G.B., 189
Bienert, H., 19, 629
Bierhoff, H.W., 700
Bigelow, A., 326
Bigelow, B.J., 688
Bigelow, D.A., 651
Binder, J.L., 623
Binet, A., 9, 450, 451, 452
Bini, L., 645
Binning, J.F., 726
Birbaumer, N., 66
Bird, E., 612
Birnbaum, D., 550
Birnbaum, I.M., 238
Birren, J.E., 391
Bisanz, G.L., 677
Bisnaire, L.M., 368
Bisson, C., 80
Bivens, J.A., 329
Bixler, E.O., 160
Bjorklund, D.F., 333
Bjorkquist, K., 471, 472
Black, J.S., 221
Blackmore, S., 135
Blade, L., 360
Blain, M.D., et al, 346
Blais, M.R., 423
Blake, R., 126, 128
Blake, R.R., 739
Blakemore, B., et al., 332
Blakeslee, S., 414
Blanchard, E.B., 629
Blanchard, K., 739
Blanchard, R., 414
Bland, R.C., 585, 586, 591, 610
Blankstein, K.R., 405, 662
Blascovich, J., 536
Blashko, C.A., 566
Blehar, M.C., 345
Bless, H., 437
Bliss, R.E., 174
Bluck, S., 391, 392, 422
Blyth, D.A., 360
Bodenhausen, G.V., 681, 755
Bodkin, J., 662
Boegman, R.J., 55
Boehne, D.M., 716
Bogard, N., 471
Bohner, G., 437
Bolduc, D., 350
Boles, D.B., 77
Bond, N.H., 13, 15
Bonin, L., 405
Bonnet, C., 95
Bonneville, F., 668
Bookbinder, M., 99
Bootzin, R., 160, 210
Borbely, A.A., 160
Borduin, C.M., 638, 639
Boreham, J., 557
Borello, G.M., 704
Borkovec, T.D., 628
Bornemann, S., 651
Bornstein, 319–20
Bornstein, R.F., 701
Bortolotti, S., 430
Boscolo, L., 638
Boshier, R., 564
Bosman, E.A., 376
Boss, M.W., 718
Botez, M.I., 66
Botzin, R.R., 626
Bouchard, T.J., 13, 83, 84, 463, 464, 466, 733,

Boudreau, G., 569
Boudreault, L., 728
Bourgeault, I.L., 391
Bourhis, R.Y., 680
Bow-Thomas, C.C., 291
Bowd, A.D., 37
Bowen, B., 524
Bower, G.H., 153, 240, 277
Bower, K.S., 168, 169
Bower, N.J.A., 331
Bower, T.G.R., 331
Bowers, T.G., 641
Bowlby, J., 345
Bowles, N., 135
Boyanowski, E.O., 483, 484
Boyce, 745
Boydell, K.M., 374
Boyes, M.C., 339, 341
Boyle, M.H., 591
Boyle, P., 556
Bozarth, M.A., 59, 172
Bradbury, T.N., 386
Bradford, J.M., 385
Bradley, B., 589
Bradley, B.P., 595, 596
Bradley, M.M., 605, 606, 607
Bradley, M.T., 431
Brady, E.M., 732
Braff, D.L., 609, 611, 613
Braiere, N.M., 423
Brand, R.J., 560
Bransford, J.D., 129
Braun, C.M., 74, 209, 434, 752
Braun, J.C., 692, 693
Braungart, 347
Braverman, N.S., 193
Bravo, M., 542
Brawley, 404
Brean, H., 98
Brecher, D., 147
Breggin, P.R., 645
Brehm, J.W., 403
Brehm, S., 637
Breland, K., 206
Breland, M., 206
Bremner, K.E., 419
Brennan, W.M., 323
Brentar, J.T., 255
Breslin, M., 137
Brett, J.M., 728
Brett, L.P., 196
Brewer, H., 410
Brewer, W.F., 255
Brickman, J., 479, 484
Bridgeman, D.L., 683, 678
Brief, A.P., 737
Briere, J., 479
Briesacher, P., 752
Briggs, R., 358
Briggs, S.R., 522
Brisson, C, 757
Britt, T.W., 154, 155
Britton, S.W., 427
Broadbent, D.E., 137
Broca, P., 72
Brockner, J., 287, 308, 387
Brodbeck, D.R., 197
Bronfen, M.I., 35
Bronfenbrenner, U., 246
Bronstein, P., 193
Brouchon, M., 107
Broughton, R.J., 162
Broussolle, E.P., 612
Brown, G., 631
Brown, G.T., 547
Brown, J., 147, 701, 730
Brown, J.D., 519, 520, 535, 666
Brown, J.M., 114
Brown, K.S., 555
Brown, N.R., 249
Brown, R., 304, 362
Brown, R.W., 237, 252
Brown, S.D., 662
Brown, W.A., 412
Browne, D.H., 369
Brugge, J.F., 111
Bruhn, J.G., 570
Brush, L.R., 479
Bryant, J., 415
Bryant, M.J., 147
Bryden, J.P., 74

Bryden, M.P., 75
Bryson, S.E., 75
Buchanan, A., 147
Bucher, B., 627
Buchsbaum, M.S., 449
Buckle, 88
Buckley, R., 651
Bulcroft, R., 360
Bullard, E.J., 422
Burack, O.R., 197
Burger, J.M., 490, 666, 692
Burgess, A., 376
Burgess, C.A., 170, 716
Burish, T.G., 196
Burke, P.J., 513
Burke, R.J., 732, 734
Burnett, W., 568
Burns, K.S., 318
Burton, I., 533
Bushman, B.J., 695
Busner, C., 620
Buss, D.M., 415, 416, 474
Butcher, J.N., 638
Butt, D.S., 389
Byblow, W.D., 747
Byers, 660
Byrne, B.M., 547, 629
Byrne, D., 412, 18, 188, 364, 369,
    402, 414, 416, 520, 629, 701,
    706, 741
Byrne, R.M.J., 270

Cacciola, J., 589
Cacioppo, J.T., 74, 673
Cafferty, T.P., 724, 730
Cain, R.L., 683
Cain, W.S., 117, 414
Cairns, K.V., 388
Caldwell, 562
Calkins, M.W., 16
Callan, V.J., 733
Calvert, C.R.X., 461
Camacho, T.C., 533, 534
Camden, C.T., 497
Came, B., 483
Campbell, E., 558
Campbell, J.D., 519, 520
Campbell, J.N., 113
Campbell, K., 347
Campbell, M., 649
Campbell, R.E., 207
Campbell, R.L., 176
Campion, M.A., 722
Candas, V., 752
Cannon, W.B., 427
Capaldi, E.J., 279
Capalid, E., 207
Cappeliez, P., 378
Carbonneau, L., 595
Cardu, B., 74
Carey, D.P., 71
Carey, M.P., 196
Cargo, M.B., 301–302, 555
Carli, L.L., 469, 690
Carlsmith, J.M., 433
Carlson, N.R., 12, 116
Carment, D.W., 680
Carnevale, P.J.D., 479
Carney, J.M., 390
Carpenter, D.J., 558
Carpenter, P.A., 104
Carr, 742
Carr, E.G., 216
Carson, R.C., 638
Carsten, J.M., 736
Carstenson, L.L., 427
Cartier, J., 114
Carver, C.M., 510
Carver, C.S., 153, 154, 155, 490,
    504, 549, 569
Case, R., 325, 330
Casper, R.C., 409
Caspi, A., 380
Castellon, C., 589
Catalan, J., 692
Catano, V.M., 547
Cattell, R.B., 445, 511, 512
Cautela, J.R., 627
Ceccadi, M., 107
Cecchin, G., 638
Ceci, S.J., 246, 444, 466
Centerwall, B.S., 220
Cerelli, E., 377
Cerone, S., 120
Chachere, J.G., 220

Chadwick, W., 714, 728
Chaiken, S., 408
Chailelson, J., 381
Challis, G.B., 196
Chandler, 328
Chaouch, A., 113
Chapman, S., 555, 556
Chappell, 547
Charest, J., 532
Charlebois, N., 434, 74
Charness, N., 378, 379, 446, 447
Charney, D.S., 588
Chase, 702
Chase, W.G., 299
Chasnoff, I. J., 318
Chassin, L., 173
Chataway, C.J., 524
Chaves, J.F., 114
Chebat, J.C., 663, 675
Cheek, J.M., 522
Chenard, J.R., 532
Cheng, M.S., 390
Cherry, E.C., 120
Chess, S., 343, 345
Cheung, F.K., 623
Childress, A.R., 200
Chilmonczyk, B.A., 557
Chipman, S.F., 479
Chipperfield, J.G., 391
Chisholm, G., 80
Chomsky, N., 299, 300
Choudhry, S., 390
Chow, K.L., 9
Christensen, A., 634
Christianson, S.A., 256
Chuang, H.T., 564
Church, A.T., 513
Church, R.M., 280
Cialdini, R.B., 687, 692, 700
Cimbolic, P., 59
Cirtos, R.C., 702
Claaren, S.K., 318
Claes, M.E., 364, 473
Clancy, S., 114
Clark, C., 81
Clark, D., 595
Clark, D.A., 631
Clark, D.M., 593
Clark, E.V., 281, 303
Clark, H.H., 299
Clark, J.N., 564
Clark, K., 685
Clark, K.B., 660
Clark, K.C., 549
Clark, L.F., 664
Clark, M.C., 240
Clark, R.W., 9
Clark, S.W., 123
Clark, W., 115
Clarke, J.T., 83
Clarke, S.W., 115, 212, 213
Claxton-Oldfield, S.P., 662
Cleveland, N.J., 726
Clifton, J., 446, 447
Clifton, R.K., 321
Clifton, T.C., 738
Cloud, J.M., 351
Clum, G.A., 641
Coan, D., 245
Coates, R.A., 564
Cobern, M.K., 678
Cochran, S.W., 351
Cockram, L.L., 567
Coe, C.L., 519
Coen, K.M., 59
Cohen, 358, 391, 744
Cohen, A.J., 322
Cohen, B.D., 580, 589, 590
Cohen, D.B., 160
Cohen, G., 450
Cohen, H.H., 749
Cohen, J., 562
Cohen, K.M., 319
Cohen, M.A., 552
Cohen, N., 546
Cohen, R.J., 459
Cohen, R.L., 240, 333
Cohen, S., 71, 539, 544, 546
Cohn, 744
Cole, C.M., 692
Cole, M., 276
Cole, R., 680
Cole, W.A., 385
Coleman, J.C., 638
Coleman, R.M., 150

Coley, 755
Coley, J., 703
Collins, J.F., 641
Colvin, C.R., 512
Colwill, N.L., 353, 662, 727
Colwill, R.M., 211, 214
Comer, P., 371
Como, P., 523
Compas, B.E., 349
Condelli, L., 465
Condon, J.W., 702
Conger, J.A., 740, 741
Connell, D.W., 217
Connelly, M.S., 738
Connoly, J., 333
Conrod, B., 376
Constanza, R.S., 570
Contrada, R.J., 560
Conway, M., 155, 520, 668
Cook, F.L., 283
Cook, R.G., 197, 279
Cook, S.W., 683
Cook, T.D., 371
Cooper, B.A., 376
Cooper, H.M., 638, 639
Cooper, J., 677
Cooper, M., 591, 592, 718
Corballis, M.C., 75
Corbett, D., 59
Cordova, D.I., 425
Coren, S., 96, 106, 126, 127, 403
Corkin, S., 260
Corkum, V., 342
Cornelius, S.W., 380
Cornelius, T., 177
Corrado, R., 591, 592
Corren, S., 432
Corrigall, W.A., 59
Corso, J.F., 376
Corter, C., 318, 319
Cossette, L., 350
Costa, P.T., Jr., 512
Cota, A.A., 727
Cote, L., 569
Cottrell, N., 386
Coulombe, A., 662
Coulter, M.E., 147
Courage, M.L., 20, 250
Courehesne, E., 611
Cousins, L.S., 332
Cousins, S.O., 376, 389
Covell, K., 343, 662
Cowan, C.L., 700
Cowan, C.P., 349
Cowan, N., 234
Cowan, P.A., 349
Cox, B.J., 593
Cox, J.E., 67
Cox, T., 534
Coyle, J.T., 55, 262
Coyne, J.C., 541
Crago, N., 626
Craig, K.D., 114, 321, 434
Craik, F.I.M., 42, 230, 378
Cram, S.J., 38
Crano, W.D., 702
Crawford, C.B., 410
Crawford, M., 467
Creese, I., 612
Criqui, M.H., 490, 513
Cristina, I.C., 558
Cristofalo, V.J., 390
Crocker, P.R., 567, 662
Crombie, G., 369
Cromwell, R.L., 579, 611, 612
Crooks, D.S., 537
Cropanzano, R., 719, 733
Cross, H.J., 171
Cross, P., 170
Crossman, J., 202, 534
Crouch, A.G., 739
Crowhurst, M., 672
Crowley, K., 335
Crownshaw, S.F., 522
Croyle, R.T., 535
Crusco, A.H., 434
Cruse, 755
Crutchfield, R.A., 690
Csikszentmihalyi, M., 363
Cubic, B.A., 410, 411, 602
Cubis, J., 368
Cullen, 431
Cumming, C.E., 80
Cumming, D.C., 80
Cuneo, D.O., 329

Cunino, G.J., 542
Cunnick, J.E., 71, 546
Cunningham, C.E., 83
Cunningham, J.B., 150
Cunningham, M.R., 700
Cwitco, G., 723
Czeisler, C.A., 150

Daher, M., 320, 321
Dahl, J.G., 716
Dahl, O., 569
Daigneault, S., 752
Dallenbach, K.M., 243
Dane, 756
Daniel, J., 145
Daniels, S.G., 435, 745
Dannals, R.F., 612
Darby, B.L., 692
Dark, V., 120
Darley, D.M., 479
Darley, J.M., 670, 699
Darling, J.R., 318
Darlington, R.B., 465
Darou, W.G., 459
Das, B., 717
Das, J.P., 447, 461, 462, 463
Dasen, P.R., 164, 255
DasGupta, B., 543
Datan, N., 375
Daubman, K.A., 296, 435, 436
Daum, I., 66
Davey, G.C.L., 198
Davey, V.A., 189
Davidio, J.F., 684
Davidson, J.K., Sr., 414
Davidson, K., 305, 434
Davidson, R.J., 427, 430, 431, 580
Davies, M.F., 279
Davis, 745
Davis, C., 410
Davis, C.G., 392
Davis, H., 422, 424
Davis, J.R., 173
Davis, K.E., 663
Davis, M.H., 508
Davis, S.W., 351
Davis, W., 362
Dawis, R.V., 13
Day, D.V., 730
de Montigny, J., 391
de Reuck, A.V.S., 72
De Villiers, J.G., 301
De Villiers, P.A., 301
de Vries, B., 391
de-Koninck, J., 144
Deaux, K., 351, 444, 467, 479
DeBono, K.G., 436, 675
DeCarufel, A., 702
DeCasper, A.J., 316
deCatanzaro, D., 316
DeCourville, N., 80
Deci, E.L., 423, 424
Deepak, N., 317
Deffenbacher, J.L., 632
DeGroot, J.M., 409
Deitz, D., 544
Delgado, P.L., 588
D'Elia, P., 430
DeLong, M.R., 55
DeLongis, A., 392, 541, 569
Demare, D., 419
Dember, W.N., 118
Dembrowski, T.M., 560
Dement, W.C., 156, 157, 158, 162
Demers, P., 75
Denis, R., 747
DeNisi, A.S., 724, 730
Denney, N.W., 380
Denning, P.J., 297
Dennis, A.M., 409
DePaulo, B.M., 277, 278, 435, 468
Dere, M., 728
Derevensky, J.L., 368
Derlega, V.J., 570, 685
Dermer, M.L., 555
Dersen, L., 213
DeRubeis, R.J., 642
Derzko, C., 374
DeScenna, P., 263
Desgent, C., 735
Desharnais, R., 662
Deszka, G., 734
Deutsch, A., 578
Deutsch, G., 74, 75
DeValois, K.K., 105

DeValois, R.L., 105
Devine, P.G., 257, 681
Devins, G.M., 564, 566
Devlin, M.C., 370
Devolder, P.A., 662
DeVries, 340
Dewhirst, B., 171
Diamond, C.P., 718
Diamond, J., 389
Dichgans, J., 66
Dickerson, C.A., 678
DiFazio, R., 668
Digman, J.M., 512
Dillabough, J.M., 662
Dillard, J.P., 31
Dimsdale, J.E., 114
Dindia, K., 509
Dingus, T.A., 748
Dion, K., 475
Dion, K.K., 499, 500, 524, 525,
    662, 681, 703, 704
Dion, K.L., 499, 500, 524, 525,
    662, 681, 687, 688, 703, 704,
    727
Dirkes, K., 318
Dirkx, E., 378
DiTecco, D., 723
Ditto, P.H., 670, 724
Dixon, R.A., 378, 379
Doane, J.A., 611
Dobbs, A.R., 379
Dobson, K.S., 38
Docherty, J.P., 147, 641
Donaldson, S., 758
Doneberg, G.R., 641
Donnerstein, E., 744
Donovan, D.M., 428
Doob, A.N., 418, 675
Dore, F.Y., 326
Dorian, P., 534
Dorsey, M.F., 217
Doty, R.L., 132
Douce, C.E., 257
Douek, E., 116
Douglas, 332
Dovidio, J.F., 682, 726
Dower, J., 317
Downey, M.K., 370
Downing, J.W., 672, 732
Downing, R., 589
Doyle, A.B., 333
Drachman, D., 702
Dragoin, W.B., 194
Drake, R.A., 672, 732
Dreger, R.M., 511
Dreidger, L., 14
Droungas, A., 196
Duais, S.T., 323
Dube, L., 666
Dubbert, P.M., 567
DuBreuil, S.C., 168, 171
Duck, S., 638
Dudek, S.Z., 382
Duffy, D.L., 552
Duffy, R.D., 20, 748
Dumais, S.T., 151
Dumas, C., 326
Dumont, F., 724
Dumont, M., 209
Duncker, K., 293
Dunkel-Schetter, C., 478, 569
Dunn, K., 651
Dunn, R., 208
Dunne, M., 368
Dunnette, M.D., 719
Durrant, 422
Durrett, M., 344
Dussault, C., 216
Dutton, D.G., 220, 428, 694
Dweck, C.S., 211
Dwarkin, E.S., 498
Dwyan, J., et al., 87
Dwyer, et al., 213
Dwyer, W.L., 678
Dyce, J., 724
Dyck, R.J., 591
Dyer, F.C., 214
Dziedzic, S., 559

Eagly, A.E., 469, 690
Eagly, A.H., 690, 31, 468, 470, 471
Earhard, B., 680
Earle, S.S., 534
Eastman, C.I., 149
Eastwood, R., 390

Ebbesen, B.L., 570
Ebbinghaus, H., 9, 228, 242
Eberhardt, C.A., 368
Eckelman, C.C., 454
Edwards, J.R., 544, 700
Efran, J.S., 498
Egeland, J.A., 588
Ehrhardt, A.A., 78
Ehrhardt, J., 450
Ehrlichman, H., 414
Ehrman, R.N., 200
Eich, J.E., 241
Eichar, D.M., 732
Eiliatrault, P., 663
Eimas, P.D., 322
Eisenberg, N., 341, 692
Eisenberg, R., 386
Ekman, P., 427, 432, 434
Eldridge, G.B., 203
Elkin, J., 641
Elkind, D., 362
Elkins, I.J., 611, 612
Elkins, L.E., 473
Ellard, J.H., 392
Eller, S.J., 211
Ellingstad, V., 750
Elliott, A.J., 301
Elliott, R., 642
Ellis, A., 630, 631
Ellis, R.J., 522, 662
Ellsworth, C.P., 342, 433
Elmer-Dewitt, P., 297
Emery, G., 589
Empsom-Warner, S., 388
Empson, J.A.C., 160, 161
Endler, N.S., 537, 645
Engel, G.L., 532
Engen, T., 116, 117
Enns, M.W., 645
Enzle, M.E., 424, 425
Epstein, J.C., 532
Epstein, S., 519
Erfurt, J.C., 544, 545
Erikson, E.H., 364, 365, 367, 372, 377
Erlenmeyer-Kimling, L., 463, 464
Erlichman, H., 126
Eron, L.D., 24, 220
Eshleman, S., 620
Eskenazi, J., 99, 635
Esses, V.M., 438, 755
Etaugh, C., 481
Evans, B.K., 547
Evans, K., 718
Evans, M.D., 642
Evans, M.G., 716, 722
Evans, N., 682, 726
Evelyn, B., 377
Everett, P.B., 212
Ewart, C.K., 552
Eyjolfsson, K., 534
Eysenck, H.J., 501, 639, 641
Eysenck, M.W., 501

Fagot, B. I., 346
Fagot, J., 280, 281
Fairburn, S., 553
Fallon, A.E., 410
Family, G., 391
Fan, L., 291
Fang, Y., 722
Farace, A., 482, 483
Faraone, S.V., 579
Farde, L., 612
Farmer, M.C., 340
Farquhar, J.W., 566, 567
Farr, J.L., 730
Fazio, R.H., 675
Feather, N.T., 560
Fechner, G.T., 9
Fein, G., 317
Feingold, A., 468, 474, 480
Feingold, A.J., 702
Feldman, 725
Feldman, D.C., 221, 734
Felner, R.D., 541
Felton, K., 559
Fennema, E., 480
Fenton, W.S., 609
Ferguson, T.J., 675
Ferguson-Pare, M., 727
Fernandez, E., 114
Ferrari, L., 662
Ferster, C.B., 207
Ferzoco, G., 483

Festinger, L., 660, 673, 675, 701
Feuerstein, M., 532
Fibiger, H.C., 58, 59, 176, 262
Field, R.H., 739
Fielder, F.E., 221
Fields, H.L., 56
Fiester, S.J., 641
Fiez, J.A., 65
Fikrig, S., 317
Filiatrault, P., 663
Fincham, F.D., 386, 706
Finchten, C.S., 432
Finegan, J.E., 672
Fink, C., 701
Finkelhor, D., 369
Finman, R., 430
Finnegan, J.P., 122
Firestone, P., 332, 368
Fischer, D.G., 547
Fischoff, B., 279, 362
Fisher, 732
Fisher, H., 706
Fisher, J.D., 363, 434, 563, 564, 741, 742, 744, 752, 753
Fisher, L., 546
Fisher, L.E., 167, 172
Fisher, R.J., 59, 469, 690, 733, 734
Fisher, R.P., 257
Fisher, W.A., 564
Fishman, H.C., 684
Fiske, S.T., 251, 424, 435, 667
Fitzgerald, 326
Fivush, R., 250
Flaherty, C.F., 214
Flanders, D., 558
Flaum, M., 450
Flavell, E.R., 327
Flavell, J.H., 326, 327, 329
Fleet, G.J., 214
Fleming, A.S., 318, 319
Fleming, D.T., 602
Fleming, I., 542
Fleming, J.A., 160
Flessati, S.L., 479
Fletcher, C., 553
Fletcher, G.J.O., 490
Fletcher, J., 177
Flett, G.L., 405, 541, 560, 662
Flor-Henry, P., 81
Floyd, R.A., 390
Flynn, D.M., 169
Flynn, J.R., 444, 465
Foderaro, L.W., 117
Foley, H.J., 104, 106, 112, 113, 118, 120, 126, 129, 130, 137
Folger, R., 424
Folkman, S., 534, 535, 541, 569
Fondacaro, R.A., 675
Foote, A., 544, 545
Ford, L., 81
Forest, M., 384
Forgas, J.P., 153, 277, 400, 435, 475
Fortin, S.P., 691
Fortinsky, R.H., 732
Fothrtgill, L.A., 56
Foti, R.J., 738
Foulkes, D., 165
Fowler, B., 63
Fox, A.J., 74
Fox, E.E., 80
Fox, N.A., 430
Fox, P.T., 72, 73
Fox, R., 323
Fozard, J.L., 376, 378
Fraczek, A., 421
Frank, M.G., 666
Franken, R.E., 387, 727
Franks, J.J., 129
Franks, P., 319
Frantz, R.L., 323
Franzoi, S.L., 508
Fraser, S.C., 692
Frecska, E., 81
Frederick, D., 284
Freedman, J., 756
Freedman, J.L., 220, 692
Freedman, L., 81
Freehan, G.G., 424
Frei, R.L., 691
French, J.L., 455
Frenkel, O.J., 675
Frese, M., 545
Freud, S., 9, 11, 22, 163, 164, 175,

244, 418, 491–505, 511, 513, 518, 579, 596, 597, 600, 620–626
Freund, K., 414
Fricko, M.A., 734
Fried, M.P., 558
Fried, P.A., 177, 316, 318
Friedman, H., 468
Friedman, H.S., 522, 569
Friedman, H.W., 490, 513
Friedman, J.K., 159
Friedman, R., 180, 544
Friesen, J.D., 662
Friesen, W.V., 427, 432
Froberg, J.E., 148
Fromhoff, F.A., 250
Frost, P.J., 739, 741
Fry, D.P., 421
Fuchs, I., 341
Fuchs, P., 746
Fuller, C.A., 145, 147
Funder, D.C., 512, 513, 671
Fung, T., 369
Furedy, J.J., 197
Furman, K., 490
Furrow, D., 483, 484
Fusco, 744

Gabora, N.J., 168, 169, 171
Gaboury, A., 209
Gaertner, S.L., 684
Gagnon, A., 680
Gaines, J., 548
Galambos, N.L., 360, 361, 364, 534
Galanter, E., 96
Galef, B.G., 194, 218, 414
Gallo, L.C., 149
Gallo, R.C., 561
Gallop, R.M., 564
Galotti, K.M., 275, 340
Gangestad, S., 522
Gannon, L., 16, 17
Ganson, H., 465
Gantz, B.J., 137
Gara, M.A., 580, 590
Garb, J.L., 196
Garcia, J., 193, 194, 196
Garcia, M.F., 726
Gardner, B.T., 305
Gardner, H., 445
Gardner, R., 158
Gardner, R.A., 305
Garfinkel, P.E., 59, 216, 409, 410
Garland, A., 620
Garland, H., 32, 288
Garner, D.M., 216
Garrett, J., 523
Garside, B., 564
Gartrell, J., 213
Garvey, A.J., 174
Gary, J.T., 250
Gatchel, R.J., 532, 542
Gates, R.D., 83
Gauthier, S., 157
Gauvain, M., 332
Gauvin, L., 568, 569
Gazzaniga, M.S., 51, 75
Gebhard, P., 413
Gee, 373
Geen, R.G., 403
Geffner, R., 678, 683
Geiselman, R.E., 257, 258
Gelinas-Chebat, C., 675
Gellatly, I.R., 718
Geller, E.S., 212, 220
George, J.M., 737
George, J.T., 217
Gerhard, D.S., 588
Gerrard, M., 369
Geschwind, N., 72
Geyer, M.A., 611
Ghesquire, K., 347, 364
Giancola, P.R., 69
Giannopoulos, C., 155, 520
Giard, N., 74
Gibb, 88
Gibbons, B., 116
Gibbons, J., 344
Gibbs, S., 349
Giberson, R., 132
Gibson, B.D., 682
Gibson, E.J., 323
Gibson, K.J., 387, 727
Gier, J.A., 433, 434

Giesen, H.A., 147
Giesler, R.B., 156, 702
Gifford, R., 542
Gilbert, A.N., 116
Gilbert, D.T., 663, 665, 681
Gill, J., 165
Gill, M.J., 564
Gilles, F.H., 557
Gillett, J., 410
Gilligan, C., 316
Gilligan, C.F., 340
Gilliland, M. A., 159
Gilliland, R.C., 567
Gillis, A.R., 743
Gilovich, T., 666, 667, 668
Ginsburg, G.P., 662
Ginthner, D., 745
Giordano, C., 524
Girgus, J.S., 126, 127
Giroux, J., 209
Gisiner, R., 307
Gist, B., 400
Gitta, M.Z., 510
Giuliano, T.A., 663
Gjedde, A., 612
Gladue, B.A., 417, 418
Glaser, R., 509, 546, 553, 559
Glass, D.R., 641
Glass, G.V., 641
Glass, K.C., 391
Glazer, S., 445
Gleaves, D.H., 410, 411, 602
Gleicher, F., 670
Glendon, A.I., 242
Glenn, N.D., 386
Globus, G.G., 159
Gloor, P., 81
Glor, J.E., 692
Goddard, E., 556
Godden, D., 241
Godfrey, D.K., 691
Goering, P.N., 651
Goethals, G.R., 519, 662, 677, 702
Gold, C.A., 147
Gold, D.P., 379, 381
Gold, E.B., 557
Goldbloom, D.S., 409, 410
Goldenberg, H., 638
Goldenberg, I., 638
Goldenring, J.M., 569
Goldman, S.J., 408
Goldstein, M.A., 726
Goldstein, M.J., 611
Goldston, R.B., 580, 589, 590
Goldwater, B., 74, 81
Goleman, D., 255
Goleman, O., 461
Golombek, H., 358, 519
Goodale, M.A., 71, 88
Goode, E., 408
Goodenough, D.R., 163
Goodman, J., 256
Goodman, J.T., 332
Goodnow, J.J., 217, 337–38
Gopnik, A., 333
Gopnik, M., 301–302
Gorchover, O., 592
Gordon, W.C., 190, 198
Gormley, E.G., 742
Gorny, B.P., 71
Gosse, V.F., 720
Gotlib, I.H., 319, 666
Gottesman, I.I., 610, 611
Gottfried, A.W., 465
Gow, C.A.,155, 400
Gowland, C.A., 376
Grace, M.C., 542
Grady, M.K., 371
Graf, 333
Graf, P., 22, 260, 379
Graffi, S., 534
Grahan, C.H., 104
Grambert, R.F., 376
Granchrow, J.R., 320, 321
Granger, D., 641
Granger, L., 10
Granholm, E., 612
Granrud, C.E., 323
Grant, D.S., 214
Grant, P.R., 679, 702
Gray, P., 705
Gray, R., 177
Gray, T.A., 67
Graziano, W.G., 469, 474, 475, 699

Green, B.L., 542
Green, D., 423
Green, J.P., 255
Green, R., 602
Green, R.G., 724
Green, S.B., 558
Green, S.G., 725
Green, T.E., 752, 753
Green, W.H., 649
Greenberg, J., 387, 406, 666, 714, 717, 720, 755
Greenberg, J.S., 181
Greenblatt, 649
Greenglass, E.R., 560, 732
Greenwald, A.G., 98, 99, 255, 635
Gregg, W., 544, 545
Gregor, P., 662
Gregory, W.L., 421
Greist-Bousquet, S., 127
Grespi, L.P., 214
Griffin, D.W., 520
Griffin, R.W., 722
Griffith, D.R., 318
Griffith, T.L., 724
Griffiths, K., 333
Grillon, C., 611
Grilly, D.M., 172, 648
Grindke, A.C., 212, 213
Grivel, F., 752
Grobe, C., 558
Groff, M.G., 454
Gross, P., 368
Grosskurth, P., 500
Groth, G.E., 476, 477
Growne, D.P., 75
Gruchy, C.G., 434, 468, 481
Gruen, R.J., 569
Gruhl, 755
Grunau, R.V., 321
Gruneberg, M.M., 243, 264
Grusec, J.E., 217, 337–38, 698, 718
Guilford, J., 296, 445
Guimond, S., 662, 666
Gunn, C., 758
Gunn, K.P., 24, 25
Gurevich, M., 541
Gurman, A.S., 637, 638
Guroff, J.J., 599
Gurstein, P., 723
Gustavson, C.R., 196
Gutek, B.A., 732, 733
Guttman, H.A., 392
Gwynn, M.I., 170

Ha, Y.W., 278
Haake, R.J., 331
Haber, F., 753
Habib, F., 371
Haccoun, R.R., 735
Haddow, J.E., 557
Hagan, J., 370, 388, 743
Hagen, E., 455
Hagen, R., 609
Hager, J.L., 196
Haier, R.J., 449
Hains, S.M., 342
Hajek, P., 165
Hakim-Larson, J., 380
Hakstain, A.R., 126, 731
Hall, 347
Hall, J.A., 434, 468, 552
Hall, W.B., 81
Hall, W.G., 407
Halldin, C., 612
Halpern, 71
Halpern, S., 723
Hamel, S., 368
Hamer, D.H., 86
Hamerman, D., 552
Hamilton, J.A., 523
Hamilton, T.E., 475
Hamilton, V.L., 695
Hammer, M., 375
Hammersmith, S.K., 85, 417
Hamovit, J.R., 147
Handfield-Jones, R., 391
Hankins, W.G., 193
Hanly, C., 401
Hans, S., 641
Hans, V.P., 695
Harder, J.W., 20, 719
Harder, L.D., 215
Hare, R.D., 606
Harlow, H.F., 317, 348–49

Harlow, M.H., 349
Harpur, T.J., 606
Harrell, W.A., 377
Harrigan, J.A., 433
Harris, J., 246
Harris, M.B., 471
Harris, P.R., 221
Harris, S.D., 549
Harrison, J.K., 222
Harrison, R.V., 544
Hart, S.D., 220
Hartel, C.E., 730, 731
Hartley, J.T., 379
Hartmann, E.L., 158
Hartup, W.W., 364
Hartwick, J., 717
Harvey, S.M., 412
Hasher, L., 378, 379, 380
Hashizume, L.G., 388
Hashmall, J.M., 662
Haskins, R., 465
Hass, K., 85
Hass, A., 85
Hasselkink, J.R., 613
Hassett, J., 414
Hastie, R., 18, 270, 279
Hatfield, D.B., 212, 213
Hatfield, E., 704, 705, 476, 701, 702, 707
Hauenstein, N.M., 726
Haugaard, J.J., 245
Haver, L.A., 691
Havercamp, 88
Hawkings, L., 387
Hawkins, W.L., 425
Hawkins, S.A., 270, 279
Hawkins, W.G., 196
Hawranik, P., 389
Hayes, N., 682
Haynes, N., 371
Hazelrigg, M.D., 638, 639
Healey, S., 160
Hearty, B., 392
Heath, C., 557
Heatherton, T.F., 507, 520, 521
Heaton, R.K., 613
Hebb, D.O., 11, 48
Hecaen, H., 72
Hedley-White, E.T., 557
Heeren, T., 537, 563
Heihold, J.W., 174
Heilbrun, L.K., 558
Heilman, M.E., 728
Heinlein, L., 660
Heinrichs, R.W., 579, 607, 609
Heirich, M.A., 544, 545
Hekinheimo, 685
Helgeson, 756
Hellige, J.B., 77
Helmreich, R.L., 479, 485
Helms, J.E., 459, 460
Hembree, E.A., 342
Hendrick, C., 637, 701, 704, 705
Hendrick, S.S., 701, 704, 705
Hendricks, S., 555
Heninger, G.R., 588
Henker, B., 332
Henna, 569
Henriques, J.B., 430, 580
Henry, J., 56
Henry, W.A., 417
Henson, R.D., 664
Heppener, P.P., 666
Herberman, R.B., 546, 559
Herling, S., 172
Herman, C.P., 408
Herman, L.M., 307
Herold, E.S., 564
Herren, L.T., 436
Herrnstein, R.J., 467
Hersey, P., 739
Hershberger, S.L., 733
Hertzog, C., 245, 378
Herz-Lazarowitz, R., 341
Hetherington, 155
Hetherington, C.R., 400
Hetu, R., 746
Hetzel, B., 550
Hewitt, E.C., 422
Hewitt, K.L., 321
Hewitt, P.L., 405, 541, 560
Heymans, S.L., 479
Hiew, C.C., 371
Higgins, A.T., 331

Higgins, E.G., 519
Higgins, E.T., 675
Hilditch, J., 392
Hilgard, E.R., 168, 169
Hill, D., 567
Hill, R., 474
Hilliard, A., 685
Hillier, L.M., 321
Hilton, A., 680
Hilton, D.J., 663
Hilton, M.E., 123
Hilton, N.Z., 370
Himelein, M.J., 652
Hines, M., 81, 467, 482
Hingson, R., 537, 563
Hinson, R.E., 190, 199
Hinsz, L.D., 602
Hinton, G.E., 297, 298
Hinz, L.D., 409
Hirsch-Pasek, K., 301
Hiscock, M., 74, 318
Hitchcock, J.L., 174
Hixon, J.G., 155, 156, 681
Hobart, C., 563
Hobson, J.A., 165
Hobson, R.W., 165
Hodges, J., 346
Hodgson, R.J., 594
Hodkin, B., 483, 484
Hoffman, D.C., 194
Hoffman, H., 147
Hoffman, L.E., 414
Hoffmann, R., 162
Hofstede, G., 499
Hogan, S.E., 83
Hogg, M.A., 680
Hogness, D.S., 105
Holden, D.J., 333
Holders, M.D., 307
Holland, H.L., 257
Holland, J.L., 734, 735
Hollon, S.D., 641, 642
Holmes, D., 245
Holmes, D.S., 180
Holmes, T.H., 539, 540, 541
Holstein, 340
Holtzworth-Munroe, A., 637
Honig, W.K., 192, 207
Honzik, C.H., 214, 215, 279
Hood, E., 643, 644
Hope, B., 134
Hopkins, B.L., 217
Hopkins, W.D., 280, 281
Hoppe, R.B., 135
Hopper, C.H., 742
Hopson, J., 79
Hopson, J. L., 305
Horner, M., 382, 422, 423
Horney, K.E., 501, 502, 503, 504
Hornick, J.P., 370
Hornorton, C., 136
Hornstein, G.A., 623
Horton, C., 134
Horvarth, P., 522
Hosman, L.A., 509
Hostetter, A.M., 588
Houfman, L.G., 103
House, M., 103
House, R.J., 739, 740
Housman, D.E., 588
Hovland, C.I., 673
Howard, G.S., 32
Howard, K.I., 641
Howe, B.L., 422, 663
Howe et al., 333
Howe, M.E., 20
Howe, M.L., 250
Howell, J.L., 739, 740, 741
Howes, J.L., 378
Howland, C., 673
Hoyseth, K., 318
Hoyt, I.P., 599
Hsia, Y., 104
Hsu, L.G., 409
Hu, N., 86
Hu, S., 86
Hubble, L.M., 454
Huber, G.P., 217
Huber, V.L., 718
Huddleston, R.J., 387
Huebner, R.R., 342
Hughes, C.F., 509
Hughes, J.R., 56
Hughes, M., 620

Hughes, P., 685
Hull, C.L., 9
Hultsch, D.F., 375, 378, 379
Hume, K.M., 202
Hummel, J.C., 341
Humphrey, 323
Humphrey et al, 322
Hundleby, J.D., 364, 410
Hunn, B.P., 748
Hunt, E.B., 20, 80, 482
Hunter, F.M., 415
Hunter, L., 555
Huntingford, F.A., 514
Hurvich, L.M., 106
Hurwitz, T.A., 81
Hutahajan, P., 134
Hutcherson, H.W., 664
Hwang, 341
Hyde, J.S., 468, 477, 480
Hyman, L.M., 433
Hyman, R., 136
Hynds, F., 135

Iacono, W.G., 431
Imber, S.D., 641
Inman, G.A., 662
Insko, C.A., 702
Intons-Peterson, M.J., 274
Irvine, M.J., 216
Irving-Neto, R.L., 535
Isabella, R.A., 347
Isen, A.M., 295, 296, 435, 436, 699, 745
Iversen, L.L., 612
Iwahashi, M., 118
Iwata, G., 217
Izard, C.E., 342, 426, 628

Jaccard, J., 370
Jacklin, C.N., 353
Jackson, 88
Jackson, D.N., 603
Jackson, E.A., 563
Jackson, R.L., 211
Jackson, S.E., 547, 548
Jacobs, A.M., 104
Jacobs, J.R., 705
Jacobsen, E., 555
Jacobson, E., 569
Jacobson, J., 317
Jacobson, L.S., 71
Jacobson, N.S., 637
Jacoby, L.L., 151, 701, 730
Jain, D., 349
Jako, R.A., 726, 731
James, K., 733
James, W., 7
James, W.J., 401
Jameson, D., 106
Jamieson, D.W., 522, 701
Jamieson, J., 479
Jang, K.L., 603, 663
Janis, I.L., 673
Jarell, K.L., 698
Jarvik, L.F., 463, 464
Jasechko, J., 701, 730
Jason, G.W., 75, 564, 745
Jefferson, D.J., 120
Jemmott, J.B., 546, 670
Jencks, D., 463
Jenkins, C.D., 559
Jenkins, E., 335
Jenkins, J.G., 243
Jenkins, J., 385
Jennings, J.M., 151
Jensen, A.R., 449, 464
Jensen-Campbell, L.A., 469, 474, 475
Jermier, J.M., 548
Jernigan, T.L., 613
Jessor, R., 371
Jevene, R., 409
Jhamandas, K., 55
Jiujias, A., 522
Jobes, D.A., 652
Jobin, J., 662
Joffe, R.T., 147, 591
Johansen, H., 589
Johansson, F., 523
John, O.P., 669
Johns, G., 722, 734, 735, 754
Johnson, C., 409
Johnson, B.T., 470
Johnson, C., 190

Johnson, D.F., 703
Johnson, E.J., 292
Johnson, L.C., 159
Johnson, N.M.S., 435
Johnson, V.E., 413, 414
Johnson-Laird, P.N., 270
Johnston, C., 532, 662
Johnston, C.C., 319, 321
Johnston, J.R., 385
Johnston, W., 120
Joiner, T.E., Jr., 589
Jones, D.M., 137
Jones, E.E., 663, 665, 691
Jones, I.L., 415
Jones, M.M., 597
Jones, P.J.H., 318
Jordan, A., 718
Jorgenson, D.O., 719
Joseph, J.A., 378
Joseph, K.M., 747
Joseph-Vanderpool, J.R., 147
Joshi, P., 349
Jourard, S.M., 508
Joy, 334
Judd, C.M., 672, 681, 726, 732
Judd, D., 432
Judge, T.A., 736
Jung, C., 501, 502, 504, 513
Jung, S.O., 80
Juscyck, P.W., 322
Jussim, L.J., 635, 636, 672
Just, M.A., 104

Kachaturian, H., 113
Kaelber, C., 584
Kafer, R., 483, 484
Kagan, J., 343, 344, 345, 430
Kahn, S.E., 534
Kahneman, D., 282, 283, 284, 285, 308, 670
Kakuchi, S., 291
Kales, A., 160
Kales, J.D., 160
Kalick, S.M., 475
Kalivas, P.W., 58
Kalsher, M.J., 20, 123, 212, 213, 748
Kamin, L.J., 191, 467
Kaniasty, K., 542
Kanner, A.D., 541
Kantz, D.S., 532
Kanungo, R.N., 717, 740
Kaplan, 354
Kaplan, H.I., 599
Kaplan, J.R., 71, 546
Kaplan, R.E., 634
Karacan, I., 163
Karasek, R., 535
Karlberg, A.M., 591, 592
Karvonen, M.J., 149
Kasian, M., 706, 707
Kasper, S.F., 147
Kassin, 741
Katz, A.N., 378, 662, 666
Katz, J., 69
Katz, N.R., 552
Kaufman, A., 213
Kaufman, A.S., 462, 482
Kaufman, K., 421, 652
Kaufmann, R., 746
Kaukiainen, A., 471, 472
Kavanaugh, K., 346
Kazarian, S., 534
Kazdin, A.E., 628, 641
Keating, L.J., 410
Keefe, R.C., 476
Keelan, J.P., 662, 703
Keesling, B., 569
Keller, L.M., 13
Kelley, C., 701, 730
Kelley, D.J., 700
Kelley, H.H., 663, 664, 667, 673, 709
Kelley, K., 364, 369, 402, 629
Kelloway, E.K., 544, 733
Kelly, B., 368
Kelly, D.D., 158
Kelly, F., 412
Kelly, K., 414, 416, 477
Kelman, H.C., 35, 695
Kelner, M.J., 391
Kelsey, F.O., 317
Kelsey, R.M., 536
Kendall-Tackett, K.A., 369

Kendler, K.S., 611, 620
Kennedy, J.M., 330
Kennedy, S., 409, 546
Kennedy, S.H., 59
Kenny, D.A., 738
Kenrick, D.T., 477, 700
Kerig, P.P., 349
Kerr, D., 14
Kerr, G., 570
Kerr, J.H., 534
Kerr, P.W., 104
Kerr, S.L., 608, 611
Kertesz, A., 71, 73, 81
Kessler, R.C., 577, 620
Ketcham, A.S., 549
Kety, S.S., 611
Keyes, 667
Keyserlingk, E., 391
Kida, T., 270, 284
Kidd, K.K., 588
Kiecolt-Glaser, J.K., 545, 546, 553, 559
Kiedinger, R.E., 280
Kienker, P.K., 298
Kieren, D.K., 360
Kierolt-Glaser, J.H.K., 509
Kiesler, C.A., 673
Kiesler, D.J., 641, 642
Kiesler, S.B., 673
Kihlstrom, J.F., 599
Kilham, W., 694
Kim, C. K., 172
Kimball, 727
Kimball, M.M., 15
Kimberly, St. J., 591
Kim,C.K., 257, 258
Kimura, D., 81
Kinder, B.N., 473
Kinsey, A.C., 413
Kirby, J.R., 447, 462, 463
Kircaali, I.G., 718
Kirchmeyer, C., 522
Kirkpatrick, S.A., 738, 739
Kirmayer, L.J., 662
Kirsch, I., 152, 167, 168
Kirwil, L., 421
Kivlahan, D.R., 428
Klaaren, K.J., 277, 278, 438
Klatzky, R.L., 708
Klayman, J., 278
Kleck, R.E., 536
Klein, H.J., 716
Klein, R., 145, 700
Kleinke, C.L., 433
Kleinman, A., 580
Kleitman, N., 162
Klentz, B., 692
Klienfeldt, S., 662
Kline, D.W., 376, 746
Kline, T.J., 376
Klonsky, B.G., 31, 470
Klotz, M.L., 20, 692, 693
Knauss, K., 280
Knauth, P., 149
Knight, G.E., 557
Kniskern, D.P., 637, 638
Knolls, 569
Knowles, J.B., 147
Knowlton, B.J., 261
Knox, S.S., 733
Kobasa, S.C., 549
Koelling, R.A., 193, 194
Koestner, R., 467, 479, 480, 490, 727
Kohlberg, L., 338–39
Kohler, I., 133
Kohn, P.M., 541
Kolarik, J., 361
Kolata, G.B., 408, 588
Kolb, B., 70, 88, 432
Kolonel, L.N., 557
Komacki, J.L., 217
Konovsky, M.A., 387
Kopala, L., 81
Kopelman, M.D., 247
Kopp, R.E., 213
Kopta, S.M., 641
Korabick, K., 470, 471
Korenblum, M., 358, 519
Kosaka, B., 74
Kosnik, W., 376
Kosslyn, S.M., 274, 375
Kost, K.A., 670
Kosterlitz, H.W., 56
Kotch, J.B., 369

Kotze, H., 752
Koulack, D., 162
Kozberg, S.F., 340
Kozlowski, L.T., 558
Kraft, D., 438
Krahn, H., 388
Krakoff, L.R., 559
Kral, P.A., 194
Kramer, K.B., 386
Kramer, M., 162
Kramp, P., 700
Krank, M.D., 199, 200
Krause, A.M., 385
Krause, M.S., 641
Krech, K.H., 319, 532
Kremen, W.S., 579
Kroger, W.S., 257
Krosnick, J.A., 732, 635, 636, 672
Kruglanski, A.W., 670
Kruk, E., 385, 387
Krumscott, S., 122
Krupka, A., 347
Kryger, B.R., 731
Kubler-Ross, E., 391, 392
Kubos, K.L., 430
Kuczaj, S.A., 307
Kuczmierczyk, A.R., 532
Kuhar, M.J., 612
Kuhn, D., 328
Kuiper, N.A., 537, 560, 589
Kulak, A.G., 479
Kulik, C.T., 719
Kulik, J., 251
Kunce, J.T., 454
Kunda, Z., 490, 729
Kunzinger, E.L., 333
Kupych, W.N., 160
Kurdek, L.A., 386
Kurtz, F., 564
Kurtz, L., 368
Kushnir, T., 547
Kutcher, S., 157
Kutchinsky, B., 245
Kwon, Y., 752

Labbe, E. E., 532
Labouvie-Vief, G.M., 380
Labrecque, R., 74
Lacroix, 433
Ladouceur, R., 209
Lafreniere, K., 541
Lagerspetz, K.M., 471, 472
Laird, J.D., 427
Lake, E.A., 509
Lalande, S., 74, 434
Lalljee, M., 662
Lalonde, M., 533
Lalonde, R.N., 66, 680, 683
Lam, R.W., 147
Lamb, J.A., 620
Lamb, M.E., 345
Lamb, R., 662
Lambert, M.J., 641, 653
Lambert, S.J., 732, 741
Lamke, T.A., 455
Lamon, M., 435, 438
Lamon, S.J., 480
Lamotte, R.H., 113
Lancee, W.J., 564, 651
Landau, S., 332
Landis, H., 588
Landreville, P., 541
Landry, T., 483, 484
Landsbergis, P.A., 544
Landum, R.W., 390
Landy, F.J., 730
Lane, M.C., 733
Laner, R.M., 83
Lang, P.J., 605, 606, 607
Lange, J.D., 412
Langley, C.M., 281–82
Langlois, J.H., 331, 703
Lanphier, C., 534
Laplante, D.P., 320
Lapsley, D.K., 362
Largen, J., 214
Larrick, R.P., 287
Larsen, R.J., 415, 416
Larson, J.R., Jr., 546
Larson, R., 363
Lashley, K.S., 9
Lassonde, M., 75
Laswell, M.E., 705
Latane, B., 699
Latham, G.P., 41, 217, 404, 439,

717, 718, 720
Lau, C.L., 59
Lau, M.A., 419
Lauer, J., 386, 637
Lauer, R., 386, 637
Laurd, J., 245
Lavallee, M., 353
LaVecchia, C., 556
Law, D.J., 20, 80, 482
Law, M.B., 77
Law, W.K., 73
Lawler, E.E., III, 736
Lawless, H., 117
Lawrence, P., 746
Lawson, K.R., 344
Lazarus, R.S., 534, 535, 541, 569
LeBegue, B., 147
Leber, W.R., 641
Lecours, A.R., 378
Ledingham, J., 369
Lee, P.C., 137
Lee, R.T., 547
Leeming, F.L., 678
Leenaars, A.A., 367, 591
Lefebvre, A., 564
LeFevre, J.A., 479
Legerstee, M., 342
Lehman, D.R., 392, 542
Lehman, H.C., 382
Leibowitz, S.F., 50
Leigh, B.C., 755
Leighton, A.H., 585
Leiter, M.P., 547
Leith, L.M., 570, 662
Leitten, C.L., 536
Lemieux, A.M., 519
Lemire, D., 651
Lempers, J.D., 327
Lempert, R.O., 18, 279
Lennon, R.T., 455
Lennox, R.D., 522
Lentz, R.J., 628
Lepper, M.R., 423, 425
Lerner, R.M., 382, 446, 703
Lero, 347
Leroux, J.A., 341
Lesgold, A.M., 240
Lester, D., 367, 591
Letourneau, J.E., 747
Lett, B., 194
Leung, A.K., 161
Levanoni, E., 732
LeVay, S., 85
Levenson, R.W., 427, 431
Levi, F., 556
Levine, D.S., 297, 298
Levine, J.M., 661, 689
Levine, S.V., 368
Levinger, G., 706, 386
Levinson, D.J., 382, 383, 384, 385
Levinton, A., 557
Levis, D.J., 627
Levitt, A.J., 147
Levy, B.A., 151
Levy, S.M., 546, 553, 559
Lewandowsky, S., 230
Lewin, K., 9
Lewin, T., 368
Lewinsohn, P.M., 409
Lewis, 351
Lewis, J.T., 427
Lewis, M., 250
Lewis, M.E., 113
Lewis, S.K., 692
Lewis, T.L., 322
Lewko, J.H., 688
Ley, P., 246
Ley, R.G., 74
Li, J., 532
Libby, R., 284
Licht, B.G., 211
Lichtenstein, P., 733
Liddell, A., 532
Liddell, F.D.K., 149
Liden, R.C., 691
Lieberman, D.A., 189
Lightdale, J.R., 472
Lin, S., 520
Lindblom, W.D., 755
Lindeis, A.E., 63
Linden, E., 306
Linden, W., 752
Lindsay, J., 390
Lindsey, S., 651
Lindsley, O., 215

Lindy, J.D., 542
Linesman, M.A., 59
Links, J.M., 612
Links, P.S., 370
Linn, M., 480
Linsenmeier, H.W.W., 691
Linton, J.M., 672
Linton, M., 247
Lippman, M., 546, 559
Lips, H.M., 727
Lipset, S.M., 702
Lisle, D.J., 438
Liss, M.B., 481
List, W., 545
Little, J.K., 351
Little, R.E., 318
Litwin, J.H., 422
Liu, S., 59
Livesley, W.J., 603
Lobsenz, N.M., 705
Locke, 732
Locke, B.Z., 551
Locke, E.A., 41, 404, 439, 717, 720, 733, 738, 739
Locker, D., 532, 563
Lockhart, R.S., 230, 239
Loewen, L.J., 753
Loftus, E.F., 242, 245, 246, 247, 255, 256, 257
Loftus, G.R., 256
Logan, G.D., 151
Logue, A.W., 196
Logue, K.R., 196
LoLordo, V.M., 196
Londorf, D., 747
Long, B.C., 385, 534, 732
Long, G.M., 376
Long, R.J., 723
Lonner, W.J., 375
Loo, R., 735
Loosen, P.T., 641, 642
Lopez, A.D., 557
Lopez, D.F., 670, 724
Lopez, R., 557
Lopez, S.R., 585
Loranger, M., 333
Lorch, E.P., 332
Lord, 725
Lord, C.G., 691
Lorrain, D., 157
Loutzenhiser, L., 714, 728
Lovaas, O.I., 216, 627
Lowell, E.L., 9
Loy, J.W., 680
Loza, W., 662
Luborsky, L., 589, 642
Lucas, D., 237
Lucchini, F., 556
Luchetta, T., 16, 17
Luchins, A.S., 293
Lundgren, S.R., 474, 475
Lupfer, M.B., 664
Lupker, S.J., 214
Luthans, F., 217
Lyall, W., 10
Lydon, J.E., 522, 701
Lykken, D.T., 84, 386, 387, 431, 464, 606
Lyman, B.J., 117
Lyness, S.A., 560
Lynn, A.R., 635, 636, 672
Lynn, S.J., 152, 153, 167, 168, 255
Lyon, J.L., 557
Lyons, S., 665
Lytton, H., 353

McAlpine, L., 333
McArthur, L.Z., 360
McCaskill, P., 567
McBurney, D.H., 601
McCain, 742
McCall, R.B., 368
McCallum, M., 392
McCandliss, B.D., 65
McCann, C.D., 675
McCanne, T.R., 427
McCarley, R.W., 165
McCarthy, 547
McCarthy, B., 370
McCarthy, G.E., 122
McCarthy, R.L., 122
McClaren, J., 391
McClearn, G.E., et al., 83
McClelland, C.L., 722
McClelland, D.C., 9, 421

Maccoby, E.E., 351, 353
Maccoby, N., 566, 567
McConkey, C., 465
McConkie, G.W., 104
McCormick, E.J., 746, 747, 751, 752
McCrae, R.R., 512
McCreath, H., 692
MacCrimmon, D.J., 81
McCulloch, T., 10
McCully, J., 199
McDaniel, M.A., 117
McDaniel, S.A., 364
McDavid, J.W., 690
MacDonald, B.H., 74
MacDonald, C., 147
McDonald, G., 371
McDonald, J., 700
MacDonald, L., 446, 447
MacDonald, M.R., 589
McDonald, R.J., 68
McDonnell, P.M., 326
McDowell, I., 390
McDown, J.M., 378
McEwan, N.H., 258
McFarland, C., 75, 80, 668, 670
McFarland, D., 177
MacFarlane, J.G., 160
McGee, R., 555
McGill, K.L., 519, 535
McGinnis, R., 474
McGlashan, T.H., 609
McGlone, J., 74, 80
McGonagle, K.A., 620
McGrath, P.J., 333
McGregor, J., 683
McGregor, S., 318
McGue, M., 84, 386, 387, 464
McGuire, G.R., 675
McGuire, J., 352
Macguire, P., 553
McIntosh, D.N., 426, 431
McIntosh, J.M., 376
McIntyre, J.S., 378
Mackay, A.V.P., 612
McKee, R., 261
McKeen, C.A., 732
McKelvey, 345
McKelvie, S.J., 264, 695, 700, 703, 755
McKendree, D.J., 392
McKenna, S.P., 242
McKenry, P.C., 369
McKey, R., 680
McKibben, B., 741
Mackie, D.M., 436, 437
McKinney, W.T., Jr., 588
MacKinnon, D.P., 257
McLachlan, A.L., 666
McLachlan, D.R., 233
McLaren, J., 75
MacLaren, R., 698
MacLean, A., 147
MacLean, A.W., 80, 160
McLennan, B., 703
MacLennan, R., 714, 728
MacLeod, G., 170
McLeod, K., 736
MacLeod, L., 479
McLeod, P.J., 343
McMahan, G.C., 722
MacMahon, B., 558
McMahon, R.J., 364
McMichael, T., 550
McMillan, M., 685
MacNamara, J. 329
McNeal, E.T., 59
MacNee, C., 318
McNeill, D., 237
MacNiven, E., 316
Macrae, C.N., 670, 671, 724
MacRae, L., 75
Macrae, P.G., 376
McReynolds, W.T., 211
McVey, G., 409
Magana-Amato, K., 611
Maggs, 348, 363
Magid, 345
Magloire, K., 546
Magnuson, V.L., 86
MaGrath, J.E., 160
Mah, K.B., 403
Mahalski, P.A., 555
Maher, B.A., 577
Maher, W.B., 577

Maier, S.F., 211
Maisonneuve, P., 556
Major, B., 479
MaKhijani, M.G., 31, 470
Malan, J.R., 593
Malat, J., 612
Malcolmson, S.A., 643, 644
Malcuit, G., 350
Malenfant, L., 216
Malinowksi, B., 164
Malkoff, S., 546
Malla, A.K., 541
Mallory, B.L., 432
Malloy, 87
Malpass, R.S., 257, 375
Maluish, A.M., 546, 559
Mamelak, M., 162
Mammone, N., 718
Mandel, D.R., 392
Mandler, J.M., 333
Mann, J., 562, 684
Mann, L., 694
Mann, L.M., 173
Mann, S.J., 559
Manning, M.R., 546
Manuck, S.B., 546
Mapletoft, S.J., 419
Maran, K.G., 347
Marchand, S., 532
Marche, T.A., 728
Margolin, G., 637
Mark, L.S., 703
Markham, M.E., 542
Marks, G., 668
Marks, I., 626
Markus, G.B., 465
Markus, H.M., 367
Marlatt, G.A., 428
Marr, D., 130
Marshall, V., 374
Marshall, V.W., 391
Martell, R.F., 728
Martin, A., 434
Martin, C., 413
Martin, C.L., 351
Martin, M., 523, 595
Martin, R.A., 537
Marton, P., 157, 358, 519
Maruyama, G., 673
Marwell, G., 520
Marzetta, B.R., 180
Maser, J.D., 584
Maslach, C., 547
Maslow, A.H., 404, 405, 406, 505, 507, 518, 526, 716
Masters, W.H., 413, 414
Masuda, M., 540
Matarazzo, J.D., 444, 447, 461
Mather, J.A., 514
Matheson, A.D., 723
Mathews, A., 589, 595, 596
Maticka-Tyndale, E., 370
Matlin, M.E., 289
Matlin, M.W., 104, 106, 112, 113, 118, 120, 126, 129, 130, 137
Matthews, K.A., 490, 560
Maturi, R., 544
Mauer, D., 323
Maunck, S.B., 71
Maupin, H.E., 469, 690
Maurer, D., 322
Mauri, M., 80
Maurice, P., 217
May, C.P., 379, 380
Mayer, R.E., 291
Mazursky, D., 18
McPherson, F.M., 567
Mechoulam, R., et al., 176
Medcof, J.W., 422
Medin, D.L., 272
Meehan, P.J., 620
Mees, H., 628
Megathlin, K.N., 557
Meglino, B.M., 724, 730
Meichenbaum, D.H., 570, 632, 633
Meier, S.T., 393
Melamed, S., 547
Meleshko, K.G.A., 509, 702
Meltzoff, A.N., 250, 321
Melzack, R., 56, 69, 95, 113
Menary, E., 171
Mendenhall, M., 221
Mendolia, M., 536

Menez, R., 317
Menzel, R., 215
Mercer, G.W., 364
Merikle, P.M., 98
Merson, M.H., 561
Merz, E., 435
Mestre, D.R., 107
Metalsky, G.I., 589
Metzger, A.M., 391
Metzler, J., 274, 280
Meuser, K.T., 608
Mewhinney, D.M.K., 564
Meyer, A.J., 566
Meyer, J.P., 714, 718, 732, 736, 737
Miceli, M.P., 733
Michelini, R.L., 755
Mikail, S., 59
Mikl, J., 568
Miles, B., 343
Milgram, S., 660, 689, 693, 694, 695
Milich, R, 332
Millan, M.J., 113
Millar, K.U., 509
Millar, M.G., 509, 700
Millar, W.J., 555
Miller, D., 678
Miller, D.J., 279
Miller, D.T., 75, 666, 668, 670
Miller, K., 702, 750
Miller, L.L., 177
Miller, M.E., 169
Miller, N., 668, 673
Miller, N.E., 37
Miller, P.H., 334
Miller, R.S., 386, 707
Miller, S.B., 559
Miller, T.J., 641
Miller-Herringer, T., 522
Millon, T., 580
Mills, D.E., 570
Milner, A.D., 71
Milner, B., 72, 74, 259, 260
Minami, H., 243
Minden, D., 564
Minden, H., 570
Minkoff, H., 317
Minnes, P., 534
Minton, M.A., 72, 73
Minuchin, P., 469
Minuchin, S., 638
Mirklowitz, D.J., 611
Mischel, W., 490
Misovich, S.J., 363, 563
Mistlberger, R.E., 146, 148
Mistler-Lachman, J.L., 299
Misumi, L., 410
Mitchell, 323
Mitchell, D.E., 133
Mitchell, D.J., 279
Mitchell, H., 568
Mitchell, O.T.R., 546
Mitchell, R.M., 400
Mitchell, T., 221
Mitchell, T.R., 691, 716, 725
Mittelstaetd, M., 651
Miura, I., 304
Moaz, B., 375
Moffat, F.L., 549
Moffitt, A., 162
Mogg, K., 595, 596
Moghaddam, F.M., 681, 683
Mohr, K., 364
Momtahan, K., 746
Money, J., 78, 414, 417
Moniz, 645
Monroe, L.R., 137
Montague, P., 459
Montplaisir, J., 157, 161
Mook, D.G., 277, 278
Moore, B.C.J., 111
Moore, C., 342
Moore, et al., 88
Moore, M.K., 321
Moore, R.J., 547
Moore, R.W., 323
Moore-Ede, M.C., 145, 147, 150
Moorman, J.E., 368
Moran, S.M., 567
Moranville, J.T., 613
Moray, N., 121
Moreland, R.L., 701
Morgan, B.A., 56
Morganstern, K.P., 198

Mori, M., 450
Morin, C., 160, 210
Morley, J.E., 67
Morris, G.B., 340, 738
Morris, B., 408
Morris, C.G., 332
Morris, H.R., 56
Morris, P., 243
Morris, S., 342
Morrison, K., 542
Morrison, R.L., 608
Morrongiello, B.A., 321
Morrow, K.B., 369
Morse, J.M., 114, 360
Morse, R.M., 114
Morton, T., 641
Moscarello, R., 542
Moscovitch,M., 233, 250
Mosher, S.W., 405
Motley, M.T., 497
Motowidlo, S.J., 546
Mottron, L., 446, 447
Moul, D.E., 147
Mouton, J.S., 739
Mrosovsky, N., 146
Mueller, H.H., 388
Muir, D.W., 133, 342, 343, 348, 349
Muir, J.E., 333
Mullaney, D.J., 159
Mullen, P.E., 415
Mumby, D.G., 207
Mumford, M.D., 738
Munsinger, H.A., 463
Murdoch, D.D., 22, 419
Murdock, B.B., Jr., 230
Murnen, S.K., 18, 706
Murphy, J.M., 585
Murphy, K.R., 726, 731
Murray, 708
Murray, C.L., 262
Murray, H.W., 465
Murray, J., 584
Murray, M.G., 147
Murrell, A., 684
Murrell, J.A., 684
Murrell, S.A., 392
Murrey, G.J., 171
Myers, R.C., 10, 11
Myers, T., 563, 564

Nadia, S., 64
Naficy, A., 677
Nagano-Nakamura, I.K., 421
Nagar, D., 744, 752, 753
Naglieri, J.A., 447
Nair, C., 589
Naitoh, P., 159
Nakajima, S., 58, 59, 202
Nanell, W.A., 699
Nanson, J.L., 318
Naranjo, C.A., 419
Nargundkar, M., 589
Nasca, P., 568
Nash, J.E., 318
Nathan, B.R., 725
Nathan, S., 606
Nathans, J., 104, 105
Nathanson, L.S., 459
Nauful, T., 245
Navarro, R., 137
NcNulty, S.E., 663
Neale, J.H., 113
Neale, J.M., 608, 611
Neale, M.A., 284, 286, 308
Neale, M.C., 86
Neale, M.S, 217
Nebeker, D.M., 723, 724
Neeb, M., 523
Needham, 99
Negri, E., 556
Neimeyer, R.A., 631, 641, 649
Neisser, U., 250, 251
Nelson, C.B., 620
Nelson, E.D., 719
Nelson, M.J., 455
Nelson, T.M., 377
Nesselroade, C.S., 382, 446
Netting, N.S., 363, 370
Neuberg, S.L., 435
Neuchterlein, K.H., 611
Neugarten, B.L., 373
Neveux, L.M., 557
Newell, A., 151

Newman, J.P., 606
Newman, S.C., 585, 586, 591, 610
Newport, S., 32
Newton, P.M., 388
Ney, P.G., 369
Nhundu, T.J., 726
Nicher, 410
Nicholls, A.L., 330
Nichols, M., 648
Nicole, S.E., 610
Niedenthal, P.M., 635
Nielson, T.A., 163
Nietzel, M.T., 652
Nilsson, L.G., 240
Nisbett, R.E., 12, 490
Nobbs, H., 390
Noble, B.P., 150
Noble, E.K., 408
Noland, S., 732
Nolen-Hoeksema, S., 469, 478, 588
Nomikos, M.S., 541
Nomura, A.M., 558
Noriega, V., 549
Norman, D.A., 151
Norman, R.M., 541
Norris, F.H., 392, 542
North, T.C., 567
Northcraft, G.B., 284, 308
Norton, A., 368
Norton, G.R., 593, 600
Novak, 547
Novalany, J., 580, 589, 590
Novick, B.E., 317
Nowicki, G.P., 296, 436
Nurius, P., 367
Nyhan, W.L., 83
Nyquist, L., 344

Oakes, P.J., 680
O'Brien, M.K., 755
O'Brien, C.P., 200
O'Brien, S.J., 376
O'Carroll, P.W., 620
O'Connor, B.P., 372, 376, 724
O'Connor, J., 738
O'Connor, M., 72
Odbert, H.S., 510
O'Farrell, B., 483
Offer, D., 364
Offord, D.R., 591
Ofir, C., 18
Ofshe, R.J., 255
Ogan, T.A., 343
Ogloff, J.R., 605
Ogrocki, P., 546
Ogus, E.D., 547
O'Heeron, R.C., 509
O'Heron, C.A., 479
Okamoto, Y., 304
Olders, H., 392
Olds, J., 50
O'Leary, D.S., 450
Oliff, M., 319
Olinger, L.J., 537, 589
Oliver, A., 81
Oliver, C.N., 390
Oliver, M.B., 468, 477
Ollove, M., 589
Olsen, J.M., 434
Olson, 326
Olson, D., 698
Olson, J.M., 434, 670, 672
Olsson, P.A., 633
Ondrack, D.A., 722
O'Neill, M.C., 746
Ophir, I., 196
Opsahl, C.A., 67
Opton, E.M., 541
Orback, I., 592
O'Regan, N.B., 58
Oren, D.A., 147
Orlinsky, D.E., 641
Orlofsky, J.L., 479
Orn, H., 585, 586, 591, 610
Ornstein, M., 478
Ornstein, P.A., 333
Orr, K.W., 563, 564
Osborne, D., 750
Oskamp, S., 697
Osterwell, Z., 421
Ostroff, C., 736, 738
Ostrom, T.M., 756
O'Sullivan, J.T., 334
Otaki, M., 344

Otis, A.S., 455
O'Touma, L.A., 612
Otto, S.R., 137
Oullette-Kobasa, S.C., 541, 549
Overbury, O., 376
Ozier, M., 340

Packard, J.S., 546
Page, J.B., 177
Page, M.M., 406, 519
Page, N.R., 732
Pain-Mantha, B.A., 542
Painter, S.L., 707
Paivio, A., 264, 273, 274
Pajurkova, E.M., 75, 564
Pak, A., 704
Pak, A.W.P., 524, 525
Palmer, A.M., 380
Palmer, C.T., 418
Palmer, D.L., 662
Palmer, S.E., 124
Palmgren, C., 362
Palomaki, G.E., 557
Pancer, S.M., 662
Pandey, J., 744, 752, 753
Papageorgiou, A.N., 320
Pappas, T.N., 407
Parasuraman, R., 118
Pardie, L., 16, 17
Pare, D., 736
Parham, T., 687
Parinello, R., 344
Park, B., 681, 701, 726
Parker, 410
Parker, E.D., 238
Parker, J.D., 537
Parker, L., 170
Parker, W.L., 425
Parloff, M.B., 641
Parsons, L.M., 298
Pascarelli, E.F., 757
Passman, R.H., 349
Pastor, D.L., 346
Patenaude, R.L., 662
Patrick, B.C., 424
Patrick, C.J., 431, 605, 606, 607
Patrick, L., 170
Pattatucci, A.J., 86
Patterson, F., 305
Paul, G.L., 628
Paul, J., 42
Paul, R., 217
Paul, S.M., 460
Pauls, D.L., 588
Paulus, P.B., 742, 753
Pavelich, J.L., 666, 666
Pavlov, I.P., 188, 192, 195, 200
Payne, 240
Pear, J.J., 203
Pearce, J.M., 197
Pearlsson, G.D., 612, 613
Pearson, D.R., 347
Peekna, H., 698
Pegg, J.E., et al., 343
Peitonen, T., 471
Pellegrino, J.W., 20, 80, 482
Pelletier, K.R., 565
Pelletier, C.N., 390
Pelletier, L.G., 155, 423
Pelletier, R., 353
Pellis, S.M., 71
Pelsser, R., 552
Penfield, W., 259
Pennebaker, J., 344
Pennebaker, J.W., 509, 550
Pennington, N., 279
Peplau, 703
Peretz, 71
Perkins, W.L., 200
Perlini, A.H., 170, 716
Perlmutter, M., 329
Perls, F.S., 625
Permaul, J.A., 392
Peronnet, F., 569
Perry, 744
Perry, R.P., 662
Persad, E., 645
Persad, S.M., 435, 589
Persaud, T.V.N., 318
Persinger, M.A., 181
Pet et al., 556
Peters, D.A., 539
Peters, J.F., 388
Peters, M., 81
Petersen, S.E., 65
Peterson, A.C., 360, 361
Peterson, C., 473, 603, 728

Peterson, J.B., 69, 419
Peterson, J.G., 566
Peterson, L.R., 237
Peterson, M.J., 237
Peterson, S.E., 72, 73
Petit, D., 157
Petit, P., 347
Peto, R., 557
Petty, M.M., 217
Petty, R.E., 74, 673, 674
Pfaffmann, C., 116
Pfeiffer, S.M., 706
Phares, V., 349
Phillips, A.G., 58, 59, 262
Phillips, B.U., 570
Phillips, D.P., 111, 176
Phillips, L.W., 235
Piaget, J., 9, 316, 323–28, 365
Picard, J., 675
Pickar, D., 612
Pickering, T., 544
Pierce, C.A., 702
Pierce, J.P., 567
Pierce, W.D., 687
Pihl, R.O., 22, 69, 419
Pilkonis, P.A., 641
Pillard, R.C., 85, 86
Pincus, A.L., 511
Pinel, J.P., 66, 80, 172, 174, 207
Pinel, P., 578
Pines, A., 80, 547
Pinker, S., 129
Pinsof, W.M., 637, 638
Pipper, W.E., 392
Pittenger, J.B., 703
Plante, C., 333
Plante, T.G., 567
Plantz, M., 465
Plechaty, M., 387
Pliner, P., 408
Plomin, R., 463, 467
Plummer, 562, 563
Polivy, J., 408, 435, 589
Polk, M., 71, 73
Pollack, E.S., 558
Pollock, N.L., 662
Pomare, M., 684
Pomerleau, A., 321, 350
Pomerleau, C.S., 555
Pomerleau, O.F., 555
Pomeroy, W., 413
Poncet, M., 107
Poole, G.D., 433, 434
Poole, R., 422
Poon, L.W., 378
Poortinga, Y.H., 164, 255
Pope, K.S., 37, 38
Popiel, 755
Popper, K., 32
Porter, B.E., 678
Porter, J., 410
Porter, L.W., 735, 736
Porter, R.H., 132, 321
Portz, J.H., 650
Posner, M.I., 65
Posner, J.I., 72, 73
Post, R.M., 599
Postersky, 219
Postman, L., 235
Potasova, A., 145
Potvin, L., 680
Poucet, B., 214
Powell, G.N., 470
Powers, R.E., 613
Powley, T.L., 67
Pozo, C., 549
Pranger, T., 547
Prata, G., 638
Pratkanis, A.R., 99, 635
Pratt, M.W., et al., 339, 340
Pratto, F., 669
Prentice, D.A., 472
Pressley, M., 662
Preston, M., 692
Pretty, G., 547
Price, D.L., 55
Price, T.R., 430
Priest, K., 369
Prigitano, G.P., 87
Prire, L.H., 588
Pritchard, R., 254
Pritchard, R.D., 719
Prkachin, K.M., 114, 432, 434, 570
Pruitt, D.G., 308

Psotka, L., 243
Ptacek, J.T., 524
Puccetti, M.C., 541, 549
Pulkkinen, M.S., 557
Pullin, W.M., 727
Purves, S., 74
Purvis, A., 563
Purvis, K.L., 332
Pussin, J.B., 578
Putnam, F.W., 599
Putrell, E., 569
Pyke, S.W., 15
Pylyshyn, Z.W., 274
Pyryt, M.C., 462
Pyszczynski, T.A., 666

Quadrel, M.J., 362
Quesney, L.F., 81
Quilter, 757
Quintanar, L.R., 74

Rabin, B.S., 71, 546
Rabin, M.D., 117
Rachman, S.J., 198, 214, 594, 627
Racicot, B.M., 748
Radloff, C.E., 519
Rae, M.S., 435
Rae, G.Q., 539
Ragland, D.R., 560
Rahav, G., 523
Rahe, R.H., 539, 541
Raichle, M.E., 72, 73
Rain, J.S., 732
Ram, B., 14
Ramirez, V., 603
Ramsey, J., 752
Ramus, S.J., 261
Randall, M.L., 719
Rankin, N.O., 541
Rao, K., 430
Raphael, B., 368
Rapson, R.L., 476, 701, 704, 707
Rasmussen, T., 72
Raso-Knott, P.A., 422
Raven, J.C., 460
Ravert, H.T., 612
Raynor, J.O., 422
Raynor, R., 198
Raz, N., 612
Raz, S., 579, 612, 613
Rea, M.S., 745
Read, D.E., 378
Reason, J.T., 237
Rechtschaffen, A., 159
Reddix, M.D., 104
Redler, 698
Reed, T.E., 449, 464
Reeder, G.D., 490
Reese, H.W., 380
Reesor, K., 59
Reeves, A., 234
Regier, D.A., 577
Reid, 326
Reid, A., 727
Reid, L.D., 59, 176, 558
Reid, R.L., 80
Reilly, A.H., 728
Reilly, S., 192
Reimold, C., 66
Reis, H.T., 473
Reiss, J.P.R., 645
Reisser-Danner, L.A., 331
Reissland, N., 321
Reitman, J.S., 237
Renrick, D.T., 476
Rensberger, B., 297
Repucci, N.D., 245
Rescorla, R.A., 195, 197, 214
Resnick, S.M., 64
Rest, J.R., 339
Rettinger, J., 431
Revusky, S., 192
Reynolds, B., 568
Reynolds, W.F., Jr., 280
Reznick, J.S., 344, 345
Rhodes, K., 16, 17
Rhue, J.W., 152, 153
Rhun, J.W., 167, 168
Ribera, J.C., 542
Rice, C.G., 137
Rice, F.P., 359
Rich, S., 84
Richard, 743
Richards, D.G., 307, 306
Richards, P., 344

Richards, S.S., 613
Richardsen, A.M., 732
Richardson, D.R., 35, 220, 418, 419, 471, 697
Richardson, J.T.E., 117, 240
Richer, F., 161
Richer, S., 351
Richer, S.D., 680
Richman, G.S., 217
Richman, S.A., 670
Rickward, J., 11
Riess, M., 676
Rigby, C.S., 424
Riley, D.A., 281–82
Riley, R., 610
Rioux, 433
Rips, L.J., 249
Risley, T., 628
Ritter, B., 629
Robbins, J.M., 662
Robbins, S.J., 200
Robert, M., 218
Roberts, D.C., 58
Roberts, P., 388
Roberts, T.A., 469, 470
Robertson, L.S., 351
Robinette, C.D., 611
Robins, L.N., 577
Robinson, D.S., 549
Robinson, D.W., 663
Robinson, G., 435
Robinson, L.A., 631, 641, 649
Robinson, R.G., 430
Robinson, T.P., 714, 728
Robson, B.E., 539
Robson, W.L., 161
Rochefort, D.A., 650, 651
Rockman et al, 347
Rodeheaver, D., 380
Rodin, G., 409
Rodin, J., 407, 409, 535, 567, 603
Rodman, M.C., 718
Roedinger, H.L., 257
Roese, N.J., 35, 434, 670
Roese, N.R., 172
Rogers, 404
Rogers, C.R., 35, 505, 506, 507, 508, 513, 518, 526, 624, 625, 626
Rogers, G., 752
Rogers, R.J., 666
Roggman, L.A., 331, 703
Rogoff, B., 332
Rokeach, M., 702
Romney, D.M., 353
Roopnarine, J.L., 349
Roper, R.G., 137
Rosch, E.H., 272, 304
Rose-Krasnor, 314
Rosen, L.N., 147
Rosenberg, L., 132
Rosenbloom, P.S., 151
Rosenfeld, A., 79
Rosenfield, D., 424
Rosengren, K.S., 329
Rosenhan, D.L., 700
Rosenman, R.H., 559
Rosenthal, C.J., 391
Rosenthal, N.E., 147, 745
Rosenthal, R.R., 468
Rosenzweig, J.M., 479
Roskies, E., 375, 560
Roskos-Ewoldsen, B.B., 274
Roskos-Ewoldsen, D.R., 675
Ross, A.S., 672, 720
Ross, B.H., 272
Ross, B.M., 117
Ross, C.A., 74, 598, 599, 600
Ross, D., 218, 419
Ross, J., 287, 288, 733
Ross, L., 520
Ross, M., 80, 666
Ross, N., 667
Ross, S., 218
Rossberg, I., 433
Rossor, M., 612
Rotenberg, 702
Rotenberg, K.G., 372
Roter, D.L., 552
Rothenberg, R., 568
Rothman, K.R., 558
Rotter, J.B., 514, 515, 516
Rouleau, J., 74
Rovee-Collier, C.K., 321
Rowlison, R.T., 541

Roxenstock, I.M., 551
Royce, J.M., 465
Rozin, P., 410
Rubio-Stipec, M., 542
Ruback, R.B., 742
Rubin, 703
Rubin, J.Z., 35, 287, 308
Ruble, D.N., 252, 343
Rudy, T.E., 114
Ruff, H.A., 344
Rule, 744
Rule, B.G., 379, 675, 677
Rumbaugh, D.M., 306
Rumbaugh, K., 523
Rumelhart, D.E., 251, 297
Rusak, B., 146
Rush, A.J., 589
Rushton, 382
Rushton, W.A.H., 105
Rusiniak, K.W., 193, 196
Russell, J.A., 432
Russell, L., 510
Russo, J.E., 279
Ryan, C.S., 681, 726
Ryan, E.B., 378, 662
Ryan, J., 454
Ryan, J.B., 103
Ryan, L., 73
Ryan, R.M., 424
Rynard, D., 368

Sabshin, M., 364
Sachdev, I., 680
Sacks, O., 133
Sadalla, E.K., 476, 477
Sadava, S.W., 555, 680
Sadock, B.J., 599
Saint-Hilaire, J.M., 74
Saks, M.J., 695, 756
Salame, P., 236
Salanova, V., 81
Sales, C.A., 732
Salmun, L.M., 557
Salovey, P., 155, 415, 535, 550
Salthouse, T.A., 378
Saltzman, L.E., 620
Sampson, P.D., 318
Samson, D., 214
Samson, H.H., 58
Samson, L.F., 317
Samson, S., 71
Samuels, M., 318
Samuels, N., 318
Sanbonmatsu, D.M., 682
Sande, G.N., 519, 662
Sandell, M., 544
Sanders, G.S., 668
Sanders, M.S., 746, 747, 751, 752
Sandler, J., 652
Santi, S., 555
Sargent, C., 114
Sauder, B., 746
Savage-Rumbaugh, E.S., 306
Savistky, J.C., 755
Savva, S., 516, 517
Scarr, S., 453, 463
Scattaregia, J.H., 726
Schab, F.R., 117
Schachar, R.J., 332
Schacter, D.L., 22, 233, 260
Schachter, S., 428, 438
Schacter, S., 701
Schaefer, C., 541
Schaeffer, A., 742
Schaeffer, M.A., 542
Schaie, K.W., 381
Schaller, G.G., 22
Schank, D., 163
Schank, R., 295
Schaur, G.B., 372
Scheier, M.F., 153, 154, 155, 490, 504, 549, 569
Schein, J.D., 432
Schell, B.H., 405, 542
Scher, S.J., 155, 677
Schettleworth, S.J., 194
Schiff, B.B., 435, 438
Schiffman, H.R., 104, 119, 127, 131, 132
Schiffman, S.S., 407
Schill, T., 368
Schlenker, B.R., 676
Schlien, B., 559
Schmidt, E., 190
Schmidt, F.N., 542

Schmidt, U., 216
Schmitt, F.O., 74
Schnall, P.L., 544
Schneider, B.H., 19
Schneider, B.M., 629
Schneider, S.L., 286
Schneider, W., 151
Schneiderman, M., 301
Schofield, W., 623
Schooler, J., 156
Schroeder, M., 698
Schroeder, M.L., 603
Schugens, M.M., 66
Schuler, R.S., 548
Schuller, R.A., 681
Schulman, P., 589
Schulz, G., 95
Schulz, P.M., 147
Schusterman, R.J., 307
Schutz, R.W., 534
Schwab, R.L., 548
Schwartz, J.E., 490, 513
Schwartz, P., 147, 317
Schwartzman, A.E., 381
Schwarz, N., 437
Schwarzwald, J., 683
Schweiger, D.M., 733
Scott, J.P., 420, 421
Scoville, W.B., 259
Scribner, S., 276
Scumacher, L.E., 298
Searle, J., 298
See, S.K., 378
Seeman, M.V., 64
Seeman, P., 64
Segal, L.D., 749
Segal, N.L., 13, 83, 84, 464, 466, 733
Segall, M.H., 164, 255
Segall, Z., 580
Segalowitz, 314, 328
Segatore, 88
Segrist, D., 16, 17
Sejinowski, T.J., 298
Sekuler, R., 126, 128, 376
Self, E.A., 403
Seligman, C., 672
Seligman, M.E.P., 196, 211, 588, 589
Selvini-Palazzaoli, M., 638
Selye, H., 534, 535, 536
Semmelroth, J., 415, 416
Semmes, J., 9
Senchak, M., 473
Senders, C.W., 137
Senecal, C., 423
Seraganian, P., 569
Sergent, J., 71, 75, 77
Seta, C.E., 682
Sevcik, R.A., 306
Sevdall, G., 612
Sevitch, D.E., 162
Seyle, H., 538, 571
Shack, M.L., 691
Shader, 649
Shaffer, D., 620
Shaffer, D.R., 31, 400, 437, 699, 700
Shafir, E., 286
Shah, A., 733
Shalker, T.E., 435
Shallice, T., 151, 298
Shaman, P., 132
Shan, A., 544
Shanab, M.E., 214, 694
Shantz, C.U., 364
Shapiro, A., 163
Shapiro, C.M., 160
Shapiro, D.A., 642, 653
Shapiro, D.H., 179
Shapiro, E. K., 469
Shapiro, I., 349
Sharabany, R., 341
Sharpe, D., 35
Shaver, K.G., 756
Shaw, B.F., 589
Shea, S.L., 323
Shea, T., 641
Shebilske, L.J., 469, 474, 475
Shell, R., 692
Shelton, B.R., 214
Shelton, R.C., 641, 642
Shepard, R.N., 128, 274, 280
Shephard, R.J., 735

Sher, K.J., 173
Sherif, M., 9
Sherman, S.J., 670
Sherman, T., 612
Sherman, W.M., 516
Sherwin, B.B., 416
Sherwin-Williams, B., 729
Shettleworth, S.J., 197, 280–82
Shevell, S.K., 249
Shieber, F., 376
Shiffrin, R.M., 151, 229, 231, 669
Shin, W.S., 405
Shirom, A., 547
Shore, B., 254
Shores, A.L., 434
Shrier, 176
Shute, V., 685
Siegel, J.M., 329
Siegel, B.V., 449
Siegel, S., 188, 199–200
Sigler, R.S., 335
Sikorski, L., 132
Silberman, E.K., 599
Silberstein, L.R., 409
Silva, C.E., 152, 167, 168
Silva, P.A., 555
Silver, S., 400
Simeon, J.G., 332
Simmonds, A.J., 720
Simmons, R.G., 360
Simon, M.C., 728
Simon, T., 9, 450, 451
Simons, R.F., 523
Simonton, D.K., 382
Simpson, J.A., 346
Simpson, M.E., 744
Simpson, S.N., 748
Singer, B., 642
Singer, J.E., 428, 438
Singer, J.L., 152
Singer, P.A., 390
Singleton, B., 217
Sinnott, J.D., 379
Sistrunk, F., 690
Sitka, C., 347
Skeels, H.M., 465
Skinner, B.F., 9, 201, 205, 206, 207, 210, 211, 212, 514
Slaby, A.E., 551
Sladen-Dew, N., 651
Slifer, K.J., 217
Sloan, E.P., 160, 210
Slobin, D.I., 300
Slochower, J., 409
Slovic, P., 279
Slugoski, B.R., 662, 663
Small, B.J., 375
Smalley, M.M., 730, 732
Smart, R.G., 57, 174, 176, 370, 555
Smart, S.A., 520
Smeaton, D., 18
Smith, A.P., 539
Smith, C.A., 714, 737
Smith, D.E., 434
Smith, E., 524
Smith, I.M., 74
Smith, J., 382
Smith, J.F., 270, 284
Smith, M.A., 385
Smith, M.C., 258
Smith, M.L., 564, 641
Smith, P.B., 13, 15
Smith, S.M., 31, 241, 400, 437
Smith, S., 35
Smith, T.W., 56, 478
Smith, W., 555, 556
Smoll, F.L., 524
Sneed, C.D., 512, 513
Snidman, N., 343, 344, 345
Snodgrass, S.E., 755
Snow, W.G., 81
Snowden, L.R., 623
Snyder, K.S., 611
Snyder, M., 522
Snyder, S.H., 113, 220, 612
Sobel, L.C., 558
Sobel, M.B., 558
Soldatos, C.R., 160
Soloman, B., 473
Soloman, R.L., 428
Solomon, D.S., 567
Solomon, S., 666
Solso, R.L., 276, 294
Somerville, S.C., 331
Sorrell, G.T., 369

Sorrentino, R.M., 422
Spacapan, S., 697
Spangenberg, E.R., 99, 635
Spangler, W.D., 740
Spanis, C.W., 263
Spanos, N.P., 168, 169, 170, 171, 716
Spearman, C.E., 445
Spector, P.E., 736
Speicher, C., 546
Speicher, H., 386
Spence, A.P., 376
Spence, J.T., 479, 485
Spencer, J., 421
Spencer, R.E., 214
Sperling, G., 234
Sperry, R.W., 51, 75
Spetch, M.L., 208, 214
Spinner, B., 660
Spirduso, W.W., 376
Spohn, C., 755
Spokes, E., 612
Springer, S.P., 74, 75
Squire, L.R., 22, 260, 261, 263
Srivastav, P., 349
Sroufe, L.A., 342
Srull, T.K., 708
Staats, M., 409
Stack, D.M., 321, 343, 348, 349
Staddon, J.E.R., 207
Stager, J.M., 360
Stalker, C.A., 510
Stam, H.J., 196
Stambrook, M., 87
Standing, L.G., 237
Stanger, C., 250, 252
Stanley, C., 291
Stanton, A.L., 478
Stanton, W.R., 555
Stapp, J.A., 479
Stark-Adamec, C., 15, 714, 727, 728
Starke-Reed, P.E., 390
Starker, S., 163
Starr, L.B., 430
Staumann, T.J., 519
Staw, B.M., 287, 288, 733
Stearns, G.M., 547
Stebloy, N.M., 692
Steers, R.M., 546, 735
Steffen, V.J., 569, 690
Steiger, H., 216
Stein, B.A., 358, 519
Stein-Seroussi, A., 156, 702
Steinbach, K., 151
Steinberg, S., 409
Steiner, D.D., 730, 732
Steiner, J.E., 320, 321
Steinfels, P., 697
Steinhilber, A., 155
Stellar, E., 407
Stemmermann, G.N., 558
Stenson, P., 369, 371
Stephan, C.W., 755
Stephan, W.G., 421, 683
Stern, J.M., 722
Sternberg, R.J., 445, 447, 448, 705
Stevenason-Hide, J., 514
Stevens, B., 321
Steward, D.E., 374
Stewart, G.G., III, 722
Stewart, M.J., 755
Stiles, W.B., 642
Stillwell, A., 667
Stillwell-Barnes, R., 514
Stingsby, J.K., 698
Stipp, D., 305
Stoltzfus, E.R., 379, 380
Stoppard, J.M., 434, 468, 481
Storm, 430
Storms, M.D., 417
Stotsky, S.M., 641
Stout, J.C., 546
Stoutjesdyk, D., 409
Strachan, A.M., 611
Strachan, C.E., 422
Strachan, H.J., 589
Stracik, F., 437
Strathman, A.J., 670
Straus, A., 430
Strauss, E., 74, 81
Strauss, K.E., 196
Strayer, J., 343, 432, 698
Strean, H.S., 622
Strickland, B.R., 478, 479, 620

Striegel-Moore, R.H., 409
Stringer, P., 681
Stroh, L.K., 728
Struckman-Johnson, C.J., 567
Struckman-Johnson, D.L., 567
Strunin, L., 537, 563
Strupp, H.H., 623
Struthers, C.W., 662
Strydom, N., 752
Stuart, R.B., 634
Stunkard, A.J., 196
Stuss, D.T., 69, 88, 155, 400
Suedfeld, P., 422, 753
Sugarman, J.H., 74
Sullivan, A.M., 720
Sullivan, K., 544
Sullivan, M.J., 59
Sullivan, M.W., 250
Sulman, J., 391
Suls, J.M., 293, 668
Sulsky, L.M., 724, 730
Sulzman, F.M., 145, 147
Summers, R.J., 662, 730
Sundstrom, E., 734, 751, 753
Sundstrom, M.G., 734, 751, 753
Surbey, M.K., 319, 359
Surridge, D.M., 147
Sussex, J.N., 588
Svec, C.M., 723, 724
Svenson, L.W., 176
Swann, W.B., Jr., 155, 156, 702
Swanson, D., 722
Swanson, G.M., 557
Swartzentruber, D., 197
Swayze, V., II, 450
Swerdlik, M.E., 459
Swets, J.A., 97
Sykes, R.N., 243
Sylvain, C., 209
Szabo, A., 569
Szalai, J., 157
Szechtman, B., 662
Sztaba, T.I., 353

Tabossi, P., 270
Taerk, G., 564
Tagalakis, V., 432
Tainturier, M.J., 378
Tajfel, H., 681
Tajika, J., 291
Takanishi, R., 368
Talukder, E., 349
Tamborini, R., 752
Tamminga, C.A., 612
Tang, C., 449
Tannock, R., 332
Tansley, B., 746
Targum, S.D., 147
Tarquinio, N., 320
Tarter, V.C., 322
Tatryn, D.J., 599
Tatum, B.C., 723, 724
Taylor, 757, 758
Taylor, B.R., 670
Taylor, D.A., 508
Taylor, D.M., 683
Taylor, J.H., 335, 339
Taylor, L., 432
Taylor, M.C., 718
Taylor, S.E., 251, 424, 534, 542, 546, 550, 551, 667
Teasdale, J.D., 589
Teicher, M.H., 147
Teichman, M., 523
Tekes, K., 81
Tellegen, A., 84, 464
Tennen, H., 211
Terenius, L., 523
Terman, L.M., 452, 461
Terman, M., 147
Terrace, H.S., 305, 280
Tesson, G., 688
Tett, R.P., 736
Teuber, H.L., 260
Teyler, T.J., 263
Theorell, T., 535
Thibault, C., 591
Thibault, C.J., 718
Thibodeau, R., 678
Thiessen, I., 385
Thomas, A., 343, 345
Thomas, D., 105
Thomas, J.L., 376, 382, 390
Thomas, M.H., 220
Thomas, S.J., 339

Thomley, J., 118, 699
Thompson, B., 704
Thompson, J.K., 409, 410, 602
Thompson, M., 662
Thompson, R.A., 348
Thompson, R.F., 263
Thompson, V.S., 685, 686
Thompson, W.C., 700
Thomson, D.M., 242
Thorndike, R.L., 455
Thorpe, L.E., 322
Threhub, S.E., 322
Thun, M., 557
Thurston, E.L., 445
Tice, D.M., 507, 520, 521
Tiffany, S.T., 173, 174
Tiggemann, M., 388
Timney, B., 323
Ting-Toomey, S., 500
Tire, D.M., 490
Tisserand, R.B., 118
Tizard, B., 347
Tobin, D.L., 409
Tobler, I., 160
Todd, R., 698
Tollestrup, P.A., 239, 256, 257, 258
Tolman, E.C., 214, 215, 279
Tomaka, J., 536
Tomasken, A.J., 430
Tomlinson-Keasey, C., 490, 513
Tompson, H.B., 221
Toneatto, T., 558
Topf, M., 744
Toufexis, A., 418
Tougas, F., 729
Toung, J.K.T., 612
Tousignant, M., 368
Towson, S.M.J., 472
Treffert, D.A., 446
Treiman, R., 301
Tremblay, M., 378
Tremblay, S., 387
Triandis, H.C., 221
Trigers, R., 474
Trinder, J., 160
Trock, G.K., 639
Tronick, E.Z., 343
Trost, M.R., 477, 476
Trqachsel, L., 160
Trudeau, M., 376
Trudel, G., 217
Trudel, M.K., 114
Trues, W.R., 177
Truscott, D., 369
Tschann, J.M., 385
Tsuang, M.T., 579
Tubbs, M.E., 716
Tucker, J.S., 490, 513
Tudiver, F., 392, 564
Tulving, E., 42, 232, 233, 242, 243, 260
Tune, L.E., 612, 613
Tunks, E., 114, 173
Turk, D.C., 114
Turkheimer, E., 482, 483
Turner, J.A., 114
Turner, J.C., 680
Turnure, J.E., 331
Tursky, B., 69
Turtle, J.W., 670
Tversky, A., 282, 283, 284, 286, 308
Tyano, S., 592
Tyler, R.B., 682, 726
Tyler, T.R., 283
Tyrrell, D.A., 539

Uhl, G.A., 542
Uhl, G.R., 113
Uhlarik, J., 747
Underwood, M., 620
Unger, R.K., 444, 467
Ungerleider, C.S., 754
Unyk, A.M., 151
Urban, M.J., 99
Urcuioli, P.J., 192
Usher, J.A., 250
Uttl, B., 379

Vaccarino, 409, 410
Valins, S., 742
Vallerand, R.J., 155, 376, 423, 424
Vallieres, E.F., 423
Vallone, R.P., 520

Valone, K., 673
Van der Walt, W., 752
Van Houten, R., 216, 217
Van Kampen, J., 410
Van Knorring, L., 523
Van Reekum, R., 370
Van Roosmalen, E.H., 364
Van Vianen, A.E., 729
Vandenbergh, J.G., 359
Vasudev, J., 341
Vauclair, J., 280, 281
Vaughan, E., 542
Veccia, E.M., 434, 468
Vernon, 382
Vernon, P.A., 449, 450, 464, 663
Verny, T.R., 535
Vertinsky, P.A., 376
Vetter, V.A., 37, 38
Vezina, J., 541
Vezina, M., 757
Vieland, V., 620
Vincente, K.J., 255
Vinet, A., 757
Vinrent, J.E., 692
Vogel, L.Z., 516, 517
Volkmer, R.E., 560
Von Senden, M., 132
Vormbrock, J.K., 20, 346
Vredenburgh, A.G., 749
Vroom, V.H., 716, 739
Vygotsky, L.S., 329

Wada, J.A., 74, 81
Wagenaar, W.A., 247, 248
Wagner, A.R., 195
Wagner, H.N., Jr., 612
Waitzkin, H., 552
Walden, T.A., 343
Walk, R.D., 323
Walker, B., 567
Walker, H., 680
Walker, L., 675
Walker, L.J., 335, 339, 340, 341, 364
Walker, M.W., 113
Walker, S., 351
Wall, A.M., 190
Wall, P.D., 56, 113
Wall, S., 345
Wallace, B., 148, 483, 490, 491
Wallace, R.K., 167, 172, 180
Wallerstein, J.S., 385
Wallersteiner, U., 746
Wallman, J., 305, 307
Walsh, G.W., 57, 370
Walsh, R.G., 555
Walsh, S., 412
Walster, E., 475, 673
Walster, G.W., 475, 704
Walton, G.E., 331
Wampold, B.E., 637
Wan, C.K., 668
Wankel, L.M., 568
Ward, L.M., 96, 106
Ward, M., 376
Waring, E.M., 510
Warm, J.S., 118
Warwick, Z.S., 407
Wasserman, D., 18, 197, 279
Wasserman, E.A., 280
Wasylenski, D.A., 651
Waters, E., 342, 345
Watkins, T.J., 641
Watkinson, B., 177, 316, 318
Watson, C., 63, 470, 471
Watson, D., 512
Watson, J.B., 12, 198, 200
Watson, J.W., 7
Watson, M., 127
Watson, S.J., 113
Watts, T., 735
Webb, N., 159
Webb, W., 156, 157, 160
Webb, W.B., 160
Webster, 755
Webster, J.D., 378
Weekes, J.R., 153, 167, 168, 255
Wegener, J.G., 422
Wehner, R., 215
Wehr, T.A., 147
Weiberger, A., 38
Weinberg, M.S., 85
Weinberg, R.A., 459, 463, 467

Weiner, B., 402, 403
Weingarten, H.P., 67
Weininger, 326
Weinstein, M., 410
Weintraub, J.K., 549, 569
Weisberg, J., 410
Weisberg, P., 349
Weisberg, R., 293
Weise, R.E., 584
Weisenberg, M., 69, 114
Weisner, T.S., 352
Weiss, B., 641
Weiss, G., 332
Weiss, M., 250
Weiss, M.J., 320
Weiss, N.S., 557
Weiss, R.A., 561
Weiss, W., 673
Weissberg, R., 344
Weisz, J.R., 641
Weithe, H., 555
Welch, S., 755
Welch, B., 147
Well, L.E., 520
Wellisch, D.K., 639
Wellman, H.M., 331
Wells, G.L., 256, 670, 675
Werker, J.F., 302, 322
Werner, C., 756
Wernicke, K., 72
West, R., 555
Western, D., 415, 416
Westhey, 741
Wetherell, M.S., 680
Wetzel, C.G., 434, 438
Whalen, C.K., 332
Wheaton, B., 388, 539
Wheeler, D., 692
Wheeler, M.A., 257
Whelan, D.T., 83
Whiffen, V.W., 319
Whipple, J., 171
Whishaw, I.Q., 71, 88
Whissell, C.M., 80, 430, 665
Whissell, R., 665
Whitaker, H.A., 74, 434
Whitcher, S.J., 434
White, G.L., 415
White, J.L., 687
White, N.M., 68
White, P.G., 410
White, R.K., 679
White, S., 672
Whorf, B.L., 304
Whybrow, P.C., 588
Whyte, G., 288
Whyte, K., 564
Wickelgren, W.A., 235
Wickett, A.R., 369
Widaman, K.F., 291
Widmeyer, W.N., 680
Widom, C.S., 220, 606
Wielkiewicz, R.M., 461
Wiesel, F., 612
Wiesel, T.N., 96, 106, 133
Wiggins, D.M., 332
Wiggins, J.S., 511
Wilcox, K.J., 84
Wilcoxon, H.C., 194
Wild, 425
Wilder, D.A., 689
Wiley, J.A., 533, 534
Wilgosh, L., 388
Wilhelm, W., 7
Wilkins, A.J., 246
Wilkinson, D., 665
Willemsem, T.M., 729
Willet, W.C., 558
Williams, 755
Williams, D.E., 406
Williams, F.A., 612
Williams, J.E., 351
Williams, L.M., 369
Williams, K., 541, 595, 596
Williams, R.B., 560
Williams, R.J., 297
Williams, R.L., 685
Williamson, D.A., 409, 410, 411, 602
Williamson, P., 157
Willis, F.N., 434
Willis, S.L., 382, 446
Willis, W.d., 113
Wills, T.A., 544
Wilson, 247, 744

Wilson, A.A., 612
Wilson, B., 432
Wilson, D.M., 479
Wilson, D.W., 699
Wilson, R.J., 216
Wilson, T.D., 156, 277, 278, 438
Wilson-Mitchell, J.E., 352
Wincze, J.P., 412
Winefield, A.H., 388
Winett, R.A., 212, 217
Wingard, D.L., 490, 513
Winocur, G., 378
Winograd, E., 246
Winstead, B.A., 570
Winter, D.G., 421, 422
Winter, J.B., 159
Winter, S.J., 732, 733
Winzenz, D., 240
Wirsching, B.A., 55
Wise, R.A., 172
Wiseman, R.L., 732
Witchen, H.U., 620
Witelson, S.F., 74, 81, 373
Wittlinger, R.P., 228
Wogalter, M.S., 20, 122, 123,
    212, 213, 748

Woike, B.A., 433
Wolberg, L.R., 620
Wolf, M., 628
Wolfe, D.A., 652
Wolfe, R.N., 522
Wolff, P.L., 700
Wolfson, C., 391
Woloshyn, N., 534
Wolpe, J., 198
Wolpert, E.A., 163
Wolz, J.P., 306, 307
Wong, D.F., 612
Wong, F.Y., 220
Wong, S., 605
Wong, T.P., 685, 706, 735
Wong, W.L., 555, 556
Wood, C., 291
Wood, E.R., 207
Wood, R.A., 717
Wood, R.S., 725
Wood, W., 220
Woodall, K.L., 490
Woodbury, M.A., 542
Woodward, J.B., 388
Woolfolk, R.L., 580, 589, 590
Woolley, R.M., 731

Woolsey, L.K., 731
Worden, F.G., 74
Worden, J.W., 391
Worth, L.T., 436, 437, 662
Wortman, C.B., 392, 691
Wotman, S.R., 667
Woycke, J., 740
Wozney, K., 600
Wright, A.L., 541
Wright, E.F., 675
Wright, J., 432
Wright, M.J., 10, 11
Wright, R.W., 116
Wrightsman, L.S., 384, 741
Wu, J.F., 390
Wyer, R.S., 708
Wylie, R., 520
Wyshak, G., 597
Wysocki, C.J., 116

Xie, J.L., 722

Yahya, K.A., 694
Yankner, J., 262
Yarmey, A.D., 755
Yeager, K., 559

Yetton, P.W., 739
Yogman, M.W., 349
Yonas, A., 323
Young, A.M., 172
Young, E., 113
Young, L.T., 643, 644
Young, R.A., 662
Young, S.L., 122, 123
Younger, J.C., 675
Yuen, 560
Yuhn, W.T.C., 450
Yuille, J.C., 239, 256, 257, 258
Yukl, G., 738, 739

Zaccaro, S.J., 738
Zacks, R.T., 378
Zajonc, R.B., 426, 431, 465, 466,
    701
Zalenski, R., 334
Zanna, M.P., 472, 522, 662, 672,
    701
Zapf, M.K., 714
Zarbatany, L., 364
Zatorre, R.J., 71
Zatzick, D.F., 114
Zeanah, C.H., 347

Zebrowitz, L.A., 468
Zebrowitz-McArthur, L., 360
Zeki, S., 106, 107
Zelazo, N.A., 319
Zelazo, P.D., 319
Zelazo, P.R., 319, 320
Zerbe, W.J., 387, 727
Zhao, S., 620
Zigler, E., 465
Zillmann, D., 414, 415, 498, 752
Zimbardo, P.G., 433
Zinger, J.T., 405
Zingle, H.W., 432
Zisook, S., 613
Zola, D., 104
Zuccaro, C., 663
Zucco, G.M., 117, 240
Zuckerman, M., 403, 490, 513,
    523
Zunz, M., 514
Zwick, W., 412
Zyzanski, S.J., 541, 559

Subject Index

Abnormal behavior, 579–80
Abreaction, 622
Absenteeism, 734–35
Absolute threshold, 96, 97
Academic Motivation Scale, 423
Academic underachievers, 368
Acceptance, as stage of dying, 391
Accommodation, 326
Acetylcholine, 55, 56, 58, 262
Achievement motivation, 421–23
Acoustic coding, 235–36
Acoustic trauma, 137
Acquisition, 188–92
Acquisitiveness, 401
ACTH, 77
Acting, 522
Action potential, 52
Action words, 303
Activational effects, 412
Active touch, 112
Acuity, 103
Adaptation to experience, 326
Addiction Research Foundation
  (ARF), 174, 176
Adolescence, 358
  in 1990s, 367
  cognitive development during,
    362
  culture and, 358–59
  family's effect on, 368–69
  high risk environment and,
    370–71
  mixed-sex interactions, 361
  physical development during,
    359–61
  sexual behavior during, 369–70
  social and emotional develop-
    ment in, 363–67
Adolescent gender intensification,
  360–61
Adolescent invulnerability, 362–63
Adolescents
  effectiveness of therapy with,
    641
  sexual behavior of, 369–70
  and smoking, 555
Adrenal androgens, 78
Adrenal cortex, 78, 79
Adrenal glands, 79
Adrenal medulla, 79
Adrenogenic insensitivity syndrome,
  78
Adult development
  crisis approach to, 372
  life event models, 372–73
Adulthood, 371–89
  cognitive change during, 378–81
  crisis of, 385–88
  early, 373–74
  gender differences in, 388–89
  physical change during, 373–77
  social change in, 382–84
Affect, 435
  influence of, on cognition,
    435–37
  positive, 296
Affective state(s), 435–38
  and information processing,
    336–37
Affirmative action programs, 729–30
Agape love, 705
Aggression
  in children, 219–20
  cultural differences in, 420–21
  definition of, 418
  factors influencing, 419
  gender differences in, 471–72
  and motivation, 418–21
  observational learning and, 219

roots of, 418–20
  temperature and, 744–45
Aggressive motivation, 418–21
Aging
  and memory, 378–79
  primary versus secondary,
    376–77
  and problem solving, 380
  theories of, 390
Agonists, 57–58
Agoraphobia, 593
Agreeableness, 512
AIDS, 561–63
  babies infected with, 317, 563
  HIV transmission, 562
  prevention programs for, 564
  psychological help for victims
    of, 564
Air, polluted, 752
Alcohol, 174, 178
  abuse of
    and aggression, 419
    blood levels of, 175
    as depressant, 174
    effects of, 178, 238–39, 258
    Korsakoff syndrome and, 262
    overconsumption of, 558
    treatment of dependence on, 59
"Alcoholic myopia," 207
Aldridge-Kimberly study, 591
Algorithms, 292
All-or-none response of neuron, 52
Altruism, 697. See also Prosocial
  behavior
Alzheimer's disease
  amnesia of, 262
  and sleep patterns, 157
Ambition, 405
American Psychiatric Association,
  582
American Sign Language (ASL), 305
Amnesia, 259
  of Alzheimer's disease, 262
  dissociative, 597–98
  from Korsakoff's syndrome, 262
  infantile, 250
  types of, 259, 597–98
Amphetamines, 58, 175, 178, 412, 612
Amplitude, 108, 109
Amygdala, 68, 260
Amyloid beta protein, 262
Anal stage, 496
Analogy, 292, 295
Anandamine, 177
Anchoring-and-adjustment
  heuristic, 284
Androgynous, 479
Anger
  in divorce, 385
  infants and, 342
  as stage of dying, 391
Angular velocity, 103
Anima, 501
Animal cognition, 279–82
Animal research
  on attachment
    with classical conditioning,
      186, 189, 191–93
    ethical issues in, 35–37
    on language, 304–307
    with operant conditioning,
      203–205, 212–13
    visual experience, 133
Animus, 501
Anomalous sentences, 307
Anorexia Nervosa, 409–410, 602, 16
Anosmia, 116
Antagonist, 58
Anterior pituitary gland, 77–78, 79

Anterograde amnesia, 259–60
Anthropocentric approach, 280–82
Antianxiety drugs, 649
Antibodies, 546
Antidepressant drugs, 59, 648–49
Antigens, 546
Antipsychotic drugs, 612, 647–48
Antisocial personality disorder,
  604–607
    and emotional reactivity,
      605–606
    learning and attention
      problems, 606–607
Anxiety, 494, 592
    drug treatment of, 649
    social, 509
    Stress Inoculation Training
      Program for, 632–33
    and subliminal processing,
      595–96
Anxiety disorders, 586
    obsessive-compulsive, 594
    panic attack, 592–93
    phobias, 593
    post-traumatic stress, 594–95
Apnea, (159)
Applied psychology, 741–745
Archetypes, 501
Arcuate fasciculus, 72
Area illusions, 127, 128
Army Alpha, 455
Army Beta, 455
Aromatherapy, 118
Arousal theory, 402–403
Artificial concepts, 271
Artificial intelligence, 296–98
Asch's line-judging task, 689
Asprin, 317
Assertiveness training, 633
Assimilation, 326
Association cortex, 71
Athletic Motivation Inventory, 423
Ativan, 649
Atkinson-Shiffrin modal model of
  memory, 230
Atlas personality, 516–17
Atmospheric perspective, 130
Attachment, 345–49
    contact comfort and, 348–49
    fathers and, 349
    measuring, 345–47
Attention
    development of, 331–32
    in observational learning, 218
    selective, 120–21, 230
Attention-deficit hyperactivity dis-
  order (ADHD), 332
Attentional load, 151
Attitudes, 672
    cognitive dissonance and,
      675–79
    persuasion in changing, 672–75
    work-related, 732–37
Attraction, interpersonal, 701–704
Attribution, 662
    bias in, 664–65
    causal, 661–63
    errors in, 725
    explaining behavior, 661–63
    fundamental error of, 665–67
Auditory cortex, 72
Auditory nerve, 108
Auditory sensitivity, and age, 376
Auditory system. See Hearing
Authority, 695
Autobiographical memory, 247–50.
    See also Episodic memory
Autobiographical memory schedule,
  247

Automatic processing, 151
Automatic vigilance, 669–71
Autonomic nervous system, 61, 428,
  430, 431
Autonomy versus shame and doubt,
  365
Availability heuristic, 283
Aversion therapy, 627
Axon, 50
Axon terminals, 50
AZT (AIDS drug), 562

Babbling, 302
Baby talk. See Infant-directed speech
Baby-facedness, 360
Backward conditioning, 189
Backward masking, 98
Balance, sense of, 119
Balding, 373
Barbiturates, 174, 178
Bargaining, as stage of dying, 391
Basal forebrain, 262
Basal metabolic rate, 408
Base rates, 284
Basil ganglia, 66
Basilar membrane, 109, 110
Beck's cognitive behavior therapy
  for depression, 630–31
Behavior
    group, 679–700
    prosocial, 697–700
Behavior therapies, 626–29, 633
Behavioral genetics, 467
Behavioral medicine, 532
Behavioral perspective, 9–10, 14. See
    also Behaviorism
Behaviorally anchored rating scales
    (BARSs), 730–31
Behaviorism, 7, 8, 201
    position in nature-nurture
      debate, 12
    See also Operant conditioning
Beliefs, 277–79, 551
Benzodiazepines, 59, 649
Bereavement, 392
Beta waves, 156
Bilingualism program in
    psychology, 10
Binocular cues, 130, 131
Biochemical interpretation of love,
    705–76
Biological clock, 146–49, 372
Biological constraints on learning,
    194. See also Instinctive drift
Biological rhythms, 144–49
    circadian, 145–49
    definition of, 144
    types of, 145
Biologically based therapies, 645–49
    drug, 646–49
    early forms of, 645
    electroconvulsive, 645–46
    psychosurgery, 646
Biopsychology, 12, 14, 48
    study of nervous system, 63
Bipolar cells, 101
Birth order, 465, 505
Bisexual, 417
Blended families, 368–69
Blind spot, 101
Blocking, 197
Bodily functions, fluctuation of, 145
Body image, distorted, 410
Body language, 433
Body temperature, 146, 147, 162
Bonnet's syndrome, 95
Bottom-up theory of pattern
    recognition, 129–30
Braille alphabet, 112

Brain
cognitive processing, 81
and condition taste aversion, 194
depression and, 588
and emotions, 74–75
gender differences in, 80–81
limbic system, 68
and motivated behavior, 67
storage of memory in, 261–62, 262–63
vision and, 106–107
See also Brain damage; Brain stem; Cerebral cortex; Thalamus
Brain damage
to cerebellum, 66
to frontal lobe, 68
to lateral hypothalamus, 67
to occipital lobe, 70
to parietal lobe, 69
to temporal lobe, 70, 71
to ventromedial hypothalamus, 67
Brain death, 390–91
Brain imaging techniques, 63–65
Brain stem, 66
Brain structure, and schizophrenia, 612
Brain-behavior relationship, research into, 48
Breast cancers, 569
Brightness, 103
Brightness constancy, 126
Bulimia, 409–410, 602, 603
Burnout, 547–48
Bystander effect, 698–99

Cafeteria-style benefit plans, 722
Caffeine, 178, 318
Canadian mental health care system, 651
Canadian Psychological Association, 10, 35, 38
Canadian psychologists, 19, 20
Canadian universities, development of psychology programs in, 0–11
Cancer, 553
Cannon-Bard theory of emotions, 426–27
Carcinogens, 553
Cardinal trait, 511
Cardiovascular disease, 554, 559
Caregiving to the terminally ill, 391–92
Case method, 22
Castration anxiety, 496
Catatonic schizophrenia, 610
Catecholamines, 559, 560
Central fissure, 68
Central nervous system, 60–61
Central route to persuasion, 674
Central traits, 511
Cerebellum, 66
Cerebral cortex
during REM sleep, 165
effects of Alzheimer's disease on, 262
emotions and, 430
frontal lobe, 68–69, 71
language and, 72–73
lateralization and, 73–77
and obsessive-compulsive disorders, 64–65
occipital lobe, 70
parietal lobe, 69
split-brain and, 75–76
temporal lobe, 70
Cerebral death, 391
Cerebral hemispheres, 68, 73–74, 430, 482
Chaining, 206
Charismatic leadership, 739–41

Child
abuse, 652
neglect, 369
Child molesters, 370
Child personality, 600
Childhood, 314
Childhood abuse, 600
Children
and acquisition of prejudices, 681
language development in, 300–303
See also Empathy; Prejudice, challenging
Chlorpromazine, 647
Choking under pressure, 155
Chromosomes, 82
Chronic illness, 376
Chronic schizophrenics, 454
Chunk, 236
Cigarette smoking, 555–57, 565–66
Circadian rhythms
disturbances in, 148–49
individual differences in, 147–48
mechanisms of, 146–47
and memory, 379–80
nature of, 145–46
sleep and, 159
Civil disobedience, 695
Clairvoyance, 135
Clark Institute, 643
Classical conditioning, 515
attitude formation and, 672
cognitive perspective on, 195–97
definition of, 186–88
and eating habits, 408
exceptions to, 193–95
of newborns, 320
Pavlov's work on, 188
phobia and, 198
and physiological response to drugs, 199–200
principles of, 188–93
role of expectation in, 195
therapies based on, 626–27
as type of learning, 186–88
versus operant, 203, 205
Client-centered therapy, 506, 624
Climacteric, 374
Clinical bias, 584–85
Clinical observation, 62
Clinical psychology, 19
Clozapine, 648
Cocaine, 58, 175–76, 178
Cochlea, 108
Cocktail party phenomenon, 121
Coefficient alpha, 456
Cognition, 270
animal, 279–82
and emotion, 435–38
and health, 553
influence of, on affect, 438
metacognition, 334–35
social, 667–71
Cognitive abilities, adaptive, 746
Cognitive Assessment System, 462
Cognitive development, 323–35
during adolescence, 362–63
during adulthood, 378–81
information-processing approach to, 330–32
Piagetian theory of, 323, 325, 326–28
variability in, 335
Cognitive disability, 461
Cognitive dissonance, 675–79
Cognitive map, 214
Cognitive perspective
on classical conditioning 195, 197
on drug abuse, 173–74
on operant conditioning, 210–11, 213–15

on persuasion, 673–75
in psychology, 10, 11, 14
Cognitive processes, 11
Cognitive psychology, 20
Cognitive sources of prejudice, 681–82
Cognitive theory
and gender identity, 350–51
of language, 300
Cognitive therapies, 629–32
Cold, absolute threshold for, 96
Collective conscious, 501
Collectivist society, love and intimacy in, 500
Color discrimination, and age, 376
Color, and mood, 745
Color vision, 104–106
Commitment in the workplace, 737
Communication skills
for doctors, 552–53
improvement of, 637
Communications approach to family therapy, 638
Compassionate love (EROS), 705
Compensation, 504
Complaining, 692
Complex skills, 242
Compliance, 690–92
Componential intelligence, 447
Computer-assisted instruction, 216
Computer-based work monitoring, 723–24
Computers, and repetitive strain injury, 757–58
Concepts, 271–73
Concrete operations stage (Piaget), 328
Concurrent validity, 457
Conditional positive regard, 506
Conditioned physiological response, 199–200
Conditioned reinforcers, 202
Conditioned response (CR), 188
Conditioned stimulus (CS), 188
Conditioned stimulus-uncondi-tioned stimulus interval, 190
Conditioned taste aversion, 194–97
Conditioning trials, 188
Conditions of worth, 623
Confidentiality, professional ethics, 37–38
Confirmation bias, 277–78
Confluence theory, 466
Conformity, 687–89, 687–90
Congenital adrenogenital syndrome, 78
Conscientiousness, 512
Consciousness
drug-altered states of, 171–79
Freud's levels of, 492–93
hypnosis, 166–71
meditation, 179–81
self-induced shifts in, 152–53
sleep, 156–60
states of, 144
waking state of, 150–56
Consensus, 663
Conservation, 327
Consistency, 663
Consolidation of memory, 260
Constancies, perceptual, 124, 126
Construct validity, 457
Construction, memory, 252, 255–58
Contact comfort, 348–49
Contact hypothesis, 683
Content validity, 457
Context-dependent memory, 241
Contextual intelligence, 447
Continuous reinforcement schedule (CRF), 207
Contrast effect, 214
Control theory of self-consciousness, 153–54

Controlled processing, 151
Controls, design of, 749–51
Conventional level (Kohnberg), 338
Convergence, 131
Convergent thinking, 295
Conversion disorder, 597
Copulins, 414
Cornea, 100
Corpus callosum, 71, 75–76, 81, 373, 482
Correlational method, 23–25, 30
Cortisone, 78
Counseling psychology, 19–20
Counterfactual thinking, 670–71
Couple therapy, 637–39
Covert desensitization, 627
Crack. See Cocaine
Cranial nerves, 61
Creativity, 294
effects of aging on innovative problem solving and, 294–96
measurement of, 296
Crib death, 557
Crises of adult life, 385–88
Crisis approach to adult development, 372
Criterion-related validity, 457
Critical thinking, 6, 42–43
Cross-era transition, 382
Cross-tolerance, 172
Crowding, 742–43
Crystallized intelligence, 381, 445
Cues
binocular, 131
monocular, 130
nonverbal, 432–35, 468
retrieval, 240–42, 246, 249, 257, 264
Cultural bias in intellience testing, 459
Cultural differences
adolescence and, 358–59
in aggression, 420–21
dream interpretations and, 163–64
in love and intimacy, 499–500
and memories, 254–55
menopause and, 375
in moral development, 341
and reaction to crowding, 743
in reasoning, 276
and in responsiveness, 319
in standards of physical attractiveness, 703–704
Culture shock, 221–22
Culture-fair tests, 460
Culture-related errors in diagnosis, 584–85
Curare, 58
Curiosity, 295

Dark adaptation, 104, 376
Day care, 347–48
Daydreams, 152–53
Death
from smoking, 554–57
leading causes of, 554–55
reactions to, 555
right to, 390–91
suicidal person's views of, 592
Debriefing, 35
Deception, 34
Deception, social, 522
Decision making, 282–88
bad, 287–88
framing in, 286–87
gender differences in
with heuristics, 282–84
planning, 331
ways to improve, 308
Declarative memory, 260
Deep processing, 239–40

Deep structure, 297
Defence mechanisms (Freud), 494–95
Deficiency needs, 405
Deinstitutionalization, 650
Delayed conditioning, 189
Delta waves, 157
Delusions, 608
Delusions of grandeur, 608
Delusions of persecution, 608
Demand characteristics, 29, 245
Dendrites, 50
Denial
        as psychological defence, 506
        as stage of dying, 391
Deoxyribonucleic acid (DNA), 82
Dependence, drug, 172
Depolarization, 55
Depressants, 174, 178
Depression, 385, 430, 478–79, 587
        in Canadian North, 644
        causes of, 588
        drug treatment of, 648–49
        ego protection and, 666
        as stage of dying, 391
Destructive obedience, 693–95
Detachment, as stage of
        bereavement, 392
Determinism, 508
Developmental psychology, 20, 314
Diagnostic Interview Schedule, 586
Diagnostic and Statistical Manual of
        Mental Disorders (DSM-IV),
        582–85
Diary studies, 247–48
Diathesis-stress model, 611
Diet, and nutrition, 558
Difference threshold, 98
Diffusion of responsibility, 288, 699
Dimensions of personality, 512–13
Direct aggression, 471
Discrete skills, 242
Discriminative stimulus, 210
Disease during pregnancy, 317
Disequilibrium, 385
Disobedience, civil, 695
Disorders of initiating and main-
        taining sleep (DIMS), 161
Disorganization and dispair, as
        stage of bereavement, 392
Disorganized (disorienated)
        attachment, 346
Disorganized subtype of schizo-
        phrenia, 610
Dissociations in consciousness,
        168–69
Dissociative
        amnensia, 598
        disorders, 597–600
        fugue, 598
        identity disorder, 589–600
Dissonance theory, 678–79
Distinctiveness, 663
Distortion, memory, 252–53, 256–58
Distortion, as psychological defence,
        506
Distress, 576
Distributional ratings of perfor-
        mance, 731–32
Disturbed interpersonal relation-
        ships, 502
Divergent thinking, 295
Divorce
        causes of, 386–87
        crisis of, 385–86
        effect on adolescents, 368
Divorce mediation, 387
Dizygotic twins, 83
Dopamine, 56, 58, 59, 408, 612
Dopamine hypothesis of schizo-
        phrenia, 612
Dopamine receptors, 194
Double standard, 477
Double-blind procedure, 29

Down's syndrome, 461
Dreams
        cognitive view of, 165–66
        culture and, 164–65
        facts on, 162–63
        physiological view of, 165
        psychodynamic view of, 163–64
        vision of future, 383, 388
Dreams of absent-minded transgres-
        sion (DAMIT), 165–66, 173–74
Dress, and compliance, 695
Drive theory, 402
Drug abuse
        contrasting views on, 172–74
        definition of, 172
Drug addiction, treatment of, 57–59
Drug therapy, 646–49
Drugs
        antianxiety, 649
        antidepressant, 648–49
        antipsychotic, 647–48
        conditioned response to,
                199–200
        consciousness-altering, 174–77
        definition of, 172
        effects of conscious-altering, 178
        pregnancy and, 317–18
        psychological effects of, 179
        types of, 174–78
        use of, to study nervous
                system, 62
Dualism, 6
Dying. See Death
Dynamic visual acuity (DVA), 103
Dysfunctional families, 369
Dysphoria, 473

Ear, 108, 119
Eardrum, 108
Early adulthood, 383
Early childhood memory, absence
        of, 250
Early chldhood sexual abuse, and
        repression of memory, 245
Eating
        habits of, 408
        regulation of, 407
Eating disorders, 409–410, 602–603
Ecolalia, 446
Ecological approach to comparative
        cognition, 280–82
Educational psychology, 20
Efferent nerve fibres, 60
Ego, 494
Ego protection, 666
Egocentrism, 327
Elaboration likelihood model
        (ELM), 674
Elaborative rehearsal, 230, 238
Electroconvulsive therapy (ECT),
        645–46, 650
Electroencephalograms (EEG),
        156–57
Electroencephalography (EEG), 63
Electromyography (EMG), 758
Embarrassment, and prosocial
        behavior, 70
Emblems, 433
Embryo, 315
Emotional stability, 512
Emotion(s), 400, 426–38
        and cognition, 435–38
        color and mood, 745
        effect of exercise on, 567
        external expressions of, 430,
                432–35
        light and mood, 745
        mood and health, 558–59
        mood and prosocial behavior,
                699–700
        nature of, 426–28
        physiology of, 428, 430, 431
        and reasoning, 277–79

temperature and violence,
        744–45
See also Social and emotional
        development
Empathetic understanding, 624
Empathy, 698
Empiricism, 6
Employee assistance programs
        (EAPs), 735–36
Encoding, 229, 240
        according to schemas, 253,
                254–55
        and memory construction, 256
Encoding specificity principle, 242
Encounter groups, 634
Endocrine glands, 77
Endocrine system, 77–79
Endorphins, 706
        function of, 56, 113
        level of, and sensation seeking,
                523
        love and, 706
        and withdrawal symtoms, 176
Environment
        and intelligence, 465–67
        as source of stress, 542–46
        workplace, 751–54
Environmental deprivation/
        enrichment, 465
Environmental psychology, 741–45
Epinephrine, 559
Episodic memory, 232, 233, 333. See
        also Autobiographical memory
Equity theory, 719–20
Ergonomics. See Human factors psy-
        chology
Erickson's stages of life, 364–67, 372
Eros (compassionate love), 705
Escalation of commitment, 287–88
Esteem needs, 405
Ethical codes and guidelines, 10, 35,
        38
Ethics
        professional, 37–38
        use of animals for research, 35
        and use of deception, 354–35
Ethological theory, 345
Euphoria, 430
Evolutionary perspective, 12–13, 14,
        418, 476
Evolutionary psychology, 12. See
        also Sociobiology
Excitement phase, 413
Exercise, 567–68
Exhaustion, 547–48
Exhibitionism, 602
Expectancies, 403, 438, 515
Expectancy theory, 403–404
        and work motivation, 716–17
Expectation in cognitive processes,
        195
Expected utility, 282
Experiential intelligence, 447
Experimental analysis of behavior
        (Skinner), (203)
Experimental method, 25–29, 30
Experimental psychology, 20
Experimentation, 30
        establishing causality, 25
        nature of, 26–28
Experimenter effects, 28
Explicit memory, 260
Externals, 516
Extinction, 192
Extrinsic motivation, intrinsic
        versus, 423–24
Extroversion, 512
Extroverts, 502
Eye
        movements, 104
        structure of, 100–101
Eyewitness testimony, 256–58

Facial expressions, 432
Facial feedback hypothesis, 427
Factor analysis, 511
False conscious effect, 66768
Family constellation, 504
Family factor, and schizophrenia, 611
Family therapy, 638–39
Fantasies, 152–53
Farsightedness, 103
Fast mapping, 303
Fathers, and divorce, 385
Feature detectors, 107
Feminine intuition, 468
Fertilization, 315
Fetal alcohol syndrome (FAS), 318
Fetus, 315
Figure-ground relationship, 123–24
Fixation, 495
Fixed-interval schedule, 208
Fixed-ratio schedule, 208
Flashbulb memories, 252
Flavor neophobia, 194
Flooding, (196)
Fluid intelligence, 381, 445
Fluoxetine, 648
Foot-in-the-door technique, 692
Forced compliance, 675
Forgetting from long-term memory,
        242–46
Formal operatons stage (Piaget),
        328, 362
Fovea, 100
Framing, 286–87
Free association, 622
Free will, 508
Free-radicals theory, 390
Frequency theory, 110
Freudian slips, 497
Freud's theory of personality, 492–97
        evaluation of, 498–99
        levels of consciousness, 492–93
        psychosexual stages of, 495
        structure of personality in,
                494–95
Friendship love, 705
Friendships
        of adolescents, 364
        gender differences in, 472–73
Frontal lobe, 68–71, 71
Frotteurism, 601
Frustration, 419
Frustration-aggression hypothesis,
        419
Fully functioning persons, 505
Functional autonomy, 511
Functional fixedness, 393
Functional MRI, 63
Functionalism, 7, 8
Fundamental attribution error, 665

GABA (gamma-anino butyric acid),
        56, 59
Gambling, compulsive, 209
Gametes, 83
Ganglion cells, 101
Ganzfield procedure, 135–36
Gazes and stares, 432–33
Gender, 350–52, 467
        bias, counteracting, 728
        identity, 350–51, 360–61
Gender constancy, 350
Gender differences
        in achievement motivation,
                422–23
        in adult years, 388–89
        in aggression, 471–72
        biological basis of, 80–81, 482
        in cognitive abilities, 480
        in color vision, 104
        in complaining, 692
        and conformity, 690
        in conversation-interruption
                behavior, 728

in decision-making style, 470
in friendships, 472–73
in leadership, 469–71
in life expectancy, 389
in mate selection, 473–75
in moral development, 339–42
origins of, 481
in perception of smell, 132
in self-disclosure, 509
in sexual behavior, 477–78
in sexual jealousy, 415–16
in social behavior, 468–75
and socialization, 481
in suicide rates, 590–95
in touching, 434
Gender identity, 479
Gender identity disorders, 601–602
Gender roles, 351, 467
Gender schema theory, 350–51
Gender stereotypes, 467, 468–69,
471, 472
Gender stereotyping, 479
Gene mutation theory, 390
General adaptation syndrome
(GAS), 535
Generalitivity, 305
Generation gap, 364
Generativity versus absorption, 372
Genetic factors
and depression, 588
and divorce, 386
and homosexuality, 85–86, 417
and job satisfaction, 733
and obesity, 406
and schizophrenia, 610–11
in sex-stereotyped behaviors,
352
and specific language impair-
ment, 301–302
Genetic linkage analysis, 86
Genetic theories of aging, 390
Genetics
and environmental effects, 84
principles of, 82–84
and sexual orientation, 84–86
Genital stage, 496
Gestalt
psychologists, 123
therapy, 624
Gestures, 433
Glands, 77–79. See also specific glands
Glial cells, 50
Goal-setting theory, 717–19
Gonadal hormones, 79
Gonads, 79, 359, 411
Graded potential, 52
Grammar, 303
Grandparents, divorce and, 386
Great person theory of leadership,
738
Group behavior, 679–700
and compliance, 690–95
prejudice, 679–87
social influence and, 687–90
Group therapies, 633–34, 637–39
Growth needs, 405
Growth spurt, 359

Habituation, 320
Hair cells, 108
Hallucinations, 152–53, 608
Hallucinogens, 176, 177. See also LSD
Halo effects, 725–26
Haptic images, 273
Hardiness, 549
Health
and emotions, 558–59
mass media and, 566–67
and personality, 559–60
self-disclosure and, 509
stress and, 539, 541, 545–46
Health belief model, 551–52
Health needs, communication of, 550

Health psychology, 532
Hearing, 96, 107–11
physical stimulus for, 108–109
pitch perception, 109–110
sound localization, 110–11
Hearing loss, 137
Height cues, 131
HEPA (high efficient particular
arresting) filters, 753
Heredity, 81
and ADHD, 332
and behavior, 82–85
and hypertension, 559
and intelligence, 463–64, 467
See also Genetics
Heroin, 58–59, 176, 178, 318
Herpes, 317
Heterosexual, 85, 417
Heuristics, 282–84
Hindsight, 278–79
Hippocampus, 68, 259, 260–62, 450
Holland Scales, 734
Holophrastic speech, 303
Homeostasis, 67, 97, 402
Homosexuality, 84–86, 416–17
Hopeless model, 589
Hormones, 77–81
circadian rhythms and, 146
definition of, 77
and gender-related behaviors,
81
and premenstrual syndrome,
79–80
and sexual behavior, 411–12
Hue, 102. See also Color vision
Human factors psychology, 715,
745–54
controls, 749–51
visual displays, 746–49
workplace environments,
751–54
Human immunodeficiency virus
(HIV), 561–62
Humanistic perspective, 12–13, 14
Humanistic theories, 505–507
evaluation of, 507–508
of Maslow, 404–406, 507
of Rogers, 505–506
Humanistic therapies, 624–32
behavior, 426–29
Gestalt, 625
for groups, 634
overview of, 625–26
person-centered, 624
Humor, and stress, 537
Hunger motivation, 406–410
Huntington's disease, 82
Hypercomplex cells, 107
Hyperpolarization, 55
Hypersomnias, 161
Hypertension, 559, 648
Hypertensive crisis, 648
Hypnosis
memory and perception and,
169–71
nature of, 168–71
susceptibility to, 148, 161,
167–68
Hypochondriasis, 597
Hypocrisy, dissonance theory and,
678–79
Hypothalamus, 67
control of biological clock by,
146
and endocrine system, 77–78
and sleep disorders, 162
Hypothesis, 24, 33
Hypothetico-deductive reasoning,
328
Hysteria, 492

Id, 494
Identity versus role confusion, 367

Illness, correlates of, 553
Illumination, 295
Illusions, 126–29
Images, 273, 274
Immune system
effect of stress on, 546
response to self-disclosure, 509
Implicit memory, 260
Impression management, 691
Incentives, 404
Incidental memory, 379
Incubation, 295
Indirect aggression, 471
Individual differences, 413–14, 422,
509
Individualist/collectivist dimension,
499–500
Individuating information, 728
Industrial/organizational psychology (I/O), 714–45
definition of, 714
performance appraisal, 724–30
reducing errors in performance
appraisals, 730–732
as subfield, 20
work motivation, 716–24
work-related attitudes, 732–38
Industry versus inferiority, 367
Infant-directed speech, 343
Infantile amnesia, 250
Infantile autism, 446
Infants
absense of autobiographical
memory in, 250
emotional development in,
342–43
memory of, 250
and pain, 342
perceptions of smell, 132
perceptual development of,
321–23
physical, 319–20
visual perception of, 132
Inferential statistics, 29
Inferior colliculi, 66
Information overload, 742
Information processing, 149, 151–52
and intelligence, 449–50,
462–63
Information-processing approach,
229
to cognitive development,
330–32
to intelligence, 447–48, 462–63
to memory, 229–30
Informed consent, 35
Ingratiation, 691
Ingroup, 680
Initiative versus guilt, 365
Innate mechanism view of language
development, 300
Inner ear, 119
Insomnia, 160
Instinct theory, 401
Instinctive drift, 206
Instincts, 401
Institute for Biodiagnostics, 63
Institute of Psychology, 10
Instrumental conditioning. See
Operant conditioning
Insulin therapy, 650
Integrity versus despair, 372
Intellectual styles, 448
Intellectually gifted, 461
Intelligence, 444–67
birth order and, 465
crystallized versus fluid, 381,
445–46
definition of, 440
effects of aging on, 381–82
environmental factors in, 463,
465–67
heredity and, 463–64, 467

measurement of, 450–59
unified versus multifaceted,
445–46
views on, 445–50
Intelligence tests
culture-fair, 460
development of, 450–51
group, 454–55
individual, 451–54
practical uses of individual,
461–63
public policy and, 459–61
reliability and validity of,
455–59
Intentional memory, 379
Interactionism, 6
Interference, and forgetting, 243
Intermittent reinforcement, 208
Internals, 516
Interpretation in psychoanalysis, 622
Intimacy, 364, 499–500
Intimacy versus isolation, 372
Intrinsic motivation, 423–25
Introverts, 501
Involuntary (eye) movements, 104
Ion channels, 51
IQ (intelligence quotient), 451–52,
453–54, 464
Iris, 120

James-Lange theory of emotions,
426–27
Jet lag, 148
Job design, 722
Job enlargement, 722
Job enrichment, 722
Job market, preparation for, 393–94
Job satisfaction, 732–37
Judgments, social, 708
Just noticeable difference (jnd), 98
Just world, belief in, 703

Kaufman Assessment Battery for
Children, 462
Kinesthesia, 118–19
Kinsey Reports, 413
Kinship studies, 465
Kitsunetsuki, 580
Kohnberg's stages of moral under-
standing, 338–39
assessment of, 339–42
Korsakoff's syndrome, 262

Language, 298–307
cerebral cortex and, 72–73
development of, 300–304
and long-term memory, 250
nature of, 298–99
in non-human species, 304–307
parallel models of, 72–73
production and comprehension
of, 72
relationship of, to thought, 304
schizophrenic disturbances in,
608
and social context of cognitive
development, 329
Language development
in Children, 300
grammar, 303–304
phonological development,
302–303
semantic development, 303
theories of, 300–301
Late adult transition, 384
Latent content of dream, 164
Later life, physical changes in,
376–77
Lateral hypothalamus, 67
Lateralization of function, 73–77
Laws of grouping, 124, 125
Leadership, 738–41
achieving, 522

gender differences in, 469–71
great person theory, 738
transformational, 739–41
Learned helplessness, 211–12
depression and, 588
Learning
biological constrains on, 194
by newborns, 320–21
cognitive processes in, 214–15
definition of, 184
See also Classical conditioning;
Observational conditioning;
Operant conditioning;
Social learning theory
Learning approaches to personality,
514–17
evaluation of, 516–17
Learning perspective, on drug
abuse, 172–73
Left temporal lobe, 71
Legal proceedings, bias in, 754–57
Leniency errors, 726
Lens, 100
Less-leads-to-more effect, 675–77
Levels of processing view of
long-term memory, 239–40
Levinson's stages of adult life, 382–84
Libido, 495
Librium, 649
Life structure, 382
Life-events models, 372
Lifestyle, 533
Light, 100
effect on mood, 745
stimulus for vision, 102, 106
Limbic system, 68
Linear perspective, 130
Lineups (queues), 688–89
Linguistic relativity hypothesis, 304
Lithium, 649
Localization, sound, 110–11
Localized neural circuits, 263
Long-term memory, 237–42
accuracy of, 237
and aging, 378–79
children's development of, 333
and cognitive effort, 239–40
effect of, on neuron structure,
363
forgetting from, 242–46
in modal model, 230
and neurotransmitters, 263
operation of, 238–40
retrieval of information from,
240–42
and structure of neurons, 263
Love, 701, 704–707
and intimacy, 499–500
LSD (lysergic acid diethylamide), 177
Ludos love, 705
Lymphocytes, 546

Macleod Report, 11
Magnetic resonance imaging (MRI),
63
Major tranquilizers, 647–48
Make-believe play, 326
Malaria, 317
Mania, 588
Mania love, 705
Manic disorders, drug treatment of,
649
Manifest content of dream, 164
Marijuana, 176–77, 178, 318
Marital therapy, 637–38
Maslow's needs hierarchy, 404–406,
507
Mastery, 388–89
Matching hypothesis, 475
Maternal deprivation, 346
Maternal responsiveness, 318–19
Mathamethics, problem-solving in,
291

Mathematics anxiety, 479
Maturation, 358
Means-ends analysis, 292
Medical perspective of psychological disorders, 578
Meditation, 179–81
Medulla, 66
Meichenbaum's stress inoculation
training program, 632–33
Melatonin, 146–47
Memory, 228
aging effects on, 378–79
alcohol effects on, 238–39, 258
Atkinson-Shiffrin modal model
of, 230
autobiographical, 247–50, 252
biological bases of, 258–63
of children, 333
circadian rhythms and, 246,
379–80
consolidation of, 259
construction in, 252, 255–56
and contextual information,
248–49
declarative, 260
development of, 333–34
disorders of, 259–62
distortion in, 252–53
forgetting from, 242–46
hypnosis and, 171, 257–58
improvement of, 264–65
incidental, 379
information-processing
approach to, 229–30
intentional, 379
in natural contexts, 247–58
for odors, 117
in parallel distributive model,
230–31
prospective, 246, 379
sensory, 233–34
storage of, in brain, 261–62,
262–63
systems of, 230
types of information in, 232–33
See also Amnesia; Long-term
memory; Short-term memory
Memory loss, 246, 250, 259
Menopause, 374
Menstrual cycle, 79, 145
Mental age, 451–52
Mental health, and personality
characteristics, 524–25
"Mental illness," 579
Mental self-government, 448
Mental set, 293–94
Mentor, 372, 383, 388
Meprobamate, 649
Meta-analysis, 31
Metacognition, 334
Method of loci, 264
Mid-life, physical changes during,
374
Mid-life transition, 384
Midbrain, 66
Middle ear, 108
Minnesota Study of Twins Raised
Apart, 464
Minor tranquilizers, 649
Minority identification, 685
Mirroring, 633
Misapplied constancy, theory of, 127
Mitosis, 83
Mnemonics, 264
Modal model of memory, 230
Modeling, 604, 628–28
Models in observational learning,
218
Monoamine oxidase (MAO)
inhibitors, 648
Monocular cues, 130–31
Monozygotic twins, 83, 84
Montreal massacre, 483–84

Mood. *See* Affective state(s);
Emotion(s)
Mood disorders, 586
bipolar, 588
depressive, 587-
lithium and, 649
Moon illusion, 127
Moral development, 335, 337–42
stages of moral understanding,
338–39
Morphemes, 298
Morphine, 58–59, 113–14, 176
Motion parallax, 131
Motivated skepticism, 669–70
Motivation, 400
achievement, 421–23
aggressive, 418–21
hunger, 406–410
intrinsic, 423–25
in observational learning, 219
and prospective memory, 246
sexual, 411–17
techniques for enhancing,
439–40
theories of, 404–406
work, 404, 716–24
Motor cortex, 68, 71
Mourning. *See* Bereavement
Muller-Lyer illusion, 127, 128
Multicultural perspective, 13. *See
also* Cultural differences
Multiple personality disorder, 598–99
Multiple requests, 692
Mumps, 317
Music
comprehension and production
of, 70–71
infants and, 322
Myelin, 50

Naltrexone, 59
Narcolepsy, 161
Narcotics Control Act, 176
National Research Council of
Canada, 63
Natural concepts, 271
Nature-nurture controversy, 12
nature of perception, 132–34
See also Cultural differences;
Gender differences; Genetics
Nearsightedness, 103
Necrophilia, 602
Negative afterimages, 105
Negative reinforcement, 202, 205
versus punishment, 204
Negative reinforcers, 202
Neo-Freudian theories, 501–504
of Adler, 503–504
evaluation of, 504
of Horney, 501–503
of Jung, 501
Neo-Freudians, 500
Neocortex, 260, 261
Neodissociation theory, 168–69
Nervous system, 60–64
damage to, 62
divisions of, 60–61
study of, 62–64
Neural circuits, 263
Neural efficiency, 449–50
Neural network, 71
Neural networks, computer system,
297
Neural transmission rates, and intel-
ligence, 450
Neurohormones, 77
Neurons, 49
function of, 51–55
structure of, 50
in visual cortex, 107
Neuropsychology, 20
Neuroscience approach, to
intelligence, 449–50

Neuroscience perspective, 12. *See
also* Biopsychological perspective
Neurotransmitters, 53, 55–59
effects of drugs on, 58
and memory, 263
types of, 55–56
See also specific transmitters
Newborns
learning abilities of, 320–21
sensory processing of, 331
See also Infants
Nicotine, 58, 555
Nicotine addiction, 565–66
See also Cigarette smoking
Night terrors, 161
Nightmares, 161
Nocturnal myoclonus, 161
Nodes of Ranvier, 52
Noise, 744, 752
Nonverbal communication, mixed
sex interactions and, 361
Nonverbal cues, 432–35, 468
Norepinephrine, 56, 58
Normative theory of leadership, 739
Normative/non-normative events,
373

Obedience, 692–95
Obesity, 407–409
Object permanence, 326
Object words, 303
Observation, clinical, 62
Observational learning, 217–22, 515
and aggression, 220
attitude formation, 672
and cross-cultural training,
221–22
gender identity and, 350
personality and, 515
principles of, 218–19
as type of learning, 186
Obsessive-compulsive disorder,
64–65, 594
Oedipus complex, 164, 496
Olfactory epithelium, 115
Olfactory senses. *See* Smell
Omission training, 203
Ontario Observational Database
(HOOD), 561
Ontario Student Survey of Drug Use
(1993), 57
Openness to experience, 512
Operant conditioning, 200–217, 515
and aggression, 220
application of, 215–17
attitude formation, 672
cognitive perspective on, 210–15
gender identity and, 350
nature of, 202–203
of newborns, 320
principles of, 203–210
therapies based on, 627–28
as type of learning, 186
Operating principles of language,
300
Opiates, 176, 178
Opioid peptides, 176. *See also*
Endorphins
Opium, 176, 178
Opponent process theory, 105–106
Opponent-process theory of
emotion, 428
Optimal arousal, 403
Optimists, 548–49
Oral stage, 496
Organizational citizenship behavior,
737
Organizing information for
retrieval, 240, 265
Orgasm disorders, 601
Orgasmic phase, 413
Otis tests, 455
Outgroup, 680

Oval window, 108
Ovaries, 79
Overlap (interpositional) monocular cue, 131
Overpathologizing women and minorities, 584
Oversight bias, 277
Ovum, 83, 315

Pain
children's understanding of, 333–34, 342
culture and perception of, 114–15
nature and control of, 112–14
Pain threshold, 114
Pancreas, 79
Panic attack disorder, 592–93
Papillae, 116
Parallel distributed processing model, 230–31
Parallel models of the neural basis of language, 72–73
Paranoid personality disorder, 603
Paranoid subtype of schizophrenia, 609
Paranormal events, 135
Paraphilias, 601
Parapsychologists, 135
Parasympathetic nervous system, 61, 430
Parathyroid, 79
Parent-absent families, adolescents growing up in, 368
Parental investment model, 474
Parenting, 353
Parietal lobe, 69, 71
Partial reinforcement, 208
Partial reinforcement effect, 208
PASS theory, 462
Passionate love, 705
Passive smoking, 557
Passive touch, 112
Pedophilia, 601
Penis envy, 496
Peptides, 55
Perception, 94, 120–136
constancies in, 124, 126
of distance, 130–31
extrasensory, 134–35
learning and experience in, 133
pattern recognition, 129–30
plasticity of, 132–33
principles of, 121, 123–24
and selective attention, 120–21
Perceptual development, 321–23
Perceptual organization, 121, 124
Performance appraisals, 724–30
error in, 725–27
reduction of error in, 730–32
as stressor, 543
Performance IQs, 453–54
Peripheral nervous system (PNS), 61
Peripheral route to persuasion, 674
Permanent threshold shift (PTS), 137
Persecutor personality, 600
Person-environment (P-E) fit, 544
Personal characteristics, and helping, 700
Personal fable, 362
Personal growth, 505
Personal identity, 364
Personal responsibility, 505
Personality, 490
and adaptation, 524–25
central dimensions of, 512–13
Freud's theories on, 492–97
and health, 559–60
humanistic theories of, 505–507
job satisfaction and, 734
job turnover and, 736
key aspects of, 517–24
learning approaches to, 514–16

Neo-Freudian theories of, 501–504
and prosocial behavior, 700
trait theories of, 510–13
Personality disorders, 603–607
paranoid personality, 603
schizoid personality, 603
Personality traits, 510
Persuasion, 672–75
Pessimists, 548–49
Phallic stage, 496
Phantom limb phenomenon, 69
Phenothiazines, 647
Phenylethylamine (PEA), 705
Phenylketonuria (PKU), 82, 412
Pheromones, 359, 414
Philosophy, 6–7
Phobias, 198, 593
Phonemes, 298
Phonological stragegies, 303
Physical abuse, and violent behavior, 369
Physical attractiveness, 474–75, 702–704
Physical development
in adolescence, 359–60
in infancy and childhood, 319–20
prenatal, 315–16
Physical growth and development, 314
Physiological death, 390
Physiological dependence on drugs, 172
Physiological psychology, 20
Piaget's theory
assessment of, 328–29
stages in, 326–28
Pineal gland, 146
Pinna, 108
Pitch, 108
Pitch perception, 109–110
Pituitary gland, 67, 77, 79
Place theory, 109–110
Placenta, 317
Plateau phase, 413
Pleasure, 389
Pleasure principle, 494
Poggendorf illusion, 127
Polluted air, 752
Polygraphs, validity of, 431–32
Pons, 66
Pornography, 415
Positive reinforcement. See Reinforcement
Positive reinforcers, 202
Positron emission tomography (PET), 63–65
Post-traumatic stress disorder, 542, 594–95
Postconventional level (Kohnberg), 339
Posterior pituitary gland, 77, 78, 79
Power motivation, 421, 422
Practice effects, 456
Pragma love, 705
Preadult era, 383
Precision teaching, 215
Precognition, 135
Preconventional level (Kohnberg), 338
Prediction, 23
Predictive validity, 457
Prefrontal cortex, 68
Prefrontal lobotomy, 646
Prejudice, 679–87
challenging, 682–84
effects of, 685
sources of bias, 679–82
Premack principle, 202
Premature ejaculation, 601
Premenstrual syndrome (PMS), 79–80

Prenatal period, 315–16
influences on development, 316–19
Preoperational stage (Piaget), 329
Prevention strategies, 565
for psychological disorders, 651–65
Primary aging, 376
Primary appraisal, 535
Primary prevention, 565–66, 651
Primary reinforcers, 202
Primary sexual characteristics, 359–60
Private self-consciousness, 154, 155
Private speech, 329
Probabilistic strategy, 272
Problem solving, 289–96
aging and, 380
aspects of, 289–90
factors interfering with, 292–94
methods for, 291–92
Procedural memory, 232
Production processes in observational learning, 218
Project Head Start, 465
Propanediol, 649
Propinquity, 701
Propositional reasoning, 328
Propositions, 273
Prosocial behavior, 697–700
Prosody, 434
Prospective memory, 246, 379
Protector personality, 600
Protest and yearning, as stage of bereavement, 392
Prototype-matching theory, 129
Prototypes, 129, 272
Protroactive interference, 243
Prozac, 648
Psi, 134–36
Psychedelics, 176, 178
Psychiatrist, 19
Psychiatry, 578
Psychoanalysis, 492–97, 493, 621–24
evaluation of, 623
See also Neo-Freudian theories
Psychobiology, 20
Psychodrama, 633
Psychodynamic perspective, 11–12, 14
on drug abuse, 173
Psychodynamic therapies, 621–23, 633
Psychokinesis, 135
Psychological defences, 494–95, 506
Psychological dependence on drugs, 172
Psychological disorders
antisocial personality, 604–607
anxiety disorders, 592–96
biological/medical perspective on, 578–79
in Canada, 585–86
in Canadian North, 644
changing conceptions of, 577–78
culture and, 580, 584–85
definition of, 576
eating, 602–603
identification of, 580–84
modern psychological approach to, 579–80
mood, 587–88
personality, 603–607
psychodynamic perspective on, 579
schizophrenia, 607–13, 607–613
sexual and gender identity, 600–602
somatoform disorders, 596–97
Psychological research
breadth of, 5
by case method, 22
by correlational method, 23–25, 30

by experimentation, 25–29, 30
by naturalistic observation, 21–22
by surveys, 22–23
cross sectional, 325
ethical issues in, 34–36
interpretation of, 29, 31
longitudinal, 324–25
longitudinal-sequential, 325
process of, 21–33
racial bias and,
role of theory in, 31–33
Psychologists, background and training of, 19
Psychology
basic questions about, 16–18
Canadian developments, 10–11, 48–49
definition of, 5
development of, 5–7
early views of, 7–8
ethical issues in, 33–34
and legal system, 754–57
perspectives in, 9–13
roots of, 6–7
subfields of, 19–20
women and minorities, 11, 14–16
Psychopharmacological methods, 62
Psychosexual stages of development (Freud), 495–97
Psychosurgery, 646, 650
Psychotherapies, 620–39
behavior, 626–29
cognitive, 629–32
culture and , 643–44
effective of, 639, 641
group, 633–39
humanistic, 624–26
psychodynamic, 621–23
successfulness of, 642–43
See also Biologically based therapies; Psychosurgery
Puberty, 359, 360–61
Public self-consciousness, 154
Pugnacity, 401
Punishers, 203
Punishment, 203, 204, 205
versus negative reinforcement, 203
Punishment-and-obedience orientation, 338
Pupil, 100
Pursuit (eye) movements, 104

Random assignment, 26
Rapid eye movement sleep (REM), 157–58, 159–60
dreams and, 165
effect of barbiturates on, 175
Rational-emotive therapy (RET), 629–30
Rationalism, 6
Raven Progressive Matrices, 449
Raven Progressive Matrices Test, 460
Reaction formation, 495
Reaction time, 376
Realistic conflict theory, 679–80
Reality principle, 494
Reasoning, 275
effects of culture on, 276
errors in, 277–79
formal versus everyday, 275–76
hypothetico-deductive, 328
propositional, 328
Recategorization, 683–84
Recency effect, 235
Reciprocity, and interpersonal attraction, 702–703
Reconditioning, 192
Recovery, as stage of bereavement, 392
Reference point, 284

Reflexes, 60–61
Refractoy phase, 413
Rehearsal
    elaborative, 230, 238
    and short-term memory, 237
    spontaneous, 333
Reinforcement, 202
    positive versus negative,
        202–203
    schedule of, 207–209
    size and delays in, 206–207
    types of, 202–203
Reinforcement value, 515
Reinforcers, 202
Rejection, and depression, 589
Relationships, 701–707
Relative size, 126
Reliability, 455
Relief, 385
Reorganization, as stage of
    bereavement, 392
Repeated exposure effect, 701
Repetitive strain injury (RSI), 757–58
Representativeness heuristic, 283–84
Repression
    and memory, 244–46
    theory of, 244
Research. See Psychological research
Reserpine, 647
Resistance in psychoanalysis, 622
Resolution phase, 413
Resting potential of neuron, 51
Reticular activating system (RAS), 66
Retina, 100
Retinal disparity (binocular
    parallax), 131
Retrieval, 229, 238, 240–42
Retrieval cues, 240–42, 246, 257, 264
Retroactive interference, 243
Retrospective forgetting, 246
Reuptake, 55
Revolving door pattern, 651
Reward delay, 207
Right temporal lobe, 71
Risk averse, 286
Risk factors, 553
Risk prone, 286
Ritalin, 332
Rites of passage, 358–59
Rods, 100
Role reversal, 633
Role-playing view of hypnosis, 168
Romantic love, 500, 704–705

Saccadic movements, 104
Sadomasochism, 415
Saturation, 103
Savant syndrome, 446–47
Schacter-Singer theory, 427
Schemas, 252, 438
    cultural, 259–60
    and memory, 252–55
    self-schema, 273
Schizoid personality disorder, 603
Schizophrenia, 454, 607–13
    and drug treatment, 612, 647
    nature of, 607–609
    negative symptoms, 609
    origins of, 610
    positive symptoms, 609
    subtypes of, 609–610
    types of, 609
Science, 6–7
Scientific methods, 16–17
Scripts, 333
Seasonal affective disorder (SAD),
    147, 745
Second-hand smoke, 557
Secondary aging, 376
Secondary appraisal, 535
Secondary prevention, 568–69, 651
Secondary traits, 511
Secure attachment, 346

"Security blankets," 348
SELA (Social and Emotional
    Loneliness Rating Scale), 660
Selective attention, 120–21, 230
Self-actualization needs, 405
Self-care, 626
Self-concept, 506, 508
    and gender schema, 351
    infants and, 250
    memory and 250
    Rogers's theory of, 505–506
    stress and, 520
    test of accuracy of, 526
    work and, 714
Self-consciousness, 153–55
    control theory of, 153–54
    effects of, 155
    heightened, 154
Self-determined goals, 515
Self-disclosure, 508–509
Self-efficacy, 515
Self-esteem, 519–21, 666
Self-evalutions of men, 469
Self-help tapes, 635–36
Self-identity, 367
Self-injurious behavior (SIB), 216–17
Self-justification, 287
Self-monitoring, 490, 521–23
Self-perception, 421, 519
Self-regulation, 515
Self-reinforcement, 515
Self-schemas, 273, 367, 589
Self-serving bias, 666–67, 719
Semantic coding, 235–36
Semantic development, 303
Semantic memory, 232
Semicircular canals, 119
Sensation, 94
    just noticeable difference in, 98
Sensation seeking, 523–25
Sensitivity-training groups, 634
Sensory abilities, and aging, 376
Sensory adaptation, 99–100
Sensory cortex, 71
Sensory hallucinations, 169–71
Sensory memory, 230, 233–34, 236
Sensory processing, 331
Sensory receptors, 95
Sensory thresholds, 95–99
Sensorymotor stage (Piaget), 326
Separation group therapy, 387
Serial position curve, 235
Serotonin, 5, 418
Serum cholesterol, 559
Sex-stereotype behavior, 350, 351–52
Sex-typed, 479
Sexism, test for, 484–85
Sexual abuse, 245, 369
Sexual arousal disorders, 601
Sexual behavior
    in adolescents, 369–70
    effects of homones on, 411–12
    gender differences in, 477–78
    phases during, 413
    risk prevention and, 563–64
    stimulation, 414–15
Sexual desire disorders, 601
Sexual dysfunctions, 601
Sexual harassment, 479
Sexual jealousy, 415
Sexual masochism, 601
Sexual motivation, 411–17
Sexual orientation, 84–86, 416–17
Sexual sadism, 601
Sexually transmitted diseases, 369
Shallow processing, 239
Shape constancy, 125
Shape illusions, 127, 128
Shaping, 206
Shift work, 148–50
Shock, as stage of bereavement, 392
Short-term memory (STM), 230
    of children, 333

children's development of
    effects on aging
    evidence for, 235–36
    limitations of
    in modal model, 230
    operation of, 236–37
Shorthand codes for improving
    memory, 265
Shyness, 508
Signal detection theory, 97–98
Similarity, and interpersonal
    attraction, 701–702
Simple cells, 107
Simultaneous conditioning, 189
Situational leadership theory, 739
Size constancy, 124, 126
Size cues, 130
Size-distance invariance, 126
Skin senses, 111–15
Sleep, 156–62
    disorders, 160–62
    functions of, 158–60
    nature of, 156–58
    study of, 156
Sleep efficiency, 159
Sleeping pills, 161
Smell, 96, 115–18
Smoking, 318. See Cigarette smoking
Social anxiety, 509
Social categorization, 689. See also
    Re-categorization
Social clock, 372–73
Social cognition, 667
    automatic vigilance, 669–71
    false consensus effect, 667–68
    positive aspects of, 671
Social cognitive theory, 515–16
Social death, 391
Social and emotional development,
    314
    in adolescence, 363–67
    of children, 342–49
    and temperament, 342–45
Social exchange model, 475–76
Social facilitation, 724
Social influence, 469
    compliance, 690–92
    conformity, 687–89
    effect of, on females, 469
    obedience and, 692–95
Social learning
    and acquisition of prejudices,
        681
    view of language development,
        300
Social norms, 687–88
Social perception deficits, 608
Social perspective, on drug abuse, 173
Social psychology, 20, 661
Social referring, 343
Social Science and Humanities
    Research Council, 35
Social selves, 367
Social smiling, 342
Social thought, 661–79
    aspects of, 667–68
    attitudes, 672–77
    attribution, 661–66
    social cognition, 667–71
Social-cognitive view of hypnosis,
    168
Social-order-maintaining
    orientation, 338
Sociobiology
    gender differences in sexual
        jealousy, 415
    and mate selection, 474
Sociocultural perspective, 13, 14
Sodium amytal, 74
Somatic form, 597
Somatic nervous system, 61
Somatization disorder, 597
Somatoform disorders, 596–97

Somatosensory cortex, 69
Somnambulism, 161
Sound shadow, 110
Sound waves, 108–109
Source traits, 511
Spatial relations, 480
Specific language impairment, 301
Speech comprehension, 297
Sperm, 83
Spinal cord, 60
Spinal nerves, 61
Split dreams, 388
Split-half reliability, 455
Spontaneous recovery, 192
Stage theories
    Erickson's, 364–67, 372
    Freud's, 495–97
    Kohlberg's, 338–39
    Levinson's, 382–84
    Piaget's, 326–28
Stanford-Binet Test, 451
Staring, 433
Starvation, 410
State-dependent retrieval, 241
Static visual acuity (SVA), 103
Stereochemical theory, 116
Stereotypes, 438
    and bias in legal proceedings,
        755
    definition of, 681
    negative effects of gender,
        727–30
    performance appraisals and,
        726
    prejudice and, 681–82
Stimulants, 175–76, 178
Stimulus, 187
    blocking of, 197
    conditioned, 188
    discriminative, 210
    familarity of, and conditioning,
        191
    intensity of, and conditioning,
        191
    unconditional, 188
Stimulus control, practical applica-
    tion of, 2120–13
Stimulus control of behavior, 209–210
Stimulus discrimination, 193
Stimulus generalization, 192
Storage, 229, 240
Strange situation test, 346
Stranger-on-the-bus effect, 508
Stress
    causes of, 539
    daily, 541
    during pregnancy, 316–17
    and eating habits, 408–409
    effects of, 545–46
    environmental sources of,
        542–43
    and health, 545–46
    management of, 569
    nature of, 534–35
    reducing workplace, 544–45
    resistance to, 548–49
    self-concept and, 529
    sense of humor and, 537
    task performance and, 546–47
    work-related, 543
Stressors, 534
    cognitive appraisal of, 535–37
    physiological responses to, 535
Striatum, 260
Striving for superiority, 504
Structural family therapy, 638
Structuralism, 7, 8
Style of life, 504
Sublimation, 495
Subliminal
    messages, 635
    perception, 98–99
    processing, 595–96

Substance abuse
     in Canadian North, 644
     disorders, 586
Substance P, 113
Sudden infant death syndrome, 557
Sugar rush, 408
Suicide, 589–92
     among native Canadians, 591
     in Canada, 590–91
     preventing, 614
Superchiasmatic nucleus, 146, 147
Superconducting quantum interfer-
     ence device (SQUID), 63
Superego, 494
Superior colliculi, 66
Suprachiasmatic nucleus, 146, 162
Surface structure, 297
Syllogistic reasoning, 275
Sympathetic nervous system, 61,
     428, 429
Sympathy, 401
Symptom perception, 550–51
Synapse, 50
Synaptic transmission, 53–55
Synaptic vesicle, 53
Synesthesia, 177
Syntax, 298, 305
Syphilis, 317
Systematic desentization, 198, 627
Systematic observation, 16

Tardive dyskinesia, 648
Target dosing, 648
Taste, 96, 116
Taste aversion. See Conditioned
     taste aversion
Taste buds, 116
Telepathy, 135
Telephone scatologia, 602
Temperament, 343–45
Temperature, 744–45, 752
Template-matching theory, 129
Templates, 129
Temporal arrangement of CS-UCS
     pairings, 189
Temporal lobe, 70, 71, 450
     left, 72
     medial, 259–60
Temporary threshold shift (TTS), 137
Teratogens, 317

Tertiary prevention, 651
Test-retest reliability, 456
Testes, 79
Testosterone, 412
Texture gradient, 130
Thalamus, 68
That's-not-all approach, 692
THC, 177
Thematic Apperception Test (TAT),
     422
Theories, 32
     role of in psychological
          research, 31–33
     See also specific theories
Therapeutic alliance, 621
Therapy
     setting for, 650–51
     successfulness of, 642–43
     See also Psychotherapies
Thinking, 270. See also Cognition;
     Thought
Thorazine, 647
Thought
     elements of, 271–78
     emergence of logical, 328
     relationship of, to language, 304
     schizophrenic disturbances in,
          608
Three-term contingency, 212
Thyroid, 79
Thyroid-hormone receptors, 332
Timbre, 109
Timing-of-life models, 372
Tinnitus, 137
"Tip of the nose" phenomenon, 117
Tip-of-the-tongue phenomenon, 237
Token economies, 628
Tolerance, drug, 172
Top-down theory of pattern
     recognition, 130
Touch, 96, 111–15
Touching, 434–35
Trace conditioning, 189
Trace-decay hypothesis, 242–43
Tracking, 751
Trait theories
     of Allport, 510–11
     of Cattell, 511
     modern framework of, 511–13
Transcendental meditation, 179–81

Transduction, 95
Transference, 623
Transformational (charismatic) lead-
     ership, 739–41
Transvestic fetishism, 602
Traumatic brain injury (TBI), 87–88
Traveling wave theory, 109–110
Trephining, 577
Trial and error, 292
Triarchic theory, 447, 448
Trichotillomania, 217
Trichromatic theory, 104–105
Tricyclics, 648
Trust versus mistrust, 365
Tuberculosis, 317
Twins, 84, 386, 464, 611, 733
Two-chair exercise, 625
Two-factor theory of emotions, 427
Type A behavior pattern, 559–60
Type B behavior pattern, 559, 560
Type I schizophrenia, 609, 611
Type II schizophrenia, 609, 611

Ultradian rhythms, 145
Unconditional positive regard, 506
Unconditioned response (UCR), 188
Unconditioned stimulus (UCS), 188
Unemployment, effects of, 387–88
Us-versus-them effect, 680–81

Validity, 457
Valium, 649
Variable-interval schedule, 208
Variable-ratio schedule, 208
Variables, 23
     confounding of, 28
     dependent, 26
     independent, 26
Ventromedial hypothalamus, 67
Verbal IQ, 453–454
Verbosity, 379
Vergence (eye) movements, 104
Version (eye) movements, 104
Vertebrae, 60
Vestibular sacs, 119
     sense, 119, 120
Violence, temperature and, 744–45
Violence against women, 478–79,
     483–84
Vision, 100–107

absolute threshold for, 96
acuity, 103
color, 104–106
dark adaptation, 104
physical stimulus for, 102–103
and vestibular information, 120
visual information, 106–107
Visual acuity, 376
Visual cortex, 107
Visual displays, 746–51
Visual imagery, and age, 379
Visual images, 264, 273
Voice, tone of, 434
Volley principle, 110
Voyeurism, 602

Warmth, absolute threshold for, 96
Warnings
     design of, 747–49
     research on, 122–23
Wavelength, 102. See also Sound
     waves
Wear and tear theories of aging, 390
Wechsler Adult Intelligence Scale,
     450, 454
Wechsler Adult Intelligence Scale
     for Children (WISC), 454
Weight, regulation of, 408–409
Wellness, promotion of, 565
Wernicke-Geschwind theory of
     speech, 72
Wisdom, 381
Withdrawal response behavior, 471
Womb envy, 501
Work, and self-concept, 714
Work motivation, 404, 716–24
Work-related
     attitudes, 732–37
     stress, 543–45
Working memory. See Short-term
     memory
Workplace environments, 751–54

X chromosome, 86, 87
Xanax, 649

Zoophilia, 602

Photo Credits

Chapter 1

13, left: Janeart, Ltd./The Image Bank. 13, right: Frank Siteman/Stock • Boston. 15: © Jeff Greenberg/PhotoEdit. 16, top: University of Guelph. 18: P. Ward/Stock • Boston. 22: © 1993/Gamma. 23: Dave Starrett. 30: Canapress. 36: Steve Winter/Black Star. 38: © Louis Bencze/AllStock. 41: © 1988 Larry Lawfer/Black Star.

Chapter 2

50, left: McGill Reporter/Public Relations, McGill University. 50, right: Ruben Garcia, San Antonio Express News. 52: © Biophoto Associates/Science Source. 57: © 1990 Kevin Morris/AllStock. 63: Monkmeyer Press/Grant. 64: Dr. Lewis Baxter/UCLA Neuropsychiatric Institute. 65, top: Julie Fiez and Steven Petersen. 65, bottom: © 1990/Custom Medical Stock Photo. 81: © Robert E. Daemmrich/The Image Works. 82: CNRI/Science Photo Library, Photo Researchers, Inc. 83: Porter/The Image Works. 87: © Charles Gupton/AllStock.

Chapter 3

99: Peter Menzel/Stock • Boston. 101: J. L. Weber/Peter Arnold, Inc. 110: PhotoEdit. 114: Alexander Tsiaras/Stock • Boston. 119: © Gerard Vandystadt/Photo Researchers, Inc. 125, top: Robert Harbison. 125, center: © Robert E. Daemmrich/Tony Stone Images, Inc. 125, bottom left: ©1989 Bill Ross/AllStock. 125, bottom right: © J & M Ibbotson/AllStock. 127, left: © 1991 Tommy L. Thompson/Black Star. 127, right: © Steve Marts/AllStock. 128, left and right: Rob Pretzer.

Chapter 4

137: Dave Starrett. 150: © C. Bruce Forster/AllStock. 151: Migdale/Stock • Boston. 153: © John Coletti. 155: Canapress. 157: Michal Heron/Woodfin Camp & Assoc. 162: Ingres/Superstock. 164: © 1985 Christopher Arnesen/AllStock. 167: © 1992 Science Photo Library/Custom Medical Stock Photo. 172: Dave Starrett. 176: Westenberger/Gamma. 178, top right: M. Ferri/The Stock Market. 178, top left: Allan Tannenbaum/ Sygma. 178, bottom left: Monkmeyer Press. 178, bottom right: The Stock Market.

Chapter 5

196: © Stan Wayman/ Photo Researchers, Inc. 198: Dr. Benjamin Harris. 203: © Tony Freeman/PhotoEdit. 204, top left: © Stephen Frisch/Stock • Boston. 204, top right: © Richard Hutchings/PhotoEdit. 204, bottom: Kevin Horan/Stock • Boston.. 206: Nina Leen/Time Warner Inc. 207: © Gerald Davis, Contact Press Images/Woodfin Camp & Assoc. 208: © Robert E. Daemmrich/Tony Stone Worldwide, Ltd. 219: Robert Harbison. 221: © 1989 Rob Nelson/ Black Star. 222: © Charles Gupton/AllStock.

Chapter 6

231, top: © 1989 Kent Wood/AllStock. 231, middle: Steven Underwood Photography. 231, bottom: © David Young-Wolff/PhotoEdit. 232: © David Young-Wolff/PhotoEdit. 234: © 1989 Kent Wood/AllStock. 239: Brian Smith. 244: © Shahn Kermani/Gamma-Liaison. 251, top left: © 1989 Kent Wood/AllStock. 251, top right: Steven Underwood Photography. 251, bottom: © David Young-Wolff/PhotoEdit. 252: Wide World Photos. 257: AP/Wide World Photos. 262: Stephen Marks.

Chapter 7

272, left and right: Bridgeman Art Library. 276: © Jeff Greenberg/ PhotoEdit. 283, top: CanadaWide. 283, middle: Japanese Tourist and Information Centre. 283: Angelika Baur. 289: Bridgeman Art Library. 296: © Ed Kashi 1984. 300, top: © Peter Pearson/Tony Stone Images, Inc. 300, bottom: Corroon/Monkmeyer Press. 305: © 1994 Michael Goldman/The Pace Gallery. 306: CNN. 308: Robert Harbison.

Chapter 8

315, left: Francis Leroy, Biocosmos/Science Photo Library, Photo Researchers. 315, middle and right: © Lennart Nilsson/Bonniers. 321: Dr. Reissland-Burghart. 323: Courtesy of J. Campos, B. Bertenthal, and R. Kermoian. 327: Tom McCarthy/Stock South. 329: © Andy Sacks/Tony Stone Images, Inc. 332: © David Young-Wolff/PhotoEdit. 341: Louis Goldman/Photo Researchers. 348: © Martin Rogers/Stock • Boston. 351: Cathlyn Melloan/TSW-Click/Chicago Ltd. 353: O. Franken/Stock • Boston.

Chapter 9

359: The Bettmann Archive. 360: J. Gerard Smith/Monkmeyer Press Photo. 362: © Nathan Benn/Stock • Boston. 364: Robert Harbison. 366, top: Robert Harbison. 366, top middle: Robert Harbison. 366, bottom middle: Robert Harbison. 366, bottom: © Charles Gupton/The Stock Market. 367: CanadaWide. 368: Culver Pictures. 371: Wendy Halonen, Northern News Service. 374: Robert A. Baron. 376: © Ed Kashi. 392: Natsuko Utsumi/Gamma-Liaison.

Chapter 10

401: © Shahn Kermani/Gamma-Liaison. 404: Duomo Photography. 406, top: Stephen Marks. 406, bottom: K. Reininger/Black Star. 407, left: Steven Underwood Photography. 407, right: © Donovan Reese/Tony Stone Worldwide, Ltd. 412: © Susan Lapides/Woodfin Camp & Assoc. 413: Underwood Photography. 426: Superstock. 429, top and bottom: CanadaWide. 431: © Hans Halberstadt/Photo Researchers, Inc. 433: © Bonnie Kamin 1988. 439: © Joel W. Rogers.

Chapter 11

448, top: Jim Pickerell. 448, middle: Laima Druskis/Stock • Boston. 448, bottom: F. Baldwin/Photo Researchers, Inc. 454: Merrim/Monkmeyer Press. 458, top: © Paul Chesley/Tony Stone Worldwide, Ltd. 458, middle: © Robert E. Daemmrich/Stock • Boston. 458, bottom: © Jon Riley/Tony Stone Images, Inc. 463, top: Mario Ruiz/Picture Group. 463, bottom: © Porterfield/Chickering, Photo Researchers, Inc. 464: © 1987 Arnold Zann/Black Star. 467: © 1991 Craig Sillitoe/Black Star. 470: R. Schleipman/Offshoot Stock.

Chapter 12

492: The Granger Collection, New York. 496: Underwood Photo Archives, SF. 499, left: © Dan Bosler/Tony Stone Images, Inc. 499, right: © Lou Jones 1994. Shooting Star. 507: CanadaWide. 509: © Robert E. Daemmrich/Stock • Boston. 513: CanadaWide. 515: Richard Hutchings/Photo Researchers, Inc. 518, middles left: B. Aron/ PhotoEdit. 518, middle right: CanadaWide. 518, bottom: F. Baldwin/ Photo Researchers, Inc. 523: © 1987 Joel W. Rogers. 526: Stephen Marks.

Chapter 13

534: © Robert Harbison. 538: AP/Wide World Photos. 540, top: David Madison 1992. 543: Robert Harbison. 544: Reuters/Bettmann. 559: © Everton/The Image Works. 562: © Ed Kashi 1993. 566: Stephen Marks. 569: Robert Harbison. 572: Elena Dorfman.

Chapter 14

576: Baum/Monkmeyer Press. 577: © Chip Clark 1993.578: Northwind Photo Archives. 579: © Anis Hamdani/Gamma Liaison. 581, top: The Granger Collection. 581, bottom: © James Wilson/ Woodfin Camp & Assoc. 585: © Michael Newman/PhotoEdit. 590, top: © Gordon Willitt/Tony Stone Worldwide/Chicago Ltd. 590, bottom: © P. Chauvel/Sygma. 593: The Bridgeman Art Library. 595: Reuters/Bettmann. 598, left and right: UPI/Bettmann. 603: Russ Kinne/Comstock. 610, top: Grunnitus/ Monkmeyer Press. 610, bottom: Courtesy of the Genain estate. 614: Suicide Information & Education Centre.

Chapter 15

622: Mary Evans/Sigmund Freud Copyrights. 627: © Richard Howard 1986. 628: W. Spunbarg/PhotoEdit. 629: © Catherine Ursillo/Photo Researchers, Inc. 634: © James Wilson/Woodfin Camp & Assoc. 638: Robert E. Daemmrich/Stock • Boston. 640, top: Mary Evans/Sigmund Freud Copyrights. 640, middle: © Richard Howard 1986. 640, bottom: © Chris Cheadle/Tony Stone Images, Inc. 644: Lyn Hancock. 645, top: Robert A. Baron. 645, bottom: © James Wilson/ Woodfin Camp & Assoc. 647: Adam Hart-Davis/Science Photo Library, Photo Researchers, Inc. 651: © Peter Southwick/Stock • Boston.

Chapter 16

654: © Louis Bencze/AllStock. 672: CanadaWide. 674: Robert Harbison. 676: © Peter Vadnai/The Stock Market. 683: © 1991 Lawrence Migdale/Photo Researchers, Inc. 694, left and right: Courtesy of the Milgram estate. 696, top: Sylvan Grandadam/Photo Researchers, Inc. 696, middle: © David J. Sams/Tony Stone Images, Inc. 696, bottom: © Bill Wisser/Liaison International. 697: Robert Harbison. 699: © Jan Halaska/Photo Researchers, Inc. 704. left: © John Curtis/Off Shoot. 704, right: © Catherine Karnow/Woodfin Camp & Assoc. 705: SuperStock. 714, left: Kathleen Bellesisles. 714, right: Tony Stone Worldwide.

Chapter 17

718: © Zigy Kalunzy/Tony Stone Worldwide. 721, top: © Ted Spiegel/Black Star. 721, bottom: CanadaWide. 723: © John Coletti. 740, left: UPI/Bettmann. 740, right: © Larry Downing/Woodfin Camp & Assoc. 747: © 1994 Brian W. Robb. 749: Human Factors & Ergonomics Society. 753, top: Robert A. Baron. 753, bottom left: © Sepp Seitz 1984/Woodfin Camp & Assoc. 753, bottom middle: © Dick Luria/Photo Researchers, Inc. 753, bottom right: © Chuck Keeler/Tony Stone Worldwide/Chicago Ltd.

Endpapers

Photo of Ken M. Prkachin: University of Northern British Columbia, Office of Communications. Photo of Sandra Byers: Joy Cummings/ University of New Brunswick Audio Visual Services.